Words of a Century

Words of a Century

The Top 100 American Speeches, 1900–1999

Stephen E. Lucas

AND

Martin J. Medhurst

New York   Oxford

OXFORD UNIVERSITY PRESS

2009

Oxford University Press, Inc., publishes works that further Oxford University's
objective of excellence in research, scholarship, and education.

Oxford   New York
Auckland   Cape Town   Dar es Salaam   Hong Kong   Karachi
Kuala Lumpur   Madrid   Melbourne   Mexico City   Nairobi
New Delhi   Shanghai   Taipei   Toronto

With offices in
Argentina   Austria   Brazil   Chile Czech   Republic France   Greece
Guatemala   Hungary   Italy   Japan   Poland   Portugal   Singapore
South Korea   Switzerland   Thailand   Turkey   Ukraine   Vietnam

Copyright © 2009 by Oxford University Press, Inc.

Published by Oxford University Press, Inc.
198 Madison Avenue, New York, New York 10016
http://www.oup.com

Oxford is a registered trademark of Oxford University Press

Library of Congress Cataloging-in Publication Data

Lucas, Stephen, 1946-
Words of a century : the top 100 American speeches, 1900-1999 / [compiled by]
Stephen E. Lucas, Martin J. Medhurst.
     p.   cm.
Includes bibliographical references and indexes.
ISBN 978-0-19-516805-1 (paper)—ISBN 978-0-19-516804-4 (cloth)   1. Speeches,
addresses, etc., American.   2. Oratory—United States—History—20th century.
3. United States—History—20th century—Sources.   4. United States—Politics and
government—20th century—Sources.   I. Medhurst, Martin J.   II. Title.
PS668.L83 2009
815.008—dc22   2008041401

Printing number: 9 8 7 6 5 4 3 2 1
Printed in the United States of America
on acid-free paper.

For my sons, Jeffrey and Ryan
SEL

For my father, Maurice Allen Medhurst, on his seventy-ninth birthday
MJM

Contents

McCarthyism, Korea, and the Nuclear Era

The Age of Camelot

Race, Poverty, and Dissension

Vietnam and Other Discontents

Watergate and Its Aftermath

Conservatism, Liberalism, and the End of the Cold War

The 1990s

Alternate Table of Contents

Speeches by Rank

Introduction

⧖

"Speech is civilization itself. The word, even the most contradictory word, preserves contact—it is silence which isolates."

Thomas Mann

"As long as there are human rights to be defended,...as long as there are great interests to be guarded, as long as the welfare of nations is a matter for discussion, so long will public speaking have its place."

William Jennings Bryan

"Oratory—the power to debate, the ability to hold an audience—will always have a prominent place in our national life, be it in campaign speeches, or from the pulpit, or in dealing with business affairs of the nation."

Al Smith

◇◇

As the twentieth century began, commentators in the United States reflected on the profound changes that had occurred during the previous hundred years and predicted what the future might have in store. Certainly not the most pressing of their concerns, but one that cropped up with regularity, was the role of oratory in American life. Following on the heels of a century that had witnessed the golden age of American oratory, it seemed to many that such glories could never again be attained. Certainly there were talented speakers in the land, but where were the likes of Abraham Lincoln, Henry Clay, Wendell Phillips, Frederick Douglass, and Daniel Webster? Magazine articles devoted to the subject carried such titles as "The Passing of the Art of Oratory," "The Neglected Art of Oratory," and "Has Oratory Declined?" It was partly to keep oratory from becoming a "lost art" that David Brewer, Chief Justice of the U.S. Supreme Court, published his ten-volume compendium, *The World's Best Orations*, in 1899.[1]

Brewer need not have worried. The next two decades produced a remarkable oratorical renaissance in which speakers such as Theodore Roosevelt, Woodrow Wilson, William Jennings Bryan, Carrie

Chapman Catt, Anna Howard Shaw, Emma Goldman, Eugene Debs, Margaret Sanger, Robert La Follette, and Clarence Darrow demonstrated that the platform remained a vital presence in American life.[2] The issues they debated included imperialism, World War I, the rise of the modern economy, woman suffrage, birth control, capital punishment, and the rights of labor. It was one of the most tumultuous periods in the nation's history, and it proved once again that in times of crisis, when great bodies of people "are stirred by intense emotion and when the wind of passion is blowing over human hearts," the contours of history will be shaped not only by the march of events but also by "the indescribable magic of the spoken word."[3]

So, too, with the Great Depression, World War II, and the emergence of the Cold War. The only person to be elected President four times, Franklin Roosevelt used his speeches to help combat fear in the face of unparalleled economic disaster and to

---

1. David J. Brewer, ed., *The World's Best Orations, from the Earliest Period to the Present Time* (St. Louis, Mo.; Ferd. P. Kaiser, 1899), 1: xi.

2. Robert Alexander Kraig, "The Second Oratorical Renaissance," in *Rhetoric and Reform in the Progressive Era*, J. Michael Hogan, ed. (East Lansing: Michigan State University Press, 2003), 1–48.

3. Harry Thurston Peck, "Some Notes on Political Oratory," *Bookman*, 4/4 (1896), 332.

lead the nation through the battle against international fascism. Friend and foe alike testified to "the magical effect of his presence and his voice upon the crowds."[4] No comparable figure dominated the rhetorical landscape after his death in 1945, but a variety of voices, including his wife, Eleanor, explored how best to deal with the troubling developments of the postwar world. No issues were more contentious than those posed by tensions with the Soviet Union and the spread of nuclear weapons, and speeches on those subjects by Harry Truman, George C. Marshall, Margaret Chase Smith, William Faulkner, Dwight Eisenhower, Douglas MacArthur, and Joseph Welch have taken their place in the nation's lore.

Every age, however, tends to judge its public discourse as inferior to that of the past. Raymond Moley, who had been one of FDR's chief speechwriters, bemoaned in 1961 the current "mediocrity of the public discourse of our political leaders and statesmen."[5] Two years later, Marie Hochmuth Nichols, observing the influence of television and advertising, wondered "whether the power of public speaking" was still "highly prized at all."[6] Yet the decade of the 1960s produced some of the most esteemed speeches in American history, including John F. Kennedy's inaugural address and Martin Luther King's "I Have a Dream." As the United States sought to deal with what Kennedy called the "long twilight struggle" against communism, to bring about racial justice for African Americans and equal rights for women, to extricate itself from the quagmire of Vietnam, and to cope with a wave of assassinations and civil uprisings, speakers of all persuasions debated these issues with passion, intensity, and often eloquence.

Nor did the rest of the century produce a respite from crisis or contention. Watergate, the resignation of a President, the denouement of the Cold War, the explosion of the space shuttle *Challenger*, the emergence of AIDS, the conservative revolution, the bombing of the Alfred P. Murrah Federal Office Building in Oklahoma City—all gave rise to speeches that possessed "the white sunlight of potent words."[7] The rhetorical achievements of Ronald Reagan brought renewed attention to oratory as an art form, as well as to its political potency, but he was not alone. Barbara Jordan, Edward Kennedy, Mario Cuomo, Jesse Jackson, Barbara Bush, Mary Fisher, and Hillary Clinton—among others—produced speeches that invigorated their listeners and are regarded as exemplars of public address.

No matter the time and place, for every rhetorical jewel there are countless sophistic baubles. Eventually, however, the dross fades into obscurity while posterity extols the exceptional. With the perspective afforded by time, it is clear that the twentieth century produced its full share of eloquent, expressive, and historically significant speeches. The tone, tenor, and topics of public address have changed over time, from the grand declamations of classical antiquity, to the set pieces of nineteenth-century oratory, to the conversational style inculcated by radio and television. Yet the fundamental human drive to use speech and language expressively and artistically remains alive and well.[8] As Brian MacArthur has stated, "Amidst the lazy illiteracy of so much modern speech, eloquent words still have the power to pierce through all the banal platitudes and make audiences stop and think and sometimes even wonder."[9]

This book is a collection of the top 100 American speeches of the twentieth century. In addition to moving audiences in their own time, more than

4. James A. Farley, *Behind the Ballots: The Personal History of a Politician* (New York: Harcourt, Brace and Company, 1938), 317.

5. Raymond Moley, "Raise the Sights," *Newsweek*, July 31, 1961, 84.

6. Marie Hochmuth Nichols, *Rhetoric and Criticism* (Baton Rouge: Louisiana State University Press, 1963), 50.

7. John S. MacIntosh, *The White Sunlight of Potent Words: An Oration* (Philadelphia: National School of Elocution and Oratory, 1882). MacIntosh attributes the phrase to Thomas Carlyle, an attribution that has been repeated by subsequent writers, but in fact it is a paraphrase from Carlyle's *Reminiscences* (New York: Harper and Brothers, 1881), 5.

8. See Stephen E. Lucas, "Public Speaking," in *Encyclopedia of Rhetoric*, Thomas O. Sloane, ed. (New York: Oxford University Press, 2001), 640–47.

9. Brian MacArthur, ed., *The Penguin Book of Twentieth-Century Speeches* (New York: Penguin, 1992), xxii.

a few of the speeches continue to resonate in ours. Notwithstanding dramatic changes in technology, demographics, political alignments, and social mores, many of the concerns we face today are not vastly different from those with which Americans grappled during the twentieth century—war and peace, individual rights and collective security, the power and obligations of the press, the rights of women and minorities, economic fluctuations, domestic versus international priorities, the role of religion in politics, national tragedy and communal sorrow. The speeches in this book open a window on the twentieth century, but they also provide a rich source to which we can turn for edification and inspiration as we make our way through the twenty-first century.

Selecting the Speeches

The genesis of this book can be traced to a national survey we conducted in October–November 1999 among scholars of rhetoric and public address to determine the top 100 American speeches of the twentieth century. Of the 282 people contacted, 137 completed and returned the survey—a response rate of 48.6 percent, far above the average for such research. In contrast with the Modern Library's rankings of the top 100 fiction and nonfiction works of the century, we drew upon the knowledge of a large number of experts rather than appointing a small panel to make the final selections. Nor did we send out a prepackaged list of nominees for people to rank.

The questionnaire asked respondents to complete three tasks. The first was to construct a list of what, in their estimation, constituted the twenty-five best public speeches of the twentieth century delivered by Americans. To be eligible for consideration, a speech need not have been presented in the United States, but the speaker had to be a U.S. resident. There were no restrictions on the genres or topics of speeches or on the number of speeches from a single speaker. We asked respondents to select speeches in light of two criteria:

- Impact: Judged by short-term impact on the immediate audience or situation and/or long-term impact

on public discourse, values, practices, policies, attitudes, perceptions, and the like.
- Artistry: Judged by the speaker's invention, argument, structure, style, delivery, ethics, and the like.

We left these criteria deliberately broad. Although students of public address have expended considerable energy over the years discussing the elements of rhetorical impact and artistry, our aim was to give respondents wide latitude to exercise their individual judgment in interpreting and applying the criteria.

Second, we asked respondents to provide two ratings for each of their twenty-five speeches. One rating considered the impact of the speech; the other its artistry. We asked for separate ratings of impact and artistry in recognition of the fact that a speech might score high on one measure but low on the other. When calculating results, we tabulated the impact and artistry scales separately before combining the results from both scales to determine an overall rating for each speech. Third, in addition to rating the speeches, we asked participants to rank what they regarded as the five top speeches of the century.[10]

The placement of speeches in the top 100 was determined according to the following decision rules: (1) the total number of points garnered by each speech on the impact and artistry ratings combined; (2) the total number of top-five ranking points; (3) the total number of times a speech was mentioned by survey respondents; (4) the total number of times a speech received the highest ranking on the impact or artistry scale. The first decision rule was applied to all speeches; subsequent rules were applied only when necessary to separate speeches that were deadlocked on the basis of the preceding decision rule.

Results of the survey were compiled in December 1999 and released to the press before the end of the year. Stories about the top 100 speeches appeared in *USA Today, Time, National Review,* the London *Independent,* the Tel Aviv *Haaretz,* and many other media outlets. The list has since been reproduced on

---

10. We are obliged to Denise Solomon for her expertise in helping us design the survey, and to Leanne Knobloch for tabulating and analyzing the data.

scores of Web sites and continues to generate interest worldwide.

For reasons of historical continuity, we reprint the speeches in chronological order. The full list is reprinted in the Alternate Table of Contents (pages xi–xiii), so readers interested primarily in the rankings can easily find where each entry is located in the book. Every speech is preceded by a headnote that provides background on the speaker, sets his or her address in historical context, and assays its significance as a rhetorical work.

Composition of the Speeches

Given the fact that almost all the speeches are political in nature, it is not surprising that some commentators detected a liberal or conservative bias in the rankings and wondered why their favorite speeches or orators were not included. Part of the answer is that the survey focused on speeches, rather than on speakers. There are individuals who are best known for the full arc of their oratorical careers, rather than for individual addresses. Billy Graham, Charles Coughlin, Marcus Garvey, W. E. B. DuBois, Claire Booth Luce, Aimee Semple McPherson, Helen Keller, Frank Church, Everett Dirksen, William Borah, and Harry Emerson Fosdick are but a few that come quickly to mind. Had we been ranking speakers, some of these would doubtless have been included.

It is also the case that speeches rise and fall in estimation with the passage of time. Regardless of the subject being ranked, any list will inevitably reflect the background, views, knowledge, and attitudes of those who compile it. The list of the top 100 speeches is a snapshot of the expert opinion of the community of scholars in rhetoric and public address at the end of the twentieth century. Had the survey queried a different set of respondents, been taken at a different point in time, or used a different methodology, the results would doubtless have been different, at least in degree. The same is true of every top 100 list compiled at the end of the twentieth century, as well as of such perennial rankings as the best and worst U.S. Presidents, which fluctuate,

sometimes dramatically, with changes in historical perspective.

When one looks at the works that are included on the list, it becomes clear that public speech in the United States was at the epicenter of many of the twentieth century's most crucial occurrences, including woman suffrage, World War I, the Great Depression, World War II, the Cold War, McCarthyism, the Korean War, the Vietnam conflict, Watergate, the civil rights and feminist movements, and the rise of conservatism. While these and other major developments of the century were shaped by a wide range of factors—political, economic, social, religious, technological—they were also influenced, often profoundly, by the public speeches identified in the top 100. Notwithstanding the complexity of the modern world and the multifarious forces that have shaped it, no complete history of the United States in the twentieth century can be written without regard to the abiding power of the spoken word.

The list also reflects far-reaching changes in the consuetudes of American political discourse, not least of which is the emergence of the rhetorical presidency. Through most of the nineteenth century, national attention was riveted on the great orators in Congress. The speeches of Webster, Clay, John C. Calhoun, Robert Hayne, Charles Sumner, Stephen Douglas, and others drew swarms of listeners to the galleries and were regularly reprinted in newspapers and magazines for all to read and discuss. Before Theodore Roosevelt transformed the White House into a "bully pulpit," chief executives usually deferred to the legislative prerogatives of Congress and seldom took to the hustings in behalf of specific policy initiatives, domestic or foreign. Even presidential candidates eschewed the extensive speech making associated with current campaigns.

After Roosevelt, however, the President increasingly became the dominant voice in American politics. The rhetorical power of the office was augmented by radio and television, which allowed the President to go over the heads of Congress and speak directly to the entire nation. Of the top 100 speeches of the twentieth century, thirty-five were delivered by sitting Presidents, while only four were presented by a Senator or Representative in the course of congressional debate.[11] In contrast, of the eighty-two American speeches from the nineteenth century printed in the volumes devoted to political oratory in the 1900 edition of Thomas B. Reed's *Modern Eloquence*, thirty-nine were delivered on the floor of the U.S. Congress, but only five came from a sitting President.[12]

Equally striking, *Modern Eloquence* did not print any addresses by women or African Americans in their volumes on political oratory, despite the fact that nineteenth-century speakers such as Frederick Douglass, Maria Stewart, Booker T. Washington, Susan B. Anthony, and Elizabeth Cady Stanton had produced works of incontestable power and artistry. In contrast, twenty-one of the speeches in this book are by women. By the end of the twentieth century, women had become so prominent on the public platform that Barbara Bush and Hillary Clinton outpolled their husbands, George H. W. Bush and Bill Clinton, in the top 100 survey, and five of the survey's seven speeches from the 1990s were by women. There are also twelve speeches by African Americans. Martin Luther King's "I Have a Dream" was deemed the finest speech of the century, while Barbara Jordan's keynote at the 1976 Democratic National Convention and Malcolm X's "The Ballot or the Bullet" were also included in the top ten. Such works manifest the rich oral tradition of the black community and the historical significance of the quest for racial justice.

There are other oppositional voices as well. Public speaking is the most democratic mode of civic communication. One need not own a newspaper, a television station, or a radio station to express one's ideas through public speech. Most of the great reform movements in American history have been propelled by the persuasive efforts of dedicated advocates who championed their causes on the public platform. Represented in this volume are speakers such as Eugene Debs, Anna Howard Shaw, Carrie Chapman Catt, Emma Goldman, Crystal Eastman, Clarence Darrow, Margaret Sanger, John L. Lewis, Elizabeth Gurley Flynn, Mario Savio, and Cesar Chavez. Their presence reminds us that public speaking has historically been the single most important mode of expression for people seeking to broaden the lines of power and privilege in American society.[13]

There is also diversity in the kinds of speeches. There are presidential inaugurals, commemorations, war messages, and farewell addresses. There are speeches delivered on the campaign trail, in Democratic and Republican national conventions, in the U.S. Congress, at the United Nations, and on three continents other than North America. Protest speeches, commencement addresses, eulogies, apologias, courtroom pleas, public lectures—all are represented. So, too, is a wide range of rhetorical styles, from the patrician eloquence of Adlai Stevenson to the populist bromides of Huey Long, the stolidity of George Marshall to the exuberance of Hubert Humphrey, the unbridled boosterism of Russell Conwell to the sobering reflections of Elie Wiesel, the meticulously composed allocutions of Carrie Chapman Catt to the extemporized exhortations of Stokely Carmichael.

It is important to emphasize that we are not seeking to create a canon of American public address. There are scores of speeches from the twentieth century other than those printed here that deserve public cognizance and scholarly scrutiny. One of our aims in conducting the survey was to invigorate the study of American public address, and we hope this book will further that objective.

---

11. When Congress did become a site for works in the top 100, it was more often for addresses by Presidents (seven) than for speeches given in the course of congressional debate. The top 100 also includes thirteen speeches delivered outside Congress by members of the House or Senate, but most of those were related to presidential campaigns, rather than to the topics of congressional debate.

12. Thomas B. Reed, ed., *Modern Eloquence*, 15 volumes (Philadelphia: J. D. Morris, 1900).

---

13. Lucas, "Public Speaking," 644.

Authenticating the Speeches

Conducting the survey turned out to be the easy part. When the opportunity arose to prepare an anthology based on the top 100, we decided to accept the challenge—and a challenge it has been. A project we thought would take two years to complete has taken seven, not least because of our decision to authenticate the text of each speech in the book. A speech is such a commonplace occurrence that most people never think much about how it comes into existence, where and under what conditions it was delivered, who first heard it, and how it was published and distributed. Yet all of those factors and more can affect what we ultimately come to know as the speech. In our case, we wanted to provide as accurate a record as possible of what the speaker actually said—not the speech as printed in the press or as revised for subsequent publication, but the speech as delivered to its immediate audience.

The first thing we discovered was a persistent lack of attention to questions of textual authenticity in existing speech anthologies. One question revolves around speeches for which there are no extant audio or video recordings and that exist only in printed form. In the current volume, this category includes the nineteen speeches presented before Franklin Roosevelt's first inaugural address of March 4, 1933, and eight delivered after that date. When printing any of these speeches, previous anthologists have typically turned to the most readily available text, which usually means the one that has been reprinted most often in the past. In few cases have they compared competing texts of the same speech to determine which is most accurate. As a result, our understanding of some of the most important public addresses in American history has been based on partial or inaccurate texts, a situation we have worked to remedy. This is not the place to review every speech—details are presented in the headnotes and in the Note on Sources (pages 659–660)—but discussing a few will help convey a sense of our methods and findings.

We can begin with Clarence Darrow's address to the court in defense of Leopold and Loeb, presented across August 22, 23, and 25, 1924. In addition to being printed on multiple occasions, though seldom in its entirety, the speech has been depicted in biographies of Darrow as well as in fictionalized accounts of the trial. Most reprints, whether complete or truncated, derive either from the 1926 pamphlet issued by the Haldeman-Julius Company of Girard, Kansas, or from Maureen McKernan's *The Amazing Crime and Trial of Leopold and Loeb*, published within a few months of the trial.[14] Both of these versions, however, were substantially revised for publication, and neither retains the oral quality of Darrow's presentation. They were meant for readers, not for the courtroom audience.

In dealing with Darrow's speech, as with the others that exist only in print, we began by searching for the text closest in time to the moment of utterance. The most obvious step was to locate a transcript of the trial. For reasons that are not altogether clear, however, there is no extant transcript for the second and third days of Darrow's speech. Fortunately, there is a transcript for the first day, which gave us a stenographic account of Darrow's words and allowed us to gauge how extensively later versions of his speech were revised for publication. The question was whether we could find a text of comparable reliability for the second and third days. We turned first to the Chicago newspapers, which had their own stenographers at the trial, but none of the papers printed Darrow's remarks in their entirety. At one point, we thought of cobbling the speech together using sections from the different newspapers and filling in any blanks with excerpts from the McKernan or Haldeman-Julius texts. The result would not have been entirely satisfactory, but it would have been an improvement over existing versions.

As matters turned out, we eventually found, among all the published versions of Darrow's speech, one that bore earmarks of having come from the original trial transcript. It was in an obscure, undated volume from the Wilson Publishing Company that

---

14. *Clarence Darrow's Plea in Defense of Loeb and Leopold* (Girard, Kans.: Haldeman-Julius Company, [1926]); Maureen McKernan, *The Amazing Crime and Trial of Leopold and Loeb* (Chicago: Plymouth Court Press, 1924), 213–305.

proved to have been released shortly after the trial.[15] Almost identical to the official transcript in reporting the first day of Darrow's summation, it also conveyed the distinctly extemporaneous flavor of his remarks on days two and three. In the end, we combined the first day of the speech as recorded in the trial transcript with the second and third days as printed in the Wilson pamphlet, with a few modifications based on the newspapers' stenographic accounts. The result is a more complete and accurate text of the speech than has appeared since the time of the trial, one that allows us to see more clearly than before the dynamics of Darrow's legendary rhetorical power.

Fortunately, not every speech proved to be as daunting as Darrow's, but neither was it a solitary instance. All the speeches that exist only in print presented their own obstacles. Our goal, however, was always the same: to find the urtext that would bring us as close as possible to the speech as delivered. In one case—Lou Gehrig's Farewell to Baseball of July 4, 1939—we found ourselves confronting a speech with multiple written texts and a few audio fragments. One of those fragments included Gehrig's famous line that he was "the luckiest man on the face of the earth" despite the debilitating disease that would take his life two years later. This line is found in all printed texts of the speech, including the one in Eleanor Gehrig's 1976 *My Luke and I*.[16] Although this has become the text most often reprinted, it is closer to what Gehrig had written at home the night before than to what he said in Yankee Stadium on the Fourth of July.

After studying all the available texts, we determined that the nearest thing to a stenographic account of Gehrig's words appeared in the *Sporting News* of July 13, 1939.[17] We say "nearest thing" because there are enough differences between this text and the

surviving audio fragments to make clear that it is not a verbatim record of the speech. After comparing the *Sporting News* version and the audio fragments with newspaper accounts, it also became clear that Gehrig referred in his remarks both to Yankees general manager Ed Barrow (missing from *Sporting News* but included by Eleanor Gehrig) and his teammate Bill Dickey (present in *Sporting News* but not in Eleanor Gehrig). In the end, we reconstructed the speech by combining the audio fragments, the *Sporting News* text, and the sentence from Eleanor Gehrig's text that mentions Ed Barrow. We will never know exactly what Lou Gehrig said that day in Yankee Stadium, but we are confident we have come as close as possible on the basis of the known evidence.

There are two other cases in which we combined portions of written texts with audio segments to produce the version printed here. One is Huey Long's "Every Man a King." Previous publications of Long's speech have reproduced the text in the *Congressional Record* of March 1, 1934, which is a substantially revised rendition of what he said in his thirty-minute radio address.[18] We discovered, however, that ten minutes and fourteen seconds of the broadcast were preserved in the Brander Matthews Collection at Columbia University and have since become part of the audio holdings at the Library of Congress. In creating our text, we blended the one-third of the speech that exists on audio with the other two-thirds from the *Congressional Record*.

We had a similar experience with Eleanor Roosevelt's "The Struggle for Human Rights," presented on September 28, 1948, at the Sorbonne in Paris, France, where Roosevelt was serving as a member of the U.S. delegation to the United Nations. The UN had been created two years earlier, and Roosevelt was chair of the commission charged with drafting the Universal Declaration of Human Rights. The official version of her speech, published by the State Department in February 1949, has been reprinted

---

15. *Attorney Clarence Darrow's Plea for Mercy and Prosecutor Robert E. Crowe's Demand for the Death Penalty in the Loeb-Leopold Case* (Chicago: Wilson Publishing Company, [1924]), 5–85.

16. Eleanor Gehrig and Joseph Durso, *My Luke and I* (New York: Crowell, 1976), 221–22.

17. "61,808 in Gehrig Tribute," *Sporting News*, July 13, 1939, 14.

18. *Congressional Record: Proceedings and Debates of the Second Session of the Seventy-Third Congress of the United States of America, Volume 78, Part 4* (Washington, D.C.: Government Printing Office, 1934), 3450–53.

many times, but it is not an accurate account of what she said.[19] Fluent in French since childhood, Roosevelt spoke in that language when she addressed her audience at the Sorbonne. In the course of our research, we discovered that the Institut National de l'Audiovisuel in Paris holds a recording of the first ten minutes and last few minutes of her speech from a French radio program broadcast a few days afterward. Our text is based on an English translation of the French audio,[20] along with the other sections of the speech as published in the State Department pamphlet. This is the first time that the parts of the speech preserved in French have been published as Roosevelt delivered them. They include an ad-libbed introduction and a number of changes in wording in the body of the speech, resulting in quite a different text from the one that has been printed in the past.

The best-case scenario, of course, was to locate complete audio or video recordings, which we were able to do in sixty-nine cases. Very few of these speeches have heretofore been published as they were delivered. Usually the advance text issued to the press has become the standard printed version, without account being taken of changes made by the speaker at the moment of presentation. While Ronald Reagan was highly disciplined in staying on text as President, for example, Franklin Roosevelt and John Kennedy were known for departing—sometimes dramatically—from their prepared remarks. Similarly, if one relied on the advance copy of Martin Luther King's "I Have a Dream," one would miss the entire dream section of the speech, which King extemporized as he faced his audience that day in 1963.

Most of the recordings we utilized are available through presidential libraries, government archives, C-SPAN, and commercial sources such as the Educational Video Group's Great American Speeches series. A good number can be listened to on the Internet at such sites as the John F. Kennedy Library and the History Place. Some were harder to track down, and in several cases we located recordings that had not been found by previous researchers. We also discovered cases in which putatively complete recordings proved to be abridged; we then set about finding versions that were fully intact. Sometimes we were rewarded with unexpected treasures.

Among them was William Faulkner's address of December 10, 1950, accepting the Nobel Prize in Literature. The fame of the speech, as well known today as any of his novels, is based on the written text published soon afterward, which is a revised version of the oral presentation. That text has been anthologized countless times, and Faulkner used it for a subsequent studio recording. We did not know whether a recording existed of Faulkner's original remarks, but we located one through the Nobel Foundation and Swedish Radio, both of whom graciously granted us permission to use it. Our text is based on that recording and is, to the best of our knowledge, the first printing of the speech as Faulkner delivered it.

There were other breakthroughs as well, not least of which was a complete recording of Huey Long's "Share Our Wealth" of March 7, 1935. As with Long's "Every Man a King," which we discussed earlier, this speech has always been reprinted from the heavily edited version published in the *Congressional Record*.[21] Now we are able to present the full speech as Long delivered it on national radio in the midst of the Great Depression. Also, due to the kindness of Newton Minow, who supplied us with a recording of his "Vast Wasteland" address (formally titled "Television and the Public Interest"), his words are being printed for the first time as he spoke them in May 1961. Other hard-to-find complete recordings that we were able to locate include Hubert Humphrey's "Sunshine of Civil Rights" from the 1948 Democratic National Convention, Joseph Welch's defense of Fred Fisher at the 1954 Army-McCarthy hearings, Robert

---

19. "The Struggle for Human Rights," in *Human Rights and Genocide: Selected Statements, United Nations Resolutions, September 21–December 12, 1948*. Department of State Publication 3416; International Organization and Conference Series III, 25 (February 1949), 1–12.

20. We are indebted to Rob Lewis and Mary Louise Roberts for providing the translation.

21. The speech was printed with the title "Our Blundering Government," *Congressional Record: Proceedings and Debates of the First Session of the Seventy-Fourth Congress of the United States of America, Volume 79, Part 3* (Washington, D.C.: Government Printing Office, 1935), 3436–39.

Kennedy's 1966 Day of Affirmation address at the University of Cape Town, Spiro Agnew's "Television News Coverage" of November 1969, and Hillary Clinton's "Women's Rights are Human Rights," presented in September 1995 at the United Nations' Fourth World Conference on Women, in Beijing, China.

One other work that deserves mention in this regard is Malcolm X's "The Ballot or the Bullet," delivered in Cleveland on April 3, 1964, and first brought to public attention in George Breitman's 1965 anthology *Malcolm X Speaks*.[22] Working from a tape recording, Breitman produced what has become the standard text of this address. Audio of a different version, titled "Ballots or Bullets" and delivered in Detroit in mid-April 1964, is available commercially, but the Cleveland recording proved to be more elusive. We eventually located one at the Schomburg Center for Research in Black Culture, in New York City. When we listened to it, we discovered that while Breitman's text was largely accurate in content, he had sanitized the speech by converting Malcolm's colloquialisms, contractions, and street dialect into "proper" English. The result was a more polished, literary work, but one that sacrificed the oral style of Malcolm's address and that dulled—albeit with the best of intentions—the sharp, angry edges of his critique of white America. In this volume, we print the speech as it was delivered. Although there is no way to convey Malcolm's riveting vocal skills on the printed page, we hope the text will give readers a better understanding of his extraordinary hold on listeners and of why Julius Lester later commented that "His clear, uncomplicated words cut through the chains on black minds like a giant blow-torch."[23]

As we worked on authenticating the speeches, we made a pair of additional discoveries, both of which can only be characterized as startling. We found that two of the top 100 works selected by our survey respondents were not in fact delivered as speeches. The first is Mary Church Terrell's "What It Means to Be Colored in the Capital of the United States." This well-known work has appeared in several books in the fields of communication, English, and women's studies over the last thirty-five years. How it ended up being identified as a speech is an interesting story. It appears to have been first anthologized when excerpted in Gerda Lerner's 1972 *Black Women in White America: A Documentary History*.[24] It was excerpted again in *We, the American Women: A Documentary History*, edited by Beth Millstein and Jeanne Bodin, as well as in Ellen Skinner's *Women and the National Experience*.[25] In 1990 the complete text appeared in Beverly Washington Jones's *Quest for Equality: The Life and Writings of Mary Eliza Church Terrell*.[26] All four of these books correctly state that Terrell's work came from the January 24, 1907, issue of the *Independent*, a popular magazine of the period, though the article did not appear over Terrell's name. It was printed anonymously, with the author identified only as "a colored woman of much culture and recognized standing."[27] Terrell's authorship was not revealed until publication of her 1940 autobiography, *A Colored Woman in a White World*, a chapter of which contained an expanded version of the 1907 article.[28]

The initial designation of "What It Means to Be Colored in the Capital of the United States" as a speech came in Judith Anderson's *Outspoken Women: Speeches*

22. George Breitman, ed., *Malcolm X Speaks: Selected Speeches and Statements* (New York: Grove, 1965), 23–44.

23. Julius Lester, "The Angry Children of Malcolm X," *Sing Out*, 16/5 (1966), 24. The same is true of Malcolm's "Message to the Grassroots," presented in Detroit on November 10, 1963. Compare the text of that speech on pages 379–388 with that in Breitman, *Malcolm X Speaks*, 3–17.

24. Gerda Lerner, ed., *Black Women in White America: A Documentary History* (New York: Pantheon, 1972), 378–82.

25. Beth Millstein and Jeanne Bodin, eds., *We, the American Women: A Documentary History* (New York: Jerome S. Ozer, 1977), 161–63; Ellen Skinner, *Women and the National Experience: Primary Sources in American History* ([Reading, Mass.]: Addison-Wesley, [1996]), 130–32.

26. Beverly Washington Jones, *Quest for Equality: The Life and Writings of Mary Eliza Church Terrell, 1863–1954* (Brooklyn, N.Y.: Carlson, 1990), 283–91.

27. "What It Means to be Colored in the Capital of the United States," *Independent*, 62 (January 24, 1907), 181–86.

28. Mary Church Terrell, *A Colored Woman in a White World* (Salem, N.H.: Ayer, 1940), 383–96. The chapter was titled "The Colored Man's Paradise."

by American Women Reformers. Published in 1984, this was the first modern anthology devoted exclusively to speeches by American women. Anderson states that Terrell's work was presented to the United Women's Club of Washington, D.C., on October 10, 1906, before being published in the *Independent* three months later.[29] In 1989 the same text appeared, with the same provenance, in Karlyn Kohrs Campbell's *Man Cannot Speak for Her: Key Texts of the Early Feminists*, thereby receiving the imprimatur of the foremost scholar of women's public address.[30] Three years after Campbell's book, Terrell's work surfaced once more as a speech, this time in Robbie Jean Walker's *The Rhetoric of Struggle: Public Address by African American Women*.[31] By this point, "What It Means to Be Colored in the Capital of the United States" had become firmly established in the literature as a speech. It showed up again in 1996 in Deborah Gillan Straub's *Voices of Multicultural America*, and in 2006 in the Library of America's *American Speeches: Political Oratory from Abraham Lincoln to Bill Clinton*.[32]

There is, however, no evidence—at least none we have been able to find—that it was presented as a speech. It certainly was not delivered on October 10, 1906, the date assigned to it by Anderson and subsequent anthologists. Terrell did speak that day, but in New York City, where she was attending the Ninth Annual Session of the National Afro-American Council. In the morning, at Mount Olivet Baptist Church, on Fifty-third Street, she presented a report in her capacity as director of the Anti-Lynching Bureau. That evening she was one of several speakers at the Cooper Union Institute on the subject "Lynching and Its Remedy."[33] Even in our current age of air travel, it would be unusual for someone to give an afternoon speech in Washington, D.C., sandwiched between morning and evening appearances in New York. In 1906 it was physically impossible.

Perhaps, we thought, Anderson had misdated the speech, so we checked to see if Terrell might have delivered "What It Means to Be Colored in the Capital of the United States" on another occasion in 1906. Although we did not find a speech with that title (in 1906 or any other year), we did discover that on November 7, 1906, in Boston, Terrell addressed members of the Twentieth Century Club and the American Peace Society on "The Colored People of Washington." A typescript of the speech is in the Mary Church Terrell Papers at the Library of Congress, and our hopes were high that it would correspond in content with "What It Means to Be Colored in the Capital of the United States." But it did not. Notwithstanding a few similar lines, the Boston speech is a different address, with a decidedly more optimistic message than "What It Means to Be Colored in the Capital of the United States."[34] We were not able to uncover any evidence whatsoever that Terrell delivered "What It Means to Be Colored in the Capital of the United States" as a speech. There is no copy of it in her collected papers at either the Library of Congress or the

29. Judith Anderson, ed., *Outspoken Women: Speeches by American Women Reformers, 1635–1935* (Dubuque, Iowa: Kendall/Hunt, 1984), 191–96.

30. Karlyn Kohrs Campbell, ed., *Man Cannot Speak for Her: Key Texts of the Early Feminists* (New York: Praeger, 1989), 421–32.

31. Robbie Jean Walker, ed., *The Rhetoric of Struggle: Public Address by African American Women* (New York: Garland, 1992), 81–93.

32. Deborah Gillan Straub, ed., *Voices of Multicultural America: Notable Speeches Delivered by African, Asian, Hispanic, and Native Americans, 1790-1995* (Detroit, Mich.: Gale Research, 1996), 1162-67; Ted Widmer, ed., *American Speeches: Political Oratory from Abraham Lincoln to Bill Clinton* (New York: Library of America, 2006), 204–12.

33. A handwritten copy of this work is in *The Papers of Mary Church Terrell* (Washington, D.C.: Library of Congress Photoduplication Service, 1977), reel 23, container 33, pp. 544–53, and Terrell refers to it in *A Colored Woman in a White World*, 182. The dates and locations of Terrell's speeches in New York are specified in the program of the Ninth Annual Session of the National Afro-American Council, in *Papers of Mary Church Terrell*, reel 29, container 41, pp. 468–72.

34. See "The Colored People of Washington," in *Papers of Mary Church Terrell*, reel 23, container 32, pp. 265–72. The speech received brief press coverage in "Good Outlook for Peace," *Boston Evening Transcript*, November 8, 1906, and was mentioned by Terrell in her autobiography, *A Colored Woman in a White World*, 183. Although there is minimal overlap between the Boston speech and "What It Means to Be Colored in the Capital of the United States," the speech does contain a fair amount of material from Terrell's article "Society Among the Colored People of Washington," *Voice of the Negro*, 1 (April 1904), 150–56.

Moorland-Spingarn Research Center at Howard University;[35] no mention of it among the many event programs, lecture announcements, and press clippings she saved over the years; no reference to it in her autobiography, which provides details of many of her other public addresses.

We contacted Professor Anderson to see if she could resolve the issue, but she said she had retired several years before and had thrown away all her notes on Terrell. She could not remember where she had found evidence of Terrell's presentation. We also contacted Professor Campbell and Professor Walker, but both had included "What It Means to Be Colored in the Capital of the United States" in their anthologies on the basis of Anderson's book.[36] Someone may yet corroborate that Terrell did indeed present "What It Means to Be Colored in the Capital of the United States" as a speech, but in light of all the evidence available to us, we had no choice but to drop it from the top 100 speeches of the century. It remains an important work in African-American rhetoric, but one that is best treated as a magazine article, not as an oral presentation.

The other work that turned out not to be a speech is Margaret Sanger's "A Moral Necessity for Birth Control." The evolution of this case is distressingly similar to that of Terrell's "What It Means to Be Colored in the Capital of the United States." The text is taken from Sanger's 1922 book *The Pivot of Civilization*, in which it appears as Chapter 9,

"A Moral Necessity." There is nothing in the book to suggest that the chapter was developed from a speech; nor is there a speech in the collected papers of Margaret Sanger that corresponds in title or content with the chapter. As with Terrell's "What It Means to Be Colored in the Capital of the United States," the entry of this work into the speech literature dates from Judith Anderson's 1984 *Outspoken Women*. Using the same text as appears in *The Pivot of Civilization*, including its decidedly unspeechlike proem from William Blake's "Garden of Love," Anderson retitled it "A Moral Necessity for Birth Control" and asserted that it "was delivered numerous times for the American Birth Control League during 1921–22" before being reprinted in Sanger's book.

Anderson provided no documentation, but that did not stop "A Moral Necessity for Birth Control" from taking on a life of its own. Eight years after showing up in Anderson's book, it was again anthologized as a speech, this time in Halford Ryan's *Contemporary American Public Discourse*. Ryan did not cite Anderson as his source, but he reiterated almost verbatim her language in stating that the address "was delivered several times during 1921–22 for the American Birth Control League."[37] In 2005 the same text, reprinted from Ryan's book, appeared in *American Rhetorical Discourse*, edited by Ronald Reid and James Klumpp, along with the now-familiar refrain that it "was delivered on numerous occasions in 1921–1922" as part of Sanger's campaign for the American Birth Control League.[38]

At least three abridged versions have also been published, the first in Robert Torricelli and Andrew Carroll's *In Our Own Words: Extraordinary Speeches of the American Century*, which silently elided the proem and the first seven paragraphs, plus an additional twenty-one paragraphs from the rest of the work. Torricelli and Carroll also replaced the title "A Moral

35. Jones, *Quest for Equality*, 283, states that Terrell's papers contain a handwritten copy of "What It Means to Be Colored in the Capital of the United States," but we have not been able to find one. Neither has Karlyn Kohrs Campbell, who states that no text of this work, other than the one published in the *Independent*, exists in either set of Terrell's collected papers. See Campbell's *Man Cannot Speak for Her: A Critical Study of Early Feminist Rhetoric* (New York: Praeger, 1989), 155.

36. Although Campbell and Walker both identify Terrell's discourse as a speech, they disagree about the audience. Campbell characterizes the United Women's Club of Washington, D.C., as Euro-American in composition, while Walker intimates that it was African-American. See Walker, *Rhetoric of Struggle*, 82; Karlyn Kohrs Campbell, "Mary Church Terrell," in *Women Public Speakers in the United States, 1925–1933: A Bio-Critical Sourcebook*, Karlyn Kohrs Campbell, ed. (Westport, Conn.: Greenwood Press, 1994), 108–19.

37. Halford Ross Ryan, ed., *Contemporary American Public Discourse: A Collection of Speeches and Critical Essays*, 3rd ed. (Prospect Heights, Ill.: Waveland, 1992), 1–11.

38. Ronald F. Reid and James F. Klumpp, eds., *American Rhetorical Discourse*, 3rd ed. (Long Grove, Ill.: Waveland, 2005), 819–30.

Necessity for Birth Control" with the words "An Ethical Necessity for Humanity" and expanded the provenance of the address by stating that Sanger delivered it "throughout the early 1920s."[39] The second abridgment, titled "The Morality of Birth Control," turned up in Maureen Harrison and Steve Gilbert's *Landmark American Speeches*. This text followed Torricelli and Carroll in expunging the proem and first seven paragraphs; it also excised nine other paragraphs. In a new wrinkle, Harrison and Gilbert have Sanger delivering the address on November 18, 1921, at the Park Theatre in New York City, rather than on multiple occasions.[40] A third redacted version appeared in *Words That Changed America*, edited by Alex Barnett, where it retains the title "A Moral Necessity for Birth Control" and is identified as "a famous address that she [Sanger] delivered many times in the early 1920s."[41]

When we started working on "A Moral Necessity for Birth Control," we never imagined that claims regarding its status as a speech could have been constructed out of whole cloth. Yet that appears to be precisely what happened. The text in Sanger's *Pivot of Civilization* does not bear any marks of an oral presentation. Almost half of its thirty-three paragraphs are composed of lengthy quotations from pro– or anti–birth control advocates, including the National Council of Catholic Women, Archbishop Patrick J. Hayes, Dean William Ralph Inge, the Fabian Society, and Lord Bertrand Dawson. There are no references to an audience, no mention of a rhetorical occasion, no signs of a speaker seeking to establish common ground

with listeners. We assumed Sanger must have revised her speech when preparing it for publication. But when we looked for evidence about its original presentation as a speech, none could be found—not in Sanger's autobiographical writings, not in the many biographies about her, not in the publications of the American Birth Control League, not in the documents collected in the Margaret Sanger Papers Microfilm Edition. We contacted Esther Katz, director of the Margaret Sanger Papers Project, who, in addition to editing the published volumes of Sanger's writings, is working on a digital edition of her speeches and articles. Professor Katz confirmed what we had come to suspect: There is no evidence that the chapter in question from *The Pivot of Civilization* had ever been presented as a speech. As with Terrell's "What It Means to Be Colored in the Capital of the United States," we faced no alternative but to expunge "A Moral Necessity for Birth Control" from the top 100 speeches of the century.

In place of these two works, we moved into the top 100 what were originally the speeches ranked number 101 and 102: Robert F. Kennedy's June 6, 1966, Day of Affirmation address at the University of Cape Town, in South Africa, and John Kerry's "Vietnam Veterans Against the War," presented before the Senate Foreign Relations Committee in Washington, D.C., on April 22, 1971. Both are worthy replacements. A work of considerable moral power and rhetorical sophistication, Kennedy's speech gave hope and support to the anti-apartheid movement at a time when other mainstream politicians in the United States were conspicuously silent about racial injustice in South Africa. Often known as Kennedy's "ripples of hope" address, it is quoted more frequently than any of his other works. Unlike Kennedy, Kerry was not a public figure when he gave his speech, but it made him one overnight and remains one of the most influential antiwar statements from the Vietnam era. Best known for its query "How do you ask a man to be the last man to die for a mistake?" it became a matter of controversy again during the 2004 presidential campaign, which Kerry lost to incumbent George W. Bush.

Editorial Methods

When we began the process of authenticating speeches, we anticipated that constructing texts of

39. Robert Torricelli and Andrew Carroll, eds., *In Our Own Words: Extraordinary Speeches of the American Century* (New York: Kodansha International, 1999), 68–70.

40. Maureen Harrison and Steve Gilbert, eds., *Landmark American Speeches, Volume III: The Twentieth Century* (Carlsbad, Calif.: Excellent Books, 2001), 173–83. This is an especially curious case. Sanger did speak at the Park Theatre on November 18, 1921, and her talk was titled "The Morality of Birth Control." Inexplicably, however, Harrison and Gilbert do not print the speech Sanger delivered on that occasion.

41. Alex Barnett, ed., *Words That Changed America: Great Speeches That Inspired, Challenged, Healed, and Enlightened* (Guilford, Conn.: Lyons Press, 2006), 176–179.

the addresses for which we located complete recordings would be a fairly straightforward task. We could not have been more wrong—which may explain why it has so seldom been attempted in previous anthologies. The older the recording, the greater the chance of passages being blurred by background noise, faulty equipment, or simply the ravages of time. But even recordings that are technologically pristine pose their own challenges. A speaker may cough or turn away from the microphone. The audience may applaud over a speaker's lines. The speaker may lose his or her place, omit a word, interject vocalized pauses, commit an error in grammar, or stumble over a phrase before regaining balance—especially when talking without benefit of notes. In some places, a speaker's imprecise articulation may make it hard to decipher his or her exact words. Then there are instances in which a speaker says the wrong thing and keeps going, perhaps unaware that he or she has misspoken. Dealing with all these circumstances required not only technical accuracy in transcription, but also the exercise of editorial judgment.

We realized early on that we would have to find a way to balance phonetic fidelity with the fact that we were creating written texts designed to be read. Including every false start, every vocalized pause (*uh, er, um*), and every hesitation would not have been productive. Such texts would be ill-suited for readers interested in the flow of political debate, the development of a speaker's arguments, and the structure of his or her discourse. Moreover, they would in some ways distort what happens when an audience listens to a speech. Oral discourse is fluid, fleeting, ephemeral—literally, words into the air—whereas print reifies a speaker's words and freezes them in time. Listeners do not fasten on a speaker's every hesitation, slip of the tongue, and vocalized pause. These and other disfluencies usually pass quickly in the flow of oral communication and are subordinated in the listener's consciousness unless they become so frequent as to distract from the speaker's message. On the printed page, however, they all arrest the eye and compel attention. In addition to being an annoyance for readers, they take on a perceptual prominence out of keeping with their status in the speech as delivered.

Yet we did not want to eliminate the uniquely oral flavor of those speeches for which we had audio or video recordings. Oral discourse *is* less tidy than expertly edited written prose. Speakers do repeat themselves; they do stop sentences and restart them; they do mispronounce words; they do make grammatical errors; they do use colloquialisms and violate standard rules of sentence structure. Although such things are usually cleaned up when speeches are edited for publication, we left the speaker's original phrasing unless doing so would render the text unintelligible. When that occurred, we corrected the text but included a footnote to indicate what the speaker actually said. The only major exceptions to this rule occurred either when a speaker uttered a vocalized pause or stumbled and quickly made a correction, usually before the next word or two. To have left in all such instances would have been needlessly distracting for readers and, we came to believe, would have done a disservice to the speakers themselves. When a speaker omitted a word or part of a word, we inserted the missing material in brackets. We have not used *sic* to highlight grammatical errors or unconventional usages.

With regard to matters of dialect and diction, we unfailingly respected the speaker's rhetorical choices. It was not uncommon for Malcolm X and Stokely Carmichael to employ both General American dialect and Black English in their speeches, and to do so as a matter of deliberate rhetorical strategy. Jesse Jackson and Martin Luther King would occasionally do the same thing. The usual approach has been to edit the texts of their speeches to accord with "proper" English. But doing so dramatically changes the tenor of their discourse and often obscures their rhetorical power. Carmichael, for example, ended his 1966 Black Power address at the University of California by saying, "Move over, or we goin' move on over you." To change Carmichael's wording so it reads "Move over, or we are going to move on over you" is to strip away the rage and defiance that were at the heart of his speech.

Other cases in point include Huey Long and Ann Richards. Part of Long's popularity came from his image as a man of the people, an image reinforced by his folksy idiom and conversational tone. Speaking extemporaneously at 180 words a minute, he sometimes produced lengthy, convoluted sentences that one can scour in vain for a corresponding subject and verb. Yet when one listens to Long's speeches, the sentences work, and there is no evidence that the millions of Americans who supported his Share Our Wealth Society were the least bit bothered by his diction or syntax. Unlike Long, who usually spoke with very few notes, Richards had a carefully prepared manuscript for her keynote address at the 1988 Democratic National Convention, but it was her decision to "talk Texan" that brought the words alive and made her speech so memorable. There is no way to capture her Texas twang on the printed page, but we did the best we could by faithfully reproducing her colloquialisms, contractions, and vernacular diction.

As we worked to provide reader-friendly texts that captured the oral—and aural—nature of the speeches, we realized we would have to confront yet another issue. All the speeches for which we had audio or video recordings already existed in print. In every case, we discovered that there were discrepancies in content—sometimes minor, sometimes major—between the existing texts and what the speakers actually said. In addition to correcting the content, however, we discovered that we would have to paragraph and punctuate the speeches in a manner that would best convey the way they were delivered. There are no paragraph breaks or punctuation marks in spoken discourse. Everything has to be communicated by the speaker's inflections, tempo, pauses, and tone of voice. Indeed, the punctuation marks of written prose originally developed as a way of conveying in print the caesuras and cadences of oral discourse. Today they exist for the convenience of readers. A phonetically unsullied text would consist of an unbroken string of words with no punctuation and no paragraphing.

The paragraphing of existing speech texts was random at best. In many cases, there was no standard paragraphing. Newspapers paragraph speeches to make them easy to read in narrow columns. Speakers (or speechwriters) may paragraph them one way when developing the speech and another way when preparing the reading copy. Anthologists who are print oriented tend to favor longer paragraphs that capture more complete units of thought. The result can be a large number of texts of the same speech, with little uniformity in paragraphing. How much does this matter? Consider just one example, from Martin Luther King's "I Have a Dream." Here is how a portion of his address is often paragraphed:

> I have a dream that my four little children will one day live in a nation where they will not be judged by the color of their skin but by the content of their character.
>
> I have a dream today. I have a dream that one day down in Alabama, with its vicious racists, with its Governor having his lips dripping with the words of interposition and nullification, one day right there in Alabama little black boys and black girls will be able to join hands with little white boys and white girls as sisters and brothers.
>
> I have a dream today. I have a dream that one day every valley shall be exalted, every hill and mountain shall be made low, the rough places will be made plane and the crooked places will be made straight, and the glory of the Lord shall be revealed and all flesh shall see it together.

This reads smoothly, but it does not capture the way King spoke. When delivering the speech, he tagged the phrase "I have a dream today" that begins paragraphs two and three on to the ends of the previous paragraphs. As anyone who has heard the speech knows, this makes all the difference in the world. It was part of the rhythm and cadence of King's address, and it was crucial to the gathering momentum of his words as he moved out of the dream section into the "My Country 'Tis of Thee" section that preceded his conclusion. Here is how we have paragraphed these passages:

> I have a dream that my four little children will one day live in a nation where they will not be judged by the color of their skin but by the content of their character. I have a dream today.
>
> I have a dream that one day down in Alabama, with its vicious racists, with its Governor having his lips dripping with the words

of interposition and nullification, one day right there in Alabama little black boys and black girls will be able to join hands with little white boys and white girls as sisters and brothers. I have a dream today.

I have a dream that one day every valley shall be exalted, every hill and mountain shall be made low, the rough places will be made plane and the crooked places will be made straight, and the glory of the Lord shall be revealed and all flesh shall see it together.

This is one small portion of a single address, but it shows how paragraphing can affect the representation of oral discourse on the printed page. Throughout the book, we have paragraphed those works for which we have recordings to reflect both the content of the speech and the structure of the speech as delivered.

Paragraphing also became an issue in speeches for which we have only printed texts. They, too, were subject to the whims of whoever transcribed or published them. Anna Howard Shaw's "The Fundamental Principle of a Republic," which runs just shy of ten thousand words, was recorded stenographically and originally published in a mere fifteen paragraphs in the *Ogdensburg Advance and St. Lawrence Weekly Democrat* of July 1, 1915. Clarence Darrow's defense of Leopold and Loeb, taken down by a stenographer, did not want for paragraphs, but those paragraphs were sometimes so arbitrary as to make it hard to follow the progress of his argument. In both cases, as in other instances in which we had stenographic texts, we paragraphed the speeches in the interest of clarity and content. At times, we also adjusted the formatting in printed speeches for which we did not have stenographic accounts to fit the layout of the book, to maintain the clarity of a speaker's argument, or to keep paragraphs from dragging on across several pages. Had we not done so, a work such as Robert La Follette's monumental "Free Speech in Wartime" might have been rendered all but unreadable.

Principles of paragraphing changed over the course of the twentieth century, but not as much as approaches to punctuation. When dealing with texts from early in the century, we sometimes faced a bewildering array of commas, dashes, semicolons, and exclamation points that did more to cloud a speaker's

meaning than to illuminate it. Conversely, some printed speeches suffered from a lack of punctuation or from misplaced punctuation marks. Although one can debate the merits of maintaining the original punctuation as opposed to modernizing it in the interests of clarity and consistency, we opted for the latter course. The same is true with regard to spelling, italics, capitalization (of initial letter or entire word), and boldface. When necessary, we also changed parentheses to dashes as needed to prevent confusion about whether the parenthetical information came from us or was part of the original text.

When printed texts contained internal headings, we eliminated them because they were added later and were not part of the speech when it was delivered. We also deleted indicators of applause in the printed texts that contained them. This was consistent with our decision not to include applause markers in the recorded speeches. Had we included them, the flow of some texts would have been interrupted so frequently as to compromise their readability. We also recognized that not all applause is created equal. It can be enthusiastic or perfunctory, momentary or sustained, subdued or thunderous. Making these kinds of distinctions, which are far from absolute, would have pulled us away from more important editorial tasks. Readers who want to know where listeners applauded can access recorded speeches on the Internet.

Annotations

Some public speeches live across the ages—Pericles' Funeral Oration, Sojourner Truth's "Ain't I a Woman," Abraham Lincoln's Gettysburg Address. Others perish almost immediately. All, however, are historically situated at the moment of delivery. The terminology, examples, events, people, and places referred to in a speech constitute a lexicon of the moment in time at which the words were uttered. Even addresses presented toward the end of the twentieth century contain references that are unknown to many people today. Although there is no way for readers to have the same associations, feelings, and responses as did listeners at the time the speeches in this volume were delivered, we have annotated the speeches to help bring them alive in a way that might not otherwise be possible.

This proved to be a massive undertaking, and nothing on a comparable scale has been attempted in previous speech anthologies. All told, the book contains more than two thousand annotations. Certain of the items we annotate will be familiar to some readers, but given the international reach of Oxford University Press, we did not want to assume that everyone who opens these pages will be equally conversant with American history or with the Western traditions that inform the speeches. The annotations are meant to help fill in the historical record and to provide greater context for understanding the speakers, their discourses, and the times in which they were delivered.

As a general rule, we sought to annotate any person, event, place, institution, law, court decision, and the like whose meaning was crucial to understanding a given speech.[42] Finding this information was often challenging, to say the least. Sometimes a speaker would make an offhand reference to something that was well known to his or her listeners but was not at all clear after the fact. We also found that speakers were not always accurate in their references. They may have misstated a name or date; they may have confused one piece of legislation with another; they may have articulated what was accepted knowledge at the time but has since been emended. When we discovered factual errors, we pointed them out in the annotations. Our sense is that the errors were usually inadvertent, but we do not attempt to make judgments about why they occurred in particular cases.

We also annotated as many quotations, paraphrases, literary allusions, and scriptural references as we could.[43] Many of these were easy to identify, but some were frustratingly elusive, and a few ended up being impossible to find. When possible, we identify both the author and the work from which a speaker quotes or paraphrases. In a few cases, we have been able to identify only the author. When there is no annotation, it means we have not been able to locate either the author or the work.

Among the things we discovered in the annotation process is that the speakers were not uniformly accurate in their quotations. When a speaker's written text included quotation marks, we kept them even though the putative quotation turned out to be a paraphrase. If the speaker's statement varied from the original by one or two inconsequential words—for example, the substitution of one demonstrative pronoun for another, or the inadvertent change of a tense—we do not identify the quotation as a paraphrase, especially given the fact that the text from which the speaker was working might itself have contained the error. However, if the change involved more than one or two words, or significantly changed the meaning of the original statement, we identify it as a paraphrase. In some cases, we found it helpful to label statements as closely paraphrased or as loosely paraphrased.

We also ran across the occasional apocryphal quotation. Over the years, spurious statements attributed to iconic figures such as Abraham Lincoln, Thomas Jefferson, William Penn, and Benjamin Franklin have become engrained in American culture. When such a statement cropped up in a speech, we noted that it could not be found in the extant writings of the person to whom it was ascribed. We also pointed out when a speaker misattributed a quotation, even though the quotation itself was genuine. Along the way, we discovered how dramatically the Internet has contributed to the proliferation of counterfeit quotations and incorrect attributions. This has come about partly through Web sites devoted to quotations; once an error takes root on one site, it is duplicated indiscriminately on others. But it has also come about through the speeches themselves. Once they are printed on the Internet, their quotations and attributions are treated as gospel. It is, for example, primarily because of Douglas MacArthur's "Duty, Honor, Country" speech at West Point in 1962 that the statement "Only the dead have seen the end of war" is widely attributed to Plato, when in fact the

---

42. With few exceptions, the annotations do not include birth and death dates for people who were alive when a speech was presented. Nor do we attempt to provide minihistories of the people and events identified in the annotations. We have tried to keep annotations as brief as possible while providing enough information to understand the importance to the speech of the item being annotated.

43. Unlike otherwise noted, all biblical citations are from the King James Version.

words were penned in 1922 by the Spanish-American philosopher George Santayana. Correcting this and other errors allows for a more accurate reading of the speeches; we can only hope it will also strike a small blow for historical veracity in general at a time when the line between fact and fiction has become increasingly blurred.[44]

Acknowledgments

No book of this scope and complexity can be completed without the help of many people. Most important on a day-to-day basis were the research assistants at the University of Wisconsin, Texas A&M University, and Baylor University who aided at various stages with scores of tasks, large and small. They include Hillary Bajema, Ashley Barrett, Pamela Conners, Terri Easley, Elizabeth Galewski, Rachel M. Harlow, Paul Hendrickson, B. Wayne Howell, Michelle Lavigne, Adam Lee, Robert McClellen, Kathryn Palmer, Maegan Parker, Heather Stur, Maia Surdam, Trina Tritz, Rebecca Watts, and Diana Winkelman. Jeffrey Lucas and Ryan Lucas also contributed during the early stages of archival research and textual authentication. We were especially fortunate to have the assistance of Paul Stob, whose participation spanned almost the entire life of the project, first as a master's student at Texas A&M and then as a doctoral candidate at Wisconsin. It is no exaggeration to say that he has been well-nigh indispensable.

Nor could we have proceeded far without the support of a wide range of public and private libraries, foundations, and other institutions that responded generously to our inquiries and requests. They include the Bentley Historical Library, University of Michigan; the Brander Matthews Collection, Columbia University; the Cesar E. Chavez Foundation; the Chicago Bar Society; the *Chicago Tribune*; the Archives Division of the Circuit Court of Cook County; C-SPAN; the Detroit Public Library; the Emma Goldman Papers; the George Bush Presidential Library and Museum;

the Graduate Theological Union; Houghton Library, Harvard University; the Jimmy Carter Presidential Library and Museum; the Eisenhower Presidential Library and Museum; the Eleanor Roosevelt Papers; the Elizabeth Glaser Pediatric AIDS Foundation; the F. W. Olin Library, Mills College; the Franklin D. Roosevelt Presidential Library and Museum; the General Douglas MacArthur Foundation; the Gerald R. Ford Presidential Library and Museum; the Hubert H. Humphrey Institute of Public Affairs; the Indiana State Historical Society; the Institut National de l'Audiovisuel; the John F. Kennedy Presidential Library and Museum; Liberty University; the Library of Congress; the Lyndon Baines Johnson Library and Museum; the Margaret Sanger Papers Project; the Charles Deering McCormick Library of Special Collections, Northwestern University; the Moorland-Spingarn Research Center, Howard University; the Museum of Television and Radio; the National Archives and Records Administration; the National Baseball Hall of Fame and Museum; the New York Public Library; the Nixon Presidential Materials Project; the Nobel Foundation; the Ogdensburg, New York, Public Library; the Papers of Benjamin Franklin; the Schomburg Center for Research in Black Culture; *Sporting News*; Tamiment Library, New York University; the Ronald Reagan Presidential Foundation and Library; Smith College; Swedish Radio, Limited; the United Nations; the United States District Court for the Southern District of New York; the United States Military Academy at West Point; the University of Cape Town; the Walter P. Reuther Library, Wayne State University; Wellesley College; Widener Library, Harvard University; the William J. Clinton Presidential Library; and the Wisconsin Historical Society.

We are also thankful to the many individuals who shared their expertise with us: Amina Adam, Assiya Akanay, Burt Altman, Robert Asen, Andrew Bandstra, James L. Baughman, Freddy Berowski, Christine Bicknell, Allida Black, Ernest G. Bormann, Steve Branch, Alan Brinkley, Ferald Bryan, Christopher Canning, John M. Cooper, Phil Costello, Christopher Decker, Vicki Denby, Erik Doxtader, Annika Ekdahl, Peter Filardo, Ed Folsom, Scott Forsythe, David A. Franz, Suzanne

---

44. Our procedure was to secure at least two verifiable sources for every annotation. We approached each piece of information with skepticism and tried to verify each fact and interpretation for ourselves, when possible through primary sources.

M. Goldberg, Cathy Moran Hajo, Robert Haveman, Kelly Hendren, Hal Higdon, Michele Hilmes, Lynne Hollander, Inga Holmberg, Robert Glenn Howard, Glen Jeansonne, Richard J. Jensen, Richard L. Johannesen, Nicholas Johnson, Esther Katz, Robert Kraig, Timothy Larsen, Elizabeth Leake, Jennifer B. Lee, Gail Malmgreen, Russell Maylone, Richard P. McBrien, Stephanie McCoy, James Briggs Murray, Scott Murray, Robert Novak, Ayala Ochert, Kate Ohno, Parker Palmer, Kimberly Parker, Barry Pateman, Bruce Perry, Sigrid P. Perry, Jane Purvis, Alison N. Quammie, Prema Ramnath, Mark Renovitch, David Ricci, Kurt Ritter, Zachary Roberts, Peter Robinson, Wendy Rogers, Kathleen Schmeling, Christel Schmidt, Romi Sison, James B. Stewart, Lawrence Tribe, Chris R. Vanden Bossche, Melissa Walker, Richard D. White Jr., Nanci A. Young, Susan Zaeske, and James M. Zobel.

J. Michael Hogan, Davis W. Houck, John M. Murphy, Angela G. Ray, and Mary E. Stuckey all read portions of the manuscript. Their comments have sharpened our accuracy and our judgment.

We are extremely fortunate that Margaret Procario was available to proofread the entire book. She did so with a close and discerning eye that saved us from more than a few factual errors and stylistic infelicities.

Rob Lewis was instrumental in helping us locate the partial recording of Eleanor Roosevelt's "The Struggle for Human Rights" at the Institut National de l'Audiovisuel. Not only did he navigate his way expertly through the Institut's collections, but he provided an initial translation of the French recording of Roosevelt's remarks. Mary Louise Roberts kindly gave of her time and expertise to collaborate on the final translation.

This book would not exist without the survey we conducted in 1999 to determine the top 100 American speeches of the twentieth century. Denise Solomon patiently educated us on the ins and outs of survey research and helped design an elegant survey instrument and analytical scheme that would produce methodologically sound results. Leanne Knobloch coded the data and produced the statistical analyses of them. And, of course, we are grateful to all the scholars who responded to the survey. Far from being a simple fill-in-the-blanks exercise, it took considerable time and effort on the part of respondents. Their collective expertise produced a set of rankings that we believe will stand the test of time.

Nor would this book exist without Peter Labella, our editor at Oxford University Press. His understanding of the project, his counsel, and his unwavering support have been invaluable. We are also grateful to Brian Black, our production editior at Oxford for his efficiency, his patience, and his attention to detail in handling all the vicissitudes involved in getting such a book properly into print.

Finally, we are indebted to our spouses, Patricia Lucas and Laurel Medhurst. This book, like our lives, is better because of them.

Russell Conwell

⧖

Acres of Diamonds

1900–1925

Throughout American history, men and women have used the lecture circuit to spread their ideas and, often, to earn a lucrative livelihood. During the period 1850–1925 alone, the roster of celebrated lecturers included Wendell Phillips, Ralph Waldo Emerson, Frederick Douglass, Elizabeth Cady Stanton, Mark Twain, Francis Willard, Anna Howard Shaw, and William Jennings Bryan. No speaker, however, was in greater demand than Russell Conwell. A star of the lecture circuit for almost six decades, he was best known for "Acres of Diamonds," which he delivered more than 6,000 times from its initial presentation in 1870 to its final reprise in 1925.

In addition to speaking in every state of the Union, Conwell gave "Acres of Diamonds" in at least a dozen foreign countries. At a time when most lecturers were getting $100 a week and paying their own expenses, he received $150 per lecture, plus expenses. His annual income from lecturing at times exceeded $50,000, and over the course of his career he may have earned as much as $1 million from "Acres of Diamonds" alone. Much of that money he plowed back into a night school he established in Philadelphia for industrious students who could not afford to attend school full time. Today that school has grown into Temple University.

The skills that made Conwell a feature attraction on the lecture circuit also made him a pulpit orator of the first rank. He was ordained as a Baptist minister in 1881, and the next year he moved to Grace Baptist Church in Philadelphia, an affiliation he would maintain until his death in 1925. Under the impetus of Conwell's preaching, Grace became the largest Baptist church in the United States. The demand to hear Conwell preach was so great that Grace had to institute a policy whereby nonmembers were required to obtain tickets for admission to Sunday services.

Given its lofty reputation, "Acres of Diamonds" sometimes strikes modern readers as a disappointment. There is no eloquence here in the grand style, no rhetorical artistry on the order of Abraham Lincoln's Gettysburg Address or Martin Luther King's "I Have a Dream." The speech consists of a series of narratives designed to illustrate the fact that the resources for success—personal and financial—are always close at hand if one is industrious enough to find them. After the opening story of Al Hafed, with which Conwell invariably began, much of the speech's structure can be rearranged without doing serious damage to the whole. Moreover, while Conwell's stories were perfectly in tune with his era, many are not well suited to twenty-first-century attitudes and sensibilities.

Nor is there any way for a printed text to bring Conwell's words to life. Dramatizing his stories with pantomime, vocal imitation, and an unerring sense of timing, he was mesmerizing on the platform. A tall, well-built man, he used all his physical and vocal resources to establish what he called "a sort of spiritual communication" with listeners. Although he never spoke from manuscript—partly to enhance the bond with his auditors, partly to ease the task of adapting to constantly changing audiences and occasions—several versions of the speech were published during his lifetime. The text printed here is from the 1905 edition.

◇◇◇◇◇◇◇◇◇◇◇◇◇◇◇◇◇◇◇◇◇◇◇◇◇◇◇◇◇◇◇◇

The acres of diamonds of which I propose to speak today are to be found in your homes, or near to them, and not in some distant land. I cannot better introduce my thought than by the relation of a little incident that occurred to a party of American travelers beyond the Euphrates River.[1]

We passed across the great Arabian Desert, coming out at Baghdad, passed down the river to the Arabian Gulf, and on our way down we hired an Arabian guide to show us all the wonderful things connected with the ancient history and scenery. And that guide was very much like the barbers whom men find in this country today—that is, he thought it was not only his duty to guide us but also to entertain us with stories both curious and weird and ancient and modern, many of which I have forgotten, and I am glad I have. But there is one I remember today. The old guide led the camel along by his halter, telling various stories, and once he took his Turkish cap from his head and swung it high in the air to give me to understand that he had something especially important to communicate, and then he told me this beautiful story:

There once lived on the banks of the Indus River[2] an ancient Persian by the name of Al Hafed.

He owned a lovely cottage on a magnificent hill, from which he could look down upon the glittering river and the glorious sea; he had wealth in abundance, fields, grain, orchards, money at interest, a beautiful wife, and lovely children, and he was contented. Contented because he was wealthy, and wealthy because he was contented.

And one day there visited this Al Hafed an ancient priest, and that priest sat down before the fire and told him how diamonds were made, and said the old priest: "If you had a diamond the size of your thumb, you could purchase a dozen farms like this, and if you had a handful, you could purchase the whole county." Al Hafed was at once a poor man. He had not lost anything. He was poor because he was discontented, and he was discontented because he thought he was poor. He said: "I want a mine of diamonds; what is the use of farming a little place like this? I want a mine and I will have it."

He could hardly sleep that night, and early in the morning he went and wakened the priest and said: "I want you to tell me where you can find diamonds." Said the old priest: "If you want diamonds, go and get them." "Won't you please tell me where I can find them?" "Well, if you go and find high mountains, with a deep river running between them, over white sand, in this white sand you will find diamonds." "Well," said he, "I will go."

So he sold his farm, collected his money, and went to hunt for diamonds. He began, very properly,

1. Running from Turkey to the Persian Gulf, the Euphrates was a vital source of water for the flowering of ancient civilizations in the Middle East.

2. Covering a distance of 1,800 miles, the Indus originates in western Tibet and flows through parts of India and Pakistan before emptying in the Arabian Sea.

with the Mountains of the Moon[3] and came down through Egypt and Palestine. Years passed. He came over through Europe, and, at last, in rags and hunger he stood a pauper on the shores of the great Bay of Barcelona. And when that great tidal wave[4] came rolling in through the Pillars of Hercules[5] he threw himself into the incoming tide and sank beneath its foaming crest, never again to rise in this life.

Here the guide stopped to fix some dislocated baggage, and I said to myself: "What does he mean by telling me this story! It was the first story I ever read in which the hero was killed in the first chapter."

But he went on: The man who purchased Al Hafed's farm led his camel one day out to the stream in the garden to drink. As the camel buried his nose in the water, the man noticed a flash of light from the white sand and reached down and picked up a black stone with a strange eye of light in it which seemed to reflect all the hues of the rainbow. He said, "It's a wonderful thing," and took it in his house, where he put it on his mantel and forgot all about it.

A few days afterwards the same old priest came to visit Al Hafed's successor. He noticed a flash of light from the mantel and, taking up the stone, exclaimed: "Here is a diamond! Has Al Hafed returned?" "Oh, no, that is not a diamond; that is nothing but a stone that we found out in the garden." "But," said the priest, "that is a diamond!" And together they rushed out into the garden and stirred up the white sands with their fingers, and there came up other more beautiful gems, and more valuable than the first.

And that was the guide's story. And it is, in the main, historically true. Thus were discovered the wonderful mines of Golconda.[6] Again the guide swung his cap and said: "Had Al Hafed remained at home and dug in his own cellar or garden or under his own wheat fields, he would have found acres of diamonds." And this discovery was the founding of the line of the Great Moguls,[7] whose magnificent palaces are still the astonishment of all travelers. He did not need to add the moral. But that I may teach by illustration, I want to tell you the story that I then told him.

We were sort of exchanging works; he would tell me a story and I would tell him one, and so I told him about the man in California, living on his ranch there, who read of the discovery of gold in the southern part of the state. He became dissatisfied and sold his ranch and started for new fields in search of gold. His successor, Colonel Sutter,[8] put a mill on the little stream below the house, and one day when the water was shut off, his little girl went down to gather some of the white sand in the race way, and she brought some of it into the house to dry it. And while she was sifting it through her fingers, a gentleman, a visitor there, noticed the first shining sands of gold ever discovered in upper California. That farm that the owner sold to go somewhere else to find gold has added eighteen millions of dollars to the circulating medium of the world; and they told me there sixteen years ago that the owner of one-third of the farm received a twenty-dollar gold piece for every fifteen minutes of his life.

That reminds me of what Professor Agassiz[9] told his summer class in mineralogy in reference to Pennsylvania. I live in Pennsylvania, but being a Yankee,[10] I enjoy telling this story. This man owned a farm, and he did just what I would do if I owned a farm in that state—sold it. Before he sold it, he concluded that he would go to Canada to collect coal oil. The professors will tell you that this stuff was first found in connection with living springs, floating on the water. This man wrote to his cousin in Canada, asking for employment collecting this oil. The cousin wrote back that he did not understand the work. The farmer then studied all the books on coal oil, and when

---

3. Ancient name for the Rwenzori Mountains of central Africa.

4. Conwell is referring to a tidal wave caused by the destruction of the legendary city of Atlantis.

5. The Rock of Gibraltar in Europe and the Jebel Musa in Africa, which lay on either side of the Strait of Gibraltar and, according to legend, were raised by Hercules.

6. The famed Golconda diamond mines were located on the lower portion of India's Kistna River.

7. Rulers of India from the 16th through the 18th centuries.

8. John Sutter; the discovery of gold on his land in 1848 set off the California gold rush.

9. Harvard scientist Louis Agassiz (1807–1873).

10. A person born or living in New England.

he knew all about it and the theories of the geologists concerning it from the formation of primitive coal beds to the present day, he removed to Canada to work for his cousin, first selling his Pennsylvania farm for eight hundred and thirty-three dollars.

The old farmer who purchased his estate went back of the barn one day to fix a place for the horses to drink and found that the previous owner had already arranged that matter. He had fixed some plank edgewise, running from one bank towards the other and resting edgewise a few inches into the water, the purpose being to throw over to one side a dreadful-looking scum that the cattle would not put their noses in, although they would drink the water below it. That man had been damming back for twenty-one years that substance, the discovery of which the official geologist pronounced to be worth to the state the sum of a hundred millions of dollars. Yet that man had sold his farm for eight hundred and thirty-three dollars. He sold one of the best oil-producing farms and went somewhere else to find—nothing.

That story brought to my mind the incident of the young man in Massachusetts. There was a young man in college studying mining and mineralogy, and while he was a student they employed him for a time as a tutor and paid him fifteen dollars a week for the special work. When he graduated, they offered him a professorship and forty-five dollars a week. When this offer came, he went home and said to his mother: "Mother, I know too much to work for forty-five dollars a week; let us go out to California, and I will stake out gold mines and copper and silver mines, and we will be rich." His mother said it was better to stay there. But as he was an only son, he had his way, and they sold out and started. But they only went to Wisconsin, where he went into the employ of the Superior Copper Mining Company at a salary of fifteen dollars a week.

He had scarcely left the old estate before the farmer who bought it was digging potatoes and bringing them through the yard in a large basket. The farms there are almost all stone-wall, and the gate was narrow, and as he was working his basket through, pulling first one side, then the other, he noticed in that stone wall a block of native silver about eight inches square. This professor of mining and mineralogy was born on that place, and when he sold out he sat on that very stone while he was making the bargain. He had passed it again and again. He had rubbed it with his sleeve until it had reflected his countenance and said, "Come, now, here is a hundred thousand dollars for digging—dig me."

I should enjoy exceedingly telling these stories, but I am not here to relate incidents so much as to bring lessons that may be helpful to you. I love to laugh at the mistakes of these men until the thought comes to me: "How do you know what that man in Wisconsin is doing—and that man in Canada?" It may be that he sits by his hearth today and shakes his sides and laughs at us for making the same mistakes and feels that after all he is in comparatively good company.

We have all made the same mistakes. Is there anyone here that has not? If there is one that says you have never made such a blunder, I can argue with you that you have. You may not have had the acres of diamonds and sold them. You may not have had wells of oil and sold them—and yet you may have done so. A teacher in the Wilkes-Barre[11] schools came to me after one of my lectures and told me that he owned a farm of fifty acres that he sold for five dollars an acre, and a few weeks before my lecture it was sold for thirty-eight thousand dollars because they had found a silver mine on it. You say you never have made any such mistakes. Are you rich today? Are you worth five million dollars? Of course not! Why not? "I never had opportunity to get it." Now you and I can talk. Let us see!

Were you ever in the mercantile business? Why didn't you get rich? "Because I couldn't; there was so much competition and all that." Now, my friend, didn't you carry on your store just as I carried on my father's store? I don't like to tell how I conducted my father's store. But when he went away to purchase goods, he would sometimes leave me in charge, and a man would come in and say, "Do you keep jackknives?" "No, we don't keep jackknives." Then another would come in and ask, "Do you keep jackknives?" "No, we don't!" And still another. "No,

---

11. City in eastern Pennsylvania.

we don't keep jackknives; why are you all bothering me about jackknives!"

Did you keep store in that way? Do you ask me what was the fault? The difficulty was that I never had learned by bitter experience the foundation of business success and that it is the same foundation that underlies all true success, the foundation that underlies Christianity and morality: that it is the whole of man's life to live for others, and he that can do the most to elevate, enrich, and inspire others shall reap the greatest reward himself.

Not only so says the Holy Book, but so says business common sense. I will go into your store and ask: Do you know neighbor A that lives over a couple of squares from your store? "Yes, he deals here." Where did he come from? "I don't know." Has he any children? "I don't know." Does he have a school in his district? Does he go to church? "I don't know." Is he a married man? "I don't know." What ticket does he vote? "I don't know, and I don't care!"

Is that the way you do business? If it is, then you have been conducting your business as I carried on my father's store! And you do not succeed and are poor? I understand it. You can't succeed and I am glad of it, and I will give five dollars to see your failure announced in the newspaper tomorrow morning. The only way to succeed is to take an interest in the people around you and honestly work for their welfare.

"But," you say, "I have no capital." I am glad you haven't. I am sorry for the rich men's sons. Young man, if you have no capital, there is hope for you. According to the statistics collected in the city of Boston twenty years ago, ninety-six of every one hundred successful merchants were born poor; and trustworthy statistics also show that of the rich men's sons not one in a thousand dies rich. I am sorry for the rich men's sons unless their fathers be wise enough to bring them up like poor children. If you haven't any capital, life is full of hope to you.

A. T. Stewart[12] started out with a dollar and a half to begin on, and he lost all but sixty-two and a half cents the first afternoon. That was before he was a schoolteacher. He purchased things the people did not want. He said, "I will never do that again," and he went around to the doors and found what the people wanted and invested his sixty-two and a half cents safely, for he knew what people wanted, and went on until he was worth forty-two millions of dollars—and what man has done men can do again.

You may say, "I can't be acquainted with every man in the county and know his wife and children in order to succeed." If you know a few fairly well, you may judge the world by them. John Jacob Astor[13] is said by one of his latest biographers to have had a mortgage on a millinery establishment. I always think when I reach this point that the ladies will say, "Fools rush in where angels fear to tread." They could not pay the interest on the mortgage, and he foreclosed and took possession. He went into partnership with the same man who failed and kept the old clerks and retained the old stock.

He went out and sat down on a bench in Union Park. What was he doing there? He was watching the women as they passed by. And when he saw a lady with her shoulders thrown back and her head up as if she didn't care if all the world was looking at her, he studied that bonnet, and before it was out of sight he knew every feather and ribbon and all about the frame, and—and—some men may be able to describe a bonnet, but I cannot. I don't believe there are words in the English language to do it. Then he went to the store and said, "Put such and such a bonnet in the window, for I know that there is one woman that likes it." And then he would go and watch for another style and return and have that put in the window with the other. And success came.

Some years ago I went into that store to find out about it for myself, and there I found the descendants of that man doing business, and it is the largest millinery firm in the world, with branch houses in all the large cities on the globe. That success was made because Astor studied into the matter and knew what the women wanted before he had the articles made.

12. Alexander Turney Stewart (1803–1876), Irish immigrant who established the first department store in New York City and became one of the wealthiest businessmen of his day.

13. German immigrant who came to the United States in 1784, set himself up in the fur business, and created one of the first great American fortunes.

But you say, "I cannot do it." You can do it. You say you have no capital—but you have a jackknife. I could not sleep if I did not have a jackknife in my pocket—a Yankee cannot. In Massachusetts there lived a man who was a carpenter and who was out of work. He sat around the stove until his wife told him to go outdoors, and he did—every man in Massachusetts is compelled by law to obey his wife! He sat down on the shore of the bay and whittled a soaked oak shingle until he made a chain that his children quarreled over. Then he whittled another.

Then a neighbor, coming in, advised him to whittle toys for sale. "I can't make toys," said he. "Yes, you can." "But I wouldn't know what to make." There is the whole thing—not in having the machinery or the capital, but in knowing what the people want. And so his friend said to the carpenter: "Why don't you ask your own children? See what they like, and perhaps other children will like the same thing."

He concluded to do so, and when his little girl came down, he said, "Mary, what kind of a toy would you like to have me make?" "Oh, a little doll cradle, and carriage, and horse," and a dozen other things. He began with his jackknife and made up these rough, unpainted toys. A friend of his sold them in a Boston shoe store at first and brought back twenty-five and fifty cents at a time, and then his wife began to be better natured. The wife always does get better natured when there is a prospect of money to divide. She came out and split up the wood while he made up the toys.

The last case I had as a lawyer before I entered the ministry, that man was on the stand, and I said to him: "When did you commence to whittle those toys?" "In 1870." "How much are the patents on those toys worth?" His answer was: Their actual value to him was seventy-eight thousand dollars, and it was a little less than seven years after the time when he began with his jackknife. And today I know that he is worth a hundred thousand dollars, and he has received it all from having consulted his own children and judging from them what other people's children wanted and trying to supply the demand. If a man takes an interest in people and knows what they need and endeavors to supply it, he must succeed.

Some of you who sit before me thinking you are poor are actually in possession of wealth, like the Baltimore lady who, fourteen years after her father's failure, found a costly diamond bracelet he had lost seventeen years before.

Many of you smile at the thought that you are in the actual possession of wealth. A shoemaker in Massachusetts sat around in the house until his wife drove him out with a broom, and then he went out into the backyard and sat down on an ash barrel. Nearby was a beautiful mountain stream, but I don't suppose that he thought of Tennyson's beautiful poem:

I chatter, chatter, as I flow,
To join the brimming river;
Men may come, and men may go,
But I go on forever.[14]

It was not a poetical situation, sitting on an ash barrel, and his wife in the kitchen with a mop. Then he saw a trout flash in the stream and hide under the bank, and he reached down and got the fish and took it into the house; and his wife took it and sent it to a friend in Worcester. The friend wrote back that he would give five dollars for another such a trout, and our shoemaker and his wife immediately started out to find it, man and wife now perfectly united, a five-dollar bill in prospect! They went up the stream to its source and followed it down to the brimming river, but there was not another trout to be found.

Then he went to the minister. That minister didn't know how trout grew, but he told them to go to the public library and, under a pile of dime novels, he would find Seth Green's book,[15] and that would give them the information they wanted. They did so and found out all about the culture of trout and began operations. They afterwards moved to the banks of the Connecticut River, and then to the Hudson, and now that man sends trout, fresh and packed in ice, all over the country and is a rich man. His wealth was in that backyard just as much twenty years before. But he did not discover it until his repeated failures had made his wife imperious.

I remember meeting, in western Pennsylvania, a distinguished professor who began as a country

---

14. From Alfred, Lord Tennyson, "The Brook" (1855).

15. *Trout Culture* (1873).

schoolteacher. He was determined to know his district, and he learned that the father of one of the boys was a maker of wagon wheels. He studied up all about making wagon wheels, and when that man's boy came to school, he told him all about it; and the boy went home and told his father, "I know more about wagon wheels than you do!" "That teacher is teaching that boy wonderfully," said the father. He told a farmer's boy all about the value of fertilizer for the soil, and he went home and told his father, and the old gentleman said, "How that boy is learning!" That teacher is now the president of a college and is a D.D., an LL.D., and a Ph.D.[16] He taught what the people wanted to know, and that made him successful.

Once I went up into the mountain region of New Hampshire to lecture, and I suffered a great deal from the cold. When I came back to Harvard, I said to a friend, who was a scientific man of great culture: "Professor, I am never going into New Hampshire to lecture again; never!" "Why?" "Because I nearly shivered the teeth out of my head." "And why did you shiver?" "Because the weather was cold." "Oh, no, no!" said my friend. "Then it was because I did not have bedclothes enough!" "No, no, it wasn't that."

Well," I said, "you are a scientific man, and I wish you would tell me, then, just why I shivered." "Well, sir," he replied, "it was because you didn't know any better." Said he: "Didn't you have in your pocket a newspaper?" "Oh, yes." "Well, why didn't you spread that over your bed? If you had, you would have been as warm as the richest man in America under all his silk coverlids; and you shivered because you did not know enough to put the two-cent paper over your bed."

How many women want divorces—and ought to have them, too! How many divorces originate something like this: A workingman comes in haste to his supper and sits down to eat potatoes that are about as hard as the rocks beside which they grew. He will chop them up and eat them in a hurry, and they won't digest well. They make him cross. He frets and scolds and perhaps he swears, he scarcely knows why, and then there is trouble.

If the good woman had only known enough of science to put in a pinch of salt, they would have come out mealy and luscious and eatable and ready to laugh themselves to pieces in edible joy, and he would have eaten them down in peace and satisfaction and with good digestion, and he would have arisen from the table with a smile on his face, and there would have been joy in that family—and all because of a pinch of salt. The lack in appreciating the value of little things often keeps us in poverty.

I want to ask the audience: Who are the great inventors of the world? Many will answer that it is a peculiar race of men, with intellects like lightning flashes and heads like bushel measures. But, in fact, inventors are usually ordinary practical thinkers. You may invent as much as they if you study on the question: What does the world need? It is not so difficult to prepare a machine, after all, as it is to find out just what people want. The Jacquard loom was invented by a working woman.[17] So was the printing roller.[18] So was the second-best cotton gin.[19] So was the mowing machine.[20]

I am out of all patience with myself because I did not invent the telephone. I had the same opportunity that the other boy[21] had. I put my ear down to the rail and heard the rumbling of the engine through the miles of track and arose and threw snowballs. The other boy arose and asked, "Why?" He discovered that it was caused by the generation of electricity

16. Doctor of Divinity, Doctor of Laws, Doctor of Philosophy.

17. Conwell is referring to the wife of Joseph Marie Jacquard (1752–1834), a French silk weaver. Although invention of the Jacquard loom is usually attributed to her husband, many have held through the years that she deserves credit as well.

18. Conwell may be referring to Elizabeth Mitton, whose role in the creation of the calico printing roller was identified in the *Monthly Review* (September 1842). Conwell's source, however, was likely Samuel Smiles's *Self-Help* (1866), which did not mention Mitton by name.

19. A reference to Catherine Littlefield Greene, who played an instrumental role in Eli Whitney's invention of the cotton gin.

20. Conwell is referring to the Manning mowing machine, patented in 1831 by William Manning but believed to have been invented by his wife, Ann Harned Manning.

21. Alexander Graham Bell.

by the wheels, and when he saw Edison's speaking machine,[22] he had the whole matter at a glance.

There was a Congressman once who resolved to talk sense; of course, he was an exception to the general rule. He was one day walking through the Treasury Department when a clerk said to him that it was a fine day. As he met other clerks, they remarked the same thing, and at last our Congressman said: "Why do you tell me that it is a fine day? I know that already. Now, if you could tell me what the weather will be tomorrow, it would be of some importance." A clerk caught the idea and began to think it over and entered into correspondence with the professor at Cincinnati.[23] That was the origin of our signal service. Soon we will know what the weather will be a week ahead. Yes, not many years hence, we will decide what weather we will have by a popular vote.

How simple all these mighty improvements and inventions seem when we study the simple steps of their evolution! Yet civilized men and women are greater today than ever before. We often think all great men are dead, and the longer they are dead, the greater they appear to have been. But, in fact, men are greater and women are nobler than ever before. We are building on the foundations of the past, and we must be exceeding[ly] small if we are not greater than they who laid them.

The world knows nothing of its greatest men. Some young man may say, "I am going to be great." "How?" "How?" "By being elected to an office." Shall the man be greater than the men who elect him? Shall the servant be greater than his master? That a man is in public office is no evidence of greatness. Even if you are great when you are in office, they will not call you great till after you die.

Another young man says, "I am going to be great when there comes a war." But success in war is not always an evidence of greatness. Historians are apt to credit a successful man with more than he really does, and with deeds that were performed by subordinates.

General Thomas[24] was one of the greatest generals of the war, yet an incident in his life illustrates this thought. After the battle of Nashville,[25] the soldiers, seeing him, cheered the hero and shouted, "Hurrah for the hero of Lookout Mountain."[26] This was distasteful to the General, and he ordered it to be stopped. Said he: "Talk about the hero of Lookout Mountain! Why, I was ordered by General Grant[27] to keep my troops at the foot of the mountain, and the enemy began to drop their shells among us, and I ordered my men to retreat, but they would not do it, and they charged and captured the works against my positive orders. Now they talk about the hero of Lookout Mountain!"

Yet as he was in command of that corps, he would naturally be credited with the victory of that charge, while the daring private or subordinate may never be mentioned in history. You can be as great at home and in private life as you can on fields of awful carnage. Greatness, in its noblest sense, knows no social or official rank.

I can see again a company of soldiers in the last war going home to be received by their native town officers. Did you ever think you would like to be a king or queen? Go and be received by your town officers, and you will know what it means. I shall never see again so proud a moment as that when, at the head of a company of troops, we were marching home to be received. I was but a boy in my teens. I can hear now distinctly the band playing, and see the people that were waiting. We marched into their town hall and were seated in the center. Then I was called to take a position on the platform with the town officers.

Then came the address of welcome. The old gentleman had never made a speech before, but he had written this, and walked up and down the pasture until he had committed it to memory. But he had

22. Conwell is referring to Thomas Edison's invention of the phonograph.

23. Cleveland Abbe, who helped pioneer the science of weather forecasting in the United States.

24. Union general George Henry Thomas (1816–1870).

25. December 15–16, 1864.

26. The Battle of Lookout Mountain, near Chattanooga, Tennessee, was fought in November 1863.

27. Ulysses S. Grant, commander in November 1863 of the Military Division of the Mississippi and soon thereafter named general in chief of all Union armies.

brought it with him and spread it out on the desk. The delivery of the speech by that good but nervous town official went something like this:

"Fellow Citizens—fellow citizens. We are—we are—we are very happy—we are—we are very happy to welcome back to our native town—these soldiers. Fellow citizens, we are very happy to welcome back to our native town these soldiers who have—who have—who have fought—who have fought and bled—and come back to their native town again. We are—we are—we are especially—especially pleased to see with us today this young hero. This young hero—to see this young hero—in imagination we have seen (remember that he said "in imagination")—we have seen him leading his troops on to battle. We have seen his—his—his shining sword, flashing in the sunshine, as he shouted to his troops, 'Come on!'"

Oh, dear, dear, dear, what did he know about war? That captain with his shining sword flashing in air, shouting to his troops, "Come on!" He never did it, never. If there had not often been a double line of flesh and blood between him and the enemy, he would not have been there that day to be received. If he had known anything about war, he would have known what any soldier in this audience can tell you—that it was next to a crime for an officer of infantry in time of danger to go ahead of his men. Do you suppose he is going out there to be shot in front by the enemy and in the back by his own men? That is no place for him.

And yet the hero of the reception hour was that boy. There stood in that house, unnoticed, men who had carried that boy on their backs through deep rivers, men who had given him their last draught of coffee, men who had run miles to get him food. And some were not there; some were sleeping their last sleep in their unknown graves. They had given their lives for the nation, but were scarcely noticed in the good man's speech. And the boy was the hero of the reception hour. Why? For no other reason under heaven but because he was an officer and these men were only private soldiers. Human nature often estimates men's greatness by the office they hold; yet office cannot make men great, nor noble, nor brave.

Any man may be great, but the best place to be great is at home. All men can make their kind better; they can labor to help their neighbors and instruct and improve the minds of the men, women, and children around them; they can make holier their own locality; they can build up the schools and churches around them; and they can make their own homes bright and sweet. These are the elements of greatness. It is here greatness begins, and if a man is not great in his own home or in his own school district, he will never be great anywhere.

William Jennings Bryan

⧖

Against Imperialism

INDIANAPOLIS, INDIANA
AUGUST 8, 1900

WHEN THE SPANISH-AMERICAN War began in April 1898, few people in the United States imagined that annexation of the Philippines might be one result. The aim of the war, as stated in the congressional resolution authorizing military action, was to ensure a free and independent Cuba. But on May 1, Commodore George Dewey defeated the Spanish fleet in Manila Bay, and the Treaty of Paris, which brought a formal end to the war in December 1898, ceded the entire Philippine Islands to the United States in exchange for $20 million. Thus the nation that had been born in revolt against British colonialism became itself a colonial power, but not without contention. Initial opposition proved so fierce that the peace treaty was barely ratified in the U.S. Senate. Debate over the Philippines remained heated for several years—especially after insurgent forces rebelled against American occupation—and even provoked a fistfight on the Senate floor in 1902.

The most prominent spokesman against imperialism was William Jennings Bryan, the "boy orator of the Platte" whose "Cross of Gold" oration had helped him capture the Democratic presidential nomination in 1896. Nominated again in 1900, he hoped to make the election a referendum on imperialism. On August 8, a month after being chosen as the party's standard-bearer at Kansas City, he presented his acceptance speech to an audience of 40,000 people at Military Park in Indianapolis. (The first major-party nominee to give his acceptance speech at the party's convention was Franklin Roosevelt in 1932.) Although Bryan spoke for ninety minutes without benefit of electronic amplification, his stentorian voice allowed him to be heard clearly throughout the vast assemblage.

Designed primarily for the national reading audience, the 8,600-word address was typeset before Bryan delivered it. Except for the extemporized second paragraph, he read the speech exactly as printed. Decrying imperialism as inconsistent with the principles of the American Revolution and free government, and portraying American rule as bringing "the thick darkness of perpetual vassalage" to the Philippines, he systematically refuted the major arguments advanced by defenders of imperialism. His conclusion, with its series of refrains beginning "Behold a republic…," is among the most eloquent in American history. Eight million copies of the speech were distributed as campaign literature. Although

Bryan lost his bid for the White House—as he would again in 1908—his speech remains a classic statement on the dangers of empire that is as applicable to our own time as it was to his.

⋄⋄⋄⋄⋄⋄⋄⋄⋄⋄⋄⋄⋄⋄⋄⋄⋄⋄⋄⋄⋄⋄⋄⋄⋄⋄⋄⋄⋄⋄⋄⋄⋄⋄⋄⋄⋄⋄

Mr. Chairman[1] and Members of the Notification Committee: I shall, at an early day and in a more formal manner, accept the nomination which you tender, and I shall at that time discuss the various questions covered by the Democratic platform.[2] It may not be out of place, however, to submit a few observations at this time upon the general character of the contest before us and upon the question which is declared to be of paramount importance in this campaign.

I feel that I owe an apology or an explanation to the people who are to listen for the fact that I must read what I am going to say. It would be more pleasant to me and more agreeable to you to speak without notes, but I want to address that larger constituency which we reach through the newspapers, for it is a thousand times as numerous as any crowd that assembles here, and it is that I might speak to all throughout the land I have committed to writing what I desire to say and will ask your indulgence while I read my speech.[3]

When I say that the contest of 1900 is a contest between democracy on the one hand and plutocracy on the other, I do not mean to say that all our opponents have deliberately chosen to give to organized wealth a predominating influence in the affairs of the government, but I do assert that on the important issues of the day the Republican Party is dominated by those influences which constantly tend to substitute the worship of mammon[4] for the protection of the rights of man.

In 1859 Lincoln said that the Republican Party believed in the man and the dollar, but that in case of conflict, it believed in the man before the dollar.[5] This is the proper relation which should exist between the two. Man, the handiwork of God, comes first; money, the handiwork of man, is of inferior importance. Man is the master, money the servant, but upon all important questions today Republican legislation tends to make money the master and man the servant.

The maxim of Jefferson, "Equal rights to all and special privileges to none,"[6] and the doctrine of Lincoln that this should be a government "of the people, by the people, and for the people,"[7] are being disregarded and the instrumentalities of government are being used to advance the interests of those who are in a position to secure favors from the government.

The Democratic Party is not making war upon the honest acquisition of wealth; it has no desire to discourage industry, economy, and thrift. On the contrary, it gives to every citizen the greatest possible stimulus to honest toil when it promises him protection in the enjoyment of the proceeds of his labor. Property rights are most secure when human rights are most respected. Democracy strives for civilization in which every member of society will share according to his merits.

No one has a right to expect from a society more than a fair compensation for the services which he renders to society. If he secures more, it is at the expense of someone else. It is no injustice to him to prevent his doing injustice to another. To him who would, either through class legislation or, in the

---

1. Congressman James D. Richardson of Tennessee, permanent chairman of the Democratic National Convention.

2. Adopted at the Democratic National Convention, held in Kansas City, Missouri, July 4–6, 1900.

3. This paragraph is from the *Indianapolis Journal*, August 9, 1900; the remainder of the text is from the pamphlet version of the speech.

4. Biblical term for avarice, riches, and worldly gain (Matthew 6:24, Luke 16:13).

5. Abraham Lincoln made this statement in a public letter of April 6, 1859.

6. Although consistent with Thomas Jefferson's philosophy, these words do not appear in his writings. They do appear in the December 1890 Ocala Platform of the Kansas Farmer's Alliance, with which Bryan was doubtless familiar.

7. From Lincoln's Gettysburg Address, November 19, 1863.

absence of necessary legislation, trespass upon the rights of another, the Democratic Party says, "Thou shalt not."[8]

Against us are arrayed a comparatively small but politically and financially powerful number who really profit by Republican policies; but with them are associated a large number who, because of their attachment to their party name, are giving their support to doctrines antagonistic to the former teachings of their own party.

Republicans who used to advocate bimetallism now try to convince themselves that the gold standard is good; Republicans who were formerly attached to the greenback are now seeking an excuse for giving national banks control of the nation's paper money;[9] Republicans who used to boast that the Republican party was paying off the national debt are now looking for reasons to support a perpetual and increasing debt; Republicans who formerly abhorred a trust[10] now beguile themselves with the delusion that there are good trusts and bad trusts, while, in their minds, the line between the two is becoming more and more obscure; Republicans who, in times past, congratulated the country upon the small expense of our standing army are now making light of the objections which are urged against a large increase in the permanent military establishment; Republicans who gloried in our independence when the nation was less powerful now look with favor upon a foreign alliance; Republicans who three years ago condemned "forcible annexation"[11] as immoral and even criminal are now sure that it is both immoral and criminal to oppose forcible annexation. That partisanship has already blinded many to present dangers is certain; how large

a portion of the Republican Party can be drawn over to the new policies remains to be seen.

For a time Republican leaders were inclined to deny to opponents the right to criticize the Philippine policy of the administration, but upon investigation they found that both Lincoln and Clay[12] asserted and exercised the right to criticize a President during the progress of the Mexican War.[13] Instead of meeting the issue boldly and submitting a clear and positive plan for dealing with the Philippine question, the Republican convention adopted a platform the larger part of which was devoted to boasting and self-congratulation.[14]

In attempting to press economic questions upon the country to the exclusion of those which involve the very structure of our government, the Republican leaders give new evidence of their abandonment of the earlier ideals of their party and of their complete subserviency to pecuniary considerations. But they shall not be permitted to evade the stupendous and far-reaching issue which they have deliberately brought into the arena of politics.

When the President, supported by a practically unanimous vote of the House and Senate, entered upon a war with Spain for the purpose of aiding the struggling patriots of Cuba,[15] the country, without regard to party, applauded. Although the Democrats realized that the administration would necessarily gain a political advantage from the conduct of a war which, in the very nature of the case, must soon end in a complete victory, they vied with the Republicans in the support which they gave to the President. When the war was over and the Republican leaders began to suggest the propriety of a colonial policy, opposition at once manifested itself. When the President finally laid before the Senate a treaty which recognized the

8. Bryan is echoing language from the Ten Commandments (Exodus 20:2–17, Deuteronomy 5:6–21).

9. These passages refer to long-standing disputes over the U.S. money supply, with most Democrats favoring bimetallism and currency expansion and most Republicans supporting the gold standard and currency contraction.

10. A corporate monopoly organized under the legal device of trusteeship; the first American trust was organized by John D. Rockefeller in 1882.

11. Bryan is referring to forcible annexation of the Philippines.

12. Henry Clay, U. S. Senator and three-time presidential candidate (1777–1852).

13. The Mexican War (1846–1848) aroused the most sustained antiwar movement in American history before the conflict in Vietnam.

14. The Republican National Convention met in Philadelphia, Pennsylvania, June 19–21, 1900.

15. The Spanish-American War of 1898.

independence of Cuba but provided for the cession of the Philippine Islands to the United States,[16] the menace of imperialism became so apparent that many preferred to reject the treaty and risk the ills that might follow, rather than take the chance of correcting the errors of the treaty by the independent action of this country.

I was among the number of those who believed it better to ratify the treaty and end the war, release the volunteers, remove the excuse for war expenditures, and then give the Filipinos the independence which might be forced from Spain by a new treaty. In view of the criticism which my action aroused in some quarters,[17] I take this occasion to restate the reasons given at that time.

I thought it safer to trust the American people to give independence to the Filipinos than to trust the accomplishment of that purpose to diplomacy with an unfriendly nation. Lincoln embodied an argument in the question when he asked, "Can aliens make treaties easier than friends can make laws?"[18] I believe that we are now in a better position to wage a successful contest against imperialism than we would have been had the treaty been rejected. With the treaty ratified, a clean-cut issue is presented between a government by consent and a government by force, and imperialists must bear the responsibility for all that happens until the question is settled.

If the treaty had been rejected, the opponents of imperialism would have been held responsible for any international complications which might have arisen before the ratification of another treaty. But whatever difference of opinion may have existed as to the best method of opposing a colonial policy, there never was any difference as to the great importance of the question and there is no difference now as to the course to be pursued.

The title of Spain being extinguished, we were at liberty to deal with the Filipinos according to American principles. The Bacon resolution, introduced a month before hostilities broke out at Manila, promised independence to the Filipinos on the same terms that it was promised to the Cubans.[19] I supported this resolution and believe that its adoption prior to the breaking out of hostilities would have prevented bloodshed, and that its adoption at any subsequent time would have ended hostilities.

If the treaty had been rejected, considerable time would have necessarily elapsed before a new treaty could have been agreed upon and ratified, and during that time the question would have been agitating the public mind. If the Bacon resolution had been adopted by the Senate and carried out by the President, either at the time of the ratification of the treaty or at any time afterwards, it would have taken the question of imperialism out of politics and left the American people free to deal with their domestic problems. But the resolution was defeated by the vote of the Republican Vice President,[20] and from that time to this a Republican Congress has refused to take any action whatever in the matter.

When hostilities broke out at Manila,[21] Republican speakers and Republican editors at once sought to lay the blame upon those who had delayed the ratification of the treaty, and, during the progress of the war, the same Republicans have accused the opponents of imperialism of giving encouragement to the Filipinos. This is a cowardly evasion of respon-

---

16. Signed on December 10, 1898, the Treaty of Paris was approved by the Senate on February 6, 1899, by one vote more than the required two-thirds majority.

17. Had Bryan not persuaded several reluctant Democrats to vote for the treaty, it probably would not have been ratified by the Senate.

18. From Lincoln's first inaugural address, March 4, 1861.

19. Introduced by Senator Augustus O. Bacon of Georgia, the resolution held that the United States had no intention of exercising "permanent sovereignty" over the Philippines and would relinquish control once "a stable and independent government" was established.

20. Garrett A. Hobart, sitting as President of the Senate, broke a 29–29 tie by voting against the Bacon resolution.

21. In February 1899 fighting began between U.S. soldiers and Filipino nationalists, who were opposed to their country becoming an American territory. Fierce hostilities continued until 1904 and intermittently thereafter until 1906, involving more than 125,000 U.S. troops and claiming 4,300 American lives, plus many times that number of Filipinos. Eventually the Philippines were granted self-government in 1916 and gained independence in 1946.

sibility. If it is right for the United States to hold the Philippine Islands permanently and imitate European empires in the government of colonies, the Republican Party ought to state its position and defend it, but it must expect the subject races to protest against such a policy and to resist to the extent of their ability.

The Filipinos do not need any encouragement from Americans now living. Our whole history has been an encouragement not only to the Filipinos, but to all who are denied a voice in their own government. If the Republicans are prepared to censure all who have used language calculated to make the Filipinos hate foreign domination, let them condemn the speech of Patrick Henry. When he uttered that passionate appeal, "Give me liberty or give me death,"[22] he expressed a sentiment which still echoes in the hearts of men. Let them censure Jefferson; of all the statesmen of history, none have used words so offensive to those who would hold their fellows in political bondage.[23] Let them censure Washington,[24] who declared that the colonists must choose between liberty and slavery. Or, if the statute of limitations has run against the sins of Henry and Jefferson and Washington, let them censure Lincoln, whose Gettysburg speech[25] will be quoted in defense of popular government when the present advocates of force and conquest are forgotten.

Someone has said that a truth once spoken can never be recalled.[26] It goes on and on, and no one can set a limit to its ever-widening influence. But if it were possible to obliterate every word written or spoken in defense of the principles set forth in the Declaration of Independence, a war of conquest would still leave its legacy of perpetual hatred, for it was God himself who placed in every human heart the love of liberty. He never made a race of people so low in the scale of civilization or intelligence that it would welcome a foreign master.

Those who would have this nation enter upon a career of empire must consider not only the effect of imperialism on the Filipinos, but they must also calculate its effects upon our own nation. We cannot repudiate the principle of self-government in the Philippines without weakening that principle here. Lincoln said that the safety of this nation was not in its fleets, its armies, its forts, but in the spirit which prizes liberty as the heritage of all men in all lands everywhere, and he warned his countrymen that they could not destroy this spirit without planting the seeds of despotism at their own doors.[27]

Even now we are beginning to see the paralyzing influence of imperialism. Heretofore this nation has been prompt to express its sympathy with those who were fighting for civil liberty. While our sphere of activity has been limited to the Western Hemisphere, our sympathies have not been bounded by the seas. We have felt it due to ourselves and to the world, as well as to those who were struggling for the right to govern themselves, to proclaim the interest which our people have, from the date of their own independence, felt in every contest between human rights and arbitrary power.

Three-quarters of a century ago, when our nation was small, the struggles of Greece aroused our people, and Webster and Clay gave eloquent expression to the universal desire for Grecian independence.[28] In 1896 all parties manifested a lively interest in the success of the Cubans, but now, when a war is in progress in South Africa which must result in the extension of

22. From Henry's speech of March 23, 1775, urging the Virginia Convention of Delegates to prepare for hostilities with Great Britain.

23. Bryan is referring to Jefferson's authorship of the Declaration of Independence (1776).

24. George Washington (1732–1799), commander in chief of American armies during the war for independence from Great Britain.

25. The Gettysburg Address, November 19, 1863.

26. From *Horace's Art of Poetry, Made English by the Right Honorable the Earl of Roscommon* (1680).

27. From Lincoln's speech in Edwardsville, Illinois, September 11, 1858.

28. Although the United States remained officially neutral, many Americans, including notable political figures such as Daniel Webster and Henry Clay, supported Greece in its successful quest during the 1820s for independence from the Ottoman Empire.

the monarchical idea or in the triumph of a republic, the advocates of imperialism in this country dare not say a word in behalf of the Boers.[29]

Sympathy for the Boers does not arise from any unfriendliness towards England; the American people are not unfriendly toward the people of any nation. This sympathy is due to the fact that, as stated in our platform,[30] we believe in the principles of self-government and reject, as did our forefathers, the claims of monarchy. If this nation surrenders its belief in the universal application of the principles set forth in the Declaration of Independence, it will lose the prestige and influence which it has enjoyed among the nations as an exponent of popular government.

Our opponents, conscious of the weakness of their cause, seek to confuse imperialism with expansion and have even dared to claim Jefferson as a supporter of their policy.[31] Jefferson spoke so freely and used language with such precision that no one can be ignorant of his views. On one occasion he declared, "If there be one principle more deeply rooted than any other in the mind of every American, it is that we should have nothing to do with conquest." And again he said, "Conquest is not in our principles; it is inconsistent with our government."[32]

The forcible annexation of territory to be governed by arbitrary power differs as much from the acquisition of territory to be built up into states as a monarchy differs from a democracy. The Democratic Party does not oppose expansion when expansion enlarges the area of the republic and incorporates land which can be settled by American citizens, or adds to our population people who are willing to become citizens and are capable of discharging their duties as such. The acquisition of the Louisiana Territory, Florida, Texas, and other tracts which have been secured from time to time enlarged the republic, and the Constitution followed the flag into the new territory. It is now proposed to seize upon distant territory already more densely populated than our own country and to force upon the people a government for which there is no warrant in our Constitution or our laws.

Even the argument that this earth belongs to those who desire to cultivate it and who have the physical power to acquire it cannot be invoked to justify the appropriation of the Philippine Islands by the United States. If the islands were uninhabited, American citizens would not be willing to go there and till the soil. The white race will not live so near the equator. Other nations have tried to colonize in the same latitude. The Netherlands have controlled Java for three hundred years, and yet today there are less than sixty thousand people of European birth scattered among the twenty-five million natives. After a century and a half of English domination in India, less than one-twentieth of 1 percent of the people of India are of English birth, and it requires an army of seventy thousand British soldiers to take care of the tax collectors. Spain had asserted title to the Philippine Islands for three centuries, and yet when our fleet entered Manila Bay there were less than ten thousand Spaniards residing in the Philippines.

A colonial policy means that we shall send to the Philippine Islands a few traders, a few taskmasters, and a few officeholders, and an army large enough to support the authority of a small fraction of the people while they rule the natives. If we have an imperial policy, we must have a great standing army as its natural and necessary complement. The spirit which will justify the forcible annexation of the Philippine Islands will justify the seizure of other islands and the domination of other people, and with wars of conquest we can expect a certain, if not rapid, growth of our military establishment.

That a large permanent increase in our regular army is intended by Republican leaders is not a matter of conjecture, but a matter of fact. In his message of December 5, 1898, the President[33] asked for authority

---

29. Bryan is referring to the Second Boer War, 1899–1902, in which Great Britain defeated the Boers and added the Transvaal and the Orange Free State to the British Empire.

30. The Democratic National Convention met in Kansas City, Missouri, July 4–6, 1900; the platform was adopted on July 5.

31. Republicans pointed to Jefferson's negotiation of the Louisiana Purchase, which added 828,000 square miles of territory to the United States.

32. From Jefferson's letters to William Short, July 28, 1791, and William Carmichael, August 2, 1790.

---

33. William McKinley.

to increase the standing army to one hundred thousand. In 1896 the army contained about twenty-five thousand. Within two years the President asked for four times that many, and a Republican House of Representatives complied with the request after the Spanish treaty had been signed and when no country was at war with the United States.[34] If such an army is demanded when an imperial policy is contemplated but not openly avowed, what may be expected if the people encourage the Republican Party by endorsing its policy at the polls?

A large standing army is not only a pecuniary burden to the people and, if accompanied by compulsory service, a constant source of irritation, but it is ever a menace to a republican form of government. The army is the personification of force, and militarism will inevitably change the ideals of the people and turn the thoughts of our young men from the arts of peace to the science of war. The government which relies for its defense upon its citizens is more likely to be just than one which has at call a large body of professional soldiers.

A small standing army and a well-equipped and well-disciplined state militia are sufficient at ordinary times, and in an emergency the nation should in the future as in the past place its dependence upon the volunteers who come from all occupations at their country's call and return to productive labor when their services are no longer required—men who fight when the country needs fighters and work when the country needs workers.

The Republican platform assumes that the Philippine Islands will be retained under American sovereignty, and we have a right to demand of the Republican leaders a discussion of the future status of the Filipino. Is he to be a citizen or a subject? Are we to bring into the body politic eight or ten million Asiatics so different from us in race and history that amalgamation is impossible? Are they to share with us in making the laws and shaping the destiny of this nation? No Republican of prominence has been bold enough to advocate such a proposition.

The McEnery resolution, adopted by the Senate immediately after the ratification of the treaty, expressly negatives this idea.[35] The Democratic platform describes the situation when it says that the Filipinos cannot be citizens without endangering our civilization. Who will dispute it? And what is the alternative? If the Filipino is not to be a citizen, shall we make him a subject? On that question the Democratic platform speaks with equal emphasis. It declares that the Filipino cannot be a subject without endangering our form of government. A republic can have no subjects. A subject is possible only in a government resting upon force; he is unknown in a government deriving its just powers from the consent of the governed.

The Republican platform says that "the largest measure of self-government consistent with their welfare and our duties shall be secured to them"— the Filipinos—"by law." This is a strange doctrine for a government which owes its very existence to the men who offered their lives as a protest against government without consent and taxation without representation.

In what respect does the position of the Republican Party differ from the position taken by the English government in 1776? Did not the English government promise a good government to the colonists? What king ever promised a bad government to his people? Did not the English government promise that the colonists should have the largest measure of self-government consistent with their welfare and English duties? Did not the Spanish government promise to give to the Cubans the largest measure of self-government consistent with their welfare and Spanish duties? The whole difference between a monarchy and a republic may be summed up in one sentence: In a monarchy the king gives to the people what he believes to be a good government; in a republic the people secure for themselves what they believe to be a good government. The Republican

---

34. The House of Representatives approved McKinley's request in March 1899.

35. Adopted on February 14, 1899, the McEnery resolution rejected permanent annexation of the Philippines and declared the intention of the United States "to establish on said islands a government suitable to the wants and conditions of the inhabitants" and "to prepare them for local self-government."

Party has accepted the European idea and planted itself upon the ground taken by George III[36] and by every ruler who distrusts the capacity of the people for self-government or denies them a voice in their own affairs.

The Republican platform promises that some measure of self-government is to be given the Filipinos by law; but even this pledge is not fulfilled. Nearly sixteen months elapsed after the ratification of the treaty before the adjournment of Congress last June and yet no law was passed dealing with the Philippine situation. The will of the President has been the only law in the Philippine Islands wherever the American authority extends.

Why does the Republican Party hesitate to legislate upon the Philippine question? Because a law would disclose the radical departure from history and precedent contemplated by those who control the Republican Party.

The storm of protest which greeted the Puerto Rican bill[37] was an indication of what may be expected when the American people are brought face to face with legislation upon this subject. If the Puerto Ricans, who welcomed annexation, are to be denied the guarantees of our Constitution, what is to be the lot of the Filipinos, who resisted our authority? If secret influences could compel a disregard of our plain duty toward friendly people living near our shores, what treatment will those same influences provide for unfriendly people seven thousand miles away? If in this country, where the people have a right to vote, Republican leaders dare not take the side of the people against the great monopolies which have grown up within the last few years, how can they be trusted to protect the Filipinos from the corporations which are waiting to exploit the islands?

Is the sunlight of full citizenship to be enjoyed by the people of the United States and the twilight of semicitizenship endured by the people of Puerto Rico, while the thick darkness of perpetual vassal-

age covers the Philippines? The Puerto Rico tariff law asserts the doctrine that the operation of the Constitution is confined to the forty-five states.[38] The Democratic Party disputes this doctrine and denounces it as repugnant to both the letter and spirit of our organic law. There is no place in our system of government for the deposit of arbitrary and irresponsible power. That the leaders of a great party should claim for any President or Congress the right to treat millions of people as mere "possessions" and deal with them unrestrained by the Constitution or the Bill of Rights shows how far we have already departed from the ancient landmarks and indicates what may be expected if this nation deliberately enters upon a career of empire.

The territorial form of government is temporary and preparatory, and the chief security a citizen of a territory has is found in the fact that he enjoys the same constitutional guarantees and is subject to the same general laws as the citizen of a state. Take away this security and his rights will be violated and his interests sacrificed at the demand of those who have political influence. This is the evil of the colonial system, no matter by what nation it is applied.

What is our title to the Philippine Islands? Do we hold them by treaty or by conquest? Did we buy them or did we take them? Did we purchase the people? If not, how did we secure title to them? Were they thrown in with the land? Will the Republicans say that inanimate earth has value but that when that earth is molded by the divine hand and stamped with the likeness of the Creator, it becomes a fixture and passes with the soil? If governments derive their just powers from the consent of the governed, it is impossible to secure title to people, either by force or by purchase.

We could extinguish Spain's title by treaty, but if we hold title, we must hold it by some method consistent with our ideas of government. When we made allies of the Filipinos and armed them to fight against Spain, we disputed Spain's title. If we buy Spain's

---

36. King of England at the time of the American Revolution.

37. Bryan is referring to the Foraker Act of April 1900, which established a civil government on Puerto Rico under control of the United States.

38. The Foraker Act placed a temporary duty on imports from Puerto Rico. Opponents charged that because Puerto Rico was now part of the United States, the tariff violated the ban against taxes on articles exported from any state. The tariff was upheld by the Supreme Court in 1901.

title, we are not innocent purchasers. There can be no doubt that we accepted and utilized the services of the Filipinos and that when we did so, we had full knowledge that they were fighting for their own independence, and I submit that history furnishes no example of turpitude baser than ours if we now substitute our yoke for the Spanish yoke.

Let us consider briefly the reasons which have been given in support of an imperialistic policy.

Some say that it is our duty to hold the Philippine Islands. But duty is not an argument; it is a conclusion. To ascertain what our duty is in any emergency, we must apply well-settled and generally accepted principles. It is our duty to avoid stealing, no matter whether the thing to be stolen is of great or little value. It is our duty to avoid killing a human being, no matter where the human being lives or to what race or class he belongs.

Everyone recognizes the obligation imposed upon individuals to observe both the human and the moral law, but as some deny the application of those laws to nations, it may not be out of place to quote the opinions of others. Jefferson, than whom there is no higher political authority, said: "I know of but one code of morality for men, whether acting singly or collectively."[39] Franklin, whose learning, wisdom, and virtue are a part of the priceless legacy bequeathed to us from the Revolutionary days, expressed the same idea in even stronger language when he said: "Justice is strictly due between neighbor nations as between neighbor citizens. A highwayman is as much a robber when he plunders in a gang as when single; and the nation that makes an unjust war is only a great gang."[40]

Many may dare to do in crowds what they would not dare to do as individuals, but the moral character of an act is not determined by the number of those who join it. Force can defend a right, but force has never yet created a right. If it was true, as declared in the resolutions of intervention[41] that the Cubans "are

and of right ought to be free and independent," language taken from the Declaration of Independence, it is equally true that the Filipinos "are and of right ought to be free and independent."

The right of the Cubans to freedom was not based upon their proximity to the United States, nor upon the language which they spoke, nor yet upon the race or races to which they belonged. Congress by a practically unanimous vote declared that the principles enunciated at Philadelphia in 1776 were still alive and applicable to the Cubans. Who will draw a line between the natural rights of the Cubans and the Filipinos? Who will say that the former has a right to liberty and that the latter has no rights which we are bound to respect? And if the Filipinos "are and of right ought to be free and independent," what right have we to force our government upon them without their consent?

Before our duty can be ascertained, their rights must be determined, and when their rights are once determined, it is as much our duty to respect those rights as it was the duty of Spain to respect the rights of the people of Cuba or the duty of England to respect the rights of the American colonists. Rights never conflict; duties never clash. Can it be our duty to usurp political rights which belong to others? Can it be our duty to kill those who, following the example of our forefathers, love liberty well enough to fight for it?

Some poet has described the terror which overcame a soldier who, in the midst of the battle, discovered that he had slain his brother.[42] It is written, "All ye are brethren."[43] Let us hope for the coming of the day when human life—which when once destroyed cannot be restored—will be so sacred that it will never be taken except when necessary to punish a crime already committed or to prevent a crime about to be committed.

It is said that we have assumed before the world obligations which make it necessary for

39. From Jefferson's letter to James Madison, August 28, 1789.

40. From Benjamin Franklin's letter to Benjamin Vaughn, March 14, 1785.

41. Bryan is referring to Congress's resolution of April 19, 1898, authorizing American military action to compel Spain to relinquish all authority in Cuba.

42. Most likely a reference to "The Sentinel," in *The Parterre of Fiction, Poetry, History, Literature, and the Fine Arts*, Vol. I (1834).

43. Matthew 23:8.

us to permanently maintain a government in the Philippine Islands. I reply, first, that the highest obligation of this nation is to be true to itself. No obligation to any particular nations, or to all the nations combined, can require the abandonment of our theory of government and the substitution of doctrines against which our whole national life has been a protest. And, second, that our obligation to the Filipinos, who inhabit the islands, is greater than any obligation which we can owe to foreigners who have a temporary residence in the Philippines or desire to trade there.

It is argued by some that the Filipinos are incapable of self-government and that, therefore, we owe it to the world to take control of them. Admiral Dewey,[44] in an official report to the Navy Department, declared the Filipinos more capable of self-government than the Cubans and said that he based his opinion upon a knowledge of both races. But I will not rest the case upon the relative advancement of the Filipinos. Henry Clay, in defending the right of the people of South America to self-government, said: "It is the doctrine of thrones that man is too ignorant to govern himself. Their partisans assert his incapacity in reference to all nations; if they cannot command universal assent to the proposition, it is then demanded to particular nations; and our pride and our presumption too often make converts of us. I contend that it is to arraign the disposition of Providence himself to suppose that he has created beings incapable of governing themselves and to be trampled on by kings. Self-government is the natural government of man."[45]

Clay was right. There are degrees of proficiency in the art of self-government, but it is a reflection upon the Creator to say that he denied to any people the capacity for self-government. Once admit that some people are capable of self-government and that others are not, and that the capable people have a right to seize upon and govern the incapable, and you make force—brute force—the only foundation of government and invite the reign of a despot. I am not willing to believe that an all-wise and an all-loving God created the Filipinos and then left them thousands of years helpless until the islands attracted the attention of European nations.

Republicans ask, "Shall we haul down the flag that floats over our dead in the Philippines?" The same question might have been asked when the American flag floated over Chapultepec[46] and waved over the dead who fell there; but the tourist who visits the City of Mexico finds there a national cemetery owned by the United States and cared for by an American citizen. Our flag still floats over our dead, but when the treaty with Mexico was signed, American authority withdrew to the Rio Grande,[47] and I venture the opinion that during the last fifty years the people of Mexico have made more progress under the stimulus of independence and self-government than they would have made under a carpetbag[48] government held in place by bayonets. The United States and Mexico, friendly republics, are each stronger and happier than they would have been had the former been cursed and the latter crushed by an imperialistic policy disguised as "benevolent assimilation."

"Can we not govern colonies?" we are asked. The question is not what we can do, but what we ought to do. This nation can do whatever it desires to do, but it must accept responsibility for what it does. If the Constitution stands in the way, the people can amend the Constitution. I repeat: The nation can do whatever it desires to do, but it cannot avoid the natural and legitimate results of its own conduct.

The young man upon reaching his majority can do what he pleases. He can disregard the teachings of his parents; he can trample upon all that he has been taught to consider sacred; he can disobey the laws of the state, the laws of society, and the laws of God. He can stamp failure upon his life and make his

44. George Dewey, who defeated the Spanish fleet at Manila Bay in May 1898.

45. From Clay's speech in the House of Representatives, March 24, 1818.

46. Site of a major battle during the Mexican War of 1846–1848.

47. Bryan is referring to a stipulation in the February 1848 Treaty of Guadalupe Hidalgo, which ended the Mexican War.

48. Derogatory term for a government controlled by outsiders who move in for the sole purpose of gaining political power or economic advantage; it is derived from the Northern carpetbaggers who moved to the South during Reconstruction after the American Civil War.

very existence a curse to his fellow men, and he can bring his father and mother in sorrow to the grave, but he cannot annul the sentence "The wages of sin is death."[49]

And so with the nation. It is of age and it can do what it pleases; it can spurn the traditions of the past; it can repudiate the principles upon which the nation rests; it can employ force instead of reason; it can substitute might for right; it can conquer weaker people; it can exploit their lands, appropriate their property, and kill their people—but it cannot repeal the moral law or escape the punishment decreed for the violation of human rights.

> Would we tread in the paths of tyranny,
>   Nor reckon the tyrant's cost?
> Who taketh another's liberty
>   His freedom is also lost.
> Would we win as the strong have ever won,
>   Make ready to pay the debt;
> For the God who reigned over Babylon
>   Is the God who is reigning yet.[50]

Some argue that American rule in the Philippine Islands will result in the better education of the Filipinos. Be not deceived. If we expect to maintain a colonial policy, we shall not find it to our advantage to educate the people. The educated Filipinos are now in revolt against us, and the most ignorant ones have made the least resistance to our domination. If we are to govern them without their consent and give them no voice in determining the taxes which they must pay, we dare not educate them, lest they learn to read the Declaration of Independence and the Constitution of the United States and mock us for our inconsistency.

The principal arguments, however, advanced by those who enter upon a defense of imperialism are:

First—That we must improve the present opportunity to become a world power and enter into international politics.

Second—That our commercial interests in the Philippine Islands and in the Orient make it necessary for us to hold the islands permanently.

Third—That the spread of the Christian religion will be facilitated by a colonial policy.

Fourth—That there is no honorable retreat from the position which the nation has taken.

The first argument is addressed to the nation's pride and the second to the nation's pocketbook. The third is intended for the church member and the fourth for the partisan.

It is sufficient answer to the first argument to say that for more than a century this nation has been a world power. For ten decades it has been the most potent influence in the world. Not only has it been a world power, but it has done more to affect the politics of the human race than all the other nations of the world combined. Because our Declaration of Independence was promulgated, others have been promulgated. Because the patriots of 1776 fought for liberty, others have fought for it. Because our Constitution was adopted, other constitutions have been adopted.

The growth of the principle of self-government planted on American soil has been the overshadowing political fact of the nineteenth century. It has made this nation conspicuous among the nations and given it a place in history such as no other nation has ever enjoyed. Nothing has been able to check the onward march of this idea. I am not willing that this nation shall cast aside the omnipotent weapon of truth to seize again the weapons of physical warfare. I would not exchange the glory of this republic for the glory of all the empires that have risen and fallen since time began.

The permanent chairman of the last Republican National Convention presented the pecuniary argument in all its baldness when he said: "We make no hypocritical pretense of being interested in the Philippines solely on account of others. While we regard the welfare of those people as a sacred trust, we regard the welfare of the American people first. We see our duty to ourselves as well as to others. We believe in trade expansion. By every legitimate means within the province of government and constitution we mean to stimulate the expansion of our trade and open new markets."[51]

---

49. Romans 6:23.

50. From "God Still Reigns," in J. Wilbur Chapman, *Present Day Parables* (1900).

---

51. From Henry Cabot Lodge's speech of June 20, 1900.

This is the commercial argument. It is based upon the theory that war can be rightly waged for pecuniary advantage and that it is profitable to purchase trade by force and violence. Franklin denied both of these propositions. When Lord Howe[52] asserted that the acts of Parliament which brought on the Revolution were necessary to prevent American trade from passing into foreign channels, Franklin replied: "To me it seems that neither the obtaining nor retaining of any trade, howsoever valuable, is an object for which men may justly spill each other's blood; that the true and sure means of extending and securing commerce are the goodness and cheapness of commodities; and that the profits of no trade can ever be equal to the expense of compelling it and holding it by fleets and armies. I consider this war against us, therefore, as both unjust and unwise."[53]

I place the philosophy of Franklin against the sordid doctrine of those who would put a price upon the head of an American soldier and justify a war of conquest upon the ground that it will pay. The Democratic Party is in favor of the expansion of trade. It would extend our trade by every legitimate and peaceful means; but it is not willing to make merchandise of human blood.

But a war of conquest is as unwise as it is unrighteous. A harbor and coaling station in the Philippines would answer every trade and military necessity, and such a concession could have been secured at any time without difficulty. It is not necessary to own people in order to trade with them. We carry on trade today with every part of the world, and our commerce has expanded more rapidly than the commerce of any European empire. We do not own Japan or China, but we trade with their people. We have not absorbed the republics of Central and South America, but we trade with them. It has not been necessary to have any political connection with Canada or the nations of Europe in order to trade with them.

Trade cannot be permanently profitable unless it is voluntary. When trade is secured by force, the cost of securing it and retaining it must be taken out of the profits, and the profits are never large enough to cover the expense. Such a system would never be defended but for the fact that the expense is borne by all the people, while the profits are enjoyed by a few.

Imperialism would be profitable to the army contractors; it would be profitable to the ship owners who would carry live soldiers to the Philippines and bring dead soldiers back; it would be profitable to those who would seize upon the franchises; and it would be profitable to the officials whose salaries would be fixed here and paid over there. But to the farmer, to the laboring man, and to the vast majority of those engaged in other occupations it would bring expenditure without return and risk without reward. Farmers and laboring men have, as a rule, small incomes, and under systems which place the tax upon consumption, pay much more than their fair share of the expenses of government. Thus the very people who receive least benefit from imperialism will be injured most by the military burdens which accompany it.

In addition to the evils which he and the farmer share in common, the laboring man will be the first to suffer if Oriental subjects seek work in the United States, the first to suffer if American capital leaves our shores to employ Oriental labor in the Philippines to supply the trade of China and Japan, the first to suffer from the violence which the military spirit arouses, and the first to suffer when the methods of imperialism are applied to our own government. It is not strange, therefore, that the labor organizations have been quick to note the approach of these dangers and prompt to protest against both militarism and imperialism.

The pecuniary argument, though more effective with certain classes, is not likely to be used so often or presented with so much enthusiasm as the religious argument. If what has been termed the "gunpowder gospel"[54] were urged against the Filipinos only, it would be a sufficient answer to say that a majority of the Filipinos are now members of one branch of the Christian church;[55] but the principle involved is

---

52. William Howe, commander in chief of British forces in America in 1776.

53. From Franklin's letter to Howe, July 20, 1776.

54. From Howard S. Taylor's poem "The Creed of the Flag" (1899).

55. Figures at the time of Bryan's speech indicated that more than 90 percent of Filipinos were Roman Catholic.

one of much wider application and challenges serious consideration.

The religious argument varies in positiveness from a passive belief that Providence delivered the Filipinos into our hands for their good and our glory to the exultation of the minister who said that we ought to "thrash the natives—Filipinos—until they understand who we are" and that "every bullet sent, every cannon shot, and every flag waved means righteousness."[56] We cannot approve of this doctrine in one place unless we are willing to apply it everywhere. If there is poison in the blood of the hand, it will ultimately reach the heart. It is equally true that forcible Christianity, if planted under the American flag in the faraway Orient, will sooner or later be transplanted upon American soil.

If true Christianity consists in carrying out in our daily lives the teachings of Christ, who will say that we are commanded to civilize with dynamite and proselyte with the sword? He who would declare the divine will must prove his authority either by Holy Writ or by evidence of special dispensation.

Imperialism finds no warrant in the Bible. The command "Go ye into all the world and preach the gospel to every creature"[57] has no Gatling-gun[58] attachment. When Jesus visited a village of Samaria and the people refused to receive him, some of the disciples suggested that fire should be called down from heaven to avenge the insult; but the Master rebuked them and said, "Ye know not what manner of spirit ye are of, for the Son of Man is not come to destroy men's lives, but to save them."[59] Suppose he had said, "We will thrash them until they understand who we are." How different would have been the history of Christianity! Compare, if you will, the swaggering, bullying, brutal doctrine of imperialism with the Golden Rule[60] and the commandment "Thou shalt love thy neighbor as thyself."[61] Love, not force, was the weapon of the Nazarene;[62] sacrifice for others, not the exploitation of them, was his method of reaching the human heart.

A missionary recently told me that the Stars and Stripes once saved his life because his assailant recognized our flag as a flag that had no blood upon it. Let it be known that our missionaries are seeking souls instead of sovereignty; let it be known that instead of being the advance guard of conquering armies, they are going forth to help and uplift, having their loins girt about with truth and their feet shod with the preparation of the gospel of peace, wearing the breastplate of righteousness and carrying the sword of the spirit;[63] let it be known that they are citizens of a nation which respects the rights of the citizens of other nations as carefully as it protects the rights of its own citizens, and the welcome given to our missionaries will be more cordial than the welcome extended to the missionaries of any other nation.

The argument made by some that it was unfortunate for the nation that it had anything to do with the Philippine Islands, but that the naval victory at Manila made the permanent acquisition of those islands necessary, is also unsound. We won a naval victory at Santiago,[64] but that did not compel us to hold Cuba. The shedding of American blood in the Philippine Islands does not make it imperative that we should retain possession forever; American blood was shed at San Juan Hill and El Caney,[65] and yet the President has promised the Cubans independence. The fact that the American flag floats over Manila does not compel us to exercise perpetual sovereignty over the islands; the American flag waves over Havana today, but the President has promised to haul it down when the flag of the Cuban republic is ready to rise in

---

56. Wayland Hoyt, quoted in *The Nation*, April 6, 1899.

57. Mark 16:15.

58. Often referred to as the first machine gun, the Gatling gun was a well-publicized element in U.S. weaponry during the Spanish-American War.

59. Luke 9:55–56.

60. "Do unto others as you would have others do unto you" (paraphrased from Matthew 7:12).

---

61. This injunction appears several places in the Bible, including Leviticus 19:18, Matthew 19:19, and Romans 13:9.

62. Jesus.

63. An allusion to Ephesians 6:14–17.

64. Bryan is referring to the battle of July 3, 1898, during the Spanish-American War.

65. Battle sites of the Spanish-American War.

its place. Better a thousand times that our flag in the Orient give way to a flag representing the idea of self-government than that the flag of this republic should become the flag of an empire.

There is an easy, honest, honorable solution of the Philippine question. It is set forth in the Democratic platform and it is submitted with confidence to the American people. This plan I unreservedly endorse. If elected, I will convene Congress in extraordinary session as soon as inaugurated and recommend an immediate declaration of the nation's purpose: first, to establish a stable form of government in the Philippine Islands, just as we are now establishing a stable form of government in Cuba; second, to give independence to the Cubans; third, to protect the Filipinos from outside interference while they work out their destiny, just as we have protected the republics of Central and South America and are, by the Monroe Doctrine, pledged to protect Cuba.[66]

A European protectorate often results in the plundering of the ward by the guardian. An American protectorate gives to the nation protected the advantage of our strength without making it the victim of our greed. For three-quarters of a century the Monroe Doctrine has been a shield to neighboring republics, and yet it has imposed no pecuniary burden upon us. After the Filipinos had aided us in the war against Spain, we could not honorably turn them over to their former masters. We could not leave them to be the victims of the ambitious designs of European nations, and since we do not desire to make them a part of us or to hold them as subjects, we propose the only alternative—namely, to give them independence and guard them against molestation from without.

When our opponents are unable to defend their position by argument, they fall back upon the assertion that it is destiny and insist that we must submit to it no matter how much it violates our moral precepts and our principles of government. This is a complacent philosophy. It obliterates the distinction between right and wrong and makes individuals and nations the helpless victims of circumstance. Destiny is the subterfuge of the invertebrate, who, lacking the courage to oppose error, seeks some plausible excuse for supporting it.

Washington said that the destiny of the republican form of government was deeply, if not finally, staked on the experiment entrusted to the American people.[67] How different Washington's definition of destiny from the Republican definition! The Republicans say that this nation is in the hands of destiny; Washington believed that not only the destiny of our own nation but the destiny of the republican form of government throughout the world was entrusted to American hands.

Immeasurable responsibility! The destiny of this republic is in the hands of its own people, and upon the success of the experiment here rests the hope of humanity. No exterior force can disturb this republic, and no foreign influence should be permitted to change its course. What the future has in store for this nation no one has authority to declare, but each individual has his own idea of the nation's mission, and he owes it to his country as well as to himself to contribute as best he may to the fulfillment of that mission.

Mr. Chairman and gentlemen of the committee: I can never fully discharge the debt of gratitude which I owe to my countrymen for the honors which they have so generously bestowed upon me; but, sirs, whether it be my lot to occupy the high office for which the convention has named me or to spend the remainder of my days in private life, it shall be my constant ambition and my controlling purpose to aid in realizing the high ideals of those whose wisdom and courage and sacrifices brought this republic into existence.

I can conceive of a national destiny surpassing the glories of the present and the past—a destiny which meets the responsibility of today and measures up to the possibilities of the future.

Behold a republic resting securely upon the foundation stones quarried by Revolutionary patriots from the mountain of eternal truth—a republic applying in practice and proclaiming to the world

---

66. The Monroe Doctrine of 1823 declared that the United States would regard any attempt on the part of European powers "to extend their system to any portion of this hemisphere as dangerous to our peace and safety."

67. From Washington's first inaugural address, April 30, 1789.

the self-evident propositions that all men are created equal, that they are endowed with inalienable rights, that governments are instituted among men to secure these rights, and that governments derive their just powers from the consent of the governed.

Behold a republic in which civil and religious liberty stimulate all to earnest endeavor and in which the law restrains every hand uplifted for a neighbor's injury—a republic in which every citizen is a sovereign but in which no one cares to wear a crown.

Behold a republic standing erect while empires all around are bowed beneath the weight of their own armaments—a republic whose flag is loved while other flags are only feared.

Behold a republic increasing in population, in wealth, in strength, and in influence, solving the problems of civilization and hastening the coming of an universal brotherhood—a republic which shakes thrones and dissolves aristocracies by its silent example and gives light and inspiration to those who sit in darkness.

Behold a republic gradually but surely becoming the supreme moral factor in the world's progress and the accepted arbiter of the world's disputes—a republic whose history, like the path of the just, "is as the shining light that shineth more and more unto the perfect day."[68]

---

68. Proverbs 4:18.

Theodore Roosevelt

⧗

The Man with the Muckrake

WASHINGTON, D.C.
APRIL 14, 1906

ALMOST ANY OCCASION can provide the setting for a significant presidential pronouncement. Such was the case with Theodore Roosevelt's "The Man with the Muckrake," delivered on April 14, 1906, at the laying of the cornerstone of a new office building for the U.S. House of Representatives. The Progressive movement was moving into high gear, fueled to no little extent by journalistic exposures of the twin evils of economic malfeasance by the Robber Barons of American industry and political corruption by their minions in state and national government. Concerned both by the material conditions of American life and the psychological and spiritual reaction to those conditions, Roosevelt took advantage of the occasion to present what would become his most enduring public address.

"The Man with the Muckrake" is best known for its warning against the excesses of journalistic sensationalism. Taking his image from John Bunyan's *Pilgrim's Progress,* Roosevelt leveled his sights on "the Man with the Muckrake, the man who…consistently refuses to see aught that is lofty and fixes his eyes with solemn intentness only on that which is vile and debasing." He charged that through their "hysterical sensationalism" and "gross and reckless assaults on character," the muckrakers—a sobriquet derived from TR's speech—performed a disservice to the public by failing to distinguish good from evil.

Contrary to the claims of his critics, however, Roosevelt did not attack all muckrakers or call for an end to the kind of crusading journalism represented in the works of writers such as Ida Tarbell, Lincoln Steffens, and Ray Stannard Baker. The speech was prepared with great care, and TR made clear that he did not intend to discourage "relentless exposure of and attack upon every evil man, every evil practice, whether in politics, in business, or in social life." He hailed as a benefactor every journalist who made such exposures, provided the writer "remembers that the attack is of use only if it is absolutely truthful."

The speech is also noteworthy for two progressive measures Roosevelt advanced after discussing the muckrakers. First, he noted that it might be necessary to adopt a national inheritance tax on inflated individual fortunes. Second, he indicated that the federal government must exercise further control over corporations engaged in interstate commerce. Although TR did not spell out specifics in either case, both proposals were radical for the day, were recognized as such by his contemporaries, and were championed by Roosevelt in subsequent addresses. "The Man with the Muckrake" is best read not as an attack on the spirit of reform, but rather as the first major expression of Roosevelt's retreat from the conservatism that had marked the first five years of his presidency. The speech was a milestone in his growing commitment to political and economic reform—commitment that would ultimately lead him to bolt the Republican Party and run for President on the Progressive ticket in 1912.

◇◇◇

Over a century ago Washington laid the cornerstone of the Capitol in what was then little more than a tract of wooded wilderness here beside the Potomac.[1] We now find it necessary to provide by great additional buildings for the business of the government. This growth in the need for the housing of the government is but a proof and example of the way in which the nation has grown and the sphere of action of the national government has grown. We now administer the affairs of a nation in which the extraordinary growth of population has been outstripped by the growth of wealth and the growth in complex interests. The material problems that face us today are not such as they were in Washington's time, but the underlying facts of human nature are the same now as they were then. Under altered external form, we war with the same tendencies toward evil that were evident in Washington's time and are helped by the same tendencies for good. It is about some of these that I wish to say a word today.

In Bunyan's *Pilgrim's Progress*[2] you may recall the description of the Man with the Muckrake, the man who could look no way but downward, with the muckrake in his hand; who was offered a celestial crown for his muckrake, but who would neither look up nor regard the crown he was offered, but continued to rake to himself the filth of the floor.

In *Pilgrim's Progress* the Man with the Muckrake is set forth as the example of him whose vision is fixed on carnal instead of on spiritual things. Yet he

---

1. President George Washington laid the cornerstone of the U.S. Capitol on September 18, 1793.

2. John Bunyan, *The Pilgrim's Progress from This World to That Which Is to Come* (1678).

also typifies the man who in this life consistently refuses to see aught that is lofty and fixes his eyes with solemn intentness only on that which is vile and debasing.

Now, it is very necessary that we should not flinch from seeing what is vile and debasing. There is filth on the floor, and it must be scraped up with the muckrake, and there are times and places where this service is the most needed of all the services that can be performed. But the man who never does anything else, who never thinks or speaks or writes save of his feats with the muckrake, speedily becomes not a help to society, not an incitement to good, but one of the most potent forces for evil.

There are in the body politic, economic and social, many and grave evils, and there is urgent necessity for the sternest war upon them. There should be relentless exposure of and attack upon every evil man, whether politician or businessman, every evil practice, whether in politics, in business, or in social life. I hail as a benefactor every writer or speaker, every man who, on the platform or in book, magazine, or newspaper, with merciless severity makes such attack, provided always that he in his turn remembers that the attack is of use only if it is absolutely truthful.

The liar is no whit better than the thief, and if his mendacity takes the form of slander, he may be worse than most thieves. It puts a premium upon knavery untruthfully to attack an honest man, or even with hysterical exaggeration to assail a bad man with untruth. An epidemic of indiscriminate assault upon character does not good, but very great harm. The soul of every scoundrel is gladdened whenever an honest man is assailed, or even when a scoundrel is untruthfully assailed.

Now, it is easy to twist out of shape what I have just said, easy to affect to misunderstand it, and, if it is slurred over in repetition, not difficult really to misunderstand it. Some persons are sincerely incapable of understanding that to denounce mudslinging does not mean the endorsement of whitewashing; and both the interested individuals who need whitewashing and those others who practice mudslinging like to encourage such confusion of ideas.

One of the chief counts against those who make indiscriminate assault upon men in business or men in public life is that they invite a reaction which is sure to tell powerfully in favor of the unscrupulous scoundrel who really ought to be attacked, who ought to be exposed, who ought, if possible, to be put in the penitentiary. If Aristides[3] is praised overmuch as just, people get tired of hearing it, and overcensure of the unjust finally and from similar reasons results in their favor.

Any excess is almost sure to invite a reaction, and unfortunately the reaction, instead of taking the form of punishment of those guilty of the excess, is very apt to take the form either of punishment of the unoffending or of giving immunity, and even strength, to offenders. The effort to make financial or political profit out of the destruction of character can only result in public calamity. Gross and reckless assaults on character, whether on the stump or in newspaper, magazine, or book, create a morbid and vicious public sentiment, and at the same time act as a profound deterrent to able men of normal sensitiveness and tend to prevent them from entering the public service at any price. As an instance in point, I may mention that one serious difficulty encountered in getting the right type of men to dig the Panama Canal[4] is the certainty that they will be exposed, both without and, I am sorry to say, sometimes within Congress to utterly reckless assaults on their character and capacity.

At the risk of repetition, let me say again that my plea is not for immunity to, but for the most unsparing exposure of, the politician who betrays his trust, of the big businessman who makes or spends his fortune in illegitimate or corrupt ways. There should be a resolute effort to hunt every such man out of the position he has disgraced. Expose the crime and hunt down the criminal, but remember that even in the case of crime, if it is attacked in sensational, lurid, and untruthful fashion, the attack may do more damage to the public mind than the crime itself. It is because I feel that there should be no rest in the endless war against the forces of evil that I ask that the war be conducted with sanity as well as with resolution.

---

3. Greek leader known as "the Just" because of his commitment to the common good (ca. 530–468 BCE).

4. Construction of the Panama Canal by the United States began in 1904; the canal opened in 1914.

The men with the muckrakes are often indispensable to the well-being of society, but only if they know when to stop raking the muck and to look upward to the celestial crown above them, to the crown of worthy endeavor. There are beautiful things above and round about them, and if they gradually grow to feel that the whole world is nothing but muck, their power of usefulness is gone. If the whole picture is painted black, there remains no hue whereby to single out the rascals for distinction from their fellows. Such painting finally induces a kind of moral color blindness, and people affected by it come to the conclusion that no man is really black and no man really white, but they are all gray. In other words, they neither believe in the truth of the attack nor in the honesty of the man who is attacked; they grow as suspicious of the accusation as of the offense; it becomes well-nigh hopeless to stir them either to wrath against wrongdoing or to enthusiasm for what is right; and such a mental attitude in the public gives hope to every knave and is the despair of honest men.

To assail the great and admitted evils of our political and industrial life with such crude and sweeping generalizations as to include decent men in the general condemnation means the searing of the public conscience. There results a general attitude either of cynical belief in and indifference to public corruption or else of a distrustful inability to discriminate between the good and the bad. Either attitude is fraught with untold damage to the country as a whole. The fool who has not sense to discriminate between what is good and what is bad is well-nigh as dangerous as the man who does discriminate and yet chooses the bad.

There is nothing more distressing to every good patriot, to every good American, than the hard, scoffing spirit which treats the allegation of dishonesty in a public man as a cause for laughter. Such laughter is worse than the crackling of thorns under a pot,[5] for it denotes not merely the vacant mind but the heart in which high emotions have been choked before they could grow to fruition.

There is any amount of good in the world, and there never was a time when loftier and more disinterested work for the betterment of mankind was being done than now. The forces that tend for evil are great and terrible, but the forces of truth and love and courage and honesty and generosity and sympathy are also stronger than ever before. It is a foolish and timid, no less than a wicked, thing to blink the fact that the forces of evil are strong, but it is even worse to fail to take into account the strength of the forces that tell for good. Hysterical sensationalism is the very poorest weapon wherewith to fight for lasting righteousness. The men who with stern sobriety and truth assail the many evils of our time, whether in the public press or in magazines or in books, are the leaders and allies of all engaged in the work for social and political betterment. But if they give good reason for distrust of what they say, if they chill the ardor of those who demand truth as a primary virtue, they thereby betray the good cause and play into the hands of the very men against whom they are nominally at war.

In his *Ecclesiastical Polity* that fine old Elizabethan divine, Bishop Hooker, wrote: "He that goeth about to persuade a multitude that they are not so well governed as they ought to be, shall never want attentive and favorable hearers because they know the manifold defects whereunto every kind of regimen is subject; but the secret lets and difficulties, which in public proceedings are innumerable and inevitable, they have not ordinarily the judgment to consider."[6]

This truth should be kept constantly in mind by every free people desiring to preserve the sanity and poise indispensable to the permanent success of self-government. Yet, on the other hand, it is vital not to permit this spirit of sanity and self-command to degenerate into mere mental stagnation. Bad though a state of hysterical excitement is, and evil though the results are which come from the violent oscillations such excitement invariably produces, yet a sodden acquiescence in evil is even worse.

At this moment we are passing through a period of great unrest—social, political, and industrial unrest. It is of the utmost importance for our future that this should prove to be not the unrest of mere

---

5. An allusion to Ecclesiastes 7:6.

6. Richard Hooker, *Of the Laws of Ecclesiastical Polity*, Book I (1594).

rebelliousness against life, of mere dissatisfaction with the inevitable inequality of conditions, but the unrest of a resolute and eager ambition to secure the betterment of the individual and the nation. So far as this movement of agitation throughout the country takes the form of a fierce discontent with evil, of a determination to punish the authors of evil, whether in industry or politics, the feeling is to be heartily welcomed as a sign of healthy life.

If, on the other hand, it turns into a mere crusade of appetite against appetite, of a contest between the brutal greed of the "have-nots" and the brutal greed of the "haves," then it has no significance for good, but only for evil. If it seeks to establish a line of cleavage, not along the line which divides good men from bad, but along that other line, running at right angles thereto, which divides those who are well off from those who are less well off, then it will be fraught with immeasurable harm to the body politic.

We can no more and no less afford to condone evil in the man of capital than evil in the man of no capital. The wealthy man who exults because there is a failure of justice in the effort to bring some trust magnate to account for his misdeeds is as bad as, and no worse than, the so-called labor leader who clamorously strives to excite a foul class feeling on behalf of some other labor leader who is implicated in murder.[7] One attitude is as bad as the other, and no worse; in each case the accused is entitled to exact justice, and in neither case is there need of action by others which can be construed into an expression of sympathy for crime.

It is a prime necessity that if the present unrest is to result in permanent good, the emotion shall be translated into action and that the action shall be marked by honesty, sanity, and self-restraint. There is mighty little good in a mere spasm of reform. The reform that counts is that which comes through steady, continuous growth; violent emotionalism leads to exhaustion.

It is important to this people to grapple with the problems connected with the amassing of enormous fortunes and the use of those fortunes, both corporate and individual, in business. We should discriminate in the sharpest way between fortunes well-won and fortunes ill-won, between those gained as an incident to performing great services to the community as a whole and those gained in evil fashion by keeping just within the limits of mere law-honesty. Of course, no amount of charity in spending such fortunes in any way compensates for misconduct in making them.

As a matter of personal conviction, and without pretending to discuss the details or formulate the system, I feel that we shall ultimately have to consider the adoption of some such scheme as that of a progressive tax on all fortunes beyond a certain amount, either given in life or devised or bequeathed upon death to any individual—a tax so framed as to put it out of the power of the owner of one of these enormous fortunes to hand on more than a certain amount to any one individual; the tax, of course, to be imposed by the national and not the state government. Such taxation should, of course, be aimed merely at the inheritance or transmission in their entirety of those fortunes swollen beyond all healthy limits.

Again, the national government must in some form exercise supervision over corporations engaged in interstate business—and all large corporations are engaged in interstate business—whether by license or otherwise, so as to permit us to deal with the far-reaching evils of overcapitalization. This year we are making a beginning in the direction of serious effort to settle some of these economic problems by the railway-rate legislation.[8] Such legislation, if so framed, as I am sure it will be, as to secure definite and tangible results, will amount to something of itself; and it will amount to a great deal more insofar as it is taken as a first step in the direction of a policy of superintendence and control over corporate wealth engaged in interstate commerce, this superintendence and control not to be exercised in a spirit of malevolence toward the men who have created the wealth, but

---

7. Roosevelt is referring to "Arouse, Ye Slaves," an article by Eugene Debs in *Appeal to Reason*, March 10, 1906, charging that William Haywood and Charles Moyer, leaders of the Western Federation of Miners, were being held illegally for the 1905 assassination of Frank Steunenberg, former Governor of Idaho.

8. Roosevelt is referring to what would become the Hepburn Act, passed by Congress in June 1906.

with the firm purpose both to do justice to them and to see that they in their turn do justice to the public at large.

The first requisite in the public servants who are to deal in this shape with corporations, whether as legislators or as executives, is honesty. This honesty can be no respecter of persons. There can be no such thing as unilateral honesty. The danger is not really from corrupt corporations; it springs from the corruption itself, whether exercised for or against corporations.

The Eighth Commandment reads, "Thou shalt not steal."[9] It does not read, "Thou shalt not steal from the rich man." It does not read, "Thou shalt not steal from the poor man." It reads simply and plainly, "Thou shalt not steal." No good whatever will come from that warped and mock morality which denounces the misdeeds of men of wealth and forgets the misdeeds practiced at their expense, which denounces bribery but blinds itself to blackmail, which foams with rage if a corporation secures favors by improper methods and merely leers with hideous mirth if the corporation is itself wronged.

The only public servant who can be trusted honestly to protect the rights of the public against the misdeeds of a corporation is that public man who will just as surely protect the corporation itself from wrongful aggression. If a public man is willing to yield to popular clamor and do wrong to the men of wealth or to rich corporations, it may be set down as certain that if the opportunity comes, he will secretly and furtively do wrong to the public in the interest of a corporation.

But in addition to honesty, we need sanity. No honesty will make a public man useful if that man is timid or foolish, if he is a hotheaded zealot or an impracticable visionary. As we strive for reform, we find that it is not at all merely the case of a long uphill pull. On the contrary, there is almost as much of breeching work as of collar work; to depend only on traces means that there will soon be a runaway and an upset.[10]

The men of wealth who today are trying to prevent the regulation and control of their business in the interest of the public by the proper government authorities will not succeed, in my judgment, in checking the progress of the movement. But if they did succeed, they would find that they had sown the wind and would surely reap the whirlwind,[11] for they would ultimately provoke the violent excesses which accompany a reform coming by convulsion instead of by steady and natural growth.

On the other hand, the wild preachers of unrest and discontent, the wild agitators against the entire existing order, the men who act crookedly whether because of sinister design or from mere puzzle-headedness, the men who preach destruction without proposing any substitute for what they intend to destroy or who propose a substitute which would be far worse than the existing evils—all these men are the most dangerous opponents of real reform. If they get their way, they will lead the people into a deeper pit than any into which they could fall under the present system. If they fail to get their way, they will still do incalculable harm by provoking the kind of reaction which in its revolt against the senseless evil of their teaching would enthrone more securely than ever the very evils which their misguided followers believe they are attacking.

More important than aught else is the development of the broadest sympathy of man for man. The welfare of the wage-worker, the welfare of the tiller of the soil, upon these depend the welfare of the entire country; their good is not to be sought in pulling down others, but their good must be the prime object of all our statesmanship.

Materially we must strive to secure a broader economic opportunity for all men so that each shall have a better chance to show the stuff of which he is made. Spiritually and ethically we must strive to bring about clean living and right thinking. We appreciate that the things of the body are important, but we appreciate also that the things of the soul are immeasurably more important. The foundation stone of national life is, and ever must be, the high individual character of the average citizen.

9. Exodus 20:15.

10. "Breeching work" and "collar work" pertain to the harnessing of work animals for pulling loads. Traces are straps that connect the collar or harness and the load.

11. An allusion to Hosea 8:7.

Eugene V. Debs

⌗

The Issue

GIRARD, KANSAS
MAY 23, 1908

B ORN IN 1855 in Terre Haute, Indiana, Eugene Victor Debs was involved
in labor unions and politics from a young age. He left school at fourteen
to work on the railroad and soon became a nationally known figure in
the Brotherhood of Railway Firemen. In 1893 he founded the American Railway
Union (ARU). The following year, he and the ARU launched a national strike
against railroads operating with Pullman cars. After President Grover Cleveland
sent federal troops to Chicago to break the strike, Debs was arrested and sentenced to six months in jail.

Soon after his release, Debs committed himself to socialism, a cause that
would sustain him for the rest of his days. Nominated for President five times
on the Socialist Party ticket, he was praised by friend and foe alike as one of
the greatest orators of his generation. His speeches combined grand predic-
tions of social revolution with appeals to basic American values of liberty,
equality, free speech, and democracy. "There he is, there he is," one woman
stood up and shouted at a 1908 rally. "Gene Debs, not the missing link but the
living link between God and man.... Here is the God consciousness, come
down to earth."

"The Issue" is characteristic of Debs's oratory—sharp in logic, rich in style,
full of heartfelt pleas for solidarity and visions of America's rebirth. Delivered in
Girard, Kansas, where Debs lived and coedited the Socialist newspaper *Appeal
to Reason* with his colleague Fred Warren, it was, for all intents and purposes, his
acceptance speech kicking off the 1908 presidential campaign. On the day of the
speech, the Socialist Party, meeting in Chicago, nominated Debs for President
for the third time. Debs had not yet learned the news when Warren entered his
office and invited him to a carnival forming in Girard's town square. The carnival turned out to be a countywide rally celebrating Debs's nomination. After
overcoming his initial embarrassment at the showing of support, Debs spoke
impromptu for more than two hours.

Declaring that he opposed "the system under which we live today because...it
is subversive of the best interests of the people," Debs looked forward to the triumph of socialism and "the grandest civilization that the human race has ever
known." He knew that while most in the audience liked him personally, they
disapproved of his politics. As always, however, he was steadfast in his belief

that "Intelligent discontent is the mainspring of civilization." "Progress," he proclaimed, "is born of agitation. It is agitation or stagnation. I have taken my choice."

Debs's speech was stenographically recorded and distributed widely by the Socialist Party. The text below is taken from the *Appeal to Reason* of May 23, 1908, and does not contain the revisions added in subsequent print versions.

◇◇

Ladies and Gentlemen: When I made some inquiry a few moments ago as to the cause for this assembling, I was told that it was the beginning of another street fair. I am quite surprised, and agreeably so, to find myself the central attraction. Allow me in the very beginning to express my heartiest appreciation of the more than kind and generous words which have been spoken here for me this afternoon. There are times when words, mere words—no matter how fitly chosen or tenderly expressed—are almost meaningless. As the rosebud under the influence of sunshine and shower opens, so does my heart receive your benedictions this afternoon.

I am a new resident of Girard, have been here but a comparatively short time, and yet I feel myself as completely at home among you, most of whom disagree with me upon very vital questions, as I do in the town in which I was born and reared and have lived all the days of my life. Since the day I first came here I have been treated with uniform kindness. I could not have been treated more hospitably anywhere. I have met practically all of your people, and all of them have taken me by the hand and treated me as cordially as if I had been neighbor and friend with them, and to say that I appreciate this is to express myself in hackneyed and very unsatisfactory manner.

The honor to which reference has been made has come to me through no fault of my own. It has been said that some men are born great, some achieve greatness, and some have greatness thrust upon them.[1] It is even so with what are called honors. Some men have honors thrust upon them. I find myself in that class. I did what little I could to prevent myself from being nominated by the convention now in session at Chicago, but the nomination

sought me out, and in spite of myself I stand in your presence this afternoon the nominee of the Socialist Party for the presidency of the United States. Long, long ago I made up my mind never again to be a candidate for any political office within the gift of the people. I was constrained to violate that vow because when I joined the Socialist Party, I was taught that the desire of the individual was subordinate to the party will and that when the party commanded it was my duty to obey.

There was a time in my life when I had the vanities of youth, when I sought that bubble called fame. I have outlived it. I have reached that point when I am capable of placing an estimate upon my own relative insignificance. I have come to realize that there is no honor in any real sense of that term to any man unless he is capable of freely consecrating himself to the service of his fellow men. To the extent that I am able to help those who are unable to help themselves, to that extent, and to that extent alone, do I honor myself and the party to which I belong. So far as the presidency of the United States is concerned, I would spurn it were it not that it conferred the power to serve the working class, and he who enters that office with any other conception prostitutes and does not honor that office.

Now, my friends, I am opposed to the system of society in which we live today, not because I lack the natural equipment to do for myself, but because I am not satisfied to make myself comfortable knowing that there are thousands upon thousands of my fellow men who suffer for the barest necessities of life. We were taught under the old ethic that man's business upon this earth was to look out for himself. That was the ethic of the jungle, the ethic of the wild beast. Take care of yourself, no matter what may become of your fellow man. Thousands of years ago the question was

---

1. From William Shakespeare, *Twelfth Night* (1623).

asked: "Am I my brother's keeper?"[2] That question has never yet been answered in a way that is satisfactory to civilized society. Yes, I am my brother's keeper. I am under a moral obligation to him that is inspired not by any maudlin sentimentality, but by the higher duty I owe to myself. What would you think of me if I were capable of seating myself at a table and gorging myself with food and saw about me the children of my fellow-beings starving to death?

Allow me to say to you, my fellow men, that nature has spread a great table bounteously for all of the children of men. There is room for all and there is a plate and a place and food for all, and any system of society that denies a single one the right and the opportunity to freely help himself to nature's bounties is an unjust and iniquitous system that ought to be abolished in the interest of a higher humanity and a civilization worthy of the name.

And here let me observe, my fellow men, that while the general impression is that human society is stationary—a finality, as it were—it is not so for a single instant. Underlying society there are great material forces that are in operation all of the circling hours of the day and night, and at certain points in the social development these forces outgrow the forms that hold them and these forms spring apart and then a new social system comes into existence and a new era dawns for the human race.

The great majority of mankind have always been in darkness. The overwhelming majority of the children of men have always been their own worst enemies. In every age of this world's history, the kings and emperors and czars and the potentates, in alliance with the priests, have sought by all the means at their command to keep the people in darkness that they might perpetuate the power in which they riot and revel in luxury while the great mass are in a state of slavery and degradation, and he who has spoken out courageously against the existing order, he who has dared to voice the protest of the oppressed and downtrodden, has had to pay the penalty, all the way from Jesus Christ of Galilee down to Fred Warren of Girard.[3]

2. Genesis 4:9.

3. Debs's colleague and coeditor of the Socialist newspaper *Appeal to Reason.*

Do you know, my friends, it is so easy to agree with the ignorant majority. It is so easy to make the people applaud an empty platitude. It takes some courage to face that beast called the majority, and tell him the truth to his teeth! Some men do so and accept the consequences of their acts as becomes men, and they live in history—every one of them. I have said so often, and I wish to repeat it on this occasion, that mankind have always crowned their oppressors, and they have as uniformly crucified their saviors, and this has been true all along the highway of the centuries. It is true today. It will not always be so. When the great majority have become enlightened, when the great mass know the truth, they will treat an honest man decently while he lives and not crucify him and then a thousand years afterward rear a monument above the dust of the hero they put to death.

I am in revolt against capitalism (and that doesn't mean to say, my friends, that I am hating you—not the slightest). I am opposed to capitalism because I love my fellow men, and if I am opposing you, I am opposing you for what I believe to be your good, and though you spat upon me with contempt, I would still oppose you to the extent of my power.

I don't hate the working man because he has turned against me. I know the poor fellow is too ignorant to understand his self-interest, and I know that as a rule the working man is the friend of his enemy and the enemy of his friend. He votes for men who represent a system in which labor is simply merchandise, in which the man who works the hardest and longest has the least to show for it. If there is a man on this earth who is entitled to all the comforts and luxuries of this life in abundance, it is the man whose labor produces them. If he is not, who is? Does he get them in the present system?

And, mark you, I am not speaking in a partisan sense this afternoon. I appreciate the fact that you have come here as Republicans and Democrats as well as Socialists to do me a personal honor, and I would be ungrateful indeed if I took advantage of such an occasion to speak to you in an offensive and partisan sense. I wish to say in the broadest possible way that I am opposing the system under which we live today because I believe it is subversive of the best interests of the people. I am not satisfied with things as they are, and I know that no matter what administration is in power, even were it a Socialist administration, I know that there will be no material change in the condition of the people until we have a new social system based upon the mutual economic interest of the people—not until you and I and all of us collectively own those things that we collectively need and use.

That is a basic economic proposition. As long as a relatively few men own the railroads, the telegraph, the telephone, own the oil fields and the gas fields and the steel mills and the sugar refineries and the leather tanneries—own, in short, the sources and means of life—they will corrupt our politics, they will enslave the working class, they will impoverish and debase society, they will do all things that are needful to perpetuate their power as the economic masters and the political rulers of the people. Not until these great agencies are owned and operated by the people can the people hope for any material improvement in their social condition.

Is the condition fair today and satisfactory to the thinking man? According to the most reliable reports at our command, as I speak here this afternoon there are at least four millions of working men vainly searching for employment. Have you ever found yourself in that unspeakably sad predicament? Have you ever had to go up the street, begging for work, in a great city thronged with surging humanity—and by the way, my friends, people are never quite so strange to each other as when they are forced into artificial, crowded, and stifled relationship.

I would rather be friendless out on the American desert than to be friendless in New York or Chicago. Have you ever walked up one side of the street and come back on the other side while your wife, Mary, was waiting at home with three or four children for you to report that you had found work? Quite fortunately for me I had an experience of somewhat similar nature to this quite early in my life. "Quite fortunately" because had I not known from my own experience just what it is to have to beg for work, just what it is to be shown the door as if I were a very offensive intruder, had I not known what it is to suffer for the want of food, had I not seen every door closed and barred in my face, had I not found myself

friendless and alone in the city as a boy looking for work, and in vain, perhaps I would not be here this afternoon. I might have grown up, as some others have who have been, as they regard themselves, fortunate. I might have waved aside my fellow men and said: "Do as I have done. If you are without work, it is your own fault. Look at me; I am self-made. No man is under the necessity of looking for work if he is willing to work."

Nothing is more humiliating than to have to beg for work, and a system in which any man has to beg for work stands condemned. No man can defend it. Now, the rights of one are just as sacred as the rights of a million. Suppose you happen to be the individual one who has no work. This republic is a failure so far as you are concerned.

Every man has the inalienable right to work. Here I stand, just as I was created. I have two hands that represent my labor power. I have some bone and muscle and sinew and some energy. I want to exchange it for food and clothing and shelter. Between my right to apply my labor to the tools with which work is done there stands a man artificially created. He says, "No, no!" Why not? "Because you cannot first make a profit for me."

Now, there has been a revolution in industry during the last fifty years, but the trouble with most people is that they haven't kept pace with it. They don't know anything about it and they are especially innocent in regard to it in the small western cities and states where the same old conditions of a century ago still prevail. Your grandfather could help himself anywhere. All he needed was some very cheap, simple, primitive tools and he could then apply his labor to the resources of nature with his individual tools and produce what he needed. That era in our history produced our greatest men.

Lincoln[4] himself sprang from this primitive state of society. People have said, "Why, he had no chance. See how great he became." Yes, but Lincoln had for his comrades great green-plumed forest monarchs. He could put his arms about them and hear their heartthrobs as they said: "Go on, Abe, a great destiny

4. Abraham Lincoln, U.S. President, 1861–1865.

awaits you." He was in partnership with nature. He associated with flowers and he was in the fields and he heard the rippling music of the laughing brooks and streams. Nature took him to her bosom. Nature nourished him, and from his unpolluted heart there sprang his noble aspirations. Had Lincoln been born in a sweatshop, he would never have been heard of.

How is it with the babe that is born in Mott Street or in the lower Bowery or in the East Side of New York City? That is where thousands, tens of thousands, and hundreds of thousands of babes are born who are to constitute our future generations. I have seen children ten years of age in New York City who had never seen a live chicken. They don't know what it is to put their tiny feet on a blade of grass. It is the most densely populated spot on earth.

You have seen your beehive—just fancy a human beehive of which yours is the miniature and you have the industrial hive under capitalism. If you have never seen this condition, you are excusable for not being a Socialist. Come to New York, Chicago, San Francisco with me; remain with me just twenty-four hours and then look into my face as I shall look into yours when I ask: "What about socialism now?" These children by hundreds and thousands are born in subcellars where a whole grown family is crowded together in one room, where modesty between the sexes is absolutely impossible. They are surrounded by filth and vermin. From their birth they see nothing but immorality and vice and crime. They are tainted in the cradle. They are inoculated by their surroundings and they are doomed from the beginning. This system takes their lives just as certainly as if a dagger were thrust into their quivering little hearts, and let me say to you that it were better for many thousands of them if they had never seen the light of day.

Now I submit, my friends, that such a condition as this is indefensible in the twentieth century. Time was when everything had to be done in a very primitive way and most men had to work all their days, all their lives, to feed themselves and shelter themselves. They had no time, they had no opportunity for a higher development, and so they were what the world calls illiterate. They had little chance. It took all their time and energy to feed the animal. But how is it today? Upon the average twenty men can today,

with the aid of modern machinery, produce as much wealth as a thousand did a half century ago. Can you think of a single thing that enters into our daily existence that cannot be easily produced in abundance for all? If you can, I wish you would do me the kindness to name it.

I don't know it all. I am simply a student of this great question, and I am serving as best I can and I know my eyes are ready for the light, and I thank that man, no matter what he be, who can add to the flame of the torch that I bear in my hand. If there is a single thing that you can think of that cannot be produced in abundance, name it. Bread, clothing, fuel—everything is here. Nature's storehouse is full to the surface of the earth. All of the raw materials are deposited here in abundance. We have the most marvelous machinery the world has ever known. Man has long since become master of the natural forces and made them work for him. Now he has but to touch a button and the wheels begin to spin and the machinery to whirr and wealth is produced on every hand in increasing abundance. Why should any man, woman, or child suffer for food, clothing, or shelter? Why? The question cannot be answered.

Don't tell me that some men are too lazy to work. Suppose they are too lazy to work; what do you think of a social system that produces men too lazy to work? If a man is too lazy to work, don't treat him with contempt. Don't look down upon him with scorn as if you were a superior being. If there is a man who is too lazy to work, there is something the matter with him. He wasn't born right or he was perverted in this system. You could not, if you tried, keep a normal man inactive, and if you did, he would go stark mad. You go to any penitentiary and you will find the men there begging for the privilege of doing work.

I know by very close study of the question exactly how men become idle. I don't repel them when I meet them. I have never yet seen the tramp I was not able to receive with open arms. He is a little less fortunate than I am. He is made the same as I am made. He is the child of the same Father. Had I been born in his environment, had I been subjected to the same things to which he was, I would have been where he is.

Can you tell me why there wasn't a tramp in the United States in 1860? In that day, if someone had said "tramp," no one would have known what was meant by it. If human nature is innately depraved and men would rather ride on brake-beams and sleep in holes and caves instead of comfortable beds, if they would do that from pure choice and from natural depravity, why were they not built that way fifty years ago? Fifty years ago capitalism was in its earlier stages. Fifty years ago work was still mainly done by hand and every boy could learn a trade and every boy could master the tools and go to work. That is why there were no tramps.

In fifty years that simple tool has become a mammoth machine. It is larger and larger all the time. It has crowded the hand tool out of production. With the machine came the capitalist. There were no capitalists; nor was there such a thing as capital before the beginning of the present system. Capitalists came with machinery. Up to the time that machinery supplanted the hand tool, the little employer was himself a working man. No matter what the shop or factory, you would find the employer sitting side by side with his men. He was a superior workman who got more orders than he could fill and employed some men to help him, but he had to pay them the equivalent of what they produced because if he did not, they would pack up their tools and go into business for themselves.

Now the individual tool has become the mammoth machine. It has multiplied production by hundreds. The old tool was individually owned and used. The modern tool, in the form of a great machine, is social in every conception of it. Look at one of these giant machines. Come to the *Appeal* office and look at the press in operation. Here the progressive conception of the ages is crystallized. What individual shall put his hand on this social machine and say, "This is mine! He who would apply labor here must first pay tribute to me."

The hand tool has been very largely supplanted by this machine. Not many tools are left. You are still producing in a very small way here in Girard, but your production is flickering out gradually. It is but a question of time until it will expire entirely. In spite of all that can be said or done to the contrary, production is organizing upon a larger and larger scale and becoming entirely cooperative. This has crowded out

the smaller competitor and gradually opened the way for a new social order.

Your material interest and mine in the society of the future will be the same. Instead of having to fight each other like animals, as we do today, and seeking to glorify the brute struggle for existence—of which every civilized human being ought to be ashamed—instead of this, our material interests are going to be mutual. We are going to jointly own these mammoth machines and we are going to operate them as joint partners and we are going to divide all the products among ourselves.

We are not going to send our surplus to the Jim Hills, Goulds, and Vanderbilts[5] of New York. We are not going to pile up a billion of dollars in John D. Rockefeller's[6] hands—a vast pyramid from the height of which he can look down with scorn and contempt upon the "common herd." John D. Rockefeller's great fortune is built upon your ignorance. When you know enough to know what your interest is, you will support the party that is organized upon the principle of collective ownership of the means of life. This party will sweep into power upon the issue of emancipation just as Republicanism swept into power upon the abolition question half a century ago.[7]

In the meantime, don't have any fear of us Socialists. We don't mean any harm! Many of you have been taught to look upon us as very dangerous people. It is amazing to what extent this prejudice has struck root. The capitalist press will tell you of a good many things that we Socialists are going to do that we never intend to do. They will tell you we are going to break up the home. Great heavens! What about the homes of the four million tramps that are looking for work today? How about the thousands and thousands of miserable shacks in New York and every great city where humanity festers? It would be

---

5. Financiers and railroad magnates James J. Hill (1838–1916), Jay Gould (1836–1892), and Cornelius Vanderbilt (1794–1877), all of whom were symbols of corrupt business practices and unbridled wealth.

6. Industrialist and president of the Standard Oil Company.

7. Debs is referring to the triumph of the Republican Party in the 1860 presidential election.

a good thing if they were torn down and obliterated completely, for they are not fit for human habitation. No, we are not going to destroy the home, but we are going to make the home possible for the first time in history.

You may think you are very comfortable. Let me make you a little comparison. You may not agree with me. I don't expect you to and I don't ask you to. I am going to ask you to remember what I say this afternoon, and perhaps before I am elected President of the United States, you will believe what I say is true. Now, there are those of you who are fairly comfortable under the present standard. Isn't it amazing to you how little the average man is satisfied with? You go out here to the edge of town and you will find a small farmer who has a small cabin with just room enough to keep himself and wife and two or three children, which has a mortgage on it, and he works early and late and gets just enough in net returns to keep him in working order, and he will deliver a lecture about the wonderful prosperity of the country. He is satisfied, and that is his calamity.

Now, the majority of you would say that is his good fortune: "It is a blessing that he is satisfied." I want to see if I can show you that it is a curse to him and to society that he is satisfied. If it had not been for the discontent of a few fellows who have not been satisfied with their condition, you would still be living in caves. You never would have emerged from the jungle. Intelligent discontent is the mainspring of civilization. Progress is born of agitation. It is agitation or stagnation. I have taken my choice.

This farmer works all day long, works hard enough to produce enough to live the life of a man—not of an animal, but of a man. Now, there is an essential difference between a man and an animal. I admire a magnificent animal in any form except in the human form. Suppose you had everything that you could possibly desire so far as your physical wants are concerned. Suppose you had a million to your credit in the bank, a palatial home, and relations to suit yourself, but no soul capacity for real enjoyment. If you were denied knowing what sorrow is, what real joy is, what music is, and literature and sculpture, and all of those subtle influences that touch the heart and quicken the pulses and fire the senses and

so lift and ennoble a man that he can feel his head among the stars and in communion with God himself—if you are denied these, no matter how sleek or fat or contented you may be, you are still as base and as corrupt and as repulsive a being as walks God's green earth.

You may have plenty of money. The poorest people on this earth are those who have [the] most money. A man is said to be poor who has none, but he is a pauper who has nothing else. Now this farmer, what does he know about literature? After his hard day's work is done, here he sits in his little shack. He is fed and his animal wants are satisfied. It is at this time that a man begins to live. It is not while you work and slave that you live. It is when you have done your work honestly, when you have contributed your share to the common fund, that you begin to live. Then, as Whitman[8] said, you take out your soul; you can commune with yourself; you can take a comrade by the hand and you can look into his eyes and down into his soul, and in that communion you live.[9] And if you don't know what that is, or if you are not at least on the edge of it, it is denied you to even look into the promised land.[10]

Now, this farmer knows nothing about the literature of the world. All its libraries are sealed to him. So far as he is concerned, Homer and Dante and Dickens[11] might as well not have lived. Beethoven, Liszt, and Wagner,[12] and all those musicians whose art makes the common atmosphere blossom with harmony, [have] never been for this farmer. He knows nothing about literature or art. Never rises above the animal plane upon which he is living. Within fifteen minutes after he has ceased to live, he is forgotten; the next generation doesn't know his name, and the

---

8. American poet Walt Whitman (1819–1892).

9. Debs is drawing on Whitman's *Democratic Vistas* (1871).

10. As told in the Bible, the land promised by God to the Israelites after their escape from bondage in Egypt.

11. Greek epic poet Homer (8th century BCE), Italian poet Dante Alighieri (1265–1321), British author Charles Dickens (1812–1870).

12. Composers Ludwig van Beethoven (1770–1827), Franz Liszt (1811–1886), and Richard Wagner (1813–1883).

world doesn't know he ever lived. This is life under the present standard.

You tell me this is all the farmer is fit for? What do I propose to do for that farmer? Nothing. I want to awaken that farmer to the fact that he is robbed every day in the week, and if I can awaken him to the fact that he is robbed under the capitalist system, he will fall into line with the Socialist movement and will march to the polls on election day, and instead of casting his vote to fasten the shackles upon his limbs more firmly, he will cast a vote for his emancipation. All I have to do is to show that farmer, that day laborer, that tramp, that they are victims of this system, that their interests are identical, that they constitute the millions and that the millions have the votes. The Rockefellers have the dollars, but we have the votes; and when we have sense enough to know how to use the votes, we will have not only the votes but the dollars for all the children of men.

This seems quite visionary to some of you, and especially to those of you who know absolutely nothing about economics. I could not begin to tell you the story of social evolution this afternoon, of how these things are doing day by day, of how the world is being pushed into socialism, and how it is bound to arrive, no matter whether you are for it or against it. It is the next inevitable phase of civilization. It isn't a scheme; it isn't a contrivance. It isn't anything that is made to order. The day is coming when you will be pushed into it by unseen hands whether you will it or not. Nothing can be introduced until the people want it, and when the majority want it, they will know how to get it.

I venture the prophecy that within the next five years you will be completely dispossessed. You are howling against the trusts, and the trusts are laughing at you. You keep on voting in the same old way, and the trusts will keep on getting what you produce. You say Congress will give you some relief. Good heavens! Who will save us from Congress? Don't you know that Congress is made up almost wholly of trust lawyers and corporation attorneys? I don't happen to have the roll of this one, but with few exceptions they are all lawyers. Now, in the competitive system, the lawyer sells himself to the highest bidder, the same as the working man does. Who is the highest bidder?

The corporation, of course. So the trust buys the best lawyer and the common herd gets the poor one.

Now, it is a fact that politics is simply the reflex of economics. The material foundation of society determines the character of all social institutions—political, educational, ethical, and spiritual. In exact proportion as the economic foundation of society changes, the character of all social institutions changes to correspond to that basis. Half of this country was in favor of chattel slavery and half was opposed to it, geographically speaking.[13] Why was the church of the South in favor of chattel slavery? Why was the church of the North opposed to chattel slavery? The Northern capitalist wasn't a bit more opposed to chattel slavery from any moral sense than was the Southern plantation owner. The South produced cotton for the market by the hand labor of Negro slaves. On the other hand, the North wasn't dependent upon cotton—could raise no cotton. In the North it was the small capitalist at the beginning of capitalism who, with the machine, had begun to manufacture and wanted cheap labor; and the sharper the competition, the cheaper he could buy his labor. Now, chattel slavery to the Southern plantation owner was the source of his wealth. He had to have slaves, and what the plantation owner had to have in economics the preacher had to justify in religion. As long as chattel slavery was necessary to the Southern plantation owner, as long as that stage of the economic condition lasted, the preachers stood up in the pulpits of the South and said it was ordained of God and proved it by the Bible. I don't know of any crime that the oppressors and their hirelings have not proven by the Bible.

Then competition between workers began as machines took the place of hand labor. Manufacturers wanted larger and larger bodies of labor, and that competition spread out here to Kansas, and I have always felt when in Kansas that I stood on sacred soil. When I hear the name of Kansas, I doff my hat in reverence. The Free-Soilers[14] came here, despised, hated,

13. Debs is referring to the situation that existed before the Civil War of 1861–1865.

14. Abolitionists who went to the Kansas Territory in the mid-1850s to prevent the establishment of slavery there.

and persecuted. They were the enemies of the human race. Why? Because they had hearts throbbing within their breasts. Because they looked with pity and compassion upon the Negro slave who received his wages in lashes applied to his naked back; who saw his crying wife torn from him and his children, pleading, snatched from his side and sold into slavery while the great mass looked on just as the great mass is looking on today, and the preachers stood up in their pulpits and said: "It is all right. It is God-ordained." And whenever an abolitionist raised his head, he was persecuted and hounded as if he had been a wild beast.

I heard the story from Wendell Phillips[15] one evening. I never can forget it. How I wish he was here this afternoon! We sat together and he said: "Debs, the world will never know with what bitter and relentless persecution the early abolitionists had to contend." Wendell Phillips was the most perfect aristocrat in everything I have ever seen; who came nearest being a perfect man; who, when he stood erect, instantly challenged respect and admiration—almost veneration. Wendell Phillips was treated as if he had been the worst felon on earth. They went to his house one night to mob him, and why? Because he protested against sending a young Negro girl and a Negro man back into slavery. They came to take them back, and the whole Commonwealth of Massachusetts said, "Take them back! Obey the law!" That is what they are everlastingly saying to us: "Obey the law!" Just above the door of the statehouse there was an inscription: "God Bless the Commonwealth of Massachusetts." Wendell Phillips said: "If Massachusetts has become a slave hunter, if Massachusetts is in alliance with the slave catchers of the South, that inscription over the portal of the doors should be changed and in place of 'God Bless the Commonwealth of Massachusetts,' it should be 'God Damn the Commonwealth of Massachusetts!'"[16] God smiled in that same instant.

All of the slave catchers and holders, all of the oppressors of man, all of the enemies of the human race, all of the rulers of Siberia, where a large part of this earth's surface has been transformed into a hell—all have spoken in the name of the Great God and in the name of the Holy Bible.

There will be a change one of these days. The world is just beginning to awaken, and is soon to sing its first anthem of freedom. All the signs of the times are cheering. Twenty-five years ago there was but a handful of Socialists; today there are a half million. When the polls are closed next fall, you will be astonished. The Socialist movement is in alliance with the forces of progress. We are today where the abolitionists were in 1858. They had a million and a quarter of votes. There was dissension in the Whig, Republican, and Free-Soil parties, but the time had come for a great change, and the Republican Party was formed in spite of the bickerings and contentions of men.[17] Lincoln made the great speech in that year that gave him the nomination and afterward made him President of the United States.[18]

If you had said to the people in 1858, "In two years from now the Republican Party is going to sweep the country and seat the President," you would have been laughed to scorn. The Socialist Party stands today where the Republican Party stood fifty years ago. It is in alliance with the forces of evolution; the one party that has a clear-cut, overmastering, overshadowing issue; the party that stands for all the people, and the only party that stands for all the people.

In this system we have one set who are called capitalists and another set who are called workers, and they are at war with each other over the division of the product. Now, we Socialists propose that society in its collective capacity shall produce, not for profit, but in abundance to satisfy human wants; that every man shall have the inalienable right to work and receive the full equivalent of all he produces; that every man may stand fearlessly erect in the pride and majesty of his own manhood. Every man and every woman will be economically free. They can, without let or hindrance, apply their labor, with the best machinery

---

15. Abolitionist leader (1811–1884) who took up the cause of labor after the Civil War.

16. Debs's narrative combines facets of public memory with dramatic embellishment and does not accord with any specific incident or speech from Phillips's life.

17. The Republican Party was formed in 1854.

18. Debs is referring to Lincoln's "House Divided" speech of June 16, 1858.

that can be devised, to all the natural resources; do the work of society and produce for all; and then receive in exchange a certificate of value equivalent to that of their production.

Then society will improve its institutions in exact proportion to the progress of invention. Whether you work in city or on farm, all things productive will be carried forward on a gigantic scale. All industry will be completely organized. Society for the first time will have a scientific foundation. Every man, by being economically free, will have some time for himself. He can then take a full and perfect breath. He can go to his wife and children because then he will have a home.

We are not going to destroy private property. We are going to introduce and establish private property—all the private property that is necessary to house man, keep him in comfort, and satisfy all his physical wants. Eighty percent of the people in the United States have no property of any kind today. A few have got it all. They have dispossessed the people, and when we get into power, we will dispossess them.

We will reduce the workday and give every man a chance. We will go to the parks, and we will have music because we will have time to play music and inclination to hear it. Is it not sad to think that not one in a thousand know what music is? Is it not pitiable to see the poor, ignorant, dumb human utterly impervious to the divine influence of music? If humanity could only respond to the higher influences! And it would if it had time. Release the animal, throw off his burden, give him a chance and he rises, as if by magic, to the plane of a man.

Man has all of these divine attributes. They are in a latent state. They are not yet developed. It does not pay now to love music. Keep your eye on the almighty dollar and your fellow man. Get the dollar and keep him down. Make him produce for you. You are not your brother's keeper in this system. Suppose he is poor! Suppose his wife is forced into prostitution! Suppose his child is deformed! And suppose he shuffles off by destroying himself! What is that to you? But you ought to be ashamed. Take the standard home and look it in the face. If you know what that standard means, and you are a success, God help the failure!

Our conduct is determined by our economic relations. If you and I must fight each other to exist, we will not love each other very hard. We can go to the same church and hear the minister tell us in good conscience that we ought to love each other, and the next day we approach the edge of some business transaction. Do we remember what the minister told us? No, it is gone until the next Sunday. Six days in the week we are following the Golden Rule[19] reversed. Now, when we approach the edge of a business transaction in competition, what is more natural than that we should try to get the better of the transaction? Get the better of our fellow man? Cheat him if we can? And if you succeed, that fixes you as a successful businessman. You have all the necessary qualifications. Don't let your conscience disturb you—that would interfere with business.

Competition was natural enough once, but do you think you are competing today? Many of you think you are competing. Against whom? Against Rockefeller? About as I would if I had a wheelbarrow and competed with the Santa Fe[20] from here to Kansas City. That is about the way you are competing, but your boys will not have even that chance—if capitalism lives that long. You hear of the "late" panic.[21] It is very late. It is going to be very late. This panic will be with us five years from now and will continue from now till then.

I am not a prophet. I can no more penetrate the future than you can. I do study the forces that underlie society and the trend of evolution. I can tell by what we have passed through about what we will have in the future; and I know that capitalism can be beaten, and the people put ultimately in possession. Now, then, when we have taken possession and we jointly own the sources and means of production, we will no longer have to fight each other to live. Our interests, instead of being competitive,

19. "Do unto others as you would have others do unto you" (paraphrased from Matthew 7:12).

20. The Atchison, Topeka & Santa Fe Railway.

21. Debs is referring to the Panic of 1907, a severe financial crisis brought on by weaknesses in the U.S. banking system.

will be cooperative. We will work side by side. Your interest shall be mine and mine will be yours. That is the economic condition from which will spring the humane social relation.

When we are in partnership and have stopped clutching each other's throats, when we have stopped enslaving each other, then we will stand together, hands clasped, and we will be friends. We will be comrades, we will be brothers, and we will begin the march to the grandest civilization that the human race has ever known.

I did not mean to keep you so long this afternoon. I am sure I appreciate the patience with which you have listened to me. From the very depths of my heart I thank you, each of you—every man, woman, and child—for this splendid testimonial, for this beautiful tribute which I shall remember with gratitude and love until memory empties its urn into forgetfulness.

Woodrow Wilson

X

First Inaugural Address

WASHINGTON, D.C.
MARCH 4, 1913

THE GREATEST CHALLENGE facing the United States from 1890 to 1915 was reconciling the perturbations brought on by massive industrialization with the traditional values and practices of American life. Beginning with the populist campaigns of the 1890s and continuing into the Progressive Era, the quest for reform won a succession of local and state battles before finally taking firm hold at the national level. In 1912 Woodrow Wilson was elected President in a three-way contest against Republican William Howard Taft and Progressive Party candidate Theodore Roosevelt. As President, Wilson secured passage of new laws that reformed the tariff, created a federal income tax, established the Federal Reserve system and the Federal Trade Commission, protected the rights of labor, established credit for farmers, and curbed the power of monopolies. It was the most sweeping series of national reform measures in American history before the New Deal.

In his first inaugural address, Wilson articulated the spirit of reform so eloquently that the Cleveland *Plain Dealer* opined that "not since Lincoln has there been a President so wonderfully gifted in the art of expression." While noting the many blessings of American life, Wilson proclaimed that "evil has come with the good, and much fine gold has been corroded." Not only had industrial growth exacted a "fearful physical and spiritual cost to the men and women and children" across the land, but the government had "too often been made use of for private and selfish purposes." Adumbrating the reform agenda he would soon present to

Congress, Wilson declared that "our duty is to cleanse, to reconsider, to restore, to correct the evil without impairing the good."

As was typical of his manuscript presentations, Wilson composed his inaugural by writing it in shorthand and then copying it on his own typewriter before making final revisions by hand. In a sense, though, he had been preparing for it his whole life. His father, a Presbyterian minister, began schooling him in the principles of effective speech before he was five. Wilson started studying the great orators of history as a youngster, participated in literary and debating societies throughout his college years, and by the time of his inauguration had become a gifted speaker whose achievements would eventually rival those of his heroes William Gladstone and Edmund Burke.

◇◇◇

There has been a change of government. It began two years ago, when the House of Representatives became Democratic by a decisive majority. It has now been completed. The Senate about to assemble will also be Democratic. The offices of President and Vice President have been put into the hands of Democrats. What does the change mean? That is the question that is uppermost in our minds today. That is the question I am going to try to answer in order, if I may, to interpret the occasion.

It means much more than the mere success of a party. The success of a party means little except when the nation is using that party for a large and definite purpose. No one can mistake the purpose for which the nation now seeks to use the Democratic Party. It seeks to use it to interpret a change in its own plans and point of view. Some old things with which we had grown familiar, and which had begun to creep into the very habit of our thought and of our lives, have altered their aspect as we have latterly looked critically upon them, with fresh, awakened eyes—have dropped their disguises and shown themselves alien and sinister. Some new things, as we look frankly upon them, willing to comprehend their real character, have come to assume the aspect of things long believed in and familiar, stuff of our own convictions. We have been refreshed by a new insight into our own life.

We see that in many things that life is very great. It is incomparably great in its material aspects, in its body of wealth, in the diversity and sweep of its energy, in the industries which have been conceived and built up by the genius of individual men and the limitless enterprise of groups of men. It is great also, very great, in its moral force. Nowhere else in the world have noble men and women exhibited in more striking forms the beauty and the energy of sympathy and helpfulness and counsel in their efforts to rectify wrong, alleviate suffering, and set the weak in the way of strength and hope. We have built up, moreover, a great system of government, which has stood through a long age as in many respects a model for those who seek to set liberty upon foundations that will endure against fortuitous change, against storm and accident. Our life contains every great thing, and contains it in rich abundance.

But the evil has come with the good, and much fine gold has been corroded. With riches has come inexcusable waste. We have squandered a great part of what we might have used and have not stopped to conserve the exceeding bounty of nature without which our genius for enterprise would have been worthless and impotent, scorning to be careful, shamefully prodigal as well as admirably efficient. We have been proud of our industrial achievements, but we have not hitherto stopped thoughtfully enough to count the human cost, the cost of lives snuffed out, of energies overtaxed and broken, the fearful physical and spiritual cost to the men and women and children upon whom the dead weight and burden of it all has fallen pitilessly the years through. The groans and agony of it all had not yet reached our ears, the solemn, moving undertone of our life, coming up out of the mines and factories and out of every home where the struggle had its intimate and familiar seat. With the great government went many deep secret things which we too long delayed to look into and scrutinize with candid, fearless eyes. The great government we loved has too often been made use of for private and selfish purposes, and those who used it had forgotten the people.

At last a vision has been vouchsafed us of our life as a whole. We see the bad with the good, the debased and decadent with the sound and vital. With this vision we approach new affairs. Our duty is to cleanse, to reconsider, to restore, to correct the evil without impairing the good, to purify and humanize every process of our common life without weakening or sentimentalizing it. There has been something crude and heartless and unfeeling in our haste to succeed and be great. Our thought has been "Let every man look out for himself, let every generation look out for itself," while we reared giant machinery which made it impossible that any but those who stood at the levers of control should have a chance to look out for themselves. We had not forgotten our morals. We remembered well enough that we had set up a polity which was meant to serve the humblest as well as the most powerful, with an eye single to the standards of justice and fair play, and remembered it with pride. But we were very heedless and in a hurry to be great.

We have come now to the sober second thought. The scales of heedlessness have fallen from our eyes. We have made up our minds to square every process of our national life again with the standards we so proudly set up at the beginning and have always carried at our hearts. Our work is a work of restoration.

We have itemized with some degree of particularity the things that ought to be altered, and here are some of the chief items: a tariff which cuts us off from our proper part in the commerce of the world, violates the just principles of taxation, and makes the government a facile instrument in the hands of private interests; a banking and currency system based upon the necessity of the government to sell its bonds fifty years ago and perfectly adapted to concentrating cash and restricting credits; an industrial system which, take it on all its sides, financial as well as administrative, holds capital in leading strings, restricts the liberties and limits the opportunities of labor, and exploits without renewing or conserving the natural resources of the country; a body of agricultural activities never yet given the efficiency of great business undertakings, or served as it should be through the instrumentality of science taken directly to the farm, or afforded the facilities of credit best suited to its practical needs; watercourses undeveloped, waste places unreclaimed, forests untended, fast disappearing without plan or prospect of renewal, unregarded waste heaps at every mine. We have studied as perhaps no other nation has the most effective means of production, but we have not studied cost or economy as we should either as organizers of industry, as statesmen, or as individuals.

Nor have we studied and perfected the means by which government may be put at the service of humanity in safeguarding the health of the nation, the health of its men and its women and its children, as well as their rights in the struggle for existence. This is no sentimental duty. The firm basis of government is justice, not pity. These are matters of justice. There can be no equality of opportunity, the first essential of justice in the body politic, if men and women and children be not shielded in their lives, their very vitality, from the consequences of great industrial and social processes which they cannot alter, control, or singly cope with. Society must see to it that it does not itself crush or weaken or damage its own constituent parts. The first duty of law is to keep sound the society it serves. Sanitary laws, pure-food laws, and laws determining conditions of labor which individuals are powerless to determine for themselves are intimate parts of the very business of justice and legal efficiency.

These are some of the things we ought to do, and not leave the others undone—the old-fashioned, never-to-be-neglected, fundamental safeguarding of property and of individual right. This is the high enterprise of the new day: to lift everything that concerns our life as a nation to the light that shines from the hearthfire of every man's conscience and vision of the right. It is inconceivable that we should do this as partisans; it is inconceivable we should do it in ignorance of the facts as they are or in blind haste. We shall restore, not destroy. We shall deal with our economic system as it is and as it may be modified, not as it might be if we had a clean sheet of paper to write upon; and step by step we shall make it what it should be, in the spirit of those who question their own wisdom and seek counsel and knowledge, not shallow self-satisfaction or the excitement of excursions whither they cannot tell. Justice, and only justice, shall always be our motto.

And yet it will be no cool process of mere science. The nation has been deeply stirred, stirred by a solemn passion, stirred by the knowledge of wrong, of ideals lost, of government too often debauched and made an instrument of evil. The feelings with which we face this new age of right and opportunity sweep across our heartstrings like some air out of God's own presence, where justice and mercy are reconciled and

the judge and the brother are one.[1] We know our task to be no mere task of politics but a task which shall search us through and through, whether we be able to understand our time and the need of our people, whether we be indeed their spokesmen and interpreters, whether we have the pure heart to comprehend and the rectified will to choose our high course of action.

This is not a day of triumph; it is a day of dedication. Here muster, not the forces of party, but the forces of humanity. Men's hearts wait upon us; men's lives hang in the balance; men's hopes call upon us to say what we will do. Who shall live up to the great trust? Who dares fail to try? I summon all honest men, all patriotic, all forward-looking men, to my side. God helping me, I will not fail them, if they will but counsel and sustain me!

---

1. An allusion to the biblical view that mercy and justice are reconciled in God's presence.

Anna Howard Shaw

⧗

The Fundamental Principle of a Republic

OGDENSBURG, NEW YORK
JUNE 21, 1915

ANNA HOWARD SHAW was the preeminent orator of the woman suffrage movement. Born in 1847 Newcastle-on-Tyne, England, she moved to Massachusetts with her family in 1851. She was captivated by the power of speech at an early age and as a child practiced speaking in the woods, where she would "stand up on stumps and address the unresponsive trees, to feel the stir of aspiration within me." Her yearning for accomplishment led her to Boston University, where she received degrees in both theology and medicine. Her real career, however, proved to be reform, and oratory was her métier.

Shaw began lecturing for the Massachusetts Woman Suffrage Association in the mid-1880s. In 1890 she was appointed national lecturer by the National American Woman Suffrage Association, which she also served as president from 1904 to 1915. For three decades she crisscrossed the country speaking on behalf of suffrage to audiences large and small, urban and rural, male and female. Despite the hardships of travel, inclement weather, and grinding fatigue, she gave several hundred speeches a year. Everywhere she went, listeners were captivated by her platform skills. After hearing her, one elderly listener in Greensboro, North Carolina, commented: "There are just two things in which I have not been disappointed—Niagara Falls and Dr. Anna Howard Shaw."

"The Fundamental Principle of a Republic" was Shaw's signature address and shows her dexterity in refuting the arguments of antisuffrage forces and exposing their many inconsistencies. Shaw invariably spoke extemporaneously, and she never composed a polished text of the speech for publication. The stenographic version printed below is from the *Ogdensburg Advance and St. Lawrence Weekly Democrat* and was delivered during the New York state suffrage campaign of 1915. It evinces the power of Shaw's logic, as well as the straightforward, colloquial style that made her, in the words of one contemporary, "simply irresistible." Newspaper accounts note that she spoke for ninety minutes and "thrilled the gathering with her oratorical powers.... She punctuated her appeal with humor and pathos, and the interest of her hearers was sustained throughout."

Like many reformers of her day, Shaw was a pacifist. As is clear from the last section of her speech, she lamented World War I and hoped the United States could escape its vortex. Once America entered the conflict, however, she chaired the Woman's Committee of the Council of National Defense. After the war she was honored for her work by becoming the first living American woman to receive the Distinguished Service Medal. She died in July 1919 after falling ill during a speaking tour in support of American entrance into the League of Nations. Not only was she "generally conceded as the greatest woman speaker who ever lived," wrote the Philadelphia *North American*, but "some believe her to have been without peer in either sex among orators of her day."

◇◇

When I came into your hall tonight, I thought of the last time I was in your city. Twenty-one years ago I came here with Susan B. Anthony,[1] and we came for exactly the same purpose as that for which we are here tonight. Boys have been born since that time and have become voters, and the women are still trying to persuade American men to believe in the fundamental principles of democracy. And I never quite feel as if it was a fair field to argue this question with men

because in doing it, you have to assume that a man who professes to believe in a republican form of government does not believe in a republican form of government, for the only thing that woman's enfranchisement means at all is that a government which claims to be a republic should be a republic, and not an aristocracy.

The difficulty with discussing this question with those who oppose us is that they make any number of arguments, but none of them have anything to do with the subject. I have never heard an argument

---

1. American suffrage leader (1820–1906).

against woman's suffrage which had anything to do with woman's suffrage; they always have something to do with something else. Therefore, the arguments which we have to make rarely ever have anything to do with the subject because we have to answer our opponents, who always escape the subject as far as possible in order to have any sort of reason in connection with what they say.

Now one of two things is true: Either a republic is a desirable form of government or else it is not. If it is, then we should have it; if it is not, then we ought not to pretend that we have it. We ought at least to be true to our ideals, and the men of New York have, for the first time in their lives, the rare opportunity, on the second day of next November, of making this state truly a part of a republic.[2] It is the greatest opportunity which has ever come to the men of the state. They have never had so serious a problem to solve before, they will never have a more serious problem to solve in any future year of our nation's life, and the thing that disturbs me more than anything else in connection with it is that so few people realize what a profound problem they have to solve on November 2. It is not merely a trifling matter; it is not a little thing that does not concern the state; it is the most vital problem we could have, and any man who goes to the polls on the second day of next November without thoroughly informing himself in regard to this subject is unworthy to be a citizen of this state and unfit to cast a ballot.

If woman's suffrage is wrong, it is a great wrong; if it is right, it is a profound and fundamental principle, and we all know, if we know what a republic is, that it is the fundamental principle upon which a republic must rise. Let us see where we are as a people, how we act here, and what we think we are.

The difficulty with the men of this country is that they are so consistent in their inconsistency that they are not aware of having been inconsistent, because their consistency has been so continuous and their inconsistency so consecutive that it has never been broken from the beginning of our nation's life

to the present time. If we trace our history back, we will find that from the very dawn of our existence as a people, men have been imbued with a spirit and a vision more lofty than they have been able to live.

They have been led by visions of the sublimest truth, both in regard to religion and in regard to government, that ever inspired the souls of men from the time the Puritans[3] left the Old World to come to this country, led by the divine ideal which is the sublimest and supremest ideal in religious freedom which men have ever known—the theory that a man has a right to worship God according to the dictates of his own conscience without the intervention of any other man or any other group of men. And it was this theory, this vision of the right of the human soul, which led men first to the shores of this country.

Now nobody can deny that they are sincere, honest, and earnest men. No one can deny that the Puritans were men of profound conviction. And yet these men, who gave up everything in behalf of an ideal, hardly established their communities in this new country before they began to practice exactly the same sort of persecutions on other men which had been practiced upon them. They settled in their communities on the New England shores, and when they formed their compacts by which they governed their local societies, they permitted no man to have a voice in the affairs unless he was a member of the church, and not a member of any church, but a member of the particular church which dominated the particular community in which he happened to be.

In Massachusetts they drove the Baptists down to Rhode Island. In Connecticut they drove the Presbyterians over to New Jersey. They burned the Quakers in Massachusetts and ducked the witches, and no colony, either Catholic or Protestant, allowed a Jew to have a voice. And so a man must worship God according to the conscience of the particular community in which he was located, and yet they called that religious freedom. They were not able to live the ideal of religious liberty, and from that time to this, the men of this government have been following along the same line of inconsistency, while they,

2. November 2 was the date of the vote on the New York woman suffrage amendment; although the amendment failed in 1915, it passed in 1917.

3. English religious separatists who emigrated to the New World during the 1630s.

too, have been following a vision of equal grandeur and power.

Never in the history of the world did it dawn upon the human mind as it dawned upon your ancestors what it would mean for men to be free. They got the vision of a government in which the people would be the supreme power; and so inspired by this vision, men wrote such documents as were sent from [the] Massachusetts legislature, from the New York legislature, and from the Pennsylvania group over to the Parliament of Great Britain which rang with the profoundest measures of freedom and justice.[4] They did not equivocate in a single word when they wrote the Declaration of Independence; no one can dream that these men had not got the sublimest ideal of democracy which had ever dawned upon the souls of men.

But as soon as the war was over and our government was formed, instead of asking the question "Who shall be the governing force in this great new republic," when they brought those thirteen little territories together, they began to eliminate instead of include the men who should be the great governing forces, and they said, "Who shall have the voice in this great new republic?" And you would have supposed that such men as fought the Revolutionary War would have been able to answer that every man who has fought, every one who has given up all he has and all he has been able to accumulate, shall be free—it never entered their minds. These excellent ancestors of yours had not been away from the Old World long enough to realize that man is of more value than his purse, so they said every man who has an estate in the government shall have a voice. And they said, "What shall that estate be?" And they answered that a man who had property valued at $250 will be able to cast a vote. And so they sang "The land of the free and the home of the brave." And they wrote into their constitution, "All males who pay taxes on $250 shall cast a vote."

And they called themselves a republic, and we call ourselves a republic, and they were not quite so much of a republic as we are, and we are not quite so much of a republic that we should be called a

republic yet. We might call ourselves angels, but that wouldn't make us angels; you have got to be an angel before you are an angel, and you have got to be a republic before you are a republic.

Now what did we do? Before the word "male" in the local compacts, they wrote the word "church member"; after that, they rubbed out "church member" and they wrote in the word "taxpayer." Then there arose a great Democrat, Thomas Jefferson,[5] who looked down into the day when you and I are living and saw that the rapidly accumulated wealth in the hands of a few men would endanger the liberties of the people. And he knew what you and I know—that no power under heaven or among men is known in a republic by which men can defend their liberties except by the power of the ballot. And so the Democratic Party took another step in the evolution of a republic out of a monarchy and they rubbed out the word "taxpayer" and wrote in the word "white." And then the Democrats thought the millennium had come, and they sang "The land of the free and the home of the brave" as lustily as the Republicans had sung it before them and spoke of the divine right of motherhood with the same thrill in their voices, and at the same time they were selling mothers' babies by the pound on the auction block and mothers apart from their babies.

Another arose who said a man is not a good citizen because he is white; he is a good citizen because he is a man.[6] And the Republican Party took out that progressive evolutionary eraser and rubbed out the word "white" from before the word "male" and could not think of another word to put in there. They were all in—black and white, rich and poor, wise and otherwise, drunk and sober—not a man left out to be put in, and so the Republicans could not write anything before the word "male," and they had to let that little word "male" stay alone by itself.

And God said in the beginning, "It is not good for man to stand alone."[7] That is why we are here

---

4. Shaw is referring to protests and petitions sent to Parliament from the colonial legislatures during the years 1765–1776.

5. President of the United States, 1801–1809.

6. Shaw is referring to Abraham Lincoln, who served as President from 1861 to 1865.

7. Closely paraphrased from Genesis 2:18.

tonight, and that is all that woman's suffrage means: just to repeat again and again that first declaration of the Divine, "It is not good for man to stand alone." And so the women of this state are asking that the word "male" shall be stricken out of the Constitution altogether and that the Constitution stand as it ought to have stood in the beginning and as it must before this state is any part of a republic. Every citizen possessing the necessary qualifications shall be entitled to cast one vote at every election and have that vote counted. We are not asking, as our antisuffrage friends think we are, for any of the awful things that we hear will happen if we are allowed to vote; we are simply asking that that government which professes to be a republic shall be a republic and not pretend to be what it is not.

Now what is a republic? Take your dictionary, encyclopedia, lexicon, or anything else you like and look up the definition and you will find that a republic is a form of government in which the laws are enacted by representatives elected by the people. Now when did the people of New York ever elect their representatives? Never in the world. The men of New York have, and I grant you that men are people—admirable people, as far as they go—but they only go halfway. There is still another half of the people who have not elected representatives, and you never read a definition of a republic in which half of the people elect representatives to govern the whole of the people. That is an aristocracy, and that is just what we are. We have been many kinds of aristocracies. We have been a hierarchy of church members, then an aristocracy of wealth, and then an oligarchy of sex.

There are two old theories which are dying today—dying hard but dying. One of them is dying on the plains of Flanders and the mountains of Galicia and Austria,[8] and that is the theory of the divine right of kings. The other is dying here in the state[s] of New York and Massachusetts and New Jersey and Pennsylvania,[9] and that is the divine right

of sex. Neither of them had a foundation in reason or justice or common sense.

Now I want to make this proposition, and I believe every man will accept it. Of course he will if he is intelligent: Whenever a republic prescribes the qualifications as applies equally to all the citizens of the republic, so that when the republic says in order to vote a citizen must be twenty-one years of age, it applies to all alike; there is no discrimination against any race or sex. When the government says that a citizen must be a native-born citizen or a naturalized citizen, that applies to all. We are either born or naturalized; somehow or other we are here. Whenever the government says that a citizen, in order to vote, must be a resident of a community a certain length of time, and of the state a certain length of time, and of the nation a certain length of time, that applies to all equally. There is no discrimination. We might go further and we might say that in order to vote the citizen must be able to read his ballot. We have not gone that far yet. We have been very careful of male ignorance in these United States.

I was much interested, as perhaps many of you, in reading the *Congressional Record* this last winter over the debate over the immigration bill.[10] And when that illiteracy clause was introduced into the immigration bill, what fear there was in the souls of men for fear we would do injustice to some of the people who might want to come to our shores.[11] And I was much interested in the language in which the President vetoed the bill, when he declared that by inserting the clause we would keep out of our shores a large body of very excellent people.[12] I could not help wondering then how it happens that male ignorance is so much less ignorant than female ignorance. When I hear people say that if women were permitted to vote, a large body of ignorant people would vote, and therefore because an ignorant woman would vote, no intelligent women should be allowed to vote,

8. Shaw is referring to World War I, which had begun in August 1914.

9. All four of these states held suffrage referenda in 1915; none was passed by the voters.

10. The Burnett Immigration Bill, which passed the House in February 1914 and the Senate in January 1915.

11. The illiteracy clause required that potential immigrants over age 16 be able to read a passage of 30 to 40 words in a language or dialect of their choice.

12. Shaw is referring to Wilson's veto message of January 28, 1915.

I wonder why we have made it so easy for male ignorance and so hard for female ignorance.

When I was a girl years ago, I lived in the backwoods[13] and there the number of votes cast at each election depended entirely upon the size of the ballot box. We had what was known as the old tissue ballots, and the man who got the most tissue in was the man elected. Now the best part of our community was very much disturbed by this method, and they did not know what to do in order to get a ballot both safe and secret. But they heard that over in Australia, where the women voted, they had a ballot which was both safe and secret. So we went over there and we got the Australian ballot and brought it here.[14]

But when we got it over, we found it was not adapted to this country because in Australia they have to be able to read their ballot. Now the question was how could we adapt it to our conditions? Someone discovered that if you should put a symbol at the head of each column, like a rooster or an eagle or a hand holding a hammer, that if a man has intelligence to know the difference between a rooster and an eagle, he will know which political party to vote for. And when the ballot was adapted, it was a very beautiful ballot; it looked like a page from *Life*.[15]

Now almost any American woman could vote that ballot; or if she had not that intelligence to know the difference between an eagle and a rooster, we could take the eagle out and put in the hen. Now when we take so much pains to adapt the ballot to the male intelligence of the United States, we should be very humble when we talk about female ignorance. Now if we should take a vote and the men had to read their ballot in order to vote it, more women could vote than men.

But when the government says not only that you must be twenty-one years of age, a resident of the community, and native-born or naturalized, those are qualifications. But when it says that an elector must be a male, that is not a qualification for citizenship, that is an insurmountable barrier between half of the people and the other half, and no government which erects an insurmountable barrier between one half of the citizens and their rights as citizens can call itself a republic. It is only an aristocracy. That barrier must be removed before that government can become a republic, and that is exactly what we are asking now—that the last step in this evolutionary process shall be taken on November second, and that this great state of New York shall become in fact, as it is in theory, a part of a government of the people, by the people, and for the people.[16]

Men know the inconsistencies themselves. They realize it in one way while they do not realize it in another, because you never heard a man make a political speech when he did not speak of this country as a whole as though the thing existed which does not exist—and that is that the people were equally free—because you hear them declare over and over again on the Fourth of July, "Under God, the people rule." They know it is not true, but they say it with a great hurrah, and then they repeat over and over again that clause from the Declaration of Independence, "Governments derive their just powers from the consent of the governed," and then they see how they can prevent half of us from giving our consent to anything.

And then they give it to us on the Fourth of July in two languages, so if [it] is not true in one, it will be in the other—"Vox populi, vox Dei, the voice of the people is the voice of God"—and the orator forgets that in the people's voice there is a soprano as well as a bass. If the voice of the people is the voice of God, how are we ever going to know what God's voice is when we are content to listen to a bass solo? Now if it is true that the voice of the people is the voice of God, we will never know what the deity's voice in government is until the bass and soprano are mingled together, the result of which will be the divine harmony. Take any of the magnificent appeals for freedom which men make and rob them of their

---

13. Shaw's family moved to northern Michigan when she was 12 years old.

14. Implemented in Australia during the 1850s, the secret ballot was widely used in the United States by the 1890s.

15. A humor and general-interest magazine published from 1883 to 1936, when it was sold to Henry Luce, who turned it into America's first photo magazine.

---

16. An echo of Lincoln's Gettysburg Address, November 19, 1863.

universal application, and you take the very life and soul out of them.

Where is the difficulty? Just in one thing and one thing only—that men are so sentimental. We used to believe that women were the sentimental sex, but they cannot hold a tallow candle compared with the arc light of the men. Men are so sentimental in their attitude about women that they cannot reason about them.

Now men are usually very fair to each other. I think the average man recognizes that he has no more right to anything at the hands of the government than has every other man. He has no right at all to anything to which every other man has not an equal right with himself. He says, "Why have I a right to certain things in the government; why have I a right to life and liberty; why have I a right to this or this?" Does he say, "Because I am a man?" Not at all—because "I am human, and being human, I have a right to everything which belongs to humanity, and every right which any other human being has, I have." And then he says of his neighbor, "And my neighbor, he also is human; therefore every right which belongs to me as a human being belongs to him as a human being, and I have no right to anything under the government to which he is not equally entitled."

And then up comes a woman, and then they say, "Now she's a woman; she is not quite human, but she is my wife, or my sister, or my daughter, or my aunt, or my cousin. She is not quite human, she is only related to a human, and being related to a human, a human will take care of her." So we have had that caretaking human being to look after us, and they have not recognized that women, too, are equally human with men. Now if men could forget for a minute (I believe the antisuffragists say that we want men to forget that we are related to them—they don't know me), if for a minute they could forget our relationship and remember that we are equally human with themselves, then they would say, "Yes, and this human being, not because she is a woman but because she is human, is entitled to every privilege and every right under the government which I as a human being am entitled to."

The only reason why men do not see as fairly in regard to women as they do in regard to each other is because they have looked upon us from an altogether different plane than what they have looked at men—that is, because women have been the homemakers while men have been the so-called protectors in the period of the world's civilization when people needed to be protected. I know that they say that men protect us now, and when we ask them what they are protecting us from, the only answer they can give is from themselves. I do not think that men need any very great credit for protecting us from themselves. They are not protecting us from any special thing from which we could not protect ourselves, except themselves. Now this old-time idea of protection was all right when the world needed this protection, but today the protection in civilization comes from within and not from without.

What are the arguments which our good Anti[17] friends give us? We know that lately they have stopped to argue and call suffragists[18] all sorts of creatures. If there is anything we believe that we do not believe, we have not heard about them, so the cry goes out of this—the cry of the infant's mind, the cry of a little child. The antisuffragists' cries are all the cries of little children who are afraid of the unborn and are forever crying, "The goblins will catch you if you don't watch out." So that anything that has not been should not be and all that is is right, when as a matter of fact if the world believed that, we would be in a statical condition and never move except back like a crab. And so the cries go on.

When suffragists are feminists, and when I ask what that is, no one is able to tell me. I would give anything to know what a feminist is. They say, "Would you like to be a feminist?" If I could find out, I would; you either have to be masculine or feminine, and I prefer feminine. Then they cry that we are Socialists and anarchists. Just how a human can be both at the same time, I really do not know. If I know what socialism means, it means absolute government,

---

17. Antisuffragists.

18. The newspaper account of Shaw's speech uses "suffragette," a derogatory word for supporters of suffrage that Shaw disliked intensely. We have replaced it with "suffragist," and its counterpart "antisuffragette" with "antisuffragist," terms that Shaw used consistently in her speeches and writings.

and anarchism means no government at all. So we are feminists, Socialists, anarchists, and Mormons or spinsters. Now that is about the list. I have not heard the last speech. Now as a matter of fact, as a unit we are nothing; as individuals we are like all other individuals.

We have our theories, our beliefs, but as suffragists we have but one belief, but one principle, but one theory, and that is the right of a human being to have a voice in the government under which he or she lives. On that we agree, if on nothing else. Whether we agree or not on religion or politics, we are not concerned. A clergyman asked me the other day, "By the way, what church does your official board belong to?" I said, "I don't know." He said, "Don't you know what religion your official board believes?" I said, "Really it never occurred to me, but I will hunt them up and see; they are not elected to my board because they believe in any particular church." We had no concern either as to what we believe as religionists or as to what we believe as women in regard to theories of government, except that one fundamental theory in the right of democracy. We do not believe in this fad or the other, but whenever any question is to be settled in any community, then the people of that community shall settle that question—the women people equally with the men people. That is all there is to it.

And yet when it comes to arguing our case, they bring up all sorts of arguments, and the beauty of it is they always answer all their own arguments. They never make an argument but they answer it. When I was asked to answer one of their debates, I said, "What is the use? Divide up their literature and let them destroy themselves."

I was followed up last year by a young married woman from New Jersey. She left her husband and home for three months to tell the women that their place was at home and that they could not leave home long enough to go to the ballot box. And she brought all her arguments out in pairs and backed them up by statistics. The antisuffragist can gather more statistics than any other person I ever saw, and there is nothing so sweet and calm as when they say, "You cannot deny this, because here are the figures, and figures never lie." Well, they don't, but some liars figure.

When they start out, they always begin the same. She started by proving that it was no use to give the women the ballot because if they did have it, they would not use it—and she had statistics to prove it. If we would not use it, then I really cannot see the harm of giving it to us; we would not hurt anybody with it and what an easy way for you men to get rid of us. No more suffrage meetings, never any nagging you again, no one could blame you for anything that went wrong with the town if it did not run right. All you would have to say is, "You have the power; why don't you go ahead and clean up?"

Then the young lady, unfortunately for her first argument, proved by statistics, of which she had many, the awful results which happened where women did have the ballot—what awful laws have been brought about by women's vote, the conditions that prevail in the homes, and how deeply women get interested in politics—because women are hysterical and we cannot think of anything else, we just forget our families, cease to care for our children, cease to love our husbands, and just go to the polls and vote and keep on voting for ten hours a day, three hundred and sixty-five days in the year, never let up; if we ever get to the polls once, you will never get us home. So that the women will not vote at all, and they will not do anything but vote. Now these are two very strong antisuffrage arguments, and they can prove them by figures.

Then they will tell you that if women are permitted to vote, it will be a great expense and no use because wives will vote just as their husbands do. Even if we have no husbands, that would not affect the result because we would vote just as our husbands would vote if we had one. How I wish the antisuffragists could make the men believe that; if they could make men believe that the women would vote just as they wanted them to, do you think we would ever have to make another speech or hold another meeting? We would have to vote whether we wanted to or not.

And then the very one who will tell you that women will vote just as their husbands do will tell you in five minutes that they will not vote as their husbands will—and then the discord in the homes, and the divorce. Why, they have discovered that in

Colorado there are more divorces than there were before women began to vote;[19] but they have forgotten to tell you that there are four times as many people in Colorado today as there were when women began to vote—and that may have some effect, particularly as these people went from the East.

Then they will tell you all the trouble that happens in the home. A gentleman told me that in California. And when he was talking, I had a wonderful thing pass through my mind because he said that he and his wife had lived together for twenty years and never had a difference in opinion in the whole twenty years, and he was afraid if women began to vote, that his wife would vote differently from him and then that beautiful harmony which they had had for twenty years would be broken. And all the time he was talking, I could not help wondering which was the idiot—because I knew that no intelligent human beings could live together for twenty years and not have differences of opinion. All the time he was talking, I looked at that splendid type of manhood and thought, how would a man feel being tagged up by a little woman for twenty years saying, "Me too, me too."

I would not want to live in a house with a human being for twenty hours who agreed with everything I said. The stagnation of a frog pond would be hilarious compared to that. What a reflection is that on men. If we should say that about men, we would never hear the last of it. Now it may be that the kind of men-being that the antisuffragists live with is that kind, but they are not the kind we live with, and we could not do it. Great big overgrown babies! Cannot be disputed without having a row! While we do not believe that men are saints by any means, we do believe that the average American man is a fairly good sort of a fellow.

In fact, my theory of the whole matter is exactly opposite, because instead of believing that men and women will quarrel, I think just the opposite thing will happen. I think just about six weeks before election a sort of honeymoon will start and it will continue until they will think they are again hanging over the gate—all in order to get each other's votes. When men want each other's votes, they do not go up and knock them down; they are very solicitous of each other if they are thirsty or need a smoke or—well, we won't worry about the home. The husband and wife who are quarreling after the vote are quarreling now.

Then the other belief that the women would not vote if they had a vote and would not do anything else; and would vote just as their husbands vote, and would not vote like their husbands; that women have so many burdens that they cannot bear another burden, and that women are the leisure class. I remember hearing Reverend Dr. Abbott[20] speak before the antisuffrage meeting in Brooklyn, and he stated that if women were permitted to vote, we could not have so much time for charity and philanthropy, and I would like to say, "Thank God, there will not be so much need of charity and philanthropy." The end and aim of the suffrage is not to furnish an opportunity for excellent old ladies to be charitable. There are two words that we ought to be able to get along without, and they are "charity" and "philanthropy." They are not needed in a republic. If we put in the word "opportunity" instead, that is what republics stand for. Our doctrine is not to extend the length of our bread lines or the size of our soup kitchens; what we need is the opportunity for men to buy their own bread and eat their own soup.

We women have used up our lives and strength in fool charities, and we have made more paupers than we have ever helped by the folly of our charities and philanthropies—the unorganized methods by which we deal with the conditions of society—and instead of giving people charity, we must learn to give them an opportunity to develop and make themselves capable of earning the bread. No human being has the right to live without toil, toil of some kind. And that old theory that we used to hear—"The world owes a man a living"—never was true and never will be true. This world does not owe anybody a living; what it does owe to every human being is the opportunity to earn a living. We have a right

---

19. In 1893 Colorado became the first state in the Union to approve woman suffrage in a referendum.

20. Lyman Abbott, pastor of Brooklyn's Plymouth Church, 1888–1898.

to the opportunity and then the right to the living thereafter. We want it. No woman, any more than a man, has the right to live an idle life in this world; we must learn to give back something for the space occupied, and we must do our duty wherever duty calls, and the woman herself must decide where her duty calls, just as a man does.

Now they tell us we should not vote because we have not the time; we are so burdened that we should not have any more burdens. Then, if that is so, I think we ought to allow the women to vote instead of the men. Since we pay a man anywhere from a third to a half more than we do women, it would be better to use up the cheap time of the women instead of the dear time of the men.

And talking about time, you would think it took about a week to vote. A dear, good friend of mine in Omaha said, "Now, Miss Shaw," and she held up her child in her arms, "is not this my job?" I said, "It certainly is." And then she said, "How can I go to the polls and vote and neglect my baby?" I said, "Has your husband a job?" And she said, "Why, you know he has." I did know it; he was a banker and a very busy one. I said, "Yet your husband said he was going to leave his bank and go down to the polls and vote." And she said, "Oh, yes, he is so very interested in election." Then I said, "What an advantage you have over your husband; he has to leave his job and you can take your job with you and you do not need to neglect your job."

Is it not strange that the only time a woman might neglect her baby is on election day, and then the dear old Antis hold up their hands and say, "You have neglected your baby." A woman can belong to a whist club and go once a week and play whist.[21] She cannot take her baby to the whist club; she has to keep whist herself without trying to keep a baby whist. She can go to the theater, to church, or a picnic and no one is worrying about that baby. But to vote and everyone cries out about the neglect. You would think on election day that a woman grabbed up her baby and started out and just dropped it anywhere and paid no attention to it.

It used to be asked, when we had the question-box,[22] "Who will take care of the babies?" I didn't know what person could be got to take care of all the babies, so I thought I would go out West and find out. So I went to Denver and I found that they took care of their babies just the same on election day as they did on every other day; they took their baby along with them. When they went to put a letter in a box, they took their baby along, and when they went to put their ballot in the box, they took their baby along. If the mother had to stand in line and the baby got restless, she would joggle the go-cart[23]—most everyone had a go-cart—and when she went in to vote, a neighbor would joggle the go-cart. And if there was no neighbor, there was the candidate, and he would joggle the cart. That is one day in the year when you could get a hundred people to take care of any number of babies. I have never worried about the babies on election day since that time.

Then the people will tell you that women are so burdened with their duties that they cannot vote, and then they will tell you that women are the leisure class and the men are worked to death, but the funniest argument of the lady who followed me about in the West: Out there they were great on the temperance question,[24] and she declared that we were not Prohibition, or she declared that we were. Now in North Dakota, which is one of the first Prohibition states[25]—and they are dry because they want to be dry—in that state she wanted to prove to them that if women were allowed to vote, they would vote North Dakota wet. And she had her figures—that women had not voted San Francisco dry or Portland dry or Chicago dry. Of course, we had not voted on the question in Chicago, but that did not matter.

---

21. The forerunner of bridge, whist was a popular card game of Shaw's time.

22. Shaw was known for her use of the question-box, into which audience members could drop questions that she would answer at intervals during a meeting.

23. A stroller, or a bottomless framework with casters in which children could learn to walk without danger of falling.

24. The temperance movement sought to prohibit the use of alcoholic beverages and was often intertwined with woman suffrage.

25. North Dakota adopted Prohibition upon achieving statehood in 1889.

Then we went to Montana, which is wet. They have it wet there because they want it wet, so that any argument that she could bring to bear upon them to prove that we would make North Dakota wet and keep it wet would have given us the state. But that would not work, so she brought out the figures out of her pocket to prove to the men of Montana that if women were allowed to vote in Montana, they would vote Montana dry. She proved that in two years in Illinois they had voted ninety-six towns dry, and that at that rate we would soon get over Montana and have it dry.

Then I went to Nebraska, and as soon as I reached there, a reporter came and asked me the question, "How are the women going to vote on the Prohibition question?" I said, "I really don't know. I know how we will vote in North Dakota—we will vote dry[26] in North Dakota; in Montana we will vote dry; but how we will vote in Nebraska, I don't know, but I will let you know just as soon as the lady from New Jersey comes."

We will either vote as our husbands vote or we will not vote as our husbands vote. We either have time to vote or we don't have time to vote. We will either not vote at all or we will vote all the time. It reminds me of the story of the old Irish woman who had twin boys, and they were so much alike that the neighbors could not tell them apart and the mother always seemed to be able to tell them apart. So one of the neighbors said, "Now Mrs. Mahoney, you have two of the finest twin boys I ever saw in all my life, but how do you know them apart?" "Oh," she says, "That's easy enough; anyone could tell them apart. When I want to know which is which, I just put my finger in Patsey's mouth, and if he bites, it is Mikey."

Now what does it matter whether the women will vote as their husbands do or will not vote? Whether they have time or have not? Or whether they will vote for Prohibition or not? What has that to do with the fundamental question of democracy, no one has yet discovered. But they cannot argue on that. They can-

not argue on the fundamental basis of our existence, so that they have to get off on all these side tracks to get anything approaching an argument.

So they tell you that democracy is a form of government. It is not. It was before governments were; it will prevail when governments cease to be. It is more than a form of government; it is a great spiritual force emanating from the heart of the Infinite, transforming human character until someday, someday in the distant future, man, by the power of the spirit of democracy, will be able to look back into the face of the Infinite and answer, as man cannot answer today, "One is our Father, even God, and all we people are the children of one family."

And when democracy has taken possession of human lives, no man will ask for himself anything which he is not willing to grant to his neighbor, whether that neighbor be a man or a woman. No man will then be willing to allow another man to rise to power on his shoulders; nor will he be willing to rise to power on the shoulders of another prostrate human being. But that has not yet taken possession of us, but someday we will be free, and we are getting nearer and nearer to it all the time; and never in the history of our country had the men and women of this nation a better right to approach it than they have today, never in the history of the nation did it stand out so splendidly as it stands today, and never ought we men and women to be more grateful for anything than that there presides in the White House today a man of peace.[27]

And so our good friends go on with one thing after another, and they say if women should vote, they will have to sit on the jury, and they ask whether we will like to see a woman sitting on a jury. I have seen some juries that ought to be sat on and I have seen some women that would be glad to sit on anything. When a woman stands up all day behind a counter, or when she stands all day doing a washing, she is glad enough to sit; and when she stands for seventy-five cents, she would like to sit for two dollars a day.

But don't you think we need some women on juries in this country? You read your paper and you

26. Perhaps a misprint in the original text; presumably Shaw meant to say "wet," since she is referring to the assertion of the antisuffragist two paragraphs earlier that women would vote North Dakota wet if they had suffrage in that state.

27. Woodrow Wilson, President from 1913 to 1921.

read that one day last week—or the week before or the week before—a little girl went out to school and never came back. Another little girl was sent on an errand and never came back. Another little girl was left in charge of a little sister and her mother went out to work, and when she returned, the little girl was not there. And you read it over and over again, and the horror of it strikes you. You read that in these United States five thousand young girls go out and never come back. Don't you think that the men and women, the vampires of our country who fatten and grow rich on the ignorance and innocence of children, would rather face Satan himself than a jury of mothers? I would like to see some juries of mothers. I lived in the slums of Boston for three years,[28] and I know the need of juries of mothers.

Then they tell us that if women were permitted to vote, that they would take office, and you would suppose that we just took office in this country. There is a difference of getting an office in this country and in Europe. In England a man stands for Parliament and in this country he runs for Congress, and so long as it is a question of running for office, I don't think women have much chance, especially with our present hobbles.[29]

There are some women who want to hold office, and I may as well own up: I am one of them. I have been wanting to hold office for more than thirty-five years. Thirty-five years ago I lived in the slums of Boston, and ever since then I have wanted to hold office. I have applied to the Mayor to be made an officer. I wanted to be the greatest officeholder in the world; I wanted the position of the man I think is to be the most envied, as far as ability to do good is concerned, and that is a policeman. I have always wanted to be a policeman, and I have applied to be appointed policeman.

And the very first question that was asked me was, "Could you knock a man down and take him to jail?" That is some people's idea of the highest

service that a policeman can render a community—knock somebody down and take him to jail. My idea is not so much to arrest criminals as it is to prevent crime. That is what is needed in the police force of every community. When I lived for three years in the back alleys of Boston, I saw there that it was needed to prevent crime, and from that day to this I believe there is no great public gathering of any sort whatever where we do not need women on the police force. We need them at every moving picture show, every dance house, every restaurant, every hotel, and every great store with a great bargain counter, and every park, and every resort where the vampires who fatten on the crimes and vices of men and women gather. We need women on the police force, and we will have them there someday.

If women vote, will they go to war? They are great on having us fight. They tell you that the government rests on force, but there are a great many kinds of force in this world, and never in the history of man were the words of the Scriptures proved to the extent that they are today—that the men of the nation that lives by the sword shall die by the sword.[30]

When I was speaking in North Dakota from an automobile with a great crowd and a great number of men gathered around, a man who had been sitting in front of a store whittling a stick called out to another man and asked if women get the vote will they go over to Germany and fight the Germans? I said, "Why, no, why should we go over to Germany and fight Germans?" I said, "Why, no, why over [t]here to fight? If German men come over here, would you fight?" I said, "Why should we women fight men? But if Germany should send an army of women over here, then we would show you what we would do. We would go down and meet them and say, 'Come on, let's go up to the opera house and talk this matter over.' It might grow wearisome, but it would not be death."

Would it not be better if the heads of the governments in Europe had talked things over? What might have happened to the world if a dozen men had gotten together in Europe and settled the awful

<hr>

28. Shaw lived in Boston while attending theology school from 1876 to 1878.

29. A reference to the then-fashionable hobble skirt, which was so narrow below the knees that it restrained the wearer's freedom of movement.

30. An allusion to Matthew 26:52: "All they that take the sword shall perish with the sword," and to Revelation 13:10: "He that killeth with the sword must be killed with the sword."

controversy which is today decimating the nations of Europe? We women got together over there last year, over in Rome, the delegates from twenty-eight different nations of women, and for two weeks we discussed problems which had like interests to us all.[31] They were all kinds of Protestants; both kinds of Catholics, Roman and Greek; three were Jews and Mohammedans; but we were not there to discuss our different religious beliefs. But we were there to discuss the things that were of vital importance to us all, and at the end of the two weeks, after the discussions were over, we passed a great number of resolutions. We discussed white slavery, the immigration laws; we discussed the spread of contagious and infectious diseases; we discussed various forms of education and various forms of juvenile criminals; every question which every nation has to meet.

And at the end of two weeks we passed many resolutions, but two of them were passed unanimously. One was presented by myself as chairman on the Committee on Suffrage, and on that resolution we called upon all civilizations of the world to give to women equal rights with men, and there was not a dissenting vote. The other resolution was on peace. We believed then, and many of us believe today, notwithstanding all the discussion that is going on, we believe and we will continue to believe that preparedness for war is an incentive to war and the only hope of permanent peace is the systematic and scientific disarmament of all the nations of the world. And we passed a resolution, and passed it unanimously, to that effect.

A few days afterward I attended a large reception given by the American ambassador,[32] and there was an Italian diplomat there, and he spoke rather superciliously and said, "You women think you have been having a very remarkable convention, and I understand that a resolution on peace was offered by the Germans, and the French women seconded it, and the British presiding officer presented it, and it was carried unanimously." We, none of us, dreamed what was taking place at that time, but he knew and

we learned it before we arrived home—that awful, awful thing that was about to sweep over the nations of the world.[33]

The American ambassador replied to the Italian diplomat and said, "Yes, Prince, it was a remarkable convention, and it is a remarkable thing that the only people who can get together internationally and discuss their various problems without acrimony and without a sword at their side are the women of the world; but we men, even when we go to the Hague to discuss peace,[34] we go with a sword dangling at our side." It is remarkable that even at this age men cannot discuss international problems and discuss them in peace.

When I turned away from that place up in North Dakota, that man in the crowd called out again, just as we were leaving, and said, "Well, what does a woman know about war anyway?" I had read my paper that morning and I knew what the awful headline was, and I saw a gentleman standing in the crowd with a paper in his pocket, and I said, "Will that gentleman hold his paper up?" And he held it up, and the headline read: "250,000 Men Killed Since the War Began."

I said: "You ask me what a woman knows about war? No woman can read that line and comprehend the awful horror, no woman knows the significance of 250,000 dead men. But you tell me that one man lay dead, and I might be able to tell you something of its awful meaning to one woman. I would know that, years before, a woman whose heart beat in unison with her love and her desire for motherhood walked day by day with her face to an open grave with courage which no man has ever surpassed. And if she did not fill that grave, if she lived and if there was laid in her arms a tiny little bit of helpless humanity, I would know that there went out from her soul such a cry of thankfulness as none save a mother could know.

"And then I would know what men have not yet learned—that women are human, that they have human hopes and human passions, aspirations, and

31. Shaw is referring to the May 1914 Congress of the International Council of Women.

32. Thomas Nelson Page.

33. World War I, which began in August 1914.

34. The Hague, Netherlands, site of international peace conventions in 1899 and 1907.

desires as men have. And I would know that that mother had laid aside all those hopes and aspirations for herself, but never for one moment did she lay them aside for her boy. And if, after years had passed by, she forgot her nights of sleeplessness and her days of fatiguing toil in her care of her growing boy, and when at last he became a man and she stood looking up into his eyes and beheld him, bone of her bone and flesh of her flesh, for out of her woman's life she had carved twenty beautiful years that went into the making of a man.

"And there he stands, the most wonderful thing in all the world, for in all the universe of God there is nothing more sublimely wonderful than a strong-limbed, clean-hearted, keen-brained, aggressive young man, standing as he does on the borderline of life, ready to reach out and grapple with its problems. Oh, how wonderful he is, and he is hers. She gave her life for him, and in an hour this country calls him out and in an hour he lies dead—that wonderful, wonderful thing lies dead—and sitting by his side, that mother looking into the dark years to come knows that when her son died, her life's hope died with him. And in the face of that wretched motherhood, what man dare ask what a woman knows of war?"

And that is not all. Read your papers; you cannot read it because it is not printable. You cannot tell it because it is not speakable; you cannot even think it because it is not thinkable—the horrible crimes perpetrated against women by the blood-drunken men of the war.

You read your paper again, and the second headline reads: "It Costs Twenty Millions of Dollars a Day." For what? To buy the material to slaughter the splendid results of civilization of the centuries, men whom it has taken centuries to build up and make into great scientific forces of brain, the flower of the manhood of the great nations of Europe, and we spend twenty millions of dollars a day to blot out all the results of civilization of hundreds and hundreds of years. And what do we do? We lay a mortgage on every unborn child for a hundred and more years to come. Mortgage his brain, his brawn, every pulse of his heart in order to pay the debt, to buy the material to slaughter the men of our country.

And that is not all. The greatest crime of war is the crime against the unborn. Read what they are doing. They are calling out every man, every young man, every virile man from seventeen to forty-five or fifty years old; they are calling them out. All the splendid scientific force and energy of the splendid, virile manhood are being called out to be food for the cannon, and they are leaving behind the degenerate, defective, imbecile, the unfit, the criminals, the diseased to be the fathers of the children yet to be born. The crime of crimes of the war is the crime against the unborn children: that we take from them what every child has a right to—that is, a virile father—and we rob women of fit mates to become the fathers of their children. In the face of these crimes against women and against children, and in the face of the fact that women are driven out of the home, shall men ask if women shall fight if they are permitted to vote?

No, we women do not want the ballot in order that we may fight, but we do want the ballot in order that we may help men to keep from fighting, whether it is in war or in peace, whether it is in the home or in the state. Just as the home is not without the man, so the state is not without the woman, and you can no more build up homes without men than you can build up the state without women. We are needed everywhere where human life is. We are needed everywhere where human problems are to solve, and men and women must go through this world together from the cradle to the grave; it is God's way and it is the fundamental principle of a republican form of government.

Carrie Chapman Catt

⧗

The Crisis

ATLANTIC CITY, NEW JERSEY
SEPTEMBER 7, 1916

BORN IN RIPON, Wisconsin, in 1859, Carrie Chapman Catt attended the Iowa State Agricultural College (now Iowa State University), where she won for women the right to speak at the Crescent Literary Society and was the only woman in her graduating class. She participated in her first suffrage convention in 1885, and by the end of the decade was acquiring a reputation for her oratorical and organizational skills. One of the movement's most dynamic figures, she served as president of the National American Woman Suffrage Association (NAWSA) from 1900 to 1904, after which she became a leader on the international stage, giving speeches in dozens of countries and attending suffrage congresses in Berlin, Copenhagen, Amsterdam, and London.

Catt's election in 1915 for a second term as NAWSA president was a turning point in the long quest to secure the vote for women. Convinced by bitter experience that the organization's traditional strategy of seeking the ballot on a state by state basis was doomed to failure, she believed the only route to success lay in an all-out campaign for a suffrage amendment to the U.S. Constitution. Central to this campaign, which became known as Catt's "Winning Plan," was a simultaneous effort in all forty-eight states to elect enough prosuffrage Representatives and Senators to ensure congressional passage of the amendment. Concurrently, states would continue their efforts, where feasible, to pass suffrage referenda.

Before her plan could be implemented, Catt had to unify the suffrage forces behind it. She called an emergency NAWSA convention to meet in Atlantic City in September 1916. At the opening session, she presented a ninety-minute address demonstrating the inherent flaws of seeking to amend each state constitution individually and arguing that the time had come to devote the movement's resources to securing a federal amendment. Galvanizing her listeners with a combination of incontestable evidence, incisive reasoning, and irresistible emotional appeal, she argued that the suffrage crusade had reached a moment of crisis that could be turned into victory with the correct strategy. Insistently repeating the conviction that "Woman's Hour Has Struck," her speech was accepted as a call to arms and set the course that, four years later, would result in ratification of the Nineteenth Amendment.

A brilliant tactician and leader, Catt used her platform skills to maximum advantage. If she did not match the sheer oratorical brilliance of Elizabeth Cady

Stanton, Susan B. Anthony, and Anna Howard Shaw, she was not far behind, especially in her powers of logic and argument. The *Boston Globe* described her by saying: "Hers is a finished speech. There isn't much left to talk about when she gets through. There is never a slip of the tongue, no hesitancy, and her arguments are piled one on another like the charge of a judge to the jury. The effect is irresistible.... And her stage presence is perfect, with a splendid voice to crown it all."

◇◇◇

I have taken for my subject "The Crisis" because I believe that a crisis has come in our movement which, if recognized and the opportunity seized with vigor, enthusiasm, and will, means the final victory of our great cause in the very near future. I am aware that some suffragists do not share this belief; they see no signs nor symptoms today which were not present yesterday, no manifestations in the year 1916 which differ significantly from those in the year 1910. To them, the movement has been a steady, normal growth from the beginning and must so continue until the end. I can only defend my claim with the plea that it is better to imagine a crisis where none exists than to fail to recognize one when it comes, for a crisis is a culmination of events which calls for new considerations and new decisions. A failure to answer the call may mean an opportunity lost, a possible victory postponed.

The object of the life of an organized movement is to secure its aim. Necessarily, it must obey the law of evolution and pass through the stages of agitation and education and finally through the stage of realization. As one has put it, "A new idea floats in the air over the heads of the people and for a long, indefinite period evades their understanding, but, by and by when through familiarity human vision grows clearer, it is caught out of the clouds and crystallized into law." Such a period comes to every movement and is its crisis. In my judgment, that crucial moment, bidding us to renewed consecration and redoubled activity, has come to our cause. I believe our victory hangs within our grasp, inviting us to pluck it out of the clouds and establish it among the good things of the world.

If this be true, the time is past when we should say, "Men and women of America, look upon that wonderful idea up there; see, one day it will come down." Instead, the time has come to shout aloud in every city, village, and hamlet, and in tones so clear and jubilant that they will reverberate from every mountain peak and echo from shore to shore: "The Woman's Hour Has Struck."[1]

Suppose suffragists as a whole do not believe a crisis has come and do not extend their hands to grasp the victory, what will happen? Why, we shall all continue to work and our cause will continue to hang, waiting for those who possess a clearer vision and more daring enterprise. On the other hand, suppose we reach out with united earnestness and determination to grasp our victory while it still hangs a bit too high? Has any harm been done? None!

Therefore, fellow suffragists, I invite your attention to the signs which point to a crisis and your consideration of plans for turning the crisis into victory.

First: We are passing through a world crisis. All thinkers of every land tell us so, and that nothing after the Great War[2] will be as it was before. Those who profess to know claim that one hundred millions of dollars are being spent on the war every day and that two years of war have cost fifty billions of dollars, or ten times more than the total expense of the American Civil War.[3] Our own country has

---

1. After the Civil War, some supporters of political rights for freedmen declared "this is the Negro's hour" and argued that equal rights for women would have to be deferred. Others argued that women were no less entitled to suffrage and other citizenship rights than were the newly freed slaves. Thus Catt's phrase "The Woman's Hour Has Struck," which she repeats throughout the speech, carried special resonance for her listeners.

2. World War I, which had begun in August 1914.

3. 1861–1865.

sent thirty-five millions of dollars abroad for relief expenses. Were there no other effects to come from the world's war, the transfer of such unthinkably vast sums of money from the usual avenues to those wholly abnormal would give so severe a jolt to organized society that it would vibrate around the world and bring untold changes in its wake.

But three and a half millions of lives have been lost. The number becomes the more impressive when it is remembered that the entire population of the American colonies was little more than three and one-half millions. Those losses have been the lives of men within the age of economic production. They have been taken abruptly from the normal business of the world, and every human activity from that of the humblest, unskilled labor to art, science, and literature has been weakened by their loss. Millions of other men will go to their homes blind, crippled, and incapacitated to do the work they once performed.

The stability of human institutions has never before suffered so tremendous a shock. Great men are trying to think out the consequences, but one and all proclaim that no imagination can find color or form bold enough to paint the picture of the world after the war. British and Russian, German and Austrian, French and Italian agree that it will lead to social and political revolution throughout the entire world. Whatever comes, they further agree that the war presages a total change in the status of women.

A simpleminded man in West Virginia, when addressed upon the subject of woman suffrage in that state, replied: "We've been so used to keepin' our women down, 'twould seem queer not to." He expressed what greater men feel but do not say. Had the wife of that man spoken in the same clear-thinking fashion, she would have said: "We women have been so used to being kept down that it would seem strange to get up. Nature intended women for 'door-mats.'" Had she so expressed herself, these two would have put the entire antisuffrage argument in a nutshell.

In Europe, from the Polar Circle to the Aegean Sea, women have risen as though to answer that argument. Everywhere they have taken the places made vacant by men, and in so doing they have grown in self-respect and in the esteem of their respective nations. In every land, the people have reverted to the primitive division of labor, and while the men have gone to war, women have cultivated the fields in order that the army and nation may be fed. No army can succeed and no nation can endure without food; those who supply it are a war power and a peace power.

Women by the thousands have knocked at the doors of munition factories and, in the name of patriotism, have begged for the right to serve their country there. Their services were accepted with hesitation, but the experiment, once made, won reluctant but universal praise. An official statement recently issued in Great Britain announced that 660,000 women were engaged in making munitions in that country alone. In a recent convention of munition workers, composed of men and women, a resolution was unanimously passed informing the government that they would forego vacations and holidays until the authorities announced that their munition supplies were sufficient for the needs of the war, and Great Britain pronounced the act the highest patriotism.

Lord Derby[4] addressed such a meeting and said, "When the history of the war is written, I wonder to whom the greatest credit will be given—to the men who went to fight or to the women who are working in a way that many people hardly believed that it was possible for them to work." Lord Sydenham[5] added his tribute. Said he, "It might fairly be claimed that women have helped to save thousands of lives and to change the entire aspect of the war. Wherever intelligence, care, and close attention have been needed, women have distinguished themselves."[6]

A writer in the London *Times* of July 18, 1916, said: "But for women, the armies could not have held the field for a month; the national call to arms could not have been made or sustained; the country would

4. Edward George Villiers Stanley, 17th Earl of Derby, director-general of recruiting.

5. George Sydenham Clarke, 1st Baron Sydenham of Combe, chairman of the Central Appeal Tribunal.

6. Catt is likely referring to speeches delivered by Derby and Sydenham at a meeting of the Young Women's Christian Association, Queen's Hall, London, July 13, 1916.

have perished of inanition and disorganization. If indeed it be true that the people have been one, it is because the genius of women has been lavishly applied to the task of reinforcing and complementing the genius of men. The qualities of steady industry, adaptability, good judgment, and concentration of mind which men do not readily associate with women have been conspicuous features."[7]

On fields of battle, in regular and improvised hospitals, women have given tender and skilled care to the wounded and are credited with the restoration of life to many, many thousands. Their heroism and self-sacrifice have been frankly acknowledged by all the governments, but their endurance, their skill, the practicality of their service seem for the first time to have been recognized by governments as "war power." So, thinking in war terms, great men have suddenly discovered that women are "war assets." Indeed, Europe is realizing, as it never did before, that women are holding together the civilization for which men are fighting. A great searchlight has been thrown upon the business of nation building, and it has been demonstrated in every European land that it is a partnership with equal but different responsibilities resting upon the two partners.

It is not, however, in direct war work alone that the latent possibilities of women have been made manifest. In all the belligerent lands, women have found their way to high posts of administration where no women would have been trusted two years ago, and the testimony is overwhelming that they have filled their posts with entire satisfaction to the authorities. They have dared to stand in pulpits (once too sacred to be touched by the unholy feet of a woman) and there, without protest, have appealed to the Father of All in behalf of their stricken lands. They have come out of the kitchen where there was too little to cook and have found a way to live by driving cabs, motors, and streetcars. Many a woman has turned her hungry children over to a neighbor and has gone forth to find food for both mothers and both families of children and has found it in strange places and occupations. Many a drawing room has been closed, and

the maid who swept and dusted it is now cleaning streets that the health of the city may be conserved. Many a woman who never before slept in a bed of her own making or ate food not prepared by paid labor, is now sole mistress of parlor and kitchen.

In all the warring countries, women are postmen, porters, railway conductors, ticket, switch, and signalmen. Conspicuous advertisements invite women to attend agricultural, milking, and motorcar schools. They are employed as police in Great Britain, and women detectives have recently been taken on the government staff. In Berlin, there are over 3,000 women streetcar conductors and 3,500 women are employed on the general railways of Germany. In every city and country, women are doing work for which they would have been considered incompetent two years ago.

The war will soon end and the armies will return to their native lands. To many a family, the men will never come back. The husband who returns to many a wife will eat no bread the rest of his life save of her earning.

What, then, will happen after the war? Will the widows left with families to support cheerfully leave their well-paid posts for those commanding lower wages? Not without protest! Will the wives who now must support crippled husbands give up their skilled work and take up the occupations which were open to them before the war? Will they resignedly say, "The woman who has a healthy husband who can earn for her has a right to tea and raisin cake, but the woman who earns for herself and a husband who has given his all to his country, must be content with butterless bread"? Not without protest! On the contrary, the economic axiom, denied and evaded for centuries, will be blazoned on every factory, counting house, and shop: "Equal pay for equal work," and common justice will slowly but surely enforce that law.

The European woman has risen. She may not realize it yet, but the woman "door-mat" in every land has unconsciously become a "door-jamb"! She will have become accustomed to her new dignity by the time the men come home. She will wonder how she ever could have been content lying across the threshold now that she discovers the upright jamb gives so much broader and more normal a vision of things. The men returning

---

7. From a letter to the editor by H. W. Massingham.

may find the new order a bit queer, but everything else will be strangely unfamiliar too, and they will soon grow accustomed to all the changes together. The "jamb" will never descend into a "door-mat" again.

The male and female antisuffragists of all lands will puff and blow at the economic change which will come to the women of Europe. They will declare it to be contrary to Nature and to God's plan and that somebody ought to do something about it. Suffragists will accept the change as the inevitable outcome of an unprecedented world's cataclysm over which no human agency had any control and will trust in God to adjust the altered circumstances to the eternal evolution of human society. They will remember that, in the long run, all things work together for good,[8] for progress, and for human weal.

The economic change is bound to bring political liberty. From every land there comes the expressed belief that the war will be followed by a mighty, on-coming wave of democracy, for it is now well known that the conflict has been one of governments—of kings and czars, kaisers and emperors—not of peoples. The nations involved have nearly all declared that they are fighting to make an end of wars. New and higher ideals of governments, and of the rights of the people under them, have grown enormously during the past two years. Another tide of political liberty, similar to that of 1848[9] but of a thousand-fold greater momentum, is rising from battlefield and hospital, from camp and munitions factory, from home and church, which, great men of many lands tell us, is destined to sweep over the world.

On the continent, the women say, "It is certain that the vote will come to men and women after the war, perhaps not immediately but soon." In Great Britain, which was the storm center of the suffrage movement for some years before the war, hundreds of bitter, active opponents have confessed their conversion on account of the war services of women. Already three great provinces of Canada—Manitoba, Alberta, and Saskatchewan—have given universal suffrage to

their women in sheer generous appreciation of their war work.[10]

Even Mr. Asquith,[11] world renowned for his immovable opposition to the parliamentary suffrage for British women, has given evidence of a change of view. Some months ago, he announced his amazement at the utterly unexpected skill, strength, and resource developed by the women and his gratitude for their loyalty and devotion.[12] Later, in reply to Mrs. Henry Fawcett,[13] who asked if woman suffrage would be included in a proposed election bill, he said that when the war should end, such a measure would be considered without prejudice carried over from events prior to the war.[14] A public statement issued by Mr. Asquith in August was couched in such terms as to be interpreted by many as a pledge to include women in the next election bill.[15]

In Great Britain, a sordid appeal which may prove the last straw to break the opposition to woman suffrage has been added to the enthusiastic appreciation of woman's patriotism and practical service and to the sudden comprehension that motherhood is a national asset which must be protected at any price. A new voters' list is contemplated. A parliamentary election should be held in September, but the voters are scattered far and wide. The whole nation is agitated over the questions involved in making a new register. At the same time, there is a constant anxiety over war funds, as is prudent in a nation spending fifty millions of dollars per day. It has been proposed that a large poll tax be assessed upon the voters of the

---

8. An allusion to Romans 8:28.

9. Catt is referring to the revolutionary ardor that swept across many European countries in 1848.

10. All three provinces passed full woman suffrage legislation in 1916.

11. Herbert Henry Asquith, British Prime Minister, 1908–1916.

12. Most likely a reference to Asquith's November 2, 1915, speech in the House of Commons.

13. Millicent Garrett Fawcett, president of Great Britain's National Union of Women's Suffrage Societies.

14. The exchange between Asquith and Fawcett took place in the first week of May 1916.

15. Catt is referring to Asquith's speech in the House of Commons, August 14, 1916.

new lists, whereupon a secondary proposal of great force has been offered, and that is that twice as much money would find its way into the public coffers were women added to the voters' lists! What nation, with compliments fresh spoken concerning women's patriotism and efficiency, could resist such an appeal?

So it happens that above the roar of cannon, the scream of shrapnel, and the whirr of aeroplanes, one who listens may hear the cracking of the fetters which have long bound the European woman to outworn conventions. It has been a frightful price to pay, but the fact remains that a womanhood, well started on the way to final emancipation, is destined to step forth from the war. It will be a bewildered, troubled, and grief-stricken womanhood with knotty problems of life to solve, but it will be freer to deal with them than women have ever been before.

"The Woman's Hour Has Struck." It has struck for the women of Europe and for those of all the world. The significance of the changed status of European women has not been lost upon the men and women of our land; our own people are not so unlearned in history nor so lacking in national pride that they will allow the republic to lag long behind the empire presided over by the descendant of George III.[16] If they possess the patriotism and the sense of nationality which should be the inheritance of an American, they will not wait until the war is ended but will boldly lead in the inevitable march of democracy, our own American specialty. Sisters, let me repeat: "The Woman's Hour Has Struck!"

Second: As the most adamantine rock gives way under the constant dripping of water, so the opposition to woman suffrage in our own country has slowly disintegrated before the increasing strength of our movement. Turn backward the pages of our history! Behold brave Abbie Kelley,[17] rotten-egged because she, a woman, essayed to speak in public. Behold the

Polish Ernestine Rose, startled that women of free America drew aside their skirts when she proposed that they should control their own property.[18] Recall the saintly Lucretia Mott and the legal-minded Elizabeth Cady Stanton, turned out of the World's Anti-Slavery Convention in London and conspiring together to free their sex from the world's stupid oppressions.[19] Remember the gentle, sweet-voiced Lucy Stone, egged because she publicly claimed that women had brains capable of education.[20] Think upon Dr. Elizabeth Blackwell,[21] snubbed and boycotted by other women because she proposed to study medicine. Behold Dr. Antoinette Brown Blackwell, standing in sweet serenity before an assembly of howling clergymen, angry that she, a woman, dared to attend a temperance convention as a delegate.[22] Revere the intrepid Susan B. Anthony, mobbed from Buffalo to Albany because she demanded fair play for women.[23] These are they who, with others, builded the foundation of political liberty for American women.

Those who came after only laid the stones in place. Yet what a wearisome task even that has been! Think of the wonderful woman who has wandered from village to village, from city to city, for a generation compelling men and women to listen and to

16. King of Great Britain at the time of the American Revolution; his great-grandson, George V, occupied the throne at the time of Catt's speech.

17. Abolitionist and pioneering women's rights advocate who broke social conventions against women speaking in public by taking to the platform during the 1830s.

18. Born in Poland, Rose came to the United States in 1836 and quickly took the lead in campaigning for the property rights of married women.

19. Mott and Stanton were denied seating as delegates at the 1840 convention because they were women; eight years later, they organized the women's rights convention at Seneca Falls, New York.

20. The first woman from Massachusetts to earn a college degree, Stone also defied social norms by keeping her name after marriage.

21. The first woman in the United States to graduate from medical school (1849).

22. Catt is referring to an incident at the World's Temperance Convention in 1853, the same year in which Blackwell became the first woman to be ordained as a Congregational minister in the United States.

23. Catt is referring to the controversy surrounding Anthony's act of voting in the 1872 presidential election, for which she was arrested and convicted of violating the New York state election statute.

reflect by her matchless eloquence. Where in all the world's history has any movement among men produced so invincible an advocate as our own Dr. Anna Howard Shaw?[24] Those whom she has led to the light are legion.

Think, too, of the consecration, the self-denial, the never-failing constancy of that other noble soul set in a frail but unflinching body—the heroine we know as Alice Stone Blackwell![25] A woman who never forgets, who detects the slightest flaw in the weapons of her adversary, who knows the most vulnerable spot in his armor, presides over the *Woman's Journal* and, like a lamp in a lighthouse, the rays of her intelligence, farsightedness, and clear thinking have enlightened the world concerning our cause. The names of hundreds of other brave souls spring to memory when we pause to review the long struggle.

The hands of many suffrage master-masons have long been stilled; the names of many who laid the stones have been forgotten. That does not matter. The main thing is that the edifice of woman's liberty nears completion. It is strong, indestructible. All honor to the thousands who have helped in the building.

The four cornerstones of the foundation were laid long years ago. We read upon the first: "We demand for women education, for not a high school or college is open to her." Upon the second: "We demand for women religious liberty, for in few churches is she permitted to pray or speak." Upon the third: "We demand for women the right to own property and an opportunity to earn an honest living. Only six, poorly paid occupations are open to her, and if she is married, the wages she earns are not hers." Upon the fourth: "We demand political freedom and its symbol, the vote."

The stones in the foundation have long been overgrown with the moss and mold of time and some there are who never knew they were laid. Of late, four

capstones at the top have been set to match those in the base, and we read upon the first: "The number of women who are graduated from high schools, colleges, and universities is legion." Upon the second: "The Christian Endeavor, that mighty, undenominational church militant, asks the vote for women, and the Methodist Episcopal Church, and many another, joins that appeal." Upon the third: "Billions of dollars worth of property are owned by women; more than eight millions of women are wage-earners. Every occupation is open to them." Upon the fourth: "Women vote in twelve states; they share in the determination of ninety-one electoral votes."[26]

After the capstones and cornice comes the roof. Across the empty spaces, the rooftree has been flung and fastened well in place. It is not made of stone but of two planks—planks in the platforms of the two majority parties, and these are well supported by planks in the platforms of all the minority parties.

And we, who are the builders of 1916, do we see no crisis? Standing upon these planks which are stretched across the topmost peak of this edifice of woman's liberty, what shall we do? Over our heads, up there in the clouds, but tantalizingly near, hangs the roof of our edifice—the vote. What is our duty? Shall we spend time in admiring the capstones and cornice? Shall we lament the tragedies which accompanied the laying of the cornerstones? Or shall we, like the builders of old, chant, "Ho! All hands, all hands, heave to! All hands, heave to!" and while we chant, grasp the overhanging roof and with "a long pull, a strong pull, and a pull all together,"[27] fix it in place for ever more?

Is the crisis real or imaginary? If it be real, it calls for action—bold, immediate, and decisive.

Let us then take measure of our strength. Our cause has won the endorsement of all political

---

24. President of the National American Woman Suffrage Association, 1904–1915. See pages 43–56 for her speech "The Fundamental Principle of a Republic."

25. Daughter of Lucy Stone, and longtime editor of the *Woman's Journal*, Blackwell helped bring about the reconciliation of rival women's rights organizations that led to creation of the National American Woman Suffrage Association in 1890.

26. Catt is referring to the 11 states that had full woman suffrage (Arizona, California, Colorado, Idaho, Kansas, Oregon, Montana, Nevada, Utah, Washington, Wyoming), plus Illinois, which had partial suffrage that allowed women to vote for President.

27. A phrase often used in the 19th century to convey the need for steady, energetic, and systematic cooperation, most often in connection with rowing a boat or pulling a rope.

parties; every candidate for the presidency is a suf-fragist. It has won the endorsement of most churches; it has won the hearty approval of all great organiza-tions of women. It has won the support of all reform movements; it has won the progressives of every vari-ety. The majority of the press in most states is with us. Great men in every political party, church, and move-ment are with us. The names of the greatest men and women of art, science, literature, philosophy, reform, religion, and politics are on our lists.

We have not won the reactionaries of any party, church, or society and we never will. From the begin-ning of things, there have been Antis. The Antis drove Moses out of Egypt; they crucified Christ, who said, "Love thy neighbor as thyself";[28] they have persecuted Jews in all parts of the world; they poi-soned Socrates, the great philosopher;[29] they cruelly persecuted Copernicus and Galileo,[30] the first great scientists; they burned Giordano Bruno[31] at the stake because he believed the world was round; they burned Savonarola,[32] who warred upon church cor-ruption; they burned Eufame MacAlyane because she used an anesthetic;[33] they burned Joan of Arc for a heretic;[34] they have sent great men and women to Siberia to eat their hearts out in isolation;[35] they burned in effigy William Lloyd Garrison;[36] they egged Abbie Kelley and Lucy Stone and mobbed Susan B. Anthony.[37]

---

28. From Leviticus 19:18.

29. Socrates was sentenced to death by drinking hemlock in 399 BCE.

30. Nicholas Copernicus (1473–1543); Galileo Galilei (1564–1642).

31. Italian philosopher and scientist (1548–1600).

32. Political and religious reformer Girolamo Savonarola (1452–1498).

33. MacAlyane was burned alive on Castle Hill, Edinburgh, in 1591 for seeking pain relief during the birth of her twin sons.

34. French heroine Jeanne d'Arc was executed in 1431.

35. During the 18th and 19th centuries, the Russian govern-ment deported more than one million prisoners to Siberia.

36. American reformer and antislavery leader (1805–1879).

37. See notes 17, 20, and 23 above.

Yet, in proportion to the enlightenment of their respective ages, these Antis were persons of intel-ligence and honest purpose. They were merely deaf to the call of progress and were enraged because the world insisted upon moving on. Antis, male and female, there still are and will be to the end of time. Give to them a prayer of forgiveness, for they know not what they do,[38] and prepare for the onward march.

We have not won the ignorant and illiterate and we never can. They are too undeveloped mentally to understand that the institutions of today are not those of yesterday nor will be those of tomorrow.

We have not won the forces of evil and we never will. Evil has ever been timorous and suspicious of all change. It is an instinctive act of self-preservation which makes it fear and consequently oppose votes for women. As the Honorable Champ Clark[39] said the other day, "Some good and intelligent people are opposed to woman suffrage, but all the ignorant and evil-minded are against it."

These three forces are the enemies of our cause. Before the vote is won, there must and will be a gigantic final conflict between the forces of progress, righteousness, and democracy and the forces of igno-rance, evil, and reaction. That struggle may be post-poned, but it cannot be evaded or avoided. There is no question as to which side will be the victor.

Shall we play the coward, then, and leave the hard knocks for our daughters or shall we throw ourselves into the fray, bare our own shoulders to the blows, and thus bequeath to them a politically liberated woman-hood? We have taken note of our gains and of our resources, and they are all we could wish. Before the final struggle, we must take cognizance of our weak-ness. Are we prepared to grasp the victory? Alas, no! Our movement is like a great Niagara[40] with a vast volume of water tumbling over its ledge but turning no wheel. Our organized machinery is set for the pro-pagandistic stage and not for the seizure of victory. Our supporters are spreading the argument for our

---

38. An echo of Jesus's words on the cross (Luke 23:34).

39. Speaker of the U.S. House of Representatives.

40. A reference to Niagara Falls, on the U.S.-Canadian border.

cause; they feel no sense of responsibility for the realization of our hopes. Our movement lacks cohesion, organization, unity, and consequent momentum.

Behind us, in front of us, everywhere about us are suffragists—millions of them, but inactive and silent. They have been "agitated and educated" and are with us in belief. There are thousands of women who have at one time or another been members of our organization, but they have dropped out because to them the movement seemed negative and pointless. Many have taken up other work whose results were more immediate. Philanthropy, charity, work for corrective laws of various kinds, temperance, relief for working women, and numberless similar public services have called them. Others have turned to the pleasanter avenues of club work, art, or literature.

There are thousands of other women who have never learned of the earlier struggles of our movement. They found doors of opportunity open to them on every side. They found well-paid posts awaiting the qualified woman, and they have availed themselves of all these blessings. Almost without exception they believe in the vote, but they feel neither gratitude to those who opened the doors through which they have entered to economic liberty nor any sense of obligation to open other doors for those who come after.

There are still others who, timorously looking over their shoulders to see if any listeners be near, will tell us they hope we will win and win soon, but they are too frightened of Mother Grundy[41] to help. There are others too occupied with the small things of life to help. They say they could find time to vote but not to work for the vote. There are men, too, millions of them, waiting to be called. These men and women are our reserves. They are largely unorganized and untrained soldiers with little responsibility toward our movement. Yet these reserves must be mobilized. The final struggle needs their numbers and the momentum those numbers will bring. Were never another convert made, there are suffragists enough in this country, if combined, to make so irresistible a driving force that victory might be seized at once.

How can it be done? By a simple change of mental attitude. If we are to seize the victory, that change must take place in this hall, here and now!

The old belief, which has sustained suffragists in many an hour of discouragement, "Woman suffrage is bound to come," must give way to the new: "The Woman's Hour Has Struck." The long, drawn-out struggle, the cruel hostility which, for years, was arrayed against our cause, have accustomed suffragists to the idea of indefinite postponement but eventual victory. The slogan of a movement sets its pace. The old one counseled patience. It said there is plenty of time; it pardoned sloth and halfhearted effort. It set the pace of an educational campaign. "The Woman's Hour Has Struck" sets the pace of a crusade which will have its way. It says, "Awake, arise, my sisters, let your hearts be filled with joy—the time of victory is here. Onward, march."

If you believe with me that a crisis has come to our movement, if you believe that the time for final action is now, if you catch the rosy tints of the coming day, what does it mean to you? Does it not give you a thrill of exaltation; does the blood not course more quickly through your veins; does it not bring a new sense of freedom, of joy, and of determination? Is it not true that you who wanted, a little time ago, to lay down the work because you were weary with long service, now, under the compelling influence of a changed mental attitude, are ready to go on until the vote is won?

The change is one of spirit! Aye, and the spiritual effect upon you will come to others. Let me borrow an expression from [the] Honorable John Finley: What our great movement needs now is a "mobilization of spirit"—the jubilant, glad spirit of victory.[42] Then let us sound a bugle call here and now to the women of the nation: "The Woman's Hour Has Struck." Let the bugle sound from the suffrage headquarters of every state at the inauguration of a state campaign. Let the call go forth again and again and yet again. Let it be repeated in every article written, in every speech made, in every conversation held. Let the bugle blow

41. A reference to Mrs. Grundy, a character in Thomas Morton's play *Speed the Plough* (1798) who became a symbol of conventionality in thought and conduct.

42. Finley was president of the University of the State of New York; the quotation is from his essay "America Needs 'Mobilization of the Spirit,'" *New York Times*, July 9, 1916.

again and yet again. The political emancipation of our sex call[s] you. Women of America, arise! Are you content that others shall pay the price of your liberty?

Women in schools and counting houses, in shops and on the farm, women in the home with babes at their breasts, and women engaged in public careers will hear. The veins of American women are not filled with milk and water. They are neither cowards nor slackers. They will come. They only await the bugle call to learn that the final battle is on.

Give heed at once to the organization of the reserves; and then to the work that they shall do. Organize in every assembly district and every voting precinct. It is the only way to make our appeal invincible. Swell the army, then set it upon the trail of every legislator and Congressman, for they alone hold the key to our political emancipation. Compel this army of lawmakers to see woman suffrage, to think woman suffrage, to talk woman suffrage every minute of every day until they heed our plea.

All this is mere preparedness for the final drive to victory. The next question is: What shall be our aim?

We have listened to an exhaustive discussion upon the three-cornered questions: Shall we concentrate on the federal amendment, shall we concentrate on state referenda, or shall we proceed as before, supporting both methods? The convention has voted to continue both forms of activity, but there is one further point which should be made clear before we adjourn, and that is the exact program to be followed in the support of the two methods. This should be so precisely defined by this convention that every member, every friend, and even every foe may understand it.

We have long known the many obstacles imposed by most state constitutions and that there are states in which women must wait a probable half century for their enfranchisement if no other avenue of escape is offered than amendment of their state constitutions. But there are other and even graver considerations which, in my judgment, should compel us to make the federal amendment our ultimate aim and work in the states [on] a program of preparedness to win nationwide suffrage by amendment of the national Constitution.

I must say in passing that this is no new opinion. I have held it for a quarter of a century, and the varying suffrage events of the passing years have only served to strengthen and emphasize my conviction. To my mind, the insistence of the enfranchisement of the women of our land by federal amendment is the only self-respecting course to pursue. My reasons, I beg the privilege of presenting.

My first campaign was that in South Dakota in the year 1890. Because I was young and all the experiences were new, every event in that campaign stands out in my memory with a vividness which does not mark later and even more important events. My first point was Mitchell, where a two days' suffrage meeting was held prior to the state Republican convention.[43] Miss Anthony was the leader; Miss Shaw "the star,"[44] and the very best women of South Dakota were there.

Of course, we wanted a plank in the Republican platform.[45] The great concession was made the suffragists of ten seats on the platform where no one could see or be seen. I was fortunate enough to be one of the ten, and being young, I did not mind standing on a chair in order to see the convention. Peeping over the heads and shoulders of those before me, I saw a man arise and move that a delegation of Sioux Indians be admitted. They had been enfranchised by the national government and, the delegate said, their votes must be won. They were admitted to the floor of the house—three blanketed, long-haired, greasy men of the plains. On the platform sat Miss Anthony, bent with the weight of her seventy years, forty of which had been unceasingly expended to secure education, property rights, and the vote for her sex. Upon her face was the expectancy born of "the hope which springs eternal in the human breast."[46] On the floor sat the Indians unmoved and unknowing.

---

43. The suffrage meeting was held on August 25–26; the Republican convention met in the same city on August 27.

44. See notes 23–24 above.

45. Suffrage forces were not successful in achieving this objective.

46. Closely paraphrased from Alexander Pope, *Essay on Man* (1733–1734).

The time came when five minutes was given the unenfranchised women, and Miss Shaw was called to speak for them. She has made many powerful addresses, but never one quite so wonderful as that. All the men who packed that big skating rink combined could not have provided so soul-stirring an appeal for any cause, but it was a prophet whose soul was lighted by a vision of truth, speaking to a mob who marveled at the power of the speaker but did not comprehend her message. With the crowd, I passed out of the door stunned by the knowledge I had gained that Americans did not understand the principles of self-government. On either side stood a man handing out papers. They were men of the lowest type, and the papers were *The Remonstrance*, published by a few rich women in Boston who were, at that date, too timid to have their names printed on the document.[47] What agent secured the men who, every person in the town knew, were henchmen of the local saloons, I never learned.

My last point in the state was Aberdeen, and there, on election day,[48] I, with other women, served as watchers. All day long, at intervals groups of five or ten Russians filed in to the order of poll workers. They, too, were saloon henchmen. These Russians could not speak English; they were totally illiterate and signed the poll book with a cross. They had no more comprehension of the sacredness of a vote than a wild man from Borneo.[49] The man who chiefly managed the affair, and who must have voted a hundred men that day, grew bold and more than once paid his men their two dollars in plain sight.

No king marshalling his army upon a battlefield could bear himself with more triumphant mien than did this political criminal whenever he entered that polling place with a new line of purchased voters. The hatred and contempt of his expression as he led them past us could not have been exceeded by an Apache chief gloating over his conquered foe. There was no remedy. South Dakota had no law to fit the case. These events at the time seemed mere local incidents, but I was to learn later that they were the early manifestation of a nationwide condition which would remain constant in our campaigns until the end and that they were to grow into an increasingly better-organized hostility to be met in every state.

Rich women, protected and serene, or women well paid by rich women have grown bolder and more skillful in their unspeakable treachery to their sex. There have been those willing to vilify their sister women from ocean to ocean and to declare them too incompetent mentally and too unclean morally to be trusted with the privilege of self-government. Their motives suffragists will never understand.

The liquor forces have developed an organized opposition, apparently supported by large funds, which has been an active factor in every campaign except two since 1890, and in those two we won. The secretary of one of the state liquor associations recently said to a man of honor that they would not allow another state to be carried for suffrage within the next ten years. Still another representative of the same force said to another man that they could gather ten millions of dollars if necessary to throw into any state which gave indications of a suffrage victory. These are doubtless wild threats, but the fact remains that a powerful force is arrayed against our cause, and it scruples at nothing.

In every precinct, there seem to be a few men willing to sell their citizen's right, and these may be numerous enough to become a balance of power which, added to the normal conservative vote, may defeat our amendments. This "triple alliance"—the women who work in the open appealing to the respectable conservative element and the liquor forces secretly conniving with the purchasable vote—forms a combined foe very difficult to combat since its attack is subterranean.

Opposition in the open which meets our arguments with arguments, our claims with defense,

---

47. Begun in 1890 by the Boston Committee of Remonstrants, *The Remonstrance* became the official organ of the Massachusetts Association Opposed to the Further Extension of Suffrage to Women when that organization was founded in 1895, and it remained a major antisuffrage periodical until ceasing publication in 1920.

48. November 4, 1890.

49. Originally a colloquialism for orangutans, who lived in the Borneo rainforest, the phrase "wild man from Borneo" was widely used in Catt's time to connote primitiveness and lack of civilization.

must always be welcome. Truth has ever followed in the wake of free and honest discussion. But an opposition which conspires behind closed doors to buy its victory with money or spoils is a criminal so black, so indescribably hideous, that it fills the soul not with discouragement for our cause, but with shame for our republic. We shall never know how many campaigns have been lost by such conspiracies, but it is my own sincere conviction that there have been several.

We know that in the Colorado campaign, the brewers of Denver printed false statements and caused them to be put under the door of every house in the city.[50] We know that in the last unsuccessful campaign in Oregon,[51] the order went out from the liquor forces to the saloons of the state to deliver a stated number of votes in opposition to the suffrage amendment. Every suffragist in Michigan seems to agree that the amendment was counted out in the first campaign and that the ballots were stuffed in the second and that the agents were the liquor forces.[52]

The Attorney General who was serving at the time of the Nebraska campaign has declared that he believes the amendment was counted out there, and again the charge lies at the same door.[53] The wet counties in Iowa certainly defeated the amendment there.[54] The Boston & Maine Railway contributed to defeat the suffrage question in the constitutional convention of New Hampshire,[55] and afterward it was found that it had been done in collusion with the liquor lobby.[56] The brewers, arrested upon the federal charge of conspiracy in elections and brought to trial in Pittsburgh this year,[57] are supposed to have contributed large sums to defeat the question in the four eastern campaign states,[58] and although this remains unproven, it is true that their business was conducted in so irregular a fashion that checkbooks and stubs had been destroyed.

It was true in New York that men visited trade unionists and told them that woman suffrage meant the certain loss of positions in all trades allied to the liquor business. It is true that in New Jersey the woman poll workers were appalled at the seemingly endless number of illiterate, drunken, and degenerate types who were lined up to vote in opposition to the amendment in that state.[59] It is true that the four men representing Texas, Indiana, Georgia, and New Jersey, respectively, who signed the minority report of the Resolutions Committee in St. Louis, which would have taken the suffrage plank out of the Democratic platform, are all well-known henchmen of the liquor interests.[60] It is well known that a group of liquor men have issued newspaper plate matter under the imprint of an alleged Farmers' Association and have sent it broadcast to rural papers, its contents purporting to be of interest to farmers but always containing antisuffrage articles.

The liquor interests have been driven to the aggressive defensive by the inroads of the Prohibition

---

50. Catt is referring to the 1893 campaign in which Colorado passed a suffrage referendum.

51. Catt is referring to the Oregon campaign of 1910; previous unsuccessful campaigns took place in 1884, 1900, 1906, and 1908. Oregon voters finally voted to enfranchise women in 1912.

52. The first Michigan referendum took place in 1874, the second in 1912. Both were defeated.

53. Catt is referring to the Nebraska campaign of 1914 and to comments from Attorney General Willis E. Reed.

54. Catt is referring to the 1916 Iowa suffrage referendum.

55. On June 20, 1912, the convention rejected a proposed constitutional amendment granting the vote to women in New Hampshire.

56. Catt is referring to a March 1916 report by the New Hampshire Public Service Commission.

57. Grand-jury indictments against the brewing companies were brought in March 1916 for violations during the 1914 elections. The companies eventually pleaded nolo contendere, and in April 1917 a total of $52,000 in fines were levied on 33 Pennsylvania breweries.

58. New York, Pennsylvania, Massachusetts, and New Jersey.

59. Catt is referring to events in the 1915 suffrage campaigns in New York and New Jersey.

60. Catt is referring to events at the Democratic National Convention, held in St. Louis, June 14–16, 1916. The men in question are James Ferguson (Texas), Stephen Fleming (Indiana), Charles Bartlett (Georgia), and James Nugent (New Jersey). Despite their efforts, the final version of the platform did include a plank supporting woman suffrage.

movement. They are obsessed by the idea that woman suffrage is only a flank Prohibition movement. They have the Americans' right to fight for their own. We cannot relieve them of their notion that woman suffrage will promote Prohibition and hence must accept their opposition as normal. But when that opposition ceases to be honest and resorts to conspiracy and bribery to gain its ends, it becomes criminal.

Since this kind of opposition has occurred to a greater or less extent in all our campaigns, suffragists must be prepared to meet it in future. What, if any, underground connection there may be between the women Antis and the liquor Antis no one knows. Some of the women are conscientious and honest, I am sure, but the obvious fact remains that these women secure what they want—that is, their own disfranchisement—by the aid and the evident conjunction of the liquor forces with the purchasable, controllable vote, and in several campaigns their posters, their literature, and buttons were circulated through saloons. This may have been done without the knowledge or consent of the women, but the fact remains that the saloons and the women Antis agree that votes in the hands of women are a "menace."

Corruption has existed since the beginning of things and will continue so long as there are dishonest men to tempt and weak ones to yield. It is a far more invidious foe to our country's weal than the bugaboos of wars with Germany, Mexico, or Japan.[61] A French philosopher said that "The corruption of each form of government commences with the decay of its principles."[62] History proves that statement to be true, and in our own land the careful student should feel genuine anxiety at the ignorance and indifference among our people concerning those truths we have called "American principles." It is through the departure from loyalty to those principles that corruption

has crept into our political life, and it is through the weakness created by internal corruption that most of the great dead nations have met their downfall.

If the suffrage amendments are defeated by illegal practices, why not demand redress, asks the novice in suffrage campaigns. Ah, there's the rub.[63] In twenty-five states no provision has been made by the election law for any form of contest or recount on a referendum. Political corrupters may, in these states, bribe voters, colonize voters, and repeat them to their hearts' content and redress of any kind is practically impossible. If clear evidence of fraud could be produced, a case might be brought to the courts and the guilty parties might be punished, but the election would stand.

In New York, in 1915, the question was submitted to the voters as to whether there should be a constitutional convention. The convention was ordered by a majority of over 1,300. It was estimated that about 800 fraudulent votes were cast. Leading lawyers discussed the question of effect upon the election, and the general opinion was that even though the entire majority and more was found to be fraudulent, the election could not be set aside. The convention was held.

In twenty states, contests on referenda seem possible under the law, but in practically every one the contest means a resort to the courts, and in only eight of these is reference made to a recount. The law is vague and incomplete in nearly all of these states. In some of these, including Michigan, where the suffrage amendment is declared to have been counted out, application for a recount must be made in each voting precinct. To have secured redress in Michigan, provided the fraud was widespread, as I understand it was, it would have been necessary to have secured definite evidence of fraud in a probable 1,000 precincts and to have instituted as many cases.[64]

In some states, the courts decide what the redress shall be, and in these no assurance is given by the law that such redress would include a correction of the

---

61. In addition to the possibility of war with Germany, which would come to pass in April 1917, there was a threat of war with Mexico as a result of clashes between American and Mexican troops in mid-1916. Japan was said to be a potential ally of Mexico.

62. Paraphrased from Charles de Secondat, Baron de Montesquieu, *De l'Esprit des Lois* (1748).

63. From William Shakespeare, *Hamlet* (1600–1601).

64. Catt is discussing the 1912 suffrage campaign in Michigan.

returns. In at least seven, the applicants must pay all costs if they fail to prove their case.

The penalties for bribery range from $5 to $2,000 and from thirty days to ten years, but only one state (Ohio) provides in terms for punishment of bribery as part of the penalty in an election contest. Just as proof of bribery does not throw out the person's vote, so the other way about—the throwing out of the purchased votes in contest cases does not bring with it automatically punishment of the purchased voter. If we may judge from this omission from the contest provisions, these bribery cases could be separate actions.

Twenty-one states in clear terms disfranchise (or give the legislature power to disfranchise) bribers and bribed, but few make provisions for the method of actually enforcing the law, and upon inquiry, the Secretary of State of many of these states reported that, so far as he knew, no man had ever been disfranchised for this offense. This was true of states which have been notorious for political corruption. With a vague, uncertain law to define their punishment in most states and no law at all in twenty-five states as a preliminary security, corrupt opponents of a woman suffrage amendment find many additional aids to their nefarious acts. A briber must make sure that the bribed carries out his part of the contract. Whenever it is easy to check up the results of the bribe, corruption may reign supreme and with little risk of being found out.

A study of some of the recent suffrage votes results in significant food for reflection. In Wisconsin, the suffrage ballot was separate and pink. It was easy to teach the most illiterate how to vote "No" and to check up returns with considerable accuracy. In New York, there were three ballots.[65] The official ballot had emblems which easily distinguished it. The other two were exactly alike in shape, size, and color and each contained three propositions, those which came from the constitutional convention and the other those which came from the legislature. The orders went forth to vote down the constitutional provisions, and it was done by a majority of 482,000, or nearly

300,000 more than the majority against woman suffrage. On the ballot containing the suffrage amendment, which was Number 1, there was Proposition Number 3, which all the political parties wanted carried. It could easily be found by all illiterate[s] as it contained more lines of printing, yet so difficult was it to teach ignorant men to vote "No" on suffrage and "Yes" on Number 3 that, despite the fact that orders had gone forth to all the state that Number 3 was to be carried, it barely squeezed through.

In Pennsylvania, there are no emblems to distinguish the tickets and, on the large ballot, the suffrage amendment would have been difficult to find by an untutored voter. In consequence, as I believe, Pennsylvania polled the largest proportional vote for the amendment of any eastern state. In Massachusetts, the ballot was small and the suffrage amendment could be easily picked out by a bribed illiterate. In Iowa, the suffrage ballot was separate and yellow, while the main ballots were white. In consequence, there were 35,000 more votes cast on the suffrage proposition than for the nomination of Governor, although the contest was an excited one. In North Dakota, the regular ballot was long and complicated and the suffrage ballot separate and small.[66] It was easy to teach the dullest illiterate how to vote "No." It might be said that it would be equally easy to teach him to vote "Yes." True, but suffragists never bribe. Both the briber and the illiterate are allies of the Antis.

The election boards are bipartisan and each party has its own machinery, not only of election officials but watchers and challengers, to see that the opposing party commits no fraud. The watchfulness of this party machinery, plus an increasingly vigilant public opinion, has corrected many of the election frauds which were once common, and many elections are probably free from all the baser forms of corruption.

When a question on referendum is sincerely espoused by both the dominant parties, it has the advantage of the watchfulness of both party machines and is doubly safeguarded from fraud. But when such

---

65. Catt is referring to the 1912 Wisconsin suffrage referendum and the 1915 New York referendum.

66. Catt is referring to ballots used in 1914 (North Dakota), 1915 (Pennsylvania and Massachusetts), and 1916 (Iowa).

a question has been espoused by no dominant party, it is utterly at the mercy of the worst forms of corruption. The election officers may even agree to wink at fraud even when plainly committed, since it is no affair of theirs. Or they may even go further and join in the pleasing game of running in as many votes against such an amendment as possible. This has not infrequently been the unhappy experience of suffrage amendments in corrupt quarters. With no one on the election board whose especial business it is to see that honesty is upheld, a suffrage amendment suffers further disaster through the fact that most states do not permit women watchers to stand guard over their own question.

When it is remembered that immigrants may be naturalized after a residence of five years; that, when naturalized, they automatically become voters by all our state constitutions; that in nine states immigrant voters are not even required to be citizens; that the right to vote is limited by an educational qualification in only seventeen states and that nine of these are Southern with special intent of disfranchising the Negro; that there is an unscrupulous body ready to engage the lowest elements of our population by fraudulent processes to oppose our amendment; that there is no authority on the election board whose business it is to see that we get a square deal; that the method of preparing the ballot is often an advantage to the enemy; that after the fraud is committed, there is practically no redress provided by election laws, it ought to be clear to all that state constitutional amendments, when unsponsored by the dominant political parties which control the election machinery, must run the gauntlet of exceedingly unfair conditions. When suffragists have been fortunate enough to overcome the obstacles imposed by the constitution of their states, they immediately enter upon the task of surmounting the infinitely greater hazards of the election law.

We are justly proud of the nine states which have been won on a referendum,[67] but these are not greater monuments to the triumphs of our cause than to the integrity of the elections in those states. I am certain that at least five other states should stand in that list. That they are not there is a reflection upon the inefficiency of the election machinery of those states.

No careful observer of the modern trend of human affairs doubts that "governments of the people" are destined to replace the monarchies of the world. No "listener in" will fail to hear the rumble of the rising tide of democracy. No watcher of events will deny that the women of all civilized lands will be enfranchised as part of "the people," and no American possessed of the least political acumen doubts woman suffrage in our land as a coming fact.

Bear these items in mind and remember that three-fourths of the men of our nation have received the vote as the direct or indirect gift of the naturalization laws; that the federal government enfranchised the Indians, assuming its authority upon the ground that they are wards of the nation; that the Negroes were enfranchised by federal amendment; that the constitutions of all states not in the list of the original thirteen automatically extended the vote to men; that in the original colonial territory the chief struggle occurred over the elimination of the landowning qualification and that a total vote necessary to give the franchise to nonlandowners did not exceed fifty or seventy-five thousand in any state.

Let us not forget that the vote is the free-will offering of our forty-eight states to any man who chooses to make this land his home. Let us not overlook the fact [that] every five years of late an average of one million immigrant voters are added to our electors' lists—a million men mainly uneducated and all molded by European traditions. To these men, women of American birth, education, and ideals must appeal for their enfranchisement. No humiliation could be more complete unless we add the sorrowful fact that leaders of Americanism in Congress and legislatures are willing to drive their wives and daughters to beg the consent of these men to their political liberty.

Let us return to South Dakota a moment. During the Civil War there was an uprising of the Sioux Indians who occupied a reservation covering a large part of the territory now comprising that state. These Indians instituted one of the cruelest and most savage massacres in our history. They committed

---

67. Arizona, California, Colorado, Idaho, Kansas, Montana, Nevada, Oregon, Washington.

atrocities upon women so indescribably indecent that they were never recorded in ordinary history.[68]

By 1890, the numerous efforts to win them to civilization had culminated in an offer of land in severalty, and if accepted in good faith, these landowners were promised the vote. Their blanketed representatives sat in the Republican convention of that year and took their first lesson in American politics. In 1916, I am reliably informed that there are 5,000 Sioux voters in the state of South Dakota and that they may prove the balance of power in November to decide whether women who have borne the burdens of pioneer life shall be permitted the vote. How much the schools have taught them of human liberty within the last quarter of a century I do not know, but I opine that they will make congenial allies to the Antis.

To my mind, the considerations aroused by such facts entirely outweigh any philosophy which supports the theory of suffrage by "state rights."

Again, let us not forget that while our struggle continues in this supposedly democratic land, women have been enfranchised within a year in three provinces of Canada nearly equal in extent to all our territory east of the Mississippi,[69] in Denmark and Iceland by majority vote of their respective parliaments.[70] All signs indicate the early enfranchisement of the women of Great Britain by the same process.[71]

Why, then, should American women be content to beg the vote on bended knee from man to man when no American male voter has been compelled to pay this price for his vote and no woman of other countries is subjected to this humiliation? Shall a republic be less generous with its womanhood than

an empire? Shall the government be less liberal with its daughters than with its sons?

The makers of the Constitution foresaw the necessity of referring important questions of state to a more intelligent body than the masses of the people and so provided for the amendment of the Constitution by referendum to the legislatures of the various states. Why should we hesitate to avail ourselves of the privileges thus created? We represent one land and one people. We have the same institutions, customs, and ideals. It is the advocates of state rights who are championing national Prohibition and child labor.[72] It will be a curious kind of logic that can uphold these measures as national and at the same time relegate woman suffrage to the states.

Our cause has been caught in a snarl of constitutional obstructions and inadequate election laws. We have a right to appeal to our Congress to extricate our cause from this tangle. If there is any chivalry left, this is the time for it to come forward and do an act of simple justice. In my judgment, the women of this land, not only have the right to sit on the steps of Congress until it acts, but it is their self-respecting duty to insist upon their enfranchisement by that route.

But let me implore you, sister women, not to imagine a federal amendment an easy process of enfranchisement. There is no quick shortcut to our liberty. The federal amendment means a simultaneous campaign in forty-eight states. It demands organization in every precinct; activity, agitation, education in every corner. It means an appeal to the voters only little less general than is required in a referendum. Nothing less than this nationwide, vigilant, unceasing campaigning will win the ratification.

Do not allow my comments to discourage you who represent the states where campaigns are pending. Your campaign may win the promise to safeguard your election from the dominant parties. It may so arouse public sentiment that any fraud may be outvoted. You

68. Most likely a reference to a series of raids led by Little Crow in August–September 1862.

69. See note 10 above.

70. Denmark established full suffrage for women in 1915; Iceland instituted conditional suffrage the same year, with full suffrage following in 1920.

71. In June 1917 the House of Commons approved extending the franchise to some, but not all, women over the age of 30; the House of Lords concurred in January 1918. Not until 1928 were British women allowed to vote on the same terms as men.

72. Southern states, which used the doctrine of states' rights to defend racial segregation, were among the strongest supporters of a federal law prohibiting the use of alcohol; opponents of laws regulating child labor argued that such legislation infringed on the rights of individual states.

are doing the best work possible. If you win, you have made federal action and ratification more certain. If you lose, you have organized an army ready for your ratification campaign and have added testimony to the need of federal action. What you have done in your state must be done in every state.

A few women here and there have dropped out from state work in the fond delusion that there is no need of work if the federal amendment is to be the aim. I hold such women to be more dangerous enemies of our cause than the known opponent. State work alone can carry the amendment through Congress and through the ratifications. There must be no shirkers, no cowards, no backsliders these coming months. The army in every state must grow larger and larger. The activity must grow livelier and even more lively. The reserves must be aroused and set to work. Let no one labor under the delusion that suffrage can be won in any other way than by the education and organization of the constituencies. Let no woman think the vote will be handed her some bright summer morning "on a golden platter at the foot of a rainbow."[73]

"The Woman's Hour Has Struck." Yet, if the call goes unheeded, if our women think it means the vote without a struggle, if they think other women can and will pay the price of their emancipation, the hour may pass and our political liberty may not be won.

Women arise: Demand the vote! The character of a man is measured, it is said, by his will. The same is true of a movement. Then will to be free. Demand the vote. Women, arise.

---

73. Most likely a reference to George Barr McCutcheon's novel *Black Is White* (1914).

Woodrow Wilson

War Message

WASHINGTON, D.C.
APRIL 2, 1917

"IT WOULD BE an irony of fate," Woodrow Wilson wrote on the eve of his inauguration as President, "if my administration had to deal chiefly with foreign affairs. All of my preparation has been in domestic affairs." Although Wilson was able to concentrate on domestic issues during most of his first term, the outbreak of war in Europe in August 1914 brought international circumstances to the forefront of his attention. He responded quickly with a proclamation of neutrality that urged Americans to be "impartial in thought as well as action." For the next two years he walked a diplomatic tightrope that balanced American honor and interests against the competing demands of the belligerent powers.

Despite Wilson's desire to keep the United States out of a conflict whose terrible toll was increasingly apparent, two events convinced him that the nation could no longer remain on the sidelines: Germany's decision of January 1917 to resume unrestricted submarine warfare against American merchant ships, and the receipt six weeks thereafter of an intercepted message from German Foreign Secretary Arthur Zimmermann offering Mexico the return of Texas, New Mexico, and Arizona if it would enter an alliance against the United States. On April 2, 1917, Wilson addressed a joint session of Congress to request a declaration of war against Germany.

Praised even by his bitter opponent Theodore Roosevelt as "one of the great state papers of our history," Wilson's war message presented a 3,600-word rationale for entering a conflict that many Americans believed should be left to Europe. At the outset, he focused on national self-interest, arguing that Germany's use of submarine warfare against civilian vessels violated "the most sacred rights of our nation and our people." It did not take him long, however, to raise the stakes to the level of universal principle. "We are but one of the champions of the rights of mankind," he declared. "We shall be satisfied when those rights have been made as secure as the faith and the freedom of nations can make them." Contending that a "steadfast concert for peace can never be maintained" by autocratic governments, he stated, in the speech's most famous line, that "the world must be made safe for democracy." In going to war, he said, America was fighting for "a universal dominion of right" that would "bring peace and safety to all nations and make the world itself at last free."

Concluding after thirty-two minutes, Wilson received thunderous applause from both sides of the aisle. He returned to the White House, where, according to his secretary, Joseph Tumulty, he said: "Think what it was they were applauding. My message today was a message of death for our young men. How strange it seems to applaud that."

◇◇

Gentlemen of the Congress: I have called the Congress into extraordinary session because there are serious, very serious, choices of policy to be made, and made immediately, which it was neither right nor constitutionally permissible that I should assume the responsibility of making.

On the third of February last, I officially laid before you the extraordinary announcement of the Imperial German Government that on and after the first day of February it was its purpose to put aside all restraints of law or of humanity and use its submarines to sink every vessel that sought to approach either the ports of Great Britain and Ireland or the western coasts of Europe or any of the ports controlled by the enemies of Germany within the Mediterranean. That had seemed to be the object of the German submarine warfare earlier in the war; but since April of last year the Imperial Government had somewhat restrained the commanders of its undersea craft in conformity with its promise then given to us that passenger boats should not be sunk and that due warning would be given to all other vessels which its submarines might seek to destroy, when no resistance was offered or escape attempted, and care taken that their crews were given at least a fair chance to save their lives in their open boats.

The precautions taken were meager and haphazard enough, as was proved in distressing instance after instance in the progress of the cruel and unmanly business, but a certain degree of restraint was observed. The new policy has swept every restriction aside. Vessels of every kind, whatever their flag, their character, their cargo, their destination, their errand, have been ruthlessly sent to the bottom without warning and without thought of help or mercy for those on board, the vessels of friendly neutrals along with those of belligerents. Even hospital ships and ships carrying relief to the sorely bereaved and stricken people of Belgium,[1] though the latter were provided with safe conduct through the proscribed areas by the German government itself and were distinguished by unmistakable marks of identity, have been sunk with the same reckless lack of compassion or of principle.

I was for a little while unable to believe that such things would in fact be done by any government that had hitherto subscribed to the humane practices of civilized nations. International law had its origin in the attempt to set up some law which would be respected and observed upon the seas, where no nation had right of dominion and where lay the free highways of the world. By painful stage after stage has that law been built up, with meager enough results, indeed, after all was accomplished that could be accomplished, but always with a clear view, at least, of what the heart and conscience of mankind demanded.

This minimum of right the German government has swept aside under the plea of retaliation and necessity and because it had no weapons which it could use at sea except these which it is impossible to employ as it is employing them without throwing to the winds all scruples of humanity or of respect for the understandings that were supposed to underlie the intercourse of the world. I am not now thinking of the loss of property involved, immense and serious as that is, but only of the wanton and wholesale destruction of the lives of noncombatants—men, women, and children—engaged in pursuits which have always, even in the darkest periods of modern history, been deemed innocent and legitimate. Property can be paid for; the lives of peaceful

and innocent people cannot be. The present German submarine warfare against commerce is a warfare against mankind.

It is a war against all nations. American ships have been sunk, American lives taken, in ways which it has stirred us very deeply to learn of, but the ships and people of other neutral and friendly nations have been sunk and overwhelmed in the waters in the same way. There has been no discrimination. The challenge is to all mankind. Each nation must decide for itself how it will meet it. The choice we make for ourselves must be made with a moderation of counsel and a temperateness of judgment befitting our character and our motives as a nation. We must put excited feeling away. Our motive will not be revenge or the victorious assertion of the physical might of the nation, but only the vindication of right, of human right, of which we are only a single champion.

When I addressed the Congress on the twenty-sixth of February last, I thought that it would suffice to assert our neutral rights with arms, our right to use the seas against unlawful interference, our right to keep our people safe against unlawful violence. But armed neutrality, it now appears, is impracticable. Because submarines are in effect outlaws when used as the German submarines have been used against merchant shipping, it is impossible to defend ships against their attacks as the law of nations has assumed that merchantmen would defend themselves against privateers or cruisers, visible craft giving chase upon the open sea. It is common prudence in such circumstances—grim necessity, indeed—to endeavor to destroy them before they have shown their own intention. They must be dealt with upon sight, if dealt with at all.

The German government denies the right of neutrals to use arms at all within the areas of the sea which it has proscribed, even in the defense of rights which no modern publicist has ever before questioned their right to defend. The intimation is conveyed that the armed guards which we have placed on our merchant ships will be treated as beyond the pale of law and subject to be dealt with as pirates would be. Armed neutrality is ineffectual enough at best. In such circumstances and in the face of such pretensions it is worse than ineffectual; it is likely only to produce what it was meant to prevent; it is practically certain

---

1. German troops invaded Belgium in August 1914 and occupied virtually the entire country throughout the war.

to draw us into the war without either the rights or the effectiveness of belligerents. There is one choice we cannot make, we are incapable of making: We will not choose the path of submission and suffer the most sacred rights of our nation and our people to be ignored or violated. The wrongs against which we now array ourselves are no common wrongs; they cut to the very roots of human life.

With a profound sense of the solemn and even tragical character of the step I am taking and of the grave responsibilities which it involves, but in unhesitating obedience to what I deem my constitutional duty, I advise that the Congress declare the recent course of the Imperial German Government to be in fact nothing less than war against the government and people of the United States; that it formally accept the status of belligerent which has thus been thrust upon it; and that it take immediate steps not only to put the country in a more thorough state of defense but also to exert all its power and employ all its resources to bring the government of the German Empire to terms and end the war.

What this will involve is clear. It will involve the utmost practicable cooperation in counsel and action with the governments now at war with Germany, and, as incident to that, the extension to those governments of the most liberal financial credits in order that our resources may, so far as possible, be added to theirs. It will involve the organization and mobilization of all the material resources of the country to supply the materials of war and serve the incidental needs of the nation in the most abundant and yet the most economical and efficient way possible. It will involve the immediate full equipment of the navy in all respects but particularly in supplying it with the best means of dealing with the enemy's submarines. It will involve the immediate addition to the armed forces of the United States already provided for by law in case of war at least 500,000 men, who should, in my opinion, be chosen upon the principle of universal liability to service, and also the authorization of subsequent additional increments of equal force so soon as they may be needed and can be handled in training. It will involve also, of course, the granting of adequate credits to the government, sustained, I hope, so far as they can

equitably be sustained by the present generation, by well-conceived taxation.

I say sustained so far as may be equitable by taxation because it seems to me that it would be most unwise to base the credits which will now be necessary entirely on money borrowed. It is our duty, I most respectfully urge, to protect our people so far as we may against the very serious hardships and evils which would be likely to arise out of the inflation which would be produced by vast loans.

In carrying out the measures by which these things are to be accomplished, we should keep constantly in mind the wisdom of interfering as little as possible in our own preparation and in the equipment of our own military forces with the duty—for it will be a very practical duty—of supplying the nations already at war with Germany with the materials which they can obtain only from us or by our assistance. They are in the field and we should help them in every way to be effective there.

I shall take the liberty of suggesting through the several executive departments of the government, for the consideration of your committees, measures for the accomplishment of the several objects I have mentioned. I hope that it will be your pleasure to deal with them as having been framed after very careful thought by the branch of the government upon which the responsibility of conducting the war and safeguarding the nation will most directly fall.

While we do these things, these deeply momentous things, let us be very clear, and make very clear to all the world, what our motives and our objects are. My own thought has not been driven from its habitual and normal course by the unhappy events of the last two months, and I do not believe that the thought of the nation has been altered or clouded by them. I have exactly the same things in mind now that I had in mind when I addressed the Senate on the twenty-second of January last, the same that I had in mind when I addressed the Congress on the third of February and on the twenty-sixth of February. Our object now, as then, is to vindicate the principles of peace and justice in the life of the world as against selfish and autocratic power and to set up amongst the really free and self-governed peoples of the world such a concert of purpose and of action as will henceforth ensure the observance of those principles.

Neutrality is no longer feasible or desirable where the peace of the world is involved and the freedom of its peoples, and the menace to that peace and freedom lies in the existence of autocratic governments backed by organized force which is controlled wholly by their will, not by the will of their people. We have seen the last of neutrality in such circumstances. We are at the beginning of an age in which it will be insisted that the same standards of conduct and of responsibility for wrong done shall be observed among nations and their governments that are observed among the individual citizens of civilized states.

We have no quarrel with the German people. We have no feeling towards them but one of sympathy and friendship. It was not upon their impulse that their government acted in entering this war. It was not with their previous knowledge or approval. It was a war determined upon as wars used to be determined upon in the old, unhappy days when peoples were nowhere consulted by their rulers and wars were provoked and waged in the interest of dynasties or of little groups of ambitious men who were accustomed to use their fellow men as pawns and tools.

Self-governed nations do not fill their neighbor states with spies or set the course of intrigue to bring about some critical posture of affairs which will give them an opportunity to strike and make conquest. Such designs can be successfully worked out only under cover and where no one has the right to ask questions. Cunningly contrived plans of deception or aggression, carried, it may be, from generation to generation, can be worked out and kept from the light only within the privacy of courts or behind the carefully guarded confidences of a narrow and privileged class. They are happily impossible where public opinion commands and insists upon full information concerning all the nation's affairs.

A steadfast concert for peace can never be maintained except by a partnership of democratic nations. No autocratic government could be trusted to keep faith within it or observe its covenants. It must be a league of honor, a partnership of opinion. Intrigue would eat its vitals away; the plottings of inner circles who could plan what they would and render account

to no one would be a corruption seated at its very heart. Only free peoples can hold their purpose and their honor steady to a common end and prefer the interests of mankind to any narrow interest of their own.

Does not every American feel that assurance has been added to our hope for the future peace of the world by the wonderful and heartening things that have been happening within the last few weeks in Russia?[2] Russia was known by those who knew it best to have been always in fact democratic at heart, in all the vital habits of her thought, in all the intimate relationships of her people that spoke their natural instinct, their habitual attitude towards life. The autocracy that crowned the summit of her political structure, long as it had stood and terrible as was the reality of its power, was not in fact Russian in origin, character, or purpose; and now it has been shaken off and the great, generous Russian people have been added in all their naive majesty and might to the forces that are fighting for freedom in the world, for justice, and for peace. Here is a fit partner for a league of honor.

One of the things that has served to convince us that the Prussian autocracy was not and could never be our friend is that from the very outset of the present war it has filled our unsuspecting communities and even our offices of government with spies and set criminal intrigues everywhere afoot against our national unity of counsel, our peace within and without, our industries, and our commerce. Indeed it is now evident that its spies were here even before the war began; and it is unhappily not a matter of conjecture but a fact proved in our courts of justice that the intrigues which have more than once come perilously near to disturbing the peace and dislocating the industries of the country have been carried on at the instigation, with the support, and even under the personal direction of official agents of the Imperial Government accredited to the government of the United States.

Even in checking these things and trying to extirpate them, we have sought to put the most generous

---

2. Czar Nicholas II abdicated the Russian throne on March 15, 1917.

interpretation possible upon them because we knew that their source lay not in any hostile feeling or purpose of the German people towards us (who were no doubt as ignorant of them as we ourselves were) but only in the selfish designs of a government that did what it pleased and told its people nothing. But they have played their part in serving to convince us at last that that government entertains no real friendship for us and means to act against our peace and security at its convenience. That it means to stir up enemies against us at our very doors the intercepted note to the German minister at Mexico City is eloquent evidence.[3]

We are accepting this challenge of hostile purpose because we know that in such a government, following such methods, we can never have a friend; and that in the presence of its organized power, always lying in wait to accomplish we know not what purpose, there can be no assured security for the democratic governments of the world. We are now about to accept gage of battle with this natural foe to liberty and shall, if necessary, spend the whole force of the nation to check and nullify its pretensions and its power.

We are glad, now that we see the facts with no veil of false pretence about them, to fight thus for the ultimate peace of the world and for the liberation of its peoples, the German peoples included; for the rights of nations great and small and the privilege of men everywhere to choose their way of life and of obedience. The world must be made safe for democracy. Its peace must be planted upon the tested foundations of political liberty. We have no selfish ends to serve. We desire no conquest, no dominion. We seek no indemnities for ourselves, no material compensation for the sacrifices we shall freely make. We are but one of the champions of the rights of mankind. We shall be satisfied when those rights have been made as secure as the faith and the freedom of nations can make them.

Just because we fight without rancor and without selfish object, seeking nothing for ourselves but what we shall wish to share with all free peoples, we shall, I feel confident, conduct our operations as belligerents without passion and ourselves observe with proud punctilio the principles of right and of fair play we profess to be fighting for.

I have said nothing of the governments allied with the Imperial Government of Germany because they have not made war upon us or challenged us to defend our right and our honor. The Austro-Hungarian government has, indeed, avowed its unqualified endorsement and acceptance of the reckless and lawless submarine warfare adopted now without disguise by the Imperial German Government, and it has therefore not been possible for this government to receive Count Tarnowski,[4] the ambassador recently accredited to this government by the Imperial and Royal Government of Austria-Hungary. But that government has not actually engaged in warfare against citizens of the United States on the seas, and I take the liberty, for the present at least, of postponing a discussion of our relations with the authorities at Vienna.[5] We enter this war only where we are clearly forced into it because there are no other means of defending our rights.

It will be all the easier for us to conduct ourselves as belligerents in a high spirit of right and fairness because we act without animus—not in enmity towards a people or with the desire to bring any injury or disadvantage upon them, but only in armed opposition to an irresponsible government which has thrown aside all considerations of humanity and of right and is running amuck. We are, let me say again, the sincere friends of the German people and shall desire nothing so much as the early reestablishment of intimate relations of mutual advantage between us—however hard it may be for them, for the time being, to believe that this is spoken from our hearts. We have borne with their present government through all these bitter months because of that friendship—exercising a patience and forbearance which would otherwise have been impossible.

We shall, happily, still have an opportunity to prove that friendship in our daily attitude and actions

3. Wilson is referring to an intercepted message from German Foreign Secretary Arthur Zimmermann offering Mexico the return of Texas, New Mexico, and Arizona if it would enter an alliance against the United States.

4. Adam Tarnowski.

5. Capital of the Austro-Hungarian Empire.

towards the millions of men and women of German birth and native sympathy who live amongst us and share our life, and we shall be proud to prove it towards all who are in fact loyal to their neighbors and to the government in the hour of test. They are, most of them, as true and loyal Americans as if they had never known any other fealty or allegiance. They will be prompt to stand with us in rebuking and restraining the few who may be of a different mind and purpose. If there should be disloyalty, it will be dealt with with a firm hand of stern repression; but, if it lifts its head at all, it will lift it only here and there and without countenance except from a lawless and malignant few.

It is a distressing and oppressive duty, gentlemen of the Congress, which I have performed in thus addressing you. There are, it may be, many months of fiery trial and sacrifice ahead of us. It is a fearful thing to lead this great peaceful people into war, into the most terrible and disastrous of all wars, civilization itself seeming to be in the balance. But the right is more precious than peace, and we shall fight for the things which we have always carried nearest our hearts—for democracy, for the right of those who submit to authority to have a voice in their own governments, for the rights and liberties of small nations, for a universal dominion of right by such a concert of free peoples as shall bring peace and safety to all nations and make the world itself at last free. To such a task we can dedicate our lives and our fortunes, everything that we are and everything that we have, with the pride of those who know that the day has come when America is privileged to spend her blood and her might for the principles that gave her birth and happiness and the peace which she has treasured. God helping her, she can do no other.

Emma Goldman

⧗

Address to the Jury

New York, New York
July 9, 1917

Born in Kovno, Russia, Emma Goldman emigrated to the United States in 1886. By 1890 she had become a dedicated anarchist who subsequently campaigned for most of the radical causes of her day, including atheism, birth control, free speech, sexual equality, free love, and the rights of labor. Though short in stature, she was fearless in the face of adversity and had a powerful sense of conviction that made her, in the words of Roger Baldwin, founder of the American Civil Liberties Union, "a great speaker—passionate, intellectual, and witty." Never before had he heard "such electric power behind words." One government attorney called Goldman "the best speaker that you perhaps ever heard," a woman whose "fiery oratory...makes her so dangerous to the peace and security of the United States."

With American entry into World War I, Goldman helped create the No-Conscription League and spoke vehemently in its behalf. Her speeches were regularly monitored by federal authorities, who regarded her as a serious threat to the war effort. On June 15, 1917, she and her colleague Alexander Berkman were arrested at the offices of their magazines *Mother Earth* and *The Blast* and charged with conspiring to obstruct the draft. They were brought to trial on June 27, Goldman's forty-eighth birthday. On the last day of the trial, Goldman, who served as her own counsel, addressed the jury in her defense.

There is no known stenographic record of Goldman's speech as delivered to the jury, but she published two versions of it after the trial. The first appeared in the July 1917 issue of *Mother Earth* and was preceded by the heading "Emma Goldman spoke substantially, as follows." The second version of the speech appeared in October as a pamphlet and was liberally revised in content and style to make a fuller, more literary statement. Even scholars who are aware of both texts usually understate the extent of the differences between them. Rather than being slightly modified representations of the same speech, they are best seen as different, albeit consanguineous, rhetorical acts with their own audiences and purposes. The pamphlet was intended to present Goldman's case in the most favorable light for a reading audience beyond the courtroom, including posterity. Although most anthologists favor the pamphlet version, we use the *Mother Earth* text because it is as close as we can get to the oral presentation made by Goldman in the courtroom. By printing it here, we hope to restore it to its rightful place in the historical record.

With regard to specific issues of the trial, Goldman concentrated on refuting the prosecution's claim that she had advocated the use of violence against the draft in a speech delivered at the Harlem River Casino on May 18. She also criticized the police for ransacking her offices without a search warrant and the court for setting excessive bail. The lasting appeal of the speech, however, comes from Goldman's spirited defense of her political principles and scathing indictment of the government's suppression of free speech. How, she asked, can America tell people "that we will give them democracy in Europe when we have no democracy here?"

The jury was not moved. After deliberating for thirty-nine minutes, it returned a guilty verdict. Goldman and Berkman were fined $10,000 and sentenced to two years in prison, after which they were deported. Although Goldman's speech failed to secure her acquittal, that has not diminished the regard in which it is held, especially when it is placed in a tradition of dissenting voices that have echoed through the ages.

◇◇

Gentlemen of the Jury: On the day after our arrest it was given out by the Marshal's office and the District Attorney's office that the two "big fish" of the no-conscription activities were now in the hands of the authorities, that there would be no more troublemakers and dangerous disturbers, that the government will be able to go on in the highly democratic method of conscripting American manhood for European slaughter. It is a great pity, it seems to me, that the Marshal and the District Attorney[1] have used such a flimsy net to make their catch. The moment they attempted to land the fish on shore, the net broke. Indeed the net proved that it was not able and strong enough to hold the fish.

The sensational arrest of the defendants and the raid of the defendants' offices would have satisfied the famous circus men Barnum and Bailey.[2] Imagine, if you can, a dozen stalwart warriors rushing up two flights of stairs to find the two defendants, Alexander Berkman and Emma Goldman, in their separate offices quietly seated at their desks, wielding not the gun or the bomb or the club or the sword, but only such a simple and insignificant thing as a pen. As a matter of fact two officers equipped with a warrant would have sufficed to arrest us two, for I take it that we are well known to the police department, and the police department will bear me out that at no time have we run away or attempted to run away, that at no time have we offered any resistance to an arrest, that at no time did we keep in hiding under the bed. We have always frankly and squarely faced the issue.

But it was necessary to stage a sensational arrest so that Marshal McCarthy and the attorney should go down to posterity and receive immortality. It was necessary to raid the offices of the *Blast* and the No-Conscription League and *Mother Earth*,[3] although without a search warrant, which was never shown to us. I ask you, gentlemen of the jury, should it be customary from the point of view of law to discriminate in the case of people merely because they have opinions which do not appeal to you? What is a scrap of paper in the form of a search warrant when it is a question of raiding the offices of anarchists or arresting anarchists? Would the gentlemen who came with Marshal McCarthy have dared to go into the offices of Morgan or of Rockefeller[4] or any of these

men without a search warrant? They never showed us the search warrant, although we asked them for it. Nevertheless, they turned our office into a battlefield, so that when they were through with it, it looked like invaded Belgium, with only the distinction that the invaders were not Prussian barbarians[5] but good patriots who were trying to make New York safe for democracy.[6]

The first act of this marvelous comedy having been properly staged by carrying off the villains in a madly rushing automobile which came near crushing life in its way, merely because Marshal McCarthy said, "I am the Marshal of the United States," he even reprimanding officers on the beat who lived up to their duty and called attention to the fact that the automobile should not have rushed at such violent speed—I say the first act having been finished by locking the villains up, the second act appeared on the scene.

And the second act, gentlemen of the jury, consisted not in prosecution but in persecution. Here are two people arrested, known to the police department, having lived in New York City for nearly thirty years, never having offered resistance to an arrest, always facing the issue. And yet we were placed under $50,000 bail,[7] although the principal witness in the Cruger case is held only on $7,000 bail.[8] Why were we placed under $50,000 bail? Because the District Attorney knew that it would be difficult to raise that bail and therefore out of personal spite made us stay in the Tombs[9] instead of enjoying our liberty.

And furthermore, not only did the District Attorney and the prosecution insist upon $50,000 bail, but when we produced a man whose property is rated at $300,000 in this city his real estate was

---

1. Federal Marshal Thomas McCarthy, who arrested Goldman; Assistant United States District Attorney Harold A. Content, who prosecuted the case for the government.

2. P.T. Barnum (1810–1891) and James Anthony Bailey (1847–1906).

3. The offices were located at 20 East 125th Street.

4. Financier J. P. Morgan; industrialist John D. Rockefeller.

5. Germany invaded Belgium in August 1914 and occupied the country throughout World War I.

6. In his speech of April 2, 1917, seeking a declaration of war against Germany, President Woodrow Wilson said, "The world must be made safe for democracy." Goldman alludes to this phrase several times in her speech.

7. Bail for Goldman and Berkman was set at $25,000 each.

8. Goldman is referring to the case of 17-year-old Ruth Cruger, whose abduction and murder made headlines through much of 1917.

9. Nickname for the Manhattan Detention Complex.

refused.[10] Why? Because the District Attorney suddenly remembered that he needed forty-eight hours to look into the man's reputation—knowing perfectly well that we were to go to trial on Wednesday, and yet not permitting the defendant Alexander Berkman to get out, although we had relied on an authentic and absolutely secure bail. So that I say that the second act, gentlemen of the jury, demonstrated that it was not only to be a case of prosecution, [but] that it was also to be a case of persecution.

And finally the third act, which was played in this court and which you, gentlemen of the jury, witnessed last week. I may say here that it is to be regretted indeed that the District Attorney knows nothing of dramatic construction, otherwise he would have supplied himself with better dramatic material; he would have used better acts in the play to sustain the continuity of the comedy. But the District Attorney is not supposed to know anything about modern drama or the construction of modern drama.

Now, then, you have already been told, and I am sure you will be charged by His Honor that the indictment against us is having conspired and having used overt acts to carry out the conspiracy to induce men of conscriptable age not to register. That is the indictment and you cannot and you may not render a verdict for anything else, no matter what material came up in this court during the last week or ten days.

As to the conspiracy: Imagine, if you please, people engaged along similar lines for thirty years, always standing out against war, whether that war was in China or Japan or Russia or England or Germany or America, always insisting with the great essayist Carlyle[11] that all wars are wars among thieves who are too cowardly to fight and who therefore induce the young manhood of the whole world to do the fighting for them.[12] That is our standing;

we have proved it by evidence, we have proved it by witnesses, we have proved it by our own position—that always and forever we have stood up against war, because we say that the war going on in the world is for the further enslavement of the people, for the further placing of them under the yoke of a military tyranny.

Imagine also people who for thirty years in succession have stood out against militarism, who claim militarism is costly and useless and brutalizing to every country; imagine us standing for years, and especially since conscription was declared in England[13] and the fight began in Australia and conscription was there defeated by the brave and determined and courageous position of the Australian people;[14] imagine that since that time we have been against conscription, then say how there can possibly be a conspiracy when people merely continue in their work which they have carried on for thirty years and for which they have spoken in different meetings and by letters! What kind of conspiracy is that? Was there any need of a conspiracy if we really had wanted to tell young men not to register? I insist that the prosecution has failed utterly, has failed miserably to prove the charge on the indictment of a conspiracy.

As to the meeting of May eighteenth:[15] It was dragged in here only for reasons known to the prosecution; otherwise I can't understand why that meeting played such an important part. No matter what we would have said at that meeting, no matter what language we would have used, that meeting cannot constitute an overt act because although it is true that the draft law was passed on the eighteenth, it is equally true that it was not made a law until the President of the United States signed that law. And the President of the United States did not sign it until late that evening, at the time when we had the

10. Goldman is referring to Michael Cohn, physician and longtime benefactor of Goldman and Berkman.

11. Scottish writer Thomas Carlyle (1795–1881).

12. This statement does not appear in Carlyle's writings; it most likely reflects Goldman's condensation of ideas in book 2, chapter 8, of Carlyle's *Sartor Resartus* (1833–1834), which she had quoted earlier in her career.

13. England introduced conscription in 1916 with passage of the Military Service Act.

14. Goldman is referring to the rejection of conscription by Australian voters in an October 1916 plebiscite.

15. Attended by some 8,000 people, the meeting was held at the Harlem River Casino to protest conscription and was addressed by a number of speakers, including Goldman.

meeting and couldn't have any idea or knowledge as to whether he was going to sign it. So the meeting of the eighteenth is utterly irrelevant.

But since the meeting came in, it is necessary to emphasize one or two points. And I mean to do so because it concerns the defendant Emma Goldman. The main thing upon which evidently the prosecution concentrated is that the reporter credited the defendant Emma Goldman with saying, "We believe in violence and we will use violence." Gentlemen of the jury, if there were no other proof to absolutely discredit this particular line and sentence and expression, there would yet be the following reasons: In the first place, I have been on the public platform for twenty-seven years and one of the things that I am particularly careful of in my speeches is that they shall be coherent and shall be logical. The speeches delivered on that evening, on May 18, absolutely excluded the necessity of using the expression, "We believe in violence and we will use violence." I couldn't have used it, as an experienced speaker, because it would merely have made the whole speech nonsensical, it would have dragged in something which was irrelevant to the body of the speech or the material used. That is one of the reasons why I never at that meeting said, "We believe in violence and we will use violence."

I am a social student. It is my business in life to ascertain the cause of our social evils and of our social difficulties. As a student of social wrongs, it is my business to diagnose a wrong. To simply condemn the man who has committed an act of political violence, in order to save my own skin, would be just as [un]pardonable as it would be on the part of the physician who is called to diagnose a case to condemn the patient because the patient had tuberculosis or cancer or any other disease. The honest, earnest, sincere physician diagnoses a case; he does not only prescribe medicine, he tries to find out the cause of the disease. And if the patient is at all capable as to means, he will tell the patient, "Get out of this putrid air, get out of the factory, get out of the place where your lungs are being infected." He will not merely give him medicines. He will tell him the cause of the disease. And that is precisely my position in regard to violence. That is what I have said on all platforms.

I have attempted to explain the cause and the reason for acts of political violence.[16]

And what is the cause? Is it conditioned in the individual who commits an act of individual violence? It is not. An act of political violence at the bottom is the culminating result of organized violence on top. It is the result of violence which expresses itself in war, which expresses itself in capital punishment, which expresses itself in courts, which expresses itself in prisons, which expresses itself in kicking and hounding people for the only crime they are guilty of—of having been born poor. So that after all when we come to consider an act of political violence committed by an individual, I take it, gentlemen of the jury, that you are conversant with history and that you know that not only a stray anarchist here and there but rebels of every movement in Ireland, in France, in Russia, in Italy, in Spain, all over the world, even in passive India, the country which has the most wonderful civilization and rests upon passive resistance, even in that country men were driven to acts of violence by organized violence on top.

So, as I said in one of the evidences we have given, we say with the greatest psychologist living, Havelock Ellis, that an act of political violence committed by an individual is the result of social wrong and social injustice and political oppression. Wherever there is political liberty—and I can demonstrate it in the Scandinavian countries: Has there been any act of violence committed in Norway, in Sweden, in Denmark, in Holland—why are there no acts of violence there? Because the government doesn't only preach free speech and free press and assembly, but lives up to it. There was no need to be driven into acts of violence. So, gentlemen, I say with Havelock Ellis[17] that the political offender or the "political criminal," as you choose to call him, is so not because of criminal tendency, not because of personal gain, not because of personal aggrandizement, but because he loves humanity too well, because he cannot face wrong and injustice and because he cannot enjoy his meal when

---

16. Goldman is referring to her essay "The Psychology of Political Violence," which she read to the court during her trial.

17. Goldman is drawing on Ellis's *The Criminal* (1890).

he knows that America is getting rich on two million wage-slave children who are ground into dust and into money and power.[18]

And so, gentlemen, I have explained the act. I have explained the act. Does that mean advocating the act? If that is your version—and I can't believe that it will be—I say, gentlemen of the jury, that you might as well condemn Jesus for having defended the prostitute Mary Magdalene, you might as well say that he advocated prostitution because he said to the mob on that occasion, "Let him among you that is without sin cast the first stone."[19] I refuse to cast the stone at the "political criminal," if he may be called so. I take his place with him because he has been driven to revolt, because his lifebreath has been choked up. And if I am to pay with prison for that, if I am to pay with my life-breath for that, gentlemen of the jury, I shall be ready at any time to take the consequences. But I refuse to be tried on trumped-up charges and I refuse to be convicted by perjured testimony for something which I haven't said when it had absolutely no relation whatever to the indictment as stated—that we conspired and agreed to conspire and used overt acts to tell people not to register.

Gentlemen of the jury, the meeting of May 18 was called for an express purpose and for that purpose only. It was called to voice the position of the conscientious objector who, as far as America is concerned, was a new type of humanity. Oh, I know that we should be expected to call the conscientious objector, just as he is being called by the papers, a "slacker," a "coward," a "shirker." These are cheap names, gentlemen of the jury. To call a man a name proves nothing whatever. What is the conscientious objector? I am a conscientious objector. What is he? He is impelled by what President Wilson said in his speech on the third of February, 1917;[20] he is impelled by the force of righteous passion for justice, which is the bulwark

and mainstay and basis of all our existence and of all our liberty.

That is the force which impels the conscientious objector: a righteous passion for justice. The conscientious objector, rightly or wrongly—that is a thing which you will have to argue with him—does not believe in war, not because he is a coward or a shirker, not because he doesn't want to stand responsible, but because he insists that, belonging to the people whence he has come and to whom he owes life, it is his place to stand on the side of the people, for the people and by the people[21] and not on the side of the governing classes. And that is what we did at that particular meeting. We voiced the position of the conscientious objector. But I reiterate once more, so you may not overlook it, that whatever we said on the eighteenth of May has no bearing whatever on the indictment for conspiracy because that meeting took place before the President signed that bill.

Gentlemen of the jury, when we examined talesmen[22] we asked whether you would be prejudiced against us when it was proved that we were engaged in an agitation for unpopular ideas. You were instructed by the court to say, "if they were within the law." But there was one thing I am sorry that the court did not tell you. It is this: that there has never been any ideal—though ever so humane and peaceful—introduced for human betterment which in its place and in its time was considered within the law.

I know that many of you believe in the teachings of Jesus. I want to call your attention to the fact that Jesus was put to death because he was not within the law. I know that all of you are Americans and patriots. Please bear in mind that those who fought and bled for whatever liberty you have—those who established the Declaration of Independence, those who established the constitutional right of free speech—that they were not within the law, that they were the anarchists of their time, that they wrote a famous document known as the Declaration of Independence, a document indeed so great that it is evidently con-

---

18. Goldman is referring to the exploitation of child labor in various sectors of the American economy.

19. Paraphrased from John 8:7.

20. Goldman is referring to Wilson's speech announcing the severing of diplomatic relations with Germany.

21. An echo of Abraham Lincoln's Gettysburg Address, November 19, 1863.

22. Potential jurors.

sidered dangerous to this day, because a boy was given ninety days in a New York court for distributing a leaflet of quotations from the Declaration of Independence.[23] They were not within the law. Those men were the rebels and the anarchists. And what is more important, they not only believed in violence but they used violence when they threw the tea into Boston Harbor.[24]

Furthermore, your country and in a measure my country—my country out of choice—is now allied with France. Need I call your attention to the fact that the French republic is due to the men who were not within the law? Why, friends, even the man who is responsible for the stirring music of the *Marseillaise*,[25] which unfortunately has been deteriorating into a war tune, even Camille Desmoulins[26] was not within the law, was considered a criminal. And finally, gentlemen, on the very day when we are tried for a conspiracy, when we are tried for overt acts, our city and its representatives were receiving with festivities and with music the Russian Commission.[27] Every one of the Russian commissioners is what you would choose to call an ex–political criminal. Every one of them had been in exile or in prison. As a matter of fact, gentlemen, the tree of Russian liberty is watered with the blood of Russian martyrs.[28]

So no great idea in its beginning can ever be within the law. How can it be within the law? The law is stationary. The law is fixed. The law is a chariot wheel which binds us all regardless of conditions or circumstances or place or time. The law does not even make an attempt to go into the complexity of the human soul which drives a man to despair or to insanity, out of hunger or out of indignation, into a political act. But progress is ever changing, progress is ever renewing, progress has nothing to do with fixity. And in its place and in its time every great ideal for human reconstruction, for a reconstruction of society and the regeneration of the race, every great idea was considered extralegal, illegal, in its time and place.

And so I must refer to Havelock Ellis when he said that the political criminal is the hero and the martyr and the saint of the new era.[29] Hence the country that locks up men and women who will stand up for an ideal—what chance is there for that country and for the future and for the young generation, a country that has not in her midst dangerous disturbers and troublemakers who can see further than their time and propagate a new idea?

Well, gentlemen, I take it that perhaps the prosecution will say that that means propagating dangerous and seditious ideas in this time of war and patriotism. Maybe it does, gentlemen of the jury. But that doesn't prove that we are responsible for the existence of such ideas. You might as well condemn the very stars that are hanging in the heavens eternally and inalienably and unchangeably for all time, as to accuse us or find us guilty because we propagate certain ideas.

Gentlemen of the jury, I wish to say right here, we respect your patriotism. We wouldn't, even if we could, want you to change one single iota of what patriotism means to you. But may there not be two kinds of patriotism, just as there are two interpretations of liberty—the kind of liberty which is real liberty in action, and the kind which has been placed on a document and is dug out once a year on the Fourth of July and is not allowed to exist for the rest of the year? And so, gentlemen, I wish to emphasize this very important fact because I know how you feel on the war, I know what patriotism means to you: that the mere accident of birth or the mere fact that you have taken out citizens' papers does not make a man necessarily a patriot. Who is the real patriot, or rather what is the kind of patriotism that we represent? The

23. Goldman is referring to the case of Harry Aurin, age 20, who was arrested on July 4, 1917.

24. A reference to the Boston Tea Party of December 16, 1773.

25. Composed during the French Revolution, the *Marseillaise* later became France's national anthem.

26. French revolutionary and journalist (1760–1794); contrary to Goldman's statement, he did not compose the *Marseillaise*.

27. Representing the provisional government that was installed after the abdication of Czar Nicholas II in March 1917, the Russian Commission was greeted in New York with a parade and other festivities on July 6, 1917.

28. An allusion to Thomas Jefferson's statement of November 13, 1787, that "The tree of liberty must be refreshed from time to time with the blood of patriots and tyrants."

29. From Ellis's *The Criminal* (1890).

kind of patriotism we represent is the kind of patriotism which loves America with open eyes. Our relation toward America is the same as the relation of a man who loves a woman, who is enchanted by her beauty, and yet who cannot be blind to her defects.

And so I wish to state here, in my own behalf and in behalf of hundreds of thousands whom you decry and state to be antipatriotic, that we love America, we love her beauty, we love her riches, we love her mountains and her forests, and above all we love the people who have produced her wealth and riches, who have created all her beauty, we love the dreamers and the philosophers and the thinkers who are giving America liberty. But that must not make us blind to the social faults of America. That cannot make us deaf to the discords in America. That cannot compel us to be inarticulate to the terrible wrongs committed in the name of patriotism and in the name of the country.

We simply insist, regardless of all protests to the contrary, that this war is not a war for democracy. If it were a war for the purpose of making democracy safe for the world, we would say that democracy must first be safe for America before it can be safe for the world. So in a measure I say, gentlemen, that we are greater patriots than those who shoot off firecrackers and say that democracy should be given to the world. By all means let us give democracy to the world. But for the present we are very poor in democracy. Free speech is suppressed. Free assemblies are broken up by uniformed gangsters, one after another. Women and girls at meetings are insulted by soldiers under this "democracy." And therefore we say that we are woefully poor in democracy at home. How can we be generous in giving democracy to the world? So we say, gentlemen of the jury, our crime, if crime there be, is not having in any way conspired to tell young men not to register or having committed overt acts. Our crime, if crime there be, consists in pointing out the real cause of the present war.

I wish to state to you here that whatever your verdict is going to be, it cannot have a possible effect upon the tremendous storm brewing in the United States. And the storm has not been created by two people, Alexander Berkman and Emma Goldman. You credit us with too much power altogether. That storm was created by the conditions themselves, by the fact that the people before election were promised that they would be kept out of war and after election they were dragged into war.[30] Gentlemen of the jury, your verdict cannot affect the growing discontent of the American people. Neither can it affect the conscientious objector to whom human life is sacred and who would rather be shot than take the life of another human being.

Of course your verdict is going to affect us. It will affect us only temporarily. And it will affect us physically; it cannot affect our spirit, gentlemen of the jury, whether we are found guilty or whether we are placed in jail. Nothing will be changed in our spirit. Nothing will be changed in our ideas. For even if we were convicted and found guilty and the penalty were to be placed against a wall and shot dead, I should nevertheless cry out with the great Luther, "Here I am and here I stand and I cannot do otherwise."[31]

And so, gentlemen, in conclusion let me tell you that my codefendant, Mr. Berkman, was right when he said the eyes of America are upon you.[32] And they are upon you not because of sympathy for us or agreement with anarchism. They are upon you because it must be decided sooner or later: Are we justified in telling people that we will give them democracy in Europe, when we have no democracy here? Shall free speech and free assemblage, shall criticism and opinion, which even the espionage bill did not include— shall that be destroyed? Shall it be a shadow of the past, the great historic American past? Shall it be trampled underfoot by any detective, any policeman, anyone who decides upon it? Or shall free speech and free press and free assemblage continue to be the heritage of the American people?

And so, gentlemen of the jury, whatever your verdict will be, as far as we are concerned, nothing

---

30. "He kept us out of war" was a prominent slogan of President Wilson's 1916 reelection campaign; less than a month after being inaugurated for a second term, he asked Congress for a declaration of war against Germany (pages 73–79).

31. Paraphrased from Martin Luther's speech at the Diet of Worms, April 18, 1521.

32. Goldman is referring to Berkman's address to the jury, which preceded hers.

will be changed. I have held ideas all my life. I have publicly held my ideas for twenty-seven years. Nothing on earth would ever make me change my ideas except one thing; and that is if you will prove to me that our position is wrong, untenable, or lacking in historic fact. But never would I change my ideas because I am found guilty. I may say in the great words of two great Americans, undoubtedly not unknown to you gentlemen of the jury, and that is Ralph Waldo Emerson and Henry David Thoreau: When Henry David Thoreau was placed in prison for refusing to pay taxes he was visited by Ralph Waldo Emerson, and Emerson said, "David, what are you doing in jail?" and Thoreau said, "Ralph, what are you doing outside, when people are in jail for their ideals?"[33]

And so, gentlemen of the jury, I do not wish to influence you. I do not wish to appeal to your passions. I do not wish to influence you by the fact that I am a woman. I have no such desires and no such designs. I take it that you are sincere enough and honest enough and brave enough to render a verdict according to your convictions, beyond the shadow of a reasonable doubt.

Please forget that we are anarchists. Forget that we said that we propagated violence. Forget that something appeared in *Mother Earth* when I was thousands of miles away three years ago.[34] Forget all that. And merely consider the evidence. Have we been engaged in a conspiracy? Has that conspiracy been proved; have we committed overt acts; have those overt acts been proved? We for the defense say they have not been proved. And therefore your verdict must be not guilty.

---

33. Thoreau was jailed overnight in 1846 for refusing to pay the Massachusetts poll tax. Although the exchange with Emerson has been recounted many times over the years, there is no evidence that it in fact occurred.

34. Goldman is referring to the July 1914 issue of *Mother Earth*, published while Goldman was out of New York on a lecture tour, which included a number of statements advocating the use of violence.

Robert M. La Follette

Free Speech in Wartime

WASHINGTON, D.C.
OCTOBER 6, 1917

As a senior at the University of Wisconsin in 1879, Robert La Follette won the annual Inter-State Oratorical Association contest with a speech on the character of Iago, the diabolical villain of Shakespeare's *Othello*. In La Follette's day such an achievement made him a hero throughout Wisconsin, and within eighteen months he had parlayed the fame of his collegiate triumph into election as District Attorney of Dane County. Propelled always by his powerful oratory—"It is the orator," he once stated, who "directs the destinies of states"—he was elected in subsequent years as U.S. Congressman,

Governor of Wisconsin, and U.S. Senator, a post he held for almost two decades. In 1924 he ran for President as the Progressive Party candidate, winning more than 16 percent of the popular vote.

Although a Republican, La Follette supported most of the reform measures advanced by Woodrow Wilson during his first administration. As the country moved toward war with Germany, however, La Follette became increasingly critical of the President, and he was one of six Senators who voted against declaring war in April 1917. Condemned for his vote by prowar publicists from one end of the country to the other, he found himself at the center of another storm of controversy when he was misquoted by the Associated Press as having said, in a September 20 speech at St. Paul, Minnesota, that America had no grievance against Germany. Enraged editorialists called for his expulsion from the Senate, or even for his arrest; angry citizens burned him in effigy; Theodore Roosevelt dubbed him a "shadow Hun" and a "sinister enemy of democracy."

On October 6 La Follette responded in the Senate chamber with one of the most memorable defenses of free expression in American history. Rather than focusing on what he did or did not say at St. Paul, he rose to the level of general principle by espousing the right of all citizens to state their beliefs fully and openly notwithstanding the existence of war. Meticulously prepared and presented from manuscript, the three-hour speech was packed with evidence supporting La Follette's position. No matter what the issue at hand, he believed effective oratory was "always a question of digging out the facts upon which to base your case." Standing calm in the face of war hysteria, he quoted from a galaxy of respected historical figures to show that in time of war, even more than in time of peace, the "precious fundamental personal rights" of free speech, expression, and assembly "should be maintained inviolable." He also developed, in the second half of the speech, an emphatic case for the power of Congress, rather than the President, to guide "the foreign policy of the nation in the present crisis."

Predictably, La Follette's opponents were not persuaded, and charges of treason continued to be hurled at him until the war's end. But he was speaking to posterity as well as to his own time, and with that audience he has fared much better. Eugene Debs, himself an object of vilification during the war (see pages 129–133), called the speech a classic and wrote to La Follette: "Let the Wall Street wolves and their prostitute press howl. The people will sustain you and history will vindicate you." Indeed, it has. In 1959 La Follette was enshrined as one of the five greatest Senators in American history.

◇◇

Mr. President,[1] I rise to a question of personal privilege. I have no intention of taking the time of the Senate with a review of the events which led to our entrance into the war except insofar as they bear upon the question of personal privilege to which I am addressing myself.

Six members of the Senate and fifty members of the House voted against the declaration of war. Immediately there was let loose upon those Senators

---

1. Thomas R. Marshall, Vice President of the United States and President of the Senate.

and Representatives a flood of invective and abuse from newspapers and individuals who had been clamoring for war, unequaled, I believe, in the history of civilized society.

Prior to the declaration of war, every man who had ventured to oppose our entrance into it had been condemned as a coward or worse, and even the President[2] had by no means been immune from these attacks. Since the declaration of war, the triumphant war press has pursued those Senators and Representatives who voted against war with malicious falsehood and recklessly libelous attacks, going to the extreme limit of charging them with treason against their country.

This campaign of libel and character assassination directed against the members of Congress who opposed our entrance into the war has been continued down to the present hour, and I have upon my desk newspaper clippings, some of them libels upon me alone, some directed as well against other Senators who voted in opposition to the declaration of war. One of these newspaper reports most widely circulated represents a federal judge in the state of Texas as saying, in a charge to a grand jury—I read the article as it appeared in the newspaper and the headline with which it is introduced:

District Judge Would Like to Take Shot at Traitors in Congress.

[BY ASSOCIATED PRESS LEASED WIRE.]

Houston, Texas, October 1, 1917

Judge Waller T. Burns, of the United States district court, in charging a federal grand jury at the beginning of the October term today, after calling by name Senators Stone of Missouri, Hardwick of Georgia, Vardaman of Mississippi, Gronna of North Dakota, Gore of Oklahoma[3], and La Follette of Wisconsin, said:

"If I had a wish, I would wish that you men had jurisdiction to return bills of indictment against these men. They ought to be tried promptly and fairly, and I believe this court could administer the law fairly; but I have a conviction, as strong as life, that this country should stand them up against an adobe wall tomorrow and give them what they deserve. If any man deserves death, it is a traitor. I wish that I could pay for the ammunition. I would like to attend the execution, and if I were in the firing squad I would not want to be the marksman who had the blank shell."

The above clipping, Mr. President, was sent to me by another federal judge, who wrote upon the margin of the clipping that it occurred to him that the conduct of this judge might very properly be the subject of investigation. He enclosed with the clipping a letter, from which I quote the following: "I have been greatly depressed by the brutal and unjust attacks that great business interests have organized against you. It is a time when all the spirits of evil are turned loose. The kaisers of high finance, who have been developing hatred of you for a generation because you have fought against them and for the common good, see this opportunity to turn the war patriotism into an engine of attack. They are using it everywhere, and it is a day when lovers of democracy, not only in the world but here in the United States, need to go apart on the mountain and spend the night in fasting and prayer.

"I still have faith that the forces of good on this earth will be found to be greater than the forces of evil, but we all need resolution. I hope you will have the grace to keep your center of gravity on the inside of you and to keep a spirit that is unclouded by hatred. It is a time for the words 'with malice toward none and charity for all.'[4] It is the office of great service to be a shield to the good man's character against malice. Before this fight is over, you will have a new revelation that such a shield is yours."

If this newspaper clipping were a single or exceptional instance of lawless defamation, I should not trouble the Senate with a reference to it. But, Mr. President, it is not.

---

2. Woodrow Wilson.

3. William S. Stone, Thomas William Hardwick, James K. Vardaman, Asle J. Gronna, and Thomas Gore—all of whom joined La Follette in voting against the declaration of war with Germany.

4. From Abraham Lincoln's second inaugural address, March 4, 1865.

In this mass of newspaper clippings which I have here upon my desk, and which I shall not trouble the Senate to read unless it is desired, and which represent but a small part of the accumulation clipped from the daily press of the country in the last three months, I find other Senators, as well as myself, accused of the highest crimes of which any man can be guilty—treason and disloyalty—and, sir, accused not only with no evidence to support the accusation, but without the suggestion that such evidence anywhere exists. It is not claimed that Senators who opposed the declaration of war have since that time acted with any concerted purpose either regarding war measures or any others. They have voted according to their individual opinions, have often been opposed to each other on bills which have come before the Senate since the declaration of war, and, according to my recollection, have never all voted together since that time upon any single proposition upon which the Senate has been divided.

I am aware, Mr. President, that in pursuance of this general campaign of vilification and attempted intimidation, requests from various individuals and certain organizations have been submitted to the Senate for my expulsion from this body, and that such requests have been referred to and considered by one of the committees of the Senate. If I alone had been made the victim of these attacks, I should not take one moment of the Senate's time for their consideration, and I believe that other Senators who have been unjustly and unfairly assailed, as I have been, hold the same attitude upon this that I do. Neither the clamor of the mob nor the voice of power will ever turn me by the breadth of a hair from the course I mark out for myself, guided by such knowledge as I can obtain and controlled and directed by a solemn conviction of right and duty.

But, sir, it is not alone members of Congress that the war party in this country has sought to intimidate. The mandate seems to have gone forth to the sovereign people of this country that they must be silent while those things are being done by their government which most vitally concern their well-being, their happiness, and their lives. Today and for weeks past honest and law-abiding citizens of this country are being terrorized and outraged in their rights by those sworn to uphold the laws and protect the rights of the people.

I have in my possession numerous affidavits establishing the fact that people are being unlawfully arrested, thrown into jail, held incommunicado for days, only to be eventually discharged without ever having been taken into court because they have committed no crime. Private residences are being invaded, loyal citizens of undoubted integrity and probity arrested, cross-examined, and the most sacred constitutional rights guaranteed to every American citizen are being violated. It appears to be the purpose of those conducting this campaign to throw the country into a state of terror, to coerce public opinion, to stifle criticism, and suppress discussion of the great issues involved in this war.

I think all men recognize that in time of war the citizen must surrender some rights for the common good which he is entitled to enjoy in time of peace. But, sir, the right to control their own government according to constitutional forms is not one of the rights that the citizens of this country are called upon to surrender in time of war. Rather, in time of war the citizen must be more alert to the preservation of his right to control his government. He must be most watchful of the encroachment of the military upon the civil power. He must beware of those precedents in support of arbitrary action by administrative officials which, excused on the plea of necessity in wartime, become the fixed rule when the necessity has passed and normal conditions have been restored.

More than all, the citizen and his Representative in Congress in time of war must maintain his right of free speech. More than in times of peace, it is necessary that the channels for free public discussion of governmental policies shall be open and unclogged. I believe, Mr. President, that I am now touching upon the most important question in this country today—and that is the right of the citizens of this country and their Representatives in Congress to discuss in an orderly way, frankly and publicly and without fear, from the platform and through the press, every important phase of this war: its causes, the manner in which it should be conducted, and the terms upon which peace should be made.

The belief which is becoming widespread in this land that this most fundamental right is being denied to the citizens of this country is a fact the tremendous significance of which those in authority have not yet begun to appreciate. I am contending, Mr. President, for the great fundamental right of the sovereign people of this country to make their voice heard and have that voice heeded upon the great questions arising out of this war, including not only how the war shall be prosecuted but the conditions upon which it may be terminated with a due regard for the rights and the honor of this nation and the interests of humanity.

I am contending for this right because the exercise of it is necessary to the welfare, to the existence, of this government, to the successful conduct of this war, and to a peace which shall be enduring and for the best interest of this country. Suppose success attends the attempt to stifle all discussion of the issues of this war, all discussion of the terms upon which it should be concluded, all discussion of the objects and purposes to be accomplished by it, and concede the demand of the war-mad press and war extremists that they monopolize the right of public utterance upon these questions unchallenged, what think you would be the consequences to this country not only during the war but after the war?

Mr. President, our government, above all others, is founded on the right of the people freely to discuss all matters pertaining to their government, in war not less than in peace, for in this government the people are the rulers in war no less than in peace. It is true, sir, that members of the House of Representatives are elected for two years, the President for four years, and the members of the Senate for six years, and during their temporary official terms these officers constitute what is called the government. But back of them always is the controlling sovereign power of the people, and when the people can make their will known, the faithful officer will obey that will.

Though the right of the people to express their will by ballot is suspended during the term of office of the elected official, nevertheless the duty of the official to obey the popular will continues throughout his entire term of office. How can that popular will express itself between elections except by meetings, by speeches, by publications, by petitions, and by addresses to the representatives of the people? Any man who seeks to set a limit upon those rights, whether in war or peace, aims a blow at the most vital part of our government. And then as the time for election approaches and the official is called to account for his stewardship—not a day, not a week, not a month, before the election, but a year or more before it, if the people choose—they must have the right to the freest possible discussion of every question upon which their representative has acted, of the merits of every measure he has supported or opposed, of every vote he has cast and every speech that he has made. And before this great fundamental right every other must, if necessary, give way, for in no other manner can representative government be preserved.

Mr. President, what I am saying has been exemplified in the lives and public discussion of the ablest statesmen of this country, whose memories we most revere and whose deeds we most justly commemorate. I shall presently ask the attention of the Senate to the views of some of these men upon the subject we are now considering.

Closely related to this subject of the right of the citizen to discuss war is that of the constitutional power and duty of the Congress to declare the purposes and objects of any war in which our country may be engaged. The authorities which I shall cite cover both the right of the people to discuss the war in all its phases and the right and the duty of the people's representatives in Congress to declare the purposes and objects of the war. For the sake of brevity, I shall present these quotations together at this point instead of submitting them separately.

Henry Clay,[5] in a memorable address at Lexington, Kentucky, on the thirteenth day of November 1847, during the Mexican War,[6] took a strong position in behalf of the right of the people to

5. During his illustrious career, Clay (1777–1852) served as Speaker of the House of Representatives, Secretary of State, U.S. Senator, and was three times nominated as the Whig Party candidate for President.

6. Beginning in April 1846 and concluding with the Treaty of Guadalupe Hidalgo in February 1848, the Mexican War produced the most vigorous antiwar movement in American history before the 20th century.

freely discuss every question relating to the war, even though the discussion involved a strong condemnation of the war policy of the Executive. He also declared it to be not only the right but the duty of the Congress to declare the objects of the war. As a part of that address, he presented certain resolutions embodying his views on these subjects. These resolutions were adopted at that meeting by the people present and were adopted at many other mass meetings throughout the country during the continuance of the Mexican War.

For introducing in this body some time ago a resolution asserting the right of Congress to declare the purposes of the present war, I have, as the newspaper clippings here will show, been denounced as a traitor and my conduct characterized as treasonable. As bearing directly upon the conduct for which I have been so criticized and condemned, I invite your attention to the language of Henry Clay in the address I have mentioned.

He said: "But the havoc of war is in progress and the no less deplorable havoc of an inhospitable and pestilential climate. Without indulging in an unnecessary retrospect and useless reproaches on the past, all hearts and heads should unite in the patriotic endeavor to bring it to a satisfactory close. Is there no way that this can be done? Must we blindly continue the conflict without any visible object or any prospect of a definite termination? This is the important subject upon which I desire to consult and to commune with you. Who in this free government is to decide upon the objects of a war at its commencement or at any time during its existence? Does the power belong to collective wisdom of the nation in Congress assembled, or is it vested solely in a single functionary of the government?

"A declaration of war is the highest and most awful exercise of sovereignty. The convention which framed our federal Constitution had learned from the pages of history that it had been often and greatly abused. It had seen that war had often been commenced upon the most trifling pretexts; that it had been frequently waged to establish or exclude a dynasty; to snatch a crown from the head of one potentate and place it upon the head of another; that it had often been prosecuted to promote alien and

other interests than those of the nation whose chief had proclaimed it, as in the case of English wars for Hanoverian interests; and, in short, that such a vast and tremendous power ought not to be confined to the perilous exercise of one single man.

"The convention therefore resolved to guard the war-making power against those great abuses of which, in the hands of a monarch, it was so susceptible. And the security against those abuses which its wisdom devised was to vest the war-making power in the Congress of the United States, being the immediate representatives of the people and the states. So apprehensive and jealous was the convention of its abuse in any other hands that it interdicted the exercise of the power to any state in the Union without the consent of Congress. Congress, then, in our system of government, is the sole depository of that tremendous power."

Mr. President, it is impossible for me to quote as extensively from this address as I should like to do and still keep within the compass of the time that I have set down for myself; but the whole of the address is accessible to every Senator here, together with all of the discussion which followed it over the country, and in these times it would seem to me worthy of the review of Senators and of newspaper editors and of those who have duties to discharge in connection with this great crisis that is upon the world.

I quote further: "The Constitution provides that Congress shall have power to declare war and grant letters of marque and reprisal, to make rules concerning captures on land and water, to raise and support armies, and provide and maintain a navy, and to make rules for the government of the land and naval forces. Thus we perceive that the principal power, in regard to war, with all its auxiliary attendants, is granted to Congress. Whenever called upon to determine upon the solemn question of peace or war, Congress must consider and deliberate and decide upon the motives, objects, and causes of the war."[7]

If that be true, is it treason for a Senator upon this floor to offer a resolution dealing with that question?

---

7. La Follette is quoting again from Clay's speech of November 13, 1847.

I quote further from Mr. Clay: "And, if a war be commenced without any previous declaration of its objects, as in the case of the existing war with Mexico, Congress must necessarily possess the authority, at any time, to declare for what purposes it shall be further prosecuted. If we suppose Congress does not possess the controlling authority attributed to it, if it be contended that a war having been once commenced, the President of the United States may direct it to the accomplishment of any object he pleases, without consulting and without any regard to the will of Congress, the convention will have utterly failed in guarding the nation against the abuses and ambition of a single individual. Either Congress or the President must have the right of determining upon the objects for which a war shall be prosecuted. There is no other alternative. If the President possess it and may prosecute it for objects against the will of Congress, where is the difference between our free government and that of any other nation which may be governed by an absolute czar, emperor, or king?"

In closing his address, Mr. Clay said: "I conclude, therefore, Mr. President and fellow citizens, with entire confidence, that Congress has the right, either at the beginning or during the prosecution of any war, to decide the objects and purposes for which it was proclaimed or for which it ought to be continued. And I think it is the duty of Congress, by some deliberate and authentic act, to declare for what objects the present war shall be longer prosecuted. I suppose the President would not hesitate to regulate his conduct by the pronounced will of Congress and to employ the force and the diplomatic power of the nation to execute that will. But if the President should decline or refuse to do so and, in contempt of the supreme authority of Congress, should persevere in waging the war for other objects than those proclaimed by Congress, then it would be the imperative duty of that body to vindicate its authority by the most stringent and effectual and appropriate measures.

"And if, on the contrary, the enemy should refuse to conclude a treaty containing stipulations securing the objects designated by Congress, it would become the duty of the whole government to prosecute the war with all the national energy until those objects

were attained by a treaty of peace. There can be no insuperable difficulty in Congress making such an authoritative declaration. Let it resolve, simply, that the war shall or shall not be a war of conquest; and, if a war of conquest, what is to be conquered. Should a resolution pass disclaiming the design of conquest, peace would follow in less than sixty days if the President would conform to his constitutional duty."

Mr. Clay, as a part of that speech, presented certain resolutions which were unanimously adopted by the meeting and which declared that the power to determine the purposes of the war rested with Congress, and then proceeded clearly to state the purposes, and the only purposes, for which the war should be prosecuted. The last one of these resolutions is so pertinent to the present discussion that I invite your attention to it at this time. It is as follows: "*Resolved*, That we invite our fellow citizens of the United States who are anxious for the restoration of the blessings of peace, or, if the existing war shall continue to be prosecuted, are desirous that its purposes and objects shall be defined and known, who are anxious to avert present and future perils and dangers with which it may be fraught, and who are also anxious to produce contentment and satisfaction at home and to elevate the national character abroad, to assemble together in their respective communities and to express their views, feelings, and opinions."

Abraham Lincoln was a member of Congress at the time of the Mexican War.[8] He strongly opposed the war while it was in progress and severely criticized President Polk[9] on the floor of the House because he did not state in his message when peace might be expected. In the course of his speech, Lincoln said: "At its beginning, General Scott[10] was by this same President driven into disfavor, if not disgrace, for intimating that peace could not be conquered in less than three or four months. But now, at the end of twenty months…this same President gives a long message, without showing us that as to the end he

---

8. Lincoln served in Congress for two years, 1847–1849.

9. James K. Polk, President, 1845–1849.

10. Winfield Scott, commander of the U.S. Army during the Mexican War.

himself has even an imaginary conception. As I have said, he knows not where he is. He is a bewildered, confounded, and miserably perplexed man. God grant he may be able to show there is not something about his conscience more painful than his mental perplexity."[11]

Writing to a friend who had objected to his opposition to Polk in relation to this power of the President in war, Lincoln said: "The provision of the Constitution giving the war-making power to Congress was dictated, as I understand it, by the following reasons: Kings had always been involving and impoverishing their people in wars, pretending generally, if not always, that the good of the people was the object. This our convention understood to be the most oppressive of all kingly oppressions, and they resolved to so frame the Constitution that no man should hold the power of bringing this oppression upon us. But your view destroys the whole matter and places our President where kings have always stood."[12]

I now quote from the speech of Charles Sumner[13] delivered at Tremont Temple, Boston, November 5, 1846. John A. Andrew, who was the great war governor of Massachusetts, as I remember, presided at this public meeting, which was in support of the independent nomination of Dr. I. G. Howe as Representative in Congress. Mr. Sumner was followed by Honorable Charles Francis Adams, who also delivered an address at this meeting. This is the view of Mr. Sumner on the Mexican War, which was then in progress, as expressed by him on this occasion: "The Mexican War is an enormity born of slavery.... Base in object, atrocious in beginning, immoral in all its influences, vainly prodigal of treasure and life, it is a war of infamy which must blot the pages of our history."

In closing his eloquent and powerful address, he said: "Even if we seem to fail in this election we shall not fail in reality. The influence of this effort will help

to awaken and organize that powerful public opinion by which this war will at last be arrested. Hang out, fellow citizens, the white banner of peace; let the citizens of Boston rally about it; and may it be borne forward by an enlightened, conscientious people, aroused to condemnation of this murderous war, until Mexico, now wet with blood unjustly shed, shall repose undisturbed beneath its folds."

Contrast this position taken by Charles Sumner at Tremont Temple with that of the Secretary of the Treasury, Mr. McAdoo.[14] He is now touring the country with all the prestige of his great financial mission and the authority of his high place in the administration. I quote the language of the authorized report of his speech before the Bankers' Association of West Virginia, September 21, 1917. According to daily press reports, he is making substantially the same denunciation in all his addresses: "America intends that those well-meaning but misguided people who talk inopportunely of peace when there can be no peace until the cancer which has rotted civilization in Europe is extinguished and destroyed forever shall be silenced. I want to say here and now and with due deliberation that every pacifist speech in this country made at this inopportune and improper time is in effect traitorous."

In these times we had better turn the marble bust of Charles Sumner to the wall. It ill becomes those who tamely surrender the right of free speech to look upon that strong, noble, patriotic face.

Mr. President, Daniel Webster,[15] then in the zenith of his power, and with the experience and knowledge of his long life and great public service in many capacities to add weight to his words, spoke at Faneuil Hall, November 6, 1846, in opposition to the Mexican War. He said: "Mr. Chairman, I wish to speak with all soberness in this respect, and I would say nothing here tonight which I would not say in my place in Congress or before the whole world. The question now is, For what purposes and to what ends is this present war to be prosecuted?"

---

11. From Lincoln's speech of January 12, 1848.

12. From Lincoln's letter to William H. Herndon, February 15, 1848.

13. U.S. Senator from Massachusetts, 1851–1874.

14. William Gibbs McAdoo.

15. U.S. Senator from Massachusetts and twice Secretary of State (1782–1852).

What will you say to the stature of the states-manship that imputes treason to his country to a member of this body who introduces a resolution having no other import than that?

Webster saw no reason why the purposes of the war in which his country was engaged should not be discussed in Congress or out of Congress by the people's representatives or by the people themselves. After referring to Mexico as a weak and distracted country, he proceeded: "It is time for us to know what are the objects and designs of our government. It is not the habit of the American people, nor natural to their character, to consider the expense of a war which they deem just and necessary"—not only just, but necessary—"but it is their habit and belongs to their character to inquire into the justice and necessity of a war in which it is proposed to involve them."

Mr. Webster discussed the Mexican War at Springfield, Massachusetts, September 29, 1847, and again, while the war was in progress, he did not hesitate to express his disapproval in plain language. Many battles had been fought and won, and our victorious armies were in the field, on foreign soil. Sir, free speech had not been suppressed. The right of the people to assemble and to state their grievances was still an attribute of American freedom. Mr. Webster said: "We are, in my opinion, in a most unnecessary and therefore a most unjustifiable war."

Whoever expects to whip men, free men, in this country into a position where they are to be denied the right to exercise the same freedom of speech and discussion that Webster exercised in that speech little understand the value which the average citizen of this country places upon the liberty guaranteed to him by the Constitution. Sir, until the sacrifices of every battlefield consecrated to the establishment of representative government and of constitutional freedom shall be obliterated from the pages of history and forgotten of men, the plain citizenship of this country will jealously guard that liberty and that freedom and will not surrender it.

To return to my text, Mr. Webster said: "We are, in my opinion, in a most unnecessary and therefore a most unjustifiable war. I hope we are nearing the close of it. I attend carefully and anxiously to every rumor and every breeze that brings to us any report

that the effusion of blood caused, in my judgment, by a rash and unjustifiable proceeding on the part of the government may cease."

He makes the charge that the war was begun under false pretexts, as follows: "Now, sir, the law of nations instructs us that there are wars of pretexts. The history of the world proves that there have been, and we are not now without proof that there are, wars waged on pretexts—that is, on pretenses, where the cause assigned is not the true cause. That I believe on my conscience is the true character of the war now waged against Mexico. I believe it to be a war of pretexts, a war in which the true motive is not distinctly avowed but in which pretenses, after-thoughts, evasions, and other methods are employed to put a case before the community which is not the true case."

Think you Mr. Webster was not within his constitutional rights in thus criticizing the character of the war, its origin, and the reasons which were given from time to time in justification of it?

Mr. Webster discusses at length what he considers some of the false pretexts of the war. Later on he says: "Sir, men there are whom we see and whom we hear speak of the duty of extending our free institutions over the whole world if possible. We owe it to benevolence, they think, to confer the blessings we enjoy on every other people. But while I trust that liberty and free civil institutions, as we have experienced them, may ultimately spread over the globe, I am by no means sure that all people are fit for them; nor am I desirous of imposing, or forcing, our peculiar forms upon any nation that does not wish to embrace them."

Taking up the subject that war does now exist, Mr. Webster asks: "What is our duty? I say for one that I suppose it to be true—I hope it to be true—that a majority of the next House of Representatives will be Whigs, will be opposed to the war. I think we have heard from the East and the West, the North and the South, some things that make that pretty clear. Suppose it to be so. What then? Well, sir, I say for one, and at once, that unless the President of the United States shall make out a case which shall show to Congress that the aim and object for which the war is now prosecuted is no purpose not connected with the safety of the Union and the just rights of the American people, then Congress ought to pass resolutions against the prosecution of the war and grant no further supplies.

"I would speak here with caution and all just limitation. It must be admitted to be the clear intent of the Constitution that no foreign war should exist without the assent of Congress. This was meant as a restraint on the executive power. But if, when a war has once begun, the President may continue it as long as he pleases, free of all control of Congress, then it is clear that the war power is substantially in his own single hand. Nothing will be done by a wise Congress hastily or rashly, nothing that partakes of the nature of violence or recklessness; a high and delicate regard must, of course, be had for the honor and credit of the nation; but, after all, if the war should become odious to the people, if they shall disapprove the objects for which it appears to be prosecuted, then it will be the bounden duty of their Representatives in Congress to demand of the President a full statement of his objects and purposes. And if these purposes shall appear to them not to be founded in the public good, or not consistent with the honor and character of the country, then it will be their duty to put an end to it by the exercise of their constitutional authority.

"If this be not so, then the whole balance of the Constitution is overthrown, and all just restraint on the executive power, in a matter of the highest concern to the peace and happiness of the country, entirely destroyed. If we do not maintain this doctrine; if it is not so—if Congress, in whom the war-making power is expressly made to reside, is to have no voice in the declaration or continuance of war; if it is not to judge of the propriety of beginning or carrying it on—then we depart at once, and broadly, from the Constitution."

Mr. Webster concluded his speech in these memorable words: "We may be tossed upon an ocean where we can see no land—nor, perhaps, the sun or stars. But there is a chart and a compass for us to study, to consult, and to obey. That chart is the Constitution of the country. That compass is an honest, single-eyed purpose to preserve the institutions and the liberty with which God has blessed us."

In 1847 Senator Tom Corwin[16] made a memorable speech in the Senate on the Mexican War. It was one of the ablest addresses made by that very able statesman, and one of the great contributions to the discussion of the subject we are now considering. At the time of Senator Corwin's address the majority in Congress were supporting the President. The people up to that time had had no chance to express their views at an election. After referring to the doctrine then preached by the dominant faction of the Senate, that after war is declared it must be prosecuted to the bitter end as the President may direct, until one side or the other is hopelessly beaten and devastated by the conflict, with one man—the President—in sole command of the destinies of the nation, Mr. Corwin said:

"With these doctrines for our guide, I will thank any Senator to furnish me with any means of escaping from the prosecution of this or any other war, for an hundred years to come, if it please the President who shall be to continue it so long. Tell me, ye who contend that, being in war, duty demands of Congress for its prosecution all the money and every able-bodied man in America to carry it on if need be, who also contend that it is the right of the President, without the control of Congress, to march your embodied hosts to Monterrey, to Yucatan, to Mexico, to Panama, to China, and that under penalty of death to the officer who disobeys him—tell me, I demand it of you—tell me, tell the American people, tell the nations of Christendom, what is the difference between your democracy and the most odious, most hateful despotism that a merciful God has ever allowed a nation to be afflicted with since government on earth began? You may call this free government, but it is such freedom, and no other, as of old was established at Babylon, at Susa, at Bactrina, or Persepolis.[17] Its parallel is scarcely to be found, when thus falsely understood, in any, even the worst, forms of civil polity in modern times. Sir, it is not so; such is not your Constitution; it is something else, something other and better than this."[18]

---

16. U.S. Senator from Ohio, 1845–1850.

17. Sites conquered by Alexander the Great (356–323 BCE).

18. From Corwin's speech of February 11, 1847.

Lincoln, Webster, Clay, Sumner—what a galaxy of names in American history! They all believed and asserted and advocated in the midst of war that it was the right—the constitutional right—and the patriotic duty of American citizens, after the declaration of war and while the war was in progress, to discuss the issues of the war and to criticize the policies employed in its prosecution and to work for the election of representatives opposed to prolonging war.

The right of Lincoln, Webster, Clay, Sumner to oppose the Mexican War, criticize its conduct, advocate its conclusion on a just basis, is exactly the same right and privilege as that possessed by every Representative in Congress and by each and every American citizen in our land today in respect to the war in which we are now engaged. Their arguments as to the power of Congress to shape the war policy and their opposition to what they believed to be the usurpation of power on the part of the Executive are potent so long as the Constitution remains the law of the land.

English history, like our own, shows that it has ever been the right of the citizen to criticize and, when he thought necessary, to condemn the war policy of his government.

John Bright[19] consistently fought the Crimean War[20] with all the power of his great personality and noble mind; he fought it inch by inch and step by step from the floor of the English Parliament. After his death Gladstone,[21] although he had been a part of the ministry that Bright had opposed because of the Crimean War, selected this as the theme for his eulogy of the great statesman, as best portraying his high character and great service to the English people.[22]

Lloyd George[23] aggressively opposed the Boer War.[24] Speaking in the House of Commons July 25, 1900, in reply to the Prime Minister,[25] he said: "He has led us into two blunders. The first was the war. But worse than the war is the change that has been effected in the purpose for which we are prosecuting the war. We went into the war for equal rights; we are prosecuting it for annexation. . . . You entered into these two republics for philanthropic purposes and remained to commit burglary. . . . A war of annexation, however, against a proud people must be a war of extermination, and that is, unfortunately, what it seems we are now committing ourselves to—burning homesteads and turning men and women out of their homes."

I am citing this language, Mr. President, as showing the length to which statesmen have gone in opposing wars which have been conducted by their governments and the latitude that has been accorded them.

"The right honorable gentleman has made up his mind that this war shall produce electioneering capital to his own side. He is in a great hurry to go to the country before the facts are known. He wants to have the judgment of the people in the very height and excitement of the fever. He wants a verdict before the pleadings are closed and before 'discovery' has been obtained. He does not want the documents to come, but he wants to have the judgment of the country upon censured news, suppressed dispatches, and unpaid bills."[26]

In a speech delivered October 23, 1901, Lloyd George charged that the English army had burned villages, blown up farmhouses, swept away the cattle, burned thousands of tons of grain, destroyed all agricultural implements, all the mills, the irrigation works, and left the territory "a blackened devastated

---

19. British statesman and orator (1811–1889).

20. Fought from 1853 to 1856 between Russia and the allied armies of France, Great Britain, Turkey, and Sardinia.

21. William Gladstone (1809–1898), three-time Prime Minister of Great Britain.

22. Gladstone's eulogy to Bright was delivered in the House of Commons, March 29, 1889.

23. David Lloyd George, British Prime Minister at the time of La Follette's speech.

24. Fought 1899–1902 between Great Britain and the Afrikaners, or Boers, of South Africa.

25. Robert Gascoyne-Cecil.

26. La Follette is again quoting from Lloyd George's speech of July 25, 1900.

wilderness." He said: "In June the death rate among the children in the Orange River Colony camps was at the rate of 192 per thousand per annum, and in Transvaal 233 per thousand per annum. In July the figures were 220 and 330 per thousand per annum, respectively. In August they had risen to 250 and 468, and in September to 442 in Orange River Colony and to 457 in the Transvaal. These are truly appalling figures. It means that at that rate in two years' time there would not be a little child left in the whole of these two new territories.

"The worst of it is that I cannot resist the conclusion that their lives could have been saved had it not been that these camps had been deliberately chosen for military purposes. In the few camps near the coast there is hardly any mortality at all"—observe that here is a criticism of the military policies of his government—"and if the children had been removed from the Orange River Colony and the Transvaal to the seacoasts, where they could have been easily fed and clothed and cared for, their lives might be saved; but as long as they were kept up in the north there was a terrible inducement offered to the Boer commanders not to attack the lines of communication.

"If I were to despair for the future of this country, it would not be because of trade competition from either America or Germany, or the ineffectiveness of its army, or anything that might happen to its ships; but rather because it used its great, hulking strength to torture a little child. Had it not been that his ministry had shown distinct symptoms of softening of the brain, I would call the torpor and indifference they are showing in face of all this criminal. It is a maddening horror, and it will haunt the Empire to its dying hour. What wonder is it that Europe should mock and hiss at us? Let any honest Britisher fearlessly search his heart and answer this question: Is there any ground for the reproach flung at us by the civilized world that, having failed to crush the men, we have now taken to killing babes?"

Mr. President, while we were struggling for our independence, the Duke of Grafton,[27] in the House of Lords, October 26, 1775, speaking against voting thanks to British officers and soldiers after the battles of Lexington and Bunker Hill, declared: "I pledge myself to your lordships and my country that if necessity should require it and my health otherwise permit it, I mean to come down to this House in a litter in order to express my full and hearty disapproval of the measures now pursued, and, as I understand from the noble lords in office, meant to be pursued."

On the same occasion, Mr. Fox[28] said: "I could not consent to the bloody consequences of so silly a contest, about so silly an object, conducted in the silliest manner that history or observation had ever furnished an instance of, and from which we are likely to derive poverty, misery, disgrace, defeat, and ruin."

In the House of Commons, May 14, 1777, Mr. Burke[29] is reported in the parliamentary debates against the war on the American colonies as saying he was, and ever would be, ready to support a just war, whether against subjects or alien enemies, but where justice or color of justice was wanting, he would ever be the first to oppose it.

Lord Chatham,[30] November 18, 1777, spoke as follows regarding the war between England and the American colonies: "I would sell my shirt off my back to assist in proper measures, properly and wisely conducted, but I would not part with a single shilling to the present ministers. Their plans are founded in destruction and disgrace. It is, my lords, a ruinous and destructive war; it is full of danger; it teems with disgrace and must end in ruin.... If I were an American, as I am an Englishman, while a foreign troop was landed in my country I never would lay down my arms! Never! Never! Never!"

Mr. President, I have made these quotations from some of the leading statesmen of England to show that the principle of free speech was no new doctrine born of the Constitution of the United States. Our Constitution merely declared the principle. It did not create it. It is a heritage of English-speaking peoples which has been won by incalculable sacrifice and

---

27. Augustus Henry Fitzroy, 3rd Duke of Grafton (1735–1811).

28. Charles James Fox (1749–1806).

29. Edmund Burke (1729–1797).

30. William Pitt the Elder, 1st Earl of Chatham (1708–1778).

which they must preserve so long as they hope to live as free men.

I say without fear of contradiction that there has never been a time for more than a century and a half when the right of free speech and free press and the right of the people to peaceably assemble for public discussion have been so violated among English-speaking people as they are violated today throughout the United States. Today, in the land we have been wont to call the free United States, governors, mayors, and policemen are preventing or breaking up peaceable meetings called to discuss the questions growing out of this war, and judges and courts, with some notable and worthy exceptions, are failing to protect the citizens in their rights.

It is no answer to say that when the war is over the citizen may once more resume his rights and feel some security in his liberty and his person. As I have already tried to point out, now is precisely the time when the country needs the counsel of all its citizens. In time of war, even more than in time of peace, whether citizens happen to agree with the ruling administration or not, these precious fundamental personal rights—free speech, free press, and right of assemblage—so explicitly and emphatically guaranteed by the Constitution should be maintained inviolable. There is no rebellion in the land, no martial law, no courts are closed, no legal processes suspended, and there is no threat even of invasion.

But more than this, if every preparation for war can be made the excuse for destroying free speech and a free press and the right of the people to assemble together for peaceful discussion, then we may well despair of ever again finding ourselves for a long period in a state of peace. With the possessions we already have in remote parts of the world, with the obligations we seem almost certain to assume as a result of the present war, a war can be made any time overnight and the destruction of personal rights now occurring will be pointed to then as precedents for a still further invasion of the rights of the citizen. This is the road which all free governments have heretofore traveled to their destruction, and how far we have progressed along it is shown when we compare the standard of liberty of Lincoln, Clay, and Webster with the standard of the present day.

This leads me, Mr. President, to the next thought to which I desire to invite the attention of the Senate, and that is the power of Congress to declare the purpose and objects of the war, and the failure of Congress to exercise that power in the present crisis. For the mere assertion of that right, in the form of a resolution to be considered and discussed, which I introduced August 11, 1917, I have been denounced throughout this broad land as a traitor to my country.[31]

Mr. President, we are in a war the awful consequences of which no man can foresee, which, in my judgment, could have been avoided if the Congress had exercised its constitutional power to influence and direct the foreign policy of this country. On the eighth day of February, 1915, I introduced in the Senate a resolution authorizing the President to invite the representatives of the neutral nations of the world to assemble and consider, among other things, whether it would not be possible to lay out lanes of travel upon the high seas and through proper negotiation with the belligerent powers have those lanes recognized as neutral territory, through which the commerce of neutral nations might pass. This, together with other provisions, constituted a resolution, as I shall always regard it, of most vital and supreme importance in the world crisis, and one that should have been considered and acted upon by Congress.

I believe, sir, that had some such action been taken, the history of the world would not be written at this hour in the blood of more than one-half of the nations of the earth, with the remaining nations in danger of becoming involved. I believe that had Congress exercised the power in this respect, which I contend it possesses, we could and probably would have avoided the present war.

Mr. President, I believe that if we are to extricate ourselves from this war and restore this country to an honorable and lasting peace, the Congress must exercise in full the war powers entrusted to it by the Constitution. I have already called your attention sufficiently, no doubt, to the opinions upon this subject

---

31. La Follette's resolution called on Congress "to determine and declare definitely the objects for which this government shall continue to participate in the European war."

expressed by some of the greatest lawyers and states-men of the country, and I now venture to ask your attention to a little closer examination of the subject viewed in the light of distinctly legal authorities and principles.

Section 8, Article I, of the Constitution provides: "The Congress shall have power to lay and collect taxes, duties, imposts, and excises to pay the debts and provide for the common defense and general welfare of the United States."

In this first sentence we find that no war can be prosecuted without the consent of the Congress. No war can be prosecuted without money. There is no power to raise the money for war except the power of Congress. From this provision alone it must fol-low absolutely and without qualification that the duty of determining whether a war shall be pros-ecuted or not, whether the people's money shall be expended for the purpose of war or not, rests upon the Congress, and with that power goes necessarily the power to determine the purposes of the war, for if the Congress does not approve the purposes of the war, it may refuse to lay the tax upon the people to prosecute it.

Again, Section 8 further provides that Congress shall have power "To declare war, grant letters of marque and reprisal, and make rules concerning cap-tures on land and water;

"To raise and support armies, but no appropria-tion of money to that use shall be for a longer term than two years;

"To provide and maintain a Navy;

"To make rules for the government and regula-tion of the land and naval forces;

"To provide for calling forth the militia to exe-cute the laws of the Union, suppress insurrection, and repel invasion;

"To provide for organizing, arming, and dis-ciplining the militia, and for governing such part of them as may be employed in the service of the United States, reserving to the States, respectively, the appointment of the officers and the authority of training the militia according to the discipline pre-scribed by Congress."

In the foregoing grants of power, which are as complete as language can make them, there is no mention of the President. Nothing is omitted from the powers conferred upon the Congress. Even the power to make the rules for the government and the regulation of all the national forces, both on land and on the sea, is vested in the Congress.

Then, not content with this, to make certain that no question could possibly arise, the framers of the Constitution declared that Congress shall have power "To make all laws which shall be necessary and proper for carrying into execution the foregoing powers, and all other powers vested by this Constitution in the government of the United States, or in any depart-ment or officer thereof."

We all know from the debates which took place in the Constitutional Convention[32] why it was that the Constitution was so framed as to vest in the Congress the entire war-making power. The framers of the Constitution knew that to give to one man that power meant danger to the rights and liberties of the people. They knew that it mattered not whether you call the man king or emperor, czar or president, to put into his hands the power of making war or peace meant despotism. It meant that the people would be called upon to wage wars in which they had no inter-est or to which they might even be opposed. It meant secret diplomacy and secret treaties. It meant that in those things most vital to the lives and welfare of the people, they would have nothing to say.

The framers of the Constitution believed that they had guarded against this in the language I have quoted. They placed the entire control of this subject in the hands of the Congress. And it was assumed that debate would be free and open, that many men representing all the sections of the country would freely, frankly, and calmly exchange their views, unafraid of the power of the Executive, uninfluenced by anything except their own convictions and a desire to obey the will of the people expressed in a consti-tutional manner.

Another reason for giving this power to the Congress was that the Congress, particularly the House of Representatives, was assumed to be directly responsible to the people and would most

---

32. The Constitutional Convention met in Philadelphia, May 25–September 17, 1787.

nearly represent their views. The term of office for a Representative was fixed at only two years. One-third of the Senate would be elected each two years. It was believed that this close relation to the people would ensure a fair representation of the popular will in the action which the Congress might take.

Moreover, if the Congress for any reason was unfaithful to its trust and declared a war which the people did not desire to support or to continue, they could in two years at most retire from office their unfaithful Representatives and return others who would terminate the war. It is true that within two years much harm could be done by an unwise declaration of war, especially a war of aggression, where men were sent abroad. The framers of the Constitution made no provision for such a condition, for they apparently never contemplated that such a condition would arise.

Moreover, under the system of voluntary enlistment, which was the only system of raising an army for use outside the country of which the framers of the Constitution had any idea, the people could force a settlement of any war to which they were opposed by the simple means of not volunteering to fight it.

The only power relating to war with which the Executive was entrusted was that of acting as commander in chief of the army and navy and of the militia when called into actual service. This provision is found in Section 2 of Article II, and is as follows: "The President shall be Commander in Chief of the Army and Navy of the United States and of the militia of the several States when called into the actual service of the United States."

Here is found the sum total of the President's war powers. After the army is raised, he becomes the general in command. His function is purely military. He is the general in command of the entire army, just as there is a general in command of a certain field of operation. The authority of each is confined strictly to the field of military service. The Congress must raise and support and equip and maintain the army which the President is to command. Until the army is raised, the President has no military authority over any of the persons that may compose it. He cannot enlist a man, or provide a uniform, or a single gun or pound of powder. The country may be invaded from

all sides and except for the command of the regular army, the President, as commander in chief of the army, is as powerless as any citizen to stem the tide of the invasion. In such case his only resort would be to the militia, as provided in the Constitution. Thus completely did the fathers of the Constitution strip the Executive of military power.

It may be said that the duty of the President to enforce the laws of the country carries with it by implication control over the military forces for that purpose, and that the decision as to when the laws are violated, and the manner in which they should be redressed, rests with the President. This whole matter was considered in the famous case of *Ex parte Milligan*[33] (4 Wall., 2).[34] The question of enforcing the laws of the United States, however, does not arise in the present discussion. The laws of the United States have no effect outside the territory of the United States. Our army in France or our navy on the high seas may be engaged in worthy enterprises, but they are not enforcing the laws of the United States, and the President derives from his constitutional obligation to enforce the laws of the country no power to determine the purposes of the present war.

The only remaining provision of the Constitution to be considered on the subject is that provision of Article II, Section 2, which provides that the President "shall have power by and with the consent of the Senate to make treaties, providing two-thirds of the Senate present concur." This is the same section of the Constitution which provides that the President "shall nominate, and by and with the advice and consent of the Senate, shall appoint ambassadors, other public ministers, consuls, judges of the Supreme Court," and so forth.

Observe, the President under this constitutional provision gets no authority to declare the purposes and objects of any war in which the country may be

---

33. In this case, which grew out of the Civil War, the U.S. Supreme Court ruled in 1866 that military jurisdiction could not supersede the civil courts in areas where the civil courts and government remained open and operational.

34. Here, as elsewhere, the parenthetical citation is part of La Follette's speech; in this instance, he is referring to the National Reporter System for Supreme Court cases.

engaged. It is true that a treaty of peace cannot be executed except the President and the Senate concur in its execution. If a President should refuse to agree to terms of peace which were proposed, for instance, by a resolution of Congress, and accepted by the parliament of an enemy nation against the will, we will say, of an emperor, the war would simply stop if the two parliaments agreed and exercised their powers respectively to withhold supplies; and the formal execution of a treaty of peace would be postponed until the people could select another President.

It is devoutly to be hoped that such a situation will never arise, and it is hardly conceivable that it should arise with both an Executive and a Senate anxious, respectively, to discharge the constitutional duties of their office. But if it should arise, under the Constitution the final authority and the power to ultimately control is vested by the Constitution in the Congress. The President can no more make a treaty of peace without the approval not only of the Senate but of two-thirds of the Senators present than he can appoint a judge of the Supreme Court without the concurrence of the Senate. A decent regard for the duties of the President, as well as the duties of the Senators, and the consideration of the interests of the people, whose servants both the Senators and the President are, requires that the negotiations which lead up to the making of peace should be participated in equally by the Senators and by the President. For Senators to take any other position is to shirk a plain duty, is to avoid an obligation imposed upon them by the spirit and letter of the Constitution and by the solemn oath of office each has taken.

As might be expected from the plain language of the Constitution, the precedents and authorities are all one way. I shall not attempt to present them all here, but only refer to those which have peculiar application to the present situation.

Watson, in his work on the Constitution, volume 2, page 915, says: "The authority of the President over the Army and Navy to command and control is only subject to the restrictions of Congress 'to make rules for the government and regulation of the land and naval forces.'... Neither can impair or invade the authority of the other. The powers of the President"

under the war clause "are only those which may be called 'military.'"[35]

The same author on the same and succeeding page points out that the President as commander in chief of the army may direct the military force in such a way as to most effectively injure the enemy. He may even direct an invasion of enemy territory. But, says the author, this can be done "temporarily, however, only until Congress has defined what the permanent policy of the country is to be."

How, then, can the President declare the purposes of the war to be to extend permanently the territory of an ally or secure for an ally damages either in the form of money or new territory?

MR. KING:[36] Mr. President, will the Senator yield for a question?

MR. LA FOLLETTE: I prefer not to yield, if the Senator will permit me to continue. I can hardly get through within the time allotted, and I am certain to be diverted if I begin to yield.

MR. KING: I just wanted to ask the Senator whether he thinks the President of the United States has contravened any constitutional powers conferred upon him thus far in the prosecution of the war?

MR. LA FOLLETTE: Well, sir, I am discussing the constitutional question here, and Senators must make their own application.

Pomeroy,[37] in his *Introduction to the Constitutional Law of the United States*, ninth edition, 1886, page 373, says: "The organic law nowhere prescribes or limits the causes for which hostilities may be waged against a foreign country. The causes of war it leaves to the discretion and judgment of the legislature."

In other words, it is for Congress to determine what we are fighting for. The President, as commander in chief of the army, is to determine the best method of carrying on the fight. But since the purposes of the war must determine what are the best methods of conducting it, the primary duty at all times rests upon Congress to declare either

---

35. David Watson, *The Constitution of the United States: Its History, Application, and Construction* (1910).

36. William H. King, Democratic Senator from Utah.

37. John Norton Pomeroy.

in the declaration of war or subsequently what the objects are which it is expected to accomplish by the war.

In Elliot's *Debates*,[38] supplement second edition, 1866, page 439, volume 5, it is said: "There is a material difference between the cases of making war and making peace. It should be more easy to get out of war than into it." In the same volume, at page 140, we find: "Mr. Sherman[39] said he considered the executive magistracy as nothing more than an institution for carrying the will of the legislature into effect."

Story, in his work on the Constitution,[40] fifth edition, 1891, page 92, says: "The history of republics has but too fatally proved that they are too ambitious of military fame and conquest and too easily devoted to the interests of demagogues, who flatter their pride and betray their interests. It should, therefore, be difficult in a republic to declare war, but not to make peace. The representatives of the people are to lay the taxes to support a war, and therefore have a right to be consulted as to its propriety and necessity."

I commend this language to those gentlemen, both in and out of public office, who condemn as treasonable all efforts, either by the people or by their representatives in Congress, to discuss terms of peace or who even venture to suggest that a peace is not desirable until such time as the President, acting solely on his own responsibility, shall declare for peace. It is a strange doctrine we hear these days that the mass of the people, who pay in money, misery, and blood all the costs of this war, out of which a favored few profit so largely, may not freely and publicly discuss terms of peace. I believe that I have shown that such an odious and tyrannical doctrine has never been held by the men who have stood for liberty and representative government in this country.

Ordronaux, in his work on constitutional legislation,[41] says: "This power"—the war-making power—"the Constitution has lodged in Congress, as the political department of the government, and more immediate representative of the will of the people" (page 495). On page 496, the same author points out that "The general power to declare war, and the consequent right to conduct it as long as the public interests may seem to require" is vested in Congress.

The right to determine when and upon what terms the public interests require that war shall cease must therefore necessarily vest in Congress.

I have already referred to the fact that Lincoln, Webster, Clay, Sumner, Corwin, and others all contended and declared in the midst of war that it was the right—the constitutional right—and the patriotic duty of American citizens, after the declaration of war, as well as before the declaration of war, and while the war was in progress, to discuss the issues of the war, to criticize the policies employed in its prosecution, and to work for the election of representatives pledged to carry out the will of the people respecting the war.

Let me call your attention to what James Madison, who became the fourth President of the United States, said on the subject in a speech at the Constitutional Convention, June 29, 1787: "A standing military force, with an overgrown Executive, will not long be safe companions to liberty. The means of defense against foreign dangers have always been the instrument of tyranny at home. Among the Romans it was a standing maxim to excite war whenever a revolt was apprehended. Throughout all Europe the armies kept up under the pretense of defending have enslaved the people. It is perhaps questionable whether the best concerted system of absolute power in Europe could maintain itself in a situation where no alarms of external danger could tame the people to the domestic yoke."

I now invite your attention to some of the precedents established by Congress, showing that it has exercised almost from the time of the first Congress

---

38. Jonathan Elliot, *The Debates in the Several State Conventions on the Adoption of the Federal Constitution.*

39. Roger Sherman (1721–1793), delegate to the Constitutional Convention from Connecticut.

40. Joseph Story, *Commentaries on the Constitution of the United States.*

41. John Ordronaux, *Constitutional Legislation in the United States: Its Origin, and Application to the Relative Powers of Congress, and of State Legislatures* (1891).

substantially the powers I am urging it should assert now. Many of the precedents to which I shall now briefly refer will be found in *Hinds' Precedents*, volume 2, chapter 49.[42] My authority for the others are the records of Congress itself as contained in the *Congressional Globe* and *Congressional Record*.

In 1811 the House originated and the Senate agreed to a resolution as follows: "Taking into view the present state of the world, the peculiar situation of Spain and of her American provinces, and the intimate relations of the territory eastward of the River Perdido adjoining the United States to their security and tranquillity: Therefore *Resolved, etc.*, That the United States cannot see with indifference any part of the Spanish Provinces adjoining the said States eastward of the River Perdido pass from the hands of Spain into those of any other foreign power."[43]

In 1821 Mr. Clay introduced the following resolution, which passed the House: "*Resolved,* That the House of Representatives participates with the people of the United States in the deep interest which they feel for the success of the Spanish Provinces of South America, which are struggling to establish their liberty and independence, and that it will give its constitutional support to the President of the United States whenever he may deem it expedient to recognize the sovereignty and independence of any of the said Provinces."[44]

In 1825 there was a long debate in the House relating to an unconditional appropriation for the expenses of the ministers to the Panama Congress.[45] According to Mr. Hinds's summary of this debate, the opposition to the amendment, led by Mr. Webster,[46]

was that "While the House had an undoubted right to express its general opinion in regard to questions of foreign policy, in this case it was proposed to decide what should be discussed by the particular ministers already appointed. If such instructions might be furnished by the House in this case they might be furnished in all, thus usurping the power of the Executive." James Buchanan and John Forsyth,[47] who argued in favor of the amendment, "contended that it did not amount to any instruction to diplomatic agents, but was a proper expression of opinion by the House. The House had always exercised the right of expressing its opinion on great questions, either foreign or domestic, and such expressions were never thought to be an improper interference with the Executive."

In April 1864 the House originated and passed a resolution declaring that "It did not accord with the policy of the United States to acknowledge a monarchical government erected on the ruins of any republican government in America under the auspices of any European power."[48] On May 23 the House passed a resolution requesting the President[49] to communicate any explanation given by the government of the United States to France respecting the sense and bearing of the joint resolution relative to Mexico. The President transmitted the correspondence to the House. The correspondence disclosed that Secretary Seward[50] had transmitted a copy of the resolution to our minister to France, with the explanation that "This is a practical and purely executive question, and the decision of its constitutionality belongs not to the House of Representatives or even to Congress but to the President of the United States."

---

42. Asher C. Hinds, *Hinds' Precedents of the House of Representatives of the United States: Including References to Provisions of the Constitution, the Laws, and Decisions of the United States Senate* (1907).

43. This resolution was passed by the House and Senate in January 1811.

44. Clay introduced this resolution on February 10, 1821; it was approved on February 11.

45. Held in 1826, the Panama Congress was the Western Hemisphere's first regionwide meeting of independent states. The debate to which La Follette refers took place in April 1825.

46. Daniel Webster, Representative from Massachusetts, 1823–1827.

---

47. Buchanan, who would be elected President in 1856, was in 1825 a Representative from Pennsylvania; Forsyth was a Representative from Georgia.

48. The resolution was passed on April 4, 1864; it opposed the impending proclamation of Austrian Archduke Ferdinand Maximilian as Emperor of Mexico, an event brought about with the military support of France, which had invaded Mexico in January 1862.

49. Abraham Lincoln.

50. Secretary of State William Seward.

After a protracted struggle, evidently accompanied with much feeling, the House of Representatives adopted the following resolution, which had been reported by Mr. Henry Winter Davis[51] from the Committee on Foreign Affairs: "*Resolved*, That Congress has a constitutional right to an authoritative voice in declaring and prescribing the foreign policy of the United States as well in the recognition of new powers as in other matters, and it is the constitutional duty of the President to respect that policy, no less in diplomatic negotiations than in the use of the national force when authorized by law."[52]

It will be observed from the language last read that it was assumed as a matter of course that Congress had an authoritative voice as to the use of the national forces to be made in time of war and that it was the constitutional duty of the President to respect the policy of the Congress in that regard, and Mr. Davis in the resolution just read argued that it was the duty of the President to respect the authority of Congress in diplomatic negotiations even as he must respect it when the Congress determined the policy of the government in the use of the national forces.

The portion of the resolution I have just read was adopted by a vote of 119 to 8. The balance of the resolution was adopted by a smaller majority, and was as follows: "And the propriety of any declaration of foreign policy by Congress is sufficiently proved by the vote which pronounces it; and such proposition, while pending and undetermined, is not a fit topic of diplomatic explanation with any foreign power."[53]

The joint resolution of 1898 declaring the intervention of the United States to remedy conditions existing in the island of Cuba is recent history and familiar to all.[54] This resolution embodied a clear declaration of foreign policy regarding Cuba as well as a declaration of war. It passed both branches of Congress and was signed by the President. After reciting the abhorrent conditions existing in Cuba, it reads as follows:

"*Resolved, etc.*, First, That the people of the island of Cuba are, and of right ought to be, free and independent.

"Second, That it is the duty of the United States to demand, and the government of the United States does hereby demand, that the government of Spain at once relinquish its authority and government in the island of Cuba and withdraw its land and naval forces from Cuba and Cuban waters.

"Third, That the President of the United States be, and he hereby is, directed and empowered to use the entire land and naval forces of the United States, and to call into the actual service of the United States the militia of the several states, to such extent as may be necessary to carry these resolutions into effect.

"Fourth, That the United States hereby disclaims any disposition or intention to exercise sovereignty, jurisdiction, or control over said island except for the pacification thereof, and asserts its determination, when that is accomplished, to leave the government and control of the island to its people."

On April 28, 1904, a joint resolution was passed by both houses of Congress in the following terms: "That it is the sense of the Congress of the United States that it is desirable in the interests of uniformity of action by maritime states in time of war that the President endeavor to bring about an understanding among the principal maritime powers with a view to incorporating into the permanent law of civilized nations the principle of the exemption of all private property at sea, not contraband of war, from capture or destruction by belligerents."

Here it will be observed that the Congress proposed by resolution to direct the President as to the policy of exempting from capture private property at sea, not contraband of war, in not only one war merely but in all wars, providing that other maritime powers could be brought to adopt the same policy. So far as I am aware, there is an unbroken line of precedents by Congress upon this subject down to the time of the present administration.

51. U.S. Representative from Maryland.

52. This resolution was originally reported on June 27, 1864, but was not acted upon. It was reported again on December 15, 1864, and approved on December 19 after the words "Executive Department" were substituted for "President."

53. This portion of the resolution passed by a vote of 68–59.

54. La Follette is referring to Congress's resolution of April 19, 1898, authorizing American military action to compel Spain to relinquish all authority in Cuba. The Spanish-American War followed.

It is true that in 1846 President Polk, without consulting Congress, assumed to send the army of the United States into territory the title of which was in dispute between the United States and Mexico, thereby precipitating bloodshed and the Mexican War.[55] But it is also true that this act was condemned as unconstitutional by the great constitutional lawyers of the country, and Abraham Lincoln, when he became a member of the next Congress, voted for and supported the resolution, called the Ashmun Amendment, which passed the House of Representatives, declaring that the Mexican War had been "Unnecessarily and unconstitutionally begun by the President of the United States."[56] See Schouler's *History of the United States*, volume 5, page 83.[57] See also Lincoln's speech in the House of Representatives, January 12, 1848.

That the full significance of this resolution was appreciated by the House of Representatives is shown by the speech of Mr. Venable,[58] Representative from North Carolina, and a warm supporter of President Polk, made in the House, January 12, 1848,[59] where, referring to this resolution, he says: "Eighty-five members of this House sustained that amendment"—referring to the Ashmun Amendment—"and it now constitutes one of our recorded acts. I will not here stop to inquire as to the moral effect upon the Mexican people and the Mexican government which will result to us from such a vote in the midst of a war. I suppose gentlemen have fully weighed this matter. Neither will I now inquire how much such a vote will strengthen our credit or facilitate the government in furnishing the necessary supply of troops.

"They"—referring to his fellow members in the House of Representatives—"have said by their votes that the President has violated the Constitution in the most flagrant manner; that every drop of blood which has been shed, every bone which now whitens the plains of Mexico, every heart-wringing agony which has been produced must be placed to his account who has so flagitiously violated the Constitution and involved the nation in the horrors of war. This the majority of this House have declared on oath. The grand inquest of the nation have asserted the fact and fixed it on their records, and I here demand of them to impeach the President."

That Mr. Lincoln was in no manner deterred from the discharge of his duty as he saw it is evidenced by the fact that on the day following the speech of Representative Venable, Lincoln replied with one of the ablest speeches of his career, the opening sentences of which I desire to quote. He said: "Some, if not all, the gentlemen of the other side of the House who have addressed the committee within the last two days have spoken rather complainingly, if I have rightly understood them, of the vote given a week or ten days ago, declaring that the war with Mexico was unnecessarily and unconstitutionally commenced by the President. I admit that such a vote should not be given in mere party wantonness and that the one given is justly censurable, if it have no other or better foundation. I am one of those who joined in that vote; and I did so under my best impression of the truth of the case."[60]

Lincoln then proceeded to demonstrate the truth of the charge as he regarded it. Evidently he did not think that patriotism in war more than in peace required the suppression of the truth respecting anything pertaining to the conduct of the war. And yet today, Mr. President, for merely suggesting a possible disagreement with the administration on any measure submitted, or the offering of amendments to increase the tax upon incomes, or on war profits, is "treason to our country and an effort to serve the enemy."

Since the Constitution vests in Congress the supreme power to determine when and for what pur-

55. In late April 1846, Mexican troops crossed the Rio Grande, entered disputed territory claimed by the United States, and attacked a small force of American soldiers. Polk, who had hoped for such an encounter, declared: "War exists...by the act of Mexico herself."

56. Introduced by Representative George Ashmun of Massachusetts, the resolution was approved on January 3, 1848.

57. James Schouler, *History of the United States of America under the Constitution*, rev. ed. (1894).

58. Abraham Watkins Venable (1799–1876).

59. La Follette misstates the date of Venable's speech, which was delivered February 11, 1848.

60. From Lincoln's speech of February 12, 1848.

pose the country will engage in war and the objects to attain which the war will be prosecuted, it seems to me to be an evasion of a solemn duty on the part of the Congress not to exercise that power at this critical time in the nation's affairs. The Congress can no more avoid its responsibility in this matter than it can in any other. As the nation's purposes in conducting this war are of supreme importance to the country, it is the supreme duty of Congress to exercise the function conferred upon it by the Constitution of guiding the foreign policy of the nation in the present crisis.

A minor duty may be evaded by Congress, a minor responsibility avoided, without disaster resulting, but on this momentous question there can be no evasion, no shirking of duty of the Congress, without subverting our form of government. If our Constitution is to be changed so as to give the President the power to determine the purposes for which this nation will engage in war, and the conditions on which it will make peace, then let that change be made deliberately by an amendment to the Constitution proposed and adopted in a constitutional manner. It would be bad enough if the Constitution clothed the President with any such power, but to exercise such power without constitutional authority cannot long be tolerated if even the forms of free government are to remain. We all know that no amendment to the Constitution giving the President the powers suggested would be adopted by the people. We know that if such an amendment were to be proposed, it would be overwhelmingly defeated.

The universal conviction of those who yet believe in the rights of the people is that the first step toward the prevention of war and the establishment of peace, permanent peace, is to give the people who must bear the brunt of war's awful burden more to say about it. The masses will understand that it was the evil of a one-man power exercised in a half dozen nations through the malevolent influences of a system of secret diplomacy that plunged the helpless peoples of Europe into the awful war that has been raging with increasing horror and fury ever since it began and that now threatens to engulf the world before it stops. No conviction is stronger with the people today than that there should be no future wars except in case of actual invasion unless supported by a referendum, a

plebiscite, a vote of ratification upon the declaration of war before it shall become effective.

And because there is no clearness of understanding, no unity of opinion in this country on the part of the people as to the conditions upon which we are prosecuting this war or what the specific objects are upon the attainment of which the present administration would be willing to conclude a peace, it becomes still more imperative each day that Congress should assert its constitutional power to define and declare the objects of this war which will afford the basis for a conference and for the establishment of permanent peace. The President has asked the German people to speak for themselves on this great world issue;[61] why should not the American people voice their convictions through their chosen representatives in Congress?

Ever since new Russia appeared upon the map[62] she has been holding out her hands to free America to come to her support in declaring for a clear understanding of the objects to be attained to secure peace. Shall we let this most remarkable revolution the world has ever witnessed appeal to us in vain?

We have been six months at war. We have incurred financial obligations and made expenditures of money in amounts already so large that the human mind cannot comprehend them. The government has drafted from the peaceful occupations of civil life a million of our finest young men—and more will be taken if necessary—to be transported 4,000 miles over the sea, with their equipment and supplies, to the trenches of Europe.

The first chill winds of autumn remind us that another winter is at hand. The imagination is paralyzed at the thought of the human misery, the indescribable suffering, which the winter months, with their cold and sleet and ice and snow, must bring to the war-swept lands, not alone to the soldiers at the front but to the noncombatants at home.

---

61. Likely a reference to Wilson's letter of August 27, 1917, responding to Pope Benedict XV's peace proposals of August 1.

62. In March 1917 Czar Nicholas II abdicated his throne in favor of a provisional government, which was in turn toppled by the Bolsheviks under the leadership of Vladimir Ilyich Lenin, a month after La Follette's speech.

To such excesses of cruelty has this war descended that each nation is now, as a part of its strategy, planning to starve the women and children of the enemy countries. Each warring nation is carrying out the unspeakable plan of starving noncombatants. Each nurses the hope that it may break the spirit of the men of the enemy country at the front by starving the wives and babes at home, and woe be it that we have become partners in this awful business and are even cutting off food shipments from neutral countries in order to force them to help starve women and children of the country against whom we have declared war.

There may be some necessity overpowering enough to justify these things, but the people of America should demand to know what results are expected to satisfy the sacrifice of all that civilization holds dear upon the bloody altar of a conflict which employs such desperate methods of warfare.

The question is: Are we to sacrifice millions of our young men, the very promise of the land, and spend billions and more billions, and pile up the cost of living until we starve—and for what? Shall the fearfully overburdened people of this country continue to bear the brunt of a prolonged war for any objects not openly stated and defined?

The answer, sir, rests, in my judgment, with the Congress, whose duty it is to declare our specific purposes in the present war and to state the objects upon the attainment of which we will make peace. And, sir, this is the ground on which I stand. I maintain that Congress has the right and the duty to declare the objects of the war and the people have the right and the obligation to discuss it.

American citizens may hold all shades of opinion as to the war; one citizen may glory in it, another may deplore it, each has the same right to voice his judgment. An American citizen may think and say that we are not justified in prosecuting this war for the purpose of dictating the form of government which shall be maintained by our enemy or our ally, and not be subject to punishment at law. He may pray aloud that our boys shall not be sent to fight and die on European battlefields for the annexation of territory or the maintenance of trade agreements and be within his legal rights. He may express the hope that

an early peace may be secured on the terms set forth by the new Russia and by President Wilson in his speech of January 22, 1917,[63] and he cannot lawfully be sent to jail for the expression of his convictions.

It is the citizen's duty to obey the law until it is repealed or declared unconstitutional. But he has the inalienable right to fight what he deems an obnoxious law or a wrong policy in the courts and at the ballot box. It is the suppressed emotion of the masses that breeds revolution.

If the American people are to carry on this great war, if public opinion is to be enlightened and intelligent, there must be free discussion. Congress, as well as the people of the United States, entered the war in great confusion of mind and under feverish excitement. The President's leadership was followed in the faith that he had some big, unrevealed plan by which peace that would exalt him before all the world would soon be achieved.

Gradually, reluctantly, Congress and the country are beginning to perceive that we are in this terrific world conflict not only to right our wrongs, not only to aid the allies, not only to share its awful death toll and its fearful tax burden, but, perhaps, to bear the brunt of the war. And so I say, if we are to forestall the danger of being drawn into years of war, perhaps finally to maintain imperialism and exploitation, the people must unite in a campaign along constitutional lines for free discussion of the policy of the war and its conclusion on a just basis.

Permit me, sir, this word in conclusion. It is said by many persons for whose opinions I have profound respect and whose motives I know to be sincere that "we are in this war and must go through to the end." That is true. But it is not true that we must go through to the end to accomplish an undisclosed purpose or to reach an unknown goal. I believe that whatever there is of honest difference of opinion concerning this war arises precisely at this point. There is, and of course can be, no real difference of opinion concerning the duty of the citizen to discharge to the last limit whatever obligation the war lays upon him.

---

63. In this speech, presented four months before America entered the war, Wilson urged the European powers to seek terms that would produce "peace without victory."

Our young men are being taken by the hundreds of thousands for the purpose of waging this war on the continent of Europe, possibly Asia or Africa, or anywhere else that they may be ordered. Nothing must be left undone for their protection. They must have the best army, ammunition, and equipment that money can buy. They must have the best training and the best officers which this great country can provide. The dependents and relatives they leave at home must be provided for not meagerly, but generously so far as money can provide for them.

I have done some of the hardest work of my life during the last few weeks on the revenue bill to raise the largest possible amount of money from surplus incomes and war profits for this war and upon other measures to provide for the protection of the soldiers and their families. That I was not able to accomplish more along this line is a great disappointment to me. I did all that I could, and I shall continue to fight with all the power at my command until wealth is made to bear more of the burden of this war than has been laid upon it by the present Congress. Concerning these matters there can be no difference of opinion. We have not yet been able to muster the forces to conscript wealth as we have conscripted men, but no one has ever been able to advance even a plausible argument for not doing so.

No, Mr. President, it is on the other point suggested where honest differences of opinion may arise. Shall we ask the people of this country to shut their eyes and take the entire war program on faith? There are no doubt many honest and well-meaning persons who are willing to answer that question in the affirmative rather than risk the dissensions which they fear may follow a free discussion of the issues of this war. With that position I do not—I cannot—agree. Have the people no intelligent contribution to make to the solution of the problems of this war? I believe that they have, and that in this matter, as in so many others, they may be wiser than their leaders and that if left free to discuss the issues of the war, they will find the correct settlement of these issues.

But it is said that Germany will fight with greater determination if her people believe that we are not in perfect agreement. Mr. President, that is the same worn-out pretext which has been used for three years to keep the plain people of Europe engaged in killing each other in this war. And, sir, as applied to this country, at least, it is a pretext with nothing to support it.

The way to paralyze the German arm, to weaken the German military force, in my opinion, is to declare our objects in this war and show by that declaration to the German people that we are not seeking to dictate a form of government to Germany or to render more secure England's domination of the seas. A declaration of our purposes in this war, so far from strengthening our enemy, I believe, would immeasurably weaken her, for it would no longer be possible to misrepresent our purposes to the German people.

Such a course on our part, so far from endangering the life of a single one of our boys, I believe, would result in saving the lives of hundreds of thousands of them by bringing about an earlier and more lasting peace by intelligent negotiation, instead of securing a peace by the complete exhaustion of one or the other of the belligerents. Such a course would also immeasurably, I believe, strengthen our military force in this country, because when the objects of this war are clearly stated and the people approve of those objects, they will give to the war a popular support it will never otherwise receive.

Then, again, honest dealing with the Entente Allies,[64] as well as with our own people, requires a clear statement of our objects in this war. If we do not expect to support the Entente Allies in the dreams of conquest we know some of them entertain, then in all fairness to them, that fact should be stated now. If we do expect to support them in their plans for conquest and aggrandizement, then our people are entitled to know that vitally important fact before this war proceeds further. Common honesty and fair dealing with the people of this country and with the nations by whose side we are fighting, as well as a sound military policy at home, requires the fullest and freest discussion before the people of every issue involved in this great war and that a plain and specific declaration of our purposes in the war be speedily made by the Congress of the United States.

---

64. Great Britain, France, and Russia.

Carrie Chapman Catt

Address to the Congress of the United States

WASHINGTON, D.C.
DECEMBER 13, 1917

NEW YORK WAS the crown jewel in the battle for woman suffrage at the state level. If suffrage forces could win in the nation's largest and most powerful state, they believed it was only a matter of time before they would succeed at the national level. When New York voters passed a suffrage referendum on November 6, 1917, Carrie Chapman Catt exulted: "The victory is not New York's alone. It's the nation's. The Sixty-fifth Congress will now pass the federal amendment." In fact, final passage did not come until the Sixty-sixth Congress, but the road to victory was now more open than it had ever been.

One month after the New York election, the National American Woman Suffrage Association held its annual convention in Washington, D.C. Standing before a packed house in Poli's Theatre, Catt delivered her presidential message in the form of a speech to Congress. Employing the classical rhetorical device of prosopopoeia—addressing an imaginary or absent auditor as if he or she were present—Catt presented a powerfully reasoned case for the morality, necessity, and inevitability of woman suffrage. "Men," she said, "should search their very souls" and bring the United States into line with its democratic principles and "the trend of world progress." Anything less would make the nation "a jest among the onward-moving peoples of the world."

Catt considered this one of the two most important speeches of her career, the other being "The Crisis," which had kicked off the winning plan that resulted in passage of the suffrage amendment (pages 57–73). "To hear her," said one listener, "was like listening to abstract thought, warmed by the fire of abstract conviction. To see her was like looking at sheer marble, flame-lit." The speech was printed in pamphlet form before Catt delivered it, and copies were hand-delivered to each member of Congress by a deputation of suffragists. Less than a month later, the House of Representatives approved the woman suffrage amendment by a vote of 274–136; the Senate would follow suit in June 1919. In August 1920, after ratification of the amendment by three-fourths of the states, American women were finally granted the right to vote.

Woman suffrage is inevitable. Suffragists knew it before November 6, 1917,[1] opponents afterward. Three distinct causes make it inevitable.

One: *The history of our country*. Ours is a nation born of revolution, of rebellion against a system of government so securely entrenched in the customs and traditions of human society that in 1776 it seemed impregnable. From the beginning of things, nations had been ruled by kings and for kings while the people served and paid the cost. The American Revolutionists boldly proclaimed the heresies: "Taxation without representation is tyranny." "Governments derive their just powers from the consent of the governed."[2]

The colonists won and the nation which was established as a result of their victory has held unfailingly that these two fundamental principles of democratic government are not only the spiritual source of our national existence but have been our chief historic pride and at all times the sheet anchor of our liberties. Eighty years after the Revolution, Abraham Lincoln welded those two maxims into a new one: "Ours is a government of the people, by the people, and for the people."[3]

Fifty years more passed and the President of the United States, Woodrow Wilson, in a mighty crisis of the nation, proclaimed to the world: "We are fighting for the things which we have always carried nearest our hearts—for democracy, for the right of those who submit to authority to have a voice in their own government."[4]

All the way between these immortal aphorisms political leaders have declared unabated faith in their truth. Not one American has arisen to question their logic in the 141 years of our national existence. However stupidly our country may have evaded the

logical application at times, it has never swerved from its devotion to the theory of democracy as expressed by those two axioms.

Not only has it unceasingly upheld the theory, but it has carried these theories into practice whenever men made application.

Certain denominations of Protestants, Catholics, Jews, nonlandholders, workingmen, Negroes, [and] Indians were at one time disfranchised in all, or in part, of our country. Class by class they have been admitted to the electorate. Political motives may have played their part in some instances, but the only reason given by historians for their enfranchisement is the unassailability of the logic of these maxims of the Declaration.

Meantime, the United States opened wide its gates to men of all the nations of earth. By the combination of naturalization granted the foreigner after a five-years' residence by our national government and the uniform provision of the state constitutions which extends the vote to male citizens, it has been the custom in our country for three generations that any male immigrant accepted by the national government as a citizen automatically becomes a voter in any state in which he chooses to reside, subject only to the minor qualifications prescribed by the state.

Justifiable exceptions to the general principle might have been entered. Men just emerging from slavery, untrained to think or act for themselves and in most cases wholly illiterate, were not asked to qualify for voting citizenship. Not even as a measure of national caution has the vote ever been withheld from immigrants until they have learned our language, earned a certificate of fitness from our schools, or given definite evidence of loyalty to our country. When such questions have been raised, political leaders have replied: "What! Tax men and in return give them no vote; compel men to obey the authority of a government to which they may not give consent! Never. That is un-American." So it happens that men of all nations and all races, except the Mongolian, may secure citizenship and automatically become voters in any state in the Union, and even the Mongolian born in this country is a citizen and has the vote.

With such a history behind it, how can our nation escape the logic it has never failed to follow

---

1. Date on which the voters of New York approved a state referendum on woman suffrage.

2. Closely paraphrased from the Declaration of Independence (1776).

3. Closely paraphrased from Lincoln's Gettysburg Address, November 19, 1863.

4. Closely paraphrased from Wilson's War Message of April 2, 1917 (pages 73–79).

when its last unenfranchised class calls for the vote? Behold our Uncle Sam floating the banner with one hand, "Taxation without representation is tyranny," and with the other seizing the billions of dollars paid in taxes by women to whom he refuses representation. Behold him again, welcoming the boys of twenty-one and the newly made immigrant citizen to "a voice in their own government" while he denies that fundamental right of democracy to thousands of women public school teachers from whom many of these men learn all they know of citizenship and patriotism, to women college presidents, to women who preach in our pulpits, interpret law in our courts, preside over our hospitals, write books and magazines, and serve in every uplifting moral and social enterprise.

Is there a single man who can justify such inequality of treatment, such outrageous discriminations? Not one.

Woman suffrage became an assured fact when the Declaration of Independence was written.[5] It matters not at all whether Thomas Jefferson and his compatriots thought of women when they wrote that immortal document. They conceived and voiced a principle greater than any man. "A Power not of themselves which makes for righteousness"[6] gave them the vision, and they proclaimed truisms as immutable as the multiplication table, as changeless as time. The Honorable Champ Clark[7] announced that he had been a woman suffragist ever since he "got the hang of the Declaration of Independence." So it must be with every other American. The amazing thing is that it has required so long a time for a people, most of whom know how to read, "to get the hang of it." Indeed, so inevitable does our history make woman suffrage that any citizen, political party, Congress, or legislature that now blocks its coming by so much as a single day contributes to the indefensible inconsistency which threatens to make our nation a jest among the onward-moving peoples of the world.

Two: *The suffrage for women already established in the United States makes woman suffrage for the nation inevitable.* When Elihu Root, as president of the American Society of International Law, at the eleventh annual meeting in Washington, April 26, 1917, said: "The world cannot be half democratic and half autocratic. it must be all democratic or all Prussian, there can be no compromise," he voiced a general truth. Precisely the same intuition has already taught the blindest and most hostile foe of woman suffrage that our nation cannot long continue a condition under which government in half its territory rests upon the consent of half the people and in the other half upon the consent of all the people, a condition which grants representation to the taxed in half its territory and denies it in the other half, a condition which permits women in some states to share in the election of the President, Senators, and Representatives and denies them that privilege in others. It is too obvious to require demonstration that woman suffrage, now covering half our territory, will eventually be ordained in all the nation. No one will deny it; the only question left is when and how will it be completely established.

Three: *The leadership of the United States in world democracy compels the enfranchisement of its own women.* The maxims of the Declaration were once called "fundamental principles of government." They are now called "American principles" or even "Americanisms." They have become the slogans of every movement toward political liberty the world around, of every effort to widen the suffrage for men or women in any land. Not a people, race, or class striving for freedom is there, anywhere in the world, that has not made our axioms the chief weapon of the struggle. More, all men and women the world around with farsighted vision into the verities of things know that the world tragedy of our day is not now being waged over the assassination of an archduke, nor commercial competition, nor national ambitions, nor the freedom of the seas—it is a death grapple between the forces which deny and those which uphold the truths of the Declaration of Independence.

Our "Americanisms" have become the issue of the great war![8] Every day the conviction grows

---

5. 1776.

6. Paraphrased from Matthew Arnold, *Literature and Dogma* (1873).

7. Speaker of the U.S. House of Representatives.

8. World War I, which the United States entered in April 1917.

deeper that a world humanity will emerge from the war demanding political liberty and accepting nothing less. In that new struggle there is little doubt that men and women will demand and attain political liberty together. Today they are fighting the world's battle for democracy together. Men and women are paying the frightful cost of war and bearing its sad and sickening sorrows together. Tomorrow they will share its rewards together in democracies which make no discriminations on account of sex.

These are new times and, as an earnest of its sincerity in the battle for democracy, the government of Great Britain has not only pledged votes to its disfranchised men and to its women, but the measure passed the House of Commons in June 1917 by a vote of seven to one and will be sent to the House of Lords in December with the assurances of Premier Lloyd George[9] that it will shortly become a national law.[10] The measure will apply to England, Scotland, Ireland, Wales, and all the smaller British islands.

Canada, too, has enfranchised the women of all its provinces stretching from the Pacific coast to northern New York, and the Premier[11] has predicted votes for all Canadian women before the next national election.

Russia, whose opposing forces have made a sad farce of the new liberty, is nevertheless pledged to a democracy which shall include women. It must be remembered that no people ever passed from absolute autocracy into a smoothly running democracy with [a] ready-made constitution and a full set of statutes to cover all conditions. Russia is no exception. She must have time to work out her destiny.[12]

Except those maxims of democracy put forth by our own country, it is interesting to note that the only one worthy of immortality is the slogan of the women of new Russia: "Without the participation of women, suffrage is not universal."[13]

France has pledged votes to its women as certainly as a republic can. Italian men have declared woman suffrage an imperative issue when the war is over and have asked its consideration before. The city of Prague (Bohemia) has appointed a commission to report a new municipal suffrage plan which shall include women. Even autocratic Germany has debated the question in the Imperial Reichstag.

In the words of Premier Lloyd George: "There are times in history when the world spins along its destined course so leisurely that for centuries it seems to be at a standstill. Then come awful times when it rushes along at so giddy a pace that the track of centuries is covered in a single year. These are the times in which we now live."[14]

It is true; democracy, votes for men and votes for women, making slow but certain progress in 1914, have suddenly become established facts in many lands in 1917. Already our onetime mother country has become the standard-bearer of our Americanisms, the principles she once denied, and—cynical fact—Great Britain, not the United States, is now leading the world on to the coming democracy.[15] Any man who has red American blood in his veins, any man who has gloried in our history and has rejoiced that our land was the leader of world democracy, will share with us the humbled national pride that our country has so long delayed action upon this question that another country has beaten us in what we thought was our especial world mission.

Is it not clear that American history makes woman suffrage inevitable? That full suffrage in

9. David Lloyd George, British Prime Minister.

10. The measure passed by the House of Commons extended the franchise to some, but not all, women over the age of 30. The House of Lords concurred in January 1918, and the bill became law on February 6. It would be another 10 years, however, until British women were allowed to vote on the same terms as men.

11. Canadian Prime Minister Robert Laird Borden.

12. After more than a decade of turmoil, Czar Nicholas II abdicated his throne in March 1917. In November, Alexander Kerensky's provisional government was overthrown by the Bolsheviks under the leadership of Vladimir Ilyich Lenin.

13. From a speech by Poliksena Shishkina-Yavein, delivered in St. Petersburg, March 20, 1917, at a mass demonstration of the Russian League for Women's Equality.

14. Paraphrased from Lloyd George's speech of April 12, 1917, to the American Club in London.

15. The pamphlet version of Catt's speech includes a lengthy footnote here on suffrage legislation in other countries; we have not printed the footnote because it was not part of Catt's address as delivered.

twelve states[16] makes its coming in all forty-eight states inevitable? That the spread of democracy over the world, including votes for the women of many countries, in each case based upon the principles our republic gave to the world, compels action by our nation? Is it not clear that the world expects such action and fails to understand its delay?

In the face of these facts, we ask you, Senators and members of the House of Representatives of the United States, is not the immediate enfranchisement of the women of our nation the duty of the hour? Why hesitate? Not an inch of solid ground is left for the feet of the opponent. The world's war has killed, buried, and pronounced the obsequies upon the hard-worked "war argument."[17] Mr. Asquith,[18] erstwhile champion antisuffragist of the world, has said so,[19] and the British Parliament has confirmed it by its enfranchisement of British women.[20] The million and fifteen thousand women of New York who signed a declaration that they wanted the vote,[21] plus the heavy vote of women in every state and country where women have the franchise, have finally and completely disposed of the familiar "they don't want it" argument. Thousands of women annually emerging from the schools and colleges have closed the debate upon the onetime serious "they don't know enough" argument. The statistics of police courts and prisons have laid the ghost of the "too bad to vote" argument.[22] The woman who demanded the book and

verse in the Bible which gave men the vote, declaring that the next verse gave it to women, brought the "Bible argument" to a sudden end.[23] The testimony of thousands of reputable citizens of our own suffrage states and of all other suffrage lands that woman suffrage has brought no harm and much positive good, and the absence of reputable citizens who deny these facts, has closed the "women only double the vote" argument. The increasing number of women wage-earners, many supporting families and some supporting husbands, has thrown out the "women are represented" argument.

One by one these pet misgivings have been relegated to the scrap heap of all rejected, cast-off prejudices. Not an argument is left. The case against woman suffrage, carefully prepared by the combined wit, skill, and wisdom of opponents, including some men of high repute, during sixty years has been closed. The jury of the New York electorate heard it all, weighed the evidence, and pronounced it "incompetent, irrelevant, and immaterial."[24] Historians tell us that the Battle of Gettysburg[25] brought our Civil War to an end, although the fighting went on a year longer because the people who directed it did not see that the end had come. Had their sight been clearer, a year's casualties of human life, desolated homes, high taxes, and bitterness of spirit might have been avoided. The battle of New York is the Gettysburg of the woman suffrage movement.

There are those too blind to see that the end has come, and others, unrelenting and unreasoning, who stubbornly deny that the end has come although they know it. These can compel the women of the nation to keep a standing suffrage army, to finance it, to fight on until these blind and stubborn ones are gathered to their fathers and men with clearer vision come to take their places, but the casualties will be sex antagonism, party antagonism, bitterness, resentment, contempt,

16. Arizona, California, Colorado, Idaho, Kansas, Montana, Nevada, New York, Oregon, Utah, Washington, Wyoming.

17. A reference to the antisuffrage argument that women should not be allowed to vote because they did not fight for their country in times of war.

18. Herbert Henry Asquith, British Prime Minister, 1908–1916.

19. Most notably in his speech to the House of Commons, August 14, 1916.

20. See note 10 above.

21. Signatures were gathered during the 1917 suffrage campaign and were publicized as the centerpiece of a massive parade in New York City on October 27.

22. Catt is referring to the claim that if suffrage were granted, "good" women would not vote, while "bad" women would, thereby reducing the quality of the electorate.

23. The Bible does not refer explicitly to the issue of suffrage, but over the years many speakers and writers refuted scriptural arguments for excluding women from the public sphere.

24. Catt is referring to passage of the New York suffrage referendum the previous month.

25. Fought in and around Gettysburg, Pennsylvania, July 1–3, 1863.

hate, and the things which grow out of a rankling grievance autocratically denied redress. These things are not mentioned in the spirit of threat, but merely to voice well-known principles of historical psychology.

Benjamin Franklin once said, "The cost of war is not paid at the time, the bills come afterwards."[26] So too the nation, refusing justice when justice is due, finds the costs accumulating and the bills presented at unexpected and embarrassing times. Think it over.

If enfranchisement is to be given to women now, how is [it] to be done? Shall it be by amendment of state constitutions or by amendment of the federal Constitution? There are no other ways. The first sends the question from the legislature by referendum to all male voters of the state; the other sends the question from Congress to the legislatures of the several states.

We elect the federal method. There are three reasons why we make this choice and three reasons why we reject the state method. We choose the federal method, one, because it is the quickest process and justice demands immediate action. If passed by the Sixty-fifth Congress, as it should be, the amendment will go to forty-one legislatures in 1919,[27] and when thirty-six have ratified, it will become a national law.[28] In 1869 Wyoming led the way,[29] and 1919 will round out half a century of the most self-sacrificing struggle any class ever made for the vote. It is enough. The British women's suffrage army will be mustered out at the end of their half century of similar endeavor. Surely men of the land of George Washington will not require a longer time than those of the land of George III[30] to discover that taxation without representation is tyranny no matter whether

it be men or women who are taxed! We may justly expect American men to be as willing to grant to the women of the United States as generous consideration as those of Great Britain have done.

Two: Every other country dignifies woman suffrage as a national question. Even Canada and Australia, composed of self-governing states like our own, so regard it. Were the precedent not established, our own national government has taken a step which makes the treatment of woman suffrage as a national question imperative. For the first time in our history, Congress has imposed a direct tax upon women[31] and has thus deliberately violated the most fundamental and sacred principle of our government, since it offers no compensating "representation" for the tax it imposes. Unless reparation is made, it becomes the same kind of tyrant as was George III.

When the exemption for unmarried persons under the income tax was reduced to $1,000, the Congress laid the tax upon thousands of wage-earning women—teachers, doctors, lawyers, bookkeepers, secretaries, and the proprietors of many businesses.[32] Such women are earning their incomes under hard conditions of economic inequalities largely due to their disfranchisement. Many of these, while fighting their own economic battle, have been contributors to the campaign for suffrage that they might bring easier conditions for all women. Now those contributions will be deflected from suffrage treasuries into government funds through taxation. Women realize the dire need of huge government resources at this time and will make no protest against the tax, but it must be understood, and understood clearly, that the protest is there just the same and that women income tax payers with few exceptions harbor a genuine grievance against the government of the United States.

26. Although often attributed to Franklin, this statement does not appear in his known writings.

27. At the time of Catt's speech, only six of the 48 state legislatures met annually. As it turned out, 43 would convene in 1919.

28. Regardless of the number of legislatures meeting in a given year, ratification by three-fourths of all 48 states was required for adoption of a constitutional amendment.

29. In 1869 the Wyoming Territorial Legislature approved a measure granting the vote to all women age 21 and above.

30. King of Great Britain at the time of the American Revolution.

31. Catt is referring to the Sixteenth Amendment to the U.S. Constitution, adopted in 1913, which allowed for a federal income tax.

32. Driven by wartime revenue needs, the annual exemption for unmarried persons was reduced in 1917 from $3,000 to $1,000, thereby increasing by $2,000 the amount of income subject to taxation. At the same time, the exemption for married persons was reduced from $4,000 to $2,000.

The national government is guilty of the violation of the principle that the tax and the vote are inseparable; it alone can make amends. Two ways are open: Exempt the women from the income tax or grant them the vote—there can be no compromise. To shift responsibility from Congress to the states is to invite the scorn of every human being who has learned to reason. A Congress which creates the law and has the power to violate a world-acknowledged axiom of just government can also command the law and the power to make reparation to those it has wronged by the violation. To you, the Congress of the United States, we must and do look for this act of primary justice.

Three: If the entire forty-eight states should severally enfranchise women, their political status would still be inferior to that of men, since no provision for national protection in their right to vote would exist. The women of California or New York are not wholly enfranchised, for the national government has not denied the states the right to deprive them of the vote. This protection can come only by federal action.[33] Therefore, since women will eventually be forced to demand congressional action in order to equalize the rights of men and women, why not take such action now and thus shorten and ease the process?

When such submission is secured, as it will be, forty-eight simultaneous state ratification campaigns will be necessary. By the state method, thirty-six states would be obliged to have individual campaigns, and those would still have to be followed by the forty-eight additional campaigns to secure the final protection in their right to vote by the national government. We propose to conserve money, time, and woman's strength by the elimination of the thirty-six state campaigns as unnecessary at this stage of the progress of the woman suffrage movement.

The three reasons why we object to the state amendment process are, one, the constitutions of many states contain such difficult provisions for amending that it is practically impossible to carry an amendment at the polls. Several states require a majority of all the votes cast at an election to ensure the passage of an amendment. As the number of persons voting on amendments is usually considerably smaller than the number voting for the head of the ticket, the effect of such provision is that a majority of those men who do not vote at all on the amendment are counted as voting against it.

For example, imagine a state casting 100,000 votes for Governor and 80,000 on a woman suffrage amendment. That proportion would be a usual one. Now suppose there were 45,000 votes in favor and 35,000 against woman suffrage. The amendment would have been carried by [a] 10,000 majority in a state which requires only a majority of the votes cast on the amendment, as in the state of New York. If, however, the state requires a majority of the votes cast at the election, the amendment would be lost by [a] 10,000 majority. The men who were either too ignorant, too indifferent, or too careless to vote on the question would have defeated it. Such constitutions have rarely been amended and then only on some noncontroversial question which the dominant powers have agreed to support with the full strength of their "machines."[34]

New Mexico, for example, requires three-fourths of those voting at an election, including two-thirds from each county. New Mexico is surrounded by suffrage states, but the women who live there probably can secure enfranchisement only by federal action. The Indiana constitution provides that a majority of all voters is necessary to carry an amendment; thus the courts may decide that registered voters who did not go to the polls at all may be counted in the number a majority of whom it is necessary to secure. The constitution cannot be amended. The courts have declared that the constitution prohibits the legislature from granting suffrage to women. What then can the women of Indiana do? They have no other hope than the federal amendment.

Several state constitutions stipulate that a definite period of time must elapse before an amendment

33. Catt is referring to the fact that the federal government controlled suffrage in the states through the Fifteenth Amendment to the Constitution. Her argument is that only an amendment explicitly granting the vote to women would provide an airtight guarantee of suffrage.

34. A reference to political organizations marked by corruption, domination of local politics, and control of voter behavior.

defeated at the polls can again be submitted. New York has no such provision and the second campaign of 1917 immediately followed the first in 1915; but Pennsylvania and New Jersey, both voting on the question in 1915, cannot vote on it again before 1920. New Hampshire has no provision for the submission of an amendment by the legislature at all. A constitutional convention alone has the right to submit an amendment, and such conventions cannot be called oftener than once in seven years. The constitutional complications in many of the states are numerous, varied, and difficult to overcome.

All careful investigators must arrive at the same conclusion that the only hope for the enfranchisement of the women of several states is through congressional action. Since this is true, we hold it unnecessary to force women to pass through any more referenda campaigns. The hazards of the state constitutional provisions which women are expected to overcome in order to get the vote, as compared with the easy process by which the vote is fairly thrust upon foreigners who choose to make their residence among us, is so offensive an outrage to one's sense of justice that a woman's rebellion would surely have been fomented long ago had women not known that the discrimination visited upon them was without deliberate intent. The continuation of this condition is, however, the direct responsibility now of every man who occupies a position authorized to right the wrong. You are such men, Honorable Senators and Representatives. To you we appeal to remove a grievance more insulting than any nation in the wide world has put upon its women.

Two: The second reason why we object to the state process is far more serious and important than the first. It is because the statutory laws governing elections are so inadequate and defective as to vouchsafe little or no protection to a referendum in most states. The need for such protection seems to have been universally overlooked by the lawmakers. Bipartisan election boards offer efficient machinery whereby the representatives of one political party may check any irregularities of the other. The interests of all political parties in an election are further protected by partisan watchers. None of these provisions is available to those interested in a referendum.

In most states women may not serve as watchers, and no political party assumes responsibility for a nonpartisan question. In the state of New York women may serve as watchers. They did so serve in 1915 and in 1917; nearly every one in the more than 5,000 polling places was covered by efficiently trained women watchers. The women believe that this fact had much to do with the favorable result.

In twenty-four states there is no law providing for a recount on a referendum. Voters may be bribed, colonized, repeated and the law provides for no possible redress. In some states corrupt voters may be arrested, tried, and punished, but that does not remove their votes from the total vote cast nor in any way change the results. When questions which are supported by men's organizations go to referendum, such as Prohibition, men interested may secure posts as election officials or party watchers and thus be in position to guard the purity of the election. This privilege is not open to women.

That corrupt influences have exerted their full power against woman suffrage, we know well. I have myself seen blocks of men marched to the polling booth and paid money in plain sight, both men and bribers flaunting the fact boldly that they were "beating the _____ women." I have myself seen men who could not speak a word of English, nor write their names in any language, driven to the polls like sheep to vote against woman suffrage, and no law at the time could punish them for the misuse of the vote so cheaply extended to them, nor change the result.

It is our sincere belief based upon evidence which has been completely convincing to us that woman suffrage amendments in several states have been won on referendum, but that the returns were juggled and the amendment counted out. We have given to such campaigns our money, our time, our strength, our very lives. We have believed the amendment carried and yet have seen our cause announced as lost. We are tired of playing the state campaign game with "the political dice loaded and the cards stacked"[35] against us before we

35. From L. F. C. Garvin, "The State Boss and How He May Be Dethroned," *Century Illustrated Monthly Magazine* (June 1903).

begin. The position of such an amendment is precisely like that of the defendant in a case brought before an inexperienced judge. After having heard the plaintiff, he untactfully remarked that he would listen to the defendant's remarks, but he was bound to tell him in advance that he proposed to give the verdict to the plaintiff. From this lower court, often unscrupulous in its unfairness, we appeal to the higher—the Congress and the legislatures of the United States.

Three: The third reason why we object to the state method is even more weighty than either or both of the others. It is because the state method fixes responsibility upon no one. The legislatures pass the question on to the voters and have no further interest in it. The political parties, not knowing how the election may decide the matter, are loath to espouse the cause of woman suffrage, lest if it loses they will have alienated from their respective parties the support of enemies of woman suffrage.

Contributors to campaign funds have at times stipulated the return service of the party machinery to defeat woman suffrage, and as such contributors are wily enough to make certain of their protection, they contribute to both dominant parties. Thousands of men in every state have become so accustomed to accept party nominations and platforms as their unquestioned guide that they refuse to act upon a political question without instruction from their leaders. When the leaders pass the word along the line to defeat a woman suffrage amendment, it is impossible to carry it. It is not submitted to an electorate of thinking voters whose reason must be convinced, but to such voters, plus political "machines" skillfully organized, servilely obedient, who have their plans laid to defeat the question at the polls even before it leaves the legislature.

From a condition where no one is responsible for the procedure of the amendment through the hazards of an election, where every enemy may effectively hide his enmity and the methods employed behind the barriers of constitutions and election laws, we appeal to a method which will bring our cause into the open where every person or party, friend or foe, involved in the campaign may be held responsible to the public. We appeal from the method which has kept the women of this country disfranchised a quarter of a century after their enfranchisement was due to the method by which the vote has been granted to the men and women of other lands. We do so with the certain assurance that every believer in fair play, regardless of party fealties, will approve our decision.

These are the three reasons why we elect the federal method and the three reasons why we reject the state method. We are so familiar with the objections congressional opponents urge against suffrage by the federal method that we know those objections also, curiously, number three.

Objection number one: *Wartime is not the proper time to consider this question.* Two neutral countries, Iceland and Denmark, and three belligerent countries, Canada, Russia and Great Britain, have enfranchised their women during wartime,[36] and they have been engaged in war for three and a half years. That which is a proper time for such countries is surely proper enough for us.

More, it is not our fault, you will admit, that this question is still unsettled in 1917. If our urgent advice had been taken, it would have been disposed of twenty-five years ago[37] and our nation would now be proudly leading the world to democracy instead of following in third place. Had Congress "got the hang of the Declaration of Independence" then, more men today would know the definition of democracy than do, and more men would understand what a world's war "to make the world safe for democracy"[38] means.

---

36. Denmark established full suffrage for women in 1915. Iceland approved conditional suffrage the same year, as did Canada and Great Britain in 1917–1918. After the fall of Czar Nicholas II in 1917, the Russian provisional government granted universal suffrage with equality for women.

37. Catt is referring to presentations of the National American Woman Suffrage Association in January 1892 before the House Judiciary Committee and the Senate Committee on Woman Suffrage in support of a constitutional amendment giving women the right to vote in all federal elections. The former committee took no action; the latter reported favorably by a vote of 3–2, but the amendment went no further in the Senate.

38. Paraphrased from President Wilson's War Message of April 2, 1917 (pages 73–79).

In 1866 an address to Congress was adopted by a suffrage convention held in New York and presented to Congress later by Susan B. Anthony and Elizabeth Cady Stanton.[39] They protested against the enfranchisement of Negro men while women remained disfranchised, and asked for congressional action.[40] That was fifty-one years ago. In 1878 the federal suffrage amendment now pending was introduced in Congress[41] at the request of the National Woman Suffrage Association[42] and has been reintroduced in each succeeding Congress.

The representatives of this association have appeared before the committees of every Congress since 1878 to urge its passage. The women who made the first appeal, brave, splendid souls, have long since passed into the Beyond, and every one died knowing that the country she loved and served classified her as a political pariah. Every Congress has seen the committee rooms packed with anxious women yearning for the declaration of their nation that they were no longer to be classed with idiots, criminals, and paupers. Every state has sent its quota of women to those committees. Among them have been the daughters of Presidents, Governors, Chief Justices, Speakers of the House, leaders of political parties, and leaders of great movements. List the women of the last century whose names will pass into history among the immortals and scarcely one is there who has not appeared before your committees—Susan B. Anthony, Elizabeth Cady Stanton, Lucy Stone, Mary A. Livermore, Lillie Devereux Blake, Julia Ward Howe, Harriet Beecher Stowe, Frances Willard, Clara

Barton,[43] and hundreds more. There are hundreds of women in the suffrage convention now sitting who have paid out more money in railroad fare to come to Washington in order to persuade men that "women are people" than all the men in the entire country ever paid to get a vote.

Perhaps you think our pleas in those committee rooms were poor attempts at logic. Ah, one chairman of the committee long ago said to a fellow member, "There is no man living or dead who could answer the arguments of those women," and then he added, "but I'd rather see my wife dead in her coffin than going to vote." Yet there are those of you who have said that women are illogical and sentimental! Since Congress has already had fifty-one years of peace in which to deal with the question of woman suffrage, we hold that a further postponement is unwarranted.

Objection number two: *A vote on this question by Congress and the legislatures is undemocratic; it should go to the "people" of the states.* You are wrong, gentlemen, as your reason will quickly tell you if you will reflect a moment. When a state submits a constitutional amendment to male voters, it does a legal, constitutional thing, but when that amendment chiefly concerns one-half the people of the state and the law permits the other half to settle it, the wildest stretch of the imagination could not describe the process as democratic. Democracy means "the rule of the people," and, let me repeat, women are people. No state referendum goes to the people; it goes to the male voters. Such referenda can never be democratic. Were the question of woman suffrage to be submitted to a vote of both sexes, the action would be democratic, but in that case it would not be legal nor constitutional.

Male voters have never been named by any constitution or statute as the representatives of women;

39. Preeminent American suffrage leaders of the 19th century.

40. "Address to Congress. Adopted by the Eleventh National Woman's Rights Convention, held in New York City, Thursday, May 10, 1866." The address was distributed to Congress in written form.

41. The amendment was introduced by Senator Aaron Augustus Sargent of California.

42. Organization founded in 1869 by Susan B. Anthony and Elizabeth Cady Stanton. In 1890 it merged with the American Woman Suffrage Association to form the National American Woman Suffrage Association.

43. In addition to being supporters of woman suffrage, all these figures were accomplished in other areas. Several, including Stanton, Anthony, and Livermore, were lyceum lecturers; Blake was a novelist; Howe wrote "The Battle Hymn of the Republic"; Beecher penned *Uncle Tom's Cabin*; Willard served as president of the Woman's Christian Temperance Union; Barton was instrumental in founding the American Red Cross.

we therefore decline to accept them in that capacity. The nearest approach to representation allowed voteless women are the members of Congress and the legislatures. These members are apportioned among the several states upon the basis of population and not upon the basis of numbers of voters.[44] Therefore every Congressman theoretically represents the women of his constituency as well as the male voters. He is theoretically responsible to them, and they may properly go to him for redress of such grievances as fall within his jurisdiction. More, every member of Congress not only represents the small constituency confined to his district but all the people of the country, since his vote upon national questions affects them all. Women, whether voters or nonvoters, may properly claim members of Congress as the only substitution for representation provided by the Constitution. We apply to you, therefore, to correct a grievous wrong which your constitutional jurisdiction gives you authority to set right.

Objection number three: *States' rights.* You pronounce it unfair that thirty-six states should determine who may vote in the remaining twelve; that possible Republican Northern states should decide who may vote in Democratic Southern states. It is no more unfair than that some counties within a state should decide who may vote in the remaining counties, no more unfair than that the Democratic city of New York should enfranchise the women of the Republican cities of Albany and Rochester, as it has just done.[45]

Forty-eight states will have the opportunity to ratify the federal amendment, and every state, therefore, will have its opportunity to enfranchise its own women in this manner. If any state fails to do it, we may agree that that state would probably not enfranchise its own women by the state method; but if it would not so enfranchise them, that state is behind the times and is holding our country up to the scorn of the nations. It has failed to catch the vision and the spirit of democracy sweeping over the world. This nation cannot, must not, wait for any state so ignorant, so backward. That state, more than all others, needs woman suffrage to shake its dry bones, to bring political questions into the home and set discussion going. It needs education, action, stimulation to prevent atrophy. In after years, posterity will utter grateful thanks that there was a method which could throw a bit of modernity into it from the outside.

It is urged that the women of some such states do not want the vote. Of course, if the thought of an entire state is antiquated, its women will share the general stagnation, but there is no state where there is not a large number of women who are working, and working hard, for the vote. The vote is permissive, a liberty extended. It is never a burden laid upon the individual, since there is no obligation to exercise the right. On the other hand, the refusal to permit those who want the vote to have and to use it is oppression, tyranny—and no other words describe the condition. When, therefore, men within a state are so ungenerous or unprogressive or stubborn as to continue the denial of the vote to the women who want it, men on the outside should have no scruples in constituting themselves the liberators of those women.

Despite these truths there are among you those who still harbor honest misgivings. Please remember that woman suffrage is coming; you know it is. In this connection, have you ever thought that the women of your own families who may tell you now that they do not want the vote are going to realize someday that there is something insincere in your protestations of chivalry, protection, and "you are too good to vote, my dear," and are going to discover that the trust, respect, and frank acknowledgment of equality which men of other states have given their women are something infinitely higher and nobler than you have ever offered them?

Have you thought that you may now bestow upon them a liberty that they may not yet realize they need but that tomorrow they may storm your castle and demand? Do you suppose that any woman in the land is going to be content with unenfranchisement when she once comprehends that men of other countries have given women the vote? Do you not

44. Catt is referring to the U.S. Constitution, Article I, Section 2, and the Fourteenth Amendment, Section 2.

45. A reference to the fact that the 1917 New York suffrage amendment was approved because it gained a majority of more than 100,000 votes in New York City, even though it did not secure a majority in the rest of the state.

see that when that time comes to her, she is going to ask why you—her husband, her father—who were so placed, perhaps, that you could observe the progress of world affairs, did not see the coming change of custom and save her from the humiliation of having to beg for that which women in other countries are already enjoying?

Have you known that no more potent influence has aroused the sheltered and consequently narrow-visioned woman into a realization that she wanted to be a part of an enfranchised class than the manner in which men treat enfranchised women? There is no patronizing "I am holier than thou" air, but the equality of "fellow citizens." One never sees that relation between men and women except where women vote. Someday that woman who doesn't know the world is moving on and leaving her behind will see and know these things. What will she say and do then? What will you do for her now?

There are many well-known men in Great Britain who frankly confess that their desire to give British women the vote is founded upon their sense of gratitude for the loyal and remarkable war service women have performed. They speak of suffrage as a reward. For years women have asked the vote as a recognition of the incontrovertible fact that they are responsible, intelligent citizens of the country and because its denial has been an outrageous discrimination against their sex. British women will receive their enfranchisement with joyous appreciation, but the joy will be lessened and the appreciation tempered by the perfect understanding that "vote as a reward" is only an escape from the uncomfortable corner into which the unanswerable logic of the women had driven the government. Mutual respect between those who give and those who receive the vote would have been promoted had the inevitable duty not been deferred. We hope American men will be wiser.

Many of you have admitted that "states' rights" is less a principle than a tradition—a tradition, however, which we all know is rooted deep in the memory of bitter and, let us say, regrettable incidents of history.[46]

But the past is gone. We are living in the present and facing the future. Other men of other lands have thrown aside traditions as tenderly revered as yours in response to the higher call of justice, progress, and democracy. Can you, too, not rise to this same call of duty? Is any good to be served by continuing one injustice in order to resent another injustice? We are one nation, and those of us who live now and make our appeal to you are, like yourselves, not of the generation whose differences created the conditions which entrenched the tradition of states' rights. We ask you, our representatives, to right the wrong done us by the law of our land as the men of other lands have done.

Our nation is in the extreme crisis of its existence and men should search their very souls to find just and reasonable causes for every thought and act. If you, making this search, shall find "states' rights" a sufficient cause to lead you to vote "No" on the federal suffrage amendment, then, with all the gentleness which should accompany the reference to a sacred memory, let us tell you that your cause will bear neither the test of time nor critical analysis and that your vote will compel your children to apologize for your act.

Already your vote has forwarded some of the measures which are far more distinctly states' rights questions than the fundamental demand for equal human rights. Among such questions are the regulation of child labor, the eight-hour law, the white slave traffic, moving pictures, questionable literature, food supply, clothing supply, Prohibition.[47] All of these acts are in the direction of the restraint of "personal liberty" in the supposed interest of the public good. Every instinct of justice, every principle of logic and ethics, is shocked at the reasoning which grants Congress the right to curtail personal liberty but no

---

46. Catt is referring to the American Civil War, 1861–1865, in which the Confederacy cited states' rights as justification for secession.

47. Catt is referring to such measures as the Keating-Owen Child Labor Act of 1916; the 1916 Adamson Act establishing an eight-hour workday for railroad workers; the 1910 White Slave Traffic Act prohibiting the transportation of women across state lines "for the purpose of prostitution or debauchery"; the Comstock Act of 1873 making it illegal to send "obscene, lewd, or lascivious" materials through the mail; the Pure Food and Drug Act and the Meat Inspection Act of 1906; and the 1913 Webb-Kenyon Act regulating the interstate shipment of alcoholic beverages.

right to extend it. "Necessity knows no law"[48] may seem to you sufficient authority to tax the incomes of women, to demand exhausting amounts of volunteer military service, to commandeer women for public work, and in other ways to restrain their liberty as war measures. But by the same token the grant of more liberty may properly be conferred as a war measure.

If other lands have been brave enough to extend suffrage to women in wartime, our own country, the mother of democracy, surely will not hesitate. We are told that a million or more American men will be on European battlefields ere many months. For every man who goes, there is one loyal woman and probably more who would vote to support to the utmost that man's cause. The disloyal men will be here to vote. Suffrage for women now as a war measure means suffrage for the loyal forces, for those who know what it means to fight "to keep the world safe for democracy."

The framers of the Constitution gave unquestioned authority to Congress to act upon woman suffrage. Why not use that authority and use it now to do the big, noble, just thing of catching pace with other nations on this question of democracy? The world and posterity will honor you for it.

In conclusion, we know, and you know that we know, that it has been the aim of both dominant parties to postpone woman suffrage as long as possible. A few men in each party have always fought with us fearlessly, but the party machines have evaded, avoided, tricked, and buffeted this question from Congress to legislatures, from legislatures to political conventions. I confess to you that many of us have a deep and abiding distrust of all existing political parties—they have tricked us so often and in such unscrupulous fashion that our doubts are natural. Some of you are leaders of those parties and all are members. Your parties, we also know, have a distrust and suspicion of new women voters. Let us counsel together. Woman suffrage is inevitable—you know it. The political parties will go on—we know it. Shall we then be enemies or friends? Can party leaders in twelve states really obtain the loyal support of women voters when those women know that the same party

is ordering the defeat of amendments in states where campaigns are pending, or delaying action in Congress on the federal amendment?

Gentlemen, we ask you to put yourselves in our places. What would you do? Would you keep on spending your money and your lives on a slow, laborious, clumsy state method, or would you use the votes you have won to complete your campaign on behalf of suffrage for all women in the nation? Would you be content to keep a standing army of women, told off for the special work of educating men in the meaning of democracy; would you raise and spend millions of dollars in the process; would you give up every other thing in life you hold dear in order to keep state campaigns going for another possible quarter of a century? Would you do this and see the women of other countries leaving you behind, or would you make "a hard pull, a long pull, and a pull all together"[49] and finish the task at once? You know you would choose the latter. We make the same choice.

Do you realize that in no other country in the world with democratic tendencies is suffrage so completely denied as in a considerable number of our own states? There are thirteen black states[50] where no suffrage for women exists, and fourteen others where suffrage for women is more limited than in many foreign countries.

Do you realize that no class of men in our own or in any other land have been compelled to ask their inferiors for the ballot?

Do you realize that when you ask women to take their cause to state referendum, you compel them to do this: that you drive women of education, refinement, achievement to beg men who cannot read for their political freedom?

Do you realize that such anomalies as a college president asking her janitor to give her a vote are overstraining the patience and driving women to desperation?

Do you realize that women in increasing numbers indignantly resent the long delay in their enfranchisement?

Your party platforms have pledged woman suffrage. Then why not be honest, frank friends of our

---

48. From the statement attributed to Publilius Syrus (1st century BCE): "Necessity knows no law except to prevail."

49. A phrase often used in the 19th century to convey the need for steady, energetic, and systematic cooperation, most often in connection with rowing a boat or pulling a rope.

50. Catt is referring to the states of the Deep South.

cause, adopt it in reality as your own, make it a party program, and "fight with us"?[51] As a party measure—a measure of all parties—why not put the amendment through Congress and the legislatures? We shall all be better friends, we shall have a happier nation, we women will be free to support loyally the party of our choice, and we shall be far prouder of our history.

"There is one thing mightier than kings and armies"—aye, than congresses and political parties—"the power of an idea when its time has come to move."[52] The time for woman suffrage has come. The woman's hour has struck.[53] If parties prefer to postpone action longer and thus do battle with this idea, they challenge the inevitable. The idea will not perish; the party which opposes it may. Every delay, every trick, every political dishonesty from now on will antagonize the women of the land more and more, and when the party or parties which have so delayed woman suffrage finally let it come, their sincerity will be doubted and their appeal to the new voters will be met with suspicion. This is the psychology of the situation. Can you afford the risk? Think it over.

We know you will meet opposition. There are a few "woman haters" left, a few "old males of the tribe," as Vance Thompson[54] calls them, whose duty they believe it to be to keep women in the places they have carefully picked out for them. Treitschke, made world famous by war literature, said some years ago: "Germany, which knows all about Germany and France, knows far better what is good for Alsace-Lorraine than that miserable people can possibly know."[55] A few American Treitschkes we have who know better than women what is good for them. There are women, too, with "slave souls" and "clinging vines" for backbones. There are female dolls and male dandies. But the world does not wait for such as these; nor does Liberty pause to heed the plaint of men and women with a grouch. She does not wait for those who have a special interest to serve, nor a selfish reason for depriving other people of freedom. Holding her torch aloft, Liberty is pointing the way onward and upward and saying to America, "Come."

To you, the supporters of our cause in Senate and House, and the number is large, the suffragists of the nation express their grateful thanks. This address is not meant for you. We are more truly appreciative of all you have done than any words can express. We ask you to make a last, hard fight for the amendment during the present session. Since last we asked a vote on this amendment, your position has been fortified by the addition to suffrage territory of Great Britain, Canada, and New York.

Some of you have been too indifferent to give more than casual attention to this question. It is worthy of your immediate consideration—a question big enough to engage the attention of our allies in wartime is too big a question for you to neglect.

Some of you have grown old in party service. Are you willing that those who take your places by and by shall blame you for having failed to keep pace with the world and thus having lost for them a party advantage? Is there any real gain for you, for your party, for the nation by delay? Do you want to drive the progressive men and women out of your party?

Some of you hold to the doctrine of states' rights as applying to woman suffrage. Adherence to that theory will keep the United States far behind all other democratic nations in action upon this question. A theory which prevents a nation from keeping up with the trend of world progress cannot be justified.

Gentlemen, we hereby petition you, our only designated representatives, to redress our grievances by the immediate passage of the federal suffrage amendment and to use your influence to secure its ratification in your own state in order that the women of our nation may be endowed with political freedom before the next presidential election and that our nation may resume its world leadership in democracy.

Woman suffrage is coming—you know it. Will you, Honorable Senators and members of the House of Representatives, help or hinder it?

51. An echo of British suffragist Christabel Pankhurst's words of April 1909 imploring delegates to the International Suffrage Congress, held in London, to "take courage, join hands, stand beside us, fight with us."

52. Paraphrased from Victor Hugo, *Histoire d'un crime* (1877–1878).

53. Catt is echoing a thematic phrase from "The Crisis," her speech of September 7, 1916 (pages 57–73).

54. American author; the quotation is from his *Woman* (1917).

55. From Heinrich von Treitschke, "Was fordern wir von Frankreich?" (1870). Catt is most likely paraphrasing from H. W. C. Davis, *The Political Thought of Heinrich von Treitschke* (1915).

Woodrow Wilson

The Fourteen Points

WASHINGTON, D.C.
JANUARY 8, 1918

WOODROW WILSON HAD been concerned about the shape of the postwar world long before the United States entered World War I. He raised the subject as early as 1915, and he redoubled his efforts after America joined the conflict in April 1917. But he was not alone in this arena. On August 1, 1917, Pope Benedict XV published his peace plan. In November the new Bolshevik government in Russia set forth its formula for peace. On January 5, 1918, British Prime Minister David Lloyd George detailed his country's war aims and peace conditions. To Wilson's consternation, Lloyd George advanced a series of measures strikingly similar to those the President was developing for his scheduled speech to Congress three days later.

When Wilson rose to address Congress, he sought not only to provide a set of principles that would guide the world toward a just and lasting peace, but to give those principles primacy on the international stage. After reviewing the stalled efforts toward peace, he announced a set of fourteen points that began by calling for "open covenants of peace, openly arrived at," and ended by proposing an international assembly of nations that would guarantee "political independence and territorial integrity to great and small states alike." Wilson did not demand reparations from the Central Powers, but otherwise there were few substantive differences between his proposals and Lloyd George's. Yet Wilson gave his Fourteen Points a sense of unity by the simple rhetorical device of enumeration. This, in combination with his lofty tone of principled idealism and moral conviction, gave them broad appeal. Franklin Roosevelt would use a similar approach with his Four Freedoms in World War II (see pages 263–268).

The Fourteen Points also became a propaganda weapon. Millions of copies were dropped behind enemy lines, where they captured the popular imagination and helped undermine German morale during the final months of war. As Wilson would discover, however, translating the Fourteen Points into reality during the treaty negotiations at Versailles proved a difficult matter. French Premier Georges Clemenceau was reported to say, "God gave us his Ten Commandments, and we broke them. Wilson gave us his Fourteen Points—and we shall see."

Gentlemen of the Congress: Once more, as repeatedly before, the spokesmen of the Central Empires[1] have indicated their desire to discuss the objects of the war and the possible bases of a general peace. Parleys have been in progress at Brest-Litovsk[2] between representatives of the Central Powers, to which the attention of all the belligerents has been invited for the purpose of ascertaining whether it may be possible to extend these parleys into a general conference with regard to terms of peace and settlement.[3] The Russian representatives presented not only a perfectly definite statement of the principles upon which they would be willing to conclude peace, but also an equally definite program of the concrete application of those principles. The representatives of the Central Powers, on their part, presented an outline of settlement which, if much less definite, seemed susceptible of liberal interpretation until their specific program of practical terms was added.

That program proposed no concessions at all either to the sovereignty of Russia or to the preferences of the populations with whose fortunes it dealt, but meant, in a word, that the Central Empires were to keep every foot of territory their armed forces had occupied—every province, every city, every point of vantage—as a permanent addition to their territories and their power. It is a reasonable conjecture that the general principles of settlement which they at first suggested originated with the more liberal statesmen of Germany and Austria, the men who have begun to feel the force of their own peoples' thought and purpose, while the concrete terms of actual settlement came from the military leaders who have no thought but to keep what they have got. The negotiations have been broken off. The Russian representatives were sincere and in earnest. They cannot entertain such proposals of conquest and domination.

The whole incident is full of significance. It is also full of perplexity. With whom are the Russian representatives dealing? For whom are the representatives of the Central Empires speaking? Are they speaking for the majorities of their respective parliaments or for the minority parties, that military and imperialistic minority which has so far dominated their whole policy and controlled the affairs of Turkey and of the Balkan states which have felt obliged to become their associates in this war? The Russian representatives have insisted, very justly, very wisely, and in the true spirit of modern democracy, that the conferences they have been holding with the Teutonic and Turkish statesmen should be held within open, not closed, doors, and all the world has been audience, as was desired.

To whom have we been listening, then? To those who speak the spirit and intention of the resolutions of the German Reichstag of the ninth of July last, the spirit and intention of the liberal leaders and parties of Germany, or to those who resist and defy that spirit and intention and insist upon conquest and subjugation?[4] Or are we listening, in fact, to both, unreconciled and in open and hopeless contradiction? These are very serious and pregnant questions. Upon the answer to them depends the peace of the world.

But whatever the results of the parleys at Brest-Litovsk, whatever the confusions of counsel and of purpose in the utterances of the spokesmen of the Central Empires, they have again attempted to acquaint the world with their objects in the war and have again challenged their adversaries to say what their objects are and what sort of settlement they would deem just and satisfactory. There is no good reason why that challenge should not be responded to, and responded to with the utmost candor. We did not wait for it. Not once, but again and again, we have laid our whole thought and purpose before the world, not in general terms only, but each time with sufficient definition to make it clear what sort of definitive terms of settlement must necessarily spring out

---

1. Germany, Austria-Hungary, Bulgaria, and the Ottoman Empire; also referred to as the Central Powers.

2. City near the present-day border of Poland and Belarus.

3. The negotiations at Brest-Litovsk culminated in March 1918 with a treaty of peace in which Russia surrendered Ukraine, Poland, Finland, and the Baltic provinces to the Central Powers. The treaty was later invalidated by the general armistice that ended World War I.

---

4. Wilson is referring to a split between propeace forces in the Reichstag, who called for a negotiated end to the war, and the German General Staff and Kaiser Wilhelm II, who insisted on a military victory.

of them. Within the last week Mr. Lloyd George[5] has spoken with admirable candor and in admirable spirit for the people and government of Great Britain.[6]

There is no confusion of counsel among the adversaries of the Central Powers, no uncertainty of principle, no vagueness of detail. The only secrecy of counsel, the only lack of fearless frankness, the only failure to make definite statement of the objects of the war, lies with Germany and her allies. The issues of life and death hang upon these definitions. No statesman who has the least conception of his responsibility ought for a moment to permit himself to continue this tragical and appalling outpouring of blood and treasure unless he is sure beyond a peradventure that the objects of the vital sacrifice are part and parcel of the very life of society and that the people for whom he speaks think them right and imperative as he does.

There is, moreover, a voice calling for these definitions of principle and of purpose which is, it seems to me, more thrilling and more compelling than any of the many moving voices with which the troubled air of the world is filled. It is the voice of the Russian people. They are prostrate and all but helpless, it would seem, before the grim power of Germany, which has hitherto known no relenting and no pity. Their power, apparently, is shattered. And yet their soul is not subservient. They will not yield either in principle or in action. Their conception of what is right, of what it is humane and honorable for them to accept, has been stated with a frankness, a largeness of view, a generosity of spirit, and a universal human sympathy which must challenge the admiration of every friend of mankind; and they have refused to compound their ideals or desert others that they themselves may be safe.

They call to us to say what it is that we desire, in what, if in anything, our purpose and our spirit differ from theirs; and I believe that the people of the United States would wish me to respond with utter simplicity and frankness. Whether their present leaders[7] believe it or not, it is our heartfelt desire and hope that some way may be opened whereby we may be privileged to assist the people of Russia to attain their utmost hope of liberty and ordered peace.

It will be our wish and purpose that the processes of peace, when they are begun, shall be absolutely open and that they shall involve and permit henceforth no secret understandings of any kind. The day of conquest and aggrandizement is gone by; so is also the day of secret covenants entered into in the interest of particular governments and likely at some unlooked-for moment to upset the peace of the world. It is this happy fact, now clear to the view of every public man whose thoughts do not still linger in an age that is dead and gone, which makes it possible for every nation whose purposes are consistent with justice and the peace of the world to avow now or at any other time the objects it has in view.

We entered this war because violations of right had occurred which touched us to the quick and made the life of our own people impossible unless they were corrected and the world secured once [and] for all against their recurrence. What we demand in this war, therefore, is nothing peculiar to ourselves. It is that the world be made fit and safe to live in; and particularly that it be made safe for every peace-loving nation which, like our own, wishes to live its own life, determine its own institutions, be assured of justice and fair dealing by the other peoples of the world as against force and selfish aggression. All the peoples of the world are in effect partners in this interest, and for our own part we see very clearly that unless justice be done to others it will not be done to us.

The program of the world's peace, therefore, is our program; and that program, the only possible program, as we see it, is this:

I. Open covenants of peace, openly arrived at, after which there shall be no private international understandings of any kind but diplomacy shall proceed always frankly and in the public view.

II. Absolute freedom of navigation upon the seas, outside territorial waters, alike in peace and in

---

5. British Prime Minister David Lloyd George.

6. Wilson is referring to Lloyd George's speech of January 5, 1918.

7. A reference to the Bolshevik government established in November 1917 under the leadership of Vladimir Ilyich Lenin.

war, except as the seas may be closed in whole or in part by international action for the enforcement of international covenants.

III. The removal, so far as possible, of all economic barriers and the establishment of an equality of trade conditions among all the nations consenting to the peace and associating themselves for its maintenance.

IV. Adequate guarantees given and taken that national armaments will be reduced to the lowest point consistent with domestic safety.

V. A free, open-minded, and absolutely impartial adjustment of all colonial claims, based upon a strict observance of the principle that in determining all such questions of sovereignty the interests of the populations concerned must have equal weight with the equitable claims of the government whose title is to be determined.

VI. The evacuation of all Russian territory and such a settlement of all questions affecting Russia as will secure the best and freest cooperation of the other nations of the world in obtaining for her an unhampered and unembarrassed opportunity for the independent determination of her own political development and national policy and assure her of a sincere welcome into the society of free nations under institutions of her own choosing; and, more than a welcome, assistance also of every kind that she may need and may herself desire. The treatment accorded Russia by her sister nations in the months to come will be the acid test of their good will, of their comprehension of her needs as distinguished from their own interests, and of their intelligent and unselfish sympathy.

VII. Belgium, the whole world will agree, must be evacuated and restored, without any attempt to limit the sovereignty which she enjoys in common with all other free nations. No other single act will serve as this will serve to restore confidence among the nations in the laws which they have themselves set and determined for the government of their relations with one another. Without this healing act, the whole structure and validity of international law is forever impaired.

VIII. All French territory should be freed and the invaded portions restored, and the wrong done to France by Prussia in 1871 in the matter of Alsace-Lorraine, which has unsettled the peace of the world for nearly fifty years, should be righted, in order that peace may once more be made secure in the interest of all.

IX. A readjustment of the frontiers of Italy should be effected along clearly recognizable lines of nationality.

X. The peoples of Austria-Hungary, whose place among the nations we wish to see safeguarded and assured, should be accorded the freest opportunity of autonomous development.

XI. Romania, Serbia, and Montenegro should be evacuated, occupied territories restored, Serbia accorded free and secure access to the sea, and the relations of the several Balkan states to one another determined by friendly counsel along historically established lines of allegiance and nationality; and international guarantees of the political and economic independence and territorial integrity of the several Balkan states should be entered into.

XII. The Turkish portions of the present Ottoman Empire should be assured a secure sovereignty, but the other nationalities which are now under Turkish rule should be assured an undoubted security of life and an absolutely unmolested opportunity of autonomous development, and the Dardanelles should be permanently opened as a free passage to the ships and commerce of all nations under international guarantees.

XIII. An independent Polish state should be erected which should include the territories inhabited by indisputably Polish populations, which should be assured a free and secure access to the sea and whose political and economic independence and territorial integrity should be guaranteed by international covenant.

XIV. A general association of nations must be formed under specific covenants for the purpose of affording mutual guarantees of political independence and territorial integrity to great and small states alike.

In regard to these essential rectifications of wrong and assertions of right we feel ourselves to be intimate partners of all the governments and peoples associated together against the Imperialists. We cannot be separated in interest or divided in purpose. We stand together until the end.

For such arrangements and covenants we are willing to fight and to continue to fight until they are achieved; but only because we wish the right to prevail and desire a just and stable peace such as can be secured only by removing the chief provocations to war, which this program does remove. We have no jealousy of German greatness, and there is nothing in this program that impairs it. We grudge her no achievement or distinction of learning or of pacific enterprise such as have made her record very bright and very enviable. We do not wish to injure her or to block in any way her legitimate influence or power. We do not wish to fight her either with arms or with hostile arrangements of trade if she is willing to associate herself with us and the other peace-loving nations of the world in covenants of justice and law and fair dealing. We wish her only to accept a place of equality among the peoples of the world—the new world in which we now live—instead of a place of mastery.

Neither do we presume to suggest to her any alteration or modification of her institutions. But it is necessary, we must frankly say, and necessary as a preliminary to any intelligent dealings with her on our part, that we should know whom her spokesmen speak for when they speak to us, whether for the Reichstag majority or for the military party and the men whose creed is imperial domination.

We have spoken now, surely, in terms too concrete to admit of any further doubt or question. An evident principle runs through the whole program I have outlined. It is the principle of justice to all peoples and nationalities and their right to live on equal terms of liberty and safety with one another, whether they be strong or weak. Unless this principle be made its foundation, no part of the structure of international justice can stand. The people of the United States could act upon no other principle, and to the vindication of this principle they are ready to devote their lives, their honor, and everything that they possess.[8]

The moral climax of this the culminating and final war for human liberty has come, and they are ready to put their own strength, their own highest purpose, their own integrity and devotion to the test.

---

8. An allusion to the Declaration of Independence (1776), whose final words pledge "our Lives, our Fortunes, and our sacred Honor."

Eugene V. Debs

Statement to the Court

WORLD WAR I was not a propitious time for civil liberties in the United States. The Wilson administration made full use of the Espionage Act (1917) and the Sedition Act (1918) to intimidate, arrest, and prosecute antiwar activists. Fourteen months after Emma Goldman was convicted by a federal jury in New York City (see pages 79–87), Eugene Debs came to trial in Cleveland for, in the words of his indictment, "attempting to cause insubordination, mutiny, disloyalty, and refusal of duty within the military forces of the United States, and the utterance of words intended to procure and incite resistance to the United States, and to promote the cause of the Imperial German Government."

Debs had been on the government's watch list for a long time and was not surprised by his arrest. On June 16, 1918, he had delivered a speech in Canton, Ohio, telling the crowd: "You need to know that you are fit for things better than slavery and cannon fodder." Among the 1,200 people in the audience was twenty-year-old Virgil Steiner, a stenographic clerk hired by the Justice Department to take notes on the speech. Although Debs mentioned the war only a few times and said nothing he had not proclaimed on countless occasions, he was arrested two weeks later.

The trial began on September 9. Although Debs retained the help of several Socialist Party attorneys, he acted largely as his own counsel. On September 12 he delivered a two-hour speech to the jury, arguing that his Canton address was constitutionally protected. "I believe in the right of free speech, in war as well as in peace," he stated. "It is far more dangerous to attempt to gag the people than allow them to speak freely of what is in their hearts." The jury did not agree and, after six hours of deliberation, brought in a guilty verdict. Unlike many others who were convicted for their antiwar activities, Debs did not assail the legal process. "The evidence was truthful," he said, "the jury was patient and attentive, and the judge's charge was masterly and scrupulously fair."

Before handing down sentence on September 14, Judge David C. Westenhaver asked Debs if he had anything to say to the court. Debs nodded and proceeded to deliver a speech with what are perhaps his most famous words: "While there is a lower class, I am in it; while there is a criminal element, I am of it; while there is a soul in prison, I am not free." Presenting his position with eloquence and dignity,

Debs reaffirmed his Socialist principles and asked for no mercy, no immunity. Eventually, he proclaimed, "the right must prevail....Let the people take heart and hope everywhere, for the cross is bending, the midnight is passing, and joy cometh with the morning."

Heywood Broun called Debs's speech "one of the most beautiful and moving passages in the English language....If anybody told me that tongues of fire danced upon his shoulders as he spoke, I would believe it." Judge Westenhaver was less impressed. Imposing the maximum penalty, he sentenced Debs to ten years in prison. While there, Debs was once again nominated for President by the Socialist Party. Running his 1920 campaign from behind bars, he received almost a million votes, the most ever received by a Socialist presidential candidate in the United States.

◇◇

Your Honor:[1] Years ago I recognized my kinship with all living beings and I made up my mind that I was not one bit better than the meanest of earth. I said then, I say now, that while there is a lower class, I am in it; while there is a criminal element, I am of it; while there is a soul in prison, I am not free.

If the law under which I have been convicted is a good law, then there is no reason why sentence should not be pronounced upon me. I listened to all that was said in this court in support and justification of this law, but my mind remains unchanged. I look upon it as a despotic enactment in flagrant conflict with democratic principles and with the spirit of free institutions.

I have no fault to find with this court or with the trial. Everything in connection with this case has been conducted upon a dignified plane and in a respectful and decent spirit—with just one exception. Your Honor, my sainted mother inspired me with a reverence for womanhood that amounts to worship. I can think with disrespect of no woman, and I can think with respect of no man who can. I resent the manner in which the names of two noble women were bandied with in this court.[2] The levity and the wantonness in this instance were absolutely inexcus-able. When I think of what was said in this connection, I feel that when I pass a woman, even though it be a sister of the street, I should take off my hat and apologize to her for being a man.

Your Honor, I have stated in this court that I am opposed to the form of our present government; that I am opposed to the social system in which we live; that I believed in the change of both—but by perfectly peaceable and orderly means.

Let me call your attention to the fact this morning that in this system 5 percent of our people own and control two-thirds of our wealth; 65 percent of the people, embracing the working class who produce all wealth, have but 5 percent to show for it.

Standing here this morning, I recall my boyhood. At fourteen, I went to work in the railroad shops; at sixteen, I was firing a freight engine on a railroad. I remember all the hardships, all the privations, of that earlier day, and from that time until now my heart has been with the working class. I could have been in Congress long ago. I have preferred to go to prison. The choice has been deliberately made. I could not have done otherwise. I have no regret.

In the struggle—the unceasing struggle—between the toilers and producers and their exploiters, I have tried, as best I might, to serve those among whom I was born, with whom I expect to share my lot until the end of my days.

I am thinking this morning of the men in the mills and factories; I am thinking of the women

---

1. U.S. District Judge David C. Westenhaver.

2. During his closing argument, U.S. District Attorney E. S. Wertz included negative comments about Rose Pastor Stokes and Kate Richards O'Hare, both of whom had previously been convicted for violating the Espionage Act.

who, for a paltry wage, are compelled to work out their lives; of the little children who, in this system, are robbed of their childhood and, in their early tender years, are seized in the remorseless grasp of Mammon[3] and forced into the industrial dungeons, there to feed the machines while they themselves are being starved body and soul. I can see them dwarfed, diseased, stunted, their little lives broken and their hopes blasted because in this high noon of our twentieth-century civilization money is still so much more important than human life.

Gold is god and rules in the affairs of men. The little girls, and there are a million of them in this country—this the most favored land beneath the bending skies, a land in which we have vast areas of rich and fertile soil, material resources in inexhaustible abundance, the most marvelous productive machinery on earth, millions of eager workers ready to apply their labor to that machinery to produce an abundance for every man, woman, and child—and if there are still many millions of our people who are the victims of poverty, whose life is a ceaseless struggle all the way from youth to age, until at last death comes to their rescue and stills the aching heart and lulls the victim to dreamless sleep, it is not the fault of the Almighty, it can't be charged to nature; it is due entirely to an outgrown social system that ought to be abolished not only in the interest of the working class, but in a higher interest of all humanity.

When I think of these little children—the girls that are in the textile mills of all description in the East, in the cotton factories of the South—when I think of them at work in a vitiated atmosphere, when I think of them at work when they ought to be at play or at school, when I think that when they do grow up, if they live long enough to approach the marriage state, they are unfit for it. Their nerves are worn out, their tissue is exhausted, their vitality is spent. They have been fed to industry. Their lives have been coined into gold. Their offspring are born tired. That is why there are so many failures in our modern life.

Your Honor, the 5 percent of the people that I have made reference to constitute that element that absolutely rules our country. They privately own all our public necessities. They wear no crowns; they wield [no] scepters; they sit upon no thrones; and yet they are our economic masters and our political rulers. They control this government and all of its institutions. They control the courts.

And, Your Honor, if you will permit me, I wish to make just one correction. It was stated here that I had charged that all federal judges are crooks. The charge is absolutely untrue. I did say that all federal judges are appointed through the influence and power of the capitalistic class and not the working class. If that statement is not true, I am more than willing to retract it.

If the 5 percent of our people who own and control all of the sources of wealth, all of the nation's industries, all of the means of our common life, it is they who declare war; it is they who make peace; it is they who control our destiny. And so long as this is true, we can make no just claim to being a democratic government—a self-governing people.

I believe, Your Honor, in common with all Socialists, that this nation ought to own and control its industries. I believe, as all Socialists do, that all things that are jointly needed and used ought to be jointly owned—that industry, the basis of life, instead of being the private property of the few and operated for their enrichment, ought to be the common property of all, democratically administered in the interest of all.

John D. Rockefeller[4] has today an income of $60 million a year, $5 million a month, $200,000 a day. He does not produce a penny of it. I make no attack upon Mr. Rockefeller personally. I do not in the least dislike him. If he were in need and it were in my power to serve him, I should serve him as gladly as I would any other human being. I have no quarrel with Mr. Rockefeller personally, nor with any other capitalist. I am simply opposing a social order in which it is possible for one man who does absolutely nothing that is useful to amass a fortune of hundreds of millions of dollars, while millions of men and women who work all of the days of their lives secure barely enough for an existence.

This order of things cannot always endure. I have registered my protest against it. I recognize

---

3. Biblical term for avarice, riches, and worldly gain (Matthew 6:24, Luke 16:13).

4. Industrialist and president of the Standard Oil Company.

the feebleness of my effort, but fortunately I am not alone. There are multiplied thousands of others who, like myself, have come to realize that before we may truly enjoy the blessings of civilized life, we must reorganize society upon a mutual and cooperative basis; and to this end we have organized a great economic and political movement that spread over the face of all the earth.

There are today upwards of sixty million Socialists, loyal, devoted adherents to this cause, regardless of nationality, race, creed, color, or sex. They are all making common cause. They are all spreading the propaganda of the new social order. They are waiting, watching, and working through all the weary hours of the day and night. They are still in the minority. They have learned how to be patient and abide their time. They feel—they know, indeed—that the time is coming, in spite of all opposition, all persecution, when this emancipating gospel will spread among all the peoples and when this minority will become the triumphant majority and, sweeping into power, inaugurate the greatest change in history.

In that day we will have the universal commonwealth—not the destruction of the nation, but, on the contrary, the harmonious cooperation of every nation with every other nation on earth. In that day war will curse this earth no more.

I have been accused, Your Honor, of being an enemy of the soldier. I hope I am laying no flattering unction to my soul when I say that I don't believe the soldier has a more sympathetic friend than I am. If I had my way, there would be no soldier. But I realize the sacrifices they are making, Your Honor. I can think of them. I can feel for them. I can sympathize with them. That is one of the reasons why I have been doing what little has been in my power to bring about a condition of affairs in this country worthy of the sacrifices they have made and that they are now making in its behalf.

Your Honor, in a local paper yesterday there was some editorial exultation about my prospective imprisonment.[5] I do not resent it in the least. I can understand it perfectly. In the same paper there appears an editorial this morning that has in it a hint of the wrong to which I have been trying to call attention: "A Senator of the United States receives a salary of $7,500–$45,000 for the six years for which he is elected. One of the candidates for Senator from a state adjoining Ohio is reported to have spent through his committee $150,000 to secure the nomination. For advertising he spent $35,000; for printing $30,000; for traveling expenses $10,000; and the rest in ways known to political managers.

"The theory is that public office is as open to a poor man as to a rich man. One may easily imagine, however, how slight a chance one of ordinary resources would have in a contest against this man who was willing to spend more than three times his six years' salary merely to secure a nomination. Were these conditions to hold in every state, the Senate would soon become again what it was once held to be—a rich men's club.

"Campaign expenditures have been the subject of much restrictive legislation in recent years, but it has not always reached the mark. The authors of primary reform have accomplished some of the things they set out to do, but they have not yet taken the bank roll out of politics."[6]

They never will take it out of politics; they never can take it out of politics in this system.

Your Honor, I wish to make acknowledgment of my thanks to the counsel for the defense.[7] They have not only defended me with exceptional legal ability, but with a personal attachment and devotion of which I am deeply sensible and which I can never forget.

Your Honor, I ask no mercy. I plead for no immunity. I realize that finally the right must prevail. I never more clearly comprehended than now the great struggle between the powers of greed on the one hand and upon the other the rising hosts of freedom.

I can see the dawn of a better day of humanity. The people are awakening. In due course of time they will come to their own.

---

5. "The Debs Verdict," *Cleveland Plain Dealer*, September 13, 1918, proclaimed that Debs "belongs in prison, and it is good news to every loyal son and daughter of the republic that he has been convicted."

6. "Too Much," *Cleveland Plain Dealer*, September 14, 1918.

7. The defense team was led by Seymour Stedman, who would be Debs's running mate in the 1920 presidential election.

When the mariner, sailing over tropic seas, looks for relief from his weary watch, he turns his eyes toward the Southern Cross,[8] burning luridly above the tempest-vexed ocean. As the midnight approaches, the Southern Cross begins to bend and the whirling worlds change their places, and with starry finger-points the Almighty marks the passage of time upon the dial of the universe, and though no bell may beat the glad tidings, the lookout knows that the midnight is passing—that relief and rest are close at hand.

Let the people take heart and hope everywhere, for the Cross is bending, the midnight is passing, and joy cometh with the morning.[9]

He's true to God who's true to man;
 wherever wrong is done,
To the humblest and the weakest,
 'neath the all-beholding sun.
That wrong is also done to us, and they
 are slaves most base,
Whose love of right is for themselves,
 and not for all their race.[10]

Your Honor, I thank you, and I thank all of this court for their courtesy, for their kindness, which I shall remember always.

I am prepared to receive your sentence.

8. A constellation used as a means of navigation in the Southern Hemisphere.

9. From Psalm 30:5.

10. From James Russell Lowell, "On the Capture of Fugitive Slaves Near Washington" (1845).

Woodrow Wilson

For the League of Nations

DES MOINES, IOWA
SEPTEMBER 6, 1919

AFTER MORE THAN four years of fighting and the loss of fourteen million lives, the guns in Europe finally fell silent with the armistice of Compiègne Forest, signed on November 11, 1918. Three weeks later, Woodrow Wilson became the first sitting President to travel to the Continent when he embarked for Paris and the peace conference that would write the Treaty of Versailles officially ending World War I. Faced with the bitterness, intransigence, and cynicism of European leaders, he was forced at Paris to compromise many of his Fourteen Points (pages 124–128) to preserve what he regarded as the most important element of an acceptable peace—an international organization that would prevent the world from ever again falling into the kind of horror it had just endured. When the treaty was formally presented to the U.S. Senate on July 10, 1919, it contained the covenant for a League of Nations, thereby touching off one of the most bitter public debates in American history. On one side were arrayed Wilson and other proponents of the league; on the other side were its opponents, the most influential of whom was Senate Majority Leader Henry Cabot Lodge.

Throughout the summer of 1919 both sides maneuvered to gain the upper hand in Congress and in the court of public opinion. With the exception of a dozen or so Senators known as Irreconcilables, who denounced ratification of the treaty in any form, most opponents were willing to accept it with a set of reservations that ameliorated its most objectionable features. Above all, they insisted on revisions to Article 10 of the covenant, which pledged signatories to protect "the territorial integrity and existing political independence" of all league nations against external aggression. In their view, the United States should not be bound to any action under Article 10 without approval from both houses of Congress. Wilson, however, adamantly opposed any alterations to Article 10, and on the evening of September 3, he left Washington, D.C., for a scheduled four-week speaking tour to rally public sentiment behind the league and to compel the Senate to ratify the treaty without reservations.

Although Wilson's tour has often been characterized as a purely idealistic quest, he had undertaken successful speaking trips both as Governor of New Jersey and as President, and he was convinced this one would be equally effective. On the night of September 6, he addressed an audience of 9,000 people in the Des Moines Coliseum. As at his other tour stops, he spoke extemporaneously from a brief set of notes. This was his favorite manner of presenting a speech—"right out of my mind as it is working at the time"—for it allowed him to connect with individual listeners more directly than was possible in a manuscript presentation. According to the *Des Moines News*, he made "an intense effort to clarify things for his audience" and "pounded home his arguments in convincing manner." Perhaps the finest of Wilson's tour speeches, his address at Des Moines reveals his earnest commitment to creating a global body that would forestall future wars and allow humanity to scale "those distant heights upon which will shine at last the serene light of justice, suffusing a whole world in blissful peace."

<hr />

Mr. Chairman and fellow countrymen: You make my heart very warm with your generous welcome, and I want to express my unaffected gratitude to your chairman for having so truly struck the note of an occasion like this. He has used almost the very words that were in my thought—that the world is inflamed and profoundly disturbed and we are met to discuss the measures by which its spirit can be quieted and its affairs turned to the right courses of human life.[1]

My fellow countrymen, the world is desperately in need of the settled conditions of peace, and it cannot wait much longer. It is waiting upon us. That is the thought, that is the burdensome thought, upon my heart tonight—that the world is waiting for the verdict of the nation to which it looked for leadership and which it thought would be the last that would ask the world to wait.

My fellow citizens, the world is not at peace. I suppose that it is difficult for one who has not had some touch of the hot passion of the other side of the sea to realize how all the passions that have been

1. Wilson is referring to the speech of introduction by James B. Weaver, president of the Des Moines Chamber of Commerce.

slumbering for ages have been uncovered and released by the tragedy of this war. We speak of the tragedy of this war, but the tragedy that lay back of it was greater than the war itself because back of it lay long ages in which the legitimate freedom of men was suppressed. Back of it lay long ages of recurrent war in which little groups of men, closeted in capitals, determined whether the sons of the land over which they ruled should go out upon the field and shed their blood.

For what? For liberty? No, not for liberty, but for the aggrandizement of those who ruled them. And this had been slumbering in the hearts of men. They had felt the suppression of it. They had felt the mastery of those whom they had not chosen as their masters. They had felt the oppression of laws which did not admit them to the equal exercise of human rights. And now all of this is released and uncovered and men glare at one another and say, "Now we are free and what shall we do with our freedom?"

What happened in Russia was not a sudden and accidental thing. The people of Russia were maddened with the suppression of Czarism. When at last the chance came to throw off those chains, they threw them off, at first with hearts full of confidence and hope,[2] and then they found out that they had been again deceived. There was no assembly chosen to frame a constitution for them, or, rather, there was an assembly chosen to choose a constitution for them and it was suppressed and dispersed, and a little group of men just as selfish, just as ruthless, just as pitiless as the agents of the Czar himself, assumed control and exercised their power by terror and not by right.[3] And in other parts of Europe the poison spread—the poison of disorder, the poison of revolt, the poison of chaos.

And do you honestly think, my fellow citizens, that none of that poison has got in the veins of this free people? Do you not know that the world is all now one single whispering gallery? Those antennae of the wireless telegraph are the symbols of our age. All the impulses of mankind are thrown out upon the air and reach to the ends of the earth, and quietly upon steamships, silently under the cover of the postal service, with the tongue of the wireless and the tongue of the telegraph, all the suggestions of disorder are spread through the world. And money coming from nobody knows where is deposited by the millions in capitals like Stockholm, to be used for the propaganda of disorder and discontent and dissolution throughout the world.

And men look you calmly in the face in America and say they are for that sort of revolution, when that sort of revolution means government by terror, government by force, not government by vote. It is the negation of everything that is American, but it is spreading, and so long as disorder continues, so long as the world is kept waiting for the answer to the question of the kind of peace we are going to have and what kind of guarantees are to be behind that peace, that poison will steadily spread more and more rapidly, spread until it may be that even this beloved land of ours will be distracted and distorted by it.

That is what is concerning me, my fellow countrymen. I know the splendid steadiness of the American people, but, my fellow citizens, the whole world needs that steadiness, and the American people are the makeweight in the fortunes of mankind. How long are we going to debate into which scale we will throw that magnificent equipoise that belongs to us? How long shall we be kept waiting for the answer whether the world may trust or despise us? They have looked to us for leadership. They have looked to us for example. They have built their peace upon the basis of our suggestions. That great volume that contains the treaty of peace is drawn along the specifications laid down by the American government, and now the world stands at amaze because an authority in America hesitates whether it will endorse an American document or not.

You know what the necessity of peace is. Why, my fellow countrymen, political liberty can exist only when there is peace. Social reform can take place only when there is peace. The settlement of every question that concerns our daily life waits for peace. I have been receiving delegations in Washington of men engaged in the service of the government temporarily in the administration of the railways,

---

2. After more than a decade of turmoil, Czar Nicholas II abdicated his throne in March 1917 and was replaced by a provisional government.

3. Wilson is referring to the Bolsheviks, under the leadership of Vladimir Ilyich Lenin, who seized power and overthrew Russia's provisional government in October 1917.

and I have had to say to them: "My friends, I cannot tell what the railways can earn until commerce is restored to its normal courses. Until I can tell what the railroads can earn, I cannot tell what the wages that the railroads can pay will be. I cannot suggest what the increase of freight and passenger rates will be to meet these increases in wages if the rates must be increased. I cannot tell yet whether it will be necessary to increase the rates or not, and I must ask you to wait."

But they are not the only people that have come to see me. There are all sorts of adjustments necessary in this country. I have asked representatives of capital and labor to come to Washington next month and confer, confer about the fundamental thing of our life at present—that is to say, the conditions of labor. Do you realize, my fellow citizens, that all through the world the one central question of civilization is, "What shall be the conditions of labor?" The profoundest unrest in Europe is due to the doubt what shall be the conditions of labor, and I need not tell you that that unrest is spreading to America. And in the midst of the treaty of peace is a Magna Carta,[4] a great guarantee for labor that labor shall have the counsels of the world devoted to the discussion of its conditions and of its betterment,[5] and labor all over the world is waiting to know whether America is going to take part in those conferences or not.

The confidence of the men who sat at Paris was such that they put it in the document that the first meeting of the labor conference under that part of the treaty should take place in Washington upon the invitation of the President of the United States. I am going to issue that invitation whether we can attend the conference or not. But think of the mortification! Think of standing by in Washington itself and seeing the world take counsel upon the fundamental matter of civilization without us. The thing is inconceivable, but it is true. The world is waiting, waiting to see not whether we will take part but whether we will serve and lead, for it has expected us to lead.

I want to say that the most touching and thrilling thing that ever happened to me was that which happened almost every day when I was in Paris.[6] Delegations from all over the world came to me to solicit the friendship of America. They frankly told us that they were not sure of anybody else that they could trust, but that they did absolutely trust us to do them justice and to see that justice was done them. Why, some of them came from countries which I have, to my shame, to admit that I never heard of before, and I had to ask as privately as possible what language they spoke. Fortunately they always had an interpreter, but I always wanted to know at least what family of languages they were speaking. But the touching thing was that from the ends of the earth, from little pocketed valleys, where I did not know that a separate people lived, there came men—men of dignity, men of intellectual parts, men entertaining in their thought and in their memories a great tradition, some of the oldest people of the world—and they came and sat at the feet of the youngest nation in the world and said, "Teach us the way to liberty."

That is the attitude of the world, and reflect, my fellow countrymen, upon the reaction, the reaction of despair, that would come if America said: "We do not want to lead you. You must do without our advice. You must shift without us." How are you going to bring about a peace, peace for which everything waits? We cannot bring it about by doing nothing. I have been very much amazed and very much amused, if I could be amused in such critical circumstances, to see that the statesmanship of some gentlemen consists in the very interesting proposition that we do nothing at all. I had heard of standing pat before, but I never had before heard of standpattism going to the length of saying it is none of our business and we do not care what happens to the rest of the world.

Your chairman made a profoundly true remark just now. The isolation of the United States is at an end—not because we chose to go into the politics of the world, but because by the sheer genius of this

4. English charter of 1215 protecting various rights of the king's subjects.

5. Wilson is referring to Articles 387–399 of the Treaty of Versailles.

6. Wilson made two trips to Paris for the peace conference. Except for a nine-day stretch in February–March 1919, he was out of the United States from December 4, 1918, to July 8, 1919.

people and the growth of our power we have become a determining factor in the history of mankind; and after you have become a determining factor, you cannot remain isolated, whether you want to or not. Isolation ended by the processes of history, not by the processes of our independent choice, and the processes of history merely fulfilled the prediction of the men who founded our republic.

Go back and read some of the immortal sentences of the men that assisted to frame this government and see how they set up a standard to which they intended that the nations of the world should rally. They said to the people of the world: "Come to us; this is the home of liberty; this is the place where mankind can learn how to govern their own affairs and straighten out their own difficulties." And the world did come to us. Look at your neighbor. Look at the statistics of the people of your state. Look at the statistics of the people of the United States. They have come, their hearts full of hope and confidence, from practically every nation in the world, to constitute a portion of our strength and our hope and a contribution to our achievement.

Sometimes I feel like taking off my hat to some of those immigrants. I was born an American. I could not help it, but they chose to be Americans. They were not born Americans. They saw this star in the west rising over the heads of the world,[7] and they said: "That is the star of hope and the star of salvation. We will set our footsteps toward the west and join that great body of men whom God has blessed with the vision of liberty." I honor those men. I say, "You made a deliberate choice which showed that you saw what the drift and history of mankind was."

I am very grateful, I may say in parenthesis, that I did not have to make that choice. I am grateful that ever since I can remember I have breathed this blessed air of freedom. I am grateful that every instinct in me, every drop of blood in me, remains and stands up and shouts at the traditions of the United States. But some gentlemen are not shouting now about that. They are saying, "Yes, we made a great promise to mankind, but it will cost too much to redeem it."

My fellow citizens, that is not the spirit of America, and you cannot have peace, you cannot have even your legitimate part in the business of the world, unless you are partners with the rest. If you are going to say to the world, "We will stand off and see what we can get out of this," the world will see to it that you do not get anything out of it. If it is your deliberate choice that, instead of being friends, you will be rivals and antagonists, then you will get just exactly what rivals and antagonists always get—just as little as can be grudgingly vouchsafed you.

And yet you must keep the world on its feet. Is there any businessman here who would be willing to see the world go bankrupt and the business of the world stop? Is there any man here who does not know that America is the only nation left by the war in a position to see that the world does go on with its business? And is it your idea that if we lend our money, as we must, to men whom we have bitterly disappointed, that that money will bring back to us the largess to which we are entitled?

I do not like to argue this thing on this basis, but if you want to talk business, I am ready to talk business. If it is a matter of how much you are going to get from your money, you will not get half as much as antagonists as you will get as partners. So think that over if you have none of that thing that is so lightly spoken of, known as altruism. And believe me, my fellow countrymen, the only people in the world who are going to reap the harvest of the future are people who can entertain ideals, who can follow ideals to the death.

I was saying to another audience today[8] that one of the most beautiful stories I know is the story that we heard in France about the first effect of the American soldiers when they got over there. The French did not believe at first, the British did not believe, that we could finally get two million men over there. The most that they hoped at first was that a few American soldiers would restore their morale, for let me say that their morale was gone.

The beautiful story to which I referred is this: The testimony that all of them rendered was that

---

7. Likely an allusion to the Star of Bethlehem, from Matthew 2:2.

8. Wilson spoke to an audience of 10,000 people in Kansas City, Missouri, earlier in the day.

they got their morale back the minute they saw the eyes of those boys. Here were not only soldiers. There was no curtain in the front of the retina of those eyes. They were American eyes. They were eyes that had seen visions. They were eyes the possessors of which had brought with them a great ardor for a supreme cause, and the reason those boys never stopped was that their eyes were lifted to the horizon. They saw a city not built with hands.[9] They saw a citadel towards which their steps were bent where dwelt the oracles of God himself. And on the battlefield were found German orders to commanders here and there to see to it that the Americans did not get lodgment in particular places, because if they ever did, you never could get them out. They had gone to Europe to go the whole way towards the realization of the teaching which their fathers had handed down to them. There never were crusaders that went to the Holy Land in the old ages that we read about that were more truly devoted to a holy cause than these gallant, incomparable sons of America.

So, my fellow citizens, you have got to make up your minds because, after all, it is you who are going to make up the minds of this country. I do not owe a report or the slightest responsibility to anybody but you. I do not mean only you in this hall, though I am free to admit that this is just as good a sample of America as you can find anywhere, and the sample looks mighty good to me. I mean you and the millions besides you—thoughtful, responsible American men and women all over this country. They are my bosses, and I am mighty glad to be their servant. I have come out upon this journey not to fight anybody, but to report to you, and I am free to predict that if you credit the report, there will be no fighting.

It is not only necessary that we should make peace with Germany and make peace with Austria and see that reasonable peace is made with Turkey and Bulgaria—that is not only not all of it, but it is a very

dangerous beginning if you do not add something to it. I said just now that the peace with Germany, and the same is true of the pending peace with Austria,[10] was made upon American specifications, not unwillingly. Do not let me leave the impression on your mind that the representatives of America in Paris had to insist and force their principles upon the rest. That is not true. Those principles were accepted before we got over there, and the men I dealt with carried them out in absolute good faith.

But they were our principles, and at the heart of them lay this—that there must be a free Poland, for example. I wonder if you realize what that means. We had to collect the pieces of Poland. For a long time one piece had belonged to Russia, and we cannot get a clear title to that yet. Another part belonged to Austria. We got a title to that. Another part belonged to Germany, and we have settled the title to that.[11] But we found Germany also in possession of other pieces of territory occupied predominately or exclusively by patriotic Poles, and we said to Germany, "You will have to give that up, too; that belongs to Poland." Not because it is ground, but because those people there are Poles and want to be part of Poland, and it is not our business to force any sovereignty upon anybody who does not want to live under it. And when we had determined the boundaries of Poland, we set it up and recognized it as an independent republic. There is a minister, a diplomatic representative, of the United States at Warsaw right now in virtue of our formal recognition of the Republic of Poland.

But upon Poland center some of the dangers of the future. And south of Poland is Bohemia, which we cut away from the Austrian combination. And below Bohemia is Hungary, which can no longer rely upon the assistant strength of Austria, and below her is an enlarged Romania. And alongside of Romania is the

---

9. An allusion to the new Jerusalem described in Revelation 21 as part of the new heaven and new earth that follow God's defeat of Satan at the end of time. Wilson's language also echoes Hebrews 11:10.

10. The Paris Peace Conference prepared five pacts. The Treaty of Versailles, signed by the conference on June 28, 1919, set the terms of peace with Germany. Peace with Austria was established by the Treaty of Saint-Germain, September 10, 1919. Subsequent treaties dealt with Bulgaria, Hungary, and Turkey.

11. First partitioned in 1772, Poland lost autonomous standing as a nation when all its remaining territory was divided among Russia, Germany, and Austria in 1795.

new Slavic kingdom that never could have won its own independence, which had chafed under the chains of Austria-Hungary but never could throw them off. We have said: "The fundamental wrongs of history center in these regions. These people have the right to govern their own country and control their own fortunes."

That is at the heart of the treaty, but, my fellow citizens, this is at the heart of the future: The business-men of Germany did not want the war that we have passed through. The bankers and the manufacturers and the merchants knew that it was unspeakable folly. Why? Because Germany by her industrial genius was beginning to dominate the world economically, and all she had to do was to wait about two more gen-erations when her credit, her merchandise, her enter-prise, would have covered all of the parts of the world that the great fighting nations did not control.

The formula of pan-Germanism,[12] you remem-ber, was Bremen to Baghdad—Bremen on the North Sea to Baghdad in Persia. These countries that we have set up as a new home of liberty lie right along that road. If we leave them there without the guaran-tee that the combined force of the world will assure their independence and their territorial integrity, we have only to wait a short generation when our recent experience will be repeated.

We did not let Germany dominate the world this time. Are we then? If Germany had known then that all the other fighting nations of the world would combine to prevent her action, she never would have dreamed of attempting it. If Germany had known— this is the common verdict of every man familiar with the politics of Europe—if Germany had known that England would go in, she never would have started it. If she had known that America would come in, she never would have dreamed of it. And now the only way to make it certain that there never will be another world war like that is that we should assist in guaranteeing the peace and its settlement.

It is a very interesting circumstance, my fellow countrymen, that the League of Nations will contain all the great nations of the world, and the little ones

too, except Germany, and Germany is merely put on probation.[13] We have practically said to Germany, "If it turns out that you really have had a change of heart and have gotten the nonsense out of your system; if it really does turn out that you have substituted a genuine self-governing republic for a kingdom where a few men on Wilhelmstrasse[14] plotted the destiny of the world, then we will let you in as partners because you will be respectable."

And in the meantime, accepting the treaty, Germany's army is reduced to 100,000 men, and she has promised to give up all the war material over and above what is necessary for 100,000 men. For a nation of sixty million! She has surrendered to the world. She has said: "Our fate is in your hands. We are ready to do what you tell us to do." And the rest of the world is combined, and the interesting circumstance is that the rest of the world, excluding us, will continue com-bined if we do not go into it. Some gentlemen seem to think they can break up this treaty and prevent this league by not going into it. Not at all.

I can give you an interesting circumstance. There is the settlement that you have heard so much discus-sed, about that rich and ancient province of Shantung in China.[15] I do not like that settlement any better than you do, but these were the circumstances: In order to induce Japan to come into the war and clear the Pacific of the German power, England and France bound themselves without any qualification to see to it that Japan got anything in China that Germany had and that Japan would take it away from her, upon the strength of which promise Japan proceeded to take Kiaochow and occupied the portions of Shantung Province which had been dominated—or rather ceded—by China for a term of years to Germany.

---

12. Political movement that sought the unification of all German-speaking people under German rule.

13. Germany was admitted to the League of Nations in 1926; it withdrew in 1933 after Adolf Hitler came to power.

14. Street in Berlin that housed many government offices, including the Reich Chancellery.

15. The treaty ceded Shantung Province, formerly a protector-ate of Germany, to Japan, which had seized it during the war. Although Wilson secured a verbal pledge from Japan that it would restore Chinese sovereignty within five years, a pledge it honored in 1922, the Shantung provision aroused intense oppo-sition in the United States.

And the most that could be got out of it was that, in view of the fact that America had nothing to do with it, the Japanese were ready to promise that they would give up every item of sovereignty which Germany would otherwise have enjoyed in Shantung Province and return it without restriction to China, and that they would retain in the province only the economic concessions such as other nations already had elsewhere in China—though you do not hear anything about that—concessions in the railway and the mines which had become attached to the railway for operative purposes.

But suppose that you say that is not enough. Very well, then, stay out of the treaty—and how will that accomplish anything? England and France are bound and cannot escape their obligation. Are you going to institute a war against Japan and France and England to get Shantung back for China? That is an enterprise which does not commend itself to the present generation.

I am putting it in brutal terms, my fellow citizens, but that is the fact. By disagreeing to that provision, we accomplish nothing for China. On the contrary, we stay out of the only combination of the counsels of nations in which we can be of service to China. With China as a member of the League of Nations, and Japan as a member of the League of Nations, and America as a member of the League of Nations, there confronts every one of them that now famous Article 10, by which every member of the league agrees to respect and preserve the territorial integrity and existing political independence of all the other member states.

Do not let anybody persuade you that you can take that article out and have a peaceful world. That cuts at the root of the German war. That cuts at the root of the outrage against Belgium. That cuts at the root of the outrage against France. That pulls that vile, unwholesome upas tree of pan-Germanism up by the roots, and it pulls all other "pans" up too. Every land-grabbing nation is served notice: "Keep on your own territory. Mind your own business. That territory belongs to those people and they can do with it what they please, provided they do not invade other people's rights by the use they make of it."

So, my fellow citizens, the thing is going to be done whether we are in it or not. If we are in it, then we are going to be the determining factor in the development of civilization. If we are out of it, we ourselves are going to watch every other nation with suspicion—and we will be justified, too—and we are going to be watched with suspicion. Every movement of trade, every relationship of manufacture, every question of raw materials, every matter that affects the intercourse of the world will be impeded by the consciousness that America wants to hold off and get something which she is not willing to share with the rest of mankind.

I am painting the picture for you because I know that it is as intolerable to you as it is to me. But do not go away with the impression, I beg you, that I think there is any doubt about the issue. The only thing that can be accomplished is delay. The ultimate outcome will be the triumphant acceptance of the treaty and the league.

And let me pay the tribute which it is only just that I should pay to some of the men who have been, I believe, misunderstood in this business. It is only a handful of men, my fellow citizens, who are trying to defeat the treaty or to prevent the league. The great majority, in official bodies and out, are scrutinizing it, as it is perfectly legitimate that they should scrutinize it, to see if it is necessary that they should qualify it in any way. And my knowledge of their conscience, my knowledge of their public principles, makes me certain that they will sooner or later see that it is safest, since it is all expressed in the plainest English that the English dictionary affords, not to qualify it—to accept it as it is. Because I have been a student of the English language all my life, and I do not see a single obscure sentence in the whole document.

Some gentlemen either have not read it or do not understand the English language, but, fortunately, on the right-hand page it is printed in English and on the left-hand page it is printed in French. Now, if they do not understand English, I hope they will get a French dictionary and dig out the meaning on that side. The French is a very precise language, more precise than the English language, I am told. I am not on a speaking acquaintance with it, but I am told that it is the most precise language in Europe and that any given phrase in French always means the same thing. That cannot be said of English. So in order to satisfy themselves, I hope these gentlemen will master the French version and then be reassured that there are no lurking monsters in that document, there are no sinister purposes, that everything is said in the frankest way.

For example, they have been very much worried at the phrase that nothing in the document shall be taken as impairing in any way the validity of such regional understandings as the Monroe Doctrine.[16] And they said: "Why put in 'such regional understandings as'? What other understandings are there? Have you got something up your sleeve? Is there going to be a Monroe Doctrine in Asia? Is there going to be a Monroe Doctrine in China?" Why, my fellow citizens, the phrase was written in perfect innocence. The men that I was associated with said: "It is not wise to put a specific thing that belongs only to one nation in a document like this. We do not know of any other regional understanding like it, we never heard of any other, we never expect to hear of any other, but there might someday be some other, and so we will say 'such regional understandings as the Monroe Doctrine,'" and their phrase was intended to give right-of-way to the Monroe Doctrine in the Western Hemisphere.

I reminded the Committee on Foreign Relations of the Senate the other day[17] that the conference I held with them was not the first conference I had held about the League of Nations. When I came back to this, our own dear country, in March last, I held a conference at the White House with the Senate Committee on Foreign Relations[18] and they made various suggestions as to how the covenant should be altered in phraseology. I carried those suggestions back to Paris, and every one of them was accepted.

I think that is a sufficient guarantee that no mischief was intended. And the whole document is of the same plain, practical, explicit sort, and it secures peace, my fellow citizens, in the only way in which peace can be secured.

I remember, if I may illustrate a very great thing with a very trivial thing, I had two acquaintances who were very much addicted to profanity. Their friends were distressed about it. It subordinated a rich vocabulary which they might otherwise have cultivated, and so we induced them to agree that they never would swear inside the corporate limits, that if they wanted to swear, they would go out of town. The first time the passion of anger came upon them, they rather sheepishly got in a streetcar and went out of town to swear, and by the time they got out of town, they did not want to swear.

And that very homely story illustrates in my mind the value of discussion. Let me remind you that every fighting nation in the world is going to belong to this league, because we are going to belong to it, and all the fighting nations make this solemn engagement with each other—that they will not resort to war in the case of any controversy until they have done one or two other things: until they have either submitted the question at issue to arbitration, in which case they promise to abide by the verdict whatever it may be, or, if they do not want to submit it to arbitration, have submitted it to discussion by the council of the league.[19]

They agree to give the council six months to discuss the matter, to supply the council with all the pertinent facts regarding it, and that, after the opinion of the council is rendered, they will not then go to war if they are dissatisfied with the opinion until three more months have elapsed. They give nine months in which to spread the whole matter before the judgment of mankind, and if they violate this promise, if any one of them violates it, the covenant prescribes that that violation shall in itself constitute an act of war against the other members of the league.

---

16. The Monroe Doctrine of 1823 declared that the United States would regard any attempt on the part of European powers "to extend their system to any portion of this hemisphere as dangerous to our peace and safety."

17. Wilson and the committee met at the White House on August 19, 1919.

18. This meeting took place on February 26, 1919, and involved members of the House and Senate Foreign Relations Committees.

19. The council's main function was to settle international disputes. Initially it was to be composed of five permanent members, one of whom would have been the United States, and four non-permanent members elected by the assembly, which included all member nations of the league.

But it does not provide that there shall be war. On the contrary, it provides for something very much more effective than war. It provides that that nation, that covenant-breaking nation, shall be absolutely cut off from intercourse of every kind with the other nations of the world—that no merchandise shall be shipped out of it or into it, that no postal messages shall go into it or come out of it, that no telegraphic messages shall cross its borders, and that the citizens of the other member states shall not be permitted to have any intercourse or transactions whatever with its citizens or its citizens with them.

There is not a single nation in Europe that can stand that boycott for six months. There is not a single nation in Europe that is self-sufficing in its resources of food or anything else that can stand that for six months. And in those circumstances we are told that this covenant is a covenant of war. It is the most drastic covenant of peace that was ever conceived, and its processes are the processes of peace. The nation that does not abide by its covenants is taboo, is put out of the society of covenant-respecting nations.

So that this is a covenant of arbitration and discussion, of compulsory arbitration or discussion, and just so soon as you discuss matters, my fellow citizens, peace looks in at the window. Did you ever really sit down and discuss matters with your neighbor when you had a difference and come away in the same temper that you went in? One of the difficulties in our labor situation is that there are some employers who will not meet their employees face to face and talk with them. And I have never known an instance in which such a meeting and discussion took place that both sides did not come away in a softened temper and with an access of respect for the other side. The processes of frank discussion are the processes of peace not only, but the processes of settlement, and those are the processes which are set up for all the powerful nations of the world.

I want to say that this is an unparalleled achievement of thoughtful civilization. To my dying day I shall esteem it the crowning privilege of my life to have been permitted to put my name to a document like that. And in my judgment, my fellow citizens, when passion is cooled and men take a sober, second thought, they are all going to feel that the supreme thing that America did was to help bring this about and then put her shoulder to the great chariot of justice and of peace which is going to lead men along in that slow and toilsome march—toilsome and full of the kind of agony that brings bloody sweat, but nevertheless going up a slow, toilsome incline to those distant heights upon which will shine at last the serene light of justice, suffusing a whole world in blissful peace.

Woodrow Wilson

Final Address for the League of Nations

THE SPEECHES ON Woodrow Wilson's tour in defense of the League of Nations were not intended solely for their immediate listeners. At each stop, his remarks were recorded by a team of stenographers under the supervision of Charles Swem. As soon as the speech was finished, official transcripts were provided for the local press and copies were distributed to 1,400 newspapers throughout the country. It was the most elaborate and sophisticated presidential public relations campaign to that point in American history. Because there was no scientific opinion polling in Wilson's day, there is no way to measure the tour's impact, but as it moved to the Pacific Coast, the crowds grew larger and more enthusiastic and many observers sensed that public sentiment was turning the President's way.

The ceaseless strain, however, was taking a frightful personal toll on Wilson. He suffered from health problems throughout his life, and by the late summer of 1919 he was on the brink of collapse. Both his wife and his personal physician had counseled against the tour, knowing how taxing it would be, but, Wilson insisted, duty demanded that he go. Beset by fatigue, blinding headaches, and breathing difficulties, he deteriorated visibly as the journey progressed.

By the time Wilson reached Pueblo, Colorado, on the afternoon of September 25, he had presented some three dozen major speeches in twenty-one days. He did not say anything new at Pueblo about the terms of the treaty itself. As with other speeches toward the end of the tour, however, he did include two elements that had not been present at the beginning. One was his penchant to question the patriotism of his adversaries by equating opposition to the treaty with disloyalty. The other was his threat to scuttle the entire treaty if the Senate did not include Article 10. "There is no middle course," he insisted. "We have got to adopt it or reject it." Recalling his visit to the cemetery at Suresnes, where thousands of American soldiers were buried, he invoked the memory of "those dear ghosts that still deploy upon the fields of France" and called for adoption of the treaty in full to "make good their redemption of the world."

Notwithstanding the powerful imagery and emotional appeal of its peroration, the Pueblo address derives its fame, as J. Michael Hogan has shown, primarily from what happened afterward. Physically unable to continue the tour, Wilson reluctantly agreed to cancel the remaining stops and to return immediately to Washington, D.C. One week later, he collapsed in the White House from a massive stroke and would remain bedridden for the rest of his presidency. No longer able to provide effective leadership in the treaty battle and unwilling to accept any compromise that would entail alterations in Article 10, he watched the treaty—and, with it, American membership in the League of Nations—go down to defeat in the Senate. As the last lengthy public speech of Wilson's life, the Pueblo address has been apotheosized in print and film as a testament of his commitment to the principles of world peace and as an exemplar of the orator heroically giving, in Abraham Lincoln's words, "the last full measure of devotion" to a righteous cause.

◇◇

Mr. Chairman and fellow countrymen: It is with a great deal of genuine pleasure that I find myself in Pueblo, and I feel it a compliment that I should be permitted to be the first speaker in this beautiful hall.[1] One of the advantages of this hall, as I look about, is that you are not too far away from me, because there is nothing so reassuring to men who are trying to express the public sentiment as getting into real personal contact with their fellow citizens.

I have gained a renewed impression as I have crossed the continent this time of the homogeneity of this great people to whom we belong. They come from many stocks, but they are all of one kind. They come from many origins, but they are all shot through with the same principles and desire the same righteous and honest things. I have received a more inspiring impression this time of the public opinion of the United States than it was ever my privilege to receive before.

The chief pleasure of my trip has been that it has nothing to do with my personal fortunes, that it has nothing to do with my personal reputation, that it has nothing to do with anything except great principles uttered by Americans of all sorts and of all parties which we are now trying to realize at this crisis of the affairs of the world.

But there have been unpleasant impressions as well as pleasant impressions, my fellow citizens, as I have crossed the continent. I have perceived more and more that men have been busy creating an absolutely false impression of what the treaty of peace and the Covenant of the League of Nations contain

and mean.[2] I find, moreover, that there is an organized propaganda against the League of Nations and against the treaty proceeding from exactly the same sources that the organized propaganda proceeded from which threatened this country here and there with disloyalty; and I want to say—I cannot say too often—any man who carries a hyphen about with him[3] carries a dagger that he is ready to plunge into the vitals of this republic whenever he gets ready. If I can catch any man with a hyphen in this great contest, I will know that I have got an enemy of the republic.

My fellow citizens, it is only certain bodies of foreign sympathies, certain bodies of sympathy with foreign nations, that are organized against this great document which the American representatives have brought back from Paris.[4] Therefore, in order to clear away the mists, in order to remove the impressions, in order to check the falsehoods that have clustered around this great subject, I want to tell you a few very simple things about the treaty and the covenant.

Do not think of this treaty of peace as merely a settlement with Germany. It is that. It is a very severe settlement with Germany, but there is not anything in it that she did not earn. Indeed, she earned more than she can ever be able to pay for, and the punishment exacted of her is not a punishment greater than she can bear, and it is absolutely necessary in

1. Wilson's speech to more than 3,000 people was the first major event held in Pueblo's new city auditorium.

2. Wilson is referring to the Treaty of Versailles, which set the terms of peace with Germany. Articles 1–26 established the Covenant of the League of Nations.

3. A reference to foreign-born Americans who, in Wilson's view, put loyalty to the land of their birth above loyalty to the United States.

4. Wilson headed the U.S. delegation to the Paris Peace Conference that produced the Treaty of Versailles.

order that no other nation may ever plot such a thing against humanity and civilization.

But the treaty is so much more than that. It is not merely a settlement with Germany; it is a readjustment of those great injustices which underlie the whole structure of European and Asiatic society. This is only the first of several treaties. They are all constructed upon the same plan. The Austrian treaty follows the same lines. The treaty with Hungary follows the same lines. The treaty with Bulgaria follows the same lines. The treaty with Turkey, when it is formulated, will follow the same lines.[5]

What are those lines? They are based upon the purpose to see that every government dealt with in this great settlement is put in the hands of the people and taken out of the hands of coteries and of sovereigns who had no right to rule over the people. It is a people's treaty that accomplishes by a great sweep of practical justice the liberation of men who never could have liberated themselves, and the power of the most powerful nations has been devoted, not to their aggrandizement, but to the liberation of people whom they could have put under their control if they had chosen to do so. Not one foot of territory is demanded by the conquerors; not one single item of submission to their authority is demanded by them. The men who sat around that table in Paris knew that the time had come when the people were no longer going to consent to live under masters, but were going to live the lives that they chose themselves, to live under such governments as they chose themselves to erect. That is the fundamental principle of this great settlement.

And we did not stop with that. We added a great international charter for the rights of labor.[6] Reject this treaty, impair it, and this is the consequence to the laboring men of the world—that there is no international tribunal which can bring the moral judgments of the world to bear upon the great labor questions of the day. What we need to do with regard to the labor questions of the day, my fellow countrymen, is to lift them into the light, is to lift them out of the haze and distraction of passion, of hostility, out into the calm spaces where men look at things without passion.

The more men you get into a great discussion, the more you exclude passion. Just as soon as the calm judgment of the world is directed upon the question of justice to labor, labor is going to have a forum such as it never was supplied with before, and men everywhere are going to see that the problem of labor is nothing more nor less than the problem of the elevation of humanity. We must see that all the questions which have disturbed the world, all the questions which have eaten into the confidence of men toward their governments, all the questions which have disturbed the processes of industry, shall be brought out where men of all points of view, men of all attitudes of mind, men of all kinds of experience, may contribute their part to the settlement of the great questions which we must settle and cannot ignore.

At the front of this great treaty is put the Covenant of the League of Nations. It will also be at the front of the Austrian treaty and the Hungarian treaty and the Bulgarian treaty and the treaty with Turkey. Every one of them will contain the Covenant of the League of Nations because you cannot work any of them without the Covenant of the League of Nations. Unless you get the united, concerted purpose and power of the great governments of the world behind this settlement, it will fall down like a house of cards. There is only one power to put behind the liberation of mankind, and that is the power of mankind. It is the power of the united moral forces of the world, and in the Covenant of the League of Nations the moral forces of the world are mobilized. For what purpose? Reflect, my fellow citizens, that the membership of this great league is going to include all the great fighting nations of the world, as well as the weak ones. It is not for the present going to include Germany,[7] but for the time being Germany is

---

5. The Treaty of Versailles with Germany was signed by the Paris Peace Conference on June 28, 1919. The pact with Austria was approved in September 1919; that with Bulgaria in November 1919; and that with Hungary in June 1920. The final treaty, with Turkey, was not initialed until August 1920.

6. Wilson is referring to Articles 387–399 of the Treaty of Versailles.

7. Germany was not admitted to the League of Nations until 1926; it withdrew in 1933 after Adolf Hitler came to power.

not a great fighting country. All the nations that have power that can be mobilized are going to be members of this league, including the United States.

And what do they unite for? They enter into a solemn promise to one another that they will never use their power against one another for aggression; that they never will impair the territorial integrity of a neighbor; that they never will interfere with the political independence of a neighbor; that they will abide by the principle that great populations are entitled to determine their own destiny and that they will not interfere with that destiny; and that no matter what differences arise amongst them, they will never resort to war without first having done one or other of two things—either submitted the matter of controversy to arbitration, in which case they agree to abide by the result without question, or submitted it to the consideration of the Council of the League of Nations, laying before that council all the documents, all the facts, agreeing that the council can publish the documents and the facts to the whole world, agreeing that there shall be six months allowed for the mature consideration of those facts by the council, and agreeing that at the expiration of the six months, even if they are not then ready to accept the advice of the council with regard to the settlement of the dispute, they will still not go to war for another three months.

In other words, they consent, no matter what happens, to submit every matter of difference between them to the judgment of mankind; and just so certainly as they do that, my fellow citizens, war will be in the far background, war will be pushed out of that foreground of terror in which it has kept the world for generation after generation, and men will know that there will be a calm time of deliberate counsel. The most dangerous thing for a bad cause is to expose it to the opinion of the world. The most certain way that you can prove that a man is mistaken is by letting all his neighbors know what he thinks, by letting all his neighbors discuss what he thinks; and if he is in the wrong, you will notice that he will stay at home, he will not walk on the street. He will be afraid of the eyes of his neighbors. He will be afraid of their judgment of his character. He will know that his cause is lost unless he can sustain it by the arguments of right

and of justice. The same law that applies to individuals applies to nations.

"But," you say, "we have heard that we might be at a disadvantage in the League of Nations." Well, whoever told you that either was deliberately falsifying or he had not read the Covenant of the League of Nations. I leave him the choice. I want to give you a very simple account of the organization of the League of Nations and let you judge for yourselves.

It is a very simple organization. The power of the league, or rather the activities of the league, lie in two bodies. There is the council, which consists of one representative from each of the principal allied and associated powers—that is to say, the United States, Great Britain, France, Italy, and Japan, along with four other representatives of smaller powers chosen out of the general body of the membership of the league. The council is the source of every active policy of the league, and no active policy of the league can be adopted without a unanimous vote of the council. That is explicitly stated in the covenant itself. Does it not evidently follow that the League of Nations can adopt no policy whatever without the consent of the United States? The affirmative vote of the representative of the United States is necessary in every case.

Now, you have heard of six votes belonging to the British Empire.[8] Those six votes are not in the council. They are in the assembly, and the interesting thing is that the assembly does not vote. I must qualify that statement a little, but essentially it is absolutely true. In every matter in which the assembly is given a voice—and there are only four or five—its vote does not count unless concurred in by the representatives of all the nations represented on the council, so that there is no validity to any vote of the assembly unless in that vote also the representative of the United States concurs. That one vote of the United States is as big as the six votes of the British Empire. I am not jealous for advantage, my fellow citizens, but I think that is a perfectly safe situation. There is no validity in a vote, either by the council or the assembly, in which

---

8. Wilson is referring to the fact that England, Canada, Australia, New Zealand, South Africa, and India would all be members of the League of Nations.

we do not concur. So much for the statements about the six votes of the British Empire.

Look at it in another aspect. The assembly is the talking body. The assembly was created in order that anybody that purposed anything wrong should be subjected to the awkward circumstance that everybody could talk about it. This is the great assembly in which all the things that are likely to disturb the peace of the world or the good understanding between nations are to be exposed to the general view, and I want to ask you if you think it was unjust, unjust to the United States, that speaking parts should be assigned to the several portions of the British Empire. Do you think it unjust that there should be some spokesman in debate for that fine little stout republic down in the Pacific, New Zealand? Do you think it was unjust that Australia should be allowed to stand up and take part in the debate—Australia, from which we have learned some of the most useful progressive policies of modern time, a little nation only five million in a great continent but counting for several times five in its activities and in its interest in liberal reform?

Do you think it unjust that that little republic down in South Africa, whose gallant resistance to being subjected to any outside authority at all we admired for so many months and whose fortunes we followed with such interest, should have a speaking part? Great Britain obliged South Africa to submit to her sovereignty, but she immediately after that felt that it was convenient and right to hand the whole self-government of that colony over to the very men whom she had beaten.[9] The representatives of South Africa in Paris were two of the most distinguished generals of the Boer Army, two of the realest men I ever met, two men that could talk sober counsel and wise advice along with the best statesmen in Europe. To exclude General Botha and General Smuts[10] from the right to stand up in the parliament of the world and say something concerning the affairs of mankind would be absurd.

And what about Canada? Is not Canada a good neighbor? I ask you: Is not Canada more likely to agree with the United States than with Great Britain? Canada has a speaking part. And then, for the first time in the history of the world, that great voiceless multitude, that throng hundreds of millions strong in India, has a voice. And I want to testify that some of the wisest and most dignified figures in the peace conference at Paris came from India, men who seemed to carry in their minds an older wisdom than the rest of us had, whose traditions ran back into so many of the unhappy fortunes of mankind that they seemed very useful counselors as to how some ray of hope and some prospect of happiness could be opened to its people.

I, for my part, have no jealousy whatever of those five speaking parts in the assembly. Those speaking parts cannot translate themselves into five votes that can in any matter override the voice and purpose of the United States. Let us sweep aside all this language of jealousy. Let us be big enough to know the facts and to welcome the facts, because the facts are based upon the principle that America has always fought for, namely, the equality of self-governing peoples, whether they were big or little—not counting men but counting rights, not counting representation but counting the purpose of that representation.

When you hear an opinion quoted, you do not count the number of persons who hold it; you ask, "Who said that?" You weigh opinions, you do not count them, and the beauty of all democracies is that every voice can be heard, every voice can have its effect, every voice can contribute to the general judgment that is finally arrived at. That is the object of democracy. Let us accept what America has always fought for, and accept it with pride that America showed the way and made the proposal. I do not mean that America made the proposal in this particular instance; I mean that the principle was an American principle, proposed by America.

When you come to the heart of the covenant, my fellow citizens, you will find it in Article 10, and I am very much interested to know that the other things have been blown away like bubbles. There is nothing in the other contentions with regard to the League of Nations, but there is something in Article 10 that you

---

9. Wilson is referring to the Boer War of 1899–1902 in which Great Britain defeated the Afrikaners, or Boers, of South Africa. In 1910 the Union of South Africa became a self-governing dominion within the British Empire.

10. Louis Botha; Jan Christian Smuts.

ought to realize and ought to accept or reject. Article 10 is the heart of the whole matter.

What is Article 10? I never am certain that I can from memory give a literal repetition of its language, but I am sure that I can give an exact interpretation of its meaning. Article 10 provides that every member of the league covenants to respect and preserve the territorial integrity and existing political independence of every other member of the league as against external aggression.

Not against internal disturbance. There was not a man at that table who did not admit the sacredness of the right of self-determination, the sacredness of the right of any body of people to say that they would not continue to live under the government they were then living under—and under Article 11 of the covenant they are given a place to say whether they will live under it or not. For following Article 10 is Article 11, which makes it the right of any member of the league at any time to call attention to anything, anywhere, that is likely to disturb the peace of the world or the good understanding between nations upon which the peace of the world depends.

I want to give you an illustration of what that would mean. You have heard a great deal—something that was true and a great deal that was false—about that provision of the treaty which hands over to Japan the rights which Germany enjoyed in the province of Shantung in China.[11] In the first place, Germany did not enjoy any rights there that other nations had not already claimed. For my part, my judgment, my moral judgment, is against the whole set of concessions. They were, all of them, unjust to China; they ought never to have been exacted; they were all exacted by duress from a great body of thoughtful and ancient and helpless people. There never was any right in any of them. Thank God, America never asked for any, never dreamed of asking for any.

But when Germany got this concession in 1898, the government of the United States made no protest whatever. That was not because the government of the United States was not in the hands of high-minded and conscientious men. It was. William McKinley was President and John Hay was Secretary of State—as safe hands to leave the honor of the United States in as any that you can cite. They made no protest because the state of international law at that time was that it was none of their business unless they could show that the interests of the United States were affected, and the only thing that they could show with regard to the interests of the United States was that Germany might close the doors of Shantung Province against the trade of the United States. They therefore demanded and obtained promises that we could continue to sell merchandise in Shantung.

Immediately following that concession to Germany, there was a concession to Russia of the same sort—of Port Arthur[12]—and Port Arthur was handed over subsequently to Japan on the very territory of the United States. Don't you remember that when Russia and Japan got into war with one another, the war was brought to a conclusion by a treaty written at Portsmouth, New Hampshire,[13] and in that treaty, without the slightest intimation from any authoritative sources in America that the government of the United States had any objection, Port Arthur—Chinese territory—was turned over to Japan.

I want you distinctly to understand that there is no thought of criticism in my mind. I am expounding to you a state of international law. Now, read Articles 10 and 11. You will see that international law is revolutionized by putting morals into it. Article 10 says that no member of the league—and that includes all these nations that have demanded these things unjustly of China—shall impair the territorial integrity or the political independence of any other member of the league. China is going to

---

11. The treaty ceded Shantung Province, formerly a protectorate of Germany, to Japan, which had seized it during the war. Although Wilson secured a verbal pledge from Japan that it would restore Chinese sovereignty within five years, a pledge it honored in 1922, the Shantung provision aroused intense opposition in the United States.

12. Now known as Lüshun, on China's Liaodong Peninsula, Port Arthur was ceded to Russia in 1898 and was occupied by Japan during the Russo-Japanese War of 1904–1905.

13. The treaty was signed on September 5, 1905.

be a member of the league. Article 11 says that any member of the league can call attention to anything that is likely to disturb the peace of the world or the good understanding between nations, and China is, for the first time in the history of mankind, afforded a standing before the jury of the world. I, for my part, have a profound sympathy for China, and I am proud to have taken part in an arrangement which promises the protection of the world to the rights of China. The whole atmosphere of the world is changed by a thing like that, my fellow citizens. The whole international practice of the world is revolutionized.

"But," you will say, "what is the second sentence of Article 10? That is what gives very disturbing thoughts." The second sentence is that the council of the league shall advise what steps, if any, are necessary to carry out the guarantee of the first sentence—namely, that the members will respect and preserve the territorial integrity and political independence of the other members. I do not know any other meaning for the word "advise" except "advise." The council advises, and it cannot advise without the vote of the United States. Why gentlemen should fear that the Congress of the United States would be advised to do something that it did not want to do, I frankly cannot imagine, because they cannot even be advised to do anything unless their own representative has participated in the advice.

It may be that that will impair somewhat the vigor of the league, but nevertheless the fact is so—that we are not obliged to take any advice except our own, which to any man who wants to go his own course is a very satisfactory state of affairs. Every man regards his own advice as best, and I dare say every man mixes his own advice with some thought of his own interest. Whether we use it wisely or unwisely, we can use the vote of the United States to make impossible drawing the United States into any enterprise that she does not care to be drawn into.

Yet Article 10 strikes at the taproot of war. Article 10 is a statement that the very things that have always been sought in imperialistic wars are henceforth foregone by every ambitious nation in the world. I would have felt very lonely, my fellow countrymen, and I would have felt very much disturbed if,

sitting at the peace table in Paris, I had supposed that I was expounding my own ideas. Whether you believe it or not, I know the relative size of my own ideas. I know how they stand related in bulk and proportion to the moral judgments of my fellow countrymen, and I proposed nothing whatever at the peace table at Paris that I had not sufficiently certain knowledge embodied the moral judgment of the citizens of the United States.

I had gone over there with, so to say, explicit instructions. Don't you remember that we laid down fourteen points which should contain the principles of the settlement?[14] They were not my points. In every one of them I was conscientiously trying to read the thought of the people of the United States, and after I uttered those points, I had every assurance given me that could be given me that they did speak the moral judgment of the United States and not my single judgment. Then when it came to that critical period just a little less than a year ago when it was evident that the war was coming to its critical end, all the nations engaged in the war accepted those fourteen principles explicitly as the basis of the armistice[15] and the basis of the peace. In those circumstances I crossed the ocean under bond to my own people and to the other governments with which I was dealing.[16] The whole specification of the method of settlement was written down and accepted beforehand, and we were architects building on those specifications.

It reassures me and fortifies my position to find how, before I went over, men whose judgment the United States has often trusted were of exactly the same opinion that I went abroad to express. Here is something I want to read from Theodore Roosevelt:[17] "The one effective move for obtaining peace is by an agreement among all the great powers in which each should pledge itself not

14. See Wilson's "Fourteen Points" speech of January 8, 1918, pages 124–128.

15. Wilson is referring to the armistice of November 11, 1918, that ended the fighting in Europe.

16. Wilson made two trips to Europe for the Paris Peace Conference. Except for a nine-day stretch in February–March 1919, he was out of the United States from December 4, 1918, to July 8, 1919.

17. President of the United States, 1901–1909.

only to abide by the decisions of a common tribunal but to back its decisions by force. The great civilized nations should combine by solemn agreement in a great world league for the peace of righteousness; a court should be established. A changed and amplified Hague court would meet the requirements, composed of representatives from each nation, whose representatives are sworn to act as judges in each case and not in a representative capacity." Now, there is Article 10. He goes on and says this: "The nations should agree on certain rights that should not be questioned, such as territorial integrity, their right to deal with their domestic affairs, and with such matters as whom they should admit to citizenship. All such guarantee each of their number in possession of these rights."[18]

Now, the other specification is in the covenant. The covenant in another portion guarantees to the members the independent control of their domestic questions. There is not a leg for these gentlemen to stand on when they say that the interests of the United States are not safeguarded in the very points where we are most sensitive. You do not need to be told again that the covenant expressly says that nothing in this covenant shall be construed as affecting the validity of the Monroe Doctrine, for example.[19] You could not be more explicit than that.

And every point of interest is covered, partly for one very interesting reason. This is not the first time that the Foreign Relations Committee of the Senate of the United States has read and considered this covenant. I brought it to this country in March last in a tentative, provisional form, in practically the form that it now has, with the exception of certain additions which I shall mention immediately. I asked the Foreign Relations Committees of both Houses to come to the White House, and we spent a long evening in the frankest discussion of every portion that they wished to discuss.[20] They made certain specific suggestions as

to what should be contained in this document when it was to be revised. I carried those suggestions to Paris, and every one of them was adopted.

What more could I have done? What more could have been obtained? The very matters upon which these gentlemen were most concerned were the right of withdrawal, which is now expressly stated; the safeguarding of the Monroe Doctrine, which is now accomplished; the exclusion from action by the league of domestic questions, which is now accomplished. All along the line, every suggestion of the United States was adopted after the covenant had been drawn up in its first form and had been published for the criticism of the world. There is a very true sense in which I can say this is a tested American document.

I am dwelling upon these points, my fellow citizens, in spite of the fact that I dare say to most of you they are perfectly well known, because in order to meet the present situation, we have got to know what we are dealing with. We are not dealing with the kind of document which this is represented by some gentlemen to be; and inasmuch as we are dealing with a document simon-pure[21] in respect of the very principles we have professed and lived up to, we have got to do one or other of two things—we have got to adopt it or reject it. There is no middle course. You cannot go in on a special-privilege basis of your own. I take it that you are too proud to ask to be exempted from responsibilities which the other members of the league will carry. We go in upon equal terms or we do not go in at all.

And if we do not go in, my fellow citizens, think of the tragedy of that result—the only sufficient guarantee to the peace of the world withheld! Ourselves drawn apart with that dangerous pride which means that we shall be ready to take care of ourselves. And that means that we shall maintain great standing armies and an irresistible navy; that means we shall have the organization of a military nation; that means we shall have a general staff, with the kind of power that the general staff of Germany had—to mobilize this great manhood of the nation

---

18. Paraphrased from "Theodore Roosevelt Writes on Helping the Cause of World Peace," *New York Times*, October 18, 1914.

19. The Monroe Doctrine of 1823 declared that the United States would regard any attempt on the part of European powers "to extend their system to any portion of this hemisphere as dangerous to our peace and safety."

20. This meeting took place on February 26, 1919.

---

21. Genuine or untainted; derived from the character Simon Pure in Susanna Centlivre's play *A Bold Stroke for a Wife* (1717).

when it pleases, all the energy of our young men drawn into the thought and preparation for war.

What of our pledges to the men that lie dead in France?[22] We said that they went over there not to prove the prowess of America or her readiness for another war, but to see to it that there never was such a war again. It always seems to make it difficult for me to say anything, my fellow citizens, when I think of my clients in this case. My clients are the children; my clients are the next generation. They do not know what promises and bonds I undertook when I ordered the armies of the United States to the soil of France, but I know, and I intend to redeem my pledges to the children; they shall not be sent upon a similar errand.

Again and again, my fellow citizens, mothers who lost their sons in France have come to me and, taking my hand, have shed tears upon it not only, but they have added, "God bless you, Mr. President!" Why, my fellow citizens, should they pray God to bless me? I advised the Congress of the United States to create the situation that led to the death of their sons. I ordered their sons overseas. I consented to their sons being put in the most difficult parts of the battle line, where death was certain, as in the impenetrable difficulties of the Forest of Argonne. Why should they weep upon my hand and call down the blessings of God upon me? Because they believe that their boys died for something that vastly transcends any of the immediate and palpable objects of the war. They believe, and they rightly believe, that their sons saved the liberty of the world. They believe that wrapped up with the liberty of the world is the continuous protection of that liberty by the concerted powers of all civilized people. They believe that this sacrifice was made in order that other sons should not be called upon for a similar gift—the gift of life, the gift of all that died.

And if we did not see this thing through, if we fulfilled the dearest present wish of Germany and now dissociated ourselves from those alongside whom we fought in the war, would not something of the halo go away from the gun over the mantelpiece, or the sword? Would not the old uniform lose something of its significance? These men were crusaders. They were not going forth to prove the might of the United States.

They were going forth to prove the might of justice and right, and all the world accepted them as crusaders, and their transcendent achievement has made all the world believe in America as it believes in no other nation organized in the modern world. There seems to me to stand between us and the rejection or qualification of this treaty the serried ranks of those boys in khaki—not only these boys who came home, but those dear ghosts that still deploy upon the fields of France.

My friends, on last Decoration Day[23] I went to a beautiful hillside near Paris, where was located the Cemetery of Suresnes, a cemetery given over to the burial of the American dead. Behind me on the slopes was rank upon rank of living American soldiers, and lying before me upon the levels of the plain was rank upon rank of departed American soldiers. Right by the side of the stand where I spoke there was a little group of French women who had adopted those graves, had made themselves mothers of those dear ghosts by putting flowers every day upon those graves, taking them as their own sons, their own beloved, because they had died in the same cause—France was free and the world was free because America had come!

I wish some men in public life who are now opposing the settlement for which these men died could visit such a spot as that. I wish that the thought that comes out of those graves could penetrate their consciousness. I wish that they could feel the moral obligation that rests upon us not to go back on those boys but to see the thing through, to see it through to the end and make good their redemption of the world. For nothing less depends upon this decision, nothing less than the liberation and salvation of the world.

You will say, "Is the league an absolute guarantee against war?" No; I do not know any absolute guarantee against the errors of human judgment or the violence of human passion. But I tell you this: With a cooling space of nine months for human passion, not much of it will keep hot.

I had a couple of friends who were in the habit of losing their tempers, and when they lost their tempers, they were in the habit of using very unparliamentary language. Some of their friends induced them to make a promise that they never would swear inside

---

22. More than 116,000 Americans lost their lives in World War I.

23. Now known as Memorial Day.

the town limits. When the impulse next came upon them, they took a streetcar to go out of town to swear, and by the time they got out of town, they did not want to swear. They came back convinced that they were just what they were—a couple of unspeakable fools—and the habit of getting angry and of swearing suffered great inroads upon it by that experience.

Now, illustrating the great by the small, that is true of the passions of nations. It is true of the passions of men however you combine them. Give them space to cool off. I ask you this: If it is not an absolute insurance against war, do you want no insurance at all? Do you want nothing? Do you want not only no probability that war will not recur, but the probability that it will recur?

The arrangements of justice do not stand of themselves, my fellow citizens. The arrangements of this treaty are just, but they need the support of the combined power of the great nations of the world. And they will have that support. Now that the mists of this great question have cleared away, I believe that men will see the truth, eye to eye and face to face. There is one thing that the American people always rise to and extend their hand to, and that is the truth of justice and of liberty and of peace. We have accepted that truth and we are going to be led by it, and it is going to lead us, and through us the world, out into pastures of quietness and peace such as the world never dreamed of before.

Crystal Eastman

Now We Can Begin

PORT WASHINGTON, NEW YORK
SEPTEMBER 10, 1920

THE NINETEENTH AMENDMENT had barely been ratified when the unity among female leaders that had been forged in the battle for suffrage began to disintegrate. With the vote in hand, they asked, what should be the movement's next objective? The most ambitious agenda for women was articulated by Crystal Eastman, a graduate of Vassar College, Columbia University, and New York University law school who first came to public attention during the years 1907–1910 because of her prominent role in developing workers' compensation laws. One of the few radical feminists who was also a Socialist, in 1913 she helped found what became the National Woman's Party, which was distinguished by its use of militant tactics such as civil disobedience and hunger strikes in the campaign for suffrage. As a speaker, Eastman was described by Freda Kirchwey, editor of *The Nation*, as "simple, direct, dramatic. Force poured from her strong body and her rich voice, and people followed where she led.... When she spoke to people—whether it was to a small committee or a swarming crowd—hearts beat faster and nerves tightened."

Eastman's "Now We Can Begin" appeared in the December 1920 issue of *The Liberator*, a magazine she edited with her brother Max. Although "Now We Can Begin" has often been reprinted, its provenance as a speech has not been clearly established. One anthologist states that Eastman delivered it several times in New York City; another claims it was presented in 1919 at the First Feminist Congress; yet another prints the text without identifying a date or occasion. As far as we are able to determine, the speech was given only once, on September 10, 1920, at a meeting of National Woman's Party officers held at the Port Washington mansion of Alva Belmont to debate the organization's future now that suffrage had been achieved.

After distinguishing the goals of feminism from "the workers' battle for industrial freedom," Eastman parted company from those feminists who placed the condition of woman's soul above material conditions. What women needed, Eastman argued, was "to create conditions of outward freedom in which a free woman's soul can be born and grow." Those conditions included giving women the same unfettered choice of occupations that men enjoyed, effacing traditional gender roles by recasting the early education of children, creating "voluntary motherhood" through the legalization of birth control, and providing government economic support for women who chose to remain home and raise children.

Eastman's program was rejected as impractical and visionary, but her speech, doubtless revised for publication, reveals the boldness of thought and expression that made her, in Kirchwey's words, "a symbol of what the free woman might be." When she died of kidney disease in 1928 at the age of forty-seven, the woman's movement lost one of its most iconoclastic voices.

◇◇◇◇◇◇◇◇◇◇◇◇◇◇◇◇◇◇◇◇◇◇◇◇◇◇◇◇◇◇◇◇◇◇◇◇◇◇◇

Most women will agree that August 23, the day when the Tennessee legislature finally enacted the federal suffrage amendment, is a day to begin with, not a day to end with.[1] Men are saying perhaps, "Thank God, this everlasting woman's fight is over!" But women, if I know them, are saying, "Now at last we can begin." In fighting for the right to vote, most women have tried to be either noncommittal or thoroughly respectable on every other subject. Now they can say what they are really after; and what they are after, in common with all the rest of the struggling world, is *freedom*.

Freedom is a large word.

Many feminists are Socialists, many are Communists, not a few are active leaders in these movements.

But the true feminist, no matter how far to the left she may be in the revolutionary movement, sees the woman's battle as distinct in its objects and different in its methods from the workers' battle for industrial freedom. She knows, of course, that the vast majority of women as well as men are without property, and are of necessity bread and butter slaves under a system of society which allows the very sources of life to be privately owned by a few, and she counts herself a loyal soldier in the working-class army that is marching to overthrow that system. But as a feminist she also knows that the whole of woman's slavery is not summed up in the profit system, nor her complete emancipation assured by the downfall of capitalism.

Woman's freedom, in the feminist sense, can be fought for and conceivably won before the gates open into industrial democracy. On the other hand, woman's freedom, in the feminist sense, is not inher-

1. Ratification by the Tennessee legislature gave the suffrage amendment the necessary number of states to become part of the U.S. Constitution.

ent in the Communist ideal. All feminists are familiar with the revolutionary leader who "can't see" the woman's movement. "What's the matter with the women? My wife's all right," he says. And his wife, one usually finds, is raising his children in a Bronx flat or a dreary suburb, to which he returns occasionally for food and sleep when all possible excitement and stimulus have been wrung from the fight. If we should graduate into communism tomorrow, this man's attitude to his wife would not be changed. The proletarian dictatorship may or may not free women. We must begin now to enlighten the future dictators.

What, then, is "the matter with women"? What is the problem of women's freedom? It seems to me to be this: how to arrange the world so that women can be human beings, with a chance to exercise their infinitely varied gifts in infinitely varied ways, instead of being destined by the accident of their sex to one field of activity—housework and child raising. And second, if and when they choose housework and child raising, to have that occupation recognized by the world as work, requiring a definite economic reward and not merely entitling the performer to be dependent on some man.

This is not the whole of feminism, of course, but it is enough to begin with. "Oh, don't begin with economics," my friends often protest. "Woman does not live by bread alone. What she needs first of all is a free soul." And I can agree that women will never be great until they achieve a certain emotional freedom, a strong healthy egotism, and some unpersonal sources of joy—that in this inner sense we cannot make woman free by changing her economic status. What we can do, however, is to create conditions of outward freedom in which a free woman's soul can be born and grow. It is these outward conditions with which an organized feminist movement must concern itself.

Freedom of choice in occupation and individual economic independence for women: How shall we approach this next feminist objective? First, by breaking down all remaining barriers, actual as well as legal, which make it difficult for women to enter or succeed in the various professions, to go into and get on in business, to learn trades and practice them, to join trades unions. Chief among these remaining barriers is inequality in pay. Here the ground is already broken. This is the easiest part of our program.

Second, we must institute a revolution in the early training and education of both boys and girls. It must be womanly as well as manly to earn your own living, to stand on your own feet. And it must be manly as well as womanly to know how to cook and sew and clean and take care of yourself in the ordinary exigencies of life. I need not add that the second part of this revolution will be more passionately resisted than the first. Men will not give up their privilege of helplessness without a struggle. The average man has a carefully cultivated ignorance about household matters—from what to do with the crumbs to the grocer's telephone number—a sort of cheerful inefficiency which protects him better than the reputation for having a violent temper. It was his mother's fault in the beginning, but even as a boy he was quick to see how a general reputation for being "no good around the house" would serve him throughout life, and half-consciously he began to cultivate that helplessness until today it is the despair of feminist wives.

A growing number of men admire the woman who has a job, and, especially since the cost of living doubled, rather like the idea of their own wives contributing to the family income by outside work. And of course for generations there have been whole towns full of wives who are forced by the bitterest necessity to spend the same hours at the factory that their husbands spend. But these breadwinning wives have not yet developed homemaking husbands. When the two come home from the factory, the man sits down while his wife gets supper, and he does so with exactly the same sense of foreordained right as if he were "supporting her." Higher up in the economic scale the same thing is true. The business or professional woman who is married perhaps engages a cook, but the responsibility is not shifted; it is still hers. She "hires and fires," she orders meals, she does the buying, she meets and resolves all domestic crises, she takes charge of moving, furnishing, settling. She may be, like her husband, a busy executive at her office all day, but unlike him, she is also an executive in a small way every night and morning at home. Her noon hour is spent in planning, and too often her Sundays and holidays are spent in "catching up."

Two businesswomen can "make a home" together without either one being overburdened or overbored. It is because they both know how and both feel responsible. But it is a rare man who can marry one of them and continue the homemaking partnership. Yet if there are no children, there is nothing essentially different in the combination. Two self-supporting adults decide to make a home together: if both are women, it is a pleasant partnership, more fun than work; if one is a man, it is almost never a partnership—the woman simply adds running the home to her regular outside job. Unless she is very strong, it is too much for her, she gets tired and bitter over it, and finally perhaps gives up her outside work and condemns herself to the tiresome half job of housekeeping for two.

Cooperative schemes and electrical devices will simplify the business of homemaking, but they will not get rid of it entirely. As far as we can see ahead people will always want homes, and a happy home cannot be had without a certain amount of rather monotonous work and responsibility. How can we change the nature of man so that he will honorably share that work and responsibility and thus make the homemaking enterprise a song instead of a burden? Most assuredly not by laws or revolutionary decrees. Perhaps we must cultivate or simulate a little of that highly prized helplessness ourselves. But fundamentally it is a problem of education, of early training—we must bring up feminist sons.

Sons? Daughters? They are born of women—how can women be free to choose their occupation, at all times cherishing their economic independence, unless they stop having children? This is a further question for feminism. If the feminist program goes to pieces on the arrival of the first baby, it is false and useless. For ninety-nine out of every hundred women want children, and seventy-five out of every hundred want to take care of their own children, or at any rate so closely superintend their care as to make any other full-time occupation impossible for at least ten or fifteen years. Is there any such thing then as freedom of choice in occupation for women? And is not the

family the inevitable economic unit and woman's individual economic independence, at least during that period, out of the question?

The feminist must have an answer to these questions, and she has. The immediate feminist program must include voluntary motherhood. Freedom of any kind for women is hardly worth considering unless it is assumed that they will know how to control the size of their families. "Birth control" is just as elementary an essential in our propaganda as "equal pay." Women are to have children when they want them; that's the first thing. That ensures some freedom of occupational choice; those who do not wish to be mothers will not have an undesired occupation thrust upon them by accident, and those who do wish to be mothers may choose in a general way how many years of their lives they will devote to the occupation of child raising.

But is there any way of ensuring a woman's economic independence while child raising is her chosen occupation? Or must she sink into that dependent state from which, as we all know, it is so hard to rise again? That brings us to the fourth feature of our program—motherhood endowment. It seems that the only way we can keep mothers free, at least in a capitalist society, is by the establishment of a principle that the occupation of raising children is peculiarly and directly a service to society, and that the mother upon whom the necessity and privilege of performing this service naturally falls is entitled to an adequate economic reward from the political government. It is idle to talk of real economic independence for women unless this principle is accepted. But with a generous endowment of motherhood provided by legislation, with all laws against voluntary motherhood and education in its methods repealed, with the feminist ideal of education accepted in home and school, and with all special barriers removed in every field of human activity, there is no reason why woman should not become almost a human thing.

It will be time enough then to consider whether she has a soul.

Clarence Darrow

Plea for Leopold and Loeb

CHICAGO, ILLINOIS
AUGUST 22, 23, AND 25, 1924

I T WAS THE crime of the century. On May 21, 1924, Bobby Franks, a fourteen-year-old boy in Chicago, was abducted in broad daylight from one of the city's most fashionable neighborhoods and murdered by nineteen-year-old Nathan Leopold and eighteen-year-old Richard Loeb. Although they demanded a $10,000 ransom, Leopold and Loeb had been raised in wealth and privilege and were animated not solely by money, but by the challenge of seeing if they could commit the perfect crime. The case quickly became a national, even international, sensation as newspapers followed every step of the investigation. Leopold and Loeb were arrested at the end of May and confessed shortly thereafter. The press and public called for swift retribution, and prosecutors announced they would seek the death penalty.

Sixty-seven years of age, perennial champion of the underdog, and a legendary courtroom pleader, Clarence Darrow agreed to defend Leopold and Loeb in hopes he could strike a blow against capital punishment. Knowing he could not secure an acquittal from any jury, on the opening day of the trial he surprised everyone by having his clients plead guilty, thereby turning the proceedings from a criminal trial to a sentencing hearing. The issue before the court now became whether Leopold and Loeb would be sentenced to death or to life in prison, a decision that would be rendered solely by the presiding judge, John R. Caverly.

On Friday, August 22, after a month of evidence and witnesses and cross-examinations, Darrow began his summation to the court. Continuing on Saturday the twenty-third and concluding on Monday the twenty-fifth, it remains the most famous closing statement in American law. Referring to his clients as "Dickie" and "Babe," Darrow portrayed them as "immature and diseased children" who could not be held responsible for their actions. For evidence he pointed to the motiveless nature of the crime, Leopold and Loeb's lack of remorse, their warped ideas about right and wrong, and the testimony of the psychologists—known in those days as alienists—he had called to the stand. Throughout, he hammered at capital punishment, claiming that the execution of his clients would be "infinitely more cold-blooded, whether justified or not, than any act that these boys have committed or can commit."

In what proved to be his most persuasive argument, Darrow contended that ever since complete records had been kept in the state of Illinois, no judge had sentenced to death any defendant under the age of twenty-one who had pled guilty. Putting the full weight of personal responsibility upon Judge Caverly, Darrow told him, "You may hang these boys; you may hang them by the neck till they are dead," but doing so would not return Bobby Franks to life and would not prevent future murders. It would only turn society "backward toward the barbarism which once possessed the world." Darrow urged Caverly to side with the future and to affirm the "faith that all life is worth saving and that mercy is the highest attribute of man." By the end, according to one reporter, "tears were streaming down the judge's face."

Caverly presented his ruling on September 10. Calling the crime one of "singular atrocity," he said he could find no mitigating circumstances "in the act itself, nor in its motive or lack of motive, nor in the antecedents of the offenders." However, because the defendants were "not of full age," he was imposing life imprisonment instead of the death penalty. Echoing Darrow's arguments, he declared the ruling was consistent with Illinois precedent and was "in accordance with the progress of criminal law all over the world and with the dictates of enlightened humanity." "This decision," Darrow told the press, "caps my career as a criminal lawyer." Except for the 1926 Scopes case on the teaching of evolution, he did little trial work after Leopold and Loeb. He died in 1938, two years after Loeb was stabbed to death by a fellow inmate at the Stateville, Illinois, penitentiary. Leopold spent three decades in prison, received parole in 1958, and died of natural causes in 1971.

Because of its length, Darrow's speech has seldom been published in its entirety. Most reprints, whether complete or truncated, are derived from the 1926 pamphlet issued by Haldeman-Julius Publications of Girard, Kansas, or from Maureen McKernan's *The Amazing Trial of Leopold and Loeb*, published within a few months of the trial. Both of these versions, however, were substantially revised for publication and neither retains the oral quality of Darrow's courtroom presentation. In the text presented below, the first day of Darrow's speech is taken from the official court transcript. The transcript for days two and three, however, no longer exists. For those days, we have turned to a little-known volume from the Wilson Publishing Company that was released shortly after the trial. Almost identical to the official transcript in reporting the first day of Darrow's summation, it possesses as well the distinctly extemporaneous flavor of his remarks on days two and three. We have supplemented the Wilson text as necessary from the daily stenographic accounts of Darrow's speech in the Chicago newspapers. Combining all these sources provides a more accurate text of the full speech than has heretofore been published and gives us a fuller view of Darrow's rhetorical power in the dynamic oral environment of the courtroom.

Friday, August 22

It has been almost three months since I first assumed the great responsibility that has devolved upon me and my associates in this case, and I am willing to confess that it has been three months of perplexity and great anxiety—a trouble which I would gladly have been spared excepting for my feelings of affection toward some of the members of one of these families. It is a responsibility that is almost too great for anyone to assume that has devolved upon me. But we lawyers can no more choose than the court can choose.[1]

Your Honor, our anxiety over this case has not been due to the facts that are connected with this most unfortunate affair, but to the almost unheard-of publicity—to the fact that newspapers all over this country have been giving it space such as they have almost never given to a case before, the fact that day after day the people of Chicago have been regaled with stories of all sorts about it until almost every person has formed an opinion.

And when the public are interested and want a punishment, no matter what the offense is, great or small, they only think of one punishment, and that is death. It may not be a question that involves the taking of human life; it may be a question of pure prejudice alone, but when the public speaks as one man, they only think of killing someone. We have been in the presence of this stress and strain for three months. We did what we could and all we could to gain the confidence of the public, who in the end really control, whether wisely or unwisely.

It was announced that there were millions of dollars to be spent on this case. Wild and extravagant stories were freely published as if they were facts. Here was to be an effort to save the lives of two boys—that should not have required an effort even—but to save their lives by the use of money in fabulous amounts such as these families never had nor could have.

We announced to the public that no excessive use of money would be made in this case—neither for lawyers, for psychiatrists,[2] or in any other way.

We have faithfully kept that promise which we made to the public. The psychiatrists, as has been shown by the evidence in this case, are receiving a per diem, and only a per diem, which is the same as is paid by the state. The attorneys of their own motion, at their own request, have agreed to take such amount as the officers of the Chicago Bar Association may think is proper in this case.[3] If we fail in this defense, it will not be for lack of money. It will be on account of money. Money has been the most serious handicap that we have met. There are times when poverty is fortunate, and this is one of those times.

I insist, Your Honor, that had this been the case of two boys of this age, unconnected with families who are supposed to have great wealth, that there is not a state's attorney in Illinois who would not at once have consented to a plea of guilty and a punishment in the penitentiary for life. Not one. No lawyer could have justified it. No prosecution could have justified it. We could have come into this court without evidence, without argument, with nothing, and this court would have given to us what every judge in the city of Chicago has given to every boy in the city of Chicago since the first capital case was tried. And we would have had no contest. We are here with the lives of two boys imperiled, with the public aroused. For what? Because, unfortunately, their parents have money. Nothing else.

I told Your Honor in the beginning that never had there been a case in Chicago where on a plea of guilty a boy under twenty-one had been sentenced to death. I will raise that age and say never has there been a case where a human being under the age of twenty-eight or thirty has been sentenced to death. And I think I am safe in saying, although I have not examined all the records and could not, but I think I am safe in saying that never has there been such a case in the state of Illinois.[4]

---

1. At this point Judge Caverly ordered a short recess while the bailiff and police quieted a commotion in the courtroom and adjoining corridors. Darrow resumed his speech after the recess.

2. The Leopold-Loeb case set precedent when Judge Caverly, over strenuous opposition from the prosecution, allowed the defense to present psychiatric evidence in support of Darrow's claim that "the condition of mind" of the defendants was a mitigating factor in the commission of their crime and constituted grounds for reducing their sentence from death to life in prison. Before this time, psychiatric evidence had been used solely to support the claim that a defendant was insane, could not be held responsible for his or her actions, and therefore should not be subject to punishment.

---

3. The families of the defendants failed to abide by this agreement and took more than a year to pay the defense attorneys. Darrow eventually received a net fee of $35,000.

4. There had been at least one such case. On January 21, 1876, Marshall Crain, age 26, was executed in Marion, Illinois, after pleading guilty to the murder of William Spence.

And yet this court is urged, aye, threatened, that he must hang two boys contrary to the precedents, contrary to the acts of every judge who ever held court in this state. Why? Tell me what public necessity there is for this. Why need the state's attorney ask for something that was never asked before? Why need a judge be urged by every argument, moderate and immoderate, to hang two boys in the face of every precedent in Illinois and in the face of the progress of the last fifty—at least twenty-five—years?

Lawyers stand here by the day and read cases from the Dark Ages where judges have said that if a man had a grain of sense left, if he was barely out of his cradle, he could be hanged because he knew the difference between right and wrong. There have been boys eighteen, seventeen, sixteen, and fourteen. Brother Marshall[5] has not half done his job. He should read his beloved Blackstone[6] again.

I have heard in the last six months[7] nothing but the cry for blood. I have heard raised from the office of the state's attorney nothing but the breath of hate. I have heard precedents quoted which would be a disgrace to a savage race. I have seen a court urged almost to the point of threats to hang two boys, in the face of science, in the face of philosophy, in the face of humanity, in the face of experience, in the face of all the better and more humane thought of the age. Why did not my friend Mr. Marshall, who dug up from the relics of the buried past these precedents that would put a blush of shame upon the face of a savage, read this from Blackstone: "Under fourteen, though an infant shall be judged to be incapable of guile prima facie, yet if it appeared to the court and the jury that he was capable of guile and could discern between good and evil he may be convicted and suffer death."[8]

Thus a girl thirteen has been burned for killing her mistress. Lord, how that would delight Dr. Krohn![9] He would lick his chops over that more than over his dastardly homicidal attempt to kill these boys. A girl of thirteen was burned because she probably didn't say "Please" to her mistress—out of my friend's beloved Blackstone. And one boy of ten and another of nine years of age, who had killed her companion, were sentenced to death and he of ten actually hanged. Why? He knew the difference between right and wrong. He had learned that in Sunday school.

Age does not count. Why, Mr. Savage[10] says age makes no difference and that if this court should do what every other court in Illinois had done since its foundation and refuse to sentence these boys to death, nobody would be hanged in Illinois any more. Well, I can imagine something worse than that. So long as this terrible tool is to be used for a plaything, without thought or consideration, in seeking to inflame the mob with the thought that a boy must be hanged, or civilization will be hanged, we ought to get rid of it and get rid of it altogether, for the protection of human life.

Blackstone, which my friend Marshall read by the page, as if it had anything to do with a fairly enlightened age, as if it had anything to do with the year 1924, as if it had anything to do with Chicago, with its boys' courts and its fairly tender protection of the young, he is called here to urge this judge to do what was never done before. Now, Your Honor, I shall discuss that more in detail a little later, and I only say it now because my friend Mr. Savage—did you pick him for his name or his ability or his learning—because my friend Mr. Savage, in as savage a speech as he knew how to make, said to this court that we pled guilty because we were afraid to do anything else. Your Honor, that is true. That is true. I want to refer to one thing in passing, and then

---

5. Assistant State's Attorney Thomas Marshall.

6. Sir William Blackstone, whose *Commentaries on the Laws of England* (1765–1769) were cited by Marshall in his argument to the court of July 31 against allowing the defense to claim mitigating circumstances as grounds for not imposing the death sentence on Leopold and Loeb.

7. Darrow meant to say "six weeks," referring to the time that had passed since the start of the trial.

8. From Blackstone's *Commentaries*, book 4, chapter 2.

9. Chicago psychiatrist William O. Krohn, former head of the department of psychology at the University of Illinois, who testified for the prosecution and whose expertise and integrity Darrow assailed relentlessly.

10. Assistant State's Attorney Joseph P. Savage, who argued vehemently for the death penalty in his summation of August 20–21.

I will discuss this age[11] in the place where I think it belongs.

It was not correct that we would have defended these boys and asked for a verdict of not guilty if we thought we could win. We would not. We believe we have been fair to this court; we believe we have been fair to the public. Anyhow we have tried, and we have tried under terribly hard conditions. We have said to the public and to this court that neither the parents nor the friends nor the attorneys would want these boys released. That they are as they are, unfortunate though it be, it is true, and those the closest to them know perfectly well that they should not be released, and that they should be permanently isolated from society. We have said that, and we mean it. We are asking this court to save their lives, which is the least and the most that a judge can do.

We did plead guilty before Your Honor because we were afraid to submit our cause to a jury. I would not for a moment deny to this court or to this community a realization of the serious danger we were in and how perplexed we were before we took this most unusual step. I can tell Your Honor why. I have found that years and experience with life tempers one's emotions and makes him more understanding of his fellow men. When my friend Savage is my age, or even of yours, he will read his address to this court with horror. I am aware that as one grows older, he is less critical. He is not so sure. He is inclined to make some allowance for his fellow man. I am aware that a court has more experience, more judgment, and more kindliness than a jury.

And then, Your Honor, it may not be hardly fair to the court, because I am aware that I have helped to place a serious burden upon your shoulders. And at that, I have always meant to be your friend. But this was not an act of friendship. I know perfectly well that where responsibility is divided by twelve, it is easy to say: "Away with him." But, Your Honor, if these boys hang, you must do it. There can be no division of responsibility here. You must do it. You can

never explain that the rest overpowered you. It must be by your deliberate, cool, premeditated act, without a chance to shift responsibility.

We did it, Your Honor. It was not a kindness to you. We placed this responsibility on your shoulders because we were mindful of the rights of our clients, and we were mindful of the unhappy families who have done no wrong.

Now, let us see, Your Honor, what we had to sustain us. Of course, I have known Your Honor for a good many years. Not intimately. I could not say that I could even guess from my experience what Your Honor might do. But I did know something. I knew, Your Honor, that ninety unfortunate human beings had been hanged by the neck until dead in the city of Chicago in our history. We would not have any civilization except for those ninety being hanged, and if we cannot make it ninety-two, we will have to shut up shop. Some ninety human beings have been hanged in the history of Chicago, and of those only three have been hanged on the plea of guilty—one of thirty.

I know that in the last ten years three hundred and fifty people have been indicted for murder in the city of Chicago and have pleaded guilty. Three hundred and fifty have pleaded guilty in the city of Chicago, and only one has been hanged. And my friend who is prosecuting this case deserves the honor of that hanging while he was on the bench.[12] But his victim was forty years old.

Your Honor will never thank me for unloading this responsibility upon you, but you know that I would have been untrue to my clients if I had not concluded to take this chance before a court instead of submitting it to a poisoned jury in the city of Chicago. I did it knowing that it would be an unheard-of thing for any court, no matter who, to sentence these boys to death. And that far, so far as that goes, Mr. Savage is right. I hope, Your Honor, that I have made no mistake. I could have wished that the state's attorney's

11. In some reprints of Darrow's speech, his wording has been changed from "age" to "phase." There can be little doubt, however, that he meant to say "age," referring to the present "enlightened age" mentioned earlier in the paragraph.

12. State's Attorney William E. Crowe, who led the prosecution against Leopold and Loeb, served as a judge of the Circuit Court of Cook County from 1916 to 1921. In October 1917 he sentenced Thomas Fitzgerald to death for the murder of a six-year-old girl.

office had met this case with the same fairness that we have met it.

It has seemed to me as I have listened to this case, five or six times repeating the story of this tragedy, spending days to urge Your Honor that a condition of mind could not mitigate, or that tender years could not mitigate, it has seemed to me that it ought to be beneath the representatives of a proud state like this to invoke the dark and cruel and bloody past to affect this court and compass these boys' death.

And, Your Honor, I must for a moment criticize the arguments that have preceded me. I can read to you in a minute my friend Marshall's argument, barring Blackstone, and I will simply call your attention to what he left out. But the rest of his arguments and the rest of brother Savage's argument I can sum up in a minute: cruel, dastardly, premeditated, fiendish, abandoned, and malignant heart—that sounds like a cancer—cowardly, cold-blooded.[13] Now that is what I have listened to for three days against two minors, two children, who could not sign a note or make a deed. I have listened to that for three days.

Cowardly? Well, I don't know. Let me tell you something that I think is cowardly, whether their acts were or not. Here is Dickie Loeb, and they object to anybody calling him Dickie, although everybody did; but they think they can hang him easier if his name is Richard, so we will call him Richard. Eighteen years old at the time. Here is Nathan Leopold Jr., nineteen. Here are three officers watching them. They are led out and in this jail and across the bridge waiting to be hanged. Not a chance to get away. Handcuffed when they get out. Not a chance. Penned like a rat in a trap, and for some lawyer with physiological eloquence to wave his fist in front of his face and shout "cowardly" does not appeal to me as a brave act. It does not commend itself to me as a proper thing for a state's attorney or his assistant—and even defendants not yet hanged have some rights with an official.

Cold-blooded? But I don't know, Your Honor. I will discuss that a little later, whether it was cold-blooded or not. Cold-blooded? Why? Because they planned and schemed and arranged and fixed? Yes.

But here are the officers of justice, so-called, with all of the power of the state, with all the influence of the press, to fan this community into a frenzy of hate with all of that, who for months have been planning and scheming and contriving and working to take these two boys' lives. You may stand them up on a scaffold, on a trap door, and choke them to death, but that act would be infinitely more cold-blooded, whether it was justified or not, than any act that these boys have committed or can commit. Cold-blooded! Let the state, who is so anxious to take these boys' lives, set an example in consideration, kindheartedness, and tenderness before they call my clients cold-blooded.

Now, another thing, Your Honor. I have heard this crime as stated—this most distressing and unfortunate homicide, as I would call it; this cold-blooded murder, as the state would call it. I call it a homicide particularly distressing because I am defending. They call it a cold-blooded murder because they want to take their lives. Call it what you will. I have heard this case talked of, and I have heard these lawyers say that this was the coldest-blooded murder that the civilized world ever knew. Of course, I don't know what they include in the civilized world. I suppose Illinois, although they talk as if they did not. But we will assume Illinois. This is the most cold-blooded murder, says the state, that ever occurred.

Now, Your Honor, I have been practicing law a good deal longer than I should have—anyhow, for forty-five or forty-six years—and during a part of that time I have tried a good many criminal cases, defending always. It does not mean that I am better. It probably means that I am more squeamish than the other fellow. It neither means I am better or worse. It means the way I am made. I can't help it. I am like the other fellow—I don't want to help it.

I have never yet tried a case where the state's attorney did not say it was the most cold-blooded, inexcusable, premeditated case that ever occurred. If it was murder, there never was such a murder. If it was robbery, there never was such a robbery. If it was a conspiracy, it was the most terrible conspiracy that ever happened since the Star Chamber passed into oblivion.[14] If it was larceny, there never was such a larceny.

---

13. Darrow is referring to the arguments by Marshall and Savage on August 19–20 and 20–21, respectively.

14. Notorious for its unfair judicial proceedings, England's Court of the Star Chamber was abolished in 1641.

Now, I am speaking moderately. All of them are the worst. Why? Well, it adds to the credit of the state's attorney to be connected with a big case. That is one thing. They can say, "Well, I tried the cold-bloodiest—is that right, cold-bloodiest?—murder case that was ever tried, and I convicted them, and they are dead." Or, "I tried the worst forgery case that was ever tried, and I won that. I never did do anything that wasn't big." Lawyers are apt to say that, anyhow.

And then there is another thing, Your Honor. Of course, I generally try cases to juries, and these adjectives always go well with juries: bloody, cold-blooded, despicable, cowardly, dastardly. The whole litany of the state's attorney's office always goes well with a jury. The twelve jurors, being good themselves, think it is a tribute to their virtue if they follow the litany of the state's attorney. I suppose it might have some effect with the court. I do not know. Anyway, those are the chances we take. When we do our best to save life and reputation, those are the chances we take.

"Here, your clients have pleaded guilty to the most cold-blooded murder that ever took place in the history of the world. And how does a judge dare to refuse to hang by the neck until dead two cowardly ruffians who committed the coldest-blooded murder in the history of the world?" Well, now, that is a good talking point. I want to give some attention to this cold-blooded murder, Your Honor.

Was it a cold-blooded murder? Was it the most terrible murder that ever happened in the state of Illinois? Was it the most dastardly act in the annals of crime? No. I insist, Your Honor, that under all fair rules and measurements, this was one of the least dastardly and cruel of any that I have known anything about.

Now, let us see how we measure it. They say that this was a cruel murder, the worst that ever happened. I say that very few murders ever occurred that were as free from it as this. Now, let's see how we measure it. There ought to be some rule to determine whether a murder is cruel or not exceedingly cruel.

Of course, Your Honor, I admit right off that I hate killing, and I hate it no matter how it is done. Whether you shoot a man through the heart or cut his head off with an axe or kill him with a chisel or tie a rope around his neck, I hate it. I always did. I always shall. But there are degrees. And if I might be permitted to make my own rules, I would say if I were estimating what was the most cruel murder, I might first consider the victim, as to his suffering. Now, probably the state would not take that rule. They would say the one that had the most attention in the newspapers. In that way they have got me beat at the start. But I would say the first thing to consider was the degree of pain to the victim.

Poor little Bobby Franks suffered very little. This is no excuse for his killing. If to hang these two boys would bring him back to life, I would say let them go, and I believe their parents would say it too. But "the moving finger writes and, having writ, moves on; nor all your piety nor wit can lure it back to cancel half a line or change one word of it."[15] Robert Franks is dead, and we cannot change that. It was all over in fifteen minutes after he got into the car, and he probably never knew it or thought of it. That does not justify it. It is the last thing I would do. I am sorry for the poor boy. I am sorry for his parents. But it is done.

Of course, I cannot say with the certainty of Mr. Savage that he would have been a great man if he had grown up. At fourteen years of age I don't know whether he would or not. Savage, I suppose, is a mind reader, and he says he would. He has a fantasy, which is hanging. So far as the cruelty to the victim is concerned, you can scarce imagine one less cruel.

Now, what else would stamp it as being a most atrocious crime? First, I put the victim, who ought not to suffer; and next I would put the attitude of those who kill. How about them? What was the attitude of these two boys? It may be the state's attorney would say it was particularly cruel to the victim because he was a boy. Well, my clients are boys, too, and if it would make more serious the offense to kill a boy, it should make less serious the offense of a boy who did the killing.

What was there in the conduct of these two boys which showed a wicked, malignant, and abandoned heart beyond that of anybody else who ever lived? Your Honor, it is simply silly. Everybody who thinks

---

15. Paraphrased from *The Rubaiyat of Omar Khayyam*, trans. Edward FitzGerald, 2nd ed. (1868).

knows the purpose of this. Counsel knows that under all the rules of the courts they have not the slightest right to ask this court to take life. Yet they urge it upon this court by falsely characterizing this as being the cruelest act that ever occurred.

What about those boys, the second cause or the second thing that would settle whether it was cruel or not? Mr. Marshall read case after case of murders and he said, "Why, those cases don't compare with yours. Yours is worse." Worse, why? What were those cases? Most of his cases were robbery cases, where a man went out with a gun to take a person's money and shot him down. Some of them were cases of hatred and of malice, where a man killed from hatred and spite and malice. Some of them were cases of special atrocities, mostly connected with money. A man kills someone to get money, he kills someone through hatred.

What is this case? This is a senseless, useless, purposeless, motiveless act of two boys. Now, let me see if I can prove it. There was not a particle of hate; there was not a grain of malice; there was not an opportunity to be cruel except as death is cruel—and death is cruel. There was absolutely no purpose in it all, no reason in it all, and no motive in it all.

Now, let me see whether I am right or not. I mean to argue this thoroughly, and it seems to me that there is not a chance for a court to hesitate upon the facts in this case. I want to try to do it honestly and plainly, and without any attempts at frills or oratory, and to state the facts of this case just as the facts exist, and nothing else.

What does the state say about it? In order to make this the most cruel thing that ever happened, of course, they must have a motive. And what, do they say, was the motive? Your Honor, if there was ever anything so foolish, so utterly futile, as the motive claimed in this case, then I have never listened to it. What did Tom Marshall say? What did Joe Savage say? "The motive was to get $10,000," say they. These two boys, neither one of whom needed a cent, scions of wealthy people, killed this little inoffensive boy to get $10,000.

Now, let us see. First let us call your attention to the opening statement of Judge Crowe,[16] where we

heard for the first time the full details of this, after a plea of guilty, and once more published in the newspapers. All right. He said these two young men were heavy gamblers, and they needed the money to pay gambling debts, or on account of gambling. Now, Your Honor, he said this was atrocious, most atrocious, and they did it to get the money because they were gamblers and needed it to pay gambling debts.

What did he prove? He put on one witness, and one only, who had played bridge with both of them in college, and he said they played for five cents a point. Now, I trust Your Honor knows better than I do how much of a game that would be. At poker I might guess, but I do not know much about bridge. But what else? He said that in that game, one of them lost ninety dollars to the other one. They were playing against each other, and one of them lost ninety dollars. Ninety dollars! Their joint money was just the same and there is not another word of evidence in this case to sustain the statement of Mr. Crowe, who pleads to hang these boys.

Your Honor, is it not trifling? It would be trifling, excepting that we, Your Honor, are dealing in human life. And we are dealing in more than that—we are dealing in the future disaster of two families. We are dealing in placing a blot upon the escutcheon of two houses that do not deserve it, for nothing. And all that they can get out of their imagination is that there was a game of bridge and one lost ninety dollars to the other, and therefore they go out and commit murder. Oh, it was not within two years of that time, or a year, anyhow.

What would I expect if on the part of the defense we would resort to a thing like that? Could I expect anyone to have the slightest confidence in anything we have said? Your Honor knows that it is utterly absurd. The evidence was absolutely worthless. The statement was made out of whole cloth, and Mr. Crowe felt like that policeman who came in here and perjured himself, as I will show you later on,[17] who said when he was talking with Nathan Leopold Jr., he told him the public were not satisfied with the motive.

16. Darrow is referring to the July 23 speech of State's Attorney Robert E. Crowe.

17. See notes 109–111 below.

I wonder if the public is satisfied with the motive. If there is any person in Chicago who, under the evidence in this case, after listening to it or knowing it, would believe that this was the motive, then he is stupid. That is all I have to say for him—just plain stupid.

But let me go further than that. Who were these two boys? How did it happen? On a certain day they killed poor little Robert Franks. I will not go over the paraphernalia, the letter demanding money, the ransom, because I will discuss that later in another connection. But they killed him. These two boys. They were not to get $10,000; they were to get $5,000 if it worked. That is, $5,000 apiece. Neither one could get more than five, and either one was risking his neck in the job. So each one of my clients was risking his neck for $5,000, if it had anything to do with it, which it did not.

Did they need the money? Why, at this very time, a few months before, Dickie Loeb had $3,000 checking account in the bank. Your Honor, I would be ashamed to talk about this except that in all seriousness—all apparent seriousness—they are asking to kill these two boys on the strength of this flimsy foolishness. At that time Richard Loeb had $3,000 checking account in the bank. He had three Liberty bonds,[18] one of which was past due, and the interest on not one of them had been collected for three years. I said, had not been collected; not a penny's interest had been collected, and the coupons were there for three years. And yet they would ask to hang him on the theory that he committed this murder because he needed money, and for money.

In addition to that, we brought his father's private secretary here, who swears that whenever he asked for it, he got a check, without ever consulting the father. She had open orders to give him a check whenever he wanted it, and that she had sent him a check in February, and he had lost it and had not cashed it. He got another in March. Your Honor, how far would this kind of an excuse go on the part of the defense? Anything is good enough to dump into a mess where

18. Interest-bearing bonds sold by the U.S. government to raise money during World War I.

the public are clamoring, and where the stage is set, and where loud-voiced young attorneys are talking about the sanctity of the law—which means killing people; anything is enough to justify a demand for hanging.

How about Leopold? Leopold was in regular receipt of $125 a month, had an automobile, paid nothing for board and clothes, expenses. He got money whenever he wanted it, and he had arranged to go to Europe and had bought his ticket and was going to leave about the time he was arrested in this case, Your Honor. He passed his examination for the Harvard Law School, was going to take a short trip to Europe before it was time for him to attend the fall term. His ticket had been bought, and his father was to give him $3,000 to make the trip.

Your Honor, jurors sometimes make mistakes, and courts do, too. If on this evidence the court is to construe a motive out of this case, then I insist, Your Honor, that human liberty is not safe and human life is not safe. A motive could be construed out of any set of circumstances and facts that might be imagined.

In addition to that, Your Honor, these boys' families were wealthy, extremely wealthy. They had been raised in luxury, they had never been denied anything—no want or desire left unsatisfied, no debts, no need of money, nothing. And yet they murdered a little boy, against whom they had nothing in the world, without malice, without reason, to get $5,000 apiece. All right. All right, Your Honor. If the court believes it, if anyone believes it, I can't help it. That is what this case rests on. It could not stand up a minute without motive. Without it, it was the senseless act of immature and diseased children, as it was—a senseless act of children wandering around in the dark and moved by some emotion that we still perhaps have not the knowledge or the insight into life to thoroughly understand.

Now, let me go on with it. What else do they claim? I want to say to Your Honor that you may cut out every expert in this case, you may cut out every lay witness in this case, you may decide this case upon the facts as they appear here alone, and there is no sort of question but what these boys were mentally diseased. I do not know, Your Honor, but I don't believe there is any man who knows this case, who has heard it, or who has carefully read, who does not know that it can only be accounted for on the theory of the mental disease of these two lads. I want to discuss that.

First, I want to refer to something else. Mr. Marshall argues to this court that you can do no such thing as to grant us the almost divine favor of saving the lives of two boys—that it is against the law, that the penalty for murder is death, and this court, who, in the fiction of the lawyers and the judges, forgets that he is a human being and becomes a court, pulseless, emotionless, devoid of those common feelings which alone make men, that this court as a human machine must hang them because they killed somebody.

Now, let us see. I do not need to ask mercy from this court—although I am willing to do it—for these clients, nor for anybody else, nor for myself. I have never yet found a person who did not need it, though. But I do not ask mercy for these boys. Your Honor may be as strict in the enforcement of the law as you please, and you cannot hang these boys. You can only hang them because back of the law and back of justice and back of the common instincts of man and back of the human feeling for the young is the hoarse voice of the mob which says, "Hang them."

I need ask nothing. What is the law of Illinois? If one is found guilty of murder in the first degree by a jury, or if he pleads guilty before a court, the court or jury may do one of three things: He may be hanged, he may be imprisoned for life, or he may be imprisoned for a term of not less than fourteen years. Now, why is that the law? Does it follow from that that a court is bound to ascertain the impossible and must necessarily measure the degrees of guilt? Not at all. He may not be able to do it. A court may act from any reason or from no reason. A jury may fix any one of these penalties as they see fit.

Why was this law passed? Undoubtedly in recognition of the growing feeling in all the forward-thinking people of the United States against capital punishment. Undoubtedly through the deep reluctance of courts and juries to take human life, they left it so that the court could do as he pleased on a plea of guilty, and a jury could do as they pleased on a conviction and find any penalty they saw fit. And without any reason whatever, without any facts whatever, Your Honor must make the choice, and you have the same

right to make one choice as another, no matter what Mr. Justice Blackstone says. It is Your Honor's province. You may do it, and I need ask nothing in order to have you do it, excepting that there is the statute.

But there is more than that in this case. We have sought to tell this court why he should not hang these boys. We have sought to tell this court, and to make this court believe, that they were diseased of mind and that they were of tender age, both.

However, before I discuss that, I ought to say another word in reference to the question of motive in this case. If there was no motive except the senseless act of immature boys, then of course there is taken from this case all of the feeling of deep guilt upon the part of these defendants. There was neither cruelty to the deceased, beyond taking his life—which is such—nor was there any depth of guilt and depravity on the part of the defendants, for it was a truly motiveless act, without the slightest feeling of hatred or revenge, done by a couple of children for no reason whatever.

But, Your Honor, we have gone further than that, and we have sought to show you, as I think we have, the condition of these boys' minds. Of course, it is not an easy job to ascertain the condition of another person's mind. These experts in the main have told you that it is impossible to ascertain what the mind is to start with—to tell how it acts.[19]

I will refer later, Your Honor, to the purpose of asking for the ransom which has been clearly testified to here. I simply so far wish to show that the money had nothing whatever to do with it. The inadequacy of it all, the risk taken for nothing, the utter lack of need, the senselessness of it all shows that it had nothing whatever to do with this crime and that the reason is the reason that has been given by the boys.

Now, I was about to say that it needs no expert, it needs nothing but a bare recitation of these facts, and a fair consideration of them, to convince any human being that this act was the act of diseased brains. The state, in their usual effort to magnify, distort, to force every construction against the defendants, have

---

19. At this point, the court ordered a five-minute recess, after which Darrow resumed his speech.

spoken about this act having its inception in their going to Ann Arbor to steal a typewriter.[20] This is on a plain par with their statement that this crime was committed for the purpose of getting $10,000.

What is the evidence? The getting of the typewriter in Ann Arbor had nothing to do with this offense, not the slightest. The evidence in this case shows that they went to Ann Arbor on the twelfth day of November. This act[21] was committed, as I recall it for the moment, on the twenty-first day of May. They went to Ann Arbor one night, after the football game in Ann Arbor, drove through in the nighttime. Nobody knew they were going and nobody knew they had been there. They knew somebody had been there the next morning because they missed things. They went there, under the evidence in this case, purely to steal something from the fraternity house. I will explain the reason for that further on.

Among the rest of the things they took was the typewriter on which these ransom letters were written. And yet the state with its fertile imagination says, "Aha, these wonderful planners," whom Dr. Krohn has told you showed such great knowledge, such active brain, such consistent action, such plans and such schemes that they must be sane. And yet a three-year-old child would not have done any of it. These wonderful planners foresaw that four months later they were going to write a ransom letter to somebody and they were going to kill a boy—nobody knew what or who or when or where or how. And in asking for a ransom they would need a typewriting machine to write it on, and so that they could not be detected, they went to Ann Arbor and stole one. That was nearly six months—it was six months, was it not?—ahead of this.

Now, let us see. There is some evidence somewhere in this record that they said on their way home from Ann Arbor that they began to discuss this question of committing a perfect crime, which had been

the fantasy for months. That was somewhere on the way home. The typewriter had nothing whatever to do with it, but to make it seem that they were schemers and planners, that they knew how to think and how to act, they argued that they went all the way to Ann Arbor in the nighttime to steal a typewriter instead of buying one here, or stealing one here, or getting one here, or using their own, or advertising for one, or securing one in any one of the hundred ways of getting a typewriter here.

Of course, it is impossible on the face of it, but let us see what the evidence is. They did bring a typewriter from Ann Arbor, and on that typewriter they wrote this so-called ransom letter, and after the boy had been killed, they threw the typewriter into the lagoon, after twisting off the letters. Why did they twist off the letters? Well, I suppose anybody knows why. Because anyone who is fairly familiar with a typewriter knows that you can always detect the writing on almost every typewriter. There will be imperfect letters, imperfect tracking, and imperfect this, that, and the other—and it is a sure thing, and probably they knew it.

But mark this: Leopold had had that typewriter in his house for six months. According to the testimony of the maid, he had written these letters on it. According to the testimony of his tutors, he had written the dope sheets[22] on it, numbers of them. These were still in existence. The state's attorney got those; the typewriter could be identified without the machine at all. It was identified without the machine; all that was needed was to show that the same machine that wrote the ransom letter wrote the dope sheets and wrote the other letters. No effort made to conceal it through all these months. All the boys knew it, the maid knew it, everybody in the house knew it. Letters were sent out broadcast and the dope sheets were made from it for the examination.

Now, what is stronger than that even in this statement? Were they trying to conceal it? Did they take a drive in the nighttime to Ann Arbor to get it, together with other stuff, so that they might be tracked, or did

20. In November 1923, Leopold and Loeb burglarized the Zeta Beta Tau fraternity house at the University of Michigan. Among the items they took was the typewriter on which they later wrote their ransom note after kidnapping Bobby Franks.

21. Darrow is referring to the murder of Bobby Franks.

22. Sheets containing notes Leopold used in studying for his law exams.

they just get it with other stuff without any thought of this thing that happened six months later?

They say, in order to make out the wonderful mental processes of these two boys, that they fixed up a plan to go to Ann Arbor to get this machine. And yet when they got ready to do this act, they went down the street a few doors from their house and bought a rope; they went around the corner and bought acid; they went somewhere else nearby and bought tape; they went down to the hotel and rented a room and then gave it up and went to another hotel and rented one there. And Dickie Loeb left his valise in the room. What was in the valise? Why, some books from the university library with his card, left in the valise in the room. Dick Loeb went to the room, took a valise containing his library card and some books from the library, left it two days in the room, until the hotel took the valise and took the books. Then he went to another hotel and rented another room. He might just as well send his card with the ransom letter—just as well.

They went to the Rent-a-Car place and rented a car. All this clumsy machinery was gone through without any need, or anything consecutive, or any thought. I submit, Your Honor, that no one, unless they had an afflicted mind, together with youth, could possibly have done it.

But let's get to something stronger than that. Were these boys in their right minds? Let's see. Here were two boys with good intellect, one eighteen and one nineteen. They had all the prospects that life could hold out for any of the young—one a graduate of Chicago and another of Ann Arbor, one who had passed his examination for the Harvard Law School and was about to take a trip in Europe, another who had passed at Ann Arbor, the youngest in his class, with money in the bank. Boys who never knew what it was to want a dollar, boys who could reach any position that was given to boys of that kind to reach, boys of distinguished and honorable fellows, of families of wealth and position, with all the world before them. And they gave it all up for nothing. For nothing! They took a little companion of one of them, on a crowded street, and killed him for nothing and sacrificed everything that could be of value in human life upon the crazy scheme of a couple of immature lads.

Now, Your Honor, you have been a boy. I have been a boy, and am proud of having been a boy. And we have known other boys. The best way to understand somebody else is to put ourselves in their place. Is it within the realm of your imagination that a boy who was right, with all the prospects of life before him, who could choose what he would, without the slightest reason in the world would lure a young companion to his death and take his place in the shadow of the gallows?

I do not care what Dr. Krohn may say; he is liable to say anything, except to tell the truth, and he is not liable to do that. There is nobody who has the process of reasoning who does not know that a boy who would do that is not right. How insane he is I care not, whether medically or legally. They did not reason; they could not reason; they committed the foolishest, most unprovoked, most purposeless, most causeless act that any two boys ever committed, and they put themselves where the rope is dangling above their heads, by their act.

There are not physicians enough in the world, if they all testified the same way, to convince any thoughtful, fair-minded man that these boys are right. Was their act one of deliberation, intellectual formality, or were they driven by some force such as Dr. White and Dr. Glueck and Dr. Healy have told this court?[23] There are only two theories: One is that their diseased brains drove them to it, the other is the old theory of possession by devils. And my friend Marshall could have read you books on that, too, but that has been pretty well given up in Illinois.

That they were intelligent and sane and sound and reasoning is unthinkable. Let me call Your Honor's attention to another thing. Why did they kill little Bobby Franks? Not for money, not for spite, not for hate. They killed him as they might kill a spider or a fly—for the experience. They killed him because they were made that way. Because somewhere in the infinite processes that go to the making up of the boy or the man something slipped, and those unfortunate

---

23. Three of America's most eminent psychiatrists, William A. White, Bernard Glueck, and William Healy were hired by the defense to examine Leopold and Loeb. Also see notes 50, 80–81 below.

lads sit here hated, despised, outcasts, and the community shouting for their blood.

Are they to blame for it? There is not any man on earth [who] can mention any purpose for it all or any reason for it all. It is one of those things that happened—that happened—and it calls not for hate but for kindness, for charity, for consideration.

I heard them talk of mothers. Mr. Savage is doing this for the mothers, and Mr. Crowe is thinking of the mothers, and I am thinking of the mothers. Mr. Savage, with the immaturity of youth and inexperience,[24] says if we hang them there will be no more killing. My God! This world has been one long slaughterhouse from the beginning until today, and killing goes on and on and on, and will forever. Why not read something, why not study something, why not think instead of blindly calling for death? Kill them! Will that prevent other senseless boys or other vicious men or vicious women? No. It would simply call upon every weak-minded person to do as they have done.

I know how easy it is to talk about mothers when you want to do something cruel, as some men talk about patriotism when they want to get something. I know all about it. But I am thinking of the mothers, too. I know that any mother might be the mother of a little Bobby Franks, who left his home and went to his school and whose life was taken and who never came back. I know that any mother might be the mother of Richard Loeb and Nathan Leopold, just the same. The trouble is this—that if she is the mother of a Nathan Leopold or of a Richard Loeb, she has to ask herself the question: "How came my children to be what they are? From what ancestry did they get this strain? How far removed was the poison that destroyed their lives? Was I the bearer of the seed that brings them to death?"

Any mother might be the mother of any of them. But these two are the victims. I remember a little poem that seems to me to illustrate the soliloquy of a boy about to be hanged, a soliloquy such as these boys might make. He says:

The night my father got me
    His mind was not on me;

He did not plague his fancy
    To muse if I should be
    The son you see.

The day my mother bore me
    She was a fool, and glad,
For all the pain I caused her,
    Because she bore the lad
    Which borne she had.

My father and my mother
    Out of the light they lie;
The warrant could not find them,
    So here am only I
    Must hang so high.

Oh, let not man remember
    The soul that God forgot,
But fetch the county sheriff,
    And noose me in a knot,
    And I will rot.

And so the game is ended,
    That should not have begun.
My father and my mother
    They had a likely son,
    But I have none.[25]

No one knows what will be the fate of the child they get or the child they bear, and the fate of the child is the last thing they think of. This weary old world goes on, begetting with birth and with living and with death, and all of it is blind from the beginning to the end. I do not know what it was made these boys do this mad act, but I do know there is a reason for it. I know they did not beget themselves. I know that any one of an infinite number of causes reaching back to the beginning might be working out in these boys' minds, whom you are asked to hang in malice and in hatred and injustice because someone in the past has sinned against them.

I am sorry for the fathers as well as the mothers: for the fathers who give their strength and their lives toward educating and protecting and creating a fortune for the boys that they love; for the mothers who go down into the shadow of death for their children, who

---

24. Savage was 29 years old at the time of the trial.

25. From A. E. Housman's "The Culprit," in *Last Poems* (1922).

nourish them and care for them, who risk their lives for them, who watch them with tenderness and fondness and longing, and who go down into [dis]honor and disgrace for the children they love. They are helpless. We are all helpless. But when you are pitying the father and the mother of poor Bobby Franks, what about the fathers and mothers of these two unfortunate boys, and what about the unfortunate boys themselves, and what about all the fathers and all the mothers and all the boys and all the girls who tread a dangerous maze in darkness from the cradle to the grave?

And do you think you can cure it by hanging these two? Do you think you can cure the hatreds and the maladjustments of the world by hanging them? You simply show your ignorance and your hate when you say it. You may here and there cure hatred with love and understanding, but you can only add fuel to the flames by hating in return.

What is my friend's idea of justice? He says to this court, whom he says he respects—and I believe he does, Your Honor—who sits here patiently, holding the lives of these two boys in your hands: "Give them the same mercy that they gave to Bobby Franks." Is that the law? Is that justice? Is this what a court should do? Is this what a state's attorney should do? For God's sake, if the state in which I live is not kinder, more human, more considerate, more intelligent than the mad act of these two mad boys, I am sorry I have lived so long.

I am sorry for these fathers and these mothers. The mother who looks into the blue eyes of her little babe cannot help but wonder what will be the end of this child—whether it will be crowned with the greatest promises which her mind can imagine or whether he may meet death from the gallows. All she can do is to raise him with care, to watch over him tenderly, to meet life with hope and trust and confidence, and to leave the rest with fate.

MR. DARROW: Your Honor, may we adjourn here?

THE COURT: We will suspend until tomorrow morning at ten o'clock.

Saturday, August 23

Your Honor, last night I was speaking about what is perfectly obvious in this case—that no human being could have done what these boys did excepting through the operation of a diseased brain. I do not propose to go through each step of it; it would take too long. But I do want to call the attention of this court to some of the other acts of these boys in this terrible and weird homicide which show conclusively that there could be no reason for their conduct.

I spoke about their registering at a hotel and leaving their names behind them, without a chance to escape. I referred to these weird letters which were written and mailed after the boy was dead. I want to come down now to the actions on that afternoon—without any excuse, without the slightest motive, not moved by money, not moved by passion or hatred, but nothing except the vague wanderings of children.

They got a machine and about four o'clock, or a little after in the afternoon, started to find somebody—not after anyone—to pick up somebody to kill. For nothing. They went over to the Harvard school. Dick's little brother was there on the playground. He went there himself in open daylight, known by all of them. Had been a pupil there himself, and he looked over the little boys.

Your Honor has been in these courts for a long time; you have listened to murder cases before. Has any such case ever appeared in any of the books? Has it ever come to the human experience of any judge or any lawyer or any person of affairs? Never once. Ordinarily there would be no sort of question of the condition of these boys' minds. The only question is raised because their parents have money.

They first pick out a little boy named Levinson, and they trail him around, or Dick does. Now, of course, that is a hard story. It is a story that shocks one: a boy bent on killing, not knowing where he would go or who he would get, but killing somebody. Here is a little boy, and the circumstances are not opportune, and so he fails to get him.

As I think of that story of Dick trailing this little boy around, there comes in my mind a picture of Dr. Krohn for sixteen years going in and out of the courtrooms in this building and other buildings, trailing victims without any regard to the victim's name or sex or age or surrounding. But he had a motive, and his motive was cash, as I will show later. One was the mad act of a child, the other the deliberate act of a man getting his living by dealing in human blood.

He abandons that lead, Dick does, and then they see the Franks boy on the street. Dick and Nathan are in the car and they see the Franks boy, and they call to him to get into the car. It is five o'clock in the afternoon, on a thickly settled street, the houses of their friends and their companions, known to everybody, automobiles on the street, and they take him in the car—for nothing.

If there had been a question of revenge, yes. If there had been a question of hate, where no one cares for his own fate, intent only on accomplishing his end, yes. But without any motive or any reason picking up this little boy right in sight of their own homes, surrounded by their neighbors. They drive a little way on a populous street where everybody could see, where eyes might be at every window on the street as they pass by, where they were known by everyone. They hit him over the head with a chisel and kill him and go on about their business, driving this car within half a block of Loeb's home, within the same distance of Frank's home, pass every neighbor that they knew, in the open highway, in broad daylight.

And still men will say that they have a bright intellect and, as Dr. Krohn puts it, can orient themselves and reason as well as he can possibly, and it is the sane act of sane men. I say again: Whatever madness and hate and frenzy may do to the human mind, there is not a single person who reasons who can believe that one of these acts was the act of men of brains that were not diseased. There is no other explanation for it. And had it not been for the wealth and the weirdness and the notoriety, they would have been sent to the psychopathic hospital for examination and been taken care of instead of demanding that this court take the last pound of flesh and the last drop of blood from two irresponsible lads.

They bring the boy back in the backseat, pull him over in the backseat, wrap him in a blanket, gag him, and this funeral car starts on its route. If ever any death vehicle went over the same route or the same kind of a route driven by sane people, I have never heard of it and I fancy no one else has ever heard of it.

This car is driven for twenty miles. First down through thickly populated streets, where everyone knew the boys and their families, had known them for years, till they come to the Midway. And then they take the main line of a street which is traveled more than any other street on the South Side except in the Loop, with automobiles that can scarcely go along on account of the number, straight down the Midway through the regular route of Jackson Park, Nathan Leopold driving this car, and Dickie Loeb on the backseat and the dead boy with him. The slightest accident, the slightest misfortune, a bit of curiosity, an arrest for speeding—anything would bring destruction.

They go down the Midway, through the park, meeting hundreds of machines, in sight of thousands of eyes, with this dead boy. For what? For nothing. The mad acts of the Fool in *King Lear* is the only thing I know of that compares with it.[26] And yet doctors will swear that it is a sane act. They know better.

They go down a thickly populated street to South Chicago, and then for three miles take the longest street to go through this city—built solid with business, with automobiles backed up on the street, with streetcars on the track, with thousands of peering eyes—one boy driving and the other on the backseat, with the corpse of poor Bobby Franks, the blood streaming from him wetting everything in the car.

And they tell me that is sanity. They tell me that the brains of these boys are not diseased. You need no experts; you need no X-rays; you need no study of the endocrines.[27] Their conduct shows exactly what it was and that this court has before him two young men who should be examined by a psychopathic hospital and treated kindly and with care.

They get through South Chicago and they take the regular automobile road down toward Hammond.[28] There is the same situation: hundreds of machines; any accident might encompass their ruin. They stop at the forks of the road and leave little Bobby Franks, soaked with blood, in the machine, and get their dinner, or get something to eat. Your Honor, we do not need to believe in miracles; we need

---

26. Darrow is referring to William Shakespeare's *King Lear* (1608).

27. Endocrine glands.

28. Indiana city 20 miles south of Chicago.

not resort to that in order to get blood. If it were any other case, there could not be a moment's hesitancy. I repeat, you may search the annals of crime and you can find no parallel. It is utterly at variance with every motive and every act and every part of conduct that influences normal people in the commission of crime. There is not a sane thing in all of this from the beginning to the end. There was not a normal act in any of it, from its inception in a diseased brain until today, when they sit here awaiting their doom.

But they say they planned. Well, what does that mean? A maniac plans; an idiot plans; an animal plans. Any brain that functions may plan. But their plans were the diseased plans of a diseased mind, of boys. Do I need to argue it? Does anybody need to more than glance at it? Is there any man with a fair intellect and a decent regard for human life and the slightest bit of heart that does not understand this situation?

And still, Your Honor, on account of its weirdness and its strangeness and its advertising, we are forced to fight. For what? Forced to plead to this court that two boys, one eighteen and the other nineteen, may be permitted to live in silence and solitude and disgrace and spend all their days in the penitentiary. Asking this court and state's attorney to be merciful enough to let these two boys be locked up in a prison until they die. I sometimes wonder if I am dreaming, if in the first quarter of the twentieth century there have come back into the hearts of men the hate and the feeling and the lust for blood which possesses the primitive savage of primitive lands.

What do they want? Tell me, is a lifetime for the young spent behind prison bars—is that not enough for this mad act? And is there any reason why this great public should be regaled by a hanging? I can't understand it, Your Honor. It would be past belief, excepting that to the four corners of the earth the news of this weird thing has been carried, and men have been stirred, and the primitive has come back, and the intellect has been destroyed, and men have been controlled by feelings and passions and hatred which should have been dead centuries ago.

My friend Savage pictured to you the putting of this dead boy in this culvert. Well, no one can minutely describe any killing and not make it shock-

ing. It is shocking. It is shocking because we love life and because we instinctively draw back from death. It is shocking if death comes into a home, if it comes to a hospital. It is shocking wherever it is and however it is, and perhaps always is almost equally shocking.

But here is the picture of a dead boy, past pain, when no harm can come to him, put in a culvert, after taking off his clothes so that the evidence would be destroyed—and that is pictured to this court as a reason for hanging. Well, Your Honor, that does not appeal to me as strongly as the hitting over the head of little Robert Franks with a chisel. The boy was dead.

I could say something about the death that, for some mysterious reason, the state wants in this case. Why do they want it? I don't know. To vindicate the law? Oh, no. The law can be vindicated without killing anyone else. It might shock the fine sensibilities of the state's counsel that this boy was put into a culvert and left after he was dead, but, Your Honor, I can think of a scene that makes this pale into insignificance.

I can think, and only think, Your Honor, of taking two boys, one eighteen and the other nineteen, irresponsible, weak, diseased, penning them in a cell, checking off the days and the hours and the minutes until they will be taken out and hanged. Wouldn't it be a glorious day for Chicago? Wouldn't it be a glorious triumph for the state's attorney? Wouldn't it be a glorious triumph for justice in this land? Wouldn't it be a glorious illustration of Christianity and kindness and charity?

I can picture them, wakened in the grey light of morning, furnished a suit of clothes by the state, led to the scaffold, their feet tied, a black cap drawn over their heads, placed on a trapdoor, and somebody pressing a spring so that it falls under them, and they are only stopped by the rope around their necks. It would surely expiate the placing of young Franks, after he was dead, in the culvert. That would bring immense satisfaction to some people. It brings a greater satisfaction because it is done in the name of justice.

I am always suspicious of righteous indignation. Nothing is more cruel than righteous indignation. To hear young men talk glibly of justice! Well, it would make me smile if it did not make me so sad. Who knows what it is? Does Mr. Savage know? Does Mr. Crowe know? Do I know? Does Your Honor know? Is there any human machinery for finding it? Is there any man who can weigh me and say what I deserve? Can Your Honor? Let us be honest. Can Your Honor express yourself and say what I deserve? Can Your Honor appraise these two young men and say what they deserve?

It may take account of infinite circumstances which a human being may not understand. If there is such a thing as justice, it could only be administered by one who knew the inmost thoughts of the man to whom they were meting it out. Aye, who knew the father and mother and the grandparents and the infinite number of people back of them. Who knew the origin of every soul that went into their body; who could understand their structure and how it acted. Who could tell how the emotions that sway the human being affected that particular frail piece of clay. It means more than that. It means that you must appraise every influence that moves them—the civilization where they live, their living, their society, all society which enters into the making of a child. If Your Honor can do it—if you can do it—you are wise, and with wisdom goes mercy.

No one with wisdom and with understanding, no one who is honest with himself and with his own life, whoever he may be, no one who has seen himself the prey and the sport and the plaything of the infinite forces that move man, no one who has tried and who has failed—and we have all tried and we have all failed—no one can tell what justice is for someone else or for themselves. And the more they try and the more responsibility they take, the more they cling to mercy as being the one thing of which they are sure.

It is not so much mercy either, Your Honor. I can hardly understand myself pleading to a court to visit mercy on two boys by shutting them in a prison for life. For life! Where is the human heart that would not be satisfied with that? Where is the man or woman who understands their own life and who has a particle of feeling that could ask for more?

Any cry for more roots back to the hyena; it roots back to the hissing serpent; it roots back to the beast from whence we came. It is not a part of man. It is not a part of that feeling which, let us hope, is

growing, though scenes like this sometimes make me doubt that it is growing. It is not a part of that feeling of mercy and pity and understanding of each other which we believe has been slowly raising man from his low estate. It is not a part of the finer instincts which are slow to develop, of the wider knowledge which is slow to come and slow to assimilate when it comes. It is not part of all that makes the best there is in man. It is not a part of all that promises any hope for the future and any justice for the present.

And must I ask that these boys get mercy by spending the rest of their lives in prison, year following year, month following month, and day following day, with nothing to look forward to but hostile guards and stone walls? It ought not to be hard to get that much mercy in any court in the year 1924.

These boys left this body down in the culvert and they came back. Telephoned first; telephoned home they would be too late for supper. Here surely was an act of consideration on the part of Leopold, telephoning home that he would be late for supper. Dr. Krohn says he must be able to think and act because he could do this. But the boy who through habit would telephone his home that he would be late for supper had not a tremor or a thought or a shudder at taking the life of little Bobby Franks for nothing, and he has not had one yet. He was in the habit of doing what he did—that was all. But in the presence of life and death, and a cruel death, he had no tremor and no thought. And I will talk to the court about why a little further on.

They came back. They got their dinner. They parked their bloody automobile in front of Leopold's house. They cleaned it to some extent that night and left it standing out in the street in front of their home. Oriented, of course. Oriented.[29] They left it there for the night so that anybody might see and might know. They took it in the barn the next day and washed it, and then poor little Dickie Loeb—I shouldn't call him Dickie, and I shouldn't call him poor, because that might be playing for sympathy, and you have no right to ask for sympathy in this world. You should

29. A reference to language used by prosecution psychiatrists William O. Krohn and Archibald Church.

ask for justice, whatever that might be, and only state's attorneys know. Sympathy has no place in it.

And then in a day or so we find Dick Loeb with his pockets stuffed with newspapers telling of the Franks' tragedy. We find him consulting with his friends in the club, with the newspaper reporters. And my experience is that the last person that a conscious criminal associates with is a reporter. He even shuns them more than he does a detective because they are smarter and less merciful. But he picks up a reporter, and he tells him he has read a great many detective stories, and he knew just how this would happen, and that the fellow who telephoned must have been down on Sixty-third Street, and the way to find him is to go down on Sixty-third Street and visit the drugstores, and he would go with him. And Dick Loeb pilots them around the drugstores where the telephoning was done, and he talks about it, and he takes the newspapers, and takes them with him, and he is having a glorious time.[30]

And yet he is "perfectly oriented," in the language of Dr. Krohn.[31] Perfectly oriented. Is there any question about the condition of his mind? Why was he doing it? He liked to hear about it. He had done something that he could not boast of directly, but he did want to hear other people talk about it, and he looked around there and helped them find the place where the telephone message was sent out.

Your Honor has had experience with criminals. I do not know just what it is, but Your Honor doubtless knows; and if you do not, you might ask the state's attorney. You have had experience with criminals and you know how they act. Was any such thing as this ever heard of before on land or sea? Does not the man who knows what he is doing, who for some reason has been overpowered and commits what is called a crime, keep as far away from it as he can? Does he not? Does he go to the reporters and help them hunt it out?

There is not a single act in this case that is not the act of a diseased mind; not one. Talk about scheming.

Yes, it is the scheme of disease; it is the scheme of infancy; it is the scheme of fools; it is the scheme of irresponsibility from the time it was conceived until the last act in the tragedy. And yet we have to talk about it and argue about it when it is obvious to anyone who cares to know the truth, perfectly obvious. But they must be hanged because everybody is talking about this case and their parents have money.

Am I asking for much in this case? Let me see for a moment now. Is it customary to get anything on a plea of guilty? How about the state's attorney? Do they not give you something on a plea of guilty? How many times has Your Honor listened to the state's attorney come into this court with a man charged with robbery with a gun, which means from ten years to life, and on condition of a plea of guilty ask to have the gun charge stricken out and get a sentence of three to twenty years, with a chance to see daylight inside of three years? How many times?

How many times has the state's attorney himself asked everything up to murder, not only with the young but even the old? How many times have they come into this court and into every court, not only here but everywhere, and asked for it? Your Honor knows. I will guarantee that three times out of four; and much more than that in murder, ninety-nine times out of one hundred; and much more than that, I would say not twice in a thousand times, have they failed to do it.

How many times has Your Honor been asked to change a sentence and not hold a man guilty of robbery with a gun, but give him a chance on a plea of guilty—and not a boy but a man? And how many times have you done it, Your Honor? How many times have others done it, over and over and over again? And it will be done so long as justice is fairly administered. And in a case of a charge of robbery with a gun, coupled with larceny, how many times have both the robbery and the gun been waived and a plea of larceny made so that one might be released in a year? How many times has all of it been waived and somebody given a year in the Bridwell?[32]

---

30. The incident Darrow describes occurred on Friday, May 23, 1924.

31. Darrow is referring to Krohn's testimony of August 18.

32. English debtor's prison and workhouse to which orphans were often sent during the 19th century.

Many, many times, because they are young, because they are immature. Many and many a time because they are boys, and youth has terrible responsibilities, and youth should have advantages. And with sane and humane people, youth, the protection of childhood, is always one of the first considerations. It is one of the first in the human heart and it is one of the first in the human mind.

How many times has rape been changed to assault and the defendant given a year, or even a Bridwell sentence? How many times has mercy come even from the state's attorney's office? I am not criticizing. It should come, and I am telling this court what this court knows. And yet, forsooth, for some reason here is a case of two immature boys of diseased mind, as plain as the light of day, and they say you can only get justice by shedding their last drop of blood. Why? I can ask the question easier than I can answer it. Why? Unheard-of, unprecedented in this court, unknown among civilized men. And yet this court is to make an example or civilization will fail.

I suppose civilization will survive if Your Honor hangs them. But it will be a terrible blow, a terrible blow. Your Honor would be turning back over the long road we have traveled. And you would be turning back from the protection of youth and infancy. Your Honor would be turning back from the treatment of children. Your Honor would be turning back to the barbarous days which brother Marshall seems to love, when they burned people thirteen years of age. You would be dealing a staggering blow to all that has been done in the city of Chicago in the last twenty years for the protection of infancy and childhood and youth.

And for what? Because the people are talking about it. Nothing else. Just because the people are talking about it. It would not mean, Your Honor, that your reason was convinced. It would mean in this land of ours, where talk is cheap, where newspapers are plenty, where the most immature expresses his opinion, and the more immature, the harder it is that a court couldn't help feeling the great pressure of public opinion which they say exists in this case.

Coming alone in this courtroom with obscure defendants, doing what has been done in this case, coming with the outside world shut off, as in most cases, and saying to this court and counsel, "I believe that these boys ought not to be at large, I believe they are immature and irresponsible, and I am willing to enter a plea of guilty and let you sentence them to life imprisonment," how long do you suppose Your Honor would hesitate? Do you suppose the state's attorneys would raise their voices in protest? You know it has been done too many times. And here, for the first time, under these circumstances this court is told that they must make an example.

Let me take some other cases. How many times has a defendant come into this court charged with burglary and larceny, and because of youth or because of something else, the state's attorney has waived the burglary and consented to a year for larceny? No more than that. Let me ask this question: How many times, Your Honor, have defendants come into this court—and I am not speaking of Your Honor's court alone; I am speaking of all the criminal courts in this country—have defendants come in charged with a burglary and larceny and been put on parole, given parole, told to go and sin no more, given another chance? It is true in almost all cases of the young except for serious aggravation.

Can you administer law without it? Can you administer what approaches justice without it? Can this court or any other court administer justice by consciously turning his heart to stone and being deaf to all the instincts which move man? Without those instincts, I wonder what would happen to the human race? Without them, if a man could judge a fellow man in coldness without taking account of their own lives, without taking account of what they knew of human life, without some understanding, how long would we have real human beings? It has taken the world a long time for man to get even where he is today. If the law was administered without any feeling whatever of sympathy or humanity or kindliness, we would begin our long, slow journey back to the jungle that was formerly our home.

How many times has assault with intent to rob or kill been changed in these courts to assault and battery? How many times has felony been waived on assault with a deadly weapon and a man or a boy given a chance? And we are asking a chance to be shut up in stone walls for life. For life! It is hard for me to think of it, but that is the mercy we are asking from this court, which we ought not to be required to ask, and which we should have as a matter of right in this court, and which I have faith to believe we will have as a matter of right.

Is this new? Why, I undertake to say that even the state's attorney's office—and if he denied it, I would like to see him bring in the records—I will undertake to say that in three cases out of four of all kinds and all degrees, leniency has been shown. Three hundred and forty murder cases in ten years with a plea of guilty in this county. All the young who pleaded guilty—every one of them—three hundred and forty in ten years with one hanging on a plea of guilty, and that a man forty years of age. And yet they say we come here with a preposterous plea for mercy.

We are not asking it. We are satisfied with justice if the court knows what justice is, or if any human being can tell what justice is. If anybody can look into the minds and hearts and the lives and the origin of these two youths and tell what justice is, that would be enough. But nobody can do it without imagination, without sympathy, without kindliness, without understanding, and I have faith that this court will take this case with his conscience and his judgment and his courage and save these boys' lives.

Now, Your Honor, let me go a little further with this. I have gone over some of the high spots in this tragedy. This tragedy has not claimed all the attention it has had on account of its atrocity. There is nothing to that. Why is it? There are two reasons and only two that I can see. First is the extreme wealth, reputed at least, of these families; not only the Loeb and Leopold families but the Franks family, and, of course, it is unusual. And next is the fact that it was weird and uncanny and motiveless. That is what attracted the attention of the world.

They may say now, many of them, they want to hang them. I may be a poor prophet, but giving the people blood is something like giving them their dinner. When they get it, they go to sleep. They may for the time being have an emotion, but they will bitterly regret it. And I undertake to say that if these two boys are sentenced to death and are hanged, on that day there will be a pall settle over the people of this land

that will be dark and deep and at least cover every humane and intelligent person in the land.

I wonder if it will do good. I wonder if it will help the children, and there is an infinite number like these. I marveled when I heard Mr. Savage talk. I do not criticize him. He is young and enthusiastic. But has he ever read anything? Has he ever thought? Was there ever any man who had studied science who has read anything of criminology or philosophy? Was there ever any man who knew himself, who could speak with the assurance with which he speaks?

What about this matter of crime and punishment, anyhow? I may know less than the rest, but I have at least tried to find out, and I am fairly familiar with the best literature that has been written on that subject in the last one hundred years. The more men study, the more they doubt the effect of severe punishment on crime. And yet Mr. Savage tells this court that if these boys are hanged, there will be no more. Mr. Savage is an optimist. He says if they are hanged, there will be no more boys like these.

I could give him a sketch of punishment beginning with the brute which hurt something because something hurt it—the punishment of the savage. If a person's injured in the tribe, they must injure somebody in the other tribe; it makes no difference who it is, but somebody. If one is killed, they must kill somebody else. You can trace it all down through the history of man. You can trace the burnings, the boilings, the drawings and quarterings, the hanging of people in England at the crossroads, carving them up and hanging them as examples for all to see. We can come down to the last century, when nearly two hundred crimes were punishable by death, and by death in every form. Not only hanging—that was too humane—but burning, boiling, cutting into pieces, torturing.

You can read the stories of the hangings on a high hill, and the populace for miles around coming out to the scene that everybody might be awed into goodness. Hanging for picking pockets—and more pockets were picked in the crowd that went to the hanging than had been known for years. Hangings for murder—and men were murdered on the way there and on the way home. Hangings for poaching, hangings for everything. And hangings in public—

not shut up cruelly and brutally in jail, out of the light of day, wakened in the nighttime and led forth and killed, but taken to the shire town on a high hill in the presence of a multitude so that they might know that the wages of sin were death.[33]

What happened? I have read the life of Lord Shaftesbury,[34] a great nobleman of England who gave his life and his labors toward modifying the penal code. I have read of the slow, painful efforts through all the ages for more humanity of man to his fellow man. I know what history says, I know what it means, and I know what flows from it, so far as we can tell, which is not definitely. I know that every step has been met and opposed by prosecutors, many times by courts. I know that when poaching and petty larceny was punishable by death in England, juries refused to convict. They were too humane to obey the law, and judges refused.

I know when the delusion of witchcraft was spreading over Europe, claiming its victims by the millions,[35] many a judge so shaped his cases that no crime of witchcraft could be punished in his court. I know that it was stopped in America because juries would no longer convict. I know that every step in the progress of the world in reference to crime has come from the human feelings of man. It has come from that deep well of sympathy that, in spite of all our training and all our conventions and all our teaching, still flows forth in the human breast. Without it there would be no life on this weary old planet. And gradually the laws have been changed and modified, and men look back with horror at the hangings and deaths of the past.

What did they find in England? That as they got rid of these barbarous statutes, crimes decreased instead of increased, and as the criminal law was modified and humanized, there was less crime instead of more. I will undertake to say, Your Honor, that you can scarcely find a single book written by a student— and I will include all the works on criminology of the

past—that has not made the statement over and over again that as the penal code was made less terrible, crimes grew less frequent.

Now let us see a little about the psychology of man. It is easy, Your Honor. Anybody can understand it if he just looks into himself. This weird tragedy occurred on the twenty-first of May. It has been heralded, broadcast through the world. How many attempted kidnappings have come since then? How many threatening letters have been sent out by weak-minded boys and weak-minded men since then? How many times have they sought to repeat again and again this same crime because of its actions upon the human mind? I can point to examples of killing and of hanging in the city of Chicago which have been repeated in detail over and over again, simply from the publicity of the newspapers and the public generally.

Let us take this case. Let's see whether we can guess about it. And it is no guess. If these two boys die on the scaffold—which I can never even yet bring myself to imagine—if they do die on the scaffold, the details of this will be spread over the world. Every newspaper in the United States will carry a full account. Every newspaper of Chicago will be filled with the gruesome details. It will enter every home and every family.

Will it make men better or make men worse? I would like to put that to the intelligence of men, at least such intelligence as they have. I would like to appeal to the feelings of human beings so far as they have feelings. Would it make the human heart softer or would it make it harder, speaking in terms not of the scientist but of the religionist? Would it harden the heart of man or would it soften it? How many men would be colder and crueler for it? How many men would enjoy the details? And you cannot enjoy human suffering without being affected for better or for worse; those who enjoyed it would be affected for the worse.

What influence would it have upon the millions of men who would read it? What impression would it have upon the millions of women? More sensitive, more expressionable, more imaginative? Would it help them if Your Honor should do what they beg you to do? What influence would it have upon the

33. An allusion to Romans 6:23.

34. Anthony Ashley Cooper, 7th Earl of Shaftesbury (1801–1885).

35. Darrow is referring to the witch hunts of the 14th through 17th centuries.

infinite number of children who would devour its details as Dickie Loeb has enjoyed reading detective stories? Would it make them better or would it make them worse?

The question needs no answer. You can answer it from the human heart. What influence, let me ask you, would it have for the unborn babes still in their mothers' wombs? And what influence would it have on the psychology of the fathers and mothers yet to come?

Do I need to argue to Your Honor that cruelty only makes cruelty? That hatred only causes hatred? That if there is any way to destroy—which perhaps there is not—if there is any way to soften this human heart, which is hard enough at its best, if there is any way to kill evil and hatred and all that goes with it, it is not through evil and hatred and cruelty; it is through charity and love and understanding?

How often do people need to be told this? Look back at the world. There is not a man who is pointed to as an example to the world who has not taught it. There is not a philosopher, there is not a religious leader, there is not a creed that has not taught it. This is a Christian community, so-called—at least it boasts of it—and yet they would hang. A Christian community.

Let me ask this court: Is there any doubt about whether these boys would be safe in the hands of the founder of the Christian religion? It would be blasphemy to say they would not. Nobody could imagine, nobody could even think of it. And yet there are men who want to hang them for a childish act, without the slightest malice toward the world.

Your Honor, I feel like apologizing for urging it so long. It is not because I doubt this court. It is not because I do not know something of the human emotions and the human heart. It is not that I do not know every feeling of logic, every page of history, every line of philosophy and religion, every precedent in this court urges this court to save life. It is not that.

I have become obsessed with this deep feeling of hate and anger that has swept across this city and this land. I have been fighting it, battling with it, until it has fairly driven me mad, until I sometimes wonder whether every righteous human emotion has

not gone down in the storm. I am not pleading so much for these boys as I am for the infinite number of others to follow, those who perhaps cannot be as well defended as they have been, those who may go down in the storm and the tempest without aid. It is of them I am thinking, and for them I am begging of this court not to turn backward toward the barbarous and the cruel past.

Now, Your Honor, who are these two boys? Leopold, with a wonderfully brilliant mind—there is no question about it. Loeb, with an unusual intelligence—there is no question about that. Both urged from their very youth, like hothouse plants, to learn more and more and more. Dr. Krohn says that they are intelligent. In spite of that, it is true—they are unusually intelligent. But it takes something besides brains to make a human being who can make his way in the world. In fact, as Dr. Church and Dr. Singer[36] regretfully admitted, brains are not the chief thing in human conduct.

There is no question about it. The things that make us live, the things that make us work or play or move us along the pathways of life, are the emotions. They are the instinctive things. In fact, intellect is a late development in life. Long before there was such a thing, the emotional life kept the organism in existence until death. Whatever our action is, it comes from the emotion, and nobody is balanced without it. The intellect does not count so much.

Let me call the attention of the court to two or three cases. Four or five years ago the world was startled by a story of a boy of eleven, the youngest boy ever turned out at Harvard, who had studied everything on earth and understood it, whose father was a physician. Simply a freak—he went through Harvard much younger than anybody else. All questions of science and philosophy he could discuss with the most learned. How he got it, nobody knows. It was prophesied that he would have a brilliant future. I do not like to mention his name, and it is not necessary. I met that young man a year or two ago, and

---

36. Archibald Church, professor of mental diseases and medical jurisprudence at Northwestern University, and Harold D. Singer, a Chicago psychiatrist in private practice, both of whom testified for the prosecution.

he was looking for a job at fifteen dollars a week, or at any figure. The fire had burned out. He was a prodigy with nothing but this marvelous brain power, which nobody understood or could understand. He was just a freak. He never was a boy; he never will be a man.[37]

Harvard had another of the same kind some years before—unbalanced, impossible, an intellectual machine. Nature works in mysterious ways.

We have all read of Blind Tom, who was an idiot, and yet a marvelous musician.[38] He never could understand music, and he never did understand music. He never knew anything about it. And yet he could go to the piano and play so that it would make people marvel and wonder.

How it comes nobody can explain. The question of intellect means the smallest part of life. Back of a man's nerves, muscles, heart, blood, and lungs is the whole organism, and the brain is the least part in human development. Without the emotional life, he is nothing.

How is it with these two boys? I insist there is not the slightest question about it. All teaching and all training appeals not only to the intellectual but to the emotional life. A child is born with no ideas of right and wrong, just a plastic brain ready for such impressions as come to it, ready to be developed. Lying, stealing, killing are not wrong. It means nothing. Gradually his parents and his teachers tell him things, teach him habits, show him that he may do this and he may not do that, teach him the difference between his and mine. No child knows that when he is born in the world. He knows nothing about property or property rights. They are given as he goes along. He is like the animal that wants something and goes out and gets it, kills it, operating purely from instinct, without training.

Now, the child is gradually taught, and we build up habits, and those habits are supposed to be strong enough so that they will make inhibitions against conduct when the emotions come in conflict with his duties of life. Dr. Singer and Dr. Church, both of them, admitted exactly what I am saying now. The child knew nothing of himself about right and wrong, and the teachings built up habits, gave him ideas, so he would be able to understand certain instincts that might surge upon him, and which surge upon everybody. If the instinct is strong enough and the habit weak enough, the habit goes down before it. Both of these eminent men admit it. There can be no question about it. It is the relative strength of the instinct and the strength of the habit that is with it.

Now, education means fixing these habits so deeply in the emotions of man that they stand him in stead when he needs them—and that is all it does mean. Now take it here. Suppose one sees a thousand-dollar bill and nobody present. He may have the impulse to take it. If he does not take it, it will be because his emotional nature revolts at it, through habit and through training. If the emotional nature does not revolt at it, he will take it. That is why people do not commit what we call crime—that and caution.

All that education means is the building of habits so that certain conduct revolts and stops you, saves you. But without an emotional nature, you can't do it. It is impossible. Some are born without it, or practically without it.

How about this case? There is no doubt about this case, Your Honor. There is not the slightest question. The state put on three experts—and Dr. Krohn. Three alienists[39] and Dr. Krohn. Two of them, Dr. Patrick[40] and Dr. Church,[41] are undoubtedly able men. One of them, Dr. Church, is a man whom I have known for forty years and for whom I have the highest regard. On Sunday, June 1, before any of the friends of these boys, or their counsel, could see them, while they

---

37. Darrow is referring to William James Sidis (1898–1944).

38. African-American composer and pianist Thomas Bethune (1849–1908), an autistic savant who dazzled audiences around the world with his musical abilities despite the fact that he lacked sight and most ordinary mental faculties.

39. "Alienist" was an early twentieth-century term for a forensic psychiatrist.

40. Hugh T. Patrick, professor emeritus of nervous and mental diseases at Northwestern University and past president of the American Neurological Association.

41. See note 36.

were in the care of the state's attorney's office, they brought them in to be examined by these alienists. I am not going to discuss that in detail as I might later on. The character of the examination—I will speak of that later. But Dr. Patrick said this: The only thing unnatural he noted about it was that they had no emotional reaction. Yes, Dr. Church said the same. These are their alienists, not ours.

And these boys could tell this gruesome story without a change of countenance, without the slightest feelings. There were no emotional reactions to it. And why haven't they? I don't know. How can I tell why? I know what causes the emotional life. I know it comes from the nerves, the muscles, the endocrine glands, the vegetative system. I know it is the most important part of life. I know it is left out of some. I know that without it, men cannot live. I know that without it, they cannot go with the rest. I know they cannot feel what you feel and what I feel, that they cannot feel the moral shocks which come to men who are educated and who have not been deprived of an emotional system or emotional feelings. I know it, and every person who has honestly studied this subject knows it as well.

Is Dickie Loeb to blame because out of the infinite forces that conspired to form him, the infinite forces that were at work producing him ages before he was born, that because out of these infinite combinations, he was born without it? If he is, then there should be a new definition for justice.

Is he to be blamed for what he did not have and never had? Is he to blame that his machine is imperfect? Who is to blame? I don't know. I have never been interested so much in my life in fixing blame as I have in relieving people from blame. I am not wise enough to fix it. I know that somewhere in the past that entered into him something missed. It may be defective nerves. It may be a defective heart, liver. It may be defective endocrine glands. I know it is something. I know that nothing happens in this world without a cause. I know, Your Honor, that if you, sitting here in this court and in this case, had infinite knowledge, you could lay your fingers on it, and I know you would not visit it on Dickie Loeb.

I asked Dr. Church and I asked Dr. Singer whether, if they were wise enough to know, they could not find the cause, and both of them said yes. I know that he and Loeb are just as they are, and that they did not make themselves.

There are at least two theories of man's responsibility. There may be more. There is the old theory that if a man does something, it is because he willfully, purposely, maliciously, and with a malignant heart sees fit to do it. And that goes back to the possession of man by devils. And the old indictments used to read that a man being possessed of a devil did so and so.

But why was he possessed with the devil? Did he invite him in? Could he help it? Very few half-civilized people believe that doctrine any more. Science has been at work, humanity has been at work, scholarship has been at work, and intelligent people know now that every human being is the product of the endless heredity back of him and the infinite environment around him. He is made as he is and he is the sport of all that goes around as applied to him. And under the same stress and storm, you might act one way and I might act another and poor Dickie Loeb another. Church said so and Singer said so and it is the truth.

Take a normal boy, Your Honor. Do you suppose he could have taken a boy into an automobile without any reason and hit him over the head and killed him? I might just as well ask you whether you thought the sun could shine at midnight in this latitude. It is not a part of normality. Something was wrong. But I am asking Your Honor not to visit the grave and dire and terrible misfortunes of Dickie Loeb and Nathan Leopold upon these two boys. I do not know where to place it. I know it is somewhere in the infinite economy of nature, if I could find it. I know it is there. And to say that because they are as they are, you should hang them is brutality and cruelty and savors of the time of fang and claw.

Now, there cannot be any question on the evidence in this case, Your Honor. Dr. Church and Dr. Patrick both testified that these boys have no emotional reactions in reference to this crime. Every one of the alienists on both sides has told this court, but no doubt this court already knew that the emotions furnish the urge and the drive to live. A man can get along without his intellect, and most people do, but he cannot get along without his emotions. When they did make a brain for man, they did not make it big enough to hurt, because emotions can still hold sway. He eats and he drinks, he works and plays and sleeps, in obedience to his emotional system. The intellectual system, the intellectual part of man, acts only as a judge over his emotions, and then he generally gets it wrong and has to rely on his instincts to save him.

These boys—I do not care what their mind is; that simply makes it worse—are emotionally defective. Every single alienist who has testified in this case has said so. The only person who did not was Dr. Krohn. While I am on that subject, lest I forget the eminent doctor, I want to refer to one or two things. In the first place, all these alienists that the state called came in and heard them tell their story of this crime, and that is all they heard. Nothing else.

Now, my associate, Mr. Bachrach,[42] might not quite have sized up my friend Judge Crowe as to his purpose for calling in those alienists. I have known the judge quite a while and I can figure out that he might have had another purpose. He might even have thought these boys were insane and had no suspicion whatever that they had diseased minds, and he might have thought that some wicked lawyer would come in and defend them on the theory that they did have diseased minds. Might not that have been the reason?

MR. CROWE: I think you have guessed it.

MR. DARROW: All right. I thought I did. Somebody might come in and claim that they are insane, which we have not done, and therefore he would take time by the forelock and get to the alienist first. I rather suspect that I am right about that, Walter.[43] Anyway, I give Bob[44] the benefit of the doubt. He thought they might get somebody who was not as conscientious as I am, and who would claim those boys were insane, and go and hire the alienists. I don't like the word, but let it go.

Now, Your Honor is familiar with Chicago the same as I am, and I am willing to admit right here and now that the two ablest alienists in Chicago are Dr. Church and Dr. Patrick. There may be abler ones, but we lawyers don't know them. And I will go further: If my friend Crowe had not got to them first, I would have tried to get them. There isn't any question about it at all. I said I would have tried to; I didn't say I would, and yet I suspect I would. I haven't got much doubt about it. And I say that, Your Honor, without casting the slightest reflection on either of them, for I really have a high regard for them, and aside from that a deep friendship for Dr. Church. And I have considerable regard for Dr. Singer. I won't go any further now.

We could not get them, and Mr. Crowe was very wise, and he deserves a great deal of credit for the industry, the research, and the thoroughness that he and his staff have used in detecting this terrible crime. What I am saying is serious; he does deserve it. He worked with intelligence and rapidity. If here and there he trampled on the edges of the Constitution, I am not going to talk about that. If he did it, he is not the first one in that office and probably will not be the last who will do it. A great many people in this world believe the end justifies the means. I don't know but I do myself. And that is the reason I never want to take the side of the prosecution, because I might harm an individual. I am sure the state will live anyhow.

On Sunday afternoon before we got a chance, he got in two alienists, Church and Patrick, and also called Dr. Krohn, and they sat around hearing these boys tell their stories, and that is all. Your Honor, they were not holding an examination. They were holding an inquest, and nothing else. It had not the slightest reference to, or earmarks of, an examination for sanity, not the slightest. It was just an inquest; a little premature, but still an inquest.

What is the truth about it? What did Patrick say? He said, no, it was not a good opportunity for examination. What did Church say? I read from his own book[45] what was necessary for an examination,

---

42. Chicago attorney Benjamin C. Bachrach, who served as Darrow's cocounsel. On July 31–August 1, Bachrach had debated State's Attorney Crowe about the reasons for involving alienists in the case.

43. Darrow's remark here is addressed to Walter Bachrach, younger brother of Benjamin Bachrach, who also assisted the defense.

44. Prosecutor Robert E. Crowe.

45. Archibald Cook and Frederick Peterson, *Nervous and Mental Diseases*, 9th ed. (1919).

and he said no, it was not a good opportunity for an examination. What did Krohn say? Fine, a fine opportunity for an examination, the best he had ever heard of, or that ever anybody had, because they were stripped naked.

WALTER BACHRACH: That the soul was naked.

MR. DARROW: Yes. Krohn is not an alienist. He is an orator. He said because their soul was naked to them. Well, if Krohn's was naked, there would not be much to show.

But Patrick and Church said that the conditions were unfavorable for an examination, that they never would choose it, that their opportunities were poor. And yet Krohn states the contrary, who for sixteen years has not been a physician but who has used a license for the sake of haunting these courts, civil and criminal, and going up and down the land peddling perjury. He has told Your Honor what he has done, and there is not a child on the street who does not know it, there is not a judge in the court who does not know it, there is not a lawyer at the bar who does not know it, there is not a physician in Chicago who does not know it, and I am willing to stake the lives of these two boys on the court knowing it—and I will throw my own in for good measure.

What else did he say in which they disputed him? Both of them say that these boys showed no emotion, no adequate emotion. Krohn said they did. One of them fainted. They had been in the hands of the state's attorney for sixty hours. They had been in the hands of policemen, lawyers, detectives, stenographers, inquisitors, and newspapermen for sixty hours, and one of them fainted.

Well, the only person who is entirely without emotion is a dead man. You cannot live without breathing, which supplies heart action, and an emotional system and some emotional responses. Krohn says, "Why, Loeb had emotion. He was polite, begged our pardon, got up from his chair." Even Dr. Krohn knows better than that. I fancy if Your Honor goes into an elevator where there is a lady or a female, he would take off his hat. I don't. I used to, but I kind of resent it. Is that out of emotion for the lady or is it habit? You say "please" and "thank you" out of habit. Emotions haven't the slightest thing to do with it.

Mr. Leopold has good manners. Mr. Loeb has good manners. They have been taught to him. He has lived them. That does not mean that they are not absolutely lacking in emotional feeling. It means training. That is all it means. And Dr. Krohn knew it. Krohn told the story of this interview and he told almost twice as much as the other two men who sat there and heard it. And how he told it, how he told it.

When he testified, my mind carried me back to the time when I was a kid, which was some time ago, and we used to eat watermelons. And I have seen little boys take a rind of watermelon and cover their whole face with water, eat it, munch it, and have the best time of their lives, up to their ears in watermelon. And when I heard Dr. Krohn testify in this case to take the blood or the lives of these two boys, I could see his mouth water with the joy it gave him, and he evinced all the delight and pleasure of myself and my young companions when we ate watermelon.

I can imagine a psychiatrist, a real one who knows the mechanics of man, who knows life and its machinery, who knows the misfortunes of youth, who knows the stress and the strain of adolescence which comes to every boy and overpowers so many, who knows the weird fantastic world that hedges around the life of a boy—I can imagine a psychiatrist who might honestly think that, under the crude definitions of the law, they were sane and know the difference between right and wrong.

But if he is a physician, a real physician, whose mission is the highest and holiest that man can practice, to save life and minister to human suffering, to save life regardless of what the life was, to prevent suffering regardless of whose suffering it is—and no mission could be higher than that—that if this was his mission instead of testifying in court, and if he were called on for an opinion that might send his fellow man to doom, I could imagine him doing it. I can imagine him doing it reluctantly, carefully, modestly, timorously, fearfully, and being careful that he did not turn one hair to the right or left more than he should and giving the advantage in favor of life and humanity and mercy. But I can never imagine a real physician who cared for life or who thought of anything excepting cash gloating over his testimony as Dr. Krohn did in this case.

Your Honor, if we may adjourn now. I am afraid I won't get through, and you are going to quit at twelve, aren't you?

THE COURT: We will suspend now until ten-thirty o'clock Monday morning.

Monday, August 25

If the court please, I have been discussing what to my mind is shown by the commission of the act itself. Without any consideration of the lives and the training of these boys, without any evidence from experts, I have tried to make a plain statement of the facts of this case, and I believe, as I have said repeatedly, that no one can honestly study the facts and conclude that anything but diseased minds was responsible for this terrible act. Let us see how far we can account for it, Your Honor.

So far we have determined whether men are diseased of mind or normal in their conduct. This line of act shows disease and this line of act shows normality. We have not been able with any satisfaction to peer into the brain and see its workings, to analyze the human system and see where it has gone awry. Science is doing something but so far has done little, and we have been compelled almost entirely to make up our minds from conduct as to the condition of the minds of men.

The mind, of course, is an elusive thing. Whether it exists or not nobody can tell. It cannot be found as you find the brain. Its relation to the brain and the nervous system is uncertain. It simply means the activity of the body which is co-coordinated with what we call brain. But when we do find from human conduct that we believe there is a diseased mind, we naturally speculate on how it came about. And we wish to find always, if possible, the reason why it is so. We may find it, we may not find it, because the unknown is infinitely wider and larger than the known, both as to the human mind and as to almost everything else.

It has not been so long since the insane were supposed to be possessed of devils and since criminals were supposed to be possessed of devils and that wise men solved intricate questions by saying that devils possessed human beings. It has not been so very long since it was supposed that diseased persons were possessed of devils, which meant simply that they be driven out to cure the disease.

We have gone further than this. We understand that there is some connection between the workings of the mind and the workings of the body. We understand something of the physical basis of life. We understand something of the intricate mechanism which may be bad in some minute parts and cause such serious habit with human conduct.

I have tried to study these two lives, the lives of these two most unfortunate boys. Three months ago, if their friends and the friends of the family had been asked to pick out the most promising boys of their acquaintance, they probably would have picked these. With every opportunity, with every advantage, with a good intellectual equipment, with plenty of wealth, they would have said that these two would succeed. In a day, by an act of madness, all this is destroyed until the best they can hope for now is a life of silence and pain, judging from their years.

How did it happen? Let us take Dickie Loeb first. I do not claim to know how it happened; I have sought to find out. I know that something, or some combination of things, is responsible for this mad act. I know that there are no accidents in nature. I know that effect follows cause. I know, if I were wise enough and knew enough about this case, I could lay my finger on it. I will do the best I can, but it is largely speculation.

The child, of course, is born without knowledge. Impressions are made upon its mind as it goes along. Dickie Loeb was a child of wealth and opportunity. Over and over in this court Your Honor has been asked, and other courts have been asked, to consider boys who have had no chance. They have been asked to consider the poor whose home had been the street, with no education and no chance, and they have done it and done it rightfully. But, Your Honor, it is just as often a great misfortune to be the child of the rich as it is the child of the poor. Wealth has its misfortunes. Too much, too great opportunity and advantage given to a child has its misfortunes, and I am asking Your

Honor to consider the rich as well as the poor, and nothing else.

Can I find what was wrong? I think I can. Here was a boy at a tender age placed in the hands of a governess—intellectual, vigorous, devoted, with a strong ambition for the welfare of this boy. He was made to study books, as plants are grown in hot-houses. He had no pleasures such as a boy should have, except in what was gained by lying and cheating. Now, I am not criticizing the nurse. I suggest some day Your Honor look at her picture. It explains her fully—forceful, brooking no interference, she loved this boy, and her ambition was that he should reach the highest possible. No time to pause, no time to stop from one book to another, no time to have those pleasures which a boy ought to have to make a normal life. And what happened?

Your Honor, what would happen? Nothing strange or unusual. This nurse was with him all the time except when he stole out at night from four to fourteen—from two to fourteen years of age—and it is instructive to read her letter to show her attitude. It speaks volumes, tells exactly the relation between these two people. He scheming and planning, as healthy boys would do, to get out from under her restraint. She putting before him the best books, which children generally do not want. And he, when she was not looking, reading detective stories, which he devoured, story after story, in his young life. Of all of this there can be no question.

What is the result? Every story he read was a story of crime. Every one. We have a statute in this state, passed only last year if I recall it, which forbids minors reading stories of crime. Why? There is only one reason. Because the legislature in its wisdom thought it would have a tendency to produce these thoughts and this life in the boys who read them. The legislature of this state has given its opinion and forbidden boys to read these books. He read them day after day. He never stopped. While he was passing through college at Ann Arbor,[46] he was still reading them. When he was a senior, he read them and almost

nothing else. Now these facts are beyond excuse. He early developed the tendency to mix with crime, to be a detective; as a little boy shadowing people on the street; and as a little child going out with his fantasy of being the head of a band of criminals and directing them on the street.

How did this go and develop in him? Let us see. It seems to me as natural as the day following the night. Every detective story is a story of a detective getting the best of it, trailing some unfortunate individual through devious ways until he is finally landed in jail or stands on the gallows. They all show how smart the detective is and where the man himself fell down—every one of them.

This boy, early in his life, conceived the idea that there could be a perfect crime, one that nobody could ever detect; that there could be one where the detective did not land his game, a perfect crime. He had been interested in the story of Charley Ross, who was kidnapped.[47] He was interested in these things all his life. He believed in his childish way that a crime could be so carefully planned that there would be no detection, and his idea was to plan a perfect crime. It would involve kidnapping and involve murder.

I might digress here just a moment because my friend Savage spoke about two crimes that were committed here—kidnapping and murder. That is, the court should hang them twice—one for each. There are more than two committed here. There are more than two crimes committed in every capital act. An attempt to extort money was committed. A conspiracy to do each was committed. Carrying arms was committed. I could probably mention half a dozen if I tried, but it is all one thing and counsel knows it is all one thing.

Is it anything new in criminal practice? Why, Your Honor, we have it every day in these courts. In almost any important crime, the state's attorney can write indictments as long as the paper lasts—not only counts, but indictments. Take a case of burning

---

46. Loeb entered the University of Chicago when he was 14, then transferred to the University of Michigan, from which he graduated one week before his 18th birthday.

47. On July 1, 1874, four-year-old Charley Ross was abducted from in front of his family's mansion in Germantown, Pennsylvania, and was never found. It was the most famous kidnapping in American history until the abduction and murder of the son of aviator Charles Lindbergh in 1932.

a building for insurance by two people. There is the crime of arson. There is the crime of burning a building to defraud an insurance company. There is conspiracy to commit arson. There is conspiracy to burn a building to defraud an insurance company. And I might mention others, all in the one act. Burglary and larceny, a number of crimes, especially if there are two. It is nothing new. This was one offense and one only. They could have made six out of it or one out of it or two out of it. It is only one thing. Just like any other important crime.

Well, now, let's see. They wanted a complete crime. There had been growing in this brain, dwarfed and twisted as every act in this case shows it was dwarfed and twisted, there had been growing this scheme, not due to any wickedness of Dickie Loeb, for he is a child. It grew as he grew; it grew from those around him; it grew from the lack of the proper training until it possessed him. He believed he could beat the police. He believed he could plan the perfect crime. He had thought of it and talked of it for years. Had talked of it as a child, had worked at it as a child, and this sorry act of his, utterly irrational and motiveless, a plan to commit a perfect crime which must contain kidnapping, and there must be ransom or else it could not be perfect, and they must get the money.

The state itself, in opening this case, said that it was largely for experience and for a thrill, which it was. In the end, they switched it on to the sorry, foolish reason of getting cash. Every fact in this case shows that cash had almost nothing to do with it except to help them commit the perfect crime; and to commit the perfect crime, there must be a kidnapping, and a kidnapping where they could get money, and that was all there was of it.

Now that is the two theories of this case, and I submit, Your Honor, under the facts in this case there can be no question but what we are right. This fantasy grew in the mind of Dickie Loeb almost before he began to read. It developed as a child just as kleptomania has developed in many a person and is clearly recognized by the courts. He tried from one thing and another and, in the main, insignificant, childish things. Finally the utterly foolish and stupid and unnecessary thing of going to Ann Arbor to steal

from a fraternity house, a fraternity of which he was a member.

And then came the planning for this crime. Murder was the least part of it; to kidnap and get the money and kill in connection with it—that was the childish scheme growing up in these childish minds. And they had it in mind for five or six months. Planning what? Planning where every step was foolish and childish, acts that could have been planned in an hour or a day. Planning this and then planning that, changing this and changing that—the weird actions of two mad brains.

Counsel have laughed at us for talking about fantasies and hallucinations. They have laughed at us in one breath but admitted it in another. Let us look at that for a moment, Your Honor. Your Honor has been a child. I well remember that I have been a child. And while youth has its advantages, it has its grievous troubles. There is an old prayer, "Let us grow old in years, but retain the heart of a child." The heart of a child with its strong emotion, with its abundant life, with its disregard of consequences, with its living in the moment and for the moment and for the moment alone, with its lack of responsibility, with its freedom from care.

The law knows and has recognized childhood for many and many a long year. What do we know about childhood? The brain of the child is the home of dreams, of castles, of visions, of illusions, and of delusions. In fact, there could be no childhood without delusions, for delusions are always more alluring than the fact. Delusions, dreams, and hallucinations are a part of the warp and woof of childhood. You know it and I know it.

I remember when I was a child the men seemed as tall as the trees and the trees as tall as the mountains. I can remember very well when, as a little boy, I do not know how old, I swam the deepest spot in the river for the first time. I swam breathlessly and landed with as much sense of glory and triumph as Julius Caesar when he led his troops across the Rubicon.[48] I have been back since and I can almost

---

48. Caesar's crossing of the Rubicon in 49 BCE touched off civil war and eventually led to his assumption of supreme power in Rome.

step across the same place, but it was almost an ocean then. And those who I thought were so wonderful died and left nothing behind them. I had lived in a dream. I had never known the real world which I met to my sorrow, to my discomfort, and to my disillusion, that dispelled many of my illusions years later.

The whole life of childhood is a dream and an illusion, and whether they take one shape or another shape depends not upon the dreamy boy but on what surrounds him. As well might I have dreamed of burglars and wished to be one as to dream of policemen and wish to be a policeman. Perhaps I was lucky, too, that I had no money. We have grown to think that the misfortune is in not having it.

The terrible misfortune in this terrible case is that they had money. That has destroyed their lives. That has given them these illusions. That has caused this mad act. And if Your Honor shall doom them to die, it will be because they are the sons of the rich. Do you suppose if they lived up here on the Northwest Side and had no money, with the evidence as clear in this case as it is, that any human being would want to hang them?

Wealth, excessive wealth, is a grievous misfortune in every step in life. When I hear foolish people, when I read malicious newspapers talking of excessive fees in this case, it makes me ill. That there is nothing else in life, that it is to be presumed that no man lives to whom money is not the first concern, that human instincts, sympathy and kindness and charity and logic, can only be used for cash—it shows how deeply money has corrupted the hearts of all people.

Now, to get to Dickie Loeb. He was a child. The books he read by day were not the books he read by night. We are all of us molded somewhat by the influences around us, and to people who read, perhaps books are the most and the strongest. I know where my life has been molded by books, amongst other things. We all know where our lives have been molded by books, amongst other things. We all know where our lives have been influenced by books. The nurse, strict and jealous and watchful, gave him one kind of books—by night he would steal off and read the other.

Do you mean to tell me that Dickie Loeb had any more to do with his making than any other prod-

uct of heredity that is born upon the earth? At this period of life it is not enough to take a boy—Your Honor, I wish I knew when to stop talking about this question that is interesting me so much—it is not enough to take a boy filled with his dreams and his fantasies and living in an unreal world, but the age of adolescence comes on him with all the rest. What does he know?

Both of these boys are in the adolescent age—both these boys whom every alienist in this case on both sides tells you is the most trying period in the life of a child; both these boys when the call of sex is new and strange; both these boys at a time seeking to adjust their young lives to the world, moved by the strongest feelings and passions that have ever moved men; both these boys at the time boys grow insane, at the time crimes are committed. All this added to all the rest of the vagaries, do you charge them with the responsibility that we may have a hanging, that we may deck Chicago in a holiday garb and let the people have their fill of blood, that you may put stains upon the heart of every man, woman, and child on that day and that the dead walls of Chicago will tell the story of blood?

For God's sake, are we crazy? In the face of history, of every line of philosophy, against the teaching of every religionist and seer and prophet the world has ever given us, we are still doing what our barbarous ancestors did when they came out of the caves and the woods!

From the age of fifteen to the age of twenty or twenty-one, the child has the burden of adolescence, of puberty and sex thrust upon him. Girls are kept at home and carefully watched. Boys without instruction are left to work it out themselves. It may lead to excess. It may lead to disease. It may lead to perversion. Who is to blame? Who did it? Did Dickie Loeb do it? Your Honor, I am almost ashamed to talk about it. I can hardly imagine we are in the nineteenth or the twentieth century. And yet there are men who seriously say that for what nature has done, for what life has done, for what training has done, take the boys' lives.

Now, there is not any mystery about this case, Your Honor. There isn't any mystery. I seem to be criticizing their parents. They had parents who were kind and good and wise in their way. But I say to you seriously that the parents of Dickie Loeb are more responsible than he. And yet few boys had better parents.

Your Honor, it is the easiest thing in the world to be a parent. We talk of motherhood, and yet every woman can be a mother. We talk of fatherhood, and yet every man can be a father. Nature takes care of that. It is easy to be a parent. But to be wise and farseeing enough to understand the boy—no, there are only a very few so wise and so farseeing as that, only a few. When I think of the light way nature has of picking out parents and populating the earth, having them born and die, I cannot hold human beings to the same degree of responsibility that young lawyers hold them when they are enthusiastic in a prosecution. I know what it means. I know there is no better citizen in Chicago than the father of this poor boy. I know there is no better woman than his mother. But I am going to be honest with this court if it is at the expense of both.

Which, think you, shaped the life of Dickie Loeb? Is there any kind of question about it? Where did it come from? A child. Was it pure maliciousness, a boy of five or six or seven—was he to blame for it? Where did he get it? He got it where we all get our ideas, and these books became a part of his dreams and a part of his life. And as he grew up, his visions became hallucinations. He went out on the street and fantastically directed his companions who were not there in their various moves to complete the perfect crime. Can there be any sort of question about it?

Suppose, Your Honor, that instead of this boy being here in this court under request of this court that he pronounce a sentence to hang him by the neck until dead, he had been taken to a pathological hospital to be analyzed and the physicians had inquired into it. What would they have said? What would they have said? There is only one thing they could possibly have said. They would have traced it all back to the gradual growth of the child.

That is not all there is to it, Your Honor. Youth is hard enough. The only good thing about youth is that it has no thought and no care; and how blindly we can do things when we are young. Where is the man who has not committed a crime in his youth?

Let us be honest with ourselves. Let us look into our own hearts. How many men [are there] today—lawyers and Congressmen and judges and even state's attorneys—who have not done something when they were young? And if they did not get caught or it was trivial, it was their good fortune, wasn't it?

We might as well be honest with ourselves, Your Honor. Before I would tie a noose around the neck of a boy, I would try to call back into my mind the emotions of youth. I would try to remember what the world looked like to me when I was a child. I would try to remember how strong were these instinctive, persistent emotions that moved my life. I would try to remember how weak and inefficient was youth in the presence of the surging, controlling feelings of the child. One that remembers it and honestly remembers it and asks himself the question and tries to unlock the door that he thinks is closed and calls back the boy—he can understand the boy.

But, Your Honor, that is not all there is to boyhood. Nature is strong and she is pitiless. She works in her own mysterious way, and we are her victims. We have not much to do with it ourselves. Nature takes this job in hand and we play our parts. In the words of old Omar Khayyam, we are only

> Impotent pieces in the game she plays
> Upon this checker board of nights and days.
> Hither and thither moves and checks and slays,
> And one by one back in the closet lays.[49]

What had this boy to do with it? He was not his own father; he was not his own mother; he was not his own grandparents. All this was handed to him. He did not surround himself with governesses and wealth. He did not make himself. And yet he is to be made to pay.

There was a time in England, running down as late as the beginning of the last century, when judges used to convene court and call juries to try a horse, a dog, a sow for crime. I have in my library a story of judges and juries, lawyers, trying and convicting an old sow for lying down on her ten pigs and killing them.

---

49. *The Rubaiyat of Omar Khayyam*, trans. Edward FitzGerald, 2nd ed. (1868).

And they stuck her. What does it mean? Animals were tried.

I know that one of two things happened to this boy: that this terrible crime was inherent in his organism and came from some ancestor, or that it came through his education and his training after he was born. Do I need to prove it? Judge Crowe said at one point in this case, when some witness spoke about his wealth, "probably that was responsible." Perhaps the judge has forgotten. To believe that any boy is responsible for himself or his early training is an absurdity that no lawyer or judge should be guilty of today.

Somewhere this came to this boy. If it came from his heredity, I do not know where or how. None of us are bred perfect and pure, and the color of our hair, the color of our eyes, our stature, the weight and fineness of our brain, and everything about us could be traced with absolute certainty somewhere; if we had the pedigree, could be traced just the same in a boy as it could in a dog, a horse, or a cow. I do not know what remote ancestor may have sent down the seed that corrupted him, and I do not know through how many ancestors it may have passed until it reached Dickie Loeb. All I know is it is true, and there is not a biologist in the world who will not say I am right.

If it did not come that way, then I know that if he was normal, if he had been understood, if he had been trained as he should have been, it would not have happened. Not that anybody may not slip, but I know it and Your Honor knows it, and every schoolhouse and every church in the land is an evidence of it. Else why build them? Every effort to protect society is an effort toward it, or why do it? Every bit of training in the world proves it—and it likewise proves it fails.

I know that if this boy had been understood and properly trained for him—and the training he got might have been the very best for someone else—but if it had been the proper training for him, he would not have been in this courtroom today with the noose above his head. If there is responsibility anywhere, it is back of him, somewhere in the infinite number of his ancestors or in his surroundings or in both. And I submit, Your Honor, that under every principle of natural justice, under every principle of conscience, of right, and of law, he should not be made responsible for the acts of somebody else, whether wise or unwise.

And I say this again, let me repeat, without finding fault with his parents, for whom I have the highest regard and who doubtless did the best they could. They might have done better if they had not had any money. I do not know. Great wealth curses everybody it touches.

This boy was sent to school. His mind worked; his emotions were dead. He could learn books, but he read detective stories. There never was a time since he was old enough to move back and forth according to what seemed to be his volition when he was not haunted with these fantasies. Never once.

They made fun of Dr. White, the ablest and, I believe, the best psychiatrist today,[50] for speaking about this boy's mind running back to teddy bears he used to play with, and in addressing somebody, he would say, "You know, Teddy." Well, Your Honor, it is nothing but the commonplace thing of the commonplace child or the ordinary man; a set of things—emotions, thoughts, feelings—take possession of the mind and we find them recurring over and over again.

I catch myself many and many a time repeating phrases of my childhood, and I have not quite got into my second childhood yet. I have caught myself doing it while I still could catch myself. It means nothing. We may have all the dreams and the visions and build all the castles we wish, but the castles of youth should be discarded with youth; and when they hang over to the time boys should have wiser things and know wiser things, then it is a diseased mind.

When I was young, I thought as a child, I spoke as a child, I understood as a child, but now I have put off childish things,[51] said the psalmist twenty centuries ago. It is when these conditions of boyhood, these fantasies of youth, still stay and the growing boy is still a child in emotion, a child in feeling, a child in hallucination, that you can say that it is the dreams and the hallucinations of childhood which are responsible for his conduct. And there is not an

---

50. Defense alienist William A. White, president of the American Psychiatric Association and superintendent of St. Elizabeth's Hospital in Washington, D.C.

51. Paraphrased from 1 Corinthians 13:11.

act in all this horrible tragedy that was not the act of a child, the act of a child wandering around in the morning of life moved by the new feelings of a boy, moved by the uncontrolled impulses which the teaching was not strong enough to take care of, moved by the dreams and the hallucinations which haunt the brain of a child.

I say, Your Honor, it would be the height of cruelty, of injustice, of wrong and barbarism to visit the penalty upon this poor boy. Your Honor, again I want to say that all parents can be criticized, grandparents, and teachers, but science is not so much interested in criticism as in finding out the causes. Sometime education will be more scientific. Sometime we will try to know the boy before we educate him and as we educate him. Sometime we will try to know what will fit him for what he knows, instead of putting them all through the same course regardless of who they are. This boy needed more home, needed more love, more affection, more direction, directing. He needed to have his emotions awakened. He needed to have guiding hands along the serious road that youth must travel. Had these been given him, he would not be here today.

Now, Your Honor, I want to speak of the other lad, Babe. Babe is somewhat older than Dick and is a boy of remarkable mind—everybody concedes that—away beyond his years. He is a sort of freak in this direction, as in others, a boy without emotions, a boy obsessed of philosophy, a boy obsessed of learning, busy every minute of his life. He went through school quickly; he went to college young;[52] he could learn faster than almost everybody else. His emotional life was lacking, as every alienist witness in this case excepting Dr. Krohn has told you. He was just a half boy, an intellect, an intellectual machine going without balance and without a governor, seeking to find out everything there was in life intellectually, seeking to solve every philosophy, but using his intellect only.

Of course, his family did not understand him; few men would. His mother died when he was young. He had plenty of money, everything given that he wanted, and too much given. Both these boys with

unlimited money, both these boys with automobiles, both of these boys with every luxury around them and in front of them. They grew up in that environment.

Babe took to philosophy. I call him "Babe" not because I want it to affect Your Honor, but because everybody else does. Being the youngest of the family, I suppose that is where he got his nickname. We will call him a man. Mr. Crowe thinks it is easier to hang a man than a boy, and so I will call him a man if I can think of it.

He grew up in this way. He became enamored of the philosophy of Nietzsche.[53] Your Honor, I have read almost everything that Nietzsche ever wrote. A man of wonderful intellect, the most original philosophy of the last century. A man who had made a deeper imprint on philosophy than any other man within a hundred years, whether right or wrong. More books have been written about him than probably all the rest of the philosophers in a hundred years. More college professors have talked about him. In a way he has reached more people and still he has been a philosopher of what we might call the intellectual cult.

He had a philosophy which was different from any other philosophy of modern times at least. He believed that sometime the superman would be born, that everybody was working toward the superman, and sometime there would be one—and he often confronted himself with the superman. He wrote one book called *Beyond Good and Evil*, which was a criticism of all moral precepts as we understand them, and a treatise that the intelligent man was beyond good and evil, that the laws for good and the laws for evil did not apply to anybody who approached the superman. He wrote on the will to power. He wrote some ten or fifteen volumes on his various philosophical ideas.

Nathan Leopold is not the only boy who has read Nietzsche. He may be the only one who was influenced in the way he was influenced, and even that is not true, most likely. I have just made a few short extracts from Nietzsche that show the things that he has read and that influenced him, and these are short and almost taken at random. It is not how it

---

52. Leopold entered the University of Chicago at age 16.

53. German philosopher Friedrich Nietzsche (1844–1900).

would affect you. It is not how it would affect me. The question is how it would affect the impressionable, visionary, dreamy mind of a boy.

At seventeen, at sixteen, at eighteen, while healthy boys were playing baseball or working on the farm or doing odd jobs, he was reading Nietzsche. A boy who never should have seen it—too early for him. But he was possessed of it, and here are some of the doctrines which Nietzsche taught: "Why so soft, oh, my brethren? Why so soft, so unresisting and yielding? Why is there so much disavowal and abnegation in your heart? Why is there so little fate in your looks? For all creators are hard and it must seem blessedness unto you to press your hand upon millenniums and upon wax. This new table, oh, my brethren, I put over you: Become hard. To be obsessed by moral consideration presupposes a very low grade of intellect. We should substitute for morality the will to our own end, and consequently to the means to accomplish that. A great man, a man whom nature has built up and invented in a grand style, is colder, harder, less cautious and more free from the fear of public opinion. He does not possess the virtues which are compatible with respectability, with being respected, nor any of those things which are counted among the virtues of the herd."[54]

A contemptuous, scornful attitude to all those things which the young are taught are important in life; a fixing of new values which are not the values by which any normal child has ever yet been raised; a philosophical dream, containing more or less truth, that was not meant by anybody to be applied to life.

Again, he says: "The morality of the master class is irritating to the taste of the present day because of its fundamental principle that a man has obligation only to his equal, that he may act to all of lower rank and to all that are foreign as he pleases."[55] In other words, man has no obligations. He may do with all other men and all other boys and all society as he

pleases—the superman, a creation of Nietzsche but which has permeated every college and university in the civilized world.

Again, quoting from a president of a university: "Although no perfect superman has yet appeared in history, Nietzsche's types are to be found in the world careers, Alexander, Napoleon,[56] in the wicked heroes such as the Borgias,[57] Wagner's *Siegfried* and Ibsen's *Brand*,[58] and the great cosmopolitan intellects such as Goethe and Stendahl.[59] These were the gods of Nietzsche's idolatry. The superman-like qualities lie not in their genius, but in their freedom from scruple. They rightly felt themselves to be above the law. What they thought was right—not because sanctioned by any law beyond themselves, but because they did it. So the superman will be a law unto himself. What he does will come from the will and superabundant power within him."[60]

Your Honor, I could read for a week from Nietzsche all to the same purpose, all to the same end. Counsel have said that because a man believes in murder, that does not excuse him. Quite right. But in cases like the anarchists' case, where a number of men, perhaps honestly believing in revolution and knowing the consequences of their act and knowing its illegal character, were held responsible for murder.[61]

Of course, the books are full of statements that the fact that a man believes in committing a crime

---

54. Darrow is running together a series of statements from several of Nietzsche's works. In the revised version of his speech prepared for publication, he described the statements as "short and taken almost at random."

55. From H. L. Mencken, *The Philosophy of Friedrich Nietzsche* (1908).

56. Greek leader Alexander the Great (365 BCE–323 BCE); French ruler Napoleon Bonaparte (1769–1821).

57. Italian Renaissance family notorious for its ruthlessness and treachery.

58. Richard Wagner's opera *Siegfried* (1876); Henrik Ibsen's play *Brand* (1866).

59. German author Johann Wolfgang von Goethe (1749–1832); French writer Marie Henri Beyle (1783–1842), who wrote over the pen name Stendhal.

60. From Ralph Barton Perry, *The Present Conflict of Ideals* (1918). Perry taught at Harvard for more than four decades, but he did not serve as a university president.

61. Darrow is referring to the 1886–1887 Haymarket Affair, in which eight Chicago anarchists were convicted of murder for a bombing that killed at least one police officer and wounded several others.

does not excuse him. That is not this case, and counsel must know that that is not this case. Here is a boy of sixteen or seventeen becoming obsessed with these doctrines. There isn't any question about the facts. Their own witnesses tell it and every one of our witnesses tell it. It was not a casual bit of philosophy with him; it was his life. He believed in a superman. He and Dickie Loeb were the supermen. There might have been others, but they were two, and two chums. The ordinary commands of society were not for him.

Many of us read it but know that it has no actual application to life, but not he. It became a part of his being. It was his philosophy. He lived it and practiced it; he thought it applied to him, and he could not have believed it excepting that it either caused a diseased mind or was the result of a diseased mind.

Now let me call your attention hastily to just a few facts in connection with it. One of the cases is a New York case, where a man named Freeman became obsessed in a very strange way of religious ideas. He read the story of Isaac and Abraham and he felt a call that he must sacrifice his son.[62] He arranged an altar in his parlor. He converted his wife to the idea. He took his little babe and put it on the altar and cut its throat. Why? Because he was obsessed of that idea. Was he sane? Was he normal? Was his mind diseased? Was this poor fellow responsible? Not in the least. And he was discharged because he was the victim of a delusion.[63]

Men are largely what their ideas make them. Boys are largely what their ideas make them. Here is a boy who by day and by night, in season and out, was talking of the superman owing no obligations to anyone, whatever gave him pleasure he should do, believing it just as another man might believe a religion or any other philosophical theory.

---

62. As told in Genesis 22:1–18, God required Abraham to sacrifice his only son, Isaac, a command Abraham was prepared to obey until God stopped him.

63. Darrow is referring to Charles F. Freeman, who murdered his younger daughter, Edith, at Pocasset, Massachusetts, in May 1879. His mention of New York is a slip of the tongue, probably due to the famous case of William Freeman, whose murder of four people in upstate New York in 1846 prompted one of the first insanity defenses in American history.

You remember I asked Dr. Church about these religious cases, and he said, "Yes, many people go to the insane asylum on account of it, that they place a literal meaning on it and believe it thoroughly." Many of them. I asked Dr. Church—whom I again say I believe to be an honest man and intelligent man—I asked him whether the same thing might be done or might have come from a philosophical belief, and he said if he believed it strong enough. And I asked him about Nietzsche. He said he knew something of Nietzsche, something of his responsibility for the war, for which he perhaps is not responsible. He said he knew something about the doctrine. I asked him what became of him, and he said he was insane for fifteen years until the time of his death. His very doctrine is a species of insanity.

Here is a man, a wise man—perhaps not wise, but brilliant—a thoughtful man, who has made his impress upon the world. Every student of philosophy knows him. His own doctrines made him a maniac. And here is a young boy in the adolescent age, harassed by everything that harasses children, who takes this philosophy and swallows it, who believes it literally, lives his life on it. It is a part of his life. It is his life. Do you suppose this mad act could have been done by him in any other way?

What did he have to get out of it? A boy with a beautiful home, with automobiles, a graduate of college, going to Europe, and then studying law at Harvard, as brilliant in intellect as any boy that you could find, a boy with every prospect that life might hold out to him, and yet he goes out and commits this weird, strange, wild, mad act, that he may die on the gallows or live in a prison cell until he dies of old age. He did it obsessed of an idea, perhaps to some extent influenced by what has not been developed publicly in this case, perversions that were present in this case. Both signs of insanity, both, together with this act, proving a diseased mind.

Is there any question about what was responsible for him? What else could be? What else? To take a boy in his youth, with every promise that the world could hold out before him—wealth and position and intellect, yes, genius, scholarship, nothing that he could not obtain—and throw it away and mount the gallows or go into a cell for life. It is too foolish to talk about. Can Your Honor imagine a sane brain doing it? Can you imagine it coming from anything but a diseased mind? Can you imagine it is any part of normality? And yet, Your Honor, you are asked to hang a boy of his age, abnormal, obsessed of dreams, visions, a philosophy that destroyed his life, when there is not any sort of question in the world as to what caused his downfall, not the slightest.

Now, I have said that, as to Loeb, if there is anybody to blame, it is back of him. Your Honor, there are lots of things happen in this world that nobody is to blame for. In fact, I am not very much for settling blame myself. If I could settle the blame on somebody else for this special act, I would wonder why that somebody else did it. And I know if I could find out, I would move it back another peg.

I know, Your Honor, that every atom of life in all this universe is bound up together. I know that a pebble cannot be thrown into the ocean without disturbing every drop of water on the earth. I know that every life is inextricably mixed and woven with every other life. I know that every influence, conscious and unconscious, acts and reacts on every living organism and that no one can fix the blame. I know that all life is a series of infinite chances, which sometimes result one way and sometimes another. I cannot tell. I have not the infinite wisdom that can fathom it; neither has any other human brain. But I do know that if back of it is a power that made it, that power alone can tell. And if there is no power, then it is an infinite chance which man alone cannot solve.

Why should this boy's life be bound up with Frederick Nietzsche, who died thirty years ago, insane, in Germany? Why? I don't know. I know it is. I know that no man who ever wrote a line that I read failed to influence me to some extent. I know that every life I ever touched influenced me, and I influenced them, and that it is not given to me to unravel the infinite causes and say this is I and this is you. I am responsible for so much and you are responsible for so much. I know—I know that in the infinite universe everything has its place and that the smallest particle is a part of all. Tell me that you can visit the wrath of fate and chance and life and eternity upon a nineteen-year-old boy! If you could, justice would be a misnomer and mercy would be a fraud.

I might say further about Nathan Leopold—where did he get this philosophy? At college? He did not make it, Your Honor. He did not write these books, and I will venture to say there are at least fifty thousand books on Nietzsche and his philosophy. I never counted them, but I will venture to say that there are that many in the libraries of the world. No other philosopher ever caused the discussion that Nietzsche has caused. There is not a university in the world where the professors are not familiar with Nietzsche, not one. There is not an intellectual man in the world whose life and feelings run to philosophy that is not more or less familiar with the Nietzschean philosophy.

Some believe it and some do not believe it. Some read it as I do and take it as a theory, a dream, a vision, mixed with good and bad, but not in any way related to human life. Some take it seriously. The universities perhaps do not all teach it, for perhaps some teach nothing in philosophy, but they give the boys the books of the masters and tell them what they think about it and they discuss it. There is not a university in the world of any high standing where the professors do not tell you about Nietzsche and discuss it, or where the books are not there. I will guarantee that you can go down to the University of Chicago today, in its big library, and find over a thousand volumes on Nietzsche, and I am sure I speak moderately.

If this boy is to blame for this, where did he get it? Is there any blame attached because somebody took Nietzsche's philosophy seriously and fashioned his life on it? And there is no question in this case but what that is true. Then who is to blame? The university would be more to blame than he is. The scholars of the world would be more to blame than he is. The publishers of the world—and Nietzsche's books are published by Macmillan, one of the biggest publishers in the world—are more to blame than he is. Your Honor, it is hardly fair to hang a nineteen-year-old boy for the philosophy that was taught him at the university. It does not meet my ideas of justice and fairness to visit upon his head the philosophy that has been taught by university men for twenty-five years.

Now, I do not want to be misunderstood about this. Even for the sake of saving the lives of my clients, I do not want to be dishonest and tell the court something that I do not honestly think in this case. I do not think that the universities are to blame. I do not think they should be held responsible. I do think, however, that they are too large and that they should keep a closer watch, if possible, upon the individual. But you cannot destroy thought because, forsooth, some brain may be deranged by thought. It is the duty of the university, as I conceive it, to be the great storehouse of the wisdom of the ages and to have its students come there and learn and choose. I have no doubt that it has meant the death of many; that we cannot help.

Every changed idea in the world has had its consequences. Every new religious doctrine has created its victims. Every new philosophy has caused suffering and death. Every new machine has carved men while it served the world. No railroad can be built without the destruction of human life. No great building can be erected but what unfortunate workmen fall to the earth and die. No great movement but what bears its toll of life and death. No great ideal but what does good and harm. And we cannot stop because it may be harmful.

It is responsible for this boy's mad act. I have no idea in this case that this act would ever have been committed or participated in by him excepting for the philosophy which he had taken literally, which belonged to older boys and older men, and which no one can take literally and practice literally and live. It cannot be done.

So, Your Honor, I do not mean to unload this on that man or this man, or this organization or that organization. I am trying to trace causes. I am trying to trace them honestly. I am trying to trace them with the light I have. I am trying to say to this court that these boys are not responsible for this and that their act was due to this and this, and this and this, and asking this court not to visit the judgment of its wrath upon them for things for which they are not to blame.

There is something else in this case, Your Honor, that is stronger still. Have you got those letters?[64] There is a large element of chance in life. I know

I will die. I don't know when; I don't know how; I don't know where; and I don't want to know. I know it will come. I know that it depends on infinite chances. Do I live to myself? Did I make myself? And control my fate? Can I fix my death unless I commit suicide? And I cannot do that because the will to live is too strong.

I know it depends on infinite chances. Take the rabbit running through the woods, and a fox meets him at a certain fence. If the rabbit had not started when it did, it would not have met the fox and would have lived longer. If the fox had started later or earlier, it would not have met the rabbit and its fate would have been different. My death will depend upon chances. It may be the breathing of a germ. It may be a pistol. It may be the decaying of my faculties and all that makes life. It may be a cancer. It may be any one of an infinite number of things. And where I am at a certain time and whether I breathe that germ and the condition of my system when I breathe it is an accident which is sealed up in the book of fate and which no human being can open.

How did these boys happen to do this? Haven't you those letters?

MR. BACHRACH: No, I haven't got the transcript.

MR. DARROW: Your Honor, I will have to pass to something else and read that afterward.

These boys, neither one of them, could possibly have committed this act excepting by joining. It was not the act of one; it was the act of two. It was the act of their planning, their conniving, their believing in each other, their thinking themselves supermen. Without it, they could not have done it. It would not have happened. Their parents happened to meet. Some sort of chemical alchemy operated so that they cared for each other, and poor Bobby Franks' dead body was found in the culvert. Neither of them could have done it alone.

I want to call your attention, Your Honor, to the two letters in this case which settle this matter to my mind conclusively—not only to the condition of these boys' minds but the terrible fate that overtook them.

Your Honor, I am sorry for poor Bobby Franks, and I think anybody who knows me knows that I am not saying it simply to speak. I am sorry for the

---

64. Darrow's question is addressed to his cocounsel Benjamin Bachrach.

bereaved father and the bereaved mother, and I would like to know what they would do with these poor unfortunate lads who are here in this court today. I know something of them, of their lives, of their charity, of their ideas, and nobody here sympathizes with them more than I.

On the twenty-first day of May, poor Bobby Franks, stripped and naked, was left in a culvert down near the Indiana line. I know it came through the mad act of mad boys. Mr. Savage told us that Franks, if he had lived, would have been a great man and accomplished much. I want to leave this thought with Your Honor before luncheon.

I do not know what Bobby Franks would have been had he grown to be a man. I do not know the laws that control one's growth. Sometimes, Your Honor, a boy of great promise is cut off in his early youth. Sometimes he dies and is placed in a culvert. Sometimes a boy of great promise stands on a trapdoor and is hanged by the neck until he is dead. Sometimes he dies of diphtheria. Death somehow pays no attention to age, sex, prospects, or wealth. It pays no attention to intellect. It comes and perhaps, perhaps—I can only say perhaps, for I never professed to unravel the mysteries of fate, and I cannot tell, but I can say perhaps—the boy who died at fourteen did as much as if he had died at seventy. And perhaps the boy who died as a babe did as much as if he had lived longer. Perhaps, somewhere in fate and chance, it might be that he lived as long as he should.

And what I want to say is this: that the death of poor little Bobby Franks should not be in vain. Would it mean anything if, on account of that death, these two boys were taken out and a rope tied around their necks and they died felons and left a blot upon the names of their families? Would that show that Bobby Franks had a purpose in his life and a purpose in his death? No.

I say this, Your Honor, that the unfortunate and tragic death of this weak young lad should mean something. It should mean an appeal to the fathers and the mothers, an appeal to the teachers, to the religious guides, to society at large. It should mean an appeal to all of them to appraise their children, to understand the emotions that control them, to understand the ideas that possess them, to teach them to dodge the pitfalls of life. It should be, to the millions of mothers who have read of this case and the millions of fathers who have read of it and the brothers and sisters who have read of it, that the death of Bobby Franks will teach them to examine their own children, their own families, their own brothers, their own sisters, to see what is in them or what may be in them or what may be avoided to prevent future tragedies like this. And society, too, should take its share of this case and make not two more tragedies, but use it as best it can to make life safer, to make childhood easier and safer, to do something to cure the cruelty, the hatred, the chance, and the willfulness of life.

If the court please, I have discussed somewhat in detail these two boys separately. Their coming together was a means of their undoing. Your Honor is familiar with the facts in reference to their association. They had a weird, almost impossible relationship. Leopold, with his idea of the superman, had repeatedly said that Loeb was his ideal of the superman. He had the attitude toward him that one has to his most devoted friend or that a man has to a lover. Without the combination of these two, nothing of this sort probably could have happened.

It is not necessary for us, Your Honor, to rely upon words to prove the condition of these boys' minds and to prove the effect of this strange and fatal relationship between these two boys. It is mostly told in a letter which the state itself has introduced in this case. Not the whole story, but enough of it, is shown so that I take it that no intelligent, thoughtful person could fail to realize what was the relation between them and how they had played upon each other to effect their downfall and their ruin.

I want to read this letter once more, a letter which was introduced by the state, and the enclosure with it, a letter dated October ninth, a month and three days before their trip to Ann Arbor. And I want the court to say in its own mind whether this letter was anything but the product of a diseased mind and if it does not show a relation that was responsible for this terrible homicide.

This was the letter written by Leopold to Loeb. Of course, they lived close together, only a few blocks from each other, saw each other every day, but Leopold wrote him this letter:[65]

October 9, 1923

Dear Dick:

In view of our former relations, I take it for granted that it is unnecessary to make any excuse for writing you at this time, and still I am going to state my reasons for so doing, as this may turn out to be a long letter, and I don't want to cause you the inconvenience of reading it all to find out what it contains if you are not interested in the subjects dealt with.

First, I am enclosing the document which I mentioned to you today, and which I will explain later. Second, I am going to tell you of a new fact which has come up since our discussion. And third, I am going to put in writing what my attitude toward our present relations, with a view of avoiding future possible misunderstandings, and in the hope (though I think it rather vain) that possibly we may have misunderstood each other, and can yet clear this matter up.

Now, as to the first, I wanted you this afternoon, and still want you, to feel that we are on an equal footing legally, and therefore, I purposely committed the same tort of which you were guilty, the only difference being that in your case the facts would be harder to prove than in mine, should I deny them. The enclosed document should secure you against changing my mind in admitting the facts, if the matter should come up, as it would prove to any court that they were true.

As to the second. On your suggestion I immediately phoned Dick Rubel,[66] and speaking from a paper prepared beforehand (to be sure of the exact wording) said: "Dick, when we were together yesterday, did I tell you that Dick (Loeb) had told me the things which I then told you, or that it was merely my opinion that I believed them to be so?"

I asked this twice to be sure he understood, and on the same answer both times (which I took down as he spoke) felt that he did understand.

He replied: "No, you did not tell me that Dick told you these things, but said that they were in your opinion true."

He further denied telling you subsequently that I had said that they were gleaned from conversation with you, and I then told him that he was quite right, that you never had told me. I further told him that this was merely your suggestion of how to settle a question of fact, that he was in no way implicated, and that neither of us would be angry with him at his reply. (I imply your assent to this.)

This of course proves that you were mistaken this afternoon in the question of my having actually and technically broken confidence, and voids my apology, which I made contingent on proof of this matter.

Now, as to the third, last, and most important question. When you came to my home this afternoon I expected either to break friendship with you or attempt to kill you unless you told me why you acted as you did yesterday.

You did, however, tell me, and hence the question shifted to the fact that I would act as before if you persisted in thinking me treacherous, either in act (which you waived if Dick's opinion went with mine) or in intention.

Now, I apprehend, though here I am not quite sure, that you said that you did not think me treacherous in intent, nor ever have, but that you considered me in the wrong and expected such a statement from me. This statement I unconditionally refused to make until such time as I may become convinced of its truth.

However, the question of our relation I think must be in your hands (unless the above conceptions are mistaken), inasmuch as you have satisfied first one and then the other requirement, upon which I agreed to refrain from attempting to kill you or refusing to continue our friendship. Hence I have no reason not to continue to be on friendly terms with you, and would under ordinary conditions continue as before.

The only question, then, is with you. You demand me to perform an act, namely, state that I acted wrongly. This I refuse. Now it is up to you to inflict the penalty for this refusal—at your discretion, to

65. The letter is not included in the Wilson Publishing Company pamphlet of Darrow's speech; we have taken it from Maureen McKernan, *The Amazing Crime and Trial of Leopold and Loeb* (1924).

66. Mutual friend of Leopold and Loeb who was one of the possible kidnapping victims they discussed before committing their crime.

break friendship, inflict physical punishment, or anything else you like, or on the other hand to continue as before.

The decision, therefore, must rest with you. This is all of my opinion on the right and wrong of the matter.

Now comes a practical question. I think that I would ordinarily be expected to, and in fact do expect to continue my attitude toward you, as before, until I learn either by direct words or by conduct on your part which way your decision has been formed. This I shall do.

Now a word of advice. I do not wish to influence your decision either way, but I do want to warn you that in case you deem it advisable to discontinue our friendship, that in both our interests extreme care must be had. The motif of "A falling out of_____
_____"[67] would be sure to be popular, which is patently undesirable and forms an irksome but unavoidable bond between us.

Therefore, it is, in my humble opinion, expedient, though our breech need be no less real in fact, yet to observe the conventionalities, such as salutation on the street and a general appearance of at least not unfriendly relations on all occasions when we may be thrown together in public.

Now, Dick, I am going to make a request to which I have perhaps no right, and yet which I dare to make also for "Auld Lang Syne."[68] Will you, if not too inconvenient, let me know your answer (before I leave tomorrow) on the last count? This, to which I have no right, would greatly help my peace of mind in the next few days when it is most necessary to me. You can if you will merely call up my home before twelve noon and leave a message saying, "Dick says yes," if you wish our relations to continue as before, and "Dick says no," if not.

It is unnecessary to add that your decision will of course have no effect on my keeping to myself our confidences of the past, and that I regret the whole affair more than I can say.

Hoping not to have caused you too much trouble in reading this, I am (for the present), as ever,

"BABE"

MR. CROWE: Mr. Darrow, I would suggest that you let the court read the exact language.[69]

MR. DARROW: Where I skipped?

MR. CROWE: Yes, where you skipped, so that he will understand what the thing is about.

THE COURT: I will read the original.

MR. CROWE: I would like to have you read it now, because it will throw a light on the whole matter.

THE COURT: All right; I will read it.

MR. DARROW: Your Honor can easily remember the few words I may have left out.

THE COURT: Yes.

MR. DARROW: The court remembers it. Now, I undertake to say that under any interpretation of this case, taking into account all the things Your Honor knows that have not been made public, or leaving them out, there is nobody can interpret that letter excepting on the theory of a diseased mind, and with it goes this strange document which was referred to in the letter: "I, Nathan F. Leopold Jr., being under no duress or compulsion, do hereby affirm and declare that on this, the ninth day of October, 1923, I, for reasons of my own, locked the door of the room in which I was with one Richard A. Loeb, with the intent of blocking his only feasible mode of egress, and that I further indicated my intention of applying physical force upon the person of the said Richard A. Loeb if necessary to carry out my design, to wit, to block his only feasible mode of egress."

There is nothing in this case, whether heard alone by the court or heard in public, that can explain these documents in the light of normal human beings, that throw any light upon the character of this relation, upon the kind of mind of these two boys.

I want to call your attention then to an extract from another letter by Babe, if I may be permitted to call him Babe up to the time of his death. This is

67. The missing words, which Darrow deleted from his reading of the letter in court, are "cock suckers." Throughout the trial, he consistently sidestepped the subject of Leopold and Loeb's sexual relationship.

68. Traditional Scottish song sung in English-speaking countries at the stroke of midnight on New Year's Day. Colloquially translated, the title refers to "times gone by."

69. Crowe is referring to Darrow's excision of the phrase "cock suckers" when he read the letter in court (see note 67 above).

written by Leopold on the 20th Century train[70] the day after the other letter was written, and in it he says: "Now, that is all that is in point to our controversy."[71]

The whole letter, I know, has been read, and I think Your Honor will probably reread it.

"But I am going to add a little more in an effort to explain my system of the Nietzschean philosophy with regard to you."

We don't need witnesses, we don't need his schoolmates, his classmates, his teacher, and all the rest about his Nietzschean philosophy. It is here in this letter: "It may not have occurred to you why a mere mistake in judgment on your part should be treated as a crime when on the part of another it should not be so considered. Here are the reasons. In formulating a superman, he is, on account of certain superior qualities inherent in him, exempt from the ordinary laws which govern ordinary men. He is not liable for anything he may do, whereas others would be, except for the one crime that it is possible for him to commit—to make a mistake."

If that is a sane expression, Your Honor, the rest of the world is crazy.

"Now obviously any code which conferred upon an individual or upon a group extraordinary responsibility would be unfair and bad. Therefore, the superman is held to have committed a crime every time he errs in judgment, a mistake excusable in others. But you may say that you have previously made mistakes which I did not treat as crimes. This is true. To cite an example, the other night you expressed the opinion, and insisted, that Marcus Aurelius Antoninus[72] was practically the founder of stoicism. In so doing you committed a crime. But it was a slight crime, and I chose to forgive it. I have, and had before that, forgiven the crime which you committed in committing the error in judgment which caused the whole train of events. I did not and do not wish to charge you

with crime, but I feel justified in using any of the consequences of your crime for which you are held responsible to my advantage. This and only this I did, so you see how careful you must be."

Is that the letter of a normal eighteen-year-old boy, or is it the letter of a diseased brain? Is that the letter of boys acting as boys should and thinking as boys should, or is it the letter of one whose philosophy has taken possession of him, who understands what the world calls crime as something that the superman may do, who believes the only crime the superman can commit is to make a mistake? He believed it. He was immature. It possessed him.

It was material in the strange, weird compact that the court already knows about between these two boys by which each was to give something. Out of that compact and out of these diseased minds grew this terrible crime. Do you tell me this was the act of a normal boy, of a boy who thinks and feels as a boy should, who has the thoughts and emotions and physical life that boys should have? There is not a thing in all of it that corresponds with normal life. There is a weird, strange, unnatural disease in all of it which is responsible for this deed.

Your Honor, it seems to be beyond argument and beyond question. I submit to you it is not the evidence of these boys alone. It is proven by the writings. It is proven by every act. It is proven by their companions, and there can be no question about it.

We brought into this courtroom a number of their boy friends whom they had known day by day, who had associated with them in the clubhouse, were their constant companions, and they tell the same stories. They tell the story that neither of these two boys was responsible for their conduct. Maremont,[73] whom the state first called, one of the oldest of the boys put on by them in the first instance, said that Leopold had never had any judgment of any sort. They talked about the superman. He argued his philosophy. It was a religion with him. But as to judgment of things in life,

---

70. The New York Central Railroad's 20th Century Limited, which ran between New York and Chicago.

71. This quotation and the ones that follow are from Leopold's letter to Loeb of October 10, 1923.

72. Roman emperor, 161–180 CE.

73. Arnold Maremont, a fellow law student at the University of Chicago, who often argued with Leopold about Nietzsche's philosophy; he testified on July 24 and August 7.

he had none. Developed intellectually, wanting emotionally, developed in those things which a boy does not need and should not have at his age, but absolutely void of the healthful feelings, of the healthful instincts of practical life, that are necessary to the child.

We called not less than ten or twelve of both of these, all of them saying the same. Here was Dickie Loeb, who was not allowed by his companions the privileges of his class because of his childishness and his lack of judgment. Nobody denies it, and yet the state's attorney makes a play here on account of this girl whose testimony was so important—Miss Nathan.[74]

What did the state's attorney do in this matter? Before we ever got to these defendants, they were called in before the grand jury, purported to issue subpoenas before the grand jury, and the state's attorneys called into their office young boys and girls just when this question broke. Without any friends, without any counsel, they were questioned in the state's attorney's office, and they were asked to say whether they had seen anything strange or insane about these boys, and they said no, several of them. Not one of them had any warning; not one of them had any chance to think; not one of them knew what it meant; not one of them had a chance to recall the lives of both. And they were in the presence of lawyers and policemen and officers—and still they seek to bind these young people by that.

Miss Nathan is quoted as saying that she never saw any mental disease about them, and yet she said they refused to put down all she said and directed the reporter not to take all she said—that she came in there from a sickbed without notice. She had no time to think about it, and then she told this court of her association with him and the strange, weird, childish things he did.

One other witness, a young man,[75] and only one other, was called in there and examined by the state's attorney on the day that this confession was made.

And we placed him on the stand and he practically tells the same story—that he had no chance to think about it, he had no chance to consider the conduct of these boys. He was called in immediately and the question was put to him. And when he was called by us and had an opportunity to consider it and know what it meant, he related to this court what has been related by every other witness in this case.

As to the condition of these boys amongst their fellows, that they were irresponsible, that they had no judgment, that they were childish, that their acts were strange, that their beliefs were impossible for boys, is beyond question in this case. And what did they do on the other side? It was given out that they had a vast array of witnesses. They called three—a professor who talked with them only upon their law studies and two others who admitted all we said, on cross-examination, and the rest were dismissed. So it leaves all of this beyond dispute and admitted in this case.

Now, both sides have called alienists, and I will refer to that for a few moments. I shall only take a little time with the alienists. The facts here are plain. When these boys had made the confession one Sunday afternoon before their counsel or their friends had any chance to see them, Mr. Crowe sent out for four men. He sent out for Dr. Patrick, who is an alienist; Dr. Church, who is an alienist; Dr. Krohn, who is a witness, a testifier; and Dr. Singer,[76] who is pretty good. I would not criticize him, but I would not class him with Patrick and with Church. I have said to Your Honor that, in my opinion, he sent for the two ablest men in Chicago as far as the public knows them, Dr. Church and Dr. Patrick. I have said to Your Honor if Judge Crowe had not got to them first, I would have tried to get them. I not only would have tried, but I say I would have succeeded.

You heard Dr. Church's testimony. Dr. Church is an honest man, though an alienist. Under cross-examination he admitted every position which I took. He admitted the failure of emotional life in these boys. He admitted its importance. He admitted the importance of belief strongly held in human conduct.

---

74. Lorraine Nathan, one of Loeb's girlfriends, who testified for the defense on August 7 about his strange and erratic behavior.

75. Max Schrayer, a fellow member with Loeb of the Zeta Beta Tau fraternity at the University of Michigan; he testified on August 7.

---

76. See note 36 above.

He said himself that if he could get at it all, he would understand what was back of this strange murder. Every single position that we have claimed in this case Dr. Church admitted.

Dr. Singer did the same. The only difference between them was this: It took me one question to get Dr. Church to admit it and it took me ten to a dozen to get Dr. Singer. He objected and hedged and ran and quibbled. There could be no mistake about it, and Your Honor heard it in this courtroom. He sought every way he could to avoid the truth, and when it came to the point where he could not dodge any longer, he admitted every proposition just exactly the same as Dr. Church admitted them. Every one of them—the value of emotional life; its effect on conduct; that it was the ruling thing in conduct, as every person knows who is familiar with psychology and who is familiar with the human system. Everybody knows it. Could there be any doubt, Your Honor, but what both these witnesses, Church and Singer, or any doubt but what Patrick would have testified for us?

Now what did they do? What kind of a chance did they have? It was perfectly obvious that they had none. Church, Patrick, and Krohn went into a room with these boys who had been in the possession of the state's attorney's office for more than two days, sixty hours; who were surrounded by policemen; who were surrounded by guards and detectives and state's attorneys, twelve or fifteen of them, and here they told their story.[77]

Of course they had a friendly attitude toward them. I know my friend, Judge Crowe, had a friendly attitude because I saw divers, various, and sundry pictures of Prosecutor Crowe taken with these boys. When I saw them, I believed it showed friendship for the boys. But now I am inclined to think he had them taken just as a lawyer who goes up in the country fishing and has his picture taken with a string of fish, or the man who goes shooting has his picture taken with a dead animal. Here was his prey.

All right. They had been led doubtless to believe that these people were friends. They were taken there

in the presence of all this crowd. What was done? They told their story and that was all. Of course, Krohn remembered a lot that did not take place—and we would expect that of him. And he forgot much that did take place—and we would expect that of him, too.

So far as the honest witnesses were concerned, they said that not a word was spoken excepting a little conversation upon birds and the relation of the story that they had already given to the state's attorney. And from that, and nothing else, both Patrick and Church said they showed no reaction as ordinary persons should show and intimated clearly that the commission of the crime itself would put them on caution as to whether these boys were right—both admitting that the condition surrounding them made the right kind of examination impossible, both admitting, according to their own books, that they needed something else. The most they said was that at this time they saw no signs of insanity.

Now, Your Honor, there have been no experts, there have been no alienists with any chance to examine who have testified that these boys were normal—none of them. Singer did a thing more marvelous still. He never saw these boys until he came into this court, excepting when they were brought down in violation of their constitutional rights to the office of Judge Crowe after they had been turned over to the jailer, and there various questions were asked them, and to all of them the boys replied they respectfully refused to answer on advice of counsel. And yet that was enough for Singer.

Your Honor, if these boys had gone to the office of any of these eminent gentlemen, been taken by their parents or gone by themselves, and the doctors had seriously tried to find out whether there was anything wrong about their minds, how would they have done it? They would have taken them patiently and carefully. They would have sought to get their story. They would listen to it in the attitude of a father listening to its child. You know it. Every doctor knows it. In no other way could they find out, and the men who are honest in connection with this question have admitted it. And yet Dr. Krohn will testify that they had the best chance in the world, when his own associates, sitting where they did, said they did not.

77. Darrow is referring to the examination of Leopold and Loeb by prosecution alienists on Sunday, June 1.

Your Honor, nobody's life or nobody's liberty or nobody's property should be taken from them upon an examination like that. It was not an examination. It was simply an effort to get witnesses, regardless of facts, who might at some time come into court and give testimony to take these boys' lives.

Now, I imagine that in closing this case Judge Crowe will say that our witnesses mainly come from abroad.[78] That is true. And he is responsible for it. I am not blaming him, but he is responsible for it. There are other alienists in Chicago, and the evidence shows that we had them examined by numerous alienists in Chicago. We wanted to get the best. Did we get them? Your Honor knows that the place a man lives does not affect him as to truthfulness or as to his ability.

We had the man who stands probably above all of them, and who certainly is far superior to anybody called upon the other side. First of all, we got Dr. White.[79] And who is he? For many years he has been superintendent of the government hospital for the insane in Washington, a man who has written more books, delivered more lectures, and had more honors, and who knows this subject better than all of their alienists put together; a man who came here plainly not for money, without any fee beyond what was set by the other side; a man who knew his subject and whose ability and truthfulness must have impressed this court. It will not do, Your Honor, to say that because Dr. White is not a resident of Chicago that he lies. No man stands higher in the United States, no man is better endorsed than Dr. White, and his appearance, his intelligence upon this witness stand, shows for itself.

Who else did we get? Do I need to say anything about Dr. Healy?[80] Is there any question about his integrity? A man who does not go into court except upon the order of the court. Your Honor was con-nected with the Municipal Court. You know that Dr. Healy was the first man who operated with the courts in the city of Chicago to give unfortunate youths whose minds were afflicted, or who deserved it, aid. No man stands higher in Chicago than Dr. Healy. No man has done so much work in the study of adolescence. No man has either read or written or thought or worked so much with children. No man knows the adolescent boy as well as Dr. Healy: beginning his research and his practice in the city of Chicago and organizing this business here in the city of Chicago, finally becoming a director of the Baker Foundation in Boston, and moving to Boston and connected with the courts of Boston ever since. His works are known wherever men study boys. His reputation is known all over the United States. Compare him and his reputation with Dr. Krohn. Compare it with any other witness that they called in this case. Nobody stands higher.

Dr. Glueck, who was for years the alienist at Sing Sing,[81] connected with all the institutions in the state of New York. He is a man of eminent attainments who would impress anybody with his worth and his learning. Nobody is his superior. And Dr. Hulbert,[82] a young man who spent nineteen days in this examination, together with an eminent doctor in his line from Boston,[83] who spent all his time getting every detail of these boys' lives and these boys' structures.

Each one of these alienists took all the time he wanted for a thorough examination, without lawyers, detectives, and policemen present, where they could get at the facts, and each one of them telling this court the story, the sad, pitiful story of the unfortunate brains of these two young lads.

---

78. By "abroad" Darrow means from outside Chicago; all his alienists came from the United States.

79. See note 50 above.

80. William Healy, director of the Judge Baker Foundation in Boston and former head of the Psychopathic Institute of the Juvenile Court in Chicago.

81. Bernard Glueck, director of the psychiatric clinic at Sing Sing prison, 1916–1918; he was in private practice at the time of the trial.

82. Harold S. Hulbert, Chicago neurologist and former instructor in nervous and mental diseases at the University of Illinois.

83. Karl M. Bowman, chief medical officer of the Boston Psychopathic Hospital. The Hulbert-Bowman report on Leopold and Loeb ran more than 300 pages and was included in the official court transcript.

I submit, Your Honor, that there can be no question about the relative value of these two sets of alienists. There can be no question of their means of understanding. There can be no question but what White, Glueck, Hulbert, and Healy knew what they were talking about, for they had every chance to find out. They are either lying to this court or their statement is true. On the other hand, not one single man called by the state had any chance to know. He was called in to see these boys the same as they would call in a hangman: "Here are boys; officer, do your duty." And that is all there was of it.

Now, Your Honor, I shall pass that subject. I think all the facts of this extraordinary case, all of the testimony of these alienists, all that Your Honor has seen and heard, all their friends and acquaintances who have come here to enlighten this court—I think all of it shows that this terrible act was the act of immature and diseased brains, the act of children. Nobody could explain it in any other way. No one could imagine it in any other way. It is not possible it could have happened in any other way. And I submit, Your Honor, that by every law of humanity, by every law of justice, by every feeling of righteousness, by every instinct of pity, mercy, and charity to boys like these, Your Honor should say that because of the condition of these boys, the condition of their minds, all of this should not be visited upon them with the vengeance that is asked by the state.

I want to discuss now another thing which this court must consider and which to my mind is absolutely conclusive in this case—that is, the age of these boys, independent of everything else. I want to discuss it more in detail than I discussed it before, and I submit, Your Honor, that it is not possible for any court to hang these two boys if he pays any attention whatever to the modern attitude toward children, if he pays any attention whatever to the precedents in this county, if he pays any attention whatever to the humane instincts which move ordinary men.

I have a list of executions in Cook County beginning in 1840, which I presume covers the first one, because I asked to have it go to the beginning. Ninety poor, unfortunate men have yielded up their lives to stop murder in Chicago, but still it goes on. Ninety men have been hanged by the neck until dead

because of the ancient superstition that in some way hanging one man keeps another from committing a crime. The ancient superstition, I say, because I defy them to point to a criminologist, a scientist, a student who has ever said it.

Still we go on with it as if human conduct was not influenced and brought about by the same law that everything else is brought about by, as if there was not a cause for it. We go on saying, "Hang them and it will end." Was there ever a crime without a cause? And yet all punishment proceeds upon the theory that there is no cause and the only way to treat it is to intimidate everyone into goodness and obedience to law. We lawyers are a long way behind.

Crime has its cause. Perhaps all crimes do not have the same cause, but they all have some cause. And people today are seeking to find out the cause. We lawyers never try to find out. Scientists are studying it, criminologists are investigating it, religionists, of course, have always believed it, but we lawyers go on and on, hanging and punishing and thinking that by general terror we can prevent crime. They used to do that with disease. If a doctor was called on to treat typhoid fever, he would probably try to find out what kind of milk or water the patient was drinking and perhaps clean out the well so that no one else would have typhoid. But if a lawyer was called on to treat a typhoid patient, he would give him thirty days in jail, and then he would think nobody else would ever have it. And if he got well in fifteen days, he would keep him because his time was not out; and if he was worse at the end of thirty days, he would let him go because his time was out.

Once in England they hanged children seven years of age—and not necessarily hanged them, because hanging was never meant for punishment; it was meant for an exhibition. If somebody committed [a] crime, he would be hanged by the head or the heels; it didn't matter much which way, yes, but hanged. Hanging was an exhibition. They were hanged on the highest hill and hanged at the crossways and hanged in public places so that all men could see. If there is any virtue in hanging, that is the way to do it because you cannot awe men into goodness unless they know about the hanging.

We have not grown better than the ancients. We have grown more squeamish. We do not like to look at it, that is all. They hanged them at seven; they hanged them again at eleven and fourteen. As I remember it, we have gotten the law in Illinois up to sixteen—anyhow, we have got it up to fourteen. In some states of the Union they raised it to twenty-one. And we have raised it. We have raised it by the humanity of courts, by the understanding of courts, by the progress in science which at last is reaching the law. And in ninety men hanged in Illinois from its beginning, not one single person under twenty-four was ever hanged upon a plea of guilty. Not one.

If Your Honor should do this, you would run against every precedent that had been set in Illinois for almost a century. There can be no excuse for it and no justification for it because this is the policy of the law which is rooted in the feelings of humanity which are deep in every human being that thinks and feels. There have been two or three cases where juries have convicted boys younger than this and where courts on convictions have refused to set aside the sentence because a jury had found it.

First, I want to call your attention, Your Honor, to the cases on pleas of guilty in the state of Illinois. Back of the year 1896 the record does not show ages. After that, which is the large part, probably sixty out of ninety, they all show the age. Not the age at which they are hanged, as my friend Marshall thought,[84] but the age at the commission of the offense, as is found today. In all the history of Illinois—I am not absolutely certain of it back of 1896, but there are so many of them that I know about from the books and otherwise, that I feel I am safe in saying there is no exception to the rule—but since 1896 everyone is recorded.

The first hanging in Illinois—the first hanging on a plea of guilty in Illinois—was May 15, 1896, when a young man twenty-four years old, a colored man,[85] was sentenced to death by Judge Baker.[86] Judge Baker

I knew very well: a man of ability, a fine fellow, but a man of moods. I do not know whether the court remembers him, but that was the first hanging on a plea of guilty to the credit of any man in Illinois—I mean in Chicago.[87] I have not got the statistics of the state, but I am satisfied they are about the same, and that boy was colored and twenty-four, either one of which should have excused him from death, but the color probably had something to do with compassing his destruction.

The next man was Julius Mannow. Now, he really was not hanged on a plea of guilty, though the records so show.[88] I will state to Your Honor just what the facts are. Joseph Windrath[89] and Julius Mannow were tried together in 1896 on a charge of murder with robbery. When the trial was nearly finished, Julius Mannow withdrew his plea of not guilty. He was defended by Elliott,[90] whom I remember very well, and probably Your Honor does. Mr. Bachrach says by Knight alone.[91] And under what he supposed was an agreement with the court, he pleaded this man guilty after the case was nearly finished.

Now, I am not here to discuss which was right or which was wrong. Judge Horton,[92] who tried this case, did not sentence him, but he waited for the jury's verdict on Windrath. And they found him guilty and sentenced him to death, and Judge Horton followed that sentence.[93] Had this case come into that court on a plea of guilty, it probably would have been different—perhaps not—but it really was not a question of a plea of guilty, and he was twenty-eight

84. Darrow is referring to statements in Marshall's summation for the prosecution, August 19–20.

85. Alfred C. Fields.

86. Francis E. Baker. Darrow errs in stating that this was the first execution in Illinois on a plea of guilty. There was at least one earlier case, Marshall Crain, who was executed in January 1876 (see note 4 above).

87. Darrow errs here as well. On September 19, 1884, Isaac Jacobson, age 54, was executed in Chicago after pleading guilty to the murder of George Bedell.

88. Mannow was executed on October 30, 1896.

89. Misspelled as "Windreth" in most published versions of Darrow's speech.

90. W. S. Elliott.

91. Darrow is referring to a comment to him from cocounsel Walter Bachrach pointing out that Mannow was defended by Thomas D. Knight, rather than by Elliott.

92. Oliver H. Horton.

93. Windrath was executed on June 5, 1896.

or thirty years old. I might say in passing as to Judge Horton—he is dead. I knew him very well. In some ways I liked him. I tried a case for him after he left the bench. But I will say this: He was never noted in Chicago for his kindness and his mercy, and anybody who remembers knows that I am stating the truth.

The next man who was hanged on a plea of guilty was Daniel McCarthy, twenty-nine years old, in 1897, by Judge Stein.[94] Well, he is dead. I am very careful about being kind to the dead, so I will say that he never knew what mercy was, at least while he lived. Whether he does now, I cannot say. Otherwise he was a good lawyer. That was in 1897.

It was twenty-two years, Your Honor, before anybody else was hanged in Cook County on a plea of guilty, old or young—twenty-two years before a judge had either the old or young walk into his court and throw himself on the mercy of the court and get the rope for it. A great many men have been tried for murder, and a great many men have been executed, and a great many have pleaded guilty and have been sentenced either to a term of years or life imprisonment, over two hundred in that twenty-two years, and no man, old or young, executed. But twenty-two years later, in 1919, Thomas Fitzgerald, a man about forty years old, sentenced for killing a little girl, pleaded guilty before my friend Judge Crowe, and he was put to death.[95] And that is all. In the history of Cook County that is all that have been put to death. That is all.

Your Honor, what excuse could you possibly have for putting these boys to death? You would have to turn your back on every precedent of the past. You would have to turn your back on the progress of the world. You would have to ignore all human sentiment and feeling, of which I know the court is full. You would have to do all this if you would hang boys of eighteen and nineteen years of age who have come into this court and thrown themselves upon your mercy. I might do it, but I would want good reason for it, which does not exist and cannot exist in this case unless publicity, worked-up feeling, strong feeling, mad hate, is the reason, and I know it is not.

Since that time one other man has been sentenced to death on a plea of guilty. That was James H. Smith, twenty-three years old, sentenced by Judge Kavanagh.[96] But we were spared his hanging through reprieve. That was in January 1923.[97] I could tell you why it was, and I will tell you later.

It is due to the cruelty that has paralyzed the hearts of men growing out of the war.[98] We are used to blood, Your Honor. It used to look mussy and make us feel squeamish. But we have not only had it shed in bucketsful, we have [had] it shed in rivers, lakes, and oceans, and we have delighted in it. We have preached it, we have worked for it, we have advised it, we have taught it to the young, encouraged the old, until the world has been drenched in blood, and it has left its stains of blood upon every human heart and upon every human mind and has almost stifled the feelings of pity and charity in humanity that have their natural home in the human heart. I do not believe Judge Kavanagh would ever have done this except for the Great War, which has left its mark on us, one of the terrible by-products of those terrible years.

This man was reprieved, but James Smith was twenty-three years old. He was old enough to vote, he was old enough to make contracts, he needed no guardian, he was old enough to do all the things that older men can do. He was not a boy—a boy that is the special ward of the state and the special ward of the court and who cannot act except in special ways because he is not mature. He was twenty-three, and he is not dead and will not die. His life was saved.

You may go over every hanging, and if Your Honor shall decorate the gallows with these two boys, Your Honor will be the first in Chicago who has ever done such a deed. And I know you will not.

Your Honor, I must hasten along, for I will close tonight. I know I should have closed before. Still there seems so much that I would like to say. I will spend a few more minutes on this record of hangings.

---

94. Philip Stein; McCarthy was executed on February 19, 1897.

95. See note 12 above.

96. Marcus A. Kavanagh.

97. Smith was sentenced in January 1923; he was twice reprieved by Illinois Governor Lennington Small, who in July 1923 commuted his sentence to life imprisonment.

98. World War I (1914–1918).

There was one boy nineteen years old, Thomas Schultz, who was convicted by a jury and executed.[99] There was one boy who has been referred to here—eighteen, Nicholas Viana,[100] who was convicted by a jury and executed.[101] No one else under twenty-one, Your Honor, has been convicted by a jury and sentenced to death, no one else. Now, let me speak a word about these. Schultz was convicted in 1912. Viana was convicted in 1920.

In 1912, this nineteen-year-old boy. Of course, I believe it should not have happened, but Your Honor knows the difference between a plea of guilty and a verdict. It is easy enough for a jury to divide the responsibility by twelve. They have not the age and the experience and the charity which is born of age and experience. It is easy for some state's attorney to influence some juries. I don't know who defended the poor boy, but I guarantee it was not the best lawyers at the bar. But doubtless a good lawyer prosecuted him, and when he was convicted, the court[102] said he had rested his fate with his jury and he would not disturb the verdict. That is all there is to it.

I do not know whether Your Honor, humane and considerate as I believe you to be, would have disturbed a jury verdict in this case, but I know that no judge in Cook County ever himself upon a plea of guilty passed judgment of death in a case below the age of twenty-three, and nobody below the age of twenty-four, and only one at the age of twenty-four was ever hanged.

Viana I have looked up, and I don't care who did it or how it was done, it was a shame and disgrace that an eighteen-year-old boy should be hanged in 1920, or a nineteen-year-old boy should be hanged in 1920, and I am assuming it is all right to hang somebody, which it is not. I have looked up the Viana case because my friend Marshall read a part where it said that Viana pleaded guilty. He

did not say it positively because he is honest, and he knew there might be a reason.[103] Viana was tried and convicted—I don't remember the name of the judge[104]—in 1920.

There were various things working against him. It was in 1920, after the war. Most anything might have happened after the war, which I will speak of later, and not much later, for I am to close tonight. He was convicted in 1920. There was a band of Italian desperadoes, so-called. I don't know. Sam Cardinelli was the leader, a man forty years of age. But their records were very bad. This boy should have been singled out from the rest. If I had been defending him, and he had not been, I never would have come into court again. But he was not. He was tried with the rest. I have looked up the records and I find that he was in the position of most of these unfortunates—he did not have a lawyer.

Your Honor, the question of whether a man is convicted or acquitted does not always depend on the evidence or entirely on the jury. The lawyer has something to do with it. And the state always has, always has at least moderately good lawyers. And the defendants have if they can get the money; and if they cannot, they have anybody. Viana, who was on trial with others for his life, had a lawyer appointed by the court. One "Ropes" O'Brien,[105] if I am rightly informed, prosecuted.[106] He had a fine chance, this poor Italian boy, tried with three or four others.

Your Honor, I have a memorandum here that Smith, who was sentenced by Judge Kavanagh, was twenty-eight instead of twenty-three. Anyway, he had two children. That can be ascertained. I will

---

99. Schultz was executed February 16, 1912.

100. Misspelled as "Viani" in most published versions of Darrow's speech.

101. Viana was convicted at age 18; he was executed on December 10, 1920, his 19th birthday.

102. Judge Adelor J. Petit.

103. Darrow is referring to a statement in Marshall's summation of August 19–20.

104. The judge was Oscar Hebel.

105. James O'Brien.

106. Viana was prosecuted by Assistant State's Attorney Edwin J. Raber. Darrow's misstatement was corrected in all pamphlet versions of his speech; the wording here comes from the stenographic account in the *Chicago Herald and Examiner*, August 26, 1924.

try to ascertain it myself and submit it to the state's attorney.[107]

But this boy, Viana, was defended by somebody whose name I never heard, who was appointed by the court.[108] He was prosecuted, as I understand it, by one of the best prosecutors—and when I say the best, I mean the cleverest. I say he was prosecuted by one of the cleverest lawyers we ever had prosecuting in these courts, and that was what happened. Neither of these young men pled guilty.

Your Honor, if in this court a boy of eighteen and a boy of nineteen should be hanged on a plea of guilty in violation of every precedent of the past, in violation of the policy of the law to take care of the young, in violation of all the progress that has been made and of the humanity that has been used in the care of the young, in violation of the policy of placing boys in reformatories instead of prisons—if Your Honor in violation of all that and in the face of all the past should stand out here in Chicago alone to hang a boy, then we are turning our faces backward toward the barbarism which once possessed the world.

If Your Honor can hang a boy of eighteen, some other judge can hang him at seventeen, or sixteen, or fourteen. Someday, someday, if there is any such thing as progress in the world, if there is any spirit of humanity that is working in the hearts of men, someday they will look back upon this as a barbarous age which deliberately turned the hands of the clock backward, which deliberately set itself in the way of all progress toward humanity and sympathy and committed an unforgivable act.

Yet Your Honor has been asked to hang, and I must refer here for a minute to something which I dislike to discuss. I hesitated whether to pass it by unnoticed or to notice it, but I felt that I must say something about it—and that was the testimony of Gortland, the policeman.[109] He came into this court,

the only witness who said that young Leopold told him that he might get into the hands of a friendly judge and succeed.[110] Your Honor, that is a blow below the belt. There isn't a word of truth in his statement, as I can prove to Your Honor in two minutes. It was carved out of the air to awe and influence the court and place him in a position where, if he saved life, someone might be malicious enough to say he was a friendly judge and, if he took it, the fear might invade the community that he did not dare do it.

I know, Your Honor, that Your Honor knows there is only one way to do in this case, and I know you will do it. You will take this case, with your judgment and your conscience, and settle it as you think it should be settled. I may approve or I may disapprove, or Judge Crowe may approve or disapprove, or the public may approve or disapprove, but you must satisfy yourself, and you will.

Now, let me take Gortland's testimony for a minute; and I am not going over the record. It is all here. He swore that on the night after the arrest of these two boys, Nathan Leopold told him, in discussing the case, that a friendly judge might save him. He is the first man who testified for the state that any of us cross-examined, if you remember. They called witness after witness to prove something that did not need to be proved under a plea of guilty. Then this came, which to me was a poisoned piece of perjury, with a purpose, and I cross-examined him:[111]

QUESTION: "Did you make any record?"
ANSWER: "Yes, I think I did."
QUESTION: "Where is it?"
ANSWER: "I think I have it."
QUESTION: "Let me see it."
ANSWER: "Yes."
MR. DARROW: There was not a word or a syllable upon that paper.
QUESTION: "Did you make any other?"
ANSWER: "Yes."
QUESTION: "When did you make it?"

107. All newspaper accounts indicate that Smith was 23 at the time of his conviction. This paragraph, which comes from the stenographic account in the *Chicago Herald and Examiner*, August 26, 1924, was deleted in all pamphlet versions of Darrow's speech.

108. Viana may have been defended by William McCabe and Francis Borrelli, who represented his codefendant Frank Campione.

109. Sergeant James J. Gortland.

110. Darrow is referring to Gortland's testimony of July 25.

111. Gortland's testimony and cross-examination occurred on July 25, 26, and 28. The portion of the cross-examination cited by Darrow occurred on July 26, though he paraphrases rather than quoting verbatim.

ANSWER: "Within two or three days of the occurrence."

QUESTION: "Let me see that."

MR. DARROW: He said he would bring it back later.

QUESTION: "Did you make another?"

ANSWER: "Yes."

QUESTION: "What was it?"

ANSWER: "A complete report to the chief of police."

QUESTION: "Is it in there?"

ANSWER: "I think so."

QUESTION: "Will you bring that?"

ANSWER: "Yes."

He brought them both into this court. They contained, all those documents together, a complete or almost complete copy of everything that happened, but not one word, not one word. He deliberately said he made that record within a few days of the time it occurred, and that he told the office about it within a few days of the time it occurred. And what did he say? Then he came back in answer to my cross-examination—or not in answer to my cross-examination, but in answer to Mr. Crowe's question—and he said he never told Judge Crowe about it until the night before Judge Crowe made his opening statement in this case. Six weeks after he heard it, six weeks after he made the report, long after the time he said he made a record of it, there was not a single word or syllable in anything he wrote about this matter.

What could he say about it, Your Honor? I am sorry to discuss it; I am sorry to embarrass this court. But what can I do? I want Your Honor to know that if in your judgment you think these boys shall hang, we will know it is your judgment. It is hard enough, God knows, for a court to sit where you sit, with the eyes of the world upon you, in the fierce heat of public opinion for and against. It is hard enough without any lawyer making it harder. I assure you it is with deep regret that I even mention what I said, and I will say no more about it, excepting that that statement was a deliberate lie made by that policeman, and his own evidence shows it.

Now, Your Honor, I have spoken about the war. I believed in it. I don't know whether I was crazy or not. Sometimes I think perhaps I was. I approved of it. I joined in the general cry of madness and despair.

I urged men to fight. I was safe because I was too old to go. I was like the rest.

What did they do? Right or wrong, justifiable or unjustifiable—which I need not discuss today—it changed the world. For four long years the civilized world was engaged in killing men. Christian against Christian, barbarians uniting with Christians to kill Christians; anything to kill. It was taught in every school, aye, in the Sunday school. The little children played at war, the toddling children on the street.

Do you suppose this world has ever been the same since? How long, Your Honor, will it take for the world to get back in its human emotions to where it stood before the war? How long will it take the calloused heart of man before the scars of hatred and cruelty shall be removed?

We read of killing one hundred thousand in a day—probably exaggerated, but what of it? We read about it and we rejoiced in it; it was the other fellows who were killed. We were fed on flesh and drank blood, even down to the prattling babe. I need not tell Your Honor this because you know. I need not tell you how many upright, honorable young boys have come into this court charged with murder, some saved and some sent to their death, boys who fought in this war and learned to place a cheap value on human life. You know it and I know it. These boys were brought up in it. The tales of death were in their homes, their playgrounds, their schools; they were in the newspapers that they read; it was part of the common frenzy. What was a life? It was nothing. It was the least sacred thing in existence, and these boys were trained to this cruelty.

It will take fifty years at least to wipe it out of the human heart, if ever. I know this, for I have studied those things, that after the Civil War in 1865 crimes of this sort increased, marvelously increased. No one needs to tell me that crime has no cause. It has as definite a cause as any other disease, and I know that out of the hatred and bitterness of the Civil War crime increased as America had never known it before. I know that growing out of the Napoleonic Wars[112] there was an era of crime such as Europe had never

---

112. Fought from 1799 to 1815, during the reign of French ruler Napoleon Bonaparte.

seen before. I know that Europe is going through it today; I know it has followed every war; and I know it has influenced these boys so that blood was not the same blood to them that it would have been if the world had not been bathed in blood.

I protest against the crimes and mistakes of society being visited upon them. All of us have our share in it. I have mine. I cannot tell and I shall never know how many words of mine might have created harshness in place of love and kindness and charity. Your Honor knows that in this very court crimes of violence have increased growing out of the war. Not necessarily by those who fought, but by those that learned that blood was cheap and human life was cheap and if the state could take it, why not the individual?

There are causes for this terrible crime. There are causes, as I have said, for everything that happens in the world. War is a part of it; education is a part of it; birth is a part of it; money is a part of it—all concentrated to wreak the destruction of these two poor boys.

Now, Your Honor, I suppose I would never close if I did not see that I should. Has the court any right to consider anything but these two boys? Yes. The state says that Your Honor has a right to consider the welfare of the community, as you have. If the welfare of the community would be benefited by taking these lives, well and good. I think it would work evil that no one could measure.

Has Your Honor a right to consider the families of these two defendants? I have been sorry, and I am sorry, for the bereavement of Mr. and Mrs. Franks and the little sister, for those broken ties that cannot be mended. All I can hope and wish is that some good may come from it. But as compared with the families of Leopold and Loeb, they are to be envied. They are to be envied, and everyone knows it.

I do not know how much salvage there is in these two boys. I hate to say it in their presence, but what is there to look forward to? I do not know but what Your Honor would be merciful if you tied a rope around their necks and let them die—merciful to them, but not merciful to civilization and not merciful to those who would be left behind. I do not know. To spend the balance of their days in prison is mighty little to look forward to, if anything. Is it anything?

They may have the hope, as the years roll around, they might be released. I do not know.

I will be honest with this court. I have tried to be from the beginning. I know that these boys are not fit to be at large. I believe they will not be until they pass through the next stage of life, at forty-five or fifty. Whether they will be then, I cannot know. I am sure of this: that I won't be here to help them. So, so far as I am concerned, it is over. I would not tell this court that I would not hope that sometime when life and age has changed their bodies, as it does, and has changed their emotions, as it does, I would not say that they would not be safe. I would be the last person on earth to close the door of hope to any human being that lived, and least of all my clients. But what have they to look forward to? Nothing. And I here think of the stanzas of Housman:

> Now hollow fires burn out to black
>   And lights are fluttering low;
> Square your shoulders and lift your pack
>   And leave your friends and go.
> Don't ever fear, lads, nought's to dread;
>   Look not to left nor right.
> In all the endless road you tread
>   There is nothing but the night.[113]

I don't care, Your Honor, whether the march begins at the gallows or when the gates of Joliet[114] close upon them, there is nothing but the night, and that is enough for any human being to ask. But there are others. Here are these two families, who have led an honest life, who will bear the name that they bear, and future generations will bear the name that they bear.

Here is Leopold's father—and this boy was the pride of his life. He watched him, he cared for him, he worked for him, he was brilliant and accomplished, he educated him, and he thought fame and position awaited him, as it should have. It is a hard thing for a father to see his life's hopes crumbling

---

113. Closely paraphrased from A. E. Housman's *A Shropshire Lad* (1896), LX.

114. Joliet State Penitentiary, where Leopold and Loeb were imprisoned after sentencing.

into the dust. Should he be considered? Should his brothers be considered? Is it going to do society any good or make your life safe or any human being's life safer that it should be handed down from generation to generation that this boy, their kin, died upon the scaffold?

And Loeb's, the same. The faithful uncle and brother, who have watched here day by day while his father and his mother are too ill to stand this terrific strain, waiting for a message which means more to them than it seems to mean to you or me. Have they got any rights? Is there any reason, Your Honor, why their proud name and all the future generations that bear it shall have this bar sinister[115] attached to it? How many boys and girls, how many unborn children, will feel it? It is bad enough as it is, God knows. It is bad enough, however it is. But it's not death by the scaffold. It's not that. And I ask, Your Honor, in addition to all I have said, to save two honorable families from a disgrace that never ends and which could be of no avail to any human being that lives.

Now, I must say a word more and then I will leave this with you where I should have left it long ago. None of us are unmindful of the public; courts are not and juries are not. We placed this in the hands of a trained court, thinking that he would be less mindful than a jury. I cannot say how people feel. I have stood here for three months as somebody might stand at the seacoast trying to sweep back the tide. I hope the seas are subsiding and the wind is falling, and I believe they are, but I wish to make no false pretense to this court.

The easy thing and the popular thing to do is to hang my clients. I know it. Men and women who do not think will applaud. The cruel and the thoughtless will approve. It will be easy today. But in Chicago and reaching out over the length and breadth of the land more and more are the fathers and mothers, the humane, the kind and the hopeful, who are gaining an understanding, are asking questions not only about these boys, but about their own. These will join in no acclaim at the death of these boys. These would ask that the shedding of blood be

stopped and that the normal feelings of man resume their sway. And as the days and the months and the years go on, they will ask it more and more. But, Your Honor, what they ask cannot count. I know the easy way.

I know Your Honor stands between the future and the past. I know the future is with me and what I stand for here—not merely for the lives of these two unfortunate lads, but for all boys and all girls, all of the young, and, as far as possible, for all of the old. I am pleading for life, understanding, charity, and kindness, and the infinite mercy that forgives all. I am pleading that we overcome cruelty with kindness and hatred with love. I know the future is on my side. Your Honor stands between the past and the future. You may hang these boys; you may hang them by the neck till they are dead. But in doing it, you will turn your face toward the past. In doing it, you are making it harder for every other boy. In doing it, you are making it harder for unborn children. You may save them, and it makes it easier for every child that sometime may sit where these boys sit. It makes it easier for every human being with an aspiration and a vision and a hope and a fate.

I am pleading for the future. I am pleading for a time when hatred and cruelty will not control the hearts of men. When we can learn by reason and judgment and understanding and faith that all life is worth saving and that mercy is the highest attribute of man.

I feel that I ought to apologize for the length of time I have taken. This may not be as important as I think it is, and I am sure I do not need to tell this court, or to tell my friend Mr. Crowe, that I would fight just as hard for the poor as for the rich. If I should succeed in saving these boys' lives and do nothing for the progress of the law, I should feel sad, indeed. If I can succeed, my greatest award and my greatest hope and my greatest compensation will be that I have done something for the tens of thousands of other boys, for the other unfortunates who must tread the same way that these poor youths have trod, that I have done something to help human understanding, to temper justice with mercy, to overcome hate with love.

115. Symbol of disgrace or infamy.

I was reading last night of the aspiration of the old Persian poet Omar Khayyam. It appealed to me as the highest that I can envision. I wish it was in my heart and I wish it was in the heart of all, and I can end no better than to quote what he said:

So I be written in the Book of Love,
   I do not care about that Book above.
Erase my name or write it as you will,
   So I be written in the Book of Love.[116]

---

116. From Richard Le Gallienne, *Rubaiyat of Omar Khayyam: A Paraphrase from Several Literal Translations* (1897).

Margaret Sanger

The Children's Era

NEW YORK, NEW YORK
MARCH 30, 1925

As THE TWENTIETH century's foremost champion of birth control, Margaret Sanger spoke to audiences around the globe in a career that spanned more than five decades. In her early years, she was often interrupted by hecklers and on more than one occasion was arrested for violating state or federal laws prohibiting the distribution of information about birth control. She also had to overcome her deep-seated fear of public speaking. Notwithstanding the calm, confident persona she projected on the platform, she wrote in her autobiography that she typically woke up on the morning of a speech with "a ghastly depression" that "did not grow better until I was on my feet and well into my subject.... All through the years it has been like a nightmare even to think of a pending speech."

One of Sanger's major arguments in support of birth control was that it would dramatically improve the lives of children, who too often were brought into the world unloved and suffered neglect, abuse, illness, and exploitation. This theme is well represented in "The Children's Era," which Sanger delivered at the Sixth International Neo-Malthusian and Birth Control Conference, held in New York City, March 25–31, 1925. Organized by Sanger, the conference brought together delegates from more than fifteen countries, received considerable press coverage, and was followed by the creation of the first international birth control organization.

Speaking to an audience of experts who were in the vanguard of thought about birth control, Sanger made a powerful call to protect "the health and happiness of the unborn child," as well as of children who have already been born. "We want," she said, "to create a real century of the child, to usher in a Children's Era." Although Sanger was eventually successful in winning for American women the right to practice birth control without interference from the state, it is a sad fact that many of the problems facing children identified in her speech remain with us today.

⬦⬦⬦⬦⬦⬦⬦⬦⬦⬦⬦⬦⬦⬦⬦⬦⬦⬦⬦⬦⬦⬦⬦⬦⬦⬦⬦⬦⬦⬦⬦⬦

Mr. Chairman, Ladies and Gentlemen: My subject is "The Children's Era." The Children's Era! This makes me think of Ellen Key's book *The Century of the Child*.[1] Ellen Key hoped that this twentieth century was to be the century of the child. The twentieth century, she said, would see this old world of ours converted into a beautiful garden of children. Well, we have already lived through a quarter of this twentieth century. What steps have we taken toward making it the century of the child? So far, very, very little.

Why does the Children's Era still remain a dream of the dim and distant future? Why has so little been accomplished in spite of all our acknowledged love of children, all our generosity, all our goodwill, all the enormous spending of millions on philanthropy and charities, all our warmhearted sentimentality, all our incessant activity and social consciousness? Why?

Before you can cultivate a garden, you must know something about gardening. You have got to give your seeds a proper soil in which to grow. You have got to give them sunlight and fresh air. You have got to give them space and the opportunity, if they are to lift their flowers to the sun, to strike their roots deep into that soil. And always—do not forget this—you have got to fight weeds. You cannot have a garden if you let weeds overrun it. So if we want to make this world a garden for children, we must first of all learn the lesson of the gardener.

So far we have not been gardeners. We have only been a sort of silly reception committee. A reception committee at the Grand Central Station[2] of life.

Trainload after trainload of children are coming in day and night—nameless refugees arriving out of the Nowhere into the Here. Trainload after trainload—many unwelcome, unwanted, unprepared for, unknown, without baggage, without passports, most of them without pedigrees. These unlimited hordes of refugees arrive in such numbers that the reception committee is thrown into a panic—a panic of sentimentality. The reception committee arouses itself heroically, establishes emergency measures: milk stations, maternity centers, settlement houses, playgrounds, orphanages, welfare leagues, and every conceivable kind of charitable effort. But still trainloads of them keep on coming—human weeds crop up that spread so fast in this sinister struggle for existence that the overworked committee becomes exhausted, inefficient, and can't think of a way out.

When I protest against this immeasurable, meaningless waste of motherhood and childlife; when I protest against the ever-mounting cost to the world of asylums, prisons, homes for the feebleminded, and such institutions for the unfit; when I protest against the disorder and chaos and tragedy of modern life; when I point out the biological corruption that is destroying the very heart of American life, I am told that I am making merely an "emotional" appeal. When I point the one immediate practical way toward order and beauty in society, the only way to lay the foundations of a society composed of happy children, happy women, and happy men, they call this idea indecent and immoral.[3]

I am proud to claim that this Sixth International Neo-Malthusian and Birth Control Conference has

1. Originally published in Swedish in 1900, Key's book was translated into many languages.

2. Railroad terminal in New York City.

3. Sanger is referring to her advocacy of birth control.

been scientific in spirit—with the possible exception of one gentleman's questionable contribution,[4] which would scarcely be considered scientific on Main Street, Gopher Prairie! We are the true scientist. We are spurred on by a real love of truth and idealism for humanity. We are more truly scientific in spirit than those so-called scientists who, shut up in their prisons of figures and percentages and statistics, are deaf to the poignant cry of universal human tragedy and blind to the vision of a possible Era of Children, which it is our supreme duty as adult men and women to create. If we refuse to join in this great task, we are false to that sacred trust imposed upon us when the human race was first endowed with the light of consciousness and the fire of intelligence.

It is not enough to clean up the filth and disorder of our overcrowded cities. It is not enough to stop the evil of child labor—even if we could! It is not enough to decrease the rate of infantile mortality. It is not enough to open playgrounds, and build more public schools in which we can standardize the minds of the young. It is not enough to throw millions upon millions of dollars into charities and philanthropies. Don't deceive ourselves that by so doing we are making the world safe for children. Toward the creation of the Children's Era we have not taken one constructive step.

Those of you who have followed the sessions of this conference must, I am sure, agree with me that the first real step toward the creation of a Children's Era must lie in providing the conditions of healthy life for children not only before birth but, even more imperatively, before conception. Human society must protect its children, yes, but prenatal care is most essential. The child-to-be, as yet not called into being, has rights no less imperative.

We have learned in the preceding sessions of this conference that, if we wish to produce strong and sturdy children, the embryo must grow in a chemically healthy medium. The bloodstream of the mother must be chemically normal. Worry, strain, shock, unhappiness, enforced maternity may all poison the blood of the enslaved mother. This chemically poi-

soned blood may produce a defective baby—a child foredoomed to idiocy or feeblemindedness, crime or failure.

Do I exaggerate? Am I taking a rare exception and making it a general rule? Our opponents declare that children are conceived in love and that every newborn baby converts its parents to love and unselfishness. My answer is to point to the asylums, the hospitals, the ever-growing institutions for the unfit. Look into the family history of those who are feebleminded or behind the bars of jails and prisons. Trace the family histories, find out the conditions under which they were conceived and born, before you attempt to persuade us that reckless breeding has nothing to do with these grave questions.

There is only one way out. We have got to fight for the health and happiness of the unborn child. And to do that in a practical, tangible way, we have got to free women from enforced, enslaved maternity. There can be no hope for the future of civilization, no certainty of racial salvation, until every woman can decide for herself whether she will or will not become a mother and when and how many children she cares to bring into this world. That is the first step.

I'd like to suggest Civil Service examinations[5] for parenthood! Prospective parents after such an examination would be given a parenthood license proving that they are physically and mentally fit to be the fathers and mothers of the next generation.

This is an interesting idea, but then arises the questions, Who is to decide? Would there be a jury, like the play jury?[6] Would a Republican administration give parenthood permits only to Republicans—or perhaps only to Democrats? The more you think of governmental interference, the less it works out, this plan of Civil Service examination for parenthood. It

---

4. Louis I. Dublin's "The Excesses of Birth Control," presented on March 26.

5. Established in 1883, the U.S. Civil Service Commission was charged with administering merit-based examinations to applicants for classified federal jobs.

6. The play jury was developed in the early 1920s as an alternative to police censorship of the New York theater. When officials received a complaint that a play posed dangers to public morality, the play would be viewed and voted upon by a jury of 12 ordinary citizens.

suggests Prohibition: there might even be bootleg-ging in babies![7]

No, I doubt the advisability of governmental sanction. The problem of bringing children into the world ought to be decided by those most seriously involved, those who run the greatest risks—in the last analysis, by the mother and the child. If there is going to be any Civil Service examination, let it be conducted by the unborn child, the child-to-be.

Just try for a moment to picture the possibilities of such an examination.

When you want a cook or housemaid, you go to an employment bureau. You have to answer questions. You have to exchange references. You have to persuade the talented cook that you conduct a proper, well-run household. Children ought to have at least the same privileges as cooks.

Sometimes in idle moments I like to think it would be a very good scheme to have a bureau of the unborn. At such a bureau of the unborn, the wise child might be able to find out a few things about its father and its mother. Just think for a moment of this bureau where prospective parents might apply for a baby. Think of the questions they would be asked to answer by the agent of the unborn or by the baby itself.

First: "A baby is an expensive luxury. Can you really afford one? Have you paid for your last baby yet?"

"How many children have you already? You must have your hands full—more than you can take care of!"

"Do you look upon children as a reward—or a penalty?"

"How are your ductless glands[8]—well balanced?"

"Can you provide a happy home for me? A sunny nursery? Proper food?"

"What's that you say? Five children already? Two dark rooms in the slums?"

"No, thank you! I don't care to be born at all if I cannot be wellborn. Good-bye!"

And if we could organize a society for the pre-vention of cruelty to unborn children, we would make it a law that children would be brought into the world only when they were welcome, invited, and wanted; that they would arrive with a clean bill of health and heritage; that they would possess healthy, happy, well-mated, and mature parents.

And there would be certain conditions of cir-cumstances which would preclude parenthood. These conditions, the presence of which would make par-enthood a crime, are the following:

1. Transmissible disease.
2. Temporary disease.
3. Subnormal children already in the family.
4. Space out between births.
5. Twenty-three years as a minimum age for parents.
6. Economic circumstances adequate.
7. Spiritual harmony between parents.

In conclusion, let me repeat: We are not trying to establish a dictatorship over parents. We want to free women from enslaved and unwilling motherhood. We are fighting for the emancipation of the moth-ers of the world, of the children of the world, and the children-to-be. We want to create a real century of the child, to usher in a Children's Era. Help us to make this conference, which has aroused so much interest, the turning point toward this era. Only so can you help in the creation of the future.

7. Sanger is referring to the Eighteenth Amendment to the U.S. Constitution, which prohibited "the manufacture, sale, or transportation of intoxicating liquors" and was widely violated through the production of illegal alcohol, a practice referred to as "bootlegging." Prohibition was repealed in 1933 upon passage of the Twenty-first Amendment.

8. Endocrine glands.

Franklin D. Roosevelt

Address to the Commonwealth Club

SAN FRANCISCO, CALIFORNIA
SEPTEMBER 23, 1932

STRICKEN WITH POLIO in 1921, Franklin Delano Roosevelt overcame his disability to become the only U.S. President elected to office four times. With the support of Democratic presidential nominee Alfred E. Smith, he was elected Governor of New York in 1928. When the stock market tumbled in October 1929, signaling the onset of the Great Depression, Roosevelt turned his gaze toward Washington. With Herbert Hoover in the White House and the economy worsening daily, FDR knew the country was looking for fresh leadership. After winning the Democratic nomination for President in July 1932, he promised "a new deal for the American people" and campaigned on a platform of "relief, recovery, and reform." Traveling aboard the Roosevelt Special train, he delivered rear-platform remarks during the day, with major speeches usually scheduled for the evening. One exception to this pattern was his address to the Commonwealth Club of San Francisco at a luncheon meeting on September 23, 1932.

The speech was drafted by Adolf A. Berle Jr., a member of FDR's "Brains Trust" of intellectuals that advised him on socioeconomic topics. It came into being after Berle inquired with Roosevelt about composing a set of remarks explaining the candidate's philosophy with regard to economic policy. In mid-September, Berle's draft, which had been much improved by the editing of his wife, Beatrice, was sent to Raymond Moley, who was coordinating FDR's campaign through the western states. As Davis W. Houck has shown, neither Moley nor Roosevelt had anticipated the need for a major address at the Commonwealth Club. By the time they realized their mistake, there was no time to prepare a speech from the ground up. Fortuitously, Berle's draft was at hand. After revising the introduction and adding a section on the social contract, Moley showed the text to Roosevelt, who made a few minor corrections on the night of September 22. It was the only time FDR laid eyes on the speech before facing his audience the next day.

The Commonwealth Club was a group of prominent business and community leaders. Because their policy barred purely partisan presentations, the occasion was ideal for a speech more reflective in tone than the usual run of campaign discourse. Roosevelt took as his topic "the relationships of government and economic life" and announced that he would "speak not of parties, but of universal principles." After tracing the historical development of the nation's economy, he turned to the crisis of the Depression. Warning his listeners that the country was moving toward "economic oligarchy," he proposed a "reappraisal of values" in which business would serve "the common interest of all" rather than merely individual advancement. He also stated that should "the unethical competitor . . . ever use its collective power contrary to public welfare, the government must be swift to enter and protect the public interest."

The historical standing of the speech is an interesting story in its own right. The address did not attract extraordinary attention when it was delivered, but once Roosevelt assumed office and the policies of the New Deal began to take shape, some observers began to find new significance in his words at the Commonwealth Club. Most important was journalist Ernest K. Lindley, who in his 1933 book, *The Roosevelt Revolution*, hailed the address as "the most significant utterance made by any major candidate for the presidency in a generation, if not in a much longer period." The reputation of the speech has continued to grow over the years, to the point that it is often seen as a blueprint for the New Deal. That is certainly an exaggeration, for FDR did not know in September 1932 the policies he would adopt as President. On the other hand, his views expressed at the Commonwealth Club about the responsibilities of government were compatible with many of the New Deal programs, and his warnings about the ethical responsibilities of big business can be seen as adumbrating his attacks on "unscrupulous moneychangers" in his first inaugural address (pages 221–224).

◇◇

My friends: I count it a privilege to be invited to address the Commonwealth Club. It has stood in the life of this city and state, and it is perhaps accurate to add, the nation, as a group of citizen leaders interested in fundamental problems of government, and chiefly concerned with achievement of progress in government through nonpartisan means. The privilege of addressing you, therefore, in the heat of a political campaign is great.

I want to respond to your courtesy in terms consistent with your policy. I want to speak not of politics, but of government. I want to speak not of parties, but of universal principles. They are not political except in that large sense in which a great American once expressed a definition of politics—that nothing in all of human life is foreign to the science of politics.[1]

I do want to give you, however, a recollection of a long life spent for a large part in public office. Some of my conclusions and observations have been deeply

accentuated in these past few weeks. I have traveled far—from Albany to the Golden Gate. I have seen many people and heard many things, and today, when in a sense my journey has reached the halfway mark, I am glad of the opportunity to discuss with you what it all means to me.

Sometimes, my friends, particularly in years such as these, the hand of discouragement falls upon us. It seems that things are in a rut, fixed, settled—that the world has grown old and tired and very much out of joint. This is the mood of depression, of dire and weary depression. But then we look around us in America and everything tells us that we are wrong. America is new. It is in the process of change and development. It has the great potentialities of youth, and particularly is this true of the great West and of this coast and of California.

I would not have you feel that I regard this as in any sense a new community. I have traveled in many parts of the world, but never have I felt the arresting thought of the change and development more than here, where the old, mystic East would seem to be

1. Paraphrased from Woodrow Wilson, "The Law and the Facts," *American Political Science Review* (February 1911).

near to us, where the currents of life and thought and commerce of the whole world meet us. This factor alone is sufficient to cause man to stop and think of the deeper meaning of things when he stands in this community.

But more than that, I appreciate that the membership of this club consists of men who are thinking in terms beyond the immediate present, beyond their own immediate tasks, beyond their own individual interest. I want to invite you, therefore, to consider with me, in the large, some of the relationships of government and economic life that go deep into our daily lives, our happiness, our future, and our security.

The issue of government has always been whether individual men and women will have to serve some system of government or economics or whether a system of government and economics exists to serve individual men and women. This question has persistently dominated the discussion of government for many generations. On questions relating to these things men have differed, and for time immemorial it is probable that honest men will continue to differ.

The final word belongs to no man; yet we can still believe in change and in progress. Democracy, as a dear old friend of mine in Indiana, Meredith Nicholson,[2] has called it, is a quest, a never-ending seeking for better things, and in the seeking for these things and the striving for them there are many roads to follow. But if we map the course of these roads, we find that there are only two general directions.

When we look about us, we are likely to forget how hard people have worked to win the privilege of government. The growth of the national governments of Europe was a struggle for the development of a centralized force in the nation, strong enough to impose peace upon ruling barons. In many instances the victory of the central government, the creation of a strong central government, was a haven of refuge to the individual. The people preferred the master far away to the exploitation and cruelty of the smaller master near at hand.

But the creators of national government were perforce ruthless men. They were often cruel in their methods, but they did strive steadily toward something that society needed and very much wanted—a strong central state able to keep the peace, to stamp out civil war, to put the unruly nobleman in his place, and to permit the bulk of individuals to live safely.

The man of ruthless force had his place in developing a pioneer country, just as he did in fixing the power of the central government in the development of the nations. Society paid him well for his services and its development. When the development among the nations of Europe, however, had been completed, ambition and ruthlessness, having served its term, tended to overstep its mark. There came a growing feeling that government was conducted for the benefit of a few who thrived unduly at the expense of all. The people sought a balancing—a limiting force. There came gradually, through town councils, trade guilds, national parliaments, by constitution and by popular participation and control, limitations on arbitrary power.

Another factor that tended to limit the power of those who ruled was the rise of the ethical conception that a ruler bore a responsibility for the welfare of his subjects. The American colonies were born in this struggle. The American Revolution was a turning point in it. After the Revolution, the struggle continued and shaped itself in the public life of the country. There were those who, because they had seen the confusion which attended the years of war for American independence, surrendered to the belief that popular government was essentially dangerous and essentially unworkable. They were honest people, my friends, and we cannot deny that their experience had warranted some measure of fear.

The most brilliant, honest, and able exponent of this point of view was Hamilton.[3] He was too impatient of slow-moving methods. Fundamentally he believed that the safety of the republic lay in the autocratic strength of its government, that the destiny of individuals was to serve that government, and that fundamentally a great and strong group of central

---

2. Journalist and author who served as U.S. ambassador to Paraguay, Venezuela, and Nicaragua during FDR's presidency.

3. Alexander Hamilton, Secretary of the Treasury, 1789–1795.

institutions guided by a small group of able and pub-lic-spirited citizens could best direct all government.

But Mr. Jefferson, in the summer of 1776, after drafting the Declaration of Independence, turned his mind to the same problem and took a differ-ent view. He did not deceive himself with outward forms. Government to him was a means to an end, not an end in itself; it might be either a refuge and a help or a threat and a danger, depending on the circumstances. We find him carefully analyzing the society for which he was to organize a government: "We have no paupers.... The great mass of our popu-lation is of laborers; our rich, who cannot live without labor, either manual or professional, being few and of moderate wealth. Most of the laboring class possess property, cultivate their own lands, have families, and from the demand for their labor are enabled to exact from the rich and the competent such prices as enable them to feed abundantly, clothe above mere decency, to labor moderately, and raise their families."[4]

These people, he considered, had two sets of rights, those of personal competency and those involved in acquiring and possessing property. By per-sonal competency he meant the right of free think-ing, freedom of forming and expressing opinions, and freedom of personal living each man according to his own lights. To ensure the first set of rights, a govern-ment must so order its functions as not to interfere with the individual. But even Jefferson realized that the exercise of the property rights might so interfere with the rights of the individual that the government, without whose assistance the property rights could not exist, must intervene—not to destroy individual-ism, but to protect it.

You are familiar with the great political duel which followed and how Hamilton and his friends, building toward a dominant centralized power, were at length defeated in the great election of 1800 by Mr. Jefferson's party. Out of that duel came the two parties, Republican and Democratic, as we know them today.[5]

So began in American political life the new day, the day of the individual against the system, the day in which individualism was made the great watch-word of American life. The happiest of economic conditions made that day long and splendid. On the western frontier land was substantially free. No one who did not shirk the task of earning a living was entirely without opportunity to do so. Depressions could, and did, come and go, but they could not alter the fundamental fact that most of the people lived partly by selling their labor and partly by extracting their livelihood from the soil, so that starvation and dislocation were practically impossible.

At the very worst there was always the possibility of climbing into a covered wagon and moving West, where the untilled prairies afforded a haven for men to whom the East did not provide a place. So great were our natural resources that we could offer this relief not only to our own people but to the distressed of all the world. We could invite immigration from Europe and welcome it with open arms. Traditionally, when a depression came, a new section of land was opened in the West. And even our temporary misfor-tune served our manifest destiny.

It was in the middle of the nineteenth cen-tury that a new force was released and a new dream created. The force was what is called the Industrial Revolution, the advance of steam and machinery and the rise of the forerunners of the modern industrial plant. The dream was the dream of an economic machine able to raise the standard of living for every-one, to bring luxury within the reach of the humblest, to annihilate distance by steam power and later by electricity, and to release everyone from the drudgery of the heaviest manual toil.

It was to be expected that this would neces-sarily affect government. Heretofore government had merely been called upon to produce conditions within which people could live happily, labor peace-fully, and rest secure. Now it was called upon to aid in the consummation of this new dream.

There was, however, a shadow over the dream. To be made real, it required use of the talents of men of tremendous will and tremendous ambition, since by no other force could the problems of financing and engineering and new developments be brought

4. Closely paraphrased from Thomas Jefferson's letter to Dr. Thomas Cooper, September 10, 1814.

5. Roosevelt is referring to the competing philosophies that char-acterize the two parties. The Democratic Party officially took its name in 1844; the Republican Party was formed in 1854.

to a consummation. So manifest were the advantages of the machine age, however, that the United States fearlessly, cheerfully, and, I think, rightly accepted the bitter with the sweet. It was thought that no price was too high to pay for the advantages which we could draw from a finished industrial system.

The history of the last half century is accordingly in large measure a history of a group of financial titans, whose methods were not scrutinized with too much care and who were honored in proportion as they produced the results, irrespective of the means they used. The financiers who pushed the railroads to the Pacific were always ruthless, often wasteful, and frequently corrupt, but they did build railroads and we have them today. It has been estimated that the American investor paid for the American railway system more than three times over in the process, but despite this fact, the net advantage was to the United States. As long as we had free land, as long as population was growing by leaps and bounds, as long as our industrial plants were insufficient to supply our own needs, society chose to give the ambitious man free play and unlimited reward, provided only that he produced the economic plant so much desired. During this period of expansion there was equal opportunity for all, and the business of government was not to interfere but to assist in the development of industry.

This was done at the request of businessmen themselves. The tariff was originally imposed for the purpose of "fostering our infant industry," a phrase I think the older among you will remember as a political issue not so long ago.[6] The railroads were subsidized, sometimes by grants of money, oftener by grants of land. Some of the most valuable oil lands in the United States were granted to assist the financing of the railroad which pushed through the Southwest. A nascent merchant marine was assisted by grants of money or by mail subsidies, so that our steam shipping might ply the seven seas.

Some of my friends tell me that they do not want the government in business. With this I agree, but

I wonder whether they realize the implications of the past. For while it has been American doctrine that the government must not go into business in competition with private enterprises, still it has been traditional, particularly in Republican administrations, for business urgently to ask the government to put at private disposal all kinds of government assistance.

The same man who tells you that he does not want to see the government interfere in business—and he means it and has plenty of good reasons for saying so—is the first to go to Washington and ask the government for a prohibitory tariff on his product. When things get just bad enough—as they did two years ago—he will go with equal speed to the United States government and ask for a loan. And the Reconstruction Finance Corporation[7] is the outcome of it. Each group has sought protection from the government for its own special interests without realizing that the function of government must be to favor no small group at the expense of its duty to protect the rights of personal freedom and of private property of all its citizens.

In retrospect we can now see that the turn of the tide came with the turn of the century. We were reaching our last frontier. There was no more free land[8] and our industrial combinations had become great, uncontrolled, and irresponsible units of power within the state. Clear-sighted men saw with fear the danger that opportunity would no longer be equal; that the growing corporation, like the feudal baron of old, might threaten the economic freedom of individuals to earn a living. In that hour our antitrust laws were born.

The cry was raised against the great corporations. Theodore Roosevelt, the first great Republican progressive,[9] fought a presidential campaign on the issue

6. Originally instituted in 1789 as a source of revenue for the new nation, the tariff became increasingly protective in nature after the War of 1812 and occasioned intense political debate throughout the 19th century.

7. Federal agency created in 1932 to combat the Depression by making emergency loans to businesses and financial institutions.

8. Roosevelt is echoing the thesis of Frederick Jackson Turner's famous 1893 essay, "The Significance of the Frontier in American History."

9. TR was President from 1901 to 1909; he ran for the office again in 1912 as the Progressive Party candidate, but lost to Democrat Woodrow Wilson.

of trust-busting[10] and talked freely about malefactors of great wealth. If the government had a policy, it was rather to turn the clock back, to destroy the large combinations, and to return to the time when every man owned his individual small business. This was impossible. Theodore Roosevelt, abandoning the idea of trust-busting, was forced to work out a difference between "good" trusts and "bad" trusts. The Supreme Court set forth the famous "rule of reason," by which it seems to have meant that a concentration of industrial power was permissible if the method by which it got its power, and the use it made of that power, was reasonable.[11]

Woodrow Wilson, elected in 1912, saw the situation more clearly. Where Jefferson had feared the encroachment of political power on the lives of individuals, Wilson knew that the new power was financial. He saw in the highly centralized economic system the despot of the twentieth century, on whom great masses of individuals relied for their safety and their livelihood and whose irresponsibility and greed, if it were not controlled, would reduce them to starvation and penury.

The concentration of financial power had not proceeded as far in 1912 as it has today, but it had grown far enough for Mr. Wilson to realize fully its implications. It is interesting now to read his speeches. What is called radical today—and I have reason to know whereof I speak—is mild compared to the campaign of Mr. Wilson. "No man can deny," he said, "that the lines of endeavor have more and more narrowed and stiffened; no man who knows anything about the development of industry in this country can have failed to observe that the larger kinds of credit are more and more difficult to obtain unless you obtain them upon terms of uniting your efforts with those who already control the industry of the country; and nobody can fail to observe that every man who tries to set himself up in competition with any process of manufacture which has taken place under the control of large combinations of capital will presently find

himself either squeezed out or obliged to sell and allow himself to be absorbed."[12]

Had there been no World War—had Mr. Wilson been able to devote eight years to domestic instead of to international affairs—we might have had a wholly different situation at the present time. However, the then distant roar of European cannon, growing ever louder, forced him to abandon the study of this issue. The problem he saw so clearly is left with us as a legacy, and no one of us on either side of the political controversy can deny that it is a matter of grave concern to the government.

A glance at the situation today only too clearly indicates that equality of opportunity as we have known it no longer exists. Our industrial plant is built; the problem just now is whether under existing conditions it is not overbuilt. Our last frontier has long since been reached and there is practically no more free land. More than half of our people do not live on the farms or on lands and cannot derive a living by cultivating their own property. There is no safety valve in the form of a western prairie to which those thrown out of work by the eastern economic machines can go for a new start. We are not able to invite the immigration from Europe to share our endless plenty. We are now providing a drab living for our own people.

Our system of constantly rising tariffs has at last reacted against us to the point of closing our Canadian frontier on the north, our European markets on the east, many of our Latin American markets to the south, and a goodly proportion of our Pacific markets on the west through the retaliatory tariffs of those countries. It has forced many of our great industrial institutions, who exported their surplus production to such countries, to establish plants in such countries, within the tariff walls. This has resulted in the reduction of the operation of their American plants and opportunity for employment.

Just as freedom to farm has ceased, so also the opportunity in business has narrowed. It still is true that men can start small enterprises, trusting to native shrewdness and ability to keep abreast of competitors;

10. A trust was a large corporate conglomerate that sought to monopolize some sector of the economy.

11. FDR is referring to the Supreme Court ruling of 1911 that dissolved the Standard Oil Trust.

12. From Wilson's *The New Freedom* (1913).

but area after area has been preempted altogether by the great corporations, and even in the fields which still have no great concerns the small man starts under a handicap. The unfeeling statistics of the past three decades show that the independent businessman is running a losing race. Perhaps he is forced to the wall; perhaps he cannot command credit; perhaps he is "squeezed out," in Mr. Wilson's words, by highly organized corporate competitors, as your corner grocery man can tell you.

Recently a careful study was made of the concentration of business in the United States.[13] It showed that our economic life was dominated by some 600-odd corporations who controlled two-thirds of American industry. Ten million small businessmen divided the other third. More striking still, it appeared that if the process of concentration goes on at the same rate, at the end of another century we shall have all American industry controlled by a dozen corporations and run by perhaps a hundred men. Put plainly, we are steering a steady course toward economic oligarchy, if we are not there already.

Clearly, all this calls for a reappraisal of values. A mere builder of more industrial plants, a creator of more railroad systems, an organizer of more corporations is as likely to be a danger as a help. The day of the great promoter or the financial titan, to whom we granted anything if only he would build or develop, is over. Our task now is not discovery or exploitation of natural resources or necessarily producing more goods. It is the soberer, less dramatic business of administering resources and plants already in hand, of seeking to reestablish foreign markets for our surplus production, of meeting the problem of underconsumption, of adjusting production to consumption, of distributing wealth and products more equitably, of adapting existing economic organizations to the service of the people. The day of enlightened administration has come.

Just as in older times the central government was first a haven of refuge and then a threat, so now in a closer economic system the central and ambitious financial unit is no longer a servant of national

desire but a danger. I would draw the parallel one step further. We did not think because national government had become a threat in the eighteenth century that therefore we should abandon the principle of national government. Nor today should we abandon the principle of strong economic units called corporations merely because their power is susceptible of easy abuse. In other times we dealt with the problem of an unduly ambitious central government by modifying it gradually into a constitutional democratic government. So today we are modifying and controlling our economic units.

As I see it, the task of government in its relation to business is to assist the development of an economic declaration of rights, an economic constitutional order. This is the common task of statesman and businessman. It is the minimum requirement of a more permanently safe order of things.

Happily, the times indicate that to create such an order not only is the proper policy of government but it is the only line of safety for our economic structures as well. We know now that these economic units cannot exist unless prosperity is uniform—that is, unless purchasing power is well distributed throughout every group in the nation. That is why even the most selfish of corporations for its own interest would be glad to see wages restored and unemployment aided and to bring the western farmer back to his accustomed level of prosperity and to assure a permanent safety to both groups. That is why some enlightened industries themselves endeavor to limit the freedom of action of each man and business group within the industry in the common interest of all; why businessmen everywhere are asking [for] a form of organization which will bring the scheme of things into balance, even though it may in some measure qualify the freedom of action of individual units within the business.

The exposition need not further be elaborated. It is brief and incomplete, but you will be able to expand it in terms of your own business or occupation without difficulty. I think everyone who has actually entered the economic struggle—which means everyone who was not born to safe wealth—knows in his own experience and his own life that we have now to apply the earlier concepts of American government to the conditions of today.

13. Adolph A. Berle Jr. and Gardiner Means, *The Modern Corporation and Private Property* (1932).

The Declaration of Independence discusses the problem of government in terms of a contract. Government is a relation of give and take—a contract, perforce, if we would follow the thinking out of which it grew. Under such a contract rulers were accorded power and the people consented to that power on consideration that they be accorded certain rights. The task of statesmanship has always been the redefinition of these rights in terms of a changing and growing social order. New conditions impose new requirements upon government and those who conduct government.

I held, for example, in proceedings before me as Governor the purpose of which was the removal of the Sheriff of New York, that under modern conditions it was not enough for a public official merely to evade the legal terms of official wrongdoing.[14] He owed a positive duty as well. I said, in substance, that if he had acquired large sums of money, he was, when accused, required to explain the sources of such wealth. To that extent, this wealth was colored with a public interest. I said that public servants should, even beyond private citizens, in financial matters be held to a stern and uncompromising rectitude.

I feel that we are coming to a view, through the drift of our legislation and our public thinking in the past quarter century, that private economic power is, to enlarge an old phrase, a public trust as well. I hold that continued enjoyment of that power by any individual or group must depend upon the fulfillment of that trust. The men who have reached the summit of American business life know this best; happily, many of these urge the binding quality of this greater social contract.

The terms of that contract are as old as the republic and as new as the new economic order. Every man has a right to life, and this means that he has also a right to make a comfortable living. He may by sloth or crime decline to exercise that right, but it may not be denied him. We have no actual famine or dearth; our industrial and agricultural mechanism can produce enough and to spare. Our government, formal and informal, political and economic, owes to every-one an avenue to possess himself of a portion of that plenty sufficient for his needs through his own work.

Every man has a right to his own property, which means a right to be assured, to the fullest extent attainable, in the safety of his savings. By no other means can men carry the burdens of those parts of life which in the nature of things afford no chance of labor—childhood, sickness, old age. In all thought of property, this right is paramount; all other property rights must yield to it. If, in accord with this principle, we must restrict the operations of the speculator, the manipulator, even the financier, I believe we must accept the restriction as needful—not to hamper individualism but to protect it.

These two requirements must be satisfied, in the main, by the individuals who claim and hold control of the great industrial and financial combinations which dominate so large a part of our industrial life. They have undertaken to be not businessmen but princes—princes of property. I am not prepared to say that the system which produces them is wrong. I am very clear that they must fearlessly and competently assume the responsibility which goes with the power. So many enlightened businessmen know this that the statement would be little more than a platitude were it not for an added implication.

This implication is, briefly, that the responsible heads of finance and industry, instead of acting each for himself, must work together to achieve the common end. They must, where necessary, sacrifice this or that private advantage, and in reciprocal self-denial must seek a general advantage. It is here that formal government—political government, if you choose—comes in. Whenever in the pursuit of this objective the lone wolf, the unethical competitor, the reckless promoter, the Ishmael[15] or Insull[16] whose hand is against every

14. Roosevelt is referring to his removal of Thomas Farley as sheriff of New York County in February 1932.

15. Son of Abraham and Hagar and half brother of Isaac, Ishmael was a quarrelsome figure whom the Bible describes as "a wild man; his hand will be against every man, and every man's hand against him" (Genesis 16:12).

16. Utilities and transportation mogul Samuel Insull (1859–1938). When Insull's economic empire collapsed during the Depression, millions of middle-class Americans lost the money they had invested in his companies. Charged with fraud and embezzlement, he fled to Greece, where he was at the time FDR spoke to the Commonwealth Club.

man's, declines to join in achieving an end recognized as being for the public welfare and threatens to drag the industry back to a state of anarchy, the government may properly be asked to apply restraint. Likewise, should the group ever use its collective power contrary to public welfare, the government must be swift to enter and protect the public interest.

The government should assume the function of economic regulation only as a last resort, to be tried only when private initiative, inspired by high responsibility, with such assistance and balance as government can give, has finally failed. As yet there has been no final failure, because there has been no attempt; and I decline to assume that this nation is unable to meet the situation.

The final term of the high contract was for liberty and the pursuit of happiness. We have learned a great deal of both in the past century. We know that individual liberty and individual happiness mean nothing unless both are ordered in the sense that one man's meat is not another man's poison. We know that the old "rights of personal competency"[17]—the right to read, to think, to speak, to choose and live a mode of life—must be respected at all hazards. We know that liberty to do anything which deprives others of those elemental rights is outside the protection of any compact, and that government in this regard is the maintenance of a balance within which every individual may have a place if he will take it, in which every individual may find safety if he wishes it, in which every individual may attain such power as his ability permits, consistent with his assuming the accompanying responsibility.

All this is a long, slow task. Nothing is more striking than the simple innocence of the men who insist, whenever an objective is present, on the prompt production of a patent scheme guaranteed to produce a result. Human endeavor is not so simple as that. Government includes the art of formulating a policy and using the political technique to attain so much of that policy as will receive general support—persuading, leading, sacrificing, teaching always, because the greatest duty of a statesman is to educate.

But in the matters of which I have spoken, we are learning rapidly in a severe school. The lessons so learned must not be forgotten even in the mental lethargy of a speculative upturn. We must build toward the time when a major depression cannot occur again; and if this means sacrificing the easy profits of inflationist booms, then let them go—and good riddance.

Faith in America, faith in our tradition of personal responsibility, faith in our institutions, faith in ourselves demands that we recognize the new terms of the old social contract. We shall fulfill them, as we fulfilled the obligation of the apparent utopia which Jefferson imagined for us in 1776 and which Jefferson, Roosevelt, and Wilson sought to bring to realization. We must do so lest a rising tide of misery, engendered by our common failure, engulf us all. But failure is not an American habit, and in the strength of great hope we must all shoulder our common load.

---

17. The phrase comes from Thomas Paine, in an undated letter to Thomas Jefferson, most likely written in 1788.

Franklin D. Roosevelt

First Inaugural Address

WASHINGTON, D.C.
MARCH 4, 1933

WITH HIS RESOUNDING victory over Herbert Hoover in the 1932 presidential election, Franklin Roosevelt came into office with a mandate that he fully intended to use. Working with speechwriter Raymond Moley on his inaugural address, FDR sought above all to restore the confidence of the American people in their government. One quarter of the adult population was out of work. Life savings had been destroyed, businesses were shuttering their doors, and banks were failing at an alarming rate. The nation's morale was as depressed as its economy. During his first hundred days in office, Roosevelt would propose a series of measures designed to redress the country's economic problems. His task on inauguration day was to create a psychological climate conducive to the actions he intended to take.

Using a line penned by advisor Louis Howe, FDR assured his audience that "the only thing we have to fear is fear itself." He declared, with his characteristic optimism, that "This great nation will endure as it has endured, will revive and will prosper." Drawing heavily on biblical imagery, he said America was "stricken by no plague of locusts." Rather, he traced the nation's problems to "unscrupulous moneychangers" and vowed to restore "the temple of our civilization ... to its ancient truths" by the application of "social values more noble than mere monetary profit."

Roosevelt also used military metaphors. He adumbrated the "lines of attack" he planned to take against the Depression and called upon the populace to "move as a trained and loyal army." The nation, he said, must proceed "with a unity of duty hitherto evoked only in times of armed strife." Stressing the need for "action, and action now," he made clear that he would, if necessary, seek "broad executive power to wage a war against the emergency, as great as the power that would be given to me if we were in fact invaded by a foreign foe."

The energy and decisiveness of Roosevelt's words were exactly what the people needed. Thousands of radio listeners sent letters and telegrams to the White House commending the President for "breathing confidence" into the nation. Referring to FDR as "an instrument in God's hands," one writer called on him to "right the wrongs that have been imposed on this country." Others spoke of "renewed confidence" and "the dawn of a new day." The *Atlanta Constitution* predicted that the speech would take its place "among the greatest of historic state papers of the nation"—as indeed it has.

◇◇

President Hoover,[1] Mr. Chief Justice,[2] my friends: This is a day of national consecration, and I am certain that on this day my fellow Americans expect that on my induction into the presidency I will address them with a candor and a decision which the present situation of our people impels. This is preeminently the time to speak the truth, the whole truth,[3] frankly and boldly. Nor need we shrink from honestly facing conditions in our country today. This great nation will endure as it has endured, will revive and will prosper.

So first of all, let me assert my firm belief that the only thing we have to fear is fear itself[4]—nameless, unreasoning, unjustified terror which paralyzes needed efforts to convert retreat into advance. In every dark hour of our national life a leadership of frankness and of vigor has met with that understanding and support of the people themselves which is essential to victory. And I am convinced that you will again give that support to leadership in these critical days.

In such a spirit on my part and on yours we face our common difficulties. They concern, thank God, only material things. Values have shrunk to fantastic levels; taxes have risen; our ability to pay has fallen; government of all kinds is faced by serious curtailment of income; the means of exchange are frozen in the currents of trade; the withered leaves of industrial enterprise lie on every side; farmers find no markets for their produce; and the savings of many years in thousands of families are gone. More important, a host of unemployed citizens face the grim problem of existence, and an equally great number toil with little return. Only a foolish optimist can deny the dark realities of the moment.

And yet our distress comes from no failure of substance. We are stricken by no plague of locusts.[5] Compared with the perils which our forefathers conquered because they believed and were not afraid, we have still much to be thankful for. Nature still offers her bounty and human efforts have multiplied it. Plenty is at our doorstep, but a generous use of it languishes in the very sight of the supply.

Primarily, this is because the rulers of the exchange of mankind's goods have failed through their own stubbornness and their own incompetence, have admitted their failure, and have abdicated. Practices of the unscrupulous moneychangers[6] stand indicted in the court of public opinion, rejected by the hearts and minds of men.

True, they have tried. But their efforts have been cast in the pattern of an outworn tradition. Faced by failure of credit, they have proposed only the lending of more money. Stripped of the lure of profit by which to induce our people to follow their false leadership, they have resorted to exhortations, pleading tearfully for restored confidence. They only know the rules of a generation of self-seekers. They have no vision, and when there is no vision, the people perish.[7]

Yes, the moneychangers have fled from their high seats in the temple of our civilization. We may now

---

1. Outgoing President Herbert Hoover.

2. Charles Evans Hughes, Chief Justice of the U.S. Supreme Court.

3. An echo of the legal oath to tell "the truth, the whole truth, and nothing but the truth."

4. Sometimes said to be a paraphrase of Henry David Thoreau's "Nothing is so much to be feared as fear" (*Journal*, September 7, 1851), though similar language can be found in the writings of Michel de Montaigne, Francis Bacon, and the Duke of Wellington. The line was inserted in the speech by FDR advisor Louis Howe, who, according to Raymond Moley, got it from a newspaper advertisement that appeared a few weeks before the inaugural.

5. An allusion to Exodus 10:1–19.

6. FDR is echoing Jesus's indictment of the moneychangers in Matthew 21:12 and Mark 11:15.

7. From Proverbs 29:18.

restore that temple to the ancient truths. The measure of that restoration lies in the extent to which we apply social values more noble than mere monetary profit. Happiness lies not in the mere possession of money; it lies in the joy of achievement, in the thrill of creative effort. The joy, the moral stimulation of work, no longer must be forgotten in the mad chase of evanescent profits. These dark days, my friends, will be worth all they cost us if they teach us that our true destiny is not to be ministered unto but to minister to ourselves, to our fellow men.[8]

Recognition of that falsity of material wealth as the standard of success goes hand in hand with the abandonment of the false belief that public office and high political position are to be valued only by the standards of pride of place and personal profit; and there must be an end to a conduct in banking and in business which too often has given to a sacred trust the likeness of callous and selfish wrongdoing. Small wonder that confidence languishes, for it thrives only on honesty, on honor, on the sacredness of obligations, on faithful protection, and on unselfish performance. Without them, it cannot live.

Restoration calls, however, not for changes in ethics alone. This nation is asking for action, and action now.

Our greatest primary task is to put people to work. This is no unsolvable problem if we face it wisely and courageously. It can be accomplished in part by direct recruiting by the government itself, treating the task as we would treat the emergency of a war, but, at the same time, through this employment accomplishing greatly needed projects to stimulate and reorganize the use of our great natural resources. Hand in hand with that we must frankly recognize the overbalance of population in our industrial centers and, by engaging on a national scale in a redistribution, endeavor to provide a better use of the land for those best fitted for the land.

Yes, the task can be helped by definite efforts to raise the values of agricultural products and, with this, the power to purchase the output of our cities. It can be helped by preventing realistically the tragedy of the growing loss through foreclosure of our small homes and our farms. It can be helped by insistence that the federal, the state, and the local governments act forthwith on the demand that their cost be drastically reduced. It can be helped by the unifying of relief activities which today are often scattered, uneconomical, unequal. It can be helped by national planning for and supervision of all forms of transportation and of communications and other utilities that have a definitely public character.

There are many ways in which it can be helped, but it can never be helped by merely talking about it. We must act. We must act quickly.

And finally, in our progress towards a resumption of work, we require two safeguards against a return of the evils of the old order: There must be a strict supervision of all banking and credits and investments—there must be an end to speculation with other people's money. And there must be provision for an adequate but sound currency.

These, my friends, are the lines of attack. I shall presently urge upon a new Congress in special session detailed measures for their fulfillment, and I shall seek the immediate assistance of the forty-eight states.

Through this program of action we address ourselves to putting our own national house in order and making income balance outgo. Our international trade relations, though vastly important, are in point of time and necessity secondary to the establishment of a sound national economy. I favor as a practical policy the putting of first things first. I shall spare no effort to restore world trade by international economic readjustment, but the emergency at home cannot wait on that accomplishment.

The basic thought that guides these specific means of national recovery is not narrowly nationalistic. It is the insistence, as a first consideration, upon the interdependence of the various elements in and parts of the United States of America—a recognition of the old and permanently important manifestation of the American spirit of the pioneer. It is the way to recovery. It is the immediate way. It is the strongest assurance that recovery will endure.

In the field of world policy, I would dedicate this nation to the policy of the good neighbor—the neighbor who resolutely respects himself and, because he does so, respects the rights of others, the neighbor

---

8. An allusion to Matthew 20:28 and Mark 10:45.

who respects his obligations and respects the sanctity of his agreements in and with a world of neighbors.

If I read the temper of our people correctly, we now realize as we have never realized before our interdependence on each other: that we cannot merely take but we must give as well; that if we are to go forward, we must move as a trained and loyal army willing to sacrifice for the good of a common discipline because without such discipline, no progress can be made, no leadership becomes effective. We are, I know, ready and willing to submit our lives and our property to such discipline because it makes possible a leadership which aims at the larger good. This I propose to offer, pledging that the larger purposes will bind upon us, bind upon us all as a sacred obligation with a unity of duty hitherto evoked only in times of armed strife.

With this pledge taken, I assume unhesitatingly the leadership of this great army of our people dedicated to a disciplined attack upon our common problems. Action in this image, action to this end is feasible under the form of government which we have inherited from our ancestors. Our Constitution is so simple, so practical that it is possible always to meet extraordinary needs by changes in emphasis and arrangement without loss of essential form. That is why our constitutional system has proved itself the most superbly enduring political mechanism the modern world has ever seen. It has met every stress of vast expansion of territory, of foreign wars, of bitter internal strife, of world relations.

And it is to be hoped that the normal balance of executive and legislative authority may be wholly equal, wholly adequate to meet the unprecedented task before us. But it may be that an unprecedented demand and need for undelayed action may call for temporary departure from that normal balance of public procedure. I am prepared under my constitutional duty to recommend the measures that a stricken nation in the midst of a stricken world may require. These measures, or such other measures as the Congress may build out of its experience and wisdom, I shall seek, within my constitutional authority, to bring to speedy adoption.

But in the event that the Congress shall fail to take one of these two courses, in the event that the national emergency is still critical, I shall not evade the clear course of duty that will then confront me. I shall ask Congress for the one remaining instrument to meet the crisis—broad executive power to wage a war against the emergency, as great as the power that would be given to me if we were in fact invaded by a foreign foe.

For the trust reposed in me, I will return the courage and the devotion that befit the time. I can do no less.

We face the arduous days that lie before us in the warm courage of national unity, with the clear consciousness of seeking old and precious moral values, with the clean satisfaction that comes from the stern performance of duty by old and young alike. We aim at the assurance of a rounded, a permanent national life.

We do not distrust the future of essential democracy. The people of the United States have not failed. In their need they have registered a mandate that they want direct, vigorous action. They have asked for discipline and direction under leadership. They have made me the present instrument of their wishes. In the spirit of the gift, I take it.

In this dedication, in this dedication of a nation, we humbly ask the blessing of God. May he protect each and every one of us. May he guide me in the days to come.

Franklin D. Roosevelt

𝕏

The Banking Crisis

WASHINGTON, D.C.
MARCH 12, 1933

B Y THE EARLY 1930s, radio had become a national medium, with stations stretching from coast to coast. As Governor of New York, Franklin Roosevelt had made regular broadcasts to his constituents in the Empire State; by the time he entered the White House, he had become a master of political radio. His voice, though not particularly deep or resonant, was distinctive, the most sought-after quality in a vehicle of communication that played to the ear. On March 4, 1933, an estimated forty million people tuned in to listen to his inaugural address. They heard a President determined to take action, and it was not long in coming.

On March 5, the day after his inauguration, Roosevelt approved two executive orders. One called Congress back into session on March 9, while the other stopped all transactions in gold and proclaimed a national bank holiday. The proclamation was an ingenious idea, since virtually all the banks had already been closed by order of the governors of the various states. Roosevelt made what had happened in most states uniform and gave the situation a pleasant-sounding name. On March 9 he sent a banking bill to Congress, where it was approved the same day. FDR signed the bill that night and made plans to explain it to a nationwide radio audience on Sunday, March 12.

In addition to explaining the bill and what it meant for the American people, Roosevelt needed to revive confidence in the nation's shattered banking system. Doing so would require simple, direct language that any citizen could understand, as well as a sense of self-assurance so emphatic that it would be infectious for listeners. Roosevelt addressed his listeners as "my friends" and talked with them in a down-to-earth manner designed to clarify the technical details of the banking crisis and the new legislation "for the benefit of the average citizen." Employing personal terms such as "you" and "I," he spoke of "checks," "deposits," and "losses," and warned the people against hiding their money "under the mattress." There was no reason, he said, to succumb to "the phantom of fear." The intelligent support of the public, in combination with a reliable financial system, would see the nation through.

Roosevelt dealt with the issues step by step, bringing them home to listeners in a straightforward manner that bred reassurance as well as understanding. When the bank holiday ended on Monday, banks began to reopen, people started redepositing money and gold, and the dollar rose in value against other currencies. The Depression was far from over, but the banking system had been saved. Few presidential addresses have generated more immediate material consequences.

This was the first of more than two dozen radio talks known as FDR's Fireside Chats. The talks were usually broadcast from the Diplomatic Reception Room in the basement of the White House, a small, cramped space that was nothing like the atmosphere evoked by Roosevelt, though there was an unlit fireplace in the room. It was not the physical setting, however, that led to the label "Fireside Chats," but the warm tone of friendliness and the sense of shared purpose generated between Roosevelt and his listeners. After Roosevelt's death, one writer expressed what many Americans felt about the Fireside Chats:

> I never saw him—
> But I *knew* him. Can you have forgotten
> How, with his voice, he came into our house,
> The President of the United States,
> Calling us friends.

◇◇

My friends: I want to talk for a few minutes with the people of the United States about banking—to talk with the comparatively few who understand the mechanics of banking, but more particularly with the overwhelming majority of you who use banks for the making of deposits and the drawing of checks. I want to tell you what has been done in the last few days and why it was done and what the next steps are going to be.

I recognize that the many proclamations from state capitals and from Washington, the legislation, the Treasury regulations, and so forth, couched for the most part in banking and legal terms, ought to be explained for the benefit of the average citizen. I owe this in particular because of the fortitude and the good temper which everybody has, with which everybody has accepted the inconvenience and the hardships of the banking holiday. And I know that when you understand what we in Washington have been about, I shall continue to have your cooperation as fully as I have had your sympathy and your help during the past week.

First of all, let me state the simple fact that when you deposit money in a bank, the bank does not put the money into a safe-deposit vault. It invests your money in many different forms of credit—in bonds and commercial paper and mortgages and in many other kinds of loans. In other words, the bank puts your money to work to keep the wheels of industry and of agriculture turning round. A comparatively small part of the money you put into the bank is kept in currency, an amount which in normal times is wholly sufficient to cover the cash needs of the average citizen. In other words, the total amount of all the currency in the country is only a comparatively small proportion of the total deposits in all the banks of the country.

What, then, happened during the last few days of February and the first few days of March? Because of undermined confidence on the part of the public, there was a general rush by a large portion of our population to turn bank deposits into currency or gold—a rush so great that the soundest banks couldn't get enough currency to meet the demand. The reason for this was that on the spur of the moment it was, of course, impossible to sell perfectly sound assets of a bank and convert them into cash except at panic prices far below their real value. By the afternoon of March 3, a week ago last Friday, scarcely a bank in the country was open to do business. Proclamations closing them in whole or in part had been issued by the governors in almost all of the states.

It was then that I issued the proclamation providing for the national bank holiday, and this was the first step in the government's reconstruction of our financial and economic fabric.

The second step, last Thursday, was the legislation promptly and patriotically passed by the Congress confirming my proclamation and broadening my powers so that it became possible in view of the requirement of time to extend the holiday and lift the ban of that holiday gradually in the days to come. This law also gave authority to develop a program of rehabilitation of our banking facilities. And I want to tell our citizens in every part of the nation that the national Congress—Republicans and Democrats alike—showed by this action a devotion to public welfare and a realization of the emergency and the necessity for speed that it is difficult to match in all our history.

The third stage has been the series of regulations permitting the banks to continue their functions to take care of the distribution of food and household necessities and the payment of payrolls.

This bank holiday, while resulting in many cases in great inconvenience, is affording us the opportunity to supply the currency necessary to meet the situation. Remember that no sound bank is a dollar worse off than it was when it closed its doors last week. Neither is any bank which may turn out not to be in a position for immediate opening. The new law allows the twelve Federal Reserve Banks to issue additional currency on good assets, and thus the banks that reopen will be able to meet every legitimate call. The new currency is being sent out by the Bureau of Engraving and Printing in large volume to every part of the country. It is sound currency because it is backed by actual, good assets.

Another question that you will ask is this: Why are all the banks not to be reopened at the same time? The answer is simple, and I know you will understand it. Your government does not intend that the history of the past few years shall be repeated. We do not want, and will not have, another epidemic of bank failures.

As a result, we start tomorrow, Monday, with the opening of banks in the twelve Federal Reserve Bank cities—those banks which on first examination by the Treasury have already been found to be all right. That will be followed on Tuesday by the resumption of all other functions by banks already found to be sound in cities where there are recognized clearinghouses. That means about 250 cities of the United States. In other words, we are moving as fast as the mechanics of the situation will allow us.

On Wednesday and succeeding days banks in smaller places all through the country will resume business, subject, of course, to the government's physical ability to complete its survey. It is necessary that the reopening of banks be extended over a period in order to permit the banks to make applications for the necessary loans, to obtain currency needed to meet their requirements, and to enable the government to make common-sense checkups.

Please let me make it clear to you that if your bank does not open the first day, you are by no means justified in believing that it will not open. A bank that opens on one of the subsequent days is in exactly the same status as the bank that opens tomorrow.

I know that many people are worrying about state banks that are not members of the Federal Reserve System. There is no occasion for that worry. These banks can and will receive assistance from member banks and from the Reconstruction Finance Corporation.[1] And, of course, they are under the immediate control of the state banking authorities. These state banks are following the same course as the national banks except that they get their licenses to resume business from the state authorities, and these authorities have been asked by the Secretary of the Treasury[2] to permit their good banks to open up on the same schedule as the national banks. And so I am confident that the state banking departments will be as careful as the national government in the policy relating to the opening of banks and will follow the same broad theory.

It is possible that when the banks resume, a very few people who have not recovered from their fear

---

1. U.S. government agency created in 1932 to combat the Depression by making emergency loans to businesses and financial institutions.

2. William H. Woodin.

may again begin withdrawals. Let me make it clear to you that the banks will take care of all needs, except, of course, the hysterical demands of hoarders, and it is my belief that hoarding during the past week has become an exceedingly unfashionable pastime in every part of our nation. It needs no prophet to tell you that when the people find that they can get their money, that they can get it when they want it for all legitimate purposes, the phantom of fear will soon be laid. People will again be glad to have their money where it will be safely taken care of and where they can use it conveniently at any time. I can assure you, my friends, that it is safer to keep your money in a reopened bank than it is to keep it under the mattress.

The success of our whole national program depends, of course, on the cooperation of the public—on its intelligent support and its use of a reliable system.

Remember that the essential accomplishment of the new legislation is that it makes it possible for banks more readily to convert their assets into cash than was the case before. More liberal provision has been made for banks to borrow on these assets at the Reserve Banks, and more liberal provision has also been made for issuing currency on the security of these good assets. This currency is not fiat currency. It is issued only on adequate security, and every good bank has an abundance of such security.

One more point before I close. There will be, of course, some banks unable to reopen without being reorganized. The new law allows the government to assist in making these reorganizations quickly and effectively and even allows the government to subscribe to at least a part of any new capital that may be required.

I hope you can see, my friends, from this essential recital of what your government is doing that there is nothing complex, nothing radical in the process. We have had a bad banking situation. Some

of our bankers had shown themselves either incompetent or dishonest in their handling of the people's funds. They had used the money entrusted to them in speculations and unwise loans. This was, of course, not true in the vast majority of our banks, but it was true in enough of them to shock the people of the United States for a time into a sense of insecurity and to put them into a frame of mind where they did not differentiate, but seemed to assume that the acts of a comparative few had tainted them all. And so it became the government's job to straighten out this situation, and to do it as quickly as possible. And that job is being performed.

I do not promise you that every bank will be reopened or that individual losses will not be suffered. But there will be no losses that possibly could be avoided, and there would have been more and greater losses had we continued to drift. I can even promise you salvation for some at least of the sorely pressed banks. We shall be engaged not merely in reopening sound banks but in the creation of more sound banks through reorganization.

It has been wonderful to me to catch the note of confidence from all over the country. I can never be sufficiently grateful to the people for the loyal support that they have given me in their acceptance of the judgment that has dictated our course, even though all our processes may not have seemed clear to them. After all, there is an element in the readjustment of our financial system more important than currency, more important than gold, and that is the confidence of the people themselves. Confidence and courage are the essentials of success in carrying out our plan.

You people must have faith. You must not be stampeded by rumors or guesses. Let us unite in banishing fear. We have provided the machinery to restore our financial system, and it is up to you to support and make it work. It is your problem, my friends, your problem no less than it is mine. Together we cannot fail.

Huey P. Long

⧗

Every Man a King

New York, New York
February 23, 1934

Five days after Franklin Roosevelt presented his initial Fireside Chat, (pages 225–228), the American radio audience heard a new voice—that of Huey P. Long, U.S. Senator from Louisiana. It was the first of eleven national radio broadcasts by Long over the next two and a half years. Those broadcasts transformed Long from a regional political figure into a household name from coast to coast. A spellbinding stump orator, he was equally mesmerizing over the airwaves. One opponent called him "the best political radio speaker in America, better even than President Roosevelt. Give him time on the air and a week to campaign in each state, and he'll sweep the country. He is the most persuasive man living."

One of the most controversial figures in the history of American politics, Long was bright, ambitious, and politically shrewd even as he cultivated the image of a country bumpkin. He ruled Louisiana with an iron fist and was often assailed, not without justification, as dictatorial. He turned corruption into an art form, yet as Governor he pursued a populist agenda that expanded social services, constructed roads, hospitals, and schools, and revised the tax code to increase the burden on corporations. He publicly bemoaned the uneven distribution of wealth as early as 1918, and it became the centerpiece of his speeches in the U.S. Senate.

On February 23, 1934, Long presented his ideas on NBC Radio. The title of his speech—"Every Man a King"—was derived from William Jennings Bryan and had been Long's slogan since his days campaigning for Governor in Louisiana. Arguing that the nation's fundamental problem was the concentration of wealth in the hands of a few "super-rich" people, he proposed to "scale down the big fortunes that we may scatter the wealth to be shared by all of the people." Each household, he said, should have a guaranteed income sufficient to ensure that "there will be no such thing as a family living in poverty and distress."

Speaking extemporaneously in a down-home idiom, Long buttressed his case with a few statistics and claimed his plan was consistent with Scripture and the Declaration of Independence. He struck a responsive chord among millions of citizens who were mired in poverty and angry at the plutocrats they blamed for their condition. Within a month, some 200,000 Americans had joined his Share Our Wealth clubs. By the end of the year, membership stood at more than three million, Long was receiving an average of 34,000 letters a day at his Senate office, and the White House was growing increasingly concerned about his hold on public opinion.

Previous publications of Long's speech have reproduced the version in the *Congressional Record* of March 1, 1934, which is an edited rendition of what he said. While there is no known recording of all of Long's words, ten minutes and fourteen seconds—one-third of the speech—were preserved at the Brander Matthews Collection at Columbia University and are now part of the audio holdings at the Library of Congress. In the following text, those ten minutes and fourteen seconds are reprinted from the recording; the remainder of the speech is taken from the *Congressional Record*. The recorded portion, demarcated with footnotes, begins in the third paragraph.

◇◇

Is that a right of life when the young children of this country are being reared into a sphere which is more owned by twelve men than it is by 120 million people?

Ladies and gentlemen, I have only thirty minutes in which to speak to you this evening, and I therefore will not be able to discuss in detail so much as I can write when I have all of the time and space that is allowed me for the subjects, but I will undertake to sketch them very briefly without manuscript or preparation, so that you can understand them so well as I can tell them to you tonight.

I contend, my friends, that we have no difficult problem to solve in America. And that is the view of nearly everyone with whom I have discussed the matter here in Washington and elsewhere throughout the United States—that we have no very difficult problem to solve. It is not the difficulty of the problem which we have. It is the fact that[1] the rich people of this country—and by the rich people I mean the super rich—will not allow us to solve the problems, or rather the one little problem that is afflicting this country, because in order to cure all our woes, it is necessary to scale down the big fortunes that we may scatter the wealth to be shared by all of the people.

We have a marvelous love for this government of ours. In fact, it is almost a religion, and it is well that it should be because we have a splendid form of government and we have a splendid set of laws. We have everything that we need here except that we have neglected the fundamental upon which the American government was principally predicated.

How many of you remember the first thing that the Declaration of Independence said? It said, "We hold these truths to be self-evident, that there are certain inalienable rights among people, that among them are life, liberty, and the pursuit of happiness." And it said further, "We hold further the view that all men are created equal."[2]

Now, what did they mean by that? Did they mean, my friends, to say that all men were created equal and that that meant that one man was born to inherit $10 billion and that another child was to be born to inherit nothin'? Did that mean, my friends, that someone coming into this world without ever having had the opportunity of course to have hit one lick of work, should be born with more than it and all of its children and children's children could ever dispose of, but that another one would have to be born into a life of starvation?

That wasn't the meaning of the Declaration of Independence when it said that all men are to be created—or that "We hold that all men are created equal." Nor was it the meaning of the Declaration of Independence when they said that they held that there were certain rights that were inalienable—the right of life, liberty, and pursuit of happiness.

---

1. The recorded portion of Long's speech begins here.

2. Long is paraphrasing the Declaration.

Is it the right of life, my friends, when the young children of this country are being reared into a sphere by which there is more owned by twelve men than there is by 120 million people? Is it, my friends, giving a fair shake of the dice, or anything like an inalienable right of life, liberty, and the pursuit of happiness, or anything resembling the fact that all people are created equal, when we have today in America thousands and hundreds of thousands and millions of children on the verge of starvation in a land that is overflowing with too much to eat and too much to wear? I don't think that they will contend it, and I don't think for a moment that you will contend it.

Now I'm going to have to ask someone in this studio to turn off the other radio that's playing here because it interrupts me and I'm afraid it's going through this microphone.

Now, my friends, let us see if we cannot return this government to the Declaration of Independence, and let's see if we're going to do anything radical in so doing. Why, my friends, should we hesitate? Why should we quibble or why should we quarrel with one another to try to find out what the difficulty is, when we know it? The Lord told us what the difficulty is. Christ told us what the difficulty is. Moses wrote it out so that a blind man could see it. It was written in the Book of James so that anyone could tell it.

And I refer, my friends, to the Scripture now and give you what it has said, not for the purpose of convincing you of the wisdom of myself, not for the purpose, ladies and gentlemen, of convincing you of the fact that I may quote the Scripture means that I am to be more believed than someone else on his own word. But I quote you the Scripture, or rather I refer you to the Scripture, because whatever you see there you may rely upon it never being disproved so long as you or your children may live. And you may further depend upon the fact that not one historical fact that the Bible has ever contained has ever yet been disproved in any scientific discovery or any invention that's been disclosed to man through his own efforts or through the wisdom that the Lord has allowed him to have.

But the Scripture says, ladies and gentlemen, that in order that a country could survive, it was necessary that we keep the wealth scattered among the people—that nothing should be permanently held by any one person, but that at certain seasons every fifty years was to be the year of jubilee in which all property would be scattered about and returned to[3] the sources from which it originally came, and that every seventh year debts should be remitted.[4]

Those two things the Almighty[5] said to be necessary—I should say he knew to be necessary, or else he would not have so prescribed that the property would be kept among the general run of the people, and that everyone would continue to share in it, so no one man would get half of it and hand it down to a son, who takes half[6] of what else was left, and then that son handed down to another one, who would get half of what else was left until, like a snowball going downhill, all the snow was off the ground except what the one snowball had. Therefore, it was the judgment and the view and the law of the Lord that we had to redistribute the wealth every so often in order that there wouldn't be people starving to death in a land of plenty, as there is in America today.

We have in America today more wealth, more goods, more food, more clothes, more houses than we've ever had. We have everything in abundance here. We have a farm problem, my friends, because we have too much cotton, and because we have too much wheat, too much corn, and too much potatoes. We have a home-loan problem because we have too many houses and nobody that can buy them and nobody to live in them.

We have trouble, my friends, in the country because we have too much—the greatest indictment that has ever been given to a civilization: that it has shown itself incapable of distributing the actual things that are here because the people haven't money enough to supply themselves with them and because the greed of a few men is such that they think that it

---

3. Long misspoke this word as "from."

4. Long is drawing from Leviticus 25:8–19, which explains the year of jubilee, and Deuteronomy 15:1–11, which commands the relaxation of debts every seven years.

5. The recording of Long's speech is interrupted briefly at this point.

6. The recording starts again here.

is necessary that they own everything and that their pleasure consists in the starvation of others and in their possessing things that they can't use and their children can't use, but that basking in the sunlight of splendor and wealth, that the darkness and despair that they compel on everyone else somehow or another they think reflects glory upon them.

So, therefore, said the Lord, foreseeing these things that have occurred and that now exist in this and other countries, there must be a constant scattering of the wealth of any country if that country is to survive. Then, said the Lord, every seventh year there shall be a remission of debt. There'll be no debts after the seventh year was the law.

Now, why? Let's take America today. We have in America today, ladies and gentlemen, $272 billion of debt. Two hundred and seventy-two billion. Two hundred and seventy-two thousand millions of dollars of debt are owed by the various people in this country today. Why, my friends, it cannot be paid. It's not possible for that kind of a debt to be paid.

The entire currency of the United States is only $6 billion. That's all the money that we've got in America today. All that you've got in all your banks, all that you've got in the government treasury, is $6 billion. And if you took all that money and paid it out today, you'd still owe 266 billion. And if you took all that money and paid again, you'd still owe 260 billion. And if you took it and paid it, my friends, twenty times, you'd still owe $155 billion. You would have to have forty-five times the entire money supply of the United States today to pay the debts of the people of America, and then you'd just have to start out from scratch, without a dime to go with.

Now, my friends, it's an impossibility to pay all these debts, and you just might as well find it out—it can't be done. The United States Supreme Court's evidently found out it can't be done because, in the Minnesota case, they held that where a state postponed the evil date of collecting debt, that it was a valid and constitutional exercise of legislative power.[7]

Now, ladies and gentlemen, if I may proceed to give you some of the words that I think you can understand—and I'm not gonna belabor you by quoting tonight—I'm going to tell you that the wise men of all ages and of all times down even to the present day have all said that you must keep the wealth of the country scattered and that you must limit the amount that any one man can own. You can't let one man own $300 billion or $400 billion. If you do, then one man can own all the wealth that the United States has in it.

Now, my friends, if you were off on an island where there were one hundred lunches, you couldn't let one man eat up the hundred lunches—or take the one hundred lunches and not let anybody else eat any of 'em—because if you did, there wouldn't be anything else for the balance of the people to consume.

So we have in America, my friends, a condition by which about twelve men dominate the field of activity in at least 85 percent of the activities of this country. They either own directly everything or they've got some kind of a mortgage on it, with a very small percent to be excepted. They own the banks, they own the steel mills, they own the railroads, they own the bonds, they own the mortgages, they own the stores, and they've chained the country from one end to the other to where there isn't any kind of a business that an independent man can go in today and make any living. Therefore, there isn't any kind of a business that an independent man can make any money to buy an automobile with.

And they are finally, gradually, steadily[8] eliminating everybody from the fields in which there is a living to be made, and still they have got little enough sense to think they ought to be able to get more business out of it anyway. If you reduce a man to the point where he is starving to death and bleeding and dying, how do you expect that man to get hold of any money to spend with you? It is not possible. Then, ladies and gentlemen, how do you expect people to live when the wherewith[al] cannot be had by the people?

---

7. Long is referring to *Home Building & Loan Association v. Blaisdell*, decided by the U.S. Supreme Court on January 8, 1934.

8. The recorded portion of Long's speech ends here. The next word in the written text is "eliminated"; we have changed it to "eliminating" since that is likely what Long would have said had the recording continued.

In the beginning, I quoted from the Scriptures. I hope you will understand that I am not quoting Scripture to you to convince you of my goodness personally, because that is a thing between me and my Maker. That is something as to how I stand with my Maker and as to how you stand with your Maker. That is not concerned with this issue except and unless there are those of you who would be so good as to pray for the souls of some of us. But the Lord gave his law, and in the Book of James they said so—that the rich should weep and howl for the miseries that had come upon them.[9] And therefore it was written that when the rich hold goods they could not use and could not consume, you will inflict punishment on them, and nothing but days of woe ahead of them.

Then we have heard of the great Greek philosopher Socrates, and the greater Greek philosopher Plato, and we have read the dialogue between Plato and Socrates in which one said that great riches brought on great poverty and would be destructive of a country.[10]

Read what they said. Read what Plato said: that you must not let any one man be too poor and you must not let any one man be too rich, that the same mill that grinds out the extra rich is the mill that will grind out the extra poor, because in order that the extra rich can become so affluent, they must necessarily take more of what ordinarily would belong to the average man. It is a very simple process of mathematics that you do not have to study and that no one is going to discuss with you.

So that was the view of Socrates and Plato. That was the view of the English statesmen. That was the view of American statesmen. That was the view of American statesmen like Daniel Webster,[11] Thomas Jefferson, Abraham Lincoln,[12] William Jennings Bryan, and Theodore Roosevelt,[13] and even as late as

Herbert Hoover and Franklin D. Roosevelt.[14] Both of these men, Mr. Hoover and Mr. Roosevelt, came out and said there had to be a decentralization of wealth, but neither one of them did anything about it. But nevertheless they recognized the principle.

The fact that neither one of them ever did anything about it is their own problem that I am not undertaking to criticize. But had Mr. Hoover carried out what he says ought to be done, he would be retiring from the President's office, very probably, three years from now instead of one year ago. And had Mr. Roosevelt proceeded along the lines that he stated were necessary for the decentralization of wealth, he would have gone, my friends, a long way already, and within a few months he would have probably reached a solution of all of the problems that afflict this country today.

But I wish to warn you now that nothing that has been done up to this date has taken one dime away from these big fortune holders. They own just as much as they did, and probably a little bit more. They hold just as many of the debts of the common people as they ever held, and probably a little bit more. And unless we, my friends, are going to give the people of this country a fair shake of the dice, by which they will all get something out of the funds of this land, there is not a chance on the topside of this God's eternal earth by which we can rescue this country and rescue the people of this country.

It is necessary to save the government of the country, but is much more necessary to save the people of America. We love this country. We love this government. It is a religion, I say. It is a kind of religion people have read of when women, in the name of religion, would take their infant babes and throw them into the burning flame, where they would be instantly devoured by the all-consuming fire, in days gone by. And there probably are some people of the world even today who, in the name of religion, throw their own babes to destruction.

But in the name of our good government, people today are seeing their own children hungry, tired,

---

9. From James 5:1.

10. Likely a reference to Plato's *Laws*, book 5, section 744.

11. U.S. Senator from Massachusetts and twice Secretary of State (1782–1852).

12. Jefferson was President from 1801 to 1809, Lincoln from 1861 to 1865.

13. Bryan was the Democratic nominee for President in 1896, 1900, and 1908; Roosevelt served as President from 1901 to 1909.

14. Herbert Hoover, President of the United States, 1929–1933; Franklin D. Roosevelt, who defeated Hoover in the 1932 presidential election.

half-naked, lifting their tear-dimmed eyes into the sad faces of their fathers and mothers who cannot give them food and clothing they both needed and which is necessary to sustain them. And that goes on day after day and night after night, when day gets into darkness and blackness, knowing those children would arise in the morning without being fed and probably go to bed at night without being fed.

Yet in the name of our government, and all alone, those people undertake and strive as hard as they can to keep a good government alive—and how long they can stand that, no one knows. If I were in their place tonight, the place where millions are, I hope that I would have what I might say—I cannot give you the word to express the kind of fortitude they have. That is the word: I hope that I might have the fortitude to praise and honor my government that had allowed me here in this land, where there is too much to eat and too much to wear, to starve in order that a handful of men can have so much more than they can ever eat or they can ever wear.

Now, we have organized a society, and we call it Share Our Wealth Society, a society with the motto "Every Man a King." Every man a king, so there would be no such thing as a man or woman who did not have the necessities of life, who would[15] be dependent upon the whims and caprices and ipse dixit[16] of the financial martyrs for a living.

What do we propose by this society? We propose to limit the wealth of big men in the country. There is an average of $15,000 in wealth to every family in America. That is right here today. We do not propose to divide it up equally. We do not propose a division of wealth, but we propose to limit the poverty that we will allow to be inflicted upon any man's family.

We will not say we are going to try to guarantee any equality, or $15,000 to families. No. But we do say that one-third of the average is low enough for any one family to hold, that there should be a guarantee of a family wealth of around $5,000—enough for a home, an automobile, a radio, and the ordinary conveniences, and the opportunity to educate their children; a fair share of the income of this land thereafter to that family so there will be no such thing as merely the select to have those things and so there will be no such thing as a family living in poverty and distress.

We have to limit fortunes. Our present plan is that we will allow no one man to own more than $50 million. We think that with that limit, we will be able to carry out the balance of the program. It may be necessary that we limit it to less than $50 million. It may be necessary, in working out of the plans, that no man's fortune would be more than $10 million or $15 million. But be that as it may, it will still be more than any one man, or any one man and his children and their children, will be able to spend in their lifetimes, and it is not necessary or reasonable to have wealth piled up beyond that point where we cannot prevent poverty among the masses.

Another thing we propose is [an] old-age pension of thirty dollars a month for everyone that is sixty years old. Now, we do not give this pension to a man making $1,000 a year, and we do not give it to him if he has $10,000 in property, but outside of that we do.

We will limit hours of work. There is not any necessity of having overproduction. I think all you have got to do, ladies and gentlemen, is just limit the hours of work to such an extent as people will work only so long as is necessary to produce enough for all of the people to have what they need.

Why, ladies and gentlemen, let us say that all of these labor-saving devices reduce hours down to where you do not have to work but four hours a day. That is enough for these people, and then praise be the name of the Lord if it gets that good. Let it be good and not a curse, and then we will have five hours a day and five days a week—or even less than that—and we might give a man a whole month off during a year, or give him two months. And we might do what other countries have seen fit to do, and what I did in Louisiana, by having schools by which adults could go back and learn the things that have been discovered since they went to school.

We will not have any trouble taking care of the agricultural situation. All you have to do is balance your production with your consumption. You simply

---

15. When delivering the speech, Long mistakenly inserted "not" here.

16. An unsupported assertion or dictum, usually from a person of standing.

have to abandon a particular crop that you have too much of, and all you have to do is store the surplus for the next year, and the government will take it over. When you have good crops in the area in which the crops that have been planted are sufficient for another year, put in your public works in the particular year when you do not need to raise any more, and by that means you get everybody employed. When the government has enough of any particular crop to take care of all of the people, that will be all that is necessary.

And in order to do all of this, our taxation is going to be to take the billion-dollar fortunes and strip them down to frying size, not to exceed $50 million. And if it is necessary to come to $10 million, we will come to $10 million. We have worked the proposition out to guarantee a limit upon property—and no man will own less than one-third the average—and guarantee a reduction of fortunes and a reduction of hours to spread wealth throughout this country.

We would care for the old people above sixty and take them away from this thriving industry and give them a chance to enjoy the necessities and live in ease, and thereby lift from the market the labor which would probably create a surplus of commodities.

Those are the things we propose to do. Every man a king. Every man to eat when there is something to eat. All to wear something when there is something to wear. That makes us all a sovereign.

You cannot solve these things through these various and sundry alphabetical codes. You can have the NRA and PWA and CWA and the UUG and GIN[17] and any other kind of dadgummed lettered code. You can wait until doomsday and see twenty-five more alphabets, but that is not going to solve this proposition. Why hide? Why quibble? You know what the trouble is. The man that says he does not know what the trouble is is just hiding his face to keep from seeing the sunlight.

God told you what the trouble was. The philosophers told you what the trouble was. And when you have a country where one man owns more than 100,000 people or a million people, and when you have a country where there are four men, as in America, that have got more control over things than all the 120 million people together, you know what the trouble is.

We had these great incomes in this country, but the farmer who plowed from sunup to sundown, who labored here from sunup to sundown for six days a week, wound up at the end of the time with practically nothing.

And we ought to take care of the veterans of the wars in this program. That is a small matter. Suppose it does cost a billion dollars a year—that means that the money will be scattered throughout this country. We ought to pay them a bonus. We can do it. We ought to take care of every single one of the sick and disabled veterans. I do not care whether a man got sick on the battlefield or did not. Every man that wore the uniform of this country is entitled to be taken care of, and there is money enough to do it.

And we need to spread the wealth of the country, which you did not do in what you call the NRA. If the NRA has done any good, I can put it all in my eye without having it hurt. All I can see that the NRA has done is to put the little man out of business—the little merchant in his store, the little Dago that is running a fruit stand, or the Greek shoe-shining stand, who has to take hold of a code of 275 pages and study it with a spirit level and compass and looking glass. He has to hire a Philadelphia lawyer to tell him what is in the code. And by the time he learns what the code is, he is in jail or out of business—and they have got a chain code system that has already put him out of business. The NRA is not worth anything, and I said so when they put it through.

Now, my friends, we have got to hit the root with the axe. Centralized power in the hands of a few, with centralized credit in the hands of a few, is the trouble.

Get together in your community tonight or tomorrow and organize one of our Share Our Wealth Societies. If you do not understand it, write me and let me send you the platform. Let me give you the proof of it.

This is Huey P. Long talking: United States Senator, Washington, D.C. Write me and let me send you the data on this proposition. Enroll with us. Let

---

17. National Recovery Administration (NRA), Public Works Administration (PWA), Civil Works Administration (CWA). Long's other acronyms are fanciful.

us make known to the people what we are going to do. I will send you a button, if I have got enough of them left. We have got a little button that some of our friends designed, with our message around the rim of the button and in the center "Every Man a King." Many thousands of them are meeting through the United States, and every day we are getting hundreds and hundreds of letters. Share Our Wealth Societies are now being organized, and people have it within their power to relieve themselves from this terrible situation.

Look at what the Mayo brothers announced this week,[18] these greatest scientists of all the world today, who are entitled to have more money than all the Morgans and the Rockefellers[19] or anyone else, and yet the Mayos turn back their big fortunes to be used for treating the sick and said they did not want to lay up fortunes in this earth[20] but wanted to turn them back where they would do some good. But the other big capitalists are not willing to do that, are not willing to do what these men, ten times more worthy, have already done, and it is going to take a law to require them to do it.

Organize your Share Our Wealth Society and get your people to meet with you and make known

18. On February 16 Charles H. Mayo and William J. Mayo announced that they were giving the University of Minnesota $500,000 for the advancement of medical research.

19. Financier J. P. Morgan (1837–1913); industrialist John D. Rockefeller (1839–1937).

20. An allusion to Matthew 6:19–20.

your wishes to your Senators and Representative in Congress.

Now, my friends, I am going to stop. I thank you for this opportunity to talk to you. I am having to talk under the auspices and by the grace and permission of the National Broadcasting System tonight, and they are letting me talk free. If I had the money—and I wish I had the money—I would like to talk to you more often on this line. But I have not got it, and I cannot expect these people to give it to me free except on some rare instance.

But, my friends, I hope to have the opportunity to talk with you, and I am writing to you, and I hope that you will get up and help in the work because the resolutions and bills are before Congress, and we hope to have your help in getting together and organizing your Share Our Wealth Society.

Now that I have but a minute left, I want to say that I suppose my family is listening in on the radio in New Orleans, and I will say to my wife and three children that I am entirely well and hope to be home before many more days. And I hope they have listened to my speech tonight, and I wish them and all of their neighbors and friends everything good that may be had.

I thank you, my friends, for your kind attention, and I hope you will enroll with us, take care of your own work in the work of this government, and share or help in our Share Our Wealth Society.

I thank you.

Huey P. Long

Share Our Wealth

NEW YORK, NEW YORK
MARCH 7, 1935

As THE NEW Deal entered its second year in 1935 without substantial signs of progress against the Great Depression, Huey Long's attacks on the Roosevelt administration grew sharper and more frequent. On March 4, Hugh S. Johnson, former head of the National Recovery Administration and no stranger to political invective, defended the President with a scathing diatribe against Long that was carried on national radio. At a banquet in New York City, Johnson called Long "the great Louisiana demagogue" whose appeals to people on the "emotional fringe" of society were leading the nation to "chaos and destruction." "You can snort at Huey Long," he warned, "but this country was never under a greater menace."

Long demanded time from NBC to defend himself. He was granted forty-five minutes, rather than the thirty minutes he received for his other broadcasts. Addressing an estimated twenty-five million listeners, the largest audience of his career, he astutely chose not to respond to Johnson in kind. He said it would do the country no good for him to "call my opponents more bitter names than they call me," and he devoted almost the whole speech to explaining his Share Our Wealth plan. Speaking as a man of reason and moderation, he calmly laid out his plan and answered objections to it.

It was a masterful performance and it sent Long's political stock soaring. Roosevelt told his advisors that he might have to "steal Long's thunder" by taking over some of his proposals. During the summer of 1935, as Long was finalizing plans for a run at the White House, a secret poll commissioned by the Democratic leadership showed he would garner from three million to four million votes as a third-party candidate—enough to swing a close election to the Republicans. Never one to settle for being a spoiler, however, Long had his eye on bigger game. If the Republicans won in 1936, he calculated, they would make a worse mess of things than Roosevelt had, leaving the door open for Long to capture the White House in 1940. It was a long shot at best, but as FDR observed, "these are not normal times; people are jumpy and very ready to run after strange gods." There is no way to know how things would have turned out. On September 7, 1935, Long was shot as he walked through the Louisiana Capitol by Carl Austin Weiss, a young Baton Rouge physician. He died three days later.

Originally titled "Our Blundering National Government and Its Spokesman General Hugh Johnson," Long's speech of March 7, 1935, was substantially revised for publication and entered in the *Congressional Record*. The version printed below is taken from a recording of the speech and, to the best of our knowledge, marks the first time that a fully accurate transcript has been made available to readers.

◇◇◇◇◇◇◇◇◇◇◇◇◇◇◇◇◇◇◇◇◇◇◇◇◇◇◇◇◇◇◇◇◇◇◇◇◇◇◇

Ladies and Gentlemen: It has been publicly announced that the White House orders of the Roosevelt administration have declared a war. The late and lamented, the pampered ex–crown prince, General Hugh S. Johnson, one of those satellites loaned by Wall Street to run the government, and who, at the end of his control over and dismissal from the ill-fated NRA,[1] and who pronounced it "as dead as a dodo," this Mr. Johnson was apparently selected to make the lead-off speech in this White House charge begun on last Monday night. The Johnson speech was followed by more fuss and fury on behalf of the administration by spellbinders and spielers[2] in and out of Congress.

In a faraway island, when a queen dies, her first favorite is done the honor to be buried alive with her. The funeral procession of the NRA—another one of these New Deal schisms and isms—is about ready to take place. It is said that General Johnson's speech of Monday night to attack me was delivered on the eve of announcing the publication of his obituary in the *Red Book* magazine. Seems, then, that soon this erstwhile prince of the deranged alphabet makes ready to appear at the funeral of NRA like unto the colored lady in Mississippi who at such a funeral asserted, "I is de wife of dese remains."

I shall undertake to cover my main subject and make answer to these gentlemen in the course of this speech. It will serve no useful purpose to our distressed people for me to call my opponents more bitter names than they can call me. Even were I able,

I have not the time to present my side of the argument and match them in billingsgate[3] or profanity.

What is the trouble with this administration of Mr. Roosevelt, and of Mr. Johnson, Mr. Farley, Mr. Astor,[4] and all their spoilers and spellbinders? They think that Huey Long is the cause of all their worry. They go gunning for me. But am I the cause of their misery? Well, they're like old Davy Crockett,[5] who went out to hunt a possum. He saw in the gleam of the moonlight that a possum in the top of the tree was going from limb to limb. So he shot, but he missed. He looked again and he saw the possum. He fired a second time and missed again. Soon he discovered that it was not a possum that he saw at all in the top of that tree. It was a louse in his own eyebrow.

I do not make this illustration to do discredit to any of these distinguished gentlemen. I make it to show how often some of us imagine that we see great trouble being done to us by someone at a distance, when in reality all it may be is a fault in our own makeup. And so is this the case of Mr. Roosevelt, of Mr. Farley, of Mr. Johnson, and of others undertaking to derange the situation today. The trouble with the Roosevelt administration is that when their schemes and isms have failed—these things I told them not to do and voted not to do—that they think it will help them to light out on those of us who warned them in the beginning that the tangled messes and experiments would not work.

---

1. National Recovery Administration. Controversial from its passage in 1933, the NRA was trimmed back by a Supreme Court ruling in January 1935 and declared unconstitutional in May 1935.

2. Colloquialism for people who talk fluently and in an exaggerated vein.

3. Foul, abusive language.

4. James Farley, U.S. Postmaster General; Vincent Astor, distant relative and confidante of President Roosevelt.

5. Legendary Tennessee backwoodsman who became a U.S. Congressman and died at the battle of the Alamo in 1836.

The Roosevelt administration has had its way for two years. They have been allowed to set up or knock down anything and everybody. There was one difference between Roosevelt and Hoover.[6] Hoover could not get the Congress to carry out the schemes he wanted to try because we managed to lick him on a roll call in the United States Senate time after time when he had both the Democratic leaders and the Republican leaders tryin' to put him over. But [it is] different with Mr. Roosevelt. He got his plans through Congress, but on cold analysis they were found to be the same things Hoover tried to pass and failed the year before.

The kitchen cabinet[7] that sat in to advise Hoover was not different from the kitchen cabinet which advises Roosevelt. Many of the persons are the same. Many more of those in Roosevelt's kitchen cabinet are of the same men or set of men who furnished the employees to sit in the kitchen cabinet to advise Mr. Hoover. Maybe you see a little change in the men waiting on the tables in the dining room, but back in the kitchen the same set of old cooks are back there fixing up the vittles and the grub for us that cooked up that mess under Hoover. There's never been even a change in the seasoning.

Why, do you think this Roosevelt plan for plowing up cotton, corn, and wheat, and for pouring milk in the river, and for destroying and burying the hogs and the cattle by the millions,[8] all while the people starve to death and go naked—do you think these plans were the original ideas of this Roosevelt administration? If you do, you're wrong. The whole idea of that kind of thing first came from Hoover's administration. Don't you remember when Mr. Hoover proposed to plow up every fourth row of cotton? We laughed him into scorn. And so we beat Mr. Hoover on his plan. But when Mr. Roosevelt started on his plan, it was not to plow up every fourth row of cotton;

it was to plow up every third row of cotton. He went Mr. Hoover one-twelfth better.

So it has been that while millions have starved and gone naked and while babies have cried and died wanting milk, so it has been that while people have begged for meat and bread to eat, Mr. Roosevelt's administration has sailed merrily along, plowing under and destroying the things to eat and wear, with tear-dimmed eyes and hungry souls made to chant for this New Deal so that even their starvation dole is not taken away from them, and meanwhile the food and clothes craved by humanity for their bodies and souls go to destruction and ruin. What do you call it? Is it government? Maybe so. It looks more like the St. Vitus dance[9] to me.

Now, since they have sallied forth with General Johnson to start this holy war on me, let us take a look at this NRA that they opened up around here about two years ago. They had parades and fascist signs just like Hitler and Mussolini.[10] They started the dictatorship here to regiment business and labor much more than anyone did in Germany or Italy. The only difference was in the sign. Hitler's[11] sign of the fascist was a black shirt. Germany's sign of the fascist was a swastika. So in America they sidetracked the Stars and Stripes, and the sign of the Blue Eagle was used instead for the NRA.

And they proceeded with the NRA. Everything from a peanut stand to a power house had to have a separate book of rules and laws to regulate what they did. If a peanut stand started to parch a sack of goobers[12] for sale, they had to be careful to go through the rule book. One slip of the man and he went to jail. A little fella who pressed a pair of pants went to jail because he charged five cents less than the price that they set up in the rule book. So they wrote their NRA rule book, codes, laws, and so forth. They got up over

---

6. Herbert Hoover, President of the United States, 1929–1933.

7. Unofficial advisors to the President.

8. Under the Agricultural Adjustment Act of 1933, farmers were paid to destroy some of their crops and animals in an effort to increase farm income by reducing the supply of agricultural products.

9. Colloquialism for involuntary movements of the body and limbs caused by Sydenham's chorea, an acute disturbance of the central nervous system.

10. Benito Mussolini, fascist leader of Italy and ally of German dictator Adolf Hitler.

11. Long meant to say "Italy's."

12. Southern idiom for peanut.

900 of 'em. One would be as thick as an unabridged dictionary and as confusing as a study of the stars. It would take forty lawyers to tell a shoe-shine merchant how to operate and be certain he didn't go to jail.

Some people came to me for advice, as a lawyer, on how to run the business. I took several days and couldn't understand it myself. The only thing I could tell them was that it couldn't be much worse in jail than it was out of jail with that kind of a thing goin' on in the country, and so to go on and do the best they could.

The whole thing of Mr. Roosevelt, as run under General Johnson, became such a national scandal that Roosevelt had to let Johnson slide out as the scapegoat. And I'm told that the day the General had to go—when they'd waited just as long as they could wait on him—that he wanted to issue a blistering statement against Mr. Roosevelt, but they finally saddled him off because they didn't know but what Wall Street might want to loan him to some other President in the future. So he left out.

It was under this NRA and the other funny alphabetical combinations which followed it that we ran the whole country into a mare's nest.[13] The Farleys and the Johnsons combed the land with agents, inspectors, supervisors, detectives, secretaries, assistants, and so forth, all of 'em armed with the power to arrest anybody and send them all to jail if they found them not living up to some one of these rules in these 900 catalogs they had out. One man, whose case reached the Supreme Court of the United States, I understand he pled guilty since he didn't know what it was all about. And when they got up to the United States Supreme Court, he was turned loose because they couldn't even find the rule book that he was supposed to have violated somethin' in it.

And now it is with the PWAs, the GWAs, the NRAs, the AAAs, the JUGs, and the GINs,[14] and every other flimsy combination that the country finds

its affairs and business tangled to where no one can recognize it. More men are now out of work than ever. The debt of the United States has gone up ten billion more dollars. There is starvation, there is homelessness, there is misery on every hand and corner, but, mind you, in the meantime Mr. Roosevelt has had his way. He's one man that can't blame any of his troubles on Huey Long. He's had his way. Back down in my part of the country if any man has the measles, he blames that on me. But there's one man that can't blame anything on anybody but himself, and that's Mr. Franklin De-La-No Roosevelt.

And now, on top of that, they order war on me because nearly four years ago I told Hoover's crowd it wouldn't do and because three years ago I told Roosevelt and his crowd it wouldn't do. In other words, they are in a rage at Huey Long because I've had to say, "I told you so."

I was not overstating the conditions now prevailing in this country. In the own words of these gentlemen, they have confessed all that I now say or ever have said. Mr. Roosevelt and Mrs. Roosevelt[15] too have lately bewailed the fact that food, clothes, and shelter have not been provided for the people. Even this General Hugh S. Johnson has said in his speech of this last Monday night that there are 80,000 babies in America who are badly hurt or wrecked by this depression. He of course includes us all in that classification of babies. Mr. Harry Hopkins, who runs the relief work,[16] says the dole roll has risen now to 22,375,000 people—the highest it has ever been.

And now what is there for the Roosevelt crowd to do but to admit the facts and admit further that they are now on their third year, making matters worse instead of better. No one is to blame except them for what is goin' on when they've had their way and they couldn't change the thing in two years. It's now bogged down worse than ever. And if they haven't been able to do any good this way they've been going, how can anyone expect any good of them in the next two years of Congress? God save us

---

13. In Long's time, a "mare's nest" could refer either to a jumbled disorder of things or a supposed discovery that turns out to be a hoax.

14. Public Works Administration (PWA), National Recovery Administration (NRA), Agricultural Adjustment Administration (AAA). Long's other acronyms appear to be fanciful.

15. First Lady Eleanor Roosevelt.

16. Hopkins headed the Federal Emergency Relief Association and the Works Progress Administration.

from two more years of the disaster that we've had under that gang.

Now, my friends, when this condition of distress and sufferin' among so many millions of our people began to develop in the Hoover administration, we knew then what was the trouble and what we would have to do to correct it. I was one of the first men to say publicly—I was the first man to say publicly—but Mr. Roosevelt followed in my tracks a few months later and said the same thing. We said that all of our trouble and woe was due to the fact that too few of our people owned too much of our wealth. We said that in our land, with too much to eat, and too much to wear, and too many houses to live in, too many automobiles to be sold, that the only trouble was that the people suffered in the land of abundance because too few controlled the money and the wealth and too many people did not have money with which to buy the things they needed for life and comfort.

So I said to the people of the United States in my speeches which I delivered in the United States Senate and over the radio in the early part of 1932 that the only way by which we could restore our people to reasonable life and comfort was to limit the size of the big men's fortune and guarantee some minimum to the fortune and comfort of the little man's family. I said then, as I have said since, that it was inhuman to have food rottin,' cotton and wool goin' to waste, houses empty, and at the same time to have millions of our people starving, naked, and homeless because they could not buy the things which other men had and for which these other men had no use.

So we convinced Mr. Franklin Delano Roosevelt that it was necessary that he announce and promise to the American people that in the event he were elected President of the United States, he would pull down the size of the big man's fortune and guarantee something to every family—enough to do away with all poverty and to give employment to those who were able to work and education to the children born into the world.

Mr. Roosevelt made those promises. He made them before he was nominated in the Chicago convention. He made them again before he was elected in November. And he went so far as to remake those

promises a day or two after he was inaugurated President of the United States, and I was one authorized to say so. And I thought for a day or two after he took the oath as President that maybe he was going through with his promises. But no heart was ever so saddened, no person's ambition was ever so blighted, as was mine when I came to the realization that the President of the United States was not going to undertake what he had said he would do, and what I knew to be necessary, if the people of America were ever [to be] saved from calamity and misery.

So now, my friends, I come to the point where I must in a few sentences describe to you just what was the cause of our trouble which became so serious in 1929 and which has been worse ever since.

The wealth in the United States was three times as much in 1910 as it was in 1890, and yet the masses of our people owned less in 1910 than they did in 1890. In the year 1916, the condition had become so bad that a committee provided for by the Congress of the United States reported that 2 percent of the people in the United States owned 60 percent of the wealth in the country and that 65 percent of the people owned less than 5 percent of the wealth. This report showed, however, that there was a middle class—some 33 percent of the people—who owned 35 percent of the wealth. This report went on to say that the trouble with the American people at that time was that too much of the wealth was in the hands of too few of the people, and recommended that something be done to correct the evil condition then existing.[17]

It was at about the same time in 1916 that many of our leading publications in America began to deplore the fact that so few people owned so much and that so many people owned so little. Among those commenting upon that deplorable situation of that day and time was the *Saturday Evening Post*, which, in an issue of September 23rd, 1916, said, quoting from the *Saturday Evening Post*, quote: "Along one statistical line you can figure out a nation bustling with wealth; along another statistical line a bloated plutocracy." They said that of America: "A bloated plutocracy comprising 1 percent of the population lording it

17. Long is referring to the *Final Report of the Commission on Industrial Relations*, published in 1915.

over a starving horde with only a thin margin of merely well-to-do in between." Close quotation from *The Saturday Evening Post*.[18]

And it was, as the *Saturday Evening Post* and the committee appointed by Congress said, it was a deplorable thing back in 1916, when it was found that 2 percent of the people owned twice as much of the wealth of this country as all of the balance of the people put together and that 65 percent of all of our people owned practically nothin'.

But what did we do to correct that condition? Instead of moving to take these big fortunes from the top and spreading them among the suffering people at the bottom, the financial masters of America moved in to take complete charge of the government for fear that our lawmakers might do something along that line. And as a result, fourteen years after the report of 1916, the Federal Trade Commission made a study to see how the wealth of this land was distributed, and did they find it still as bad as it was in 1916? They found it worse. They found that 1 percent of the people owned 59 percent of the wealth,[19] which was almost twice as bad as what was said to be an intolerable condition in 1916, when 2 percent of the people owned 60 percent of the wealth.

And as a result of foreclosures of mortgages and bankruptcies which began to happen during the last years, it is the estimate of the conservative statistician that 75 percent of the people in the United States don't own anything today—that is, not even enough to pay their debts—and that 4 percent of the people, or maybe less than 4 percent of the people, own from 85 to 90 percent of all the wealth in the United States.

Remember, in 1916 there was a middle class—33 percent of the people—who owned 35 percent of the wealth. That middle class is practically gone today. It no longer exists. They have dropped into the ranks of the poor. The thriving man of independent business standing is fast fading. The corner grocery store is becoming a thing of the past. Concentrated chain merchandise stores and chain banking systems have laid waste to all middlemen opportunity. That thin margin of merely well-to-do in between, which the *Saturday Evening Post* mentioned on September 23rd, 1916, is no longer thin. No, it's dwindled to no margin at all at this late date. Those suffering on the bottom and the few lords of finance on the top are all that's left. There's no middle class. Lords at the top, masses at the bottom.

It became apparent that the billionaires and multimillionaires began to squeeze out the common ordinary millionaires. In other words, the whales began to eat up the goggle-eye[20] after they had taken all the minnows into account, closing in and takin' their properties and wrecking their businesses. And so we arrived, and we're still there, at the place that in abundant America where we have everything for which a human heart can pray, the hundreds of millions—or, as General Johnson says, the 80 million—of our people are crying in misery for want of the things which they need for life, notwithstanding the fact that the country has had and can have more than the entire human race can consume.

The 125 million people of America have seated themselves at the barbecue table to eat the products which have been given to them by their Lord and Creator. There is provided by the Almighty what it takes for all of them to eat—yea, more. There has been provided for the people of America who have been called to this barbecue table more than is needed for all to eat. But the financial masters of America have taken off of the barbecue table 90 percent of the food placed thereon by the Lord even before the feast began, and there is left on that table for 125 million people about what is needed for 10 million people. In other words, there is not enough to feed one out of twelve.

What has become of the balance of those vittles placed on the table by the Lord for the use of us all? They're in the hands of the Morgans, the Rockefellers, the Mellons, the Baruchs, the Bakers, the Astors, and

---

18. Long is quoting from an article titled "Are We Rich or Poor?"

19. Long is referring to figures in *National Wealth and Income: A Report by the Federal Trade Commission* (1926). He misstates the date of the report.

20. Colloquialism for freshwater fish with prominent eyes, most often perch or bass.

the Vanderbilts[21]—600 families at the most either possessing or controlling the entire 90 percent of all that is in America. These big men cannot eat all the food, they cannot wear all the clothes, so they destroy it. They have it rotted, they plow it up, they pour it in the rivers. They bring destruction through the acts of mankind to let humanity suffer, to let humanity go naked, to let humanity go homeless, so that nothing may occur that will do harm to their vanity and to their greed. Like the dog in the manger, they command a wagonload of hay, which the dog would not allow the cow to eat, though he could not eat it himself.

So now, ladies and gentlemen, I introduce myself again for fear that the some who have just tuned in do not know who it is that is talking. This is Huey P. Long, United States Senator from Louisiana, talking over radio station, the NBC hookup from Washington, D.C.

We come to that plan of mine now for which I have been so recently and roundly condemned and denounced by the Roosevelt administration and by such men as Mr. Farley and Mr. Robinson[22] and General Hugh S. Johnson and other spielers and speakers and spoilers. It is for the redistribution of wealth and for guaranteeing comforts and conveniences to all humanity out of this abundance in our country.

I hope none would be horror stricken when they hear me say that we must limit the size of the big men's fortunes in order to guarantee a minimum of fortune, life, and comfort to the little man. But if you are horror stricken at my making mention of that fact, think first that such is the declaration on which Mr. Roosevelt rode into the nomination and election as President of the United States.

While my urgings are declared by some to be the ravings of a madman, and by such men as General

Johnson as insincere bait of a pied piper, if you will listen to me, you will find that it is restating the law handed down by God to man. You will find that it was the exact provision of the contract and law of the Pilgrim Fathers who landed at Plymouth in 1620. Now, just for the benefit of some of these gentlemen, I'm gonna read to you from the contract of those Pilgrim Fathers who landed at Plymouth in 1620. I'm reading [to] you from the contract of the Pilgrim Fathers, paragraph five: "That at the end of the seven years, the capital and profits—that is, the houses, lands, goods, and chattels—be equally divided betwixt the adventurers and planters; which done, every man shall be free from other of them of any debt or detriment concerning this adventure." [23]

In other words, these birds who are undertaking to tell you of the bad things I have done and am advocating, they have failed to note that I not only have the Bible back of me, but that this nation was founded by the Pilgrim Father[s] not to do just what I said, but to go and do all the balance—divide up equally every seven years and cancel out all debts. And they had the authority of the Bible for doing that. On the other hand, mine does not go near so far, but it will save this country as the Pilgrims intended it should be saved.

You will find that what I am advocating is the cornerstone on which nearly every religion since the beginning of man has been founded. You will find that it was urged by Lord Bacon, by Milton, and by Shakespeare in England;[24] by Socrates, Plato, Theognis,[25] and the other wisest of the philosophers of ancient Greece; by Pope Pius XI in the Vatican;[26] by the world's greatest inventor, Marconi in Italy;[27] by

---

21. Long is referring to the families of J. P. Morgan (1837–1913), John D. Rockefeller (1839–1937), Andrew W. Mellon (1855–1937), Bernard Baruch (1870–1965), George F. Baker (1840–1931), John Jacob Astor (1763–1848), and Cornelius Vanderbilt (1794–1877).

22. Joseph T. Robinson, U.S. Senator from Arkansas, with whom Long often sparred.

23. From William Bradford, *Of Plymouth Plantation* (1856).

24. Francis Bacon (1561–1626); John Milton (1608–1674); William Shakespeare (1564–1616),

25. Greek poet of the 6th century BCE. Long may have meant Diogenes, who reputedly walked the streets of ancient Athens in daylight with a lamp looking for an honest man.

26. Pius XI served as Pope from 1922 to 1939.

27. Guglielmo Marconi, inventor of the radio and corecipient of the 1909 Nobel Prize in Physics.

Daniel Webster,[28] Ralph Waldo Emerson,[29] Abraham Lincoln, Andrew Jackson,[30] William Jennings Bryan, and Theodore Roosevelt[31] in the United States, as well as by nearly all of the thousands of great men whose names are mentioned in history.

And the only great man who's ever deigned forth to dispute these things from the Bible on down is this marvelous General Hugh S. Johnson, who labels himself a soldier and a lawyer. He is a great soldier, though he never smelt powder nor heard a cap snap, and is a great lawyer, though he never tried a lawsuit. And I will not be willing to transact business on the lines that everybody else must be forgotten whom I follow and that I should fall into such footsteps as was arranged for this combination of alphabetical propositions.

The principle was not only—that is, the principle that I'm advocating that I'll give you in detail in a minute—that principle was not only the mainspring of the Roosevelt nomination and election, but in the closing speech of Herbert Hoover at Madison Square Garden in November 1932, even Hoover said, quote: "My conception of America is a land where men and women may walk in ordered liberty, where they may enjoy the advantages of wealth not concentrated in the hands of the few but diffused through the lives of all."[32] End quote. So there you have it, ladies and gentlemen. Both Hoover and Roosevelt swallowed the Huey Long doctrine and never made one single complaint before the election occurred on November 8th, 1932.

So now I come to give you again that plan, taken from these leaders of all times and from the Bible, for the sponsoring of which I am labeled America's menace and madman and pied piper and demagogue.

So I give you that plan of our Share Our Wealth Society.

I propose first that every big fortune would be cut down immediately. We'll cut that down by a capital levy tax to where no one will own more than a few millions of dollars—as a matter of fact, to where no one can very long own a fortune in excess of about three to four millions of dollars. Just between me and you, I think that's too much, but we figure that we can allow that size of a fortune and give prosperity to all the people even though it is done. I propose that the surplus of all the big fortunes, above the few millions to any one person at the most, shall go into the United States ownership.

Now, how would we get all these surplus fortunes into the United States Treasury, Mr. Johnson wants to know. Well now, if he'll listen, he won't have any trouble finding out. It's not hard to do. We would not do it by making everyone sell what he owned. No, we would send everyone a questionnaire just like they did during the war when they was takin' us over there to make the world safe for democracy so that they might come back here and make America safe for autocracy.[33] On that questionnaire the man to whom it was sent would list the properties he owns—the lands, the houses, stocks and bonds, factories, and patents. Every man would place his appraisal on his property, which the government would review and maybe change. On that appraisal the big fortune holder would say out of what property he would retain the few millions allowed to him, the balance to go to the United States.

Let's say that Mr. Henry Ford should show that he owned all the stock of the Ford Motor Company, say, and that's worth $2 billion, we'll say. He would claim, say, $4 million of the Ford stock, but one billion nine hundred and ninety-six million dollars would go to the United States. Say the Rockefeller fortune was listed at ten billions of dollars in oil stocks, bank stocks, money, and storehouses. Each Rockefeller could say whether he wanted his limit in either the money, the oil, or bank stocks, but about nine billion

---

28. U.S. Senator from Massachusetts and twice Secretary of State (1782–1852).

29. Transcendentalist philosopher and author (1803–1882).

30. Lincoln was President of the United States from 1861 to 1865; Jackson was President from 1829 to 1837.

31. Bryan was the Democratic nominee for President in 1896, 1900, and 1908; Roosevelt served as President from 1901 to 1909.

32. From Hoover's speech of October 31, 1932.

33. A reference to World War I, which President Wilson defined in his War Message of April 2, 1917, as a war to make the world safe for democracy (pages 73–79).

and eight hundred million would be left, and that would go to the United States government.

And so, in this way, the government of the United States would come into the possession of about two-fifths of its wealth, which on normal values would be worth from 165 billion to 175 billion. Then we would turn to the inventories of the 25 million families of America. All those who showed properties and money clear of debts that were above $5,000 and up to the limit of a few million—we wouldn't touch them. In other words, we wouldn't draw down a fortune that wasn't bigger than a few million, and if a man had over $5,000, then he would have his guaranteed minimum.

But those showing less than $5,000 for the family free of debt would be added to, so that every family would start life again with homestead possessions of at least a home and the comforts needed for a home, including such things as a radio and an automobile. Those things would go to every family as a homestead, not to be sold either for debts or for taxes or even by consent of the owner except [when] the government would allow it, and then only on condition that the court hold it—that is, hold the money that was received for it—to be spent for the purpose of buying another home and the comforts thereof. Such would mean that 165 billion or more taken from big fortunes would have about 100 billion of it used to provide everybody with the comforts of home. The government might have to issue warrants for claim and location, or even currency to be retired from such property as it was claimed, but all that is a detail not impractical to get these homes into the hands of the people.

So America would start again with millionaires, but with no multimillionaires or billionaires. We'd start with some poor, but they wouldn't be so poor that they wouldn't have the comforts of life. The lowest a man could go would not take away his home and the home comforts from him. America, however, would still have about $65 billion balance after providing these homes. Now, what do we do with that? Wait a minute and I'll tell you.

Next we propose, second, that after homes and comforts of homes have been set up for the families of the country, that we will turn our attention to the children and to the youth of the land, providing first for their education and training. We would not have to worry about the problem of child labor, because the very first thing which we would place in front of every child would be not only a comfortable home during his early years but the opportunity for education and training—not only through the grammar school and the high school but through college and to include vocational and professional training for every child. If necessary, that would include the living cost of that child while he attended a college if there wasn't a college close enough for him to live at home and conveniently attend it, and that would be the case with many of those living in rural areas and we'd have to pay their living cost while they went away to college.

We now have an educational system, and in states like Louisiana, which has the best one, schoolbooks are furnished free to every child and transportation is given free by bus to every student. However far he may live from a schoolhouse in Louisiana, they take him in a bus and take him until he graduates from high school. But when it comes to a matter of college education, except in a few cases the right to a college education is determined by the financial ability of the father and mother to pay for the cost of the college education. It don't make any difference how brilliant a boy or a girl may be, that don't give them the right to a college education in America today. The only thing that gives them a right to a college education is having parents with enough money to pay their expenses away from home to go to school.

Now, General Hugh Johnson says I am indeed a very smart demagogue; he says I'm a wise and dangerous menace. Well, wise as he says I am and smart as he says I am—and I oughtn't to be made to deny that—with all that credit given to me, I am one of those who didn't have the opportunity to secure a college education or training. We propose that the right to education and the extent of education will be determined and gauged not so much by the ability of the parents to pay money, but by the mental ability and energy of a child to absorb the learning at a college. This should appeal to General Johnson, who says I am a smart man, since, had I enjoyed the learning and college training which my plan would provide for others, I might not have fallen into the path of the dangerous menace and demagogue that he now finds me to be.

Remember, after providing for everyone to have a home, we have $65 billion to account for that will lie in the hands of the United States. We will use a large part of it immediately to expand particularly the colleges and universities of this country. You wouldn't know the great institutions like Yale, Harvard, and Louisiana State University. Get ready for a surprise. College enrollments would multiply 1,000 percent. We would immediately call in the architects and engineers, the idle professors and scholars of learning. We would send out a hurry call because the problem of providing college education for all of the youth would start a fusillade[34] of employment which might suddenly and immediately make it impossible for us to shorten the hours of labor, even as we contemplate in the balance of our program.

And how happy the youth of this land would be tomorrow morning if they knew instantly that their right to a home and the comforts of a home and to complete college and professional training and education were assured to every one of them. I know how happy they would be because I know how I would have felt had such a message been delivered to my door. I cannot deliver that promise to the youth of this land tonight, but I am doing my part. I'm standing the blows; I'm hearing the charges hurled from the four quarters of the country.

It is the same fight which was made against me in Louisiana when I was undertaking to provide the free schoolbooks, the free buses, the cheap university facilities, and things of that kind to educate the youth of that state. It is the same blare which I heard when I was undertaking to provide for the sick and afflicted in Louisiana, where they are provided for as nowhere else in the whole world. When the youth of this land, however, realizes what is meant and what is contemplated in the Share Our Wealth program—that it means absolute, complete training and education for them regardless of their financial means—then the billingsgate and the profanity of all the Farleys and Johnsons in America can't prevent the light of truth

from hurling itself in understandable letters against the dark canopy of the sky.

Now, when we have landed at the place where homes and comforts are provided for all families and complete education and training for all young men and women has been furnished, the next problem is to have an income to sustain our people thereafter. How shall that be arranged? Well, here's what we propose.

We'll shorten the hours of labor by law so much as may be necessary so that none will be worked too long and there'll be none unemployed. We'll cut the hours of toil to thirty hours a week, and maybe less. We'll cut the working year to eleven months of the year and have a month's vacation, and maybe less than eleven months if it's necessary. But if our great improvement programs show we need more labor than we have, we'll have to lengthen the hours as the conveniences and circumstances require. One year it might be thirty hours, another year it might be twenty-eight, another year it might be thirty-two hours a week. At all events, the hours for production would be gauged to meet the market for consumption. We will need all our machinery for many years because we have much improvement to do; the more use that we make of machinery, the less toil will be required of our people.

Now, a minimum earning would be established for any person with a family to support. It would be such a living [by] which one already owning a home could maintain a family in comfort—of not less than around $2,500 per year to every family.

And now by reason of false statements made, particularly by Mr. Arthur Brisbane[35] and General Hugh S. Johnson, I must make answer to show you that there is more than enough in this country and more than enough raised and made every year to do what I propose.

Mr. Arthur Brisbane says that I am proposing to give every person $15,000 for a home and its comforts, and he says that that would mean that the United States would have to be worth over a trillion dollars to do it. Well, why make that untrue statement, Mr. Arthur

---

34. Long misspoke this word as "fulissade."

35. Nationally known newspaper editor and syndicated columnist.

Brisbane? You know that is not so. I do not propose any home and comfort of $15,000 to each person. It is proposed by our plan a minimum of $5,000 to every family, which would be less than $125 billion, and that is less than one-third of this nation's wealth in normal times, when it is at least $400 billion.

General Johnson says that my proposal is for $5,000 guaranteed earning to each family every year, which he says would cost from four to five hundred millions of dollars per year, which he says is four times more than our whole national income has ever been. Why make such an untruthful statement as that, General Johnson? Must you turn and be a false witness in order to make that kind of a point?

I do not propose $5,000 to each family as an income every year as a guaranteed minimum. I propose a minimum of from $2,000 to $2,500 to each family after they've had their home and the comforts furnished to them. For 25 million families, that minimum income per family would require from $50 million—or 50 billion to $60 billion—per year. In the prosperous days we have had already, nearly double that income has already been made in some years. That would allow plenty of excess for the fortunes and excess incomes of the financially affluent. But with the unheard-of prosperity which we would have if all of our people could buy what they need, our national income would be double.

Now, let's see if I'm tryin' to give too much. Here is a letter from that eminent writer of Wall Street writing in these books and these statistics who says that there would be an income of $10,000 to every family if there were a fair distribution and everybody was allowed to work. Wow! Now, if that's true—and this is a gentleman writing in a Hearst paper and in the *Wall Street Journal*, Mr. Bascom, and his figures are accepted by them all—why are they quarreling when I'm only guaranteeing the minimum of $2,500, just one-fourth as much as they say would be available?[36] Why don't Mr. Brisbane get together with his

other men that he's got working for him—or that, rather, he may be working for?

And now I come to the balance of the plan. We propose, number four, the agricultural production will be cared for in the manner specified in the Bible. We would plow up no crops; we would burn no corn; we'd spill no milk in the river. We would shoot no hogs; we would slaughter no cattle to be rotted. We'd raise all the cotton we needed. If we raised more than we needed, we'd store the surplus in the government warehouses for the next year. And if we got to where we had more than twelve months' supply of any crops, then we wouldn't raise any of that crop the next year. And that'd be the year we'd put our government and state public works in that territory widening roads, providing for floods, extending the power lines into the rural areas. And if we had any time left, some of us who've grown old would go back to school and learn some of the things that we forgot since we've become grown and maybe learn some of the things now that they didn't know anything about when we were young and were able to go to school.

Now, ladies and gentlemen, I'm not going to detail to you more except to say this: that we propose to provide, after we've given to everybody homes and comforts of a home, an old-age pension for those above sixty, who not only would have their homes and the home comforts but a sufficient revenue to maintain them at a reasonable state of decency and respect during the declining days of their lives. We also include in our program that we'll not quibble about the soldier's bonus or the obligations which our government owes to the soldiers of our wars, but that we will discharge that obligation and care for them completely.

Now, my friends, this is our program of the Share Our Wealth Society. This country cannot continue to go as it is at this time. There is such misery as ought to reach the heart of every man, and it's doing more than that—it's reaching up into the very functions of all the life of nearly every man in this country. I have letters before me, and they come to my office by the hundreds and by the thousands, and they describe conditions more pitiful than there have ever been.

Here is a letter from the center of the cotton section, where more cotton is raised than any other place in America. Here is a woman in the cotton country.

---

36. Long may have meant journalist Bascom Timmons, but mention of "Mr. Bascom" was deleted from published versions of the speech, which mentioned only an unnamed "Wall Street writer and statistician."

They won't allow this woman and her children to raise cotton, and now she's begging me to send whatever old clothes that I may be able to spare so that she can cut 'em up and make clothes for other people. They won't allow the woman to raise cotton and she hasn't got money to buy clothes—that's her condition.

Now, I have a letter here from Little Rock, Arkansas. Here's a poor woman tryin' to get something to do. She wants to work herself. Says: "I can't make a living. I wanted to get a job where I could be at home when the boy come from school, and I do want to finish him at school. He is in the eighth-A grade. God would surely bless you if you will help me get a job. I have no money to live on. Sincerely." That's just a letter from a mother.

Here's a letter from a poor nigger down in our country. They're no worse off there than they are anywhere else. This poor nigger says: "Extreme distress and actual hunger suffering by not only myself but my wife and child compel me to make this most urgent appeal to you for some help because I have been out of employment most of the time for the past two or three years. Could get only a little work now and then, and less than four weeks all last year by the CWA.[37] And now I have exhausted all sources of employment or help, I decided I would have to ask you to help us—myself and little family—in this time's extreme hunger and actual distress. I pray you, Mr. Long, do help me now. James Stuart."

I'm not reading you all this letter. This poor colored person—it would appeal to anybody. And I want to say this: He's in Louisiana. I can't help him all that I would like to, but I'll help every one of these white and colored people to some extent in my state. I can't help them much, but I am undertaking to make the fight here that will relieve that poverty.

Here is another letter from a poor woman. She says this: "We do not have shoes and clothing to keep us warm. You go to the ERA[38] office to ask for help, they look at you slant eyed just as good to say, 'What sort of a creature are you and what zoo did you escape from?' The office help are always well dressed and drive good cars, while we are hungry and naked."

And that's what's going on—the plight of America today, ladies and gentlemen. And we're going on and on and on with the St. Vitus dance of the Roosevelt Depression. More people unemployed, twenty-odd million people unemployed; the national debt up to twenty-nine to thirty billions of dollars; the plight becoming worse and worse as time goes on. The only relief that we have in sight is to share our wealth. Won't you write me tonight? Won't you write me tomorrow? Won't you organize a Share Our Wealth Society?

If you want a copy of my speech, write to me. If you want the statistics to prove anything I have said, write to me. Organize a Share Our Wealth Society in your community. Write to me, Huey P. Long, United States Senate, in Washington, D.C. I'll send you the credentials; I'll send you the material.

But get out. Organize your friends. Let's make the fight. Let's make the politicians keep the promises, or vote somebody into office that will keep the promises that in this land of abundance none shall have too much, none shall have too little. That in the land of too much to eat and too much to wear and too many homes to live in and too many automobiles to ride in that we'll see that the blessings of this land, given to us by God and by mankind, shall be reasonably shared by all our people.

I thank you.

---

37. Civil Works Administration.

38. Emergency Relief Administration.

John L. Lewis

✠

Labor and the Nation

WASHINGTON, D.C.
SEPTEMBER 3, 1937

JOHN L. LEWIS WAS the most powerful labor leader in the United States during the mid-1930s. As president of the United Mine Workers, in 1935 he led that organization and nine other unions out of the American Federation of Labor (AFL) to form the Committee for Industrial Organization (CIO). He thereupon began efforts to organize entire industries, starting with the automotive and steel industries. He was so successful that by 1937 membership of the CIO eclipsed that of the AFL.

This success was not without its costs. After negotiating a pact with the United States Steel Corporation in March 1937, the CIO was not able to reach agreement with five other corporations known collectively as "Little Steel." Strikes against these companies in the spring and summer of 1937 met fierce resistance and resulted in the deaths and maiming of numerous strikers. Having supported Franklin D. Roosevelt in the 1936 presidential election, Lewis expected him to weigh in on the side of labor. But Roosevelt, though urging all sides to negotiate in good faith, remained neutral, even going so far as to utter, at one point, "a plague on both your houses."

Against this backdrop, Lewis's speech of September 3, 1937, was broadcast coast to coast on the CBS radio network. To ensure maximum news coverage, it was presented three days before Labor Day, so as to get the jump on other orators who would fill the airwaves on labor's designated national holiday. After hailing the growth and achievements of the CIO, Lewis excoriated the "Little Steel" companies and the public officials he held responsible for the violence against strikers. Finally, he took on Roosevelt himself, issuing a not-so-subtle warning to labor's "so-called friends...who chant their praises of democracy but who lose no chance to drive their knives into labor's defenseless back." In words whose meaning could not be mistaken, he exclaimed: "It ill behooves one who has supped at labor's table and who has been sheltered in labor's house to curse with equal fervor and fine impartiality both labor and its adversaries when they become locked in deadly embrace."

Regarded by posterity as a classic prolabor manifesto, Lewis's speech fared less well in its own time. It was attacked by the AFL, condemned by congressional Democrats, questioned by liberal editorial opinion, and found no succor in Roosevelt's Labor Day comments. Keeping to the line he had adopted

249

throughout the preceding months, FDR lamented the "mutual distrust and bitter recrimination" that had engulfed negotiations between labor and management. Pointedly reinforcing the stance of neutrality that Lewis attacked in his speech, the President reiterated his view that "both sides have made mistakes."

In many ways "Labor and the Nation" represented the zenith of Lewis's influence. He fought with Roosevelt from that moment forward and endorsed Republican candidate Wendell Wilkie in the 1940 presidential election. When Wilkie went down to defeat, Lewis resigned as president of the CIO, though he remained as head of the mine workers until 1960, a diminished but still-formidable public figure, instantly recognizable with his bushy eyebrows, fedora, cane, shiny shoes, and ever-present cigar.

◇◇

Out of the agony and travail of economic America the Committee for Industrial Organization[1] was born. To millions of Americans, exploited without stint by corporate industry and socially debased beyond the understanding of the fortunate, its coming was as welcome as the dawn to the night watcher. To a lesser group of Americans, infinitely more fortunately situated, blessed with larger quantities of the world's goods, and insolent in their assumption of privilege, its coming was heralded as a harbinger of ill, sinister of purpose, of unclean methods and nonvirtuous objectives.

But the Committee for Industrial Organization is here. It is now and henceforth a definite instrumentality destined greatly to influence the lives of our people and the internal course of the republic. This is true only because the purposes and objectives of the Committee for Industrial Organization find economic, social, political, and moral justification in the hearts of the millions who are its members and the millions more who support it. The organization and constant onward sweep of this movement exemplifies the resentment of the many toward the selfishness, greed, and the neglect of the few.

The workers of the nation were tired of waiting for corporate industry to right their economic wrongs, to alleviate their social agony, and to grant them their

political rights. Despairing of fair treatment, they resolved to do something for themselves. They therefore have organized a new labor movement, conceived within the principles of the national Bill of Rights[2] and committed to the proposition[3] that the workers are free to assemble in their own forums, voice their own grievances, declare their own hopes, and contract on even terms with modern industry for the sale of their only material possession—their labor.

The Committee for Industrial Organization has a numerical enrollment of 3,718,000 members. It has thirty-two affiliated national and international unions. Of this number, eleven unions account for 2,765,000 members. This group is organized in the textile, auto, garment, lumber, rubber, electrical manufacturing, power, steel, coal, and transport industries. The remaining membership exists in the maritime, oil production and refining, shipbuilding, leather, chemical, retail, meatpacking, vegetable canning, metalliferous mining, miscellaneous manufacturing, agricultural labor, and several miscellaneous industries. Some 200,000 workers are organized into 507 chartered local unions not yet attached to a national industrial union.

This record bespeaks progress. It is a development without precedent in our own country. Some

1. Formed by Lewis and other labor leaders in 1935, the CIO changed its name in 1938 to the Congress of Industrial Organizations and competed with the American Federation of Labor for the right to represent various unions. The two groups merged in 1955 to form the AFL-CIO.

2. The first 10 amendments to the U.S. Constitution, which were ratified by the states in 1791.

3. An echo of Abraham Lincoln's Gettysburg Address, November 19, 1863.

of this work was accomplished with the enlightened cooperation or the tolerant acquiescence of employers who recognized that a new labor movement was being forged and who were not disposed, in any event, to flout the law of the land. On the other hand, much of this progress was made in the face of violent and deadly opposition which reached its climax in the slaughter of workers paralleling the massacres of Ludlow[4] and Homestead.[5]

In the steel industry, the corporations generally have accepted collective bargaining and negotiated wage agreements with the Committee for Industrial Organization.[6] Eighty-five percent of the industry is thus under contract and a peaceful relationship exists between the management and the workers. Written wage contracts have been negotiated with 399 steel companies covering 510,000 men. One thousand thirty-one local lodges in 700 communities have been organized.

Five of the corporations in the steel industry elected to resist collective bargaining and undertook to destroy the steel workers' union.[7] These companies filled their plants with industrial spies, assembled depots of guns and gas bombs, established barricades, controlled their communities with armed hirelings, leased the police power of cities, and mobilized the military power of a state to guard them against the intrusion of collective bargaining within their plants.

During this strike eighteen steel workers were either shot to death or had their brains clubbed out by police or armed hirelings in the pay of the steel companies. In Chicago, Mayor Kelly's[8] police force was successful in killing ten strikers before they could escape the fury of the police, shooting eight of them in the back. One hundred and sixty strikers were maimed and injured by police clubs, riot guns, and gas bombs and were hospitalized. Hundreds of strikers were arrested, jailed, treated with brutality while incarcerated, and harassed by succeeding litigation.[9] None but strikers were murdered, gassed, injured, jailed, or maltreated. No one had to die except the workers who were standing for the right guaranteed them by the Congress and written in the law.

Governor Davey of Ohio,[10] successful in the last election because of his reiterated promises of fair treatment to labor, used the military power of the commonwealth on the side of the Republic Steel Company and the Youngstown Sheet and Tube Company. Nearly half of the staggering military expenditure incident to the crushing of this strike in Ohio[11] was borne by the federal government through the allocation of financial aid to the military establishment of the state.

The steel workers have now buried their dead, while the widows weep and watch their orphaned children become objects of public charity. The murder of these unarmed men has never been publicly rebuked by any authoritative officer of the state or federal government. Some of them, in extenuation, plead lack of jurisdiction, but crime against the moral code can always be rebuked without regard to the niceties of legalistic jurisdiction by those who profess to be the keepers of the public conscience.

---

4. The Ludlow Massacre occurred on April 20, 1914, when a tent city occupied by striking coal miners and their families was attacked by Colorado militiamen, coal company guards, and strikebreakers, resulting in the deaths of 20 men, women, and children.

5. On July 6, 1892, striking workers at the Carnegie Steel Company plant in Homestead, Pennsylvania, engaged in an all-day battle with agents of the Pinkerton Detective Agency who had been hired to dislodge the strikers. Scores of people were injured and more than a dozen were killed.

6. Lewis is referring to an agreement signed in March 1937 between the Steel Workers Organizing Committee and the United States Steel Corporation.

7. The five corporations were Bethlehem Steel, Republic Steel, Youngstown Sheet and Tube, National Steel, and Inland Steel.

8. Edward Joseph Kelly.

9. Lewis is referring to events of May 30, 1937, during the strike against the Republic Steel South Chicago plant.

10. Martin L. Davey. The prepared text of Lewis's speech referred to Davey as "infamous," wording that was deleted at the urging of CBS officials. Lewis retained it, however, in the text published in *Vital Speeches*, September 15, 1937, as well as in the pamphlet version released later in September by the CIO. The broadcast speech also left out a paragraph excoriating Tom Girdler, president of Republic Steel; that paragraph did not appear in the pamphlet, but it was included in *Vital Speeches*.

11. The Ohio strike, which focused on Republic Steel plants in several cities, ran May–August 1937.

Shortly after Kelly's police force in Chicago had indulged in their bloody orgy, Kelly came to Washington looking for political patronage. That patronage was forthcoming, and Kelly must believe that the killing of the strikers is no liability in partisan politics.

Meanwhile, the steel puppet Davey is still Governor of Ohio, but not for long, I think, not for long. The people of Ohio may be relied upon to mete out political justice to one who has betrayed his state, outraged the public conscience, and besmirched the public honor.

While the men of the steel industry were going through blood and gas in defense of their rights and their homes and their families, elsewhere on the far-flung CIO front the hosts of labor were advancing, and intelligent and permanent progress was being made. In scores of industries, plant after plant and company after company were negotiating sensible working agreements. The men in the steel industry who sacrificed their all were not merely aiding their fellows at home but were adding strength to the cause of their comrades in all industry. Labor was marching toward the goal of industrial democracy and contributing constructively toward a more rational arrangement of our domestic economy.

Labor does not seek industrial strife. It wants peace, but a peace with justice. In the long struggle for labor's rights, it has been patient and forbearing. Sabotage and destructive syndicalism have had no part in the American labor movement. Workers have kept faith in American institutions. Most of the conflicts which have occurred have been when labor's right to live has been challenged and denied. If there is to be peace in our industrial life, let the employer recognize his obligation to his employees, at least to the degree set forth in existing statutes. Ordinary problems affecting wages, hours, and working conditions, in most instances, will quickly respond to negotiation in the council room.

The United States Chamber of Commerce, the National Association of Manufacturers, and similar groups representing industry and financial interests are rendering a disservice to the American people in their attempts to frustrate the organization of labor and in their refusal to accept collective bargaining as one of our economic institutions. These groups are encouraging a systematic organization of vigilante groups to fight unionization under the sham pretext of local interests. They equip these vigilantes with tin hats, wooden clubs, gas masks, and lethal weapons and train them in the arts of brutality and oppression. They bring in snoops, finks, hatchet gangs, and Chowderhead Cohens[12] to infest their plants and disturb the communities.

Fascist organizations have been launched and financed under the shabby pretext that the CIO movement is communistic. The real breeders of discontent and alien doctrines of government and philosophies subversive of good citizenship are such as these who take the law into their own hands. No tin-hat brigade of goose-stepping[13] vigilantes or bibble-babbling[14] mob of blackguarding and corporation-paid scoundrels will prevent the onward march of labor or divert its purpose to play its natural and rational part in the development of the economic, political, and social life of our nation.

Unionization, as opposed to communism, presupposes the relation of employment; it is based upon the wage system and it recognizes fully and unreservedly the institution of private property and the right to investment profit. It is upon the fuller development of collective bargaining, the wider expansion of the labor movement, the increased influence of labor in our national councils that the perpetuity of our democratic institutions must largely depend. The organized workers of America, free in their industrial life, conscious partners in production, secure in their homes, and enjoying a decent standard of living, will prove the finest bulwark against the intrusion of alien doctrines of government.

Do those who have hatched this foolish cry of communism in the CIO fear the increased influence of labor in our democracy? Do they fear its influence

12. Chowderhead Cohen was a notorious strikebreaker who offered his services to corporations that were experiencing labor problems.

13. Method of marching associated with Nazi troops.

14. Idle talking.

will be cast on the side of shorter hours, a better system of distributed employment, better homes for the underprivileged, social security for the aged, a fairer distribution of the national income?

Certainly the workers that are being organized want a voice in the determination of these objectives of social justice. Certainly labor wants a fairer share in the national income. Assuredly labor wants a larger participation in increased productive efficiency. Obviously the population is entitled to participate in the fruits of the genius of our men of achievement in the field of the material sciences.

Labor has suffered, just as our farm population has suffered, from a viciously unequal distribution of the national income. In the exploitation of both classes of workers has been the source of panic and depression, and upon the economic welfare of both rests the best assurance of a sound and permanent prosperity.

In this connection let me call attention to the propaganda which some of our industrialists are carrying on among the farmers. By pamphlets in the milk cans or attached to machinery and in countless other ways of direct and indirect approach, the farmers of the nation are being told that the increased price of farm machinery and farm supplies is due to the rising wage level brought about by the Committee for Industrial Organization.

And yet it is the industrial millions of the country who constitute the substantial market for all agricultural products. The interests of the two groups are mutually dependent. It is when the payroll goes down that the farmer's realization is diminished, so that his loans become overdue at the bank and the arrival of the tax collector is awaited with fear. On the other hand, it is the prosperity of the farmer that quickens the tempo of manufacturing activities and brings buying power to the millions of urban and industrial workers.

As we view the years that have passed, this has always been true, and it becomes increasingly imperative that the farm population and the millions of workers in industry must learn to combine their strength for the attainment of mutual and desirable objectives and at the same time learn to guard themselves against the sinister propaganda of those who would divide and exploit them.

Under the banner of the Committee for Industrial Organization, American labor is on the march. Its objectives today are those it had in the beginning: to strive for the unionization of our unorganized millions of workers and for the acceptance of collective bargaining as a recognized American institution. It seeks peace with the industrial world. It seeks cooperation and mutuality of effort with the agricultural population. It would avoid strikes. It would have its rights determined under the law by the peaceful negotiations and contract relationships that are supposed to characterize American commercial life. Until an aroused public opinion demands that employers accept that rule, labor has no recourse but to surrender its rights or struggle for their realization with its own economic power.

The objectives of this movement are not political in a partisan sense. Yet it is true that a political party which seeks the support of labor and makes pledges of good faith to labor must, in equity and good conscience, keep that faith and redeem those pledges. The spectacle of august and dignified members of Congress, servants of the people and agents of the republic, skulking in hallways and closets, hiding their faces in a party caucus to prevent a quorum from acting upon a labor measure, is one that emphasizes the perfidy of politicians and blasts the confidence of labor's millions in politicians' promises and statesmen's vows.[15]

Labor next year cannot avoid the necessity of a political assay of the work and deeds of its so-called friends and its political beneficiaries. It must determine who are its friends in the arena of politics, as elsewhere. It feels that its cause is just and that its friends should not view its struggle with neutral detachment or intone constant criticism of its activities. Those who chant their praises of democracy but who lose no chance to drive their knives into labor's defenseless back must feel the weight of labor's woe, even as its open adversaries must ever feel the thrust of labor's power.

---

15. Lewis is referring to the failure of the House of Representatives to pass a wage-and-hour bill, previously approved by the Senate, during the most recent session of Congress. The bill eventually became law in 1938 as the Fair Labor Standards Act.

Labor, like Israel, has many sorrows. Its women weep for their fallen and they lament for the future of the children of the race.[16] It ill behooves one who has supped at labor's table and who has been sheltered in labor's house to curse with equal fervor and fine impartiality both labor and its adversaries when they become locked in deadly embrace.

I repeat that labor seeks peace and guarantees its own loyalty, but the voice of labor, insistent upon its rights, should not be annoying to the ears of justice nor offensive to the conscience of the American people.

---

16. An allusion to the biblical story of Rachel weeping for the children of Israel (Jeremiah 31:15–16).

Lou Gehrig

Farewell to Baseball

New York, New York
July 4, 1939

Lou Gehrig's Farewell to Baseball is the Gettysburg Address of American sports. Known as the "Iron Horse," Gehrig played in 2,130 consecutive games and was twice named the American League's Most Valuable Player. When he was forced to retire at the peak of his career because of a fatal neurological condition, people from all walks of life were shocked and saddened. A man of unimpeachable character as well as exceptional athletic talent, Gehrig stood, as one columnist wrote, "for everything that makes sports important in the American scene."

On July 4, 1939, a tribute to Gehrig was held at Yankee Stadium between games of a doubleheader with the Washington Senators. Standing hat in hand in front of a microphone set up at home plate, Gehrig called himself "the luckiest man on the face of the earth" despite the "bad break" he had been dealt. His grace, humility, and courage touched even the most hardened of spectators among the 62,000 in attendance. Gehrig's life was apotheosized in the 1942 movie *Pride of the Yankees*, and his speech has become firmly ensconced in popular lore. On June 2, 1941, seventeen days before his thirty-eighth birthday, he died of the disease that now bears his name.

According to Gehrig's wife, Eleanor, he wrote the speech the night before but did not rehearse it. When he stepped to the microphone, he spoke without notes, covering essentially the same ground as in his prepared text but choosing his words as he went. The version of the speech usually reprinted is drawn from

Eleanor Gehrig's 1976 *My Luke and I* and probably reflects what Gehrig had written more than what he actually said.

The text printed below is based primarily on the *Sporting News* of July 13, 1939, which contains the nearest thing that exists to a stenographic account of Gehrig's words. Only a few fragments of the speech are known to have been preserved in recorded form—most of the first and second sentences, all of the fourth sentence, and most of the last two sentences. We have substituted those fragments for the wording in the *Sporting News*. In addition, we have included one phrase—referring to Yankees general manager Ed Barrow—from Eleanor Gehrig's text. Although Barrow is not mentioned in the *Sporting News*, there is little doubt, on the basis of other newspaper accounts, that Gehrig named him in the speech. Although we will never know exactly what Gehrig said that day in Yankee Stadium, the words that follow are as close as we are likely to get.

◇◇◇

Fans, for the past two weeks you've been reading about a bad break I got. Yet today I consider myself the luckiest man on the face of the earth. I have been in ballparks sixteen years and have never received anything but kindness and encouragement from you fans. When you look around, wouldn't you consider it a privilege to associate yourself with such[1] fine-looking men as are standing in uniform in this ballpark today?

Sure, I'm lucky. Who wouldn't consider it an honor to have known Jake Ruppert;[2] also the builder of baseball's greatest empire, Ed Barrow;[3] to have spent six years with such a grand little fellow as Miller Huggins;[4] to have spent nine years with that smart student of psychology, the best manager in baseball today, Joe McCarthy?[5] Who wouldn't feel lucky to room with such a grand guy as Bill Dickey?[6]

When the New York Giants, a team you would give your right arm to beat, and vice versa, send a gift—that's something.

When the ground keepers and office staff and writers and old-timers and players and concessionaires all remember you with trophies—that's something.

When you have a wonderful mother-in-law who takes sides with you in squabbles against her own daughter—that's something.

When you have a father and mother who work all their lives so that you can have an education and build your body—it's a blessing.

When you have a wife who has been a tower of strength and shown more courage than you dreamed existed—that's the finest I know.

So I close in saying that I might have been given a bad break, but I've got an awful lot to live for.

Thank you.

1. When delivering the speech, Gehrig inserted "a" here.

2. Jacob Ruppert Jr., owner of the New York Yankees, 1915–1939.

3. During his career with the Yankees from 1920 to 1946, Barrow held a number of posts, including business manager, president, and chairman of the board.

4. Yankees' manager, 1918–1929.

5. Yankees' manager, 1931–1946.

6. Yankees' catcher who was Gehrig's best friend on the team and his roommate on road trips.

Franklin D. Roosevelt

The Arsenal of Democracy

WASHINGTON, D.C.
DECEMBER 29, 1940

WELL BEFORE NOVEMBER 1940, when he won election to a third term as President, Franklin Roosevelt had begun turning his attention from the nation's economic woes to the increasingly perilous state of world affairs. The growth of militarism in Japan, the triumph of Adolf Hitler's Nationalist Socialist Party in Germany, and Benito Mussolini's Fascist rule in Italy undermined stability and threatened free institutions around the globe. In January 1939 Roosevelt urged Congress to adopt measures "short of war, but stronger and more effective than mere words," but he could not easily overcome the country's traditional isolationist sentiment. Few people wanted any part of what they considered Europe's wars, and they were even less concerned about events in Asia.

Attitudes began to change in September 1939 when Germany invaded Poland and Great Britain responded by declaring war on Germany, but still there remained a strong isolationist impulse, backed by Congress's passage of the Neutrality Act of November 1939. The scope of the war widened in 1940, as Denmark, Norway, Belgium, Luxembourg, France, and the Netherlands fell before the German onslaught and Great Britain struggled to retain its freedom. Japan joined with Germany and Italy in September to form the third spoke of the Axis powers. In a victory for Roosevelt and other advocates of preparedness, the United States responded in October by instituting its first peacetime draft, though opposition from isolationists limited the service of draftees to the Western Hemisphere and U.S. Territories.

Seeking both to aid Great Britain and to convince Americans of their stake in the war raging about them, Roosevelt spoke to the nation via radio on the evening of December 29, 1940. The speech was also broadcast internationally by shortwave in six languages. Arguing that American civilization had never been in such danger, FDR painted a vivid picture of the Axis powers' nefarious ambitions—ambitions, he warned, that included conquest in the Western Hemisphere. He stated, as he had on previous occasions, that his aim was to keep the United States out of war, but he argued that Americans could best ensure their own safety by providing aid that would enable the British to fight "for their liberty and for our security." America must become "the great arsenal of democracy" by producing "more ships, more guns, more planes—more of everything" to assist Britain in its defense of freedom.

Eighty million Americans listened to Roosevelt's address, giving it the largest radio audience in U.S. history to that time. Afterward, 99 percent of letters to the White House ran in favor of the President's position, and public opinion polls showed approval from 80 percent of listeners. In response to FDR's speech, industries began transforming themselves from producers of goods to manufacturers of the tools of war. This transformation would take months to accomplish, but it started in earnest following Roosevelt's call for courage, sacrifice, and action to aid the British, and it would prove of immeasurable value when, just less than a year later, the United States was drawn into war by the Japanese attack on Pearl Harbor.

◇◇

My friends: This is not a Fireside Chat on war. It is a talk on national security, because the nub of the whole purpose of your President is to keep you now, and your children later, and your grandchildren much later out of a last-ditch war for the preservation of American independence and all of the things that American independence means to you and to me and to ours.

Tonight, in the presence of a world crisis, my mind goes back eight years to a night in the midst of a domestic crisis. It was a time when the wheels of American industry were grinding to a full stop, when the whole banking system of our country had ceased to function. I well remember that while I sat in my study in the White House, preparing to talk with the people of the United States, I had before my eyes the picture of all those Americans with whom I was talking. I saw the workmen in the mills, the mines, the factories, the girl behind the counter, the small shopkeeper, the farmer doing his spring plowing, the widows and the old men wondering about their life's savings. I tried to convey to the great mass of American people what the banking crisis meant to them in their daily lives.[1]

Tonight I want to do the same thing, with the same people, in this new crisis which faces America. We met the issue of 1933 with courage and realism. We face this new crisis, this new threat to the security of our nation, with the same courage and realism.

Never before since Jamestown and Plymouth Rock[2] has our American civilization been in such danger as now. For on September 27th, 1940—this year—by an agreement signed in Berlin, three powerful nations, two in Europe and one in Asia, joined themselves together in the threat that if the United States of America interfered with or blocked the expansion program of these three nations—a program aimed at world control—they would unite in ultimate action against the United States.[3]

The Nazi masters of Germany have made it clear that they intend not only to dominate all life and thought in their own country but also to enslave the whole of Europe and then to use the resources of Europe to dominate the rest of the world. It was only three weeks ago that their leader stated this: "There are two worlds that stand opposed to each other." And then in defiant reply to his opponents he said this: "Others are correct when they say, 'With this world we cannot ever reconcile ourselves.' I can beat any other power in the world."[4] So said the leader of the Nazis.

In other words, the Axis not merely admits but the Axis proclaims that there can be no ultimate peace between their philosophy—their philosophy

2. A reference to the initial settlements of British colonists at Jamestown, Virginia, in 1607, and at Plymouth Bay, Massachusetts, in 1620.

3. FDR is referring to Japan's joining Germany and Italy as the third member of the Axis powers.

4. From Adolf Hitler's speech of December 10, 1940.

1. FDR is referring to his March 12, 1933, Fireside Chat on the banking crisis (pages 225–228).

of government—and our philosophy of government. In view of the nature of this undeniable threat, it can be asserted, properly and categorically, that the United States has no right or reason to encourage talk of peace until the day shall come when there is a clear intention on the part of the aggressor nations to abandon all thought of dominating or conquering the world.

At this moment the forces of the states that are leagued against all peoples who live in freedom are being held away from our shores. The Germans and the Italians are being blocked on the other side of the Atlantic by the British and by the Greeks and by thousands of soldiers and sailors who were able to escape from subjugated countries. In Asia the Japanese are being engaged by the Chinese nation in another great defense. In the Pacific Ocean is our fleet.

Some of our people like to believe that wars in Europe and in Asia are of no concern to us. But it is a matter of most vital concern to us that European and Asiatic war makers should not gain control of the oceans which lead to this hemisphere.

One hundred and seventeen years ago the Monroe Doctrine[5] was conceived by our government as a measure of defense in the face of a threat against this hemisphere by an alliance in continental Europe. Thereafter, we stood guard in the Atlantic, with the British as neighbors. There was no treaty. There was no unwritten agreement. And yet there was the feeling, proven correct by history, that we as neighbors could settle any disputes in peaceful fashion. And the fact is that during the whole of this time the Western Hemisphere has remained free from aggression from Europe or from Asia.

Does anyone seriously believe that we need to fear attack anywhere in the Americas while a free Britain remains our most powerful naval neighbor in the Atlantic? And does anyone seriously believe, on the other hand, that we could rest easy if the Axis powers were our neighbors there?

If Great Britain goes down, the Axis powers will control the continents of Europe, Asia, Africa, Australasia, and the high seas. And they will be in a position to bring enormous military and naval resources against this hemisphere. It is no exaggeration to say that all of us in all the Americas would be living at the point of a gun—a gun loaded with explosive bullets, economic as well as military. We should enter upon a new and terrible era in which the whole world, our hemisphere included, would be run by threats of brute force. And to survive in such a world, we would have to convert ourselves permanently into a militaristic power on the basis of war economy.

Some of us like to believe that even if Britain falls, we are still safe because of the broad expanse of the Atlantic and of the Pacific. But the width of those oceans is not what it was in the days of clipper ships. At one point between Africa and Brazil the distance is less than it is from Washington to Denver, Colorado—five hours for the latest type of bomber. And at the north end of the Pacific Ocean, America and Asia almost touch each other. Why, even today we have planes that could fly from the British Isles to New England and back again without refueling. And remember that the range of the modern bomber is ever being increased.

During the past week many people in all parts of the nation have told me what they wanted me to say tonight. Almost all of them expressed a courageous desire to hear the plain truth about the gravity of the situation. One telegram, however, expressed the attitude of the small minority who want to see no evil and hear no evil, even though they know in their hearts that evil exists. That telegram begged me not to tell again of the ease with which our American cities could be bombed by any hostile power which had gained bases in this Western Hemisphere. The gist of that telegram was: "Please, Mr. President, don't frighten us by telling us the facts."

Frankly and definitely there is danger ahead—danger against which we must prepare. But we well know that we cannot escape danger, or the fear of danger, by crawling into bed and pulling the covers over our heads.

---

5. The Monroe Doctrine of 1823 declared that the United States would regard any attempt on the part of European powers "to extend their system to any portion of this hemisphere as dangerous to our peace and safety."

Some nations of Europe were bound by solemn nonintervention pacts with Germany. Other nations were assured by Germany that they need never fear invasion. Nonintervention pact or not, the fact remains that they were attacked, overrun, thrown into modern slavery at an hour's notice—or even without any notice at all. As an exiled leader of one of these nations said to me the other day, "The notice was a minus quantity. It was given to my government two hours after German troops had poured into my country in a hundred places." The fate of these nations tells us what it means to live at the point of a Nazi gun.

The Nazis have justified such actions by various pious frauds. One of these frauds is the claim that they are occupying a nation for the purpose of restoring order. Another is that they are occupying or controlling a nation on the excuse that they are protecting it against the aggression of somebody else.

For example, Germany has said that she was occupying Belgium to save the Belgians from the British.[6] Would she then hesitate to say to any South American country: "We are occupying you to protect you from aggression by the United States"? Belgium today is being used as an invasion base against Britain, now fighting for its life. And any South American country, in Nazi hands, would always constitute a jumping-off place for German attack on any one of the other republics of this hemisphere.

Analyze for yourselves the future of two other places even nearer to Germany if the Nazis won. Could Ireland hold out? Would Irish freedom be permitted as an amazing pet exception in an unfree world? Or the islands of the Azores, which still fly the flag of Portugal after five centuries? You and I think of Hawaii as an outpost of defense in the Pacific. And yet the Azores are closer to our shores in the Atlantic than Hawaii is on the other side.

There are those who say that the Axis powers would never have any desire to attack the Western Hemisphere. That is the same dangerous form of wishful thinking which has destroyed the powers of resistance of so many conquered peoples. The plain

facts are that the Nazis have proclaimed, time and again, that all other races are their inferiors and therefore subject to their orders. And most important of all, the vast resources and wealth of this American hemisphere constitute the most tempting loot in all of the round world.

Let us no longer blind ourselves to the undeniable fact that the evil forces which have crushed and undermined and corrupted so many others are already within our own gates. Your government knows much about them and every day is ferreting them out. Their secret emissaries are active in our own and in neighboring countries. They seek to stir up suspicion and dissension, to cause internal strife. They try to turn capital against labor, and vice versa. They try to reawaken long-slumbering racial and religious enmities which should have no place in this country. They are active in every group that promotes intolerance. They exploit for their own ends our own natural abhorrence of war. These trouble breeders have but one purpose. It is to divide our people—to divide them into hostile groups and to destroy our unity and shatter our will to defend ourselves.

There are also American citizens, many of them in high places, who, unwittingly in most cases, are aiding and abetting the work of these agents. I do not charge these American citizens with being foreign agents. But I do charge them with doing exactly the kind of work that the dictators want done in the United States. These people not only believe that we can save our own skins by shutting our eyes to the fate of other nations. Some of them go much further than that. They say that we can and should become the friends and even the partners of the Axis powers. Some of them even suggest that we should imitate the methods of the dictatorships. But Americans never can and never will do that.

The experience of the past two years has proven beyond doubt that no nation can appease the Nazis. No man can tame a tiger into a kitten by stroking it. There can be no appeasement with ruthlessness. There can be no reasoning with an incendiary bomb. We know now that a nation can have peace with the Nazis only at the price of total surrender. Even the people of Italy have been forced to become accomplices of the Nazis; but at this moment they do not

6. Belgium was invaded by Germany on May 10, 1940, and surrendered before the end of the month.

know how soon they will be embraced to death by their allies.

The American appeasers ignore the warning to be found in the fate of Austria, Czechoslovakia, Poland, Norway, Belgium, the Netherlands, Denmark, and France.[7] They tell you that the Axis powers are going to win anyway, that all of this bloodshed in the world could be saved, that the United States might just as well throw its influence into the scale of a dictated peace and get the best out of it that we can.

They call it a negotiated peace. Nonsense! Is it a negotiated peace if a gang of outlaws surrounds your community and on threat of extermination makes you pay tribute to save your own skins? For such a dictated peace would be no peace at all. It would be only another armistice, leading to the most gigantic armament race and the most devastating trade wars in all history. And in these contests the Americas would offer the only real resistance to the Axis power[s].

With all their vaunted efficiency, with all their parade of pious purpose in this war, there are still in their background the concentration camp and the servants of God in chains. The history of recent years proves that the shootings and the chains and the concentration camps are not simply the transient tools but the very altars of modern dictatorships. They may talk of a new order in the world, but what they have in mind is only a revival of the oldest and the worst tyranny. In that there is no liberty, no religion, no hope.

The proposed new order is the very opposite of a United States of Europe or a United States of Asia. It is not a government based upon the consent of the governed. It is not a union of ordinary, self-respecting men and women to protect themselves and their freedom and their dignity from oppression. It is an unholy alliance of power and pelf to dominate and to enslave the human race.

The British people and their allies today are conducting an active war against this unholy alliance. Our own future security is greatly dependent on the outcome of that fight. Our ability to keep out of war

is going to be affected by that outcome. Thinking in terms of today and tomorrow, I make the direct statement to the American people that there is far less chance of the United States getting into war if we do all we can now to support the nations defending themselves against attack by the Axis than if we acquiesce in their defeat, submit tamely to an Axis victory, and wait our turn to be the object of attack in another war later on.

If we are to be completely honest with ourselves, we must admit that there is risk in any course we may take. But I deeply believe that the great majority of our people agree that the course that I advocate involves the least risk now and the greatest hope for world peace in the future.

The people of Europe who are defending themselves do not ask us to do their fighting. They ask us for the implements of war—the planes, the tanks, the guns, the freighters—which will enable them to fight for their liberty and for our security. Emphatically, we must get these weapons to them, get them to them in sufficient volume and quickly enough so that we and our children will be saved the agony and suffering of war which others have had to endure. Let not the defeatists tell us that it is too late. It will never be earlier. Tomorrow will be later than today.

Certain facts are self-evident:

In a military sense Great Britain and the British Empire are today the spearhead of resistance to world conquest. And they are putting up a fight which will live forever in the story of human gallantry.

There is no demand for sending an American expeditionary force outside our own borders. There is no intention by any member of your government to send such a force. You can therefore nail—nail—any talk about sending armies to Europe as deliberate untruth.

Our national policy is not directed toward war. Its sole purpose is to keep war away from our country and away from our people.

Democracy's fight against world conquest is being greatly aided, and must be more greatly aided, by the rearmament of the United States and by sending every ounce and every ton of munitions and supplies that we can possibly spare to help the defenders who are in the front lines. And it is no more unneutral for

---

7. All these countries fell under Nazi rule between spring 1938 and autumn 1940.

us to do that than it is for Sweden, Russia, and other nations near Germany to send steel and ore and oil and other war materials into Germany every day in the week.

We are planning our own defense with the utmost urgency, and in its vast scale we must integrate the war needs of Britain and the other free nations which are resisting aggression. This is not a matter of sentiment or of controversial personal opinion. It is a matter of realistic, practical military policy, based on the advice of our military experts who are in close touch with existing warfare. These military and naval experts and the members of the Congress and the administration have a single-minded purpose: the defense of the United States.

This nation is making a great effort to produce everything that is necessary in this emergency, and with all possible speed. And this great effort requires great sacrifice. I would ask no one to defend a democracy which in turn would not defend everyone in the nation against want and privation. The strength of this nation shall not be diluted by the failure of the government to protect the economic well-being of its citizens.

If our capacity to produce is limited by machines, it must ever be remembered that these machines are operated by the skill and the stamina of the workers. As the government is determined to protect the rights of the workers, so the nation has a right to expect that the men who man the machines will discharge their full responsibilities to the urgent needs of defense. The worker possesses the same human dignity and is entitled to the same security of position as the engineer or the manager or the owner. For the workers provide the human power that turns out the destroyers and the planes and the tanks.

The nation expects our defense industries to continue operation without interruption by strikes or lockouts. It expects and insists that management and workers will reconcile their differences, by voluntary or legal means, to continue to produce the supplies that are so sorely needed. And on the economic side of our great defense program, we are, as you know, bending every effort to maintain stability of prices and with that the stability of the cost of living.

Nine days ago I announced the setting up of a more effective organization to direct our gigantic efforts to increase the production of munitions.[8] The appropriation of vast sums of money and a well-coordinated executive direction of our defense efforts are not in themselves enough. Guns, planes, ships, and many other things have to be built in the factories and the arsenals of America. They have to be produced by workers and managers and engineers with the aid of machines which in turn have to be built by hundreds of thousands of workers throughout the land. In this great work there has been splendid cooperation between the government and industry and labor. And I am very thankful.

American industrial genius, unmatched throughout all the world in the solution of production problems, has been called upon to bring its resources and its talents into action. Manufacturers of watches, of farm implements, of linotypes and cash registers and automobiles and sewing machines and lawn mowers and locomotives are now making fuses and bomb-packing crates and telescope mounts and shells and pistols and tanks.

But all of our present efforts are not enough. We must have more ships, more guns, more planes—more of everything. And this can be accomplished only if we discard the notion of business as usual. This job cannot be done merely by superimposing on the existing productive facilities the added requirements of the nation for defense.

Our defense efforts must not be blocked by those who fear the future consequences of surplus plant capacity. The possible consequences of failure of our defense efforts now are much more to be feared. And after the present needs of our defense are past, a proper handling of the country's peacetime needs will require all of the new productive capacity, if not still more. No pessimistic policy about the future of America shall delay the immediate expansion of those industries essential to defense. We need them.

I want to make it clear that it is the purpose of the nation to build now with all possible speed every

---

8. FDR is referring to the Office for Production Management for Defense, which he announced at a press conference on December 20.

machine, every arsenal, every factory that we need to manufacture our defense material. We have the men, the skill, the wealth, and, above all, the will. I am confident that if and when production of consumer or luxury goods in certain industries requires the use of machines and raw materials that are essential for defense purposes, then such production must yield, and will gladly yield, to our primary and compelling purpose.

So I appeal to the owners of plants, to the managers, to the workers, to our own government employees to put every ounce of effort into producing these munitions swiftly and without stint. With this appeal, I give you the pledge that all of us who are officers of your government will devote ourselves to the same wholehearted extent to the great task that lies ahead. As planes and ships and guns and shells are produced, your government, with its defense experts, can then determine how best to use them to defend this hemisphere. The decision as to how much shall be sent abroad and how much shall remain at home must be made on the basis of our overall military necessities.

We must be the great arsenal of democracy. For us this is an emergency as serious as war itself. We must apply ourselves to our task with the same resolution, the same sense of urgency, the same spirit of patriotism and sacrifice as we would show were we at war. We have furnished the British great material support and we will furnish far more in the future. There will be no bottlenecks in our determination to aid Great Britain. No dictator, no combination of dictators, will weaken that determination by threats of how they will construe that determination.

The British have received invaluable military support from the heroic Greek army and from the forces of all the governments in exile. Their strength is growing. It is the strength of men and women who value their freedom more highly than they value their lives.

I believe that the Axis powers are not going to win this war. I base that belief on the latest and best of information. We have no excuse for defeatism. We have every good reason for hope—hope for peace, yes, and hope for the defense of our civilization and for the building of a better civilization in the future.

I have the profound conviction that the American people are now determined to put forth a mightier effort than they have ever yet made to increase our production of all the implements of defense to meet the threat to our democratic faith. As President of the United States, I call for that national effort. I call for it in the name of this nation which we love and honor and which we are privileged and proud to serve. I call upon our people with absolute confidence that our common cause will greatly succeed.

Franklin D. Roosevelt

⌛

The Four Freedoms

WASHINGTON, D.C.
JANUARY 6, 1941

J UST ONE WEEK after his "Arsenal of Democracy" speech (256–262), Franklin Roosevelt reported to the nation in his annual State of the Union address, the only specific communication from the President to the Congress required by the Constitution. Although George Washington and John Adams had delivered their addresses in person, Thomas Jefferson sent his to Congress in writing, a custom that remained in place until Woodrow Wilson returned to the original practice of presenting the address as a speech. As with every President since Wilson, FDR spoke in the chamber of the House of Representatives when, on January 6, 1941, he presented what has become the most celebrated State of the Union address in American history.

Roosevelt spoke to the assembled lawmakers at a moment of peril he described as "unprecedented in the history of the Union." With Secret Service agents swarming the building, Speaker of the House Sam Rayburn called the afternoon session of Congress to order—and promptly broke his gavel in two. FDR spoke in slow and somber tones, once again calling for America to become the arsenal for those countries battling the enemies of democracy, and setting forth the rationale for what would become the Lend-Lease program. Under that program, the United States would lend or lease war matériel to nations resisting the Axis powers with no expectation of repayment until after the end of hostilities. Calling for cooperation from all sectors of American society, Roosevelt stressed the need for sacrifice, speed, and efficiency to ensure that "defense preparations of any kind" would be pursued in keeping with "the national need."

In closing his address, Roosevelt envisioned a world founded upon four essential human freedoms: freedom of speech and expression, freedom of worship, freedom from want, and freedom from fear. He offered those ideals both as expressions of American values and as touchstones for a postwar international order. As with Woodrow Wilson's Fourteen Points during World War I (pages 124–128), FDR's Four Freedoms captured the public imagination. They were popularized in a series of illustrations by Norman Rockwell, they were used by the Treasury Department in a campaign that raised more than $130 million through the sale of war bonds, they found expression in the Atlantic Charter and the founding documents of the United Nations, and they remain a statement of principle that voices the most fundamental aspirations of freedom-seeking people everywhere.

◇◇◇◇◇◇◇◇◇◇◇◇◇◇◇◇◇◇◇◇◇◇◇◇◇◇◇◇◇◇◇◇◇◇◇◇◇

Mr. Speaker, members of the Seventy-seventh Congress: I address you, the members of this new Congress, at a moment unprecedented in the history of the Union. I use the word "unprecedented" because at no previous time has American security been as seriously threatened from without as it is today.

Since the permanent formation of our government under the Constitution in 1789, most of the periods of crisis in our history have related to our domestic affairs. And, fortunately, only one of these—the four-year War Between the States—ever threatened our national unity.[1] Today, thank God, 130 million Americans in forty-eight states have forgotten points of the compass in our national unity.

It is true that prior to 1914 the United States often had[2] been disturbed by events in other continents. We had even engaged in two wars with European nations[3] and in a number of undeclared wars—in the West Indies, in the Mediterranean, and in the Pacific—for the maintenance of American rights and for the principles of peaceful commerce.[4] But in no case had a serious threat been raised against our national safety or our continued independence.

What I seek to convey is the historic truth that the United States as a nation has at all times maintained opposition—clear, definite opposition—to any attempt to lock us in behind an ancient Chinese wall while the procession of civilization went past. Today, thinking of our children and of their children, we oppose enforced isolation for ourselves or for any other part of the Americas.

That determination of ours, extending over all these years, was proved, for example, in the early days during the quarter century of wars following the French Revolution. While the Napoleonic struggles did threaten interests of the United States because of the French foothold in the West Indies and in Louisiana, and while we engaged in the War of 1812 to vindicate our right to peaceful trade, it is nevertheless clear that neither France nor Great Britain nor any other nation was aiming at domination of the whole world.

And in like fashion, from 1815 to 1914—ninety-nine years—no single war in Europe or in Asia constituted a real threat against our future or against the future of any other American nation. Except in the Maximilian interlude in Mexico,[5] no foreign power sought to establish itself in this hemisphere. And the strength of the British fleet in the Atlantic has been a friendly strength; it is still a friendly strength. Even when the World War broke out in 1914, it seemed to contain only small threat of danger to our own American future. But as time went on, as we remember, the American people began to visualize what the downfall of democratic nations might mean to our own democracy.

We need not overemphasize imperfections in the Peace of Versailles.[6] We need not harp on failure of the democracies to deal with problems of world reconstruction. We should remember that the peace of 1919 was far less unjust than the kind of pacification which began even before Munich[7] and which is being carried on under the new order of tyranny

---

1. The Civil War took place from 1861 to 1865.

2. FDR misspoke this word as "has."

3. FDR is referring to the War of 1812, fought against Great Britain, and to the Spanish-American War of 1898.

4. Among the conflicts Roosevelt may have had in mind are the 1798–1800 Quasi-War with France; the First Barbary War of 1801–1805; and the Philippine-American War of 1899–1902.

5. Ferdinand Maximilian Joseph, Archduke of Austria, became Emperor of Mexico in 1864 as part of a deal between Napoleon III and Mexican conservatives; he was deposed and executed in 1867.

6. The Treaty of Versailles (1919) brought an official end to World War I.

7. FDR is referring to the Munich Pact of September 1938, which ceded the Sudetenland, then a part of Czechoslovakia, to Germany.

that seeks to spread over every continent today. The American people have unalterably set their faces against that tyranny.

I suppose that every realist knows that the democratic way of life is at this moment being directly assailed in every part of the world—assailed either by arms or by secret spreading of poisonous propaganda by those who seek to destroy unity and promote discord in nations that are still at peace. During sixteen long months this assault has blotted out the whole pattern of democratic life in an appalling number of independent nations, great and small. And the assailants are still on the march, threatening other nations, great and small.

Therefore, as your President, performing my constitutional duty to "give to the Congress information of the state of the Union,"[8] I find it unhappily necessary to report that the future and the safety of our country and of our democracy are overwhelmingly involved in events far beyond our borders.

Armed defense of democratic existence is now being gallantly waged in four continents. If that defense fails, all the population and all the resources of Europe and Asia and Africa and Australasia will be dominated by conquerors. And let us remember that the total of those populations in those four continents, the total of those populations and their resources greatly exceed the sum total of the population and the resources of the whole of the Western Hemisphere—yes, many times over.

In times like these it is immature—and, incidentally, untrue—for anybody to brag that an unprepared America, single-handed and with one hand tied behind its back, can hold off the whole world. No realistic American can expect from a dictator's peace international generosity or return of true independence or world disarmament or freedom of expression or freedom of religion or even good business. Such a peace would bring no security for us or for our neighbors. Those who would give up essential liberty to purchase a little temporary safety deserve neither liberty nor safety.[9]

As a nation we may take pride in the fact that we are softhearted, but we cannot afford to be softheaded. We must always be wary of those who with sounding brass and a tinkling cymbal preach the ism of appeasement. We must especially beware of that small group of selfish men who would clip the wings of the American eagle in order to feather their own nests.

I have recently pointed out how quickly the tempo of modern warfare could bring into our very midst the physical attack which we must eventually expect if the dictator nations win this war.[10] There is much loose talk of our immunity from immediate and direct invasion from across the seas. Obviously, as long as the British navy retains its power, no such danger exists. Even if there were no British navy, it is not probable that any enemy would be stupid enough to attack us by landing troops in the United States from across thousands of miles of ocean until it had acquired strategic bases from which to operate.

But we learn much from the lessons of the past years in Europe—particularly the lesson of Norway, whose essential seaports were captured by treachery and surprise built up over a series of years.[11] The first phase of the invasion of this hemisphere would not be the landing of regular troops. The necessary strategic points would be occupied by secret agents and by their dupes—and great numbers of them are already here and in Latin America.

As long as the aggressor nations maintain the offensive, they, not we, will choose the time and the place and the method of their attack. And that is why the future of all the American republics is today in serious danger. That is why this annual message to the Congress is unique in our history. That is why every member of the executive branch of the government and every member of the Congress face great responsibility, great accountability. The need of the moment is that our actions and our policy should be devoted primarily—almost exclusively—to meeting

8. From Article II, Section 3, of the U.S. Constitution.

9. This sentence repeats Benjamin Franklin's famous statement in his November 11, 1755, message from the Pennsylvania Assembly to Governor Robert Hunter Morris.

10. A reference to Roosevelt's speech of December 29, 1940 (pages 256–262).

11. Norway was invaded by Germany on April 9, 1940, and it surrendered two months later.

this foreign peril. For all our domestic problems are now a part of the great emergency.

Just as our national policy in internal affairs has been based upon a decent respect for the rights and the dignity of all of our fellow men within our gates, so our national policy in foreign affairs has been based on a decent respect for the rights and the dignity of all nations, large and small. And the justice of morality must and will win in the end.

Our national policy is this: First, by an impressive expression of the public will and without regard to partisanship, we are committed to all-inclusive national defense.

Secondly, by an impressive expression of the public will and without regard to partisanship, we are committed to full support of all those resolute people everywhere who are resisting aggression and are thereby keeping war away from our hemisphere. By this support we express our determination that the democratic cause shall prevail, and we strengthen the defense and the security of our own nation.

Third, by an impressive expression of the public will and without regard to partisanship, we are committed to the proposition that principles of morality and considerations for our own security will never permit us to acquiesce in a peace dictated by aggressors and sponsored by appeasers. We know that enduring peace cannot be bought at the cost of other people's freedom.

In the recent national election, there was no substantial difference between the two great parties in respect to that national policy.[12] No issue was fought out on this line before the American electorate. And today it is abundantly evident that American citizens everywhere are demanding and supporting speedy and complete action in recognition of obvious danger.

Therefore the immediate need is a swift and driving increase in our armament production. Leaders of industry and labor have responded to our summons. Goals of speed have been set. In some cases, these goals are being reached ahead of time. In some cases, we are on schedule; in other cases, there are slight but not serious delays. And in some cases—and, I am sorry to say, very important cases—we are all concerned by the slowness of the accomplishment of our plans.

The army and navy, however, have made substantial progress during the past year. Actual experience is improving and speeding up our methods of production with every passing day. And today's best is not good enough for tomorrow.

I am not satisfied with the progress thus far made. The men in charge of the program represent the best in training, in ability, and in patriotism. They are not satisfied with the progress thus far made. None of us will be satisfied until the job is done. No matter whether the original goal was set too high or too low, our objective is quicker and better results.

To give you two illustrations: We are behind schedule in turning out finished airplanes. We are working day and night to solve the innumerable problems and to catch up. We are ahead of schedule in building warships, but we are working to get even further ahead of that schedule. To change a whole nation from a basis of peacetime production of implements of peace to a basis of wartime production of implements of war is no small task. And the greatest difficulty comes at the beginning of the program, when new tools, new plant facilities, new assembly lines, new shipways must first be constructed before the actual material begins to flow steadily and speedily from them.

The Congress, of course, must rightly keep itself informed at all times of the progress of the program. However, there is certain information, as the Congress itself will readily recognize, which, in the interests of our own security and those of the nations that we are supporting, must of needs be kept in confidence.

New circumstances are constantly begetting new needs for our safety. I shall ask of this Congress for greatly increased new appropriations and authorizations to carry on what we have begun. I also ask this Congress for authority and for funds sufficient to manufacture additional munitions and war supplies of many kinds, to be turned over to those nations which are now in actual war with aggressor nations. Our most useful and immediate role is to act as an arsenal for them as well as for ourselves. They do not need manpower, but they do need billions of dollars worth of the weapons of defense.

---

12. FDR is referring to the election of November 5, 1940, in which he won a third term in the White House.

The time is near when they will not be able to pay for them all in ready cash. We cannot, and we will not, tell them that they must surrender merely because of present inability to pay for the weapons which we know they must have. I do not recommend that we make them a loan of dollars with which to pay for these weapons—a loan to be repaid in dollars. I recommend that we make it possible for those nations to continue to obtain war materials in the United States, fitting their orders into our own program. And nearly all of their material would, if the time ever came, be useful in our own defense.

Taking counsel of expert military and naval authorities, considering what is best for our own security, we are free to decide how much should be kept here and how much should be sent abroad to our friends who, by their determined and heroic resistance, are giving us time in which to make ready our own defense. For what we send abroad, we shall be repaid, repaid within a reasonable time following the close of hostilities, repaid in similar materials or, at our option, in other goods of many kinds which they can produce and which we need.

Let us say to the democracies: We Americans are vitally concerned in your defense of freedom. We are putting forth our energies, our resources, and our organizing powers to give you the strength to regain and maintain a free world. We shall send you, in ever-increasing numbers, ships, planes, tanks, guns. That is our purpose and our pledge.

In fulfillment of this purpose, we will not be intimidated by the threats of dictators that they will regard as a breach of international law or as an act of war our aid to the democracies which dare to resist their aggression. Such aid, such aid is not an act of war, even if a dictator should unilaterally proclaim it so to be.

And when the dictators—if the dictators—are ready to make war upon us, they will not wait for an act of war on our part. They did not wait for Norway or Belgium or the Netherlands to commit an act of war.[13] Their only interest is in a new one-way international law which lacks mutuality in its observance

and therefore becomes an instrument of oppression. The happiness of future generations of Americans may well depend on how effective and how immediate we can make our aid felt. No one can tell the exact character of the emergency situations that we may be called upon to meet. The nation's hands must not be tied when the nation's life is in danger.

Yes, and we must prepare, all of us prepare, to make the sacrifices that the emergency—almost as serious as war itself—demands. Whatever stands in the way of speed and efficiency in defense, in defense preparations of any kind, must give way to the national need.

A free nation has the right to expect full cooperation from all groups. A free nation has the right to look to the leaders of business, of labor, and of agriculture to take the lead in stimulating effort—not among other groups, but within their own groups. The best way of dealing with the few slackers or troublemakers in our midst is, first, to shame them by patriotic example, and, if that fails, to use the sovereignty of government to save government.

As men do not live by bread alone,[14] they do not fight by armaments alone. Those who man our defenses and those behind them who build our defenses must have the stamina and the courage which come from unshakeable belief in the manner of life which they are defending. The mighty action that we are calling for cannot be based on a disregard of all the things worth fighting for.

The nation takes great satisfaction and much strength from the things which have been done to make its people conscious of their individual stake in the preservation of democratic life in America. Those things have toughened the fiber of our people, have renewed their faith, and strengthened their devotion to the institutions we make ready to protect. Certainly this is no time for any of us to stop thinking about the social and economic problems which are the root cause of the social revolution which is today a supreme factor in the world, for there is nothing mysterious about the foundations of a healthy and strong democracy.

---

13. Norway, Belgium, and the Netherlands were invaded by Germany in the spring of 1940.

14. This principle is expressed in Deuteronomy 8:3, Matthew 4:4, and Luke 4:4.

The basic things expected by our people of their political and economic systems are simple. They are: Equality of opportunity for youth and for others. Jobs for those who can work. Security for those who need it. The ending of special privilege for the few. The preservation of civil liberties for all. The enjoyment, the enjoyment of the fruits of scientific progress in a wider and constantly rising standard of living.

These are the simple, the basic things that must never be lost sight of in the turmoil and unbelievable complexity of our modern world. The inner and abiding strength of our economic and political systems is dependent upon the degree to which they fulfill these expectations.

Many subjects connected with our social economy call for immediate improvement. As examples: We should bring more citizens under the coverage of old-age pensions and unemployment insurance. We should widen the opportunities for adequate medical care. We should plan a better system by which persons deserving or needing gainful employment may obtain it.

I have called for personal sacrifice, and I am assured of the willingness of almost all Americans to respond to that call. A part of the sacrifice means the payment of more money in taxes. In my budget message I will recommend that a greater portion of this great defense program be paid for from taxation than we are paying for today. No person should try—or be allowed—to get rich out of the program. And the principle of tax payments in accordance with ability to pay should be constantly before our eyes to guide our legislation. If the Congress maintains these principles, the voters, putting patriotism ahead of pocketbooks, will give you their applause.

In the future days which we seek to make secure, we look forward to a world founded upon four essential human freedoms.

The first is freedom of speech and expression—everywhere in the world.

The second is freedom of every person to worship God in his own way—everywhere in the world.

The third is freedom from want, which, translated into world terms, means economic understandings which will secure to every nation a healthy peacetime life for its inhabitants—everywhere in the world.

The fourth is freedom from fear, which, translated into world terms, means a worldwide reduction of armaments to such a point and in such a thorough fashion that no nation will be in a position to commit an act of physical aggression against any neighbor—anywhere in the world.

That is no vision of a distant millennium. It is a definite basis for a kind of world attainable in our own time and generation. That kind of world is the very antithesis of the so-called new order of tyranny which the dictators seek to create with the crash of a bomb. To that new order we oppose the greater conception—the moral order.

A good society is able to face schemes of world domination and foreign revolutions alike without fear. Since the beginning of our American history we have been engaged in change—in a perpetual, peaceful revolution, a revolution which goes on steadily, quietly, adjusting itself to changing conditions without the concentration camp or the quicklime in the ditch. The world order which we seek is the cooperation of free countries working together in a friendly, civilized society.

This nation has placed its destiny in the hands and heads and hearts of its millions of free men and women, and its faith in freedom under the guidance of God. Freedom means the supremacy of human rights everywhere. All our support goes to those who struggle to gain those rights and keep them. Our strength is our unity of purpose. To that high concept there can be no end save victory.

Franklin D. Roosevelt

⧗

War Message

WASHINGTON, D.C.
DECEMBER 8, 1941

O N THE MORNING of Sunday, December 7, 1941, the Empire of Japan launched a surprise attack on the American naval base at Pearl Harbor in the Hawaiian Islands. Arriving in two waves, the Japanese airplanes destroyed or crippled eight battleships, put out of commission more than 150 American planes, and killed or wounded over 4,000 American military personnel. With a single stroke, the attack brought to a halt the debate between U.S. internationalists and isolationists, between the advocates of preparedness and those who sought to ignore what had already become a global conflict.

When Franklin Roosevelt convened an emergency joint session of Congress on December 8, there was no doubt that the outcome would be a declaration of war against Japan. Yet no one knew exactly what he would say. When Woodrow Wilson delivered his war message to Congress in April 1917 (pages 73–79), he presented a document of more than 3,600 words reviewing the development of events and justifying the move to hostilities. But no such length was necessary in 1941. A model of concision as well as eloquence, FDR's message accomplished everything it needed in 518 words.

Seven of those words—"a date which will live in infamy"—are among the most famous in the history of American oratory. Stating that the Empire of Japan had deliberately deceived the U.S. government with false hopes of peace even as it was planning the attack on Pearl Harbor, Roosevelt underscored the treacherous and malevolent nature of the enemy. Using the rhetorical device of climax, he also made clear that Pearl Harbor was only part of Japan's military operations throughout the Pacific area. Starting with "yesterday," then moving to "last night," and ending with "this morning," the movement of his language mirrored the movement of the enemy—constantly getting closer to the present moment.

As in so many of his speeches, FDR gave voice to the emotions of the American people, ninety million of whom heard him live on radio. By his words, tone, and demeanor, he sought to instill national confidence in the face of war, just as he had instilled confidence in the face of economic depression. Notwithstanding the grave losses of December 7, there was no equivocation in

FDR's message. "No matter how long it may take," he declared, the American people "will win through to absolute victory."

◇◇◇

Mr. Vice President,[1] Mr. Speaker,[2] members of the Senate and of the House of Representatives: Yesterday, December 7th, 1941—a date which will live in infamy—the United States of America was suddenly and deliberately attacked by naval and air forces of the Empire of Japan.

The United States was at peace with that nation and, at the solicitation of Japan, was still in conversation with its government and its Emperor looking toward the maintenance of peace in the Pacific. Indeed, one hour after Japanese air squadrons had commenced bombing in the American island of Oahu, the Japanese ambassador to the United States and his colleague delivered to our Secretary of State[3] a formal reply to a recent American message. And while this reply stated that it seemed useless to continue the existing diplomatic negotiations, it contained no threat or hint of war or of armed attack.

It will be recorded that the distance of Hawaii from Japan makes it obvious that the attack was deliberately planned many days or even weeks ago. During the intervening time, the Japanese government has deliberately sought to deceive the United States by false statements and expressions of hope for continued peace.

The attack yesterday on the Hawaiian Islands has caused severe damage to American naval and military forces. I regret to tell you that very many American lives have been lost. In addition, American ships have been reported torpedoed on the high seas between San Francisco and Honolulu.

Yesterday the Japanese government also launched an attack against Malaya.

Last night Japanese forces attacked Hong Kong.

Last night Japanese forces attacked Guam.

Last night Japanese forces attacked the Philippine Islands.

Last night the Japanese attacked Wake Island.

And this morning the Japanese attacked Midway Island.

Japan has, therefore, undertaken a surprise offensive extending throughout the Pacific area. The facts of yesterday and today speak for themselves. The people of the United States have already formed their opinions and well understand the implications to the very life and safety of our nation.

As commander in chief of the army and navy, I have directed that all measures be taken for our defense. But always will our whole nation remember the character of the onslaught against us. No matter how long it may take us to overcome this premeditated invasion, the American people in their righteous might will win through to absolute victory.

I believe that I interpret the will of the Congress and of the people when I assert that we will not only defend ourselves to the uttermost, but will make it very certain that this form of treachery shall never again endanger us.

Hostilities exist. There is no blinking at the fact that our people, our territory, and our interests are in grave danger. With confidence in our armed forces, with the unbounding determination of our people, we will gain the inevitable triumph—so help us God.

I ask that the Congress declare that since the unprovoked and dastardly attack by Japan on Sunday, December 7th, 1941, a state of war has existed between the United States and the Japanese Empire.

1. Henry A. Wallace.

2. Sam Rayburn, Speaker of the House of Representatives.

3. Cordell Hull.

⌛

The Truman Doctrine

WASHINGTON, D.C.
MARCH 12, 1947

HARRY TRUMAN WAS not a great orator, but when he wanted to say something, he did so plainly and forcefully. After serving as Vice President for less than three months, he was elevated to the White House with the death of Franklin D. Roosevelt on April 12, 1945. "I felt," he said at the time, "like the moon, the stars, and all the planets had fallen on me." Despite his trepidation, Truman proved to be an effective President, leading the nation through the end of World War II and the early crises of the Cold War. In 1948 he was elected in his own right after a canvass highlighted by a series of "whistle-stop" speeches delivered from the back of his campaign train. Of all his speeches as President, however, none was more important than his address to a joint session of Congress on March 12, 1947, in which he announced what quickly became known as the Truman Doctrine.

Although the United States, Great Britain, and the Soviet Union were still allies when World War II ended in 1945, they soon divided over postwar policy. A chief point of contention was the refusal of the USSR to withdraw from the countries of Central and Eastern Europe that it had occupied during the war. Poland, Czechoslovakia, Bulgaria, Rumania, Albania, Hungary, and eastern Germany found themselves, in the words of Winston Churchill, behind an "iron curtain" of Soviet domination. Relations between the USSR and the Western democracies continued to deteriorate through 1946 and early 1947. With Soviet troops occupying Eastern Europe, indigenous Communist parties, some of them supported by Moscow, began to challenge for political power in Western Europe. In Greece, Communist guerilla fighters took up arms in an effort to topple the pro-Western government. In Turkey, the Soviet Union sought to establish a military presence at the Dardanelles and the Bosporus straits. Faced with its own economic crisis, Great Britain informed the State Department in February 1947 that it was stopping economic aid to Greece and was withdrawing 40,000 troops from that country.

Faced with these developments, Truman let it be known in advance of his speech that he was going to request $400 million in aid to Greece and Turkey. Otherwise, few people knew what to expect. In addition to being carried live by radio and television, his words were conducted by shortwave to Europe and the

Middle East and, on a delayed basis, to Latin America and the Far East. The speech was translated for broadcast into eight languages, with summaries transmitted in twenty-five more. This was clearly a message that Truman wanted the world to hear.

At stake, he argued, were the same human freedoms for which World War II had been waged. Without mentioning the Soviet Union by name, he noted that the postwar world was divided into two camps—one that supported free institutions and representative government, and one that was based on "terror and oppression." The duty of America in such a world was to create "conditions in which we and other nations will be able to work out a way of life free from coercion." Providing assistance to Greece and Turkey was consistent with this duty, but Truman was announcing a general principle as well as presenting a specific request for aid. Neither international peace nor American security could be maintained, he warned, if "aggressive movements" were allowed to impose totalitarian regimes in country after country. "It must be the policy of the United States to support free peoples who are resisting attempted subjugation by armed minorities or by outside pressures."

With the example of World War II in mind, newspapers such as the *Hartford Courant* supported the President by editorializing that "it pays to act earlier, to insure survival for freedom without waiting for Armageddon." Others, including the *Dallas Morning News*, worried that the speech amounted to nothing less than "the establishment and maintenance of a Pax Americana." Truman emphasized economic and financial aid, rather than military armaments, but what stuck in people's minds was his designation of the United States as the leader of the free world. In the span of nineteen minutes, he articulated a far-reaching change in national identity and foreign policy that would shape American attitudes and actions for decades to come.

◇◇◇◇◇◇◇◇◇◇◇◇◇◇◇◇◇◇◇◇◇◇◇◇◇◇◇◇◇◇◇◇◇◇◇◇◇

Mr. President,[1] Mr. Speaker,[2] members of the Congress of the United States: The gravity of the situation which confronts the world today necessitates my appearance before a joint session of the Congress. The foreign policy and the national security of this country are involved. One aspect of the present situation, which I present to you at this time for your consideration and decision, concerns Greece and Turkey.

The United States has received from the Greek government an urgent appeal for financial and economic assistance. Preliminary reports from the American Economic Mission now in Greece and reports from the American ambassador in Greece[3] corroborate the statement of the Greek government that assistance is imperative if Greece is to survive as a free nation. I do not believe that the American people and the Congress wish to turn a deaf ear to the appeal of the Greek government.

Greece is not a rich country. Lack of sufficient natural resources has always forced the Greek people to work hard to make both ends meet. Since 1940 this industrious, peace-loving country has suffered

1. Arthur H. Vandenberg, President Pro Tempore of the Senate.

2. Joseph W. Martin Jr., Speaker of the House of Representatives.

3. Lincoln MacVeagh.

invasion, four years of cruel enemy occupation, and bitter internal strife. When forces of liberation entered Greece, they found that the retreating Germans had destroyed virtually all the railways, roads, port facilities, communications, and merchant marine. More than a thousand villages had been burned. Eighty-five percent of the children were tubercular. Livestock, poultry, and draft animals had almost disappeared. Inflation had wiped out practically all savings.

As a result of these tragic conditions, a militant minority, exploiting human want and misery, was able to create political chaos which, until now, has made economic recovery impossible. Greece is today without funds to finance the importation of those goods which are essential to bare subsistence. Under these circumstances the people of Greece cannot make progress in solving their problems of reconstruction. Greece is in desperate need of financial and economic assistance to enable it to resume purchases of food, clothing, fuel, and seeds. These are indispensable for the subsistence of its people and are obtainable only from abroad. Greece must have help to import the goods necessary to restore internal order and security so essential for economic and political recovery.

The Greek government has also asked for the assistance of experienced American administrators, economists, and technicians to ensure that the financial and other aid given to Greece shall be used effectively in creating a stable and self-sustaining economy and in improving its public administration.

The very existence of the Greek state is today threatened by the terrorist activities of several thousand armed men, led by Communists, who defy the government's authority at a number of points, particularly along the northern boundaries. A commission appointed by the United Nations Security Council is at present investigating disturbed conditions in northern Greece and alleged border violations along the frontiers between Greece on the one hand and Albania, Bulgaria, and Yugoslavia on the other. Meanwhile, the Greek government is unable to cope with the situation. The Greek army is small and poorly equipped. It needs supplies and equipment if it is to restore authority to the government throughout Greek territory.

Greece must have assistance if it is to become a self-supporting and self-respecting democracy. The United States must supply this assistance. We have already extended to Greece certain types of relief and economic aid, but these are inadequate. There is no other country to which democratic Greece can turn.

No other nation is willing and able to provide the necessary support for a democratic Greek government. The British government, which has been helping Greece, can give no further financial or economic aid after March 31st. Great Britain finds itself under the necessity of reducing or liquidating its commitments in several parts of the world, including Greece. We have considered how the United Nations might assist in this crisis. But the situation is an urgent one requiring immediate action, and the United Nations and its related organizations are not in a position to extend help of the kind that is required.

It is important to note that the Greek government has asked for our aid in utilizing effectively the financial and other assistance we may give to Greece, and in improving its public administration. It is of the utmost importance that we supervise the use of any funds made available to Greece in such a manner that each dollar spent will count toward making Greece self-supporting and will help to build an economy in which a healthy democracy can flourish.

No government is perfect. One of the chief virtues of a democracy, however, is that its defects are always visible and under democratic processes can be pointed out and corrected. The government of Greece is not perfect. Nevertheless, it represents 85 percent of the members of the Greek parliament who were chosen in an election last year. Foreign observers, including 692 Americans, considered this election to be a fair expression of the views of the Greek people.

The Greek government has been operating in an atmosphere of chaos and extremism. It has made mistakes. The extension of aid by this country does not mean that the United States condones everything that the Greek government has done or will do. We have condemned in the past, and we condemn now, extremist measures of the right or the left. We have in the past advised tolerance, and we advise tolerance now.

Greek's neighbor Turkey also deserves our attention. The future of Turkey as an independent and economically sound state is clearly no less important to the freedom-loving peoples of the world than the future of Greece. The circumstances in which Turkey finds itself today are considerably different from those of Greece. Turkey has been spared the disasters that have beset Greece. And during the war, the United States and Great Britain furnished Turkey with material aid.

Nevertheless, Turkey now needs our support. Since the war Turkey has sought additional financial assistance from Great Britain and the United States for the purpose of effecting that modernization necessary for the maintenance of its national integrity. That integrity is essential to the preservation of order in the Middle East. The British government has informed us that, owing to its own difficulties, it can no longer extend financial or economic aid to Turkey. As in the case of Greece, if Turkey is to have the assistance it needs, the United States must supply it. We are the only country able to provide that help.

I am fully aware of the broad implications involved if the United States extends assistance to Greece and Turkey, and I shall discuss these implications with you at this time.

One of the primary objectives of the foreign policy of the United States is the creation of conditions in which we and other nations will be able to work out a way of life free from coercion. This was a fundamental issue in the war with Germany and Japan. Our victory was won over countries which sought to impose their will, and their way of life, upon other nations.

To ensure the peaceful development of nations free from coercion, the United States has taken a leading part in establishing the United Nations.[4] The United Nations is designed to make possible lasting freedom and independence for all its members. We shall not realize our objectives, however, unless we are willing to help free peoples to maintain their free institutions and their national integrity against aggressive movements that seek to impose upon them totalitarian regimes. This is no more than a

frank recognition that totalitarian regimes imposed upon free peoples by direct or indirect aggression undermine the foundations of international peace and hence the security of the United States.

The peoples of a number of countries of the world have recently had totalitarian regimes forced upon them against their will. The government of the United States has made frequent protests against coercion and intimidation in violation of the Yalta agreement[5] in Poland, Rumania, and Bulgaria. I must also state that in a number of other countries there have been similar developments.

At the present moment in world history nearly every nation must choose between alternative ways of life. The choice is too often not a free one. One way of life is based upon the will of the majority and is distinguished by free institutions, representative government, free elections, guarantees of individual liberty, freedom of speech and religion, and freedom from political oppression. The second way of life is based upon the will of a minority forcibly imposed upon the majority. It relies upon terror and oppression, a controlled press and radio, fixed elections, and the suppression of personal freedoms.

I believe that it must be the policy of the United States to support free peoples who are resisting attempted subjugation by armed minorities or by outside pressures. I believe that we must assist free peoples to work out their own destinies in their own way. I believe that our help should be primarily through economic and financial aid which is essential to economic stability and orderly political processes.

The world is not static, and the status quo is not sacred. But we cannot allow changes in the status quo in violation of the Charter of the United Nations by such methods as coercion or by such subterfuges as political infiltration. In helping free and independent nations to maintain their freedom, the United States will be giving effect to the principles of the Charter of the United Nations.

4. The United Nations was founded in 1945.

5. Signed by the Soviet Union, Great Britain, and the United States in February 1945, the Yalta accords included a commitment to assist the countries formerly under the control of Nazi Germany "to create democratic institutions of their own choice."

It is necessary only to glance at a map to realize that the survival and integrity of the Greek nation are of grave importance in a much wider situation. If Greece should fall under the control of an armed minority, the effect upon its neighbor Turkey would be immediate and serious. Confusion and disorder might well spread throughout the entire Middle East.

Moreover, the disappearance of Greece as an independent state would have a profound effect upon those countries in Europe whose peoples are struggling against great difficulties to maintain their freedoms and their independence while they repair the damages of war. It would be an unspeakable tragedy if these countries, which have struggled so long against overwhelming odds, should lose that victory for which they sacrificed so much. Collapse of free institutions and loss of independence would be disastrous not only for them but for the world. Discouragement and possibly failure would quickly be the lot of neighboring peoples striving to maintain their freedom and independence.

Should we fail to aid Greece and Turkey in this fateful hour, the effect will be far reaching to the West as well as to the East. We must take immediate and resolute action. I therefore ask the Congress to provide authority for assistance to Greece and Turkey in the amount of $400 million for the period ending June 30th, 1948. In requesting these funds, I have taken into consideration the maximum amount of relief assistance which would be furnished to Greece out of the $350 million which I recently requested that the Congress authorize for the prevention of starvation and suffering in countries devastated by the war.[6]

In addition to funds, I ask the Congress to authorize the detail of American civilian and military personnel to Greece and Turkey, at the request of those countries, to assist in the tasks of reconstruction and for the purpose of supervising the use of such financial and material assistance as may be furnished. I recommend that authority also be provided for the instruction and training of selected Greek and Turkish personnel.

Finally, I ask that the Congress provide authority which will permit the speediest and most effective use, in terms of needed commodities, supplies, and equipment, of such funds as may be authorized. If further funds, or further authority, should be needed for the purposes indicated in this message, I shall not hesitate to bring the situation before the Congress. On this subject the executive and legislative branches of the government must work together.

This is a serious course upon which we embark. I would not recommend it except that the alternative is much more serious. The United States contributed, the United States contributed $341 billion toward winning World War II. This is an investment in world freedom and world peace. The assistance that I'm recommending for Greece and Turkey amounts to a little more than one-tenth of 1 percent of this investment. It is only common sense that we should safeguard this investment and make sure that it was not in vain.

The seeds of totalitarian regimes are nurtured by misery and want. They spread and grow in the evil soil of poverty and strife. They reach their full growth when the hope of a people for a better life has died. We must keep that hope alive. The free peoples of the world look to us for support in maintaining their freedoms. If we falter in our leadership, we may endanger the peace of the world and we shall surely endanger the welfare of this nation.

Great responsibilities have been placed upon us by the swift movement of events. I am confident that the Congress will face these responsibilities squarely.

---

6. Truman requested these funds in a special message of February 21, 1947.

George C. Marshall

⧗

The Marshall Plan

CAMBRIDGE, MASSACHUSETTS
JUNE 5, 1947

THE RECIPIENTS OF honorary degrees at Harvard University in 1947 included such luminaries as physicist J. Robert Oppenheimer, poet T. S. Eliot, and General Omar Bradley. To the crowd of 7,000 people gathered at Harvard Yard, however, they were all overshadowed by George C. Marshall, who was revered as a national hero. Chief of Staff of the U.S. Army during World War II, he was deemed the "true organizer of victory" by Winston Churchill. No less effusive in his praise, President Truman called Marshall "the great one of his age" and appointed him Secretary of State in January 1947. Marshall had declined two previous requests from Harvard to bestow an honorary degree upon him, but this time he accepted—not out of vainglory, but because the timing of Harvard's commencement provided a perfect occasion for him to introduce the broad outlines of what would become the European Recovery Program, known to history as the Marshall Plan.

At the time of Marshall's speech, specifics of the plan had yet to be formulated. Indeed, he would say later that what he presented at Harvard was "something between a hint and a suggestion." What had been agreed upon was the need for a comprehensive effort to rebuild the European economies shattered by World War II. Three weeks before Marshall appeared at Harvard, Churchill had described Europe as "a rubble-heap, a charnel house, a breeding ground of pestilence and hate." Marshall's language was less colorful and was typical, in Truman's words, of the man himself: "Matter-of-fact and without oratorical flourishes, compact and to the point." Noting that without "the return of normal economic health in the world...there can be no political stability and no assured peace," Marshall offered aid to "any government that is willing to assist in the task of recovery." The initiative, he said, must come from Europe, but the United States would help "so far as it may be practical for us to do so." In his most quoted words, he declared that the new American policy was "directed not against any country or doctrine, but against hunger, poverty, desperation, and chaos." It was such sentiments that led British Foreign Secretary Ernest Bevin to remark that "the speech may well rank as one of the greatest in the world's history."

Many people were involved in creating the European Recovery Program, not least President Truman, but the press instantly referred to it as the Marshall Plan. This was fine with Truman, who believed Marshall's name would improve its chances of getting through the House and Senate. Although the Soviet Union and the occupied states of Eastern Europe declined to participate in the plan, it was a godsend to the nations who did take part. Passed by Congress in March 1948, it pumped $13 billion of aid into Western Europe, helped put a battle-scarred continent on the road to recovery, earned Marshall the 1953 Nobel Peace Prize, and remains one of the most successful initiatives in the history of American foreign policy.

Some previous printings of Marshall's speech do not include the opening paragraph and the final three paragraphs, which were not part of the prepared text released to the press. Working from an audio recording, we have restored the missing portions, which together make up 20 percent of the text.

◇◇

Mr. President,[1] Dr. Conant,[2] members of the Board of Overseers, ladies and gentlemen: I'm profoundly grateful, touched by the great distinction and honor, great compliment accorded me by the authorities of Harvard this morning.[3] I'm overwhelmed, as a matter of fact, and I'm rather fearful of my inability to maintain such a high rating as you've been generous enough to accord to me. In these historic and lovely surroundings, this perfect day, and this very wonderful assembly, it is a tremendously impressive thing to an individual in my position.

But to speak more seriously, I need not tell you that the world situation is very serious. That must be apparent to all intelligent people. I think one difficulty is that the problem is one of such enormous complexity that the very mass of facts presented to the public by press and radio make it exceedingly difficult for the man in the street to reach a clear appraisement of the situation. Furthermore, the people of this country are distant from the troubled areas of the earth, and it is hard for them to comprehend the plight and consequent reactions of the long-suffering peoples of Europe and the effect of those reactions on their governments in connection with our efforts to promote peace in the world.

In considering the requirements for the rehabilitation of Europe, the physical loss of life, the visible destruction of cities, factories, mines, and railroads was correctly estimated, but it has become obvious during recent months that this visible destruction was probably less serious than the dislocation of the entire fabric of [the] European economy. For the past ten years conditions have been highly abnormal.

The feverish preparation for war and the more feverish maintenance of the war effort engulfed all aspects of national economies. Machinery has fallen into disrepair or is entirely obsolete. Under the arbitrary and destructive Nazi rule, virtually every possible enterprise was geared into the German war machine. Long-standing commercial ties, private institutions, banks, insurance companies, and shipping companies disappeared through loss of capital, absorption through nationalization, or by simple destruction. In many countries, confidence in the local currency has been severely shaken.

The breakdown of the business structure of Europe during the war was complete. Recovery has been seriously retarded by the fact that two years after the close of hostilities a peace settlement with Germany and Austria has not been agreed upon. But even given a more prompt solution of these difficult problems, the rehabilitation of the economic structure of Europe quite evidently will require a much longer time and greater effort than has been foreseen.

There is a phase of this matter which is both interesting and serious. The farmer has always produced the foodstuffs to exchange with the city dweller for the other necessities of life. This division of labor

---

1. Leonard Bell, president of the Harvard Alumni Association.

2. James Bryant Conant, president of Harvard.

3. Marshall was awarded an honorary degree at the commencement ceremonies that morning.

is the basis of modern civilization. At the present time it is threatened with breakdown. The town and city industries are not producing adequate goods to exchange with the food-producing farmer. Raw materials and fuel are in short supply. Machinery, as I have said, is lacking or worn out. The farmer or the peasant cannot find the goods for sale which he desires to purchase. So the sale of his farm produce for money, which he cannot use, seems to him an unprofitable transaction. He therefore has withdrawn many fields from crop cultivation and is using them for grazing. He feeds more grain to stock and finds for himself and his family an ample supply of food, however short he may be on clothing and the other ordinary gadgets of civilization.

Meanwhile, people in the cities are short of food and fuel, and in some places approaching the starvation level. So their governments are forced to use their foreign money and credit to procure these necessities abroad. This process exhausts funds which are urgently needed for reconstruction. Thus a very serious situation is rapidly developing which bodes no good for the world. The modern system of the division of labor upon which the exchange of products is based is in danger of breaking down.

The truth of the matter is that Europe's requirements for the next three or four years of foreign food and other essential products, principally from America, are so much greater than her present ability to pay that she must have substantial additional help or face economic, social, and political deterioration of a very grave character.

The remedy seems to lie in breaking the vicious circle and restoring the confidence of the people of Europe in the economic future of their own countries and of Europe as a whole. The manufacturer and the farmer throughout wide areas must be able and willing to exchange their products for currencies, the continuing value of which is not open to question.

Aside from the demoralizing effect on the world at large and the possibilities of disturbances arising as a result of the desperation of the people concerned, the consequences to the economy of the United States should be apparent to all. It is logical that the United States should do whatever it is able to do to assist in the return of normal economic health in the world, without which there can be no political stability and no assured peace.

Our policy is directed not against any country or doctrine, but against hunger, poverty, desperation, and chaos. Its purpose should be the revival of a working economy in the world so as to permit the emergence of political and social conditions in which free institutions can exist. Such assistance, I am convinced, must not be on a piecemeal basis as various crises develop. Any assistance that this government may render in the future should provide a cure rather than a mere palliative.

Any government that is willing to assist in the task of recovery will find full cooperation, I am sure, on the part of the United States government. Any government which maneuvers to block the recovery of other countries cannot expect help from us. Furthermore, furthermore, governments, political parties, or groups which seek to perpetuate human misery in order to profit therefrom politically or otherwise will encounter the opposition of the United States.

It is already evident that before the United States government can proceed much further in its efforts to alleviate the situation and help start the European world on its way to recovery, there must be some agreement among the countries of Europe as to the requirements of the situation and the parts those countries themselves will take in order to give a proper effect to whatever action might be undertaken by this government. It would be neither fitting nor efficacious for our government to undertake to draw up unilaterally a program designed to place Europe on its feet economically. This is the business of the Europeans. The initiative, I think, must come from Europe. The role of this country should consist of friendly aid in the drafting of a European program and of later support of such a program so far as it may be practical for us to do so. The program should be a joint one, agreed to by a number, if not all, European nations.

An essential part of any successful action on the part of the United States is an understanding on the part of the people of America of the character of the problem and the remedies to be applied. Political passion and prejudice should have no part.

With foresight and a willingness on the part of our people to face up to the vast responsibilities which history has clearly placed upon our country, the difficulties I have outlined can and will be overcome.

I am sorry that on each occasion I have said something publicly in regard to our international situation, I have been forced by the necessities of the case to enter into rather technical discussions. But to my mind, it is of vast importance that our people reach some general understanding of what the complications really are, rather than react from a passion or a prejudice or an emotion of the moment.

As I said more formally a moment ago, we are remote from the scene of these troubles. It is virtually impossible at this distance merely by reading or listening or even seeing photographs and motion pictures, to grasp at all the real significance of the situation. And yet the whole world of the future hangs on a proper judgment. It hangs, I think, to a large extent on the realization of the American people of just what are the various dominant factors. What are the reactions of the people? What are the justifications of those reactions? What are the sufferings? What is needed? What can best be done? What must be done?

Thank you very much.

Hubert H. Humphrey

⧗

The Sunshine of Human Rights

PHILADELPHIA, PENNSYLVANIA
JULY 14, 1948

O NE OF THE most voluble American politicians of the twentieth century, Hubert Humphrey had what Lyndon Johnson called "the greatest coordination of mind and tongue of anybody I know." Elected three times to the U.S. Senate, he served as Johnson's Vice President and was the Democratic Party's presidential nominee in 1968. Today he is best remembered for his rousing address in support of civil rights at the 1948 Democratic National Convention, a speech that first brought him to national prominence, forced the Democratic Party to confront the issue of equal rights for African Americans, and helped propel him from the plains of Minnesota to the corridors of power in Washington, D.C.

Just three weeks before the Democrats convened in Philadelphia, the Republicans had adopted a progressive civil rights plank at their national convention. Would the Democrats do the same or would they follow the dictates of the party's Southern wing, which had long used the doctrine of states' rights to deny blacks their basic citizenship rights? The issue came to a head when a group of Northern liberals led by Humphrey, then Mayor of Minneapolis, demanded that the party platform incorporate language supporting the "basic and funda-mental rights" of full political participation, equal opportunity of employment, security of person, and equal treatment in the armed forces.

After trying, and failing, to get the desired language in the report of the platform committee, Humphrey and his allies filed a minority report, which they succeeded in bringing to the floor of the convention for a vote. Speaking in sup-port of the minority report, Humphrey urged the delegates to commit themselves to American principles that held forth the "promise of a land where all men are truly free and equal." To those who argued that each state should be allowed to decide which rights would be granted to or withheld from citizens within its borders, Humphrey responded by saying, "The time has arrived in America for the Democratic Party to get out of the shadows of states' rights and to walk forthrightly into the bright sunshine of human rights."

The speech lasted less than ten minutes, but it left the convention in a state of near hysteria. Liberal delegates started a demonstration in the aisles in support of Humphrey's position, while Southerners waved their placards and screamed for recognition from convention chairman Sam Rayburn. When order was restored, the question was called and Humphrey's minority plank was adopted. Ignoring the Southern delegations, Rayburn recognized a delegate from Massachusetts, who promptly moved to recess. Humphrey had carried the day.

After the two-hour recess, the entire Mississippi delegation and half the Alabama delegation walked out of the convention. Three days later, disgrun-tled Southern Democrats formed the States' Rights Democratic Party, popu-larly known as the Dixiecrats, and nominated South Carolina Governor Strom Thurmond for President. With Thurmond running to his right and Progressive Party candidate Henry Wallace running to his left, most observers predicted that incumbent President Harry Truman would not be able to muster enough votes to defeat Republican candidate Thomas Dewey. But Truman proved them wrong, and later analysis showed that the strong civil rights plank championed by Humphrey was a factor in his victory.

◇◇◇

Mr. Chairman,[1] fellow Democrats, fellow Americans: I realize that in speaking in behalf of the minority report on civil rights as presented by Congressman Biemiller of Wisconsin[2] that I am dealing with a charged issue, with an issue which has been confused by emotionalism on all sides of the fence. I realize that there are here today friends and colleagues of mine, many of them, who feel just as deeply and keenly as I do about this issue and who are yet in complete dis-agreement with me.

My respect and admiration for these men and their views was great when I came to this conven-tion. It is now far greater because of the sincerity, the courtesy, and the forthrightness with which many of them have argued in our prolonged discussions in the platform committee.

Because of this very great respect and because of my profound belief that we have a challenging task

---

1. Sam Rayburn, Speaker of the U.S. House of Representatives and permanent chairman of the convention.

2. Andrew John Biemiller, chief architect of the minority report supported by Humphrey.

to do here, because good conscience, decent morality, demands it, I feel I must rise at this time to support a report—the minority report—a report that spells out our democracy, a report that the people of this country can and will understand, and a report that they will enthusiastically acclaim on the great issue of civil rights.

Now, let me say this at the outset—that this proposal is made for no single region. Our proposal is made for no single class, for no single racial or religious group in mind. All of the regions of this country, all of the states have shared in our precious heritage of American freedom. All the states and all the regions have seen at least some of the infringements of that freedom. All people—get this, all people, white and black, all groups, all racial groups—have been the victims at time[s] in this nation of, let me say, vicious discrimination.

The masterly statement of our keynote speaker, the distinguished United States Senator from Kentucky Alben Barkley, made that point with great force. Speaking of the founder of our party, Thomas Jefferson, he said this, and I quote from Alben Barkley: "He did not proclaim that all the white or the black or the red or the yellow men are equal, that all Christian or Jewish men are equal, that all Protestant and Catholic men are equal, that all rich and poor men are equal, that all good and bad men are equal. What he declared was that all men are equal, and the equality which he proclaimed was the equality in the right to enjoy the blessings of free government in which they may participate and to which they have given their support."[3]

Now these words of Senator Barkley's are appropriate to this convention, appropriate to this convention of the oldest, the most truly progressive political party in America. From the time of Thomas Jefferson, the time when that immortal American doctrine of individual rights under just and fairly administered laws, the Democratic Party has tried hard to secure expanding freedoms for all citizens. Oh, yes, I know other political parties may have talked more about civil rights, but the Democratic Party has surely done more about civil rights.

We have made progress; we've made great progress in every part of this country. We've made great progress in the South; we've made it in the West, in the North, and in the East. But we must now focus the direction of that progress towards the, towards the realization of a full program of civil rights to all. This convention must set out more specifically the direction in which our party efforts are to go.

We can be proud that we can be guided by the courageous trailblazing of two great Democratic Presidents. We can be proud of the fact that our great and beloved immortal leader Franklin Roosevelt gave us guidance.[4] And we can be proud of the fact, we can be proud of the fact that Harry Truman[5] has had the courage to give to the people of America the new Emancipation Proclamation.[6]

It seems to me, it seems to me that the Democratic Party needs to make definite pledges of the kinds suggested in the minority report to maintain the trust and the confidence placed in it by the people of all races and all sections of this country. Sure, we're here as Democrats. But, my good friends, we're here as Americans. We're here as the believers in the principle and the ideology of democracy, and I firmly believe that as men concerned with our country's future, we must specify in our platform the guarantees which we have mentioned in the minority report.

Yes, this is far more than a party matter. Every citizen in this country has a stake in the emergence of the United States as a leader in a free world. That world is being challenged by the world of slavery.[7] For us to play our part effectively, we must be in a morally sound position. We can't use a double

<hr/>

3. Barkley spoke on July 12.

4. Roosevelt was President from 1933 to 1945.

5. Truman became President upon Franklin Roosevelt's death on April 12, 1945.

6. The Emancipation Proclamation was issued by Abraham Lincoln in January 1963. Humphrey's mention of a "new Emancipation Proclamation" refers to Truman's commitment, in a February 1948 special message to Congress, to desegregate all U.S. armed services. The policy was effected through Executive Order 9981, issued twelve days after Humphrey's speech.

7. A reference to the Cold War between the United States and the Soviet Union.

standard—there's no room for double standards in American politics—for measuring our own and other people's policies. Our demands for democratic practices in other lands will be no more effective than the guarantee of those practices in our own country.

Friends, delegates, I do not believe that there can be any compromise on the guarantees of the civil rights which we have mentioned in the minority report. In spite, in spite of my desire for unanimous agreement on the entire platform, in spite of my desire to see everybody here in honest and unanimous agreement, there are some matters which I think must be stated clearly and without qualification. There can be no hedging; the newspaper headlines are wrong.[8] There will be no hedging and there will be no watering down, if you please, of the instruments and the principles of the civil rights program.

To those who say, my friends, to those who say that we are rushing this issue of civil rights, I say to them we are 172 years late. To those who say, to those who say that this civil rights program is an infringement on states' rights, I say this: The time has arrived in America for the Democratic Party to get out of the shadows of states' rights and to walk forthrightly into the bright sunshine of human rights.

People, people—human beings: This is the issue of the twentieth century. People of all kinds, all sorts of people, and these people are looking to America

for leadership, and they're looking to America for precept and example.

My good friends, my fellow Democrats, I ask you for a calm consideration of our historic opportunity. Let us not forget the evil, but let us do forget the evil passions and the blindness of the past. In these times of world economic, political, and spiritual—above all, spiritual—crisis, we cannot, and we must not, turn from the path so plainly before us. That path has already led us through many valleys of the shadow of death.[9] And now is the time to recall those who were left on that path of American freedom.

For all of us here, for the millions who have sent us, for the whole two billion members of the human family, our land is now, more than ever before, the last best hope on earth.[10] And I know that we can—and I know that we shall—begin[11] here the fuller and richer realization of that hope, that promise of a land where all men are truly free and equal and each man uses his freedom and equality wisely well.

My good friends, I ask my party, I ask the Democratic Party to march down the high road of progressive democracy. I ask this convention, I ask this convention to say in unmistakable terms that we proudly hail and we courageously support our President and leader Harry Truman in his great fight for civil rights in America.

8. On the morning of Humphrey's speech, headlines in the *Philadelphia Inquirer* referred to the platform committee's "watered-down civil rights plank."

9. An allusion to Psalm 23:4.

10. An echo of language often used by the American Revolutionaries and later by Abraham Lincoln.

11. Humphrey misspoke this word as "began."

Eleanor Roosevelt

The Struggle for Human Rights

PARIS, FRANCE
SEPTEMBER 28, 1948

DESPITE BEING PAINFULLY shy as a child and suffering from low self-esteem into early adulthood, Eleanor Roosevelt became one of the leading public figures of her time. She gave her first political speech in 1922, and when her husband, Franklin Delano Roosevelt, was elected President ten years later, she became the most visible—and controversial—first lady to that point in American history. In addition to using her influence on behalf of equal rights for women, workers, and African Americans, she was much in demand as a public speaker, wrote a nationally syndicated column, held regular press conferences, and in 1940 became the first President's spouse to address the national convention of a major political party. When critics called her "Madam President" or "Empress Eleanor," she held fast to her convictions and said that women in public life needed "a skin as thick as a rhinoceros hide."

Eleanor Roosevelt was long an advocate of international cooperation. President Harry Truman made her a member of the U.S. delegation to the newly created United Nations, which held its first session in London in January 1946. As chair of the UN's Human Rights Commission, she played a central role in creating the Universal Declaration of Human Rights, a document often referred to as the Magna Carta of mankind. Of all the challenges she faced in the two years it took to draft the declaration and guide it to passage by the General Assembly, none was more daunting than dealing with the Soviet Union at a time when tensions between the United States and its former ally seemed to escalate daily. Although she was initially optimistic about the prospects of cooperation with Moscow, Roosevelt came to regard Soviet obstructionism as the greatest barrier to approval of the declaration. In August 1948, President Truman and Secretary of State George C. Marshall consulted with her about the upcoming UN meetings in Paris. They urged her to make a major address highlighting the different conceptions of human rights held by the United States and the Soviet bloc. As Roosevelt worked on the speech, she characterized it as setting a "keynote" for what she anticipated would be the climactic deliberations on the Declaration of Human Rights.

On September 28, 1948, less than a week after the opening of the UN's fall session in Paris, Roosevelt addressed a packed house of 2,500 people at the amphitheatre of the Sorbonne. Her speech reflected the friction that had emerged during deliberations on the Declaration of Human Rights, but it ended by expressing hope that "with mutual good faith in the principles of the United Nations Charter," it was still possible to "find a common basis of understanding" through "the fundamental democratic practices of honest discussion and negotiation." Although she usually spoke from a brief set of notes, on this occasion she used a manuscript, which had been carefully prepared in consultation with the State Department. The official version of the speech, published by the State Department in February 1949, is based on Roosevelt's manuscript and has been reprinted many times, but it is not an accurate text of what she said.

When she delivered the speech, Roosevelt, who had been fluent in French since childhood, spoke in that language, rather than in English. Although the full speech was broadcast by French radio, there is no known complete recording of it. However, part of the speech was rebroadcast a few days later as part of a program on all the proceedings at the Sorbonne. A recording of that program is available at the Institut National de l'Audiovisuel in Paris. It contains the first ten minutes and last few minutes of Roosevelt's address as delivered in French. The middle portion is summarized by the announcer. The remainder of the thirty-minute program contains a description of the setting for the speech, as well as remarks by the speakers who preceded Roosevelt.

It is clear from the program that there are two major differences between the speech as published by the State Department and Roosevelt's actual words. First, when Roosevelt addressed her audience, she ad-libbed an introduction in which she thanked France for its contributions to the United States over the years and praised French delegate René Cassin for his work on the Human Rights Commission. Second, when she reached her prepared text, she remained faithful to its structure and ideas but introduced a number of changes in wording as she rendered it in French. In the text printed below, the portions of Roosevelt's speech presented on the broadcast are translated from that source. The middle section is from the State Department text. This is the first time that the parts of the speech preserved in French have been published as Roosevelt delivered them.

◇◇◇

I am very moved to come chat with you here. I'm afraid to not give a speech worthy of the Sorbonne. Still, if I can tell you all that I have in my heart tonight, I believe that we will understand each other very well.

I have known France for a long time; I have loved France for a long time. And when one forgets that today the United States is sending some aid to France and to other countries in Europe,[1] I would like to say that, regarding France, the United States will always recognize that it can return but a little of what France has done for us, not only in aiding us as a young country[2] but always throughout all the years. What France has been for us—that has given us something for which we could never give you enough thanks.

I would like to say a word to my colleague on the Commission for Human Rights.[3] He aids us a lot; believe me, he often seduces us with his speeches.

1. A reference to the European Recovery Program, popularly known as the Marshall Plan (see pages 276–279).

2. Roosevelt is referring to French support during the American Revolution, without which the colonies may well have failed in their quest for independence from Great Britain.

3. René Cassin, who preceded Roosevelt to the platform at the Sorbonne.

He is impassioned about human rights. And if we are to succeed, we need to have colleagues who are impassioned in his manner because it is not easy to win something so new as the enthusiasm of people for an idea. And I believe that we owe much, within our commission, to Professor René Cassin for the enthusiasm that he brings to us. As for me, I always apply what he says. I know that he knows much more than I do.

I have made my excuses to you. And if I make errors in French, I hope you will make excuses for me.[4]

I have come this evening to talk with you on one of the greatest issues of our time—that of the preservation of human freedom. I am happy to be able to give my little speech here in France, at the Sorbonne, because French soil knows liberty well. It has already been many years that the roots of the tree of liberty have run across this nourishing earth and have found the necessary elements for them to flourish there. It was here the Declaration of the Rights of Man was proclaimed[5] and the great slogans of the French Revolution—liberty, equality, fraternity—fired the imagination of men. I have chosen to discuss this issue in Europe because it is in Europe that the greatest battles between liberty and tyranny have been fought. I have chosen to discuss it in the early days of the General Assembly because liberty is a decisive question for the settlement of the principal political differences between peoples and governments today. And in consequence it is a decisive question that will have an influence on the future of the United Nations.

The decisive importance of this question was fully recognized by the founders of the United Nations at San Francisco.[6] Concern for the preservation and promotion of human rights and fundamental freedoms stands at the heart of the United Nations. Its charter is distinguished by its preoccupation with the rights and welfare of individual men and women.[7] The United Nations has made it clear that it intends to uphold human rights and to protect the dignity of the human personality. The preamble to the charter establishes the guiding idea in these terms: "We the peoples of the United Nations determined . . . to reaffirm faith in fundamental human rights, in the dignity and worth of the human person, in the equal rights of men and women and of nations large and small, and . . . to promote social progress and better standards of life in larger freedom." The charter thus poses the principle that peace and the security of mankind are tightly linked to the respect of each individual for the rights and freedoms of all.

One of the purposes of the United Nations is declared in Article 1 in these words: "To achieve international cooperation in solving international problems of an economic, social, cultural, or humanitarian character, and in promoting and encouraging respect for human rights and for fundamental freedoms for all without distinction as to race, sex, language, or religion."

This thought is repeated at several points, and notably in Articles 55 and 56 the members pledge themselves to take joint and separate action in cooperation with the United Nations for the promotion of "universal respect for, and observance of, human rights and fundamental freedoms for all without distinction as to race, sex, language, or religion."[8]

Our first task, the most important one that the Human Rights Commission was given, was to prepare an international bill of human rights. The first fruits of the work of the commission in this regard, that is to say the International Declaration of Human Rights,[9] will be presented to the General Assembly in the midst of its third session, which opened a few days ago in Paris. This declaration was finally completed after much work during the last session of

---

4. A reference to the fact that Roosevelt was speaking in French.

5. The declaration was approved by France's National Constituent Assembly on August 26, 1789.

6. On April 25, 1945, delegates from 50 countries convened for the United Nations Conference on International Organization. During the next two months, they established the UN's principles and organizational structure.

---

7. The UN Charter was signed in San Francisco on June 26, 1945. The UN officially came into existence in October 1945, after the charter was ratified by the required number of signatories.

8. From Article 55 of the UN Charter.

9. Original working title of what became the Universal Declaration of Human Rights.

the Human Rights Commission in New York in the spring of 1948.[10] The Economic and Social Council has sent it without recommendation to the General Assembly, together with other documents transmitted by our commission.

The Human Rights Commission decided that an international bill of rights should contain two parts. First, a declaration which could be presented to the General Assembly for the approval of the member states of the United Nations. This declaration will have great moral force and will declare to the peoples of the world: "This is what we hope to see accepted as fundamental human rights in the years to come." We have put down here the rights that we consider as fundamental for all individual human beings the world over, and with them the full development of the individual's personality is, in our opinion, possible.

Secondly, we have joined to the declaration a pact that should be in the form of a treaty, and submitted to the nations of the world. The Human Rights Commission was not able to finish this second part of its work, due to a lack of time. Each nation would ratify this covenant as it is prepared to do so, and the covenant would become binding on the nations which had adhered to it. Each nation that would ratify it would be then obligated to modify its laws whenever they did not conform to the covenant.[11]

This covenant, of course, would have to be a simpler document. It could not state aspirations, which we feel to be permissible in the declaration. It could only state rights which could be assured by law, and it must contain methods of implementation, and no state ratifying the covenant could be allowed to disregard it. The methods of implementation have not yet been agreed upon; nor have they been given adequate consideration by the commission at any of its meetings. There certainly should be discussion on the entire question of this world bill of human rights and there may be acceptance by this assembly of the declaration if they come to agreement on it. The acceptance of the declaration, I think, should encourage every

nation in the coming months to discuss its meaning with its people so that they will be better prepared to accept the covenant with a deeper understanding of the problems involved when that is presented, we hope, a year from now and, we hope, accepted.[12]

The declaration has come from the Human Rights Commission with unanimous acceptance except for four abstentions—the USSR, Yugoslavia, Ukraine, and Byelorussia. The reason for this is a fundamental difference in the conception of human rights as they exist in these states and in certain other member states in the United Nations.

In the discussion before the assembly, I think it should be made crystal clear what these differences are, and tonight I want to spend a little time making them clear to you. It seems to me there is a valid reason for taking the time today to think carefully and clearly on the subject of human rights because in the acceptance and observance of these rights lies the root, I believe, of our chance for peace in the future and for the strengthening of the United Nations organization to the point where it can maintain peace in the future.

We must not be confused about what freedom is. Basic human rights are simple and easily understood: freedom of speech and a free press; freedom of religion and worship; freedom of assembly and the right of petition; the right of men to be secure in their homes and free from unreasonable search and seizure and from arbitrary arrest and punishment.

We must not be deluded by the efforts of the forces of reaction to prostitute the great words of our free tradition and thereby to confuse the struggle. Democracy, freedom, human rights have come to have a definite meaning to the people of the world which we must not allow any nation to so change that they are made synonymous with suppression and dictatorship.

There are basic differences that show up even in the use of words between a democratic and a totalitarian country. For instance, "democracy" means one thing to the USSR and another to the USA and,

---

10. The commission met at Lake Success, New York, May 24–June 18, 1948.

11. The next 34 paragraphs are based on the printed version of Roosevelt's speech.

12. The Universal Covenant on Civil and Political Rights was not approved by the UN until 1966 and was not ratified by the requisite number of nations until 1976.

I know, in France. I have served since the first meeting of the nuclear commission on the Human Rights Commission,[13] and I think this point stands out clearly.

The USSR representatives assert that they already have achieved many things which we, in what they call the "bourgeois democracies," cannot achieve because their government controls the accomplishment of these things. Our government seems powerless to them because, in the last analysis, it is controlled by the people. They would not put it that way—they would say that the people in the USSR control their government by allowing their government to have certain absolute rights. We, on the other hand, feel that certain rights can never be granted to the government but must be kept in the hands of the people.

For instance, the USSR will assert that their press is free because the state makes it free by providing the machinery, the paper, and even the money for salaries for the people who work on the paper. They state that there is no control over what is printed in the various papers that they subsidize in this manner, such, for instance, as a trade union paper. But what would happen if a paper were to print ideas which were critical of the basic policies and beliefs of the Communist government? I am sure some good reason would be found for abolishing the paper.

It is true that there have been many cases where newspapers in the USSR have criticized officials and their actions and have been responsible for the removal of those officials, but in doing so they did not criticize anything which was fundamental to Communist beliefs. They simply criticized methods of doing things. So one must differentiate between things which are permissible, such as criticism of any individual or of the manner of doing things, and the criticism of a belief which would be considered vital to the acceptance of communism.

What are the differences, for instance, between trade unions in the totalitarian states and in the democracies? In the totalitarian state, a trade union is an instrument used by the government to enforce duties, not to assert rights. Propaganda material which the government desires the workers to have is furnished to the trade unions to be circulated to their members.

Our trade unions, on the other hand, are solely the instrument of the workers themselves. They represent the workers in their relations with the government and with management, and they are free to develop their own opinions without government help or interference. The concepts of our trade unions and those in totalitarian countries are drastically different. There is little mutual understanding.

I think the best example one can give of this basic difference of the use of terms is "the right to work." The Soviet Union insists that this is a basic right which it alone can guarantee because it alone provides full employment by the government. But the right to work in the Soviet Union means the assignment of workers to do whatever task is given to them by the government without an opportunity for the people to participate in the decision that the government should do this. A society in which everyone works is not necessarily a free society and may indeed be a slave society; on the other hand, a society in which there is widespread economic insecurity can turn freedom into a barren and vapid right for millions of people.

We in the United States have come to realize it means freedom to choose one's job, to work or not to work as one desires. We in the United States have come to realize, however, that people have a right to demand that their government will not allow them to starve because as individuals they cannot find work of the kind they are accustomed to doing, and this is a decision brought about by public opinion which came as a result of the Great Depression,[14] in which many people were out of work. But we would not consider in the United States that we had gained any

13. The nuclear commission was a nine-member group appointed in early 1946 to make recommendations about the UN's permanent Commission on Human Rights. Chaired by Roosevelt, it met in New York City April 29–May 20, 1946, and advised that the commission's first project should be to write a bill of human rights.

14. Economic downturn that affected the entire world, at various times and in various ways, from 1929 through most of World War II.

freedom if we were compelled to follow a dictatorial assignment to work where and when we were told. The right of choice would seem to us an important, fundamental freedom.

I have great sympathy with the Russian people. They love their country and have always defended it valiantly against invaders. They have been through a period of revolution, as a result of which they were for a time cut off from outside contact.[15] They have not lost their resulting suspicion of other countries, and the great difficulty is today that their government encourages this suspicion and seems to believe that force alone will bring them respect.

We, in the democracies, believe in a kind of international respect and action which is reciprocal. We do not think others should treat us differently from the way they wish to be treated. It is interference in other countries that especially stirs up antagonism against the Soviet government. If it wishes to feel secure in developing its economic and political theories within its territory, then it should grant to others that same security. We believe in the freedom of people to make their own mistakes. We do not interfere with them, and they should not interfere with others.

The basic problem confronting the world today, as I said in the beginning, is the preservation of human freedom for the individual and consequently for the society of which he is a part. We are fighting this battle again today as it was fought at the time of the French Revolution and at the time of the American Revolution. The issue of human liberty is as decisive now as it was then. I want to give you my conception of what is meant in my country by freedom of the individual.

Long ago in London during a discussion with Mr. Vyshinsky,[16] he told me there was no such thing as freedom for the individual in the world. All freedom of the individual was conditioned by the rights of other individuals. That, of course, I granted. I said: "We approach the question from a different point of view; we here in the United Nations are trying

to develop ideals which will be broader in outlook, which will consider first the rights of man, which will consider what makes man more free: not governments, but man."

The totalitarian state typically places the will of the people second to decrees promulgated by a few men at the top.

Naturally there must always be consideration of the rights of others; but in a democracy this is not a restriction. Indeed, in our democracies we make our freedoms secure because each of us is expected to respect the rights of others and we are free to make our own laws.

Freedom for our peoples is not only a right, but also a tool. Freedom of speech, freedom of the press, freedom of information, freedom of assembly—these are not just abstract ideals to us; they are tools with which we create a way of life, a way of life in which we can enjoy freedom.

Sometimes the processes of democracy are slow, and I have known some of our leaders to say that a benevolent dictatorship would accomplish the ends desired in a much shorter time than it takes to go through the democratic processes of discussion and the slow formation of public opinion. But there is no way of ensuring that a dictatorship will remain benevolent or that power once in the hands of a few will be returned to the people without struggle or revolution. This we have learned by experience, and we accept the slow processes of democracy because we know that shortcuts compromise principles on which no compromise is possible.

The final expression of the opinion of the people with us is through free and honest elections, with valid choices on basic issues and candidates. The secret ballot is an essential to free elections, but you must have a choice before you. I have heard my husband[17] say many times that a people need never lose their freedom if they kept their right to a secret ballot and if they used that secret ballot to the full.

Basic decisions of our society are made through the expressed will of the people. That is why when we see these liberties threatened, instead of falling

15. Roosevelt is referring to the Russian Revolution of 1917 and events of succeeding years.

16. Soviet Deputy Foreign Minister Andrei Vyshinsky.

17. Franklin D. Roosevelt, President of the United States, 1933–1945.

apart, our nation becomes unified and our democracies come together as a unified group in spite of our varied backgrounds and many racial strains.

In the United States we have a capitalistic economy. That is because public opinion favors that type of economy under the conditions in which we live. But we have imposed certain restraints; for instance, we have antitrust laws. These are the legal evidence of the determination of the American people to maintain an economy of free competition and not to allow monopolies to take away the people's freedom.

Our trade unions grow stronger because the people come to believe that this is the proper way to guarantee the rights of the workers and that the right to organize and to bargain collectively keeps the balance between the actual producer and the investor of money and the manager in industry who watches over the man who works with his hands and who produces the materials which are our tangible wealth.

In the United States we are old enough not to claim perfection. We recognize that we have some problems of discrimination,[18] but we find steady progress being made in the solution of these problems. Through normal democratic processes we are coming to understand our needs and how we can attain full equality for all our people. Free discussion on the subject is permitted. Our Supreme Court has recently rendered decisions to clarify a number of our laws to guarantee the rights of all.

The USSR claims it has reached a point where all races within her borders are officially considered equal and have equal rights, and they insist they have no discrimination where minorities are concerned.

This is a laudable objective, but there are other aspects of the development of freedom for the individual which are essential before the mere absence of discrimination is worth much, and these are lacking in the Soviet Union. Unless they are being denied freedoms which they want and which they see other people have, people do not usually complain of discrimination. It is these other freedoms—the basic freedoms of speech, of the press, of religion and conscience, of assembly, of fair trial and freedom from

arbitrary arrest and punishment—which a totalitarian government cannot safely give its people and which give meaning to freedom from discrimination.

It is my belief, and I am sure it is also yours, that the struggle for democracy and freedom is a critical struggle, for their preservation is essential to the great objective of the United Nations to maintain international peace and security.

Among free men the end cannot justify the means. We know the patterns of totalitarianism—the single political party, the control of schools, press, radio, the arts, the sciences, and the church to support autocratic authority. These are the age-old patterns against which men have struggled for 3,000 years. These are the signs of reaction, retreat, and retrogression.

The United Nations must hold fast to the heritage of freedom won by the struggle of its peoples; it must help us to pass it on to generations to come.

The development of the ideal of freedom and its translation into the everyday life of the people in great areas of the earth is the product of the efforts of many peoples. It is the fruit of a long tradition of vigorous thinking and courageous action. No one race and no one people can claim to have done all the work to achieve greater dignity for human beings and greater freedom to develop human personality. In each generation and in each country there must be a continuation of the struggle and new steps forward must be taken since this is preeminently a field in which to stand still is to retreat.

The field of human rights is not one in which compromise[s] on fundamental principles are possible. The work of the Commission on Human Rights is illustrative. The Declaration of Human Rights provides: "Everyone has the right to leave any country, including his own."[19] The Soviet representative said he would agree to this right if a single phrase was added to it: "in accordance with the procedure laid down in the laws of that country." It is obvious that to accept this would be not only to compromise but to nullify the right stated. This case forcefully illustrates the importance of the proposition that we must

18. A reference to racial, social, and economic discrimination faced by African Americans.

19. This language became part of Article 13 in the final version of the declaration.

ever be alert not to compromise fundamental human rights merely for the sake of reaching unanimity and thus lose them.

As I see it, it is not going to be easy to attain unanimity with respect to our different concepts of government and human rights. The struggle is bound to be difficult and one in which we must be firm but patient.[20] If we adhere faithfully to our principles, I think it is possible for us to maintain freedom and to do so peacefully and without recourse to force.

The future must see the broadening of human rights throughout the world. People who have glimpsed freedom will never be content until they have secured it for themselves. In a true sense, human rights are a fundamental object of law and government in a just society. Human rights exist to the degree that they are respected by people in relations with each other and by governments in relations with their citizens.[21]

The world at large is aware of the tragic consequences for human beings ruled by totalitarian systems. If we examine Hitler's rise to power, we see how the chains are forged which keep the individual a slave, and we can establish numerous parallels with what is taking place in other countries. Men must be free to discuss and to obtain as many facts as possible from the political point of view. And in all countries there must be at least two political parties because when there is only one political party, too many things can be subordinated to the interests of that one party, which then becomes a tyrant and not an instrument of democratic government.

The propaganda we have witnessed in past years, like that which we perceive currently, seeks to attack, to undermine, and to destroy the liberty and independence of peoples. Such propaganda leads people to doubt their heritage of rights and consequently compromises the principles by which they live. Or instead they rise to the challenge, redouble their vigilance, and stand steadfast to continue the struggle to maintain and enlarge human freedoms. People who continue to be denied the respect to which they are entitled as human beings will not acquiesce forever in such denial.

The Charter of the United Nations is the torch that lights the way leading to the achievement of human rights and fundamental freedoms on a universal scale. What matters now is not only the extent to which human rights and freedoms have been achieved, but the direction in which the world is oriented. Will the goals of the charter be faithfully pursued if some countries continue to restrain human rights and freedoms instead of promoting their general application and a universal respect for them, as is stipulated in the charter?

It is in the forum of the United Nations that the question of human rights must be debated. The United Nations as an organization has been set up to serve as the meeting ground for nations, to permit them to examine their mutual problems together and to take advantage of the differences in their experiences. It is because we are firmly attached to the principles of democracy and freedom that we stand always ready to use the fundamental democratic practices of honest discussion and negotiation. We now hope, as we have always done, that despite the marked differences in approach that we are facing in the world today, we can, with mutual good faith in the principles of the United Nations Charter, find a common basis of understanding.

We are here to take part in the meetings of this great international assembly which is meeting in your beautiful capital. Individual liberty is an inseparable part of the traditions cherished by France. In my capacity as a member of the delegation from the United States, I pray God to aid us to win another victory here for the rights and the freedoms of all men. And I know that France and the French people will always fight alongside us for those rights and that liberty.

---

20. Roosevelt's notes for her speech include the following statement: "When I was bringing up children I thought I understood well the full significance of patience. Children usually develop that quality in us, but I never knew in the faintest degree what it meant to really have patience until I served on the Human Rights Commission with delegates from the USSR." There is no way to know whether she used these exact words, but Durward Sandifer, director of the State Department's Office of UN Affairs, who was present at the Sorbonne, wrote that she "got a big laugh" when she extemporized words to this effect, most likely at this point in her address.

21. The remainder of the text is based on the recording of Roosevelt's remarks.

Eleanor Roosevelt

✕

Adoption of the Universal Declaration of Human Rights

B Y THE TIME the Universal Declaration of Human Rights was introduced for debate on the floor of the United Nations General Assembly on December 9, 1948, it had been through a six-stage drafting process in which all member states had been free to participate. Though at times unwieldy and often producing sharp debate, this process ensured that the declaration had broad support. Only one substantive change to it was made by the General Assembly, and shortly before midnight on December 10 it was approved, with forty-eight nations voting in favor, eight abstaining, and none voting in opposition. The lack of nays was especially gratifying to Eleanor Roosevelt, who, as chair of the Human Rights Commission, worried to the end that the Soviet bloc would line up against the declaration.

Roosevelt was one of more than thirty delegates who spoke on the declaration at the General Assembly. She averred that it was not perfect from the U.S. point of view but stated that it was "a good document—even a great document." It was, she acknowledged, only a declaration and did not carry the force of law; yet it provided "a common standard of achievement for all peoples of all nations" and marked a "great event…in the life of mankind." Echoing Abraham Lincoln's Gettysburg Address, she urged members of the UN to "rededicate ourselves to the unfinished task which lies before us" of creating an international covenant on human rights and measures for the implementation of human rights.

Roosevelt was enough of a realist to know the declaration could not, by itself, change the behavior of nations, but she was enough of an optimist to hope it would provide a moral compass for future generations. She remained a member of the U.S. delegation until 1953, after which she traveled widely and worked for a variety of humanitarian causes. By the time she died in 1962 at age seventy-eight, she was known as "the first lady of the world." Although she was often dismayed by the course of events during the Cold War, she regarded her work on the Universal Declaration of Human Rights as her greatest legacy, a judgment shared by her biographers. Perhaps the most eloquent tribute to her was paid by Adlai Stevenson, who said, "She would rather light a candle than curse the darkness, and her glow has warmed the world."

◇◇◇

The long and meticulous study and debate of which this Universal Declaration of Human Rights is the product means that it reflects the composite views of the many men[1] and governments who have contributed to its formulation. Not every man nor every government can have what he wants in a document of this kind. There are of course particular provisions in the declaration before us with which we are not fully satisfied. I have no doubt this is true of other delegations, but taken as a whole the delegation of the United States believes that this a good document— even a great document—and we propose to give it our full support. The position of the United States on the various parts of the declaration is a matter of record in the Third Committee.[2] I shall not burden the assembly, and particularly my colleagues of the Third Committee, with a restatement of that position here.

Certain provisions of the declaration are stated in such broad terms as to be acceptable only because of the limitations in Article 29 providing for limitation on the exercise of the rights for the purpose of meeting the requirements of morality, public order, and the general welfare.[3] An example of this is the provision that everyone has the right of equal access to the public service in his country.[4] The basic principle of equality and of nondiscrimination as to public employment is sound, but it cannot be accepted without limitations. My government, for example, would consider that this is unquestionably subject to limitation in the interest of public order and the general welfare. It would not consider that the exclusion from public employment of persons holding subversive political beliefs and not loyal to the basic principles and practices of the constitution and laws of the country would in any way infringe upon this right.

Likewise, my government has made it clear in the course of the development of the declaration that it does not consider that the economic and social and cultural rights stated in the declaration imply an obligation on governments to assure the enjoyment of these rights by direct governmental action. This was made quite clear in the Human Rights Commission text of Article 23, which served as a so-called umbrella article to the articles on economic and social rights.[5] We consider that the principle has not been affected by the fact that this article no longer contains a reference to the articles which follow it. This in no way affects our wholehearted support for the basic principles of economic, social, and cultural rights set forth in these articles.

---

1. Roosevelt uses "man" and "men" throughout her speech to refer to males and females alike, as does the declaration itself. When this issue was raised in the drafting committee in June 1947, she stated: "I have always considered myself a feminist, but I really have no objection to the use of the word [men] as the committee sees it....When we say 'all men are brothers,' we mean that all human beings are brothers, and we are not differentiating between men and women."

2. The UN's Third Committee on Social, Humanitarian and Cultural Concerns began its review of the draft of the declaration on September 28, 1948, and on December 7 approved it for submission to the General Assembly.

3. Article 29, Section 2, states: "In the exercise of his rights and freedoms, everyone shall be subject only to such limitations as are determined by law solely for the purpose of securing due recognition and respect for the rights and freedoms of others and of meeting the just requirements of morality, public order and the general welfare in a democratic society."

4. This provision is stated in Article 21, Section 2.

5. Roosevelt is referring to Article 20 in the draft approved by the Human Rights Commission in June 1948 at its meeting in Lake Success, New York: "Everyone, as a member of society, has the right to social security and is entitled to the realization, through national effort and international cooperation, and in accordance with the organization and resources of each state, of the economic, social, and cultural rights set out below." After revision, this became Article 22 in the final version of the declaration. The reference to Article 23 in Roosevelt's speech may have resulted from a typographical error in the printed text, which appeared initially in the December 19, 1948, *Department of State Bulletin*.

In giving our approval to the declaration today, it is of primary importance that we keep clearly in mind the basic character of the document. It is not a treaty; it is not an international agreement. It is not and does not purport to be a statement of law or legal obligation. It is a declaration of basic principles of human rights and freedoms, to be stamped with the approval of the General Assembly by formal vote of its members and to serve as a common standard of achievement for all peoples of all nations.

We stand today at the threshold of a great event both in the life of the United Nations and in the life of mankind—that is the approval by the General Assembly of the Universal Declaration of Human Rights recommended by the Third Committee. This declaration may well become the international Magna Carta[6] of all men everywhere. We hope its proclamation by the General Assembly will be an event comparable to the proclamation of the declaration of the Rights of Man by the French people in 1789,[7] the adoption of the Bill of Rights[8] by the people of the United States, and the adoption of comparable declarations at different times in other countries.

At a time when there are so many issues on which we find it difficult to reach a common basis of agreement, it is a significant fact that fifty-eight states have found such a large measure of agreement in the complex field of human rights. This must be taken as testimony of our common aspiration first voiced in the Charter of the United Nations to lift men everywhere to a higher standard of life and to a greater enjoyment of freedom. Man's desire for peace lies behind this declaration. The realization that the flagrant violation of human rights by Nazi and Fascist countries sowed the seeds of the last world war has supplied the impetus for the work which brings us to the moment of achievement here today.[9]

In a recent speech in Canada, Gladstone Murray said: "The central fact is that man is fundamentally a moral being, that the light we have is imperfect does not matter so long as we are always trying to improve it.... We are equal in sharing the moral freedom that distinguishes us as men. Man's status makes each individual an end in himself. No man is by nature simply the servant of the state or of another man.... The ideal and fact of freedom—and not technology—are the true distinguishing marks of our civilization."[10]

This declaration is based upon the spiritual fact that man must have freedom in which to develop his full stature and through common effort to raise the level of human dignity. We have much to do to fully achieve and to assure the rights set forth in this declaration. But having them put before us with the moral backing of fifty-eight nations will be a great step forward.

As we here bring to fruition our labors on this Declaration of Human Rights, we must at the same time rededicate ourselves to the unfinished task which lies before us.[11] We can now move on with new courage and inspiration to the completion of an international covenant on human rights[12] and of measures for the implementation of human rights.

In conclusion, I feel that I cannot do better than to repeat the call to action by Secretary

---

6. Issued in 1215 during the reign of King John, Magna Carta is regarded as a cornerstone of British constitutional liberty.

7. Approved by the National Constituent Assembly in August 1789, the Declaration of the Rights of Man and of the Citizen pronounced the French Revolution's principles of liberty and equality.

8. The first 10 amendments to the U.S. Constitution; ratified by the states in 1791.

9. The final four paragraphs of the speech are inexplicably omitted from *The Eleanor Roosevelt Papers, Vol. I: The Human Rights Years, 1945–1948* (2007).

10. Murray was a Canadian journalist and public intellectual. We have not been able to identify the source from which Roosevelt drew Murray's quotation, but he used the same passage in a speech to the Empire Club of Canada, in Toronto, February 17, 1949.

11. An allusion to Abraham Lincoln's Gettysburg Address, November 19, 1863.

12. The adoption of UN covenants based on the Universal Declaration of Human Rights did not occur until 1966.

Marshall[13] in his opening statement to this assembly: "Let this third regular session of the General Assembly approve by an overwhelming majority the Declaration of Human Rights as a standard of conduct for all; and let us, as members of the United Nations, conscious of our own shortcomings and imperfections, join our effort in good faith to live up to this high standard."[14]

---

13. Secretary of State George C. Marshall.

14. From Marshall's speech of September 23, 1948.

Margaret Chase Smith

Declaration of Conscience

WASHINGTON, D.C.
JUNE 1, 1950

SPEAKING TO THE Republican Women's Club in Wheeling, West Virginia, on February 9, 1950, U.S. Senator Joseph McCarthy claimed to have in his hand a list of 205 known members of the Communist Party who were employed in the State Department. Exhibiting his typical lack of regard for accuracy or consistency, in a radio interview the next day he changed the number to fifty-seven. Either figure was alarming, however, and McCarthy's charge was headline material. Thus began his meteoric rise as the nation's most notorious anti-Communist. Virtually unknown outside his home state of Wisconsin before the Wheeling speech, he soon became a national political force and "McCarthyism" entered America's political vocabulary.

In addition to being synonymous with anti-communism, McCarthyism was marked by the bullying tactics and reckless disregard for truth of its chief practitioner. Even the U.S. Senate wilted in the face of McCarthy's onslaught. At a time when no public official wanted to be stigmatized as soft on communism, most Senators were unwilling openly to challenge McCarthy. One of the few exceptions was Maine's Margaret Chase Smith, who had been elected in 1948 after serving eight years in the House of Representatives. The only woman in the Senate and, at the time, the only woman in U.S. history to sit in both houses of Congress, Smith had impeccable anti-Communist credentials, but she was deeply troubled by McCarthy's methods as well as by the fact, as she said later, that he had "the Senate paralyzed with fear."

Working with her chief aide, William Lewis, Smith drafted a five-point statement deploring both the Truman administration's "lack of effective leadership" against communism and the use of "totalitarian techniques" by "certain elements of the Republican Party" who sought to exploit legitimate concerns about communism for political gain. A Republican herself, Smith privately enlisted six other moderate Senate Republicans to join her in signing the statement. On June 1, 1950, with no advance publicity, she introduced the statement in a speech on the Senate floor.

In deference to the rules of senatorial courtesy, Smith did not mention McCarthy by name, but there could be no doubt about her meaning when she referred in her speech to the "hate and character assassination" that were undermining free expression in Congress and out. The record of the Truman administration, she said, provided more than enough ammunition for its critics without resorting to political smears. In the most memorable line of the speech, she stated: "I do not want to see the Republican Party ride to political victory on the Four Horsemen of Calumny—Fear, Ignorance, Bigotry, and Smear." It was vital, she declared, that the nation recapture "the strength and unity" it had in World War II, "when we fought the enemy instead of ourselves."

Although the press called Smith's speech "a public document of great significance" that brought "a fresh breeze in the fear-ridden atmosphere" of the Senate, it was not enough to slow the McCarthy juggernaut. All but one of Smith's cosigners on the statement recanted their positions in fairly short order, only a few Democrats lined up behind her, and it would take another four years for the Senate to repudiate McCarthy (see pages 328–332). Smith, however, stood her ground and became widely admired for her courage and independence. She remained in the Senate until 1972, and in 1964 became the first American woman to have her name placed in nomination for the presidency at the convention of a major political party.

◇◇

Mr. President,[1] I would like to speak briefly and simply about a serious national condition. It is a national feeling of fear and frustration that could result in national suicide and the end of everything that we Americans hold dear. It is a condition that comes from the lack of effective leadership either in the legislative branch or the executive branch of our government. That leadership is so lacking that serious and responsible proposals are being made that national advisory commissions be appointed to provide such critically needed leadership.

I speak as briefly as possible because too much harm has already been done with irresponsible words of bitterness and selfish political opportunism. I speak as simply as possible because the issue is too great to be obscured by eloquence. I speak simply and briefly in the hope that my words will be taken to heart.

Mr. President, I speak as a Republican. I speak as a woman. I speak as a United States Senator. I speak as an American.

The United States Senate has long enjoyed worldwide respect as the greatest deliberative body in the world. But recently that deliberative character has too often been debased to the level of a forum of hate

---

1. Kenneth McKellar, President pro tempore of the Senate.

and character assassination sheltered by the shield of congressional immunity.

It is ironical that we Senators can in debate in the Senate, directly or indirectly, by any form of words, impute to any American who is not a Senator any conduct or motive unworthy or unbecoming an American—and without that non-Senator American having any legal redress against us—yet if we say the same thing in the Senate about our colleagues, we can be stopped on the grounds of being out of order.

It is strange that we can verbally attack anyone else without restraint and with full protection, and yet we hold ourselves above the same type of criticism here on the Senate floor. Surely the United States Senate is big enough to take self-criticism and self-appraisal. Surely we should be able to take the same kind of character attacks that we "dish out" to outsiders.

I think that it is high time for the United States Senate and its members to do some real soul-searching and to weigh our consciences as to the manner in which we are performing our duty to the people of America and the manner in which we are using or abusing our individual powers and privileges.

I think it is high time that we remembered that we have sworn to uphold and defend the Constitution. I think it is high time that we remembered that the Constitution, as amended, speaks not only of the freedom of speech but also of trial by jury instead of trial by accusation.[2] Whether it be a criminal prosecution in court or a character prosecution in the Senate, there is little practical distinction when the life of a person has been ruined.

Those of us who shout the loudest about Americanism in making character assassinations are all too frequently those who, by our own words and acts, ignore some of the basic principles of Americanism—the right to criticize, the right to hold unpopular beliefs, the right to protest, the right of independent thought.

The exercise of these rights should not cost one single American citizen his reputation or his right to a livelihood. Nor should he be in danger of losing his reputation or livelihood merely because he happens to know someone who holds unpopular beliefs. Who of us does not? Otherwise none of us could call our souls our own. Otherwise thought control would have set in.

The American people are sick and tired of being afraid to speak their minds lest they be politically smeared as Communists or Fascists by their opponents. Freedom of speech is not what it used to be in America. It has been so abused by some that it is not exercised by others.

The American people are sick and tired of seeing innocent people smeared and guilty people whitewashed. But there have been enough proved cases such as the *Amerasia* case,[3] the Hiss case,[4] the Coplon case,[5] the Gold case,[6] to cause nationwide distrust and strong suspicion that there may be something to the unproved, sensational accusations.

As a Republican, I say to my colleagues on this side of the aisle that the Republican Party faces a challenge today that is not unlike the challenge that it faced back in Lincoln's day. The Republican Party so successfully met that challenge that it emerged from the Civil War as the champion of a united nation in addition to being a party which unrelentingly fought loose spending and loose programs.

Today our country is being psychologically divided by the confusion and the suspicions that are bred in the United States Senate to spread like cancerous tentacles of "know nothing, suspect everything" attitudes. Today we have a Democratic administration which has developed a mania for loose spending and loose programs. History is repeating

---

2. Smith is referring to the Sixth Amendment to the U.S. Constitution.

3. In June 1945 six people associated with *Amerasia* magazine, three of them government employees, were arrested on espionage charges. By the time of Smith's speech, three of the six had been cleared, charges had been dropped against one, and two had been assessed fines on reduced charges.

4. Accused of transmitting government documents to the Soviet Union, Alger Hiss was found guilty in January 1950 of perjury, for which he served a five-year prison term.

5. Judith Coplon, a Justice Department employee, was arrested in 1949 and convicted of passing secrets to the Soviet Union.

6. A longtime Soviet agent in the United States, Harry Gold was arrested and confessed to his activities in the spring of 1950.

itself, and the Republican Party again has the opportunity to emerge as the champion of unity and prudence.

The record of the present Democratic administration has provided us with sufficient campaign issues without the necessity of resorting to political smears. America is rapidly losing its position as leader of the world simply because the Democratic administration has pitifully failed to provide effective leadership.

The Democratic administration has completely confused the American people by its daily contradictory grave warnings and optimistic assurances, which show the people that our Democratic administration has no idea of where it is going.

The Democratic administration has greatly lost the confidence of the American people by its complacency to the threat of communism here at home and the leak of vital secrets to Russia through key officials of the Democratic administration. There are enough proved cases to make this point without diluting our criticism with unproved charges.

Surely these are sufficient reasons to make it clear to the American people that it is time for a change and that a Republican victory is necessary to the security of the country. Surely it is clear that this nation will continue to suffer as long as it is governed by the present ineffective Democratic administration.

Yet to displace it with a Republican regime embracing a philosophy that lacks political integrity or intellectual honesty would prove equally disastrous to the nation. The nation sorely needs a Republican victory. But I do not want to see the Republican Party ride to political victory on the Four Horsemen of Calumny[7]—Fear, Ignorance, Bigotry, and Smear.

I doubt if the Republican Party could do so, simply because I do not believe the American people will uphold any political party that puts political exploitation above national interest. Surely we Republicans are not so desperate for victory.

I do not want to see the Republican Party win that way. While it might be a fleeting victory for the Republican Party, it would be a more lasting defeat for the American people. Surely it would ultimately be suicide for the Republican Party and the two-party system that has protected our American liberties from the dictatorship of a one-party system.

As members of the minority party, we do not have the primary authority to formulate the policy of our government. But we do have the responsibility of rendering constructive criticism, of clarifying issues, of allaying fears by acting as responsible citizens.

As a woman, I wonder how the mothers, wives, sisters, and daughters feel about the way in which members of their families have been politically mangled in Senate debate—and I use the word "debate" advisedly.

As a United States Senator, I am not proud of the way in which the Senate has been made a publicity platform for irresponsible sensationalism. I am not proud of the reckless abandon in which unproved charges have been hurled from this side of the aisle. I am not proud of the obviously staged, undignified countercharges which have been attempted in retaliation from the other side of the aisle.

I do not like the way the Senate has been made a rendezvous for vilification, for selfish political gain at the sacrifice of individual reputations and national unity. I am not proud of the way we smear outsiders from the floor of the Senate and hide behind the cloak of congressional immunity and still place ourselves beyond criticism on the floor of the Senate.

As an American, I am shocked at the way Republicans and Democrats alike are playing directly into the Communist design of confuse, divide, and conquer. As an American, I do not want a Democratic administration whitewash or cover-up any more than I want a Republican smear or witch hunt.

As an American, I condemn a Republican Fascist just as much as I condemn a Democrat Communist. I condemn a Democrat Fascist just as much as I condemn a Republican Communist. They are equally dangerous to you and me and to our country. As an

7. Smith is alluding to the Four Horsemen of the Apocalypse discussed in Revelation 6:2–8: Conquest, War, Famine, and Death.

American, I want to see our nation recapture the strength and unity it once had when we fought the enemy instead of ourselves.

It is with these thoughts that I have drafted what I call a Declaration of Conscience. I am gratified that the Senator from New Hampshire, the Senator from Vermont, the Senator from Oregon, the Senator from New York, the Senator from Minnesota, and the Senator from New Jersey[8] have concurred in that declaration and have authorized me to announce their concurrence.

---

8. Charles W. Tobey (New Hampshire), George D. Aiken (Vermont), Wayne L. Morse (Oregon), Irving M. Ives (New York), Edward J. Thye (Minnesota), Robert C. Hendrickson (New Jersey).

William Faulkner

Speech Accepting the Nobel Prize in Literature

STOCKHOLM, SWEDEN
DECEMBER 10, 1950

WHEN WILLIAM FAULKNER learned he had won the Nobel Prize in Literature, he reported that he would not be traveling to Stockholm to accept the award in person. It was, he said, too far from his home in Oxford, Mississippi: "I am a farmer down here and I can't get away." Faulkner's response was doubtless fueled as well by his aversion to public speaking. Only at the last minute did he agree to go, but not before starting on a drinking binge whose effects were compounded by a high fever and the grippe. Still shaky at the awards ceremony, he was at times so hard to hear that, one listener reported, "we did not know what he said until the next morning."

Faulkner's speech reflected the angst of the nuclear age, yet voiced the optimism that "man...will prevail." The speech was widely reprinted, and it captured the imagination of people around the globe. Today it is as well known as any of his novels and remains a classic statement of the writer's duty "to help man endure by lifting his heart." The fame of the speech is based on the written text published soon afterward, which is a revised version of the oral presentation. That text has been anthologized countless times, and Faulkner used it for a subsequent studio recording. What appears below is the speech as Faulkner presented it on December 10, 1950, transcribed from a recording made at the awards banquet. As with other speeches in the volume, we have not included those moments when Faulkner stumbled over a word and corrected himself, which he did several times. This is, to the best of our knowledge, the first printing of the speech in this form.

◇◇

Ladies and Gentlemen: I feel that this award was not made to me as a man, but to my work—a life's work in the agony and sweat of the human spirit, not for glory, but to make out of the material of the human spirit something which was not there before. So that this award is only mine in trust. It will not be hard to find a dedication for the money part of it commensurate with the purpose and significance of its origin. But I would like to do the same with the acclaim too, by using this fine moment as a pinnacle from which I might be listened to by the young men and young women already dedicated to the same anguish and travail, among whom is the one who may someday stand where I stood this afternoon.[1]

Our tragedy today is a general and universal physical fear so long sustained by now that we can even bear it. There are no longer problems of the spirit. There is only one question: When will I be blown up? Because of this, the young man, young woman writing today has forgotten the problems of the human heart in conflict with itself which alone can make good writing, because only that is worth writing about, worth the agony and the sweat.

He must learn them again. He must teach himself that the basest of all things is to be afraid; and, teaching himself that, forget it forever, leaving no room in his workshop for anything but the old verities and truths of the heart, the old universal truths lacking which any story is ephemeral and doomed—love and honor and pity and pride and compassion and sacrifice. Until he does so, he lives under a curse. He writes not of love but of lust, of defeats in which nobody loses anything of value, of victories without hope and, worst of all, without pity or compassion. His griefs grieve on no universal bones, leaving no scars. He writes not of the heart but of the glands.

Until he relearns these things, he will write as though he stood among and watched the end of man. I decline to accept the end of man. It is easy enough to say that man is immortal simply because he[2] still endures: that when the last ding-dong of doom has clanged and faded from the last worthless rock hanging tideless in the last red and dying evening, that even then there will still be one more sound—that of his puny, inexhaustible voice, still talking.

I believe more than this. I believe that man will not merely endure; he will prevail. He is immortal not because he alone among creatures has an inexhaustible voice, but because he has a soul, a spirit capable of compassion and sacrifice and endurance. The poet, the writer's duty is to write about these things. It is his privilege to help man endure by lifting his heart, by reminding him of courage and honor and hope and pride and compassion and pity. The poet's voice need not merely be the record of man, it can be one of the props to help him endure and prevail.

1. Faulkner had received his prize earlier in the day at Stockholm's concert hall; his speech was presented at a banquet held in the town hall.

2. Faulkner mistakenly inserted "must" here when delivering the speech.

Douglas MacArthur

✕

Old Soldiers Never Die

WASHINGTON, D.C.
APRIL 19, 1951

THE COLD WAR turned hot on June 25, 1950, when thousands of North Korean troops stormed across the thirty-eighth parallel and pushed deep into South Korea. Within a week, the United Nations Security Council condemned the invasion and President Harry Truman ordered American ground forces to the Korean Peninsula. On July 7 General Douglas MacArthur was appointed supreme commander of all UN operations in Korea. The most decorated American combat soldier of World War I, MacArthur served as Army Chief of Staff during the 1930s and as commander of army forces in the Pacific during World War II. After accepting the Japanese surrender in September 1945, he headed the postwar occupation that transformed Japan into a democratic nation and laid the foundation for its future prosperity.

In a stroke of military genius, MacArthur stemmed the North Korean advance with an amphibious landing at Inchon in September 1950, after which he pursued the enemy toward the Yalu River. When hundreds of thousands of Chinese troops joined the contest in late 1950 and early 1951, MacArthur lobbied to expand the war into China but was rebuffed by Truman. After MacArthur publicly denounced the President's strategy as "ludicrous," Truman removed him from command on April 11, 1951. MacArthur flew back to the United States, where he received a hero's welcome. On April 19 he defended his views before a joint session of Congress and a national radio and television audience.

The Korean conflict was America's first experience with limited warfare, and it did not sit well with MacArthur. After reviewing the changes that had swept Asia since the end of the colonial era, he stated that the decision to intervene in Korea was sound and that victory was in sight until China intervened with "numerically superior ground forces." Retooling a line he had used when exhorting the West Point football team in 1945, he declared that "In war there is no substitute for victory." Any other course would risk the loss of South Korea and could even scuttle all of the Pacific. Concluding with a powerful surge of emotion, MacArthur recalled the old barracks ballad that proclaimed, "Old soldiers never die; they just fade away." Like that old soldier, he said, "I now close my military career and just fade away." He left the rostrum to wave after wave of applause.

It was a virtuoso performance by a master orator. One member of Congress declared that the whole nation was on "a great emotional binge," and the next day several million people turned out to see MacArthur's motorcade in New York City. In the long run, however, public opinion gradually turned to Truman's side, and the 1952 Republican presidential nomination that MacArthur coveted went to Dwight Eisenhower. Although MacArthur's position on Korea has led to his enduring image as a Cold War hawk, he was by rule pragmatic rather than ideological in his judgments. Toward the end of his life, he urged both Presidents Kennedy and Johnson not to commit American ground forces in Vietnam. It was, as Geoffrey Perret has written, "sterling advice, sadly ignored."

◇◇

Mr. President,[1] Mr. Speaker,[2] and distinguished members of the Congress: I stand on this rostrum with a sense of deep humility and great pride—humility in the wake of those great American architects of our history who have stood here before me, pride in the reflection that this home of legislative debate represents human liberty in the purest form yet devised. Here are centered the hopes and aspirations and faith of the entire human race.

I do not stand here as advocate for any partisan cause, for the issues are fundamental and reach quite beyond the realm of partisan considerations. They must be resolved on the highest plane of national interest if our course is to prove sound and our future protected. I trust, therefore, that you will do me the justice of receiving that which I have to say as solely expressing the considered viewpoint of a fellow American. I address you with neither rancor nor bitterness in the fading twilight of life, with one but—with but one—purpose in mind: to serve my country.

The issues are global and so interlocked that to consider the problems of one sector oblivious to those of another is but to court disaster for the whole. While Asia is commonly referred to as the gateway to Europe, it is no less true that Europe is the gateway to Asia, and the broad influence of the one cannot fail to have its impact upon the other. There are those who claim our strength is inadequate to protect on both fronts—that we cannot divide our effort. I can think of no greater expression of defeatism. If a potential enemy can divide his strength on two fronts, it is for us to counter his effort. The Communist threat is a global one. Its successful advance in one sector threatens the destruction of every other sector. You cannot appease or otherwise surrender to communism in Asia without simultaneously undermining our efforts to halt its advance in Europe.

Beyond pointing out these general truisms, I shall confine my discussion to the general areas of Asia. Before one may objectively assess the situation now existing there, he must comprehend something of Asia's past and the revolutionary changes which have marked her course up to the present. Long exploited by the so-called colonial powers, with little opportunity to achieve any degree of social justice, individual dignity, or a higher standard of life such as guided our own noble administration in the Philippines, the peoples of Asia found their opportunity in the war just past[3] to throw off the shackles of colonialism and now see the dawn of new opportunity, a heretofore unfelt dignity, and the self-respect of political freedom. Mustering half of the earth's population and 60 percent of its natural resources, these peoples are rapidly consolidating a new force, both moral and material, with which to raise the living standard and erect adaptations of the design of modern progress to their own distinct cultural environments.

1. Alben W. Barkley, Vice President of the United States and President of the U.S. Senate.

2. Sam Rayburn, Speaker of the U.S. House of Representatives.

3. World War II.

Whether one adheres to the concept of colonization or not, this is the direction of Asian progress and it may not be stopped. It is a corollary to the shift of the world economic frontiers as the whole epicenter of world affairs rotates back toward the area whence it started. In this situation, it becomes vital that our own country orient its policies in consonance with this basic evolutionary condition, rather than pursue a course blind to the reality that the colonial era is now past and the Asian peoples covet the right to shape their own free destiny.

What they seek now is friendly guidance, understanding, and support, not imperious direction—the dignity of equality and not the shame of subjugation. Their prewar standard of life, pitifully low, is infinitely lower now in the devastation left in war's wake. World ideologies play little part in Asian thinking and are little understood. What the peoples strive for is the opportunity for a little more food in their stomachs, a little better clothing on their backs, a little firmer roof over their heads, and the realization of the normal nationalist urge for political freedom.

These political-social conditions have but an indirect bearing upon our own national security, but do form a backdrop to contemporary planning which must be thoughtfully considered if we are to avoid the pitfalls of unrealism. Of more direct and immediate bearing upon our national security are the changes wrought in the strategic potential of the Pacific Ocean in the course of the past war.

Prior thereto the western strategic frontier of the United States lay on the littoral line of the Americas, with an exposed island salient extending out through Hawaii, Midway, and Guam to the Philippines. That salient proved not an outpost of strength but an avenue of weakness along which the enemy could and did attack. The Pacific was a potential area of advance for any predatory force intent upon striking at the bordering land areas.

All this was changed by our Pacific victory. Our strategic frontier then shifted to embrace the entire Pacific Ocean, which became a vast moat to protect us as long as we held it. Indeed, it acts as a protective shield for all of the Americas and all free lands of the Pacific Ocean area. We control it to the shores of Asia by a chain of islands extending in an arc from the Aleutians to the Marianas held by us and our free allies. From this island chain we can dominate with sea and air power every Asiatic port from Vladivostok to Singapore—with sea and air power every port, as I said, from Vladivostok to Singapore—and prevent any hostile movement into the Pacific. Any predatory attack from Asia must be an amphibious effort. No amphibious force can be successful without control of the sea lanes and the air over those lanes in its avenue of advance. With naval and air supremacy and modest ground elements to defend bases, any major attack from continental Asia toward us or our friends [in the] Pacific would be doomed to failure.

Under such conditions, the Pacific no longer represents menacing avenues of approach for a prospective invader. It assumes, instead, the friendly aspect of a peaceful lake. Our line of defense is a natural one and can be maintained with a minimum of military effort and expense. It envisions no attack against anyone, nor does it provide the bastions essential for offensive operations, but, properly maintained, would be an invincible defense against aggression.

The holding of this littoral defense line in the western Pacific is entirely dependent upon holding all segments thereof, for any major breach of that line by an unfriendly power would render vulnerable to determined attack every other major segment. This is a military estimate as to which I have yet to find a military leader who will take exception. For that reason, I have strongly recommended in the past, as a matter of military urgency, that under no circumstances must Formosa[4] fall under Communist control. Such an eventuality would at once threaten the freedom of the Philippines and the loss of Japan and might well force our western frontier back to the coast of California, Oregon, and Washington.

To understand the changes which now appear upon the Chinese mainland, one must understand the changes in Chinese character and culture over the past fifty years. China up to fifty years ago was completely nonhomogeneous, being compartmented into groups divided against each other. The warmaking tendency was almost nonexistent, as they still

---

4. Taiwan.

followed the tenets of the Confucian ideal of pacifist culture. At the turn of the century, under the regime of Chang Tso-lin,[5] efforts toward greater homogeneity produced the start of a nationalist urge. This was further and more successfully developed under the leadership of Chiang Kai-shek,[6] but has been brought to its greatest fruition under the present regime to the point that it has now taken on the character of a united nationalism of increasingly dominant aggressive tendencies.

Through these past fifty years, the Chinese people have thus become militarized in their concepts and in their ideals. They now constitute excellent soldiers, with competent staffs and commanders. This has produced a new and dominant power in Asia which, for its own purposes, is allied with Soviet Russia but which in its own concepts and methods has become aggressively imperialistic, with a lust for expansion and increased power normal to this type of imperialism. There is little of the ideological concept either one way or another in the Chinese makeup. The standard of living is so low and the capital accumulation has been so thoroughly dissipated by war that the masses are desperate and eager to follow any leadership which seems to promise the alleviation of local stringencies.

I have from the beginning believed that the Chinese Communists' support of the North Koreans was the dominant one. Their interests are at present parallel to those of the Soviet, but I believe that the aggressiveness recently displayed not only in Korea but also in Indochina and Tibet[7] and pointing potentially toward the south reflects predominantly the same lust for the expansion of power which has animated every would-be conqueror since the beginning of time.

The Japanese people since the war have undergone the greatest reformation recorded in modern history. With a commendable will, eagerness to learn, and marked capacity to understand, they have from the ashes left in war's wake erected in Japan an edifice dedicated to the primacy of individual liberty and personal dignity, and in the ensuing process there has been created a truly representative government committed to the advance of political morality, freedom of economic enterprise, and social justice.

Politically, economically, and socially Japan is now abreast of many free nations of the earth and will not again fail the universal trust. That it may be counted upon to wield a profoundly beneficial influence over the course of events in Asia is attested by the magnificent manner in which the Japanese people have met the recent challenge of war, unrest, and confusion surrounding them from the outside and checked communism within their own frontiers without the slightest slackening in their forward progress. I sent all four of our occupation divisions to the Korean battlefront without the slightest qualms as to the effect of the resulting power vacuum upon Japan. The results fully justified my faith. I know of no nation more serene, orderly, and industrious, nor in which higher hopes can be entertained for future constructive service in the advance of the human race.

Of our former ward, of our former ward, the Philippines, we can look forward in confidence that the existing unrest will be corrected and a strong and healthy nation will grow in the longer aftermath of war's terrible destructiveness. We must be patient and understanding and never fail them—as in our hour of need they did not fail us.[8] A Christian nation, the Philippines stand as a mighty bulwark of Christianity in the Far East, and its capacity for high moral leadership in Asia is unlimited.

On Formosa, the government of the Republic of China[9] has had the opportunity to refute by action much of the malicious gossip which so undermined the strength of its leadership on

5. Inspector general of Manchuria who sought to extend his rule southward and briefly won control of Beijing before being defeated by Chiang Kai-shek in 1926.

6. Nationalist leader of China from 1928 to 1949, when he was deposed by the Communist revolution led by Mao Zedong.

7. Chinese forces invaded Tibet in late 1950.

8. MacArthur is referring to the Philippines's decision to send troops in support of South Korea.

9. Led by Chiang Kai-shek (see note 6), who had fled the mainland in 1949 after the establishment of the People's Republic of China and his defeat by Communist forces.

the Chinese mainland. The Formosan people are receiving a just and enlightened administration with majority representation on the organs of government, and politically, economically, and socially they appear to be advancing along sound and constructive lines.

With this brief insight into the surrounding areas, I now turn to the Korean conflict. While I was not consulted prior to the President's decision to intervene in support of the Republic of Korea, that decision, from a military standpoint, proved a sound one as we—as I say, it proved a sound one—as we hurled back the invader and decimated his forces. Our victory was complete and our objectives within reach when Red China intervened with numerically superior ground forces. This created a new war and an entirely new situation, a situation not contemplated when our forces were committed against the North Korean invaders, a situation which called for new decisions in the diplomatic sphere to permit the realistic adjustment of military strategy. Such decisions have not been forthcoming.

While no man in his right mind would advocate sending our ground forces into continental China—and such was never given a thought—the new situation did urgently demand a drastic revision of strategic planning if our political aim was to defeat this new enemy as we had defeated the old. Apart from the military need, as I saw it, to neutralize the sanctuary protection given the enemy north of the Yalu, I felt that military necessity in the conduct of the war made necessary, first, the intensification of our economic blockade against China; two, the imposition of a naval blockade against the China coast; three, removal of restrictions on air reconnaissance of China's coastal areas and of Manchuria; four, removal of restrictions on the forces of the Republic of China on Formosa, with logistical support to contribute to their effective operations against the common enemy.

For entertaining these views—all professionally designed to support our forces committed to Korea and bring hostilities to an end with the least possible delay and at a saving of countless American and allied lives—I have been severely criticized in lay circles, principally abroad, despite my understanding that

from a military standpoint the above views have been fully shared in [the] past by practically every military leader concerned with the Korean campaign, including our own Joint Chiefs of Staff.

I called for reinforcements but was informed that reinforcements were not available. I made clear that if not permitted to destroy the enemy-built-up bases north of the Yalu, if not permitted to utilize the friendly Chinese force of some 600,000 men on Formosa, if not permitted to blockade the China coast to prevent the Chinese Reds from getting succor from without, and if there were to be no hope of major reinforcements, the position of the command from the military standpoint forbade victory. We could hold in Korea by constant maneuver and at an approximate area where our supply-line advantages were in balance with the supply-line disadvantages of the enemy, but we could hope at best for only an indecisive campaign with its terrible and constant attrition upon our forces if the enemy utilized his full military potential.

I have constantly called for the new political decisions essential to a solution. Efforts have been made to distort my position. It has been said in effect that I was a warmonger. Nothing could be further from the truth. I know war as few other men now living know it, and nothing to me—and nothing to me—is more revolting. I have long advocated its complete abolition, as its very destructiveness on both friend and foe has rendered it useless as a means of settling international disputes.

Indeed, on the second day of September 1945, just following the surrender of the Japanese nation on the battleship *Missouri*, I formally cautioned as follows: "Men since the beginning of time have sought peace. Various methods through the ages have been attempted to devise an international process to prevent or settle disputes between nations. From the very start, workable methods were found insofar as individual citizens were concerned, but the mechanics of an instrumentality of larger international scope have never been successful. Military alliances, balances of power, leagues of nations all in turn failed, leaving the only path to be by way of the crucible of war. The utter destructiveness of war now blocks out this alternative. We have had our last chance. If we will not devise some greater and more equitable system, Armageddon[10] will be at our door. The problem basically is theological and involves a spiritual recrudescence[11] and improvement of human character that will synchronize with our almost matchless advances in science, art, literature, and all material and cultural developments of the past two thousand years. It must be of the spirit if we are to save the flesh."

But once war is forced upon us, there is no other alternative than to apply every available means to bring it to a swift end. War's very object is victory, not prolonged indecision. In war there is no substitute for victory.[12]

There are some who, for varying reasons, would appease Red China. They are blind to history's clear lesson, for history teaches with unmistakable emphasis that appeasement but begets new and bloodier war. It points to no single instance where this end has justified that means, where appeasement has led to more than a sham peace. Like blackmail, it lays the basis for new and successively greater demands until, as in blackmail, violence becomes the only other alternative.

Why, my soldiers asked of me, surrender military advantages to an enemy in the field? I could not answer. Some may say to avoid spread of the conflict into an all-out war with China. Others to avoid Soviet intervention. Neither explanation seems valid, for China is already engaging with the maximum power it can commit, and the Soviet will not necessarily mesh its actions with our moves. Like a cobra, any new enemy will more likely strike whenever it feels that the relativity in military or other potential is in its favor on a worldwide basis.

The tragedy of Korea is further heightened by the fact that as military action is confined to its territorial limits, it condemns that nation, which it is our purpose to save, to suffer the devastating impact of full naval and air bombardment while the enemy's sanctuaries are fully protected from such attack and devastation. Of the nations of the world, Korea alone, up to now, is the sole one which has risked its all against communism. The magnificence of the courage and fortitude of the Korean people defies description. They, they have chosen to risk death rather than slavery. Their last words to me were, "Don't scuttle the Pacific."

I have just left your fighting sons in Korea. They have met all tests there, and I can report to you without reservation that they are splendid in every way. It was my constant effort to preserve them and end this savage conflict honorably and with the least loss of time and a minimum sacrifice of life. Its growing bloodshed has caused me the deepest anguish and anxiety. Those gallant men will remain often in my thoughts and in my prayers always.

I am closing my fifty-two years of military service. When I joined the army, even before the turn of the century, it was the fulfillment of all of my boyish hopes and dreams. The world has turned over many times since I took the oath on the Plain[13] at West Point, and the hopes and dreams have long since vanished. But I still remember the refrain of one of the most popular barrack ballads of that day, which proclaimed most proudly that "Old soldiers never die, they just fade away."[14] And like the old soldier of that ballad, I now close my military career and just fade away—an old soldier who tried to do his duty as God gave him the light to see that duty.

Good-bye.

---

10. In the Bible, the scene of a final battle between the forces of good and evil, prophesied to occur at the end of the world; used secularly to refer to a catastrophic conflict with the potential to destroy the human race.

11. MacArthur misspoke this word as "recrudescent."

12. Sometimes misquoted as "In war there can be no substitute for victory," which MacArthur had in his written text but altered when delivering the speech.

13. Forty-acre terrace overlooking the Hudson River.

14. From an early 20th-century British soldiers' song set to the tune of "Kind Thoughts Can Never Die." The song was copyrighted with the title "Old Soldiers Never Die" by J. Foley in 1920.

Adlai E. Stevenson

⌛

Let's Talk Sense to the American People

CHICAGO, ILLINOIS
JULY 26, 1952

URBANE, ERUDITE, AND possessing a Jeffersonian gift for felicity of expression, Adlai Stevenson was Governor of Illinois when he was drafted in 1952 as the Democratic nominee for President of the United States. A relative newcomer to the national stage, he persistently stated that he was not interested in running for the Oval Office after only four years in the statehouse. Despite being urged by outgoing President Harry Truman to enter the race, he stayed on the sidelines and insisted that he was not a candidate even as the party's convention opened on July 21. It quickly became apparent, however, that the majority of delegates favored Stevenson, especially after he delivered an eloquent speech of welcome on the opening day of the convention. Four days later, without openly declaring himself a candidate, he was selected on the third ballot as his party's standard-bearer.

It was pushing 3:00 a.m. when he finally delivered his acceptance speech. Most people had long since gone to bed. Yet those in the convention hall, and those who would read the speech later that morning, found in Stevenson's words an inspiring defense of the Democratic Party's stewardship and its commitment to those who "dream the dreams and see the visions of a better America and a better world." Eschewing traditional campaign bromides, Stevenson said it was time to "talk sense to the American people" and "tell them the truth, that there are no gains without pains." "Better we lose the election," he declared, "than mislead the people."

Replete with complex sentences, restrictive clauses, and other markers of literary prose seldom heard from the political platform in mid-twentieth-century America, Stevenson's speech received high praise for its aesthetic merits and contrasted sharply with the more prosaic discourse of Dwight D. Eisenhower, his opponent in the fall election. Yet there lay Stevenson's greatest weakness as well as his greatest strength. As the campaign proceeded, he was often called an "egghead," an epithet that underscored his professorial demeanor and penchant for elevated language. Despite losing to Eisenhower in 1952 and again in 1956, however, he prefigured a political idiom that, when simplified in tone and combined with the magnetism of a young, telegenic candidate, would help carry John F. Kennedy to the White House in 1960.

◇◇◇◇◇◇◇◇◇◇◇◇◇◇◇◇◇◇◇◇◇◇◇◇◇◇◇◇◇◇◇◇◇◇◇◇◇◇◇

Mr. President,[1] ladies and gentlemen of the convention, my fellow citizens: I accept your nomination and your program. I should have preferred to hear those words uttered by a stronger, a wiser, a better man than myself. But after listening to the President's speech, I even feel better about myself. None of you, my friends, can wholly appreciate what is in my heart. I can only hope that you understand my words. They will be few.

I have not sought the honor you have done me. I could not seek it because I aspired to another office, which was the full measure of my ambition, and one does not treat the highest office within the gift of the people of Illinois as an alternative or as a consolation prize.

I would not seek your nomination for the presidency because the burdens of that office stagger the imagination. Its potential for good or evil, now and in the years of our lives, smothers exultation and converts vanity to prayer. I have asked the Merciful Father, the Father of us all, to let this cup pass from me, but from such dread responsibility one does not shrink in fear, in self-interest, or in false humility. So "If this cup may not pass from me, except I drink it, Thy will be done."[2]

That my heart has been troubled, that I have not sought this nomination, that I could not seek it in good conscience, that I would not seek it in honest self-appraisal, is not to say that I value it the less. Rather, it is that I revere the office of the presidency of the United States. And now, my friends, that you have made your decision, I will fight to win that office with all my heart and my soul. And with your help, I have no doubt that we will win.

You have summoned me to the highest mission within the gift of any people. I could not be more proud. Better men than I were at hand for this mighty task, and I owe to you and to them every resource of mind and of strength that I possess to make your deed today a good one for our country and for our party. I am confident, too, that your selection for—of

a candidate for—Vice President[3] will strengthen me and our party immeasurably in the hard, the implacable work that lies ahead of all of us.

I know you join me in gratitude and in respect for the great Democrats and the leaders of our generation whose names you have considered here in this convention, whose vigor, whose character, whose devotion to the republic we love so well have won the respect of countless Americans and have enriched our party. I shall need them; we shall need them because I have not changed in any respect since yesterday.

Your nomination, awesome as I find it, has not enlarged my capacities, so I am profoundly grateful and emboldened by their comradeship and their fealty, and I have been deeply moved by their expressions of goodwill and of support. And I cannot, my friends, resist the urge to take the one opportunity that has been afforded me to pay my humble respects to a very great and good American whom I am proud to call my kinsman, Alben Barkley of Kentucky.[4]

Let me say, too, that I have been heartened by the conduct of this convention. You have argued and disagreed because, as Democrats, you care and you care deeply. But you have disagreed and argued without calling each other liars and thieves, without despoiling our best traditions. You have not spoiled our best traditions in any naked struggles for power.

And you have written a platform that neither equivocates, contradicts, nor evades. You have restated our party's record, its principles, and its purposes in language that none can mistake and with a firm confidence in justice, freedom, and peace on earth that will raise the hearts and the hopes of mankind for that distant day when no one rattles a saber and no one drags a chain.

For all these things I am grateful to you. But I feel no exultation, no sense of triumph. Our troubles are all ahead of us. Some will call us appeasers; others will say that we are the war party. Some will say we are reactionary; others will say that we stand for socialism. There will be inevitable, the inevitable cries

1. U.S. President Harry S. Truman, who spoke on behalf of Stevenson immediately before his acceptance speech.

2. Matthew 26:42.

3. The next day, John Sparkman, U.S. Senator from Alabama, was chosen by the convention as Stevenson's running mate.

4. Truman's Vice President, Barkley had been a U.S. Senator for more than 20 years and was a contender for the presidential nomination in 1952.

of "Throw the rascals out," "It's time for a change," and so on and so on.

We'll hear all those things and many more besides. But we will hear nothing that we have not heard before. I'm not too much concerned with partisan denunciation, with epithets and abuse, because the workingman, the farmer, the thoughtful businessman all know that they are better off than ever before, and they all know that the greatest danger to free enterprise in this country died with the Great Depression under the hammer blows of the Democratic Party.

Nor am I afraid that the precious two-party system is in danger. Certainly the Republican Party looked brutally alive a couple of weeks ago, and I mean both Republican Parties.[5] Nor am I afraid that the Democratic Party is old and fat and indolent. After a hundred and fifty years, it has been old for a long time, and it will never be indolent as long as it looks forward and not back, as long as it commands the allegiance of the young and the hopeful who dream the dreams and see the visions of a better America and a better world.

You will hear many sincere and thoughtful people express concern about the continuation of one party in power for twenty years. I don't belittle this attitude. But change for the sake of change has no absolute merit in itself.

If our greatest hazard, if our greatest hazard is preservation of the values of Western civilization, in our self-interest alone, if you please, it is the part—is it the part—of wisdom to change for the sake of change to a party with a split personality, to a leader whom we all respect but who has been called upon to minister to a hopeless case of political schizophrenia? If the fear is corruption in official position, do you believe with Charles Evans Hughes[6] that guilt is personal and knows no party? Do you doubt the power of any political leader, if he has the will to do so, to set his own house in order without his neighbors having to burn it down?

What does concern me, in common with thinking partisans of both parties, is not just winning this election but how it is won, how well we can take advantage of this great quadrennial opportunity to debate issues sensibly and soberly. I hope and pray that we Democrats, win or lose, can campaign not as a crusade to exterminate the opposing party, as our opponents seem to prefer, but as a great opportunity to educate and elevate a people whose destiny is leadership, not alone of a rich and prosperous, contented country, as in the past, but of a world in ferment.

And, my friends, even more important than winning the election is governing the nation. That is the test of a political party—the acid, final test. When the tumult and the shouting die, when the bands are gone and the lights are dimmed, there is the stark reality of responsibility in an hour of history haunted with those gaunt, grim specters of strife, dissension, and materialism at home and ruthless, inscrutable, and hostile power abroad.

The ordeal of the twentieth century, the bloodiest, most turbulent era of the whole Christian age, is far from over. Sacrifice, patience, understanding, and implacable purpose may be our lot for years to come. Let's face it. Let's talk sense to the American people. Let's tell them the truth: that there are no gains without pains; that there, that we are now on the eve of great decisions, not easy decisions like resistance when you're attacked, but a long, patient, costly struggle which alone can assure triumph over the great enemies of man—war, poverty, and tyranny—and the assaults upon human dignity which are the most grievous consequences of each.

Let's tell them that the victory to be won in the twentieth century, this portal to the Golden Age, mocks the pretensions of individual acumen and ingenuity, for it is a citadel guarded by thick walls of ignorance and of mistrust which do not fall before the trumpets' blast or the politicians' imprecations or

---

5. Stevenson is referring to the division at the Republican National Convention between the internationalist wing that supported Dwight Eisenhower in his successful bid for the presidential nomination and the isolationist wing that preferred Ohio Senator Robert A. Taft.

6. Stevenson is referring to a January 1920 statement submitted to the New York State Assembly Judiciary Committee by Hughes on behalf of a special committee of the Association of the Bar of the City of New York.

even a general's baton.[7] They are, they are, my friends, walls that must be directly stormed by the hosts of courage, of morality, and of vision, standing shoulder to shoulder, unafraid of ugly truth, contemptuous of lies, half truths, circuses, and demagoguery.

The people are wise, wiser than the Republicans think. And the Democratic Party is the people's party—not the labor party, not the farmers' party, not the employers' party. It is the party of no one because it is the party of everyone.

That, that, I think, is our ancient mission. Where we have deserted it, we have failed. With your help, there will be no desertion now. Better we lose the election than mislead the people, and better we lose than misgovern the people. Help me to do the job in this autumn of conflict and of campaign, help me to do the job in these years of darkness, of doubt, and of crisis which stretch beyond the horizon of tonight's happy vision, and we will justify our glorious past and the loyalty of silent millions who look to us for compassion, for understanding, and for honest purpose. Thus we will serve our great tradition greatly.

I ask of you all you have. I will give you all I have, even as he who came here tonight and honored me, as he has honored you, the Democratic Party, by a lifetime of service and bravery that will find him an imperishable page in the history of the republic and of the Democratic Party—President Harry S. Truman.

And finally, my friends, in this staggering task that you have assigned me, I shall always try "to do justly, to love mercy, and to walk humbly with my God."[8]

---

7. A reference to Republican presidential nominee Dwight Eisenhower, who was supreme commander of Allied forces during the invasion of Normandy on D-Day in World War II.

---

8. Closely paraphrased from Micah 6:8.

Richard M. Nixon

Checkers

HOLLYWOOD, CALIFORNIA
SEPTEMBER 23, 1952

TWICE ELECTED TO the House of Representatives, thirty-nine-year-old Richard Nixon was serving his first term in the U.S. Senate when he was tapped by Dwight Eisenhower as his vice-presidential running mate in the 1952 election. The political calculus seemed perfect. Eisenhower was older, Nixon younger; Eisenhower was from Kansas, Nixon from California; Eisenhower was associated with the eastern, moderate wing of the party; Nixon with the more conservative western and midwestern wings; Eisenhower had fought the Nazis, Nixon was battling the Communists.

Then, on the morning of September 18, 1952, a front-page headline in the *New York Post* screamed, "Secret Nixon Fund!" while an interior headline announced, "Secret Rich Men's Trust Fund Keeps Nixon in Style Far Beyond His Salary." In fact, the fund was not secret, was not used for personal expenses, and was smaller and more carefully administered than many similar funds maintained by other politicians. The story created a sensation, however, especially in light of Eisenhower's commitment to clean up the "mess" in Washington. Battling corruption was supposed to be Eisenhower's issue, and now his partner on the ticket was being accused of improper use of funds.

Many of Eisenhower's advisors urged him to drop Nixon, but he knew that if Nixon was guilty of something, then the man who had chosen Nixon was also guilty—of bad judgment. So it was agreed that the Republican National Committee would purchase thirty minutes of airtime on NBC immediately following *Texaco Star Theater* starring Milton Berle, then the most popular program on television. Eisenhower told Nixon to tell the public "everything there is to tell, everything you can remember since the day you entered public life. Tell them about any money you have ever received." An estimated sixty million viewers would see Nixon's speech and millions more would listen on radio.

The pressure on Nixon was ratcheted up even further when, an hour before he was scheduled to leave for the broadcast, he received a phone call from top Eisenhower advisor Thomas Dewey telling him that he should announce his resignation from the ticket at the end of the speech. In his account of the incident in *Six Crises*, Nixon recalled moving around in a daze as he thought about what to do in light of Dewey's command. He would not resign, and he would ask the audience to wire and phone their decision about his fate to the Republican National Committee, rather than to Eisenhower himself. Under the circumstances, he could not have been optimistic about the outcome, but it was his only chance, and it required a speech that would succeed almost beyond imagination.

Seated behind a desk on the stage of the El Capitan Theatre in Hollywood, Nixon spoke extemporaneously with five pages of notes spread out before him. No one else was in the 750-seat theater except his wife, Pat, who was seated a few feet away, and the cameramen and electricians. Nixon denied any moral or legal wrongdoing. He explained the origins and purposes of the fund, produced an official audit in support of his position, and disclosed the details of his financial life in a manner unprecedented in American politics. Assuming the stance of a man who has been wrongfully accused and has provided the evidence to prove his innocence, he capped off his defense with a heart-tugging story about the family dog, Checkers, which one of his daughters had received as a gift. Then he rose from his chair and moved in front of the desk as he concluded with a litany of Republican attacks on communism, corruption, and President Truman's handling of the Korean War.

Nixon aimed his speech at Republicans, and he hit the mark unerringly. More than a million telegrams, letters, postcards, and petitions poured in from all parts of the country urging Eisenhower to keep Nixon on the ticket. Although far from eloquent in the classic sense and often caricatured by Nixon's detractors, ggg⁸

the speech was a rhetorical masterstroke that saved his career. At a time when Americans were beginning to fall in love with television, it also demonstrated the potential power of the new medium for political communication, a development fraught with implications for the future of American public discourse and civic life.

◇◇

My fellow Americans: I come before you tonight as a candidate for the vice presidency and as a man whose honesty and integrity has been questioned.

Now, the usual political thing to do when charges are made against you is to either ignore them or to deny them without giving details. I believe we've had enough of that in the United States, particularly with the present administration in Washington, D.C. To me, the office of the vice presidency of the United States is a great office, and I feel that the people have got to have confidence in the integrity of the men who run for that office and who might obtain it. I have a theory, too, that the best and only answer to a smear or to an honest misunderstanding of the facts is to tell the truth. And that's why I'm here tonight. I want to tell you my side of the case.

I'm sure that you have read the charge, and you've heard it, that I, Senator Nixon, took $18,000 from a group of my supporters. Now, was that wrong? And let me say that it was wrong.[1] I'm saying it, incidentally, that it was wrong, not just illegal, because it isn't a question of whether it was legal or illegal—that isn't enough. The question is: Was it morally wrong? I say that it was morally wrong if any of that $18,000 went to Senator Nixon for my personal use. I say that it was morally wrong if it was secretly given and secretly handled. And I say that it was morally wrong if any of the contributors got special favors for the contributions that they made.

And now to answer those questions, let me say this: Not one cent of the $18,000 or any other money of that type ever went to me for my personal use. Every penny of it was used to pay for political expenses that I did not think should be charged to the taxpayers of the United States.

It was not a secret fund. As a matter of fact, when I was on *Meet the Press*—some of you may have seen it last Sunday—Peter Edson[2] came up to me after the program, and he said, "Dick, what about this fund we hear about?" And I said, "Well, there's no secret about it. Go out and see Dana Smith,[3] who was the administrator of the fund." And I gave him his address. And I said, "You will find that the purpose of the fund simply was to defray political expenses that I did not feel should be charged to the government."

And third, let me point out—and I want to make this particularly clear—that no contributor to this fund, no contributor to any of my campaigns, has ever received any consideration that he would not have received as an ordinary constituent. I just don't believe in that, and I can say that never, while I have been in the Senate of the United States, as far as the people that contributed to this fund are concerned, have I made a telephone call for them to an agency or have I gone down to an agency in their behalf. And the records will show that, the records which are in the hands of the administration.

Well, then, some of you will say, and rightly, "Well, what did you use the fund for, Senator? Why did you have to have it?"

Let me tell you in just a word how a Senate office operates. First of all, a Senator gets $15,000 a year in salary. He gets enough money to pay for one trip a year, a round trip, that is, for himself and his family between his home and Washington, D.C. And then he gets an allowance to handle the people that work in his office to handle his mail. And the allowance for my state of California is enough to hire thirteen

1. Nixon did not mean to say he had done anything wrong. He misspoke as he worked toward the question raised two sentences later of whether the fund was morally wrong.

2. Washington, D.C., columnist for the Newspaper Enterprise Association.

3. California attorney who administered the fund for Nixon.

people. And let me say, incidentally, that that allowance is not paid to the Senator. It's paid directly to the individuals that the Senator puts on his payroll. But all of these people and all of these allowances are for strictly official business—business, for example, when a constituent writes in and wants you to go down to the Veterans Administration and get some information about his GI policy. Items of that type, for example.

But there are other expenses which are not covered by the government, and I think I can best discuss those expenses by asking you some questions. Do you think that when I or any other Senator makes a political speech, has it printed, should charge the printing of that speech and the mailing of that speech to the taxpayers? Do you think, for example, when I or any other Senator makes a trip to his home state to make a purely political speech that the cost of that trip should be charged to the taxpayers? Do you think when a Senator makes political broadcasts or political television broadcasts, radio or television, that the expense of those broadcasts should be charged to the taxpayers?

Well, I know what your answer is. It's the same answer that audiences give me whenever I discuss this particular problem. The answer is no. The taxpayers shouldn't be required to finance items which are not official business but which are primarily political business.

Well, then the question arises, you say: "Well, how do you pay for these and how can you do it legally?" And there are several ways that it can be done, incidentally, and that it is done legally in the United States Senate and in the Congress. The first way is to be a rich man. I don't happen to be a rich man, so I couldn't use that one.

Another way that is used is to put your wife on the payroll. Let me say, incidentally, that my opponent, my opposite number for the vice presidency on the Democratic ticket,[4] does have his wife on the payroll and has had it—her—on his payroll for the ten years, for the past ten years. Now, just let me say this: That's his business, and I'm not critical of him

for doing that. You will have to pass judgment on that particular point.

But I have never done that for this reason: I have found that there are so many deserving stenographers and secretaries in Washington that needed the work that I just didn't feel it was right to put my wife on the payroll. My wife's sitting over here. She's a wonderful stenographer. She used to teach stenography and she used to teach shorthand in high school. That was when I met her. And I can tell you, folks, that she's worked many hours at night and many hours on Saturdays and Sundays in my office, and she's done a fine job, and I am proud to say tonight that in the six years I've been in the House and the Senate of the United States, Pat Nixon has never been on the government payroll.

Well, there are other ways that these finances can be taken care of. Some who are lawyers, and I happen to be a lawyer, continue to practice law, but I haven't been able to do that. I am so far away from California that I've been so busy with my senatorial work that I have not engaged in any legal practice. And also, as far as law practice was concerned, it seemed to me that the relationship between an attorney and the client was so personal that you couldn't possibly represent a man as an attorney and then have an unbiased view when he presented his case to you in the event that he had one before the government.

And so I felt that the best way to handle these necessary political expenses of getting my message to the American people and the speeches I made—the speeches that I had printed for the most part concerned this one message of exposing this administration, the communism in it, the corruption in it—the only way that I could do that was to accept the aid which people in my home state of California who contributed to my campaign and who continued to make these contributions after I was elected were glad to make.

And let me say I am proud of the fact that not one of them has ever asked me for a special favor. I am proud of the fact that not one of them has ever asked me to vote on a bill other than of my own conscience would dictate. And I am proud of the fact that the taxpayers, by subterfuge or otherwise, have never paid one dime for expenses which I thought were political and shouldn't be charged to the taxpayers.

4. Alabama Senator John Sparkman.

Let me say, incidentally, that some of you may say, "Well, that's all right, Senator, that's your explanation, but have you got any proof?" And I'd like to tell you this evening that just an hour ago we received an independent audit of this entire fund. I suggested to Governor Sherman Adams, who is the chief of staff for the Dwight Eisenhower campaign, that an independent audit and legal report be obtained, and I have that audit here in my hands. It's an audit made by the Price Waterhouse and Company firm, and the legal opinion by Gibson, Dunn, and Crutcher, lawyers in Los Angeles, the biggest law firm, and, incidentally, one of the best ones in Los Angeles.

I am proud to be able to report to you tonight that this audit and this legal opinion is being forwarded to General Eisenhower. And I'd like to read to you the opinion that was prepared by Gibson, Dunn, and Crutcher and based on all the pertinent laws and statutes, together with the audit report prepared by the certified public accountants. Quote: "It is our conclusion that Senator Nixon did not obtain any financial gain from the collection and disbursement of the fund by Dana Smith; that Senator Nixon did not violate any federal or state law by reason of the operation of the fund; and that neither the portion of the fund paid by Dana Smith directly to third persons, nor the portion paid to Senator Nixon, to reimburse him for designated office expenses, constituted income to the Senator which was either reportable or taxable as income under applicable tax laws." Signed: Gibson, Dunn, and Crutcher, by Elmo H. Conley.

Now that, my friends, is not Nixon speaking, but that's an independent audit which was requested because I want the American people to know all the facts and I'm not afraid of having independent people go in and check the facts, and that is exactly what they did.

But then I realized that there are still some who may say, and rightfully so—and let me say that I recognize that some will continue to smear regardless of what the truth may be—but that there has been understandably some honest misunderstanding on this matter, and there are some that will say: "Well, maybe you were able, Senator, to fake this thing. How can we believe what you say? After all, is there a possibility that maybe you got some sums in cash? Is

there a possibility that you may have feathered your own nest?"

And so now what I am going to do—and, incidentally, this is unprecedented in the history of American politics—I am going at this time to give to this television and radio audience a complete financial history: everything I've earned, everything I've spent, everything I owe. And I want you to know the facts.

I'll have to start early. I was born in 1913. Our family was one of modest circumstances, and most of my early life was spent in the store out in East Whittier. It was a grocery store, one of those family enterprises. The only reason we were able to make it go was because my mother and dad had five boys and we all worked in the store.

I worked my way through college and, to a great extent, through law school. And then in 1940 probably the best thing that ever happened to me happened: I married Pat, who's sitting over here. We had a rather difficult time after we were married, like so many of the young couples who may be listening to us. I practiced law. She continued to teach school.

Then in 1942 I went into the service. Let me say that my service record was not a particularly unusual one. I went to the South Pacific; I guess I'm entitled to a couple of battle stars; I got a couple of letters of commendation. But I was just there when the bombs were falling. And then I returned, returned to the United States, and in 1946 I ran for the Congress.

When we came out of the war, Pat and I—Pat during the war had worked as a stenographer and in a bank and as an economist for a government agency—and when we came out, the total of our savings from both my law practice, her teaching, and all the time that I was in the war, the total for that entire period was just a little less than $10,000. Every cent of that, incidentally, was in government bonds.

Well, that's where we start when I go into politics. Now, what have I earned since I went into politics? Well, here it is. I've jotted it down. Let me read the notes.

First of all, I've had my salary as a Congressman and as a Senator. Second, I have received a total in this past six years of $1,600 from estates which were in my law firm at the time that I severed my connection with it. And, incidentally, as I said before,

I have not engaged in any legal practice and have not accepted any fees from business that came into the firm after I went into politics. I have made an average of approximately $1,500 a year from nonpolitical speaking engagements and lectures. And then, fortunately, we've inherited a little money. Pat sold her interest in her father's estate for $3,000 and I inherited $1,500 from my grandfather.

We lived rather modestly. For four years we lived in an apartment in Parkfairfax, in Alexandria, Virginia. The rent was $80 a month. And we saved for the time that we could buy a house.

Now, that was what we took in. What did we do with this money? What do we have today to show for it? This will surprise you because it is so little, I suppose, as standards generally go of people in public life.

First of all, we've got a house in Washington, which cost $41,000 and on which we owe $20,000. We have a house in Whittier, California, which cost $13,000 and on which we owe $3,000. My folks are living there at the present time. I have just $4,000 in life insurance plus my GI policy, which I've never been able to convert and which will run out in two years. I have no life insurance whatever on Pat. I have no life insurance on our two youngsters, Tricia and Julie. I own a 1950 Oldsmobile car. We have our furniture. We have no stocks and bonds of any type. We have no interest of any kind, direct or indirect, in any business.

Now, that's what we have. What do we owe? Well, in addition to the mortgage—the $20,000 mortgage on the house in Washington, the $10,000 one on the house in Whittier—I owe $4,500 to the Riggs Bank in Washington, D.C., with interest four and a half percent. I owe $3,500 to my parents, and the interest on that loan, which I pay regularly because it's the part of the savings they made through the years they were working so hard, I pay regularly 4 percent interest. And then I have a $500 loan which I have on my life insurance.

Well, that's about it. That's what we have and that's what we owe. It isn't very much, but Pat and I have the satisfaction that every dime that we've got is honestly ours. I should say this: that Pat doesn't have a mink coat. But she does have a respectable

Republican cloth coat, and I always tell her that she'd look good in anything.

One other thing I probably should tell you because if I don't, they'll probably be saying this about me too. We did get something, a gift, after the election. A man down in Texas heard Pat on the radio mention the fact that our two youngsters would like to have a dog. And believe it or not, the day before we left on this campaign trip, we got a message from Union Station in Baltimore saying they had a package for us. We went down to get it. You know what it was? It was a little cocker spaniel dog in a crate that he'd sent all the way from Texas, black and white, spotted, and our little girl Tricia, the six-year-old, named it Checkers. And you know, the kids, like all kids, love the dog, and I just want to say this right now: that regardless of what they say about it, we're gonna keep it.[5]

It isn't easy to come before a nationwide audience and bare your life as I've done. But I want to say some things before I conclude that I think most of you will agree on. Mr. Mitchell,[6] the Chairman of the Democratic National Committee, made the statement that if a man couldn't afford to be in the United States Senate, he shouldn't run for the Senate. And I just want to make my position clear: I don't agree with Mr. Mitchell when he says that only a rich man should serve his government in the United States Senate or in the Congress. I don't believe that represents the thinking of the Democratic Party, and I know that it doesn't represent the thinking of the Republican Party.

I believe that it's fine that a man like Governor Stevenson,[7] who inherited a fortune from his father, can run for President. But I also feel that it's essential in this country of ours that a man of modest means can also run for President because, you know,

---

5. In his *Six Crises* (1962), Nixon explained that his decision to mention Checkers was inspired by President Franklin D. Roosevelt's speech of September 23, 1944, in which he deflected criticism from Republicans by charging that they were now resorting to attacks on "my little dog, Fala."

6. Stephen A. Mitchell.

7. Adlai Stevenson, Governor of Illinois and the 1952 Democratic presidential nominee.

remember Abraham Lincoln. You remember what he said: "God must've loved the common people—he made so many of them."[8]

And now I'm going to suggest some courses of conduct. First of all, you have read in the papers about other funds now. Mr. Stevenson apparently had a couple, one of them in which a group of business-people paid and helped to supplement the salaries of state employees. Here is where the money went directly into their pockets. And I think that what Mr. Stevenson should do should be to come before the American people, as I have, give the names of the people that contributed to that fund, give the names of the people who put this money into their pockets at the same time that they were receiving money from their state government, and see what favors, if any, they gave out for that. I don't condemn Mr. Stevenson for what he did, but until the facts are in, there is a doubt that will be raised.

And as far as Mr. Sparkman is concerned, I would suggest the same thing. He's had his wife on the payroll. I don't condemn him for that, but I think that he should come before the American people and indicate what outside sources of income he has had. I would suggest that under the circumstances both Mr. Sparkman and Mr. Stevenson should come before the American people, as I have, and make a complete financial statement as to their financial history. And if they don't, it will be an admission that they have something to hide.[9]

And I think you will agree with me because, folks, remember, a man that's to be President of the United States, a man that's to be Vice President of the United States, must have the confidence of all the people. And that's why I'm doing what I'm doing. And that's why I suggest that Mr. Stevenson and Mr. Sparkman, since they are under attack, should do what they're doing.

Now let me say this: I know that this is not the last of the smears. In spite of my explanation tonight,

other smears will be made. Others have been made in the past. And the purpose of the smears, I know, is this: to silence me, to make me let up.

Well, they just don't know who they're dealing with. I'm going to tell you this: I remember in the dark days of the Hiss case[10] some of the same columnists, some of the same radio commentators who are attacking me now and misrepresenting my position, were violently opposing me at the time I was after Alger Hiss. But I continued to fight because I knew I was right, and I can say to this great television and radio audience that I have no apologies to the American people for my part in putting Alger Hiss where he is today. And as far as this is concerned, I intend to continue to fight.

Why do I feel so deeply? Why do I feel that in spite of the smears, the misunderstanding, the necessity for a man to come up here and bare his soul as I have, why is it necessary for me to continue this fight? And I want to tell you why. Because, you see, I love my country. And I think my country is in danger. And I think the only man that can save America at this time is the man that's running for President on my ticket—Dwight Eisenhower.

You say, "Why do I think it's in danger?" And I say, "Look at the record." Seven years of the Truman-Acheson administration,[11] and what's happened? Six hundred million people lost to the Communists[12] and a war in Korea in which we have lost 117,000 American casualties.[13] And I say to all of you that a policy that results in the loss of 600 million people to

8. Although frequently attributed to Lincoln, this sentiment does not appear in his extant writings.

9. Stevenson made available a summary of his fund at the end of September, along with his income tax returns for the previous 10 years. Sparkman and Eisenhower followed suit in October.

10. Nixon is referring to Alger Hiss, a former State Department official who was accused in 1948 of spying for the Soviet Union during the 1930s. Although the statute of limitations for espionage had run out, Hiss was tried for perjury in his testimony before the House Un-American Activities Committee. After his first trial ended in a hung jury, he was retried and convicted in early 1950. The case was highly controversial and brought Nixon, then a Congressman and one of Hiss's most persistent accusers, to national attention.

11. A reference to President Harry S. Truman and his Secretary of State, Dean Acheson, who was a target of repeated criticism by Republicans.

12. Nixon is referring to the triumph of Chinese Communists, who came to power in 1949 under the leadership of Mao Zedong.

13. The Korean War began in June 1950.

the Communists and a war which costs us 117,000 American casualties isn't good enough for America. And I say that those in the State Department that made the mistakes which caused that war and which resulted in those losses should be kicked out of the State Department just as fast as we get them out of there. And let me say that I know Mr. Stevenson won't do that because he defends the Truman policy. And I know that Dwight Eisenhower will do that and that he will give America the leadership that it needs.

Take the problem of corruption.[14] You've read about the mess in Washington. Mr. Stevenson can't clean it up because he was picked by the man, Truman, under whose administration the mess was made. You wouldn't trust the man who made the mess to clean it up—that's Truman. And by the same token, you can't trust the man who was picked by the man that made the mess to clean it up—and that's Stevenson. And so I say Eisenhower, who owed nothing to Truman, nothing to the big-city bosses—he is the man that can clean up the mess in Washington.

Take communism. I say that as far as that subject is concerned, the danger is great to America. In the Hiss case they got the secrets which enabled them to break the American secret State Department code. They got secrets in the atomic bomb case[15] which enabled them to get the secret of the atomic bomb five years before they would have gotten it by their own devices. And I say that any man who called the Alger Hiss case a red herring isn't fit to be President of the United States.[16]

I say that a man who, like Mr. Stevenson, has pooh-poohed and ridiculed the Communist threat in the United States—he said that they are phantoms among ourselves, he has accused us that have

attempted to expose the Communists of looking for Communists in the Bureau of Fisheries and Wildlife—I say that a man who says that isn't qualified to be President of the United States.

And I say that the only man who can lead us in this fight to rid the government of both those who are Communists and those who have corrupted this government is Eisenhower, because Eisenhower, you can be sure, recognizes the problem and he knows how to deal with it.

Now let me say that finally this evening I want to read to you just briefly excerpts from a letter which I received, a letter which after all this is over no one can take away from us. It reads as follows: "Dear Senator Nixon: Since I am only nineteen years of age, I can't vote in this presidential election, but believe me if I could, you and General Eisenhower would certainly get my vote. My husband is in the Fleet Marines in Korea. He's a corpsman on the front lines and we have a two-month-old son he's never seen. And I feel confident that with great Americans like you and General Eisenhower in the White House, lonely Americans like myself will be united with their loved ones now in Korea. I only pray to God that you won't be too late. Enclosed is a small check to help you in your campaign. Living on $85 a month, it is all I can afford at present, but let me know what else I can do."

Folks, it's a check for $10, and it's one that I will never cash.

And just let me say this: We hear a lot about prosperity these days, but I say why can't we have prosperity built on peace, rather than prosperity built on war? Why can't we have prosperity and an honest government in Washington, D.C., at the same time? Believe me, we can. And Eisenhower is the man that can lead this crusade to bring us that kind of prosperity.

And now, finally, I know that you wonder whether or not I am going to stay on the Republican ticket or resign. Let me say this: I don't believe that I ought to quit, because I'm not a quitter. And, incidentally, Pat's not a quitter. After all, her name was Patricia Ryan and she was born on St. Patrick's Day,[17] and you know the Irish never quit.

---

14. Allegations of corruption and influence-peddling in the Truman administration were reiterated by Republicans throughout the 1950 presidential campaign.

15. Nixon is referring to the arrest of Klaus Fuchs, Julius Rosenberg, Ethel Rosenberg, and several others on charges of selling U.S. atomic secrets to the Soviet Union. The most controversial case involved the Rosenbergs, who were convicted in March 1951 and sentenced to death.

16. Nixon is referring to a remark by President Truman in an April 1948 news conference.

17. Pat Nixon was actually born on March 16, one day before St. Patrick's Day.

But the decision, my friends, is not mine. I would do nothing that would harm the possibilities of Dwight Eisenhower to become President of the United States. And for that reason I am submitting to the Republican National Committee tonight through this television broadcast the decision which it is theirs to make. Let them decide whether my position on the ticket will help or hurt. And I'm going to ask you to help them decide. Wire and write the Republican National Committee whether you think I should stay on or whether I should get off. And whatever their decision is, I will abide by it.

But just let me say this last word: Regardless of what happens, I'm going to continue this fight. I'm going to campaign up and down in America until we drive the crooks and the Communists and those that defend them out of Washington. And remember, folks, Eisenhower is a great man, believe me. He's a great man. And a vote for Eisenhower is a vote for what's good for America.

Elizabeth Gurley Flynn

⧗

Statement at the Smith Act Trial

NEW YORK, NEW YORK
FEBRUARY 2, 1953

BORN IN 1890 to radical Irish immigrants, Elizabeth Gurley Flynn spent her life agitating for economic and political causes. By 1906 she had become a Socialist, and the next year she dropped out of high school to become an organizer for the International Workers of the World. A leading figure in some of the most dramatic labor conflicts of the early century, she was known as "The Rebel Girl." After World War I, she chaired the Workers' Defense Union, was instrumental in bringing the case of Sacco and Vanzetti to public attention, and helped found the American Civil Liberties Union. In 1937 she joined the Communist Party, rose quickly to a leadership position, and for twenty-six years wrote a regular column for the *Daily Worker*. In 1961 she became the first female chair of the party in the United States.

Even as a child, Flynn showed the flair for public speaking that made her almost irresistible on the platform. She won a gold medal in grammar school for a speech on woman suffrage and began her public career at age sixteen with an address to the Harlem Socialist Club. Over the years she gave thousands of speeches and at one point taught public speaking at the School of Marxist Studies in New York City. "I agitate a listener," she said. "I know how to get the power out of my diaphragm instead of my vocal chords and I'm happy to be free to give capitalism hell." One listener reported that when Flynn spoke, "the excitement of the crowd became a visible thing.... It was as though a spurt of flame had gone through the audience, something stirring and powerful."

In June 1951, at age sixty, Flynn was arrested and charged with violating the Smith Act, which made it illegal to advocate or teach the forcible overthrow of the U.S. government. She was tried and convicted with twelve other defendants in proceedings that began the last of day of March 1952 and ran for ten months. On the morning of February 2, 1953, Flynn, who acted as her own counsel, addressed the court before receiving sentence. Immediately after her prepared speech, Judge Edward J. Dimock, reiterating a suggestion he had made to the prosecutor earlier in the day, asked Flynn whether she might prefer spending the rest of her days in the Soviet Union to serving a jail sentence. Flynn rejected the proposal, saying the defendants "would merely consider ourselves traitors to the American people if we turned our back on this country and considered only our own freedom from jail."

In a comment that presumably included Flynn's address to the court, Dimock later remarked that some of the defendants' speeches were "magnificent and deserve to be recorded in the reports of state trials." Flynn was sentenced to three years at the Federal Reformatory for Women in Alderson, West Virginia. After her release, she made two trips to the Soviet Union, where she died on September 5, 1964. She received a state funeral in Red Square, and part of her ashes were deposited under the Kremlin wall. The remainder were returned to the United States, where they were buried in Chicago, not far from the grave site of Emma Goldman.

◇◇◇◇◇◇◇◇◇◇◇◇◇◇◇◇◇◇◇◇◇◇◇◇◇◇◇◇◇◇◇◇◇◇◇◇◇◇◇

Your Honor,[1] my first impulse was to remain silent during this last act of our trial, which I feel could have been foretold in April 1952. I had had many opportunities as a pro se counsel to speak and to testify at length. The time available here today really belongs to my comrades, who thus far have not been heard. Your Honor undoubtedly has the list of our names and sentences already in mind, and this procedure will probably cause no change.

In spite of a sense of futility which grew with every passing day of this frustrating trial, I must speak out, however. Silence might be construed as an acceptance of a verdict justified neither by the so-called evidence of a motley array of bought-and-paid-for informers, stool pigeons, and renegades as unworthy of belief as a Judas Iscariot[2] or a Benedict Arnold,[3] nor by the law as expounded in your charge to the jury. Therefore, I say again, Your Honor, that I and none of my comrades are guilty of any conspiracy to advocate overthrow of the United States government by force and violence. Silence might be construed as defeatism, when the truth is that I am so serene in our consciousness of innocence of any crimes, that I can be imprisoned but I cannot be corrected, reformed, or changed. My body can be incarcerated, but my thoughts will remain free and unaffected.

All human history has demonstrated that ideas, thoughts, cannot be put in prison. They can only

---

1. Federal District Judge Edward Dimock.

2. Apostle who betrayed Jesus Christ.

3. Traitor who plotted during the American Revolutionary War to turn West Point over to the British.

be met in the forum of public discussion. Someone sent me a picture of Thomas Jefferson, which now adorns my cell in the House of Detention. It says: "Difference of opinion leads to enquiry, and enquiry to truth. We value too much freedom of opinion not to cherish its exercise."[4]

The political, industrial, and social conditions under capitalism which created our ideas remain. They will produce similar ideas in the minds of countless others and further strengthen them in ours. Never did prison affect resolute people who live and work and die, if necessary, by their ideas. We Communists are such people.

I have faith in the ultimate justice of the American people once the fog of lies, hysteria, prejudice, and, worst of all, fear is swept away. It is a terrible thing to see one's country in the grip of fear—needless, stupid, foolish fear; fear of imaginary enemies; fear of our allies and friends; fear of the accusing fingers of stool pigeons; fear of losing one's job or one's citizenship or one's place in a community. The whole governmental bureaucracy, wasting billions of dollars, boasting, bragging, bullying, is whistling in the dark and fear, trying to make the whole world afraid of us. But some bright morning the American people, Your Honor, will come out of this fog and remember the wise words of Franklin Delano Roosevelt: "We have nothing to fear but fear itself."[5] It has happened before. They will ask themselves, "Who is afraid?"

And now it is from a small handful of frightened rich that this contagion has spread—the men of the trusts who never loved their country more than their stocks and bonds, whose patriotism is always on a percentage basis, who would rule and exploit and use violence against not only their fellow countrymen but the human race. They would plunge the world into a sea of blood by atomic warfare in order to maintain their own mean and mercenary rule, their way of life, and foist it upon other people who want none of it.

Great as the danger looms, I have faith that fascism will never come to pass in our country. I am proud of the role that our party has played in signalizing that danger since 1935. American Communists shed their blood in Spain[6] and in every theater of action during World War II against fascism. Great as the threat of war looms, I am confident it is not inevitable, and I am proud of the role of the Communists who were throughout the world in the struggle for peace.

We defendants tried for many months to present what we really stand for and do—our intent. The scales were weighted against us. The government seeks to convict, and thwarts all efforts to present the facts. The voice of truth is stifled here by precedents, procedures, laws of evidence. Sometimes, for a few moments, it breaks through like the synthetic sunlight that occasionally is reflected here from the upper-story windows, but life and progress moves on outside, Your Honor.

You know our analysis of the jury system. I will not attempt to repeat it. How impossible it was for a single juror to enter that box with an open mind or a courageous spirit. Poisoned with prejudice, fearful of their futures, incapable of assimilating scientific concept[s], hypnotized by legalistic language, smothered in data they could neither remember nor comprehend, they grasped the straw man of the government's case to their bosoms as set forth in its closing summation. It was all they cared to remember.

It is no illusion, however, for us to say confidently, Your Honor, we are on the winning side. We have the welfare of our country and its people at heart. We know that millions of Americans hate fascism and want peace, that the working class of our country moves forward, that the Negro people are on the march for their full democratic rights and will not turn back.

Time was when the Communists alone raised slogans for peace, for security, for jobs, for democracy, for unionism that are on the minds and lips of millions

4. Paraphrased from Jefferson's letter to P. H. Wendover, March 13, 1815.

5. Paraphrased from Roosevelt's first inaugural address (pages 221–224).

6. A reference to the Spanish civil war of the 1930s.

of Americans today. Our lives, our work, our aspirations are part of the American scene for the past half century. Our predecessors go back a century and more. Somewhere and soon the Smith Act will go into the discard as did the alien and sedition laws of 1800,[7] the fugitive slave laws of the '60s,[8] the criminal syndicalist laws of the '20s.[9]

The fog-engulfing courtrooms, middle-class juries, and the press will lift among the masses of plain people, the ones who never get on federal juries because their appearance and manner doesn't satisfy a hard-boiled political appointee who splits his infinitives, doubles his negatives, and toadies to the prosperous. A people's movement is arising in our country like a strong, fresh prairie wind against repressive legislation, loyalty oaths, congressional investigations, witch hunts, political trials, and the like. They will repeal the Smith Act and see that its victims are released, and those will be long before a transition to socialism, Your Honor.

It is a hard and bitter path that American reaction is plotting out for the American people, but they will not go far along that path. Our voices have been and will be raised in protest at every step of the way. If our individual voices are silenced, others will be raised.

I asked you a question on Friday, Your Honor, which I now repeat: If the Communist Party is not illegal, its membership and officership is not illegal, if advocating socialism is not illegal, if advocating a day-to-day program of "good deeds," as the government cynically calls it, is not illegal, what in all conscience is illegal here? Of what are we guilty?

In all my long life—and Mr. Lane[10] did not do justice to it; I think I did better on the witness stand,

Your Honor, and that you know me better, and that everything that there is in my life there that I myself testified to—in all my long life I never expected that I would go to jail for books, and not even whole books but scraps and pieces. And if I return to my normal life of the last forty-seven years, of working and speaking on unionism, democratic rights, the rights of Negro people, of women, on peace and against fascism and war, and on socialism, what happens then, Your Honor? Does the government tote out all the by-then tattered and torn books, the trained marionettes of aging stool pigeons, and the whole thing start over again?

Does this question not demonstrate that constitutional rights are tied up in the Smith Act, not only for Communists, but for any who speak out on these matters?

Your Honor, all the material property I possess, as far as a fine is concerned, are books accumulated since I first bought a paper-covered copy of Tom Paine's *Common Sense*[11] at the age of sixteen. They are good books—poetry, drama, history, political economy, fiction, philosophy, art, music, travel, literature. Marx and Engels[12] are there besides Shakespeare, Shaw, Emerson, Hegel,[13] Mark Twain; Lenin and Stalin[14] are there besides Thoreau, Jefferson,[15] the Beards, the Webbs,[16] Hugo, Hardy,[17] and many others. What happens to them, Your Honor, my guilt-by-association partners that I use for my speeches and my articles?

---

7. Passed in 1798, the Alien and Sedition Acts were the last peacetime antisedition legislation enacted by Congress until the Smith Act in 1940.

8. Flynn is referring to the Fugitive Slave Act of 1850, which instituted stringent measures to abet the return of escaped slaves to their owners.

9. Such laws prohibited the advocacy or abetting of "crime, violence, sabotage, or other unlawful methods as a means of industrial or political reform" and were used mainly against the International Workers of the World.

10. U.S. Attorney Myles J. Lane, who prosecuted the case against Smith.

11. (1776).

12. Karl Marx and Friedrich Engels, authors of *The Communist Manifesto* (1848).

13. British playwright William Shakespeare (1564–1616); British writer and iconoclast George Bernard Shaw (1856–1950); American transcendentalist Ralph Waldo Emerson (1803–1882); German philosopher Georg Wilhelm Friedrich Hegel (1770–1831).

14. Russian revolutionary Vladimir Ilyich Lenin (1870–1924); Soviet leader Joseph Stalin (1879–1953).

15. Henry David Thoreau, author of *Civil Disobedience* (1849); Thomas Jefferson, author of the Declaration of Independence (1776).

16. American historians Charles and Mary Beard; British reformers Sidney and Beatrice Webb.

17. French author and republican Victor Hugo (1802–1885); British novelist and poet Thomas Hardy (1840–1928).

There is force and violence on those shelves, but not where the government looked for it. It is in Irish history—Connolly, O'Casey,[18] and others telling of the long and bloody struggle against British rule. It is in American labor history—in Colorado, West Virginia, Homestead, South Chicago, and on the Embarcadero of San Francisco.[19] It is in American history—the Revolution, the wars against the American Indians, the Civil War, the Spanish-American War. It is in the struggles of the Negro people. It is in the Bible, too—which is on my shelf, Your Honor—against the Jewish tribes and the old prophets, against Jesus and his disciples and the early Christian martyrs. And it all proves our thesis that force and violence comes from the ruling class and not from the people.

There is a Homeric irony,[20] Your Honor, in the ending of this hollow and costly Pyrrhic victory[21] for the government: that the books, the ideas, the thoughts remain outside, spreading on the wings of the morning, while only we, a few individuals, go to prison, and that history will write a different verdict and will agree that we are many and they are few.

THE COURT: Well, that is the way I thought you felt, Miss Flynn. I am afraid that if you go to prison, you will come out feeling just exactly as you do now, and it was that thought that made me wonder whether there was any alternative. If something like spending the rest of your life in Russia could be worked out as a substitute for prison, would that interest you at all?

FLYNN: It would not, Your Honor. I am an American; I want to live and work in the United States of America. I am not interested in going anyplace else, and I would reject any such proposition.

[At this point, there is a brief discussion between Judge Dimock and U.S. Attorney Lane about Pettis Perry, another defendant. The transcript then resumes as follows.]

FLYNN: There is one other aspect of this that bothers me considerably, and Your Honor asked me the question so suddenly that I really didn't answer it as fully as I should have done, and that is that the question is susceptible of a double meaning, and I can see the headlines in tomorrow's papers—"Communists Prefer Jail to Soviet Union"—and all the dishonest deductions that will be drawn from our refusal. And I think therefore, in justice to the defendants, it has to be said further that we reject the concept of political exile or banishment from our country. And while I say that, I wish to say that our refusal is in no way a reflection upon the Soviet Union, which I, for one, have never visited; and though I certainly would like to visit the Soviet Union, I certainly would not be given a passport.

The point is we do not want to leave our country. It is like a proposition made to a Christian who believed in heaven: "Well, do you want to go there right away?" Certainly no one would want to answer yes to that question, although their belief in heaven would be great. The Emperor Nero, without asking that question, took them at their word, as history records.[22]

There are many rich American expatriates who enjoy the comforts of the Riviera[23] and evade all their responsibilities and even their taxes here in the United States, and we have no desire to emulate their example—to enjoy the fruits of socialism in a land where we did not work for it. We feel that we belong here and we have political responsibilities here. And I think that has to be said in addition to what Mr. McTernan[24] has said so that there will be no misunderstanding of our

18. Insurgent James Connolly (1868–1916); playwright Sean O'Casey (1880–1964).

19. Flynn is referring to the Ludlow, Colorado, massacre of April 20, 1914; the 1921 Battle of Blair Mountain in Logan County, West Virginia; the violent suppression of the 1892 steel strike at Homestead, Pennsylvania; the bloody assault on workers at the Republic Steel South Chicago plant on May 30, 1937; and the July 1934 battles between police and striking dock workers in San Francisco.

20. A reference to the use of irony in the *Iliad* and the *Odyssey*, attributed to the ancient Greek poet Homer.

21. A victory with ruinous consequences for the victor; derived from the triumph of Pyrrhus of Epirus over the Romans in 280–279 BCE.

22. A reference to the persecution of Christians by the Roman Emperor Nero (37–68 CE).

23. Resort area along the southeast coast of France.

24. John T. McTernan, chief counsel for the defense.

position since now you are not going to ask any of the other defendants the same question. We would merely consider ourselves traitors to the American people if we turned our back on this country and considered only our own freedom from jail.

In other words, while none of us want to go to jail, we are not martyrs and we consider it a frightful waste of time. Nevertheless, if that is part of our contribution to the awakening of the people of this country, well, we feel that we must make that contribution. We have no desire to avoid or evade our responsibilities by this proposal which you made, and it certainly is a purely hypothetical question, Your Honor, because Mr. Lane in his official capacity should have informed you, I believe, that the Soviet Union has not for years issued visas in American deportation cases, and as for the other—

THE COURT: Let me interrupt you there. There has never been such a thing in my mind as exile. And let's not go into the law of this thing because we are not going to do it. What I had in mind would not involve a form of deportation.

FLYNN: Well, it is the first time in American history that such a proposal was made to American citizens, and I think it shows how far we have gone down the road to fascism, and I am very glad that Your Honor is going to abandon it.

Dwight D. Eisenhower

Atoms for Peace

NEW YORK, NEW YORK
DECEMBER 8, 1953

ALARMED BY THE potential for nuclear annihilation as a result of the arms race between the United States and the Soviet Union, Dwight Eisenhower made the subject one of his first priorities after entering the White House in January 1953. During May, June, and July, administration speechwriters worked on drafts of an address warning the American public about the growing arsenal of atomic weapons and the possible consequences, but Eisenhower found them all too dark and foreboding. He wanted Americans to understand the dangers of the nuclear age, but he also wanted to provide something positive and reassuring to offset their fears.

Then Eisenhower came up with an idea. If the atomic powers would agree to donate a small percentage of their weapons-grade nuclear materials to an International Atomic Energy Agency, the amount of fissionable materials available for war making would be reduced and the donated materials could be used for research into peaceful applications of nuclear technology. It would be a small step away from the nuclear precipice and might, in time, pave the way for nuclear disarmament. A new round of speech writing was set in motion, with eleven distinct drafts eventually produced. In the process, the audience broadened from the

American people to the international community and the venue changed from the Oval Office to the United Nations General Assembly.

Eisenhower put the final touches on his remarks while flying to New York from a meeting with British and French leaders in Bermuda. Using what he called the "new language" of atomic warfare, he warned that a major nuclear attack would cause such degradation and destruction as to efface "the irreplaceable heritage of mankind handed down to us generation from generation." He called on the Soviet Union to join with Western nuclear powers in seeking a mutually acceptable solution to the arms race, and he presented his Atoms for Peace program as a way to turn "the greatest of destructive forces...into a great boon for the benefit of all mankind." The United States, he pledged, was committed to solving "the fearful atomic dilemma" so "the miraculous inventiveness of man shall not be dedicated to his death but consecrated to his life."

After Eisenhower concluded, the 3,500 delegates erupted in cascades of applause, with even the Soviets participating, and his words received favorable commentary around the world. The hostilities of the Cold War, however, could not be dissipated with a single speech, and nuclear disarmament proved to be a perennially elusive goal. Yet the Atoms for Peace program provided a hopeful alternative to the grim realities of nuclear weaponry, spurred a number of concrete initiatives, and was one of the most important accomplishments of the Eisenhower presidency.

◇◇

Madam President,[1] members of the General Assembly: When Secretary General Hammarskjöld's[2] invitation to address this General Assembly reached me in Bermuda, I was just beginning a series of conferences with the Prime Ministers and Foreign Ministers of Great Britain and of France.[3] Our subject was some of the problems that beset our world. During the remainder of the Bermuda Conference, I had constantly in mind that ahead of me lay a great honor. That honor is mine today as I stand here, privileged to address the General Assembly of the United Nations.

At the same time that I appreciate the distinction of addressing you, I have a sense of exhilaration as I look upon this assembly. Never before in history has so much hope for so many people been gathered together in a single organization. Your deliberations and decisions during these somber years have already realized part of those hopes.

But the great tests and the great accomplishments still lie ahead. And in the confident expectation of those accomplishments, I would use the office which, for the time being, I hold to assure you that the government of the United States will remain steadfast in its support of this body. This we shall do in the conviction that you will provide a great share of the wisdom, of the courage, and the faith which can bring to this world lasting peace for all nations and happiness and well-being for all men.

Clearly, it would not be fitting for me to take this occasion to present to you a unilateral American report on Bermuda. Nevertheless, I assure you that in

1. Vijaya Lakshmi Pandit, President of the UN General Assembly.

2. UN Secretary General Dag Hammarskjöld.

3. The Bermuda Conference began on December 4 and included Eisenhower, British Prime Minister Winston Churchill, and French Premier Joseph Laniel.

our deliberations on that lovely island, we sought to invoke those same great concepts of universal peace and human dignity which are so cleanly etched in your charter. Neither would it be a measure of this great opportunity merely to recite, however hopefully, pious platitudes. I therefore decided that this occasion warranted my saying to you some of the things that have been on the minds and hearts of my legislative and executive associates and on mine for a great many months—thoughts I had originally planned to say primarily to the American people.

I know that the American people share my deep belief that if a danger exists in the world, it is a danger shared by all; and equally, that if hope exists in the mind of one nation, that hope should be shared by all. Finally, if there is to be advanced any proposal designed to ease even by the smallest measure the tensions of today's world, what more appropriate audience could there be than the members of the General Assembly of the United Nations?

I feel impelled to speak today in a language that in a sense is new—one which I, who have spent so much of my life in the military profession, would have preferred never to use. That new language is the language of atomic warfare.

The atomic age has moved forward at such a pace that every citizen of the world should have some comprehension, at least in comparative terms, of the extent of this development of the utmost significance to every one of us. Clearly, if the peoples of the world are to conduct an intelligent search for peace, they must be armed with the significant facts of today's existence. My recital of atomic danger and power is necessarily stated in United States terms, for these are the only incontrovertible facts that I know. I need hardly point out to this assembly, however, that this subject is global, not merely national, in character.

On July 16th, 1945, the United States set off the world's first atomic explosion.[4] Since that date in 1945, the United States of America has conducted forty-two test explosions. Atomic bombs today are more than twenty-five times as powerful as the weapons with which the atomic age dawned, while hydro-

gen weapons are in the ranges of millions of tons of TNT equivalent.

Today the United States's stockpile of atomic weapons, which, of course, increases daily, exceeds by many times the total equivalent of the total of all bombs and all shells that came from every plane and every gun in every theater of war in all of the years of World War II. A single air group, whether afloat or land based, can now deliver to any reachable target a destructive cargo exceeding in power all the bombs that fell on Britain in all of World War II.

In size and variety the development of atomic weapons has been no less remarkable. The development has been such that atomic weapons have virtually achieved conventional status within our armed services. In the United States, the army, the navy, the air force, and the marine corps are all capable of putting this weapon to military use.

But the dread secret, and the fearful engines of atomic might, are not ours alone. In the first place, the secret is possessed by our friends and allies, Great Britain and Canada, whose scientific genius made a tremendous contribution to our original discoveries and the designs of atomic bombs. The secret is also known by the Soviet Union. The Soviet Union has informed us that, over recent years, it has devoted extensive resources to atomic weapons. During this period, the Soviet Union has exploded a series of atomic devices, including at least one involving thermonuclear reactions. If at one time the United States possessed what might have been called a monopoly of atomic power, that monopoly ceased to exist several years ago.

Therefore, although our earlier start has permitted us to accumulate what is today a great quantitative advantage, the atomic realities of today comprehend two facts of even greater significance: First, the knowledge now possessed by several nations will eventually be shared by others—possibly all others. Second, even a vast superiority in numbers of weapons, and a consequent capability of devastating retaliation, is no preventive, of itself, against the fearful material damage and toll of human lives that would be inflicted by surprise aggression.

The free world, at least dimly aware of these facts, has naturally embarked on a large program of warning and defense systems. That program will be accelerated and expanded. But let no one think that

---

4. Eisenhower is referring to a test explosion at Alamogordo, New Mexico.

the expenditure of vast sums for weapons and systems of defense can guarantee absolute safety for the cities and citizens of any nation. The awful arithmetic of the atomic bomb does not permit of any such easy solution. Even against the most powerful defense, an aggressor in possession of the effective minimum number of atomic bombs for a surprise attack could probably place a sufficient number of his bombs on the chosen targets to cause hideous damage.

Should such an atomic attack be launched against the United States, our reactions would be swift and resolute. But for me to say that the defense capabilities of the United States are such that they could inflict terrible losses upon an aggressor, for me to say that the retaliation capabilities of the United States are so great that such an aggressor's land would be laid waste, all this, while fact, is not the true expression of the purpose and the hope of the United States.

To pause there would be to confirm the hopeless finality of a belief that two atomic colossi are doomed malevolently to eye each other indefinitely across a trembling world. To stop there would be to accept helplessly the probability of civilization destroyed, the annihilation of the irreplaceable heritage of mankind handed down to us generation from generation, and the condemnation of mankind to begin all over again the age-old struggle upward from savagery toward decency and right and justice.

Surely no sane member of the human race could discover victory in such desolation. Could anyone wish his name to be coupled by history with such human degradation and destruction? Occasional pages of history do record the faces of the "Great Destroyers," but the whole book of history reveals mankind's never-ending quest for peace and mankind's God-given capacity to build.

It is with the book of history, and not with isolated pages, that the United States will ever wish to be identified. My country wants to be constructive, not destructive. It wants agreements, not wars, among nations. It wants itself to live in freedom and in the confidence that the people of every other nation enjoy equally the right of choosing their own way of life. So my country's purpose is to help us move out of the dark chamber of horrors into the light, to find a way by which the minds of men, the hopes of men, the souls of men everywhere can move forward toward peace and happiness and well-being.

In this quest, I know that we must not lack patience. I know that in a world divided, such as ours today, salvation cannot be attained by one dramatic act. I know that many steps will have to be taken over many months before the world can look at itself one day and truly realize that a new climate of mutually peaceful confidence is abroad in the world. But I know, above all else, that we must start to take these steps now.

The United States and its allies Great Britain and France have, over the past months, tried to take some of these steps. Let no one say that we shun the conference table. On the record has long stood the request of the United States, Great Britain, and France to negotiate with the Soviet Union the problems of a divided Germany.[5] On that record has long stood the request of the same three nations to negotiate an Austrian peace treaty.[6] On the same record still stands the request of the United Nations to negotiate the problems of Korea.[7]

Most recently, we have received from the Soviet Union what is in effect an expression of willingness to hold a Four Power Meeting. Along with our allies, Great Britain and France, we were pleased to see that this note did not contain the unacceptable preconditions previously put forward. As you already know from our joint Bermuda communiqué, the United States, Great Britain, and France have agreed promptly to meet with the Soviet Union.[8]

---

5. Germany had been divided since the end of World War II, with the Soviet Union occupying the eastern half of the country and the United States, France, and Great Britain occupying the western half.

6. At the time of Eisenhower's speech, some 40,000 Soviet troops remained in Austria, along with a small number of Western forces. Efforts to end the occupation finally bore success with the State Treaty of 1955.

7. Partitioned at the 38th parallel after the surrender of Japan in World War II, the Korean Peninsula was formally divided into North Korea and South Korea in 1948. North Korea invaded the South in June 1950, touching off the Korean War, which lasted until July 1953 and whose repercussions were still a matter of considerable tension at the time of Eisenhower's speech.

8. The Four Power Meeting of the United States, Great Britain, France, and the Soviet Union convened in Berlin in January 1954 but concluded without substantial progress.

The government of the United States approaches this conference with hopeful sincerity. We will bend every effort of our mind to the single purpose of emerging from that conference with tangible results toward peace—the only true way of lessening international tension.

We never have, we never will, propose or suggest that the Soviet Union surrender what is rightfully theirs. We will never say that the peoples of Russia are an enemy with whom we have no desire ever to deal or mingle in friendly and fruitful relationship. On the contrary, we hope that this coming conference may initiate a relationship with the Soviet Union which will eventually bring about a free intermingling of the peoples of the East and of the West—the one sure, human way of developing the understanding required for confident and peaceful relations.

Instead of the discontent which is now settling upon Eastern Germany, occupied Austria, and the countries of Eastern Europe,[9] we seek a harmonious family of free European nations, with none a threat to the other and least of all a threat to the peoples of Russia. Beyond the turmoil and strife and misery of Asia, we seek peaceful opportunity for these peoples to develop their natural resources and to elevate their lives.

These are not idle words or shallow visions. Behind them lies a story of nations lately come to independence not as a result of war, but through free grant or peaceful negotiation. There is a record already written of assistance gladly given by nations of the West to needy peoples and to those suffering the temporary effects of famine, drought, and natural disaster. These are deeds of peace. They speak more loudly than promises or protestations of peaceful intent.

But I do not wish to rest either upon the reiteration of past proposals or the restatement of past deeds. The gravity of the time is such that every new avenue of peace, no matter how dimly discernible, should be explored. There is at least one new avenue of peace

which has not yet been well explored—an avenue now laid out by the General Assembly of the United Nations. In its resolution of November 18th, 1953, this General Assembly suggested, and I quote, "that the Disarmament Commission study the desirability of establishing a subcommittee consisting of representatives of the powers principally involved, which should seek in private an acceptable solution…and report such a solution to the General Assembly and to the Security Council not later than September 1, 1954."

The United States, heeding the suggestion of the General Assembly of the United Nations, is instantly prepared to meet privately with such other countries as may be "principally involved" to seek "an acceptable solution" to the atomic armaments race which overshadows not only the peace, but the very life, of the world. We shall carry into these private or diplomatic talks a new conception. The United States would seek more than the mere reduction or elimination of atomic materials for military purposes. It is not enough to take this weapon out of the hands of the soldiers. It must be put into the hands of those who will know how to strip its military casing and adapt it to the arts of peace.

The United States knows that if the fearful trend of atomic military buildup can be reversed, this greatest of destructive forces can be developed into a great boon for the benefit of all mankind. The United States knows that peaceful power from atomic energy is no dream of the future. That capability, already proved, is here now—today. Who can doubt if the entire body of the world's scientists and engineers had adequate amounts of fissionable material with which to test and develop their ideas, that this capability would rapidly be transformed into universal, efficient, and economic usage?

To hasten the day when fear of the atom will begin to disappear from the minds of people and the governments of the East and West, there are certain steps that can be taken now. I therefore make the following proposals: The governments principally involved, to the extent permitted by elementary prudence, to begin now and continue to make joint contributions from their stockpiles of normal uranium and fissionable materials to an International Atomic

---

9. Eisenhower is referring to the countries of Eastern Europe that were occupied by the USSR at the end of World War II and remained under Soviet control.

Energy Agency.[10] We would expect that such an agency would be set up under the aegis of the United Nations. The ratios of contributions, the procedures, and other details would properly be within the scope of the private conversations I have referred to earlier.

The United States is prepared to undertake these explorations in good faith. Any partner of the United States acting in the same good faith will find the United States a not unreasonable or ungenerous associate.

Undoubtedly initial and early contributions to this plan would be small in quantity. However, the proposal has the great virtue that it can be undertaken without the irritations and mutual suspicions incident to any attempt to set up a completely acceptable system of worldwide inspection and control. The Atomic Energy Agency could be made responsible for the impounding, storage, and protection of the contributed fissionable and other materials. The ingenuity of our scientists will provide special, safe conditions under which such a bank of fissionable materials can be made essentially immune to surprise seizure.

The more important responsibility of this Atomic Energy Agency would be to devise methods whereby this fissionable material would be allocated to serve the peaceful pursuits of mankind. Experts would be mobilized to apply atomic energy to the needs of agriculture, medicine, and other peaceful activities. A special purpose would be to provide abundant electrical energy in the power-starved areas of the world. Thus the contributing powers would be dedicating some of their strength to serve the needs rather than the fears of mankind.

The United States would be more than willing—it would be proud—to take up with others "principally involved" the development of plans whereby such peaceful use of atomic energy would be expedited. Of

those "principally involved," the Soviet Union must, of course, be one. I would be prepared to submit to the Congress of the United States, and with every expectation of approval, any such plan that would:

First, encourage worldwide investigation into the most effective peacetime uses of fissionable material, and with the certainty that they had all the material needed for the conduct of all experiments that were appropriate;

Second, begin to diminish the potential destructive power of the world's atomic stockpiles;

Third, allow all peoples of all nations to see that, in this enlightened age, the great powers of the earth, both of the East and of the West, are interested in human aspirations first rather than in building up the armaments of war;

Fourth, open up a new channel for peaceful discussion and initiate at least a new approach to the many difficult problems that must be solved in both private and public conversations if the world is to shake off the inertia imposed by fear and is to make positive progress toward peace. Against the dark background of the atomic bomb, the United States does not wish merely to present strength but also the desire and the hope for peace.

The coming months will be fraught with fateful decisions. In this assembly, in the capitals and military headquarters of the world, in the hearts of men everywhere, be they governed or governors, may they be the decisions which will lead this world out of fear and into peace. To the making of these fateful decisions the United States pledges before you—and therefore before the world—its determination to help solve the fearful atomic dilemma, to devote its entire heart and mind to find the way by which the miraculous inventiveness of man shall not be dedicated to his death but consecrated to his life.

I again thank the delegates for the great honor they have done me in inviting me to appear before them and in listening to me so courteously. Thank you.

---

10. Eisenhower's speech provided the impetus for such an agency, which was established in 1957.

Joseph Welch

Defense of Fred Fisher at the Army-McCarthy Hearings

Washington, D.C.
June 9, 1954

T HE GREATEST IRONY of McCarthyism is that it took place at a time when the Communist threat in the United States was lower than it had been at any point since the end of World War II. By the early 1950s, most of the Communists in the State Department had been rooted out, the KGB's spy network in the United States was in decline, and the American Communist Party was a shadow of its former self. Yet the public's fear of subversion was so great that Joseph McCarthy's relentless charges of Communist influence in government made him the most feared elected official in American politics from 1950 to 1954. A master of vituperation, invective, and innuendo, he had a pathological disregard for truth and turned character assassination into an art form. As chairman of the Senate's Permanent Subcommittee on Investigations, he hectored witnesses, intimidated his colleagues, and ran roughshod over anyone who stood in his way.

McCarthy's demise, when it occurred, was as swift as his ascent had been (see pages 294–298). After a series of exchanges between McCarthy and Secretary of the Army Robert T. Stevens, the Army accused McCarthy and his aides Roy Cohn and Frank Carr of seeking preferential treatment for G. David Schine, an unpaid committee consultant who had been drafted in November 1953. In return, McCarthy accused the Army of holding Schine "hostage" in order block an investigation of military security. The conflict came to a head in the Army-McCarthy hearings, which began on April 22, 1954, and continued until June 17.

Broadcast live on the ABC and DuMont television networks, the hearings gave the nation a chance to view McCarthy up close, and most Americans did not like what they saw. Although the rules of the hearings forbade McCarthy from participating other than to cross-examine witnesses, he repeatedly interjected himself into the proceedings by raising points of order. As the days passed, McCarthy revealed himself more and more as a rhetorical bully for whom no accusation, no insinuation, no twisting of the truth was off limits. The climax of the hearings came on June 9, when Joseph Welch, chief attorney for the Army, dealt McCarthy a blow from which he would never recover.

Welch was a brilliant lawyer with a droll wit and folksy charm. He was cross-examining Cohn and ridiculing him for being lax in pursuing Communists at

Fort Monmouth, the Army Signal Corps facility in New Jersey, when McCarthy interrupted. His words dripping with derision, McCarthy accused Welch of hypocrisy and charged that he had tried to secure a committee position for a young man from his law firm named Fred Fisher, who had known ties to the Communist Party. Refusing to let up after Welch exculpated Fisher, McCarthy returned to the attack even as Cohn shook his head urging him to stop. Finally, his eyes brimming with tears, Welch rebuked McCarthy by asking, "Have you no sense of decency, sir, at long last? Have you left no sense of decency? . . . If there is a God in heaven, it will do neither you nor your cause any good."

It was a moment of high drama, and the sixty-three-year-old Welch, who later appeared in the film *Anatomy of a Murder*, played his role to perfection. By the time the hearings ended just over a week later, public opinion had turned against McCarthy, and in mid-July a motion to censure him was introduced by Ralph E. Flanders, Republican Senator from Vermont. The decision for censure was approved on December 2 by a vote of 67–22. Stripped of his power and ravaged by alcoholism, McCarthy died in May 1957 at age forty-eight.

◇◇

WELCH: Mr. Cohn, tell me once more: Every time you learn of a Communist or a spy anywhere, is it your policy to get them out as fast as possible?

COHN: Surely we want them out as fast as possible, sir.

WELCH: And whenever you learn of one from now on, Mr. Cohn, I beg of you, will you tell somebody about them quick?

COHN: Mr. Welch, sir, with great respect, I work for the committee here. They know how we go about handling situations of Communist infiltration and failure to act on FBI information about Communist infiltration. If they are displeased with the speed with which I and the group of men who work with me proceed at, if they are displeased with the order in which we move, I am sure they will give me appropriate instructions along those lines, and I will follow any which they give me.

WELCH: And may I add my small voice, sir, and say whenever you know about a subversive or a Communist or a spy, please hurry. Will you remember those words?

McCARTHY: Mr. Chairman.

COHN: Mr. Welch, I can assure you, sir, that as far as I'm concerned, and certainly as far as the chairman

of this committee[1] and the members and the members of the staff are concerned, we are a small group, but we proceed as expeditiously as is humanly possible to get out Communists and traitors and to bring to light the mechanism by which they have been permitted to remain where they were for so long a period of time.

McCARTHY: Mr. Chairman, Mr. Chairman, in view of that question—

MUNDT:[2] Do you have a point of order?

McCARTHY: Not exactly, Mr. Chairman. But in view of Mr. Welch's request that the information be given once we know of anyone who might be performing any work for the Communist Party, I think we should tell him that he has in his law firm a young man named Fisher whom he recommended, incidentally, to do the work on this committee, who has been for a number of years a member of an organization which was named, oh, years and years ago, as the legal bulwark of the Communist Party,

---

1. Cohn is referring to Senator McCarthy.

2. Karl E. Mundt, Republican Senator from South Dakota and temporary chair of the Subcommittee on Investigations that conducted the Army–McCarthy hearings. McCarthy was the permanent chair.

an organization which always springs to the defense of anyone who dares to expose Communists.[3]

I certainly assume that Mr. Welch did not know this young man at the time he recommended him as the assistant counsel for this committee, but he has such terror and such a great desire to know where anyone is located who may be serving the Communist cause, Mr. Welch, that I thought we should just call to your attention the fact that your Mr. Fisher, who is still in your law firm today, whom you asked to have down here looking over the secret and classified material, is a member of an organization, not named by me but named by various committees, named by the Attorney General, as I recall, and I think I quote this verbatim, as "the legal bulwark of the Communist Party."[4] He belonged to that for a sizable number of years, according to his own admission. He belonged to it long after it had been exposed as the legal arm of the Communist Party.

Knowing that, Mr. Welch, I just felt that I had a duty to respond to your urgent request that before sundown, when we know of anyone serving the Communist cause, we let the agency know. We're now letting you know that your man did belong to this organization for either three or four years, belonged to it long after he was out of law school. And I don't think you can find anyplace, anywhere, an organization which has done more to defend Communists—I'm again quoting the report—to defend Communists, to defend espionage agents, and to aid the Communist cause than the man whom you originally wanted down here at your right hand instead of Mr. St. Clair.[5]

Now, I have hesitated bringing that up, but I have been rather bored with your phony requests

to Mr. Cohn here that he personally get every Communist out of government before sundown. Therefore, we will give you the information about the young man in your own organization.

Now, I'm not asking you at this time to explain why you tried to foist him on this committee. That you did, the committee knows. Whether you knew he was a member of that Communist organization or not, I don't know. I assume you did not, Mr. Welch, because I get the impression that while you are quite an actor, you play for a laugh, I don't think you have any conception of the danger of the Communist Party. I don't think you, yourself, would ever knowingly aid the Communist cause. I think you're unknowingly aiding it when you try to burlesque this hearing in which we are attempting to bring out the facts, however.

WELCH: Mr. Chairman—

MUNDT: The Chair should say that he has no recognition or no memory of Mr. Welch recommending either Mr. Fisher or anybody else as counsel for this committee. I will recognize Mr. Welch.

McCARTHY: I refer to the record, Mr. Chairman, the news, the news story on that.

WELCH: Mr. Chairman, under these circumstances, I must myself have something approaching a personal privilege.

MUNDT: You may have it, sir. It will not be taken out of your time.

WELCH: Senator McCarthy, I did not know— Senator, Senator, sometimes you say, "May I have your attention."

McCARTHY: I'm listening.

WELCH: May I have your attention?

McCARTHY: I can listen with one ear and talk with the other.

WELCH: Now this time, sir, I want you to listen with both.

McCARTHY: Yes.

WELCH: Senator McCarthy, I think until this moment—

McCARTHY: Just a minute. Let me ask Jim.[6] Jim, will you get the news story to the effect that this

---

3. McCarthy is referring to the National Lawyers Guild. He meant to say that it had a history of defending people who were accused of being Communists.

4. During the summer of 1953, Attorney General Herbert Brownell Jr. called the Lawyers Guild the "legal mouthpiece" of the Communist Party and announced his intention to list it as a subversive organization. The phrase McCarthy quotes, however, is not from Brownell but from the September 1950 *Report on the National Lawyers Guild* by the House of Representatives Committee on Un-American Activities.

5. James D. St. Clair, who later served as special counsel to President Richard Nixon during the Watergate investigation.

6. McCarthy aide James Juliana.

man belonged to the—to this—Communist front organization?

WELCH: I will tell you that he belonged to it.

McCARTHY: Jim, will you get the citations, one of the citations, showing that this was the legal arm of the Communist Party, and the length of time that he belonged, and the fact that he was recommended by Mr. Welch? I think that should be in the record as well.

WELCH: Senator, you won't need anything in the record when I finish telling you this. Until this moment, Senator, I think I never really gauged your cruelty or your recklessness.

Fred Fisher is a young man who went to the Harvard Law School and came into my firm and is starting what looks to be a brilliant career with us. When I decided to work for this committee, I asked Jim St. Clair, who sits on my right, to be my first assistant. I said to Jim, "Pick somebody in the firm to work under you that you would like." He chose Fred Fisher, and they came down on an afternoon plane.

That night, when we had taken a little stab at trying to see what the case is about, Fred Fisher and Jim St. Clair and I went to dinner together. I then said to these two young men, "Boys, I don't know anything about you, except I've always liked you, but if there's anything funny in the life of either one of you that would hurt anybody in this case, you speak up quick."

And Fred Fisher said, "Mr. Welch, when I was in the law school, and for a period of months after, I belonged to the Lawyers Guild"—as you have suggested, Senator. He went on to say, "I am Secretary of the Young Republicans League in Newton with the son of Massachusetts's Governor, and I have the respect and admiration of my community, and I'm sure I have the respect and admiration of the twenty-five lawyers or so in Hale and Dorr."

And I said, "Fred, I just don't think I'm gonna ask you to work on the case. If I do, one of these days that will come out and go over national television and it will just hurt like the dickens." And so, Senator, I asked him to go back to Boston.

Little did I dream you could be so reckless and so cruel as to do an injury to that lad. It is true he is still with Hale and Dorr. It is true that he will continue to be with Hale and Dorr. It is, I regret to say, equally true that I fear he shall always bear a scar needlessly inflicted by you. If it were in my power to forgive you for your reckless cruelty, I would do so. I like to think I'm a gentle man, but your forgiveness will have to come from someone other than me.

McCARTHY: Mr. Chairman, Mr. Chairman, may I say that Mr. Welch talks about this being cruel and reckless. He was just baiting, he has been baiting Mr. Cohn here for hours, requesting that Mr. Cohn, before sundown, get out of any department of the government anyone who is serving the Communist cause. Now I just give this man's record, and I want to say, Mr. Welch, that it had been labeled long before he became a member, as early as 1944—

WELCH: Senator, may we not drop this? We know he belonged to the Lawyers Guild. And Mr. Cohn nods his head at me. I did you, I think, no personal injury, Mr. Cohn?

COHN: No, sir.

WELCH: I meant to do you no personal injury, and if I did, I beg your pardon. Let us not assassinate this lad further, Senator. You've done enough. Have you no sense of decency, sir, at long last? Have you left no sense of decency?

McCARTHY: I know this hurts you, Mr. Welch.

WELCH: I'll say it hurts.

McCARTHY: But may I say, Mr. Chairman, as a point of personal privilege, I'd like to finish this.

WELCH: Senator, I think it hurts you, too, sir.

McCARTHY: I'd like to finish this. Mr. Welch here has been filibustering this hearing; he has been talking day after day about the way he wants to get anyone tainted with communism out before sundown.

I know Mr. Cohn would rather not have me go into this. I intend to, however. And Mr. Welch talks about any sense of decency. If I say anything which is not the truth, then I would like to know about it. This organization has been named as the, this organization has been named as the foremost, and I quote, "the foremost legal bulwark of the Communist Party, its front organizations, and controlled unions," and which "since its inception has never failed to rally to the legal defense of the Communist Party and individual members thereof, including known espionage agents."[7] Now, that is not the language of Senator McCarthy. That is the language of the Un-American Activities Committee. And I can go on with, I can go on with many more citations.

It seems that Mr. Welch is pained so deeply he thinks it's improper for me to give the record, the Communist front record, of the man whom he wanted to foist upon this committee. But it doesn't pain him at all, there's no pain in his chest, about the unfounded charges against Mr. Frank Carr.[8] There's no pain there about the attempt to destroy the reputation and to take the jobs away from the young men who are working on my committee.

And, Mr. Welch, if I have said anything here which is untrue, then tell me. I have heard you and everyone else talk so much about laying the truth upon the table that when I heard—it's completely phony, Mr. Welch, I've listened to you now for a long time—to say now before sundown you must get these people out of government. So I just want to have it very clear, very clear that you were not so serious about that when you tried to recommend this man for this committee.

And may I say, Mr. Welch, in fairness to you I have reason to believe that you did not know about his Communist front record at the time you recommended him. I don't think you would have recommended him to the committee if you knew that. I think it's entirely possible you learned that after he came on the, after you recommended him. But the point is—

MUNDT: The Chair would like to say again that he does not believe Mr. Welch recommended Mr. Fisher as counsel for this committee because he has, through his office, all the recommendations that have been made and does not recall any of them coming from Mr. Welch, and that would include Mr. Fisher.

McCARTHY: Well, let me ask Mr. Welch. You brought him down, did you not, to act as your assistant?

WELCH: Mr. McCarthy, I will not discuss this further with you. You have sat within six feet of me and could ask—could have asked—me about Fred Fisher. You have seen fit to bring it out, and, if there is a God in heaven, it will do neither you nor your cause any good. I will not discuss it further. I will not ask Mr. Cohn any more questions.[9] You, Mr. Chairman, may, if you will, call the next witness.

---

7. From *Report on the National Lawyers Guild: Legal Bulwark of the Communist Party* (September 1950), issued by the Committee on Un-American Activities, U.S. House of Representatives.

8. Executive director of the Subcommittee on Investigations. In addition to being charged by the Army, along with McCarthy and Cohn, of seeking special treatment for G. David Schine, Carr came under fire during the hearings for irregularities in his handling of subcommittee documents.

---

9. Welch misspoke this word as "witnesses."

John F. Kennedy

⌛

Speech to the Greater Houston Ministerial Association

HOUSTON, TEXAS
SEPTEMBER 12, 1960

THE 1960 PRESIDENTIAL election was one of the closest in American history, with John F. Kennedy defeating Richard Nixon by two-tenths of one percent of the popular vote. Of all the issues in the campaign, none aroused more passion than Kennedy's religion. Anti-Catholicism ran deep in American history, and no major party nominated a Catholic for President until the Democrats ran Al Smith in 1928. He lost in a landslide to Herbert Hoover. Thirty-two years later, it was still not clear whether a Catholic could win enough votes to claim the White House. "Roman Catholicism is not only a religion," one Baptist pastor told his radio audience, "it is a political tyranny." Robert Kennedy, who served as his brother's campaign manager, believed that "religion is the biggest issue in the South, and in the country." One estimate suggested that fears of a Catholic President could cost John Kennedy as many as 1.5 million votes.

The issue came into sharp relief on September 7, when a group of 150 prominent Protestant ministers and laymen, operating under the banner of an organization called the National Conference of Citizens for Religious Freedom, issued a public proclamation questioning the ability of any Catholic officeholder to resist influence from the Vatican and to maintain the separation of church and state. This was a challenge Kennedy could not ignore. But it also gave him an opportunity to tackle the religious question head-on, rather than allowing it to fester under the surface. Five days later, on Monday, September 12, he addressed some 300 members of the Greater Houston Ministerial Association, meeting in the Crystal Ballroom of the Rice Hotel. Working with speechwriter Ted Sorensen, he spent the weekend preparing. "We can win or lose the election right there in Houston on Monday night," Sorensen told a friend.

Kennedy responded by giving the best speech of his campaign. In lines that quickly became famous, he stated that "contrary to common newspaper usage, I am not the Catholic candidate for President. I am the Democratic Party's candidate for President who happens also to be a Catholic." After affirming his unequivocal commitment to the separation of church and state, he deftly turned the tables on his opponents by redefining the issue as one of tolerance versus intolerance. Should he lose on the real issues, he said, he would return to the Senate satisfied that he had been fairly judged. But should the election be "decided on the basis that forty million Americans lost their chance of being President on the day they were baptized, then it is the whole nation that will be the loser in the eyes of Catholics and non-Catholics around the world, in the eyes of history, and in the eyes of our own people."

In the words of Theodore H. White, Kennedy "defined the personal doctrine of a modern Catholic in a democratic society…more fully and explicitly than any other thinker of his faith." The Houston speech was so effective that clips from it were used nationally in Kennedy ads through the rest of the campaign. It did not gain him a majority of the Protestant vote—he received 46 percent—but it defused the religious issue enough for him to win the election, and it remains a classic statement of the need for religious toleration in the American republic.

◇◇

Reverend Meza,[1] Reverend Reck,[2] I am grateful for your generous invitation to state my views.

While the so-called religious issue is necessarily and properly the chief topic here tonight, I want to emphasize from the outset that I believe that we have far more critical issues in the 1960 campaign: the spread of Communist influence until it now festers only ninety miles from the coast of Florida;[3] the humiliating treatment of our President and Vice President by those who no longer respect our power;[4] the hungry children I saw in West Virginia;[5] the old people who cannot pay their doctor's bills; the families forced to give up their farms; an America with too many slums, with too few schools, and too late to the moon and outer space.[6]

These are the real issues which should decide this campaign. And they are not religious issues, for war and hunger and ignorance and despair know no religious barrier. But because I am a Catholic and no Catholic has ever been elected President, the real issues in this campaign have been obscured, perhaps deliberately, in some quarters less responsible than this. So it is apparently necessary for me to state once again not what kind of church I believe in, for that should be important only to me, but what kind of America I believe in.

I believe in an America where the separation of church and state is absolute; where no Catholic prelate would tell the President, should he be Catholic, how to act, and no Protestant minister would tell his parishioners for whom to vote; where no church or church school is granted any public funds or political preference; and where no man is denied public office merely because his religion differs from the President who might appoint him or the people who might elect him.

I believe in an America that is officially neither Catholic, Protestant, nor Jewish; where no public official either requests or accepts instructions on public policy from the Pope, the National Council of Churches,[7] or any other ecclesiastical source; where no religious body seeks to impose its will, directly or indirectly, upon the general populace or the public acts of its officials; and where religious liberty is so

---

1. Herbert Meza, vice president of the Greater Houston Ministerial Association.

2. George Reck, president of the Greater Houston Ministerial Association.

3. A reference to the Cuban Revolution of 1959, which brought Fidel Castro to power.

4. In May 1958 Vice President Richard Nixon faced violent protests during his trip to Latin America. Two years later, President Dwight Eisenhower was forced to cancel a goodwill trip to Japan because of predicted protests and was publicly rebuked by USSR leader Nikita Khrushchev, who stormed out of a summit meeting in Paris after a U.S. spy plane was shot down over Soviet territory.

5. Kennedy is referring to his experiences during the 1960 West Virginia Democratic presidential primary campaign.

6. Throughout the campaign, Kennedy argued that the United States should commit itself to a vigorous program of space exploration to keep up with the Soviet Union.

---

7. The leading mainstream organization of Protestant denominations in the United States.

indivisible that an act against one church is treated as an act against all.

For while this year it may be a Catholic against whom the finger of suspicion is pointed, in other years it has been, and may someday be again, a Jew or a Quaker or a Unitarian or a Baptist. It was Virginia's harassment of Baptist preachers, for example, that led to Jefferson's Statute of Religious Freedom.[8] Today I may be the victim, but tomorrow it may be you—until the whole fabric of our harmonious society is ripped apart at a time of great national peril.

Finally, I believe in an America where religious intolerance will someday end; where all men and all churches are treated as equals; where every man has the same right to attend or not to attend the church of his choice; where there is no Catholic vote, no anti-Catholic vote, no bloc voting of any kind; and where Catholics, Protestants, and Jews, at both the lay and the pastoral levels, will refrain from those attitudes of disdain and division which have so often marred their works in the past, and promote instead the American ideal of brotherhood.

That is the kind of America in which I believe. And it represents the kind of presidency in which I believe—a great office that must be neither humbled by making it the instrument of any religious group nor tarnished by arbitrarily withholding it, its occupancy, from the members of any one religious group. I believe in a President whose views on religion are his own private affair, neither imposed upon him by the nation nor imposed by the nation upon him as a condition to holding that office.

I would not look with favor upon a President working to subvert the First Amendment's guarantees of religious liberty; nor would our system of checks and balances permit him to do so. And neither do I look with favor upon those who would work to subvert Article VI of the Constitution[9] by requiring a religious test—even by indirection—for if they

disagree with that safeguard, they should be openly working to repeal it.

I want a chief executive whose public acts are responsible to all and obligated to none; who can attend any ceremony, service, or dinner his office may appropriately require him to fulfill; and whose fulfillment of his presidential office is not limited or conditioned by any religious oath, ritual, or obligation.

This is the kind of America I believe in—and this is the kind of America I fought for in the South Pacific and the kind my brother died for in Europe.[10] No one suggested then that we might have a "divided loyalty," that we did "not believe in liberty," or that we belonged to a disloyal group that threatened, I quote, "the freedoms for which our forefathers died."[11]

And in fact this is the kind of America for which our forefathers did die when they fled here to escape religious test oaths that denied office to members of less-favored churches; when they fought for the Constitution, the Bill of Rights, the Virginia Statute of Religious Freedom; and when they fought at the shrine I visited today—the Alamo.[12] For side by side with Bowie and Crockett[13] died Fuentes and McCafferty and Bailey and Bedillio and Carey—but no one knows whether they were Catholics or not, for there was no religious test there.

I ask you tonight to follow in that tradition, to judge me on the basis of fourteen years in the Congress—on my declared stands against an ambassador to the Vatican, against unconstitutional aid to parochial schools, and against any boycott of the public schools, which I attended myself. And instead of doing this, do not judge me on the basis of these

---

8. Passed by the Virginia legislature in 1786, the statute became a model for the freedom of religion clause in the First Amendment to the U.S. Constitution.

9. Article VI states that "no religious test shall ever be required as a qualification to any office or public trust under the United States."

10. Kennedy's older brother, Joseph Kennedy Jr., was killed in combat during World War II.

11. Kennedy is quoting from among the many anonymous anti-Catholic publications circulated during the campaign. Contrary to some reports, the quotations did not come from the September 7 statement issued by the National Conference of Citizens for Religious Freedom.

12. Site of a 13-day battle during the Texas Revolution of 1835–1836.

13. Adventurer Jim Bowie and frontiersman Davy Crockett, the two most famous American heroes of the Battle of the Alamo.

pamphlets and publications we have all seen that carefully select quotations out of context from the statements of Catholic Church leaders, usually in other
countries, frequently in other centuries, and rarely
relevant to any situation here—and always omitting,
of course, the statement of the American bishops in
1948[14] which strongly endorsed church-state separation and which more nearly reflects the views of
almost every American Catholic. I do not consider
these other quotations binding upon my public acts.
Why should you?

But let me say, with respect to other countries,
that I am wholly opposed to the state being used
by any religious group—Catholic or Protestant—to
compel, prohibit, or prosecute the free exercise of any
other religion. And that goes for any persecution at
any time by anyone in any country.

And I hope that you and I condemn with equal
fervor those nations which deny their presidency
to Protestants and those which deny it to Catholics.
And rather than cite the misdeeds of those who differ,
I would also cite the record of the Catholic Church in
such nations as France and Ireland, and the independence of such statesmen as de Gaulle and Adenauer.[15]

But let me stress again that these are my views.
For contrary to common newspaper usage, I am
not the Catholic candidate for President. I am the
Democratic Party's candidate for President who happens also to be a Catholic. I do not speak for my
church on public matters, and the church does not
speak for me.

Whatever issue may come before me as President,
if I should be elected—on birth control, divorce, censorship, gambling, or any other subject—I will make
my decision in accordance with these views, in accordance with what my conscience tells me to be in the
national interest, and without regard to outside religious pressure or dictates. And no power or threat of
punishment could cause me to decide otherwise.

But if the time should ever come—and I do not
concede any conflict to be remotely possible—when
my office would require me to either violate my conscience or violate the national interest, then I would
resign the office, and I hope any other conscientious
public servant would do likewise.

But I do not intend to apologize for these views
to my critics of either Catholic or Protestant faith.
Nor do I intend to disavow either my views or my
church in order to win this election.

If I should lose on the real issues, I shall return
to my seat in the Senate satisfied that I tried my best
and was fairly judged. But if this election is decided
on the basis that forty million Americans lost their
chance of being President on the day they were baptized, then it is the whole nation that will be the loser
in the eyes of Catholics and non-Catholics around
the world, in the eyes of history, and in the eyes of
our own people.

But if, on the other hand, I should win this election, then I shall devote every effort of mind and spirit
to fulfilling the oath of the presidency—practically
identical, I might add, with the oath I have taken
for fourteen years in the Congress.[16] For without
reservation, I can, and I quote, "solemnly swear that
I will faithfully execute the office of President of the
United States and will to the best of my ability preserve, protect, and defend the Constitution. So help
me God."[17]

14. *The Christian in Action*, adopted by the Administrative Board
of the National Catholic Welfare Conference in November
1948.

15. Charles de Gaulle, President of France, and Konrad
Adenauer, Chancellor of West Germany, both of whom were
Catholic.

16. Kennedy was elected to the House of Representatives in
1946, and to the Senate in 1952.

17. The phrase "So help me God" is not part of the oath of office
as prescribed by the Constitution. It was added spontaneously
by George Washington at his first inauguration and has been
repeated by Presidents since that time.

Dwight D. Eisenhower

Farewell Address

WASHINGTON, D.C.
JANUARY 17, 1961

AT THE TIME he left office, Dwight Eisenhower was only the fifth President in American history to present a formal farewell address. (The others had been George Washington, Andrew Jackson, Andrew Johnson, and Harry Truman.) Delivered from the White House three days before the inauguration of John F. Kennedy, Ike's speech is best known for its warning about the potential dangers of the "military-industrial complex." Over the years, this phrase has taken on a life of its own, usually with little understanding of the context that gave it birth.

Supreme Allied commander in Europe during World War II, Eisenhower was one of the creators of the military-industrial complex, a series of interlocking relationships that linked American munitions makers, engineering firms, and defense contractors to the armed forces. He believed such linkage was necessary to make sure the United States would not repeat the experience of both world wars: being unprepared at the moment of crisis and having to take months or years to gear up for the mass production of weaponry. What concerned him by 1961 was not the existence of a military-industrial complex per se, but the imbalance created by defense contractors who pressured military and legislative leaders to purchase the latest weapons systems at a cost of billions of dollars, dollars that would undermine economic stability by throwing the national budget out of balance. To Eisenhower, a strong national defense and a strong economy were two sides of the same coin. One could not be sacrificed in favor of the other; both must be kept in balance.

In fact, the overarching theme of Eisenhower's farewell address is balance. In addition to discussing the military-industrial complex, he cautioned against the domination of scientific research by government contracts and called upon the nation to "avoid the impulse to live only for today, plundering, for our own ease and convenience, the precious resources of tomorrow." The great task of leadership, he stated, was "to mold, to balance, and to integrate" the complex forces of modern life "within the principles of our democratic system, ever aiming toward the supreme goals of our free society."

Although not a dynamic speaker, Eisenhower communicated a sense of trust, integrity, and goodwill that made him one of the most popular chief executives in

American history. As with Washington's classic valedictory of 1796, Ike's farewell address speaks to abiding issues in the American republic, and its counsel resonates across the passage of time.

◇◇

Good evening, my fellow Americans: First I should like to express my gratitude to the radio and television networks for the opportunities they have given me over the years to bring reports and messages to our nation. My special thanks go to them for the opportunity of addressing you this evening.

Three days from now, after half a century in the service of our country, I shall lay down the responsibilities of office as, in traditional and solemn ceremony, the authority of the presidency is vested in my successor. This evening I come to you with a message of leave-taking and farewell, and to share a few final thoughts with you, my countrymen.

Like every other citizen, like every other citizen, I wish the new President,[1] and all who will labor with him, Godspeed. I pray that the coming years will be blessed with peace and prosperity for all.

Our people expect their President and the Congress to find essential agreement on issues of great moment, the wise resolution of which will better shape the future of the nation. My own relations with the Congress, which began on a remote and tenuous basis when, long ago, a member of the Senate appointed me to West Point,[2] have since ranged to the intimate during the war and immediate postwar period and finally to the mutually interdependent during these past eight years. In this final relationship, the Congress and the administration have, on most vital issues, cooperated well to serve the nation[al] good rather than mere partisanship, and so have assured that the business of the nation should go forward. So my official relationship with the Congress ends in a feeling, on my part, of gratitude that we have been able to do so much together.

We now stand ten years past the midpoint of a century that has witnessed four major wars among great nations.[3] Three of these involved our own country. Despite these holocausts, America is today the strongest, the most influential, and most productive nation in the world. Understandably proud of this preeminence, we yet realize that America's leadership and prestige depend not merely upon our unmatched material progress, riches, and military strength, but on how we use our power in the interests of world peace and human betterment.

Throughout America's adventure in free government, our basic purposes have been to keep the peace, to foster progress in human achievement, and to enhance liberty, dignity, and integrity among peoples and among nations. To strive for less would be unworthy of a free and religious people. Any failure traceable to arrogance or our lack of comprehension or readiness to sacrifice would inflict upon us grievous hurt both at home and abroad.

Progress toward these noble goals is persistently threatened by the conflict now engulfing the world.[4] It commands our whole attention, absorbs our very beings. We face a hostile ideology—global in scope, atheistic in character, ruthless in purpose, and insidious[5] in method. Unhappily the danger it poses promises to be of indefinite duration. To meet it successfully there is called for, not so much the emotional and transitory sacrifices of crisis, but rather those which enable us to carry forward steadily, surely, and without complaint the burdens of a prolonged and complex struggle—with liberty the stake. Only thus shall we remain, despite every provocation, on our

---

1. John F. Kennedy, who took office three days after Eisenhower's address.

2. Eisenhower attended West Point from 1911 to 1915.

3. The Russo-Japanese War (1904–1905), World War I (1914–1918), World War II (1937–1945), the Korean War (1950–1953).

4. Eisenhower is referring to the Cold War.

5. Eisenhower misspoke this word as "insiduous."

charted course toward permanent peace and human betterment.

Crises there will continue to be. In meeting them, whether foreign or domestic, great or small, there is a recurring temptation to feel that some spectacular and costly action could become the miraculous solution to all current difficulties. A huge increase in newer elements of our defenses, development of unrealistic programs to cure every ill in agriculture, a dramatic expansion in basic and applied research—these and many other possibilities, each possibly promising in itself, may be suggested as the only way to the road we wish to travel.

But each proposal must be weighed in the light of a broader consideration: the need to maintain balance in and among national programs, balance between the private and the public economy, balance between the cost and hoped-for advantages, balance between the clearly necessary and the comfortably desirable, balance between our essential requirements as a nation and the duties imposed by the nation upon the individual, balance between actions of the moment and the national welfare of the future. Good judgment seeks balance and progress; lack of it eventually finds imbalance and frustration.

The record of many decades stands as proof that our people and their government have, in the main, understood these truths and have responded to them well in the face of threat and stress. But threats, new in kind or degree, constantly arise. Of these, I mention two only.

A vital element in keeping the peace is our military establishment. Our arms must be mighty, ready for instant action, so that no potential aggressor may be tempted to risk his own destruction. Our military organization today bears little relation to that known by[6] any of my predecessors in peacetime, or indeed by the fighting men of World War II or Korea. Until the latest of our world conflicts, the United States had no armaments industry. American makers of plowshares could, with time and as required, make swords as well.[7] But we can no longer risk emergency improvisation of national defense; we have been compelled to create a permanent armaments industry of vast proportions. Added to this, three and a half million men and women are directly engaged in the defense establishment. We annually spend on military security alone more than the net income of all United States corporations.

Now, this conjunction of an immense military establishment and a large arms industry is new in the American experience. The total influence—economic, political, even spiritual—is felt in every city, every statehouse, every office of the federal government. We recognize the imperative need for this development. Yet we must not fail to comprehend its grave implications. Our toil, resources, and livelihood are all involved; so is the very structure of our society.

In the councils of government, we must guard against the acquisition of unwarranted influence, whether sought or unsought, by the military-industrial complex. The potential for the disastrous rise of misplaced power exists and will persist. We must never let the weight of this combination endanger our liberties or democratic processes. We should take nothing for granted. Only an alert and knowledgeable citizenry can compel the proper meshing of the huge industrial and military machinery of defense with our peaceful methods and goals so that security and liberty may prosper together.

Akin to, and largely responsible for, the sweeping changes in our industrial-military posture has been the technological revolution during recent decades. In this revolution, research has become central; it also becomes more formalized, complex, and costly. A steadily increasing share is conducted for, by, or at the direction of the federal government. Today the solitary inventor tinkering in his shop has been overshadowed by task forces of scientists in laboratories and testing fields. In the same fashion, the free university, historically the fountainhead of free ideas and scientific discovery, has experienced a revolution in the conduct of research. Partly because of the huge costs involved, a government contract becomes virtually a substitute for intellectual curiosity. For every old blackboard there are now hundreds of new electronic computers.

The prospect of domination of the nation's scholars by federal employment, project allocations, and

---

6. Eisenhower misspoke this word as "of."

7. An allusion to Isaiah 2:4: "and they shall beat their swords into plowshares."

the power of money is ever present—and is gravely to be regarded. Yet in holding scientific research and discovery in respect, as we should, we must also be alert to the equal and opposite danger that public policy could itself become the captive of a scientific-technological elite. It is the task of statesmanship to mold, to balance, and to integrate these and other forces, new and old, within the principles of our democratic system, ever aiming toward the supreme goals of our free society.

Another factor in maintaining balance involves the element [of] time. As we peer into society's future, we—you and I and our government—must avoid the impulse to live only for today, plundering, for our own ease and convenience, the precious resources of tomorrow. We cannot mortgage the material assets of our grandchildren without risking the loss also of their political and spiritual heritage. We want democracy to survive for all generations to come, not to become the insolvent phantom of tomorrow.

During the long lane of the history yet to be written, America knows that this world of ours, ever growing smaller, must avoid becoming a community of dreadful fear and hate, and be instead a proud confederation of mutual trust and respect. Such a confederation must be one of equals. The weakest must come to the conference table with the same confidence as do we, protected as we are by our moral, economic, and military strength. That table, though scarred by many past frustrations, cannot be abandoned for the certain agony of the battlefield.[8]

Disarmament, with mutual honor and confidence, is a continuing imperative. Together we must learn how to compose differences, not with arms, but with intellect and decent purpose. Because this need is so sharp and apparent, I confess that I lay down my official responsibilities in this field with a definite sense of disappointment. As one who has witnessed the horror and the lingering sadness of war, as one who knows that another war could utterly destroy this civilization which has been so slowly and painfully built over thousands of years, I wish I could say tonight that a lasting peace is in sight.

Happily, I can say that war has been avoided. Steady progress toward our ultimate goal has been made. But so much remains to be done. As a private citizen, I shall never cease to do what little I can to help the world advance along that road.

So in this, my last good night to you as your President, I thank you for the many opportunities you have given me for public service in war and in peace. I trust that in that service you find some things worthy; as for the rest of it, I know you will find ways to improve performance in the future.

You and I, my fellow citizens, need to be strong in our faith that all nations, under God, will reach the goal of peace with justice. May we be ever unswerving in devotion to principle, confident but humble with power, diligent in pursuit of the nation's great goals.

To all the peoples of the world, I once more give expression to America's prayerful and continuing aspiration: We pray that peoples of all faiths, all races, all nations may have their great human needs satisfied; that those now denied opportunity shall come to enjoy it to the full; that all who yearn for freedom may experience its spiritual blessings; [that] those who have freedom will understand also its heavy responsibility; that all who are insensitive to the needs of others will learn charity; and that the scourges of poverty, disease, and ignorance will be made [to] disappear from the earth; and that, in the goodness of time, all peoples will come to live together in a peace guaranteed by the binding force of mutual respect and love.[9]

Now, on Friday noon, I am to become a private citizen. I am proud to do so. I look forward to it.

Thank you, and good night.

---

8. Because of difficulties with the teleprompter, Eisenhower stumbled over the delivery of this sentence. We have printed the sentence without the stumbles.

9. Eisenhower closes his presidency with a prayer, just as he had begun with a prayer in his first inaugural address, January 20, 1953.

John F. Kennedy

Inaugural Address

Washington, D.C.
January 20, 1961

Unlike other great presidential inaugural addresses—George Washington's first, Thomas Jefferson's first, both of Lincoln's, Franklin Roosevelt's first—John F. Kennedy's was not delivered in a moment of national crisis. Tensions with the Soviet Union were high, as they would be throughout the Cold War, but no American troops were in combat on foreign soil, the economy was performing solidly if not spectacularly, and outgoing President Dwight Eisenhower remained the most admired man in America.

Yet there was a special sense of excitement in the air on the day of Kennedy's inauguration, notwithstanding the snowdrifts, below-freezing temperatures, and twenty-mile-an-hour winds that buffeted Washington, D.C. Kennedy had adopted "The New Frontier" as his campaign slogan, and he wanted his speech to reinforce his image as part of a new generation that would bring vigor and vision to the challenges of a world divided. The inaugural would be crucial in setting the tone for his administration, but Kennedy also knew he was performing on the grandest of political stages, upon which the right speech could gain not only immediate applause but lasting esteem.

In preparation, he instructed speechwriter Ted Sorensen to read all previous presidential inaugurals and to study the secret of Abraham Lincoln's Gettysburg Address. He wanted a speech that was short, eloquent, and memorable. Because the occasion was ceremonial, he had more freedom than would otherwise have been the case to cultivate an elevated tone through rhetorical devices such as repetition, parallelism, antithesis, alliteration, and chiasmus. The result was a speech more in the grand style of classical oratory than any presidential address of the twentieth century.

There has been much debate about the extent to which Kennedy crafted the words himself and the extent to which they came from Sorensen. In fact, a number of people contributed to the address, including Adlai Stevenson, John Kenneth Galbraith, Gore Vidal, and Walter Lippmann. The speech also echoes ideas and words from previous addresses by Kennedy, who had a sharp eye for concision and a keen ear for the rhythms of language. He was especially fond of Winston Churchill, whose speeches he used to recite out loud, and there is a discernibly Churchillian ring to the inaugural.

Ultimately, all the pieces were put together by Sorensen, but Kennedy continued to tinker with the speech even after the official reading copy was prepared. There are more than thirty changes in the speech as delivered when compared with the reading copy. There is no way to know how many of those changes were extemporized by Kennedy at the moment of presentation and how many were penned on the reading copy beforehand, but as Thurston Clarke notes in his study of the speech, "all made grammatical or logical sense, or rendered his sentences tighter or smoother."

Focusing almost solely on international affairs, Kennedy's inaugural fused elegant phraseology and lofty idealism with a square-eyed recognition of the realities of Cold War politics. Broadcast internationally by radio and widely reprinted in other nations, it stirred millions in the United States and abroad. It was immediately hailed as one of the finest speeches by an American President, and it has retained its standing in the court of history.

◇◇◇◇◇◇◇◇◇◇◇◇◇◇◇◇◇◇◇◇◇◇◇◇◇◇◇◇◇◇◇◇◇◇◇◇◇◇

Vice President Johnson,[1] Mr. Speaker,[2] Mr. Chief Justice,[3] President Eisenhower, Vice President Nixon, President Truman,[4] Reverend Clergy, fellow citizens: We observe today not a victory of party, but a celebration of freedom[5]—symbolizing an end as well as a beginning, signifying renewal as well as change. For I have sworn before you and Almighty God the same solemn oath our forebears prescribed nearly a century and three-quarters ago.

The world is very different now. For man holds in his mortal hands the power to abolish all forms of human poverty and all forms of human life. And yet the same revolutionary beliefs for which our forebears fought are still at issue around the globe—the belief that the rights of man come not from the generosity of the state but from the hand of God.

We dare not forget today that we are the heirs of that first revolution. Let the word go forth from this time and place, to friend and foe alike, that the torch has been passed to a new generation of Americans—born in this century, tempered by war, disciplined by a hard and bitter peace, proud of our ancient heritage, and unwilling to witness or permit the slow undoing of those human rights to which this nation has always been committed and to which we are committed today at home and around the world.

Let every nation know, whether it wishes us well or ill, that we shall pay any price, bear any burden, meet any hardship, support any friend, oppose any foe to assure the survival and the success of liberty. This much we pledge—and more.

To those old allies whose cultural and spiritual origins we share, we pledge the loyalty of faithful friends. United, there is little we cannot do in a host of cooperative ventures. Divided, there is little we can do, for we dare not meet a powerful challenge at odds and split asunder.

To those new states whom we welcome to the ranks of the free, we pledge our word that one form of colonial control shall not have passed away merely to be replaced by a far more iron tyranny. We shall not always expect to find them supporting our view. But we shall always hope to find them strongly supporting their own freedom—and to remember that, in the

---

1. Lyndon B. Johnson, elected with John F. Kennedy in 1960.

2. Sam Rayburn, Speaker of the House of Representatives.

3. Earl Warren, Chief Justice of the U.S. Supreme Court.

4. Outgoing President Dwight D. Eisenhower; outgoing Vice President Richard M. Nixon; former President Harry S. Truman.

5. An echo of Woodrow Wilson's first inaugural address (pages 40–43).

past, those who foolishly sought power by riding the back of the tiger ended up inside.[6]

To those people in the huts and villages of half the globe struggling to break the bonds of mass misery, we pledge our best efforts to help them help themselves for whatever period is required—not because the Communists may be doing it, not because we seek their votes, but because it is right. If a free society cannot help the many who are poor, it cannot save the few who are rich.

To our sister republics south of our border, we offer a special pledge: to convert our good words into good deeds in a new alliance for progress to assist free men and free governments in casting off the chains of poverty. But this peaceful revolution of hope cannot become the prey of hostile powers. Let all our neighbors know that we shall join with them to oppose aggression or subversion anywhere in the Americas. And let every other power know that this hemisphere intends to remain the master of its own house.

To that world assembly of sovereign states, the United Nations, our last best hope in an age where the instruments of war have far outpaced the instruments of peace, we renew our pledge of support—to prevent it from becoming merely a forum for invective, to strengthen its shield of the new and the weak, and to enlarge the area in which its writ may run.

Finally, to those nations who would make themselves our adversary, we offer not a pledge but a request: that both sides begin anew the quest for peace before the dark powers of destruction unleashed by science engulf all humanity in planned or accidental self-destruction.

We dare not tempt them with weakness. For only when our arms are sufficient beyond doubt can we be certain beyond doubt that they will never be employed.

But neither can two great and powerful groups of nations take comfort from our present course—both sides overburdened by the cost of modern weapons, both rightly alarmed by the steady spread of the deadly atom, yet both racing to alter that uncertain balance of terror that stays the hand of mankind's final war.

So let us begin anew, remembering on both sides that civility is not a sign of weakness and sincerity is always subject to proof. Let us never negotiate out of fear. But let us never fear to negotiate.

Let both sides explore what problems unite us instead of belaboring those problems which divide us.

Let both sides, for the first time, formulate serious and precise proposals for the inspection and control of arms—and bring the absolute power to destroy other nations under the absolute control of all nations.

Let both sides seek to invoke the wonders of science instead of its terrors. Together let us explore the stars, conquer the deserts, eradicate disease, tap the ocean depth[s], and encourage the arts and commerce.

Let both sides unite to heed in all corners of the earth the command of Isaiah to "undo the heavy burdens" and "let the oppressed go free."[7]

And if a beachhead of cooperation may push back the jungle of suspicion, let both sides join in creating a new endeavor—not a new balance of power, but a new world of law where the strong are just and the weak secure and the peace preserved.

All this will not be finished in the first one hundred days. Nor will it be finished in the first one thousand days, nor in the life of this administration, nor even perhaps in our lifetime on this planet. But let us begin.

In your hands, my fellow citizens, more than mine,[8] will rest the final success or failure of our course. Since this country was founded, each generation of Americans has been summoned to give testimony to its national loyalty. The graves of young Americans who answered the call to service surround the globe.

6. Perhaps an allusion to Winston Churchill's "Armistice—Or Peace," *Evening Standard*, November 11, 1937: "Dictators ride to and fro on tigers which they dare not dismount. And the tigers are getting hungry." Similar imagery, without the political connotations, appears in a 1901 limerick attributed to British poet Cosmo Monkhouse, as well as in Chinese and Hindu proverbs. Churchill's statement is usually misattributed to his World War II speeches or to *While England Slept* (1938).

7. Isaiah 58:6.

8. An echo of Abraham Lincoln's first inaugural address, March 4, 1861.

Now the trumpet summons us again—not as a call to bear arms, though arms we need, not as a call to battle, though embattled we are—but a call to bear the burden of a long twilight struggle, year in and year out, "rejoicing in hope, patient in tribulation,"[9] a struggle against the common enemies of man: tyranny, poverty, disease, and war itself. Can we forge against these enemies a grand and global alliance—North and South, East and West—that can assure a more fruitful life for all mankind? Will you join in that historic effort?

In the long history of the world, only a few generations have been granted the role of defending freedom in its hour of maximum danger. I do not shrink from this responsibility—I welcome it. I do not believe that any of us would exchange places with any other people or any other generation. The energy, the faith, the devotion which we bring to this endeavor will light our country and all who serve it—and the glow from that fire can truly light the world.

And so, my fellow Americans, ask not what your country can do for you—ask what you can do for your country.[10]

My fellow citizens of the world, ask not what America will do for you, but what together we can do for the freedom of man.

Finally, whether you are citizens of America or citizens of the world, ask of us here the same high standards of strength and sacrifice which we ask of you. With a good conscience our only sure reward, with history the final judge of our deeds, let us go forth to lead the land we love, asking his blessing and his help, but knowing that here on earth God's work must truly be our own.

---

9. Romans 12:12.

10. The ideas and antithetical structure of this sentence have numerous antecedents, but the final formulation is unique to Kennedy's speech.

Newton N. Minow

Television and the Public Interest

WASHINGTON, D.C.
MAY 9, 1961

NEWTON MINOW WAS one of the "New Frontiersmen" brought to Washington, D.C., with the election of John F. Kennedy. A former aide to Adlai Stevenson in the 1952 and 1956 presidential campaigns, Minow joined the Kennedy forces in 1960. After taking office, Kennedy made him chairman of the Federal Communications Commission (FCC). Only thirty-five years old and a lawyer by training, Minow seemed an unusual choice for such an important position. But he had developed an interest in television during the 1950s—particularly its political possibilities and its impact on children—and he wasted no time in taking charge of the commission.

Less than four months into his appointment, Minow spoke to the annual convention of the National Association of Broadcasters, an organization of radio and television executives. Often such speeches are back-patting exercises, liberally sprinkled with praise for the titans of the industry. Instead, Minow lambasted the executives for failing to live up to their responsibilities as keepers of a public trust. During the course of his remarks, which grew out of several months of planning, drafting, and revising, he asked the executives to sit in front of their televisions and watch a whole day of programming. What they would see, he said, was a "vast wasteland" filled with game shows, violence, soap operas, banal comedies, and endless commercials.

Rebuking broadcasters for being driven by profits, Minow declared that "It is not enough to cater to the nation's whims; you must also serve the nation's needs." He challenged the networks and station owners to provide intelligence and leadership, rather than persisting "in a relentless search for the highest rating and the lowest common denominator." What the industry needed was "imagination in programming, not sterility; creativity, not imitation; experimentation, not conformity; excellence, not mediocrity." Speaking of television's influence on young viewers, Minow deplored the "massive doses of cartoons, violence, and more violence" on children's shows. He called on broadcasters to use their medium "to teach, to inform, to uplift, to stretch, to enlarge the capacities of our children." Many of his words ring as true today as they did in 1961.

At the end of World War II, there were fewer than 7,000 television sets in the United States. By the time President Kennedy took office, there were more than fifty million. Many Americans found themselves simultaneously enamored with and troubled by the ubiquitous new medium. Minow's description of television as a vast wasteland immediately entered the public vocabulary and touched off a national debate about the quality of programming and the responsibility of broadcasters to serve the public interest. Minow spent only two years as chairman of the FCC, but it has been estimated that he generated more column-inches of news coverage during that time than any member of the Kennedy administration other than the President himself.

◇◇◇

Governor Collins,[1] distinguished guests, ladies and gentlemen: Governor Collins, you are much too kind, as all of you have been to me the last few days.[2] It's been a great pleasure and an honor for me to meet so many of you. And I want to thank you for this opportunity to meet with you today.

As you know, this is my first public address since I took over my new job. When the New Frontiersmen rode into town, I locked myself in my office to do my homework and get my feet wet. But apparently I haven't managed yet to stay out of hot water. I seem to have detected a very nervous apprehension about what I might say or do when I emerged from that locked office for this, my maiden station break.

So first let me begin by dispelling a rumor. I was not picked for this job because I regard myself as the fastest draw on the New Frontier. Second, let

1. Thomas LeRoy Collins, Governor of Florida, 1955–1961, and president of the National Association of Broadcasters (NAB), 1961–1964.

2. The NAB convention had begun on May 7.

me start a rumor. Like you, I have carefully read President Kennedy's messages about the regulatory agencies, conflict of interest, and the dangers of ex parte contacts.[3] And, of course, we at the Federal Communications Commission will do our part. Indeed, I may even suggest that we change the name of the FCC to The Seven Untouchables![4]

It may also come as a surprise to some of you, but I want you to know that you have my admiration and my respect. Yours is a most honorable profession. Anyone who is in the broadcasting business has a tough row to hoe. You earn your bread by using public property. When you work in broadcasting, you volunteer for public service, public pressure, and public regulation. You must compete with other attractions and other investments, and the only way you can do it is to prove to us every three years that you should have been in business in the first place.[5] I can think of easier ways to make a living, but I cannot think of more satisfying ways.

I admire your courage, but that doesn't mean that I would make life any easier for you. Your license lets you use the public's airwaves as trustees for 180 million Americans. The public is your beneficiary. If you want to stay on as trustees, you must deliver a decent return to the public, not only to your stockholders. So as a representative of the public, your health and your product are among my chief concerns.

As to your health, let's talk only of television today. Nineteen-sixty gross broadcast revenues of the television industry were over $1,268,000,000. Profit before taxes was $243,900,000, an average return on revenue of 19.2 percent. Compare these with 1959, when gross broadcast revenues were $1,163,900,000, and profit before taxes was 222,300,000, an average

return on revenue of 19.1 percent. So the percentage increase of total revenues from '59 to '60 was 9 percent, and the percentage increase of profit was 9.7 percent. This, despite a recession throughout the country. For your investors, the price has indeed been right.[6]

So I have confidence in your health. But not in your product. It is with this and much more in mind that I come before you today.

One editorialist in the trade press wrote that "the FCC of the New Frontier is going to be one of the toughest FCCs in the history of broadcast regulation."[7] If he meant that we intend to enforce the law in the public interest, let me make it perfectly clear that he is right—we do. If he meant that we intend to muzzle or censor broadcasting, he is dead wrong. It wouldn't surprise me if some of you had expected me to come here today and say to you, in effect: "Clean up your own house or the government will do it for you." Well, in a limited sense, you would be right because I've just said it.

But I want to say to you as earnestly as I can that it is not in that spirit that I come before you today. Nor is it in that spirit that I intend to serve the FCC. I am in Washington to help broadcasting, not to harm it; to strengthen it, not weaken it; to reward it, not to punish it; to encourage it, not threaten it; and to stimulate it, not censor it. Above all, I am here to uphold and protect the public interest.

Now, what do we mean by the public interest? Some say the public interest is merely what interests the public. I disagree. And so does your distinguished president, Governor Collins. In a recent speech—and, of course, as [he] also told you yesterday—in a recent speech, he said: "Broadcasting, to serve the public interest, must have a soul and a conscience, a burning desire to excel, as well as to sell; the urge to build the character, citizenship, and intellectual stature of people, as well as to expand the gross national product.... By no means do I imply that broadcasters

3. Minow is referring to John F. Kennedy's April 13, 1961, Message to Congress on the Regulatory Agencies and his April 27 Message on Conflict-of-Interest Legislation and on Problems of Ethics in Government.

4. A reference to the seven members of the FCC; *The Untouchables* was a popular TV series that aired from 1959 to 1963.

5. In 1961 licenses for television stations were reviewed for renewal by the FCC every three years; the time period was changed to eight years in 1966.

6. A reference to the game show *The Price is Right*, which debuted in 1956.

7. From "Hard Life on the New Frontier," *Broadcasting*, March 27, 1961.

disregard the public interest.... But a much better job can be done and should be done."[8]

I could not agree more with Governor Collins. And I would add that in today's world, with chaos in Laos and the Congo aflame, with Communist tyranny on our Caribbean doorstep, relentless pressures on our Atlantic alliance, with social and economic problems at home of the gravest nature, yes, and with the technological knowledge that makes it possible, as our President has said,[9] not only to destroy our world but to destroy poverty around the world in a time of peril and opportunity, the old complacent, unbalanced fare of action-adventure and situation comedies is simply not good enough.

Your industry possesses the most powerful voice in America. It has an inescapable duty to make that voice ring with intelligence and with leadership. In a few years, this exciting industry has grown from a novelty to an instrument of overwhelming impact on the American people. It should be making ready for the kind of leadership that newspapers and magazines assumed years ago—to make our people aware of their world.

Ours has been called the jet age, the atomic age, the space age. It is also, I submit, the television age. And just as history will decide whether the leaders of today's world employed the atom to destroy the world or rebuild it for mankind's benefit, so will history decide whether today's broadcasters employed their powerful voice to enrich the people or to debase them.

If I seem today to address myself chiefly to the problems of television, I don't want any of you radio broadcasters to think that we've gone to sleep at your switch—we haven't. We still listen. But in recent years most of the controversies and crosscurrents in broadcast programming have swirled around television. And so my subject today is the television industry and the public interest.

Like everybody, I wear more than one hat. I am the chairman of the FCC, but I am also a television

viewer and the husband and father of other television viewers. I have seen a great many programs that seemed to me eminently worthwhile, and I'm not talking about the much-bemoaned good old days of *Playhouse 90* and *Studio One*.[10] I'm talking about this past season. Some were wonderfully entertaining, such as *The Fabulous Fifties*, *The Fred Astaire Show*, and *The Bing Crosby Special*. Some were dramatic and moving, such as Conrad's *Victory*[11] and *Twilight Zone*. Some were marvelously informative, such as *The Nation's Future*, *CBS Reports*, *The Valiant Years*. I could list many more—programs that I am sure everyone here felt enriched his own life and that of his family. When television is good, nothing—not the theater, not the magazines or newspapers—nothing is better.

But when television is bad, nothing is worse. I invite each of you to sit down in front of your own television set when your station goes on the air and stay there for a day without a book, without a magazine, without a newspaper, without a profit-and-loss sheet or rating book to distract you. Keep your eyes glued to that set until the station signs off. I can assure you that what you will observe is a vast wasteland.

You will see a procession of game shows, formula comedies about totally unbelievable families, blood and thunder, mayhem, violence, sadism, murder, western bad men, western good men, private eyes, gangsters, more violence, and cartoons. And, endlessly, commercials—many screaming, cajoling, and offending. And most of all, boredom. True, you'll see a few things you will enjoy. But they will be very, very few. And if you think I exaggerate, I only ask you to try it.

Is there one person in this room who claims that broadcasting can't do better? Well, a glance at next season's proposed programming can give us little heart. Of seventy-three and a half hours of prime evening time, the networks have tentatively scheduled fifty-nine hours of categories of action-adventure, situation comedy, variety, quiz, and movies. Is there one network president in this room who claims he

8. From Collins's speech to the Radio and Television Executives Society of New York, March 15, 1961.

9. Minow is referring to President Kennedy's inaugural address of January 20, 1961 (pages 341–344).

10. *Playhouse 90* and *Studio One* were live dramatic anthology programs aired during the 1950s.

11. Minow is referring to the television adaptation of Joseph Conrad's 1915 novel *Victory: An Island Tale*.

can't do better? Well, is there at least one network president who believes that the other networks can do better? Gentlemen, your trust accounting with your beneficiaries is long overdue. Never have so few owed so much to so many.[12]

Why is so much of television so bad? I've heard many answers. Demands of your advertisers, competition for ever-higher ratings, the need always to attract a mass audience, the high cost of television programs, the insatiable appetite for programming material—these are some of the reasons. Unquestionably these are tough problems not susceptible to easy answers. But I am not convinced that you have tried hard enough to solve them. I do not accept the idea that the present overall programming is aimed accurately at the public taste.

The ratings tell us only that some people have their television sets turned on and, of that number, so many are tuned to one channel and so many to another. They don't tell us what the public might watch if they were offered half a dozen additional choices. A rating, at best, is an indication of how many people saw what you gave them. Unfortunately, it does not reveal the depth of the penetration or the intensity of reaction, and it never reveals what the acceptance would have been if what you gave them had been better—if all the forces of art and creativity and daring and imagination had been unleashed. I believe in the people's good sense and good taste, and I'm not convinced that the people's taste is as low as some of you assume.

My concern with the rating services is not with their accuracy. Perhaps they're accurate; I really don't know. What, then, is wrong with the ratings? It's not been their accuracy—it's been their use.

Certainly I hope you will agree that ratings should have little influence where children are concerned. The best estimates indicate that during the hours of 5:00 to 6:00 p.m., 60 percent of your audience is composed of children under twelve. And most young children today, believe it or not, spend as much time watching television as they do in the schoolroom. I repeat—let that sink in, ladies and gentlemen—most young children today spend as much time watching television as they do in the schoolroom. It used to be said that there were three great influences on a child—home, school, and church. Today there is a fourth great influence, and you ladies and gentlemen in this room control it.

If parents, teachers, and ministers conducted their responsibility by following the ratings, children would have a steady diet of ice cream, school holidays, and no Sunday school. What about your responsibilities? Is there no room on television to teach, to inform, to uplift, to stretch, to enlarge the capacities of our children? Is there no room for programs deepening their understanding of children in other lands? Is there no room for a children's news show explaining something to them about the world at their level of understanding? Is there no room for reading the great literature of the past or teaching them the great traditions of freedom?

There are some fine children's shows, but they are drowned out in the massive doses of cartoons, violence, and more violence. Must these be your trademarks? Search your consciences and see if you cannot offer more to your young beneficiaries whose future you guide so many hours each and every day.

Now, what about adult programming and ratings? You know, newspaper publishers take popularity ratings too. And the answers are pretty clear. It is almost always the comics, followed by advice-to-the-lovelorn columns. But, ladies and gentlemen, the news is still on the front page of all newspapers, the editorials are not replaced by more comics, and the newspapers have not become one long collection of advice to the lovelorn. Yet newspapers do not even need a license from the government to be in business—they do not use public property.

But in television, where your responsibilities as public trustees are so plain, the moment that the ratings indicate that westerns[13] are popular, there are new imitations of westerns on the air faster than the old coaxial cable could take us from Hollywood to

---

12. A play on Winston Churchill's statement of August 20, 1940, about the heroism of the Royal Air Force during the Battle of Britain: "Never in the field of human combat was so much owed by so many to so few."

---

13. Shows set in the American West, usually of the late 19th century, and a staple of early television programming.

New York. Broadcasting cannot continue to live by the numbers. Ratings ought to be the slave of the broadcaster, not his master. And you and I both know, you and I both know that the rating services themselves would agree.

Let me make clear that what I am talking about is balance. I believe that the public interest is made up of many interests. There are many people in this great country, and you must serve all of us. You will get no argument from me if you say that, given a choice between a western and a symphony, more people will watch the western. I like westerns too, but a steady diet for the whole country is obviously not in the public interest. We all know that people would more often prefer to be entertained than stimulated or informed. But your obligations are not satisfied if you look only to popularity as a test of what to broadcast.

You are not only in show business. You are free to communicate ideas as well as relaxation. And as Governor Collins said to you yesterday when he encouraged you to editorialize,[14] as you know, the FCC has now encouraged editorializing for years. We want you to do this. We want you to editorialize, take positions. We only ask that you do it in a fair and a responsible manner. Those stations that have editorialized have demonstrated to you that the FCC will always encourage a fair and responsible clash of opinions. You must provide a wider range of choices, more diversity, more alternatives. It is not enough to cater to the nation's whims; you must also serve the nation's needs.

And I would add this: that if some of you persist in a relentless search for the highest rating and the lowest common denominator, you may very well lose your audience. Because, to paraphrase a great American who was recently my law partner,[15] the people are wise, wiser than some of the broadcasters—and politicians—think.

As you may have gathered, I would like to see television improved. But how is this to be brought about? By voluntary action by the broadcasters themselves? By direct government intervention? Or how?

Let me address myself now to my role not as a viewer, but as chairman of the FCC. I could not, if I would, chart for you this afternoon in detail all of the actions I contemplate. Instead I want to make clear some of the fundamental principles which guide me.

First, the people own the air. And they own it as much in prime evening time as they do at six o'clock Sunday morning. For every hour that the people give you, you owe them something. And I intend to see that your debt is paid with service.

Second, I think it would be foolish and wasteful for us to continue any worn-out wrangle over the problems of payola,[16] rigged quiz shows,[17] and other mistakes of the past. There are laws on the books which we will enforce. But there's no chip on my shoulder. We live together in perilous, uncertain times; we face together staggering problems; and we must not waste much time now by rehashing the clichés of past controversy. To quarrel over the past is to lose the future.

Third, I believe in the free-enterprise system. I want to see broadcasting improved, and I want you to do the job. I am proud to champion your cause. It is not rare for American businessmen to serve a public trust. Yours is a special trust because it is imposed by law.

Fourth, I will do all I can to help educational television. There are still not enough educational stations, and major centers of the country still lack usable educational channels. If there were a limited number of printing presses in this country, you may be sure that a fair proportion of them would be put to educational use. Educational television has an enormous contribution to make to the future, and I intend to give it a hand along the way. If there is not a nationwide educational television system in this country, it will not be the fault of the FCC.[18]

---

14. Newton is referring to Collins's presidential address, delivered on May 8.

15. Adlai Stevenson, Governor of Illinois, 1948–1952, and twice the Democratic nominee for President.

16. The paying of cash or gifts in exchange for airplay, mention, or advocacy of a product.

17. During the late 1950s, it was discovered that popular quiz shows such as *Twenty-One* and *The $64,000 Question* had rigged their outcomes to produce higher ratings.

18. Although it occurred after Minow left the FCC, creation of the Corporation for Public Broadcasting in the late 1960s was partly the result of his efforts in behalf of national noncommercial television.

Fifth, I'm unalterably opposed to governmental censorship. There will be no suppression of programming which does not meet with bureaucratic tastes. Censorship strikes at the very taproot of our free society.

Sixth, I did not come to Washington to idly observe the squandering of the public's airwaves. The squandering of our airwaves is no less important than the lavish waste of any precious natural resource. I intend to take the job of chairman of the FCC very seriously. I happen to believe in the gravity of my own particular sector of the New Frontier. There will be times perhaps when you will consider that I take myself or my job too seriously. Frankly, I don't care if you do, for I am convinced that either one takes this job seriously or one can be seriously taken.

Now, how will these principles be applied? Clearly, at the heart of the FCC's authority lies its power to license, to renew or fail to renew, or to revoke a license. As you know, when your license comes up for renewal, your performance is compared with your promises. I understand that many people feel that in the past, licenses were often renewed pro forma. I say to you now: Renewal will not be pro forma in the future. There is nothing permanent or sacred about a broadcast license.

But simply matching promises and performance is not enough. I intend to do more. I intend to find out whether the people care. I intend to find out whether the community which each broadcaster serves believes he has been serving the public interest. When a renewal is set down for a hearing, I intend whenever possible to hold a well-advertised public hearing right in the community you have promised to serve. I want the people who own the air and the homes that television enters to tell you and the FCC what's been going on. I want the people—if they're truly interested in the service you give them—to make notes, document cases, tell us the facts. And for those few of you who really believe that the public interest is merely what interests the public, I hope that these hearings will arouse no little interest. The FCC has a fine reserve of monitors—almost 180 million Americans gathered around fifty-six million sets. If you want those monitors to be your friends at court, it's up to you.

Now, some of you may say, "Yes, but I still do not know where the line is between a grant of a renewal and the hearing you just spoke of." My answer is: "Why should you want to know how close you can come to the edge of the cliff?"

What the commission asks of you is to make a conscientious, good-faith effort to serve the public interest. Every one of you serves a community in which the people would benefit by educational and religious, instructive and other public-service programming. Every one of you serves an area which has local needs—as to local elections, controversial issues, local news, local talent. Make a serious, genuine effort to put on that programming. And when you do, you will not be playing brinkmanship with the public interest.

Now, what I've been saying applies to the broadcast stations. Now a station break for the networks, and it will last even longer than forty seconds.[19] You networks know your importance in this great industry. Today more than one-half of all hours of television station programming comes from the networks; in prime time, this rises to more than three-fourths of the available hours. You know that the FCC has been studying network operations for some time. I intend to press this to a speedy conclusion with useful results.

I can tell you right now, however, that I'm deeply concerned with the concentration of power in the hands of the networks. As a result, too many local stations have foregone any efforts at local programming, with little use of live talent and local service. Too many local stations operate with one hand on the network switch and the other on a projector loaded with old movies. We want the individual stations to be free to meet their legal responsibilities to serve their communities.

I join Governor Collins in his views so well expressed to the advertisers who use the public air.[20] And I urge the networks to join him and undertake a very special mission in behalf of this industry. You

---

19. Forty seconds was the length of the standard station break between network programs in 1961.

20. Minow is referring to Collins's April 22, 1961, speech to the American Association of Advertising Agencies.

can tell your advertisers: "This is the high quality we are going to serve—take it or other people will. If you think you can find a better place to move automobiles, cigarettes, and soap, then go ahead and try." Tell your sponsors to be less concerned with costs per thousand and more concerned with understanding per millions. And remind your stockholders that an investment in broadcasting is buying a share in public responsibility. The networks can start this industry on the road to freedom from the dictatorship of numbers.

But there is more to the problem than network influences on stations or advertiser influences on networks. I know the problems networks face in trying to clear some of their best programs—the informational programs that exemplify public service. They are your finest hours. Whether sustaining or commercial, whether regularly scheduled or special, these are the signs that broadcasting knows the way to leadership. They make the public's trust in you a wise choice. They should be seen.

As you know, we are readying for use new forms by which broadcast stations will report their programming to the commission. You probably also know that special attention will be paid in these forms to reports of public-service programming. I believe that stations taking network service should also be required to report the extent of the local clearance of network public-service programs, and when they fail to clear them, they should explain why. If it is to put on some outstanding local program, this is one reason. But if it is simply to run an old movie, that's an entirely different matter. And the commission should consider such clearance reports carefully when making up its mind about the licensee's overall programming.

We intend to move. And as you know, and as I want to say publicly, the FCC was rapidly moving in other new areas before the new administration arrived in Washington. And I want to pay my public respects to my very able predecessor, Fred Ford,[21] and to my colleagues on the commission, each of whom has welcomed me to the FCC with warmth and cooperation.

We have approved an experiment with pay-TV, and in New York we are testing the potential of UHF[22] broadcasting. Either or both of these may revolutionize television. Only a foolish prophet would venture to guess the direction they will take, and their effect. But we intend that they shall be explored fully, for they are part of broadcasting's new frontier. The questions surrounding pay-TV are largely economic. The questions surrounding UHF are largely technological. We are going to give the infant pay-TV a chance to prove whether it can offer a useful service. We are going to protect it from those who would strangle it in its crib.

As for UHF, I'm sure you know about our test in the canyons of New York City.[23] We will take every possible positive step to break through the allocations barrier into UHF. We will put this sleeping giant to use, and in the years ahead we may have twice as many channels operating in cities where now there are only two or three. We may have half a dozen networks instead of three.

I have told you that I believe in the free enterprise system. I believe that most of television's problems stem from lack of competition. This is the importance of UHF to me. With more channels in the air, we will be able to provide every community with enough stations to offer service to all parts of the public. Programs with a mass-market appeal required by mass-product advertisers certainly will still be available. But other stations will recognize the need to appeal to more limited markets and to special tastes. In this way, we can all have a much wider range of programs. Television should thrive on this competition and the country should benefit from alternative sources of service to the public. And, Governor Collins, I hope the NAB will benefit from many new members.

Another and perhaps the most important frontier: Television will rapidly join the parade into space. International television will be with us soon. No one knows how long it will be until a broadcast from a

---

21.   Frederick W. Ford, FCC chairman, 1960–1961.

22.   Ultrahigh frequency.

23.   The test began on November 1, 1961, with station WUHF transmitting from the Empire State Building.

studio in New York will be viewed in India as well as in Indiana, will be seen in the Congo as it is seen in Chicago. But as surely as we are meeting here today, that day will come—and once again our world will shrink. What will the people of other countries think of us when they see our western bad men and good men punching each other in the jaw in between the shooting? What will the Latin American or African child learn of America from this great communications industry? We cannot permit television in its present form to be our voice overseas.

There is your challenge to leadership. You must reexamine some fundamentals of your industry. You must open your minds and open your hearts to the limitless horizons of tomorrow.

I can suggest some words that should serve to guide you: "Television and all who participate in it are jointly accountable to the American public for respect for the special needs of children, for community responsibility, for the advancement of education and culture, for the acceptability of the program materials chosen, for decency and decorum in production, and for propriety in advertising. This responsibility cannot be discharged by any given group of programs, but can be discharged only through the highest standards of respect for the American home, applied to every moment of every program presented by television.... Program materials should enlarge the horizons of the viewer, provide him with wholesome entertainment, afford helpful stimulation, and remind him of the responsibilities which the citizen has toward his society."

Now, those are not my words. They are yours. They are taken literally verbatim from your own Television Code.[24] They reflect the leadership and aspirations of your own great industry. I urge you to respect them as I do. And I urge you to respect the intelligent and farsighted leadership of Governor LeRoy Collins and to make this meeting a creative act. I urge you at this meeting and, after you leave, back home at your stations and your networks, to strive ceaselessly to improve your product and to better serve your viewers, the American people.

I hope that we at the FCC will not allow ourselves to become so bogged down in the mountain of papers, hearings, memoranda, orders, and the daily routine that we close our eyes to this wider view of the public interest. And I hope that you broadcasters will not permit yourselves to become so absorbed in the daily chase for ratings, sales, and profits that you lose this wider view. Now, more than ever before in broadcasting's history, the times demand the best of all of us. We need imagination in programming, not sterility; creativity, not imitation; experimentation, not conformity; excellence, not mediocrity. Television is filled with creative, imaginative people. You must strive to set them free.

Television in its young life has had many hours of greatness—its *Victory at Sea*, its Army-McCarthy hearings,[25] its *Peter Pan*, its *Kraft Theatre*s, its *See It Now*, its *Project 20*, the World Series, its political conventions and campaigns, and the Great Debates.[26] And it's had its endless hours of mediocrity and its moments of public disgrace. There are estimates today that the average viewer spends about two hundred minutes daily with television, while the average reader spends thirty-eight minutes with magazines, forty minutes with newspapers. Television has grown faster than a teenager, and now it is time to grow up. What you gentlemen broadcast through the people's air affects the people's taste, their knowledge, their opinions, their understanding of themselves and their world. And their future.

Just think for a moment of the impact of broadcasting in the past few days. Yesterday was one of the great days of my life. Last week the President asked me to ride over with him when he came to speak here at the NAB.[27] And when I went to the White House, he said: "Do you think it would be a good

24. The Code of Practices for Television Broadcasters, adopted in December 1951.

25. Held in the spring of 1954, the Army-McCarthy hearings were broadcast live on nationwide television and had a decisive impact on public opinion regarding Senator Joseph McCarthy (see pages 328–332).

26. A reference to the televised debates between Richard M. Nixon and John F. Kennedy during the 1960 presidential campaign.

27. President Kennedy addressed the NAB on May 8, the day before Minow's speech.

idea to take Commander Sheppard?"[28] And of course I said it would be magnificent, and I was privileged to ride here yesterday in the car with the President and the Vice President[29] [and] Commander and Mrs. Sheppard. This was an unexpected, unscheduled stop, and Commander Sheppard said to me: "Where are we going? What is this group?" And I said: "This is the National Association of Broadcasters at its annual convention. This is the group, this is the industry that made it possible for millions of Americans to share with you that great moment in history."

His gallant flight was witnessed by millions of anxious Americans who saw in it an intimacy which they could have achieved through no other medium, in no other way. It was one of your finest hours. The depth of broadcasting's contribution to public under-

standing of that event cannot be measured. And it thrilled me as a representative of the government that deals with this industry to say to Commander Sheppard the group that he was about to see.

I say to you, ladies and gentlemen, I remind you what the President said in his stirring inaugural. He said, "Ask not what America can do for you; ask what you can do for America."[30] I say to you, ladies and gentlemen: Ask not what broadcasting can do for you; ask what you can do for broadcasting. And ask what broadcasting can do for America. I urge you, I urge you to put the people's airwaves to the service of the people and the cause of freedom. You must help prepare a generation for great decisions. You must help a great nation fulfill its future. Do this—I pledge you our help.

Thank you.

---

28. Alan B. Sheppard Jr., who on May 5, 1961, became the first American to journey into space.

29. Lyndon B. Johnson.

30. Kennedy's exact words were "Ask not what your country can do for you—ask what you can do for your country" (see page 344).

Douglas MacArthur

Duty, Honor, Country

WEST POINT, NEW YORK
MAY 12, 1962

AMERICA'S GREATEST MILITARY commander of the twentieth century, Douglas MacArthur was also an accomplished stylist. As superintendent of the U.S. Military Academy at West Point after World War I, he encouraged the study of public speaking, required all cadets to write poetry, and regarded English as the most important subject for an officer's advancement. Although his written prose strikes some modern readers as florid and melodramatic, listeners found him spellbinding in conversation as well as in formal speeches. When the veteran *New York Times* correspondent Cyrus L. Sulzberger visited MacArthur in Tokyo after World War II, he was determined to resist the General's well-known powers of persuasion. "How long did it take MacArthur to get you in his pocket?" Sulzberger was asked later. "About thirty seconds," he confessed.

On May 12, 1962, MacArthur returned to West Point to receive the Sylvanus Thayer Award for service to his country. Seriously ill at age eighty-two, he made the trip over the objections of his wife and doctor. "I will attend the Thayer Award ceremony," he vowed, "if I have to crawl there on my hands and knees." Back on the Plain where he had been a student six decades earlier, MacArthur presented the most eloquent public address of his long career. Some of his images and phrases were recycled from previous occasions, but he wove them seamlessly with new ideas and a fresh structure to create a masterpiece that was literally a lifetime in the making.

Meticulously prepared but presented without notes, the speech seemed as if it were being coined on the spot. Using the West Point motto of "Duty, Honor, Country" as a leitmotif, MacArthur paid tribute to the American soldier and the school he loved so dearly. In poetic tones and elevated diction more characteristic of the nineteenth century than the twentieth, he reminded the 2,200 cadets of the hallowed traditions of the Long Gray Line and the sacred nature of their calling as those "who hold the nation's destiny in their hands the moment the war tocsin sounds." His slow, measured cadences reinforced the solemnity of his words and imbued them with an Olympian majesty. As he had concluded his military career on an unforgettable note in his "Old Soldiers Never Die" speech (pages 300–305), he now took leave of the public stage altogether. "The shadows are lengthening for me," he said. "The twilight is here.... Today marks my final roll call with you." Knowing he had once again spun his oratorical magic, he took his seat as many in the audience watched with tears in their eyes.

◇◇◇◇◇◇◇◇◇◇◇◇◇◇◇◇◇◇◇◇◇◇◇◇◇◇◇◇◇◇◇◇◇◇◇◇◇◇

General Westmoreland,[1] General Groves,[2] distinguished guests, and gentlemen of the Corps: As I was leaving the hotel this morning, a doorman asked me, "Where are you bound for, General?" And when I replied, "West Point," he remarked, "Beautiful place—have you ever been there before?"

No human being could fail to be deeply moved by such a tribute as this. Coming from a profession I have served so long and a people I have loved so well, it fills me with an emotion I cannot express. But this award is not intended primarily to honor a personality, but to symbolize a great moral code—the code of conduct and chivalry of those who guard this beloved land of culture and ancient descent. That is the animation of this medallion. For all eyes and for all time, it is an expression of the ethics of the American soldier. That I should be integrated in this way with so noble an ideal arouses a sense of pride and yet of humility which will be with me always.

Duty, Honor, Country: Those three hallowed words reverently dictate what you ought to be, what you can be, what you will be. They are your rallying points: to build courage when courage seems to fail; to regain faith when there seems to be little cause for faith; to create hope when hope becomes forlorn.

Unhappily, I possess neither that eloquence of diction, that poetry of imagination, nor that brilliance of metaphor to tell you all that they mean. The unbeliever will say they are but words, but a slogan, but a

---

1. William Westmoreland, superintendent of West Point.

2. Leslie R. Groves, president of West Point's Association of Graduates, who presented the Thayer Award to MacArthur.

flamboyant phrase. Every pedant, every demagogue, every cynic, every hypocrite, every troublemaker, and, I am sorry to say, some others of an entirely different character will try to downgrade them even to the extent of mockery and ridicule.

But these are some of the things they do. They build your basic character; they mold you for your future roles as the custodians of the nation's defense; they make you strong enough to know when you are weak, and brave enough to face yourself when you are afraid.

They teach you to be proud and unbending in honest failure but humble and gentle in success; not to substitute words for actions; not to seek the path of comfort but to face the stress and spur of difficulty and challenge; to learn to stand up in the storm but to have compassion on those who fall; to master yourself before you seek to master others; to have a heart that is clean, a goal that is high; to learn to laugh yet never forget how to weep; to reach into the future yet never neglect the past; to be serious yet never to take yourself too seriously; to be modest so that you will remember the simplicity of true greatness, the open mind of true wisdom, the meekness of true strength.

They give you a temper of the will, a quality of the imagination, a vigor of the emotions, a freshness of the deep springs of life, a temperamental predominance of courage over timidity, of an appetite for adventure over love of ease.

They create in your heart the sense of wonder, the unfailing hope of what next, and the joy and inspiration of life. They teach you in this way to be an officer and a gentleman.

And what sort of soldiers are those you are to lead? Are they reliable? Are they brave? Are they capable of victory? Their story is known to all of you. It is the story of the American man-at-arms. My estimate of him was formed on the battlefield many, many years ago and has never changed. I regarded him then as I regard him now, as one of the world's noblest figures—not only as one of the finest military characters but also as one of the most stainless. His name and fame are the birthright of every American citizen. In his youth and strength, his love and loyalty, he gave all that mortality can give. He needs no eulogy from me or from any other man. He has

written his own history, and written it in red on his enemy's breast.

But when I think of his patience under adversity, of his courage under fire, and of his modesty in victory, I am filled with an emotion of admiration I cannot put into words. He belongs to history as furnishing one of the greatest examples of successful patriotism. He belongs to posterity as the instructor of future generations in the principles of liberty and freedom. He belongs to the present—to us—by his virtues and by his achievements. In twenty campaigns, on a hundred battlefields, around a thousand campfires, I have witnessed that enduring fortitude, that patriotic self-abnegation, and that invincible determination which have carved his statue in the hearts of his people. From one end of the world to the other, he has drained deep the chalice of courage.

As I listened to those songs,[3] in memory's eye I could see those staggering columns of the First World War, bending under soggy packs on many a weary march from dripping dusk to drizzling dawn, slogging ankle-deep through the mire of shell-shocked roads to form grimly for the attack, blue-lipped, covered with sludge and mud, chilled by the wind and rain, driving home to their objective, and, for many, to the judgment seat of God. I do not know the dignity of their birth, but I do know the glory of their death. They died unquestioning, uncomplaining, with faith in their hearts, and on their lips the hope that we would go on to victory. Always for them Duty, Honor, Country; always their blood and sweat and tears as we sought the way and the light and the truth.[4]

And twenty years after, on the other side of the globe, again the filth of murky foxholes, the stench of ghostly trenches, the slime of dripping dugouts; those boiling suns of relentless heat, those torrential rains of devastating storms; the loneliness and utter desolation of jungle trails, the bitterness of long separation from those they loved and cherished, the deadly pestilence of tropical disease, the horror of stricken areas of war;

---

3. MacArthur is referring to the World War I songs performed by the West Point Glee Club before his speech.

4. An echo of John 14:6.

their resolute and determined defense, their swift and sure attack, their indomitable purpose, their complete and decisive victory—always victory. Always through the bloody haze of their last reverberating shot, the vision of gaunt, ghastly men reverently following your password of Duty, Honor, Country.

The code which those words perpetuate embraces the highest moral laws and will stand the test of any ethics or philosophies ever promulgated for the uplift of mankind. Its requirements are for the things that are right, and its restraints are from the things that are wrong. The soldier, above all other men, is required to practice the greatest act of religious training—sacrifice. In battle and in the face of danger and death, he discloses those divine attributes which his Maker gave when he created man in his own image. No physical courage and no brute instinct can take the place of the divine help which alone can sustain him. However horrible the incidents of war may be, the soldier who is called upon to offer and to give his life for his country is the noblest development of mankind.

You now face a new world, a world of change. The thrust into outer space of the satellite, spheres, and missiles marked the beginning of another epoch in the long story of mankind. In the five or more billions of years the scientists tell us it has taken to form the earth, in the three or more billion years of development of the human race, there has never been a more abrupt or staggering evolution. We deal now not with things of this world alone but with the illimitable distances and as yet unfathomed mysteries of the universe. We are reaching out for a new and boundless frontier.

We speak in strange terms: of harnessing the cosmic energy; of making winds and tides work for us; of creating unheard synthetic materials to supplement or even replace our old standard basics; to purify seawater for our drink; of mining ocean floors for new fields of wealth and food; of disease preventatives to expand life into the hundred[s] of years; of controlling the weather for a more equitable distribution of heat and cold, of rain and shine; of spaceships to the moon; of the primary target in war no longer limited to the armed forces of an enemy, but instead to include his civil populations; of ultimate conflict between a united human race and the sinister forces of some other planetary galaxy; of such dreams and fantasies as to make life the most exciting of all time.

And through all this welter of change and development, your mission remains fixed, determined, inviolable. It is to win our wars. Everything else in your professional career is but corollary to this vital dedication. All other public purposes, all other public projects, all other public needs, great or small, will find others for their accomplishment. But you are the ones who are trained to fight. Yours is the profession of arms: the will to win, the sure knowledge that in war there is no substitute for victory; that if you lose, the nation will be destroyed; that the very obsession of your public service must be Duty, Honor, Country.

Others will debate the controversial issues, national and international, which divide men's minds. But serene, calm, aloof, you stand as the nation's war guardian, as its lifeguard from the raging tides of international conflict, as its gladiator in the arena of battle. For a century and a half you have defended, guarded, and protected its hallowed traditions of liberty and freedom, of right and justice.

Let civilian voices argue the merits or demerits of our processes of government; whether our strength is being sapped by deficit financing indulged in too long, by federal paternalism grown too mighty, by power groups grown too arrogant, by politics grown too corrupt, by crime grown too rampant, by morals grown too low, by taxes grown too high, by extremists grown too violent; whether our personal liberties are as thorough and complete as they should be. These great national problems are not for your professional participation or military solution. Your guidepost stands out like a tenfold beacon in the night: Duty, Honor, Country.

You are the leaven which binds together the entire fabric of our national system of defense. From your ranks come the great captains who hold the nation's destiny in their hands the moment the war tocsin sounds. The Long Gray Line has never failed us. Were you to do so, a million ghosts in olive drab, in brown khaki, in blue and gray, would rise from their white crosses thundering those magic words: Duty, Honor, Country.

This does not mean that you are warmongers. On the contrary, the soldier, above all other people, prays for peace, for he must suffer and bear the deepest wounds and scars of war. But always in our ears ring the ominous words of Plato, that wisest of all philosophers: "Only the dead have seen the end of war."[5]

The shadows are lengthening for me. The twilight is here. My days of old have vanished. Tone and tint, they have gone glimmering through the dreams of things that were. Their memory is one of wondrous beauty watered by tears and coaxed and caressed by the smiles of yesterday. I listen vainly, but with thirsty ear, for the witching melody of faint bugles blowing reveille, of far drums beating the long roll. In my dreams, I hear again the crash of guns, the rattle of musketry, the strange, mournful mutter of the battlefield. But in the evening of my memory, always I come back to West Point. Always there echoes and reechoes: Duty, Honor, Country.

Today marks my final roll call with you, but I want you to know that when I cross the river, my last conscious thoughts will be of the Corps, and the Corps, and the Corps. I bid you farewell.

---

5. This quotation appears in George Santayana's *Soliloquies in England and Later Soliloquies* (1922), as well as on the wall of the Imperial War Museum in London. Although often attributed to Plato, it has not been found in his works.

John F. Kennedy

Address on the Cuban Missile Crisis

WASHINGTON, D.C.
OCTOBER 22, 1962

A GOOD DEAL OF presidential speech making falls into traditional genres: inaugurals, State of the Union addresses, veto messages, and the like There is one genre, however, that most Presidents use but none can predict: the crisis speech. Crises—sudden, unpredictable, and often of epic import—provide the ultimate test of presidential leadership and rhetorical skill.

Of all the crises faced by American Presidents during the twentieth century, none was more perilous than that which confronted John F. Kennedy in October 1962, when he learned that the Soviet Union had begun installing medium- and intermediate-range ballistic missiles in Cuba. With a range of 1,100 miles to 2,200 miles, such missiles were clearly offensive (as opposed to short-range defensive missiles) and could strike virtually anywhere on the eastern seaboard of the United States, including Washington, D.C. Although American intelligence had reported the movement of Soviet ships to Cuba in late July, their cargo was not verified until mid-October, when aerial reconnaissance revealed the presence of four operational missile-launching sites in Cuba, with more under construction.

President Kennedy kept the information secret, and on October 16 he convened an ad hoc group of senior advisors to determine how to respond. After several days of intense debate, a decision was reached on October 20. Kennedy would deliver a nationally televised speech describing the situation to the American people and calling on Soviet leader Nikita Khrushchev to remove the missiles from Cuba. He would also announce that the United States was imposing a blockade on Cuba to prevent any further missiles or nuclear warheads from being delivered. However, because a blockade was technically an act of war (and conjured up the Soviet Union's effort to bring West Berlin to its knees early in the Cold War), it would be called a "quarantine," a term used famously by Franklin Roosevelt in an October 1937 speech alerting Americans to the dangers of international aggression by Japan and Nazi Germany.

Kennedy addressed the nation from the Oval Office at 7:00 p.m. on Monday, October 22. Speaking for seventeen and a half minutes, he called the "secret, swift, extraordinary buildup" of missiles in Cuba a deliberately provocative act that could not be accepted by the United States "if our courage and our commitments are ever to be trusted again by either friend or foe." His ultimatum to Khrushchev was clear: Remove the missiles or risk nuclear war. At the same time, Kennedy was careful not to impose any demands other than removal of the missiles. Nor did he define what actions the United States would take if Soviet ships tried to break through the blockade. His combination of firmness and flexibility eventually proved vital in resolving the crisis short of war.

What the outcome would be, however, was far from clear when Kennedy finished his speech. Construction of the missile sites continued, more than two dozen Soviet ships continued on course to Cuba, and the United States prepared for military action. It was not until October 28 that a breakthrough occurred, when Khrushchev signaled that work on the sites would stop and that the missiles would be returned to the Soviet Union. For its part, the United States made a public pledge not to invade Cuba and a private promise to remove American missiles from Turkey. It was a face-saving solution that allowed both nations, in Kennedy's words, "to move the world back from the abyss of destruction."

◇◇

Good evening, my fellow citizens: This government, as promised, has maintained the closest surveillance of the Soviet military buildup on the island of Cuba. Within the past week, unmistakable evidence has established the fact that a series of offensive missile sites is now in preparation on that imprisoned island. The purpose of these bases can be none other than to provide a nuclear strike capability against the Western Hemisphere.

Upon receiving the first preliminary hard information of this nature last Tuesday morning at 9:00 a.m., I directed that our surveillance be stepped up. And having now confirmed and completed our evaluation of the evidence and our decision on a course of action, this government feels obliged to report this new crisis to you in fullest detail.

The characteristics of these new missile sites indicate two distinct types of installations. Several of them include medium-range ballistic missiles capable of carrying a nuclear warhead for a distance of more than 1,000 nautical miles. Each of these missiles, in short, is capable of striking Washington, D.C., the

Panama Canal, Cape Canaveral, Mexico City, or any other city in the southeastern part of the United States, in Central America, or in the Caribbean area.

Additional sites not yet completed appear to be designed for intermediate-range ballistic missiles capable of traveling more than twice as far and thus capable of striking most of the major cities in the Western Hemisphere, ranging as far north as Hudson's Bay, Canada, and as far south as Lima, Peru. In addition, jet bombers capable of carrying nuclear weapons are now being uncrated and assembled in Cuba, while the necessary air bases are being prepared.

This urgent transformation of Cuba into an important strategic base—by the presence of these large, long-range, and clearly offensive weapons of sudden mass destruction—constitutes an explicit threat to the peace and security of all the Americas, in flagrant and deliberate defiance of the Rio Pact of 1947,[1] the traditions of this nation and hemisphere,[2] the joint resolution of the Eighty-seventh Congress,[3] the Charter of the United Nations, and my own public warnings to the Soviets on September 4th and 13th.[4] This action also contradicts the repeated assurances of Soviet spokesmen, both publicly and privately delivered, that the arms buildup in Cuba would retain its original defensive character and that the Soviet Union had no need or desire to station strategic missiles on the territory of any other nation.

The size of this undertaking makes clear that it has been planned for some months. Yet only last month, after I had made clear the distinction between any introduction of ground-to-ground missiles and the existence of defensive antiaircraft missiles, the

Soviet government publicly stated on September eleventh that, and I quote, "the armament and military equipment sent to Cuba are designed exclusively for defensive purposes." Unquote. "That there is," and I quote the Soviet government, "there is no need for the Soviet government to shift its weapons for a retaliatory blow to any other country—for instance, Cuba." Unquote. And that, and I quote their government, "the Soviet Union has so powerful rockets to carry these nuclear warheads that there is no need to search for sites for them beyond the boundaries of the Soviet Union." Unquote. That statement was false.

Only last Thursday, as evidence of this rapid offensive buildup was already in my hand, Soviet Foreign Minister Gromyko[5] told me in my office that he was instructed to make it clear once again, as he said his government had already done, that Soviet assistance to Cuba, and I quote, "pursued solely the purpose of contributing to the defense capabilities of Cuba." Unquote. That, and I quote him, "training by Soviet specialists of Cuban nationals in handling defensive armaments was by no means offensive, and if it were otherwise," Mr. Gromyko went on, "the Soviet government would never become involved in rendering such assistance." Unquote. That statement also was false.

Neither the United States of America nor the world community of nations can tolerate deliberate deception and offensive threats on the part of any nation, large or small. We no longer live in a world where only the actual firing of weapons represents a sufficient challenge to a nation's security to constitute maximum peril. Nuclear weapons are so destructive and ballistic missiles are so swift that any substantially increased possibility of their use or any sudden change in their deployment may well be regarded as a definite threat to peace.

For many years both the Soviet Union and the United States, recognizing this fact, have deployed strategic nuclear weapons with great care, never upsetting the precarious status quo which ensured that these weapons would not be used in the absence

---

1. Signed by the United States and 19 Latin American countries on September 2, 1947, the Rio Pact affirmed the principle that an attack on any member would be considered an attack on all.

2. A reference to the Monroe Doctrine (1823), which declared that the United States would regard any attempt on the part of European powers "to extend their system to any portion of this hemisphere as dangerous to our peace and safety."

3. Senate Joint Resolution 230, approved October 3, 1962, declared that the United States would use force, if necessary, to halt the spread of communism in the Western Hemisphere.

4. Kennedy is referring to presidential statements presented on September 4 and 13 by Press Secretary Pierre Salinger.

---

5. Andrei Gromyko.

of some vital challenge. Our own strategic missiles have never been transferred to the territory of any other nation under a cloak of secrecy and deception, and our history—unlike that of the Soviets since the end of World War II—demonstrates that we have no desire to dominate or conquer any other nation or impose our system upon its people.

Nevertheless, American citizens have become adjusted to living daily on the bull's-eye of Soviet missiles located inside the USSR or in submarines. In that sense, missiles in Cuba add to an already clear and present danger, although it should be noted the nations of Latin America have never previously been subjected to a potential nuclear threat.

But this secret, swift, extraordinary buildup of Communist missiles in an area well known to have a special and historical relationship to the United States and the nations of the Western Hemisphere, in violation of Soviet assurances, and in defiance of American and hemispheric policy—this sudden, clandestine decision to station strategic weapons for the first time outside of Soviet soil—is a deliberately provocative and unjustified change in the status quo which cannot be accepted by this country if our courage and our commitments are ever to be trusted again by either friend or foe.

The 1930s taught us a clear lesson: Aggressive conduct, if allowed to go unchecked and unchallenged, ultimately leads to war. This nation is opposed to war. We are also true to our word. Our unswerving objective, therefore, must be to prevent the use of these missiles against this or any other country and to secure their withdrawal or elimination from the Western Hemisphere.

Our policy has been one of patience and restraint, as befits a peaceful and powerful nation which leads a worldwide alliance. We have been determined not to be diverted from our central concerns by mere irritants and fanatics. But now further action is required—and it is under way. And these actions may only be the beginning. We will not prematurely or unnecessarily risk the costs of worldwide nuclear war in which even the fruits of victory would be ashes in our mouth—but neither will we shrink from that risk at any time it must be faced.

Acting, therefore, in the defense of our own security and of the entire Western Hemisphere, and under the authority entrusted to me by the Constitution as endorsed by the resolution of the Congress,[6] I have directed that the following initial steps be taken immediately.

First: To halt this offensive buildup, a strict quarantine on all offensive military equipment under shipment to Cuba is being initiated. All ships of any kind bound for Cuba from whatever nation or port will, if found to contain cargoes of offensive weapons, be turned back. This quarantine will be extended, if needed, to other types of cargo and carriers. We are not at this time, however, denying the necessities of life as the Soviets attempted to do in their Berlin blockade of 1948.[7]

Second: I have directed the continued and increased close surveillance of Cuba and its military buildup. The foreign ministers of the OAS,[8] in their communiqué of October sixth, rejected secrecy in such matters in this hemisphere. Should these offensive military preparations continue, thus increasing the threat to the hemisphere, further action will be justified. I have directed the armed forces to prepare for any eventualities, and I trust that in the interest of both the Cuban people and the Soviet technicians at the sites, the hazards to all concerned of continuing this threat will be recognized.

Third: It shall be the policy of this nation to regard any nuclear missile launched from Cuba against any nation in the Western Hemisphere as an attack by the Soviet Union on the United States, requiring a full retaliatory response upon the Soviet Union.

Fourth: As a necessary military precaution, I have reinforced our base at Guantanamo,[9] evacuated today the dependents of our personnel there, and ordered additional military units to be on a standby alert basis.

---

6. Kennedy is referring to the resolution of October 3, 1962 (see note 3).

7. The Soviet Union imposed a blockade on West Berlin from June 1948 to May 1949.

8. Organization of American States.

9. U.S. naval base at Guantanamo Bay, Cuba.

Fifth: We are calling tonight for an immediate meeting of the Organization of Consultation,[10] under the Organization of American States, to consider this threat to hemispheric security and to invoke Articles 6 and 8 of the Rio Treaty in support of all necessary action.[11] The United Nations Charter allows for regional security arrangements, and the nations of this hemisphere decided long ago against the military presence of outside powers. Our other allies around the world have also been alerted.

Sixth: Under the Charter of the United Nations we are asking tonight that an emergency meeting of the Security Council be convoked without delay to take action against this latest Soviet threat to world peace. Our resolution will call for the prompt dismantling and withdrawal of all offensive weapons in Cuba, under the supervision of UN observers, before the quarantine can be lifted.

Seventh and finally: I call upon Chairman Khrushchev[12] to halt and eliminate this clandestine, reckless, and provocative threat to world peace and to stable relations between our two nations. I call upon him further to abandon this course of world domination and to join in an historic effort to end the perilous arms race and to transform the history of man. He has an opportunity now to move the world back from the abyss of destruction—by returning to his government's own words that it had no need to station missiles outside its own territory and withdrawing these weapons from Cuba, by refraining from any action which will widen or deepen the present crisis, and then by participating in a search for peaceful and permanent solutions.

This nation is prepared to present its case against the Soviet threat to peace, and our own proposals for a peaceful world, at any time and in any forum—in the OAS, in the United Nations, or in any other meeting that could be useful—without limiting our freedom of action. We have in the past made strenuous efforts to limit the spread of nuclear weapons. We have proposed the elimination of all arms and military bases in a fair and effective disarmament treaty. We are prepared to discuss new proposals for the removal of tensions on both sides, including the possibilities of a genuinely independent Cuba, free to determine its own destiny.

We have no wish to war with the Soviet Union, for we are a peaceful people who desire to live in peace with all other peoples. But it is difficult to settle or even discuss these problems in an atmosphere of intimidation. That is why this latest Soviet threat—or any other threat which is made either independently or in response to our actions this week—must and will be met with determination. Any hostile move anywhere in the world against the safety and freedom of peoples to whom we are committed—including in particular the brave people of West Berlin[13]—will be met by whatever action is needed.

Finally, I want to say a few words to the captive people of Cuba, to whom this speech is being directly carried by special radio facilities. I speak to you as a friend, as one who knows of your deep attachment to your fatherland, as one who shares your aspirations for liberty and justice for all. And I have watched, and the American people have watched, with deep sorrow how your nationalist revolution was betrayed and how your fatherland fell under foreign domination.[14]

Now your leaders are no longer Cuban leaders inspired by Cuban ideals. They are puppets and agents of an international conspiracy which has turned Cuba against your friends and neighbors in the Americas and turned it into the first Latin American country

---

10. Kennedy meant to say "Organ of Consultation," which was composed of the Ministers of Foreign Affairs of all nations belonging to the Organization of American States.

11. Article 6 of the Rio Treaty states that the Organ of Consultation shall meet to consider the measures to be taken in response to aggression that might endanger the peace of the Americas; Article 8 lists what those measures might entail.

12. Soviet leader Nikita Khrushchev.

13. Located more than 100 miles inside East Germany, enclosed by the Berlin Wall, and surrounded by hostile forces, West Berlin was a flashpoint of international tension and a powerful symbol of the Cold War.

14. The Cuban Revolution overthrew the dictatorship of Fulgencio Batista and brought Fidel Castro to power in 1959. After turning back the Bay of Pigs invasion of April 1961 by U.S.-armed Cuban exiles, Castro turned to the Soviet Union for advice and armaments.

to become a target for nuclear war, the first Latin American country to have these weapons on its soil.

These new weapons are not in your interest. They contribute nothing to your peace and well-being. They can only undermine it. But this country has no wish to cause you to suffer or to impose any system upon you. We know that your lives and land are being used as pawns by those who deny your freedom.

Many times in the past the Cuban people have risen to throw out tyrants who destroyed their liberty. And I have no doubt that most Cubans today look forward to the time when they will be truly free—free from foreign domination, free to choose their own leaders, free to select their own system, free to own their own land, free to speak and write and worship without fear or degradation. And then shall Cuba be welcomed back to the society of free nations and to the associations of this hemisphere.

My fellow citizens, let no one doubt that this is a difficult and dangerous effort on which we have set out. No one can foresee precisely what course it will take or what costs or casualties will be incurred. Many months of sacrifice and self-discipline lie ahead—months in which both our patience and our will will be tested, months in which many threats and denunciations will keep us aware of our dangers.

But the greatest danger of all would be to do nothing. The path we have chosen for the present is full of hazards—as all paths are—but it is the one most consistent with our character and courage as a nation and our commitments around the world. The cost of freedom is always high, but Americans have always paid it. And one path we shall never choose, and that is the path of surrender or submission.

Our goal is not the victory of might, but the vindication of right—not peace at the expense of freedom, but both peace and freedom, here in this hemisphere and, we hope, around the world. God willing, that goal will be achieved.

Thank you, and good night.

John F. Kennedy

⌛

Speech at American University

WASHINGTON, D.C.
JUNE 10, 1963

THE CUBAN MISSILE crisis of October 1962 had convinced both the United States and the Soviet Union that nuclear standoffs were not the best way to conduct international diplomacy (pages 357–362). From the outset of his presidency, John F. Kennedy had sought some form of nuclear test-ban treaty with the Soviets. But seeking and obtaining proved to be two different things. The chief stumbling blocks to all such proposals were the number and extent of on-site inspections. The Soviet Union opposed inspections as pretexts for espionage. The U.S. Senate, which would have to ratify any treaty, insisted on inspections.

With the scare of the missile crisis seared into public memory, both sides began to seek a middle ground. By the spring of 1963, Soviet Premier Nikita Khrushchev had agreed to three on-site inspections. Kennedy said his "rock-bottom number" was six. That's where matters stood when, in early April, Norman Cousins, editor of the *Saturday Review*, was contacted by JFK before leaving on a trip to the Soviet Union, where he was scheduled to meet with Premier Khrushchev. Kennedy asked Cousins to deliver a message to the Soviet leader. The message, in brief, was to let the past be past and to seek a fresh start toward disarmament. Kennedy wanted Khrushchev to know "that I am acting in good faith and that I genuinely want a test-ban treaty."

Cousins delivered the message on April 12 and found Khrushchev receptive if the United States were genuinely interested. "You can tell the President I accept his explanation," he told Cousins. "But the next move is up to him." After returning to the United States, Cousins suggested to the President that he deliver a peace speech of his own before Khrushchev could make recommendations to the annual meeting of the Soviet Central Committee, scheduled for mid-June. Thus was born the idea for what became Kennedy's American University address of June 10, 1963. The subject was so tightly guarded that neither Secretary of Defense Robert McNamara nor Secretary of State Dean Rusk were shown a draft of the speech until the day before its presentation.

Speaking under a bright sun to a commencement-day audience of 10,000 people, Kennedy proposed a "strategy of peace" that could help break the "vicious and dangerous" cycle of the Cold War. Part of the strategy required changes in habitual patterns of thought in the United States and the Soviet Union, changes that would allow both nations to recognize their common interests and find peaceful ways of resolving their differences. The strategy also entailed changes in policy, including moving forward with a nuclear test-ban treaty. Such action, Kennedy declared, would be in the interest of both superpowers, for "in the final analysis, our most basic common link is that we all inhabit this small planet. We all breathe the same air. We all cherish our children's futures. And we are all mortal."

It was the most significant presidential pronouncement on breaking the nuclear impasse of the Cold War since Dwight D. Eisenhower's "Atoms for Peace" speech ten years earlier (pages 322–327). Although it was overshadowed at home by Kennedy's civil rights address of the next day (pages 369–372), the speech was lauded abroad as "one of the great state papers of American history," and some scholars consider it Kennedy's finest public address. Its message was heard clearly in the Soviet Union. Khrushchev called it "the best speech by any President since Roosevelt," and the official Soviet newspapers *Pravda* and *Izvestia* published the entire text, something that had not happened since Kennedy's inaugural address, two and a half years earlier. Equally telling, the Kremlin allowed all but one paragraph of the speech to be broadcast to the Russian people by the Voice of America. The Soviets' position on nuclear inspections softened almost immediately, and progress toward a limited test-ban treaty picked up speed. A pact was initialed in Moscow less than two months later.

◇◇

President Anderson;[1] members of the faculty; Board of Trustees; distinguished guests; my old colleague Senator Bob Byrd,[2] who has earned his degree through many years of attending night law school, while I am earning mine in the next thirty minutes; distinguished guests; ladies and gentlemen:

It is with great pride that I participate in this ceremony of the American University, sponsored by the Methodist Church, founded by Bishop John Fletcher Hurst, and first opened by President Woodrow Wilson in 1914.[3] This is a young and growing university, but it has already fulfilled Bishop Hurst's enlightened hope for the study of history and public affairs in a city devoted to the making of history and to the conduct of the public's business. By sponsoring this institution of higher learning for all who wish to learn, whatever their color or their creed, the Methodists of this area and the nation deserve the nation's thanks, and I commend all those who are today graduating.

Professor Woodrow Wilson once said that every man sent out from a university should be a man of his nation as well as a man of his time,[4] and I am confident that the men and women who carry the honor of graduating from this institution will continue to give from their lives, from their talents, a high measure of public service and public support.

"There are few earthly things more beautiful than a university," wrote John Masefield in his tribute to English universities—and his words are equally true today. He did not refer to towers or to campuses. He admired the splendid beauty of a university because it was, he said, "a place where those who hate igno-rance may strive to know, where those who perceive truth may strive to make others see."[5] I have, therefore, chosen this time and place to discuss a topic on which ignorance too often abounds and the truth [is] too rarely perceived. And that is the most important topic on earth: peace.

What kind of a peace do I mean and what kind of a peace do we seek? Not a Pax Americana[6] enforced on the world by American weapons of war. Not the peace of the grave or the security of the slave. I am talking about genuine peace, the kind of peace that makes life on earth worth living, the kind that enables men and nations to grow and build a better life for their children—not merely peace for Americans but peace for all men and women, not merely peace in our time but peace in all time.

I speak of peace because of the new face of war. Total war makes no sense in an age where great powers can maintain large and relatively invulnerable nuclear forces and refuse to surrender without resort to those forces. It makes no sense in an age where a single nuclear weapon contains almost ten times the explosive force delivered by all the allied air forces in the Second World War. It makes no sense in an age when the deadly poisons produced by a nuclear exchange would be carried by wind and water and soil and seed to the far corners of the globe and to generations yet unborn.

Today the expenditure of billions of dollars every year on weapons acquired for the purpose of making sure we never need them is essential to the keeping of peace. But surely the acquisition of such idle stockpiles—which can only destroy and never create—is not the only, much less the most efficient, means of assuring peace.

1. Hurst Robins Anderson, president of American University.

2. Robert C. Byrd, U.S. Senator from West Virginia.

3. Wilson officially dedicated the university in 1914, the year in which it admitted its first students.

4. From "University Training and Citizenship" (1894), published while Wilson was a professor at Princeton University.

5. Masefield was an English poet and novelist; the quotation is from his speech at the University of Sheffield, June 25, 1946.

6. An allusion to the Pax Romana of the first and second centuries CE.

I speak of peace, therefore, as the necessary, rational end of rational men. I realize the pursuit of peace is not as dramatic as the pursuit of war, and frequently the words of the pursuers fall on deaf ears. But we have no more urgent task.

Some say that it is useless to speak of peace or world law or world disarmament, and that it will be useless until the leaders of the Soviet Union adopt a more enlightened attitude. I hope they do. I believe we can help them do it.

But I also believe that we must reexamine our own attitudes, as individuals and as a nation, for our attitude is as essential as theirs. And every graduate of this school, every thoughtful citizen who despairs of war and wishes to bring peace, should begin by looking inward, by examining his own attitude towards the possibilities of peace, towards the Soviet Union, towards the course of the Cold War, and towards freedom and peace here at home.

First, examine our attitude towards peace itself. Too many of us think it is impossible. Too many think it is unreal. But that is a dangerous, defeatist belief. It leads to the conclusion that war is inevitable, that mankind is doomed, that we are gripped by forces we cannot control.

We need not accept that view. Our problems are man-made. Therefore, they can be solved by man. And man can be as big as he wants. No problem of human destiny is beyond human beings. Man's reason and spirit have often solved the seemingly unsolvable, and we believe they can do it again. I am not referring to the absolute, infinite concept of universal peace and goodwill of which some fantasies and fanatics dream. I do not deny the value of hopes and dreams, but we merely invite discouragement and incredulity by making that our only and immediate goal.

Let us focus instead on a more practical, more attainable peace—based not on a sudden revolution in human nature but on a gradual evolution in human institutions, on a series of concrete actions and effective agreements which are in the interest of all concerned. There is no single, simple key to this peace—no grand or magic formula to be adopted by one or two powers. Genuine peace must be the product of many nations, the sum of many acts. It must be dynamic, not static, changing to meet the challenge of each new generation. For peace is a process—a way of solving problems.

With such a peace, there will still be quarrels and conflicting interests, as there are within families and nations. World peace, like community peace, does not require that each man love his neighbor—it requires only that they live together in mutual tolerance, submitting their disputes to a just and peaceful settlement. And history teaches us that enmities between nations, as between individuals, do not last forever. However fixed our likes and dislikes may seem, the tide of time and events will often bring surprising changes in the relations between nations and neighbors.

So let us persevere. Peace need not be impracticable, and war need not be inevitable. By defining our goal more clearly, by making it seem more manageable and less remote, we can help all people to see it, to draw hope from it, and to move irresistibly towards it.

And second, let us reexamine our attitude towards the Soviet Union. It is discouraging to think that their leaders may actually believe what their propagandists write. It is discouraging to read a recent authoritative Soviet text on military strategy and find, on page after page, wholly baseless and incredible claims, such as the allegation that "American imperialist circles are preparing to unleash different types of war, ... that there is a very real threat of a preventative war being unleashed by American imperialists against the Soviet Union," and that the political aims—and I quote—"of the American imperialists ... are to enslave economically and politically the European and other capitalist countries and ... to achieve world domination by means of aggressive war."[7] Unquote.

Truly, as it was written long ago: "The wicked flee when no man pursueth."[8] Yet it is sad to read these Soviet statements, to realize the extent of the gulf between us. But it is also a warning—a warning to the American people not to fall into the same trap as the Soviets, not to see only a distorted and desperate

---

7. The quotations are from Vasilii D. Sokolovskii's *Military Strategy*, published in the Soviet Union in 1962 and translated into English the next year under the title *Soviet Military Strategy*.

8. Proverbs 28:1.

view of the other side, not to see conflict as inevitable, accommodation as impossible, and communication as nothing more than an exchange of threats. No government or social system is so evil that its people must be considered as lacking in virtue. As Americans, we find communism profoundly repugnant as a negation of personal freedom and dignity. But we can still hail the Russian people for their many achievements—in science and space, in economic and industrial growth, in culture, in acts of courage.

Among the many traits the peoples of our two countries have in common, none is stronger than our mutual abhorrence of war. Almost unique among the major world powers, we have never been at war with each other. And no nation in the history of battle ever suffered more than the Soviet Union in the Second World War. At least twenty million lost their lives. Countless millions of homes and families were burned or sacked. A third of the nation's territory, including two-thirds of its industrial base, was turned into a wasteland—a loss equivalent to the destruction of this country east of Chicago.

Today, should total war ever break out again—no matter how—our two countries will be the primary target. It is an ironic but accurate fact that the two strongest powers are the two in the most danger of devastation. All we have built, all we have worked for, would be destroyed in the first twenty-four hours.

And even in the Cold War, which brings burdens and dangers to so many countries, including this nation's closest allies, our two countries bear the heaviest burdens. For we are both devoting massive sums of money to weapons that could be better devoted to combat ignorance, poverty, and disease. We are both caught up in a vicious and dangerous cycle, with suspicion on one side breeding suspicion on the other, and new weapons begetting counterweapons.

In short, both the United States and its allies, and the Soviet Union and its allies, have a mutually deep interest in a just and genuine peace and in halting the arms race. Agreements to this end are in the interests of the Soviet Union as well as ours. And even the most hostile nations can be relied upon to accept and keep those treaty obligations, and only those treaty obligations, which are in their own interest.

So let us not be blind to our differences, but let us also direct attention to our common interests and the means by which those differences can be resolved. And if we cannot end now our differences, at least we can help make the world safe for diversity. For in the final analysis, our most basic common link is that we all inhabit this small planet. We all breathe the same air. We all cherish our children's futures. And we are all mortal.

Third, let us reexamine our attitude towards the Cold War, remembering we're not engaged in a debate, seeking to pile up debating points. We are not here distributing blame or pointing the finger of judgment. We must deal with the world as it is, and not as it might have been had the history of the last eighteen years been different.

We must, therefore, persevere in the search for peace in the hope that constructive changes within the Communist bloc might bring within reach solutions which now seem beyond us. We must conduct our affairs in such a way that it becomes in the Communists' interest to agree on a genuine peace. And above all, while defending our own vital interests, nuclear powers must avert those confrontations which bring an adversary to a choice of either a humiliating retreat or a nuclear war. To adopt that kind of course in the nuclear age would be evidence only of the bankruptcy of our policy—or of a collective death wish for the world.

To secure these ends, America's weapons are nonprovocative, carefully controlled, designed to deter, and capable of selective use. Our military forces are committed to peace and disciplined in self-restraint. Our diplomats are instructed to avoid unnecessary irritants and purely rhetorical hostility. For we can seek a relaxation[9] of tensions without relaxing our guard. And, for our part, we do not need to use threats to prove we are resolute. We do not need to jam foreign broadcasts out of fear our faith will be eroded.[10] We are unwilling to impose our system on any unwilling people, but we are willing

---

9. Kennedy misspoke this word as "relaxtion."

10. Kennedy is referring to the Soviets' jamming of broadcasts from Radio Free Europe, Radio Liberty, and the Voice of America.

and able to engage in peaceful competition with any people on earth.

Meanwhile, we seek to strengthen the United Nations, to help solve its financial problems, to make it a more effective instrument for peace, to develop it into a genuine world security system—a system capable of resolving disputes on the basis of law, of ensuring the security of the large and the small, and of creating conditions under which arms can finally be abolished.

At the same time, we seek to keep peace inside the non-Communist world, where many nations, all of them our friends, are divided over issues which weaken Western unity, which invite Communist intervention, or which threaten to erupt into war. Our efforts in West New Guinea, in the Congo, in the Middle East, and the Indian subcontinent[11] have been persistent and patient despite criticism from both sides. We have also tried to set an example for others by seeking to adjust small but significant differences with our own closest neighbors in Mexico and Canada.

Speaking of other nations, I wish to make one point clear. We are bound to many nations by alliances. These alliances exist because our concern and theirs substantially overlap. Our commitment to defend Western Europe and West Berlin, for example, stands undiminished because of the identity of our vital interests. The United States will make no deal with the Soviet Union at the expense of other nations and other peoples—not merely because they are our partners, but also because their interests and ours converge.

Our interests converge, however, not only in defending the frontiers of freedom but in pursuing the paths of peace. It is our hope, and the purpose of allied policy, to convince the Soviet Union that she, too, should let each nation choose its own future, so long as that choice does not interfere with the choices of others. The Communist drive to impose their political and economic system on others is the primary cause of world tension today. For there can be no doubt that if all nations could refrain from inter-

fering in the self-determination of others, the peace would be much more assured.

This will require a new effort to achieve world law, a new context for world discussions. It will require increased understanding between the Soviets and ourselves. And increased understanding will require increased contact and communication. One step in this direction is the proposed arrangement for a direct line between Moscow and Washington, to avoid on each side the dangerous delays, misunderstandings, and misreadings of others' actions which might occur at a time of crisis.[12]

We have also been talking in Geneva about our first-step measures of arm controls,[13] designed to limit the intensity of the arms race and reduce the risk of accidental war.[14] Our primary long-range interest in Geneva, however, is general and complete disarmament, designed to take place by stages, permitting parallel political developments to build the new institutions of peace which would take the place of arms. The pursuit of disarmament has been an effort of this government since the 1920s. It has been urgently sought by the past three administrations. And however dim the prospects are today, we intend to continue this effort—to continue it in order that all countries, including our own, can better grasp what the problems and the possibilities of disarmament are.

The only major area of these negotiations where the end is in sight, yet where a fresh start is badly needed, is in a treaty to outlaw nuclear tests. The conclusion of such a treaty, so near and yet so far, would check the spiraling arms race in one of its most dangerous areas. It would place the nuclear powers in a position to deal more effectively with one of the greatest hazards which man faces in 1963—the further spread of nuclear arms. It would increase our security. It would decrease the prospects of war.

11. These were all areas of international tension at the time of Kennedy's speech.

12. A reference to the U.S.-Soviet "hotline," which went into operation in August 1963.

13. Kennedy meant to say "arms control."

14. The Geneva Conference on the Discontinuance of Nuclear Weapons Tests had begun in October 1958, during the Eisenhower administration, but without result. Talks reopened in March 1961 and were in progress at the time of Kennedy's speech.

Surely this goal is sufficiently important to require our steady pursuit, yielding neither to the temptation to give up the whole effort nor the temptation to give up our insistence on vital and responsible safeguards.

I'm taking this opportunity, therefore, to announce two important decisions in this regard. First, Chairman Khrushchev,[15] Prime Minister Macmillan,[16] and I have agreed that high-level discussions will shortly begin in Moscow looking towards early agreement on a comprehensive test-ban treaty.[17] Our hope must be tempered, our hopes must be tempered with the caution of history—but with our hopes go the hopes of all mankind.

Second, to make clear our good faith and solemn convictions on this matter, I now declare that the United States does not propose to conduct nuclear tests in the atmosphere so long as other states do not do so. We will not, we will not be the first to resume. Such a declaration is no substitute for a formal binding treaty, but I hope it will help us achieve one. Nor would such a treaty be a substitute for disarmament, but I hope it will help us achieve it.

Finally, my fellow Americans, let us examine our attitude towards peace and freedom here at home. The quality and spirit of our own society must justify and support our efforts abroad. We must show it in the dedication of our own lives—as many of you who are graduating today will have an opportunity to do by serving without pay in the Peace Corps abroad or in the proposed National Service Corps here at home.[18]

But wherever we are, we must all, in our daily lives, live up to the age-old faith that peace and freedom walk together. In too many of our cities today, the peace is not secure because freedom is incomplete. It is the responsibility of the executive branch at all levels of government—local, state, and national—to provide and protect that freedom for all of our citizens by all means within our authority. It is the responsibility of the legislative branch at all levels, wherever the authority is not now adequate, to make it adequate. And it is the responsibility of all citizens in all sections of this country to respect the rights of others and respect the law of the land.[19]

All this, all this is not unrelated to world peace. "When a man's way[s] please the Lord," the Scriptures tell us, "he maketh even his enemies to be at peace with him."[20] And is not peace, in the last analysis, basically a matter of human rights—the right to live out our lives without fear of devastation, the right to breathe air as nature provided it, the right of future generations to a healthy existence?

While we proceed to safeguard our national interests, let us also safeguard human interests. And the elimination of war and arms is clearly in the interests of both. No treaty, however much it may be to the advantage of all, however tightly it may be worded, can provide absolute security against the risks of deception and evasion. But it can—if it is sufficiently effective in its enforcement, and it is sufficiently in the interests of its signers—offer far more security and far fewer risks than an unabated, uncontrolled, unpredictable arms race.

The United States, as the world knows, will never start a war. We do not want a war. We do not now expect a war. This generation of Americans has already had enough—more than enough—of war and hate and oppression. We shall be prepared if others wish it. We shall be alert to try to stop it. But we shall also do our part to build a world of peace where the weak are safe and the strong are just. We are not helpless before that task or hopeless of its success. Confident and unafraid, we must labor on—not towards a strategy of annihilation, but towards a strategy of peace.

15. Soviet leader Nikita Khrushchev.

16. British Prime Minister Harold Macmillan.

17. Khrushchev had agreed to the talks on June 8, two days before Kennedy's speech.

18. The Peace Corps was founded in 1961; Kennedy proposed the National Service Corps (NSC) in 1963. After Kennedy's assassination, President Lyndon Johnson incorporated the NSC into the 1964 Economic Opportunity Act and renamed the program Volunteers in Service to America (VISTA).

19. Kennedy is referring to the racial protests and confrontations that gripped many American cities at the time of his speech. See his "Civil Rights: A Moral Issue," June 11, 1963 (pages 369–372).

20. Proverbs 16:7.

John F. Kennedy

Civil Rights: A Moral Issue

WASHINGTON, D.C.
JUNE 11, 1963

As THE COLD War raged abroad during the early 1960s, the civil rights movement continued to heat up in the United States. It had begun in December 1955 with the Montgomery bus boycott and by June 1963 had come to overshadow all other domestic issues. Although sympathetic to the plight of African Americans, John F. Kennedy was two years into his presidency before he fully committed the power and prestige of his office to the cause of equal rights—two years that saw the arrest of African American students for the crime of sitting at a department store lunch counter in North Carolina, the beating of freedom riders in Alabama, the repeated flouting of federal court orders throughout the South, and the brutal suppression of nonviolent protesters in Birmingham, Alabama, during the weeks just before Kennedy's speech.

On June 11, one day after Kennedy's peace address at American University (pages 362–368), events in Alabama heated up again when Governor George C. Wallace stood in the doorway to Foster Auditorium at the University of Alabama, symbolically blocking the entrance of African American students Vivian Malone and James Hood. A similar action by Mississippi Governor Ross Barnett the previous September had touched off an explosion of mob violence in opposition to the admission of James Meredith to the University of Mississippi. It had taken several thousand U.S. Army troops to restore order, and Kennedy was determined not to have a replay in Alabama. He promptly federalized the Alabama National Guard, and the students' registration proceeded peacefully.

That evening, Kennedy addressed the nation from the Oval Office. The decision to speak had been made that afternoon, partly at the urging of Attorney General Robert F. Kennedy, the President's brother. Ted Sorensen, working with Robert Kennedy and Burke Marshall, quickly cobbled together a draft, which JFK received five minutes before going on the air at 8:00 p.m. Moving back and forth between the draft and the notes he had written in longhand, Kennedy delivered one of the most powerful speeches of his presidency, telling the country: "We are confronted primarily with a moral issue. It is as old as the Scriptures and is as clear as the American Constitution." He outlined the civil rights legislation he would send to Congress the next week, but he also stressed the responsibility of every American to further the cause of racial justice: "This nation, for all its hopes and all its boasts, will not be fully free until all its citizens are free."

In the eyes of some white Americans, Kennedy was pushing too hard. In the eyes of some blacks, he did not push hard enough. For the first time, however, his speech put the moral weight of his presidency squarely behind the civil rights movement. On June 19 he sent a comprehensive civil rights package to Congress. Martin Luther King, who was often exasperated by Kennedy's cautious approach to race issues, called it "the most sweeping and forthright" civil rights legislation "ever presented by an American president." It would eventually be passed in 1964 under the leadership of Lyndon Johnson, who ascended to the White House after Kennedy's assassination.

◇◇◇

Good evening, my fellow citizens: This afternoon, following a series of threats and defiant statements, the presence of Alabama National Guardsmen was required on the University of Alabama to carry out the final and unequivocal order of the United States District Court of the Northern District of Alabama. That order called for the admission of two clearly qualified young Alabama residents who happen to have been born Negro. That they were admitted peacefully on the campus is due in good measure to the conduct of the students of the University of Alabama, who met their responsibilities in a constructive way.

I hope that every American, regardless of where he lives, will stop and examine his conscience about this and other related incidents. This nation was founded by men of many nations and backgrounds. It was founded on the principle that all men are created equal and that the rights of every man are diminished when the rights of one man are threatened.

Today we are committed to a worldwide struggle to promote and protect the rights of all who wish to be free. And when Americans are sent to Vietnam or West Berlin,[1] we do not ask for whites only. It ought to be possible, therefore, for American students of any color to attend any public institution they select

without having to be backed up by troops. It ought to be possible for American consumers of any color to receive equal service in places of public accommodation, such as hotels and restaurants and theaters and retail stores, without being forced to resort to demonstrations in the street. And it ought to be possible for American citizens of any color to register and to vote in a free election without interference or fear of reprisal.

It ought to be possible, in short, for every American to enjoy the privileges of being American without regard to his race or his color. In short, every American ought to have the right to be treated as he would wish to be treated, as one would wish his children to be treated.

But this is not the case. The Negro baby born in America today, regardless of the section of the state[2] in which he is born, has about one-half as much chance of completing a high school as a white baby born in the same place on the same day, one-third as much chance of completing college, one-third as much chance of becoming a professional man, twice as much chance of becoming unemployed, about one-seventh as much chance of earning $10,000 a year, a life expectancy which is seven years shorter, and the prospects of earning only half as much.

This is not a sectional issue. Difficulties over segregation and discrimination exist in every city, in

---

1. By 1963, the United States had 16,000 military advisors in South Vietnam and continued to support the people and government of West Berlin, which was surrounded by Soviet-controlled East Germany.

2. Kennedy meant to say "nation."

every state of the Union, producing in many cities a rising tide of discontent that threatens the public safety. Nor is this a partisan issue. In a time of domestic crisis men of goodwill and generosity should be able to unite regardless of party or politics. This is not even a legal or legislative issue alone. It is better to settle these matters in the courts than on the streets, and new laws are needed at every level, but law alone cannot make men see right.

We are confronted primarily with a moral issue. It is as old as the Scriptures and is as clear as the American Constitution. The heart of the question is whether all Americans are to be afforded equal rights and equal opportunities, whether we are going to treat our fellow Americans as we want to be treated. If an American, because his skin is dark, cannot eat lunch in a restaurant open to the public, if he cannot send his children to the best public school available, if he cannot vote for the public officials who represent him, if, in short, he cannot enjoy the full and free life which all of us want, then who among us would be content to have the color of his skin changed and stand in his place? Who among us would then be content with the counsels of patience and delay?

One hundred years of delay have passed since President Lincoln freed the slaves,[3] yet their heirs, their grandsons, are not fully free. They are not yet freed from the bonds of injustice. They are not yet freed from social and economic oppression. And this nation, for all its hopes and all its boasts, will not be fully free until all its citizens are free.

We preach freedom around the world, and we mean it, and we cherish our freedom here at home. But are we to say to the world and, much more importantly, to each other that this is a land of the free except for the Negroes; that we have no second-class citizens except Negroes; that we have no class or caste system, no ghettos, no master race, except with respect to Negroes?

Now the time has come for this nation to fulfill its promise. The events in Birmingham and elsewhere[4] have so increased the cries for equality that no city or state or legislative body can prudently choose to ignore them. The fires of frustration and discord are burning in every city, North and South. Where legal remedies are not at hand, redress is sought in the streets—in demonstrations, parades, and protests which create tensions and threaten violence and threaten lives.

We face, therefore, a moral crisis as a country and a people. It cannot be met by repressive police action. It cannot be left to increased demonstrations in the streets. It cannot be quieted by token moves or talk. It is a time to act in the Congress, in your state and local legislative body, and, above all, in all of our daily lives.

It is not enough to pin the blame on others, to say this is a problem of one section of the country or another, or deplore the facts that we face. A great change is at hand, and our task, our obligation, is to make that revolution, that change, peaceful and constructive for all. Those who do nothing are inviting shame as well as violence. Those who act boldly are recognizing right as well as reality.

Next week I shall ask the Congress of the United States to act—to make a commitment it has not fully made in this century to the proposition that race has no place in American life or law. The federal judiciary has upheld that proposition in a series of forthright cases. The executive branch has adopted that proposition in the conduct of its affairs, including the employment of federal personnel, the use of federal facilities, and the sale of federally financed housing. But there are other necessary measures which only the Congress can provide, and they must be provided at this session.

The old code of equity law under which we live commands for every wrong a remedy, but in too many communities, in too many parts of the country, wrongs are inflicted on Negro citizens and there are no remedies at law. Unless the Congress acts, their only remedy is the street.

3. Kennedy is referring to the Emancipation Proclamation of January 1, 1863.

4. Civil rights protests in Birmingham, Alabama, during April and May had attracted international attention when local authorities turned fire hoses and police dogs against protesters. Racial demonstrations and confrontations also occurred in dozens of other cities, North and South.

I am therefore asking the Congress to enact legislation giving all Americans the right to be served in facilities which are open to the public—hotels, restaurants, theaters, retail stores, and similar establishments. This seems to me to be an elementary right. Its denial is an arbitrary indignity that no American in 1963 should have to endure—but many do.

I have recently met with scores of business leaders urging them to take voluntary action to end this discrimination, and I've been encouraged by their response. And in the last two weeks, over seventy-five cities have seen progress made in desegregating these kinds of facilities. But many are unwilling to act alone, and for this reason nationwide legislation is needed if we are to move this problem from the streets to the courts.

I'm also asking Congress to authorize the federal government to participate more fully in lawsuits designed to end segregation in public education. We have succeeded in persuading many districts to desegregate voluntarily. Dozens have admitted Negroes without violence. Today a Negro is attending a state-supported institution in every one of our fifty states, but this pace is very slow. Too many Negro children entering segregated grade schools at the time of the Supreme Court's decision nine years ago[5] will enter segregated high schools this fall having suffered a loss which can never be restored. The lack of an adequate education denies the Negro a chance to get a decent job. The orderly implementation of the Supreme Court decision, therefore, cannot be left solely to those who may not have the economic resources to carry the legal action or who may be subject to harassment.

Other features will be also requested, including greater protection for the right to vote. But legislation, I repeat, cannot solve this problem alone. It must be solved in the homes of every American in every community across our country. In this respect, I want to pay tribute to those citizens, North and South, who've been working in their communities to make life better for all. They are acting not out of [a] sense of legal duty, but out of a sense of human decency. Like our

soldiers and sailors in all parts of the world, they are meeting freedom's challenge on the firing line, and I salute them for their honor and their courage.

My fellow Americans, this is a problem which faces us all, in every city of the North as well as the South. Today there are Negroes unemployed, two or three times as many compared to whites, inadequate [in] education, moving into the large cities, unable to find work; young people, particularly, out of work, without hope, denied equal rights, denied the opportunity to eat at a restaurant or a lunch counter or go to a movie theater, denied the right to a decent education, denied almost today the right to attend a state university, even though qualified. It seems to me that these are matters which concern us all—not merely Presidents or Congressmen or Governors, but every citizen of the United States.

This is one country. It has become one country because all of us, and all the people who came here, had an equal chance to develop their talents. We cannot say to 10 percent of the population that you can't have that right; your children can't have the chance to develop whatever talents they have; that the only way that they're going to get their rights is to go in the street and demonstrate. I think we owe them and we owe ourselves a better country than that.

Therefore, I'm asking for your help in making it easier for us to move ahead and provide the kind of equality of treatment which we would want ourselves—to give a chance for every child to be educated to the limit of his talents. As I've said before, not every child has an equal talent or an equal ability or equal motivation, but they should have the equal right to develop their talent and their ability and their motivation to make something of themselves.

We have a right to expect that the Negro community will be responsible, will uphold the law. But they have a right to expect that the law will be fair, that the Constitution will be color-blind, as Justice Harlan said at the turn of the century.[6] This is what we're talking about and this is a matter which concerns this country and what it stands for; and in meeting it, I ask the support of all of our citizens.

Thank you very much.

5. Kennedy is referring to *Brown v. Topeka, Kansas, Board of Education* (1954), in which the Court declared that segregated public schools denied black children the equal protection of the laws guaranteed by the Fourteenth Amendment to the U.S. Constitution.

6. Kennedy is referring to the dissenting opinion of U.S. Supreme Court Justice John Harlan in the 1896 case of *Plessy v. Ferguson.*

John F. Kennedy

✠

Ich Bin ein Berliner

WEST BERLIN, GERMANY
JUNE 26, 1963

LOCATED MORE THAN one hundred miles inside East Germany, Berlin had long been a flashpoint of international tension. After World War II, it was divided into a Soviet-occupied eastern sector and a western sector under jurisdiction of the United States, Great Britain, and France. In 1948 the Soviets attempted to gain control of the whole city by imposing a blockade on the western section, but they were thwarted by a massive allied airlift. During the 1950s some four million East Berliners emigrated to the West in search of political freedom and better living conditions. To stop this exodus, in 1961 Soviet Premier Nikita Khrushchev ordered construction of the Berlin Wall, a twenty-eight-mile barrier of concrete and barbed wire between East and West Berlin. Guards were ordered to shoot anyone who tried to escape to the West, and the wall quickly became the most powerful symbol of the Cold War.

On June 26, 1963, President John F. Kennedy visited Berlin as part of a weeklong European trip. Only two weeks earlier he had offered an olive branch to the Soviet Union in his speech at American University (pages 362–368), but on this day he returned to the bellicose idiom of the Cold Warrior. Deciding on his flight into Berlin to scrap his original remarks, which had the twin defects of being dull and long, he prepared a new speech praising the heroism of West Berliners and deriding the wall as "an offense not only against history but an offense against humanity." He wanted to emphasize his identification with the city's people, and so he asked aide McGeorge Bundy how to say "I am a Berliner" in German. "Ich bin ein Berliner," McBundy told him. In fact, the correct phrasing was "Ich bin Berliner," since "ein Berliner" referred to a popular jelly doughnut, but it did not matter to the sea of humanity gathered at the city hall plaza. They understood perfectly what JFK meant, and they roared in approval.

More than a million people lined Kennedy's parade route, and perhaps 250,000 jammed the plaza for his speech, chanting his name and cheering his words with one great burst of emotion after another. It was an exhilarating experience for speaker and audience alike, and it remains an iconic moment in the history of the Cold War. Afterward, on board Air Force One, Kennedy told Ted Sorensen, "We'll never have another day like this one as long as we live."

◇◇◇◇◇◇◇◇◇◇◇◇◇◇◇◇◇◇◇◇◇◇◇◇◇◇◇◇◇◇◇◇◇◇◇◇

Thank you. I am proud to come to this city as the guest of your distinguished Mayor,[1] who has symbolized throughout the world the fighting spirit of West Berlin. And I am proud, and I am proud to visit the Federal Republic with your distinguished Chancellor,[2] who for so many years has committed Germany to democracy and freedom and progress, and to come here in the company of my fellow American, General Clay,[3] who has been in this city during its great moments of crisis and will come again if ever needed.

Two thousand years ago, two thousand years ago the proudest boast was *Civis Romanus sum.*[4] Today, in the world of freedom, the proudest boast is *Ich bin ein Berliner.*

I, I, I appreciate, I appreciate my interpreter translating my German.

There are many people in the world who really don't understand, or say they don't, what is the great issue between the free world and the Communist world. Let them come to Berlin.

There are some who say, there are some who say that communism is the wave of the future. Let them come to Berlin.

And there are some who say, in Europe and elsewhere, we can work with the Communists. Let them come to Berlin.

And there are even a few who say that it's true that communism is an evil system, but it permits us to make economic progress. *Lass' sie nach Berlin kommen*: Let them come to Berlin.

Freedom has many difficulties and democracy is not perfect, but we have never had to put a wall up to keep our people in, to prevent them from leaving us.

I want to say, on behalf of my countrymen, who live many miles away on the other side of the Atlantic, who are far distant from you, that they take the greatest pride that they have been able to share with you, even from a distance, the story of the last eighteen years. I know of no town, no city, that has been besieged for eighteen years that still lives with the vitality and the force and the hope and the determination of the city of West Berlin.

While the wall is the most obvious and vivid demonstration of the failures of the Communist system, for all the world to see, we take no satisfaction in it, for it is, as your Mayor has said, an offense not only against history but an offense against humanity—separating families, dividing husbands and wives and brothers and sisters, and dividing a people who wish to be joined together.

What is true of this city is true of Germany—real, lasting peace in Europe can never be assured as long as one German out of four is denied the elementary right of free men, and that is to make a free choice. In eighteen years of peace and good faith, this generation of Germans has earned the right to be free, including the right to unite their families and their nation in lasting peace with goodwill to all people.

You live in a defended island of freedom, but your life is part of the main. So let me ask you, as I close, to lift your eyes beyond the dangers of today to the hopes of tomorrow, beyond the freedom merely of this city of Berlin or your country of Germany to the advance of freedom everywhere, beyond the wall to the day of peace with justice, beyond yourselves and ourselves to all mankind.

Freedom is indivisible, and when one man is enslaved, all are not free. When all are free, then we can look forward to that day when this city will be joined as one and this country and this great continent of Europe in a peaceful and hopeful globe. When that day finally comes, as it will, the people of West Berlin can take sober satisfaction in the fact that they were in the front lines for almost two decades.

All, all free men, wherever they may live, are citizens of Berlin, and therefore as a free man, I take pride in the words *Ich bin ein Berliner.*

---

1. Willy Brandt, Mayor of West Berlin, 1957–1966.

2. Konrad Adenauer, Chancellor of West Germany, 1949–1963.

3. Lucius D. Clay, Military Governor of Germany during the Berlin airlift of 1948–1949.

4. "I am a Roman citizen."

Martin Luther King Jr.

I Have a Dream

WASHINGTON, D.C.
AUGUST 28, 1963

THE MOST MEMORABLE words in the twentieth century's greatest public address were almost never uttered. Speaking at the epic civil rights march of August 28, 1963, Martin Luther King was approaching the end of his prepared text when, as he recalled later, "all of a sudden this thing came to me that...I'd used many times before, that thing about 'I have a dream'—and I just felt that I wanted to use it here. I don't know why. I hadn't thought about it before the speech." And so, facing an audience of 200,000 people plus millions more on television and radio, King left his manuscript and extemporized the dream section of his address. Whatever the source of his inspiration—James Farmer deemed it divine—it transformed an estimable speech into an exquisite one.

One hundred years after Abraham Lincoln held out the promise in his Gettysburg Address of a new birth of freedom for a nation wracked by civil war, King gave the United States a vision of itself reborn and cleansed of the stain of racial discrimination. His rich baritone voice marked by the fervor of the crusader and modulated by the cadences of the black Baptist preacher, he stood before the huge throng and, like a biblical prophet, offered them a vision of the Promised Land, a vision so striking in its imagery, so irresistible in its optimism, so transcendent in its grandeur that it has come to surpass in the public mind even the vision offered by Lincoln at Gettysburg. King's speech is studied and admired around the world, and its "I have a dream" refrain has become part of the global lexicon.

The March on Washington marked the high water point of the nonviolent civil rights movement that had begun eight years earlier with the boycott of segregated buses in Montgomery, Alabama. A twenty-seven-year-old minister at Montgomery's Dexter Avenue Baptist Church, King became the chief spokesman for the boycott and began to emerge as a national figure. In 1957 he helped found the Southern Christian Leadership Conference to coordinate civil rights activities throughout the South. His stirring oratory, commitment to interracial coalition, and belief in the transformative power of nonviolence made him the best-known African American leader of his time. In April 1963 he led massive demonstrations against segregation in Birmingham, Alabama, during which he wrote his classic *Letter from Birmingham Jail*. At the end of 1963 he was named *Time* magazine's Man of the Year; in 1964 he received the Nobel Peace Prize.

Of all King's speeches, none is more artistic than "I Have a Dream" in its use of imagery and metaphor to make the abstract principles of liberty and equality clear and compelling. His language is rich in scriptural connotation, his phrasing formal and uplifting. Repetition and parallel structure provide a poetic quality and quicken the impress of his ideas. Unifying and vitalizing every element of the speech is King's nonpareil delivery. He began slowly, at ninety-two words a minute. By the end, his rate was up to 145 words a minute, with his voice rising and falling in perfect concord with his words and sentence structure until the speech reached a majestic crescendo in its final words: "Free at last, free at last, thank God almighty we are free at last." One of King's biographers has called "I Have a Dream" the rhetorical achievement of a lifetime. More than that, it was a rhetorical achievement for the ages.

◇◇◇

I am happy to join with you today in what will go down in history as the greatest demonstration for freedom in the history of our nation.

Five score years ago, a great American in whose symbolic shadow we stand today[1] signed the Emancipation Proclamation.[2] This momentous decree came as a great beacon light of hope to millions of Negro slaves who had been seared in the flames of withering injustice. It came as a joyous daybreak to end the long night of their captivity.[3]

But one hundred years later, the Negro still is not free. One hundred years later, the life of the Negro is still sadly crippled by the manacles of segregation and the chains of discrimination. One hundred years later, the Negro lives on a lonely island of poverty in the midst of a vast ocean of material prosperity. One hundred years later, the Negro is still languished in the corners of American society and finds himself an exile in his own land. And so we've come here today to dramatize a shameful condition.

In a sense we've come to our nation's Capitol to cash a check. When the architects of our republic wrote the magnificent words of the Constitution and the Declaration of Independence, they were signing a promissory note to which every American was to fall heir. This note was a promise that all men—yes, black men as well as white men—would be guaranteed the unalienable rights of life, liberty, and the pursuit of happiness.[4]

It is obvious today that America has defaulted on this promissory note insofar as her citizens of color are concerned. Instead of honoring this sacred obligation, America has given the Negro people a bad check, a check which has come back marked "insufficient funds."

But we refuse to believe that the bank of justice is bankrupt. We refuse to believe that there are insufficient funds in the great vaults of opportunity of this nation. And so we've come to cash this check, a check that will give us upon demand the riches of freedom and the security of justice.

We have also come to this hallowed spot to remind America of the fierce urgency of now. This is no time to engage in the luxury of cooling off or to take the tranquilizing drug of gradualism. Now is the time to make real the promises of democracy. Now is the time to rise from the dark and desolate valley of segregation to the sunlit path of racial justice. Now is the time to lift our nation from the quicksands of racial injustice to the solid rock of brotherhood. Now

---

1. Abraham Lincoln. King spoke from the steps of the Lincoln Memorial, with the audience spread out in the vast area between the Lincoln Memorial and the Washington Monument.

2. Document of January 1, 1863, that freed the slaves in areas still under control of the Confederacy.

3. A reference to the biblical account of the freeing of the Jews from their captivity in ancient Egypt.

4. An echo of the Declaration of Independence (1776).

is the time to make justice a reality for all of God's children.

It would be fatal for the nation to overlook the urgency of the moment. This sweltering summer of the Negro's legitimate discontent[5] will not pass until there is an invigorating autumn of freedom and equality. Nineteen sixty-three is not an end, but a beginning. Those who hope that the Negro needed to blow off steam and will now be content will have a rude awakening if the nation returns to business as usual. There will be neither rest nor tranquility in America until the Negro is granted his citizenship rights. The whirlwinds of revolt will continue to shake the foundations of our nation until the bright day of justice emerges.

But there is something that I must say to my people, who stand on the warm threshold which leads into the palace of justice. In the process of gaining our rightful place, we must not be guilty of wrongful deeds. Let us not seek to satisfy our thirst for freedom by drinking from the cup of bitterness and hatred. We must forever conduct our struggle on the high plain of dignity and discipline. We must not allow our creative protest to degenerate into physical violence. Again and again we must rise to the majestic heights of meeting physical force with soul force.

The marvelous new militancy which has engulfed the Negro community must not lead us to a distrust of all white people, for many of our white brothers, as evidenced by their presence here today, have come to realize that their destiny is tied up with our destiny. They have come to realize that their freedom is inextricably bound to our freedom. We cannot walk alone.

And as we walk, we must make the pledge that we shall always march ahead. We cannot turn back. There are those who are asking the devotees of civil rights, "When will you be satisfied?" We can never be satisfied as long as the Negro is the victim of the unspeakable horrors of police brutality. We can never be satisfied as long as our bodies, heavy with the fatigue of travel, cannot gain lodging in the motels of the highways and the hotels of the cities. We cannot be satisfied as long as the Negro's basic mobility is from a smaller ghetto to a larger one. We can never be satisfied as long as our children are stripped of their selfhood and robbed of their dignity by signs stating "For Whites Only." We cannot be satisfied as long as a Negro in Mississippi cannot vote and a Negro in New York believes he has nothing for which to vote. No, no, we are not satisfied and we will not be satisfied until justice rolls down like waters and righteousness like a mighty stream.[6]

I am not unmindful that some of you have come here out of great trials and tribulations. Some of you have come fresh from narrow jail cells. Some of you have come from areas where your quest for freedom left you battered by the storms of persecution and staggered by the winds of police brutality. You have been the veterans of creative suffering. Continue to work with the faith that unearned suffering is redemptive.

Go back to Mississippi, go back to Alabama, go back to South Carolina, go back to Georgia, go back to Louisiana, go back to the slums and ghettos of our Northern cities knowing that somehow this situation can and will be changed. Let us not wallow in the valley of despair.

I say to you today, my friends, so even though we face the difficulties of today and tomorrow, I still have a dream. It is a dream deeply rooted in the American dream.

I have a dream that one day this nation will rise up and live out the true meaning of its creed, "We hold these truths to be self-evident, that all men are created equal."[7]

I have a dream that one day on the red hills of Georgia the sons of former slaves and the sons of former slave owners will be able to sit down together at the table of brotherhood.

I have a dream that one day even the state of Mississippi, a state sweltering with the heat of injustice, sweltering with the heat of oppression, will be transformed into an oasis of freedom and justice.

---

5. A play on the opening words of Shakespeare's *Richard III*: "Now is the winter of our discontent."

6. An echo of Amos 5:24.

7. From the Declaration of Independence.

I have a dream that my four little children will one day live in a nation where they will not be judged by the color of their skin but by the content of their character. I have a dream today.

I have a dream that one day down in Alabama, with its vicious racists, with its Governor[8] having his lips dripping with the words of interposition and nullification,[9] one day right there in Alabama little black boys and black girls will be able to join hands with little white boys and white girls as sisters and brothers. I have a dream today.

I have a dream that one day every valley shall be exalted, every hill and mountain shall be made low, the rough places will be made plain and the crooked places will be made straight, and the glory of the Lord shall be revealed and all flesh shall see it together.[10]

This is our hope. This is the faith that I go back to the South with. With this faith we will be able to hew out of the mountain of despair a stone of hope. With this faith we will be able to transform the jangling discords of our nation into a beautiful symphony of brotherhood. With this faith we will be able to work together, to pray together, to struggle together, to go to jail together, to stand up for freedom together knowing that we will be free one day.

This will be the day, this will be the day when all of God's children will be able to sing with new meaning: "My country 'tis of thee, sweet land of liberty, of thee I sing. Land where my fathers died, land of the pilgrim's pride; from every mountainside, let freedom ring."[11] And if America is to be a great nation, this must become true.

And so let freedom ring from the prodigious hilltops of New Hampshire. Let freedom ring from the mighty mountains of New York. Let freedom ring from the heightening Alleghenies of Pennsylvania. Let freedom ring from the snowcapped Rockies of Colorado. Let freedom ring from the curvaceous slopes of California.

But not only that. Let freedom ring from Stone Mountain of Georgia. Let freedom ring from Lookout Mountain of Tennessee. Let freedom ring from every hill and molehill of Mississippi. From every mountainside, let freedom ring.

And when this happens, when we allow freedom ring—when we let it ring from every village and every hamlet, from every state and every city—we will be able to speed up that day when all of God's children, black men and white men, Jews and Gentiles, Protestants and Catholics, will be able to join hands and sing in the words of the old Negro spiritual, "Free at last! Free at last! Thank God almighty, we are free at last!"[12]

---

8. George C. Wallace.

9. Interposition asserts the right of a state to stand between its citizens and actions by the federal government that exceed the powers granted to it by the Constitution. Nullification holds that a state has the right to prevent the enforcement within its borders of federal laws that the state deems unconstitutional. Both doctrines were used by Southern states to justify secession from the Union during the Civil War.

10. Closely paraphrased from Isaiah 40:4–5.

---

11. From "My Country 'Tis of Thee," lyrics by Samuel Francis Smith (1831).

12. Paraphrased from the spiritual "Free at Last."

Malcolm X

Message to the Grassroots

DETROIT, MICHIGAN
NOVEMBER 10, 1963

UNLIKE MARTIN LUTHER King, whose rhetoric echoed the imagery and cadences of the pulpit, Malcolm X's reflected the idiom and anger of the streets. Born Malcolm Little in 1925, he changed his name when he converted to the Nation of Islam during the mid-1940s while serving a prison term for burglary. He was mesmerized by the teachings of the Nation's leader, Elijah Muhammad, and soon began converting other inmates. Recognizing the deficiencies in his education and linguistic skills, he became a regular in the prison library, copied the dictionary word by word to increase his vocabulary, and became hooked on debating, which, he said, "was as exhilarating to me as the discovery of knowledge through reading had been."

After leaving prison in 1952, Malcolm became a minister and organizer for the Nation of Islam. Proselytizing in parks, on street corners, and anywhere else he could muster an audience, he soon created enough converts to establish temples in Boston, Detroit, and Philadelphia. In 1954 he became minister of the Harlem temple, and before the end of the decade he had eclipsed Elijah Muhammad as the Nation of Islam's dominant public figure. At times he seemed ubiquitous, speaking everywhere from black communities to college campuses to radio talk shows to made-for-television debates. Always he was the agitator, stating his positions defiantly, stridently, and uncompromisingly in language that rang with loathing of white racism and scorn for blacks who adopted half measures in combatting it.

On November 10, 1963, Malcolm addressed an audience of 2,000 people at the King Solomon Baptist Church for the closing rally of the Northern Negro Grassroots Leadership Conference, a radical alternative to the moderate Northern Negro Leadership Conference being held in Detroit at the same time. "Message to the Grass Roots" is typical of Malcolm's discourse in its identification of the white man as the inveterate enemy of dark-skinned people the world over. The only way to deal with this enemy, he said, is through genuine revolution, which must be based on land and is inherently bloody. He assailed the civil rights movement for its emphasis on nonviolence and, in one of his favorite set pieces, compared its leaders to the house Negroes of slavery days who loved their masters better than they loved themselves. Even the March on Washington, which had taken place seven months earlier, was, in Malcolm's view, no more than "a circus, with clowns and all," a pathetic performance in which blacks danced to the tune of their white masters, who "acted like they really loved Negroes."

Because Malcolm always spoke extemporaneously, he left behind no manuscripts of his speeches. The text of "Message to the Grassroots" is based on a tape recording, which contains about half of what he said in his ninety-minute address. Although most editors of Malcolm's speeches have "corrected" his colloquial diction and grammar, we have rendered his words—here and in "The Ballot or the Bullet" (pages 392–405)—as accurately as possible so as to reflect the tone and temper of his spoken discourse. What Malcolm said and how he said it were both the result of deliberate rhetorical choices and often changed depending on the audience he was addressing and the effect he wanted to create. Even when he spoke softly, as he often did for emphasis, his language was sharp and aggressive, his tone edgy and informal, his connection with his audience electric and visceral. As Julius Lester later observed, "Malcolm X said aloud those things which Negroes had been saying among themselves. He even said those things Negroes had been afraid to say to each other. His clear, uncomplicated words cut through the chains on black minds like a giant blowtorch."

◇◇◇◇◇◇◇◇◇◇◇◇◇◇◇◇◇◇◇◇◇◇◇◇◇◇◇◇◇◇◇◇

And during the few moments that we have left, we wanna have just an off-the-cuff chat between you and me—us. We wanna talk right down to earth in a language that everybody here can easily understand. We all agree tonight, all of the speakers have agreed, that America has a very serious problem. Not only does America have a very serious problem, but our people have a very serious problem.

America's problem is us. We're her problem. The only reason she has a problem is she doesn't want us here. And every time you look at yourself—be you black, brown, red or yellow, a so-called Negro—you are, you represent a person who poses such a serious problem for America because you're not wanted. Once you face this as a fact, then you can start plotting a course that will make you appear intelligent, instead of unintelligent.

What you and I need to do is learn to forget our differences. When we come together, we don't come together as Baptists or Methodists. You don't catch hell 'cause you're a Baptist, and you don't catch hell 'cause you're a Methodist. You don't, you don't catch hell 'cause you're a Methodist or a Baptist; you don't catch hell because you're a Democrat or a Republican; you don't catch hell because you're a

Mason or an Elk;[1] and you sure don't catch hell 'cause you're an American, 'cause if you was an American, you wouldn't catch no hell. You catch hell 'cause you're a black man. You catch hell, all of us catch hell, for the same reason.

So we are all black people: so-called Negroes, second-class citizens, ex-slaves. You are nothin' but a ex-slave. You don't like to be told that. But what else are you? You are ex-slave[s]. You didn't come here on the *Mayflower*. You came here in a slave ship, in chains, like a horse or a cow or a chicken. And you were brought here by the people who came here on the *Mayflower*. You were brought here by the so-called Pilgrims, or Founding Fathers. They were the ones who brought you here.[2]

We have a common enemy. We have this in common. We have a common oppressor, a common exploiter, and a common discriminator. So once we all realize that we have this common enemy, then we

---

1. A Freemason or a member of the Benevolent and Protective Order of Elks.

2. There were no slaves on the *Mayflower*, which landed in America in September 1620; the first Africans had been imported into Virginia a year earlier.

unite on the basis of what we have in common. And what we have foremost in common is that enemy—the white man. He's an enemy to all of us. I know some of you all think that some of 'em aren't enemies. Time will tell.

In Bandung back in, I think, 1954 was the first unity meeting in centuries of black people.[3] And once you study what happened at the Bandung Conference and the results of the Bandung Conference, it actually serves as a model for the same procedure you and I can use to get our problems solved. At Bandung all the nations came together. There were dark nations from Africa and Asia. Some of them were Buddhists, some of them were Muslim, some of them were Christians, some of them were Confucianists, some were atheists. Despite their religious differences, they came together. Some were Communists, some were Socialists, some were capitalists. Despite, despite their economic and political differences, they came together. All of them were black, brown, red, or yellow.

The number-one thing that was not allowed to attend the Bandung Conference was the white man. He couldn't come. Once they excluded the white man, they found that they could get together. Once they kept him out, everybody else fell right in and fell in line. This is the thing that you and I have to understand. And these people who came together didn't have nuclear weapons; they didn't have jet planes; they didn't have all of the heavy armaments that the white man has. But they had unity. They were able to submerge their little petty differences and agree on one thing: that though one African came from Kenya and was being colonized by the Englishman, and another African came from the Congo and was being colonized by the Belgian, and another African came from Guinea and was being colonized by the French, and another came from Angola and was being colonized by the Portuguese, when they came to the Bandung Conference, they looked at the Portuguese and at the Frenchman and at the Englishman and at the Dutchman and learned, or realized, that the one thing that all of 'em had in common—they were

all from Europe. They were all from—they were all Europeans: blonde, blue-eyed, and white skin.

They began to recognize who their enemy was. The same man that was colonizing our people in Kenya was colonizing our people in the Congo. The same one in the Congo was colonizing our people in South Africa, and in Southern Rhodesia, and in Burma, and in India, and in Afghanistan, and in Pakistan. They realized all over the world where a dark man was being oppressed, he was being oppressed by the white man. Where the dark man was being exploited, he was being exploited by the white man. So they got together under this basis: that they had a common enemy.

And when you and I here in Detroit and in Michigan and in America who have been awakened today look around us, we, too, realize here in America we all have a common enemy. Whether he's in Georgia or Michigan, whether he's in California or New York, he's the same man: blue eyes and blonde hair and pale skin. Same man.

So what we have to do is what they did. They agreed to stop quarreling among themselves. Any little spat that they had, they'd settle it among themselves. Go into a huddle; don't let the enemy know that you got a disagreement. Instead of us airing our differences in public, we have to realize we're all the same family. And when you have a family squabble, you don't get out on the sidewalk. If you do, everybody calls you uncouth, unrefined, uncivilized, savage. If you don't make it at home, you settle it at home. You get in the closet, argue it out behind closed doors, and then when you come out on the street, you pose a common front, a united front. And this is what we need to do in the community and in the city and in the state. We need to stop airing our differences in front of the white man—put the white man out of our meeting, number one, and then sit down and talk shop with each other. That's all you gotta do.

I would like to make a few comments concerning the difference between the black revolution and the Negro revolution. There's a difference. Are they both the same? And if they're not, what is the difference? What is the difference between a black revolution and a Negro revolution?

---

3. Malcolm is referring to the meeting of 29 African and Asian nations held at Bandung, Indonesia, in April 1955.

First, what is a revolution? Sometimes I'm inclined to believe that many of our people are using this word "revolution" loosely, without taking careful consideration [of] what this word actually means and what its historic characteristics are. When you study the historic nature of revolutions, the motive of a revolution, the objective of a revolution, and the result of a revolution, and the methods used in a revolution, you may change words. You may devise another program, you may change your goal, and you may change your mind.

Look at the American Revolution in 1776. That revolution was for what? For land. How was it—why did they want land? Independence. How was it carried out? Bloodshed. Number one, it was based on land—the basis of independence. And the only way they could get it was bloodshed.

The French Revolution,[4] what was it based on? The landless against the landlord. What was it for? Land. How did they get it? Bloodshed. Was no love lost, was no compromise, was no negotiation. I'm telling you, you don't know what a revolution is, 'cause when you find out what it is, you'll get back in the alley, you'll get out of the way.

The Russian Revolution,[5] what was it based on? Land: the landless against the landlord. How did they bring it about? Bloodshed. You haven't got a revolution that doesn't involve bloodshed. And you're afraid to bleed.

I said you're afraid to bleed. Long as the white man send you to Korea, you bled. He sent you to Germany, you bled. He sent you to the South Pacific to fight the Japanese, you bled.[6] You bleed for white people, but when it comes time to seeing your own churches being bombed and little black girls murdered,[7] you haven't got no blood. You bleed when the white man says bleed, you bite when the white man says bite, and you bark when the white man says bark. I hate to say this about us, but it's true. How you goin' be nonviolent in Mississippi, as violent as you were in Korea? How can you justify being nonviolent in Mississippi and Alabama when your churches are being bombed and your little girls are being murdered, and at the same time you gonna get violent with Hitler and Tojo[8] and somebody else that you don't even know?

If violence is wrong in America, violence is wrong abroad. If it's wrong to be violent defending black women and black children and black babies and black men, then it's wrong for America to draft us and make us violent abroad in defense of her. And if it is right for America to draft us and teach us how to be violent in defense of her, then it is right for you and me to do whatever is necessary to defend our own people right here in this country.

The Chinese Revolution,[9] they wanted land. They threw the British out, along with the Uncle Tom[10] Chinese. Yeah, they did. They set a good example. When I was in prison, I read a article in—don't be shocked when I say I was in prison; you still in prison. That's what America means: prison. When I was in prison, I read an article in *Life* magazine showing [a] little Chinese girl, nine years old. Her father was on his hands and knees and she was pullin' the trigger 'cause he was a Uncle Tom Chinaman. When they had the revolution over there, they took a whole generation of Uncle Toms—just wiped 'em out. And within ten years that little girl [had] become a full-grown woman. No more Toms in China. And today,

<hr>

4. The French Revolution of 1788–1789 toppled the monarchy, overturned the established social order, and eventually pulled much of Europe into its vortex.

5. The Russian Revolution brought about the abdication of Czar Nicholas II in 1917, the seizure of power by the Bolsheviks under the leadership of Vladimir Ilyich Lenin, and the creation of the Soviet Union in 1922.

6. Malcolm is referring to the Korean War of 1950–1953 and the European and Pacific theaters of World War II.

7. A reference to the September 1963 bombing that killed four black girls as they attended Sunday school in Birmingham, Alabama.

8. Tojo Hideki, Japanese Premier who ordered the attack on Pearl Harbor in 1941.

9. The Chinese Revolution occurred over several decades and culminated in 1949 with the establishment of Communist rule under the leadership of Mao Zedong.

10. Disparaging term for a black person who is seen as submissive to white people; derived from the title character of Harriet Beecher Stowe's *Uncle Tom's Cabin* (1852).

today it's one of the toughest, roughest, most feared countries on this earth by the white man 'cause there are no Uncle Toms over there.

Of all our studies, history is best qualified to reward all research. And when you see that you got problems, all you have to do is examine the historic method used all over the world by others who had problems similar to yours. And once you see how they got theirs straight, then you know how you can get yours straight.

There's been a revolution, a black revolution, going on in Africa. In Kenya, the Mau Mau were revolutionaries;[11] they were the ones who made the word "Uhuru."[12] They were the ones who brought it to the fore. The Mau Mau, they were revolutionaries, they believed in scorched earth, they knocked everything aside that got in their path. And their revolution also was based on land, a desire for land.

In Algeria, the northern part of Africa, a revolution took place.[13] The Algerians were revolutionists; they wanted land. France offered to let them be integrated into France. They told France, "To hell with France." They wanted some land, not some France. And they engaged in a bloody battle.

So I cite these various revolutions, brothers and sisters, to show you you don't have a peaceful revolution. You don't have a turn-the-other-cheek revolution. There's no such thing as a nonviolent revolution. Only thing, only kind of revolution that's nonviolent is the Negro revolution. The only revolution based on lovin' your enemy is the Negro revolution, the only revolution in which the goal is a desegregated lunch counter, a desegregated theater, a desegregated park, and a desegregated public toilet. You can sit down next to white folks on the toilet. That's no revolution. Revolution is based on land. Land is the basis of all independence. Land is the basis of freedom, justice, and equality.

The white man knows what a revolution is. He knows that the black revolution is worldwide in scope and in nature. The black revolution is sweeping Asia, sweeping Africa, it's rearing its head in Latin America. The Cuban Revolution—that's a revolution.[14] They overturned the system. Revolution is in Asia, revolution is in Africa, and the white man is screaming because he sees revolution in Latin America. How do you think he'll react to you when you learn what a real revolution is?

You don't know what a revolution is. If you did, you wouldn't use that word. A revolution is bloody; revolution is hostile; revolution knows no compromise; revolution overturns and destroys everything that gets in its way. And you sittin' around here like a knot on the wall sayin', "I'm goin' love these folks no matter how much they hate me." No, you need a revolution. Whoever heard of a revolution where they lock arms, as Reverend Cleage[15] was pointing out beautifully, singin' "We Shall Overcome"?[16] Just tell me. You don't do that in a revolution. You don't do any singin'—you're too busy swinging.

It's based on land. A revolutionary wants land so he can set up his own nation, an independent nation. These Negroes aren't askin' for no nation; they tryin' to crawl back on the plantation.

When you want a nation, that's called nationalism. When the white man became involved in a revolution in this country against England, what was it for? He wanted this land so he could set up another white nation. That's white nationalism. The American Revolution was white nationalism. The French Revolution was white nationalism. The Russian Revolution, too—yes, it was—white nationalism. You don't think so? Why you think Khrushchev and Mao[17] can't get their heads together? White nationalism.

11. The Mau Mau led an uprising against British rule during the 1950s.

12. "Uhuru" means "freedom" in Swahili. Malcolm's reference to the term here may have been prompted by the fact that a black nationalist group named UHURU had been founded in Detroit in March 1963.

13. The Algerian Revolution of 1954–1962 resulted in Algeria's independence from France.

14. The Cuban Revolution overthrew the dictatorship of Fulgencio Batista and brought Fidel Castro to power in 1959.

15. Albert B. Cleage Jr., pastor of Detroit's Central Congregational Church, who preceded Malcolm on the platform.

16. Unofficial anthem of the civil rights movement.

17. Nikita Khrushchev and Mao Zedong, leaders of the Soviet Union and China, respectively. Malcolm is referring to the diplomatic split between the two nations that emerged in the late 1950s.

All the revolutions that's goin' on in Asia and Africa today are based on what? Black nationalism. A revolutionary is a black nationalist. He wants a nation. I was reading some beautiful words by Reverend Cleage pointing out why he couldn't get together with someone else here in the city because all of them were afraid of being identified with black nationalism. If you're afraid of black nationalism, you're afraid of revolution. And if you love revolution, you love black nationalism.[18]

To understand this, you have to go back to what young brother here referred to as the house Negro and the field Negro back during slavery. There was two kind of slaves; there was the house Negro and the field Negro. The house Negro, they lived in the house with master, they dressed pretty good, they ate good 'cause they ate his food—what he left. They lived in the attic or the basement, but still they lived near their master, and they loved their master more than the master loved himself. They would, they would give their life to save their master's house quicker than the master would. The house Negro, if the master said, "We got a good house here," the house Negro [would] say, "Yeah, we got a good house here." Whenever the master said "we," he said "we." That's how you can tell a house Negro.

If the master's, if the master's house caught on fire, the house Negro would fight harder to put the blaze out than the master would. If the master got sick, the house Negro would say, "What's the matter, boss, we sick?" We sick! He identified himself with his master more than his master identified with himself. And if you came to the house Negro and said, "Let's run away, let's escape, let's separate," that house Negro would look at you and say, "Man, you crazy. What you mean, separate? Where is there a better house than this? Where can I wear better clothes than this? Where can I eat better food than this?"

That was that house Negro. In those days he was called a "house nigger." And that's what we call him today 'cause we still got some house niggers running around here. This modern house Negro loves his master. He wants to live near him. He'll pay three times

as much as the house is worth just to live near his master and then brag about, "I'm the only Negro out here; I'm the only one on my job; I'm the only one in this school." You're nothin' but a house Negro.

And if someone come to you right now and say, "Let's separate," you say the same thing that the house Negro said on the plantation: "What you mean, separate? From America? This good white man? Where you going to get a better job than you get here?" I mean, this is what you say. "I ain't left nothing in Africa"—that's what you say. Why, you left your mind in Africa.

On that same plantation, there was the field Negro. The field Negro, those were the masses. There was always more Negroes in the field than there was Negroes in the house. The Negro in the field caught hell. He ate leftovers. In the house they ate high up on the hog. The Negro in the field didn't get nothin' but what was left of the insides of the hog. They call 'em chitlings nowadays. In those days they called 'em what they were—guts. That's what you were: a gut-eater. And some of you all still gut-eaters.

The field Negro was beaten from mornin' till night. He lived in a shack, in a hut. He wore cast-off clothes. And he hated his master. I say, he hated his master. He was intelligent. That house Negro loved his master, but that field Negro—remember, they were in the majority, and they hated the master. When the house caught on fire, he didn't try and put it out; that field Negro prayed for a wind, for a breeze. When the master got sick, the field Negro prayed that he'd die. If someone come to the field Negro and said, "Let's separate, let's run," he didn't say, "Where we going?" He'd say, "Any place is better than here."

You got field Negroes in America today. I'm a field Negro. The masses are the field Negroes. When they see this man's house on fire, you don't hear these little Negroes talking about "Our government is in trouble." They say, "The government is in trouble." Imagine a Negro: "Our government"! I even heard one say "Our astronauts." They won't even let him near the plant[19]—and "Our astronauts"! "Our navy"! That's a Negro that's out of his mind. That's a Negro that's out of his mind.

---

18. There is a break of unknown duration in the recording at this point.

19. Malcolm may have meant to say "plane."

Just as the slave master in that day used Tom, the house Negro, to keep the field Negroes in check, the same old slave master today has Negroes who are nothin' but modern Uncle Toms, twentieth-century Uncle Toms, to keep you and me in check, keep us under control, keep us passive and peaceful and non-violent. That's Tom makin' you nonviolent.

It's like when you go to the dentist and the man is goin' take your tooth. You gonna fight him when he start pullin'. So they squirts some stuff in your jaw called Novocain to make you think they not doin' anything to you. So you sit there, and 'cause you've got all that Novocain in your jaw, you suffer peacefully. Ha, ha, ha, ha. Blood runnin' all down your jaw and you don't know what's happenin' 'cause someone has taught you to suffer peacefully.

The white man do the same thing to you in the street when he wanna put knots on your head and take advantage of you and don't have to be afraid of you fightin' back. To keep you from fightin' back, he get[s] these old religious Uncle Toms to teach you and me. They're just like Novocain: Suffer peacefully. Don't stop suffering, just suffer peacefully. As Reverend Cleage pointed out, let your blood flow in the streets. This is a shame. And you know he's a Christian preacher. If it's a shame to him, you know what it is to me.

There's nothin' in our book, the Koran—as you call it, Koh-ran—teaches us to suffer peacefully. Our religion teaches us to be intelligent, be peaceful, be courteous, obey the law, respect everyone; but if someone puts his hand on you, send him to the cemetery. That's a good religion. In fact, that's that old-time religion. That's the one that Ma and Pa used to talk about: an eye for an eye, and a tooth for a tooth, and a head for a head, and a life for a life. That's a good religion. And then anybody—no one resents that kind of religion being taught but a wolf, who intends to make you his meal.

This is the way it is with the white man in America. He's a wolf and you a sheep. Any time a shepherd, a pastor, teach[es] you and me not to run from the white man and, at the same time, teaches don't fight the white man, he's a traitor to you and me. Don't lay down our life all by itself. No, preserve your life; it's the best thing you got. And if you got to give it up, let it be even-Steven.

The slave master took Tom and dressed him well and fed him well and even gave him a little education—a little education—gave him a long coat and a top hat and made all the other slaves look up to him. Then he used Tom to control them. The same strategy that was used in those days is used today by the same white man. He take a Negro, a so-called Negro, and make him prominent, build him up, publicize him, make him a celebrity. And then he becomes a spokesman for Negroes, and a Negro leader.

I would like to just mention one thing else quickly, and that is the method that the white man uses, how the white man uses these "big guns," or Negro leaders, against the black revolution. They are not a part of the black revolution. They're used against the black revolution.

When Martin Luther King failed to desegregate Albany, Georgia, the civil rights struggle in America reached its low point.[20] King became bankrupt, almost, as a leader. Plus, even financially the Southern Christian Leadership Conference[21] was in financial trouble. Plus it was in trouble, period, with the people when they failed to desegregate Albany, Georgia. Other Negro civil rights leaders of so-called national stature became fallen idols. As they became fallen idols, began to lose their prestige and influence, local Negro leaders began to stir up the masses. In Cambridge, Maryland, Gloria Richardson.[22] In Danville, Virginia,[23] and other parts of the country local leaders began to stir up our people at the grassroots level. This was never done by these Negroes whom you recognize of national stature. They controlled you, but they never incited you or excited you. They controlled you. They contained you. They kept you on the plantation.

---

20. The 1961 Albany campaign was perhaps King's greatest defeat.

21. Civil rights organization founded by King and others in 1957.

22. Leader of the Cambridge Nonviolent Action Committee during civil rights protests in 1962–1963. Richardson was in the audience for Malcolm's speech.

23. Site of brutal police violence against civil rights protesters in June 1963.

As soon as King failed in Birmingham,[24] Negroes took to the streets. King got out and went out to California to a big rally and raised about I don't know how many thousands of dollars.[25] Come to Detroit and had a march and raised some more thousands of dollars.[26] And recall, right after that, Wilkins[27] attacked King, accused King and the CORE[28] of startin' trouble everywhere and then makin' the NAACP get 'em out of jail and spend a lot of money. And then they accused King and CORE of raisin' all the money and not payin' it back. This happened. I got it in documented evidence in the newspaper. Roy started attackin' King, and King started attackin' Roy, and Farmer[29] started attackin' both of 'em.

And as these Negroes of national stature begin to attack each other, they begin to lose their control of the Negro masses. And Negroes was out there in the streets. They was talkin' about we goin' march on Washington. By the way, right at that time Birmingham had exploded, and the Negroes in Birmingham—remember, they also exploded—they began to stab the crackers[30] in the back and bust 'em up side the head. Yes, they did. That's when Kennedy[31] sent in the troops down in Birmingham.

So, and right after that, Kennedy got on the television and said, "This is a moral issue."[32] That's when he said he goin' put out a civil rights bill. And when he mentioned civil rights bill and the Southern crackers start[ed] talkin' about they were gonna boycott it—or

filibuster it—then the Negroes started talkin' about what? We goin' march on Washington, march on the Senate, march on the White House, march on the Congress and tie it up, bring it to a halt, don't let the government proceed. They even said they was gonna go out to the airport and lay down on the runway and don't let no airplanes land. I'm tellin' you what they said.

That was revolution. That was revolution. That was the black revolution. It was the grassroots out there in the street. Scared the white man to death; scared the white power structure in Washington, D.C., to death. I was there. When they found out that this black steamroller was gonna come down on the capital, they called in Wilkins. They called in Randolph.[33] They called in these national Negro leaders that you respect and told 'em, "Call it off."

Kennedy said, "Look, you all lettin' this thing go too far." And Old Tom said, "Boss, I can't stop it 'cause I didn't start it." I'm tellin' you what they said. They said, "I'm not even in it, much less at the head of it." They said, "These Negroes are doin' things on their own; they runnin' ahead of us." And that old shrewd fox, he said: "Well, if you all aren't in it, I'll put you in it. I'll put you at the head of it. I'll endorse it. I'll welcome it. I'll help it. I'll join it."

The very—a matter of hours went by. They had a meeting at the Carlyle Hotel in New York City. The Carlyle Hotel is owned by the Kennedy family. That's the hotel Kennedy spent the night at two nights ago—belongs to his family. A philanthropic society headed by a white man named Stephen Currier[34] called all the top civil rights leaders together at the Carlyle Hotel and told them that "By you all fightin' each other, you're destroying the civil rights movement. And since you're fightin' over money from white liberals, let us set up what's known as the Council for United Civil Rights Leadership. Let's form this council, and all the civil rights organizations will belong to it, and we'll use it for fundraising purposes."

---

24. Malcolm is referring to the Birmingham desegregation campaign of April–May 1963; he calls it a failure because King accepted a compromise agreement with city leaders.

25. King's speech in Los Angeles on May 26, 1963, helped raise $75,000 for the civil rights movement.

26. An estimated 125,000 people participated in the Detroit march of June 23, 1963.

27. Roy Wilkins, head of the National Association for the Advancement of Colored People (NAACP).

28. Congress of Racial Equality.

29. James Farmer Jr., national director of CORE.

30. Disparaging term for white people.

31. President John F. Kennedy.

32. Malcolm is referring to Kennedy's speech of June 11, 1963 (pages 369–372).

---

33. A. Philip Randolph, president of the Brotherhood of Sleeping Car Porters.

34. President of the Taconic Foundation.

Let me show you how tricky the white man is. And as soon as they got it formed, they elected Whitney Young[35] as the chairman. And who you think became the cochairman? Stephen Currier, the white man, a millionaire. Powell[36] was talkin' about it down at the Cobo[37] today. This is what he was talkin' about. Powell knows it happened. Randolph knows it happened. Wilkins knows it happened. King knows it happened. Every one of that so-called Big Six, they know what happened.

Once they formed it, with the white man over it, he promised them and gave them $800,000 to split up between the Big Six and told them that after the march was over, they'd give 'em $700,000. A million and a half dollars, split up between the leaders that you've been followin', goin' to jail for, cryin' crocodile tears for. And they ain't nothin' but Frank James and Jesse James and the whatcha-call-it brothers.[38]

Soon as they got the setup organized, the white man made available to them top public relations experts, opened the news media across the country at their disposal, and then they begin to project these Big Six as the leaders of the march. Originally they weren't even in the march. You was talkin' this march talk on Hastings Street—is Hastings Street still here?—on Hastings Street. You was talkin' the march talk on Lenox Avenue and out on whatcha-call-it, Fillmore Street, and Central Avenue and Forty-second Street and Sixty-third Street. That's where the march talk was being talked.

But the white man put the Big Six ahead of it, made them the march. They became the march. They took it over. And the first move they made after they took it over, they invited Walter Reuther,[39] a white man. They invited a priest, a rabbi, and a ol'

white preacher[40]—yes, a ol' white preacher. The same white element that put Kennedy in power—labor, the Catholics, the Jews, and liberal Protestants—same clique that put Kennedy in power joined the March on Washington.[41]

It's just like when you got some coffee that's too black, which means it's too strong, what you do? You integrate it with cream; you make it weak. If you pour too much cream in, you won't even know you ever had coffee. It used to be hot; it becomes cool. It used to be strong; it becomes weak. It used to wake you up; now it'll put you to sleep. This is what they did with the March on Washington. They joined it. They didn't integrate it; they infiltrated it. They joined it, became a part of it, took it over.

And as they took it over, it lost its militancy. They ceased to be angry; they ceased to be hot; they ceased to be uncompromising. Why, it even ceased to be a march. It became a picnic, a circus. Nothin' but a circus, with clowns and all. You had one right here in Detroit—I saw it on television—with clowns leadin' it, white clowns and black clowns. I know you don't like what I'm sayin', but I'm gonna tell you anyway 'cause I can prove what I'm saying. If you think I'm tellin' you wrong, you bring me Martin Luther King and A. Philip Randolph and James Farmer and those other three and see if they'll deny it over a microphone.

No, it was a sellout. It was a takeover. When James Baldwin[42] came in from Paris, they wouldn't let him talk 'cause they couldn't make him go by the script. Burt Lancaster read the speech that Baldwin was supposed to make.[43] They wouldn't let Baldwin get up there 'cause they know Baldwin [is] liable to say anything. They controlled it so tight, they told those Negroes what time to hit town, how to come,

---

35. Executive director of the National Urban League.

36. Adam Clayton Powell Jr., U.S. Representative from Harlem.

37. Detroit's Cobo Hall, site of the Northern Negro Leadership Conference meeting.

38. The James brothers led a notorious band of bank and train robbers from 1866 to 1882.

39. President of the United Auto Workers.

40. Mathew Ahmann, executive director of the National Catholic Conference for Interracial Justice; Rabbi Joachim Prinz; and Reverend Eugene Carson Blake.

41. Malcolm is referring to the August 28, 1963, march at which Martin Luther King delivered "I Have a Dream" (pages 375–378).

42. Author of *Go Tell It on the Mountain* (1953) and *Notes of a Native Son* (1955).

43. Although Lancaster attended the March on Washington, Baldwin's speech was read by Charlton Heston.

where to stop, what sign to carry, what song to sing, what speech they could make and what speech they couldn't make, and then told 'em to get out of town by sundown. And every one of those Toms were out of town by sundown.

Now, I know you don't like my sayin' this, but I can back it up. It was a circus, a performance. It beat anything Hollywood could ever do—the performance of the year. Reuther and those other three devils should get a Academy Award for the best actors 'cause they acted like they really loved Negroes and fooled a whole lot of Negroes. And the six Negro leaders should get an award, too, for the best supporting casts.

Lyndon B. Johnson

Let Us Continue

WASHINGTON, D.C.
NOVEMBER 27, 1963

ON NOVEMBER 22, 1963, John F. Kennedy was assassinated while riding in an open car in Dallas, Texas. Three days later, he was laid to rest at Arlington National Cemetery. The images of that period are indelibly burned into the nation's memory: President Kennedy recoiling from the impact of the bullets; his motorcade dashing from Dealey Plaza to Parkland Hospital; Jacqueline Kennedy in her bloodstained suit; Lyndon Johnson taking the presidential oath of office aboard *Air Force One*; suspected assassin Lee Harvey Oswald being shot by Jack Ruby at Dallas police headquarters; the riderless horse at Kennedy's funeral parade; the black caisson bearing the President's flag-draped coffin; three-year-old John F. Kennedy Jr. saluting the caisson as it passed. The nation, shocked and disbelieving, mourned openly.

It also waited to hear from newly sworn President Lyndon Johnson. But when, and how, would he speak? Following in the footsteps of Harry Truman, who had addressed the House and Senate four days after Franklin D. Roosevelt's funeral in April 1945, Johnson called a special joint session of Congress to convene at noon on November 27. It was the perfect setting for Johnson, who had spent eleven years in the House of Representatives and twelve in the Senate before becoming Kennedy's Vice President.

Johnson's speech was part eulogy, part inaugural, and part State of the Union address. Its main themes were continuity and action. Praising Kennedy as the "greatest leader of our time," Johnson pledged to "continue the forward thrust of America that he began." He reassured America's allies that it would keep its commitments around the globe, ready always to "defend the national interest and to negotiate the common interest." The Kennedyesque tone of such passages was not accidental. Written by Ted Sorensen, JFK's chief wordsmith, the speech established a sense of rhetorical continuity with the slain President.

The sense of continuity was substantive as well. "Let us continue," Johnson declared, as he called upon Congress to enact Kennedy's proposals for civil rights legislation, tax reform, improved education, and care for the elderly. By making Kennedy's priorities his own, Johnson turned the country's attention from "this evil moment" to the future and "the destiny that history has set for us." The speech could not have been better suited for the situation. It allowed Johnson, as Doris Kearns Goodwin has noted, to serve both as the "faithful agent of Kennedy's intentions and the healing leader of a stunned and baffled nation."

◇◇◇

Mr. Speaker,[1] Mr. President,[2] members of the House, members of the Senate, my fellow Americans: All I have I would have given gladly not to be standing here today.

The greatest leader of our time has been struck down by the foulest deed of our time. Today John Fitzgerald Kennedy lives on in the immortal words and works that he left behind. He lives on in the mind and memories of mankind. He lives on in the hearts of his countrymen. No words are sad enough to express our sense of loss. No words are strong enough to express our determination to continue the forward thrust of America that he began.

The dream of conquering the vastness of space, the dream of partnership across the Atlantic and across the Pacific as well, the dream of a Peace Corps in less-developed nations, the dream of education for all of our children, the dream of jobs for all who seek them and need them, the dream of care for our elderly, the dream of an all-out attack on mental illness, and, above all, the dream of equal rights for all Americans, whatever their race or color—these and other American dreams have been vitalized by his drive and by his dedication. And now the ideas and the ideals which he so nobly represented must and will be translated into effective action.

Under John Kennedy's leadership, this nation has demonstrated that it has the courage to seek peace, and it has the fortitude to risk war. We have proved that we are a good and reliable friend to those who seek peace and freedom. We have shown that we can also be a formidable foe to those who reject the path of peace and those who seek to impose upon us or our allies the yoke of tyranny.

This nation will keep its commitments from South Vietnam to West Berlin.[3] We will be unceasing in the search for peace, resourceful in our pursuit of areas of agreement even with those with whom we differ, and generous and loyal to those who join with us in common cause. In this age when there can be no losers in peace and no victors in war, we must recognize the obligation to match national strength with national restraint. We must be prepared at one and the same time for both the confrontation of power and the limitation of power. We must be ready to defend the national interest and to negotiate the common interest.

This is the path that we shall continue to pursue. Those who test our courage will find it strong, and

---

1. John W. McCormack, Speaker of the House of Representatives.

2. Carl T. Hayden, President Pro Tempore of the Senate.

3. By 1963 the United States had 16,000 military advisors in South Vietnam and continued to support the people and government of West Berlin, which was surrounded by Soviet-controlled East Germany.

those who seek our friendship will find it honorable. We will demonstrate anew that the strong can be just in the use of strength and the just can be strong in the defense of justice.

And let all know we will extend no special privilege and impose no persecution. We will carry on the fight against poverty and misery and disease and ignorance in other lands and in our own. We will serve all the nation—not one section or one sector or one group, but all Americans.

These are the United States—a united people with a united purpose. Our American unity does not depend upon unanimity. We have differences, but now, as in the past, we can derive from those differences strength, not weakness, wisdom, not despair. Both as a people and a government, we can unite upon a program, a program which is wise and just, enlightened and constructive.

For thirty-two years Capitol Hill has been my home.[4] I have shared many moments of pride with you, pride in the ability of the Congress of the United States to act, to meet any crisis, to distill from our differences strong programs of national action. An assassin's bullet has thrust upon me the awesome burden of the presidency. I am here today to say I need your help; I cannot bear this burden alone. I need the help of all Americans, and all America.

This nation has experienced a profound shock, and in this critical moment it is our duty, yours and mine, as the government of the United States, to do away with uncertainty and doubt and delay and to show that we are capable of decisive action—that from the brutal loss of our leader we will derive not weakness but strength, that we can and will act and act now.

From this chamber of representative government, let all the world know and none misunderstand that I rededicate this government to the unswerving support of the United Nations, to the honorable and determined execution of our commitments to our allies, to the maintenance of military strength second to none, to the defense of the strength and the stability of the dollar, to the expansion of our foreign trade, to the reinforcement of our programs of mutual assistance and cooperation in Asia and Africa, and to our Alliance for Progress[5] in this hemisphere.

On the twentieth day of January in 1961, John F. Kennedy told his countrymen that our national work would not be finished "in the first thousand days, nor in the life of this administration, nor even perhaps in our lifetime on this planet." "But," he said, "let us begin."[6] Today, in this moment of new resolve, I would say to all my fellow Americans: Let us continue. This is our challenge—not to hesitate, not to pause, not to turn about and linger over this evil moment, but to continue on our course so that we may fulfill the destiny that history has set for us.

Our most immediate tasks are here on this hill. First, no memorial oration or eulogy could more eloquently honor President Kennedy's memory than the earliest possible passage of the civil rights bill for which he fought so long.[7] We have talked long enough in this country about equal rights. We have talked for a hundred years or more. It is time now to write the next chapter, and to write it in the books of law. I urge you again, as I did in 1957 and again in 1960,[8] to enact a civil rights law so that we can move forward to eliminate from this nation every trace of discrimination and oppression that is based upon race or color. There could be no greater source of strength to this nation, both at home and abroad.

And second, no act of ours could more fittingly continue the work of President Kennedy than the early passage of the tax bill for which he fought all

---

4. Johnson was secretary to Representative Richard Kleberg, 1931–1935; he was elected to the House in 1937 and to the Senate in 1948, where he served until becoming Vice President in 1961.

5. An assistance program for Latin America initiated by President Kennedy in 1961.

6. From Kennedy's inaugural address, January 20, 1961 (pages 341–344).

7. Kennedy had proposed a comprehensive civil rights bill in his speech of June 11, 1963 (pages 369–372). It was sent to Congress on June 19, 1963, and eventually became the Civil Rights Act of 1964.

8. As Senate Majority Leader, Johnson helped secure passage of the Civil Rights Act of 1957 and the Civil Rights Act of 1960, both of which were signed into law by President Dwight D. Eisenhower.

this long year.[9] This is a bill designed to increase our national income and federal revenues and to provide insurance against recession. That bill, if passed without delay, means more security for those now working, more jobs for those now without them, and more incentive for our economy.

In short, this is no time for delay. It is a time for action—strong, forward-looking action on the pending education bills to help bring the light of learning to every home and hamlet in America; strong, forward-looking action on youth employment opportunities; strong, forward-looking action on the pending foreign aid bill, making clear that we are not forfeiting our responsibilities to this hemisphere or to the world, nor erasing executive flexibility in the conduct of our foreign affairs; and strong, prompt, and forward-looking action on the remaining appropriation bills.

In this new spirit of action, the Congress can expect the full cooperation and support of the executive branch. And in particular I pledge that the expenditures of your government will be administered with the utmost thrift and frugality. I will insist that the government get a dollar's value for a dollar spent. The government will set an example of prudence and economy. This does not mean that we will not meet our unfilled needs or that we will not honor our commitments. We will do both.

As one who has long served in both houses of the Congress, I firmly believe in the independence and the integrity of the legislative branch. And I promise you that I shall always respect this. It is deep in the marrow of my bones. With equal firmness, I believe in the capacity and I believe in the ability of the Congress, despite the divisions of opinions which characterize our nation, to act—to act wisely, to act vigorously, to act speedily when the need arises. The need is here. The need is now. I ask your help.

We meet in grief, but let us also meet in renewed dedication and renewed vigor. Let us meet in action, in tolerance, and in mutual understanding. John Kennedy's death commands what his life conveyed—that America must move forward. The time has come for Americans of all races and creeds and political beliefs to understand and to respect one another. So let us put an end to the teaching and the preaching of hate and evil and violence. Let us turn away from the fanatics of the far left and the far right, from the apostles of bitterness and bigotry, from those defiant of law and those who pour venom into our nation's bloodstream.

I profoundly hope that the tragedy and the torment of these terrible days will bind us together in new fellowship, making us one people in our hour of sorrow. So let us here highly resolve that John Fitzgerald Kennedy did not live—or die—in vain.[10] And on this Thanksgiving eve, as we gather together to ask the Lord's blessing[11] and give him our thanks, let us unite in those familiar and cherished words:

> America, America,
> God shed His grace on thee,
> And crown thy good
> With brotherhood
> From sea to shining sea.[12]

---

9. Kennedy formally proposed a permanent reduction in U.S. income tax rates in his January 1963 State of the Union address.

10. An echo of Abraham Lincoln's Gettysburg Address, November 19, 1863.

11. From the opening line of the traditional Thanksgiving hymn "We Gather Together."

12. From "America the Beautiful," lyrics by Katharine Lee Bates.

Malcolm X

The Ballot or the Bullet

CLEVELAND, OHIO
APRIL 3, 1964

IN MARCH 1964 Malcolm X left the Nation of Islam and formed his own organization, the Muslim Mosque, Inc. In a series of speeches, he moved to articulate a modified approach to racial issues, one that set matters of religion to the side and focused on what he called black nationalism. On April 3 he spoke at the Cory Methodist Church in Cleveland as part of a symposium sponsored by the Congress of Racial Equality on "The Negro Revolt—What Comes Next?" Following CORE representative Louis Lomax to the microphone, he spoke about "The Ballot or the Bullet." The words of the title can be traced back at least to the abolitionist movement before the Civil War, but the ideas were vintage Malcolm.

As in Malcolm's "Message to the Grassroots" (pages 379–388), his extemporaneous delivery, defiant language, and colloquial diction reinforced the piercing content of his speech and created a powerful bond with his audience. After uniting blacks around opposition to their common enemy, the white man, he introduced his main theme: that 1964 was the year of the ballot or the bullet, the year in which white America would finally take meaningful steps to solve its race problem or witness an explosion of rage from the black community. He attacked white liberals, the Democratic Party, established civil rights leaders, and the federal government with equal fury. Rather than continuing to turn the other cheek to white violence, he said, blacks needed to stand up for their rights. As usual, he was careful not to advocate the use of violence except in self-defense, but that distinction was lost on many people, black and white alike, in the light of such statements as "Die for what you believe in. But don't die alone. Let your dying be reciprocal.... What's good for the goose is good for the gander."

Blending ideas promoted by Marcus Garvey earlier in the century and subsequently modified by Elijah Muhammad, Malcolm promoted the economic, social, and political philosophy of black nationalism. Because he believed that the conscience of white America was morally bankrupt, he also called for shifting the focus of race relations from civil rights to human rights, which would allow blacks to take their case before the United Nations, where dark-skinned people made up a voting majority. It was time, he declared, to expose Uncle Sam's hypocrisy to the world, time to show "how bloody his hands are." At the time, even militant blacks who might have been expected to be Malcolm's allies shied away from his ideas, but many of those ideas would later find expression in the speeches of Black Power leaders such as Stokely Carmichael (see pages 441–452).

Nine days after speaking in Cleveland, Malcolm left for Africa and the Middle East, where he undertook a much-publicized pilgrimage to Mecca that confirmed his growing conviction that the true teachings of Islam had been distorted by Elijah Muhammad. He also advanced the apostasy that some white people might not be inherently racist. How fully his view of whites had changed, however, and where the ideas of "The Ballot or the Bullet" would have taken him remain open questions. While speaking in New York City's Audubon Ballroom in February 1965, he was shot to death by three members of the Nation of Islam. At his funeral he was eulogized by Ozzie Davis, who proclaimed him "a prince, our own shining black prince, who didn't hesitate to die, because he loved us so." The apotheosis of Malcolm that would take him from the feared, polemical figure he had been in his lifetime to the iconic status he now occupies in public memory had begun.

◇◇

Mr. Moderator, Brother Lomax,[1] brothers and sisters, friends and enemies: I just can't believe everyone in here is a friend and I don't wanna leave anybody out. The question tonight, as I understand it, "The Negro Revolt, and Where Do We Go From Here?" or "What Next?" in my little humble way of understanding it, it points toward either the ballot or the bullet.

Before we try and explain what is meant by the ballot or the bullet, I would like to clarify something concerning myself. I'm still a Muslim, my religion is still Islam. That's my personal belief. Just as Adam Clayton Powell[2] is a Christian minister who heads the Abyssinian Baptist Church in New York, but at the same time takes part in the political struggles to try and bring about rights to black people in this country; and Dr. Martin Luther King is also a Christian minister down in Atlanta, Georgia, who heads another organization[3] fighting for the civil rights of black people in this country; and Reverend Galamison,[4] I guess you've heard of him, [is] another Christian minister in New York who has been deeply involved in the school boycotts to eliminate segregated edu-

cation; well, I myself am a minister, not a Christian minister, but a Muslim minister, and I believe in action on all fronts by whatever means necessary.

Although I'm still a Muslim, I'm not here tonight to discuss my religion. I'm not here to try and change your religion. I'm not here to argue or to discuss anything that we differ about, because it's time for us to submerge our differences and realize that it is best for us to first see that we have the same problem, a common problem, a problem that will make you catch hell whether you're a Baptist or a Methodist or a Muslim or a nationalist. Whether you're educated or illiterate, whether you live on the boulevard or in the alley, you're gonna catch hell just like I am. We're all in the same boat, and we all are going to catch the same hell from the same man. He just happens to be a white man. All of us have suffered here, in this country, political oppression at the hands of the white man, economic exploitation at the hands of the white man, and social degradation at the hands of the white man.

Now, in speaking like this, [it] doesn't mean that we're antiwhite, but it does mean we're antiexploitation, we're antidegradation, we're antioppression. And if the white man doesn't want us to be anti-him, let him stop oppressing and exploiting and degrading us.

Whether we are Christians or Muslims or nationalists or agnostics or atheists, we must first learn to forget our differences. If we have differences, let us differ in the closet; when we come out in front, let us not have anything to argue about until we get finished

---

1. Representative of the Congress of Racial Equality who had preceded Malcolm on the platform.

2. Adam Clayton Powell Jr., U.S. Representative from Harlem.

3. Southern Christian Leadership Conference.

4. Milton A. Galamison, minister of the Siloam Presbyterian Church in Brooklyn.

arguing with the Man. If the late President Kennedy[5] could get together with Khrushchev[6] and exchange some wheat,[7] we certainly have more in common with each other than Kennedy and Khrushchev had with each other.

If we don't do something real soon, I think you'll have to agree we're going to be forced either to use the ballot or the bullet. It's one or the other in 1964. It isn't that time is running out—time has run out. Nineteen sixty-four threatens to be the most explosive year America has ever witnessed. The most explosive year. Why? It's also a political year. It's the year when all the white politicians will be back in the so-called Negro community jiving you and me for some votes. It's the year when all of the white political crooks will be right back—right back in your and my community with their false promises, building up our hopes for a letdown, building up our frustrations, nourishing our dissatisfactions. And as they with their trickery and their treachery, with their false promises which they don't intend to keep, as they nourish these dissatisfactions, it can only lead to one thing—an explosion.

And now we have the type of black man on the scene in America today—I'm sorry, Brother Lomax—who just doesn't intend to turn the other cheek any longer. Don't let anybody tell you anything about the odds are against you. If they draft you, they send you to Korea and make you face 800 million Chinese.[8] If you can be brave over there, you be brave right here. These odds aren't as great as those odds. And if you fight here, you will at least know what you're fighting for.

I'm not a politician, not even a student of politics; in fact, I'm not a student of much of anything. I'm not a Democrat. I'm not a Republican. I don't even consider myself an American. If you and I were

Americans, there'd be no problem. Those Hunkies[9] that just got off the boat, they're already Americans; the Polacks are already Americans; the Italian refugees are already Americans. Everything that came out of Europe, everything, every blue-eyed thing, is already an American. And as long as you been over here, as long as you and I have been over here, we aren't Americans yet.

Well, I am one who doesn't believe in deluding myself. I'm not going to sit at your table and watch you eat, with nothing on my plate, and call myself a diner. Sitting at the table doesn't make you a diner. You must be eating some of what's on that plate. Being here in America doesn't make you an American. Being born here in America doesn't make you an American. Why, if birth made you American, you wouldn't need any legislation, you wouldn't need any amendments to the Constitution, you wouldn't be faced with civil rights filibustering in Washington, D.C., right now.[10] They don't have to pass civil rights legislation to make a Polack an American.

No, I'm not an American. I'm one of the twenty-two million black people who are the victims of Americanism. One of the twenty-two million black people who are the victims of democracy, nothing but disguised hypocrisy. So I'm not standing here speaking to you as an American or a patriot or a flag-saluter or a flag-waver—no, not I. I'm speaking as a victim of this American system. And I see America through the eyes of a victim. I don't see any American dream; I see an American nightmare.

These twenty-two million victims are waking up. Their eyes are coming open. They're beginning to see what they used to only look at. They're becoming politically mature. They are realizing that there are new political trends from coast to coast. And as

5. John F. Kennedy, who was assassinated in November 1963.

6. Nikita Khrushchev, First Secretary of the Communist Party of the Soviet Union.

7. In October 1963 President Kennedy approved the sale of excess U.S. wheat to the Soviet Union to help offset shortfalls in the Soviet grain harvest. When completed in 1964, the sale amounted to 65 million bushels at a cost of $140 million.

8. Malcolm is referring to the Korean War of 1950–1953, in which North Korea was supported by China.

9. Disparaging term for a person from eastern or central Europe.

10. On March 9, 1964, the Senate began consideration of a civil rights bill previously approved by the House of Representatives. A group of Southern Senators launched a filibuster to prevent passage of the bill. The filibuster lasted until June 10, when the Senate brought it to an end by voting for cloture, paving the way for passage of the 1964 Civil Rights Act.

they see these new political trends, it's possible for them to see that every time there's an election, they have to have a recount when the races are so close. In Massachusetts, when they were running for Governor recently, they had to recount to see who was going to be Governor, it was so close.[11] It was the same way in Rhode Island, in Minnesota,[12] and in many other parts of the country. And the same with Kennedy and Nixon when they ran for President; it was so close they had to count all over again.[13] Well, what does this mean? It means that when white people are evenly divided and black people have a block of votes of their own, it is left up to them to determine who's gonna sit in the White House and who's gonna be in the dog house.

It was the black man's vote who put the present administration in Washington, D.C. Your vote, your dumb vote, your ignorant vote, your wasted vote put an administration in Washington, D.C., who has seen fit to pass every kind of legislation imaginable. They save you until last and then they filibuster on top of that. And your and my leaders have the audacity to run around clappin' their hands and talk about how much progress we're making and how what a good President we have.[14] If he wasn't good in Texas,[15] he sure can't be good in Washington, D.C. Texas is a lynch state. It is in the same breath as Mississippi, no different; they only lynch you in Texas with a Texas accent and lynch you in Mississippi with a Mississippi accent. And these Negro leaders have the audacity to go and have some coffee in the White House with

a Texan, a Southern cracker[16]—that's all he is—and then come out and tell you and me that he's going to be better for us because, since he's from the South, he knows how to deal with the Southerners. What kind of logic is that? Let Eastland[17] be President. He's from the South too. He should be better able to deal with them than Johnson.

In this present administration they have in the House of Representatives 257 Democrats to only 177 Republicans. They control two-thirds of the House vote. Why can't they pass something that will help you and me? In the Senate, there are sixty-seven Senators who are of the Democratic Party. Only thirty-three of them are Republicans. Why, the Democrats got the government sewed up, and you're the one who sewed it up for them. And what have they given you for it? Four years in office and just now getting around to some civil rights legislation. Just now, after everything else is gone, out of the way, they gonna sit down now and play with you all summer long—some old giant con game that they call filibuster.

All of 'em are in cahoots together. Don't you ever think they're not in cahoots together. The man that is heading, the man that is heading the civil rights filibuster is a man from Georgia named Richard Russell.[18] When Johnson became President, the first man he asked for when he got back to D.C. was "Dicky"—that's how tight they are. That's his boy, that's his pal, that's his buddy. But they're playing that old con game. One of 'em makes believe he's for you, and he's got it fixed where the other one is so tight against you, he never has to keep his promise.

No, it's time in 1964 to wake up. And when you see them coming up with that kind of conspiracy, let 'em know your eyes are open. And let 'em know you got something else that's wide open too. It's got to be the ballot or the bullet. The ballot or the bullet. If you're afraid to use an expression like that, you should

---

11. Malcolm is referring to the 1962 election, in which Democrat Endicott Peabody defeated Republican John Volpe.

12. John H. Chafee was elected Governor of Rhode Island in 1962 by 398 votes, while Karl Rolvaag won in Minnesota by 91 votes.

13. In 1960 John F. Kennedy defeated Richard Nixon in the popular vote by less than two-tenths of a percentage point, but there was not a recount of the vote.

14. Malcolm is referring to Lyndon B. Johnson, who became President after the assassination of John F. Kennedy in November 1963.

15. Born and raised in Texas, Johnson represented that state in the U.S. Congress for more than two decades before becoming Vice President in 1961.

---

16. Disparaging term for a white person.

17. James O. Eastland, U.S. Senator from Mississippi and a notorious segregationist.

18. U.S. Senator from Georgia.

get on out of the country, you should get back in the cotton patch, you should get back in the alley.

The Democrats do, they get all the Negro vote, and after they get it, the Negro gets nothing in return. All they did when they got to Washington was give a few big Negroes big jobs. Those big Negroes didn't even need big jobs; they already had jobs. That's camouflage, that's trickery, that's treachery, window dressing. I'm not tryin' to knock out the Democrats for the Republicans; we get to them in a minute. But it is you—you put the Democrats first and the Democrats put you last.

Look at it the way it is. What alibi do they use, since they control Congress and the Senate? What alibi do they use when you and I ask, "Well, when you gonna keep your promise?" They blame the Dixiecrats.[19] What is a Dixiecrat? A Democrat. A Dixiecrat is nothin' but a Democrat in disguise. The titular head of the Democrats is also the head of the Dixiecrats, because the Dixiecrats are a part of the Democratic Party. Mind you, the Democrats have never kicked the Dixiecrats out of the party. The Dixiecrats bolted themselves once, but the Democrats didn't put them out. Imagine, these low-down Southern segregationists puttin' the Northern Democrats down. But the Northern Democrats have never put the Dixiecrats down. No, look at that thing the way it is. They got a con game going on, a political con game, and you and I are in the middle. And it's time for you and me to wake up and start looking at it like it is and trying to understand it like it is. Then we can deal with it like it is.

The Dixiecrats in Washington, D.C., control the key committees that run this government. And the only reason the Dixiecrats control those committees is because they have seniority. The only reason they have seniority is because they come from states where Negroes can't vote. This is not even a government that's based on democracy. It's not a

government that is made up of the representatives of the people. Half of the people live in the South, and half of the people in the South can't even vote. Eastland is not even supposed to be in Washington. Half of the Senators and the Congressmen who occupy these key positions in Washington, D.C., are there illegally, are there unconstitutionally.

I was in Washington, D.C., a week ago Thursday when they were debating whether or not they should let the bill come onto the floor. And in the back of the room where the Senate meets, there's a huge map of the United States, and on that map it shows the location of Negroes in this country, how they are located throughout the country. And it shows that the Southern section of the country is more heavily populated with Negroes. And in the states where the Negroes are in the majority, these states are the ones that have Senators and Congressmen standing up in the Senate filibustering and doing all other kind[s] of trickery to keep the Negro from being able to vote. This is pitiful. But it's not pitiful for us any longer. It's actually pitiful for the white man because soon now, when the Negro awakens a little more and sees the vise that he's in, sees the bag that he's in, sees the real game that he's in, then the Negro's gonna develop some new tactics.[20]

These Senators and Congressmen actually violate the constitutional amendments that guarantee the people of that particular state or county the right to vote. And the Constitution itself has within it the machinery set up to expel any representative from a state where the voting rights of the people are violated. You don't even need new legislation. Any person in Congress right now who is there from a state or a district where the rights of the people—voting rights of the people—are violated, that particular person should be expelled from Congress. And when you expel him, you've removed one of the obstacles in the path of any real meaningful legislation in this country. In fact, when you expel them, you don't need new legislation because when you expel them, they will be replaced by black representatives from counties and

---

19. Originally, "Dixiecrats" referred to the States' Rights Party formed in 1948 after some three dozen Southern Democrats walked out of the Democratic National Convention in protest of its adoption of a strong civil rights plank (see pages 279–282). By the 1960s, the term was used to refer to any Southern supporter of racial segregation.

20. At this point, Malcolm inserted an aside, "Must be an integrationist playing with these lights," in reference to some momentary lighting problems in the auditorium.

districts where the black man is in the majority, not in the minority.

If the black man in these Southern states had his full voting rights, the key Dixiecrats in Washington, D.C., which means the key Democrats in Washington, D.C., would lose their seats. The Democratic Party itself would lose its power; it would cease to be powerful as a party. When you see the amount of power that would be lost by the Democratic Party if it were to lose the Dixiecrat wing or branch or element, you can see where it's against the interests of the Democrats to give voting rights to Negroes in states where the Democrats have been in complete power and authority ever since the Civil War.[21] You just can't belong to that party without analyzing it.

And as I say again, I'm not anti-Democrat, I'm not anti-Republican, I'm not anti-anything. I'm just questioning their sincerity and some of the strategy that they've been using on our people by promising them promises that they don't intend to keep. When you keep the Democrats in power, when you keep the Democrats in power, you're keeping the Dixiecrats in power. I doubt that my good Brother Lomax will deny that. A vote for a Democrat is a vote for a Dixiecrat. That's why in 1964 it's time now for you and me to become more politically mature and realize what the ballot is for; what we're supposed to get when we cast a ballot; and if we don't cast a ballot, it's going to end up into a situation where we're going to have to cast a bullet. It's either a ballot or a bullet.

In the North, they do it a different way. They, they have a system that's known as gerrymandering, whatever that means. It means when Negroes become too heavily concentrated in a certain area and begin to gain too much political power, the white man comes along and changes the district lines. That's all. You may say, "Why you keep sayin' white man?" Because it's the white man who does it. I haven't ever seen any Negro changing any lines. They don't let him get near the line. It's the white man who does this. And usually it's the white man who grins at you the most and pats you on the back and is supposed to be your friend. He may be friendly, but he's not your friend.

So what I'm trying to impress upon you in essence is this: You and I in America are faced not with a segregationist conspiracy, we're faced with a government conspiracy. Almost everybody, everyone who's filibustering is a Senator—that's the government. Everyone who's finagling in Washington, D.C., is a Congressman—that's the government. You don't have anybody puttin' blocks in your path but people who are a part of the government. The same government that you go abroad to fight for and die for is the government that has been in a conspiracy to deprive you of your voting rights, deprive you of your economic opportunity, deprive you of decent housing, deprive you of decent education. You don't need to go to the employer alone. It is the government itself, the government of America, that is responsible for the oppression and the exploitation and the degradation of black people in this country. And when you drop it in their lap, this government has failed the Negro. This so-called democracy has failed the Negro. And all these white liberals have definitely failed the Negro.

So where do we go from here? First, we need some new friends; we need some new allies. The entire civil rights struggle needs a new interpretation, a broader interpretation. We need to look at this civil rights thing from another angle, from the inside as well as from the outside. To those of us whose philosophy is black nationalism, the only way we can get involved in the civil rights struggle is give it a new interpretation. That old interpretation excluded us; it kept us out. So we're giving a new interpretation to the civil rights struggle, an interpretation that will enable us to come into it, take part in it. And these handkerchief-heads[22] who have been dillydallyin' and pussyfootin' and compromisin'—we don't intend to let them pussyfoot and dillydally and compromise any longer.

How can you thank a man for givin' you what's already yours? How, then, can you thank him for giving you only part of what's already yours? You haven't even made progress if what's being given to you, you should have had it already. That's not progress. And I love my Brother Lomax, the way he pointed out

---

21. 1861–1865.

22. Slang for sycophantic African Americans.

we're right back where we were in 1954. We're not even as far up as we were in 1954. We're behind where we were in 1954. There's more segregation now than there was in 1954. There's more, there's more racial animosity, more racial hatred, more racial violence today in 1964 than there was in 1954. Where is the progress?

And now you're facing a situation where the young Negro's comin' up. They don't wanna hear that turn-the-other-cheek stuff. No. In Jacksonville, those were teenagers; they were throwing Molotov cocktails.[23] Negroes have never done that before. But it shows you there's a new deal comin' in. There's a new thinkin' comin' in. There's new strategy comin' in. It'll be Molotov cocktails this month, hand grenades next month, and somethin' else next month. It'll be ballots or it'll be bullets. It'll be liberty or it will be death.[24]

The only difference between this kind of death, it'll be reciprocal. You know what is meant by "reciprocal"? That's one of Brother Lomax's words; I stole it from him. I don't usually deal with those big words 'cause I don't usually deal with big people. I deal with small people. I find you can get a whole lot of small people and whip hell out of a whole lot of big people. They haven't got anything to lose, and they got everything to gain. And they'll let you know in a minute: "It takes two to tango. When I go, you go."

The black nationalists, those whose philosophy is black nationalism, in bringing about this new interpretation to the entire meaning of civil rights look upon it as meaning, as Brother Lomax has pointed out, equality of opportunity. Well, we're justified in seeking civil rights if it means equality of opportunity, because all we're doing there is trying to collect for our investment. Our mothers and fathers invested sweat and blood. Three hundred and ten years we worked in this country without a dime in return. I mean without a dime in return. You let the white man walk around here talkin' about how rich this country is, but you never stop to think how it got rich so quick. It got rich—you made it rich.

You take the people who are in this audience right now. They're poor; we're all poor as individuals. Our weekly salary individually amounts to hardly anything. But if you take the salary of everyone in here collectively, it'll fill up a whole lot of baskets. It's a lot of wealth. If you can collect the wages of just these people right here for a year, you'll be rich, richer than rich. When you look at it like that, think how rich Uncle Sam had to become, not with this handful, but millions of black people—your and my mother and father, who didn't work a eight-hour shift, but worked from "can't see" in the morning until "can't see" at night and worked for nothing, makin' the white man rich, makin' Uncle Sam rich.

This is our investment. This is our contribution—our blood. Not only did we give of our free labor, we gave of our blood. Every time he had a call to arms, we were the first ones in uniform. We died on every battlefield the white man had. We have made a greater sacrifice than anybody who's standing up in America today. We have made a greater contribution and have collected less—have collected less. Civil rights, to those of us whose philosophy is black nationalism, means: "Give it to us now. Don't even wait [for] next year. Give it to us yesterday, and that's not fast enough."

I might stop right here to point out one thing. Whenever you're going after something that belongs to you, anyone who's depriving you of the right to have it is a criminal. Understand that. Whenever you are going after something that is yours, you are within your legal rights to lay claim to it. And anyone who puts forth any effort to deprive you of that which is yours is breaking the law, is a criminal. And this was pointed out by the Supreme Court decision.[25] It outlawed segregation. Which means segregation is against the law. Which means a segregationist is breakin' the law. A segregationist is a criminal—can't label him as anything other than that. And when you demonstrate against segregation, the law is on your side. The Supreme Court is on your side.

---

23. Malcolm is referring to protests that took place in Jacksonville, Florida, in March 1964.

24. A play on Patrick Henry's "Liberty or Death" speech of March 23, 1775.

---

25. Malcolm is referring to the 1954 *Brown v. Topeka, Kansas, Board of Education* decision that declared segregation in the public schools to be unconstitutional.

Now, who is it that opposes you in carrying out the law? The police department itself, with police dogs and clubs. Whenever you demonstrate against segregation, whether it is segregated education, segregated housing, segregated anything else, the law is on your side, and anyone who stands in your way is not the law any longer. They are breaking the law; they are not representatives of the law. Any time you demonstrate against segregation and a man has the audacity to put a police dog on you, kill that dog. Kill him. I'm telling you—kill that dog. I say it, if they put me in jail tomorrow, kill that dog. Then you'll put a stop to it. Now, if these white people in here don't want to see that kind of action, get down and tell the mayor to tell the police department to pull the dogs in. That's all you have to do. If you don't do it, someone else will.

If you don't take this kind of stand, your little children will grow up and look at you and think, "Shame." If you don't take an uncompromising stand—I don't mean, I don't mean go out and get violent; but at the same time you should never be nonviolent unless you run into some nonviolence. I'm nonviolent with those who are nonviolent with me. And I'll get insane and violent. When you drop that violence on me, then you've made me go insane, and I'm not responsible for what I do. And that's the way every Negro should get. Any time you know you're within the law, within your legal rights, within your moral rights, in accord with justice, then die for what you believe in. But don't die alone. Let your dying, let your dying be reciprocal. That's what is meant by equality: What's good for the goose is good for the gander.

So when we begin to get in this area, we need new friends, we need new allies. We need to expand the civil rights struggle to a higher level—to the level of human rights. Whenever you are in a civil rights struggle, whether you know it or not, you are confining yourself to the jurisdiction of Uncle Sam. No one from the outside world can speak out in your behalf as long as your struggle is a civil rights struggle. Civil rights comes within the domestic affairs of this country. All of our African brothers and our Asian brothers and our Latin American brothers cannot open their mouths and interfere in the domestic affairs of the United States. And as long as it's civil rights, this comes under the jurisdiction of Uncle Sam.

But the United Nations has what's known as the charter on human rights;[26] it has a committee that deals in human rights. You may wonder why, of all of the atrocities that have been committed in Africa and in Hungary[27] and in Asia and in Latin America, why do they bring it before the UN and never the Negro problem before the UN. This is part of the conspiracy. This old, tricky, blue-eyed liberal who is supposed to be your and my friend, supposed to be in our corner, supposed to be subsidizing our struggle, and supposed to be acting in the capacity of an adviser, never tells you anything about human rights. They keep you wrapped up in civil rights. And you spend so much time barkin' up the civil rights tree, you don't even know there's a human rights tree on the same floor.

When you expand the civil rights struggle to the level of human rights, you can then take the case of the black man in this country before the nations in the UN. You can take it before the General Assembly. You can take it, you can take Uncle Sam before a world court. But the only level you can do it on is the level of human rights. Civil rights keeps you under his restriction, under his jurisdiction. Civil rights keeps you in his pocket. Civil rights means you're asking Uncle Sam to treat you right. Human rights are somethin' you were born with. Human rights are your God-given rights. Human rights are the rights that are recognized by all nations of this earth. And any time anyone violates your human rights, you can take them to [the] World Court.[28]

Uncle Sam's hands are drippin' with blood, drippin' with the blood of the black man in this country. He's the earth's number-one hypocrite. Yes, he is. Imagine him posing as the leader of the free world. The free world! And you are over here singing "We Shall Overcome."[29] Expand the civil rights struggle to the level of human rights. Take it into the United

---

26. The Universal Declaration of Human Rights, adopted in December 1948 (see pages 291–294).

27. A reference to the Soviet Union's violent suppression of the 1956 Hungarian Revolution.

28. Formally known as the International Court of Justice, the primary judicial organ of the United Nations.

29. Unofficial anthem of the civil rights movement.

Nations where our African brothers can throw their weight on our side, where our Asian brothers can throw their weight on our side, where our Latin American brothers can throw their weight on our side, and where 800 million Chinamen are sittin' there waitin' to throw their weight on our side.

When you take your case to Washington, D.C., you're taking it to the criminal who's responsible. It's like running from the wolf to the fox. They're all in cahoots together. They all work political chicanery and make you look like a chump before the eyes of the world. Here you are walkin' around in America, getting ready to be drafted and sent abroad like a tin solder, and when you get over there, people ask you what are you fightin' for, and you have to stick your tongue in your cheek. No, take Uncle Sam to court, take him before the world. Let the world know how bloody his hands are. Let the world know the hypocrisy that's practiced over here. Let it be the ballot or the bullet. And let him know that it must be the ballot or the bullet.

By ballot I only mean freedom. Don't you know—I disagree with Lomax on this issue—that the ballot is more important than the dollar? Can I prove it? Yes, look in the UN. There are poor nations in the UN, but yet those poor nations can get together with their voting power and keep the rich nations from makin' a move. They have one nation, one vote. Everyone has an equal vote. And when those brothers from Asia and Africa and the darker parts of this earth get together, their voting power is sufficient to hold Sam in check or Russia in check or some other section of the earth in check.

So the ballot is most important. And right now in this country, if you and I, twenty-two million African Americans—that's what we are, Africans who are in America. You're nothin' but Africans, nothin' but Africans. In fact, you'd get farther calling yourself a African than calling yourself Negro. African[s] don't catch no hell. You're the only one catch hell. They don't have to pass civil rights bills for Africans. An African can go anywhere he wants right now. All you've got to do is tie your head up. That's right, go anywhere you want. Just stop being a Negro. Change your name to Hoogagagooba. That'll show you how silly the white man is. You dealin' with a silly man.

A friend of mine who's very dark put a turban on his head and went into a restaurant in Atlanta before they called themselves desegregated. And he went in a white restaurant, he sat down, they served him, and he said, "What would happen if a Negro come in here?" And he's sitting up there black as night. But because he had his head wrapped up, the waitress looked back at him and says, "Why, wouldn't no nigger dare come in here."

So you're dealing with a man, you're dealing with a man whose bias and prejudice is making him lose his mind, his intelligence, every day. He's frightened. He looks around and sees what's taking place on this earth, and he sees that the pendulum of time is swinging in your direction. The dark people are waking up. They're losing their fear of the white man. No place right now where he's fighting is he winning. Everywhere he's fighting, he's fighting someone your and my complexion. And they're beating him. He can't win anymore.

He has won his last battle. He failed to win the Korean War. He couldn't win it; he had to sign a truce. That's a loss. Any time Uncle Sam, with all his machinery for warfare, is held to a draw by some rice eaters, why, he lost the battle. He had to sign a truce. America's not supposed to sign a truce. She's supposed to be bad. But she's not bad anymore. She's bad as long as she can use her hydrogen bomb, but she can't use hers for fear Russia might use hers. Russia can't use hers for fear that Sam might use hers. So both of them are weaponless. They can't use the weapon because each other's weapon nullifies the weapon itself.

So the only [place] where action can take place is on the ground. And the white man can't win another war fightin' on the ground. His days are over. Yes, the black man knows it, the brown man knows it, the red man knows it, and the yellow man knows it. So they engage him in guerrilla warfare. That's not his style. You got to have heart to be a guerrilla warrior, and he hasn't got any heart. I'm telling you now. I just wanna give you a little briefing on guerrilla warfare because before you know it, before you know it[30]—

---

30. Instead of finishing this sentence verbally, Malcolm slowed his rate and used his tone of voice to imply that guerilla warfare might arise between blacks and whites in the United States.

It takes heart to be a guerrilla warrior 'cause you're on your own. In conventional warfare you have tanks and a whole lotta other people with you to back you up, and planes over your head and all that kind of stuff. But a guerrilla is on his own. All you have is a rifle, some sneakers, and a bowl of rice. And that's all you need—and a lot of heart. The Japanese on some of those islands in the Pacific, when the American soldiers landed, one Japanese sometimes could hold the whole army of 'em off.[31] He'd just wait until the sun went down, and when the sun went down, they were all equal. He would take his little blade and slip from bush to bush and from American to American. The white soldiers couldn't cope with that. Whenever you see a white soldier that fought in the Pacific, he has the shakes, he has a nervous condition, 'cause they scared him to death.

The same thing happened to the French up in French Indochina. People who just a few years previously were rice farmers got together and ran the heavily mechanized French army out of Indochina.[32] You don't need it; this modern warfare today won't work. This is the day of the guerrilla. They did the same thing in Algeria. Algerians, who were nothing but Bedouins, took a rifle and sneaked off to the hills, and de Gaulle[33] and all of his highfalutin war machinery couldn't defeat those guerrillas.[34]

Nowhere on this earth does the white man win in a guerrilla warfare. It's not his speed. Just as guerrilla warfare is prevailing in Asia and in parts of Africa and in parts of Latin America, you've got to be mighty naive, or you've got to play the black man cheap, if you don't think someday he's goin' wake up and find that it's got to be the ballot or the bullet.

I would like to say, in closing, concerning us, the Muslim Mosque, Incorporated, which fate compelled me to establish recently in New York City,[35] it's true we're Muslims and our religion is Islam, but we don't mix our religion with our politics and our economics and our social and civic activities—not any more. We keep our religion in our mosque. After our religious services are over, then as Muslims we become involved in political action, economic action, and social and civic action. We become involved with anybody, anywhere, any time, and in any manner that's designed to eliminate the evils, the political and economic and social evils that are afflicting the people of our community.

The political philosophy of black nationalism means that the black man should control the politics and the politicians in his own community—no more. The black man in the black community has to be reeducated into the science of politics so he will know what politics is supposed to bring him in return. Don't be throwing out any ballots. A ballot is like a bullet. You don't throw your ballot until you see a target, and if that target is not within your reach, keep your ballot in your pocket.

The political philosophy of black nationalism is being taught in the Christian church. It's being taught in the NAACP.[36] It's being taught in CORE[37] meetings. It's being taught in SNCC[38] meetings. It's being taught in Muslim meetings. It's being taught where nothing but atheists and agnostics come together. It's being taught everywhere. Black people are fed up with the dillydallyin', pussyfootin', compromisin' approach that we've been using toward getting our freedom. We want freedom now, but we're not gonna get it singin' "We Shall Overcome." We got to fight until we overcome.

The economic philosophy of black nationalism is pure and simple. It only means that we should control the economy of our community. Why should white people be running all the stores in our

---

31. Malcolm is referring to operations in the Pacific theater during World War II.

32. Malcolm is referring to the Indochina War of 1946–1954, in which Vietnam won its independence from France.

33. French President Charles de Gaulle.

34. Malcolm is referring to the Algerian War of Independence, 1954–1962.

35. Malcolm founded the Muslim Mosque, Incorporated, in March 1964, shortly after he left the Nation of Islam.

36. National Association for the Advancement of Colored People.

37. Congress of Racial Equality.

38. Student Nonviolent Coordinating Committee.

community? Why should white people be running the banks of our community? Why should they, why should the economy of our community be in the hands of the white man? Why? For [if] a black man can't move his store into a white community, you tell me why a white man should move his store into a black community.

The political philosophy of black nationalism involves a reeducation program in the black community in regards to economics. Our people have to be made to see that anytime you take your dollar out of your community and spend it in a community where you don't live, the community where you live will get poorer and poorer, the community where you spend your money will get richer and richer, and then you wonder why where you live is always a ghetto or a slum area. And where you and I are concerned, not only when we spend it out of the community do we lose it, but the white man got all our stores in the community tied up, so that though we spend it in the community, at sundown the man who runs the store takes it over crosstown somewhere. He's got us in a vise.

So the economic philosophy of black nationalism is pure and simple. It means in every church, in every civic organization, in every fraternal order, it is time now for our people to become conscious of the importance of controlling the economy of our community. If we own the stores, if we operate the businesses, if we try and establish some industry in our own community, then we are developing to the position where we are creating employment for our own kind. Once you gain control of the economy of your own community, then you don't have to picket and boycott and beg some cracker downtown for a job in his business.

The social philosophy of black nationalism only means that we have to get together and remove the evils, the vices—alcoholism, drug addiction, and other evils—that are destroying the moral fiber of our community. We ourselves have to lift the level of our community, the standard of our community, to a higher level, make our own society beautiful so that we will be satisfied in our own social circles and won't be runnin' around here trying to knock our way into a social circle where we're not wanted.

So I say, in my conclusion, in spreading a gospel such as black nationalism, which is designed to make the black man not reevaluate the white man—you know him already—but make the black man reevaluate himself. Don't change the white man's mind; you can't change his mind. And that whole thing about appealing to the moral conscience of America, America's conscience is bankrupt. She lost all conscience [a] long time ago. No, Uncle Sam has no conscience. They don't know what morals are. They don't try and eliminate an evil because it's evil or because it's illegal or because it's immoral. They eliminate it only when it threatens their existence. So you wastin' your time appealing to the moral consciousness of a bankrupt man like Uncle Sam. If he had a conscience, he'd straighten this thing out with no more pressure being put upon him.

So it is not necessary to change the white man's mind. We have to change our own mind. You can't change his mind about us. We got to change our own minds about each other. We have to see each other with new eyes. We have to see each other as brothers and sisters. We have to come together with warmth so we can develop [the] unity and harmony that's necessary to get this problem solved ourselves.

How can we do that? How can we avoid jealousy? How can we avoid the suspicion and the divisions that exist in the community? I watched how Billy Graham[39] comes into a city, spreading what he calls the gospel of Christ, which is only white nationalism. That's what he is; Billy Graham is a white nationalist. I'm a black nationalist. But since it's the natural tendency for leaders to be jealous and look upon a popular figure like Graham with suspicion and envy, how is it possible for him to come into a city and get the cooperation of all the church leaders? And don't think 'cause they're church leaders that they don't have weaknesses that make 'em envious and jealous—no, everybody got it. It's not an accident that when they want to choose a cardinal[40] over there in Rome, that they get in a closet so you can't hear 'em cussin' and fightin' and carryin' on.

---

39. America's foremost Christian evangelist during the second half of the 20th century.

40. Malcolm may have meant to say "pope."

Billy Graham comes in preaching the gospel of Christ. He evangelizes the gospel, he stirs everybody up, but he never tries to start a church. If he came in trying to start a church, all the churches would be against him. So what he does, he just comes in talking about Christ and tells everybody who gets Christ, he tells 'em, "Go to any church where Christ is." And in this way the church cooperates with him. So we're goin' take a page from his book.

Our gospel is black nationalism. We're not tryin' to threaten the existence of any organization, but we're spreading the gospel of black nationalism. And anywhere there's a church that is also preaching and practicing the gospel of black nationalism, join that church. If the NAACP is preachin' and practicin' the gospel of black nationalism, join the NAACP. If CORE is spreadin' and practicin' the gospel of black nationalism, join CORE. Join any organization that has the gospel in it that's for the upliftment of the black man. And when you get into it and see them pussyfootin' or compromisin', pull out of it 'cause that's not black nationalism. Go find another one.

And in this manner, the organizations will increase in number and in quantity and in quality, and by August it is then our intention to have a black nationalist convention which will consist of delegates from all over the country who are interested in the political, economic, and social philosophy of black nationalism.[41] And after these delegates convene, we will hold seminars, we will hold discussions, we will listen to everyone. We want to hear new ideas and new solutions and new answers. And at that time, if we see fit then to form a black nationalist party, we'll form a black nationalist party. If it's necessary to form a black nationalist army, we'll form a black nationalist army. It'll be the ballot or the bullet. It'll be liberty or it'll be death.

It's time for you and me to stop sittin' in this country, lettin' some cracker Senators, Northern crackers and Southern crackers, sit down in Washington, D.C., and come to a conclusion in their mind that you and I are supposed to have civil rights. There no white man tell me anything about my rights. Brothers and

sisters, always remember: If it doesn't take Senators and Congressmen and presidential proclamations to give freedom to the white man, it is not necessary for legislation or proclamations or Supreme Court decisions to give freedom to the black man. You let that white man know if this is a country of freedom, let it be a country of freedom. And if it's not a country of freedom, change it.

We will work with anybody, anywhere, at any time who is genuinely interested in tackling the problem head-on—nonviolently as long as the enemy is nonviolent, but get violent when the enemy gets violent. We'll work with you on the voters' registration drive, we'll work with you on rent strikes, we'll work with you on school boycotts.

And I don't believe in any kind of integration. I'm not even worried about it, but I know you not gonna get it anyway. You not gonna get it 'cause you afraid to die. You gotta die. Try and force yourself on the white man; he'll get just as violent as those crackers in Mississippi—right here in Cleveland. But we will still work with you on the school boycotts because we're against a segregated school system.[42] A segregated school system produces children who, when they graduate, graduate with crippled minds. But this does not mean because a school is all black, it's segregated. A segregated school means a school that is controlled by people who have no real interest in it whatsoever.

Just let me explain what I mean. A segregated district or community is a community in which people live but outsiders control the politics and the economy of that community. They never refer to the white section as a segregated community. It's the all-Negro section that's a segregated community. Why? The white man controls his own school, his own banks, his own economy, his own politics, his own everything, his own community. But he also controls yours. So when you're under someone else's control, you're segregated. They'll always give you the lowest or the worst that there is to offer, but because you

41. Such a convention was not held.

42. At the time of Malcolm's speech, civil rights organizations were planning a one-day boycott of the Cleveland public schools to support demands for fuller school integration; the boycott was held on April 20.

have your own, it doesn't mean you're segregated. But you've got to control your own. Just like the white man has control of his, you need to control yours.

Now, you know the best way to get rid of segregation? The white man is more afraid of separation than he is of integration. Segregation means that he puts you away from him, but not far enough for you to be out of his jurisdiction. Separation means you gone. And the white man, the white man will integrate faster than he'll let you separate. So we will work with you against the segregated school system because it's criminal and what it does absolutely is destructive in every way imaginable to the minds of the children who have to be exposed to that type of crippling education.

Last but not least, I must say this concerning the great controversy over rifles and shotguns:[43] The only thing that I've ever said is that in areas where the government has proven itself either unwilling or unable to defend the lives and the property of Negroes, it's time for Negroes to defend themselves. Article Number Two of the constitutional amendments[44] provides you and me the right to own a rifle or a shotgun. It's constitutionally legal to own a shotgun or a rifle. This doesn't mean you're gonna get a rifle and form battalions and go out lookin' for white folks, although you'd be within your rights. I mean you'd be justified, but that would be illegal, and we don't do anything illegal.

If the white man doesn't want the black man buying rifles and shotguns, then let the government do its job. That's all. And don't let the white man come to you and ask you what do you think about what Malcolm says. Why, you old Uncle Tom.[45] He wouldn't never ask you if he thought you were goin' say, "Amen!" No, he is making a Tom out of you.

So this doesn't mean you form rifle clubs and going out lookin' for people. But it is time in 1964, if you're a man, to let that man know: If he's not gonna do his job in running the government and providing you and me with the protection that our taxes are supposed to be for, since he spends how many billions for defense? Since he spends all that money for his defense budget, he certainly can't grudge you and me spending twelve or fifteen dollars for a single-shot or a double-action.

I hope you understand. Don't go out shooting people. But anytime, brothers and sisters, and especially the men in this audience—you and I in 1963,[46] some of you all wearin' Congressional Medals of Honor, got shoulders this wide, chests this big, muscles that big—sit around and read where they bomb a church and murder in cold blood, not some grown-ups, but four little girls while they were praying to the same god the white man taught 'em to pray to,[47] and you and I see the government go down there and can't find who did it.

Why, this man found, they found Eichmann[48] while he was hiding down in Argentina somewhere. Two or three American soldiers who are minding somebody else's business way over in South Vietnam[49] can get killed and he'll send battleships, stickin' his nose in their business. He wanted to send troops down to Cuba and make 'em have what he calls some free elections,[50] and this old cracker don't have free elections in this country. No, if you don't never see me another time in your life, if I die in the mornin', I'll die sayin' one thing: The ballot or the bullet. The ballot or the bullet.

---

43. When Malcolm announced his separation from the Nation of Islam three weeks before this speech, he stated that "it is legal and lawful to own a shotgun or rifle" and that blacks should form rifle clubs to defend their lives and property in times of emergency.

44. The Bill of Rights.

45. Disparaging term for a black person who is seen as submissive to white people; derived from the title character of Harriet Beecher Stowe's *Uncle Tom's Cabin* (1852).

46. Malcolm meant to say 1964.

47. Malcolm is referring to the September 15, 1963, bombing of the 16th Street Baptist Church in Birmingham, Alabama, that took the lives of four African American girls aged 11 to 14.

48. Adolf Eichmann, Nazi war criminal captured by Israeli Mossad agents in May 1960.

49. Although the massive buildup of American forces would not begin until 1965, there were more than 20,000 U.S. military personnel in Vietnam in 1964.

50. Most likely a reference to the unsuccessful Bay of Pigs invasion of April 1961.

If a Negro in 1964 has to sit around and wait for some cracker Senators to filibuster when it comes to the rights of black people, why, you and I should hang our heads in shame. You talk about a March on Washington in 1963, you haven't seen anything. There's some more goin' down in '64. And this time they're not goin' like they went last year. They not goin' singing "We Shall Overcome." They not goin' with white friends. They not goin' with placards already painted for them. They not goin' with round-trip tickets. They goin' with one-way tickets.

And if they don't want that non-nonviolent army going down there, tell 'em: "Bring the filibuster to a halt." The black nationalists aren't gonna wait. Lyndon B. Johnson is the head of the Democratic Party. If he's for civil rights, let him go into the Senate next week and declare himself. Let him go in there right now and declare himself. Let him go in there and denounce the Southern branch of his party. Let him go in there right now and take a moral stand—right now, not later. Tell him, "Don't wait until election time." If he waits too long, brothers and sisters, he will be responsible for letting a condition develop in this country which will create a climate that will bring seeds up out of the ground with vegetation on the end of 'em lookin' like something these people never dreamt of. In 1964 it's the ballot or the bullet.

Thank you.

Lyndon B. Johnson

The Great Society

Ann Arbor, Michigan
May 22, 1964

By the spring of 1964, the initial trauma associated with the assassination of John F. Kennedy was beginning to subside. President Johnson had repeatedly paid homage to the fallen leader both rhetorically and programmatically. He urged Congress to continue the Kennedy legacy and vowed to see JFK's civil rights bill through to passage, which he would do in July 1964. In the meantime, another issue had to be addressed: the upcoming presidential election. Having spent the previous three years in Kennedy's shadow, Johnson needed to go beyond the former President's agenda and define for the electorate who he was and what he stood for. As JFK had invited voters to endorse his New Frontier in 1960, LBJ would lay before the electorate his vision of the Great Society.

Johnson first employed the phrase "great society" at a fund-raising dinner in Chicago on April 23, 1964. There followed in quick succession seven more speeches in which he used it, but the media did not pick up on it. So Johnson decided to devote an entire speech to the subject. That speech was delivered on May 22, 1964, during graduation exercises at the University of Michigan.

Talking to 85,000 people in America's largest football stadium, Johnson said the United States had "the opportunity to move not only toward the rich society and the powerful society, but upward to the Great Society." Such a society would rebuild America's cities, preserve the environment, put an end to poverty, ensure equal rights for all citizens, and create an educational system in which every child could realize his or her dreams. Its ultimate objective, however, was moral as well as material. Economic abundance, Johnson said, "is only the foundation on which we will build a richer life of mind and spirit." For the first time, it was possible to "build a society where the demands of morality and the needs of the spirit can be realized in the life of the nation."

From this point on, the media began to tag LBJ's vision for America as the "Great Society," giving him a pithy slogan for the election campaign. That fall, Johnson won in a landslide against Republican Barry Goldwater. In keeping with the theme of the Great Society, most voters expected his presidency to focus on domestic issues and on improving life in the United States. Less than three months after his inauguration in January 1965, however, he began a massive buildup of U.S. troops in Vietnam—despite pledging in the election campaign not to do so—and the promise of the Great Society would soon prove evanescent as America became more and more entangled in the jungles of Southeast Asia.

◇◇◇◇◇◇◇◇◇◇◇◇◇◇◇◇◇◇◇◇◇◇◇◇◇◇◇◇◇◇◇◇◇◇◇◇

President Hatcher,[1] Governor Romney,[2] Senators McNamara and Hart,[3] Congressmen Meader and Staebler,[4] and other members of the fine Michigan delegation, members of the graduating class, my fellow Americans: It is a great pleasure to be here today.

This university has been coeducational since 1870, but I do not believe it was on the basis of your accomplishments that a Detroit high-school girl said, and I quote: "In choosing a college, you first have to decide whether you want a coeducational school or an educational school." Well, we can find both here at Michigan, although perhaps at different hours.

I came out here today very anxious to meet the Michigan student whose father told a friend of mine that his son's education had been a real value: It stopped his mother from bragging about him.

I have come today from the turmoil of your capital[5] to the tranquility of your campus to speak about the future of your country.

The purpose of protecting the life of our nation and preserving the liberty of our citizens is to pursue the happiness of our people. Our success in that pursuit is the test of our success as a nation.

For a century we labored to settle and to subdue a continent. For half a century we called upon unbounded invention and untiring industry to create an order of plenty for all of our people. The challenge of the next half century is whether we have the wisdom to use that wealth to enrich and elevate our national life and to advance the quality of our American civilization. Your imagination and your initiative and your indignation will determine whether we build a society where progress is the servant of our needs or a society where old values and new visions are buried under unbridled growth. For in your time

1. University of Michigan President Harlan Hatcher.

2. Michigan Governor George Romney.

3. Patrick McNamara and Philip Hart, U.S. Senators from Michigan.

4. George Meader and Neil Staebler.

5. Johnson is referring to the ongoing debate in the U.S. Senate to end a filibuster against what would eventually become the 1964 Civil Rights Act.

we have the opportunity to move not only toward the rich society and the powerful society, but upward to the Great Society.

The Great Society rests on abundance and liberty for all. It demands an end to poverty and racial injustice, to which we're totally committed in our time. But that is just the beginning. The Great Society is a place where every child can find knowledge to enrich his mind and to enlarge his talents. It is a place where leisure is a welcome chance to build and reflect, not a feared cause of boredom and restlessness. It is a place where the city of man serves not only the needs of the body and the demands of commerce but the desire for beauty and the hunger for community. It is a place where man can renew contact with nature. It is a place which honors creation for its own sake and for what it adds to the understanding of the race. It is a place where men are more concerned with the quality of their goals than the quantity of their goods.

But most of all, the Great Society is not a safe harbor, a resting place, a final objective, a finished work. It is a challenge constantly renewed, beckoning us toward a destiny where the meaning of our lives matches the marvelous products of our labor. So I want to talk to you today about three places where we begin to build the Great Society—in our cities, in our countryside, and in our classrooms.

Many of you will live to see the day, perhaps fifty years from now, when there will be four hundred million Americans, four-fifths of them in urban areas. In the remainder of this century urban population will double, city land will double, and we will have to build homes and highways and facilities equal to all those built since this country was first settled. So in the next forty years we must rebuild the entire urban United States.

Aristotle said: "Men come together in cities in order to live, but they remain together in order to live the good life."[6] It is harder and harder to live the good life in American cities today. The catalog of ills is long. There is the decay of the centers and the despoiling of the suburbs. There's not enough housing for our people or transportation for our traffic. Open land is vanishing and old landmarks are violated. Worst of all, expansion is eroding these precious and

time-honored values of community with neighbors and communion with nature. The loss of these values breeds loneliness and boredom and indifference.

And our society will never be great until our cities are great. Today the frontier of imagination and innovation is inside those cities and not beyond their borders. New experiments are already going on. It will be the task of your generation to make the American city a place where future generations will come not only to live but to live the good life.

And I understand that if I stayed here tonight, I would see that Michigan students are really doing their best to live the good life. This is the place where the Peace Corps was started.[7] It is inspiring to see how all of you, while you're in this country, are trying so hard to live at the level of the people.

A second place where we begin to build the Great Society is in our countryside. We have always prided ourselves on being not only America the strong and America the free, but America the beautiful. Today that beauty is in danger. The water we drink, the food we eat, the very air that we breathe are threatened with pollution. Our parks are overcrowded, our seashores overburdened. Green fields and dense forests are disappearing.

A few years ago we were greatly concerned about the ugly American.[8] Today we must act to prevent an ugly America. For once the battle is lost, once the battle is lost, once our natural splendor is destroyed, it can never be recaptured. And once man can no longer walk with beauty or wonder at nature, his spirit will wither and his sustenance be wasted.

A third place to build the Great Society is in the classrooms of America. There your children's lives will be shaped. Our society will not be great until every young mind is set free to scan the farthest reaches of thought and imagination. We are still far from that goal. Today, eight million adult Americans, more

6. *Politics*, book 3, chapter 6.

7. Johnson is referring to an October 14, 1960, speech at the University of Michigan in which John F. Kennedy introduced the idea that would later culminate in the founding of the Peace Corps.

8. An allusion to the 1958 bestseller *The Ugly American*, which maintained that the United States was losing Indochina to communism because of arrogance, incompetence, and corruption.

than the entire population of Michigan, have not finished five years of school. Nearly twenty million have not finished eight years of school. Nearly fifty-four million—more than one-quarter of all America—have not even finished high school. Each year more than one hundred thousand high-school graduates, with proved ability, do not enter college because they cannot afford it. And if we cannot educate today's youth, what will we do in 1970, when elementary-school enrollment will be five million greater than 1960? And high-school enrollment will rise by five million? And college enrollment will increase by more than three million?

In many places, classrooms are overcrowded and curricula are outdated. Most of our qualified teachers are underpaid, and many of our paid teachers are unqualified. So we must give every child a place to sit and a teacher to learn from. Poverty must not be a bar to learning, and learning must offer an escape from poverty.

But more classrooms and more teachers are not enough. We must seek an educational system which grows in excellence as it grows in size. And this means better training for our teachers. It means preparing youth to enjoy their hours of leisure as well as their hours of labor. It means exploring new techniques of teaching to find new ways to stimulate the love of learning and the capacity for creation.

These are three of the central issues of the Great Society. While our government has many programs directed at those issues, I do not pretend that we have the full answer to those problems. But I do promise this: We are going to assemble the best thought and the broadest knowledge from all over the world to find those answers for America. I intend to establish working groups to prepare a series of White House conferences and meetings—on the cities, on natural beauty, on the quality of education, and on other emerging challenges. And from these meetings and from this inspiration and from these studies we will begin to set our course toward the Great Society.

The solution to these problems [does] not rest on a massive program in Washington; nor can it rely solely on the strained resources of local authority. They require us to create new concepts of cooperation, a creative federalism, between the national capital and the leaders of local communities.

Woodrow Wilson once wrote: "Every man sent out from his university should be a man of his nation as well as a man of his time."[9] Within your lifetime powerful forces already loosed will take us toward a way of life beyond the realm of our experience, almost beyond the bounds of our imagination. For better or for worse, your generation has been appointed by history to deal with those problems and to lead America toward a new age. You have the chance never before afforded to any people in any age. You can help build a society where the demands of morality and the needs of the spirit can be realized in the life of the nation.

So will you join in the battle to give every citizen the full equality which God enjoins and the law requires, whatever his belief or race or the color of his skin?

Will you join in the battle to give every citizen an escape from the crushing weight of poverty?

Will you join in the battle to make it possible for all nations to live in enduring peace—as neighbors and not as mortal enemies?

Will you join in the battle to build the Great Society, to prove that our material progress is only the foundation on which we will build a richer life of mind and spirit?

There are those timid souls that say this battle cannot be won, that we are condemned to a soulless wealth. I do not agree. We have the power to shape the civilization that we want. But we need your will and your labor and your hearts if we are to build that kind of society.

Those who came to this land sought to build more than just a new country. They sought a new world. So I have come here today to your campus to say that you can make their vision our reality. So let us from this moment begin our work so that in the future men will look back and say: It was then, after a long and weary way, that man turned the exploits of his genius to the full enrichment of his life.

Thank you. Good-bye.

---

9. From Wilson's "University Training and Citizenship" (1894).

Barry Goldwater

Speech Accepting the Republican Presidential Nomination

SAN FRANCISCO, CALIFORNIA
JULY 16, 1964

B Y TRADITION, SPEECHES accepting a political party's presidential nomination seek to bind up lingering wounds from the primary election battles, to unify the disparate elements of the party, and to set forth a vision around which the entire party, as well as independent voters, can rally. But when Barry Goldwater stepped to the rostrum at the 1964 Republican National Convention, he was in no mood for conciliation.

Even before the primaries began, it was clear that the nomination process would be a war for the heart and soul of the Republican Party. On one side stood Goldwater, U.S. Senator from Arizona, whose rock-hard conservative principles helped him secure a solid majority of the delegates going into the convention. On the other side stood the party's moderate-liberal wing, represented by Pennsylvania Governor William Scranton and New York Governor Nelson Rockefeller. For a month before the convention, Scranton and Rockefeller continued their attacks on Goldwater, calling him a dangerous reactionary who would gut social programs and whose finger could not be trusted on the nuclear trigger. Although it was clear that Goldwater had the nomination sewed up, the convention was marked by repeated confrontations between his supporters and Scranton-Rockefeller backers. In the most notorious incident, Rockefeller was shouted down as he stood at the podium and associated the Goldwater forces with "goon squads, bomb threats,... and Nazi methods."

When it came time for his acceptance speech, Goldwater did not offer an olive branch. "This Republican Party," he declared, "is a party for free men, not for blind followers and not for conformists.... Those who do not care for our cause, we don't expect to enter our ranks in any case." He lashed the "false security of governmental paternalism" and reaffirmed his commitment to stop Communists from leading new nations down "the dark alleys of tyranny or the dead-end streets of collectivism."

What made the speech instantly famous, however, was its declaration that "extremism in the defense of liberty is no vice" and that "moderation in the pursuit of justice is no virtue." The statement was penned by Harry V. Jaffa, a professor at Ohio State University and one of the architects of the speech. Goldwater's supporters cheered it so wildly that he had to pause for almost a minute after the "extremism" line, but it did not play well in the rest of the country. Goldwater had already been charged with extremism by Democrats and the press, as well as by the Scranton-Rockefeller wing of his own party. Now here he was, with the nation watching, saying that extremism was "no vice."

No matter what Goldwater meant by the statement—and he certainly did not mean it as an endorsement of political extremism—it was a rhetorical and political disaster. Richard Nixon, who was in the audience at the Cow Palace, said if Goldwater "ever had a chance to win the presidency, he lost it that night with that speech.... I felt almost physically sick as I sat there." In November Goldwater gained only 39 percent of the popular vote, one of the most lopsided defeats in American history. In the long view, however, his campaign was far from a failure. By energizing the conservative wing of the Republican Party, it paved the way for the ascension of Ronald Reagan and the emergence of conservatism as a dominant force in American politics.

◇◇◇

To my good friend and great Republican, Dick Nixon,[1] and your charming wife, Pat; my running mate, that wonderful Republican who has served us so well for so long, Bill Miller,[2] and his wife, Stephanie; to Thruston Morton,[3] who's done such a commendable job in chairmanning this convention; to Mr. Herbert Hoover,[4] whom I hope is watching; and to that, that great American and his wife, General and Mrs. Eisenhower;[5] to my own wife, my family, and to all of my fellow Republicans here assembled, and Americans across this great nation: From this moment, united and determined, we will go forward together, dedicated to the ultimate and undeniable greatness of the whole man. Together, together we will win.

I accept your nomination with a deep sense of humility. I accept, too, the responsibility that goes with it, and I seek your continued help and your continued guidance. My fellow Republicans, our cause is too great for any man to feel worthy of it. Our task would be too great for any man did he not have with him the hearts and the hands of this great Republican Party. And I promise you tonight that every fiber of my being is consecrated to our cause—that nothing shall be lacking from the struggle that can be brought to it by enthusiasm, by devotion, and plain hard work. In this world no person, no party can guarantee anything, but what we can do and what we shall do is to deserve victory, and victory will be ours.

The good Lord raised this mighty republic to be a home for the brave and to flourish as the land of the free—not to stagnate in the swampland of collectivism, not to cringe before the bullying of communism. Now, my fellow Americans, the tide has been running against freedom. Our people have followed false prophets. We must, and we shall, return to proven ways—not because they are old, but because they are true. We must, and we shall, set the tides running again in the cause of freedom. And this party, with its every action, every word, every breath, and every heartbeat, has but a single resolve, and that

1. Richard M. Nixon, Vice President of the United States, 1953–1961, who spoke immediately before Goldwater.

2. William Miller, Goldwater's vice-presidential pick, served in the U.S. House of Representatives from 1951 to 1965.

3. U.S. Senator from Kentucky.

4. President of the United States, 1929–1933.

5. Dwight Eisenhower, President of the United States, 1953–1961, who addressed the convention on July 14.

is freedom—freedom made orderly for this nation by our constitutional government, freedom under a government limited by the laws of nature and of nature's God,[6] freedom balanced so that order lacking liberty will not become the slavery of the prison cell,[7] balanced so that liberty lacking order will not become the license of the mob and of the jungle.

Now, we Americans understand freedom. We have earned it, we have lived for it, and we have died for it. This nation and its people are freedom's model in a searching world. We can be freedom's missionaries in a doubting world. But, ladies and gentlemen, first we must renew freedom's mission in our own hearts and in our own homes.

During four futile years, the administration which we shall replace has, has distorted and lost that vision. It has talked and talked and talked and talked the words of freedom, but it has failed and failed and failed in the works of freedom. Now failures cement the wall of shame in Berlin.[8] Failures blot the sands of shame at the Bay of Pigs.[9] Failures mark the slow death of freedom in Laos. Failures infest the jungles of Vietnam.[10] And failures haunt the houses of our once-great alliances and undermine the greatest bulwark ever erected by free nations—the NATO[11] community. Failures proclaim lost leadership, obscure purpose, weakening will, and the risk of inciting our sworn enemies to new aggressions and to new excesses.

And because of this administration, we are tonight a world divided, we are a nation becalmed. We have lost the brisk pace of diversity and the genius of individual creativity. We are plodding along

at a pace set by centralized planning, red tape, rules without responsibility, and regimentation without recourse. Rather than useful jobs in our country, our people have been offered bureaucratic "make work"; rather than moral leadership, they have been given bread and circuses. They have been given spectacles and, yes, they've even been given scandals.

Tonight there is violence in our streets, corruption in our highest offices, aimlessness amongst our youth, anxiety among our elders, and there is a virtual despair among the many who look beyond material success for the inner meaning of their lives. And where examples of morality should be set, the opposite is seen. Small men, seeking great wealth or power, have too often and too long turned even the highest levels of public service into mere personal opportunity. Now, certainly, simple honesty is not too much to demand of men in government. We find it in most; Republicans demand it from everyone. They demand it from everyone no matter how exalted or protected his position might be.

The growing menace in our country tonight—to personal safety, to life, to limb and property, in homes, in churches, on the playgrounds and places of business, particularly in our great cities—is the mounting concern, or should be, of every thoughtful citizen in the United States.[12] Security from domestic violence, no less than from foreign aggression, is the most elementary and fundamental purpose of any government, and a government that cannot fulfill this purpose is one that cannot long command the loyalty of its citizens. History shows us, it demonstrates that nothing, nothing prepares the way for tyranny more than the failure of public officials to keep the streets safe from bullies and marauders.

Now, we Republicans see all this as more, much more, than the result of mere political differences or mere political mistakes. We see this as the result of a fundamentally and absolutely wrong view of man—his nature and his destiny. Those who seek to live your lives for you, to take your liberties in return for relieving you of yours, those who elevate the state and downgrade the citizen must see ultimately a world

6. An echo of the Declaration of Independence (1776).

7. Goldwater misspoke this word as "shell."

8. Goldwater is referring to the Berlin Wall, which was erected in 1961.

9. Location where U.S.-trained Cuban exiles launched an abortive invasion of Cuba in April 1961.

10. During his campaign, Goldwater frequently charged that the Johnson administration was not taking strong enough measures to combat communism in Laos and Vietnam.

11. North Atlantic Treaty Organization, founded in the wake of World War II.

12. Goldwater is referring to the race riots that affected many American cities during 1963–1964.

in which earthly power can be substituted for divine will. And this nation, this nation was founded upon the rejection of that notion and upon the acceptance of God as the author of freedom.

Now, those who seek absolute power, even though they seek it to do what they regard as good, are simply demanding the right to enforce their own version of heaven on earth. And let me remind you, they are the very ones who always create the most hellish tyrannies. Absolute power does corrupt,[13] and those who seek it must be suspect and must be opposed. Their mistaken course stems from false notions, ladies and gentlemen, of equality. Equality, rightly understood, as our Founding Fathers understood it, leads to liberty and to the emancipation of creative differences. Wrongly understood, as it has been so tragically in our time, it leads first to conformity and then to despotism.

Fellow Republicans, it is the cause of Republicanism to resist concentrations of power, private or public, which, which enforce such conformity and inflict such despotism. It is the cause of Republicanism to ensure that power remains in the hands of the people, and, so help us God, that is exactly what a Republican President will do with the help of a Republican Congress.

It is further the cause of Republicanism to restore a clear understanding of the tyranny of man over man in the world at large. It is our cause to dispel the foggy thinking which avoids hard decisions in the delusion that a world of conflict will somehow mysteriously resolve itself into a world of harmony if we just don't rock the boat or irritate the forces of aggression—and this is hogwash.

It is further the cause of Republicanism to remind ourselves and the world that only the strong can remain free, that only the strong can keep the peace. Now, I needn't remind you or my fellow Americans, regardless of party, that Republicans have shouldered this hard responsibility and marched in this cause before.

It was Republican leadership under Dwight Eisenhower that kept the peace and passed along to this administration the mightiest arsenal for defense the world has ever known. And I needn't remind you that it was the strength and the believable will of the Eisenhower years that kept the peace by using our strength, by using it in the Formosa Straits[14] and in Lebanon[15] and by showing it courageously at all times. It was during those Republican years that the thrust of Communist imperialism was blunted. It was during those years of Republican leadership that this world moved closer not to war, but closer to peace, than at any other time in the last three decades.

And I needn't remind you, but I will, that it's been during Democratic years that our strength to deter war has stood still and even gone into a planned decline. It has been during Democratic years that we have weakly stumbled into conflict, timidly refusing to draw our own lines against aggression, deceitfully refusing to tell even our own people of our full participation, and tragically letting our finest men die on battlefields unmarked by purpose, unmarked by pride or the prospect of victory. Yesterday it was Korea.[16] Tonight it is Vietnam. Make no bones of this. Don't try to sweep this under the rug. We are at war in Vietnam.[17] And yet the President, who is the commander in chief of our forces, refuses to say—refuses to say, mind you—whether or not the objective over there is victory. And his Secretary of Defense[18] continues to mislead and misinform the American people, and enough of it's gone by.

And I needn't remind you, but I will, it has been during Democratic years that a billion persons were cast into Communist captivity and their fate

---

13. An echo of Lord Acton's famous dictum that "power tends to corrupt and absolute power corrupts absolutely" (from a letter to Bishop Mandell Creighton, April 5, 1887).

14. Eisenhower sent a large naval contingent to the Formosa Strait in 1958 to discourage the People's Republic of China from attacking Taiwan, then also called Formosa.

15. In July 1958 Eisenhower landed U.S. forces in Lebanon to support the pro-Western government of President Camille Chamoun.

16. A reference to the Korean War of 1950–1953.

17. Although the massive buildup of American forces would not begin until 1965, there were more than 20,000 U.S. military personnel in Vietnam by the end of 1964.

18. Robert S. McNamara.

cynically sealed. Today, today in our beloved country we have an administration which seems eager to deal with communism in every coin known—from gold to wheat,[19] from consulates to confidences,[20] and even human freedom itself.

Now, the Republican cause demands that we brand communism as the principal disturber of peace in the world today. Indeed, we should brand it as the only significant disturber of the peace. And we must make clear that until its goals of conquest are absolutely renounced and its relations with all nations tempered, communism and the governments it now controls are enemies of every man on earth who is or wants to be free.

Now, we here in America can keep the peace only if we remain vigilant and only if we remain strong. Only if we keep our eyes open and keep our guard up can we prevent war. And I want to make this abundantly clear: I don't intend to let peace or freedom be torn from our grasp because of lack of strength or lack of will—and that I promise you, Americans.

I believe that we must look beyond the defense of freedom today to its extension tomorrow. I believe that the communism which boasts it will bury us[21] will instead give way to the forces of freedom. And I can see in the distant and yet recognizable future the outlines of a world worthy of our dedication, our every risk, our every effort, our every sacrifice along the way. Yes, a world that will redeem the suffering of those who will be liberated from tyranny. I can see, and I suggest that all thoughtful men must contemplate, the flowering of an Atlantic civilization, the whole of Europe reunified and freed, trading openly across its borders, communicating openly across the world.

Now, this is a goal far, far more meaningful than a moon shot. It's a, it's a truly inspiring goal for all free men to set for themselves during the latter half of the twentieth century. I can see, and all free men must thrill to, the events of this Atlantic civilization joined by its great ocean highway to the United States. What a destiny, what a destiny can be ours to stand as a great central pillar linking Europe, the Americas, and the venerable and vital peoples and cultures of the Pacific. I can see a day when all the Americas, North and South, will be linked in a mighty system, a system in which the errors and misunderstandings of the past will be submerged one by one in a rising tide of prosperity and interdependence.

We know that the misunderstandings of centuries are not to be wiped away in a day or wiped away in an hour. But we pledge, we pledge that human sympathy—what our neighbors to the south call an attitude of *simpatico*—no less than enlightened self-interest will be our guide. And I can see this Atlantic civilization galvanizing and guiding emergent nations everywhere.

Now, I know that freedom is not the fruit of every soil. I know that our own freedom was achieved through centuries, by unremitting efforts of brave and wise men. And I know that the road to freedom is a long and a challenging road; and I know also that some men may walk away from it, that some men resist challenge, accepting the false security of governmental paternalism. And I, and I pledge that the America I envision in the years ahead will extend its hand in health, in teaching, and in cultivation so that all new nations will be at least encouraged, encouraged to go our way, so that they will not wander down the dark alleys of tyranny or the dead-end streets of collectivism. My fellow Republicans, we do no man a service by hiding freedom's light under a bushel of mistaken humility.[22]

I seek an America proud of its past, proud of its ways, proud of its dreams, and determined actively to proclaim them. But our example to the world must, like charity, begin at home.[23] In our vision of a good

19. In 1964 the United States sold $140 million worth of excess wheat to the Soviet Union, which financed the deal in part by gold sales in the West.

20. The United States and the Soviet Union signed a new consular treaty on June 1, 1964, and were exploring other ways of expanding contacts between the two nations.

21. Goldwater is referring to a boast made by Soviet Premier Nikita Khrushchev at a reception at the Polish Embassy in Moscow on November 18, 1956.

22. An echo of Matthew 5:14–15.

23. An allusion to the aphorism of Roman playwright Terence (ca. 190–159 BCE).

and decent future, free and peaceful, there must be room, room for the liberation of the energy and the talent of the individual; otherwise our vision is blind at the outset. We must assure a society here which, while never abandoning the needy or forsaking the helpless, nurtures incentives and opportunities for the creative and the productive. We must know the whole good is the product of many single contributions. And I cherish a day when our children once again will restore as heroes the sort of men and women who, unafraid and undaunted, pursue the truth, strive to cure disease, subdue and make fruitful our natural environment, and produce the inventive engines of production, science, and technology.

This nation, whose creative people have enhanced this entire span of history, should again thrive upon the greatness of all those things which we—we as individual citizens—can and should do. And during Republican years, this again will be a nation of men and women, of families proud of their roles, jealous of their responsibilities, unlimited in their aspirations—a nation where all who can will be self-reliant.

We Republicans see in our constitutional form of government the great framework which assures the orderly but dynamic fulfillment of the whole man, and we see the whole man as the great reason for instituting orderly government in the first place. We see, we see in private property and an economy based upon and fostering private property, the one way to make government a durable ally of the whole man, rather than his determined enemy. We see in the sanctity of private property the only durable foundation for constitutional government in a free society.

And, and beyond that we see and cherish[24] diversity of ways, diversity of thoughts, of motives, and accomplishments. We don't seek to live anyone's life for him. We only seek, only seek to secure his rights, guarantee him opportunity, guarantee him opportunity to strive, with government performing only those needed and constitutionally sanctioned tasks which cannot otherwise be performed.

We Republicans seek a government that attends to its inherent responsibilities of maintaining a stable monetary and fiscal climate, encouraging a free and a competitive economy, and enforcing law and order. Thus do we seek inventiveness, diversity, and creative difference within a stable order. For we Republicans define government's role where needed at many, many levels, preferably, though, the one closest to the people involved—our towns and our cities, then our counties, then our states, then our regional compacts, and only then the national government. That, let me remind you, is the ladder of liberty built by decentralized power. On it also we must have balance between the branches of government at every level.

Balance, diversity, creative difference—these are the elements of the Republican equation. Republicans agree, Republicans agree heartily to disagree on many, many of their applications, but we have never disagreed on the basic fundamental issues of why you and I are Republicans. This is a party, this Republican Party is a party for free men, not for blind followers and not for conformists.

In fact, in 1858 Abraham Lincoln said this of the Republican Party, and I, I quote him because he probably could have said it during the last week or so: It was composed of "strange, discordant, and even hostile elements."[25] End of the quote in 1958.[26] Yet, yet all of these elements agreed on one paramount objective: to arrest the progress of slavery and place it in the course of ultimate extinction.

Today, as then, but more urgently and more broadly than then, the task of preserving and enlarging freedom at home and of safeguarding it from the forces of tyranny abroad is great enough to challenge all our resources and to require all our strength. Anyone who joins us in all sincerity, we welcome. Those, those who do not care for our cause, we don't expect to enter our ranks in any case.

And let our Republicanism, so focused and so dedicated, not be made fuzzy and futile by unthinking and stupid labels. I would remind you that extremism in the defense of liberty is no

---

24. Goldwater misspoke here by saying "in cherished."

25. From Lincoln's "House Divided" speech of June 16, 1858.

26. Goldwater meant to say "1858."

vice.[27] Thank you. Thank you. Thank you. Thank you. Thank you. And let me remind you also that moderation in the pursuit of justice is no virtue.

The beauty of the very system we Republicans are pledged to restore and revitalize, the beauty of this federal system of ours, is in its reconciliation of diversity with unity. We must not see malice in honest differences of opinion, and no matter how great, so long as they are not inconsistent with the pledges we have given to each other in and through our Constitution.

Our Republican cause is not to level out the world or make its people conform in computer-regimented sameness. Our Republican cause is to free our people and light the way for liberty throughout the world. Ours is a very human cause for very humane goals. This party, its good people, and its unquenchable devotion to freedom will not fulfill the purposes of this campaign which we launch here and now until our cause has won the day, inspired the world, and shown the way to a tomorrow worthy of all our yesteryears.

I repeat: I accept your nomination with humbleness, with pride, and you and I are going to fight for the goodness of our land.

Thank you.

27. According to Harry V. Jaffa, who wrote this portion of the speech, the inspiration came from Thomas Paine's *The Rights of Man*, part 2 (1792): "Moderation in temper is always a virtue; but moderation in principle is always a vice."

Ronald Reagan

A Time for Choosing

LOS ANGELES, CALIFORNIA
OCTOBER 27, 1964

THE TWO MOST important speeches of the 1964 presidential election were delivered in a losing cause. The first was Barry Goldwater's ill-fated acceptance speech at the Republican National Convention (pages 409–415). The second was "A Time for Choosing," an October television address by Ronald Reagan in support of Goldwater. Both sounded the trumpet of conservatism, but while Goldwater's doomed his campaign, Reagan's set him on a road that, sixteen years later, would lead him to the White House.

Reagan was a sports announcer in the Midwest during the 1930s, and he parlayed his good looks and resonant voice into a Hollywood screen test. By 1937 he was appearing in the movies, eventually starring alongside Errol Flynn, Humphrey Bogart, Jane Wyman, and other Hollywood legends. When his film career stalled in the early 1950s, he turned to the new medium of television, playing host for the popular *General Electric Theater*. His politics changed as well. A Democrat for two decades, he became increasingly conservative and outspokenly anti-Communist. As a spokesman for General Electric, he toured the country giving what became known as The Speech, in which he warned about "encroaching government control" and the "swiftly rising tide of collectivism" that were stifling individual liberty and the free-enterprise system.

In 1964 Reagan served as cochairman of California Citizens for Goldwater. Using The Speech, with a few adaptations to the current presidential contest, he stumped the state in support of Goldwater. On October 1 he addressed an audience of 800 people at the Coconut Grove in downtown Los Angeles. Afterward, several high-powered Republicans asked Reagan if he would reprise his speech on national television if they raised money for the broadcast. He agreed, and several days later he found himself in a large NBC studio with an audience numbering in the hundreds. He delivered his speech as the cameras rolled, recording the performance. It was broadcast nationally on the evening of October 27.

Lambasting the administration of President Lyndon Johnson and liberalism in general, Reagan decried the growth of big government and the appeasement of communism. Americans, he argued, faced a choice between "the ant heap of totalitarianism" and "individual freedom consistent with law and order." The speech generated such a positive response among Republicans that the Goldwater campaign ran it nationally two more times and distributed 300 copies to local television markets around the country. They also used excerpts in campaign ads for Goldwater, and the Republican National Committee published the text in pamphlet form. According to biographer Lou Cannon, Reagan's performance raised close to a million dollars, more than any political speech to that time.

"A Time for Choosing" could not save Goldwater, but, as Reagan said later, it "changed my entire life." Unlike Goldwater, who looked and sounded angry in his acceptance speech, Reagan, articulating essentially the same ideas, came across as reasonable and personable—qualities that helped him become Governor of California two years later and would prove essential to his popularity as President. In their study of Republicanism during the 1960s, David S. Broder and Stephen Hess called "A Time for Choosing" the "most successful national political debut" since William Jennings Bryan's legendary "Cross of Gold" speech at the 1896 Democratic National Convention, and "it made Reagan a political star overnight."

◇◇◇

Thank you. Thank you very much. Thank you, and good evening. The sponsor has been identified, but unlike most television programs, the performer hasn't been provided with a script. As a matter of fact, I have been permitted to choose my own words and discuss my own ideas regarding the choice that we face in the next few weeks.

I have spent most of my life as a Democrat. I recently have seen fit to follow another course. I believe that the issues confronting us cross party lines. Now, one side in this campaign has been telling us that the issues of this election are the maintenance of peace and prosperity. The line has been used: "We've never had it so good!"

But I have an uncomfortable feeling that this prosperity isn't something on which we can base our hopes for the future. No nation in history has ever survived a tax burden that reached a third of its national income. Today thirty-seven cents out of every dollar earned in this country is the tax collector's share, and yet our government continues to spend $17 million a day more than the government takes in. We haven't balanced our budget twenty-eight out of the last thirty-four years. We've raised our debt limit three times in the last twelve months, and now our national debt is one and a half times bigger than all the combined debts of all the nations of the world. We have $15 billion in gold in our treasury; we don't own an ounce. Foreign dollar claims are $27.3 billion, and we've just had announced that the dollar of 1939 will now purchase forty-five cents in its total value.

As for the peace that we would preserve, I wonder who among us would like to approach the wife or mother whose husband or son has died in South Vietnam[1] and ask them if they think this is a peace that should be maintained indefinitely. Do they mean peace, or do they mean we just want to be left in peace? There can be no real peace while one American is dying someplace in the world for the rest of us. We're at war with the most dangerous enemy that has ever faced mankind in his long climb from the swamp to the stars, and it's been said if we lose that war, and in so doing lose this way of freedom of ours, history will record with the greatest astonishment that those who had the most to lose did the least to prevent its happening. Well, I think it's time we ask ourselves if we still know the freedoms that were intended for us by the Founding Fathers.

Not too long ago, two friends of mine were talking to a Cuban refugee, a businessman who had escaped from Castro,[2] and in the midst of his story one of my friends turned to the other and said, "We don't know how lucky we are." And the Cuban stopped and said, "How lucky you are? I had someplace to escape to." And in that sentence he told us the entire story. If we lose freedom here, there's no place to escape to. This is the last stand on earth.

And this idea that government is beholden to the people, that it has no other source of power except the sovereign people, is still the newest and the most unique idea in all the long history of man's relation to man. This is the issue of this election: whether we believe in our capacity for self-government or whether we abandon the American Revolution and confess that a little intellectual elite in a far-distant capital can plan our lives for us better than we can plan them ourselves.

You and I are told increasingly we have to choose between a left or right. Well, I'd like to suggest there is no such thing as a left or right. There's only an up or down—man's age-old dream,[3] the ultimate in individual freedom consistent with law and order, or down to the ant heap of totalitarianism. And regardless of their sincerity, their humanitarian motives, those who would trade our freedom for security have embarked on this downward course.

In this vote-harvesting time they use terms like the Great Society, or as we were told a few days ago by the President,[4] we must accept a "greater government activity in the affairs of the people." But they've been a little more explicit in the past and among themselves, and all of the things I now will quote have appeared in print—these are not Republican accusations.

For example, they have voices that say "the Cold War will end through our acceptance of a not-undemocratic socialism."[5] Another voice says the profit motive has become outmoded, it must be replaced by the incentives of the welfare state; or our traditional system of individual freedom is incapable of solving the complex problems of the twentieth century. Senator Fulbright[6] has said at Stanford University that the Constitution is outmoded. He referred to the President as our moral teacher and our leader, and he says he is hobbled in his task by the restrictions of power imposed on him by this antiquated document. He must be freed so that he can do for us what he knows is best. And Senator Clark of Pennsylvania,[7] another articulate spokesman,

---

1. Four hundred U.S. military personnel had died in Vietnam by the end of 1964.

2. Cuban President Fidel Castro.

3. When delivering the speech, Reagan misspoke these words as man's "old, old-age dream."

4. Lyndon B. Johnson, whose domestic program was labeled the Great Society.

5. In a speech of November 4, 1962, Reagan attributed this quotation to an unidentified "government advisor."

6. J. William Fulbright; the speech Reagan refers to was delivered July 28, 1961.

7. Joseph S. Clark Jr.

defines liberalism as "meeting the material needs of the masses through the full power of centralized government."

Well, I for one resent it when a representative of the people refers to you and me, the free men and women of this country, as "the masses." This is a term we haven't applied to ourselves in America. But beyond that, "the full power of centralized government"—this was the very thing the Founding Fathers sought to minimize. They knew that governments don't control things. A government can't control the economy without controlling people. And they know when a government sets out to do that, it must use force and coercion to achieve its purpose. They also knew, those Founding Fathers, that outside of its legitimate functions, government does nothing as well or as economically as the private sector of the economy.

Now, we have no better example of this than government's involvement in the farm economy over the last thirty years. Since 1955 the cost of this program has nearly doubled. One-fourth of farming in America is responsible for 85 percent of the farm surplus. Three-fourths of farming is out on the free market and has known a 21 percent increase in the per capita consumption of all its produce. You see, that one-fourth of farming—that's regulated and controlled by the federal government. In the last three years we've spent $43 in the feed grain program for every dollar bushel of corn we don't grow.

Senator Humphrey[8] last week charged that Barry Goldwater as President would seek to eliminate farmers. He should do his homework a little better because he'll find out that we've had a decline of five million in the farm population under these government programs. He'll also find that the Democratic administration has sought to get from Congress extension of the farm program to include that three-fourths that is now free. He'll find that they've also asked for the right to imprison farmers who wouldn't keep books as prescribed by the federal government. The Secretary of Agriculture[9] asked for the right to

seize farms through condemnation and resell them to other individuals. And contained in that same program was a provision that would have allowed the federal government to remove two million farmers from the soil.

At the same time there's been an increase in the Department of Agriculture employees. There's now one for every thirty farms in the United States, and still they can't tell us how sixty-six shiploads of grain headed for Austria disappeared without a trace,[10] and Billie Sol Estes[11] never left shore.

Every responsible farmer and farm organization has repeatedly asked the government to free the farm economy, but who are farmers to know what's best for them? The wheat farmers voted against a wheat program. The government passed it anyway. Now the price of bread goes up; the price of wheat to the farmer goes down.

Meanwhile, back in the city, under urban renewal the assault on freedom carries on. Private property rights [are] so diluted that public interest is almost anything a few government planners decide it should be. In a program that takes from the needy and gives to the greedy, we see such spectacles as in Cleveland, Ohio, a million-and-a-half-dollar building completed only three years ago must be destroyed to make way for what government officials call a "more compatible use of the land." The President tells us he's now going to start building public housing units in the thousands where heretofore we've only built them in the hundreds. But FHA[12] and the Veterans Administration tell us they have 120,000 housing units they've taken back through mortgage foreclosure.

For three decades we've sought to solve the problems of unemployment through government planning, and the more the plans fail, the more the planners plan. The latest is the Area Redevelopment

---

8. Hubert Humphrey, U.S. Senator from Minnesota and the Democratic candidate for Vice President in 1964.

9. Orville L. Freeman.

10. Reagan is referring to an ongoing investigation of the illegal diversion of more than half a million metric tons of U.S. feed grain intended for Austria under the foreign aid program between 1959 and 1962.

11. Texas businessman convicted in 1963 of swindling the federal government of millions of dollars in crop subsidies.

12. Federal Housing Administration.

Agency.[13] They've just declared Rice County, Kansas, a depressed area. Rice County, Kansas, has 200 oil wells, and the 14,000 people there have over $30 million on deposit in personal savings in their banks. When the government tells you you're depressed, lie down and be depressed.

We have so many people who can't see a fat man standing beside a thin one without coming to the conclusion the fat man got that way by taking advantage of the thin one. So they're going to solve all the problems of human misery through government and government planning. Well, now, if government planning and welfare had the answer, and they've had almost thirty years of it, shouldn't we expect government to read the score to us once in a while? Shouldn't they be telling us about the decline each year in the number of people needing help? The reduction in the need for public housing?

But the reverse is true. Each year the need grows greater, the program grows greater. We were told four years ago that seventeen million people went to bed hungry each night. Well, that was probably true. They were all on a diet! But now we're told that 9.3 million families in this country are poverty-stricken on the basis of earning less than $3,000 a year. Welfare spending—ten times greater than it was in the dark depths of the Depression. We're spending $45 billion on welfare. Now, do a little arithmetic and you'll find that if we divided the $45 billion up equally among those nine million poor families, we'd be able to give each family $4,600 a year. And this added to their present income should eliminate poverty. Direct aid to the poor, however, is only running about $600 per family. It would seem that someplace there must be some overhead.

Now, so now we declare war on poverty, or "You, too, can be a Bobby Baker!"[14] Now do they honestly expect us to believe that if we add $1 billion to the $45 billion we're spending, one more program

to the thirty-odd we have—and remember, this new program doesn't replace any, it just duplicates existing programs—do they believe that poverty is suddenly going to disappear by magic?

Well, in all fairness I should explain there is one part of the new program that isn't duplicated. This is the youth feature. We are now going to solve the dropout problem, juvenile delinquency, by reinstituting something like the old CCC camps,[15] and we're going to put our young people in these camps. But again we do some arithmetic, and we find that we're going to spend each year, just on room and board for each young person we help, $4,700 a year. We can send them to Harvard for $2,700. Of course, don't get me wrong. I'm not suggesting Harvard is the answer to juvenile delinquency.

But seriously, what are we doing to those we seek to help? Not too long ago, a judge called me here in Los Angeles. He told me of[16] a young woman who had come before him for a divorce. She had six children, was pregnant with her seventh. Under his questioning, she revealed her husband was a laborer earning $250 a month. She wanted a divorce to get an $80 raise. She's eligible for $330 a month in the Aid to Dependent Children program. She got the idea from two women in her neighborhood who'd already done that very thing.

Yet any time you and I question the schemes of the do-gooders, we're denounced as being against their humanitarian goals. They say we're always against things, we're never for anything. Well, the trouble with our liberal friends is not that they're ignorant, it's just that they know so much that isn't so.

Now, we're for a provision that destitution should not follow unemployment by reason of old age, and to that end we've accepted Social Security as a step toward meeting the problem. But we're against those entrusted with this program when they practice deception regarding its fiscal shortcomings, when they charge that any criticism of the program

13. Created in 1961, the agency distributed more than $300 million between 1961 and 1965 for redevelopment in locales with high levels of unemployment.

14. Former aide to President Johnson who resigned his position in October 1963 while under investigation for fraud and influence-peddling.

15. Reagan is referring to the Civilian Conservation Corps, a New Deal program that put more than 3 million young men to work on conservation-related projects. Participants lived in camps and were paid $1 per day.

16. Reagan misspoke this word as "that."

means that we want to end payments to those people who depend on them for a livelihood. They've called it "insurance" to us in a hundred million pieces of literature. But then they appeared before the Supreme Court and they testified it was a welfare program. They only use the term "insurance" to sell it to the people.

And they said Social Security dues are a tax for the general use of the government, and the government has used that tax. There is no fund, because Robert Byers,[17] the actuarial head, appeared before a congressional committee and admitted that Social Security as of this moment is $298 billion in the hole. But he said there should be no cause for worry because as long as they had the power to tax, they could always take away from the people whatever they needed to bail them out of trouble. And they're doing just that.

A young man, twenty-one years of age, working at an average salary, his Social Security contribution would, in the open market, buy him an insurance policy that would guarantee $220 a month at age sixty-five. The government promises 127. He could live it up until he's thirty-one and then take out a policy that would pay more than Social Security. Now, are we so lacking in business sense that we can't put this program on a sound basis so that people who do require those payments will find they can get them when they're due—that the cupboard isn't bare? Barry Goldwater thinks we can.

At the same time, can't we introduce voluntary features that would permit a citizen who can do better on his own to be excused upon presentation of evidence that he had made provision for the non-earning years? Should we not allow a widow with children to work and not lose the benefits supposedly paid for by her deceased husband? Shouldn't you and I be allowed to declare who our beneficiaries will be under this program, which we cannot do?

I think we're for telling our senior citizens that no one in this country should be denied medical care because of a lack of funds. But I think we're against forcing all citizens, regardless of need, into a compulsory government program,[18] especially when we have such examples, as was announced last week, when France admitted that their Medicare program is now bankrupt. They've come to the end of the road.

In addition, was Barry Goldwater so irresponsible when he suggested that our government give up its program of deliberate planned inflation so that when you do get your Social Security pension, a dollar will buy a dollar's worth, and not forty-five cents' worth?

I think we're for an international organization where the nations of the world can seek peace. But I think we're against subordinating American interests to an organization[19] that has become so structurally unsound that today you can muster a two-thirds vote on the floor of the General Assembly among nations that represent less than 10 percent of the world's population. I think we're against the hypocrisy of assailing our allies because here and there they cling to a colony while we engage in a conspiracy of silence and never open our mouths about the millions of people enslaved in the Soviet colonies in the satellite nations.

I think we're for aiding our allies by sharing of our material blessings with those nations which share in our fundamental beliefs, but we're against doling out money government to government, creating bureaucracy, if not socialism, all over the world. We set out to help nineteen countries.[20] We're helping one hundred and seven. We've spent $146 billion. With that money, we bought a $2 million yacht for Haile Selassie.[21] We bought dress suits for Greek undertakers, extra wives for Kenya government officials. We bought a thousand TV sets for a place where they have no electricity. In the last six years, fifty-two nations have bought $7 billion worth of our gold, and

18. Reagan is referring to Medicare, which had received a favorable vote in the U.S. Senate on September 2, 1964, though final approval from both houses of Congress would not occur until July 1965.

19. The United Nations.

20. Most likely a reference to the Marshall Plan, which helped rebuild Western Europe after World War II.

21. Emperor of Ethiopia.

all fifty-two are receiving foreign aid from this country. No government ever voluntarily reduces itself in size. So government programs, once launched, never disappear. Actually, a government bureau is the nearest thing to eternal life we'll ever see on this earth.

Federal employees, federal employees number 2.5 million, and federal, state, and local, one out of six of the nation's workforce employed by government. These proliferating bureaus with their thousands of regulations have cost us many of our constitutional safeguards. How many of us realize that today federal agents can invade a man's property without a warrant? They can impose a fine without a formal hearing, let alone a trial by jury. And they can seize and sell his property at auction to enforce the payment of that fine. In Chicot County, Arkansas, James Wier overplanted his rice allotment. The government obtained a $17,000 judgment, and a U.S. marshal sold his 960-acre farm at auction. The government said it was necessary as a warning to others to make the system work.

Last February nineteenth, at the University of Minnesota, Norman Thomas, six times candidate for President on the Socialist Party ticket, said: "If Barry Goldwater became President, he would stop the advance of socialism in the United States." I think that's exactly what he will do.

But as a former Democrat, I can tell you Norman Thomas isn't the only man who has drawn this parallel to socialism with the present administration. Because back in 1936, Mister Democrat himself, Al Smith,[22] a great American, came before the American people and charged that the leadership of his party was taking the party of Jefferson, Jackson, and Cleveland[23] down the road under the banners of Marx, Lenin, and Stalin.[24] And he walked away from his party and he never returned till the day he died, because to this day the leadership of that party has been taking

that party, that honorable party, down the road in the image of the Labor Socialist Party of England.

Now, it doesn't require expropriation or confiscation of private property or business to impose socialism on a people. What does it mean whether you hold the deed or the title to your business or property if the government holds the power of life and death over that business or property? And such machinery already exists. The government can find some charge to bring against any concern it chooses to prosecute. Every businessman has his own tale of harassment. Somewhere a perversion has taken place. Our natural, unalienable rights are now considered to be a dispensation of government, and freedom has never been so fragile, so close to slipping from our grasp as it is at this moment.

Our Democratic opponents seem unwilling to debate these issues. They want to make you and I believe that this is a contest between two men—that we're to choose just between two personalities. Well, what of this man[25] that they would destroy? And in destroying, they would destroy that which he represents, the ideas that you and I hold dear.

Is he the brash and shallow and trigger-happy man they say he is? Well, I've been privileged to know him "when." I knew him long before he ever dreamed of trying for high office, and I can tell you personally I've never known a man in my life I believe so incapable of doing a dishonest or dishonorable thing.

This is a man who, in his own business, before he entered politics, instituted a profit sharing plan before unions had ever thought of it. He put in health and medical insurance for all his employees. He took 50 percent of the profits before taxes and set up a retirement program, a pension plan for all his employees. He sent monthly checks for life to an employee who was ill and couldn't work. He provides nursing care for the children of mothers who work in the stores. When Mexico was ravaged by the floods in the Rio Grande, he climbed in his airplane and flew medicine and supplies down there.

An ex-GI told me how he met him. It was the week before Christmas during the Korean War, and he was at the Los Angeles airport trying to get a ride

22. Elected Governor of New York four times, Smith was the Democratic Party's nominee for President in 1928.

23. U.S. Presidents Thomas Jefferson, Andrew Jackson, and Grover Cleveland.

24. Communist icons Vladimir Ilyich Lenin, Karl Marx, and Joseph Stalin.

25. Republican presidential nominee Barry Goldwater.

home to Arizona for Christmas, and he said that a lot of servicemen [were] there and no seats available on the planes. And then a voice came over the loudspeaker and said, "Any men in uniform wanting a ride to Arizona, go to runway such-and-such." And they went down there, and there was a fellow named Barry Goldwater sitting in his plane. Every day in those weeks before Christmas, all day long, he'd load up the plane, fly it to Arizona, fly them to their homes, fly back over to get another load.

During the hectic, split-second timing of a campaign, this is a man who took time out to sit beside an old friend who was dying of cancer. His campaign managers were understandably impatient, but he said, "There aren't many left who care what happens to her. I'd like her to know I care."

This is a man who said to his nineteen-year-old son: "There is no foundation like the rock of honesty and fairness, and when you begin to build your life on that rock, with the cement of the faith in God that you have, then you have a real start." This is not a man who could carelessly send other people's sons to war. And that is the issue of this campaign that makes all the other problems I've discussed academic, unless we realize we're in a war that must be won.

Those who would trade our freedom for the soup kitchen of the welfare state have told us they have a utopian solution of peace without victory. They call their policy "accommodation," and they say if we'll only avoid any direct confrontation with the enemy, he'll forget his evil ways and learn to love us. All who oppose them are indicted as warmongers. They say we offer simple answers to complex problems. Well, perhaps there is a simple answer—not an easy answer, but simple, if you and I have the courage to tell our elected officials that we want our national policy based on what we know in our hearts is morally right.

We cannot buy our security, our freedom from the threat of the bomb by committing an immorality so great as saying to a billion human beings now enslaved behind the Iron Curtain: "Give up your dreams of freedom because to save our own skins, we're willing to make a deal with your slave masters." Alexander Hamilton said: "A nation which can

prefer disgrace to danger is prepared for a master and deserves one."[26] Now let's set the record straight. There's no argument over the choice between peace and war, but there's only one guaranteed way you can have peace, and you can have it in the next second: Surrender.

Admittedly there's a risk in any course we follow other than this, but every lesson of history tells us that the greater risk lies in appeasement. And this is the specter our well-meaning liberal friends refuse to face: that their policy of accommodation is appeasement, and it gives no choice between peace and war, only between fight or surrender. If we continue to accommodate, continue to back and retreat, eventually we have to face the final demand—the ultimatum.

And what then, when Nikita Khrushchev[27] has told his people he knows what our answer will be? He has told them that we are retreating under the pressure of the Cold War, and someday, when the time comes to deliver the final ultimatum, our surrender will be voluntary because by that time we will have been weakened from within spiritually, morally, and economically. He believes this because from our side he's heard voices pleading for "peace at any price" or "better Red than dead," or, as one commentator put it, he'd rather "live on his knees than die on his feet."[28]

And therein lies the road to war, because those voices don't speak for the rest of us. You and I know and do not believe that life is so dear and peace so sweet as to be purchased at the price of chains and slavery.[29] If nothing in life is worth dying for, when did this begin—just in the face of this enemy? Or should Moses have told the children of Israel to live in slavery under the pharaohs? Should Christ have refused the cross? Should the patriots at Concord Bridge have

---

26. From Hamilton's "The Warning, No. III" (February 21, 1797).

27. Premier of the Soviet Union.

28. An inversion of Franklin D. Roosevelt's World War II declaration in a speech at Oxford University, June 19, 1941, that Americans "would rather die on our feet than live on our knees."

29. An echo of Patrick Henry's "Give Me Liberty or Give Me Death" speech of March 23, 1775.

thrown down their guns and refused to fire the shot heard round the world?[30] The martyrs of history were not fools, and our honored dead who gave their lives to stop the advance of the Nazis didn't die in vain.

Where, then, is the road to peace? Well, it's a simple answer after all. You and I have the courage to say to our enemies: "There is a price we will not pay. There is a point beyond which they must not advance." And this, this is the meaning, in the phrase of Barry Goldwater, "Peace through strength."

Winston Churchill said: "The destiny of man is not measured by material computations. When great forces are on the move in the world, . . . we learn we're spirits, not animals." And, he said, there's something "going on in time and space, and beyond time and space, which, whether we like it or not, spells duty."[31] You and I have a rendezvous with destiny.[32] We'll preserve for our children this, the last, best hope of man on earth,[33] or we'll sentence them to take the last step into a thousand years of darkness.

We will keep in mind and remember that Barry Goldwater has faith in us. He has faith that you and I have the ability and the dignity and the right to make our own decisions and determine our own destiny.

Thank you very much.

---

30. The battles of Concord and Lexington, April 19, 1775, were the opening military clashes of the American Revolutionary War.

31. From Churchill's radio broadcast of June 16, 1941.

32. From Franklin D. Roosevelt's acceptance speech at the Democratic National Convention, June 27, 1936.

33. From Abraham Lincoln's second annual message to Congress, December 1, 1862.

Mario Savio

An End to History

BERKELEY, CALIFORNIA
DECEMBER 2, 1964

THE FREE SPEECH Movement at the University of California in the fall of 1964 jolted the nation and prefigured the campus protests that would command headlines for the next decade. Best known among the movement's leaders was Mario Savio, a philosophy major who had spent the previous summer as a civil rights worker in Mississippi. When the university administration decided in September to enforce a ban on political activities on campus, Savio and other student activists responded by organizing rallies, protests, and sit-ins in defense of free speech. The administration would not budge, however, and tensions escalated throughout the semester, coming to a head on December 2, when more than 800 students occupied Sproul Hall, the main administration building, and settled in for the night. Shortly before 4:00 a.m., police arrived and began hauling the students off to jail. A campuswide boycott of classes followed, and after a month of discussions involving students, faculty, administrators, and the Board of Regents, the university announced new rules that opened parts of the campus to political activities.

Savio first burst into public view in early October, when he gave a speech from the top of a police car that had been surrounded by a crowd of 2,000 people in front of Sproul Hall. He suffered from a serious stammer through high school but worked hard to overcome it and showed no signs of it during the Free Speech Movement. In addition to the moral and philosophical meaning of the protest movement, he said, it signified at a personal level "the free movement" of his own speech. A fiery orator, he electrified listeners with words that were unfailingly forceful and often eloquent. Before the students entered Sproul Hall on December 2, he rallied them by famously exclaiming: "There's a time when the operation of the machine becomes so odious, makes you so sick at heart, that you can't take part, you can't even passively take part, and you've got to put your bodies upon the gears and upon the wheels, upon the levers, upon all the apparatus, and you've got to make it stop."

Often confused with Savio's speech outside Sproul Hall, "An End to History" was delivered inside the building, where it was tape-recorded. A polished version was published a few days later in *Humanity: An Arena of Critique and Commitment* and was widely reprinted thereafter. It remains the best-known articulation of the ideals of the Free Speech Movement and of the alienation from established institutions that underlay much of the student Left during the 1960s. As for Savio, he shunned the celebrity he acquired as a result of the movement and slipped quickly out of the limelight. He eventually earned bachelor's and master's degrees from San Francisco State University and was teaching at Sonoma State University when he died of heart failure in 1996.

Last summer I went to Mississippi to join the struggle there for civil rights. This fall I am engaged in another phase of the same struggle, this time in Berkeley. The two battlefields may seem quite different to some observers, but this is not the case. The same rights are at stake in both places—the right to participate as citizens in [a] democratic society and the right to due process of law. Further, it is a struggle against the same enemy. In Mississippi an autocratic and powerful minority rules through organized violence to suppress the vast, virtually powerless majority. In California the privileged minority manipulates the university bureaucracy to suppress the students' political expression. That "respectable" bureaucracy masks the financial plutocrats; that impersonal bureaucracy is the efficient enemy in a *Brave New World*.[1]

In our free speech fight at the University of California, we have come up against what may emerge as the greatest problem of our nation—depersonalized, unresponsive bureaucracy. We have encountered the organized status quo in Mississippi, but it is the same in Berkeley. Here we find it impossible usually to meet with anyone but secretaries. Beyond that, we find functionaries who cannot make policy but can only hide behind the rules. We have discovered total lack of response on the part of the policy makers. To

---

1. Aldous Huxley's classic 1932 novel, in which the state exerts control over all aspects of human life.

grasp a situation which is truly Kafkaesque,[2] it is necessary to understand the bureaucratic mentality. And we have learned quite a bit about it this fall, more outside the classroom than in.

As bureaucrat, an administrator believes that nothing new happens. He occupies an ahistorical point of view. In September, to get the attention of this bureaucracy which had issued arbitrary edicts suppressing student political expression and refused to discuss its action, we held a sit-in on the campus.[3] We sat around a police car and kept it immobilized for over thirty-two hours.[4] At last, the administrative bureaucracy agreed to negotiate. But instead, on the following Monday, we discovered that a committee had been appointed, in accordance with usual regulations, to resolve the dispute. Our attempt to convince any of the administrators that an event had occurred, that something new had happened, failed. They saw this simply as something to be handled by normal university procedures.

The same is true of all bureaucracies. They begin as tools, means to certain legitimate goals, and they end up feeding their own existence. The conception that bureaucrats have is that history has in fact come to an end. No events can occur now that the Second World War is over which can change American society substantially. We proceed by standard procedures as we are.

The most crucial problems facing the United States today are the problem of automation and the problem of racial injustice. Most people who will be put out of jobs by machines will not accept an end to events, this historical plateau, as the point beyond which no change occurs. Negroes will not accept an end to history here. All of us must refuse to accept history's final judgment that in America there is no place in society for people whose skins are dark. On campus students are not about to accept it as fact that the university has ceased evolving and is in its

final state of perfection, that students and faculty are respectively raw material and employees, or that the university is to be autocratically run by unresponsive bureaucrats.

Here is the real contradiction: The bureaucrats hold history [h]as ended. As a result significant parts of the population both on campus and off are dispossessed, and these dispossessed are not about to accept this ahistorical point of view. It is out of this that the conflict has occurred with the university bureaucracy and will continue to occur until that bureaucracy becomes responsive or until it is clear the university cannot function.

The things we are asking for in our civil rights protests have a deceptively quaint ring. We are asking for the due process of law. We are asking for our actions to be judged by committees of our peers. We are asking that regulations ought to be considered as arrived at legitimately only from the consensus of the governed. These phrases are all pretty old, but they are not being taken seriously in America today; nor are they being taken seriously on the Berkeley campus.

I have just come from a meeting with the Dean of Students. She notified us that she was aware of certain violations of university regulations by certain organizations. University friends of SNCC,[5] which I represent, was one of these. We tried to draw from her some statement on these great principles, consent of the governed, jury of one's peers, due process. The best she could do was to evade or to present the administration party line. It is very hard to make any contact with the human being who is behind these organizations.

The university is the place where people begin seriously to question the conditions of their existence and raise the issue of whether they can be committed to the society they have been born into. After a long period of apathy during the '50s, students have begun not only to question but, having arrived at answers, to act on those answers. This is part of a growing understanding among many people in America that history

2. A condition marked by surreal distortion and a sense of impending danger; derived from the writings of novelist Franz Kafka (1883–1924).

3. Savio is referring to the September 30 sit-in at Sproul Hall.

4. These events took place on October 1–2.

5. Student Nonviolent Coordinating Committee, founded in 1960 to mobilize and organize student efforts in support of the civil rights movement.

426 WORDS OF A CENTURY

has not ended, that a better society is possible and that it is worth dying for.

This free speech fight points up a fascinating aspect of contemporary campus life. Students are permitted to talk all they want so long as their speech has no consequences.

One conception of the university, suggested by a classical Christian formulation, is that it be in the world but not of the world.[6] The conception of Clark Kerr[7] by contrast is that the university is part and parcel of this particular stage in the history of American society; it stands to serve the need of American industry; it is a factory that turns out a certain product needed by industry or government. Because speech does often have consequences which might alter this perversion of higher education, the university must put itself in a position of censorship. It can permit two kinds of speech, speech which encourages continuation of the status quo and speech which advocates changes in it so radical as to be irrelevant in the foreseeable future. Someone may advocate radical change in all aspects of American society, and this I am sure he can do with impunity. But if someone advocates sit-ins to bring about changes in discriminatory hiring practices, this cannot be permitted because it goes against the status quo of which the university is a part. And that is how the fight began here.

The administration of the Berkeley campus has admitted that external, extralegal groups have pressured the university not to permit students on campus to organize picket lines, not to permit on campus any speech with consequences. And the bureaucracy went along. Speech with consequences, speech in the area of civil rights, speech which some might regard as illegal, must stop.

---

6. John 17:11–16.

7. President of the University of California, Berkeley.

Many students here at the university, many people in society, are wandering aimlessly about. Strangers in their own lives, there is no place for them. They are people who have not learned to compromise, who, for example, have come to the university to learn to question, to grow, to learn—all the standard things that sound like clichés because no one takes them seriously. And they find at one point or other that for them to become part of society, to become lawyers, ministers, businessmen, people in government, that very often they must compromise those principles which were most dear to them. They must suppress the most creative impulses that they have; this is a prior condition for being part of the system. The university is well structured, well tooled, to turn out people with all the sharp edges worn off, the well-rounded person. The university is well equipped to produce that sort of person, and this means that the best among the people who enter must for four years wander aimlessly much of the time questioning why they are on campus at all, doubting whether there is any point in what they are doing, and looking toward a very bleak existence afterward in a game in which all of the rules have been made up, which one cannot really amend.

It is a bleak scene, but it is all a lot of us have to look forward to. Society provides no challenge. American society in the standard conception it has of itself is simply no longer exciting. The most exciting things going on in America today are movements to change America. America is becoming ever more the utopia of sterilized, automated contentment. The "futures" and "careers" for which American students now prepare are for the most part intellectual and moral wastelands. This chrome-plated consumers' paradise would have us grow up to be well-behaved children. But an important minority of men and women coming to the front today have shown that they will die rather than be standardized, replaceable, and irrelevant.

Lyndon B. Johnson

✠

We Shall Overcome

WASHINGTON, D.C.
MARCH 15, 1965

D ESPITE THE CIVIL Rights Act of 1964, Southern blacks remained largely stripped of the right to vote. In Alabama, only 19 percent of voting-age blacks were on the rolls; in Mississippi, the figure was 6 percent. By 1965 the campaign for voting rights had moved to the forefront of the civil rights movement. As was often the case, white opposition turned violent. Nowhere was that violence more clearly on display than in Selma, Alabama, where only 2 percent of eligible blacks were registered to vote. Martin Luther King had targeted Selma as the center of his voting-rights activities, and tensions had been rising steadily since the beginning of the year. They would explode on Sunday, March 7.

In mid-afternoon, more than 500 nonviolent civil rights protesters began walking across Selma's Edmund Pettus Bridge, headed for the state capital in Montgomery. On the other side of the bridge waited a phalanx of state troopers and local posse men. As the marchers reached the end of the bridge, they were ordered to turn back. When they refused to do so, the troopers and posse men rushed forward, some on foot, some on horseback. They smashed into the protesters, searing them with electric cattle prods and beating them with nightsticks, bullwhips, and flails of rubber hose studded with spikes. Teargas was fired into the crowd as troopers wearing gas masks pursued the fleeing marchers. All this was conveyed to the nation by television.

A year earlier, President Lyndon Johnson had cajoled Congress into passing the 1964 Civil Rights Act over intense opposition from the Southern wing of his own party. Now he was waiting for the right moment to introduce a voting rights bill. The crisis at Selma gave him the opening he needed. Eight days after "Bloody Sunday," in the finest speech of his life, drafted primarily by Richard Goodwin, he presented to a joint session of Congress what would become the Voting Rights Act of 1965. The proceedings were broadcast in prime time to a nationwide television and radio audience.

Speaking in his soft Texas accent, with what one reporter described as "an intensity and purposefulness not soon to be forgotten," Johnson declared there could be no compromise with the fundamental principle that "every American citizen must have an equal right to vote." Johnson had served in Congress for more than two decades before becoming President, and now he spoke without equivocation to the body he knew so well. He called on the House and Senate to pass the voting rights bill without delay, hesitation, or compromise, for "outside this chamber is the outraged conscience of a nation" and "the harsh judgment of history." The most memorable moment came when Johnson appropriated the words of the civil rights anthem "We Shall Overcome." The symbolism could not have been more plain—or more powerful. A President born and bred in the South was unequivocally identifying himself and his office with the civil rights movement. Martin Luther King sent Johnson a telegram terming his speech "the most moving, eloquent, unequivocal, and passionate plea for human rights ever made by a President of this nation."

Notwithstanding Johnson's appeal, Southern Senators and Representatives did what they could to scuttle the voting rights bill, as they had with the Civil Rights Act of 1964. In the end, however, the bill passed with its key provisions intact, and Johnson signed it into law on August 6. One hundred years after the end of the Civil War, the federal government had finally committed itself to safeguarding for African Americans the most fundamental right of citizens in a democratic society.

◇◇◇

Mr. Speaker,[1] Mr. President,[2] members of the Congress: I speak tonight for the dignity of man and the destiny of democracy. I urge every member of both parties, Americans of all religions and of all colors, from every section of this country, to join me in that cause.

At times, history and fate meet at a single time in a single place to shape a turning point in man's unending search for freedom. So it was at Lexington and Concord.[3] So it was a century ago at Appomattox.[4] So it was last week in Selma, Alabama. There long-suffering men and women peacefully protested the denial of their rights as Americans. Many were brutally assaulted. One good man, a man of God, was killed.[5]

There is no cause for pride in what has happened in Selma. There is no cause for self-satisfaction in the long denial of equal rights of millions of Americans. But there is cause for hope and for faith in our democracy in what is happening here tonight. For the cries of pain and the hymns and protests of oppressed people have summoned into convocation all the majesty of this great government, the government of the greatest nation on earth. Our mission is at once the oldest and the most basic of this country—to right wrong, to do justice, to serve man.

In our time we have come to live with the moments of great crisis. Our lives have been marked with debate about great issues—issues of war and peace, issues of prosperity and depression. But rarely in any time does an issue lay bare the secret heart of America itself. Rarely are we met with a challenge, not to our growth or abundance, or our welfare or our security, but rather to the values and the purposes and the meaning of our beloved nation.

The issue of equal rights for American Negroes is such an issue. And should we defeat every enemy, and should we double our wealth and conquer the stars and still be unequal to this issue, then we will have failed as a people and as a nation. For with a country

---

1. John McCormack, Speaker of the House of Representatives.

2. Hubert H. Humphrey, Vice President of the United States and President of the Senate.

3. Sites of the opening battles of the American Revolution.

4. Appomattox, Virginia, where Confederate General Robert E. Lee surrendered in April 1865, ending the Civil War.

5. James Reeb, a Unitarian minister from Boston who had gone to Selma to support the marchers, died on March 11 after being beaten by a group of white men two days before.

as with a person, "What is a man profited if he shall gain the whole world, and lose his own soul?"[6]

There is no Negro problem. There is no Southern problem. There is no Northern problem. There is only an American problem. And we are met here tonight as Americans—not as Democrats or Republicans—we're met here as Americans to solve that problem.

This was the first nation in the history of the world to be founded with a purpose. The great phrases of that purpose still sound in every American heart, North and South: "All men are created equal," "Government by consent of the governed," "Give me liberty or give me death."[7]

Well, those are not just clever words, or those are not just empty theories. In their name Americans have fought and died for two centuries, and tonight around the world they stand there as guardians of our liberty, risking their lives. Those words are promised to every citizen that he shall share in the dignity of man. This dignity cannot be found in a man's possessions. It cannot be found in his power or in his position. It really rests on his right to be treated as a man equal in opportunity to all others. It says that he shall share in freedom. He shall choose his leaders, educate his children, provide for his family according to his ability and his merits as a human being.

To apply any other test, to deny a man his hopes because of his color or race or his religion or the place of his birth is not only to do injustice, it is to deny America and to dishonor the dead who gave their lives for American freedom. Our fathers believed that if this noble view of the rights of man was to flourish, it must be rooted in democracy. The most basic right of all was the right to choose your own leaders.

The history of this country in large measure is the history of the expansion of that right to all of our people. Many of the issues of civil rights are very complex and most difficult. But about this there can and should be no argument: Every American citizen must have an equal right to vote. There is no reason

which can excuse the denial of that right. There is no duty which weighs more heavily on us than the duty we have to ensure that right.

Yet the harsh fact is that in many places in this country men and women are kept from voting simply because they are Negroes. Every device of which human ingenuity is capable has been used to deny this right. The Negro citizen may go to register only to be told that the day is wrong or the hour is late or the official in charge is absent. And if he persists, and if he manages to present himself to the registrar, he may be disqualified because he did not spell out his middle name or because he abbreviated a word on the application. And if he manages to fill out an application, he is given a test. The registrar is the sole judge of whether he passes this test. He may be asked to recite the entire Constitution or explain the most complex provisions of state law.

And even a college degree cannot be used to prove that he can read and write. For the fact is that the only way to pass these barriers is to show a white skin. Experience has clearly shown that the existing process of law cannot overcome systematic and ingenuous[8] discrimination. No law that we now have on the books—and I have helped to put three of them there[9]—can, can ensure the right to vote when local officials are determined to deny it. In such a case, our duty must be clear to all of us.

The Constitution says that no person shall be kept from voting because of his race or his color. We have all sworn an oath before God to support and to defend that Constitution. We must now act in obedience to that oath. Wednesday I will send to Congress a law designed to eliminate illegal barriers to the right to vote. The broad principles of that bill will be in the hands of the Democratic and Republican leaders tomorrow. After they have reviewed it, it will come here formally as a bill.

I am grateful for this opportunity to come here tonight at the invitation of the leadership to reason

6. Matthew 16:26.

7. The first two phrases echo the Declaration of Independence; the third is from Patrick Henry's speech of March 23, 1775.

8. Johnson meant to say "ingenious."

9. A reference to the Civil Rights Acts of 1957, 1960, and 1964. Johnson was Majority Leader of the U.S. Senate when the first two were passed; he signed the third during his presidency.

with my friends, to give them my views, and to visit with my former colleagues.[10] I've had prepared a more comprehensive analysis of the legislation which I had intended to transmit to the clerk tomorrow, but which I will submit to the clerks tonight. But I want to really discuss with you now briefly the main proposals of this legislation.

This bill will strike down restrictions to voting in all elections—federal, state, and local—which have been used to deny Negroes the right to vote. This bill will establish a simple, uniform standard which cannot be used, however ingenious the effort, to flout our Constitution. It will provide for citizens to be registered by officials of the United States government if the state officials refuse to register them. It will eliminate tedious, unnecessary lawsuits which delay the right to vote. Finally, this legislation will ensure that properly registered individuals are not prohibited from voting.

I will welcome the suggestions from all the members of Congress—I have no doubt that I will get some—on ways and means to strengthen this law and to make it effective. But experience has plainly shown that this is the only path to carry out the command of the Constitution.

To those who seek to avoid action by their national government in their home communities, who want to and who seek to maintain purely local control over elections, the answer is simple: Open your polling places to all your people; allow men and women to register and vote whatever the color of their skin; extend the rights of citizenship to every citizen of this land.

There is no constitutional issue here. The command of the Constitution is plain. There is no moral issue. It is wrong—deadly wrong—to deny any of your fellow Americans the right to vote in this country. There is no issue of states' rights or national rights. There is only the struggle for human rights.

I have not the slightest doubt what will be your answer. But the last time a President sent a civil rights bill to the Congress, it contained a provision to protect voting rights in federal elections. That civil rights

bill was passed after eight long months of debate. And when that bill came to my desk from the Congress for my signature, the heart of the voting provision had been eliminated.[11]

This time, on this issue, there must be no delay or no hesitation or no compromise with our purpose. We cannot, we must not, refuse to protect the right of every American to vote in every election that he may desire to participate in. And we ought not, and we cannot, and we must not wait another eight months before we get a bill. We have already waited a hundred years and more, and the time for waiting is gone.

So I ask you to join me in working long hours and nights and weekends, if necessary, to pass this bill. And I don't make that request lightly, for from the window where I sit with the problems of our country, I recognize that from outside this chamber is the outraged conscience of a nation, the grave concern of many nations, and the harsh judgment of history on our acts.

But even if we pass this bill, the battle will not be over. What happened in Selma is part of a far larger movement which reaches into every section and state of America. It is the effort of American Negroes to secure for themselves the full blessings of American life. Their cause must be our cause too. Because it's not just Negroes, but really it's all of us who must overcome the crippling legacy of bigotry and injustice. And we shall overcome.[12]

As a man whose roots go deeply into Southern soil,[13] I know how agonizing racial feelings are. I know how difficult it is to reshape the attitudes and the structure of our society. But a century has passed—more than a hundred years—since the Negro was freed. And he is not fully free tonight. It was more than a hundred years ago that Abraham Lincoln, a great President of another party, signed the Emancipation Proclamation.[14] But emancipation

---

10. Before becoming Vice President, Johnson served in the House of Representatives for 11 years and in the Senate for 12 years.

11. Johnson is referring to the Civil Rights Act of 1964.

12. An echo of "We Shall Overcome," the unofficial anthem of the civil rights movement.

13. Johnson was born and raised in Texas.

14. Lincoln, the first Republican President, issued the Emancipation Proclamation on January 1, 1863.

is a proclamation and not a fact. A century has passed—more than a hundred years—since equality was promised, and yet the Negro is not equal. A century has passed since the day of promise, and the promise is unkept.

The time of justice has now come, and I tell you that I believe sincerely that no force can hold it back. It is right in the eyes of man and God that it should come, and when it does, I think that day will brighten the lives of every American. For Negroes are not the only victims. How many white children have gone uneducated? How many white families have lived in stark poverty? How many white lives have been scarred by fear because we wasted our energy and our substance to maintain the barriers of hatred and terror?

And so I say to all of you here, and to all in the nation tonight, that those who appeal to you to hold on to the past do so at the cost of denying you your future. This great, rich, restless country can offer opportunity and education and hope to all—all, black and white; all, North and South; sharecropper and city dweller.

These are the enemies: poverty, ignorance, disease. They are our enemies—not our fellow man, not our neighbor. And these enemies too—poverty, disease, and ignorance—we shall overcome.

Now, let none of us in any section look with prideful righteousness on the troubles in another section or the problems of our neighbors. There's really no part of America where the promise of equality has been fully kept. In Buffalo as well as in Birmingham, in Philadelphia as well as Selma, Americans are struggling for the fruits of freedom.

This is one nation. What happens in Selma or in Cincinnati is a matter of legitimate concern to every American. But let each of us look within our own hearts and our own communities and let each of us put our shoulder to the wheel to root out injustice wherever it exists.

As we meet here in this peaceful historic chamber tonight, men from the South, some of whom were at Iwo Jima,[15] men from the North who have carried Old Glory to far corners of the world and brought it back without a stain on it, men from the East and from the West are all fighting together without regard to religion or color or region in Vietnam.[16] Men from every region fought for us across the world twenty years ago. And now in these common dangers, in these common sacrifices, the South made its contribution of honor and gallantry no less than any other region in the great republic—and in some instances, a great many of them, more.

And I have not the slightest doubt that good men from everywhere in this country, from the Great Lakes to the Gulf of Mexico, from the Golden Gate to the harbors along the Atlantic, will rally now together in this cause to vindicate the freedom of all Americans. For all of us owe this duty, and I believe that all of us will respond to it. Your President makes that request of every American.

The real hero of this struggle is the American Negro. His actions and protests, his courage to risk safety and even to risk his life, have awakened the conscience of this nation. His demonstrations have been designed to call attention to injustice, designed to provoke change, designed to stir reform. He has called upon us to make good the promise of America. And who among us can say that we would have made the same progress were it not for his persistent bravery and his faith in American democracy? For at the real heart of [the] battle for equality is a deep-seated belief in the democratic process. Equality depends not on the force of arms or teargas, but depends upon the force of moral right; not on recourse to violence, but on respect for law and order.

And there have been many pressures upon your President, and there will be others as the days come and go. But I pledge you tonight that we intend to fight this battle where it should be fought—in the courts and in the Congress and in the hearts of men.

We must preserve the right of free speech and the right of free assembly. But the right of free speech does not carry with it, as has been said, the right to holler "Fire!" in a crowded theater.[17] We must preserve

15. Site of one of the last major battles of World War II; the photograph of U.S. troops raising the flag on Iwo Jima is among the best-known images in American history.

16. At the time of Johnson's speech, there were close to 30,000 U.S. troops in Vietnam.

17. An allusion to the famous doctrine coined by Justice Oliver Wendell Holmes Jr. in *Schenck v. United States* (1919).

the right to free assembly. But free assembly does not carry with it the right to block public thoroughfares to traffic.[18] We do have a right to protest, and a right to march under conditions that do not infringe the constitutional rights of our neighbors. And I intend to protect all those rights as long as I am permitted to serve in this office.

We will guard against violence, knowing it strikes from our hands the very weapons which we seek—progress, obedience to law, and belief in American values. In Selma, as elsewhere, we seek and pray for peace. We seek order, we seek unity, but we will not accept the peace of stifled rights or the order imposed by fear or the unity that stifles protest—for peace cannot be purchased at the cost of liberty.[19]

In Selma tonight—and we had a good day there—as in every city, we are working for a just and peaceful settlement. And we must all remember that after this speech I'm making tonight, after the police and the FBI[20] and the marshals have all gone, and after you have promptly passed this bill, the people of Selma and the other cities of the nation must still live and work together. And when the attention of the nation has gone elsewhere, they must try to heal the wounds and to build a new community. This cannot be easily done on a battleground of violence, as the history of the South itself shows. It is in recognition of this that men of both races have shown such an outstandingly impressive responsibility in recent days—last Tuesday, again today.[21]

The bill that I am presenting to you will be known as a civil rights bill. But in a larger sense,

most of the program I am recommending is a civil rights program. Its object is to open the city of hope to all people of all races because all Americans just must have the right to vote, and we are going to give them that right. All Americans must have the privileges of citizenship regardless of race, and they are going to have those privileges of citizenship regardless of race.

But I would like to caution you and remind you that to exercise these privileges takes much more than just legal right. It requires a trained mind and a healthy body. It requires a decent home and the chance to find a job and the opportunity to escape from the clutches of poverty. Of course, people cannot contribute to the nation if they are never taught to read or write, if their bodies are stunted from hunger, if their sickness goes untended, if their life is spent in hopeless poverty, just drawing a welfare check. So we want to open the gates to opportunity. But we're also going to give all our people, black and white, the help that they need to walk through those gates.

My first job after college was as a teacher in Cotulla, Texas, in a small Mexican American school. Few of them could speak English, and I couldn't speak much Spanish. My students were poor and they often came to class without breakfast, hungry. And they knew even in their youth the pain of prejudice. They never seemed to know why people disliked them, but they knew it was so, because I saw it in their eyes.

I often walked home late in the afternoon after the classes were finished, wishing there was more that I could do. But all I knew was to teach them the little that I knew, hoping that it might help them against the hardships that lay ahead. And somehow you never forget what poverty and hatred can do when you see its scars on the hopeful face of a young child.

I never thought then, in 1928, that I would be standing here in 1965. It never even occurred to me in my fondest dreams that I might have the chance to help the sons and daughters of those students and to help people like them all over this country. But now I do have that chance. And I'll let you in on a

18. Most likely a reference to protesters who blocked traffic in front of the White House three days before Johnson's speech.

19. An allusion to Patrick Henry's speech of March 23, 1775: "Is life so dear, or peace so sweet, as to be purchased at the price of chains and slavery?"

20. Federal Bureau of Investigation.

21. "Last Tuesday" refers to March 9, when peaceful protest marches occurred throughout the country.

secret—I mean to use it. And I hope that you will use it with me.

This is the richest and the most powerful country which ever occupied this globe. The might of past empires is little compared to ours. But I do not want to be the President who built empires or sought grandeur or extended dominion.

I want to be the President who educated young children to the wonders of their world.

I want to be the President who helped to feed the hungry and to prepare them to be taxpayers instead of tax-eaters.

I want to be the President who helped the poor to find their own way and who protected the right of every citizen to vote in every election.

I want to be the President who helped to end hatred among his fellow men and who promoted love among the people of all races and all regions and all parties.

I want to be the President who helped to end war among the brothers of this earth.

And so, at the request of your beloved Speaker and the Senator from Montana, the Majority Leader;[22] and [the] Senator from Illinois, the Minority Leader;[23] Mr. McCulloch,[24] and other members of both parties, I came here tonight—not as President Roosevelt came down one time in person to veto a bonus bill, not as President Truman came down one time to urge the passage of a railroad bill[25]—but I came down here to ask you to share this task with me. And to share it with the people that we both work for. I want this to be the Congress, Republicans and Democrats alike, which did all these things for all these people.

Beyond this great chamber, out yonder in fifty states, are the people that we serve. Who can tell what deep and unspoken hopes are in their hearts tonight as they sit there and listen? We all can guess, from our own lives, how difficult they often find their own pursuit of happiness, how many problems each little family has. They look most of all to themselves for their future, but I think that they also look to each of us.

Above the pyramid on the Great Seal of the United States, it says in Latin: "God has favored our undertaking."[26] God will not favor everything that we do. It is rather our duty to divine his will. But I cannot help believing that he truly understands and that he really favors the undertaking that we begin here tonight.

---

22. Mike Mansfield.

23. Everett M. Dirksen.

24. William McCulloch, ranking Republican member of the Judiciary Committee and a principal author of the House version of the 1964 Civil Rights Act.

---

25. Roosevelt spoke on May 22, 1935; Truman on May 25, 1946.

26. The Latin phrase is *Annuit Cœptis*.

Robert F. Kennedy

✕

Day of Affirmation

CAPE TOWN, SOUTH AFRICA
JUNE 6, 1966

AFTER SERVING AS Attorney General during the presidency of his brother John F. Kennedy, Robert Kennedy was elected to the U.S. Senate in 1964. A supporter of the American civil rights movement, he was also concerned about the condition of racial minorities abroad. In June 1966 he traveled to South Africa in response to an invitation from the antiapartheid National Union of South African Students to deliver its annual Day of Affirmation speech at the University of Cape Town. Kennedy's visit was not welcomed by the South African government, which took five months to issue his visa and refused to meet with him or to provide security once he arrived. He was going, as one of his aides wrote, "into a terribly explosive and delicate situation."

Kennedy followed advice from his contacts in South Africa and did not attack apartheid directly. Instead, he framed his speech around freedom, individual liberty, and human dignity—the "sacred rights of Western society." Doing all he could to avoid a holier-than-thou posture, he conceded that the United States had long struggled with the implementation of these rights. Yet, he said, "with painful slowness" the country had "extended and enlarged the meaning and the practice of freedom to all of our people." The unstated—but inescapable—message was that South Africa should do the same. In the most memorable lines of the speech, Kennedy called the youth of the world its best hope for a better future and affirmed the power of individuals to change their societies: "Every time a man stands up for an ideal or acts to improve the lot of others or strikes out against injustice, he sends forth a tiny ripple of hope, and crossing each other from a million different centers of energy and daring, those ripples build a current which can sweep down the mightiest walls of oppression and resistance."

When Kennedy finished speaking, he was greeted with an almost reverential silence followed by several minutes of applause from the audience of 15,000 that had crammed into the auditorium to hear him. The *London Daily Telegraph* called it "the most stirring and memorable address ever to come from a foreigner in South Africa," and many scholars regard it as Kennedy's finest speech. At a time when the outside world showed little interest in combatting apartheid, the *Rand Daily Mail* wrote, his visit was "the best thing that has happened to South Africa for years. It is as if a window has been flung open and a gust of fresh air has swept into a room in which the atmosphere has become stale and fetid. Suddenly it is possible to breathe again without feeling choked."

◇◇

Mr. Chancellor,[1] Mr. Vice Chancellor,[2] Professor Robertson,[3] Mr. Diamond,[4] Mr. Daniel,[5] and ladies and gentlemen: I come here this evening because of my deep interest and affection for a land settled by the Dutch in the mid-seventeenth century, then taken over by the British, and at last independent; a land in which the native inhabitants were at first subdued but relations with whom remain a problem to this day; a land which defined itself on a hostile frontier; a land which has tamed rich natural resources through the energetic application of modern technology; a land which was once the importer of slaves and now must struggle to wipe out the last traces of that former bondage. I refer, of course, to the United States of America.

But I am glad to come here, and my wife and I and all of our party are glad to come here to South Africa, and we are glad to come here to Cape Town. I am already greatly enjoying my stay and my visit here. I am making an effort to meet and exchange views with people of all walks of life and all segments of South African opinion, including those who represent the views of the government.

Today I am glad to meet with the National Union of South African Students. For a decade, NUSAS has stood and worked for the principles of the Universal Declaration of Human Rights[6]—principles which embody the collective hopes of men of goodwill all around the globe. Your work at home and in international student affairs has brought great credit to yourselves and to your country. I know the National Student Association in the United States feels a particularly close relationship with this organization.

And I wish to thank especially Mr. Ian Robertson, who first extended the invitation on behalf of NUSAS. I wish to thank him for his kindness to me in inviting me. I am very sorry that he cannot be with us here this evening. I was happy to have had the opportunity to meet and speak with him earlier this evening, and I presented him with a copy of *Profiles in Courage*, which was a book that was written by President John Kennedy and was signed to him by President Kennedy's widow, Mrs. John Kennedy.[7]

This is a day of affirmation, a celebration of liberty. We stand here in the name of freedom. At the heart of that Western freedom and democracy is the belief that the individual man, the child of God, is the touchstone of value, and all society, all groups and states, exist for that person's benefit. Therefore, the enlargement of liberty for individual human beings must be the supreme goal and the abiding practice of any Western society.

The first element of this individual liberty is the freedom of speech: the right to express and communicate ideas, to set one's self apart from the dumb beasts of field and forest; the right to recall governments to their duties and to their obligations; above all, the right to affirm one's membership and allegiance to the body politic—to society—to the men with whom we share our land, our heritage, and our children's future.

Hand in hand with freedom of speech goes the power to be heard, to share in the decisions of government which shape men's lives. Everything that makes man's life worthwhile—family, work, education, a

---

1. Albert van de Sandt Centlivres.

2. J. P. Duminy.

3. H. M. Robertson, chairman of the Academic Freedom Committee.

4. Charles Diamond, head of the Students' Representative Council.

5. John Daniel, vice president of the National Union of South African Students (NUSAS).

6. Adopted by the United Nations on December 10, 1948 (see pages 291–294).

7. Shortly before Kennedy's visit to South Africa, Robertson, president of NUSAS, was placed under an edict that banned him from political activity for five years. Kennedy met with Robertson at his apartment in Cape Town.

place to rear one's children and a place to rest one's head—all this depends on the decisions of government; all can be swept away by a government which does not heed the demands of its people, and I mean all of its people. Therefore, this essential humanity of man can be protected and preserved only where government must answer not just to the wealthy, not just to those of a particular religion, not just to those of a particular race, but to all of the people.

And even government by the consent of the governed, as in our own constitution, must be limited in its power to act against its people so that there may be no interference with the right to worship, but also no interference with the security of the home, no arbitrary imposition of pains or penalty on an ordinary citizen by officials high or low, no restriction on the freedom of men to seek education or to seek work or opportunity of any kind, so that each man may become all that he is capable of becoming.

These are the sacred rights of Western society. These were the essential differences between us and Nazi Germany, as they were between Athens and Persia.[8] They are the essence of our differences with communism today. I am unalterably opposed to communism because it exalts the state over the individual and over the family and because its system contains a lack of freedom of speech, of protest, of religion, and of the press, which is characteristic of a totalitarian regime.

The way of opposition to communism, however, is not to imitate its dictatorship, but to enlarge individual human freedom. There are those in every land who would label as Communist every threat to their privilege. But may I say to you, as I have seen on my travels in all sections of the world, reform is not communism. And the denial of freedom in whatever name only strengthens the very communism it claims to oppose.

Many nations have set forth their own definitions and declarations of these principles. And there have often been wide and tragic gaps between promise and performance, ideal and reality. Yet the great ideals have constantly recalled us to our own duties. And—with painful slowness—we in the United States have extended and enlarged the meaning and

the practice of freedom to all of our people. For two centuries my own country has struggled to overcome the self-imposed handicap of prejudice and discrimination based on nationality, on social class, or race—discrimination profoundly repugnant to the theory and to the command of our Constitution.

Even as my father[9] grew up in Boston, Massachusetts, signs told him "No Irish Need Apply." Two generations later President Kennedy became the first Irish Catholic, and the first Catholic, to head the nation. But how many men of ability had, before 1961, been denied the opportunity to contribute to the nation's progress because they were Catholic, or because they were of Irish extraction? How many sons of Italian or Jewish or Polish parents slumbered in the slums—untaught, unlearned, their potential lost forever to our nation and to the human race? Even today, what price will we pay before we have assured full opportunity to millions of Negro Americans?

In the last five years we have done more to assure equality to our Negro citizens and to help the deprived, both white and black, than in the hundred years before that time. But much, much more remains to be done. For there are millions of Negroes untrained for the simplest of jobs, and thousands every day denied their full and equal rights under the law, and the violence of the disinherited, the insulted, the injured looms over the streets of Harlem and of Watts and of the South Side of Chicago.

But a Negro American trains now as an astronaut,[10] one of mankind's first explorers into outer space; another is the chief barrister of the United States government,[11] and dozens sit on the benches of our court[s]; and another, Dr. Martin Luther King, is the second man of African descent to win the Nobel Peace Prize, for his nonviolent efforts for social justice between all of the races.[12] We have passed laws prohibiting, we have passed laws prohibiting

---

8. Kennedy is referring to the Greco-Persian wars of the 5th century BCE.

9. Joseph P. Kennedy, who served as U.S. ambassador to Great Britain, 1938–1940.

10. Robert H. Lawrence Jr., who was killed in a plane crash in 1967 before he could get into space.

11. U.S. Solicitor General Thurgood Marshall.

12. King was awarded the Peace Prize in 1964.

discrimination in education, in employment, in housing, but these laws alone cannot overcome the heritage of centuries—of broken families and stunted children and poverty and degradation and pain.

So the road toward equality of freedom is not easy, and great cost and danger march alongside all of us. We are committed to peaceful and nonviolent change, and that is important for[13] all to understand—though change is unsettling. Still, even in the turbulence of protest and struggle is greater hope for the future as men learn to claim and achieve for themselves the rights formerly petitioned from others.

And most important of all, all of the panoply of government power has been committed to the goal of equality before the law, as we are now committing ourselves to the achievement of equal opportunity in fact.[14] We must recognize the full human equality of all of our people before God, before the law, and in the councils of government. We must do this not because it is economically advantageous, although it is; not because the laws of God command it, although they do; not because people in other lands wish it so. We must do it for the single and fundamental reason that it is the right thing to do.

We recognize that there are problems and obstacles before the fulfillment of these ideals in the United States, as we recognize that other nations—in Latin America and in Asia and in Africa—have their own political, economic, and social problems, their unique barriers to the elimination of injustices. In some, there is concern that change will submerge the rights of a minority, particularly where that minority is of a different race than that of the majority. We in the United States believe in the protection of minorities. We recognize the contributions that they can make and the leadership that they can provide, and we do not believe that any people—whether majority or minority or individual human being—are expendable in the cause of theory or policy.

We recognize also that justice between men and nations is imperfect and that humanity sometimes progresses very slowly indeed. All do not develop in the same manner and at the same pace. Nations, like men, often march to the beat of different drummers, and the precise solutions of the United States can neither be dictated nor transplanted to others, and that is not our intention. What is important, however, is that all nations must march toward increasing freedom, toward justice for all, toward a society strong and flexible enough to meet the demands of all of its people, whatever their race, and the demands of[15] the world of immense and dizzying change that face us all.

In a few hours, the plane that brought me to this country crossed over oceans and countries which have been a crucible of human history. In minutes we traced migrations of men over thousands of years; seconds, the briefest glimpse, and we passed battlefields on which millions of men once struggled and died. We could see no national boundaries, no vast gulfs or high walls dividing people from people—only nature and the works of man, homes and factories and farms, everywhere reflecting man's common effort to enrich his life.

Everywhere new technology and communications brings men and nations closer together; the concerns of one inevitably become the concerns of all. And our new closeness is stripping away the false masks, the illusion of differences, which is the root of injustice and of hate and of war. Only earthbound man still clings to the dark and poisoning superstition that his world is bounded by the nearest hill, his universe ends at river's shore, his common humanity is enclosed in the tight circle of those who share his town or his views and the color of his skin.

It is your job, the task of young people in this world, to strip the last remnants of that ancient, cruel belief from the civilization of man. Each nation has different obstacles and different goals, shaped by the vagaries of history and of experience. Yet as I talk to young people around the world, I am impressed not by the diversity but by the closeness of their goals, their desires, and their concerns and their hope for the future.

13. Kennedy misspoke this word as "to."

14. Kennedy is referring to such statutes as the 1964 Civil Rights Act and the 1965 Voting Rights Act.

15. Kennedy misspoke this word as "that."

There is discrimination in New York, the racial inequality of apartheid in South Africa, and serfdom in the mountains of Peru. People starve to death in the streets of India, a former prime minister is summarily executed in the Congo,[16] intellectuals go to jail in Russia, and thousands are slaughtered in Indonesia.[17] Wealth is lavished on armaments everywhere in the world. These are different evils, but they are the common works of man. They reflect the imperfections of human justice, the inadequacy of human compassion, the defectiveness of our sensibility toward the sufferings of our fellows. They mark the limit of our ability to use knowledge for the well-being of our fellow human beings throughout the world. And therefore they call upon common qualities of conscience and indignation, a shared determination to wipe away the unnecessary sufferings of our fellow human beings at home and around the world. It is these qualities which make of our youth today the only true international community.

More than this, I think that we could agree on what kind of a world we would all want to build. It would be a world of independent nations moving toward international community, each of which protected and respected the basic human freedoms. It would be a world which demanded of each government that it accept its responsibility to ensure social justice. It would be a world of constantly accelerating economic progress—not material welfare as an end in itself, but as a means to liberate the capacity of every human being to pursue his talents and to pursue his hopes. It would, in short, be a world that we would all be proud to have built.

Just to the north of here are lands of challenge and of opportunity rich in natural resources—land and minerals and people. Yet they are also lands confronted by the greatest odds—overwhelming ignorance, internal tensions and strife, and great obstacles of climate and geography. Many of these nations, as colonies, were oppressed and were exploited. Yet they have not estranged themselves from the broad traditions of the West; they are hoping, and they are gambling their progress and their stability on the chance that we will meet our responsibility to them to help them overcome their poverty.

In the world we would like to build, South Africa could play an outstanding role, and a role of leadership in that effort. This country is without question a preeminent repository of the wealth and the knowledge and the skill of this continent. Here are the greater part of Africa's research scientists and steel production, most of its reservoirs of coal and of electric power. Many South Africans have made major contributions to African technical development and world science; the names of some are known wherever men seek to eliminate the ravages of tropical disease and of pestilence. In your faculties and councils, here in this very audience, are hundreds and thousands of men and women who could transform the lives of millions for all time to come.

But the help and the leadership of South Africa, or of the United States, cannot be accepted if we—within our own countries or in our relationships with others—deny individual integrity, human dignity, and the common humanity of man. If we would lead outside our own borders, if we would help those who need our assistance, if we would meet our responsibilities to mankind, we must first, all of us, demolish the borders which history has erected between men within our own nations—barriers of race and religion, social class and ignorance.

Our answer is the world's hope; it is to rely on youth. The cruelties and the obstacles of this swiftly changing planet will not yield to obsolete dogmas and outworn slogans. It cannot be moved by those who cling to a present which is already dying, who prefer the illusion of security to the excitement and danger which comes with even the most peaceful progress. This world demands the qualities of youth: not a time of life but a state of mind, a temper of the will, a quality of the imagination, a predominance of courage over timidity, of the appetite for adventure over the life of ease—a man like the chancellor of this university.[18] It is a revolutionary world that we all live in, and thus, as I have said, in Latin America and in Asia and in Europe and in my own country,

16. A reference to Patrice Lumumba, who was killed in January 1961.

17. At least 300,000 people lost their lives in 1965–1966 during an anti-Communist purge by Indonesian leader Suharto.

18. Albert van de Sandt Centlivres.

the United States, it is the young people who must take the lead. Thus you and your young compatriots everywhere have had thrust upon you a greater burden of responsibility than any generation that has ever lived.

"There is," said an Italian philosopher, "nothing more difficult to take in hand, more perilous to conduct, or more uncertain in its success than to take the lead in the introduction of a new order of things."[19] Yet this is the measure of the task of your generation, and the road is strewn with many dangers.

First is the danger of futility: the belief there is nothing one man or one woman can do against the enormous array of the world's ills—against misery, against ignorance, or injustice and violence. Yet many of the world's great movements of thought and action have flowed from the work of a single man. A young monk began the Protestant Reformation,[20] a young general extended an empire from Macedonia to the borders of the earth,[21] and a young woman reclaimed the territory of France.[22] It was a young Italian explorer who discovered the New World,[23] and thirty-two-year-old Thomas Jefferson who proclaimed that all men are created equal.[24] "Give me a place to stand," said Archimedes,[25] "and I will move the world." These men moved the world, and so can we all.

Few will have the greatness to bend history, but each of us can work to change a small portion of the events, and in the total of all those acts will be written the history of this generation.[26] Thousands of Peace Corps volunteers are making a difference in the isolated villages and the city slums of dozens of countries.[27] Thousands of unknown men and women in Europe resisted the occupation of the Nazis, and many died, but all added to the ultimate strength and freedom of their countries. It is from numberless diverse acts of courage and belief such as these that human history is shaped.[28]

Each time a man stands up for an ideal or acts to improve the lot of others or strikes out against injustice, he sends forth a tiny ripple of hope, and crossing each other from a million different centers of energy and daring, those ripples build a current which can sweep down the mightiest walls of oppression and resistance. "If Athens shall appear great to you," said Pericles, "consider then that her glories were purchased by valiant men, and by men who learned their duty."[29] That is the source of all greatness in all societies, and it is the key to progress in our time.

The second danger is that of expediency, of those who say that hopes and beliefs must bend before immediate necessities. Of course, if we must act effectively, we must deal with the world as it is. We must get things done. But if there was one thing that President Kennedy stood for that touched the most profound feeling of young people around the world, it was the belief that idealism, high aspirations, and deep convictions are not incompatible with the most practical and efficient of programs—that there is no basic inconsistency between ideals and realistic possibility, no separation between the deepest desires of heart and of mind and the rational application of human effort to human problems.

It is not realistic or hardheaded to solve problems and take action unguided by ultimate moral aims and values, although we all know some who claim that it is so. In my judgment, it is thoughtless folly. For it ignores the realities of human faith and of passion and of belief—forces ultimately more powerful than all the calculations of our economists or of our generals.

---

19. Niccolo Machiavelli, *The Prince* (1532).

20. Martin Luther (1483–1546).

21. Alexander the Great (356–323 BCE).

22. Jeanne d'Arc (ca. 1412–1431).

23. Christopher Columbus (1451–1506).

24. A reference to Jefferson's authorship of the Declaration of Independence (1776).

25. Greek mathematician (ca. 287–212 BCE).

26. When delivering the speech, Kennedy misspoke the last part of this sentence as: "in the total, all of these acts will be written in the history of this generation."

---

27. The Peace Corps was founded in 1961, during the presidency of John F. Kennedy.

28. When delivering the speech, Kennedy misspoke this sentence by saying: "It is from numberless diverse acts of courage such as these that the belief that human history is thus shaped."

29. Closely paraphrased from Pericles' Funeral Oration, in Thucydides, *History of the Peloponnesian War* (431–413 BCE).

Of course, to adhere to standards, to idealism, to vision in the face of immediate dangers takes great courage and takes self-confidence. But we also know that only those who dare to fail greatly can ever achieve greatly. It is this new idealism which is also, I believe, the common heritage of a generation which has learned that while efficiency can lead to the camps at Auschwitz[30] or the streets of Budapest,[31] only the ideals of humanity and love can climb the hills of the Acropolis.[32]

And a third danger is timidity. Few men are willing to brave the disapproval of their fellows, the censure of their colleagues, the wrath of their society. Moral courage is a rarer commodity than bravery in battle or great intelligence. Yet it is the one essential, vital quality for those who seek to change the world, which yields most painfully to change. Aristotle tells us: "At the Olympic games it is not the finest or the strongest men who are crowned, but those who enter the lists.... So too in the life of the honorable and the good, it is they who act rightly who win the prize."[33] I believe that in this generation those with the courage to enter the conflict will find themselves with companions in every corner of the world.

For the fortunate amongst us, the fourth danger, my friends, is comfort: the temptation to follow the easy and familiar path of personal ambition and financial success so grandly spread before those who have the privilege of an education. But that is not the road history has marked out for us. There is a Chinese curse which says, "May he live in interesting times."[34]

Like it or not, we live in interesting times. They are times of danger and uncertainty, but they are also the most creative of any time in the history of mankind. And everyone here will ultimately be judged—will ultimately judge himself—on the efforts he has contributed to building a new world society and the extent to which his ideals and goals have shaped that effort.

So we part, I to my country and you to remain. We are, if a man of forty can claim the privilege, fellow members of the world's largest younger generation. Each of us have our own work to do.

I know at times you must feel very alone with your problems and with your difficulties. But I want to say how impressed I am with what you stand for and for the effort that you are making—and I say this not just for myself but men and women all over the world. And I hope you will often take heart from the knowledge that you are joined with your fellow young people in every land, they struggling with their problems and you with yours, but all joined in a common purpose; that like the young people of my own country and of every country that I have visited, you are all in many ways more closely united to the brothers of your time than to the older generation in any of these nations.

You are determined to build a better future. President Kennedy was speaking to the young people of America, but beyond them to young people everywhere, when he said, "The energy, the faith, the devotion which we bring to this endeavor will light our country and all who serve it, and the glow from that fire can truly light the world." And, he added, "With a good conscience our only sure reward, with history the final judge of our deeds, let us go forth to lead the land we love, asking his blessing and his help, but knowing that here on earth God's work must truly be our own."[35]

I thank you.

---

30. Located in Poland, Auschwitz was the most notorious of the Nazi death camps.

31. Kennedy is referring to the Soviet Union's suppression of the 1956 Hungarian Revolution.

32. Site of the Parthenon, the Acropolis was the most important spot in ancient Athens.

33. From Aristotle's *Nicomachean Ethics*, book I, chapter 8.

34. Although usually labeled as a Chinese curse, this saying appears to have originated in the West.

35. From John F. Kennedy's inaugural address, January 20, 1961 (pages 341–344).

Stokely Carmichael

Black Power

BERKELEY, CALIFORNIA
OCTOBER 29, 1966

LTHOUGH STOKELY CARMICHAEL did not coin the phrase "Black Power," he made it part of the national lexicon. Speaking at a civil rights march in Greenwood, Mississippi, he exclaimed that it was time to stop asking for "Freedom Now" and to start demanding "Black Power." The crowd chanted the refrain over and over, bringing the long-simmering tensions between followers of Martin Luther King and more radical blacks fed up with nonviolence into the national spotlight. Almost overnight Carmichael was vaulted to national prominence and the meaning of Black Power was debated from coast to coast. To Carmichael and others of like mind, it meant African Americans were going to achieve self-determination and self-identity in the same manner as other ethnic groups before them. To King and his fellow mainstream civil rights leaders, it meant a public relations disaster that would fragment the movement and drive away white supporters. As King predicted, most whites saw Black Power as a racial call to arms and responded with alarm.

Born in Trinidad in 1941, Carmichael moved to New York City at the age of eleven. As a college student, he participated in the 1961 Freedom Rides against segregated transportation in the South. After graduating in 1964, he became a full-time organizer for the Student Nonviolent Coordinating Committee (SNCC). As part of a campaign to register black voters in Mississippi, he helped create the Lowndes County Freedom Organization, whose black panther symbol was later adopted by the ultramilitant Black Panther Party. Carmichael was originally committed to nonviolence but grew increasingly radical as peaceful protesters were brutalized and sometimes killed by defenders of segregation. He raised the call for Black Power a month after being chosen to head SNCC in May 1966.

Described by one reporter as "cocky enough" to look "like he was strutting when standing still," Carmichael was a spellbinding orator who was equally fluent in street jive and formal academic English. Using a mixture of the two, he explained Black Power to an audience of more than 10,000 people at the University of California's Greek Theatre in late October 1966. He spoke without notes, lambasting the United States for everything from its racial policies to the war in Vietnam. He ridiculed President Lyndon Johnson as a "buffoon" and California gubernatorial candidates Ronald Reagan and Pat Brown as "a pair of clowns." In its behavior at home and abroad, he exclaimed, the United States was "uncivilized,... a nation of thieves... on the brink of becoming a nation of murderers." If white people were not willing to eliminate racism, blacks would have no choice but to say, "Move over, or we goin' move on over you."

The speech drew applause and laughter from the predominantly student audience, but it was far from the more scholarly exposition Carmichael gave his subject the next year in *Black Power: The Politics of Liberation*, written with Charles V. Hamilton. The speech as printed below also differs from the stylistically polished version Carmichael published in his 1971 anthology *Stokely Speaks*. It is transcribed from a tape recording and is printed exactly as Carmichael uttered it. The syntax is at times awkward and there are occasional grammatical errors, but both are in keeping with the fluid, extemporaneous nature of Carmichael's presentation. Readers will also notice that Carmichael periodically uses the word "that" where it would not customarily appear in written prose. This can be disconcerting when reading the speech, but there is no evidence that it was troublesome for listeners.

Carmichael's descent was as meteoric as his rise had been. SNCC severed ties with him in 1967. After a brief association with the Black Panthers, he moved to Guinea, West Africa, where he changed his name to Kwame Ture and lived until his death from cancer in 1998. To the end, he answered his phone with the greeting "Ready for the revolution!"

◇◇◇

Thank you very much. It's a privilege and an honor to be in the white intellectual ghetto of the West. We wanted to do a couple of things before we started. The first is that based on the fact that SNCC,[1] through the articulation of its program by its chairman, has been able to win elections in Georgia, Alabama, Maryland,[2] and, by our appearance here, will win an election in California, in 1968 I'm gonna run for President of the United States. I just can't make it 'cause I wasn't born in the United States; that's the only thing holding me back.

We wanted to say that this is a student conference, as it should be, held on a campus—and that we're not ever to be caught up in the intellectual masturbation of the question of Black Power. That's a function of people who are advertisers that call

themselves reporters. Oh, for my members and friends of the press, my self-appointed white critics, I was reading Mr. Bernard Shaw two days ago and I came across a very important quote, which I think is most apropos for you. He says, "All criticism is a autobiography."[3] Dig yourself. Okay.

The philosophers Camus and Sartre[4] raise the question whether or not a man can condemn himself. The black existentialist philosopher who was pragmatic, Frantz Fanon,[5] answered the question. He said that man could not. Camus and Sartre do not.[6] We in SNCC tend to agree with Camus and Sartre that a man cannot condemn himself. Were he to condemn

---

1. Student Nonviolent Coordinating Committee (pronounced "SNICK"); Carmichael was chairman at the time of his speech.

2. SNCC's successes in these states included voter registration drives and the election of Julian Bond, a founding member of the organization, to the Georgia state legislature in 1965.

3. This aphorism does not appear in Shaw's writings. It is derived from Oscar Wilde, who stated in the preface to *The Picture of Dorian Gray* (1891): "The highest, as the lowest, form of criticism is a mode of autobiography."

4. Albert Camus (1913–1960), Jean-Paul Sartre (1905–1980).

5. Author of *Black Skins, White Masks* and *The Wretched of the Earth*, Fanon died in 1961.

6. Carmichael misspoke these words as "does not."

himself, he would then have to inflict punishment upon himself.

An example would be the Nazis. Any prisoner who, any of the Nazi prisoners who admitted, after he was caught and incarcerated, that he committed crimes, that he killed all the many people that he killed—he committed suicide. The only ones who were able to stay alive were the ones who never admitted that they committed crimes against people—that is, the ones who rationalized that Jews were not human beings and deserved to be killed, or that they were only following orders. On a more immediate scene, the officials and the population of, the white population in, Neshoba County, Mississippi—that's where Philadelphia is—could not, could not condemn Rainey, his deputies, and the other fourteen men that killed three human beings.[7] They could not because they elected Mr. Rainey to do precisely what he did; and that for them to condemn him, would be for them to condemn themselves.

In a much larger view, SNCC says that white America cannot condemn herself. And since we are liberal, we have done it. You stand condemned. Now a number of things that arise[8] from that answer of how do you condemn yourselves. It seems to me that the institutions that function in this country are clearly racist and that they're built upon racism. And the question then is: How can black people inside of this country move? And then how can white people who say they're not a part of those institutions begin to move? And how then do we begin to clear away the obstacles that we have in this society that make us live like human beings? How can we begin to build institutions that will allow people to relate with each other as human beings? This country has never done that, especially around the country[9] of white or black.

Now, several people have been upset because we've said that integration was irrelevant when initiated by blacks and that in fact it was a subterfuge, an insidious subterfuge, for the maintenance of white supremacy. Now we maintain that in the past six years or so this country has been feeding us a thalidomide[10] drug of integration and that some Negroes have been walking down a dream street talking about sitting next to white people, and that that does not begin to solve the problem; that when we went to Mississippi, we did not go to sit next to Ross Barnett,[11] we did not go to sit next to Jim Clark,[12] we went to get them out of our way; and that people ought to understand that—that we were never fighting for the right to integrate. We were fighting against white supremacy.

Now, then, in order to understand white supremacy, we must dismiss the fallacious notion that white people can give anybody their freedom. No man can give anybody his freedom. A man is born free. You may enslave a man after he is born free, and that is in fact what this country does. It enslaves black people after they're born. So that the only act that white people can do is to stop denying black people their freedom. That is, they must stop denying freedom; they never give it to anyone.

Now, we want to take that to its logical extension so that we could understand then what its relevancy would be in terms of new civil rights bills. I maintain that every civil rights bill in this country was passed for white people, not for black people. For example, I am black. I know that. I also know that while I am black, I am a human being. Therefore, I have the right to go into any public place. White people didn't know that. Every time I tried to go into a place, they stopped me. So some boys had to write a bill to tell that white man, "He's a human being; don't stop him." That bill was for that white man, not for me. I knew it all the time. I knew it all the time.

---

7. In August 1964 the bodies of three murdered civil rights workers were discovered in an earthen dam near Philadelphia, Mississippi. Although charges against Neshoba County Sheriff Lawrence Rainey and seventeen other men were initially dismissed, the case finally went to trial in October 1967 and resulted in the conviction of seven defendants.

8. Carmichael misspoke this words as "arises."

9. Carmichael meant to say "issue."

---

10. Thalidomide was banned in the early 1960s when it was linked to birth defects in thousands of babies worldwide.

11. Segregationist governor of Mississippi, 1960–1964.

12. Sheriff of Dallas County, Alabama, who led several violent assaults on civil rights marchers in 1964–1965.

I knew that I could vote and that that wasn't a privilege—it was my right. Every time I tried, I was shot, killed, or jailed, beaten, or economically deprived. So somebody had to write a bill for white people to tell them, "When a black man comes to vote, don't bother him." That bill again was for white people, not for black people.

So that when you talk about open occupancy, I know I can live anyplace I want to live. It is white people across this country who are incapable of allowing me to live where I wanna live. You need a civil rights bill—not me. I know I can live where I wanna live. So that the failure to pass a civil rights bill isn't because of Black Power, isn't because of the Student Nonviolent Coordinating Committee, is not because of the rebellions that are occurring in the major cities. It is [the] incapability of whites to deal with their own problems inside their own communities—that is the problem of the failure of the civil rights bill.

And so in a larger sense we must then ask: How is it that black people move? And what do we do? But the question in a greater sense is: How can white people, who are the majority and who are responsible for making democracy work, make it work? They have miserably failed to this point. They have never made democracy work, be it inside the United States, Vietnam, South Africa, the Philippines, South America, Puerto Rico. Wherever America has been, she has not been able to make democracy work. So that in a larger sense, we not only condemn the country for what is done internally, but we must condemn it for what it does externally. We see this country trying to rule the world, and someone must stand up and start articulating that this country is not God and cannot rule the world.

Now, then, before we move on, we ought to develop the white supremacy attitudes that we're either conscious or subconscious of and how they run rampant through the society today. For example, the missionaries were sent to Africa. They went with the attitude that blacks were automatically inferior. As a matter of fact, the first act the missionaries did, you know, when they got[13] to Africa, was to make us cover up our bodies because they said it got them excited.

We couldn't go bare-breasted any more because they got excited. Now, when the missionaries came to civilize us because we were uncivilized, educate us because we were uneducated, and give us some literate studies because we were illiterate, they charged a price. The missionaries came with the Bible and we had the land. When they left, they had the land and we still have the Bible.

And that has been the rationalization for Western civilization as it moves across the world and stealing and plundering and raping everybody in its path. Their one rationalization is that the rest of the world is uncivilized and they are in fact civilized; and they are un-civi-lized.

And that runs on today, you see, because what we have today is that we have what we call modern-day Peace Corps—missionaries. And they come into our ghettos and they Head Start, Upward Lift, Bootstrap, and Upward Bound[14] us into white society. 'Cause they don't want to face the real problem, which is a man is poor for one reason and one reason only—'cause he does not have money, period. If you want to get rid of poverty, you give people money, period. And you ought not to tell me about people who don't work and you can't give people money without working, 'cause if that were true, you'd have to start stopping Rockefeller, Bobby Kennedy, Lyndon Baines Johnson, Lady Bird Johnson,[15] the whole of Standard Oil, the Gulf Corp—all of 'em, including probably a large number of the board of trustees of this university.

So the question, then, clearly is not whether or not one can work. It's who has power. Who has power to make his or her acts legitimate? That is all. And that [in] this country that power's invested in the hands of white people, and they make their acts legitimate. It is now, therefore, for black people to make our acts legitimate.

---

13. Carmichael misspoke this word as "get."

14. Head Start and Upward Bound were federal programs initiated during the presidency of Lyndon B. Johnson. Operation Bootstrap was a self-help training program begun in Los Angeles in 1965.

15. New York Governor Nelson Rockefeller; U.S. Senator Robert F. Kennedy; President Lyndon Johnson; First Lady Claudia Alta (Lady Bird) Johnson.

Now, we are engaged in a psychological struggle in this country, and that is whether or not black people will have the right to use the words they want to use without white people giving their sanction to it. And that we maintain whether they like it or not, we gonna use the word "Black Power" and let them address themselves to that. But that we are not gonna wait for white people to sanction Black Power. We're tired waiting.

Every time black people move in this country, they're forced to defend their position before they move. It's time that the people who are supposed to be defending their position do that—that's white people. They ought to start defending themselves as to why they have oppressed and exploited us.

Now, it is clear that when this country started to move in terms of slavery, the reason for a man being picked as a slave was one reason—because of the color of his skin. If one was black, one was automatically inferior, inhuman, and therefore fit for slavery. So that the question of whether or not we are individually suppressed is nonsensical, and it's a downright lie. We are oppressed as a group because we are black—not because we're lazy, not because we're apathetic, not because we're stupid, not because we smell, not because we eat watermelon and have good rhythm. We are oppressed because we are black.

And in order to get out of that oppression, one must wield the group power that one has—not the individual power which this country then sets [as] the criteria under which a man may come into it. That is what is called in this country as integration: "You do what I tell you to do and then we'll let you sit at the table with us." And that we are saying that we have to be opposed to that. We must now set a criteria, and that if there's going to be any integration, it's gonna be a two-way thing. If you believe in integration, you can come live in Watts. You can send your children to the ghetto schools. Let's talk about that. If you believe in integration, then we going to start adopting us some white people to live in our neighborhood.

So it is clear that the question is not one of integration or segregation. Integration is a man's ability to want to move in there by himself. If someone wants to live in a white neighborhood and he is black, that is his choice. It should be his right. It is not, because white people will not allow him. So vice versa, if a black man wants to live in the slums, that should be his right. Black people will let him—that is the difference. And it's a difference on which this country makes a number of logical mistakes when they begin to try to criticize a program articulated by SNCC.

Now, we maintain that we cannot be—afford to be—concerned about 6 percent of the children in this country, black children who you allow to come into white schools. We have 94 percent who still live in shacks. We are gonna be concerned about those 94 percent. You ought to be concerned about them too. The question is: Are we willing to be concerned about those 94 percent? Are we willing to be concerned about the black people who will never get to Berkeley, who will never get to Harvard and cannot get an education, so you'll never get a chance to rub shoulders with them and say, "Well, he's almost as good as we are; he's not like the others"?

The question is: How can white society begin to move to see black people as human beings? I am black, therefore I am. Not that I am black and I must go to college to prove myself. I am black, therefore I am. And don't deprive me of anything and say to me that you must go to college before you gain access to X, Y, and Z. It is only a rationalization for one's oppression.

The political parties in this country do not meet the needs of people on a day-to-day basis. The question is: How can we build new political institutions that will become the political expressions of people on a day-to-day basis? The question's: How can you build political institutions that will begin to meet the needs of Oakland, California? And the needs of Oakland, California, is not 1,000 policemen with submachine guns.[16] They don't need that. They need that least of all. The question is: How can we build institutions where those people can begin to function on a day-to-day basis, where they can get decent jobs, where they can get decent houses, and where they can

---

16. Most likely a reference to the efforts of police to clear the streets during an eruption of violence in East Oakland on the night of October 19. Newspaper reports indicate that 200 police in riot gear took part.

begin to participate in the policy and major decisions that affect their lives? That's what they need—not Gestapo[17] troops, because this is not 1942, and if you play like Nazis, we playing back with you this time around. Get hip to that.

The question, then, is: How can white people move to start making the major institutions that they have in this country function the way it is supposed to function? That is the real question. And can white people move inside their own community and start tearing down racism where in fact it does exist? Where it exists. It is you who live in Cicero and stopped us from living there.[18] It is white people who stopped us from moving into Grenada.[19] It is white people who make sure that we live in the ghettos of this country. It is white institutions that do that. They must change. In order, in order for America to really live on a basic principle of human relationships, a new society must be born. Racism must die, and the economic exploitation by[20] this country of nonwhite peoples around the world must also die. Must also die.

Now, there're several programs that we have in the South among some poor white communities. We're trying to organize poor whites on a base where they can begin to move around the question of economic exploitation and political disfranchisement. We know; we've heard the theory several times. But few people are willing to go into there.

The question is: Can the white activist not try to be a Pepsi generation[21] who comes alive in the black community, but can he be a man who's willing to move into the white community and start organizing where the organization is needed? Can he do that? The question is: Can the white society—or the white activist—disassociate himself with two clowns who waste time parrying with each other rather than talking about the problems that are facing people in this state?[22] Can you disassociate yourself with those clowns and start to build new institutions that will eliminate all idiots like them?

And the question is: If we are going to do that, when and where do we start and how do we start? We maintain that we must start doing that inside the white community. Our own personal position politically is that we don't think the Democratic Party represents the needs of black people. We know it don't. And that if in fact white people really believe that, the question is: If they're gonna move inside that structure, how are they gonna organize around a concept of whiteness based on true brotherhood and based on stopping exploitation—economic exploitation—so that there will be a coalition base for black people to hook up with? You cannot form a coalition based on national sentiment. That is not a coalition. If you need a coalition to address[23] itself to real changes in this country, white people must start building those institutions inside the white community. And that is the real question, I think, facing the white activists today: Can they in fact begin to move into and tear down the institutions which have put us all in a trick bag that we've been into for the last hundred years?

I don't think that we should follow what many people say—that we should fight to be leaders of tomorrow. Frederick Douglass[24] said that the youth should fight to be leaders today. And God knows we need to be leaders today 'cause the men who run this country are sick—are sick. So that can we, on a larger sense, begin now today to start building those institutions and to fight to articulate our position, to fight to be able to control our universities (we need to be able to do that), and to fight to control the basic institutions which perpetuate racism by destroying them and building new ones? That's the real question that

17. Secret police of Nazi Germany under Adolf Hitler.

18. A 1965 campaign to desegregate housing in Cicero, an all-white suburb of Chicago, was met with violence that Martin Luther King called more hostile and hateful than anything he had seen in the South.

19. Grenada, Mississippi, where efforts to desegregate the public schools in 1966 were met with violent opposition that attracted worldwide attention.

20. Carmichael misspoke this word as "of."

21. Targeted toward youth, "Pepsi Generation" was a well-known advertising slogan during the 1960s.

22. Carmichael is referring to the 1966 California gubernatorial campaign between Edmund G. Brown and Ronald Reagan.

23. Carmichael misspoke this word as "redress."

24. Nineteenth-century African American leader (1817–1895).

face[s] us today, and it is a dilemma because most of us do not know how to work, and that the excuse that most white activists find is to run into the black community.

Now, we've maintained that we cannot have white people working in the black community, and we've made it on a psychological ground. The fact is that all black people often question whether or not they are equal to whites because every time they start to do something, white people are around showing them how to do it. If we are going to eliminate that for the generation that comes after us, then black people must be seen in positions of power, doing and articulating for themselves—for themselves.

That is not to say that one is a reverse racist. It is to say that one is moving in[to] a healthy ground. It is to say what the philosopher Sartre says: One is becoming an antiracist racist.[25] And this country can't understand that. Maybe it's because it's all caught up in racism, but I think what you have in SNCC is an antiracist racism. We are against racists. Now, if everybody who's white see themselves as a racist and then see us against them, they're speaking from their own guilt position, not ours—not ours.

Now, then, the question is: How can we move to begin to change what's going on in this country? I maintain, as we have in SNCC, that the war in Vietnam is an illegal and immoral war.[26] And the question is: What can we do to stop that war? What can we do to stop the people who, in the name of our country, are killing babies, women, and children? What can we do to stop that? And I maintain that we do not have the power in our hands to change that institution, to begin to re-create it so that they learn to leave the Vietnamese people alone, and that the only power we have is the power to say, "Hell, no!" to the draft.

We have to say, we have to say to ourselves that there is a higher law than the law of a racist named McNamara, there is a higher law than the law of a fool named Rusk, and there's a higher law [than] the law of a buffoon named Johnson.[27] It's the law of each of us. It's the law of each of us. It is the law of each of us saying that we will not allow them to make us hired killers. We will stand pat. We will not kill anybody that they say kill, and if we decide to kill, we're gonna decide who we gonna kill. And this country will only be able to stop the war in Vietnam when the young men who are made to fight it begin to say, "Hell, no, we ain't goin."

Now, then, there's a failure because the peace movement has been unable to get off the college campuses, where everybody has a 2 S[28] and not gonna get drafted anyway. And the question is: How can you move out of that into the white ghettos of this country and begin to articulate a position for those white students who do not want to go? We cannot do that. It is sometimes ironic that many of the peace groups are[29] beginning to call us violent and say they can no longer support us, and we are in fact the most militant organization—peace or civil rights or human rights—against the war in Vietnam in this country today. There isn't one organization that has begun to meet our stance on the war in Vietnam, 'cause we not only say we are against the war in Vietnam, we are against the draft. We are against the draft. No man has the right to take a man for two years and train him to be a killer. A man should decide what he wants to do with his life.

So the question, then, is it becomes crystal clear for black people, because we can easily say that anyone fighting in the war in Vietnam is nothing but a black mercenary, and that's all he is. Any time a black man leaves a country where he can't vote to supposedly deliver the vote for somebody else, he's a black mercenary. Any time, any time a black man leaves this country, gets shot in Vietnam on foreign ground, and returns home, and you won't give him a burial in his own homeland, he's a black mercenary—a black mercenary.

25. From Sartre's "Orphée Noir" (1948).

26. By the time of Carmichael's speech, there were close to 400,000 U.S. military personnel in Vietnam.

27. Secretary of Defense Robert McNamara, Secretary of State Dean Rusk, President Lyndon Johnson.

28. Student deferment.

29. Carmichael misspoke this word as "have."

And that even if I were to believe the lies of Johnson, if I were to believe his lies that we're fighting to give democracy to the people in Vietnam, as a black man living in this country I wouldn't fight to give this to anybody. I wouldn't give it to anybody. So that we have to use our bodies and our minds in the only way that we see fit. We must begin, like the philosopher Camus, to come alive by saying no.[30] That is the only act in which we begin to come alive, and we have to say no to many, many things in this country.

This country is a nation of thieves. It has stole[n] everything it has, beginnin' with black people—beginnin' with black people. And that the question is: How can we move to start changing this country from what it is, a nation of thieves? This country cannot justify any longer its existence. We have become the policemen of the world. The marines are at our disposal to always bring democracy, and if the Vietnamese don't want democracy, well, damn it, we'll just wipe them the hell out 'cause they don't deserve to live if they won't have our way of life.

There is, then, in a larger sense: What do you do on your university campus? Do you raise questions about the hundred black students who were kicked off campus a couple of weeks ago? Eight hundred? Eight hundred?[31] And how does that question begin to move? Do you begin to relate to people outside of the ivory tower and university wall? Do you think you're capable of building those human relationships as the country now stands? You're fooling yourself. It is impossible for white and black people to talk about building a relationship based on humanity when the country is the way it is, when the institutions are clearly against us.

We have taken all the myths of this country and we've found them to be nothing but downright lies. This country told us that if we worked hard, we would

succeed. And if that were true, we would own this country lock, stock, and barrel. Lock, stock, and barrel. Lock, stock, and barrel. It is we who have picked the cotton for nothing. It is we who are the maids in the kitchens of liberal white people. It is we who are the janitors, the porters, the elevator men. It's we who sweep up your college floors. Yes, it is we who are the hardest workers and the lowest paid—and the lowest paid.

And that it is nonsensical for people to start talking about human relationships until they are willing to build new institutions. Black people are economically insecure. White liberals are economically secure. Can you begin to build an economic coalition? Are the liberals willing to share their salaries with the economically insecure black people they so much love? Then if you're not, are you willing to start building new institutions that will provide economic security for black people? That's the question we wanna deal with. That's the question we wanna deal with.

We have to seriously examine the histories that we have been told, but we have something more to do than that. American students are perhaps the most politically unsophisticated students in the world—in the world, in the world. Across every country in this world, while we were growing up, students were leading the major revolutions of their countries. We have not been able to do that. They have been politically aware of their existence. In South America, our neighbors down below the border have one every twenty-four hours just to remind us that they're politically aware. And that we have been unable to grasp it because we've always moved in a field of morality and love while people have been politically jiving with our lives.

And the question is: How do we now move politically and stop trying to move morally? You can't move morally against a man like Brown and Reagan. You've got to move politically to cut 'em out of business. You've got to move politically. You can't move morally against Lyndon Baines Johnson because he is an immoral man. He doesn't know what it's all about. So you've got to move politically. You've got to move politically. And that we have to begin to develop a political sophistication which is not to be a parrot: "The two-party system is the best party in the world." There is a difference between being a

30. Carmichael is referring to Camus's *The Rebel: An Essay on Man in Revolt* (1951).

31. Carmichael is responding to comments from the audience. The incident in question occurred on October 21, 1966, when 800 students taking part in a boycott of Oakland high schools were barred from using facilities at the University of California campus to hold "freedom classes."

parrot and being politically sophisticated. We have to raise questions about whether or not we do need new types of political institutions in this country, and we in SNCC maintain that we need them now. We need new political institutions in this country.

Any time, any time Lyndon Baines Johnson can head a party which has in it Bobby Kennedy, Wayne Morse,[32] Eastland, Wallace,[33] and all those other supposed-to-be-liberal cats, there's something wrong with that party. They're moving politically, not morally. And that if that party refuses to seat black people from Mississippi and goes ahead and seats racists like Eastland and his clique,[34] it is clear to me that they're moving politically and that one cannot begin to talk morality to people like that. We must begin to think politically and see if we can have the power to impose and keep the moral values that we hold high.

We must question the values of this society, and I maintain that black people are the best people to do that because we have been excluded from that society. And the question is: We ought to think whether or not we want to become a part of that society. That's what we want. And that that is precisely what it seems to me that the Student Nonviolent Coordinating Committee is doing. We are raising questions about this country. I do not wanna be a part of the American pie. The American pie means raping South Africa, beating Vietnam, beating South America, raping the Philippines, raping every country you've been in. I don't want any of your blood money. I don't want it, don't want to be part of that system. And the question's: How do we raise those questions? How do we raise them as activists? How do we begin to raise them?

We have grown up and we are the generation that has found this country to be a world power, that has found this country to be the wealthiest country in the world. We must question how she got her wealth. That's what we're questioning—and whether or not we want this country to continue being the wealthiest country in the world at the price of raping everybody else across the world. That's what we must begin to question. And that because black people are saying we do not now want to become a part of you, we are called reverse racists. Ain't that a gas?

Now, then, we wanna touch on nonviolence because we see that again as the failure of white society to make nonviolence work. I was always surprised at Quakers who came to Alabama[35] and counseled me to be nonviolent but didn't have the guts to start talking to James Clark[36] to be nonviolent. That is where nonviolence needs to be preached—to Jim Clark, not to black people. They have already been nonviolent too many years. The question is: Can white people conduct their nonviolent schools in Cicero,[37] where they belong to be conducted, not among black people in Mississippi? Can they conduct it among the white people in Grenada?[38] Six-foot-two men who kick little black children; can you conduct nonviolent schools there? That is the question that we must raise—not that you conduct nonviolence among black people. Can you name me one black man today who has killed anybody white and is still alive? Even after rebellion, when some black brothers throw some bricks and bottles, ten thousands of 'em has to pay the crime 'cause when the white policeman comes in, anybody who's black is arrested because we all look alike.

So that we have to raise those questions. We, the youth of this country, must begin to raise those questions. And we must begin to move to build new institutions that's gonna speak to the needs of people who need it. We are gonna have to speak to change the foreign policy of this country. One of the problems with the peace movement is that it's just too caught up in Vietnam, and that if we pulled out the troops

32. U.S. Senator from Oregon.

33. James Eastland, U.S. Senator from Mississippi; George Wallace, Governor of Alabama.

34. Carmichael is referring to the exclusion of the Mississippi Freedom Democratic Party delegation from the 1964 Democratic National Convention in favor of the all-white Mississippi delegation.

35. Members of the Society of Friends, known as Quakers, lent substantial support to the civil rights movement.

36. See note 12 above.

37. See note 18 above.

38. See note 19 above.

from Vietnam this week, next week you'd have to get another peace movement for Santo Domingo.[39]

And the question is: How do you begin to articulate needs to change the foreign policy of this country, a policy that is decided upon rape, a policy in which decisions are made upon getting economic wealth at any price—at any price? Now, we articulate that we therefore have to hook up with black people around the world. And that that hook-up is not only psychological, but becomes very real. If South America today were to rebel and black people were to shoot the hell out of all the white people there—as they should, as they should—then Standard Oil would crumble tomorrow. If South Africa were to go today, Chase Manhattan Bank would crumble tomorrow. If Zimbabwe, which is called Rhodesia by white people, were to go tomorrow, General Electric would cave in on the East Coast.

The question is: How do we stop those institutions that are so willing to fight against Communist aggression but closes their eye to racist oppression? That is the question that you raise. Can this country do that? Now, many people talk about pulling out of Vietnam. What will happen? If we pull out of Vietnam, there will be one less aggressor in there. We won't be there. We won't be there. And so the question is: How do we articulate those positions? And we cannot begin to articulate them from the same assumptions that the people in the country speak 'cause they speak from different assumptions than I assume what the youth in this country are talking about.

That we're not talking about a policy or aid or sending Peace Corps people in to teach people how to read and write and build houses while we steal their raw materials from them. Is that what we're talkin' about? 'Cause that's all we do. What underdeveloped countries need are information about how to become industrialized, so they can keep their raw materials where they have it, produce 'em, and sell it to this country for the price it's supposed to pay—not that we produce it and sell it back to them for a

profit and keep sending our modern-day missionaries in, calling 'em the sons of Kennedy.[40] And that if the youth are gonna participate in that program, how do you raise those questions where you begin to control that Peace Corps program? How do you begin to raise 'em?

How do you raise the questions of poverty? The assumption for this country is that if someone is poor, they are poor because of their own individual blight, or they weren't born on the right side of town, they had too many children, they went in the army too early, their father was a drunk, they didn't care about school, they made a mistake. That's a lotta nonsense. Poverty is well calculated in this country. It is well calculated, and the reason why the poverty program[41] won't work is because the calculators of poverty are administering it. That's why it won't work.

So how can we, as the youth in the country, move to start tearing those things down? We must move into the white community. We are in the black community; we have developed a movement in the black community. The challenge is that the white activist has failed miserably to develop the movement inside of his community. And the question is: Can we find white people who are gonna have the courage to go into white communities and start organizing them? Can we find them? Are they here? And are they willing to do that? Those are the questions that we must raise for the white activist.

And we're never gonna get caught up in questions about power. This country knows what power is. It knows it very well. And it knows what Black Power is 'cause it's deprived black people of it for four hundred years. So it knows what Black Power is. But the question of why do black people—why do white people—in this country associate Black Power with violence? And the answer[42] is: Because of their own inability to deal with blackness. If we had said "Negro

---

39. In April 1965 the United States intervened in the Dominican Republic's civil war, eventually sending more than 20,000 troops to restore order and to secure the capital, Santo Domingo.

40. President John F. Kennedy, who established the Peace Corps in 1961.

41. A reference to the War on Poverty, which was launched in 1964 during the Johnson administration.

42. Carmichael misspoke this word as "question."

Power," nobody would get scared. Everybody would support it. If we said "Power for Colored People," everybody'd be for that. But it is the word "black," it is the word "black" that bothers people in this country—and that's their problem, not mine. Their problem. Their problem.

Now, there's one modern-day lie that we want to attack and then move on very quickly—and that is the lie that says anything all black is bad. Now, you're all a college-university crowd. You've taken your basic logic course; you know about a major premise and minor premise. So people have been telling me anything all black is bad. Let's make that our major premise. Major premise: Anything all black is bad. Minor premise or particular premise: I am all black. Therefore—[43]

I'm never gonna be put in that trick bag. I am all black and I'm all good. Anything all black is not necessarily bad. Anything all black is only bad when you use force to keep whites out. Now, that's what white people have done in this country, and they're projecting their same fears and guilt on us, and we won't have it. We won't have it. Let them handle their own fears and their own guilt. Let them find their own psychologists. We refuse to be the therapy for white society any longer. We have gone mad trying to do it. We have gone stark, raving mad trying to do it.

I look at Dr. King[44] on television every single day. And I say to myself, "Now there is a man who's desperately needed in this country. There is a man full of love. There is a man full of mercy. There is a man full of compassion." But every time I see Lyndon[45] on television, I said, "Martin, baby, you got a long way to go."

So that the question stands as to what we are willing to do. How [are] we willing to say no, to withdraw from that system and begin within our community to start to function and to build new institutions that will speak to our needs? In Lowndes County we

developed something called the Lowndes County Freedom Organization.[46] It is a political party. The Alabama law says that if you have a party, you must have an emblem. We chose for the emblem a black panther—a beautiful black animal which symbolizes the strength and dignity of black people, an animal that never strike[s] back until he's backed so far into the wall he's got nothing to do but spring out. And when he springs, he does not stop.

Now, there is a party in Alabama called the Alabama Democratic Party. It is all white. It has as its emblem a white rooster and the words, "White Supremacy for the Right." Now, the gentlemen of the press, because they're advertisers and because most of them are white and because they're produced by that white institution, never calls the Lowndes County Freedom Organization by its name. But rather they call it the Black Panther Party. Our question is: Why don't they call the Alabama Democratic Party the White Cock Party? It's clear to us, clear to us. It is clear to me that that just points out America's problem with sex and color—not our problem, not our problem. And it is now white America who's gonna deal with those problems of sex and color.

If we were to be real and to be honest, we would have to admit, we would have to admit that most people in this country see things black and white. We have to do that—all of us do. We live in a country that's geared that way. White people would have to admit that they are afraid to go into a black ghetto at night. They are afraid. That's a fact. They're afraid because they'd be "beat up," "lynched," "looted," "cut up," et cetera, et cetera.

That happens to black people inside the ghetto every day, incidentally, and white people are afraid of that. So you get a man to do it for you—a policeman. And now you figure his mentality, where he's afraid of black people. The first time a black man jumps, that white man gonna shoot him. He's gonna shoot him. So police brutality is going to exist on that level because of the incapability of that white man to see black people come together and to live in the conditions.

43. Instead of finishing this sentence verbally, Carmichael used his tone of voice to imply the conclusion to the syllogism: "Therefore, I am all bad."

44. Martin Luther King.

45. President Lyndon Johnson.

46. Independent political party cofounded by Carmichael in 1965 to support African American voting rights in Lowndes County, Alabama.

This country is too hypocritical, and that we cannot adjust ourselves to its hypocrisy. The only time I hear people talk about nonviolence is when black people move to defend themselves against white people. Black people cut themselves every night in the ghetto—don't anybody talk about nonviolence. Lyndon Baines Johnson is busy bombing the hell out of Vietnam—don't nobody talk about nonviolence. White people beat up black people every day—don't nobody talk about nonviolence. But as soon as black people start to move, the double standard comes into being. "You can't defend yourself." That's what you're saying, 'cause you show me a man who would advocate aggressive violence that would be able to live in this country. Show him to me.

The double standard's again come into itself. Isn't it ludicrous and hypocritical for the political chameleon who calls himself a Vice President in this country[47] to stand up before this country and say, "Looting never got anybody anywhere"? Isn't it hypocritical for Lyndon to talk about looting, that you can't accomplish anything by looting, and you must accomplish it by the legal ways? What does he know about legality? Ask Ho Chi Minh[48]—he'll tell you.

So that in conclusion we wanna say that, number one, it is clear to me that we have to wage a psychological battle on the right for black people to define their own terms, define themselves as they see fit, and organize themselves as they see it. Now, the question is: How is the white community gonna begin to allow for that organizing? Because once they start to do that, they will also allow for the organizing that they wanna do inside their community. It doesn't make a difference 'cause we gonna organize our way anyway. We goin' do it.

_____

47. Hubert H. Humphrey.

48. President of North Vietnam.

The question is how we're gonna facilitate those matters—whether it's gonna be done with a thousand policemen with submachine guns, or whether or not it's gonna be done in a context where it is allowed to be done by white people warding off those policemen. That is the question. And the question is: How are white people who call themselves activists ready to start [to] move into the white communities on two counts—on building new political institutions to destroy the old ones that we have, and to move around the concept of white youth refusing to go into the army, so that we can start then to build a new world?

It is ironic to talk about civilization in this country. This country is uncivilized. It needs to be civilized. It needs to be civilized. And that we must begin to raise those questions of civilization—what it is and who [will] do it. And so we must urge you to fight now to be the leaders of today, not tomorrow. We've got to be the leaders of today. This country, this country is a nation of thieves. It stands on the brink of becoming a nation of murderers. We must stop it. We must stop it. We must stop it. We must stop it.

And then, therefore, in a larger sense there's the question of black people. We are on the move for our liberation. We have been tired of trying to prove things to white people. We are tired of trying to explain to white people that we're not gonna hurt them. We are concerned with getting the things we want, the things that we have to have, to be able to function. The question is: Can white people allow for that in this country? The question is: Will white people overcome their racism and allow for that to happen in this country? If that does not happen, brothers and sisters, we have no choice but to say very clearly, "Move over, or we goin' move on over you."

Thank you.

Martin Luther King Jr.

⌛

Speech at Riverside Church

NEW YORK, NEW YORK
APRIL 4, 1967

MARTIN LUTHER KING began to voice concern about the war in Vietnam soon after the first official deployment of American ground troops in March 1965, but he muted his criticism for fear it would alienate President Lyndon Johnson and draw attention away from civil rights. As the number of troops and casualties mounted, King decided he could no longer remain on the sidelines of the antiwar movement. By the end of 1966, the United States had 485,000 military personnel in Vietnam, had lost more than 6,500 lives, and was spending $22 billion a year on the war. In February 1967 King delivered his first major speech devoted solely to the war. The next month he participated in his first antiwar march. Then, on April 4, one year to the day before his death, he took the most momentous step of his journey toward antiwar activism when he addressed a meeting of the Clergy and Laity Concerned About Vietnam held in New York City's Riverside Church.

Historian Taylor Branch has untangled the process by which King's speech was created. Because of his unrelenting schedule, King had time only to give his assistant Andrew Young a four-part outline of the speech before heading to Chicago on March 24 for a mix of civil rights and antiwar activities. Young enlisted Spelman University's Vincent Harding and Wesleyan University's John Maguire to work on a draft, to which King turned his attention on April 2; major contributions also came from Young and Al Lowenstein. When delivering the speech, King extemporized new opening and closing paragraphs; otherwise, he stuck closely to his prepared text.

King presented a searing denunciation of the war on moral, political, and economic grounds, telling the audience of 3,900 people that his conscience left him no other choice. Not only was the war diverting precious resources that could be better used to combat poverty at home, but it was taking the lives of the poor in disproportionate numbers. America's government, he charged, had become "the greatest purveyor of violence in the world today," destroying the villages and families of Vietnam in reckless pursuit of misguided objectives. For America to save its soul, "this madness must cease." King urged the nation to recapture its revolutionary spirit so as not to be "dragged down the long, dark, and shameful corridors of time reserved for those who possess power without compassion, might without morality, and strength without sight."

King's address, delivered in the media capital of the world, was the balefire of his commitment to the antiwar movement. For his efforts he was scathingly denounced by most of the mainstream press, the Johnson administration, and other civil rights leaders. *Life* magazine assailed the speech as "a demagogic slander that sounded like a script for Radio Hanoi," and the NAACP called it "a serious tactical mistake." King knew his position would be unpopular, but he believed it was the only moral action he could take. Before the year was out, many of his critics had come to agree with him and antiwar sentiment had grown to the point that it would eventually drive Lyndon Johnson out of the White House.

◇◇

Mr. Chairman, ladies, and gentlemen: I need not pause to say how very delighted I am to be here tonight and how very delighted I am to see you expressing your concern about the issues that will be discussed tonight by turning out in such large numbers. I also want to say that I consider it a great honor to share this program with Dr. Bennett, Dr. Commager, and Rabbi Heschel,[1] some of the distinguished leaders and personalities of our nation. And, of course, it's always good to come back to Riverside Church. Over the last eight years I have had the privilege of preaching here almost every year in that period, and it is always a rich and rewarding experience to come to this great church and this great pulpit.

I come to this magnificent house of worship tonight because my conscience leaves me no other choice. I join you in this meeting because I am in deepest agreement with the aims and work of the organization which has brought us together: Clergy and Laymen Concerned About Vietnam. The recent statements of your executive committee are the sentiments of my own heart, and I found myself in full accord when I read its opening lines: "A time comes when silence is betrayal."[2] That time has come for us in relation to Vietnam.

The truth of these words is beyond doubt, but the mission to which they call us is a most difficult one. Even when pressed by the demands of inner truth, men do not easily assume the task of opposing their government's policy, especially in time of war. Nor does the human spirit move without great difficulty against all the apathy of conformist thought within one's own bosom and in the surrounding world. Moreover, when the issues at hand seem as perplexing as they often do in the case of this dreadful conflict, we are always on the verge of being mesmerized by uncertainty. But we must move on.

Some of us who have already begun to break the silence of the night have found that the calling to speak is often a vocation of agony, but we must speak. We must speak with all the humility that is appropriate to our limited vision, but we must speak. And we must rejoice as well, for surely this is the first time in our nation's history that a significant number of its religious leaders have chosen to move beyond the prophesying of smooth patriotism to the high grounds of a firm dissent based upon the mandates of conscience and the reading of history. Perhaps a new spirit is rising among us. If it is, let us trace its movements and pray that our own inner being may be sensitive to its guidance, for we are deeply in need of a new way beyond the darkness that seems so close around us.

Over the past two years, as I have moved to break the betrayal of my own silences and to speak from the burnings of my own heart, as I have called for radical departures from the destruction of Vietnam, many persons have questioned me about the wisdom of my path. At the heart of their concerns this query has often loomed large and loud: "Why are you speaking about the war, Dr. King? Why are you joining the voices of dissent?" "Peace and civil rights don't mix," they say. "Aren't you hurting the cause of your people?" they ask.

And when I hear them, though I often understand the source of their concern, I am nevertheless greatly saddened, for such questions mean that the inquirers have not really known me, my commitment,

1. Union Theological Seminary president John C. Bennett, historian Henry Steele Commager, Rabbi Abraham Joshua Heschel.

2. From *The Religious Community and the War in Vietnam* (February 1967).

or my calling. Indeed, their questions suggest that they do not know the world in which they live. In the light of such tragic misunderstanding, I deem it of signal importance to try to state clearly, and I trust concisely, why I believe that the path from Dexter Avenue Baptist Church—the church in Montgomery, Alabama, where I began my pastorate—leads clearly to this sanctuary tonight.

I come to this platform tonight to make a passionate plea to my beloved nation. This speech is not addressed to Hanoi[3] or to the National Liberation Front.[4] It is not addressed to China or to Russia. Nor is it an attempt to overlook the ambiguity of the total situation and the need for a collective solution to the tragedy of Vietnam. Neither is it an attempt to make North Vietnam or the National Liberation Front paragons of virtue, nor to overlook the role they must play in the successful resolution of the problem. While they both may have justifiable reasons to be suspicious of the good faith of the United States, life and history give eloquent testimony to the fact that conflicts are never resolved without trustful give and take on both sides. Tonight, however, I wish not to speak with Hanoi and the National Liberation Front, but rather to my fellow Americans.

Since I am a preacher by calling, I suppose it is not surprising that I have seven major reasons for bringing Vietnam into the field of my moral vision.

There is at the outset a very obvious and almost facile connection between the war in Vietnam and the struggle I and others have been waging in America. A few years ago there was a shining moment in that struggle. It seemed as if there was a real promise of hope for the poor, both black and white, through the poverty program.[5] There were experiments, hopes, new beginnings. Then came the buildup in Vietnam, and I watched this program broken and eviscerated as if it were some idle political plaything of a society gone mad on war, and I knew that America

would never invest the necessary funds or energies in rehabilitation of its poor so long as adventures like Vietnam continued to draw men and skills and money like some demonic destructive suction tube. So I was increasingly compelled to see the war as an enemy of the poor and to attack it as such.

Perhaps a more tragic recognition of reality took place when it became clear to me that the war was doing far more than devastating the hopes of the poor at home. It was sending their sons and their brothers and their husbands to fight and to die in extraordinarily high proportions relative to the rest of the population. We were taking the black young men who had been crippled by our society and sending them 8,000 miles away to guarantee liberties in Southeast Asia which they had not found in southwest Georgia and East Harlem. So we have been repeatedly faced with the cruel irony of watching Negro and white boys on TV screens as they kill and die together for a nation that has been unable to seat them together in the same schools. So we watch them in brutal solidarity burning the huts of a poor village, but we realize that they would hardly live on the same block in Chicago. I could not be silent in the face of such cruel manipulation of the poor.

My third reason moves to an even deeper level of awareness, for it grows out of my experience in the ghettos of the North over the last three years—especially the last three summers. As I have walked among the desperate, rejected, and angry young men, I have told them that Molotov cocktails[6] and rifles would not solve their problems. I have tried to offer them my deepest compassion while maintaining my conviction that social change comes most meaningfully through nonviolent action. But they asked, and rightly so, what about Vietnam? They asked if our own nation wasn't using massive doses of violence to solve its problems, to bring about the changes it wanted. Their questions hit home, and I knew that I could never again raise my voice against the violence

---

3. Capital of North Vietnam.

4. Formed in 1960 with direction from North Vietnam, the National Liberation Front conducted the guerilla war against the Saigon government and the United States.

5. A reference to the War on Poverty initiated under President Lyndon B. Johnson.

---

6. Bottles filled with liquid, typically gasoline, that can be ignited and thrown at targets. The name originated during World War II when Finnish soldiers utilized such weapons to resist invasion by the Soviet Union, whose Commissar for Foreign Relations was Vyacheslav Molotov.

of the oppressed in the ghettos without having first spoken clearly to the greatest purveyor of violence in the world today—my own government. For the sake of those boys, for the sake of this government, for the sake of the hundreds of thousands trembling under our violence, I cannot be silent.

For those who ask the question, "Aren't you a civil rights leader?" and thereby mean to exclude me from the movement for peace, I have this further answer. In 1957, when a group of us formed the Southern Christian Leadership Conference,[7] we chose as our motto, "To save the soul of America." We were convinced that we could not limit our vision to certain rights for black people, but instead affirmed the conviction that America would never be free or saved from itself until the descendants of its slaves were loosed completely from the shackles they still wear. In a way, we were agreeing with Langston Hughes, that black bard of Harlem, who had written earlier:

> O, yes, I say it plain,
> America never was America to me,
> And yet I swear this oath—
> America will be![8]

Now, it should be incandescently clear that no one who has any concern for the integrity and life of America today can ignore the present war. If America's soul becomes totally poisoned, part of the autopsy must read "Vietnam." It can never be saved so long as it destroys the deepest hopes of men the world over. So it is that those of us who are yet determined that "America will be"[9] are led down the path of protest and dissent, working for the health of our land.

As if the weight of such a commitment to the life and health of America were not enough, another burden of responsibility was placed upon me in 1954,[10]

and I cannot forget that the Nobel Peace Prize was also a commission, a commission to work harder than I had ever worked before for the brotherhood of man. This is a calling that takes me beyond national allegiances.

But even if it were not present, I would yet have to live with the meaning of my commitment to the ministry of Jesus Christ. To me the relationship of this ministry to the making of peace is so obvious that I sometimes marvel at those who ask me why I am speaking against the war. Could it be that they do not know that the good news was meant for all men—for Communist and capitalist, for their children and ours, for black and for white, for revolutionary and conservative? Have they forgotten that my ministry is in obedience to the one who loved his enemies so fully that he died for them? What, then, can I say to the Vietcong[11] or to Castro or to Mao[12] as a faithful minister of this one? Can I threaten them with death, or must I not share with them my life?

Finally, as I try to explain for you and for myself the road that leads from Montgomery to this place, I would have offered all that was most valid if I simply said that I must be true to my conviction that I share with all men the calling to be a son of the living God. Beyond the calling of race or nation or creed is this vocation of sonship and brotherhood, and because I believe that the Father is deeply concerned, especially for his suffering and helpless and outcast children. I come tonight to speak for them. This I believe to be the privilege and the burden of all of us who deem ourselves bound by allegiances and loyalties which are broader and deeper than nationalism and which go beyond our nation's self-defined goals and positions. We are called to speak for the weak, for the voiceless, for the victims of our nation, for those it calls "enemy," for no document from human hands can make these humans any less our brothers.

---

7. King served as president of this organization from its founding until his death in 1968.

8. From Hughes's "Let America Be America Again" (1936).

9. King mistakenly inserted "allowed" here when delivering the speech.

10. King meant to say 1964, the year he received the Nobel Peace Prize.

11. Contraction for Viet Nam Cong San, meaning "Vietnamese Communist." By the mid-1960s, it had become synonymous in popular parlance with the National Liberation Front, which had been formed with direction from North Vietnam to conduct the guerilla war against South Vietnam and the United States.

12. Cuban president Fidel Castro; Chinese leader Mao Zedong.

And as I ponder the madness of Vietnam and search within myself for ways to understand and respond in compassion, my mind goes constantly to the people of that peninsula. I speak now not of the soldiers of each side, not of the ideologies of the Liberation Front, not of the junta in Saigon, but simply of the people who have been living under the curse of war for almost three continuous decades now. I think of them, too, because it is clear to me that there will be no meaningful solution there until some attempt is made to know them and hear their broken cries.

They must see Americans as strange liberators. The Vietnamese people proclaimed their own independence in 1954—in 1945, rather—after a combined French and Japanese occupation and before the Communist revolution in China. They were led by Ho Chi Minh.[13] Even though they quoted the American Declaration of Independence in their own document of freedom,[14] we refused to recognize them. Instead, we decided to support France in its reconquest of her former colony.[15]

Our government felt then that the Vietnamese people were not ready for independence, and we again fell victim to the deadly Western arrogance that has poisoned the international atmosphere for so long. With that tragic decision we rejected a revolutionary government seeking self-determination, and a government that had been established not by China—for whom the Vietnamese have no great love—but by clearly indigenous forces that included some Communists. For the peasants this new government meant real land reform, one of the most important needs in their lives.

For nine years following 1945 we denied the people of Vietnam the right of independence. For nine years we vigorously supported the French in their abortive effort to recolonize Vietnam. Before the end of the war we were meeting 80 percent of the French war costs. Even before the French were defeated at Dien Bien Phu,[16] they began to despair of their reckless action, but we did not. We encouraged them with our huge financial and military supplies to continue the war even after they had lost the will. Soon we would be paying almost the full cost of this tragic attempt at recolonization.

After the French were defeated, it looked as if independence and land reform would come again through the Geneva agreement.[17] But instead there came the United States, determined that Ho should not unify the temporarily divided nation, and the peasants watched again as we supported one of the most vicious modern dictators—our chosen man, Premier Diem.[18]

The peasants watched and cringed as Diem ruthlessly rooted out all opposition, supported their extortionist landlords, and refused even to discuss reunification with the North. The peasants watched as all of this was presided over by United States influence and then by increasing numbers of United States troops who came to help quell the insurgency that Diem's methods had aroused. When Diem was overthrown, they may have been happy, but the long line of military dictators seemed to offer no real change, especially in terms of their need for land and peace.

The only change came from America as we increased our troop commitments in support of governments which were singularly corrupt, inept, and without popular support. All the while the people read our leaflets and received the regular promises of peace and democracy and land reform. Now they languish under our bombs and consider us—not their

---

13. Founder of the Democratic Republic of Vietnam in 1945, Ho led North Vietnam in the war against South Vietnam and the United States during the 1960s.

14. Declaration of Independence of the Democratic Republic of Vietnam (1945).

15. A French colony since the mid-19th century, Vietnam came under Japanese control during World War II. After the war, it asserted its independence as the Democratic Republic of Vietnam, but France sought to restore colonial rule, resulting in the Indochina War of 1946–1954.

16. Last battle of the Indochina War of 1946–1954.

17. The Geneva Accords of 1954 partitioned the newly independent Vietnam at the 17th parallel. Although the partition was supposed to end in 1956 after elections to choose a new national government, the elections were never held and the country remained divided into North Vietnam and South Vietnam until 1975.

18. Ngo Dinh Diem, who ruled South Vietnam from 1954 to his assassination in 1963.

fellow Vietnamese—the real enemy. They move sadly and apathetically as we herd them off the land of their fathers into concentration camps where minimal social needs are rarely met. They know they must move on or be destroyed by our bombs.

So they go, primarily women and children and the aged. They watch as we poison their water, as we kill a million acres of their crops. They must weep as the bulldozers roar through their areas preparing to destroy the precious trees. They wandered into the hospitals, with at least twenty casualties from American firepower for one Vietcong-inflicted injury. So far we may have killed a million of them, mostly children. They wander into the towns and see thousands of the children—homeless, without clothes, running in packs on the streets like animals. They see the children degraded by our soldiers as they beg for food. They see the children selling their sisters to our soldiers, soliciting for their mothers.

What do the peasants think as we ally ourselves with the landlords and as we refuse to put any action into our many words concerning land reform? What do they think as we test out our latest weapons on them, just as the Germans tested out new medicine and new tortures in the concentration camps of Europe? Where are the roots of the independent Vietnam we claim to be building? Is it among these voiceless ones?

We have destroyed their two most cherished institutions, the family and the village. We have destroyed their land and their crops. We have cooperated in crushing, in the crushing of the nation's only non-Communist revolutionary political force, the unified Buddhist church. We have supported the enemies of the peasants of Saigon. We have corrupted their women and children and killed their men.

Now there is little left to build on, save bitterness. Soon the only solid physical foundations remaining will be found at our military bases and in the concrete of the concentration camps we call fortified hamlets. The peasants may well wonder if we plan to build our new Vietnam on such grounds as these. Could we blame them for such thoughts? We must speak for them and raise the questions they cannot raise. These, too, are our brothers.

Perhaps a more difficult but no less necessary task is to speak for those who have been designated as our enemies. What of the National Liberation Front, that strangely anonymous group we call VC[19] or Communists? What must they think of the United States of America when they realize that we permitted the repression and cruelty of Diem which helped to bring them into being as a resistance group in the South? What do they think of our condoning the violence which led to their own taking up of arms? How can they believe in our integrity when now we speak of "aggression from the North" as if there were nothing more essential to the war? How can they trust us when now we charge them with violence after the murderous reign of Diem and charge them with violence while we pour every new weapon of death into their land?

Surely we must understand their feelings even if we do not condone their actions. Surely we must see that the men we supported pressed them to their violence. Surely we must see that our own computerized plans of destruction simply dwarf their greatest acts.

How do they judge us when our officials know that their membership is less than 25 percent Communist and yet insist on giving them the blanket name? What must they be thinking when they know that we are aware of their control of major sections of Vietnam and yet we appear ready to allow national elections in which this highly organized political parallel government will not have a part? They ask how we can speak of free elections when the Saigon press is censored and controlled by the military junta. And they are surely right to wonder what kind of new government we plan to help form without them, the only party in real touch with the peasants. They question our political goals and they deny the reality of a peace settlement from which they will be excluded. Their questions are frighteningly relevant. Is our nation planning to build on political myth again and then shore it up from the power of a new violence?

Here is the true meaning and value of compassion and nonviolence—when it helps us to see the enemy's point of view, to hear his questions, to know

---

19. Vietcong (see note 11 above).

his assessment of ourselves. For from his view we may indeed see the basic weaknesses of our own condition, and if we are mature, we may learn and grow and profit from the wisdom of the brothers who are called the opposition.

So, too, with Hanoi. In the North, where our bombs now pummel the land and our mines endanger the waterways, we are met by a deep but understandable mistrust. To speak for them is to explain this lack of confidence in Western words, and especially their distrust of American intentions now.

In Hanoi are the men who led the nation to independence against the Japanese and the French, the men who sought membership in the French Commonwealth and were betrayed by the weakness of Paris and the willfulness of the colonial armies. It was they who led a second struggle against French domination at tremendous costs and then were persuaded to give up the land they controlled between the thirteenth and seventeenth parallel as a temporary measure at Geneva.[20] After 1954 they watched us conspire with Diem to prevent elections which could have surely brought Ho Chi Minh to power over a united Vietnam, and they realized they had been betrayed again. When we ask why they do not leap to negotiate, these things must be remembered.

Also, it must be clear that the leaders of Hanoi considered the presence of American troops in support of the Diem regime to have been the initial military breach of the Geneva agreements concerning foreign troops, and they remind us that they did not begin to send troops in large numbers and even supplies into the South until American forces had moved into the tens of thousands. Hanoi remembers how our leaders refused to tell us the truth about the earlier North Vietnamese overtures for peace, how the President[21] claimed that none existed when they had clearly been made.

Ho Chi Minh has watched as America has spoken of peace and built up its forces, and now he has surely heard the increasing international rumors of American plans for an invasion of the North. He knows the bombing and shelling and mining we are doing are part of traditional preinvasion strategy. Perhaps only his sense of humor and of irony can save him when he hears the most powerful nation of the world speaking of aggression as it drops thousands of bombs on a poor weak nation more than 800—or, rather, 8,000—miles away from its shores.

At this point I should make it clear that while I have tried in these last few minutes to give a voice to the voiceless in Vietnam, to understand the arguments of those who are called "enemy," I am as deeply concerned about our own troops there as anything else. For it occurs to me that what we are submitting them to in Vietnam is not simply the brutalizing process that goes on in any war where armies face each other and seek to destroy. We are adding cynicism to the process of death, for they must know after the short period there that none of the things we claim to be fighting for are really involved. Before long they must know that their government has sent them into a struggle among Vietnamese, and the more sophisticated surely realize that we are on the side of the wealthy and the secure while we create a hell for the poor.

Somehow this madness must cease. We must stop now. I speak as a child of God and brother to the suffering poor of Vietnam. I speak for those whose land is being laid waste, whose homes are being destroyed, whose culture is being subverted. I speak for the poor of America who are paying the double price of smashed hopes at home and death and corruption in Vietnam. I speak as a citizen of the world for the world as it stands aghast at the path we have taken. I speak as one who loves America to the leaders of our own nation. The great initiative in this war is ours. The initiative to stop it must be ours.

This is the message of the great Buddhist leaders of Vietnam. Recently one of them wrote these words, and I quote: "Each day the war goes on, the hatred increases in the heart of the Vietnamese and in the hearts of those of humanitarian instinct. The Americans are forcing even their friends into becoming their enemies. It is curious that the Americans, who calculate so carefully on the possibilities of military victory, do not realize that in the process they are incurring deep psychological and political defeat. The image of America will never again be the image

---

20. See notes 15 and 17 above.

21. Lyndon B. Johnson.

of revolution, freedom, and democracy, but the image of violence and militarism." Unquote.

If we continue, there will be no doubt in my mind and in the mind of the world that we have no honorable intentions in Vietnam. If we do not stop our war against the people of Vietnam immediately, the world will be left with no other alternative than to see this as some horrible, clumsy, and deadly game we have decided to play. The world now demands a maturity of America that we may not be able to achieve. It demands that we admit that we have been wrong from the beginning of our adventure in Vietnam, that we have been detrimental to the life of the Vietnamese people. The situation is one in which we must be ready to turn sharply from our present ways.

In order to atone for our sins and errors in Vietnam, we should take the initiative in bringing a halt to this tragic war. I would like to suggest five concrete things that our government should do immediately to begin the long and difficult process of extricating ourselves from this nightmarish conflict.

Number one: End all bombing in North and South Vietnam.

Number two: Declare a unilateral cease-fire in the hope that such action will create the atmosphere for negotiation.

Three: Take immediate steps to prevent other battlegrounds in Southeast Asia by curtailing our military buildup in Thailand[22] and our interference in Laos.[23]

Four: Realistically accept the fact that the National Liberation Front has substantial support in South Vietnam and must thereby play a role in any meaningful negotiations and any future Vietnam government.

Five: Set a date that we will remove all foreign troops from Vietnam in accordance with the 1954 Geneva agreement.

Part of our ongoing, part of our ongoing commitment might well express itself in an offer to grant asylum to any Vietnamese who fears for his life under

the new regime which included the Liberation Front. Then we must make what reparations we can for the damage we have done. We must provide the medical aid that is badly needed, making it available in this country if necessary.

Meanwhile, meanwhile we in the churches and synagogues have a continuing task while we urge our government to disengage itself from a disgraceful commitment. We must continue to raise our voices and our lives if our nation persists in its perverse ways in Vietnam. We must be prepared to match actions with words by seeking out every creative method of protest possible. As we counsel young men concerning military service, we must clarify for them our nation's role in Vietnam and challenge them with the alternative of conscientious objection. I am pleased to say that this is the path now chosen by more than seventy students at my own alma mater, Morehouse College, and I recommend it to all who find the American course in Vietnam a dishonorable and unjust one.

Moreover, I would encourage all ministers of draft age to give up their ministerial exemptions and seek status as conscientious objectors. These are the times for real choices and not false ones. We are at the moment when our lives must be placed on the line if our nation is to survive its own folly. Every man of humane convictions must decide on the protest that best suits his convictions, but we must all protest.

Now, there is something seductively tempting about stopping there and sending us all off on what in some circles has become a popular crusade against the war in Vietnam. I say we must enter that struggle, but I wish to go on now to say something even more disturbing.

The war in Vietnam is but a symptom of a far deeper malady within the American spirit. And if we ignore this sobering reality, and if we ignore this sobering reality, we will find ourselves organizing clergy-and-laymen-concerned committees for the next generation. They will be concerned about Guatemala and Peru. They will be concerned about Thailand and Cambodia. They will be concerned about Mozambique and South Africa.[24] We will be marching for these and a dozen other names and attending rallies without end

---

22. Thailand was used as a staging area for American troops in Vietnam.

23. The United States had been involved in anti-Communist operations in Laos since 1961.

24. All six countries faced revolutionary insurgencies that were opposed by the United States.

unless there is a significant and profound change in American life and policy. So such thoughts take us beyond Vietnam, but not beyond our calling as sons of the living God.

In 1957 a sensitive American official overseas said that it seemed to him that our nation was on the wrong side of a world revolution. During the past ten years we have seen emerge a pattern of suppression which has now justified the presence of U.S. military advisors in Venezuela. This need to maintain social stability for our investments accounts for the counterrevolutionary action of American forces in Guatemala. It tells why American helicopters are being used against guerrillas in Cambodia and why American napalm and Green Beret forces have already been active against rebels in Peru.

It is with such activity in mind that the words of the late John F. Kennedy come back to haunt us. Five years ago he said, "Those who make peaceful revolution impossible will make violent revolution inevitable."[25] Increasingly, by choice or by accident, this is the role our nation has taken, the role of those who make peaceful revolution impossible by refusing to give up the privileges and the pleasures that come from the immense profits of overseas investments.

I am convinced that if we are to get on the right side of the world revolution, we as a nation must undergo a radical revolution of values. We must rapidly begin, we must rapidly begin the shift from a thing-oriented society to a person-oriented society. When machines and computers, profit motives and property rights, are considered more important than people, the giant triplets of racism, extreme materialism, and militarism are incapable of being conquered.

A true revolution of values will soon cause us to question the fairness and justice of many of our past and present policies. On the one hand we are called to play the Good Samaritan on life's roadside, but that will be only an initial act. One day we must come to see that the whole Jericho Road must be transformed so that men and women will not be constantly beaten and robbed as they make their journey on life's highway.[26] True compassion is more than flinging a coin to a beggar. It comes to see that an edifice which produces beggars needs restructuring.

A true revolution of values will soon look uneasily on the glaring contrast of poverty and wealth. With righteous indignation, it will look across the seas and see individual capitalists of the West investing huge sums of money in Asia, Africa, and South America, only to take the profits out with no concern for the social betterment of the countries, and say, "This is not just." It will look at our alliance with the landed gentry of South America and say, "This is not just." The Western arrogance of feeling that it has everything to teach others and nothing to learn from them is not just.

A true revolution of values will lay hand on the world order and say of war, "This way of settling differences is not just." This business of burning human beings with napalm, of filling our nation's homes with orphans and widows, of injecting poisonous drugs of hate into the veins of peoples normally humane, of sending men home from dark and bloody battlefields physically handicapped and psychologically deranged cannot be reconciled with wisdom, justice, and love. A nation that continues year after year to spend more money on military defense than on programs of social uplift is approaching spiritual death.

America, the richest and most powerful nation in the world, can well lead the way in this revolution of values. There is nothing except a tragic death wish to prevent us from reordering our priorities so that the pursuit of peace will take precedence over the pursuit of war. There is nothing to keep us from molding a recalcitrant status quo with bruised hands until we have fashioned it into a brotherhood.

This kind of positive revolution of values is our best defense against communism. War is not the answer. Communism will never be defeated by the use of atomic bombs or nuclear weapons. Let us not join those who shout war and, through their misguided passions, urge the United States to relinquish its participation in the United Nations. These are days

---

25. From Kennedy's remarks to Latin American diplomats, Washington, D.C., March 12, 1962.

26. King is alluding to the parable of the Good Samaritan (Luke 10:25–37), which takes place on the road from Jerusalem to Jericho.

which demand wise restraint and calm reasonableness. We must not engage in a negative anti-communism, but rather in a positive thrust for democracy, realizing that our greatest defense against communism is to take offensive action in behalf of justice. We must with positive action seek to remove those conditions of poverty, insecurity, and injustice which are the fertile soil in which the seed of communism grows and develops.

These are revolutionary times. All over the globe men are revolting against old systems of exploitation and oppression, and out of the wombs of a frail world new systems of justice and equality are being born. The shirtless and barefoot people of the land are rising up as never before. The people who sat in darkness have seen a great light.[27] We in the West must support these revolutions.

It is a sad fact that because of comfort, complacency, a morbid fear of communism, and our proneness to adjust to injustice, the Western nations that initiated so much of the revolutionary spirit of the modern world have now become the arch antirevolutionaries. This has driven many to feel that only Marxism has the revolutionary spirit. Therefore, communism is a judgment against our failure to make democracy real and follow through on the revolutions that we initiated.

Our only hope today lies in our ability to recapture the revolutionary spirit and go out into a sometimes hostile world declaring eternal hostility to poverty, racism, and militarism. With this powerful commitment, we shall boldly challenge the status quo and unjust mores and thereby speed the day when every valley shall be exalted and every mountain and hill shall be made low, the crooked shall be made straight and the rough places plain.[28]

A genuine revolution of values means in the final analysis that our loyalties must become ecumenical rather than sectional. Every nation must now develop an overriding loyalty to mankind as a whole in order to preserve the best in their individual societies. This call for a worldwide fellowship that lifts neighborly concern beyond one's tribe, race, class, and nation is in reality a call for an all-embracing and unconditional love for all mankind. This oft-misunderstood, this oft-misinterpreted concept, so readily dismissed by the Nietzsches[29] of the world as a weak and cowardly force, has now become an absolute necessity for the survival of man.

When I speak of love, I am not speaking of some sentimental and weak response. I'm not speaking of that force which is just emotional bosh. I am speaking of that force which all of the great religions have seen as the supreme unifying principle of life. Love is somehow the key that unlocks the door which leads to ultimate reality. This Hindu-Moslem-Christian-Jewish-Buddhist belief about ultimate reality is beautifully summed up in the first epistle of Saint John: "Let us love one another, for love is God; and everyone that loveth is born of God, and knoweth God. He that loveth not knoweth not God, for God is love.... If we love one another, God dwelleth in us, and his love is perfected in us."[30]

Let us hope that this spirit will become the order of the day. We can no longer afford to worship the god of hate or bow before the altar of retaliation. The oceans of history are made turbulent by the ever-rising tides of hate. History is cluttered with the wreckage of nations and individuals that pursued this self-defeating path of hate. As Arnold Toynbee[31] says, "Love is the ultimate force that makes for the saving choice of life and good against the damning choice of death and evil. Therefore the first hope in our inventory... must be the hope that love is going to have the last word."[32] Unquote.

We are now faced with the fact, my friends, that tomorrow is today. We are confronted with the fierce urgency of now. In this unfolding conundrum of life and history there is such a thing as being too late. Procrastination is still the thief of time. Life often leaves us standing bare, naked, and dejected with a

27. An echo of Isaiah 9:2.

28. From Isaiah 40:4.

29. German philosopher Friedrich Nietzsche (1844–1900).

30. 1 John 4:7–8, 12.

31. Renowned British historian and antiwar activist.

32. From Toynbee's "Conditions of Survival," *Saturday Review*, August 29, 1964.

lost opportunity. The tide in the affairs of men does not remain at flood; it ebbs. We may cry out desperately for time to pause in her passage, but time is adamant to every plea and rushes on. Over the bleached bones and jumbled residues of numerous civilizations are written the pathetic words, "Too late." There is an invisible book of life that faithfully records our vigilance or our neglect. Omar Khayyam is right: "The moving finger writes and, having writ, moves on."[33]

We still have a choice today: nonviolent coexistence or violent co-annihilation. We must move past indecision to action. We must find new ways to speak for peace in Vietnam and justice throughout the developing world, a world that borders on our doors. If we do not act, we shall surely be dragged down the long, dark, and shameful corridors of time reserved for those who possess power without compassion, might without morality, and strength without sight.

Now let us begin. Now let us rededicate ourselves to the long and bitter, but beautiful, struggle for a new world. This is the calling of the sons of God, and our brothers wait eagerly for our response. Shall we say the odds are too great? Shall we tell them the struggle is too hard? Will our message be that the forces of American life militate against their arrival as full men and we send our deepest regrets? Or will there be another message—of longing, of hope, of solidarity with their yearnings, of commitment to their cause, whatever the cost?

The choice is ours, and though we might prefer it otherwise, we must choose in this crucial moment of human history. As that noble bard of yesterday, James Russell Lowell, eloquently stated:

> Once to every man and nation
>   Comes the moment to decide,
> In the strife of truth and falsehood,
>   For the good or evil side;
> Some great cause, God's new Messiah,
>   Offering each the bloom or blight—
> And the choice goes by forever
>   'Twixt that darkness and that light....
>
> Though the cause of evil prosper,
>   Yet 'tis truth alone is strong;
> Though her portion be the scaffold,
>   And upon the throne be wrong—
> Yet that scaffold sways the future,
>   And, behind the dim unknown,
> Standeth God within the shadow,
>   Keeping watch above his own.[34]

And if we will only make the right choice, we will be able to transform this pending cosmic elegy into a creative psalm of peace. If we will make the right choice, we will be able to transform the jangling discords of our world into a beautiful symphony of brotherhood. If we will but make the right choice, we will be able to speed up the day, all over America and all over the world, when justice will roll down like waters and righteousness like a mighty stream.[35]

---

33. From Edward FitzGerald, *The Rubaiyat of Omar Khayyam* (1859).

34. From the hymn "Once to Every Man and Nation," published in 1896 by W. Garrett Horder using passages selected, rearranged, and, in some cases, modified from Lowell's 1845 poem "The Present Crisis."

35. From Amos 5:24.

Cesar Chavez

Speech on Breaking His Fast

DELANO, CALIFORNIA
MARCH 10, 1968

GROWING UP IN a migratory family during the Great Depression, Cesar Chavez knew well the poverty and exploitation of farm workers. In 1962, after a decade honing his skills as an organizer in the Community Services Organization, an activist group for Mexican Americans, he moved to Delano and created the National Farm Workers Organization, which later became the United Farm Workers. Three years later he launched a strike against the grape growers that would last five years and include a nationwide boycott of table grapes before ending in victory for the workers.

In February 1968, as the strike dragged on, Chavez could feel the workers' commitment to nonviolence waning in the face of fierce resistance from the growers and their allies. Inspired by Mahatma Gandhi, Chavez undertook a fast to bring his followers back to the principles of nonviolence and sacrifice. Called by one magazine "an epic struggle against the masters of the land," the fast drew international attention. Workers from California's farm communities came to Delano to be near Chavez, to show loyalty to the cause, and to pray at the daily Mass. When Chavez finally broke his fast after three weeks, he had lost more than thirty-five pounds and was so weak he could barely walk.

On March 11 more than 6,000 people gathered at the Delano county park to celebrate the end of the fast. A flatbed truck had been converted into an altar and a speaker's platform. Chavez sat in an overstuffed chair next to U.S. Senator Robert F. Kennedy, who had flown in to show his support for the cause. Chavez's speech was read for him, first in Spanish, then in English, as the crowd responded with cheers of "Viva la Causa! Viva Chavez!" The speech does not waste a word; it is pellucid, uncluttered, and plainspoken. Of its 488 words, more than 90 percent have only one or two syllables, close to the same ratio as the Lord's Prayer and Abraham Lincoln's Gettysburg Address, proving once again that eloquence requires neither large words nor a large number of words.

◇◇

I have asked the Reverend James Drake to read this statement to you because my heart is so full and my body too weak to be able to say what I feel.

My warm thanks to all of you for coming today. Many of you have been here before, during the fast. Some have sent beautiful cards and telegrams and made offerings at the Mass. All of these expressions of your love have strengthened me, and I am grateful.

We should all express our thanks to Senator Kennedy for his constant work on behalf of the poor, for his personal encouragement to me, and for taking the time to break bread with us today.

I do not want any of you to be deceived about the fast. The strict fast of water only which I undertook on February 15 ended after the twenty-first day because of the advice of our doctor, James McKnight, and other physicians. Since that time I have been taking liquids in order to prevent serious damage to my kidneys.

We are gathered here today not so much to observe the end of the fast but because we are a family bound together in a common struggle for justice. We are a union family celebrating our unity and the nonviolent nature of our movement. Perhaps in the future we will come together at other times and places to break bread and to renew our courage and to celebrate important victories.

The fast has had different meanings for different people. Some of you may still wonder about its meaning and importance. It was not intended as a pressure against any growers. For that reason we have suspended negotiations and arbitration proceedings and relaxed the militant picketing and boycotting of the strike during this period. I undertook this fast because my heart was filled with grief and pain for the sufferings of farm workers. The fast was first for me and then for all of us in this union. It was a fast for nonviolence and a call to sacrifice.

Our struggle is not easy. Those who oppose our cause are rich and powerful and they have many allies in high places. We are poor. Our allies are few. But we have something the rich do not own. We have our own bodies and spirits and the justice of our cause as our weapons.

When we are really honest with ourselves we must admit that our lives are all that really belong to us. So, it is how we use our lives that determines what kind of men we are. It is my deepest belief that only by giving our lives do we find life. I am convinced that the truest act of courage, the strongest act of manliness is to sacrifice ourselves for others in a totally nonviolent struggle for justice.

To be a man is to suffer for others. God help us to be men!

Lyndon B. Johnson

Address on Not Seeking Reelection

WASHINGTON, D.C.
MARCH 31, 1968

AFTER COMING INTO office upon John Kennedy's assassination in November 1963, Lyndon Johnson was elected President in his own right in 1964. The next two years saw a flurry of domestic legislation almost unprecedented in American history, including Medicare, two landmark civil rights bills, and a host of educational, employment, conservation, and antipoverty programs. All these were part of Johnson's vision for the Great Society (see pages 405–408).

But even as the Great Society programs were being put into place, Johnson was steadily escalating the number of U.S. troops in Vietnam, which ultimately totaled more than 540,000. Each new escalation brought increased protest and civil disobedience against the war. In April 1967 Martin Luther King added his voice to the antiwar movement (see pages 453–463). By March 1968 the war had claimed some 25,000 American lives and Johnson's overall approval rating in the Gallup poll had plummeted to 36 percent. On March 12 he almost lost the New Hampshire Democratic presidential primary to U.S. Senator Eugene McCarthy. Less than a week later, Robert Kennedy announced his candidacy for the nomination.

For three years, Johnson had tried everything he could think of to win the war. He had bombed enemy sanctuaries, mined the North Vietnamese harbor at Haiphong, sent troops on search-and-destroy missions, defoliated the jungles using Agent Orange, initiated village pacification programs, made repeated efforts to negotiate, even offered aid to North Vietnam in exchange for a peace treaty—all to no avail. An unpopular President waging an even more unpopular war, he faced a revolt inside his own ranks and a reinvigorated Republican Party that was sure to make Vietnam the central issue of the fall campaign. He could soldier on or he could step aside and let a Democrat with less baggage carry the torch.

Johnson's speech to the nation on March 31 was another in a long line of presidential reports on the war. When he began, only a handful of people knew what was coming at the end. Indeed, Johnson had not fully made up his mind until that afternoon. After discussing the progress of military efforts and ongoing efforts to end the war, he looked into the camera and announced that he would not seek, and would not accept, the Democratic nomination for another four years in the White House. The announcement was so brief and so unexpected that millions of Americans watching on television wondered if they had heard correctly.

In stepping aside, Johnson regained a measure of the public esteem he had long since lost. Even his critics praised the speech as the "act of a very great patriot" that "lifted the office of the presidency to its proper place, far above politics." Johnson himself seemed liberated. One aide noted that when he finished speaking, he "bounded from his chair in the Oval Office" with "the air of a prisoner let free." For the next seven months, he would continue to work for peace, ultimately without result, while others contended for the reins of power.

<><><><><><><><><><><><><><><><><><><><><><><><><><>

Good evening, my fellow Americans. Tonight I want to speak to you of peace in Vietnam and Southeast Asia. No other question so preoccupies our people. No other dream so absorbs the 250 million human beings who live in that part of the world. No other goal motivates American policy in Southeast Asia.

For years, representatives of our governments and others have traveled the world seeking to find a basis for peace talks. Since last September, they have carried the offer that I made public at San Antonio.[1]

---

1. Johnson is referring to his speech at the National Legislative Conference, September 29, 1967.

And that offer was this: that the United States would stop its bombardment of North Vietnam when that would lead promptly to productive discussions—and that we would assume that North Vietnam would not take military advantage of our restraint.

Hanoi[2] denounced this offer, both privately and publicly. Even while the search for peace was going on, North Vietnam rushed their preparations for a savage assault on the people, the government, and the allies of South Vietnam.

Their attack—during the Tet holidays[3]—failed to achieve its principal objective. It did not collapse the elected government of South Vietnam or shatter its army, as the Communists had hoped. It did not produce a general uprising among the people of the cities as they had predicted. The Communists were unable to maintain control of any of the more than thirty cities that they attacked. And they took very heavy casualties.

But they did compel the South Vietnamese and their allies to move certain forces from the countryside into the cities. They caused widespread disruption and suffering. Their attacks, and the battles that followed, made refugees of half a million human beings.

The Communists may renew their attack any day. They are, it appears, trying to make 1968 the year of decision in South Vietnam—the year that brings, if not final victory or defeat, at least a turning point in the struggle.

This much is clear: If they do mount another round of heavy attacks, they will not succeed in destroying the fighting power of South Vietnam and its allies. But tragically, this is also clear: Many men—on both sides of the struggle—will be lost. A nation that has already suffered twenty years of warfare will suffer once again.[4] Armies on both sides will take new casualties. And the war will go on.

There is no need for this to be so. There is no need to delay the talks that could bring an end to this long and this bloody war. Tonight I renew the offer I made last August to stop the bombardment of North Vietnam.[5] We ask that talks begin promptly, that they be serious talks on the substance of peace. We assume that during those talks Hanoi will not take advantage of our restraint.

We are prepared to move immediately toward peace through negotiations. So tonight, in the hope that this action will lead to early talks, I am taking the first step to deescalate the conflict. We are reducing—substantially reducing—the present level of hostilities. And we are doing so unilaterally, and at once.

Tonight I have ordered our aircraft and our naval vessels to make no attacks on North Vietnam except in the area north of the demilitarized zone[6] where the continuing enemy buildup directly threatens allied forward positions and where the movement of their troops and supplies are clearly related to that threat. The area in which we are stopping our attacks includes almost 90 percent of North Vietnam's population and most of its territory. Thus there will be no attacks around the principal populated areas or in the food-producing areas of North Vietnam.

Even this very limited bombing of the North could come to an early end if our restraint is matched by restraint in Hanoi. But I cannot in good conscience stop all bombing so long as to do so would immediately and directly endanger the lives of our men and our allies. Whether a complete bombing halt becomes possible in the future will be determined by events.

Our purpose in this action is to bring about a reduction in the level of violence that now exists. It is to save the lives of brave men and to save the lives of innocent women and children. It is to permit the contending forces to move closer to a political settlement. And tonight I call upon the United Kingdom and I call upon the Soviet Union, as cochairmen of

2. Capital of North Vietnam.

3. Vietnamese New Year. Typically referred to as the Tet offensive, the North Vietnamese attack started on January 30, 1968.

4. Fighting among the various factions in Vietnam, then part of French Indochina, started shortly after the end of World War II.

5. In August 1967 Johnson offered, through diplomatic channels, to stop the bombing if North Vietnam would agree promptly to "productive discussions."

6. Originally created in 1954 as a temporary dividing line between North and South Vietnam, the demilitarized zone saw some of the fiercest fighting of the war.

the Geneva Conferences[7] and as permanent members of the United Nations Security Council, to do all they can to move from the unilateral act of deescalation that I have just announced toward genuine peace in Southeast Asia.

Now, as in the past, the United States is ready to send its representatives to any forum, at any time, to discuss the means of bringing this ugly war to an end. I am designating one of our most distinguished Americans, Ambassador Averell Harriman,[8] as my personal representative for such talks. In addition, I have asked Ambassador Llewellyn Thompson,[9] who returned from Moscow for consultation, to be available to join Ambassador Harriman at Geneva or any other suitable place just as soon as Hanoi agrees to a conference.

I call upon President Ho Chi Minh[10] to respond positively, and favorably, to this new step toward peace. But if peace does not come now through negotiations, it will come when Hanoi understands that our common resolve is unshakable and our common strength is invincible.

Tonight we and the other allied nations are contributing 600,000 fighting men to assist 700,000 South Vietnamese troops in defending their little country. Our presence there has always rested on this basic belief: The main burden of preserving their freedom must be carried out by them—by the South Vietnamese themselves. We and our allies can only help to provide a shield behind which the people of South Vietnam can survive and can grow and develop. On their efforts—on their determinations and resourcefulness—the outcome will ultimately depend.

That small, beleaguered nation has suffered terrible punishment for more than twenty years. I pay tribute once again tonight to the great courage and the endurance of its people. South Vietnam supports armed forces tonight of almost 700,000 men—and I call your attention to the fact that that is the equivalent of more than ten million in our own population. Its people maintain their firm determination to be free of domination by the North.

There has been substantial progress, I think, in building a durable government during these last three years. The South Vietnam of 1965 could not have survived the enemy's Tet offensive of 1968. The elected government of South Vietnam survived that attack and is rapidly repairing the devastation that it wrought.

The South Vietnamese know that further efforts are going to be required: to expand their own armed forces, to move back into the countryside as quickly as possible, to increase their taxes, to select the very best men that they have for civil and military responsibilities, to achieve a new unity within their constitutional government, and to include in the national effort all those groups who wish to preserve South Vietnam's control over its own destiny.

Last week President Thieu[11] ordered the mobilization of 135,000 additional South Vietnamese. He plans to reach, as soon as possible, a total military strength of more than 800,000 men. To achieve this, the government of South Vietnam started the drafting of nineteen-year-olds on March first. On May first, the government will begin the drafting of eighteen-year-olds. Last month, 10,000 men volunteered for military service—that was two and a half times the number of volunteers during the same month last year. Since the middle of January, more than 48,000 South Vietnamese have joined the armed forces, and nearly half of them volunteered to do so. All men in the South Vietnamese armed forces have had their tours of duty extended for the duration of the war, and reserves are now being called up for immediate active duty.

President Thieu told his people last week—I quote: "We must make greater efforts. We must

7. Great Britain and the Soviet Union were cochairs of the 1954 Geneva Conference that ended the Indochina War. During the 1960s there were a number of proposals to reconvene the conference in an effort to end the fighting in Vietnam.

8. Longtime American diplomat who served as ambassador at large through most of the Johnson administration.

9. Former ambassador to the Soviet Union who served as ambassador at large for President John F. Kennedy and then for Johnson.

10. President of North Vietnam.

11. South Vietnamese President Nguyen Van Thieu.

accept more sacrifices because, as I have said many times, this is our country. The existence of our nation is at stake, and this is mainly a Vietnamese responsibility."[12] He warned his people that a major national effort is required to root out corruption and incompetence at all levels of government.

We applaud this evidence of determination on the part of South Vietnam. Our first priority will be to support their effort. We shall accelerate the re-equipment of South Vietnam's armed forces in order to meet the enemy's increased firepower. And this will enable them progressively to undertake a larger share of combat operations against the Communist invaders.

On many occasions I have told the American people that we would send to Vietnam those forces that are required to accomplish our mission there. So with that as our guide, we have previously authorized a force level of approximately 525,000. Some weeks ago, to help meet the enemy's new offensive, we sent to Vietnam about 11,000 additional marine and airborne troops. They were deployed by air in forty-eight hours, on an emergency basis. But the artillery and the tank and the aircraft and medical and other units that were needed to work with and to support these infantry troops in combat could not then accompany them by air on that short notice.

In order that these forces may reach maximum combat effectiveness, the Joint Chiefs of Staff have recommended to me that we should prepare to send, during the next five months, the support troops totaling approximately 13,500 men. A portion of these men will be made available from our active forces. The balance will come from reserve component units which will be called up for service.

The actions that we have taken since the beginning of the year to re-equip the South Vietnamese forces, to meet our responsibilities in Korea[13] as well as our responsibilities in Vietnam, to meet price increases

and the cost of activating and deploying these reserve forces, to replace helicopters and provide the other military supplies we need—all of these actions are going to require additional expenditures. The tentative estimate of those additional expenditures is two and a half billion dollars in this fiscal year and two billion, six hundred million in the next fiscal year.

These projected increases in expenditures for our national security will bring into sharper focus the nation's need for immediate action, action to protect the prosperity of the American people and to protect the strength and the stability of our American dollar. On many occasions I have pointed out that without a tax bill or decreased expenditures, next year's deficit would again be around twenty billion. I have emphasized the need to set strict priorities in our spending. I have stressed that failure to act—and to act promptly and decisively—would raise very strong doubts throughout the world about America's willingness to keep its financial house in order.

Yet Congress has not acted. And tonight we face the sharpest financial threat in the postwar era—a threat to the dollar's role as the keystone of international trade and finance in the world. Last week, at the monetary conference in Stockholm, the major industrial countries decided to take a big step toward creating a new international monetary asset that will strengthen the international monetary system.[14] And I am very proud of the very able work done by Secretary Fowler and Chairman Martin of the Federal Reserve Board.[15]

But to make this system work the United States just must bring its balance of payments to—or very close to—equilibrium. We must have a responsible fiscal policy in this country. The passage of a tax bill now, together with expenditure control that the Congress may desire and dictate, is absolutely necessary to protect this nation's security and to continue our prosperity and to meet the needs of our people.

---

12. From Thieu's speech of March 21, 1968.

13. There were 50,000 U.S. troops in South Korea at the time of Johnson's speech. Tensions had increased in January 1968 when North Korea captured the *USS Pueblo*, an American intelligence ship operating in international waters in the Sea of Japan. The crew of the *Pueblo* remained in captivity for 11 months before being released.

14. In an effort to stabilize the world's monetary system, the conference proposed creating new reserve assets to supplement the gold and dollar holdings of central banks.

15. Henry H. Fowler, Secretary of the Treasury; William McChesney Martin Jr., chairman of the Board of Governors of the Federal Reserve System.

Now, what is at stake is seven years of unparalleled prosperity. In those seven years, the real income of the average American, after taxes, rose by almost 30 percent—a gain as large as that of the entire preceding nineteen years. So the steps that we must take to convince the world are exactly the steps that we must take to sustain our own economic strength here at home. In the past eight months, prices and interest rates have risen because of our inaction. We must therefore now do everything we can to move from debate to action, from talking to voting. And there is, I believe—I hope there is—in both houses of the Congress a growing sense of urgency that this situation just must be acted upon and must be corrected.

My budget in January, we thought, was a tight one. It fully reflected our evaluation of most of the demanding needs of this nation. But in these budgetary matters the President does not decide alone. The Congress has the power and the duty to determine appropriations and taxes. And the Congress is now considering our proposals, and they are considering reductions in the budget that we submitted. As part of a program of fiscal restraint that includes the tax surcharge, I shall approve appropriate reductions in the January budget when and if Congress so decides that that should be done.

One thing is unmistakably clear, however: Our deficit just must be reduced. Failure to act could bring on conditions that would strike hardest at those people that all of us are trying so hard to help.

So these times call for prudence in this land of plenty. And I believe that we have the character to provide it, and tonight I plead with the Congress and with the people to act promptly to serve the national interest and thereby serve all of our people.

Now let me give you my estimate of the chances for peace—the peace that will one day stop the bloodshed in South Vietnam, that will [let] all the Vietnamese people be permitted to rebuild and develop their land, that will permit us to turn more fully to our own tasks here at home.

I cannot promise that the initiative that I have announced tonight will be completely successful in achieving peace any more than the thirty others that we have undertaken and agreed to in recent years. But it is our fervent hope that North Vietnam, after years of fighting that has left the issue unresolved, will now cease its efforts to achieve a military victory and will join with us in moving toward the peace table. And there may come a time when South Vietnamese—on both sides—are able to work out a way to settle their own differences by free political choice rather than by war.

As Hanoi considers its course, it should be in no doubt of our intentions. It must not miscalculate the pressures within our democracy in this election year. We have no intention of widening this war. But the United States will never accept a fake solution to this long and arduous struggle and call it peace.

No one can foretell the precise terms of an eventual settlement. Our objective in South Vietnam has never been the annihilation of the enemy. It has been to bring about a recognition in Hanoi that its objective—taking over the South by force—could not be achieved. We think that peace can be based on the Geneva Accords of 1954,[16] under political conditions that permit the South Vietnamese—all the South Vietnamese—to chart their course free of any outside domination or interference, from us or from anyone else. So tonight I reaffirm the pledge that we made at Manila: that we are prepared to withdraw our forces from South Vietnam as the other side withdraws its forces to the North, stops the infiltration, and the level of violence thus subsides.[17]

Our goal of peace and self-determination in Vietnam is directly related to the future of all of Southeast Asia, where much has happened to inspire confidence during the past ten years. And we have done all that we knew how to do to contribute and to help build that confidence.

A number of its nations have shown what can be accomplished under conditions of security. Since 1966, Indonesia, the fifth-largest nation in all the

---

16. Agreement at the end of the French Indochina War that partitioned the newly independent Vietnam at the 17th parallel. The partition was supposed to end in 1956 after elections to choose a new national government, but the elections were never held and Vietnam was not unified until 1975.

17. Johnson made this pledge on more than one occasion; here he is referring to his reiteration of it at the Manila Conference of October 24–25, 1966.

world, with a population of more than a hundred million people, has had a government that's dedicated to peace with its neighbors and the improved conditions for its own people. Political and economic cooperation between nations has grown rapidly, and I think every American can take a great deal of pride in the role that we have played in bringing this about in Southeast Asia. We can rightly judge, as responsible Southeast Asians themselves do, that the progress of the past three years would have been far less likely—if not completely impossible—if America's sons and others had not made their stand in Vietnam.

At Johns Hopkins University, about three years ago,[18] I announced that the United States would take part in the great work of developing Southeast Asia, including the Mekong Valley, for all the people of that region. Our determination to help build a better land, a better land for men on both sides of the present conflict, has not diminished in the least. Indeed, the ravages of war, I think, have made it more urgent than ever. So I repeat on behalf of the United States again tonight what I said at Johns Hopkins: that North Vietnam could take its place in this common effort just as soon as peace comes.

Over time, a wider framework of peace and security in Southeast Asia may become possible. The new cooperations of the nations of the area could be a foundation stone. Certainly friendship with the nations of such a Southeast Asia is what the United States seeks—and that is all that the United States seeks.

One day, my fellow citizen, there will be peace in Southeast Asia. It will come because the people of Southeast Asia want it—those whose armies are at war tonight, those who, though threatened, have thus far been spared. Peace will come because Asians were willing to work for it and to sacrifice for it and to die by the thousands for it.

Let it never be forgotten: Peace will come also because America sent her sons to help secure it. It has not been easy—far from it. During the past four and a half years, it has been my fate and my responsibility to be commander in chief. I have lived daily and nightly with the cost of this war. I know the pain that it has inflicted. I know, perhaps better than anyone, the misgivings that it has aroused. And throughout this entire, long period, I have been sustained by a single principle: that what we are doing now in Vietnam is vital not only to the security of Southeast Asia, but it is vital to the security of every American.

Surely we have treaties which we must respect. Surely we have commitments that we are going to keep. Resolutions of the Congress testify to the need to resist aggression in the world and in Southeast Asia. But the heart of our involvement in South Vietnam—under three different Presidents,[19] three separate administrations—has always been America's own security. And the larger purpose of our involvement has always been to help the nations of Southeast Asia become independent and stand alone, self-sustaining, as members of a great world community, at peace with themselves, at peace with all others. And with such an Asia, our country—and the world—will be far more secure than it is tonight.

I believe that a peaceful Asia is far nearer to reality because of what America has done in Vietnam. I believe that the men who endure the dangers of battle there—fighting there for us tonight—are helping the entire world avoid far greater conflicts, far wider wars, far more destruction, than this one.

The peace that will bring them home someday will come. Tonight I have offered the first in what I hope will be a series of mutual moves toward peace. I pray that it will not be rejected by the leaders of North Vietnam. I pray that they, they will accept it as a means by which the sacrifices of their own people may be ended. And I ask your help and your support, my fellow citizens, for this effort to reach across the battlefield toward an early peace.

Finally, my fellow Americans, let me say this: Of those to whom much is given, much is asked.[20] I cannot say—and no man could say—that no more will be asked of us. Yet I believe that now, no less than when the decade began, this generation of Americans is willing to "pay any price, bear any burden, meet any

---

18. Johnson is referring to his speech "Peace Without Conquest," April 7, 1965.

19. Johnson, Kennedy, and Dwight D. Eisenhower.

20. From Luke 12:48.

hardship, support any friend, oppose any foe to assure the survival and the success of liberty."[21] Since those words were spoken by John F. Kennedy, the people of America have kept that compact with mankind's noblest cause. And we shall continue to keep it.

Yet I believe that we must always be mindful of this one thing, whatever the trials and the tests ahead: The ultimate strength of our country and our cause will lie not in powerful weapons or infinite resources or boundless wealth, but will lie in the unity of our people. This I believe very deeply.

Throughout my entire public career I have followed the personal philosophy that I am a free man, an American, a public servant, and a member of my party—in that order always and only. For thirty-seven years in the service of our nation, first as a Congressman, as a Senator, and as Vice President, and now as your President,[22] I have put the unity of the people first. I have put it ahead of any divisive partisanship. And in these times, as in times before, it is true that a house divided against itself by the spirit of faction, of party, of region, of religion, of race, is a house that cannot stand.[23]

There is division in the American house now. There is divisiveness among us all tonight. And holding the trust that is mine, as President of all the people, I cannot disregard the peril to the progress of the American people and the hope and the prospects of peace for all peoples. So I would ask all Americans, whatever their personal interests or concern, to guard against divisiveness and all of its ugly consequences.

Fifty-two months and ten days ago, in a moment of tragedy and trauma, the duties of this office fell upon me.[24] I asked then for your help, and God's, that we might continue America on its course, binding up our wounds, healing our history, moving forward in new unity, to clear the American agenda and to keep the American commitment for all of our people.[25] United we have kept that commitment. And united we have enlarged that commitment. And through all time to come I think America will be a stronger nation, a more just society, a land of greater opportunity and fulfillment because of what we have all done together in these years of unparalleled achievement. Our reward will come in the life of freedom and peace and hope that our children will enjoy through ages ahead.

What we won when all of our people united just must not now be lost in suspicion and distrust and selfishness and politics among any of our people. And believing this as I do, I have concluded that I should not permit the presidency to become involved in the partisan divisions that are developing in this political year. With American sons in the fields far away, with America's future under challenge right here at home, with our hopes and the world's hopes for peace in the balance every day, I do not believe that I should devote an hour or a day of my time to any personal partisan causes or to any duties other than the awesome duties of this office—the presidency of your country. Accordingly, I shall not seek, and I will not accept, the nomination of my party for another term as your President.

But let men everywhere know, however, that a strong and a confident and a vigilant America stands ready tonight to seek an honorable peace—and stands ready tonight to defend an honored cause—whatever the price, whatever the burden, whatever the sacrifice that duty may require.

Thank you for listening. Good night, and God bless all of you.

---

21. From President Kennedy's inaugural address, January 20, 1961 (pages 341–344).

22. Johnson served in the House of Representatives from 1937 to 1949, the U.S. Senate from 1949 to 1961, as Vice President from 1961 to 1963, and as President from 1963 to 1969.

23. An allusion to Abraham Lincoln's "House Divided" speech of June 16, 1858, whose central trope echoed the language of Matthew 12:25 and Mark 3:25.

24. Johnson came into office upon the assassination of John F. Kennedy on November 22, 1963.

25. See Johnson's "Let Us Continue," November 27, 1963 (pages 388–391).

Martin Luther King

I've Been to the Mountaintop

MEMPHIS, TENNESSEE
APRIL 3, 1968

A T THE END of 1967, Martin Luther King announced plans for a Poor People's March in Washington, D.C., to be held the next April. Reflecting his belief that "the evils of capitalism are as real as the evils of militarism and the evils of racism," the march aimed to build an interracial coalition to combat the scourge of poverty. In the midst of preparing for the march, King was invited to Memphis, Tennessee, whose sanitation workers, almost all of whom were black, had gone on strike in February 1968. After an initial visit on March 18, King returned ten days later for what he believed would be a nonviolent march in support of the strikers, but it turned into a bloody melee that injured more than fifty people and cost one black youth his life. Stung by criticism of his leadership, King made the fateful decision to go to Memphis yet again, this time on Wednesday, April 3. The next evening, while standing on his balcony at the Lorraine Hotel, he was killed by a single bullet to the head fired by James Earl Ray.

The night before his death, King addressed an audience of 2,000 people at the Mason Temple. As was often the case when speaking to black audiences during the civil rights movement, he spent the bulk of his time seeking to bolster the optimism of his listeners that their efforts would be successful and that the bright day of justice would arrive. As he moved toward the end of his remarks, he took a more introspective turn, talking about his near-fatal stabbing in a Harlem department store ten years earlier. But it was his concluding words that were most arresting. Like anyone, he said, he would like to lead a long life, but that didn't concern him now, for God had allowed him to go up to the mountain and see the Promised Land. "I may not get there with you," he declared, but "we as a people will get to the Promised Land. And so I'm happy tonight. I'm not worried about anything. I'm not fearing any man. Mine eyes have seen the glory of the coming of the Lord."

These words have led to much speculation as to whether King had a premonition of his impending death, but such a conclusion seems far-fetched. King faced the threat of assassination every day, and he had used much the same words on other occasions. While the situation in Memphis was volatile, it did not appear to be any more dangerous than many he had faced in previous years. He had been in a despondent mood for several months, but he seemed happy and relaxed after the speech. When King's peroration is read closely, the tone is essentially uplifting and reinforces the main theme of the speech: that African Americans will indeed get to the Promised Land. The tragedy is that while King's words proved to be prophetic with regard to his own fate, they were less so with regard to the cause for which he gave his life.

◇◇

Thank you very kindly, my friends. As I listened to Ralph Abernathy[1] and his eloquent and generous introduction and then thought about myself, I wondered who he was talking about. It's always good to have your closest friend and associate to say something good about you. And Ralph Abernathy is the best friend that I have in the world.

I'm delighted to see each of you here tonight in spite of a storm warning. You reveal that you are determined to go on anyhow. Something is happening in Memphis; something is happening in our world.

And you know, if I were standing at the beginning of time with the possibility of taking a kind of general and panoramic view of the whole of human history up to now, and the Almighty said to me, "Martin Luther King, which age would you like to live in?" I would take my mental flight by Egypt, and I would watch God's children in their magnificent trek from the dark dungeons of Egypt through—or rather across—the Red Sea, through the wilderness, on toward the Promised Land.[2] And in spite of its magnificence, I wouldn't stop there.

I would move on by Greece, and take my mind to Mount Olympus. And I would see Plato, Aristotle, Socrates, Euripides, and Aristophanes assembled around the Parthenon,[3] and I would watch them around the Parthenon as they discussed the great and eternal issues of reality. But I wouldn't stop there.

I would go on even to the great heyday of the Roman Empire, and I would see developments around there through various emperors and leaders. But I wouldn't stop there.

I would even come up to the day of the Renaissance and get a quick picture of all that the Renaissance did for the cultural and aesthetic life of man. But I wouldn't stop there.

I would even go by the way that the man for whom I'm named had his habitat, and I would watch Martin Luther as he tacked his ninety-five theses on the door at the church of Wittenberg.[4] But I wouldn't stop there.

I would come on up even to 1863 and watch a vacillating President by the name of Abraham Lincoln finally come to the conclusion that he had to sign the Emancipation Proclamation.[5] But I wouldn't stop there.

I would even come up to the early '30s and see a man grappling with the problems of the bankruptcy of his nation and come with an eloquent cry that we have nothing to fear but fear itself.[6] But I wouldn't stop there.

Strangely enough, I would turn to the Almighty and say, "If you allow me to live just a few years in the second half of the twentieth century, I will be happy." Now, that's a strange statement to make because the world is all messed up. The nation is sick. Trouble is in the land, confusion all around. That's a strange statement.

But I know somehow that only when it is dark enough can you see the stars. And I see God working in this period of the twentieth century in a way that

---

1. Longtime associate of King and vice president of the Southern Christian Leadership Conference (SCLC), the civil rights organization founded by King and others in 1957.

2. King is referring to the Jews' escape from ancient Egypt as told in the biblical book of Exodus.

3. Built atop the Acropolis, the Parthenon was the most imposing structure of ancient Athens.

4. This event, which helped touch off the Protestant Reformation, occurred in 1517.

5. Document of January 1, 1863, that freed the slaves in areas still under control of the Confederacy.

6. King is referring to Franklin D. Roosevelt's first inaugural address, March 4, 1933 (pages 221–224).

men, in some strange way, are responding. Something is happening in our world. The masses of people are rising up. And wherever they are assembled today, whether they are in Johannesburg, South Africa; Nairobi, Kenya; Accra, Ghana; New York City; Atlanta, Georgia; Jackson, Mississippi; or Memphis, Tennessee, the cry is always the same: "We want to be free."

And another reason that I'm happy to live in this period is that we have been forced to a point where we're gonna have to grapple with the problems that men have been trying to grapple with through history, but the demands didn't force them to do it. Survival demands that we grapple with 'em. Men for years now have been talking about war and peace. But now no longer can they just talk about it. It is no longer a choice between violence and nonviolence in this world; it's nonviolence or nonexistence. That is where we are today.

And also, in the human rights revolution, if something isn't done, and done in a hurry, to bring the colored peoples of the world out of their long years of poverty, their long years of hurt and neglect, the whole world is doomed. Now, I'm just happy that God has allowed me to live in this period, to see what is unfolding. And I'm happy that he's allowed me to be in Memphis.

I can remember, I can remember when Negroes were just goin' around, as Ralph has said so often, scratchin' where they didn't itch and laughin' when they were not tickled. But that day is all over. We mean business now, and we are determined to gain our rightful place in God's world. And that's all this whole thing is about. We aren't engaged in any negative protest and in any negative arguments with anybody. We are saying that we are determined to be men; we are determined to be people. We are saying, we are saying that we are God's children. And that [since] we are God's children, we don't have to live like we are forced to live.

Now, what does all of this mean in this great period of history? It means that we've got to stay together. We've got to stay together and maintain unity. You know, whenever Pharaoh wanted to prolong the period of slavery in Egypt, he had a favorite, favorite formula for doing it. What was that? He kept the slaves fightin' among themselves. But whenever the slaves get together, something happens in Pharaoh's court, and he cannot hold the slaves in slavery. When the slaves get together, that's the beginning of gettin' out of slavery. Now let us maintain unity.

Secondly, let us keep the issues where they are. The issue is injustice. The issue is the refusal of Memphis to be fair and honest in its dealings with its public servants who happen to be sanitation workers. Now, we've got to keep attention on that. That's always the problem with a little violence. You know what happened the other day, and the press dealt only with the window breaking.[7] I read the articles. They very seldom got around to mentioning the fact that 1,300 sanitation workers are on strike and that Memphis is not being fair to them and that Mayor Loeb[8] is in dire need of a doctor. They didn't get around to that.

Now, we're gonna march again, and we've gotta march again, in order to put the issue where it is supposed to be and force everybody to see that there are 1,300 of God's children here suffering, sometimes goin' hungry, going through dark and dreary nights wondering how this thing is gonna come out. That's the issue. And we've got to say to the nation, "We know how it's coming out." For when people get caught up with that which is right and they are willing to sacrifice for it, there is no stopping point short of victory.

We aren't gonna let any mace stop us. We are masters in our nonviolent movement in disarming police forces. They don't know what to do; I've seen 'em so often. I remember in Birmingham, Alabama, when we were in that majestic struggle there,[9] we would move out of the Sixteenth Street Baptist Church day after day. By the hundreds we would move out, and Bull Connor[10] would tell 'em to send the dogs forth, and they did come. But we just went

---

7. Six days before King's speech, a march in support of the sanitation workers turned violent when some black youths began breaking windows and looting stores. Police responded with force, and by the time the melee was over, dozens of people had been injured and one had been killed.

8. Memphis Mayor Henry Loeb.

9. The Birmingham demonstrations took place in the spring of 1963.

10. Commissioner of public safety in Birmingham.

before the dogs singin' "Ain't Gonna Let Nobody Turn Me Around."[11]

Bull Connor next would say, "Turn the fire hoses on." And as I said to you the other night, Bull Connor didn't know history. He knew a kind of physics that somehow didn't relate to the transphysics that we knew about. And that was the fact that there was a certain kind of fire that no water could put out. And we went before the fire hoses. We had known water. If we were Baptist or some other denomination, we had been immersed. If we were Methodist and some others, we had been sprinkled. But we knew water— that couldn't stop us.

And we just went on before the dogs, and we would look at them; and we'd go on before the water hoses, and we would look at it; and we'd just go on singin' "Over my head I see freedom in the air."[12] And then we would be thrown in the paddy wagons, and sometimes we were stacked in there like sardines in a can. And they would throw us in, and old Bull would say, "Take 'em off." And they did, and we would just go on in the paddy wagon singin' "We Shall Overcome."[13]

And every now and then we'd get in jail, and we'd see the jailers looking through the windows being moved by our prayers and being moved by our words and our songs. And there was a power there which Bull Connor couldn't adjust to. And so we ended up transforming Bull into a steer, and we won our struggle in Birmingham.

Now, we've got to go on in Memphis just like that. I call upon you to be with us when we go out Monday.

Now, about injunctions. We have an injunction, and we're goin' into court tomorrow morning to fight this illegal, unconstitutional injunction.[14] All we say

to America is, "Be true to what you said on paper." If I lived in China or even Russia or any totalitarian country, maybe I could understand some of these illegal injunctions. Maybe I could understand the denial of certain basic First Amendment privileges, because they hadn't committed themselves to that over there. But somewhere I read of the freedom of assembly. Somewhere I read of the freedom of speech. Somewhere I read of the freedom of press.[15] Somewhere I read that the greatness of America is the right to protest for right. And so just as I say we aren't gonna let any dogs or water hoses turn us around, we aren't gonna let any injunction turn us around. We are goin' on. We need all of you.

And you know what's beautiful to me is to see all of these ministers of the Gospel. It's a marvelous picture. Who is it that is supposed to articulate the longings and aspirations of the people more than the preacher? Somehow the preacher must have a kind of fire shut up in his bones, and whenever injustice is around, he must tell it. Somehow the preacher must be an Amos, who said, "When God speaks, who can but prophesy?"[16] Again with Amos: "Let justice roll down like waters and righteousness like a mighty stream."[17] Somehow the preacher must say with Jesus: "The spirit of the Lord is upon me, because he has anointed me."[18] And he's anointed me to deal with the problems of the poor.

And I want to commend the preachers, under the leadership of these noble men: James Lawson,[19] one who has been in this struggle for many years. He's been to jail for struggling; he's been kicked out of Vanderbilt University for this strugglin', but he's still going on, fighting for the rights of his people. Reverend Ralph Jackson, Billy Kyles[20]—I could just

---

11. Traditional Baptist spiritual often sung by civil rights protesters.

12. Civil rights refrain adapted from the spiritual lyric "Over my head I see Jesus in the air."

13. Based on a combination of older songs, "We Shall Overcome" was sung during a 1945 strike by the Negro Food and Tobacco Union in Charleston, South Carolina, and later became the unofficial anthem of the civil rights movement.

14. On April 3, U.S. District Judge Bailey Brown issued a temporary restraining order against the SCLC demonstration scheduled for April 5.

15. Freedom of speech, press, and assembly are all protected under the First Amendment to the U.S. Constitution.

16. Paraphrased from Amos 3:8.

17. Paraphrased from Amos 5:24.

18. Luke 4:18.

19. Pastor of Centenary Methodist Church in Memphis.

20. H. Ralph Jackson of the American Methodist Episcopal church in Memphis; Samuel B. "Billy" Kyles, pastor of Memphis's Monumental Baptist Church.

go right on down the list, but time will not permit. But I want to thank all of 'em. And I want you to thank 'em because so often preachers aren't concerned about anything but themselves.

And I'm always happy to see a relevant ministry. It's all right to talk about long white robes over yonder,[21] in all of its symbolism. But ultimately people want some suits and dresses and shoes to wear down here. It's all right to talk about streets flowin' with milk and honey,[22] but God has commanded us to be concerned about the slums down here and his children who can't eat three square meals a day. It's all right to talk about the new Jerusalem,[23] but one day God's preacher must talk about the new New York, the new Atlanta, the new Philadelphia, the new Los Angeles, the new Memphis, Tennessee. This is what we have to do.

Now, the other thing we'll have to do is this: always anchor our external direct action with the power of economic withdrawal. Now, we are poor people. Individually we are poor when you compare us with white society in America. We are poor. Never stop and forget that collectively—that means all of us together—collectively we are richer than all the nations in the world with the exception of nine. Did you ever think about that? After you leave the United States, Soviet Russia, Great Britain, West Germany, France, and I could name the others, the American Negro collectively is richer than most nations of the world. We have an annual income of more than $30 billion a year, which is more than all of the exports of the United States and more than the national budget of Canada. Did you know that? That's power right there, if we know how to pool it.

We don't have to argue with anybody. We don't have to curse and go around acting bad with our words. We don't need any bricks and bottles; we don't need any Molotov cocktails.[24] We just need to go around to these stores, and to these massive industries in our country, and say: "God sent us by here to say to you that you're not treating his children right. And we've come by here to ask you to make the first item on your agenda fair treatment where God's children are concerned. Now, if you are not prepared to do that, we do have an agenda that we must follow. And our agenda calls for withdrawing economic support from you."

And so, as a result of this, we are asking you tonight to go out and tell your neighbors not to buy Coca-Cola in Memphis. Go by and tell them not to buy Sealtest milk. Tell them not to buy—what is the other bread?—Wonder Bread. And what is the other bread company, Jesse?[25] Tell 'em not to buy Hart's bread. As Jesse Jackson has said, up to now only the garbage men have been feeling pain. Now, we must kind of redistribute the pain. We are choosing these companies because they haven't been fair in their hiring policies; and we are choosing them because they can begin the process of saying they are gonna support the needs and the rights of these men who are on strike. And then they can move on downtown and tell Mayor Loeb to do what is right.

And not only that, we've got to strengthen black institutions. I call upon you to take your money out of the banks downtown and deposit your money in Tri-State Bank.[26] We want a bank-in movement[27] in Memphis. Go by the savings and loan association. I'm not askin' you something that we don't do ourselves in SCLC. Judge Hooks[28] and others will tell you that we have an account here in the savings and loan association from the Southern Christian

---

21. An allusion to the gospel song "Just Over Yonder," lyrics by Roscoe Reed.

22. An echo of Exodus 3:8.

23. In Revelation 21, the new Jerusalem is described as part of the new heaven and new earth that follow God's defeat of Satan at the end of time.

24. Bottles filled with liquid, typically gasoline, that can be ignited and thrown at targets. The name originated during World War II, when Finnish soldiers utilized such weapons to resist invasion by the Soviet Union, whose Commissar for Foreign Relations was Vyacheslav Molotov.

25. Jesse Jackson, who was with King in Memphis.

26. Black-owned bank founded in 1946.

27. An allusion to the sit-in campaigns used to desegregate Southern lunch counters during the early 1960s.

28. Benjamin Hooks, who in 1965 had become the first black criminal court judge in Tennessee.

Leadership Conference. We are telling you to follow what we're doing: Put your money there. You have six or seven black insurance companies here in the city of Memphis. Take out your insurance there. We want to have an insurance-in.

Now, these are some practical things that we can do. We begin the process of building a greater economic base, and at the same time we are puttin' pressure where it really hurts. And I ask you to follow through here.

Now, let me say as I move to my conclusion that we've got to give ourselves to this struggle until the end. Nothing would be more tragic than to stop at this point in Memphis. We've got to see it through. And when we have our march, you need to be there. If it means leaving work, if it means leaving school, be there. Be concerned about your brother. You may not be on strike. But either we go up together, or we go down together.

Let us develop a kind of dangerous unselfishness. One day a man came to Jesus, and he wanted to raise some questions about some vital matters of life. At points he wanted to trick Jesus and show him that he knew a little more than Jesus knew and throw him off base.[29] Now, that question could have easily ended up in a philosophical and theological debate. But Jesus immediately pulled that question from midair and placed it on a dangerous curve between Jerusalem and Jericho. And he talked about a certain man who fell among thieves. You remember that a Levite[30] and a priest passed by on the other side; they didn't stop to help him. And finally, a man of another race came by. He got down from his beast, decided not to be compassionate by proxy. But he got down with him, administered first aid, and helped the man in need.[31] Jesus ended up saying this was the good man, this was the great man, because he had the capacity to project the "I" into the "thou" and to be concerned about his brother.[32]

Now, you know we use our imagination a great deal to try to determine why the priest and the Levite didn't stop. At times we say they were busy going to a church meeting, an ecclesiastical gathering, and they had to get on down to Jerusalem so they wouldn't be late for their meeting. At other times we would speculate that there was a religious law that one who was engaged in religious ceremonials was not to touch a human body twenty-four hours before the ceremony. And every now and then we begin to wonder whether maybe they were not going down to Jerusalem—or down to Jericho, rather—to organize a Jericho Road Improvement Association.[33] That's a possibility. Maybe they felt that it was better to deal with the problem from the causal root, rather than to get bogged down with an individual effect.

But I'm going to tell you what my imagination tells me. It's possible that those men were afraid. You see, the Jericho road is a dangerous road. I remember when Mrs. King and I were first in Jerusalem. We rented a car and drove from Jerusalem down to Jericho. And as soon as we got on that road, I said to my wife, "I can see why Jesus used this as the setting for his parable." It's a winding, meandering road. It's really conducive for ambushing. You start out in Jerusalem, which is about 1,200 miles—or, rather 1,200 feet—above sea level. And by the time you get down to Jericho fifteen or twenty minutes later, you're about 2,200 feet below sea level. That's a dangerous road. In the days of Jesus it came to be known as the Bloody Pass.

And you know it's possible that the priest and the Levite looked over that man on the ground and wondered if the robbers were still around. Or it's possible that they felt that the man on the ground was merely fakin', and he was acting like he had been robbed and hurt in order to seize them over there, lure them there for quick and easy seizure. And so the first question that the priest asked, the first question that the Levite asked, was: "If I stop to help this man, what will happen to me?" But then the Good Samaritan came by,

---

29. There is a brief interruption in the recording at this point.

30. A descendant of the Hebrew tribe of Levi, usually used to designate males who served as assistants to the temple priests.

31. King is discussing the parable of the Good Samaritan (Luke 10:25–37), which takes place on the road from Jerusalem to Jericho.

32. A reference to Martin Buber's *Ich und Du* (1923).

33. A play on the Montgomery Improvement Association, which King headed during the Montgomery bus boycott of 1955–1956.

and he reversed the question: "If I do not stop to help this man, what will happen to him?"

That's the question before you tonight. Not "If I stop to help the sanitation workers, what will happen to my job?" Not "If I stop to help the sanitation workers, what will happen to all of the hours that I usually spend in my office every day and every week as a pastor?" The question is not "If I stop to help this man in need, what will happen to me?" The question is "If I do not stop to help the sanitation workers, what will happen to them?" That's the question.

Let us rise up tonight with a greater readiness. Let us stand with a greater determination. And let us move on in these powerful days, these days of challenge, to make America what it ought to be. We have an opportunity to make America a better nation.

And I want to thank God once more for allowing me to be here with you. You know, several years ago[34] I was in New York City autographing the first book that I had written. And while sitting there autographing books, a demented black woman came up. The only question I heard from her was, "Are you Martin Luther King?" And I was looking down writing, and I said, "Yes." The next minute I felt something beating on my chest. Before I knew it, I had been stabbed by this demented woman. I was rushed to Harlem Hospital. It was a dark Saturday afternoon. And that blade had gone through, and the X-rays revealed that the tip of the blade was on the edge of my aorta, the main artery. And once that's punctured, you're drowned in your own blood—that's the end of you. It came out in the *New York Times* the next morning that if I had merely sneezed, I would have died.

Well, about four days later they allowed me, after the operation, after my chest had been opened and the blade had been taken out, to move around in the wheelchair in the hospital. They allowed me to read some of the mail that came in—and from all over the states and the world kind letters came in. I read a few, but one of them I will never forget. I had received one from the President and the Vice President;[35] I've

forgotten what those telegrams said. I'd received a visit and a letter from the Governor of New York,[36] but I've forgotten what that letter said.

But there was another letter that came from a little girl, a young girl who was a student at the White Plains High School. And I looked at that letter, and I'll never forget it. It said simply: "Dear Dr. King, I am a ninth-grade student at the White Plains High School." She said: "While it should not matter, I would like to mention that I'm a white girl. I read in the paper of your misfortune and of your suffering. And I read that if you had sneezed, you would have died. And I'm simply writing you to say that I'm so happy that you didn't sneeze."

And I want to say tonight, I want to say tonight that I, too, am happy that I didn't sneeze. Because if I had sneezed, I wouldn't have been around here to 1960, when students all over the South started sitting-in at lunch counters.[37] And I knew that as they were sitting-in, they were really standing up for the best in the American dream and taking the whole nation back to those great wells of democracy which were dug deep by the Founding Fathers in the Declaration of Independence and the Constitution.

If I had sneezed, I wouldn't have been around here to 1961, when we decided to take a ride for freedom and ended segregation in interstate travel.[38]

If I had sneezed, I wouldn't have been around here in 1962, when Negroes in Albany, Georgia, decided to straighten their backs up.[39] And whenever men and women straighten their backs up, they are going somewhere, because a man can't ride your back unless it is bent.

If I had sneezed, if I had sneezed, I wouldn't have been here in 1963, when the black people of Birmingham, Alabama, aroused the conscience of this nation and brought into being the civil rights bill.[40]

---

34. 1958.

35. President Dwight D. Eisenhower; Vice President Richard M. Nixon.

36. Averell Harriman.

37. See note 27 above.

38. King is referring to the Freedom Rides that took place in the South during the summer of 1961.

39. A reference to the Albany desegregation campaign of 1961–1962.

40. King is referring to the Civil Rights Act of 1964.

If I had sneezed, I wouldn't have had a chance later that year, in August, to try to tell America about a dream that I had had.[41]

If I had sneezed, I wouldn't have been down in Selma, Alabama, to see the great movement there.[42]

If I had sneezed, I wouldn't have been in Memphis to see a community rally around those brothers and sisters who are suffering. I'm so happy that I didn't sneeze.

And they were telling me.[43]

Now, it doesn't matter now. It really doesn't matter what happens now. I left Atlanta this morning, and as we got started on the plane—there were six of us—the pilot said over the public address system: "We are sorry for the delay, but we have Dr. Martin Luther King on the plane. And to be sure that all of the bags were checked, and to be sure that nothing would be wrong on the plane, we had to check out everything carefully. And we've had the plane protected and guarded all night."

And then I got into Memphis. And some began to say the threats, or talk about the threats that were out of what would happen to me from some of our sick white brothers.

Well, I don't know what will happen now. We've got some difficult days ahead. But it really doesn't matter with me now because I've been to the mountaintop. And I don't mind. Like anybody, I would like to live a long life. Longevity has its place. But I'm not concerned about that now. I just want to do God's will. And he's allowed me to go up to the mountain. And I've looked over, and I've seen the Promised Land. I may not get there with you. But I want you to know tonight that we as a people will get to the Promised Land. And so I'm happy tonight. I'm not worried about anything. I'm not fearing any man. Mine eyes have seen the glory of the coming of the Lord.

---

41. A reference to King's "I Have a Dream," August 28, 1963 (pages 375–378).

42. The Selma protests, especially the March 7, 1965, attack on civil rights marchers at the Edmund Pettis Bridge, helped spur passage of the Voting Rights Act later that year (see pages 427–433).

43. King, who delivered this speech without notes, stopped in mid-sentence and paused briefly before shifting the direction of his ideas.

Robert F. Kennedy

Statement on the Assassination of Martin Luther King Jr.

INDIANAPOLIS, INDIANA
APRIL 4, 1968

OPPOSED TO THE war in Vietnam and distressed by growing polarization within the United States, Robert Kennedy announced in March 1968 that he would seek the Democratic nomination for President. On April 4 he was boarding a plane for a campaign stop in Indianapolis when he learned that Martin Luther King had been shot outside his hotel room in Memphis,

Tennessee. Soon after the plane landed, word came that King had died. Kennedy was slated to speak in the toughest section of Indianapolis's black community. The chief of police urged him to cancel and said he could not provide a police escort into the ghetto. Never one to fear danger—indeed, he often seemed to seek it out—Kennedy proceeded as planned.

When he arrived at the speech site, the crowd did not know King had been shot. It fell to Kennedy to inform them, to solace them in their grief, and to assuage their anger. Standing on the back of a flatbed truck, his face, in the words of a television reporter, "gaunt and distressed and full of anguish," he spoke slowly and somberly, with barely a glance at the brief notes he held in his hand. The crowd gasped and screamed when he told them of King's death. Mentioning King's commitment to nonviolence and reminding the audience that his own brother had been slain by an assassin, Kennedy bemoaned the division and hatred rampant in the land and called for "love and wisdom and compassion toward one another." The crowd dispersed quietly and returned to their homes. That night there were riots in more than a hundred American cities, but in Indianapolis the streets remained peaceful.

After King's funeral, Hosea Williams expressed the thoughts of many African Americans when he said, "The thing that kept us going was that maybe Bobby Kennedy would come up with some answers for the country." Those hopes were dashed two months later when Kennedy also fell victim to an assassin's bullet.

◇◇◇

Ladies and Gentlemen: I'm only going to talk to you just for a minute or so this evening because I have some very sad news for all of you. Could you lower those signs please?[1] I have some very sad news for all of you and, I think, sad news for all of our fellow citizens and people who love peace all over the world, and that is that Martin Luther King was shot and was killed tonight in Memphis, Tennessee.

Martin Luther King dedicated his life to love and to justice between fellow human beings. He died in the cause of that effort.

In this difficult day, in this difficult time for the United States, it's perhaps well to ask what kind of a nation we are and what direction we want to move in. For those of you who are black—considering the evidence evidently is that there were white people who

were responsible—you can be filled with bitterness and with hatred and a desire for revenge.

We can move in that direction as a country, in greater polarization—black people amongst blacks, and white amongst whites, filled with hatred toward one another. Or we can make an effort, as Martin Luther King did, to understand and to comprehend, and replace that violence, that stain of bloodshed that has spread across our land, with an effort to understand, compassion, and love.

For those of you who are black and are tempted to fill with—to be filled with—hatred and mistrust of the injustice of such an act, against all white people, I would only say that I can also feel in my own heart the same kind of feeling. I had a member of my family killed, but he was killed by a white man. But we have to make an effort in the United States, we have to make an effort to understand, to get beyond or go beyond these rather difficult times.

---

1. A reference to signs in the crowd supporting Kennedy's presidential candidacy.

My favorite poem—my favorite poet—was Aeschylus, and he once wrote: "Even in our sleep, pain which cannot forget falls drop by drop upon the heart until, in our own despair, against our will, comes wisdom through the awful grace of God."[2]

What we need in the United States is not division. What we need in the United States is not hatred. What we need in the United States is not violence and lawlessness, but is love and wisdom and compassion toward one another, and a feeling of justice toward those who still suffer within our country, whether they be white or whether they be black. So I ask you tonight to return home, to say a prayer for the family of Martin Luther King. That's true, but more importantly to say a prayer for our own country, which all of us love—a prayer for understanding and that compassion of which I spoke.

We can do well in this country. We will have difficult times. We've had difficult times in the past. And we will have difficult times in the future. It is not the end of violence; it is not the end of lawlessness; and it's not the end of disorder. But the vast majority of white people and the vast majority of black people in this country want to live together, want to improve the quality of our life, and want justice for all human beings that abide in our land.

[Let us] dedicate ourselves to what the Greeks wrote so many years ago: to tame the savageness of man and make gentle the life of this world. Let us dedicate ourselves to that and say a prayer for our country and for our people.

Thank you very much.

---

2. Paraphrased from Aeschylus's *Agamemnon* (458 BCE). As translated in Edith Hamilton's *Three Greek Plays* (1937), the lines read: "Drop, drop—in our sleep, upon the heart sorrow falls, memory's pain, and to us, though against our very will, even in our own despite, comes wisdom by the awful grace of God."

Edward M. Kennedy

Eulogy to Robert F. Kennedy

NEW YORK, NEW YORK
JUNE 8, 1968

SHORTLY AFTER MIDNIGHT on June 5, 1968, Robert Kennedy left the ballroom of the Ambassador Hotel in Los Angeles after addressing a boisterous crowd celebrating his victory in California's Democratic presidential primary. As Kennedy walked through the kitchen, Sirhan Sirhan, a Christian Palestinian reportedly unhappy with Kennedy's support for Israel, opened fire with a .22-caliber pistol. Kennedy was hit three times, once in the brain. He died twenty-five hours later.

On Saturday, June 8, Edward (Ted) Kennedy eulogized his brother in a memorial service at St. Patrick's Cathedral in New York City. Perhaps because it was easier emotionally than talking about Robert's life, Ted Kennedy quoted extensively from his brother's words to illustrate the principles for which he had stood. The longest section of the eulogy was taken from RFK's 1966 Day of Affirmation speech in South Africa (pages 434–440) as redacted in the postscript of his 1967 book *To Seek a Newer World*. Along the way a few minor changes in wording were introduced for stylistic purposes, and two of the paragraphs represented as being from the Day of Affirmation address were actually from a speech Robert Kennedy had delivered in Cleveland two months before his death.

The best-known part of the eulogy is its closing line, which RFK used often on the campaign trail: "Some men see things as they are and say why; I dream things that never were and say why not." The words are paraphrased from George Bernard Shaw's 1921 play, *Back to Methuselah*, in which they were uttered by the serpent in its dialogue with Eve that led to banishment from the Garden of Eden. As employed by Robert Kennedy, and then again in his brother's eulogy, they were associated with idealism and high purpose, showing both how context shapes meaning and how memorable phrases can assume a life of their own when stripped from their original context.

◇◇

Your Eminences, Your Excellencies, Mr. President[1]: On behalf of Mrs. Kennedy,[2] her children, the parents and sisters of Robert Kennedy, I want to express what we feel to those who mourn with us today in this cathedral and around the world.

We loved him as a brother and as a father and as a son. From his parents and from his older brothers and sisters—Joe and Kathleen and Jack[3]—he received an inspiration which he passed on to all of us. He gave us strength in time of trouble, wisdom in time of uncertainty, and sharing in time of happiness. He will always be by our side.

Love is not an easy feeling to put into words. Nor is loyalty, or trust or joy. But he was all of these. He loved life completely and he lived it intensely.

A few years back, Robert Kennedy wrote some words about his own father which expresses the way we in his family felt about him. He said of what his father meant to him, and I quote: "What it really all adds up to is love—not love as it is described with such facility in popular magazines, but the kind of love that is affection and respect, order and encouragement and support. Our awareness of this was an incalculable source of strength, and because real love is something unselfish and involves sacrifice and giving, we could not help but profit from it."

And he continued: "Beneath it all he has tried to engender a social conscience. There were wrongs which needed attention. There were people who were poor and needed help.... And we have a responsibility to them and to this country. Through no virtues and accomplishments of our own, we have been fortunate enough to be born in the United States under the most comfortable conditions. We, therefore, have a responsibility to others who are less well-off."[4]

That is what Robert Kennedy was given. What he leaves to us is what he said, what he did, and what he stood for. A speech he made to the young people

---

1. U.S. President Lyndon B. Johnson.

2. Robert Kennedy's wife, Ethel.

3. Joseph Kennedy Jr. was killed in combat during World War II; Kathleen Kennedy died in a plane crash in May 1948; President John F. Kennedy was assassinated in November 1963.

4. These words from RFK appeared in *The Fruitful Bough: A Tribute to Joseph P. Kennedy*, privately printed in 1965. The verb tenses in the second paragraph were altered slightly in Edward Kennedy's eulogy.

of South Africa on their Day of Affirmation in 1966 sums it up the best, and I would like to read it now:[5]

"There is discrimination in this world and slavery and slaughter and starvation. Governments repress their people, millions are trapped in poverty while the nation grows rich, and wealth is lavished on armaments everywhere.

"These are differing evils, but they are the common works of man. They reflect the imperfection of human justice, the inadequacy of human compassion, our lack of sensibility towards the suffering of our fellows.

"But we can perhaps remember—even if only for a time—that those who live with us are our brothers, that they share with us the same short moment of life, that they seek, as we do, nothing but the chance to live out their lives in purpose and happiness, winning what satisfaction and fulfillment they can.[6]

"Surely this bond of common faith, this bond of common goal, can begin to teach us something. Surely we can learn at least to look at those around us as fellow men. And surely we can begin to work a little harder to bind up the wounds among us and to become in our own hearts brothers and countrymen once again.

"The answer is to rely on youth—not a time of life but a state of mind, a temper of the will, a quality of imagination, a predominance of courage over timidity, of the appetite for adventure over the love of ease. The cruelties and obstacles of this swiftly changing planet will not yield to the obsolete dogmas and outworn slogans. They cannot be moved by those who cling to a present that is already dying, who prefer the illusion of security to the excitement and danger that come with even the most peaceful progress. It is a revolutionary world we live in, and this generation at home and around the world has had thrust upon it a greater burden of responsibility than any generation that has ever lived.

"Some believe there is nothing one man or one woman can do against the enormous array of the world's ills. Yet many of the world's great movements of thought and action have flowed from the work of a single man. A young monk began the Protestant Reformation, a young general extended an empire from Macedonia to the borders of the earth, a young woman reclaimed the territory of France. And it was a young Italian explorer who discovered the New World, and the thirty-two-year-old Thomas Jefferson who proclaimed that all men are created equal.

"These men moved the world, and so can we all. Few will have the greatness to bend history itself, but each of us can work to change a small portion of events, and in the total of all those acts will be written the history of this generation.... Each time a man stands up for an ideal or acts to improve the lot of others or strikes out against injustice, he sends forth a tiny ripple of hope, and crossing each other from a million different centers of energy and daring, those ripples build a current that can sweep down the mightiest walls of oppression and resistance.

"Few are willing to brave the disapproval of their fellows, the censure of their colleagues, the wrath of their society. Moral courage is a rarer commodity than bravery in battle or great intelligence. Yet it is the one essential, vital quality for those who seek to change a world that yields most painfully to change. And I believe that in this generation those with the courage to enter the moral conflict will find themselves with companions in every corner of the globe.

"For the fortunate among us, there is the temptation to follow the easy and familiar paths of personal ambition and financial success so grandly spread before those who enjoy the privilege of education. But that is not the road history has marked out for us. Like it or not, we live in times of danger and uncertainty. But they are also more open to the creative energy of men than any other time in history. All of us will ultimately be judged—and as the years pass, we will surely judge ourselves—on the effort we have contributed to building a new world society and the extent to which our ideals and goals have shaped that event.

"Our future may lie beyond our vision, but it is not completely beyond our control. It is the shaping

5. What follows are excerpts from Robert Kennedy's speech of June 6, 1966, as printed in his *To Seek a Newer World* (1967). For the full text of the speech as delivered, see pages 434–440.

6. This and the following paragraph are from a speech Robert Kennedy delivered in Cleveland, April 5, 1968.

impulse of America that neither fate nor nature nor the irresistible tides of history but the work of our own hands, matched to reason and principle, that will determine our destiny. There is pride in that, even arrogance, but there is also experience and truth. In any event, it is the only way we can live."[7]

That is the way he lived. And that is what he leaves us. My brother need not be idealized or enlarged in death beyond what he was in life to be remembered

simply as a good and decent man who saw wrong and tried to right it, saw suffering and tried to heal it, saw war and tried to stop it. Those of us who loved him and who take him to his rest today pray that what he was to us and what he wished for others will someday come to pass for all the world.

As he said many times in many parts of this nation to those he touched and who sought to touch him: "Some men see things as they are and say why; I dream things that never were and say why not."[8]

---

7. This paragraph was not part of Robert Kennedy's Day of Affirmation speech; it was added at the end of the postscript of his *To Seek a Newer World* (1967).

8. Paraphrased from George Bernard Shaw's *Back to Methuselah* (1921).

Edward M. Kennedy

Chappaquiddick

Hyannis Port, Massachusetts
July 25, 1969

WITH THE DEATH of Robert Kennedy, the mantle of family leadership passed to thirty-six-year-old Edward M. (Ted) Kennedy. So, too, did the hopes of those who dreamed of another Camelot. Unlike his older brothers, however, Kennedy enjoyed the U.S. Senate, to which he had been elected in 1962. He went about his work there with energy and dedication and was in no hurry to run for the White House. But neither did he foreclose the possibility, and few doubted that in time he would become a candidate, perhaps as early as 1972.

All that changed shortly after 11:00 p.m. on July 18, 1969. After leaving a party on Massachusetts's Chappaquiddick Island with Mary Jo Kopechne, a former aide in Robert Kennedy's Senate office, Ted Kennedy drove his Oldsmobile into a pond off a small, unlit bridge. He managed to get out alive, but Kopechne did not. When the car and body were discovered early the next day, Kennedy had not yet reported the accident. When he finally met with the police, ten hours after the fact, he dictated a statement acknowledging that he had been the driver, saying he had been exhausted and in shock from the accident and from trying to rescue Kopechne, and declaring that he had not "fully realized what had happened" until morning.

On July 25 Kennedy appeared in court, pleaded guilty to leaving the scene of an accident, and was given a suspended sentence. That evening he addressed the people of Massachusetts and a national television audience from his father's house at the Kennedy compound in Hyannis Port. With his political life on the line, Kennedy called in the family's most trusted wordsmiths, including Ted Sorensen, who had written most of President John F. Kennedy's major speeches. After denying the "ugly speculation" that he had a "private relationship of any kind" with Kopechne, Kennedy reiterated the essence of his police statement, with the addition of dramatic details such as feeling water enter his lungs as he made "immediate and repeated efforts to save Mary Jo by diving into the strong and murky current." In a carefully worded mea culpa, he said: "I do not seek to escape responsibility for my actions by placing the blame either on the physical and emotional trauma brought on by the accident, or on anyone else." Then he went on to do just that, invoking even the notion that "some awful curse" might "actually hang over all the Kennedys." He ended by asking the voters of Massachusetts to help him decide whether or not he should resign from the Senate, though he made it clear that the final decision would be his alone.

The reaction in Massachusetts was predictably positive, with letters, telegrams, and phone calls running heavily in favor of Kennedy staying in office. Nationally, the response was more skeptical with regard to Kennedy's explanation of the accident, his response to it, and his judgment under stress. The speech saved Kennedy's Senate seat, but the shadow of Chappaquiddick would hang over him for the rest of his career.

◇◇◇

My fellow citizens: I have requested this opportunity to talk to the people of Massachusetts about the tragedy which happened last Friday evening.

This morning I entered a plea of guilty to the charge of leaving the scene of an accident. Prior to my appearance in court it would have been [im]proper for me to comment on these matters, but tonight I am free to tell you what happened and to say what it means to me.

On the weekend of July eighteenth, I was on Martha's Vineyard Island participating with my nephew, Joe Kennedy, as for thirty years my family has participated, in the annual Edgartown Sailing Regatta. Only reasons of health prevented my wife from accompanying me.

On Chappaquiddick Island, off Martha's Vineyard, I attended on Friday evening, July eighteenth, a cookout I had encouraged and helped sponsor for a devoted group of Kennedy campaign secretaries. When I left the party around 11:15 p.m., I was accompanied by one of these girls, Miss Mary Jo Kopechne. Mary Jo was one of the most devoted members of the staff of Senator Robert Kennedy.[1] She worked for him for four years and was broken up over his death. For this reason and because she was such a gentle, kind, and idealistic person, all of us tried to help her feel that she still had a home with the Kennedy family.

There is no truth, no truth whatever, to the widely circulated suspicions of immoral conduct that have been leveled at my behavior and hers regarding that evening. There has never been a private relationship between us of any kind. I know of nothing in Mary Jo's conduct on that or any other occasion—and the same is true of the other girls at that party—that would lend any substance to such ugly speculation

---

1. Robert Kennedy served as U.S. Senator from New York from March 1966 until his assassination in June 1968.

about their character. Nor was I driving under the influence of liquor.

Little over one mile away, the car that I was driving on an unlit road went off a narrow bridge which had no guardrails and was built on a left angle to the road. The car overturned in a deep pond and immediately filled with water. I remember thinking, as the cold water rushed in around my head, that I was for certain drowning. Then water entered my lungs and I actually felt the sensation of drowning, but somehow I struggled to the surface alive. I made immediate and repeated efforts to save Mary Jo by diving into the strong and murky current, but succeeded only in increasing my state of utter exhaustion and alarm.

My conduct and conversations during the next several hours, to the extent that I can remember them, make no sense to me at all. Although my doctors inform me that I suffered a cerebral concussion as well as shock, I do not seek to escape responsibility for my actions by placing the blame either on the physical and emotional trauma brought on by the accident, or on anyone else.

I regard as indefensible the fact that I did not report the accident to the police immediately. Instead of looking directly for a telephone after lying exhausted in the grass for an undetermined time, I walked back to the cottage where the party was being held and requested the help of two friends, my cousin Joseph Gargan and Paul Markham, and directed them to return immediately to the scene with me—this was sometime after midnight—in order to undertake a new effort to dive down and locate Miss Kopechne. Their strenuous efforts, undertaken at some risk to their own lives, also proved futile.

All kinds of scrambled thoughts—all of them confused, some of them irrational, many of them which I cannot recall, and some of which I would not have seriously entertained under normal circumstances—went through my mind during this period. They were reflected in the various inexplicable, inconsistent, and inconclusive things I said and did, including such questions as whether the girl might still be alive somewhere out of that immediate area, whether some awful curse did actually hang over all the Kennedys, whether there was some justifiable reason for me to doubt what had happened and to

delay my report, whether somehow the awful weight of this incredible incident might in some way pass from my shoulders. I was overcome, I'm frank to say, by a jumble of emotions: grief, fear, doubt, exhaustion, panic, confusion, and shock.

Instructing Gargan and Markham not to alarm Mary Jo's friends that night, I had them take me to the ferry crossing. The ferry having shut down for the night, I suddenly jumped into the water and impulsively swam across, nearly drowning once again in the effort, and returned to my hotel about 2:00 a.m. and collapsed in my room. I remember going out at one point and saying something to the room clerk. In the morning, with my mind somewhat more lucid, I made an effort to call a family legal advisor, Burke Marshall, from a public telephone on the Chappaquiddick side of the ferry, and then belatedly reported the accident to the Martha's Vineyard police.

Today, as I mentioned, I felt morally obligated to plead guilty to the charge of leaving the scene of an accident. No words on my part can possibly express the terrible pain and suffering I feel over this tragic incident. This last week has been an agonizing one for me and for the members of my family, and the grief we feel over the loss of a wonderful friend will remain with us the rest of our lives.

These events, the publicity, innuendo, and whispers which have surrounded them, and my admission of guilt this morning raises the question in my mind of whether my standing among the people of my state has been so impaired that I should resign my seat in the United States Senate.

If at any time the citizens of Massachusetts should lack confidence in their Senator's character or his ability, with or without justification, he could not, in my opinion, adequately perform his duties and should not continue in office. The people of this state—the state which sent John Quincy Adams and Daniel Webster and Charles Sumner and Henry Cabot Lodge and John Kennedy to the United States Senate—are entitled to representation in that body by men who inspire their utmost confidence. For this reason I would understand full well why some might think it right for me to resign.

For me this will be a difficult decision to make. It has been seven years since my first election to the Senate. You and I share many memories. Some of them have been glorious, some have been very sad. The opportunity to work with you and serve Massachusetts has made my life worthwhile. And so I ask you tonight, the people of Massachusetts, to think this through with me. In facing this decision, I seek your advice and opinion. In making it, I seek your prayers. For this is a decision that I will have finally to make on my own.

It has been written: "A man does what he must—in spite of personal consequences, in spite of obstacles and dangers and pressures—and that is the basis of all human morality.... Whatever may be the sacrifices he faces if he follows his conscience—the loss of his friends, his fortune, his contentment, even

the esteem of his fellow men—each man must decide for himself the course he will follow. The stories of the past courage...cannot supply courage itself. For this each man must look into his own soul."[2]

I pray that I can have the courage to make the right decision. Whatever is decided, whatever the future holds for me, I hope that I shall be able to put this most recent tragedy behind me and make some further contribution to our state and mankind, whether it be in public or private life.

Thank you, and good night.

---

2. From the closing paragraphs of John F. Kennedy's *Profiles in Courage* (1956).

Richard M. Nixon

The Great Silent Majority

WASHINGTON, D.C.
NOVEMBER 3, 1969

AFTER LOSING TO John F. Kennedy in the 1960 presidential election, Richard Nixon returned to his native California, where he ran an unsuccessful campaign for Governor in 1962. Five days later, ABC television aired a program titled "The Political Obituary of Richard Nixon." It proved to be more than a bit premature. By the mid-1960s, Nixon was moving back onto the national stage, and in 1968 he captured the White House by defeating Lyndon Johnson's Vice President, Hubert Humphrey. The dominant images of the campaign were of U.S. soldiers fighting in Vietnam and of violent protests against the war in the streets of America.

During the election, Nixon had claimed that he had a "secret plan" for peace. Yet by autumn 1969, eight months into his administration, the war continued with no end in sight. There were still 475,000 U.S. troops in Vietnam, and the number of combat deaths had risen to more than 35,000. Antiwar groups called for a series of monthly moratoriums to protest the fighting, with the first one scheduled for October 15. Two days before the moratorium, Nixon announced that he would make a major policy address on Vietnam three weeks hence, on November 3. Despite this announcement, hundreds of thousands of protesters filled the streets of major cities across the country in the largest antiwar protests in American history. *Washington Post* columnist David Broder wrote that "the men and the movement that broke Lyndon B. Johnson's authority" appeared likely to succeed in breaking Nixon's as well.

During the next three weeks, Nixon labored over his speech, which he composed without the assistance of speechwriters. Knowing this would be a defining moment for his presidency, he prepared at least a dozen drafts and kept everyone but his closest advisors in the dark about what he would say. There were no advance copies for either the press or congressional leaders. As Nixon explained later, speculation about the speech reached a "fever pitch" as November 3 approached: "I welcomed this because I knew that the more it was talked about, the bigger the audience would be."

Speaking to the nation from the Oval Office, Nixon appealed to "the great silent majority" of Americans who did not support the antiwar protesters and who wanted America to find a just and lasting peace in Vietnam. To achieve that goal, he set forth a policy of Vietnamization, whereby the fighting would gradually be turned over to South Vietnamese troops, thereby allowing for the slow withdrawal of American forces. He contrasted this policy with "precipitate withdrawal," which would result in the "first defeat in our nation's history" and a "collapse of confidence in American leadership" throughout the world. Appealing to patriotism and national honor, he called for an end to division and discord at home. "North Vietnam cannot defeat or humiliate the United States," he declared. "Only Americans can do that."

The speech was controversial at the time and has remained so since, but there can be no doubting its effectiveness. It received positive marks from 77 percent of those who heard it, while Nixon's approval rating shot up twelve points in the Gallup poll, to 68 percent. By appealing to "the great silent majority," Nixon gave a sense of identity to those Americans who were repelled by the antiwar movement and the radical counterculture they associated with it. They became his constituency, provided a bedrock of support through the remaining years of the war, and helped ensure that his presidency, unlike Johnson's, would not founder on Vietnam.

◇◇◇

Good evening, my fellow Americans: Tonight I want to talk to you on a subject of deep concern to all Americans and to many people in all parts of the world—the war in Vietnam.

I believe that one of the reasons for the deep division about Vietnam is that many Americans have lost confidence in what their government has told them about our policy. The American people cannot and should not be asked to support a policy which involves the overriding issues of war and peace unless they know the truth about that policy.

Tonight, therefore, I would like to answer some of the questions that I know are on the minds of many of you listening to me: How and why did America get involved in Vietnam in the first place? How has this administration changed the policy of the previous administration? What has really happened in the negotiations in Paris[1] and on the battlefront in Vietnam? What choices do we have if we are to end the war? What are the prospects for peace?

Now, let me begin by describing the situation I found when I was inaugurated on January 20. The war had been going on for four years. Thirty-one thousand Americans had been killed in action. The training program for the South Vietnamese was behind schedule. Five hundred and forty thousand Americans were in Vietnam with no plans to reduce the number. No progress had been made at the negotiations in Paris, and the United States had not put forth a comprehensive peace proposal. The war was causing deep division at home and criticism from many of our friends, as well as our enemies, abroad.

In view of these circumstances, there were some who urged that I end the war at once by ordering the immediate withdrawal of all American forces. From a political standpoint this would have been a popular and easy course to follow. After all, we became involved in the war while my predecessor was in office. I could blame the defeat which would be the result of my action on him and come out as the peacemaker. Some put it to me quite bluntly: This was the only way to avoid allowing Johnson's war to become Nixon's war.

But I had a greater obligation than to think only of the years of my administration and of the next election. I had to think of the effect of my decision on the next generation and on the future of peace and freedom in America and in the world. Let us all understand that the question before us is not whether some Americans are for peace and some Americans are against peace. The question at issue is not whether Johnson's war becomes Nixon's war. The great question is: How can we win America's peace?

Well, let us turn now to the fundamental issue. Why and how did the United States become involved in Vietnam in the first place? Fifteen years ago North Vietnam, with the logistical support of Communist China and the Soviet Union, launched a campaign to impose a Communist government on South Vietnam

by instigating and supporting a revolution. In response to the request of the government of South Vietnam, President Eisenhower[2] sent economic aid and military equipment to assist the people of South Vietnam in their efforts to prevent a Communist takeover. Seven years ago, President Kennedy sent 16,000 military personnel to Vietnam as combat advisers. Four years ago, President Johnson sent American combat forces to South Vietnam.

Now, many believe that President Johnson's decision to send American combat forces to South Vietnam was wrong. And many others—I among them—have been strongly critical of the way the war has been conducted. But the question facing us today is: Now that we are in the war, what is the best way to end it?

In January[3] I could only conclude that the precipitate withdrawal of all American forces from Vietnam would be a disaster not only for South Vietnam but for the United States and for the cause of peace.

For the South Vietnamese, our precipitate withdrawal would inevitably allow the Communists to repeat the massacres which followed their takeover in the North fifteen years before. They then murdered more than 50,000 people, and hundreds of thousands more died in slave labor camps. We saw a prelude of what would happen in South Vietnam when the Communists entered the city of Hue last year. During their brief rule there, there was a bloody reign of terror in which 3,000 civilians were clubbed, shot to death, and buried in mass graves. With the sudden collapse of our support, these atrocities of Hue would become the nightmare of the entire nation, and particularly for the million and a half Catholic refugees who fled to South Vietnam when the Communists took over in the North.

For the United States, this first defeat in our nation's history would result in a collapse of confidence in American leadership, not only in Asia but throughout the world. Three American Presidents have recognized the great stakes involved in Vietnam and understood what had to be done. In 1963

---

1. Official peace talks had begun in Paris in May 1968 but quickly stalled; they resumed in January 1969.

2. Dwight D. Eisenhower, President from 1953 to 1961.

3. Nixon is referring to his inauguration as President on January 20, 1969.

President Kennedy, with his characteristic eloquence and clarity, said: "We want to see a stable government there, carrying on the struggle to maintain its national independence. We believe strongly in that. We are not going to withdraw from that effort. In my opinion, for us to withdraw from that effort would mean a collapse not only of South Vietnam, but Southeast Asia. So we're going to stay there."[4] President Eisenhower and President Johnson[5] expressed the same conclusion during their terms of office.

For the future of peace, precipitate withdrawal would be a disaster of immense magnitude. A nation cannot remain great if it betrays its allies and lets down its friends. Our defeat and humiliation in South Vietnam without question would promote recklessness in the councils of those great powers who have not yet abandoned their goals of world conquest. This would spark violence wherever our commitments help maintain the peace—in the Middle East, in Berlin, eventually even in the Western Hemisphere. Ultimately, this would cost more lives. It would not bring peace; it would bring more war.

For these reasons, I rejected the recommendation that I should end the war by immediately withdrawing all of our forces. I chose instead to change American policy on both the negotiating front and the battlefront.

In order to end a war fought on many fronts, I initiated a pursuit for peace on many fronts. In a television speech on May 14, in a speech before the United Nations,[6] on a number of other occasions, I set forth our peace proposals in great detail. We have offered the complete withdrawal of all outside forces within one year. We have proposed a cease-fire under international supervision. We have offered free elections under international supervision with the Communists participating in the organization and conduct of the elections as an organized political force. And the Saigon government has pledged to accept the result of the election.

We have not put forth our proposals on a take-it-or-leave-it basis. We have indicated that we're willing to discuss the proposals that have been put forth by the other side. We have declared that anything is negotiable except the right of the people of South Vietnam to determine their own future. At the Paris Peace Conference, Ambassador Lodge[7] has demonstrated our flexibility and good faith in forty public meetings. Hanoi has refused even to discuss our proposals. They demand our unconditional acceptance of their terms, which are that we withdraw all American forces immediately and unconditionally and that we overthrow the government of South Vietnam as we leave.

We have not limited our peace initiatives to public forums and public statements. I recognized in January that a long and bitter war like this usually cannot be settled in a public forum. That is why, in addition to the public statements and negotiations, I have explored every possible private avenue that might lead to a settlement. Tonight I am taking the unprecedented step of disclosing to you some of our other initiatives for peace—initiatives we undertook privately and secretly because we thought we thereby might open a door which publicly would be closed.

I did not wait for my inauguration to begin my quest for peace. Soon after my election, through an individual who is directly in contact on a personal basis with the leaders of North Vietnam, I made two private offers for a rapid, comprehensive settlement. Hanoi's replies called, in effect, for our surrender before negotiations.

Since the Soviet Union furnishes most of the military equipment for North Vietnam, Secretary of State Rogers,[8] my Assistant for National Security Affairs, Dr. Kissinger,[9] Ambassador Lodge, and I personally have met on a number of occasions with representatives of the Soviet government to enlist their assistance in getting meaningful negotiations started. In addition, we have had extended discussions

4. From John F. Kennedy's news conference of July 17, 1963.

5. Lyndon B. Johnson, President from 1963 to 1969.

6. Nixon addressed the UN General Assembly on September 18, 1969.

7. Henry Cabot Lodge Jr., former ambassador to South Vietnam and chief U.S. negotiator at the Paris peace talks in 1969.

8. William P. Rogers.

9. Henry Kissinger.

directed toward that same end with representatives of other governments which have diplomatic relations with North Vietnam. None of these initiatives have to date produced results.

In mid-July, I became convinced that it was necessary to make a major move to break the deadlock in the Paris talks. I spoke directly in this office, where I am now sitting, with an individual who had known Ho Chi Minh[10] on a personal basis for twenty-five years. Through him I sent a letter to Ho Chi Minh. I did this outside of the usual diplomatic channels with the hope that with the necessity of making statements for propaganda removed, there might be constructive progress toward bringing the war to an end. Let me read from that letter to you now: "Dear Mr. President: I realize that it is difficult to communicate meaningfully across the gulf of four years of war. But precisely because of this gulf, I wanted to take this opportunity to reaffirm in all solemnity my desire to work for a just peace. I deeply believe that the war in Vietnam has gone on too long and delay in bringing it to an end can benefit no one—least of all the people of Vietnam.... The time has come to move forward at the conference table toward an early resolution of this tragic war. You will find us forthcoming and open-minded in a common effort to bring the blessings of peace to the brave people of Vietnam. Let history record that at this critical juncture, both sides turned their face toward peace rather than toward conflict and war."

I received Ho Chi Minh's reply on August 30, three days before his death. It simply reiterated the public position North Vietnam had taken at Paris and flatly rejected my initiative. The full text of both letters is being released to the press.

In addition to the public meetings that I have referred to, Ambassador Lodge has met with Vietnam's chief negotiator in Paris[11] in eleven private sessions. And we have taken other significant initiatives which must remain secret to keep open some channels of communications which may still prove to be productive.

But the effect of all the public, private, and secret negotiations which have been undertaken since the bombing halt a year ago and since this administration came into office on January twentieth can be summed up in one sentence: No progress whatever has been made except agreement on the shape of the bargaining table.

Well, now, who is at fault? It's become clear that the obstacle in negotiating an end to the war is not the President of the United States. It is not the South Vietnamese government. The obstacle is the other side's absolute refusal to show the least willingness to join us in seeking a just peace. And it will not do so while it is convinced that all it has to do is to wait for our next concession, and our next concession after that one, until it gets everything it wants. There can now be no longer any question that progress in negotiation depends only on Hanoi's deciding to negotiate, to negotiate seriously.

I realize that this report on our efforts on the diplomatic front is discouraging to the American people, but the American people are entitled to know the truth—the bad news as well as the good news—where the lives of our young men are involved.

Now let me turn, however, to a more encouraging report on another front. At the time we launched our search for peace I recognized we might not succeed in bringing an end to the war through negotiation. I therefore put into effect another plan to bring peace—a plan which will bring the war to an end regardless of what happens on the negotiating front. It is in line with a major shift in U.S. foreign policy which I described in my press conference at Guam on July 25. Let me briefly explain what has been described as the Nixon Doctrine, a policy which not only will help end the war in Vietnam but which is an essential element of our program to prevent future Vietnams.

We Americans are a do-it-yourself people. We're an impatient people. Instead of teaching someone else to do a job, we like to do it ourselves. And this trait has been carried over into our foreign policy. In Korea[12] and again in Vietnam, the United States furnished most of the money, most of the arms, and most of

10. President of North Vietnam.

11. Tran Buu Kiem.

12. Nixon is referring to the Korean War of 1950–1953.

the men to help the people of those countries defend their freedom against Communist aggression.

Before any American troops were committed to Vietnam, a leader of another Asian country expressed this opinion to me when I was traveling in Asia as a private citizen. He said: "When you are trying to assist another nation defend its freedom, U.S. policy should be to help them fight the war but not to fight the war for them."

Well, in accordance with this wise counsel, I laid down in Guam three principles as guidelines for future American policy toward Asia.[13] First, the United States will keep all of its treaty commitments. Second, we shall provide a shield if a nuclear power threatens the freedom of a nation allied with us or of a nation whose survival we consider vital to our security. Third, in cases involving other types of aggression, we shall furnish military and economic assistance when requested in accordance with our treaty commitments. But we shall look to the nation directly threatened to assume the primary responsibility of providing the manpower for its defense.

After I announced this policy, I found that the leaders of the Philippines, Thailand, Vietnam, South Korea, [and] other nations which might be threatened by Communist aggression welcomed this new direction in American foreign policy. The defense of freedom is everybody's business—not just America's business. And it is particularly the responsibility of the people whose freedom is threatened.

In the previous administration, we Americanized the war in Vietnam. In this administration, we are Vietnamizing the search for peace. The policy of the previous administration not only resulted in our assuming the primary responsibility for fighting the war, but, even more significant, did not adequately stress the goal of strengthening the South Vietnamese so that they could defend themselves when we left.

The Vietnamization plan was launched following Secretary Laird's[14] visit to Vietnam in March. Under the plan, I ordered first a substantial increase in the training and equipment of South Vietnamese

forces. In July, on my visit to Vietnam,[15] I changed General Abrams'[16] orders so that they were consistent with the objectives of our new policies. Under the new orders, the primary mission of our troops is to enable the South Vietnamese forces to assume the full responsibility for the security of South Vietnam. Our air operations have been reduced by over 20 percent.

And now we have begun to see the results of this long-overdue change in American policy in Vietnam. After five years of Americans going into Vietnam, we are finally bringing American men home. By December 15, over 60,000 men will have been withdrawn from South Vietnam, including 20 percent of all of our combat forces. The South Vietnamese have continued to gain in strength. As a result they've been able to take over combat responsibilities from our American troops.

Two other significant developments have occurred since this administration took office. Enemy infiltration, infiltration which is essential if they are to launch a major attack, over the last three months is less than 20 percent of what it was over the same period last year. And most important, United States casualties have declined during the last two months to the lowest point in three years.

Let me now turn to our program for the future. We have adopted a plan which we have worked out in cooperation with the South Vietnamese for the complete withdrawal of all U.S. combat ground forces and their replacement by South Vietnamese forces on an orderly scheduled timetable. This withdrawal will be made from strength and not from weakness. As South Vietnamese forces become stronger, the rate of American withdrawal can become greater.

I have not and do not intend to announce the timetable for our program. And there [are] obvious reasons for this decision which I am sure you will understand. As I've indicated on several occasions, the rate of withdrawal will depend on developments on three fronts. One of these is the progress which can be or might be made in the Paris talks.

---

13. Nixon spoke in Guam on July 25, 1969.

14. Secretary of Defense Melvin Laird.

15. Nixon visited South Vietnam on July 30, 1969.

16. Creighton Abrams Jr., U.S. commander in Vietnam, 1968–1972.

An announcement of a fixed timetable for our withdrawal would completely remove any incentive for the enemy to negotiate an agreement. They would simply wait until our forces had withdrawn and then move in.

The other two factors on which we will base our withdrawal decisions are the level of enemy activity and the progress of the training programs of the South Vietnamese forces. And I am glad to be able to report tonight progress on both of these fronts has been greater than we anticipated when we started the program in June for withdrawal. As a result, our timetable for withdrawal is more optimistic now than when we made our first estimates in June. Now, this clearly demonstrates why it is not wise to be frozen in on a fixed timetable. We must retain the flexibility to base each withdrawal decision on the situation as it is at that time rather than on estimates that are no longer valid.

Along with this optimistic estimate, I must in all candor leave one note of caution. If the level of enemy activity significantly increases, we might have to adjust our timetable accordingly.

However, I want the record to be completely clear on one point. At the time of the bombing halt just a year ago,[17] there was some confusion as to whether there was an understanding on the part of the enemy that if we stopped the bombing of North Vietnam, they would stop the shelling of cities in South Vietnam. I want to be sure that there is no misunderstanding on the part of the enemy with regard to our withdrawal program. We have noted the reduced level of infiltration, the reduction of our casualties, and are basing our withdrawal decisions partially on those factors. If the level of infiltration or our casualties increase while we are trying to scale down the fighting, it will be the result of a conscious decision by the enemy.

Hanoi could make no greater mistake than to assume that an increase in violence will be to its advantage. If I conclude that increased enemy action jeopardizes our remaining forces in Vietnam, I shall not hesitate to take strong and effective measures to deal with that situation. This is not a threat. This is

a statement of policy, which as commander in chief of our armed forces, I am making in meeting my responsibility for the protection of American fighting men wherever they may be.

My fellow Americans, I am sure you can recognize from what I have said that we really only have two choices open to us if we want to end this war. I can order an immediate, precipitate withdrawal of all Americans from Vietnam without regard to the effects of that action. Or we can persist in our search for a just peace through a negotiated settlement if possible, or through continued implementation of our plan for Vietnamization if necessary—a plan in which we will withdraw all of our forces from Vietnam on a schedule in accordance with our program as the South Vietnamese become strong enough to defend their own freedom. I have chosen this second course. It is not the easy way. It is the right way. It is a plan which will end the war and serve the cause of peace—not just in Vietnam but in the Pacific and in the world.

In speaking of the consequences of a precipitate withdrawal, I mentioned that our allies would lose confidence in America. Far more dangerous, we would lose confidence in ourselves. Oh, the immediate reaction would be a sense of relief that our men were coming home. But as we saw the consequences of what we had done, inevitable remorse and divisive recrimination would scar our spirit as a people. We have faced other crises in our history, and we have become stronger by rejecting the easy way out and taking the right way in meeting our challenges. Our greatness as a nation has been our capacity to do what has to be done when we knew our course was right.

I recognize that some of my fellow citizens disagree with the plan for peace I've chosen. Honest and patriotic Americans have reached different conclusions as to how peace should be achieved. In San Francisco a few weeks ago, I saw demonstrators carrying signs reading: "Lose in Vietnam, bring the boys home." Well, one of the strengths of our free society is that any American has a right to reach that conclusion and to advocate that point of view.

But as President of the United States, I would be untrue to my oath of office if I allowed the policy of this nation to be dictated by the minority who hold that point of view and who try to impose it on the

---

17. President Johnson ordered that the bombing of North Vietnam be halted on November 1, 1968.

nation by mounting demonstrations in the street. For almost 200 years the policy of this nation has been made under our Constitution by those leaders in the Congress and the White House elected by all the people. If a vocal minority, however fervent its cause, prevails over reason and the will of the majority, this nation has no future as a free society.

And now I would like to address a word, if I may, to the young people of this nation who are particularly concerned—and I understand why they are concerned—about this war. I respect your idealism. I share your concern for peace. I want peace as much as you do.

There are powerful personal reasons I want to end this war. This week I will have to sign eighty-three letters to mothers, fathers, wives, and loved ones of men who have given their lives for America in Vietnam. It's very little satisfaction to me that this is only one-third as many letters as I signed the first week in office. There is nothing I want more than to see the day come when I do not have to write any of those letters.

I want to end the war to save the lives of those brave young men in Vietnam. But I want to end it in a way which will increase the chance that their younger brothers and their sons will not have to fight in some future Vietnam someplace in the world.

And I want to end the war for another reason. I want to end it so that the energy and dedication of you, our young people, now too often directed into bitter hatred against those responsible for the war, can be turned to the great challenges of peace, a better life for all Americans, a better life for all people on this earth.

I have chosen a plan for peace. I believe it will succeed. If it does not succeed, what the critics say now won't matter.[18] Or if it does succeed, what the critics say now won't matter. If it does not succeed, anything I say then won't matter.

I know it may not be fashionable to speak of patriotism or national destiny these days, but I feel it is appropriate to do so on this occasion. Two hundred

years ago this nation was weak and poor. But even then, America was the hope of millions in the world. Today we have become the strongest and richest nation in the world. And the wheel of destiny has turned so that any hope the world has for the survival of peace and freedom will be determined by whether the American people have the moral stamina and the courage to meet the challenge of free-world leadership. Let historians not record that when America was the most powerful nation in the world, we passed on the other side of the road[19] and allowed the last hopes for peace and freedom of millions of people to be suffocated by the forces of totalitarianism.

And so tonight, to you, the great silent majority of my fellow Americans, I ask for your support. I pledged in my campaign for the presidency to end the war in a way that we could win the peace. I have initiated a plan of action which will enable me to keep that pledge. The more support I can have from the American people, the sooner that pledge can be redeemed, for the more divided we are at home, the less likely the enemy is to negotiate at Paris.

Let us be united for peace. Let us also be united against defeat. Because let us understand: North Vietnam cannot defeat or humiliate the United States. Only Americans can do that.

Fifty years ago, in this room and at this very desk, President Woodrow Wilson spoke words which caught the imagination of a war-weary world.[20] He said: "This is the war to end wars."[21] His dream for peace after World War I was shattered on the hard realities of great power politics, and Woodrow Wilson died a broken man.[22]

---

18. This sentence was not in Nixon's written text. He misspoke by accidentally combining parts of each of his next two sentences.

19. An allusion to the parable of the Good Samaritan (Luke 10:25–37).

20. A dramatization on Nixon's part. Wilson, in an age before radio or television, did not deliver public speeches from the Oval Office. Nor was the desk at which Nixon spoke the same one used by President Wilson; it had belonged to Henry Wilson, U.S. Vice President, 1873–1875.

21. Although often attributed to Wilson, these words echo the title of British writer H. G. Wells's *The War That Will End War* (1914).

22. See Wilson's speeches on World War I and the League of Nations, pages 73–79, 124–128, and 133–152.

Tonight I do not tell you that the war in Vietnam is the war to end wars. But I do say this: I have initiated a plan which will end this war in a way that will bring us closer to that great goal to which Woodrow Wilson and every American President in our history has been dedicated—the goal of a just and lasting peace.

As President I hold the responsibility for choosing the best path to that goal and then leading the nation along it. I pledge to you tonight that I shall meet this responsibility with all of the strength and wisdom I can command in accordance with your hopes, mindful of your concerns, sustained by your prayers.

Thank you, and good night.

Spiro T. Agnew

Television News Coverage

DES MOINES, IOWA
NOVEMBER 13, 1969

WHEN RICHARD NIXON ran for the presidency in 1968, he chose as his running mate little-known Maryland Governor Spiro Agnew. Although Agnew would eventually be forced to resign the vice presidency in October 1973 after pleading no contest to charges of income tax evasion, he became a household name in Nixon's first administration for his spirited speeches assailing the President's critics. On one occasion, he called antiwar protesters "an effete corps of impudent snobs." On another, he attacked them as "nattering nabobs of negativism." His job was to say those things the President could not say, and he performed it with gusto.

On November 13, 1969, he addressed the Midwestern Regional Republican Conference in Des Moines, Iowa. He had declined the group's original invitation to speak, but everything changed after Nixon's November 3 speech on the Vietnam War (pages 488–496). Although Nixon's speech was generally well received by the public, television analysts began immediately to dissect its logic and to find weaknesses in its arguments. A few days later, White House speechwriter Patrick Buchanan sent Nixon a draft of an address attacking the network commentators for their bias and insularity. Nixon liked what he saw, edited the draft himself, and agreed that the speech should be delivered by Agnew, who added his own touches to the final version.

At one level, the speech was a hard-hitting political attack on the television news networks (at that time limited to ABC, NBC, and CBS) for their "hostile prejudices" in reporting on Nixon's address of November 3. Employing his usual colorful language, Agnew lambasted the networks for subjecting the President's words to "querulous criticism" by a "gaggle of commentators" before the American people had a chance to judge those words for themselves. The people had a right, Agnew insisted, to respond to the President without having his remarks "chewed over by a roundtable of critics" and "self-appointed analysts." He questioned the patriotism of such coverage in time of war and indirectly threatened retaliation at the time of license renewal for network-affiliated stations.

At another level, the speech had elements of a white paper on television news broadcasting. Noting the reliance of most Americans on television as their primary source of news, Agnew stated that the networks held "a concentration of power over American public opinion unknown in history." He questioned the objectivity of television news and, quoting Walter Lippmann, noted the difference between the diversity of print news and the homogeneity of television, in which three or four stations "control virtually all that can be received over the air by ordinary television sets." No less problematic, Agnew argued, was the networks' "endless pursuit of controversy," which threatened to undermine the "spirit of compromise...essential to the functioning of a democratic society."

These were not new concerns. They had all been raised in one form or another by scholars, journalists, and commentators long before Agnew's appearance at Des Moines. Coming from the Vice President, however, they became politically charged, especially in a discourse patently designed to diminish press criticism of the administration's Vietnam policies. Ironically, it was the same broadcasters attacked by Agnew that made his speech a national phenomenon. Broadcast live by all three networks, it reached a prime-time audience of more than forty million people. Opinion surveys showed strong support for Agnew's position, and at the end of the year the Gallup poll identified him as the third most respected man in America.

◇◇◇

Thank you. Thank you very much. Thank you very much. Thank you very much Governor Ray, Governor Ogilvie, Governor Tiemann,[1] Mr. Boyd, Mr. Peterson,[2] the many distinguished officials of the Republican Party gathered for this Midwest regional meeting. It's indeed a pleasure for me to be here tonight. I had intended to make all three of the regional meetings that have been scheduled thus far, but unfortunately I had to scrub the Western one— Hawaii was a little far at the moment, at that time.

But I'm glad to be here tonight, and I look forward to attending the others.

I think it's obvious from the cameras here that I didn't come to discuss the ban on cyclamates or DDT.[3] I have a subject I think is of great interest to the American people. Tonight I want to discuss the importance of the television medium to the American people. No nation depends more on the intelligent judgment of its citizens, and no medium has a more profound influence over public opinion. Nowhere in our system are there fewer checks on such vast power.

1. Robert D. Ray, Richard B. Ogilvie, Norbert T. Tiemann, Governors of Iowa, Illinois, and Nebraska, respectively.

2. McGill Boyd, Republican state committeeman from Kansas; Peter G. Peterson, chief executive officer of Bell and Howell.

3. Agnew is referring to two controversial substances banned by the U.S. government: artificial sweeteners made from cyclamates, and DDT, a powerful insecticide.

So nowhere should there be more conscientious responsibility exercised than by the news media. The question is: Are we demanding enough of our television news presentations? And are the men of this medium demanding enough of themselves?

Monday night a week ago, President Nixon delivered the most important address of his administration, one of the most important of our decade. His subject was Vietnam. My hope, as his at that time, was to rally the American people to see the conflict through to a lasting and just peace in the Pacific. For thirty-two minutes he reasoned with a nation that has suffered almost a third of a million casualties in the longest war in its history. When the President completed his address—an address, incidentally, that he spent weeks in the preparation of—his words and policies were subjected to instant analysis and querulous criticism. The audience of seventy million Americans—gathered to hear the President of the United States—was inherited by a small band of network commentators and self-appointed analysts, the majority of whom expressed in one way or another their hostility to what he had to say.

It was obvious that their minds were made up in advance. Those who recall the fumbling and groping that followed President Johnson's dramatic disclosure of his intention not to seek another term[4] have seen these men in a genuine state of nonpreparedness. This was not it. One commentator, one commentator twice contradicted the President's statement about the exchange of correspondence with Ho Chi Minh.[5] Another challenged the President's abilities as a politician. A third asserted that the President was following a Pentagon line. Others, by the expressions on their faces, the tone of their questions, and the sarcasm of their responses, made clear their sharp disapproval.

To guarantee in advance that the President's plea for national unity would be challenged, one network trotted out Averell Harriman[6] for the occasion.

Throughout the President's address, he waited in the wings. When the President concluded, Mr. Harriman recited perfectly. He attacked the Thieu[7] government as unrepresentative; he criticized the President's speech for various deficiencies; he twice issued a call to the Senate Foreign Relations Committee to debate Vietnam once again; he stated his belief that the Vietcong[8] or North Vietnamese did not really want a military takeover of South Vietnam; and he told a little anecdote about a "very, very responsible" fellow he had met in the Vietnamese delegation. All in all, Mr. Harriman offered a broad range of gratuitous advice challenging and contradicting the policies outlined by the President of the United States. Where the President had issued a call for unity, Mr. Harriman was encouraging the country not to listen to him.

A word about Mr. Harriman. For ten months he was America's chief negotiator at the Paris peace talks[9]—a period in which the United States swapped some of the greatest military concessions in the history of warfare for an enemy agreement on the shape of the bargaining table. Like Coleridge's Ancient Mariner,[10] Mr. Harriman seems to be under some heavy compulsion to justify his failures to anyone who will listen. And the networks have shown themselves willing to give him all the airtime he desires.

Now, every American has a right to disagree with the President of the United States and to express publicly that disagreement. But the President of the United States has a right to communicate directly with the people who elected him. And the people of this country have the right to make up their own minds and form their own opinions about

---

4. Agnew is referring to Lyndon B. Johnson's speech of March 31, 1968 (pages 465–472).

5. President of North Vietnam.

6. Longtime diplomat who served as chief U.S. negotiator at the Paris peace talks on Vietnam during the Johnson administration.

7. Nguyen Van Thieu, president of South Vietnam, 1967–1975.

8. Contraction for Viet Nam Cong San, meaning "Vietnamese Communist." By the mid-1960s, it had become synonymous in popular parlance with the National Liberation Front, which had been formed with direction from North Vietnam to conduct the guerilla war against South Vietnam and the United States.

9. The talks began in May 1968 and remained officially in progress, though in fact often deadlocked, until the signing of a peace agreement in January 1973.

10. An allusion to Samuel Taylor Coleridge's "Rime of the Ancient Mariner" (1798).

a presidential address without having a President's words and thoughts characterized through the prejudices of hostile critics before they can even be digested.

When Winston Churchill[11] rallied public opinion to stay the course against Hitler's Germany, he didn't have to contend with a gaggle of commentators raising doubts about whether he was reading public opinion right or whether Britain had the stamina to see the war through. When President Kennedy rallied the nation in the Cuban missile crisis, his address to the people was not chewed over by a roundtable of critics who disparaged the course of action he'd asked America to follow.[12]

The purpose of my remarks tonight is to focus your attention on this little group of men who not only enjoy a right of instant rebuttal to every presidential address, but, more importantly, wield a free hand in selecting, presenting, and interpreting the great issues in our nation.

First, let's define that power. At least forty million Americans every night, it's estimated, watch the network news. Seven million of them view ABC, the remainder being divided between NBC and CBS. According to Harris polls and other studies, for millions of Americans the networks are the sole source of national and world news. In Will Rogers's[13] observation, what you knew was what you read in the newspaper. Today, for growing millions of Americans, it's what they see and hear on their television sets.

Now, how is this network news determined? A small group of men, numbering perhaps no more than a dozen anchormen, commentators, and executive producers, settle upon the twenty minutes or so of film and commentary that's to reach the public. This selection is made from the ninety to 180 minutes that may be available. Their powers of choice are broad. They decide what forty to fifty million Americans will learn of the day's events in the nation and in the world.

We cannot measure this power and influence by the traditional democratic standards, for these men can create national issues overnight. They can make or break, by their coverage and commentary, a moratorium on the war. They can elevate men from obscurity to national prominence within a week. They can reward some politicians with national exposure and ignore others. For millions of Americans, the network reporter who covers a continuing issue—like the ABM[14] or civil rights—becomes, in effect, the presiding judge in a national trial by jury.

It must be recognized that the networks have made important contributions to the national knowledge. Through news, documentaries, and specials they have often used their power constructively and creatively to awaken the public conscience to critical problems. The networks made hunger and black lung disease national issues overnight. The TV networks have done what no other medium could have done in terms of dramatizing the horrors of war. The networks have tackled our most difficult social problems with a directness and an immediacy that's the gift of their medium. They focus the nation's attention on its environmental abuses—on pollution in the Great Lakes and the threatened ecology of the Everglades. But it was also the networks that elevated Stokely Carmichael[15] and George Lincoln Rockwell[16] from obscurity to national prominence.

Nor is their power confined to the substantive. A raised eyebrow, an inflection of the voice, a caustic remark dropped in the middle of a broadcast can raise doubts in a million minds about the veracity of a public official or the wisdom of a government policy. One Federal Communications Commissioner considers the powers of the networks equal to that of local, state, and federal governments all combined.[17]

---

11. Prime Minister of Great Britain 1940–1945, 1951–1955.

12. Agnew is referring to John F. Kennedy's speech of October 22, 1962 (pages 357–362).

13. American humorist known for his political satire (1879–1935).

14. A reference to ongoing discussions with the Soviet Union about an antiballistic missile treaty; such a treaty was eventually signed in 1972.

15. Black Power leader (see pages 441–452).

16. Founder of the American Nazi Party.

17. Perhaps a reference to Nicholas Johnson's "The Media Barons and the Public Interest: An FCC Commissioner's Warning," *Atlantic Monthly* (June 1968).

Certainly it represents a concentration of power over American public opinion unknown in history.

Now, what do Americans know of the men who wield this power? Of the men who produce and direct the network news, the nation knows practically nothing. Of the commentators, most Americans know little other than that they reflect an urbane and assured presence seemingly well informed on every important matter.

We do know that to a man these commentators and producers live and work in the geographical and intellectual confines of Washington, D.C., or New York City, the latter of which James Reston[18] terms the most unrepresentative community in the entire United States. Both communities bask in their own provincialism, their own parochialism. We can deduce that these men read the same newspapers. They draw their political and social views from the same sources. Worse, they talk constantly to one another, thereby providing artificial reinforcement to their shared viewpoints.

Do they allow their biases to influence the selection and presentation of the news? David Brinkley[19] states: "Objectivity is impossible to normal human behavior." Rather, he says, we should "strive for fairness." Another anchorman on a network news show[20] contends, and I quote: "You can't expunge all your private convictions just because you sit in a seat like this and a camera starts to stare at you. I think your program has to reflect what your basic feelings are. I'll plead guilty to that."[21]

Less than a week before the 1968 election, this same commentator charged that President Nixon's campaign commitments were no more durable than campaign balloons. He claimed that were it not for the fear of a hostile reaction, Richard Nixon would be giving in to, and I quote him exactly, "his natural instinct... to smash the enemy with a club or go after him with a meat axe."[22] Had this slander been made by one political candidate about another, it would have been dismissed by most commentators as a partisan attack. But this attack emanated from the privileged sanctuary of a network studio and therefore had the apparent dignity of an objective statement.

The American people would rightly not tolerate this concentration of power in government. Is it not fair and relevant to question its concentration in the hands of a tiny, enclosed fraternity of privileged men elected by no one and enjoying a monopoly sanctioned and licensed by government?

The views of the majority of this fraternity do not—and I repeat, not—represent the views of America. That is why such a great gulf existed between how the nation received the President's address and how the networks reviewed it. Not only did the country receive the President's address more warmly than the networks, but so also did the Congress of the United States. Yesterday, the President was notified that three hundred individual Congressmen and fifty Senators of both parties had endorsed his efforts for peace. As with other American institutions, perhaps it is time that the networks were made more responsive to the views of the nation and more responsible to the people they serve.

Now, I want to make myself perfectly clear. I'm not asking for government censorship or any other kind of censorship. I am asking whether a form of censorship already exists when the news that forty million Americans, when the news that forty million Americans receive each night is determined by a handful of men responsible only to their corporate employers and is filtered through a handful of commentators who admit to their own set of biases.

The questions I'm raising here tonight should have been raised by others long ago. They should have been raised by those Americans who have traditionally considered the preservation of freedom of speech and freedom of the press their special provinces of responsibility. They should have been raised by those Americans who share the view of the late Justice

---

18. Pulitzer Prize–winning journalist with the *New York Times*.

19. Coanchor of NBC's nightly news.

20. ABC's Frank Reynolds.

21. The statements by Brinkley and Reynolds are from *The Whole World Is Watching*, a Public Broadcasting Laboratory program that aired December 22, 1968. Reynolds is quoted verbatim; Brinkley is paraphrased.

22. Frank Reynolds, ABC evening news broadcast, October 30, 1968.

Learned Hand[23] that right conclusions are more likely to be gathered out of a multitude of tongues than through any kind of authoritative selection.

Advocates for the networks have claimed a First Amendment right to the same unlimited freedoms held by the great newspapers of America. But the situations are not identical. Where the *New York Times* reaches 800,000 people, NBC reaches twenty times that number on its evening news. Nor can the tremendous impact of seeing television film and hearing commentary be compared with reading the printed page.

A decade ago, before the network news acquired such dominance over public opinion, Walter Lippmann[24] spoke to the issue. He said: "There's an essential and radical difference between television and printing.... The three or four competing television stations control virtually all that can be received over the air by ordinary television sets. But besides the mass-circulation dailies, there are weeklies, monthlies, out-of-town newspapers, and books. If a man doesn't like his newspaper, he can read another from out of town or wait for a weekly news magazine. It's not ideal, but it's infinitely better than the situation in television. There, if a man doesn't like what the networks are showing, all he can do is turn them off and listen to a phonograph." "Networks," he stated, "which are few in number, have a virtual monopoly of a whole medium of communication. The newspaper[s] of mass circulation have no monopoly on the medium of print."[25]

Now, a virtual monopoly of a whole medium of communication is not something that democratic people should blindly ignore. And we are not going to cut off our television sets and listen to the phonograph just because the airways belong to the networks. They don't. They belong to the people. As Justice Byron White wrote in his landmark opinion six months ago, "It's the right of the viewers and listeners, not the right of the broadcasters, which is paramount."[26]

Now, it's argued that this power presents no danger in the hands of those who have used it responsibly. But as to whether or not the networks have abused the power they enjoy, let us call, as our first witness, former Vice President Humphrey and the city of Chicago.[27] According to Theodore White, television's intercutting of the film from the streets of Chicago with the "current proceedings on the floor of the convention...created the most striking and false political picture of 1968—the nomination of a man for the American presidency by the brutality and violence of merciless police."[28]

If we are to believe a recent report of the House of Representatives Commerce Committee, then television's presentation of the violence in the streets worked an injustice on the reputation of the Chicago police. According to the committee findings, one network in particular presented, and I quote, "a one-sided picture which in large measure exonerates the demonstrators and protesters."[29] Film of provocations of police that was available never saw the light of day, while the film of a police response which the protesters provoked was shown to millions. Another network showed virtually the same scene of violence from three separate angles without making clear it was the same scene. And while the full report is reticent in drawing conclusions, it is not a document to inspire confidence in the fairness of the network news.

Our knowledge of the impact of network news on the national mind is far from complete,[30] but

23. Judge of the Federal Court of Appeals for the Second Circuit, 1924–1951.

24. Pulitzer Prize–winning journalist and political commentator.

25. From Lippmann's column "Television and Press," March 3, 1960.

26. From White's opinion in the U.S. Supreme Court's ruling in *Red Lion Broadcasting Company v. Federal Communications Commission* (1969).

27. Vice President under Lyndon Johnson, Hubert Humphrey won the 1968 Democratic presidential nomination at the party's convention in Chicago, where violent clashes between police and antiwar protesters dominated the news.

28. From White's *The Making of the President 1968* (1969).

29. From *Television Coverage of the Democratic National Convention, Chicago, Illinois, 1968* (1969), issued by the Commerce Committee's Special Subcommittee on Investigations.

30. When delivering the speech, Agnew misspoke this work as "incomplete."

some early returns are available. Again, we have enough information to raise serious questions about its effect on a democratic society. Several years ago Fred Friendly,[31] one of the pioneers of network news, wrote that its missing ingredients were conviction, controversy, and a point of view. The networks have compensated with a vengeance. And in the networks' endless pursuit of controversy, we should ask what is the end value: to enlighten or to profit? What is the end result: to inform or to confuse? How does the ongoing exploration for more action, more excitement, more drama serve our national search for internal peace and stability?

Gresham's Law[32] seems to be operating in the network news. Bad news drives out good news. The irrational is more controversial than the rational. Concurrence can no longer compete with dissent. One minute of Eldridge Cleaver[33] is worth ten minutes of Roy Wilkins.[34] The labor crisis settled at the negotiating table is nothing compared to the confrontation that results in a strike or, better yet, violence along the picket lines. Normality has become the nemesis of the network news.

Now, the upshot of all this controversy is that a narrow and distorted picture of America often emerges from the televised news. A single, dramatic piece of the mosaic becomes in the minds of millions the entire picture. The American who relies upon television for his news might conclude that the majority of American students are embittered radicals, that the majority of black Americans feel no regard for their country, that violence and lawlessness are the rule rather than the exception on the American campus.

We know that none of these conclusions is true. Perhaps the place to start looking for a credibility gap is not in the offices of the government in Washington, but in the studios of the networks in New York. Television may have destroyed the old stereotypes, but has it not created new ones in their places?

What has this passionate pursuit of controversy done to the politics of progress through local compromise essential to the functioning of a democratic society? The members of Congress or the Senate who follow their principles and philosophy quietly in a spirit of compromise are unknown to many Americans, while the loudest and most extreme dissenters on every issue are known to every man in the street. How many marches and demonstrations would we have if the marchers did not know that the ever-faithful TV cameras would be there to record their antics for the next news show?

We've heard demands that Senators and Congressmen and judges make known all their financial connections so that the public will know who and what influences their decisions and their votes. Strong arguments can be made for that view. But when a single commentator or producer, night after night, determines for millions of people how much of each side of a great issue they are going to see and hear, should he not first disclose his personal views on the issue as well? In this search for excitement and controversy, has more than equal time gone to the minority of Americans who specialize in attacking the United States—its institutions and its citizens?

Tonight, I've raised questions. I've made no attempt to suggest the answers. The answers must come from the media men. They are challenged to turn their critical powers on themselves—to direct their energy, their talent, and their conviction toward improving the quality and objectivity of news presentation. They are challenged to structure their own civic ethics to relate to the great responsibilities they hold.[35]

And the people of America are challenged, too—challenged to press for responsible news presentations. The people can let the networks know that they want their news straight and objective. The people

---

31. President of CBS News, 1964–1966.

32. The principle that bad money drives good money out of circulation; named after Thomas Gresham (1519–1579).

33. Author of *Soul on Ice* (1968) and prominent member of the radical Black Panthers.

34. Head of the National Association for the Advancement of Colored People.

---

35. Agnew misspoke the end of this sentence as: "to relate their great feeling with the great responsibilities they hold."

can register their complaints on bias through mail to the networks and phone calls to local stations. This is one case where the people must defend themselves, where the citizen—not the government—must be the reformer, where the consumer can be the most effective crusader.

By way of conclusion, let me say that every elected leader in the United States depends on these men of the media. Whether what I've said to you tonight will be heard and seen at all by the nation is not my decision, it's not your decision, it's their decision. In tomorrow's edition of the *Des Moines Register*, you'll be able to read a news story detailing what I've said tonight. Editorial comment will be reserved for the editorial page, where it belongs. Should not the same wall of separation exist between news and comment on the nation's networks?

Now, my friends, we'd never trust such power as I've described over public opinion in the hands of an elected government. It's time we questioned it in the hands of a small and unelected elite. The great networks have dominated America's airwaves for decades. The people are entitled to a full accounting of their stewardship.

Richard M. Nixon

Address on the Cambodian Incursion

Washington, D.C.
April 30, 1970

WHEN PRESIDENT RICHARD Nixon announced his Vietnamization plan during his address of November 3, 1969 (pages 488–496 above), he explained that his aim was to reduce American casualties by gradually replacing U.S. personnel with South Vietnamese forces. By the end of 1969, American troop levels in Vietnam had been reduced by 115,000. On April 20, 1970, Nixon announced that another 150,000 would return home during the coming year. Vietnamization appeared to be working. Then, ten days later, Nixon shocked the nation by going on national television to announce a military incursion into the officially neutral country of Cambodia, where, he said, North Vietnam had occupied military sanctuaries all along the border with South Vietnam.

In actuality, the presence of enemy troops in Cambodia had long been known to Nixon, and the United States had been conducting clandestine bombing raids there since March 1969. None of this had been communicated to the general public, however, and most Americans were focused on getting out of Vietnam, not on expanding the war to another country. In defense of his decision, Nixon argued that Vietnamization could not work—and more American troops could not be brought home—unless the North Vietnamese sanctuaries were removed. More than that, he argued, the credibility of the United States was on the line: "If, when the chips are down, the world's most powerful nation...acts like a pitiful, helpless giant, the forces of totalitarianism and anarchy will threaten free nations and free institutions throughout the world."

It was, as National Security Advisor Henry Kissinger said, "a very tough speech," and it touched off a storm of protest, especially on college campuses, which had long been centers of antiwar activity. On the following Monday, May 4, members of the Ohio National Guard fired upon student demonstrators at Kent State University, killing four and wounding eight. By the end of the week, there had been protests at more than 1,100 campuses, two million students had gone on strike, and some 450 schools had closed. In Congress, antiwar Senators moved to cut off funding for operations in Cambodia, and even some longtime supporters began to criticize the President. Three of Kissinger's White House aides resigned in protest.

Nixon's "silent majority" did not desert him, however. In a Gallup poll taken a fortnight after the shootings at Kent State, only 11 percent of respondents blamed the National Guard, while 58 percent put responsibility on the students. By the end of June, the last American ground troops had left Cambodia and the turmoil on college campuses had been replaced by the calm of summer break. The war in Vietnam was far from over, but Nixon had survived another crisis.

◇◇

Good evening, my fellow Americans: Ten days ago, in my report to the nation on Vietnam,[1] I announced the decision to withdraw an additional 150,000 Americans from Vietnam over the next year. I said then that I was making that decision despite our concern over increased enemy activity in Laos, in Cambodia, and in South Vietnam. And at that time, I warned that if I concluded that increased enemy activity in any of these areas endangered the lives of Americans remaining in Vietnam, I would not hesitate to take strong and effective measures to deal with that situation.

Despite that warning, North Vietnam has increased its military aggression in all these areas, and particularly in Cambodia. After full consultation with the National Security Council, Ambassador

Bunker,[2] General Abrams,[3] and my other advisers, I have concluded that the actions of the enemy in the last ten days clearly endanger the lives of Americans who are in Vietnam now and would constitute an unacceptable risk to those who will be there after withdrawal of another 150,000.

To protect our men who are in Vietnam and to guarantee the continued success of our withdrawal and Vietnamization programs, I have concluded that the time has come for action. Tonight I shall describe the actions of the enemy, the actions I have ordered to deal with that situation, and the reasons for my decision.

Cambodia, a small country of seven million people, has been a neutral nation since the Geneva agree-

1. Nixon is referring to a 15-minute televised address of April 20.

2. Ellsworth Bunker, ambassador to South Vietnam.

3. Creighton Abrams Jr., commanding general of U.S. forces in Vietnam.

ment of 1954—an agreement, incidentally, which was signed by the government of North Vietnam.[4] American policy since then has been to scrupulously respect the neutrality of the Cambodian people. We have maintained a skeleton diplomatic mission of fewer than fifteen in Cambodia's capital, and that only since last August. For the previous four years, from 1965 to 1969, we did not have any diplomatic mission whatever in Cambodia, and for the past five years, we have provided no military assistance whatever and no economic assistance to Cambodia.

North Vietnam, however, has not respected that neutrality. For the past five years, as indicated on this map that you see here,[5] North Vietnam has occupied military sanctuaries all along the Cambodian frontier with South Vietnam. Some of these extend up to twenty miles into Cambodia. The sanctuaries are in red and, as you note, they are on both sides of the border. They are used for hit-and-run attacks on American and South Vietnamese forces in South Vietnam.

These Communist-occupied territories contain major base camps, training sites, logistics facilities, weapons and ammunition factories, airstrips, and prisoner-of-war compounds. And for five years, neither the United States nor South Vietnam has moved against these enemy sanctuaries because we did not wish to violate the territory of a neutral nation.[6] Even after the Vietnamese Communists began to expand these sanctuaries four weeks ago, we counseled patience to our South Vietnamese allies and imposed restraints on our own commanders.

In contrast to our policy, the enemy in the past two weeks has stepped up his guerrilla actions, and he is concentrating his main forces in these sanctuaries that you see on this map where they are building up to launch massive attacks on our forces and those of South Vietnam. North Vietnam in the last two weeks has stripped away all pretense of respecting the sovereignty or the neutrality of Cambodia. Thousands of their soldiers are invading the country from the sanctuaries; they are encircling the capital of Phnom Penh. Coming from these sanctuaries, as you see here, they have moved into Cambodia and are encircling the capital.

Cambodia, as a result of this, has sent out a call to the United States, to a number of other nations, for assistance. Because if this enemy effort succeeds, Cambodia would become a vast enemy staging area and a springboard for attacks on South Vietnam along 600 miles of frontier—a refuge where enemy troops could return from combat without fear of retaliation. North Vietnamese men and supplies could then be poured into that country, jeopardizing not only the lives of our own men but the people of South Vietnam as well.

Now, confronted with this situation, we have three options. First, we can do nothing. Well, the ultimate result of that course of action is clear. Unless we indulge in wishful thinking, the lives of Americans remaining in Vietnam after our next withdrawal of 150,000 would be gravely threatened. Let us go to the map again. Here is South Vietnam. Here is North Vietnam. North Vietnam already occupies this part of Laos. If North Vietnam also occupied this whole band in Cambodia, or the entire country, it would mean that South Vietnam was completely outflanked and the forces of Americans in this area, as well as the South Vietnamese, would be in an untenable military position.

Our second choice is to provide massive military assistance to Cambodia itself. Now, unfortunately, while we deeply sympathize with the plight of seven million Cambodians whose country is being invaded, massive amounts of military assistance could not be rapidly and effectively utilized by the small Cambodian army against the immediate threat. With other nations, we shall do our best to provide the small arms and other equipment which the Cambodian army of 40,000 needs and can use for its defense. But the aid we will provide will be limited to the purpose of enabling Cambodia to defend its neutrality and not for the purpose of making it an active belligerent on one side or the other.

---

4. The Geneva Accords brought an end to the First Indochina War and were signed by France and North Vietnam; they were not signed by either South Vietnam or the United States.

5. Nixon pointed to a large map behind him that had been prepared especially for the telecast.

6. In fact, the United States had carried out 13 months of secret bombing in Cambodia before Nixon's speech.

Our third choice is to go to the heart of the trouble. And that means cleaning out major North Vietnamese- and Vietcong[7]-occupied territories, these sanctuaries which serve as bases for attacks on both Cambodia and American and South Vietnamese forces in South Vietnam. Some of these, incidentally, are as close to Saigon[8] as Baltimore is to Washington. This one, for example, is called the Parrot's Beak. It's only thirty-three miles from Saigon.

Now, faced with these three options, this is the decision I have made: In cooperation with the armed forces of South Vietnam, attacks are being launched this week to clean out major enemy sanctuaries on the Cambodian-Vietnam border. A major responsibility for the ground operations is being assumed by South Vietnamese forces. For example, the attacks in several areas, including the Parrot's Beak that I referred to a moment ago, are exclusively South Vietnamese ground operations under South Vietnamese command, with the United States providing air and logistical support.

There is one area, however, immediately above Parrot's Beak, where I have concluded that a combined American and South Vietnamese operation is necessary. Tonight, American and South Vietnamese units will attack the headquarters for the entire Communist military operation in South Vietnam. This key control center has been occupied by the North Vietnamese and Vietcong for five years in blatant violation of Cambodia's neutrality.

This is not an invasion of Cambodia. The areas in which these attacks will be launched are completely occupied and controlled by North Vietnamese forces. Our purpose is not to occupy the areas. Once enemy forces are driven out of these sanctuaries and once their military supplies are destroyed, we will withdraw.

These actions are in no way directed to the security interests of any nation. Any government that chooses to use these actions as a pretext for harming

relations with the United States will be doing so on its own responsibility and on its own initiative, and we will draw the appropriate conclusions.

And now let me give you the reasons for my decision. A majority of the American people, a majority of you listening to me, are for the withdrawal of our forces from Vietnam. The action I have taken tonight is indispensable for the continuing success of that withdrawal program. A majority of the American people want to end this war rather than to have it drag on interminably. The action I have taken tonight will serve that purpose. A majority of the American people want to keep the casualties of our brave men in Vietnam at an absolute minimum. The action I take tonight is essential if we are to accomplish that goal.

We take this action not for the purpose of expanding the war into Cambodia, but for the purpose of ending the war in Vietnam and winning the just peace we all desire. We have made, we will continue to make, every possible effort to end this war through negotiation at the conference table rather than through more fighting on the battlefield.

Let's look again at the record. We've stopped the bombing of North Vietnam. We have cut air operations by over 20 percent. We've announced withdrawal of over 250,000 of our men. We've offered to withdraw all of our men if they will withdraw theirs. We've offered to negotiate all issues with only one condition—and that is that the future of South Vietnam be determined not by North Vietnam and not by the United States, but by the people of South Vietnam themselves.

The answer of the enemy has been intransigence at the conference table, belligerence at Hanoi, massive military aggression in Laos and Cambodia, and stepped-up attacks in South Vietnam designed to increase American casualties. This attitude has become intolerable. We will not react to this threat to American lives merely by plaintive diplomatic protests. If we did, the credibility of the United States would be destroyed in every area of the world where only the power of the United States deters aggression.

Tonight, I again warn the North Vietnamese that if they continue to escalate the fighting when the United States is withdrawing its forces, I shall meet my responsibility as commander in chief of our armed forces to take the action I consider nec-

7. Contraction for Viet Nam Cong San, meaning "Vietnamese Communist." By the mid-1960s, it had become synonymous in popular parlance with the National Liberation Front, which had been formed with direction from North Vietnam to conduct the guerilla war against South Vietnam and the United States.

8. Capital of South Vietnam.

essary to defend the security of our American men. The action that I have announced tonight puts the leaders of North Vietnam on notice that we will be patient in working for peace. We will be conciliatory at the conference table. But we will not be humiliated. We will not be defeated. We will not allow American men by the thousands to be killed by an enemy from privileged sanctuaries.

The time came long ago to end this war through peaceful negotiations. We stand ready for those negotiations. We've made major efforts, many of which must remain secret. I say tonight: All the offers and approaches made previously remain on the conference table whenever Hanoi is ready to negotiate seriously. But if the enemy response to our most conciliatory offers for peaceful negotiation continues to be to increase its attacks and humiliate and defeat us, we shall react accordingly.

My fellow Americans, we live in an age of anarchy, both abroad and at home. We see mindless attacks on all the great institutions which have been created by free civilizations in the last 500 years. Even here in the United States, great universities are being systematically destroyed.[9] Small nations all over the world find themselves under attack from within and from without. If, when the chips are down, the world's most powerful nation, the United States of America, acts like a pitiful, helpless giant, the forces of totalitarianism and anarchy will threaten free nations and free institutions throughout the world.

It is not our power but our will and character that is being tested tonight. The question all Americans must ask and answer tonight is this: Does the richest and strongest nation in the history of the world have the character to meet a direct challenge by a group which rejects every effort to win a just peace, ignores our warning, tramples on solemn agreements, violates the neutrality of an unarmed people, and uses our prisoners as hostages? If we fail to meet this challenge, all other nations will be on notice that despite its overwhelming power, the United States, when a real crisis comes, will be found wanting.

During my campaign for the presidency, I pledged to bring Americans home from Vietnam. They are coming home. I promised to end this war. I shall keep that promise. I promised to win a just peace. I shall keep that promise. We shall avoid a wider war. But we are also determined to put an end to this war.

In this room,[10] Woodrow Wilson made the great decisions which led to victory in World War I. Franklin Roosevelt made the decisions which led to our victory in World War II. Dwight D. Eisenhower made decisions which ended the war in Korea[11] and avoided war in the Middle East.[12] John F. Kennedy, in his finest hour, made the great decision which removed Soviet nuclear missiles from Cuba and the Western Hemisphere.[13]

I have noted that there's been a great deal of discussion with regard to this decision that I have made, and I should point out that I do not contend that it is in the same magnitude as these decisions that I have just mentioned. But between those decisions and this decision there is a difference that is very fundamental. In those decisions, the American people were not assailed by counsels of doubt and defeat from some of the most widely known opinion leaders of the nation. I have noted, for example, that a Republican Senator has said that this action I have taken means that my party has lost all chance of winning the November elections. And others are saying today that this move against enemy sanctuaries will make me a one-term President.

No one is more aware than I am of the political consequences of the action I have taken. It is tempting to take the easy political path—to blame this war on previous administrations and to bring all of our men home immediately, regardless of the consequences, even though that would mean defeat for the United States; to desert eighteen million South Vietnamese people, who have put their trust in us; to expose

9. College campuses had long been a major hub of antiwar activity, and violent confrontations between students and law-enforcement officials occurred at a number of major universities.

10. The Oval Office of the White House.

11. Fighting in the Korean War ended in July 1953, during Eisenhower's first administration.

12. Nixon is referring to Eisenhower's exertion of pressure on France and Great Britain to accept a cease-fire during the Suez Canal crisis of 1956–1957.

13. See Kennedy's speech of October 22, 1962 (pages 357–362).

them to the same slaughter and savagery which the leaders of North Vietnam inflicted on hundreds of thousands of North Vietnamese who chose freedom when the Communists took over North Vietnam in 1954; to get peace at any price now, even though I know that a peace of humiliation for the United States would lead to a bigger war or surrender later.

I have rejected all political considerations in making this decision. Whether my party gains in November is nothing compared to the lives of 400,000 brave Americans fighting for our country and for the cause of peace and freedom in Vietnam. Whether I may be a one-term President is insignificant compared to whether, by our failure to act in this crisis, the United States proves itself to be unworthy to lead the forces of freedom in this critical period in world history. I would rather be a one-term President and do what I believe is right than to be a two-term President at the cost of seeing America become a second-rate power and to see this nation accept the first defeat in its proud 190-year history.

I realize that in this war there are honest and deep differences in this country about whether we should have become involved. That there are differences as to how the war should have been conducted. But the decision I announce tonight transcends those differences, for the lives of American men are involved. The opportunity for 150,000 Americans to come home in the next twelve months is involved. The future of eighteen million people in South Vietnam and seven million people in Cambodia is involved. The possibility of winning a just peace in Vietnam and in the Pacific is at stake.

It is customary to conclude a speech from the White House by asking support for the President of the United States. Tonight, I depart from that precedent. What I ask is far more important. I ask for your support for our brave men fighting tonight halfway around the world—not for territory, not for glory, but so that their younger brothers and their sons and your sons can have a chance to grow up in a world of peace and freedom and justice.

Thank you, and good night.

Shirley Chisholm

For the Equal Rights Amendment

WASHINGTON, D.C.
AUGUST 10, 1970

AFFIRMING THAT "EQUALITY of rights under the law shall not be denied or abridged by the United States or by any state on account of sex," the Equal Rights Amendment became a subject of intense public debate during the 1970s. Although such an amendment had been introduced in Congress as early as 1923, it took almost fifty years to get it approved by both the Senate and the House of Representatives.

The first black woman elected to the House, Shirley Chisholm was one of the amendment's most articulate supporters. She won the seat of New York's Twelfth Congressional District in 1968 and eventually served seven terms. Manifesting an independent spirit consistent with her slogan "Unbought and Unbossed," she was a respected voice for progressive causes and in 1972 became the first African American to make a bid for the Democratic presidential nomination. She stayed in the race until the party's national convention and received more than 150 votes on the first ballot. As a student at Brooklyn College, she had been trained in debate, and she captured listeners with speeches that relied predominantly on evidence, reasoning, and a strong sense of moral conviction.

Chisholm spoke in favor of the Equal Rights Amendment the day before it came to a vote in the House, arguing that discrimination against women was founded on "outmoded views of society" and "prescientific beliefs about psychology and physiology." The time had come, she declared, "to sweep away these relics of the past and set future generations free of them." Affirming the benefits of the ERA and refuting the objections of its opponents, she urged her colleagues to go on record "for the fullest expression of that equality of opportunity which our Founding Fathers professed."

The amendment passed in the House with only fifteen dissenting votes and was sent to the Senate, where it was not acted upon until the next session of Congress. After being approved by both chambers in 1971–1972, it was sent to the states for ratification. Despite a series of early victories, it remained three states short of the thirty-eight needed at the end of the seven-year deadline stipulated by the Constitution. The deadline was extended another three years, but no more states ratified during that period, and the amendment expired in 1982 without going into effect.

◇◇

Mr. Speaker:[1] House Joint Resolution 264, before us today, which provides for equality under the law for both men and women, represents one of the most clear-cut opportunities we are likely to have to declare our faith in the principles that shaped our Constitution. It provides a legal basis for attack on the most subtle, most pervasive, and most institutionalized form of prejudice that exists. Discrimination against women, solely on the basis of their sex, is so widespread that it seems to many persons normal, natural, and right. Legal expression of prejudice on the grounds of religious or political belief has become a minor problem in our society. Prejudice on the basis of race is, at least, under systematic attack. There is reason for optimism that it will start to die with the present older generation. It is time we act to assure full equality of opportunity to those citizens who, although in a majority, suffer the restrictions that are more commonly imposed on minorities—to women.

The argument that this amendment will not solve the problem of sex discrimination is not relevant. If the argument were used against a civil rights bill—as it has been used in the past—the prejudice that lies behind it would be embarrassing. Of course laws will not eliminate prejudice from the hearts of human beings. But that is no reason to allow prejudice to continue to be enshrined in our laws—to perpetuate injustice through inaction.

The amendment is necessary to clarify countless ambiguities and inconsistencies in our legal system. For instance, the Constitution guarantees due process of law in the Fifth and Fourteenth Amendments. But the applicability of due process to sex distinctions is not clear: Women are excluded from some state colleges and universities. In some states, restrictions

1. John W. McCormack, Speaker of the House of Representatives.

are placed on a married woman who engages in an independent business. Women may not be chosen for some juries. Women even receive heavier criminal penalties than men who commit the same crime.

What would the legal effects of the Equal Rights Amendment really be? The Equal Rights Amendment would govern only the relationship between the state and its citizens—not relationships between private citizens.

The amendment would be largely self-executing—that is, any federal or state laws in conflict would be ineffective one year after date of ratification without further action by the Congress or state legislatures.

Opponents of the amendment claim its ratification would throw the law into a state of confusion and would result in much litigation to establish its meaning. This objection overlooks the influence of legislative history in determining intent and the recent activities of many groups preparing for legislative changes in this direction.

State labor laws applying only to women, such as those limiting hours of work and weights to be lifted, would become inoperative unless the legislature amended them to apply to men. As of early 1970 most states would have some laws that would be affected. However, changes are being made so rapidly as a result of Title VII of the Civil Rights Act of 1964,[1] it is likely that by the time the Equal Rights Amendment would become effective, no conflicting state laws would remain.

In any event, there has for years been great controversy as to the usefulness to women of these state labor laws. There has never been any doubt that they worked a hardship on women who need or want to work overtime and on women who need or want better-paying jobs, and there has been no persuasive evidence as to how many women benefit from the archaic policy of the laws. After the Delaware hours law was repealed in 1966,[2] there were no complaints from women to any of the state agencies that might have been approached.

Jury service laws not making women equally liable for jury service would have to be revised.

The Selective Service Law would have to include women, but women would not be required to serve in the armed forces where they are not fitted, any more than men are required to serve. Military service, while a great responsibility, is not without benefits, particularly for young men with limited education or training. Since October 1966, 246,000 young men who did not meet the normal mental or physical requirements have been given opportunities for training and correcting physical problems. This opportunity is not open to their sisters. Only girls who have completed high school and meet high standards on the educational test can volunteer. Ratification of the amendment would not permit application of higher standards to women.

Survivorship benefits would be available to husbands of female workers on the same basis as to wives of male workers. The Social Security Act and the civil service and military service retirement acts are in conflict.

Public schools and universities could not be limited to one sex and could not apply different admission standards to men and women. Laws requiring longer prison sentences for women than men would be invalid, and equal opportunities for rehabilitation and vocational training would have to be provided in public correctional institutions.

Different ages of majority based on sex would have to be harmonized.

Federal, state, and other governmental bodies would be obligated to follow nondiscriminatory practices in all aspects of employment, including public school teachers and state university and college faculties.

What would be the economic effects of the Equal Rights Amendment? Direct economic effects would be minor. If any labor laws applying only to women still remained, their amendment or repeal would provide opportunity for women in better-paying jobs in manufacturing. More opportunities in public vocational and graduate schools for women would also tend to open up opportunities in better jobs for women.

Indirect effects could be much greater. The focusing of public attention on the gross legal, economic, and social discrimination against women by hearings

---

1. Title VII protected individuals against employment discrimination based on race, color, religion, sex, or national origin.

2. Chisholm is referring to legislation, originally passed in 1915 and revised in 1935, regulating the hours and conditions of work for women laborers in Delaware.

and debates in the federal and state legislatures would result in changes in attitude of parents, educators, and employers that would bring about substantial economic changes in the long run.

Sex prejudice cuts both ways. Men are oppressed by the requirements of the Selective Service Act, by enforced legal guardianship of minors, and by alimony laws. Each sex, I believe, should be liable when necessary to serve and defend this country. Each has a responsibility for the support of children.

There are objections raised to wiping out laws protecting women workers. No one would condone exploitation. But what does sex have to do with it? Working conditions and hours that are harmful to women are harmful to men; wages that are unfair for women are unfair for men. Laws setting employment limitations on the basis of sex are irrational, and the proof of this is their inconsistency from state to state. The physical characteristics of men and women are not fixed, but cover two wide spans that have a great deal of overlap. It is obvious, I think, that a robust woman could be more fit for physical labor than a weak man. The choice of occupation would be determined by individual capabilities, and the rewards for equal work should be equal.

This is what it comes down to: Artificial distinctions between persons must be wiped out of the law. Legal discrimination between the sexes is, in almost every instance, founded on outmoded views of society and the prescientific beliefs about psychology and physiology. It is time to sweep away these relics of the past and set future generations free of them.

Federal agencies and institutions responsible for the enforcement of equal opportunity laws need the authority of a constitutional amendment. The 1964 Civil Rights Act and the 1963 Equal Pay Act are not enough; they are limited in their coverage—for instance, one excludes teachers, and the other leaves out administrative and professional women. The Equal Employment Opportunity Commission has not proven to be an adequate device, with its powers limited to investigation, conciliation, and recommendation to the Justice Department. In its cases involving sexual discrimination, it has failed in more than one-half. The Justice Department has been even less effective. It has intervened in only one case involving

discrimination on the basis of sex, and this was on a procedural point. In a second case, in which both sexual and racial discrimination were alleged, the racial bias charge was given far greater weight.

Evidence of discrimination on the basis of sex should hardly have to be cited here. It is in the Labor Department's employment and salary figures for anyone who is still in doubt. Its elimination will involve so many changes in our state and federal laws that without the authority and impetus of this proposed amendment, it will perhaps take another 194 years. We cannot be parties to continuing a delay. The time is clearly now to put this House on record for the fullest expression of that equality of opportunity which our Founding Fathers professed.

They professed it, but they did not assure it to their daughters, as they tried to do for their sons. The constitution they wrote was designed to protect the rights of white, male citizens. As there were no black Founding Fathers, there were no Founding Mothers—a great pity, on both counts. It is not too late to complete the work they left undone. Today, here, we should start to do so.

In closing, I would like to make one point. Social and psychological effects will be initially more important than legal or economic results. As Leo Kanowitz has pointed out: "Rules of law that treat of the sexes per se inevitably produce far-reaching effects upon social, psychological, and economic aspects of male-female relations beyond the limited confines of legislative chambers and courtrooms. As long as organized legal systems, at once the most respected and most feared of social institutions, continue to differentiate sharply, in treatment or in words, between men and women on the basis of irrelevant and artificially created distinctions, the likelihood of men and women coming to regard one another primarily as fellow human beings and only secondarily as representatives of another sex will continue to be remote. When men and women are prevented from recognizing one another's essential humanity by sexual prejudices, nourished by legal as well as social institutions, society as a whole remains less than it could otherwise become."[3]

---

3. From Kanowitz's *Women and the Law: The Unfinished Revolution* (1969).

John F. Kerry

☒

Vietnam Veterans Against the War

WASHINGTON, D.C.
APRIL 22, 1971

JOHN KERRY WAS twenty-seven years old when he spoke before the Senate Foreign Relations Committee on April 22, 1971. A Yale graduate who had enlisted in the navy, he received three Purple Hearts, a Bronze Star for bravery, and a Silver Star for valor in combat during his tour of duty as a Swift boat commander in Vietnam from November 1968 through March 1969. By the time he left the service in January 1970, however, he was convinced that the purposes and conduct of the war were fundamentally misguided.

Soon thereafter, he joined Vietnam Veterans Against the War (VVAW). A stirring speech at a VVAW rally in Valley Forge, Pennsylvania, in September 1970 vaulted him to a position of leadership in the organization. In late January and early February 1971, he attended VVAW's "Winter Soldier" symposium in Detroit, where some 150 veterans testified to atrocities they had seen or had committed in Vietnam. Kerry did not speak, but he would incorporate part of what he heard into his Senate address three months later. That address came about because of an invitation from Arkansas Senator J. William Fulbright, an outspoken critic of the war who chaired the Foreign Relations Committee and saw Kerry as someone who might give effective voice to dissent from a veteran's perspective.

Kerry more than justified Fulbright's confidence. At the time, 300,000 American military personnel were deployed in Vietnam and more than 50,000 had been killed. Opposition to the conflict had driven Lyndon Johnson out of the White House, and antiwar protests had escalated in size and intensity since Richard Nixon's inauguration in January 1969. In April 1971 attention was focused on the nation's capital because of the VVAW demonstrations being held there. When Kerry reached the committee chamber, it was jammed with spectators, reporters, and television cameras. Dressed in green fatigues and wearing his medals and ribbons, he spoke calmly yet movingly about atrocities committed by U.S. troops in Vietnam, about the futility of American military policy, and about the sense of betrayal felt by veterans at the hands of the nation's political leaders. "How," he queried, "do you ask a man to be the last man to die in Vietnam? How do you ask a man to be the last man to die for a mistake?"

Kerry was little known outside antiwar circles before the speech, but he became a national figure after it. Lengthy clips were shown on all the television networks, Kerry was profiled in the *New York Times* and newsweeklies, and his speech was widely reprinted. The *Chicago Daily News* said he was "so eloquent and moving that a couple grizzled Senators bit their lips.... Print cannot convey the cool anguish of this tall young man with a handsome face." Recognizing that the antiwar movement had a new luminary, President Nixon told aides that Kerry was "extremely effective" and had been the "real star" of the committee hearing.

Buoyed by his newfound public standing, Kerry came close to winning a seat in Congress the next year. After working as a lawyer and assistant district attorney, he was elected Lieutenant Governor of Massachusetts in 1982. Two years later, he won a seat in the U.S. Senate. Often mentioned as a possible presidential candidate, he received the Democratic nomination in 2004 but was unable to unseat incumbent George W. Bush.

◇◇◇◇◇◇◇◇◇◇◇◇◇◇◇◇◇◇◇◇◇◇◇◇◇◇◇◇◇◇◇◇◇◇◇

Thank you very much, Senator Fulbright, Senator Javits, Senator Symington, Senator Pell.[1] I would like to say for the record that, and also for the men behind me who are also wearing the uniform and their medals, that my sitting up here is really symbolic. I'm not here as John Kerry. I'm here as one member of a group of 1,000,[2] which is a small representation of a very much larger group of veterans in this country, and were it possible for all of them to sit at this table, they would be here and have the same kind of testimony.

I would simply like to speak in very general terms. I apologize if my statement is general because I received notification yesterday you would hear me, and I'm afraid because of the injunction[3] I was up most of the night and haven't had a great deal of chance to prepare.

I would like to talk, representing all those veterans, and say that several months ago in Detroit we had an investigation at which over 150 honorably discharged and many very highly decorated veterans testified to war crimes committed in Southeast Asia—not isolated incidents, but crimes committed on a day-to-day basis with the full awareness of officers at all levels of command. It's impossible to describe to you exactly what did happen in Detroit—the emotions in the room, the feelings of the men who were reliving their experiences in Vietnam. But they did; they relived the absolute horror of what this country, in a sense, made them do.

They told the stories of times that they had personally raped, cut off ears, cut off heads, taped wires from portable telephones to human genitals and turned up the power, cut off limbs, blown up bodies, randomly shot at civilians, razed villages in fashion reminiscent of Genghis Khan,[4] shot cattle and dogs for fun, poisoned food stocks, and generally ravaged the countryside of South Vietnam—in addition to the normal ravage[s] of war and the normal and very particular ravaging which is done by the applied bombing power of this country.

We call this investigation the Winter Soldier Investigation. The term "Winter Soldier" is a play on words of Thomas Paine's in 1776, when he spoke of the sunshine patriot and summertime soldiers who deserted at Valley Forge because the going was rough.[5] And we who have come here to Washington have come here because we feel we have to be winter soldiers now. We could come back to this country and we could be quiet; we could hold our silence; we could not tell what went on in Vietnam. But we feel because of what threatens this country—the fact that

1. J. William Fulbright, Jacob K. Javits, Stuart Symington, Claiborne Pell.

2. Vietnam Veterans Against the War (VVAW).

3. The Nixon administration had obtained an injunction prohibiting VVAW members and supporters from "camping" in the Washington Mall.

4. Mongol conqueror (ca. 1162–1227).

5. A reference to the opening lines of the first installment of Thomas Paine's "The American Crisis," December 19, 1776.

the crimes threaten it, not Reds, not redcoats, but the crimes which we're committing are what threaten it—and we have to speak out.

I would like to talk to you a little bit about what the result is of the feelings these men carry with them after coming back from Vietnam. The country doesn't know it yet, but it's created a monster, a monster in the form of millions of men who have been taught to deal and to trade in violence and who are given the chance to die for the biggest nothing in history, men who have returned with a sense of anger and a sense of betrayal which no one has yet grasped.

As a veteran and one who feels this anger, I'd like to talk about it. We're angry because we feel we have been used in the worst fashion by the administration of this country. In 1970, at West Point, Vice President Agnew said, "Some glamorize the criminal misfits of society while our best men die in Asian rice paddies to preserve the freedoms which those misfits abuse,"[6] and this was used as a rallying point for our effort in Vietnam. But for us, as boys in Asia whom the country was supposed to support, his statement is a terrible distortion from which we can only draw a very deep sense of revulsion. And hence the anger of some of the men who are here in Washington today.

It's a distortion because we in no way considered ourselves the best men of this country, because those he calls "misfits" were standing up for us in a way that nobody else in this country dared to, because so many who have died would have returned to this country to join the "misfits" in their efforts to ask for an immediate withdrawal from South Vietnam, because so many of those best men have returned as quadriplegics and amputees and they lie forgotten in Veterans Administration's hospitals in this country which fly the flag which so many have chosen as their own personal symbol. And we cannot consider ourselves America's best men when we were ashamed of and hated what we were called on to do in Southeast Asia.

In our opinion, and from our experience, there is nothing in South Vietnam, nothing which could happen, that realistically threatens the United States

of America. And to attempt to justify the loss of one American life in Vietnam, Cambodia, or Laos by linking such loss to the preservation of freedom, which those "misfits" supposedly abuse, is to us the height of criminal hypocrisy—and it's that kind of hypocrisy which we feel has torn this country apart.

But we are probably much more angry than that, and I don't want to go into the foreign policy aspects because I'm outclassed here. I know that all of you have talked about every possible, every possible alternative of getting out of Vietnam. We understand that. We know that you've considered the seriousness of the aspects to the utmost level, and I'm not gonna try and deal on that. But I want to relate to you the feeling which many of the men who have returned to this country express, because we are probably angriest about all that we were told about Vietnam and about the mystical war against communism.

We found that not only was it a civil war, an effort by a people who had for years been seeking their liberation from any colonial influence whatsoever, but also we found that the Vietnamese whom we had enthusiastically molded after our own image were hard put to take up the fight against the threat we were supposedly saving them from.

We found that most people didn't even know the difference between communism and democracy. They only wanted to work in rice paddies without helicopters strafing them and bombs with napalm burning their villages and tearing their country apart. They wanted everything to do with the war—particularly with this foreign presence of the United States of America—to leave them alone in peace, and they practiced the art of survival by siding with whichever military force was present at a particular time, be it Vietcong,[7] North Vietnamese, or American.

We found also that all too often American men were dying in those rice paddies for want of support from their allies. We saw firsthand how monies from

<hr>

6. Paraphrased from Agnew's speech of June 3, 1970.

7. Contraction for Viet Nam Cong San, meaning "Vietnamese Communist." By the mid-1960s, it had become synonymous in popular parlance with the National Liberation Front, which had been formed with direction from North Vietnam to conduct the guerilla war against South Vietnam and the United States.

American taxes was used for a corrupt dictatorial regime. We saw that many people in this country had a one-sided idea of who was kept free by our flag, as blacks provided the highest percentage of casualties. We saw Vietnam ravaged equally by American bombs, as well as by search-and-destroy missions, as well as by Vietcong terrorism, and yet we listened while this country tried to blame all of the havoc on the Vietcong.

We rationalized destroying villages in order to save them. We saw America lose her sense of morality as she accepted very coolly a My Lai[8] and refused to give up the image of American soldiers that hand out chocolate bars and chewing gum.

We learnt the meaning of free-fire zones—shoot anything that moves—and we watched while America placed a cheapness on the lives of Orientals. We watched the United States' falsification of body counts—in fact, the glorification of body counts. We listened while month after month we were told the back of the enemy was about to break.

We fought using weapons against Oriental human beings—with quotation marks around that[9]—we fought using weapons against those people which I do not believe this country would dream of using were we fighting in a European theater or, let us say, a non-Third-World-people theater.

And so we watched while men charged up hills because a general said, "That hill has to be taken," and after losing one platoon or two platoons they marched away to leave the hill for the reoccupation of the North Vietnamese; because, because we watched pride allow the most unimportant of battles to be blown into extravaganzas; because we couldn't lose and we couldn't retreat and because it didn't matter how many American bodies were lost to prove that point. And so there were Hamburger Hills and Khe Sanhs and Hill 881s and Fire Base 6s[10] and so many others.

And now we're told that the men who fought there must watch quietly while American lives are lost so that we can exercise the incredible arrogance of Vietnamizing the Vietnamese.[11] Each day, each—[Applause]

SENATOR FULBRIGHT: I hope you won't interrupt. He is making a very significant statement. Let him proceed.

KERRY: Each day to facilitate the process by which the United States washes her hands of Vietnam someone has to give up his life so that the United States doesn't have to admit something that the entire world already knows, so that we can't say that we've made a mistake. Someone has to die so that President Nixon won't be, and these are his words, "the first President to lose a war."[12] And we are asking Americans to think about that, because how do you ask a man to be the last man to die in Vietnam? How do you ask a man to be the last man to die for a mistake?

But we're trying to do that, and we're doing it with thousands of rationalizations. And if you read carefully the President's last speech to the people of this country, you can see that he says, and says clearly, "But the issue, gentlemen, the issue is communism, and the question is whether or not we will leave that country to the Communists or whether or not we will try to give it hope to be a free people."[13] But the point is they're not a free people now, under us. They're not a free people, and we cannot fight communism all over the world, and I think we should've learnt that lesson by now.

But the problem of veterans goes beyond this personal problem, because you think about a poster in this country with a picture of Uncle Sam, and the picture says, "I want you." And a young man comes out of high school and says, "That's fine. I'm gonna serve my country." And he goes to Vietnam and he

---

8. In March 1968 U.S. soldiers murdered more than 300 Vietnamese civilians in the village of My Lai.

9. Kerry's statement "with quotation marks around that" was meant to emphasize his belief that many U.S. military personnel did not accord "Oriental human beings" the same respect they accorded other human beings.

10. Sites of major battles in Vietnam.

11. Kerry is referring to Richard Nixon's policy of Vietnamization, in which the war was gradually turned over to the South Vietnamese while the United States reduced its military presence. See Nixon's address of November 3, 1969 (pages 488–496).

12. Nixon expressed this sentiment on a number of occasions, as did President Lyndon Johnson before him.

13. Loosely paraphrased from Nixon's speech of April 7, 1971.

shoots and he kills and he does his job. Or maybe he doesn't kill; maybe he just goes and he comes back. And when he gets back to this country, he finds that he isn't really wanted, because the largest unemployment figure in the country—it varies depending on who you get it from, the Veterans Administration 15 percent, various other sources 22 percent—but the largest figure of unemployed in this country are veterans of this war, and of those veterans, 33 percent of the unemployed are black. That means one out of every ten of the nation's unemployed is a veteran of Vietnam.

The hospitals across the country won't—or can't—meet their demands. It's not a question of not trying. They haven't got the appropriations. A man recently died after he had a tracheotomy in California, not because of the operation, but because there weren't enough personnel to clean the mucous out of his tube and he suffocated to death. Another young man just died in a New York VA hospital the other day. A friend of mine was lying in a bed two beds away and tried to help him, but he couldn't. They rang a bell and there was no one there to service that man, and so he died of convulsions.

Fifty-seven percent—I understand 57 percent—of all those entering VA hospitals talk about suicide, and some 27 percent have tried. And they try because they come back to this country and they have to face what they did in Vietnam, and then they come back and find the indifference of a country that doesn't really care—that doesn't really care.

Suddenly we're faced with a very sickening situation in this country because there's no moral indignation, and if there is, it comes from people who are almost exhausted by their past indignancies—and I know that many of them are sitting in front of me.[14] The country seems to have lain down and accepted something as serious as Laos,[15] just as we calmly

shrugged off the loss of 700,000 lives in Pakistan, the so-called greatest disaster of all times.[16]

We are here as veterans to say that we think we are in the midst of the greatest disaster of all times now because they are still dying over there—and not just Americans, Vietnamese—and we are rationalizing leaving that country so that those people can go on killing each other for years to come. Americans seem to have accepted the idea that the war is winding down, at least for Americans, and they have also allowed the bodies which were once used by a President for statistics to prove that we were winning this war to be used as evidence against a man who followed orders and who interpreted those orders no differently than hundreds of other men in South Vietnam.[17]

We veterans can only look with amazement on the fact that this country has not been able to see that there's absolutely no difference between a ground troop and a helicopter crew, and yet people have accepted a differentiation fed them by the administration. No ground troops are in Laos, so it's all right to kill Laotians by remote control. But, believe me, the helicopter crews fill the same body bags and they wreak the same kind of damage on the Vietnamese and Laotian countryside as anyone else, and the President is talking about allowing that to go on for many years to come. And one can only ask if we will really be satisfied when the troops march into Hanoi.

We are asking here in Washington for some action, action from the Congress of the United States of America, which has the power to raise and maintain armies and which, by the Constitution, also has the power to declare war. We've come here, not to the President, because we believe that this body can be responsive to the will of the people, and we believe that the will of the people says that we should be out of Vietnam now.

14. Members of the Senate Foreign Relations Committee present for Kerry's testimony.

15. In February 1971, 20,000 South Vietnamese troops, supported by American air and artillery, invaded Laos, where the United States had conducted secret bombing raids since 1964.

16. Kerry is referring to a cyclone that struck East Pakistan in November 1970; subsequent estimates put the number of deaths at 250,000–500,000.

17. Kerry is speaking of Lieutenant William Calley, who was convicted of murder for his role in the My Lai massacre (see note 8 above).

We're here in Washington also to say that the problem of this war is not just a question of war and diplomacy. It's part and parcel of everything that we are trying as human beings to communicate to people in this country. The question of racism, which is rampant in the military, and so many other questions also—the use of weapons, the hypocrisy in our taking umbrage in the, in the Geneva Conventions[18] and using that as justification for a continuation of this war when we are more guilty than any other body of violations of those Geneva Conventions in the use of free-fire zones, harassment-interdiction fire, search-and-destroy missions, the bombings, the torture of prisoners, the killing of prisoners, accepted policy by many units in South Vietnam. That's what we're trying to say: It's part and parcel of everything.

An American Indian friend of mine who lives in the Indian Nation of Alcatraz[19] put it to me very succinctly. He told me how as a boy on an Indian reservation he had watched television and he used to cheer the cowboys when they came in and shot the Indians. And then suddenly one day he stopped in Vietnam and he said, "My God, I'm doing to these people the very same thing that was done to my people." And he stopped. And that's what we're trying to say: that we think this thing has to end.

We're also here to ask, we are here to ask—and we're here to ask vehemently—where are the leaders of our country? Where is the leadership? We're here to ask where are McNamara, Rostow, Bundy, Gilpatrick[20] and so many others? Where are they now that we, the men whom they sent off to war, have returned? These are commanders who have deserted their troops, and there is no more serious crime in the law of war. The army says they never leave their wounded. The marines say they never leave even their dead. These men have left all the casualties and retreated behind a pious shield of public rectitude. They've left the real stuff of their reputations bleaching behind them in the sun in this country.

And finally, this administration has done us the ultimate dishonor. They have attempted to disown us and the sacrifices we made for this country. In their blindness and fear they have tried to deny that we are veterans or that we served in 'Nam. We do not need their testimony. Our own scars and stumps of limbs are witness enough for others and for ourselves.

We wish that a merciful God could wipe away our own memories of that service as easily as this administration has wiped their memories of us. But all that they have done and all that they can do by this denial is to make more clear than ever our own determination to undertake one last mission: to search out and destroy the last vestige of this barbaric war, to pacify our own hearts, to conquer the hate and fear that have driven this country these last ten years and more, and so when thirty years from now our brothers go down the street without a leg, without an arm or a face, and small boys ask why, we will be able to say "Vietnam" and not mean a desert, not a filthy obscene memory, but mean instead the place where America finally turned and where soldiers like us helped it in the turning.

Thank you.

---

18. Kerry is referring to the Conventions for the Protection of Victims of War, adopted in 1949.

19. Name taken by American Indians who occupied Alcatraz Island, in San Francisco Bay, from November 1969 to June 1971 in protest of the government's treatment of Native Americans.

20. Robert McNamara, Secretary of Defense, 1961–1968; Walt Rostow, National Security Advisor, 1966–1969; McGeorge Bundy, National Security Advisor, 1961–1966; Roswell Gilpatrick, Deputy Secretary of Defense, 1961–1964.

Barbara Jordan

⧗

Statement on the Articles of Impeachment Against Richard M. Nixon

WASHINGTON, D.C.
JULY 25, 1974

BORN AND RAISED in Houston, Texas, Barbara Jordan was a championship orator and debater in high school and college. She received a law degree from Boston University in 1959 and returned to Houston, where, after passing the state bar exam, she acquired a taste for politics. After two losing campaigns, in 1966 she became the first African American elected to the Texas Senate in almost a century. Six years later, she became the first black woman from a Southern state to win a seat in the U.S. House of Representatives.

The election that sent Jordan to Congress also returned Richard Nixon for a second term as President. Few people during the campaign had paid attention when five men were arrested on the night of June 16–17 for breaking into the Democratic National Committee headquarters, located in the Watergate complex in Washington, D.C. By the end of the year, however, investigative reports by *Washington Post* writers Robert Woodward and Carl Bernstein had exposed a trail of money, dirty tricks, and a possible cover-up that led directly from Watergate to the White House. In February 1973 a Senate Select Committee began its own investigation. By the time public hearings opened on May 17, Nixon's two top aides—Chief of Staff H. R. Haldeman and Domestic Affairs Advisor John Ehrlichman—had resigned and it appeared the scandal might reach to the President himself.

The biggest bombshell of the hearings occurred in July, when Alexander Butterfield revealed the existence of a secret tape-recording system in the Oval Office. Knowing that the tapes—especially one from June 23, 1972—contained unequivocal evidence that he had obstructed justice, Nixon refused to release them, even after they were subpoenaed. The crisis escalated further in October 1973 when Nixon fired Special Prosecutor Archibald Cox. In February 1974 the House of Representatives, by a vote of 410–4, directed the Judiciary Committee to decide whether there were grounds for impeachment of the President.

After five months of investigations and closed-door meetings, the committee began public debates on July 24 with a nationwide television audience looking on in prime time. Each member of the committee had fifteen minutes for an opening statement. As a junior member, Jordan was slated to speak on July 25. No one could have predicted the impact her speech would have. Arguing in classic debate style, she set forth the criteria for impeachment as established by the Founders at the time they created the Constitution. She then showed how Nixon's actions were impeachable when weighed against those criteria. "If the impeachment provision in the Constitution of the United States will not reach the offenses charged here," she concluded, "then perhaps that eighteenth-century Constitution should be abandoned to a twentieth-century paper shredder."

Jordan's speech focused on one of the major issues that had confronted the committee throughout its deliberations, an issue that was also paramount in the public mind. No President had been impeached since Andrew Johnson in 1868, and the American people wanted to know whether Nixon's actions merited impeachment under the Constitution. Citing the *Federalist Papers*, as well as speeches from the state ratification debates of 1788, Jordan presented what one reporter called "a lecture in constitutional law." Her gravitas, sonorous voice, and exaggerated enunciation all lent credence and dramatic effect to her words, so much so that during her speech Senator Lloyd Bentsen said he "looked down to see if she were reading from stone tablets."

All thirty-eight members of the Judiciary Committee made opening statements, but it was Jordan who captured the nation's imagination. Her speech was printed in the *Washington Post* two days later and has been widely anthologized. Almost all published versions, however, are variations on the text in the *Post* and do not reflect the changes Jordan extemporized. The speech is printed here exactly as Jordan presented it.

◇◇◇

Thank you, Mr. Chairman.[1] Mr. Chairman, I join my colleague Mr. Rangel[2] in thanking you for giving the junior members of this committee the glorious opportunity of sharing the pain of this inquiry. Mr. Chairman, you are a strong man, and it has not been easy, but we have tried as best we can to give you as much assistance as possible.

Earlier today we heard the beginning of the Preamble to the Constitution of the United States: "We, the people." It's a very eloquent beginning. But when that document was completed on the seventeenth of September in 1787, I was not included in that "We, the people." I felt somehow for many years that George Washington and Alexander Hamilton just left me out by mistake. But through the process of amendment, interpretation, and court decision, I have finally been included in "We, the people."

Today I am an inquisitor, and hyperbole would not be fictional and would not overstate the solemnness that I feel right now. My faith in the Constitution is whole, it is complete, it is total. And I am not going to sit here and be an idle spectator to the diminution, the subversion, the destruction of the Constitution.

"Who can so properly be the inquisitors for the nation as the representatives of the nation themselves?...The subjects of its jurisdiction are those offenses which proceed from the misconduct of public men."[3] And that's what we're talking about—in other words, from the abuse or violation of some public trust.

It is wrong, I suggest it is a misreading of the Constitution for any member here to assert that for a member to vote for an article of impeachment means that that member must be convinced that the President should be removed from office. The Constitution doesn't say that. The powers relating to impeachment

---

1. Peter Rodino, chairman of the House Judiciary Committee.

2. Charles B. Rangel, Representative from New York, who was the first speaker of the evening.

3. From "The Federalist No. 65" (March 7, 1788).

are an essential check in the hands of the body, the legislature, against and upon the encroachments of the executive, the division between the two branches of the legislature, the House and the Senate, assigning to the one the right to accuse and to the other the right to judge. The framers of this Constitution were very astute. They did not make the accusers and the judgers—and the judges—the same person.

We know the nature of impeachment. We've been talking about it a while now. It is chiefly designed for the President and his high ministers to somehow be called into account.[4] It is designed to "bridle" the executive if he engages in excesses. It is "designed as a method of national inquest into the conduct of public men."[5] The framers confided in the Congress the power, if need be, to remove the President in order to strike a delicate balance between a President swollen with power and grown tyrannical and preservation of the independence of the executive.

The nature of impeachment [is] a narrowly channeled exception to the separation-of-powers maxim; the federal convention of 1787 said that.[6] It limited impeachment to high crimes and misdemeanors and discounted and opposed the term "maladministration." It is to be used only for "great misdemeanors"—so it was said in the North Carolina ratification convention.[7] And in the Virginia ratification convention: "We do not trust our liberty to a particular branch. We need one branch to check the other."[8] "No one need be afraid"—the North Carolina ratification convention—"No one need be afraid that officers who commit oppression will pass with immunity."[9]

Prosecutions of impeachments "will seldom fail to agitate the passions of the whole community," said Hamilton in the *Federalist Papers*, number 65. We divide "into parties more or less friendly or inimical to the accused."[10] I do not mean political parties in that sense.[11]

The drawing of political lines goes to the motivation behind impeachment, but impeachment must proceed within the confines of the constitutional term "high crime[s] and misdemeanors." Of the impeachment process, it was Woodrow Wilson who said that "nothing short of the grossest offenses against the plain law of the land will suffice to give them speed and effectiveness. Indignation so great as to overgrow party interest may secure a conviction; but nothing else can."[12]

Common sense would be revolted if we engaged upon this process for petty reasons. Congress has a lot to do—appropriations, tax reform, health insurance, campaign finance reform, housing, environmental protection, energy sufficiency, mass transportation. Pettiness cannot be allowed to stand in the face of such overwhelming problems. So today we're not being petty. We're trying to be big because the task we have before us is a big one.

This morning, in a discussion of the evidence, we were told that the evidence which purports to support the allegations of misuse of the CIA by the President is thin. We're told that that evidence is insufficient. What that recital of the evidence this morning did not include is what the President did know on June the twenty-third, 1972.[13] The President did know that

4. Some printed versions attribute this sentence to "The Federalist No. 65," but its language does not appear in any of the *Federalist Papers*.

5. From "The Federalist No. 65" (March 7, 1788).

6. Jordan is referring to the Constitutional Convention, which met in Philadelphia, May 25–September 17, 1787.

7. Paraphrased from Samuel Johnston's speech of July 25, 1788.

8. Paraphrased from Edmund Randolph's speech of June 10, 1788.

9. Paraphrased from Samuel Johnston's speech of July 25, 1788.

10. From "The Federalist No. 65" (March 7, 1788).

11. Jordan is referring to the fact that there were not political parties in the modern sense during the 1780s; "party," at that time, was used synonymously with "faction."

12. From Wilson's *Congressional Government* (1885); Jordan misstates the final phrase, which reads: "nothing less can."

13. Jordan is referring to an Oval Office conversation in which Nixon and Chief of Staff H. R. Haldeman discussed a plan for using the CIA to undermine the FBI's investigation of the Watergate burglary. A tape recording of this conversation, often referred to as the "smoking gun" that conclusively proved Nixon's guilt, was among the items that the U.S. Supreme Court ordered the White House to turn over to the special prosecutor on July 24, 1972 (see note 20 below).

it was Republican money, that it was money from the Committee for the Re-Election of the President,[14] which was found in the possession of one of the burglars arrested on June the seventeenth.[15] What the President did know on the twenty-third of June was the prior activities of E. Howard Hunt,[16] which included his participation in the break-in of Daniel Ellsberg's psychiatrist,[17] which included Howard Hunt's participation in the Dita Beard–ITT affair,[18] which included Howard Hunt's fabrication of cables designed to discredit the Kennedy administration.[19]

We were further cautioned today that perhaps these proceedings ought to be delayed because certainly there would be new evidence forthcoming from the President of the United States. There has not even been an obfuscated indication that this committee would receive any additional materials from the President. The committee subpoena is outstanding, and if the President wants to supply that material, the committee sits here. The fact is that on yesterday, the American people waited with great anxiety for eight hours, not knowing whether their President would obey an order of the Supreme Court of the United States.[20]

At this point I would like to juxtapose a few of the impeachment criteria with some of the actions the President has engaged in.

Impeachment criteria. James Madison, from the Virginia ratification convention: "If the President be connected in any suspicious manner with any person and there be grounds to believe that he will shelter him, he may be impeached."[21] We have heard time and time again that the evidence reflects the payment to defendants—money. The President had knowledge that these funds were being paid and these were funds collected for the 1972 presidential campaign. We know that the President met with Mr. Henry Petersen[22] twenty-seven times to discuss matters related to Watergate and immediately thereafter met with the very persons who were implicated in the information Mr. Petersen was receiving. The words are: "If the President is connected in any suspicious manner with any person and there be grounds to believe that he will shelter that person, he may be impeached."

Justice Story:[23] "Impeachment is attended—is intended—for occasional and extraordinary cases where a superior power acting for the whole people is put into operation to protect their rights and rescue their liberties from violations." We know about the Huston plan.[24] We know about the break-in of

14. In addition to raising campaign funds, the committee, headed by former U.S. Attorney General John Mitchell, organized a wide range of spying operations and other activities of dubious legality.

15. The burglars were carrying $2,400 when arrested, $1,300 of it in new $100 bills.

16. A former CIA officer who was involved in the Watergate break-in and other shady activities on behalf of President Nixon.

17. Ellsberg was a defense analyst who leaked a top-secret study of U.S. decision making in Vietnam, popularly known as the Pentagon Papers, to the *New York Times* in 1971. The office of his psychiatrist, Lewis Fielding, was broken into in an attempt to find information that could be used against Ellsberg.

18. A lobbyist for International Telephone and Telegraph (ITT), Beard wrote a memo in June 1971 linking a $400,000 donation to the Republican Party to the Nixon administration's quick settlement of an antitrust case against ITT. In March 1972, two weeks after the memo was made public by columnist Jack Anderson, Hunt, in disguise, visited Beard in the hospital and persuaded her to issue a statement saying the memo was a fraud.

19. Hunt had fabricated State Department cables to make it appear that President John F. Kennedy had ordered the assassination of South Vietnamese President Ngo Dinh Diem in November 1963.

20. Issued on July 24, the day the Judiciary Committee began its public hearings, the Supreme Court's ruling in *U.S. v. Nixon* ordered the President to turn over subpoenaed tape recordings and documents covering 64 conversations related to the Watergate investigation. After debating how to respond, Nixon decided late in the day to comply.

21. From Madison's speech of June 18, 1788.

22. Assistant Attorney General who was in charge of the Watergate investigation until the appointment of Special Prosecutor Archibald Cox in May 1973.

23. Joseph Story, Justice of the Supreme Court, 1811–1845; the quotation is from his *Commentaries on the Constitution* (1833).

24. A plan developed, but never implemented, for interagency domestic surveillance of radical groups and individuals; the plan was developed, at Nixon's direction, by White House aide Tom Charles Huston.

the psychiatrist's office.[25] We know that there was absolute, complete direction on September 3 when the President indicated that a surreptitious entry had been made in Dr. Fielding's office, after having met with Mr. Ehrlichman[26] and Mr. Young.[27] "Protect their rights...rescue their liberties from violation."

The Carolina ratification convention impeachment criteria: Those are impeachable "who behave amiss or betray their public trust."[28] Beginning shortly after the Watergate break-in and continuing to the present time, the President has engaged in a series of public statements and actions designed to thwart the lawful investigation by government prosecutors. Moreover, the President has made public announcements and assertions bearing on the Watergate case which the evidence will show he knew to be false. These assertions, false assertions, impeachable: Those who misbehave, those who "behave amiss or betray the public trust."

---

25. See note 17 above.

26. John Ehrlichman, Nixon's domestic policy advisor.

27. David Young, who helped set up the "Plumbers" unit in the White House that orchestrated the break-in at the office of Daniel Ellsberg's psychiatrist and that hired G. Gordon Liddy and the burglars who broke into the Democratic National Headquarters at the Watergate complex.

28. From Charles Cotesworth Pinckney's speech of January 17, 1788, in the South Carolina convention.

James Madison, again at the Constitutional Convention: A President is impeachable if he "attempts to subvert the Constitution."[29] The Constitution charges the President with the task of taking care that the laws be faithfully executed, and yet the President has counseled his aides to commit perjury, willfully disregard the secrecy of grand jury proceedings, conceal surreptitious entry, attempt to compromise a federal judge, while publicly displaying his cooperation with the processes of criminal justice. A President is impeachable if he "attempts to subvert the Constitution."

If the impeachment provision in the Constitution of the United States will not reach the offenses charged here, then perhaps that eighteenth-century Constitution should be abandoned to a twentieth-century paper shredder.

Has the President committed offenses and planned and directed and acquiesced in a course of conduct which the Constitution will not tolerate? That's the question. We know that. We know the question. We should now forthwith proceed to answer the question. It is reason, and not passion, which must guide our deliberations, guide our debate, and guide our decision.

I yield back the balance of my time, Mr. Chairman.

---

29. From Madison's *Notes of the Debates in the Federal Convention* for September 8, 1787; Madison attributes the phrase to Virginia delegate George Mason.

Richard M. Nixon

⧗

Address Resigning the Presidency

WASHINGTON, D.C.
AUGUST 8, 1974

O N JULY 24, 1974, the House Judiciary Committee began public debates on whether to impeach President Richard Nixon (see pages 518–522). On Saturday the twenty-seventh, it approved an article of impeachment accusing Nixon of endeavoring to obstruct justice in the Watergate investigation. On Monday the twenty-ninth, it passed a second article that cited specific abuses of power, including unlawful use of the Secret Service, the Central Intelligence Agency, the Federal Bureau of Investigation, and the Internal Revenue Service. On Tuesday the thirtieth, the committee approved a third article, this one for ignoring the committee's subpoenas for tapes and other items relating to the Watergate investigation. In each article, the committee stated that Nixon's conduct warranted "impeachment and trial, and removal from office."

It was one of the most stunning reversals of fortune in the history of American politics. Only eighteen months earlier, Nixon had won reelection in a landslide over Democrat George McGovern. During his first term, he had opened the door to China, begun the process of détente with the Soviet Union, and reduced U.S. troop levels in Vietnam by close to 500,000. When he was sworn in for a second term in January 1973, he was on the brink of securing a negotiated end to the war and his approval rating stood at 68 percent.

What followed was a steady accumulation of revelations about Watergate that brought the finger of suspicion ever closer to the President. The nation watched as former presidential counsel John Dean told a Senate investigating committee that Nixon was personally involved in covering up the Watergate affair; as the President refused to obey subpoenas from the Senate, House, and special prosecutor; as more than a dozen of his former aides were sentenced to prison for various Watergate-related crimes; and as Nixon himself was named an unindicted coconspirator by a federal grand jury. By the time the House Judiciary Committee wrapped up its debates, 66 percent of the American people favored impeachment and Nixon had few allies left in Congress, even among Republicans. He was left with only two choices—resign or be removed from office in a Senate trial. He chose to resign.

On the evening of August 8, some 110 million people watched Nixon's resignation speech on television, but they were not his primary audience. Above all, he was addressing posterity. The speech was essentially an apologia, the first step in what would be a twenty-year effort on Nixon's part to rehabilitate his image and to improve his standing in the eyes of history. He did not admit guilt for any of his actions—not for obstructing justice, not for abusing the power of his office, not for repeatedly lying to the country. He took responsibility for nothing other than unspecified errors in judgment. The only stated reason for his resignation was a loss of political support in Congress. More than a third of the speech was devoted to reviewing his accomplishments as President, especially in foreign policy. Nixon wanted those accomplishments to stand as his legacy, but they have yet to wipe away the stain of Watergate.

◇◇

Good evening. This is the thirty-seventh time I have spoken to you from this office,[1] where so many decisions have been made that shaped the history of this nation. Each time I have done so to discuss with you some matter that I believe affected the national interest.

In all the decisions I have made in my public life, I have always tried to do what was best for the nation. Throughout the long and difficult period of Watergate, I have felt it was my duty to persevere, to make every possible effort to complete the term of office to which you elected me.

In the past few days, however, it has become evident to me that I no longer have a strong enough political base in the Congress to justify continuing that effort. As long as there was such a base, I felt strongly that it was necessary to see the constitutional process through to its conclusion, that to do otherwise would be unfaithful to the spirit of that deliberately difficult process and a dangerously destabilizing precedent for the future. But with the disappearance of that base, I now believe that the constitutional purpose has been served and there is no longer a need for the process to be prolonged.

I would have preferred to carry through to the finish, whatever the personal agony it would have involved, and my family unanimously urged me to do so. But the interest of the nation must always come before any personal considerations. From the discussions I have had with congressional and other leaders, I have concluded that because of the Watergate matter, I might not have the support of the Congress that I would consider necessary to back the very difficult decisions and carry out the duties of this office in the way the interests of the nation would require.

I have never been a quitter. To leave office before my term is completed is abhorrent to every instinct in my body. But as President I must put the interest of America first. America needs a full-time President and a full-time Congress, particularly at this time with problems we face at home and abroad. To continue to fight through the months ahead for my personal vindication would almost totally absorb the time and attention of both the President and the Congress in a period when our entire focus should be on the great issues of peace abroad and prosperity without inflation at home.

Therefore, I shall resign the presidency effective at noon tomorrow. Vice President Ford[2] will be sworn in as President at that hour in this office.

As I recall the high hopes for America with which we began this second term, I feel a great sadness that I will not be here in this office working on your behalf to achieve those hopes in the next two and a half years. But in turning over direction of the government to Vice President Ford, I know, as I told the nation when I nominated him for that office ten months ago, that the leadership of America will be in good hands. In passing this office to the Vice President, I also do so with the profound sense of the weight of responsibility that will fall on his shoulders tomorrow and therefore of the understanding, the patience, the cooperation he will need from all Americans. As he assumes that responsibility, he will deserve the help and the support of all of us.

---

1. The Oval Office of the White House.

2. Gerald R. Ford.

As we look to the future, the first essential is to begin healing the wounds of this nation, to put the bitterness and divisions of the recent past behind us, and to rediscover those shared ideals that lie at the heart of our strength and unity as a great and as a free people. By taking this action, I hope that I will have hastened the start of that process of healing which is so desperately needed in America. I regret deeply any injuries that may have been done in the course of the events that led to this decision. I would say only that if some of my judgments were wrong—and some were wrong—they were made in what I believed at the time to be the best interest of the nation.

To those who have stood with me during these past difficult months—to my family, my friends, to many others who joined in supporting my cause because they believed it was right—I will be eternally grateful for your support.

And to those who have not felt able to give me your support, let me say I leave with no bitterness toward those who have opposed me, because all of us, in the final analysis, have been concerned with the good of the country, however our judgments might differ. So let us all now join together in affirming that common commitment and in helping our new President succeed for the benefit of all Americans.

I shall leave this office with regret at not completing my term but with gratitude for the privilege of serving as your President for the past five and a half years. These years have been a momentous time in the history of our nation and the world. They have been a time of achievement in which we can all be proud—achievements that represent the shared efforts of the administration, the Congress, and the people. But the challenges ahead are equally great, and they too will require the support and the efforts of the Congress and the people working in cooperation with the new administration.

We have ended America's longest war,[3] but in the work of securing a lasting peace in the world, the goals ahead are even more far-reaching and more difficult. We must complete a structure of peace so

that it will be said of this generation—our generation of Americans—by the people of all nations, not only that we ended one war but that we prevented future wars.

We have unlocked the doors that for a quarter of a century stood between the United States and the People's Republic of China.[4] We must now ensure that the one-quarter of the world's people who live in the People's Republic of China will be and remain, not our enemies, but our friends.

In the Middle East, one hundred million people in the Arab countries, many of whom have considered us their enemy for nearly twenty years, now look on us as their friends.[5] We must continue to build on that friendship so that peace can settle at last over the Middle East and so that the cradle of civilization will not become its grave.

Together with the Soviet Union we have made the crucial breakthroughs that have begun the process of limiting nuclear arms.[6] But we must set as our goal not just limiting but reducing and finally destroying these terrible weapons so that they cannot destroy civilization and so that the threat of nuclear war will no longer hang over the world and the people. We have opened the new relation with the Soviet Union.[7] We must continue to develop and expand that new relationship so that the two strongest nations of the world will live together in cooperation rather than confrontation.

Around the world—in Asia, in Africa, in Latin America, in the Middle East—there are millions of people who live in terrible poverty, even starvation.

---

3. The Treaty of Paris, signed on January 27, 1973, brought an end to the Vietnam War; the last U.S. troops left Vietnam two months later.

4. Nixon's visit to China in February 1972 reopened relations between the two nations.

5. American efforts to help broker the disengagement of Israeli, Syrian, and Egyptian forces after the 1973 Yom Kippur War produced a temporary thaw in relations with the Arab world, especially in Egypt, where Nixon received a warm welcome from President Anwar Sadat and was cheered by huge crowds during his visit in June 1974.

6. The United States and the Soviet Union signed an antiballistic missile treaty in 1972 during Nixon's visit to Moscow.

7. U.S.-Soviet relations improved considerably during the last two years of Nixon's administration, ushering in an era of détente between the superpowers.

We must keep as our goal turning away from production for war and expanding production for peace so that people everywhere on this earth can at last look forward in their children's time, if not in our own time, to having the necessities for a decent life.

Here in America we are fortunate that most of our people have not only the blessings of liberty but also the means to live full and good and, by the world's standards, even abundant lives. We must press on, however, toward a goal not only of more and better jobs but of full opportunity for every American and of what we are striving so hard right now to achieve—prosperity without inflation.

For more than a quarter of a century in public life I have shared in the turbulent history of this era. I have fought for what I believed in. I have tried to the best of my ability to discharge those duties and meet those responsibilities that were entrusted to me. Sometimes I have succeeded. And sometimes I have failed. But always I have taken heart from what Theodore Roosevelt once said about the man in the arena, "whose face is marred by dust and sweat and blood, who strives valiantly, who errs and comes short again and again because there is not effort without error and shortcoming, but who does actually strive to do the deed, who knows the great enthusiasms, the great devotions, who spends himself in a worthy cause, who at the best knows in the end the triumphs of high achievements and, with the worst, if he fails, at least fails while daring greatly."[8]

I pledge to you tonight that as long as I have a breath of life in my body, I shall continue in that spirit. I shall continue to work for the great causes to which I have been dedicated throughout my years as a Congressman, a Senator, Vice President, and President: the cause of peace—not just for America, but among all nations—prosperity, justice, and opportunity for all of our people.

There is one cause above all to which I have been devoted and to which I shall always be devoted for as long as I live. When I first took the oath of office as President five and a half years ago, I made this sacred commitment: to "consecrate my office, my energies, and all the wisdom I can summon to the cause of peace among nations."[9] I've done my very best in all the days since to be true to that pledge.

As a result of these efforts, I am confident that the world is a safer place today, not only for the people of America but for the people of all nations, and that all of our children have a better chance than before of living in peace rather than dying in war. This, more than anything, is what I hoped to achieve when I sought the presidency. This, more than anything, is what I hope will be my legacy to you, to our country, as I leave the presidency.

To have served in this office is to have felt a very personal sense of kinship with each and every American. In leaving it, I do so with this prayer: May God's grace be with you in all the days ahead.

---

8. From Roosevelt's speech "The Man in the Arena: Citizenship in a Republic," April 23, 1910.

9. From Nixon's first inaugural address, January 20, 1969.

Gerald R. Ford

Our Long National Nightmare Is Over

Washington, D.C.
August 9, 1974

AT 12:03 P.M. on August 9, 1974, Gerald R. Ford became the only person to take office as President of the United States without having been elected to either the vice presidency or the presidency. A thirteen-term Congressman from Michigan, he was nominated by Richard Nixon on October 12, 1973, to replace Vice President Spiro Agnew, who had stepped down two days earlier under threat of prosecution for income tax evasion. After confirmation by the Senate, Ford became Vice President in December 1973 as the Watergate scandal was drawing ever closer to the Oval Office. Eight months later, he became the nation's thirty-eighth President when Nixon resigned rather than face impeachment by the House of Representatives and conviction in the Senate (see pages 523–526).

Immediately after being administered the oath of office in the East Room of the White House by Warren Burger, Chief Justice of the Supreme Court, Ford spoke to the nation in a live broadcast. It was not an inaugural address per se, but, like an inaugural, it marked the transition of power. After almost two years of investigations, speeches, discord, and debate over Watergate, the country did not need a lot of words from its new President, but it needed the right ones.

Speaking with a sense of candor and personal authenticity that stood in marked contrast to his predecessor, Ford called his speech "a little straight talk among friends." He acknowledged the unusual circumstances of his elevation to the presidency, pledged to work for the welfare of all the people regardless of party, promised devotion to the truth, and prayed that "brotherly love" might "purge our hearts of suspicion and of hate." In his most memorable words, he spoke exactly what the nation yearned to hear: "Our long national nightmare is over. Our Constitution works. Our great republic is a government of laws and not of men." The country had survived its gravest constitutional crisis since the Civil War.

Mr. Chief Justice,[1] my dear friends, my fellow Americans: The oath that I have taken is the same oath that was taken by George Washington and by every President under the Constitution. But I assume the presidency under extraordinary circumstances never before experienced by Americans. This is an hour of history that troubles our minds and hurts our hearts. Therefore, I feel it is my first duty to make an unprecedented compact with my countrymen: not an inaugural address, not a fireside chat,[2] not a campaign speech, just a little straight talk among friends. And I intend it to be the first of many.

I am acutely aware that you have not elected me as your President by your ballots, so I ask you to confirm me as your President with your prayers. And I hope that such prayers will also be the first of many.

If you have not chosen me by secret ballot, neither have I gained office by any secret promises. I have not campaigned either for the presidency or the vice presidency. I have not subscribed to any partisan platform. I am indebted to no man and only to one woman, my dear wife, as I begin this very difficult job.

I have not sought this enormous responsibility, but I will not shirk it. Those who nominated and confirmed me as Vice President were my friends and are my friends. They were of both parties, elected by all the people and acting under the Constitution in their name. It is only fitting, then, that I should pledge to them and to you that I will be the President of all the people.

Thomas Jefferson said the people are the only sure reliance for the preservation of our liberty.[3] And down the years, Abraham Lincoln renewed this American article of faith, asking, Is there any better way or equal hope in the world?[4] I intend, on next Monday next,[5] to request of the Speaker of the House

of Representatives[6] and the President Pro Tempore of the Senate[7] the privilege of appearing before the Congress to share with my former colleagues and with you, the American people, my views on the priority business of the nation and to solicit your views and their views. And may I say to the Speaker and the others, if I could meet with you right after these remarks, I would appreciate it.

Even though this is late in an election year,[8] there is no way we can go forward except together and no way anybody can win except by serving the people's urgent needs. We cannot stand still or slip backwards. We must go forward now together.

To the peoples and the governments of all friendly nations, and I hope that could encompass the whole world, I pledge an uninterrupted and sincere search for peace. America will remain strong and united, but its strength will be—will remain—dedicated to the safety and sanity of the entire family of man as well as to our own precious freedom.

I believe that truth is the glue that holds government together—not only our government but civilization itself. That bond, though stained,[9] is unbroken at home and abroad. In all my public and private acts as your President, I expect to follow my instincts of openness and candor with full confidence that honesty is always the best policy in the end.

My fellow Americans, our long national nightmare is over. Our Constitution works. Our great republic is a government of laws and not of men. Here the people rule.

But there is a higher power, by whatever name we honor him, who ordains not only righteousness but love, not only justice but mercy. As we bind up the internal wounds of Watergate, more painful and more poisonous than those of foreign wars, let us restore the

---

1. Warren Burger, Chief Justice of the U.S. Supreme Court.

2. A reference to President Franklin D. Roosevelt's radio addresses known as the Fireside Chats (see pages 225–228).

3. From Jefferson's letter to James Madison, December 20, 1787.

4. From Lincoln's first inaugural address, March 4, 1861.

5. Ford misspoke by adding an extra "next." He meant the coming Monday, August 12, 1974.

---

6. Carl Albert.

7. James O. Eastland.

8. Ford is referring to the fact that elections for the U.S. House and Senate would be held in three months; the next presidential election occurred in 1976.

9. Ford meant to say "strained."

Golden Rule[10] to our political process, and let brotherly love purge our hearts of suspicion and of hate.

In the beginning, I asked you to pray for me. Before closing, I ask again your prayers, for Richard Nixon and for his family. May our former President, who brought peace to millions, find it for himself. May God bless and comfort his wonderful wife and daughters, whose love and loyalty will forever be a shining legacy to all who bear the lonely burdens of the White House. I can only guess at those burdens, although I have witnessed at close hand the tragedies that befell three Presidents[11] and the lesser trials of others.

With all the strength and all the good sense I have gained from life, with all the confidence[12] my family, my friends, and my dedicated staff impart to me, and with the goodwill of countless Americans I have encountered in recent visits to forty states, I now solemnly reaffirm my promise I made to you last December sixth:[13] to uphold the Constitution, to do what is right as God gives me to see the right,[14] and to do the very best I can for America. God helping me, I will not let you down.

Thank you.

---

10. "Do unto others as you would have others do unto you"; derived from Matthew 7:12.

11. Nixon, John F. Kennedy, and Lyndon B. Johnson.

12. Ford mistakenly inserted "of" here when delivering the speech.

13. Ford is referring to his speech of December 6, 1973, upon becoming Vice President.

14. An echo of Abraham Lincoln's second inaugural address, March 4, 1865.

Gerald R. Ford

Address on Pardoning Richard M. Nixon

Washington, D.C.
September 8, 1974

Once Richard Nixon resigned the presidency (see pages 523–526), he was no longer subject to impeachment. Now the question was whether he would be prosecuted on criminal charges for obstructing justice during the Watergate investigations. No former President had ever been charged with a crime for activities undertaken during his term in office. Would Nixon be indicted by the Watergate special prosecutor? If so, would he stand trial? What would happen if he were convicted? Might he end up in jail? Regardless of the outcome of legal proceedings against Nixon, what would be the effect on the country of a protracted and divisive trial?

These were among the issues new President Gerald Ford weighed during his first three weeks in office. Following an August 28 press conference that was dominated by questions about Nixon's future and the possibility of a presidential pardon for any crimes he might have committed, Ford concluded that the country would not be able to move forward until he put the issue to rest. At 11:00 a.m. on Sunday, September 8, he announced his decision on national television. Pointing to the uniqueness of the case, his constitutional responsibilities, and the dictates of his own conscience, Ford stated that it was time to bring an end to the "American tragedy" of Watergate. Therefore, he was granting a "full, free, and absolute pardon" to Richard Nixon for all legal offenses against the United States that he may have committed during his presidency.

As Ford anticipated, the pardon unleashed a torrent of criticism. It was called a "disgrace," a "sham," and a "gross misuse" of power. Ford's approval rating dropped 21 points in less than a week, and even many Republican leaders joined the chorus of condemnation. Polls showed that a majority of the public opposed the pardon, and the issue dogged Ford all the way through the 1976 presidential election, which he lost narrowly to Georgia Governor Jimmy Carter. Contrary to some allegations, there is no evidence that a secret deal had been struck before Nixon's resignation, and Ford never wavered in the judgment that his actions were in the national interest. He wrote later: "You can't pull a bandage off slowly, and I was convinced that the sooner I issued the pardon, the better it would be for the country."

◇◇

Ladies and Gentlemen: I have come to a decision which I felt I should tell you and all of my fellow American citizens as soon as I was certain in my own mind and in my own conscience that it is the right thing to do.

I have learned already in this office that the difficult decisions always come to this desk. I must admit that many of them do not look at all the same as the hypothetical questions that I have answered freely and perhaps too fast on previous occasions.

My customary policy is to try and get all the facts and to consider the opinions of my countrymen and to take counsel with my most valued friends. But these seldom agree, and, in the end, the decision is mine. To procrastinate, to agonize, and to wait for a more favorable turn of events that may never come or more compelling external pressures that may as well be wrong as right, is itself a decision of sorts and a weak and potentially dangerous course for a President to follow.

I have promised to uphold the Constitution, to do what is right as God gives me to see the right,[1]

and to do the very best that I can for America. I have asked your help and your prayers—not only when I became President,[2] but many times since.

The Constitution is the supreme law of our land, and it governs our actions as citizens. Only the laws of God, which govern our consciences, are superior to it. As we are a nation under God, so I am sworn to uphold our laws with the help of God. And I have sought such guidance and searched my own conscience with special diligence to determine the right thing for me to do with respect to my predecessor in this place, Richard Nixon, and his loyal wife and family. Theirs is an American tragedy in which we all have played a part. It could go on and on and on, or someone must write the end to it. I have concluded that only I can do that, and if I can, I must.

There are no historic or legal precedents to which I can turn in this matter, none that precisely fit the circumstances of a private citizen who has resigned the presidency of the United States. But it is common knowledge that serious allegations and accusations hang like a sword over our former President's head,

1. An echo of Abraham Lincoln's second inaugural address, March 4, 1865.

2. See Ford's speech of August 9, 1974 (pages 527–529).

threatening his health as he tries to reshape his life, a great part of which was spent in the service of this country and by the mandate of its people.

After years of bitter controversy and divisive national debate, I have been advised, and I am compelled to conclude, that many months and perhaps more years will have to pass before Richard Nixon could obtain a fair trial by jury in any jurisdiction of the United States under governing decisions of the Supreme Court.

I deeply believe in equal justice for all Americans, whatever their station or former station. The law, whether human or divine, is no respecter of persons, but the law is a respecter of reality. The facts, as I see them, are that a former President of the United States, instead of enjoying equal treatment with any other citizen accused of violating the law, would be cruelly and excessively penalized either in preserving the presumption of his innocence or in obtaining a speedy determination of his guilt in order to repay a legal debt to society.

During this long period of delay and potential litigation, ugly passions would again be aroused and our people would again be polarized in their opinions. And the credibility of our free institutions of government would again be challenged at home and abroad. In the end, the courts might well hold that Richard Nixon had been denied due process, and the verdict of history would even more be inconclusive with respect to those charges arising out of the period of his presidency of which I am presently aware.

But it is not the ultimate fate of Richard Nixon that most concerns me, though surely it deeply troubles every decent and every compassionate person. My concern is the immediate future of this great country. In this, I dare not depend upon my personal sympathy as a longtime friend of the former President, nor my professional judgment as a lawyer, and I do not. As President, my primary concern must always be the greatest good of all the people of the United States, whose servant I am. As a man, my first consideration is to be true to my own convictions and my own conscience.

My conscience tells me clearly and certainly that I cannot prolong the bad dreams that continue to reopen a chapter that is closed. My conscience tells me that only I, as President, have the constitutional power to firmly shut and seal this book. My conscience tells me it is my duty not merely to proclaim domestic tranquility, but to use every means that I have to ensure it.

I do believe that the buck stops here,[3] that I cannot rely upon public opinion polls to tell me what is right. I do believe that right makes might[4] and that if I am wrong, ten angels swearing I was right would make no difference.[5] I do believe, with all my heart and mind and spirit, that I, not as President but as a humble servant of God, will receive justice without mercy if I fail to show mercy.[6]

Finally, I feel that Richard Nixon and his loved ones have suffered enough and will continue to suffer, no matter what I do, no matter what we, as a great and good nation, can do together to make his goal of peace come true.

Now,[7] therefore, I, Gerald R. Ford, President of the United States, pursuant to the pardon power conferred upon me by Article II, Section 2, of the Constitution, have granted and by these presents do grant a full, free, and absolute pardon unto Richard Nixon for all offenses against the United States which he, Richard Nixon, has committed or may have committed or taken part in during the period from July 20, 1969,[8] through August 9, 1974.[9] In witness whereof, I have hereunto set my hand this eighth day of September, in the year of our Lord nineteen hundred and seventy-four, and of the independence of the United States of America the one hundred and ninety-ninth.

---

3. A colloquialism associated with President Harry S. Truman, who kept a sign reading "The Buck Stops Here" on his desk in the Oval Office.

4. From Abraham Lincoln's speech at Cooper Union, February 27, 1860.

5. Attributed to Lincoln in F. B. Carpenter, *Six Months at the White House with Abraham Lincoln* (1866).

6. Paraphrased from James 2:13.

7. At this point, Ford began reading from the proclamation of pardon, which was on his desk.

8. Ford misspoke; he meant to say January 20, 1969, the date on the pardon and the date on which Nixon's presidency began.

9. At this point, Ford paused to sign the pardon before reading the rest of it.

Barbara Jordan

Who Then Will Speak for the Common Good?

NEW YORK, NEW YORK
JULY 12, 1976

BARBARA JORDAN HAD become a national figure in 1974 as a result of her opening speech during the House Judiciary Committee hearings on the impeachment of President Richard Nixon (pages 518–522). Two years later, as America celebrated its bicentennial, the Democratic Party tabbed Jordan to deliver a keynote address at its national convention. Following the same tack as in her impeachment speech, she began on a personal note that highlighted the historical significance of her presence, as an African American woman, on the platform. The power of her voice, the drama of her delivery, and the weight of her words instantly captured the audience. Describing the start of Jordan's speech, Stan McClelland wrote: "Barbara is so dramatic... and the audience goes nuts; they go wild. And from that point on you could hear a pin drop.... Barbara electrified everyone."

Jordan eschewed the partisan attacks on the opposition that are a standard part of most keynotes, Democrat and Republican alike. Instead, she focused on healing the national divisions that had persisted since the Watergate crisis. She praised the Democratic Party for its historical commitment to equality, inclusiveness, and innovation, but she also urged the party to acknowledge its own mistakes. Adopting the mantle of a stateswoman, rather than that of a party advocate, she devoted the second half of her address to exploring how the American people as a whole could "restore the belief that we share a sense of national community." One step was for the citizenry to "define the common good and begin again to shape a common future." Another was for elected officials, regardless of party affiliation, to "hold ourselves strictly accountable" and to "provide the people with a vision of the future." Ultimately, she concluded, "a spirit of harmony will survive in America only... if each of us remembers, when self-interest and bitterness seem to prevail, that we share a common destiny."

It was an inspiring message, and it resonated as fully with the national audience as with the delegates at Madison Square Garden. As Mary Beth Rogers has noted, the speech on paper was lifeless without the power of Jordan's voice, whose "instrumentation, pacing, pauses, repetitions, swells, and crescendos conveyed a meaning that did not rely solely on words." Jordan's appeal to the common good demonstrated the performative power of oratory at its best and touched a deep nerve in a nation riven with partisanship. No less a figure than former Republican presidential candidate Barry Goldwater called it "the most electrifying speech I've ever heard."

Jordan would retire from politics two years later, primarily because of the multiple sclerosis that had, unknown to all but a few of her closest associates, been diagnosed at the time of the Watergate investigations. Through the rest of her life she remained one of the most respected people in America, transcending political, racial, and social lines. Speaking at Jordan's funeral in 1996, Ann Richards echoed the sentiments of millions when she said, "There was simply something about her that made you proud to be a part of the country that produced her."

◇◇

Thank you, ladies and gentlemen, for a very warm reception. It was 144 years ago that members of the Democratic Party first met in convention to select a presidential candidate. Since that time, Democrats have continued to convene once every four years and draft a party platform and nominate a presidential candidate. And our meeting this week is a continuation of that tradition.

But there is something different about tonight. There is something special about tonight. What is different? What is special? I, Barbara Jordan, am a keynote speaker. A lot of years passed since 1832, and during that time it would have been most unusual for any national political party to ask a Barbara Jordan to deliver a keynote address. But tonight here I am. And I feel, I feel that, notwithstanding the past, that my presence here is one additional bit of evidence that the American dream need not forever be deferred.

Now, now that I have this grand distinction, what in the world am I supposed to say?

I could easily spend this time praising the accomplishments of this party and attacking the Republicans, but I don't choose to do that.

I could list the many problems which Americans have. I could list the problems which cause people to feel cynical, angry, frustrated—problems which include lack of integrity in government, the feeling that the individual no longer counts, the reality of material and spiritual poverty, the feeling that the grand American experiment is failing or has failed. I could recite these problems and then I could sit down and offer no solutions. But I don't choose to do that either.

The citizens of America expect more. They deserve and they want more than a recital of problems.

We are a people in a quandary about the present. We are a people in search of our future. We are a people in search of a national community. We are a people trying not only to solve the problems of the present—unemployment, inflation—but we are attempting on a larger scale to fulfill the promise of America. We are attempting to fulfill our national purpose, to create and sustain a society in which all of us are equal.

Throughout, throughout our history, when people have looked for new ways to solve their problems and to uphold the principles of this nation, many times they have turned to political parties. They have often turned to the Democratic Party. What is it, what is it about the Democratic Party that makes it the instrument the people use when they search for ways to shape their future? Well, I believe the answer to that question lies in our concept of governing. Our concept of governing is derived from our view of people. It is a concept deeply rooted in a set of beliefs firmly etched in the national conscience of all of us.

Now, what are these beliefs? First, we believe in equality for all and privileges for none. This is a belief, this is a belief that each American regardless of background has equal standing in the public forum—all of us. Because, because we believe this idea so firmly, we are an inclusive rather than an exclusive party. Let everybody come.

I think it no accident that most of those emigrating to America in the nineteenth century identified with the Democratic Party. We are a heterogeneous party made up of Americans of diverse backgrounds. We believe that the people are the source of all governmental power, that the authority of the people is to be extended, not restricted. This, this can be accomplished only by providing each citizen with every opportunity to participate in the management of the government. They must have that.

We believe, we believe that the government which represents the authority of all the people—not just one interest group, but all the people—has an obligation to actively, underscore "actively," seek to remove those obstacles which would block individual achievement, obstacles emanating from race, sex, economic condition. The government must remove them, seek to remove them.

We, we are a party, we are a party of innovation. We do not reject our traditions, but we are willing to adapt to changing circumstances when change we must. We are willing to suffer the discomfort of change in order to achieve a better future. We have a positive vision of the future founded on the belief that the gap between the promise and reality of America can one day be finally closed. We believe that.

This, my friends, is the bedrock of our concept of governing. This is a part of the reason why Americans have turned to the Democratic Party. These are the foundations upon which a national community can be built. Let all understand that these guiding principles cannot be discarded for short-term political gains. They represent what this country is all about. They are indigenous to the American idea. And these are principles which are not negotiable.

In other times, in other times I could stand here and give this kind of exposition on the beliefs of the Democratic Party and that would be enough. But today that is not enough. People want more. That is not sufficient reason for the majority of the people of this country to decide to vote Democratic. We have made mistakes. We realize that. We admit our mistakes. In our haste to do all things for all people, we did not foresee the full consequences of our actions. And when the people raised their voices, we didn't hear.

But our deafness was only a temporary condition and not an irreversible condition. Even as I stand here and admit that we have made mistakes, I still believe that as the people of America sit in judgment on each party, they will recognize that our mistakes were mistakes of the heart. They'll recognize that.

And now, now we must look to the future. Let us heed the voice of the people and recognize their common sense. If we do not, we not only blaspheme our political heritage, we ignore the common ties that bind all Americans.

Many fear the future. Many are distrustful of their leaders and believe that their voices are never heard. Many seek only to satisfy their private work wants, to satisfy their private interests. But this is the great danger America faces: that we will cease to be one nation and become instead a collection of interest groups—city against suburb, region against region, individual against individual. Each seeking to satisfy private wants.

If that happens, who then will speak for America? Who then will speak for the common good? This is the question which must be answered in 1976. Are we to be one people bound together by common spirit, sharing in a common endeavor, or will we become a divided nation?

For all of its uncertainty, we cannot flee the future. We must not become the new Puritans[1] and reject our society. We must address and master the future together. It can be done if we restore the belief that we share a sense of national community, that we share a common national endeavor. It can be done.

There is no executive order, there is no law, that can require the American people to form a national community. This we must do as individuals, and if we do it as individuals, there is no President of the United States who can veto that decision.[2]

As a first step, as a first step we must restore our belief in ourselves. We are a generous people—so why can't we be generous with each other? We need to take to heart the words spoken by Thomas Jefferson: "Let us restore the social intercourse, let us restore to social intercourse that harmony and that affection

1. English religious separatists who emigrated to the New World during the 1630s.

2. A reference to Gerald Ford, who issued 66 vetoes during his presidency.

without which liberty and even life are but dreary things."[3]

A nation is formed by the willingness of each of us to share in the responsibility for upholding the common good. A government is invigorated when each one of us is willing to participate in shaping the future of this nation. In this election year we must define the common good and begin again to shape a common future. Let each person do his or her part. If one citizen is unwilling to participate, all of us are going to suffer. For the American idea, though it is shared by all of us, is realized in each one of us.

And now, what are those of us who are elected public officials supposed to do? We call ourselves public servants, but I'll tell you this: We, as public servants, must set an example for the rest of the nation. It is hypocritical for the public official to admonish and exhort the people to uphold the common good if we are derelict in upholding the common good.

More is required, more is required of public officials than slogans and handshakes and press releases. More is required. We must hold ourselves strictly accountable. We must provide the people with a vision of the future. If we promise as public officials, we must deliver. If, if we as public officials propose, we must produce. If we say to the American people it is time for you to be sacrificial—sacrifice. If the public official says that, we must be the first to give. We must be.

And again, if we make mistakes, we must be willing to admit them. We have to do that. What we have to do is strike a balance between the idea that government should do everything and the idea, the belief, that government ought to do nothing. Strike a balance.

Let there be no illusions about the difficulty of forming this kind of a national community. It's tough, difficult, not easy. But a spirit of harmony will survive in America only if each of us remembers that we share a common destiny—if each of us remembers, when self-interest and bitterness seem to prevail, that we share a common destiny.

I have confidence that we can form this kind of national community. I have confidence that the Democratic Party can lead the way. I have that confidence. We cannot improve on the system of government handed down to us by the founders of the republic; there is no way to improve upon that. But what we can do is to find new ways to implement that system and realize our destiny.

Now, I began this speech by commenting to you on the uniqueness of a Barbara Jordan making the keynote address. Well, I am going to close my speech by quoting a Republican President. And I ask you that as you listen to these words of Abraham Lincoln, relate them to the concept of a national community in which every last one of us participates: "As I would not be a slave, so I would not be a master. This, this, this expresses my idea of democracy. Whatever differs from this, to the extent of the difference, is no democracy."[4]

Thank you.

---

3. From Jefferson's first inaugural address, March 4, 1801.

4. Written in Lincoln's hand on an unsigned scrap of paper that was in the possession of his wife, Mary Todd Lincoln.

Jimmy Carter

⧗

Energy and the Crisis of Confidence

JIMMY CARTER BECAME President of the United States on January 20, 1977, after winning a close election over incumbent Gerald R. Ford. During the campaign, Carter promised Americans "a government as good as its people" and titled his autobiography *Why Not the Best?* With the bitter memories of Vietnam and Watergate still vivid in the public mind, Carter exploited his status as a Washington outsider and offered a rhetoric of moral rectitude at home and respect for human rights abroad. From the outset, however, his administration encountered a series of problems that eroded his support and ultimately made him a one-term President.

No problem aroused more public ire than the energy crisis of 1979. For the first time since World War II, gasoline was in short supply. Some drivers had to wait in line an hour or more to fill their tanks. Gas stations began closing on Sundays, then shortening their weekday hours, and finally imposing limits on the number of gallons that could be pumped. "Out of Gas" signs began to appear across the country. At one point, more than 90 percent of the gas stations in New York City were closed. Sporadic violence broke out as drivers became increasingly irate. Many long-haul truckers went on strike, bringing shipments of meat and fresh produce nearly to a standstill. With inflation running more than 12 percent annually and the price of oil increasing monthly, Carter's approval rating stood at 26 percent in June 1979.

In an effort to recoup his losses, Carter sequestered himself for ten days early in July at Camp David, the presidential retreat in the Maryland mountains. During this time he invited close to 150 leaders from across American society to meet with him. Each was asked to give his or her views on the problems facing the nation and how to solve them. In addition, Carter was strongly influenced by a seventy-five-page memorandum titled "Of Crisis and Opportunity" prepared by his pollster Patrick Caddell, who believed the country's concerns ran deeper than inflation, gas prices, and energy policy. The real problem, Caddell held, was a trauma of spirit and confidence that had sapped the American people of their can-do attitude. "America is a nation deep in crisis," he wrote. "Psychological more than material, it is a crisis marked by a dwindling faith in the future."

Not everyone in the administration agreed with this analysis, but after hearing many of the same themes emerge from his visitors at Camp David, Carter, at Caddell's urging, decided to make a presidential speech unlike any in American history, a jeremiad that the *Los Angeles Times* likened to a "scolding" by "a pastor with a profligate flock." Lambasting Americans for worshipping "self-indulgence and consumption," Carter declared that "owning things and consuming things does not satisfy our longing for meaning…piling up material goods cannot fill the emptiness of lives which have no confidence or purpose." Officially titled "Energy and the Crisis of Confidence," the thirty-three-minute address soon became known as the malaise speech, even though Carter did not use the word "malaise" at any point. In fact, the speech was actually two discourses—one on the crisis of confidence and one on energy policy—which were woven into a single text by making the crisis of confidence the problem and adoption of Carter's energy program the first step in finding a solution.

Initial reaction to the speech was positive. Carter's approval rating went up eleven points, and 79 percent of the public agreed that the nation faced a "crisis of confidence." By the end of July, however, his poll numbers had plummeted again, as he demanded that all cabinet members and senior members of his staff submit letters of resignation so he could choose whom to keep and whom to dismiss, once again creating the impression of a presidency in disarray. Sixteen months later, with inflation and energy concerns still plaguing the nation and fifty-two Americans held hostage in Iran a year after being seized by militants, Carter was soundly beaten in his bid for reelection by Ronald Reagan.

◇◇◇

Good evening. This is a special night for me. Exactly three years ago, on July 15, 1976, I accepted the nomination of my party to run for President of the United States. I promised you a President who is not isolated from the people, who feels your pain and who shares your dreams and who draws his strength and his wisdom from you.

During the past three years I've spoken to you on many occasions about national concerns—the energy crisis, reorganizing the government, our nation's economy, and issues of war and especially peace. But over those years the subjects of the speeches, the talks, and the press conferences have become increasingly narrow, focused more and more on what the isolated world of Washington thinks is important. Gradually, you've heard more and more about what the government thinks or what the government should be doing and less and less about our nation's hopes, our dreams, and our vision of the future.

Ten days ago I had planned to speak to you again about a very important subject—energy. For the fifth time I would have described the urgency of the problem and laid out a series of legislative recommenda-

tions to the Congress. But as I was preparing to speak, I began to ask myself the same question that I now know has been troubling many of you: Why have we not been able to get together as a nation to resolve our serious energy problem?

It's clear that the true problems of our nation are much deeper—deeper than gasoline lines or energy shortages, deeper even than inflation or recession. And I realize more than ever that as President I need your help. So I decided to reach out and to listen to the voices of America. I invited to Camp David people from almost every segment of our society—business and labor, teachers and preachers, governors, mayors, and private citizens. And then I left Camp David to listen to other Americans, men and women like you. It has been an extraordinary ten days, and I want to share with you what I've heard.

First of all, I got a lot of personal advice. Let me quote a few of the typical comments that I wrote down.

This from a southern Governor: "Mr. President, you are not leading this nation—you're just managing the government."

"You don't see the people enough any more."

"Some of your cabinet members don't seem loyal. There is not enough discipline among your disciples."

"Don't talk to us about politics or the mechanics of government, but about an understanding of our common good."

"Mr. President, we're in trouble. Talk to us about blood and sweat and tears."[1]

"If you lead, Mr. President, we will follow."

Many people talked about themselves and about the condition of our nation. This from a young woman in Pennsylvania: "I feel so far from government. I feel like ordinary people are excluded from political power."

And this from a young Chicano: "Some of us have suffered from recession all our lives."

"Some people have wasted energy, but others haven't had anything to waste."

And this from a religious leader: "No material shortage can touch the important things like God's love for us or our love for one another."

And I like this one particularly, from a black woman who happens to be the mayor of a small Mississippi town: "The big shots are not the only ones who are important. Remember, you can't sell anything on Wall Street unless someone digs it up somewhere else first."

This kind of summarized a lot of other statements: "Mr. President, we are confronted with a moral and a spiritual crisis."

Several of our discussions were on energy, and I have a notebook full of comments and advice. I'll read just a few.

"We can't go on consuming 40 percent more energy than we produce."

"When we import oil, we are also importing inflation plus unemployment."

"We've got to use what we have. The Middle East has only 5 percent of the world's energy, but the United States has 24 percent."

And this is one of the most vivid statements: "Our neck is stretched over the fence and OPEC[2] has a knife."

"There will be other cartels and other shortages. American wisdom and courage right now can set a path to follow in the future."

This was a good one: "Be bold, Mr. President. We may make mistakes, but we are ready to experiment."

And this one from a labor leader got to the heart of it: "The real issue is freedom. We must deal with the energy problem on a war footing."

And the last that I'll read: "When we enter the moral equivalent of war, Mr. President, don't issue us BB guns."

These ten days confirmed my belief in the decency and the strength and the wisdom of the American people, but it also bore out some of my longstanding concerns about our nation's underlying problems.

I know, of course, being President, that government actions and legislation can be very important. That's why I've worked hard to put my campaign promises into law, and, I have to admit, with just mixed success. But after listening to the American people, I have been reminded again that all the legislation in the world can't fix what's wrong with America. So I want to speak to you first tonight about a subject even more serious than energy or inflation. I want to talk to you right now about a fundamental threat to American democracy.

I do not mean our political and civil liberties. They will endure. And I do not refer to the outward strength of America, a nation that is at peace tonight everywhere in the world, with unmatched economic power and military might. The threat is nearly invisible in ordinary ways. It is a crisis of confidence. It is a crisis that strikes at the very heart and soul and spirit of our national will. We can see this crisis in the growing doubt about the meaning of our own lives and in the loss of a unity of purpose for our nation. The erosion of our confidence in the future is threatening to destroy the social and the political fabric of America.

---

1. An allusion to Winston Churchill's speech of May 13, 1940, in which he said, upon becoming Prime Minister of Great Britain during World War II, "I have nothing to offer but blood, toil, tears, and sweat."

---

2. Organization of the Petroleum Exporting Countries, whose policies led to a fourfold increase in oil prices during the 1970s.

The confidence that we have always had as a people is not simply some romantic dream or a proverb in a dusty book that we read just on the Fourth of July. It is the ideal which founded our nation and has guided our development as a people. Confidence in the future has supported everything else—public institutions and private enterprise, our own families, and the very Constitution of the United States. Confidence has defined our course and has served as a link between generations. We've always believed in something called progress. We've always had a faith that the days of our children would be better than our own.

Our people are losing that faith, not only in government itself but in the ability as citizens to serve as the ultimate rulers and shapers of our democracy. As a people we know our past and we are proud of it. Our progress has been part of the living history of America, even the world. We always believed that we were part of a great movement of humanity itself called democracy, involved in the search for freedom, and that belief has always strengthened us in our purpose. But just as we are losing our confidence in the future, we are also beginning to close the door on our past.

In a nation that was proud of hard work, strong families, close-knit communities, and our faith in God, too many of us now tend to worship self-indulgence and consumption. Human identity is no longer defined by what one does, but by what one owns. But we've discovered that owning things and consuming things does not satisfy our longing for meaning. We've learned that piling up material goods cannot fill the emptiness of lives which have no confidence or purpose.

The symptoms of this crisis of the American spirit are all around us. For the first time in the history of our country a majority of our people believe that the next five years will be worse than the past five years. Two-thirds of our people do not even vote. The productivity of American workers is actually dropping, and the willingness of Americans to save for the future has fallen below that of all other people in the Western world. As you know, there is a growing disrespect for government and for churches and for schools, the news media, and other institutions. This is not a message of happiness or reassurance, but it is the truth and it is a warning.

These changes did not happen overnight. They've come upon us gradually over the last generation, years that were filled with shocks and tragedy. We were sure that ours was a nation of the ballot, not the bullet, until the murders of John Kennedy and Robert Kennedy and Martin Luther King Jr.[3] We were taught that our armies were always invincible and our causes were always just, only to suffer the agony of Vietnam.[4] We respected the presidency as a place of honor until the shock of Watergate.[5] We remember when the phrase "sound as a dollar" was an expression of absolute dependability until ten years of inflation began to shrink our dollar and our savings. We believed that our nation's resources were limitless until 1973, when we had to face a growing dependence on foreign oil.

These wounds are still very deep. They have never been healed. Looking for a way out of this crisis, our people have turned to the federal government and found it isolated from the mainstream of our nation's life. Washington, D.C., has become an island. The gap between our citizens and our government has never been so wide. The people are looking for honest answers, not easy answers; clear leadership, not false claims and evasiveness and politics as usual.

What you see too often in Washington and elsewhere around the country is a system of government that seems incapable of action. You see a Congress twisted and pulled in every direction by hundreds of well-financed and powerful special interests. You see every extreme position defended to the last vote, almost to the last breath, by one unyielding group or another. You often see a balanced and a fair approach that demands sacrifice, a little sacrifice from everyone, abandoned like an orphan without support and without friends. Often you see paralysis and stagnation and drift. You don't like it, and neither do I.

---

3. John Kennedy was killed in November 1963, King in April 1968, and Robert Kennedy in June 1968.

4. More than 58,000 Americans lost their lives in Vietnam and more than 300,000 were wounded.

5. As a result of the Watergate scandal, President Richard Nixon resigned in August 1974.

What can we do? First of all, we must face the truth and then we can change our course. We simply must have faith in each other, faith in our ability to govern ourselves, and faith in the future of this nation. Restoring that faith and that confidence to America is now the most important task we face. It is a true challenge of this generation of Americans. One of the visitors to Camp David last week put it this way: "We've got to stop crying and start sweating, stop talking and start walking, stop cursing and start praying. The strength we need will not come from the White House, but from every house in America."

We know the strength of America. We are strong. We can regain our unity. We can regain our confidence. We are the heirs of generations who survived threats much more powerful and awesome than those that challenge us now. Our fathers and mothers were strong men and women who shaped a new society during the Great Depression, who fought world wars, and who carved out a new charter of peace for the world.[6] We ourselves are the same Americans who just ten years ago put a man on the moon.[7] We are the generation that dedicated our society to the pursuit of human rights and equality. And we are the generation that will win the war on the energy problem and in that process rebuild the unity and confidence of America.

We are at a turning point in our history. There are two paths to choose. One is a path I've warned about tonight—the path that leads to fragmentation and self-interest. Down that road lies a mistaken idea of freedom, the right to grasp for ourselves some advantage over others. That path would be one of constant conflict between narrow interests ending in chaos and immobility. It is a certain route to failure.

All the traditions of our past, all the lessons of our heritage, all the promises of our future point to another path—the path of common purpose and the restoration of American values. That path leads to true freedom for our nation and ourselves. We can take the first steps down that path as we begin to solve our energy problem. Energy will be the immediate test of our ability

to unite this nation, and it can also be the standard around which we rally. On the battlefield of energy we can win for our nation a new confidence, and we can seize control again of our common destiny.

In little more than two decades we've gone from a position of energy independence to one in which almost half the oil we use comes from foreign countries at prices that are going through the roof. Our excessive dependence on OPEC has already taken a tremendous toll on our economy and our people. This is the direct cause of the long lines which have made millions of you spend aggravating hours waiting for gasoline. It's a cause of the increased inflation and unemployment that we now face. This intolerable dependence on foreign oil threatens our economic independence and the very security of our nation.

The energy crisis is real. It is worldwide. It is a clear and present danger to our nation. These are facts and we simply must face them. What I have to say to you now about energy is simple and vitally important.

Point one: I am tonight setting a clear goal for the energy policy of the United States. Beginning this moment, this nation will never use more foreign oil than we did in 1977. Never. From now on, every new addition to our demand for energy will be met from our own production and our own conservation. The generation-long growth in our dependence on foreign oil will be stopped dead in its tracks right now and then reversed as we move through the 1980s, for I am tonight setting the further goal of cutting our dependence on foreign oil by one-half by the end of the next decade—a saving of over four and a half million barrels of imported oil per day.

Point two: To ensure that we meet these targets, I will use my presidential authority to set import quotas. I'm announcing tonight that for 1979 and 1980 I will forbid the entry into this country of one drop of foreign oil more than these goals allow. These quotas will ensure a reduction in imports even below the ambitious levels we set at the recent Tokyo summit.[8]

Point three: To give us energy security, I am asking for the most massive peacetime commitment of funds and resources in our nation's history to develop America's own alternative sources of fuel—from coal,

6. A reference to the Charter of the United Nations, signed in June 1945.

7. The first lunar landing occurred on July 20, 1969.

8. The G7 Summit of June 28–29, 1979.

from oil shale, from plant products for gasohol, from unconventional gas, from the sun.

I propose the creation of an energy security corporation to lead this effort to replace two and a half million barrels of imported oil per day by 1990. The corporation will issue up to five billion dollars in energy bonds, and I especially want them to be in small denominations so that average Americans can invest directly in America's energy security. Just as a similar synthetic rubber corporation helped us win World War II,[9] so will we mobilize American determination and ability to win the energy war.

Moreover, I will soon submit legislation to Congress calling for the creation of this nation's first solar bank, which will help us achieve the crucial goal of 20 percent of our energy coming from solar power by the year 2000.

These efforts will cost money, a lot of money, and that is why Congress must enact the windfall profits tax[10] without delay. It will be money well spent. Unlike the billions of dollars that we ship to foreign countries to pay for foreign oil, these funds will be paid by Americans to Americans. These funds will go to fight, not to increase, inflation and unemployment.

Point four: I'm asking Congress to mandate, to require as a matter of law, that our nation's utility companies cut their massive use of oil by 50 percent within the next decade and switch to other fuels—especially coal, our most abundant energy source.

Point five: To make absolutely certain that nothing stands in the way of achieving these goals, I will urge Congress to create an energy mobilization board which, like the War Production Board in World War II,[11] will have the responsibility and authority to cut through the red tape, the delays, and the endless roadblocks to completing key energy projects. We will protect our environment. But when this nation critically needs a refinery or a pipeline, we will build it.

Point six: I'm proposing a bold conservation program to involve every state, county, and city, and every average American in our energy battle. This effort will permit you to build conservation into your homes and your lives at a cost you can afford.

I ask Congress to give me authority for mandatory conservation and for standby gasoline rationing. To further conserve energy, I'm proposing tonight an extra ten billion dollars over the next decade to strengthen our public transportation systems. And I'm asking you, for your good and for your nation's security, to take no unnecessary trips, to use carpools or public transportation whenever you can, to park your car one extra day per week, to obey the speed limit, and to set your thermostats to save fuel. Every act of energy conservation like this is more than just common sense. I tell you, it is an act of patriotism.

Our nation must be fair to the poorest among us, so we will increase aid to needy Americans to cope with rising energy prices.

We often think of conservation only in terms of sacrifice. In fact, it is the most painless and immediate way of rebuilding our nation's strength. Every gallon of oil each one of us saves is a new form of production. It gives us more freedom, more confidence, that much more control over our own lives. So the solution of our energy crisis can also help us to conquer the crisis of the spirit in our country. It can rekindle our sense of unity, our confidence in the future, and give our nation and all of us individually a new sense of purpose.

You know we can do it. We have the natural resources. We have more oil in our shale alone than several Saudi Arabias. We have more coal than any nation on earth. We have the world's highest level of technology. We have the most skilled work force, with innovative genius. And I firmly believe that we have the national will to win this war.

I do not promise you that this struggle for freedom will be easy. I do not promise a quick way out of our nation's problems, when the truth is that the only way out is an all-out effort. What I do promise you is that I will lead our fight and I will enforce fairness in our struggle and I will ensure honesty. And, above all,

---

9. Created by President Franklin Roosevelt in June 1940, the Rubber Reserve Company oversaw the massive production of synthetic rubber that was essential to the U.S. war effort.

10. In April 1979 Carter called for a tax on windfall profits earned by oil companies after removal of the price controls that had been instituted during the Nixon administration; the tax eventually became law in April 1980.

11. Established in January 1942, the War Production Board had broad powers in directing the acquisition and production of materials needed to fight World War II.

I will act. We can manage the short-term shortages more effectively—and we will—but there are no short-term solutions to our long-range problems. There is simply no way to avoid sacrifice.

Twelve hours from now I will speak again in Kansas City, to expand and to explain further our energy program. Just as the search for solutions to our energy shortages has now led us to a new awareness of our nation's deeper problems, so our willingness to work for those solutions in energy can strengthen us to attack those deeper problems.

I will continue to travel this country, to hear the people of America. You can help me to develop a national agenda for the 1980s. I will listen and I will act. We will act together. These were the promises I made three years ago, and I intend to keep them.

Little by little we can and we must rebuild our confidence. We can spend until we empty our treasuries, and we may summon all the wonders of science. But we can succeed only if we tap our greatest resources—America's people, America's values, and America's confidence. I have seen the strength of America in the inexhaustible resources of our people. In the days to come, let us renew that strength in the struggle for an energy-secure nation.

In closing, let me say this: I will do my best, but I will not do it alone. Let your voice be heard. Whenever you have a chance, say something good about our country. With God's help and for the sake of our nation, it is time for us to join hands in America. Let us commit ourselves together to a rebirth of the American spirit. Working together, with our common faith, we cannot fail.

Thank you, and good night.

Edward M. Kennedy

The Dream Shall Never Die

NEW YORK, NEW YORK
AUGUST 12, 1980

THERE IS LITTLE in American politics that is more difficult than wresting the presidential nomination from an incumbent chief executive of one's own party. Yet just as Robert Kennedy sought to unseat Lyndon Johnson in 1968, so Edward (Ted) Kennedy decided to take on Jimmy Carter in 1980. With the economy ravaged by double-digit inflation and polls showing Kennedy holding a two-to-one lead among Democrats, he began his campaign from a position of strength. Within two months, however, Carter had pulled ahead as the seizure of the U.S. embassy in Tehran and the Soviet invasion of Afghanistan shifted attention from economic issues to foreign policy. Nor did Kennedy help himself. Especially disastrous was a national television interview in which he fumbled questions about Chappaquiddick (see pages 485–488) and failed to provide a convincing explanation of why he wanted to be President. Though he kept the race close with victories in a few large primaries, he could not overtake Carter, who went to the Democratic convention in New York City with enough delegates to ensure his renomination.

On August 12, two nights before Carter was to present his acceptance speech, Kennedy addressed the convention in the midst of its platform debates. Reprising the theme that had been at the heart of his campaign, Kennedy presented himself as the standard-bearer of the party's progressive principles. As he invoked Democratic icons from Thomas Jefferson and Andrew Jackson to Franklin Roosevelt and John Kennedy, he called on the party to renew its commitment to economic justice and "the cause of the common man and the common woman." Training his sights on the Republicans, he brought the crowd to its feet with a scathing attack on Ronald Reagan for trying to appropriate Democratic principles and slogans, but he quickly returned to the issues on which he had campaigned for the nomination. In one of the finest conclusions in the long history of convention oratory, he ended by invoking the memory of his slain brothers and proclaiming that while his quest for the nomination had come to an end, "the work goes on, the cause endures, the hope still lives, and the dream shall never die."

It was old-fashioned, stem-winding political oratory at its finest. Early in his career, Kennedy liked to read anthologies of orations, and he developed an ear for the music and rhythm of speech. No one of his generation was better at speaking from a manuscript, and Kennedy was at the top of his game in New York. With his voice rising and falling in perfect accord with the carefully crafted cadences of lead speechwriter Robert Shrum, he was by turns tempered, passionate, humorous, sarcastic, lyrical, and poignant. The speech was interrupted repeatedly by applause, set off a boisterous demonstration afterward, and remains a classic of its genre. Still, it was a bittersweet moment for Kennedy, who refused to raise Carter's hand on the podium at the end of the convention and would not contend again for the White House.

◇◇

Thank you, thank you very much, Barbara Mikulski,[1] for your very eloquent, your eloquent introduction. Distinguished legislator, great spokeswoman for economic democracy and social justice in this country, I thank you for your eloquent introduction.

Well, things worked out a little different from the way I thought, but let me tell you, I still love New York. My fellow Democrats and my fellow Americans, I have come here tonight not to argue as a candidate, but to affirm a cause. I'm asking you, I am asking you

to renew the commitment of the Democratic Party to economic justice. I am asking you to renew our commitment to a fair and lasting prosperity that can put America back to work.

This is the cause that brought me into the campaign and that sustained me for nine months across a hundred thousand miles in forty different states. We had our losses, but the pain of our defeats is far, far less than the pain of the people that I have met. We have learned that it is important to take issues seriously, but never to take ourselves too seriously.

The serious issue before us tonight is the cause for which the Democratic Party has stood in its finest hours, the cause that keeps our party young and

1. In 1980, Mikulski was a member of the U.S. House of Representatives from Maryland; she was elected to the U.S. Senate in 1986.

makes it, in the second century of its age, the largest political party in this republic and the longest-lasting political party on this planet. Our cause has been, since the days of Thomas Jefferson,[2] the cause of the common man and the common woman. Our commitment has been, since the days of Andrew Jackson, to all those he called "the humble members of society—the farmers, mechanics, and laborers."[3] On this foundation we have defined our values, refined our policies, and refreshed our faith.

Now I take the unusual step of carrying the cause and the commitment of my campaign personally to our national convention. I speak out of a deep sense of urgency about the anguish and anxiety I have seen across America. I speak out of a deep belief in the ideals of the Democratic Party and in the potential of that party and of a President to make a difference. And I speak out of a deep trust in our capacity to proceed with boldness and a common vision that will feel and heal the suffering of our time and the divisions of our party.

The economic plank of this platform on its face concerns only material things,[4] but it is also a moral issue that I raise tonight. It has taken many forms over many years. In this campaign and in this country that we seek to lead, the challenge in 1980 is to give our voice and our vote for these fundamental Democratic principles: Let us pledge that we will never misuse unemployment, high interest rates, and human misery as false weapons against inflation. Let us pledge that employment will be the first priority of our economic policy. Let us pledge that there will be security for all those who are now at work, and let us pledge that there will be jobs for all who are out of work—and we will not compromise on the issues of jobs.

These are not simplistic pledges. Simply put, they are the heart of our tradition and they have been the soul of our party across the generations. It is the glory and the greatness of our tradition to speak for those who have no voice, to remember those who are forgotten, to respond to the frustrations and fulfill the aspirations of all Americans seeking a better life in a better land. We dare not forsake that tradition. We cannot let the great purposes of the Democratic Party become the bygone passages of history. We must not permit the Republicans to seize and run on the slogans of prosperity.

We heard the orators at their convention all trying to talk like Democrats.[5] They proved that even Republican nominees can quote Franklin Roosevelt[6] to their own purpose.[7] The Grand Old Party[8] thinks it has found a great new trick. But forty years ago an earlier generation of Republicans attempted the same trick and Franklin Roosevelt himself replied: "Most Republican leaders... have bitterly fought and blocked the forward surge of average men and women in their pursuit of happiness. Let us not be deluded that overnight those leaders have suddenly become the friends of average men and women." "You know," he continued, "very few of us are that gullible."[9]

And four years later, when the Republicans tried that trick again, Franklin Roosevelt asked, "Can the Old Guard pass itself off as the New Deal? I think not. We have all seen many marvelous stunts in the circus, but no performing elephant could turn a handspring without falling flat on its back."[10]

The 1980 Republican convention was awash with crocodile tears for our economic distress, but it is by their long record and not their recent words that you shall know them.[11]

---

2. President of the United States, 1801–1809.

3. From President Jackson's message of July 10, 1832, vetoing a bill for renewing the charter of the Bank of the United States.

4. An echo of Franklin D. Roosevelt's first inaugural address (pages 221–224).

---

5. The Republican National Convention met July 14–17 in Detroit, Michigan.

6. President of the United States, 1933–1945.

7. In his acceptance speech of July 17, 1980, Ronald Reagan quoted several passages from Roosevelt's addresses to the 1932 and 1936 Democratic National Conventions.

8. Nickname for the Republican Party; often abbreviated as GOP.

9. From Roosevelt's campaign address in Brooklyn, November 1, 1940.

10. From Roosevelt's speech at a Teamsters Union banquet, September 23, 1944; the meaning of his statement is based on the fact that the Republican Party's symbol is an elephant.

11. An allusion to Matthew 7:20: "Wherefore by their fruits ye shall know them."

The same Republicans who are talking about the crisis of unemployment have nominated a man who once said, and I quote: "Unemployment insurance is a prepaid vacation plan for freeloaders."[12] And that nominee is no friend of labor.

The same Republicans who are talking about the problems of the inner cities have nominated a man who said, and I quote: "I have included in my morning and evening prayers every day the prayer that the federal government not bail out New York."[13] And that nominee is no friend of this city and our great urban centers across this nation.

The same Republicans who are talking about security for the elderly have nominated a man who said, just four years ago, that participation in Social Security should be made voluntary.[14] And that nominee is no friend of the senior citizens of this nation.

The same Republicans who are talking about preserving the environment have nominated a man who last year made the preposterous statement, and I quote: "Eighty percent of our air pollution comes...from plants and trees."[15] And that nominee is no friend of the environment.

And the same Republicans who are invoking Franklin Roosevelt have nominated a man who said in 1976, and these are his exact words: "Fascism was really the basis of the New Deal."[16] And that nominee, whose name is Ronald Reagan, has no right to quote Franklin Delano Roosevelt.

The great adventures which our opponents offer is a voyage into the past. Progress is our heritage, not theirs. What is right for us as Democrats is also the right way for Democrats to win.

The commitment I seek is not to outworn views, but to old values that will never wear out. Programs may sometimes become obsolete, but the ideal of fairness always endures. Circumstances may change, but the work of compassion must continue. It is surely correct that we cannot solve problems by throwing money at them, but it is also correct that we dare not throw out our national problems onto a scrap heap of inattention and indifference. The poor may be out of political fashion, but they are not without human needs. The middle class may be angry, but they have not lost the dream that all Americans can advance together.

The demand, the demand of our people in 1980 is not for smaller government or bigger government, but for better government. Some say that government is always bad and that spending for basic social programs is the root of our economic evils. But we reply: The present inflation and recession cost our economy $200 billion a year. We reply: Inflation and unemployment are the biggest spenders of all.

The task of leadership in 1980 is not to parade scapegoats or to seek refuge in reaction, but to match our power to the possibilities of progress. While others talked of free enterprise, it was the Democratic Party that acted, and we ended excessive regulation in the airline and trucking industry and we restored competition to the marketplace. And I take some satisfaction that this deregulation [was] legislation that I sponsored and passed in the Congress of the United States.[17]

As Democrats, we recognize that each generation of Americans has a rendezvous with a different reality.[18] The answers of one generation become the questions of the next generation. But there is a guiding star in the American firmament. It is as old as the revolutionary belief that all people are created equal and as clear as the contemporary condition of Liberty City and the South Bronx. Again and again Democratic leaders have followed that star, and they

---

12. Reagan made comments to this effect during the 1966 California gubernatorial campaign.

13. From Reagan's speech at the Colony Theater, Cleveland, Ohio, October 7, 1975, as reported in the *Cleveland Plain Dealer* of October 8.

14. Reagan spoke often on this topic during his unsuccessful 1976 bid for the Republican presidential nomination.

15. From a radio address given by Reagan in January–February 1979.

16. From an interview in *Time*, May 17, 1976.

17. Kennedy is referring to the 1978 Airline Deregulation Act and the 1980 Motor Carrier Act.

18. An evocation of Franklin Roosevelt's declaration to the Democratic National Convention, June 27, 1936, that "This generation of Americans has a rendezvous with destiny."

have given new meaning to the old values of liberty and justice for all.

We are the party, we are the party of the New Freedom, the New Deal, and the New Frontier.[19] We have always been the party of hope. So this year let us offer new hope—new hope to an America uncertain about the present but unsurpassed in its potential for the future.

To all those who are idle in the cities and industries of America, let us provide new hope for the dignity of useful work. Democrats have always believed that a basic civil right of all Americans is[20] their right to earn their own way. The party of the people must always be the party of full employment.

To all those who doubt the future of our economy, let us provide new hope for the reindustrialization of America. And let our vision reach beyond the next election or the next year to a new generation of prosperity. If we could rebuild Germany and Japan after World War II, then surely we can reindustrialize our own nation and revive our inner cities in the 1980s.

To all those who work hard for a living wage, let us provide new hope that their price of their employment shall not be an unsafe workplace and a death at an earlier age.

To all those who inhabit our land from California to the New York Island, from the redwood forest to the Gulf Stream waters,[21] let us provide new hope that prosperity shall not be purchased by poisoning the air, the rivers, and the natural resources that are the greatest gift of this continent. We must insist that our children and our grandchildren shall inherit a land which they can truly call America the beautiful.

To all those who see the worth of their work and their savings taken by inflation, let us offer new hope for a stable economy. We must meet the pressures of the present by invoking the full power of government to master increasing prices. In candor, we must say that the federal budget can be balanced only by policies that bring us to a balanced prosperity of full employment and price restraint.

And to all those overburdened by an unfair tax structure, let us provide new hope for real tax reform. Instead of shutting down classrooms, let us shut off tax shelters. Instead of cutting out school lunches, let us cut off tax subsidies for expensive business lunches that are nothing more than food stamps for the rich.

The tax cut of our Republican opponents takes the name of tax reform in vain. It is a wonderfully Republican idea that would redistribute income in the wrong direction. It's good news for any of you with incomes over $200,000 a year. For the few of you, it offers a pot of gold worth $14,000. But the Republican tax cut is bad news for the middle-income families. For the many of you, they plan a pittance of $200 a year—and that is not what the Democratic Party means when we say tax reform.

The vast majority of Americans cannot afford this panacea from a Republican nominee who has denounced the progressive income tax as the invention of Karl Marx.[22] I am afraid he has confused Karl Marx with Theodore Roosevelt, that obscure Republican President who sought and fought for a tax system based on ability to pay.[23] Theodore Roosevelt was not Karl Marx, and the Republican tax scheme is not tax reform.

Finally, we cannot have a fair prosperity in isolation from a fair society. So I will continue to stand for a national health insurance. We must, we must not surrender, we must not surrender to the relentless medical inflation that can bankrupt almost anyone and that may soon break the budgets of government at every level. Let us insist on real controls over what doctors and hospitals can charge, and let us resolve that the state of a family's health shall never depend on the size of a family's wealth.

---

19. A reference to the presidencies of Woodrow Wilson (New Freedom), Franklin Roosevelt (New Deal), and John F. Kennedy (New Frontier).

20. When delivering the speech, Kennedy inserted an extraneous "that" here.

21. Kennedy uses words from Woody Guthrie's populist song "This Land Is Your Land," which was adopted as an anthem of the environmental movement. It was also the theme song of Robert F. Kennedy's 1968 campaign for the Democratic presidential nomination.

22. Coauthor of *The Communist Manifesto* (1848).

23. At a time when there was no federal income tax, Roosevelt called for a progressive inheritance tax in his 1906 speech "The Man with the Muckrake" (pages 24–29).

The President, the Vice President, the members of Congress have a medical plan that meets their needs in full, and whenever Senators and Representatives catch a little cold, the Capitol Physician will see them immediately, treat them promptly, fill a prescription on the spot. We do not get a bill even if we ask for it. And when do you think was the last time a member of Congress asked for a bill from the federal government? And I say again, as I have before, if health insurance is good enough for the President, the Vice President, the Congress of the United States, then it's good enough for you and every family in America.

There were some, there were some who said we should be silent about our differences on issues during this convention, but the heritage of the Democratic Party has been a history of democracy. We fight hard because we care deeply about our principles and purposes. We did not flee this struggle. We welcome the contrast with the empty and expedient spectacle last month in Detroit where no nomination was contested, no question was debated, and no one dared to raise any doubt or dissent. Democrats can be proud that we chose a different course and a different platform.

We can be proud that our party stands for investment in safe energy instead of a nuclear future that may threaten the future itself. We must not permit the neighborhoods of America to be permanently shadowed by the fear of another Three Mile Island.[24]

We can be proud that our party stands for a fair housing law to unlock the doors of discrimination once and for all. The American house will be divided against itself[25] so long as there is prejudice against any American buying or renting a home.

And we can be proud that our party stands plainly and publicly and persistently for the ratification of the Equal Rights Amendment.[26] Women hold their rightful place at our convention, and women must have their rightful place in the Constitution of the United States. On this issue we will not yield, we will not equivocate, we will not rationalize, explain, or excuse.[27] We will stand for ERA and for the recognition at long last that our nation was made up of Founding Mothers as well as Founding Fathers.

A fair prosperity and a just society are within our vision and our grasp, and we do not have every answer. There are questions not yet asked, waiting for us in the recesses of the future. But of this much we can be certain because it is the lesson of all of our history: Together a President and the people can make a difference. I have found that faith still alive wherever I have traveled across this land. So let us reject the counsel of retreat and the call to reaction. Let us go forward in the knowledge that history only helps those who help themselves.

There will be setbacks and sacrifices in the years ahead, but I am convinced that we as a people are ready to give something back to our country in return for all it has given to us. Let this, let this be our commitment: Whatever sacrifices must be made will be shared and shared fairly. And let this be our confidence: At the end of our journey, and always before us, shines that ideal of liberty and justice for all.

In closing, let me say a few words to all those that I have met and to all those who have supported me at this convention and across the country. There were hard hours on our journey, and often we sailed against the wind. But always we kept our rudder true, and there were so many of you who stayed the course and shared our hope.

You gave your help, but, even more, you gave your hearts. And because of you, this has been a happy campaign. You welcomed Joan,[28] me, and our family into your homes and neighborhoods, your churches, your campuses, your union halls. And when I think back of all the miles and all the months and all the

24. In a highly publicized incident, a nuclear reactor at the Three Mile Island power plant near Middletown, Pennsylvania, suffered a partial meltdown in March 1979.

25. An allusion to Abraham Lincoln's June 16, 1858, description of the United States as a "house divided against itself" over the issue of slavery.

26. Approved by Congress in 1971–1972, the Equal Rights Amendment providing for legal equality of the sexes failed to achieve ratification by three-fourths of the states by the deadline of June 30, 1982.

27. An echo of William Lloyd Garrison's declaration in the first issue of *The Liberator*, January 1, 1831, that in the battle against slavery, "I will not equivocate, I will not excuse, I will not retreat a single inch, and I will be heard."

28. Kennedy's wife, Joan Bennett Kennedy.

memories, I think of you and I recall the poet's words, and I say, what "golden friends I had."[29]

Among you, my golden friends across this land, I have listened and learned. I have listened to Kenny Dubois, a glassblower in Charleston, West Virginia, who has ten children to support but has lost his job after thirty-five years, just three years short of qualifying for his pension.

I have listened to the Trachta family, who farm in Iowa and who wonder whether they can pass the good life and the good earth on to their children.

I have listened to the grandmother in East Oakland who no longer has a phone to call her grandchildren because she gave it up to pay the rent on her small apartment.

I have listened to young workers out of work, to students without the tuition for college, and to families without the chance to own a home. I have seen the closed factories and the stalled assembly lines of Anderson, Indiana, and South Gate, California, and I have seen too many—far too many—idle men and women desperate to work. I have seen too many—far too many—working families desperate to protect the value of their wages from the ravages of inflation.

Yet I have also sensed a yearning for new hope among the people in every state where I have been. And I have felt it in their handshakes, I saw it in their faces, and I shall never forget the mothers who carried children to our rallies. I shall always remember the elderly who have lived in an America of high purpose and who believe that it can all happen again. Tonight, in their name, I have come here to speak for them. And for their sake, I ask you to stand with them. On their behalf, I ask you to restate and reaffirm the timeless truth of our party.

29. From A. E. Housman, *A Shropshire Lad* (1896).

I congratulate President Carter on his victory here. I am, I am confident that the Democratic Party will reunite on the basis of Democratic principles and that together we will march towards a Democratic victory in 1980.

And someday, long after this convention, long after the signs come down and the crowds stop cheering and the bands stop playing, may it be said of our campaign that we kept the faith. May it be said of our party in 1980 that we found our faith again. And may it be said of us, both in dark passages and in bright days, in the words of Tennyson that my brothers[30] quoted and loved and that have special meaning for me now:

I am a part of all that I have met...
Too much is taken, much abides...
That which we are, we are;
One equal temper of heroic hearts...strong in will
To strive, to seek, to find, and not to yield.[31]

For me, a few hours ago this campaign came to an end. For all those whose cares have been our concern, the work goes on, the cause endures, the hope still lives, and the dream shall never die.[32]

30. Joseph Kennedy Jr., who was killed in World War II; John F. Kennedy, who was assassinated in 1963; Robert F. Kennedy, who was assassinated in 1968.

31. From Alfred, Lord Tennyson, "Ulysses" (1842). When delivering the speech, Kennedy misspoke the opening word of line two, which should have been "Tho" rather than "Too."

32. This sentence was reworked from Kennedy's speech at the dedication of the John F. Kennedy Library in October 1979, in which he said: "In dedicating this library to Jack, we recall those years of grace, that time of hope. The spark still glows. The journey never ends. The dream shall never die." He would rework the line again in his August 25, 2008, speech at the Democratic National Convention.

Ronald Reagan

✕

First Inaugural Address

WASHINGTON, D.C.
JANUARY 20, 1981

ROM THE TIME Ronald Reagan delivered his "Time for Choosing" speech
in October 1964 (pages 415–423), conservative Republicans had been
grooming him for the White House. After failing to gain the party's
nomination in 1968 and 1976, he became, at age sixty-nine, the oldest person
elected President when he triumphed over incumbent Jimmy Carter in 1980.
More than any chief executive of the twentieth century, his rise to power, his
personal popularity, and his ability to govern were predicated on his abilities as
a public speaker.

Trained first as a radio announcer and then as an actor, he had a warm
baritone voice with relaxed, conversational inflections. Over the years he developed a keen sense of timing, plus the ability to convey a panorama of meanings
through fine modulations of tone, rate, pitch, and body language. No matter the size of his audience, there was always a sense of personal intimacy in
his speeches. Much of his appeal as a speaker grew out of the fact that he
did not sound like a political orator. As with his rhetorical model, Franklin
D. Roosevelt, he came across as talking with people, rather than haranguing
them. He exuded warmth, sincerity, and a genuine sense of conviction. Dubbed
the Great Communicator by the press, he had a 63 percent approval rating
when he left office, higher than any outgoing President in the second half of
the twentieth century.

Always attentive to the power of political symbolism. Reagan delivered
his inaugural address from the back of the U.S. Capitol, facing west, instead
of from the front, where it had been presented for a century and a half. The
message was unmistakable: Reagan was a conservative, but his administration
was going to mark a change in national direction. The country, he said, faced "an
economic affliction of great proportions"—inflation, unemployment, overtaxa-
tion, and deficit spending—but the solution lay in less government rather than
in more. It was time to make government "work with us, not over us; to stand
by our side, not ride on our back." Drawing a distinction between himself and
President Carter, who had discerned a crisis of national confidence (see pages
536–542), Reagan denied that the United States was "doomed to an inevitable decline." He called for "an era of national renewal" that would unleash
the strength, courage, and creative energy of the American people and restore
respect abroad.

These ideas were vintage Reagan, but his inaugural address gave them fresh expression. Like FDR's first inaugural, which Reagan subtly echoed several times, his speech exuded optimism, hope, change, and renewal. It also showed Reagan's penchant for invoking heroic exemplars to represent the American spirit. In this case, it was Martin Treptow, a World War I soldier who had sacrificed his life for the freedom of others. The story was not accurate in every particular—including the fact that Treptow was buried in Bloomer, Wisconsin, rather than at Arlington Cemetery—but Reagan, with his Hollywood background, understood well the concept of dramatic license. What mattered to him—and to most citizens—was the need to believe in American heroes and to believe that America itself could be heroic again.

◇◇

Thank you. Thank you. Senator Hatfield,[1] Mr. Chief Justice, Mr. President,[2] Vice President Bush, Vice President Mondale,[3] Senator Baker, Speaker O'Neill,[4] Reverend Moomaw,[5] and my fellow citizens:

To a few of us here today, this is a solemn and most momentous occasion; and yet, in the history of our nation, it is a commonplace occurrence. The orderly transfer of authority as called for in the Constitution routinely takes place as it has for almost two centuries and few of us stop to think how unique we really are. In the eyes of many in the world, this every-four-year ceremony we accept as normal is nothing less than a miracle.

Mr. President, I want our fellow citizens to know how much you did to carry on this tradition. By your gracious cooperation in the transition process, you have shown a watching world that we are a united people pledged to maintaining a political system which guarantees individual liberty to a greater degree than any other, and I thank you and your people for all your help in maintaining the continuity which is the bulwark of our republic.

The business of our nation goes forward. These United States are confronted with an economic affliction of great proportions. We suffer from the longest and one of the worst sustained inflations in our national history. It distorts our economic decisions, penalizes thrift, and crushes the struggling young and the fixed-income elderly alike. It threatens to shatter the lives of millions of our people. Idle industries have cast workers into unemployment, human misery, and personal indignity. Those who do work are denied a fair return for their labor by a tax system which penalizes successful achievement and keeps us from maintaining full productivity.

But great as our tax burden is, it has not kept pace with public spending. For decades we have piled deficit upon deficit, mortgaging our future and our children's future for the temporary convenience of the present. To continue this long trend is to guarantee tremendous social, cultural, political, and economic upheavals. You and I, as individuals, can, by borrowing, live beyond our means, but for only a limited period of time. Why, then, should we think that collectively, as a nation, we are not bound by that same limitation? We must act today in order to preserve tomorrow. And let there be no misunderstanding: We are going to begin to act, beginning today.

---

1. Mark O. Hatfield, U.S. Senator from Oregon and head of the Joint Congressional Committee on Inaugural Ceremonies.

2. Warren Burger, Chief Justice of the U.S. Supreme Court; outgoing President Jimmy Carter.

3. Reagan's Vice President, George H. W. Bush; outgoing Vice President Walter F. Mondale.

4. Howard Baker Jr., Majority Leader of the U.S. Senate; Thomas P. "Tip" O'Neill Jr., Speaker of the U.S. House of Representatives.

5. Donn Moomaw, pastor of the Bel Air Presbyterian Church in Los Angeles, where the Reagans worshipped, who gave the invocation and benediction.

The economic ills we suffer have come upon us over several decades. They will not go away in days, weeks, or months, but they will go away. They will go away because we, as Americans, have the capacity now, as we've had in the past, to do whatever needs to be done to preserve this last and greatest bastion of freedom.

In this present crisis, government is not the solution to our problem; government is the problem. From time to time, we've been tempted to believe that society has become too complex to be managed by self-rule, that government by an elite group is superior to government for, by, and of the people.[6] But if no one among us is capable of governing himself, then who among us has the capacity to govern someone else?[7] All of us together, in and out of government, must bear the burden. The solutions we seek must be equitable, with no one group singled out to pay a higher price.

We hear much of special interest groups. Well, our concern must be for a special interest group that has been too-long neglected. It knows no sectional boundaries or ethnic and racial divisions, and it crosses political party lines. It is made up of men and women who raise our food, patrol our streets, man our mines and factories, teach our children, keep our homes, and heal us when we're sick—professionals, industrialists, shopkeepers, clerks, cabbies, and truck drivers. They are, in short, "We, the people,"[8] this breed called Americans.

Well, this administration's objective will be a healthy, vigorous, growing economy that provides equal opportunities for all Americans, with no barriers born of bigotry or discrimination. Putting America back to work means putting all Americans back to work. Ending inflation means freeing all Americans from the terror of runaway living costs. All must share in the productive work of this new beginning and all must share in the bounty of a revived economy. With the idealism and fair play which are the core of our system and our strength, we can have a strong and prosperous America at peace with itself and the world.

So as we begin, let us take inventory. We are a nation that has a government—not the other way around. And this makes us special among the nations of the earth. Our government has no power except that granted it by the people. It is time to check and reverse the growth of government which shows signs of having grown beyond the consent of the governed. It is my intention to curb the size and influence of the federal establishment and to demand recognition of the distinction between the powers granted to the federal government and those reserved to the states or to the people. All of us, all of us need to be reminded that the federal government did not create the states; the states created the federal government.

Now, so there will be no misunderstanding, it's not my intention to do away with government. It is, rather, to make it work—work with us, not over us; to stand by our side, not ride on our back. Government can and must provide opportunity, not smother it; foster productivity, not stifle it.

If we look to the answer as to why, for so many years, we achieved so much, prospered as no other people on earth, it was because here, in this land, we unleashed the energy and individual genius of man to a greater extent than has ever been done before. Freedom and the dignity of the individual have been more available and assured here than in any other place on earth. The price for this freedom at times has been high, but we have never been unwilling to pay that price. It is no coincidence that our present troubles parallel and are proportionate to the intervention and intrusion in our lives that result from unnecessary and excessive growth of government.

It is time for us to realize that we are too great a nation to limit ourselves to small dreams. We are not, as some would have us believe, doomed to an inevitable decline. I do not believe in a fate that will fall on us no matter what we do. I do believe in a fate that will fall on us if we do nothing. So with all the creative energy at our command, let us begin an era

---

6. An echo of Abraham Lincoln's Gettysburg Address, November 19, 1863.

7. An allusion to Thomas Jefferson's first inaugural address, March 4, 1801: "Sometimes it is said that man cannot be trusted with the government of himself. Can he, then, be trusted with the government of others?"

8. Opening words of the U.S. Constitution.

of national renewal. Let us renew our determination, our courage, and our strength. And let us renew our faith and our hope.

We have every right to dream heroic dreams. Those who say that we're in a time when there are no heroes, they just don't know where to look. You can see heroes every day going in and out of factory gates. Others, a handful in number, produce enough food to feed all of us and then the world beyond. You meet heroes across a counter—and they're on both sides of that counter. There are entrepreneurs with faith in themselves and faith in an idea who create new jobs, new wealth, and opportunity. They're individuals and families whose taxes support the government and whose voluntary gifts support church, charity, culture, art, and education. Their patriotism is quiet, but deep. Their values sustain our national life.

Now, I have used the words "they" and "their" in speaking of these heroes. I could say "you" and "your" because I am addressing the heroes of whom I speak—you, the citizens of this blessed land. Your dreams, your hopes, your goals are going to be the dreams, the hopes, and the goals of this administration, so help me God.

We shall reflect the compassion that is so much a part of your makeup. How can we love our country and not love our countrymen, and, loving them, reach out a hand when they fall, heal them when they're sick, and provide opportunity to make them self-sufficient so they will be equal in fact and not just in theory?

Can we solve the problems confronting us? Well, the answer is an unequivocal and emphatic yes. To paraphrase Winston Churchill, I did not take the oath I've just taken with the intention of presiding over the dissolution of the world's strongest economy.[9]

In the days ahead I will propose removing the roadblocks that have slowed our economy and reduced productivity. Steps will be taken aimed at restoring the balance between the various levels of government. Progress may be slow—measured in inches and feet, not miles—but we will progress.

It is time to reawaken this industrial giant, to get government back within its means, and to lighten our punitive tax burden. And these will be our first priorities, and on these principles there will be no compromise.

On the eve of our struggle for independence, a man who might have been one of the greatest among the Founding Fathers, Dr. Joseph Warren, President of the Massachusetts Congress, said to his fellow Americans: "Our country is in danger, but not to be despaired of.... On you depend the fortunes of America. You are to decide the important question upon which rests the happiness and the liberty of millions yet unborn. Act worthy of yourselves."[10]

Well, I believe we, the Americans of today, are ready to act worthy of ourselves, ready to do what must be done to ensure happiness and liberty for ourselves, our children, and our children's children. And as we renew ourselves here in our own land, we will be seen as having greater strength throughout the world. We will again be the exemplar of freedom and a beacon of hope for those who do not now have freedom.

To those neighbors and allies who share our freedom, we will strengthen our historic ties and assure them of our support and firm commitment. We will match loyalty with loyalty. We will strive for mutually beneficial relations. We will not use our friendship to impose on their sovereignty, for our own sovereignty is not for sale.

As for the enemies of freedom, those who are potential adversaries, they will be reminded that peace is the highest aspiration of the American people. We will negotiate for it, sacrifice for it; we will not surrender for it, now or ever.

Our forbearance should never be misunderstood. Our reluctance for conflict should not be misjudged as a failure of will. When action is required to preserve our national security, we will act. We will maintain sufficient strength to prevail if need be, knowing that if we do so, we have the best chance of never having to use that strength.

---

9. In his speech of November 10, 1942, Churchill stated: "I have not become the King's First Minister in order to preside over the liquidation of the British Empire."

10. From Warren's Boston Massacre Oration, March 6, 1775.

Above all, we must realize that no arsenal, or no weapon in the arsenals of the world, is so formidable as the will and moral courage of free men and women. It is a weapon our adversaries in today's world do not have. It is a weapon that we as Americans do have. Let that be understood by those who practice terrorism and prey upon their neighbors.

I'm, I'm told that tens of thousands of prayer meetings are being held on this day, and for that I am deeply grateful. We are a nation under God, and I believe God intended for us to be free. It would be fitting and good,[11] I think, if on each inaugural day in future years it should be declared a day of prayer.

This is the first time in our history that this ceremony has been held, as you've been told, on this west front of the Capitol.[12] Standing here, one faces a magnificent vista, opening up on this city's special beauty and history. At the end of this open mall are those shrines to the giants on whose shoulders we stand.[13]

Directly in front of me, the monument to a monumental man: George Washington, father of our country. A man of humility who came to greatness reluctantly, he led America out of Revolutionary victory into infant nationhood. Off to one side, the stately memorial to Thomas Jefferson. The Declaration of Independence flames with his eloquence. And then, beyond the reflecting pool, the dignified columns of the Lincoln Memorial. Whoever would understand in his heart the meaning of America will find it in the life of Abraham Lincoln.

Beyond those monuments to heroism is the Potomac River, and on the far shore the sloping hills of Arlington National Cemetery with its row upon row of simple white markers bearing crosses or Stars of David. They add up to only a tiny fraction of the price that has been paid for our freedom.

Each one of those markers is a monument to the kind of hero I spoke of earlier. Their lives ended in places called Belleau Wood, the Argonne,[14] Omaha Beach, Salerno, and halfway around the world on Guadalcanal, Tarawa,[15] Pork Chop Hill, the Chosin Reservoir,[16] and in a hundred rice paddies and jungles of a place called Vietnam.

Under one such marker lies a young man, Martin Treptow, who left his job in a small-town barber shop in 1917 to go to France with the famed Rainbow Division.[17] There, on the western front, he was killed trying to carry a message between battalions under heavy artillery fire. We're told that on his body was found a diary. On the flyleaf, under the heading "My Pledge," he had written these words: "America must win this war. Therefore, I will work, I will save, I will sacrifice, I will endure, I will fight cheerfully and do my utmost, as if the issue of the whole struggle depended on me alone."[18]

The crisis we are facing today does not require of us the kind of sacrifice that Martin Treptow and so many thousands of others were called upon to make. It does require, however, our best effort and our willingness to believe in ourselves and to believe in our capacity to perform great deeds, to believe that together, with God's help, we can and will resolve the problems which now confront us. And, after all, why shouldn't we believe that? We are Americans.

God bless you, and thank you. Thank you very much.

11. A play on "fitting and proper," from Lincoln's Gettysburg Address.

12. Inaugurations had traditionally been held on the East Portico of the Capitol.

13. An echo of language used most famously by Isaac Newton in a letter to Robert Hooke, February 5, 1675/1676.

14. World War I battle sites.

15. World War II battle sites.

16. Korean War battle sites.

17. Composed of units from 26 states and the District of Columbia, the 42nd Infantry Division was called the Rainbow Division after Douglas MacArthur, who later became its commander, said it would "stretch like a rainbow across the United States."

18. Killed in action in July 1918, Treptow penned these words in his diary on December 31, 1917, under the heading "1918 Resolution." He did not write "My Pledge," and he is buried in Bloomer, Wisconsin, rather than at Arlington National Cemetery.

Ronald Reagan

⧗

The Evil Empire

ORLANDO, FLORIDA
MARCH 8, 1983

FOR TWO DECADES Ronald Reagan had been proclaiming the moral bankruptcy of the Soviet system, and he was not about to desist after being elected to the White House. In June 1982, during his first presidential trip to Europe, he told the British Parliament, meeting at the Palace of Westminster, that "the march of freedom and democracy...will leave Marxist-Leninism on the ash heap of history, as it has left other tyrannies which stifle the freedom and muzzle the self-expression of the people." It was one of Reagan's best speeches, but it attracted more attention abroad than at home.

Not so with his "Evil Empire" speech of March 8, 1983. Speaking at the annual meeting of the National Association of Evangelicals, Reagan switched from the secular idiom of his Westminster address to a mode of discourse suffused with religious themes and imagery. He called the Soviet Union an "evil empire" whose quest to dominate "all peoples on the earth" made it "the focus of evil in the modern world." And he declared communism to be no more than "another sad, bizarre chapter in human history" that could not survive the spiritual quest for human freedom. Nearly every liberal media outlet in America condemned the President's language as needlessly provocative, but it was fully in keeping with his long-standing goal of stripping away the veneer of moral legitimacy from Soviet totalitarianism.

The timing of the speech was not coincidental. By the spring of 1983 the nuclear freeze movement had gained enough momentum that it seemed close to achieving its objective of passing House and Senate resolutions against the testing, production, and further deployment of nuclear weapons by both the United States and the Soviet Union. Because such resolutions could not bind the Soviet Union, in Reagan's view they were akin to unilateral disarmament and would undercut his administration's negotiating position on arms control. He was also dismayed that religious groups such as the National Council of Churches and the National Conference of Catholic Bishops had expressed support for a freeze. By speaking to the National Association of Evangelicals, an organization that represented more than fifty denominations and organizations with a combined membership of thirty million people, Reagan was assured a predominantly receptive audience that would counter the perception that all religious and moral leaders endorsed the nuclear freeze movement.

He was also assured an audience favorably disposed toward his views about government and religion. Although some commentators see the last third of the speech, the "evil empire" section, as tagged on to the first two-thirds, which deal with domestic policy, the speech is thematically unified by Reagan's belief that "freedom prospers only where the blessings of God are avidly sought and humbly accepted." Domestically, he argued, the greatest danger facing America was "a modern-day secularism" that discarded "the tried and time-tested values upon which our very civilization is based." Internationally, the struggle against communism was ultimately "a test of moral will and faith" that could not be won as long as the West was "indifferent to God" and collaborated in "communism's attempt to make man stand alone without God." Never had a twentieth-century President spoken in such evangelical tones about the importance of faith in the political arena. Religious conservatives heard well, and they would rally to Reagan's side throughout his administration.

◇◇

Thank you. Thank you very much. Thank you very much. Thank you very much. Thank you very much. And reverend clergy all, Senator Hawkins,[1] distinguished members of the Florida congressional delegation, and all of you: I can't tell you how you have warmed my heart with your welcome. I'm delighted to be here today.

Those of you in the National Association of Evangelicals are known for your spiritual and humanitarian work. And I would be especially remiss if I didn't discharge right now one personal debt of gratitude. Thank you for your prayers. Nancy and I have felt their presence many times, in many ways. And believe me, for us they've made all the difference.

The other day in the East Room of the White House at a meeting there, someone asked me whether I was aware of all the people out there who were praying for the President. And I had to say, "Yes, I am. I've felt it. I believe in intercessionary prayer." But I couldn't help but say to that questioner after he'd asked the question that—or at least say to them that if sometimes when he was praying he got a busy signal, it was just me in there ahead of him. I think I understand how Abraham Lincoln felt when he said, "I have been driven many times

to my knees by the overwhelming conviction that I had nowhere else to go."[2]

From the joy and the good feeling of this conference, I go to a political reception. Now, I don't know why, but that bit of scheduling reminds me of a story which I'll share with you.

An evangelical minister and a politician arrived at heaven's gate one day together. And St. Peter, after doing all the necessary formalities, took them in hand to show them where their quarters would be. And he took them to a small, single room with a bed, a chair, and a table and said this was for the clergyman. And the politician was a little worried about what might be in store for him. And he couldn't believe it then when St. Peter stopped in front of a beautiful mansion with lovely grounds, many servants, and told him that these would be his quarters.

And he couldn't help but ask. He said, "But wait, how—there's something wrong—how do I get this mansion while that good and holy man only gets a single room?" And St. Peter said, "You have to understand how things are up here. We've got thousands and thousands of clergy. You're the first politician who ever made it."

---

1. Paula Hawkins, U.S. Senator from Florida.

2. Attributed to Lincoln by Noah Brooks, "Personal Recollections of Abraham Lincoln," *Harper's New Monthly Magazine* (July 1865).

But I don't want to contribute to a stereotype. So I tell you there are a great many God-fearing, dedicated, noble men and women in public life, present company included. And, yes, we need your help to keep us ever mindful of the ideas and the principles that brought us into the public arena in the first place. The basis of those ideals and principles is a commitment to freedom and personal liberty that itself is grounded in the much deeper realization that freedom prospers only where the blessings of God are avidly sought and humbly accepted.

The American experiment in democracy rests on this insight. Its discovery was the great triumph of our Founding Fathers, voiced by William Penn when he said: "If we will not be governed by God, we must be governed by tyrants."[3] Explaining the inalienable rights of men, Jefferson said: "The God who gave us life, gave us liberty at the same time."[4] And it was George Washington who said that "of all the dispositions and habits which lead to political prosperity, religion and morality are indispensable supports."[5]

And finally, that shrewdest of all observers of American democracy, Alexis de Tocqueville, put it eloquently after he had gone on a search for the secret of America's greatness and genius. And he said: "Not until I went into the churches of America and heard her pulpits aflame with righteousness did I understand the greatness and the genius of America. America is good. And if America ever ceases to be good, America will cease to be great."[6]

Well, I'm pleased to be here today with you who are keeping America great by keeping her good. Only through your work and prayers and those of millions of others can we hope to survive this perilous century and keep alive this experiment in liberty, this last, best hope of man.[7] I want you to know that this administration is motivated by a political philosophy that sees the greatness of America in you, her people, and in your families, churches, neighborhoods, communities—the institutions that foster and nourish values like concern for others and respect for the rule of law under God.

Now, I don't have to tell you that this puts us in opposition to, or at least out of step with, a prevailing attitude of many who have turned to a modern-day secularism, discarding the tried and time-tested values upon which our very civilization is based. No matter how well intentioned, their value system is radically different from that of most Americans. And while they proclaim that they're freeing us from superstitions of the past, they've taken upon themselves the job of superintending us by government rule and regulation. Sometimes their voices are louder than ours, but they are not yet a majority.

An example of that vocal superiority is evident in a controversy now going on in Washington. And since I'm involved, I've been waiting to hear from the parents of young America. How far are they willing to go in giving to government their prerogatives as parents?

Let me state the case as briefly and simply as I can. An organization of citizens, sincerely motivated, deeply concerned about the increase in illegitimate births and abortions involving girls well below the age of consent, some time ago established a nationwide network of clinics to offer help to these girls and, hopefully, alleviate this situation. Now, again let me say I do not fault their intent. However, in their well-intentioned effort, these clinics have decided to provide advice and birth control drugs and devices to underage girls without the knowledge of their parents.

For some years now, the federal government has helped with funds to subsidize these clinics. In providing for this, the Congress decreed that every effort would be made to maximize parental participation.

3. Though often attributed to Penn, these words do not appear in his extant writings.

4. From Thomas Jefferson, *A Summary View of the Rights of British America* (1774).

5. From Washington's Farewell Address, September 19, 1796.

6. Attributed to Tocqueville in Sherwood Eddy's *The Kingdom of God and the American Dream* (1941), these sentences do not appear in Tocqueville's extant works.

7. Reagan is echoing language used by the American Revolutionaries and later by Abraham Lincoln.

Nevertheless, the drugs and devices are prescribed without getting parental consent or giving notification after they've done so. Girls termed "sexually active"— and that has replaced the word "promiscuous"—are given this help in order to prevent illegitimate birth or abortion.

Well, we have ordered clinics receiving federal funds to notify the parents such help has been given. One of the nation's leading newspapers has created the term "squeal rule" in editorializing against us for doing this,[8] and we're being criticized for violating the privacy of young people. A judge has recently granted an injunction against an enforcement of our rule.[9] I've watched TV panel shows discuss this issue, seen columnists pontificating on our error, but no one seems to mention morality as playing a part in the subject of sex.

Is all of Judeo-Christian tradition wrong? Are we to believe that something so sacred can be looked upon as a purely physical thing with no potential for emotional and psychological harm? And isn't it the parents' right to give counsel and advice to keep their children from making mistakes that may affect their entire lives?

Many of us in government would like to know what parents think about this intrusion in their family by government. We're going to fight in the courts. The right of parents and the rights of family take precedence over those of Washington-based bureaucrats and social engineers.

But the fight against parental notification is really only one example of many attempts to water down traditional values and even abrogate the original terms of American democracy. Freedom prospers when religion is vibrant and the rule of law under God is acknowledged. When our Founding Fathers passed the First Amendment, they sought to protect churches from government interference.[10]

They never intended to construct a wall of hostility between government and the concept of religious belief itself.[11]

The evidence of this permeates our history and our government. The Declaration of Independence mentions the Supreme Being no less than four times. "In God We Trust" is engraved on our coinage. The Supreme Court opens its proceedings with a religious invocation. And the members of Congress open their sessions with a prayer. I just happen to believe the schoolchildren of the United States are entitled to the same privileges as Supreme Court Justices and Congressmen.

Last year, I sent the Congress a constitutional amendment to restore prayer to public schools. Already this session, there's growing bipartisan support for the amendment, and I am calling on the Congress to act speedily to pass it and to let our children pray.

Perhaps some of you read recently about the Lubbock school case,[12] where a judge actually ruled that it was unconstitutional for a school district to give equal treatment to religious and nonreligious student groups, even when the group meetings were being held during the students' own time. The First Amendment never intended to require government to discriminate against religious speech.

Senators Denton and Hatfield[13] have proposed legislation in the Congress on the whole question of prohibiting discrimination against religious forms of student speech.[14] Such legislation could go far to restore freedom of religious speech for public school students. And I hope the Congress considers these bills quickly. And with your help, I think it's possible we could also get the constitutional amendment through the Congress this year.

---

8. *New York Times*, January 12, 1983.

9. The injunction was granted on February 14, 1983, by Federal District Judge Henry F. Werker.

10. The First Amendment to the U.S. Constitution includes the statement that "Congress shall make no law respecting an establishment of religion, or prohibiting the free exercise thereof."

11. A play on Thomas Jefferson's metaphor of "a wall of separation between church and state," from his letter to the Danbury Baptist Association, January 1, 1802.

12. *Lubbock Civil Liberties Union v. Lubbock Independent School District* (1982).

13. Jeremiah Denton and Mark O. Hatfield.

14. This proposed legislation eventually became the Equal Access Act of 1984.

More than a decade ago, a Supreme Court decision literally wiped off the books of fifty states statutes protecting the rights of unborn children.[15] Abortion on demand now takes the lives of up to one and a half million unborn children a year. Human life legislation ending this tragedy will someday pass the Congress, and you and I must never rest until it does. Unless and until it can be proven that the unborn child is not a living entity, then its right to life, liberty, and the pursuit of happiness[16] must be protected.

You, you may remember that when abortion on demand began, many, and indeed I'm sure, many of you, warned that the practice would lead to a decline in respect for human life, that the philosophical premises used to justify abortion on demand would ultimately be used to justify other attacks on the sacredness of human life—infanticide or mercy killing. Tragically enough, those warnings proved all too true. Only last year a court permitted the death by starvation of a handicapped infant.[17]

I have directed the Health and Human Services Department to make clear to every health-care facility in the United States that the Rehabilitation Act of 1973 protects all handicapped persons against discrimination based on handicaps, including infants. And we have taken the further step of requiring that each and every recipient of federal funds who provides health-care services to infants must post, and keep posted in a conspicuous place, a notice stating that "discriminatory failure to feed and care for handicapped infants in this facility is prohibited by federal law." It also lists a twenty-four-hour, toll-free number so that nurses and others may report violations in time to save the infant's life.[18]

In addition, recent legislation introduced by—in the Congress—by Representative Henry Hyde of Illinois not only increases restrictions on publicly financed abortions, it also addresses this whole problem of infanticide.[19] I urge the Congress to begin hearings and to adopt legislation that will protect the right of life to all children, including the disabled or handicapped.

Now, I'm sure that you must get discouraged at times, but there you've done better than you know, perhaps. There's a great spiritual awakening in America, a renewal of the traditional values that have been the bedrock of America's goodness and greatness. One recent survey by a Washington-based research council concluded that Americans were far more religious than the people of other nations; 95 percent of those surveyed expressed a belief in God and a huge majority believed the Ten Commandments had real meaning in their lives. And another study has found that an overwhelming majority of Americans disapprove of adultery, teenage sex, pornography, abortion, and hard drugs. And this same study showed a deep reverence for the importance of family ties and religious belief.

I think the items that we've discussed here today must be a key part of the nation's political agenda. For the first time the Congress is openly and seriously debating and dealing with the prayer and abortion issues, and that's enormous progress right there. I repeat: America is in the midst of a spiritual awakening and a moral renewal. And with your biblical keynote, I say today, "Yes, let justice roll on like a river, righteousness like a never-failing stream."[20]

Now, obviously much of this new political and social consensus I've talked about is based on a positive view of American history, one that takes pride in our country's accomplishments and record. But we must never forget that no government schemes are

---

15. Reagan is referring to the decision in *Roe v. Wade* (1973).

16. An echo of the Declaration of Independence (1776).

17. Reagan is referring to the Baby Doe case in Bloomington, Indiana. Born on April 9, 1982, with Down syndrome and esophageal atresia, the baby died on April 15 when the Indiana courts upheld the parents' right to withhold medical treatment.

18. Reagan is referring to the interim final rule issued by Margaret Heckler, Secretary of Health and Human Services, on March 7, 1983.

---

19. Hyde's Respect Human Life Act was introduced in January 1983.

20. Amos 5:24 (New International Version). This verse was cited in the program as part of the scriptural mandate for the theme of that year's NAE convention: "Change Your World."

going to perfect man. We know that living in this world means dealing with what philosophers would call the phenomenology of evil, or, as theologians would put it, the doctrine of sin.

There is sin and evil in the world, and we're enjoined by Scripture and the Lord Jesus to oppose it with all our might. Our nation, too, has a legacy of evil with which it must deal. The glory of this land has been its capacity for transcending the moral evils of our past. For example, the long struggle of minority citizens for equal rights, once a source of disunity and civil war, is now a point of pride for all Americans. We must never go back. There is no room for racism, anti-Semitism, or other forms of ethnic and racial hatred in this country.

I know that you've been horrified, as have I, by the resurgence of some hate groups preaching bigotry and prejudice. Use the mighty voice of your pulpits and the powerful standing of your churches to denounce and isolate these hate groups in our midst. The commandment given us is clear and simple: "Thou shalt love thy neighbor as thyself."[21]

But whatever sad episodes exist in our past, any objective observer must hold a positive view of American history, a history that has been the story of hopes fulfilled and dreams made into reality. Especially in this century, America has kept alight the torch of freedom—but not just for ourselves, but for millions of others around the world.

And this brings me to my final point today. During my first press conference as President, in answer to a direct question, I pointed out that, as good Marxist-Leninists, the Soviet leaders have openly and publicly declared that the only morality they recognize is that which will further their cause, which is world revolution. I think I should point out I was only quoting Lenin, their guiding spirit, who said in 1920 that they repudiate all morality that proceeds from supernatural ideas—that's their name for religion—or ideas that are outside class conceptions.[22] Morality is entirely subordinate to the inter-

ests of class war. And everything is moral that is necessary for the annihilation of the old, exploiting social order and for uniting the proletariat.

Well, I think the refusal of many influential people to accept this elementary fact of Soviet doctrine illustrates an historical reluctance to see totalitarian powers for what they are. We saw this phenomenon in the 1930s.[23] We see it too often today.

This doesn't mean we should isolate ourselves and refuse to seek an understanding with them. I intend to do everything I can to persuade them of our peaceful intent, to remind them that it was the West that refused to use its nuclear monopoly in the forties and fifties for territorial gain and which now proposes [a] 50 percent cut in strategic ballistic missiles and the elimination of an entire class of land-based, intermediate-range nuclear missiles.

At the same time, however, they must be made to understand we will never compromise our principles and standards. We will never give away our freedom. We will never abandon our belief in God. And we will never stop searching for a genuine peace. But we can assure none of these things America stands for through the so-called nuclear freeze solutions proposed by some.[24]

The truth is that a freeze now would be a very dangerous fraud, for that is merely the illusion of peace. The reality is that we must find peace through strength. I would agree to a freeze if only we could freeze the Soviets' global desires. A freeze at current levels of weapons would remove any incentive for the Soviets to negotiate seriously in Geneva[25] and virtually end our chances to achieve the major arms reductions which we have proposed. Instead, they would achieve their objectives through the freeze.

---

21. Matthew 22:39.

22. A reference to Lenin's speech "The Tasks of the Youth League," October 2, 1920.

23. Reagan is referring to efforts to appease Germany and Japan before World War II.

24. The nuclear freeze campaign began in 1980 and called on the United States and the Soviet Union to mutually suspend testing, producing, and deploying nuclear weapons.

25. Reagan is referring to negotiations then in progress with the Soviet Union on the reduction of intermediate-range nuclear missiles.

A freeze would reward the Soviet Union for its enormous and unparalleled military buildup. It would prevent the essential and long-overdue modernization of United States and allied defenses and would leave our aging forces increasingly vulnerable. And an honest freeze would require extensive prior negotiations on the systems and numbers to be limited and on the measures to ensure effective verification and compliance. And the kind of a freeze that has been suggested would be virtually impossible to verify. Such a major effort would divert us completely from our current negotiations on achieving substantial reductions.

A number of years ago, I heard a young father, a very prominent young man in the entertainment world,[26] addressing a tremendous gathering in California. It was during the time of the Cold War, and communism and our own way of life were very much on people's minds. And he was speaking to that subject. And suddenly, though, I heard him saying, "I love my little girls more than anything." And I said to myself, "Oh, no, don't. You can't—don't say that." But I had underestimated him. He went on: "I would rather see my little girls die now, still believing in God, than have them grow up under communism and one day die no longer believing in God."

There were thousands of young people in that audience. They came to their feet with shouts of joy. They had instantly recognized the profound truth in what he had said with regard to the physical and the soul and what was truly important.

Yes, let us pray for the salvation of all of those who live in that totalitarian darkness—pray they will discover the joy of knowing God. But until they do, let us be aware that while they preach the supremacy of the state, declare its omnipotence over individual man, and predict its eventual domination of all peoples on the earth, they are the focus of evil in the modern world.

It was C. S. Lewis who, in his unforgettable *Screwtape Letters*, wrote: "The greatest evil is not done now in those sordid 'dens of crime' that

Dickens[27] loved to paint. It is not even done in concentration camps and labor camps. In those we see its final result. But it is conceived and ordered; moved, seconded, carried, and minuted in clear, carpeted, warmed, and well-lighted offices by quiet men with white collars and cut fingernails and smooth-shaven cheeks who do not need to raise their voice."[28]

Well, because these quiet men do not raise their voices, because they sometimes speak in soothing tones of brotherhood and peace, because, like other dictators before them, they're always making their final territorial demand,[29] some would have us accept them at their word and accommodate ourselves to their aggressive impulses. But if history teaches anything, it teaches that simpleminded appeasement or wishful thinking about our adversaries is folly. It means the betrayal of our past, the squandering of our freedom.

So I urge you to speak out against those who would place the United States in a position of military and moral inferiority. You know, I've always believed that old Screw Tape reserved his best efforts for those of you in the church. So in your discussions of the nuclear freeze proposals, I urge you to beware the temptation of pride—the temptation of blithely declaring yourselves above it all and label both sides equally at fault, to ignore the facts of history and the aggressive impulses of an evil empire, to simply call the arms race a giant misunderstanding and thereby remove yourself from the struggle between right and wrong and good and evil. I ask you to resist the attempts of those who would have you withhold your support for our efforts, this administration's efforts, to keep America strong and free while we negotiate real and verifiable reductions in the world's nuclear arsenals and one day, with God's help, their total elimination.

---

26. Singer Pat Boone.

27. British author Charles Dickens (1812–1870).

28. From the introduction to the revised edition of Lewis's *Screwtape Letters* (1952).

29. An allusion to Adolf Hitler, who, after seizing the Sudetenland in September 1938, declared that it was his final territorial demand.

While America's military strength is important, let me add here that I've always maintained that the struggle now going on for the world will never be decided by bombs or rockets, by armies or military might. The real crisis we face today is a spiritual one; at root, it is a test of moral will and faith.

Whittaker Chambers,[30] the man whose own religious conversion made him a witness to one of the terrible traumas of our time, the Hiss-Chambers case,[31] wrote that the crisis of the Western world exists to the degree in which the West is indifferent to God, the degree to which it collaborates in communism's attempt to make man stand alone without God. And then he said, for Marxism-Leninism is actually the second-oldest faith, first proclaimed in the Garden of Eden with the words of temptation, "Ye shall be as gods."[32] The Western world can answer this challenge, he wrote, "but only provided that its faith in God and the freedom he enjoins is as great as communism's faith in Man."[33]

I believe we shall rise to the challenge. I believe that communism is another sad, bizarre chapter in human history whose last, last pages even now are being written. I believe this because the source of our strength in the quest for human freedom is not material, but spiritual. And because it knows no limitation, it must terrify and ultimately triumph over those who would enslave their fellow man. For in the words of Isaiah: "He giveth power to the faint; and to them that have no might He increased strength.... But they that wait upon the Lord shall renew their strength; they shall mount up with wings as eagles; they shall run, and not be weary."[34]

Yes, change your world. One of our Founding Fathers, Thomas Paine, said: "We have it within our power to begin the world over again."[35] We can do it, doing together what no one church could do by itself.

God bless you, and thank you very much.

---

30. Journalist and former Soviet spy turned Christian convert.

31. Testifying before Congress in 1948, Chambers accused Alger Hiss, a former State Department official, of spying for the Soviet Union during the 1930s. Although the statute of limitations for espionage had run out, Hiss was indicted for perjury in testimony he had given to the House Un-American Activities Committee. After his first trial resulted in a hung jury, he was retried and convicted in January 1950.

32. Genesis 3:5.

33. From the foreword to Chambers's *Witness* (1952).

34. Isaiah 40:29, 31.

35. From the second edition of Paine's *Common Sense* (1776).

Ursula K. Le Guin

✕

A Left-Handed Commencement Address

OAKLAND, CALIFORNIA
MAY 22, 1983

COMMENCEMENT ADDRESSES HAVE been part of graduation ceremonies at American colleges and universities since the eighteenth century. As with some of the speeches in this volume, they have provided Presidents and others a forum for major pronouncements on issues such as rebuilding Europe after World War II, combating poverty in the United States, and pursuing arms-control agreements during the Cold War (pages 276–279, 362–368, and 405–408). Usually, however, commencement addresses offer reflections on some aspect of human affairs or current events, along with at least a modicum of advice for the graduating class. This was the pattern for Ursula Le Guin's speech at Mills College on May 22, 1983. Le Guin accepted the invitation to speak at Mills, she wrote later, because "it is one of the few remaining colleges for women, and I had a few things I wanted to say to young women."

The title of Le Guin's speech alludes to her 1969 science fiction classic *The Left Hand of Darkness*, which explores sexual mores and gender roles through the prism of life on an androgynous world. It was one of three books by Le Guin to receive the Nebula Award of the Science Fiction and Fantasy Writers of America, and it received the Hugo Award of the World Science Fiction Society. In addition, Le Guin won a National Book Award for *The Farthest Shore*, the last volume of her *Earthsea Trilogy*.

As with Barbara Bush's 1990 commencement address at Wellesley College (pages 634–637), Le Guin deals with gender issues, but from a very different perspective. Using the speech as an opportunity "to speak aloud in public in the language of women," she encourages women to live life on their terms and to reject "the so-called man's world of institutionalized competition, aggression, violence, authority, and power." Everyone, she says, will meet with failure, will find themselves "in dark places, alone, and afraid." But those dark places are ultimately a source of strength. "What hope we have lies there.... Not in the light that blinds, but in the dark that nourishes, where human beings grow human souls." More poetic than argumentative, lyrical rather than didactic, the speech rings with honest sentiment and won an enthusiastic response from Le Guin's audience.

◇◇◇

I imagine one reason you invited me to speak to you is that I'm a woman, and I know I accepted because you offered me a rare chance: to speak aloud in public in the language of women.

I know there are men getting graduate degrees, and I don't mean to exclude them—far from it. There is a Greek tragedy where the Greek says to the foreigner, "If you don't understand Greek, please signify by nodding." Since he says it in Greek[1]—

Anyhow, commencements are usually operated under the unspoken agreement that everybody graduating is either male or ought to be. That's why we are all wearing these twelfth-century dresses that look so great on men and make women look either like a mushroom or a pregnant stork. Intellectual tradition is male. Public speaking is done in the public tongue, the national or tribal language, and the language of our tribe is the men's language.

Of course, women learn it. We're not dumb. If you can tell Margaret Thatcher[2] from Ronald Reagan,[3] or Indira Gandhi[4] from General Somoza,[5] by anything they say or think, tell me how. This is a man's world, so it talks a man's language. The words are all words of power. You've come a long way, baby,[6] but no way is long enough. You can only get there by selling yourself out: because there is theirs, not yours.

Maybe we've had enough words of power, and stuff about the battle of life. Maybe we need some words of weakness. Instead of saying now that I hope you will all go forth from this ivory tower (ha, ha) of college into the real world (ha, ha) and forge a triumphant career, or help your husband to, and keep our country strong and wish you success in

---

1. Instead of finishing this sentence verbally, Le Guin used her tone of voice to convey the idea that the foreigner could not respond to the question because he did not speak Greek.

2. Prime Minister of Great Britain.

3. President of the United States.

4. Prime Minister of India.

5. Anastasio Somoza, President of Nicaragua, 1967–1980.

6. Introduced in 1968 as part of an advertising campaign for Virginia Slims cigarettes, the phrase "You've come a long way, baby," soon became a staple of American popular culture.

everything—instead of talking power, what if I talked like a woman right here in public? It won't sound right. It's going to sound terrible. What if I said what I hope for you is, first, if—only if—you want kids, I hope you have them. Not hordes of them. A couple, enough. I hope they're beautiful. I hope you and they have enough to eat, and a place to be warm and clean in, and friends, and work you like doing. Well, is that what you went to college for? Is that all? What about success?

Success is somebody else's failure. Success is the American dream we can keep dreaming because most people in most places, including thirty million of ourselves, live wide awake in the terrible reality of poverty. No, I do not wish you success. I don't even want to talk about it. I want to talk about failure.

Because you are human beings, you are going to meet failure. You are going to meet disappointment, injustice, betrayal, and irreparable loss. You will find you're weak where you thought yourself strong. You'll work for possessions and then find they possess you. You will find yourself—as I know you already have—in dark places, alone, and afraid. What I hope for you, for all my sisters and daughters, brothers and sons, is that you will be able to live there, in the dark place. To live in the place that our rationalizing culture of success denies, calling it a place of exile, uninhabitable, foreign.

Well, we're already foreigners. Women as women are excluded from, alien to, the self-declared male norms of this society, where human beings are called Man, the only respectable god is male, and the only direction is Up.

So, that's their country; let's explore our own. I'm not talking about sex; that's a whole other universe, where every man and woman is on their own. I'm talking about society, the so-called man's world of institutionalized competition, aggression, violence, authority, and power. If we want to live as women, some separatism is forced upon us. Mills College is a wise embodiment of that separatism. The war-games world wasn't made by us or for us; we can't even breathe the air there without masks. And if you put the mask on, you'll have a hard time getting it off.

So how about going on doing things our own way, as to some extent you did here at Mills? Not for men and the male power hierarchy—that's their game. Not against men, either—that's still playing by their rules. But with any men who are with us—that's our game. Why should a free woman with a college education either fight Mr. Machoman or serve him? Why should she live her life on his terms?

Machoman is afraid of our terms, which are not all rational, positive, competitive, etc. And so he has taught us to despise and deny them. In our society, women have lived, and have been despised for living, the whole side of life which includes and takes responsibility for helplessness, weakness, and illness, for the irrational and the irreparable, for all that is obscure, passive, uncontrolled, animal, unclean—the valley of the shadow, the deep, the depths of life. All that the Warrior denies and refuses is left to us and the men who share it with us and therefore, like us, can't play doctor, only nurse; can't be warriors, only civilians; can't be chiefs, only Indians.

Well, so that is our country. The night side of our country. If there is a day side to it—High Sierras, prairies of bright grass—we only know pioneers' tales about it; we haven't got there yet. We're never going to get there by imitating Machoman. We are only going to get there by going our own way, by living there, by living through the night in our own country.

So what I hope for you is that you live there not as prisoners, ashamed of being women, consenting captives of a psychopathic social system, but as natives. That you will be at home there, keep house there, be your own mistress with a room of your own.[7]

That you will do your work there, whatever you're good at—art or science or tech or running a company or sweeping under the beds—and when they tell you that it's second-class work because a woman is doing it, I hope you tell them to go to hell and while they're going to give you equal pay for equal time.

I hope you live without the need to dominate, and without the need to be dominated. I hope you are never victims, but I hope you have no power over other people. And when you fail and are defeated, and in pain, and in the dark, then I hope you will remember that darkness is your country, where you live, where no wars are fought and no wars are won, but where the future is. Our roots are in the dark; the earth is our country. What hope we have lies there. Not in the sky full of orbiting spy-eyes and weaponry, but in the earth we have despised. Not from above, but from below. Not in the light that blinds, but in the dark that nourishes, where human beings grow human souls.

---

7. An allusion to Virginia Woolf's *A Room of One's Own* (1929).

Edward M. Kennedy

Tolerance and Truth in America

LYNCHBURG, VIRGINIA
OCTOBER 3, 1983

T HE BEST KNOWN of the Christian political action groups created in the late 1970s, Jerry Falwell's Moral Majority lent strong support to conservative candidates across the country and helped put Ronald Reagan in the White House. As a result of a computer error, in 1983 it mailed a membership card to Senator Edward (Ted) Kennedy with an invitation to join the fight against "ultraliberals such as Ted Kennedy." When news of the slipup became public, an aide to Falwell sent a facetious note telling Kennedy he could keep the membership card and inviting him to visit Liberty Baptist College (now Liberty University), which Falwell had founded in 1971. Kennedy accepted and offered to speak as well. Thus came about one of the least likely public appearances of the twentieth century.

With Falwell sitting near him onstage, Kennedy received a warm welcome from the audience of 5,000 students and townspeople. After a good-humored introduction, he turned to the relationship between "faith and country, tolerance and truth, in America." It was imperative, he said, to respect the integrity of religion, but it was just as important to maintain the separation of church and state. Tempting as it might be to use government to impose one group's religious values over another's, he warned, "once we succumb to that temptation, we step onto a slippery slope where everyone's freedom is at risk." He condemned name-calling on both sides of the political spectrum and called for an America "where we can all contend freely and vigorously, but where we will treasure and guard those standards of civility which alone make this nation safe for both democracy and diversity."

Kennedy spoke with firm conviction but avoided a confrontational tone, and his audience interrupted him sixteen times with applause. "You may have won a few souls," Falwell told him afterward, "but I'll get them back next Sunday." The two men gained a measure of respect for each other, and Falwell soon stopped attacking Kennedy in the Moral Majority's mailings.

The political stakes were nowhere near those faced by John Kennedy in his address to the Houston Ministerial Association during the 1960 presidential campaign (pages 333–336), but the Liberty Baptist speech deserves equal respect for its thoughtful examination of a perennially contentious issue. That examination extends even to the title of the speech, which in previous anthologies has been mistakenly rendered as "Truth and Tolerance in America." We use Kennedy's original title, which emphasizes the importance of tolerance when competing versions of truth contend in the public arena.

◇◇◇◇◇◇◇◇◇◇◇◇◇◇◇◇◇◇◇◇◇◇◇◇◇◇◇◇◇◇◇◇◇◇◇◇◇◇

Thank you very much Professor Combee[1] for that generous introduction, and let me say that I never expected to hear such kind words from Dr. Falwell.[2] So in return I have an invitation of my own. On January 20th 1985, I hope Dr. Falwell will say a prayer at the inauguration of the next Democratic President of the United States. Now, Dr. Falwell, I'm not sure exactly how you feel about that. You might not appreciate the President, but the Democrats certainly would appreciate the prayer.

Actually, a number of people in Washington were surprised that I was invited to speak here and even more surprised when I accepted the invitation. They seem to think that it's easier for a camel to pass through the eye of a needle than for a Kennedy to come to the campus of Liberty Baptist College.[3] In honor of our meeting, I have asked Dr. Falwell as your chancellor to permit all the students an extra hour next Saturday night before curfew. And in return I have promised to watch *The Old Time Gospel Hour*[4] next Sunday morning.

I realize that my visit may be a little controversial, but as many of you have heard, Dr. Falwell recently sent me a membership in the Moral Majority and I didn't even apply for it—and I wonder if that means I'm a member in good standing.

FALWELL: Somewhat.

KENNEDY: Somewhat, he says.

This is, of course, a nonpolitical speech, which is probably best under the circumstances. Since I'm not a candidate for President, it would certainly be inappropriate to ask for your support in this election,

and probably inaccurate to thank you for it in the last one.[5]

I have come here to discuss my beliefs about faith and country, tolerance and truth in America. I know we begin with certain disagreements, and I strongly suspect at the end of the evening some of our disagreements will remain. But I also hope that tonight and in the months and years ahead we will always respect the right of others to differ, that we will never lose sight of our own fallibility, and that we will view ourselves with a sense of perspective and a sense of humor. After all, in the New Testament even the disciples had to be taught to look first to the beam in their own eyes and only then to the mote in their neighbor's eyes.[6]

I am mindful of that counsel. I am an American and a Catholic. I love my country and treasure my faith. But I do not assume that my conception of patriotism or policy is invariably correct, or that my convictions about religion should command any greater respect than any other faith in this pluralistic society. I believe there surely is such a thing as truth, but who among us can claim a monopoly on it?

There are those who do, and their own words testify to their intolerance. For example, because the Moral Majority has worked with members of different denomination[s], one fundamentalist group has denounced Dr. Falwell for hastening the ecumenical church and for yoking together with Roman Catholics, Mormons, and others.[7] I am relieved that

---

1. Jerry H. Combee, professor of political science.

2. Jerry Falwell, president of the Moral Majority and founder of Liberty Baptist College, who spoke before Kennedy.

3. Kennedy is playing on the words of Jesus that "It is easier for a camel to go through the eye of a needle, than for a rich man to enter into the kingdom of God" (Matthew 19:24; Mark 10:25).

4. Falwell's weekly television program.

5. Kennedy had campaigned unsuccessfully for the Democratic presidential nomination in 1980. For his speech at that year's Democratic National Convention, see pages 542–548.

6. "Thou hypocrite, first cast out the beam out of thine own eye; and then shalt thou see clearly to cast out the mote out of thy brother's eye" (Matthew 7:5).

7. *The Revivalist*, December 1980, charged Falwell, among others, with "yoking together Roman Catholics, liberals, and new evangelicals and others." The reference to yoking echoes 2 Corinthians 6:14: "Be ye not unequally yoked together with unbelievers."

Dr. Falwell does not regard that as a sin—and on this issue he, himself, has become the target of narrow prejudice. When people agree on public policy, they ought to be able to work together even while they worship in diverse ways. For truly, for truly we are all yoked together as Americans, and the yoke is the happy one of individual freedom and mutual respect.

But in saying that, we cannot and should not turn aside from a deeper and more pressing question, which is whether and how religion should influence government. A generation ago, a presidential candidate had to prove his independence of undue religious influence in public life, and he had to do so partly at the insistence of the evangelical Protestants. John Kennedy said at that time, "I believe in an America where there is no religious bloc voting of any kind."[8] Only twenty years later, another candidate was appealing to a[n] evangelical meeting as a religious bloc. Ronald Reagan said to 15,000 evangelicals at the Roundtable in Dallas: "I know that you can't endorse me. I want you to know I endorse you and what you are doing."[9]

To many Americans, that pledge was a sign and a symbol of a dangerous breakdown in the separation of church and state. Yet this principle, as vital as it is, is not a simplistic and rigid command. Separation of church and state cannot mean an absolute separation between moral principles and political power. The challenge, the challenge today is to recall the origin of the principle, to define its purpose, and refine its application to the politics of the present.

The founders of our nation had long and bitter experience with the state as both the agent and the adversary of particular religious views. In colonial Maryland, Catholics paid a double land tax, and in Pennsylvania they had to list their names on a public roll—an ominous precursor to the first Nazi laws against the Jews. And Jews in turn faced discrimination in all of the thirteen original colonies.

Massachusetts exiled Roger Williams and his congregation for contending that civil government had no right to enforce the Ten Commandments.[10] Virginia harassed Baptist teachers and also established a religious test for public service, writing into the law that no "Popish followers" could hold any office.

But during the Revolution, Catholics, Jews, and nonconformists all rallied to the cause and fought valiantly for the American commonwealth, for John Winthrop's "city upon a hill."[11] Afterwards, when the Constitution was ratified and then amended, the framers gave freedom for all religion—and from any established religion—the very first place in the Bill of Rights.

Indeed, the framers themselves professed very different faiths. Washington was an Episcopalian, Jefferson a deist, and Adams a Calvinist. And although he had earlier opposed toleration, John Adams later contributed to the building of Catholic churches, and so did George Washington. Thomas Jefferson said his proudest achievement was not the presidency or the writing of the Declaration of Independence, but drafting the Virginia Statute of Religious Freedom. He stated the vision of the first Americans and the First Amendment very clearly: "The God who gave us life gave us liberty at the same time."[12]

The separation of church and state can sometimes be frustrating for women and men of religious faith. They may be tempted to misuse government in order to impose a value which they cannot persuade others to accept. But once we succumb to that temptation, we step onto a slippery slope where everyone's freedom is at risk. Those who favor censorship should recall that one of the first books ever burned was the first English translation of the Bible. As President Eisenhower warned in 1953, "Don't join the book burners.... The right to say ideas, the right to record them, and the right to have them accessible to others

---

8. Paraphrased from John F. Kennedy's September 12, 1960, address to the Greater Houston Ministerial Association (pages 333–336).

9. Reagan made his remarks on August 22, 1980; the Roundtable was a nondenominational group that supported conservative causes.

10. Banished from Massachusetts in 1636, Williams founded Providence and what subsequently became the colony of Rhode Island.

11. From Winthrop's sermon "A Model of Christian Charity" (1630).

12. From Jefferson's *Summary View of the Rights of British America* (1774).

is unquestioned, or this isn't America."[13] And if that right is denied, at some future day the torch can be turned against any other book or any other belief. Let us never forget. Today's Moral Majority could become tomorrow's persecuted minority.

The danger is as great now as when the founders of the nation first saw it. In 1789 their fear was of factional strife among dozens of denominations. Today there are hundreds, and perhaps even thousands, of faiths and millions of Americans who are outside any fold. Pluralism obviously does not and cannot mean that all of them are right, but it does mean that there are areas where government cannot and should not decide what is wrong to believe, to think, to read, and to do. As Professor Larry Tribe, one of the nation's leading constitutional scholars, has written, "Law in a nontheocratic state cannot measure religious truth"—nor can the state impose it.[14]

The real transgression occurs when religion wants government to tell citizens how to live uniquely personal parts of their lives. The failure of Prohibition proves the futility of such an attempt when a majority—or even a substantial minority—happens to disagree.[15] Some questions may be inherently individual ones or people may be sharply divided about whether they are. In such cases like Prohibition and abortion, the proper role of religion is to appeal to the conscience of the individual, not the coercive power of the state.

But there are other, but there are other questions which are inherently public in nature, which we must decide together as a nation and where religion and religious values can and should speak to our common conscience. The issue of nuclear war is a compelling example. It is a moral issue; it will be decided by government, not by each individual. And to give any effect to the moral values of their creed, people of faith must speak directly about public policy. The Catholic bishops[16] and the Reverend Billy Graham[17] have every right to stand for the nuclear freeze[18]—and Dr. Falwell has every right to stand against it.

There must be standards for the exercise of such leadership so that the obligations of belief will not be debased into an opportunity for mere political advantage. But to take a stand at all when a question is both properly public and truly moral is to stand in a long and honored tradition. Many of the great evangelists of the 1800s were in the forefront of the abolitionist movement. In our own time, the Reverend William Sloane Coffin challenged the morality of the war in Vietnam.[19] Pope John XXIII renewed the Gospel's call to social justice.[20] And Dr. Martin Luther King Jr., who was the greatest prophet of this century, awakened our nation and its conscience to the evil of racial segregation.[21]

Their words have blessed our world. And who now wishes that they had been silent? Who would bid Pope John Paul[22] to quiet his voice against the oppression in Eastern Europe, the violence in Central America, or the crying needs of the landless, the hungry, and those who are tortured in so many of the dark political prisons of our time?

13. Closely paraphrased from Eisenhower's commencement address at Dartmouth College, June 14, 1953.

14. From Tribe's *American Constitutional Law* (1978). When delivering the speech, Kennedy misspoke these words as, "Law is not theocratic in a nontheocratic state cannot measure religious truth—nor can the state impose it."

15. Prohibition went into effect in 1920 with the Eighteenth Amendment to the U.S. Constitution, which forbade "the manufacture, sale, or transportation of intoxicating liquors." It was repealed in 1933 upon passage of the Twenty-first Amendment.

16. The National Conference of Catholic Bishops.

17. The leading American evangelist of the 20th century, Graham preached during his career to live audiences of more than 200 million people in 185 countries and reached millions more via television.

18. The nuclear-freeze campaign began in 1980 and called on the United States and the Soviet Union to mutually suspend testing, producing, and deploying nuclear weapons.

19. Chaplain of Yale University from 1958 to 1975, Coffin was a major figure in the antiwar movement.

20. John XXIII served as Pope from 1958 to 1963. His 1961 encyclical, *Mater et Magistra*, advocated social reform and economic justice, and the Second Vatican Council, which he called in 1962, explored ways to renew the church in the modern world.

21. See the speeches by King on pages 375–378, 453–463, and 473–480.

22. John Paul II, elected to the papacy in 1978.

President Kennedy, who said that no religious body should seek to impose its will, also urged religious leaders to state their views and give their commitment when the public debate involved ethical issues. In drawing the line between imposed will and essential witness, we keep church and state separate, and at the same time we recognize that the City of God[23] should speak to the civic duties of men and women.

There are four tests which draw that line and define the difference.

First, we must respect the integrity of religion itself. People of conscience should be careful how they deal in the word of their Lord. In our own history, religion has been falsely invoked to sanction prejudice, even slavery, to condemn labor unions and public spending for the poor. I believe that the prophecy "the poor you have always with you"[24] is an indictment, not a commandment. And I respectfully suggest that God has taken no position on the Department of Education and that a balanced budget constitutional amendment is a matter of economic analysis and not heavenly appeals.

Religious values cannot be excluded from every public issue, but not every public issue involves religious values. And how ironic it is when those very values are denied in the name of religion. For example, we are sometimes told that it is wrong to feed the hungry, but that mission is an explicit mandate given to us in the twenty-fifth chapter of Matthew.[25]

Second, we must respect the independent judgments of conscience. Those who proclaim moral and religious values can offer counsel, but they should not casually treat a position on a public issue as a test of fealty to faith. Just as I disagree with the Catholic bishops on tuition tax credits—which I oppose—so other Catholics can and do disagree with the hierarchy, on the basis of honest conviction, on the question of the nuclear freeze.

Thus the controversy about the Moral Majority arises not only from its views, but from its name, which, in the minds of many seems to imply that only one set of public policies is moral and only one majority can possibly be right. Similarly, people are and should be perplexed when the religious lobbying group Christian Voice publishes a morality index of congressional voting records which judges the morality of Senators by their attitude towards Zimbabwe and Taiwan.

Let me offer another illustration. Dr. Falwell has written, and I quote: "To stand against Israel is to stand against God."[26] Now, there is no one in the Senate who has stood more firmly for Israel than I have. Yet I do not doubt the faith of those on the other side. Their error is not one of religion but of policy, and I hope to be able to persuade them that they are wrong in terms of both America's interest and the justice of Israel's cause.

Respect for conscience is most in jeopardy—and the harmony of our diverse society is most at risk—when we reestablish, directly or indirectly, a religious test for public office. That relic of the colonial era, which is specifically prohibited in the Constitution,[27] has reappeared in recent years. After the last election, the Reverend James Robison[28] warned President Reagan not to surround himself, as Presidents before him had, "with the counsel of the ungodly."[29] I utterly reject any such standard for any position anywhere in public service.

Two centuries ago the victims were Catholics and Jews. In the 1980s the victims could be atheists. In some other day or decade they could be the members of the Thomas Road Baptist Church.[30] Indeed,

---

23. An allusion to Augustine of Hippo's 5th-century work *The City of God Against the Pagans.*

24. John 12:8.

25. Kennedy is referring to Matthew 25:31–46.

26. From Falwell's *The Fundamentalist Phenomenon: The Resurgence of Conservative Christianity* (1981).

27. Article VI of the Constitution states that "no religious test shall ever be required as a qualification to any office or public trust under the United States."

28. Founder and president of LIFE Outreach International and host of the syndicated television program *LIFE Today.*

29. An echo of Psalm 1:1.

30. Falwell's church, which he founded in Lynchburg, Virginia, in 1956.

in 1976 I regarded it as unworthy and un-American when some people said or hinted that Jimmy Carter should not be President because he was a born-again Christian. We must never judge the fitness of individuals to govern on the base[31] of where they worship, whether they follow Christ or Moses, or whether they are called "born again" or "ungodly."

Where it is right to apply moral values to public life, let all of us avoid the temptation to be self-righteous and absolutely certain of ourselves. And if that temptation, and if that temptation ever comes, let us recall Winston Churchill's humbling description of an intolerant and inflexible colleague: "There, but for the grace of God, goes God."[32]

Third, in applying religious values, we must respect the integrity of public debate. In that debate, faith is no substitute for facts. Critics may oppose the nuclear freeze for what they regard as moral reasons. They have every right to argue that any negotiation with the Soviets is wrong, or that any accommodation with them sanctions their crimes, or that no agreement can be good enough and therefore all agreements only increase the chance of war. I do not believe that, but it surely does not violate the standard of fair public debate to say it.

What does violate that standard, what the opponents of the nuclear freeze have no right to do, is to assume that they are infallible and so any argument against the freeze will do, whether it is false or true. The nuclear-freeze proposal is not unilateral but bilateral, with equal restraints on the United States and the Soviet Union. The nuclear freeze does not require that we trust the Russians, but demands full and effective verification. The nuclear freeze does not concede a Soviet lead in nuclear weapons, but recognizes that human beings in each great power already have in their fallible hands the overwhelming capacity to remake into a pile of radioactive rubble the earth which God has made.

There is no morality, there is no morality in the mushroom cloud. The black rain of nuclear ashes will fall alike on the just and the unjust.[33] And then it will be too late to wish that we had done the real work of this atomic age—which is to seek a world that is neither Red nor dead.

I'm perfectly prepared to debate the nuclear freeze on policy grounds or moral ones. But we should not be forced to discuss phantom issues or false charges. They only deflect us from the urgent task of deciding how best to prevent a planet divided from becoming a planet destroyed.

And it does not advance the debate to contend that the arms race is more divine punishment than human problem—or that, in any event, the final days are near. As Pope John said two decades ago at the opening of the Second Vatican[34] Council, "We must beware of those who burn with zeal, but are not endowed with much sense. We must disagree with the prophets of doom, who are always forecasting disasters, as though the end of the earth was at hand."[35] The message which echoes across the years is very clear: The earth is still here, and if we wish to keep it, a prophecy of doom is no alternative to a policy of arms control.

Fourth and finally, we must respect the motives of those who exercise their right to disagree. We sorely test our ability to live together if we readily question each other's integrity. It may be harder to restrain our feelings when moral principles are at stake, for they go to the deepest wellsprings of our being. But the more our feelings diverge, the more deeply felt they are, the greater is our obligation to grant the sincerity and essential decency of our fellow citizens on the other side.

Those who favor ERA[36] are not "antifamily" or "blasphemers," and their purpose is not "an attack on the Bible." Rather, we believe this is the best way to

31. Kennedy meant to say "basis."

32. Churchill reputedly made this statement about Labor Party politician Stafford Cripps.

33. An allusion to Matthew 5:45.

34. Kennedy misspoke this word as "Vatical."

35. Loosely paraphrased from Pope John XXIII's speech of October 11, 1962.

36. Kennedy is referring to the Equal Rights Amendment providing for legal equality of the sexes. Though approved by Congress in 1971–1972, the amendment failed to achieve ratification by three-fourths of the states.

fix in our national firmament the ideal that not only all men, but all people, are created equal. Indeed, my mother, who strongly favors ERA, would be surprised to hear that she is antifamily. For my part, I think of the amendment's opponents as wrong on the issue, but not lacking in moral character.

I could multiply the instances of name-calling, sometimes on both sides. Dr. Falwell is not a "warmonger," and liberal clergymen are not, as the Moral Majority suggested in a recent letter, equivalent to "Soviet sympathizers." The critics of official prayer in public schools are not "Pharisees."[37] Many of them are both civil libertarians and believers who think that families should pray more at home with their children and attend church and synagogue more faithfully. And people are not "sexist" because they stand against abortion, and they are not "murderers" because they believe in free choice.

Nor does it help anyone, nor does it help anyone's cause to shout such epithets or to try and shout a speaker down, which is what happened last April when Dr. Falwell was hissed and heckled at Harvard.[38] So I'm doubly grateful for your courtesy here this evening. That was not Harvard's finest hour, but I'm happy to say that the loudest applause from the Harvard audience came in defense of Dr. Falwell's right to speak.

In short, I hope for an America where neither "fundamentalist" nor "humanist" will be a dirty word, but a fair description of the different ways in which people of goodwill look at life and into their own souls.

I hope for an America where no President, no public official, no individual will ever be deemed a greater or lesser American because of religious doubt or religious belief.

I hope for an America where the power of faith will always burn brightly, but where no modern Inquisition[39] of any kind will ever light the fires of fear, coercion, or angry division.

I hope for an America where we can all contend freely and vigorously, but where we will treasure and guard those standards of civility which alone make this nation safe for both democracy and diversity.

Twenty years ago this fall, in New York City, President Kennedy met for the last time with a Protestant assembly. The atmosphere had been transformed since his earlier address during the 1960 campaign to the Houston Ministerial Association.[40] He had spoken there to allay suspicions about his Catholicism and to answer those who claimed that on the day of his baptism he was somehow disqualified from becoming President. His speech in Houston, and then his election, drove that prejudice from the center of our national life.

Now, three years later, in November of 1963 he was appearing before the Protestant Council of New York City to reaffirm what he regarded as some fundamental truths. On that occasion, John Kennedy said: "The family of man is not limited to a single race or religion, to a single city or country. The family of man is nearly three billion strong. Most of its members are not white, and most of them are not Christian." And as President Kennedy reflected on that reality, he restated an ideal for which he had lived his life: that "the members of this family should be at peace with one another."[41]

That ideal shines across all the generations of our history and all the ages of our faith, carrying with it the most ancient dream. For as the Apostle Paul wrote long ago in Romans, "If it be possible, as much as it lieth in you, live peaceably with all men."[42]

I believe it is possible; the choice lies within us. As fellow citizens, let us live peaceably with each other. As fellow human beings, let us strive to live peaceably with men and women everywhere. Let that be our purpose and our prayer—yours and mine—for ourselves, for our country, and for all the world.

Thank you.

---

37. A Jewish sect discussed in the New Testament as enemies of Jesus.

38. This incident occurred when Falwell spoke at the Kennedy School of Government on April 25, 1983.

39. Notorious for its arbitrary methods and brutal punishments, the Inquisition was used by the Catholic Church to discover and eradicate heresy during the Middle Ages and early Renaissance.

---

40. JFK spoke to the Houston Ministerial Association on September 12, 1960 (pages 333–336).

41. Paraphrased from President Kennedy's speech of November 8, 1963.

42. Romans 12:18.

Ronald Reagan

⧖

Address on the Fortieth Anniversary of D-Day

POINTE DU HOC, FRANCE
JUNE 6, 1984

O N JUNE 6, 1944, Allied forces under the command of General Dwight D. Eisenhower launched Operation Overlord, the invasion of Europe that would result eleven months later in the defeat of Nazi Germany. At Normandy, France, a force of more than 150,000 men stormed the beaches, led by Ranger battalions whose job was to scale the hundred-foot-high cliffs to Pointe du Hoc and take out the German guns positioned there. Forty years later, standing on that promontory overlooking Omaha Beach and the English Channel, in front of a granite monument honoring the U.S. Army's Second Ranger Battalion, Ronald Reagan delivered one of the most inspiring presidential speeches in American history.

The immediate audience was composed largely of World War II veterans and their families, including sixty-two surviving Rangers from the assault at Pointe du Hoc. Reagan's primary purpose was to commemorate their valor and heroism, but like the aged Revolutionary War veterans at Daniel Webster's first Bunker Hill Address fifty years after the battles of Lexington and Concord, their presence became part of the rhetorical event itself. "These," said Reagan, "are the boys of Pointe du Hoc. These are the men who took the cliffs. These are the champions who helped free a continent. And these are the heroes who helped end a war." Addressing the soldiers directly, he stated: "You were young the day you took these cliffs. Some of you were hardly more than boys, with the deepest joys of life before you. Yet you risked everything here."

Penned primarily by Peggy Noonan, who would later be the chief architect of Reagan's eulogy to the *Challenger* astronauts (pages 611–612), the words were worthy of the epochal event they commemorated. The emotion they generated among those at the scene was shared by millions of Americans who saw the speech on television. (Originally scheduled for late afternoon, it was moved forward three hours so it could be broadcast live on the U.S. morning news shows.) With the cameras cutting between Reagan's words and the tear-streaked faces of the veterans seated in front of him, the speech helped reawaken America to the gallantry and glory of the soldiers who fought and won World War II. In the next decade a spate of books and movies would apotheosize what Tom Brokaw called the Greatest Generation, replacing in public memory the bitter legacy of Vietnam with the warm luster of the noble battle for freedom during World War II.

Like another great presidential discourse delivered at a wartime cemetery, Reagan's speech at Pointe du Hoc also included a lesson for the future. The task of Americans during the Civil War was, in Abraham's Lincoln's immortal locution at Gettysburg, to dedicate themselves to ensuring that "government of the people, by the people, for the people shall not perish from the earth." The task of Americans and the European democracies during the Cold War, Reagan declared, was to stand fast against Soviet dictatorship with the same unity and sense of purpose that had turned the tide of history on D-Day: "Here, in this place where the West held together, let us make a vow to our dead.... Strengthened by their courage, heartened by their value, and borne by their memory, let us continue to stand for the ideals for which they lived and died." As historian David Brinkley has pointed out, Reagan's affinity for "monumental pro-democracy eloquence" was inspired by Franklin Roosevelt. Its roots, however, lay deep in the American tradition.

◇◇

We're here to mark that day in history when the Allied armies joined in battle to reclaim this continent to liberty. For four long years, much of Europe had been under a terrible shadow. Free nations had fallen, Jews cried out in the camps, millions cried out for liberation. Europe was enslaved, and the world prayed for its rescue. Here in Normandy the rescue began. Here the Allies stood and fought against tyranny in a giant undertaking unparalleled in human history.

We stand on a lonely, windswept point on the northern shore of France. The air is soft, but forty years ago at this moment, the air was dense with smoke and the cries of men, and the air was filled with the crack of rifle fire and the roar of cannon. At dawn on the morning of the sixth of June, 1944, 225 Rangers jumped off the British landing craft and ran to the bottom of these cliffs.[1] Their mission was one of the most difficult and daring of the invasion: to climb these sheer and desolate cliffs and take out the enemy guns. The Allies had been told that some of the mightiest of these guns were here and they would be trained on the beaches to stop the Allied advance.

The Rangers looked up and saw the enemy soldiers [at] the edge of the cliffs shooting down at them with machine guns and throwing grenades. And the American Rangers began to climb. They shot rope ladders over the face of these cliffs and began to pull themselves up. When one Ranger fell, another would take his place. When one rope was cut, a Ranger would grab another and begin his climb again. They climbed, shot back, and held their footing. Soon, one by one, the Rangers pulled themselves over the top, and in seizing the firm land at the top of these cliffs, they began to seize back the continent of Europe. Two hundred and twenty-five came here. After two days of fighting, only ninety could still bear arms.

Behind me is a memorial that symbolizes the Ranger daggers that were thrust into the top of these cliffs. And before me are the men who put them there. These are the boys of Pointe du Hoc. These are the men who took the cliffs. These are the champions who helped free a continent. And these are the heroes who helped end a war. Gentlemen, I look at you and I think of the words of Stephen Spender's poem. You are men who in your, quote, "lives fought for life... and left the vivid air signed with your honor."[2]

I think I know what you may be thinking right now—thinking we were just part of a bigger effort; everyone was brave that day. Well, everyone was.

---

1. Because of accidents that sank two craft before they could reach the beach, only about 180 Rangers actually landed at Pointe du Hoc.

2. From Spender's "I Think Continually of Those Who Were Truly Great." Reagan changed the penultimate word from "their" to "your."

Do you remember the story of Bill Millin of the 51st Highlanders?[3] Forty years ago today, British troops were pinned down near a bridge,[4] waiting desperately for help. Suddenly, they heard the sound of bagpipes, and some thought they were dreaming. Well, they weren't. They looked up and saw Bill Millin with his bagpipes, leading the reinforcements and ignoring the smack of the bullets into the ground around him.

Lord Lovat[5] was with him—Lord Lovat of Scotland, who calmly announced when he got to the bridge, "Sorry, I'm a few minutes late," as if he'd been delayed by a traffic jam, when in truth he'd just come from the bloody fighting on Sword Beach, which he and his men had just taken.

There was the impossible valor of the Poles, who threw themselves between the enemy and the rest of Europe as the invasion took hold, and the unsurpassed courage of the Canadians, who had already seen the horrors of war on this coast. They knew what awaited them there, but they would not be deterred. And once they hit Juno Beach, they never looked back.

All of these men were part of a roll call of honor with names that spoke of a pride as bright as the colors they bore: the Royal Winnipeg Rifles, Poland's 24th Lancers, the Royal Scots Fusiliers, the Screaming Eagles, the Yeomen of England's armored divisions, the forces of Free France, the Coast Guard's "Matchbox Fleet," and you, the American Rangers.

Forty summers have passed since the battle that you fought here. You were young the day you took these cliffs; some of you were hardly more than boys, with the deepest joys of life before you. Yet you risked everything here. Why? Why did you do it? What impelled you to put aside the instinct for self-preservation and risk your lives to take these cliffs? What inspired all the men of the armies that

met here? We look at you and somehow we know the answer. It was faith and belief; it was loyalty and love.

The men of Normandy had faith that what they were doing was right, faith that they fought for all humanity, faith that a just God would grant them mercy on this beachhead or on the next. It was the deep knowledge—and pray God we have not lost it—that there is a profound moral difference between the use of force for liberation and the use of force for conquest. You were here to liberate, not to conquer, and so you and those others did not doubt your cause. And you were right not to doubt.

You all knew that some things are worth dying for. One's country is worth dying for, and democracy is worth dying for, because it's the most deeply honorable form of government ever devised by man. All of you loved liberty. All of you were willing to fight tyranny, and you knew the people of your countries were behind you.

The Americans who fought here that morning knew word of the invasion was spreading through the darkness back home. They fought—or felt—in their hearts, though they couldn't know in fact—that in Georgia they were filling the churches at 4:00 a.m., in Kansas they were kneeling on their porches and praying, and in Philadelphia they were ringing the Liberty Bell.

Something else helped the men of D-Day: their rock-hard belief that Providence would have a great hand in the events that would unfold here, that God was an ally in this great cause. And so the night before the invasion, when Colonel Wolverton[6] asked his parachute troops to kneel with him in prayer, he told them: Do not bow your heads, but look up so you can see God and ask his blessing in what we're about to do. Also that night, General Matthew Ridgway[7] on his cot, listening in the darkness for the promise God made to Joshua: "I will not fail thee, nor forsake thee."[8]

---

3. Bagpiper for the 1st Special Service Brigade, under the command of Lord Lovat.

4. Pegasus Bridge, where the 2nd Battalion of the Oxfordshire and Buckinghamshire Light Infantry Regiment, British 6th Airborne Division, awaited reinforcements.

5. Commander of the 1st Special Service Brigade, who defied orders from the British War Office banning bagpipers in combat.

6. Lt. Colonel Robert Wolverton, commander of the 3rd Battalion of the 506th Parachute Infantry Regiment, 101st Airborne Division, was killed on D-Day.

7. Commander of the 82nd Airborne Division on D-Day; he later became Chief of Staff of the U.S. Army.

8. Joshua 1:5.

These are the things that impelled them; these are the things that shaped the unity of the Allies.

When the war was over, there were lives to be rebuilt and governments to be returned to the people. There were nations to be reborn. Above all, there was a new peace to be assured. These were huge and daunting tasks. But the Allies summoned strength from the faith, belief, loyalty, and love of those who fell here. They rebuilt a new Europe together.

There was first a great reconciliation among those who had been enemies, all of whom had suffered so greatly. The United States did its part, creating the Marshall Plan[9] to help rebuild our allies and our former enemies. The Marshall Plan led to the Atlantic alliance—a great alliance that serves to this day as our shield for freedom, for prosperity, and for peace.[10]

In spite of our great efforts and successes, not all that followed the end of the war was happy or planned. Some liberated countries were lost. The great sadness of this loss echoes down to our own time in the streets of Warsaw, Prague, and East Berlin. Soviet troops that came to the center of this continent did not leave when peace came. They're still there, uninvited, unwanted, unyielding, almost forty years after the war. Because of this, Allied forces still stand on this continent. Today, as forty years ago, our armies are here for only one purpose—to protect and defend democracy. The only territories we hold are memorials like this one and graveyards where our heroes rest.[11]

We in America have learned bitter lessons from two world wars: It is better to be here ready to protect the peace than to take blind shelter across the sea, rushing to respond only after freedom is lost. We've learned that isolationism never was and never will be an acceptable response to tyrannical governments with an expansionist intent.

But we try always to be prepared for peace, prepared to deter aggression, prepared to negotiate the reduction of arms, and, yes, prepared to reach out again in the spirit of reconciliation. In truth, there is no reconciliation we would welcome more than a reconciliation with the Soviet Union, so together we can lessen the risks of war, now and forever.

It's fitting to remember here the great losses also suffered by the Russian people during World War II. Twenty million perished, a terrible price that testifies to all the world the necessity of ending war. I tell you from my heart that we in the United States do not want war. We want to wipe from the face of the earth the terrible weapons that man now has in his hands. And I tell you we are ready to seize that beachhead. We look for some sign from the Soviet Union that they are willing to move forward, that they share our desire and love for peace, and that they will give up the ways of conquest. There must be a changing there that will allow us to turn our hope into action.

We will pray forever that someday that changing will come. But for now, particularly today, it is good and fitting[12] to renew our commitment to each other, to our freedom, and to the alliance that protects it. We are bound today by what bound us forty years ago—the same loyalties, traditions, and beliefs. We're bound by reality. The strength of America's allies is vital to the United States, and the American security guarantee is essential to the continued freedom of Europe's democracies. We were with you then; we are with you now. Your hopes are our hopes and your destiny is our destiny.

Here, in this place where the West held together, let us make a vow to our dead. Let us show them by our actions that we understand what they died for. Let our actions say to them the words for which Matthew Ridgway listened: "I will not fail thee, nor forsake thee." Strengthened by their courage, heartened by their valor,[13] and borne by their memory, let us continue to stand for the ideals for which they lived and died.

Thank you very much, and God bless you all.

---

9. Popular name for the European Economic Recovery Program that helped rebuild Europe after World War II. It was unveiled by Secretary of State George C. Marshall in a June 5, 1947, speech at Harvard University (pages 276–279).

10. Reagan is referring to the North Atlantic Treaty Organization (NATO), the military alliance between North America and Western Europe created after World War II to block Soviet aggression in Europe.

11. There are 20 permanent U.S. cemeteries in Europe for soldiers killed in World War I or World War II.

---

12. An allusion to "fitting and proper" from Abraham Lincoln's Gettysburg Address, November 19, 1863.

13. Reagan misspoke this word as "value."

Mario Cuomo

A Tale of Two Cities

SAN FRANCISCO, CALIFORNIA
JULY 17, 1984

HE HAD TROUBLE speaking English until he was eight years old, but Mario Cuomo went on to become one of the best political orators of the late twentieth century. After being elected Governor of New York in 1982, he came to national prominence as a result of his keynote speech at the 1984 Democratic National Convention, which was praised by conservative and liberal commentators alike. William Safire called it the best-delivered keynote since Alben Barkley's rousing address of 1948 won him the Democrats' vice-presidential nomination. Anthony Lewis said the speech "was as electrifying as any I remember, and I have been going to political conventions for thirty years." The *New York Times* called it a "brilliant performance, with every word, gesture, expression, and pause in harmony."

Cuomo patterned the speech partly on his 1982 gubernatorial inaugural address, which sounded the same themes of family, compassion, and the responsibility of government to help those who, through no fault of their own, cannot provide for themselves. Unlike an inaugural, however, which marks the start of a new administration after an election, a keynote must sound the tocsin for the campaign ahead. Cuomo did so by taking as his text President Ronald Reagan's words that the United States was "a shining city on a hill." This was one of Reagan's favorite expressions, and he used it in any number of speeches. Cuomo countered with his own view of America, drawn from the title of Charles Dickens's 1859 novel *A Tale of Two Cities*.

It was a brilliant move, totally out of keeping with the banalities of most keynotes, and it provided a framework for everything that followed. As the speech progressed, Cuomo subjected Reagan's policies to a barrage of predictable Democratic criticisms, but he coupled the criticisms with a passionate call for Democrats to unite around their historic mission of making America "one city, indivisible, shining for all of its people." In Cuomo's vision, no one in the American family needed to be left out; rather than emphasizing survival of the fittest, society would best be served by "mutuality, the sharing of benefits and burdens for the good of all." He concluded, as he had in his inaugural address of two years earlier, by turning to the experience of his own family. But whereas in that speech he had talked about his mother, here he presented his father as a symbol of democracy, the American dream, the principles of the Democratic Party, and the "struggle to live with dignity" that constituted "the real story of the shining city."

As with all his major speeches, Cuomo wrote the keynote himself, and it was a deeply personal statement of political belief as well as a call to party unity and action. Afterward, he downplayed it by saying, "It wasn't a great speech, a powerful speech, but it was exactly what they wanted to hear." His wife, Matilda, was closer to the mark when she said, "He spilled his guts out in that speech.... You can't forget a person who says those things and believes them with all his heart and soul."

◇◇

Thank you very much. On behalf of the great Empire State and the whole family of New York, let me thank you for the great privilege of being able to address this convention. Please allow me to skip the stories and the poetry and the temptation to deal in nice but vague rhetoric. Let me instead use this valuable opportunity to deal immediately with the questions that should determine this election and that we all know are vital to the American people.

Ten days ago President Reagan admitted that although some people in this country seemed to be doing well nowadays, others were unhappy, even worried, about themselves, their families, and their futures. The President said that he didn't understand that fear. He said, "Why, this country is a shining city on a hill."[1] And the President is right. In many ways we are a shining city on a hill. But the hard truth is that not everyone is sharing in this city's splendor and glory. A shining city is perhaps all the President sees from the portico of the White House and the veranda of his ranch,[2] where everyone seems to be doing well.

But there's another city, there's another part to the shining city, the part where some people can't pay their mortgages and most young people can't afford one, where students can't afford the education they need and middle-class parents watch the dreams they hold for their children evaporate. In this part of the city, there are more poor than ever, more families in trouble, more and more people who need help but can't find it. Even worse, there are elderly people who tremble in the basements of the houses there, and there are people who sleep in the city's streets, in the gutter, where the glitter doesn't show. There are ghettos where thousands of young people without a job or an education give their lives away to drug dealers every day.

There is despair, Mr. President, in the faces that you don't see, in the places that you don't visit in your shining city. In fact, Mr. President, this is a nation— Mr. President, you ought to know that this nation is more a "Tale of Two Cities"[3] than it is just a "shining city on a hill."

Maybe, maybe, Mr. President, if you visited some more places. Maybe if you went to Appalachia, where some people still live in sheds. Maybe if you went to Lackawanna,[4] where thousands of unemployed steelworkers wonder why we subsidize foreign steel. Maybe, maybe, Mr. President, if you stopped in at a shelter in Chicago and spoke to the homeless there. Maybe, Mr. President, if you asked a woman who had been denied the help she needed to feed her children because you said you needed the money for a tax break for a millionaire or for a missile we couldn't afford to use.

---

1. Paraphrased from Reagan's speech to the Texas State Bar Association, July 6, 1984. Based on an allusion to Matthew 5:14, the notion of America as a "city on a hill" originated in John Winthrop's 1630 sermon "A Model of Christian Charity," preached on board the *Arbella* as it sailed toward the New World. Reagan used the locution many times during his presidency.

2. Cuomo is referring to Reagan's California ranch, which served as the Western White House when he was away from Washington, D.C.

3. Cuomo is borrowing from the title of Charles Dickens's 1859 novel.

4. City in New York State where the closure of the Bethlehem Steel plant in 1983 eliminated more than 7,000 jobs among a population of 21,700 people.

Maybe, maybe, Mr. President, but I'm afraid not. Because the truth is, ladies and gentlemen, that this is how we were warned it would be. President Reagan told us from the very beginning that he believed in a kind of Social Darwinism,[5] survival of the fittest.[6] Government can't do everything, we were told, so it should settle for taking care of the strong and hope that economic ambition and charity will do the rest. Make the rich richer and what falls from the table[7] will be enough for the middle class and those who are trying desperately to work their way into the middle class.

You know, the Republicans called it "trickle-down" when Hoover[8] tried it. Now they call it "supply-side."[9] But it's the same shining city for those relative few who are lucky enough to live in its good neighborhoods. But for the people who are excluded, for the people who are locked out, all they can do is stare from a distance at that city's glimmering towers.

It's an old story; it's as old as our history. The difference between Democrats and Republicans has always been measured in courage and confidence. The Republicans, the Republicans believe that the wagon train will not make it to the frontier unless some of the old, some of the young, some of the weak are left behind by the side of the trail. The strong—the strong, they tell us—will inherit the land.[10]

We Democrats believe in something else. We Democrats believe that we can make it all the way

with the whole family intact. And we have more than once—ever since Franklin Roosevelt lifted himself from his wheelchair to lift this nation from its knees.[11] Wagon train after wagon train to new frontiers[12] of education, housing, peace. The whole family aboard. Constantly reaching out to extend and enlarge that family. Lifting them up into the wagon on the way—blacks and Hispanics and people of every ethnic group and Native Americans, all those struggling to build their families and claim some small share of America.

For nearly fifty years we carried them all to new levels of comfort and security and dignity, even affluence. And remember this: Some of us in this room today are here only because this nation had that kind of confidence, and it would be wrong to forget that.

So here we are at this convention to remind ourselves where we come from and to claim the future for ourselves and for our children. Today our great Democratic Party, which has saved this nation from depression, from fascism, from racism, from corruption, is called upon to do it again—this time to save the nation from confusion and division, from the threat of eventual fiscal disaster, and, most of all, from the fear of a nuclear holocaust.

That's not going to be easy. Mo Udall[13] is exactly right: It won't be easy. And in order to succeed, we must answer our opponent's polished and appealing rhetoric with a more telling reasonableness and rationality. We must win this case on the merits. We must get the American public to look past the glitter, beyond the showmanship, to the reality, the hard substance of things. And we'll do it not so much with speeches that sound good as with speeches that are good and sound. Not so much with speeches that will bring people to their feet as with speeches that will bring people to their senses.

We must make, we must make the American people hear our "Tale of Two Cities." We must

5. A philosophy developed during the 19th century holding that Charles Darwin's theory of evolution in the natural world can be applied to human society.

6. Usually attributed to Charles Darwin, this famous phrase was coined by Herbert Spencer in his *Principles of Biology* (1864–1867).

7. An allusion to Luke 16:21, in which the beggar Lazarus desired to eat "the crumbs which fell from the rich man's table."

8. Herbert Hoover, President of the United States, 1929–1933, who was in office when the Great Depression began.

9. Supply-side economics, which called for reducing high marginal tax rates, was at the heart of economic policy during Reagan's presidency.

10. An inversion of Matthew 5:5: "Blessed are the meek: for they shall inherit the earth."

11. Cuomo is referring to President Roosevelt's efforts to combat the Great Depression.

12. An allusion to the theme of John F. Kennedy's presidential campaign and administration.

13. U.S. Congressman Morris K. Udall, who addressed the convention earlier on the evening of Cuomo's speech.

convince them that we don't have to settle for two cities, that we can have one city, indivisible,[14] shining for all of its people.

Now, we will have no chance to do that if what comes out of this convention is a babble of arguing voices. If that's what's heard throughout the campaign, dissonant sounds from all sides, we will have no chance to tell our message. To succeed we will have to surrender some small parts of our individual interests to build a platform that we can all stand on at once, and comfortably, proudly singing out. We need a platform we can all agree to so that we can sing out the truth for the nation to hear, in chorus, its logic so clear and commanding that no slick Madison Avenue commercial, no amount of geniality, no martial music will be able to muffle the sound of the truth.

And we Democrats must unite, we Democrats must unite so that the entire nation can unite, because surely the Republicans won't bring this country together. Their policies divide the nation into the lucky and the left out, into the royalty and the rabble. The Republicans are willing to treat that division as victory. They would cut this nation in half, into those temporarily better off and those worse off than before, and they would call that division "recovery."

Now, we should not, we should not be embarrassed or dismayed or chagrined if the process of unifying is difficult, even wrenching at times. Remember that, unlike any other party, we embrace men and women of every color, every creed, every orientation, every economic class. In our family are gathered everyone from the abject poor of Essex County in New York to the enlightened affluent of the gold coasts at both ends of the nation. And in between is the heart of our constituency, the middle class—the people not rich enough to be worry-free but not poor enough to be on welfare. The middle class—those people who work for a living because they have to, not because some psychiatrist told them it was a convenient way to fill the interval between birth and eternity. White collar and blue collar, young professionals, men and women in small business, desperate for the capital and contracts that they need to prove their worth.

We speak for the minorities who have not yet entered the mainstream. We speak for ethnics who want to add their culture to the magnificent mosaic that is America.

We speak, we speak for women who are indignant that this nation refuses to etch into its governmental commandments the simple rule, "Thou shalt not sin against equality." A rule so simple, I was going to say, and I perhaps dare not, but I will: It's a commandment so simple it can be spelled in three letters—ERA.[15]

We speak, we speak for young people demanding an education and a future. We speak for senior citizens, we speak for senior citizens who are terrorized by the idea that their only security, their Social Security, is being threatened. We speak for millions of reasoning people fighting to preserve our environment from greed and from stupidity.

And we speak for reasonable people who are fighting to preserve our very existence from a macho intransigence that refuses to make intelligent attempts to discuss the possibility of nuclear holocaust with our enemy. They refuse, they refuse because they believe we can pile missiles so high that they will pierce the clouds and the sight of them will frighten our enemies into submission.

Now, we're proud of this diversity as Democrats. We're grateful for it. We don't have to manufacture it the way the Republicans will next month in Dallas[16] by propping up mannequin delegates on the convention floor.

But we, while we're proud of this diversity, we pay a price for it. The different people that we represent have different points of view, and sometimes they compete, and even debate, and even argue. That's what our primaries were all about. But now the primaries are over, and it is time when we pick our candidates and our platform here to lock arms and move into this campaign together.

---

14. An echo of the Pledge of Allegiance, which refers to "one nation, indivisible."

15. Cuomo is referring to the Equal Rights Amendment providing for legal equality of the sexes. Although approved by Congress in 1971–1972, the amendment failed to achieve ratification by three-fourths of the states.

16. The Republican National Convention met in Dallas, Texas, August 20–23.

If you need any more inspiration to put some small part of your own difference aside to create this consensus, then all you need to do is to reflect on what the Republican policy of divide and cajole has done to this land since 1980. Now, the President has asked the American people to judge him on whether or not he's fulfilled the promises he made four years ago. I believe, as Democrats, we ought to accept that challenge, and just for a moment let us consider what he has said and what he's done.

Inflation, inflation is down since 1980, but not because of the supply-side miracle promised to us by the President. Inflation was reduced the old-fashioned way, with a recession, the worst since 1932. Now, how did we—we could've brought inflation down that way. How did he do it? Fifty-five thousand bankruptcies, two years of massive unemployment, 250,000 farmers and ranchers forced off the land, more homeless, more homeless than at any time since the Great Depression in 1932. More hungry in this world of enormous affluence, the United States of America, more hungry, more poor, most of them women.

And, and he paid one other thing—a nearly $200 billion deficit threatening our future. Now, we must make the American people understand this deficit, because they don't. The President's deficit is a direct and dramatic repudiation of his promise in 1980 to balance the budget by 1983.

How large is it? The deficit is the largest in the history of the universe. President Carter's last budget had a deficit less than one-third of this deficit.[17] It is a deficit that, according to the President's own fiscal advisor, may grow to as much as $300 billion a year for as far as the eye can see.[18] And, ladies and gentlemen, it is a debt so large that almost one-half of the money we collect from the personal income tax each year goes just to pay the interest. It is a

mortgage on our children's future that can be paid only in pain and that could bring this nation to its knees.

Now, don't take my word for it. I'm a Democrat. Ask the Republican investment bankers on Wall Street what they think the chances of this recovery being permanent are. You see, if they're not too embarrassed to tell you the truth, they'll say that they're appalled and frightened by the President's deficit. Ask them what they think of our economy now that it's been driven by the distorted value of the dollar back to its colonial condition, now [that] we're exporting agricultural products and importing manufactured ones. Ask those Republican investment bankers what they expect the rate of interest to be a year from now. And ask them; if they dare tell you the truth, you'll learn from them what they predict for the inflation rate a year from now because of the deficit.

Now, how important is this question of the deficit? Think about it practically. What chance would the Republican candidate have had in 1980 if he had told the American people that he intended to pay for his so-called economic recovery with bankruptcies, unemployment, more homeless, more hungry, and the largest government debt known to humankind? If he had told the voters in 1980 that truth, would American voters have signed the loan certificate for him on election day? Of course not. That was an election won under false pretenses. It was won with smoke and mirrors and illusions, and that's the kind of recovery we have now as well.

Now, what about foreign policy? They said that they would make us and the whole world safer. They say they have. By creating the largest defense budget in history, one that even they now admit is excessive. By escalating to a frenzy the nuclear arms race. By incendiary rhetoric. By refusing to discuss peace with our enemies. By the loss of 279 young Americans in Lebanon in pursuit of a plan and a policy that no one can find or describe.[19]

---

17. Jimmy Carter served as President from 1977 to 1981.

18. Testifying before the House of Representatives Budget Committee in February 1984, Martin S. Feldstein, Chairman of the Council of Economic Advisors, said the annual budget deficit could grow to more than $300 billion by the end of the decade, depending on economic conditions.

---

19. American military personnel were in Lebanon as part of a multinational force from August 1982 to February 1984. Most of the deaths occurred on October 23, 1983, when 241 marines were killed by a truck-bomb attack on their barracks in Beirut.

We give money to Latin American governments that murder nuns and then we lie about it.[20] We have been less than zealous in support of our only real friend, it seems to me, in the Middle East, the one democracy there, our flesh-and-blood ally, the state of Israel. Our, our policy, our foreign policy drifts with no real direction other than an hysterical commitment to an arms race that leads nowhere if we're lucky, and if we're not, it could lead us into bankruptcy or war.

Of course, we must have a strong defense. Of course, Democrats are for a strong defense. Of course, Democrats believe that there are times that we must stand and fight. And we have. Thousands of us have paid for freedom with our lives. But always, when this country has been at its best, our purposes were clear. Now they're not. Now our allies are as confused as our enemies. Now we have no real commitment to our friends or to our ideals—not to human rights, not to the refuseniks,[21] not to Sakharov,[22] not to Bishop Tutu[23] and the others struggling for freedom in South Africa.

We, we have in the last few years spent more than we can afford. We have pounded our chests and made bold speeches. But we lost 279 young Americans in Lebanon and we live behind sandbags in Washington. How can anyone say that we are safer, stronger, or better?

That, that is the Republican record. That its disastrous quality is not more fully understood by the American people I can only attribute to the President's amiability and the failure by some to separate the salesman from the product. And now, now, now it's up to us. Now it's up to you and to me to make the case to America and to remind Americans that if they are not happy with all that the President has done so far, they should consider how much worse it will be if he is left to his radical proclivities for another four years unrestrained—unrestrained.

Now if, if July, if July brings back Anne Gorsuch Burford,[24] what can we expect of December? Where would, where would another four years take us? Where would four years more take us? How much larger will the deficit be? How much deeper the cuts in programs for the struggling middle class and the poor to limit that deficit? How high will the interest rates be? How much more acid rain killing our forests and fouling our lakes?

And, ladies and gentlemen, please think of this, the nation must think of this: What kind of Supreme Court will we have? We, we must ask ourselves what kind of court and country will be fashioned by the man who believes in having government mandate people's religion and morality. The man who believes that trees pollute the environment. The man that believes that the laws against discrimination against people go too far. A man who threatens Social Security and Medicaid and help for the disabled.

How high will we pile the missiles? How much deeper will the gulf be between us and our enemies? And, ladies and gentlemen, will four years more make meaner the spirit of the American people?

This election will measure the record of the past four years. But more than that, it will answer the question of what kind of people we want to be. We Democrats still have a dream.[25] We still believe in this nation's future, and this is our answer to the question. This is our credo:

We believe in only the government we need, but we insist on all the government we need.

We believe in a government that is characterized by fairness and reasonableness, a reasonableness that

---

20. In December 1980, during the presidency of Jimmy Carter, three American nuns and one lay missionary were murdered by military death squads during the civil war in El Salvador. Cuomo is criticizing Reagan for providing covert support to the Salvadoran government.

21. Russian Jews who were denied permission to emigrate by Soviet authorities.

22. Andrei Sakharov, Russian dissident and Nobel Peace Prize winner who was under internal exile in the Soviet Union.

23. Desmond Tutu, Anglican Archbishop of Cape Town and a leader in the battle against apartheid.

24. Director of the Environmental Protection Agency who resigned in March 1983 because of scandals in the agency; 12 days before Cuomo's speech, President Reagan appointed her to chair the National Advisory Committee on Oceans and Atmosphere.

25. Cuomo is identifying with Martin Luther King's "I Have a Dream" speech of August 28, 1963 (pages 375–378).

goes beyond labels, that doesn't distort or promise to do things that we know we can't do.

We believe in a government strong enough to use words like "love" and "compassion" and smart enough to convert our noblest aspirations into practical realities.

We believe in encouraging the talented, but we believe that while survival of the fittest may be a good working description of the process of evolution, a government of humans should elevate itself to a higher order. We, our, our government, our government should be able to rise to the level where it can fill the gaps that are left by chance or by a wisdom we don't fully understand. We would rather have laws written by the patron of this great city, the man called the world's most sincere democrat, St. Francis of Assisi,[26] than laws written by Darwin.[27]

We believe, we believe as Democrats that a society as blessed as ours, the most affluent democracy in the world's history, one that can spend trillions on instruments of destruction, ought to be able to help the middle class in its struggle, ought to be able to find work for all who can do it, room at the table, shelter for the homeless, care for the elderly and infirm, and hope for the destitute. And we proclaim as loudly as we can the utter insanity of nuclear proliferation and the need for a nuclear freeze,[28] if only to affirm the simple truth that peace is better than war because life is better than death.

We believe in firm, we believe in firm but fair law and order.

We believe proudly in the union movement.

We believe, we believe in privacy for people, openness by government.

And we believe in civil rights, and we believe in human rights.

We believe in a single, we believe in a single fundamental idea that describes better than most

textbooks, and any speech that I could write, what a proper government should be—the idea of family. Mutuality. The sharing of benefits and burdens for the good of all. Feeling one another's pain. Sharing one another's blessings. Reasonably, honestly, fairly, without respect to race or sex or geography or political affiliation.

We believe we must be the family of America, recognizing that at the heart of the matter we are bound one to another. That the problems of a retired schoolteacher in Duluth are our problems. That the future of the child, that the future of the child in Buffalo is our future, that the struggle of a disabled man in Boston to survive and live decently is our struggle. That the hunger of a woman in Little Rock is our hunger. That the failure anywhere to provide what reasonably we might to avoid pain is our failure.

Now, for fifty years, for fifty years we Democrats created a better future for our children using traditional democratic principles as a fixed beacon, giving us direction and purpose but constantly innovating, adapting to new realities: Roosevelt's alphabet programs,[29] Truman's NATO[30] and the GI Bill of Rights,[31] Kennedy's intelligent tax incentives[32] and the Alliance for Progress,[33] Johnson's civil rights,[34] Carter's human rights and the nearly miraculous Camp David Peace Accord.[35] Democrats did it. Democrats did it, and Democrats can do it again.

We can build a future that deals with our deficit. Remember this: that fifty years of progress under

---

26. Founder of the Franciscan Order in the 13th century.

27. Charles Darwin (1809–1882), foremost proponent of the theory of evolution; also see notes 5–6 above.

28. The nuclear-freeze campaign called on the United States and the Soviet Union to mutually suspend testing, producing, and deploying nuclear weapons.

29. Cuomo is referring to the many programs instituted by President Franklin Roosevelt during the Great Depression that came to be known by their acronyms.

30. North Atlantic Treaty Organization, established in 1949 during the administration of President Harry S. Truman.

31. Program that provided educational benefits and low-interest housing loans for veterans returning from World War II.

32. President Kennedy introduced tax-reform proposals in 1963.

33. U.S. assistance program for Latin America begun in 1961.

34. Cuomo is referring to the 1964 Civil Rights Act and the 1965 Voting Rights Act signed by President Lyndon B. Johnson.

35. September 1978 peace agreement between Israel and Egypt mediated by President Jimmy Carter.

our principles never cost us what the last four years of stagnation have. And we can deal with the deficit intelligently, by shared sacrifice, with all parts in the nation's family contributing, building partnerships with the private sector, providing a sound defense without depriving ourselves of what we need to feed our children and care for our people. We can have a future that provides for all the young of the present by marrying common sense and compassion.

We know we can because we did it for nearly fifty years before 1980. And we can do it again if we do not forget, if we do not forget that this entire nation has profited by these progressive principles. That they helped lift up generations to the middle class and higher. That they gave us a chance to work, to go to college, to raise a family, to own a house, to be secure in our old age, and before that to reach heights that our own parents would not have dared dream of.

That struggle to live with dignity is the real story of the shining city. And it's a story, ladies and gentlemen, that I didn't read in a book or learn in a classroom. I saw it and lived it. Like many of you.

I watched a small man with thick calluses on both his hands work fifteen and sixteen hours a day. I saw him once literally bleed from the bottoms of his feet, a man who came here uneducated, alone, unable to speak the language, who taught me all I needed to know about faith and hard work by the simple eloquence of his example. I learned about our kind of democracy from my father.

And I learned about our obligation to each other from him and my mother. They asked only for a chance to work and to make the world better for their children, and they, they asked to be protected in those moments when they would not be able to protect themselves. This nation and this nation's government did that for them. And that they were able to build a family and live in dignity and see one of their children go from behind their little grocery store in South Jamaica,[36] on the other side of the tracks, where he was born, to occupy the highest seat in the greatest state in the greatest nation in the only world we know is an ineffably beautiful tribute to the democratic process.

And, and, ladies and gentlemen, on January 20, 1985,[37] it will happen again—only on a much, much grander scale. We will have a new President of the United States, a Democrat born not to the blood of kings but to the blood of pioneers and immigrants. And we will have America's first woman Vice President,[38] the child of immigrants, and she, she, she will open with one magnificent stroke a whole new frontier for the United States.

Now, it will happen, it will happen if we make it happen, if you and I make it happen. And I ask you now, ladies and gentlemen, brothers and sisters, for the good of all of us, for the love of this great nation, for the family of America, for the love of God, please make this nation remember how futures are built.

Thank you, and God bless you.

---

36. New York City neighborhood where Cuomo was raised.

37. Presidential inauguration date.

38. Cuomo is referring to the Democratic Party's vice-presidential nominee, Geraldine Ferraro.

Jesse Jackson

⧖

The Rainbow Coalition

San Francisco, California
July 18, 1984

B Y THE 1980s, Jesse Jackson had become the best-known African American leader since Martin Luther King. After working with King's Southern Christian Leadership Conference during the late 1960s, in 1971 Jackson started his own organization, People United to Save Humanity (PUSH), which began as a social ministry focusing on economic justice and empowerment but soon expanded to include nationwide rallies at inner-city schools promoting discipline, self-reliance, and educational excellence. Looking beyond the domestic horizon, Jackson traveled in 1979 to South Africa, where he was greeted by huge crowds. Trips to the Middle East and Western Europe followed, with Jackson gaining visibility and public stature at every step. In November 1983, at age forty-two and without having held any previous elective office, he announced his candidacy for President of the United States.

Despite starting late and having a ramshackle campaign organization, Jackson fared better than even he had predicted. Combining progressive political programs with Gospel preachments, he appealed to what he called the Rainbow Coalition—a name he borrowed from Mel King's 1983 Boston mayoral campaign and that had been used in the late 1960s by Chicago Black Panther leader Fred Hampton. He arrived at the Democratic National Convention in San Francisco having garnered 3.5 million votes—21 percent of the total cast in primaries and caucuses—and with 384 delegates committed to him. Only former Vice President Walter Mondale, who had enough delegates to guarantee him the nomination, and U.S. Senator Gary Hart had greater totals. Because Mondale would need the black voters Jackson had registered and brought to the polls, Jackson was offered a prime-time speaking slot at the convention.

Addressing the delegates one night after Mario Cuomo's electrifying keynote (pages 576–583), Jackson cast his own rhetorical spell in what one commentator likened to "a populist tent-revival sermon." Speaking in a cadenced, evangelical style, with a text heavy in biblical allusions, Jackson coaxed wave after wave of applause from the 20,000 people in the convention center. "Our flag is red, white, and blue," he proclaimed, "but our nation is rainbow—red, yellow, brown, black, and white, we're all precious in God's sight." Lacing his speech with rhyme, repetition, and alliteration, he combined a stinging critique of Ronald Reagan's presidency with the verbal virtuosity of African American pulpit oratory. As Jackson spoke, the number of television viewers rose steadily, making him, according to CBS, the biggest draw of the convention. Many in the hall were moved to tears by the time he finished his emotional peroration. Florida Governor Bob Graham summed up their feelings when he remarked: "If you are a human being and weren't affected by what you just heard, you may be beyond redemption."

◇◇

Thank you very much. Tonight we come together bound by our faith in a mighty God, with genuine respect and love for our country, and inheriting the legacy of a great party, the Democratic Party, which is the best hope for redirecting our nation on a more humane, just, and peaceful course.

This is not a perfect party. We're not a perfect people. Yet we are called to a perfect mission—our mission to feed the hungry, to clothe the naked, to house the homeless,[1] to teach the illiterate, to provide jobs for the jobless, and to choose the human race over the nuclear race. We are gathered here this week to nominate a candidate and adopt a platform which will expand, unify, direct, and inspire our party and the nation to fulfill this mission.

My constituency is the desperate, the damned, the disinherited, the disrespected, and the despised. They are restless and seek relief. They have voted in record numbers. They have invested the faith, hope, and trust that they have in us. The Democratic Party must send them a signal that we care. I pledge my best not to let them down.

There is the call of conscience, redemption, expansion, healing, and unity. Leadership must heed the call of conscience, redemption, expansion, healing, and unity, for they are the key to achieving our mission. Time is neutral and does not change things. With courage and initiative, leaders change things.

No generation can choose the age or circumstance in which it is born, but through leadership it can choose to make the age in which it is born an age of enlightenment, an age of jobs and peace and justice. Only leadership—that intangible combination of gifts, the discipline, the information, circumstance, courage, timing, will, and divine inspiration—can lead us out of

the crisis in which we find ourselves. Leadership can mitigate the misery of our nation. Leadership can part the waters and lead our nation in the direction of the Promised Land.[2] Leadership can lift the boats stuck at the bottom.

I've had the rare opportunity to watch seven men, and then two, pour out their souls, offer their service, and heal—and heed—the call of duty to direct the course of our nation.[3] There is a proper season for everything. There is a time to sow and a time to reap.[4] There's a time to compete and a time to cooperate.

I ask for your vote on the first ballot as a vote for a new direction for this party and this nation—a vote of conviction, a vote of conscience. But I will be proud to support the nominee of this convention for the presidency of the United States of America. Thank you.

I have, I've watched the leadership of our party develop and grow. My respect for both Mr. Mondale and Mr. Hart is great. I've watched them struggle with the crosswinds and cross fires of being public servants, and I believe they will both continue to try to serve us faithfully. I'm elated by the knowledge that for the first time in our history a woman, Geraldine Ferraro,[5] will be recommended to share our ticket.

Throughout this campaign I have tried to offer leadership to the Democratic Party and the nation. If, in my high moments, I have done some good, offered

---

1. An allusion to Matthew 25:35–45.

2. An allusion to the biblical story of Moses parting the Red Sea and leading the children of Israel toward the Promised Land.

3. Jackson is referring to the seven men who contended for the Democratic Party's presidential nomination, and to Gary Hart and Walter Mondale, the two leading candidates coming into the convention.

4. An echo of Ecclesiastes 3:2.

5. U.S. Congresswoman from New York who was chosen as the party's vice-presidential candidate (see pages 593–597).

some service, shed some light, healed some wounds, rekindled some hope, or stirred someone from apathy and indifference, or in any way along the way helped somebody, then this campaign has not been in vain.[6] For friends who loved and cared for me, and for a God who spared me, and for a family who understood, I am eternally grateful.

If, in my low moments, in word, deed, or attitude, through some error of temper, taste, or tone, I've caused anyone discomfort, created pain, or revived someone's fears, that was not my truest self. If there were occasions when my grape turned into a raisin and my joy bell lost its resonance,[7] please forgive me. Charge it to my head and not to my heart—my head, so limited in its finitude; my heart, which is boundless in its love for the human family. I am not a perfect servant. I am a public servant doing my best against the odds. As I develop and serve, be patient. God is not finished with me yet.

This campaign has taught me much: that leaders must be tough enough to fight, tender enough to cry, human enough to make mistakes, humble enough to admit them, strong enough to absorb the pain, and resilient enough to bounce back and keep on moving. For leaders, the pain is often intense. But you must smile through your tears and keep moving with the faith that there's a brighter side somewhere.

I went to see Hubert Humphrey[8] three days before he died. He had just called Richard Nixon[9] from his dying bed, and many people wondered why. And I asked him. He said: "Jesse, from this vantage point, the sun setting in my life, all of the speeches, the political conventions, the crowds, and the great fights are behind me now. At a time like this you are forced to deal with your irreducible essence, forced to grapple with that which is really important to you. And what I've concluded about life," Hubert Humphrey said, "when all is said and done, we must forgive each other and redeem each other and move on."

Our party's emerging from one of its most hard-fought battles for the Democratic Party's presidential nomination in our history. But our healthy competition should make us better, not bitter. We must use, we must use the insight, wisdom, and experience of the late Hubert Humphrey as a balm for the wounds in our party, this nation, and the world. We must forgive each other, redeem each other, regroup and move on. Our flag is red, white, and blue, but our nation is rainbow—red, yellow, brown, black, and white, we're all precious in God's sight.[10]

America, America's not like a blanket—one piece of unbroken cloth, the same color, the same texture, the same size. America's more like a quilt—many patches, many pieces, many colors, many sizes, all woven and held together by a common thread. The white, the Hispanic, the black, the Arab, the Jew, the woman, the Native American, the small farmer, the businessperson, the environmentalist, the peace activist, the young, the old, the lesbian, the gay, and the disabled make up the American quilt. Even in our fractured state, all of us count and fit somewhere. We have proven that we can survive without each other. But we have not proven that we can win and make progress without each other. We must come together.

From Fannie Lou Hamer in Atlantic City in 1964[11] to the Rainbow Coalition[12] in San Francisco today, from the Atlantic to the Pacific, we have experienced pain but progress as we ended American apartheid laws, we got public accommodation, we secured voting rights, we obtained open housing, as young people got the right to

6. An allusion to Alma B. Androzzo's hymn "If I Can Help Somebody" (1945).

7. Likely an echo of the hymn "You May Have the Joy-Bells," lyrics by J. Edward Ruark (1899).

8. Vice President of the United States, 1965–1969, and the Democratic Party's presidential nominee in 1968.

9. President of the United States, 1969–1974; Nixon defeated Humphrey in the 1968 election.

10. An echo of the hymn "Jesus Loves the Little Children," lyrics by C. Herbert Woolston.

11. Hamer gained national attention for her speech challenging the seating of the all-white Mississippi delegation at the 1964 Democratic National Convention in Atlantic City.

12. Name used by Jackson during his campaign for the informal coalition of groups to whom he appealed; after the campaign, he created a formal organization called the National Rainbow Coalition.

vote. We lost Malcolm, Martin, Medgar, Bobby, John, and Viola.[13] The team that got us here must be expanded, not abandoned.

Twenty years ago tears welled up in our eyes as the bodies of Schwerner, Goodman, and Chaney were dredged from the depths of a river in Mississippi.[14] Twenty years later, our communities—black and Jewish—are in anguish, anger, and pain. Feelings have been hurt on both sides.[15] There is a crisis in communications. Confusion is in the air. But we cannot afford to lose our way. We may agree to agree or agree to disagree on issues; we must bring back civility to these tensions.

We are copartners in a long and rich religious history—the Judeo-Christian traditions. Many blacks and Jews have a shared passion for social justice at home and peace abroad. We must seek a revival of the spirit, inspired by a new vision and new possibilities. We must return to higher ground.

We are bound by Moses and Jesus, but also connected with Islam and Mohammed. These three great religions—Judaism, Christianity, and Islam—were all born in the revered and holy city of Jerusalem.

We are bound by Dr. Martin Luther King Jr. and Rabbi Abraham Heschel,[16] crying out from their graves for us to reach common ground. We are bound by shared blood and shared sacrifices. We are much too intelligent; much too bound by our Judeo-Christian heritage; much too victimized by racism, sexism, militarism, and anti-Semitism; much too threatened as historical scapegoats to go on divided one from another.

We must turn from finger pointing to clasped hands. We must share our burdens and our joys with each other once again. We must turn to each other and not on each other, and choose higher ground. Twenty years later, twenty years later we cannot be satisfied by just restoring the old coalition. Old wine skins must make room for new wine.[17] We must heal and expand.

The Rainbow Coalition is makin' room for Arab Americans. They, too, know the pain and hurt of racial and religious rejection. They must not continue to be made pariahs.

The Rainbow Coalition is makin' room for Hispanic Americans, who this very night are living under the threat of the Simpson-Mazzoli bill,[18] and farm workers from Ohio who are fighting the Campbell Soup Company with a boycott to achieve legitimate workers' rights.[19]

The Rainbow is makin' room for the Native American, the most exploited people of all, a people with the greatest moral claim amongst us. We support them as they seek the restoration of their ancient land and claim amongst us. We support them as they seek the restoration of land and water rights, as they seek to preserve their ancestral homelands and the beauty of a land that was once all theirs. They can never receive a fair share for all they have given us. They must finally have a fair chance to develop their great resources and to preserve their people and their culture.

The Rainbow Coalition includes Asian Americans, now being killed in our streets, scapegoats for the failures of corporate, industrial, and economic policies.[20]

The Rainbow is makin' room for the young Americans. Twenty years ago our young people were

---

13. Malcolm X, Martin Luther King, Medgar Evers, Robert F. Kennedy, John F. Kennedy, and Viola Liuzzo, all of whom were murdered.

14. Civil rights workers Michael Schwerner, Andrew Goodman, and James Chaney, who were murdered in June 1964 near Philadelphia, Mississippi.

15. Jackson is referring to the controversy created by his long-standing support of the Palestinian cause and to his use, in an early 1984 interview, of "Hymie" and "Hymietown" to refer to New York's Jewish community.

16. Jewish theologian and civil rights activist (1907–1972).

17. An allusion to Luke 5:37.

18. Immigration legislation presented in Congress by Senator Alan Simpson and Representative Romano Mazzoli. One of its proposals called for sanctions against employers who hired illegal aliens.

19. Led by Baldemar Velasquez, head of the Farm Labor Organizing Committee, the boycott began in 1979 and remained in place until 1986.

20. Jackson is referring to Vincent Chin, a Chinese American beaten to death in Detroit in June 1982 by two unemployed white auto workers who blamed Japanese car manufacturers for the loss of U.S. jobs.

dying in a war for which they could not even vote.[21] Twenty years later young America has the power to stop a war in Central America[22] and the responsibility to vote in great numbers. Young America must be politically active in 1984. The choice is war or peace. We must make room for young America.

The Rainbow includes disabled veterans. The color scheme fits in the Rainbow. The disabled have their handicap revealed and their genius concealed, while the able-bodied have their genius revealed and their disability concealed. But ultimately we must judge people by their values and their contribution. Don't leave anybody out. I would rather have Roosevelt in a wheelchair[23] than Reagan on a horse.[24]

The Rainbow is makin' room for small farmers. They have suffered tremendously under the Reagan regime. They will either receive 90 percent parity or 100 percent charity.[25] We must address their concerns and make room for them.

The Rainbow includes lesbians and gays. No American citizen ought [to] be denied equal protection under the law.

We must be unusually committed and caring as we expand our family to include new members. All of us must be tolerant and understanding, as the fears and anxieties of the rejected and the party leadership express themselves in many different ways. Too often what we call hate—as if it were some deeply rooted philosophy or strategy—is simply ignorance, anxiety, paranoia, fear, and insecurity. To be strong leaders, we must be long-suffering as we seek to right the wrongs

of our party and our nation. We must expand our party, heal our party, and unify our party. That is our mission in 1984.

We are often reminded that we live in a great nation—and we do. But it can be greater still. The Rainbow is mandating a new definition of greatness. We must not measure greatness from the mansion down but the manger up.[26] Jesus said that we should not be judged by the bark we wear but by the fruit that we bear. Jesus said that we must measure greatness by how we treat the least of these.[27]

President Reagan says the nation is in recovery. Those 90,000 corporations that made a profit last year but paid no federal taxes are recovering. The 37,000 military contractors who have benefited from Reagan's more than doubling the military budget in peacetime—surely they are recovering. The big corporations and rich individuals who received the bulk of the three-year, multibillion tax cut from Mr. Reagan are recovering. But no such recovery is under way for the least of these. Rising tides don't lift all boats,[28] particularly those stuck at the bottom.

For the boats stuck at the bottom there's a misery index.[29] This administration has made life more miserable for the poor. Its attitude has been contemptuous. Its policies and programs have been cruel and unfair to workin' people. They must be held accountable in November for increasing infant mortality among the poor. In Detroit, one of the great cities of the Western world, babies are dying at the same rate as Honduras, the most undeveloped nation in our hemisphere.

This administration must be held accountable for policies that have contributed to the growing poverty in America. There are now 34 million people in poverty, 15 percent of our nation. Twenty-three million are white, 11 million black, Hispanic, Asian, and others, mostly women and children. By the end of this

---

21. During most of the Vietnam War, the federal voting age was 21; it was lowered to 18 in 1971 upon adoption of the Twenty-sixth Amendment to the U.S. Constitution.

22. At the time of Jackson's speech, both Nicaragua and El Salvador were in the throes of civil war.

23. Franklin D. Roosevelt, President of the United States, 1933–1945, was confined to a wheelchair because of polio.

24. Ronald Reagan, President at the time of Jackson's speech, was often photographed riding a horse at his California ranch, which served as the Western White House when he was away from Washington, D.C.

25. Institutionalized during the New Deal, the parity program was designed to prop up agricultural prices; the higher the rate of parity, the more income provided for farmers.

26. An allusion to Jesus being placed in a manger as an infant.

27. Allusions to Matthew 7:16–20 and Matthew 25:40, 45.

28. An allusion to the aphorism that "a rising tide lifts all boats."

29. Based on the inflation rate added to the unemployment rate, the "misery index" was created in the 1970s by economist Robert Barro.

year, there will be 41 million people in poverty. We cannot stand idly by. We must fight for change now.

Under this regime, we look at Social Security. The '81 budget cuts included nine permanent Social Security benefit cuts totaling $20 billion over five years. Small businesses have suffered on the Reagan tax cuts. Only 18 percent of total business tax cuts went to them, 82 percent to big business. Health care under Mr. Reagan has been sharply cut. Education under Mr. Reagan has been cut 25 percent. Under Mr. Reagan there are now 9.7 million female-head families. They represent 16 percent of all families. Half of all of them are poor. Seventy percent of all poor children live in a house headed by a woman, where there is no man. Under Mr. Reagan the administration's cleaned up only six of 546 priority toxic waste dumps. Farmers' real net income was only about half its level in 1979.

Many say that the race in November will be decided in the South. President Reagan is depending on the conservative South to return him to office. But the South, I tell you, is unnaturally conservative. The South is the poorest region in our nation and therefore [has] the least to conserve. In his appeal to the South, Mr. Reagan is trying to substitute flags and prayer cloths[30] for food and clothing and education, health care and housing.

Mr. Reagan will ask us to pray, and I believe in prayer. I've come this way by the power of prayer.[31] But, then, we must watch false prophecy. He cuts energy assistance to the poor, cut breakfast programs from children, cut lunch programs from children, cut job training from children, and then say[s] to an empty table, "Let us pray." Apparently he is not familiar with the structure of a prayer. You thank the Lord for the food that you're about to receive, not the food that just left. I think that we should pray, but don't pray for the food that left. Pray for the man that took the food to leave. We need a change. We need a change in November.

Under Mr. Reagan the misery index has risen for the poor; the danger index has risen for every-body. Under this administration we've lost the lives of our boys in Central America and Honduras,[32] in Grenada,[33] in Lebanon,[34] in nuclear standoff in Europe. Under this administration one-third of our children believe they will die in a nuclear war. The danger index is increasing in this world. All the talk about the defense against Russia, the Russian submarines are closer and their missiles are more accurate. We live in a world tonight more miserable and a world more dangerous.

While Reaganomics[35] and Reaganism is talked about often, so often we miss the real meaning. Reaganism is a spirit and Reaganomics represents the real economic facts of life. In 1980 Mr. George Bush, a man with reasonable access to Mr. Reagan, did an analysis of Mr. Reagan's economic plan. Mr. George Bush concluded that Reagan's plan was "voodoo economics."[36] He was right. Third-party candidate John Anderson said "a combination of military spending, tax cuts, and a balanced budget by '84 would be accomplished with blue smoke and mirrors."[37] They were both right.

Mr. Reagan talks about a dynamic recovery. There's some measure of recovery. Three and a half years later, unemployment has inched just below where it was when he took office in '81. There are still 8.1 million people officially unemployed, 11 million working only part-time. Inflation has come down,

---

30. A piece of cloth that a person or group prays over and gives to a sick person for help in healing.

31. Jackson is referring to his background as a minister.

32. During the mid-1980s there were 10,000–12,000 U.S. troops in Honduras to support anti-Leftist forces in neighboring Nicaragua and El Salvador.

33. Nineteen Americans were killed in the October 1983 invasion of Grenada.

34. On October 23, 1983, 241 marines were killed by a truck-bomb attack on their barracks in Beirut.

35. A term used by opponents of President Reagan's economic policies.

36. Reagan's Vice President, George H. W. Bush made this statement on April 10, 1980, while campaigning against Reagan for the Republican presidential nomination.

37. Anderson's exact words, from a campaign debate in Des Moines, Iowa, on January 5, 1980, were: "How do you balance the budget, cut taxes, and increase defense spending at the same time? It's very simple. You do it with mirrors."

but let's analyze for a moment who has paid the price for this superficial economic recovery.

Mr. Reagan curbed inflation by cutting consumer demand. He cut consumer demand with conscious and callous fiscal and monetary policies. He used the federal budget to deliberately induce unemployment and curb social spending. He then weighed and supported tight monetary policies of the Federal Reserve Board to deliberately drive up interest rates, again to curb consumer demand created through borrowing. Unemployment reached 10.7 percent. We experienced skyrocketing interest rates. Our dollar inflated abroad. There were record bank failures, record farm foreclosures, record business bankruptcies, record budget deficits, record trade deficits.

Mr. Reagan brought inflation down by destabilizing our economy and disrupting family life. He promised, he promised in 1980 a balanced budget. But instead we now have a record $200 billion budget deficit. Under Mr. Reagan the cumulative budget deficit for his four years is more than the sum total of deficits from George Washington through Jimmy Carter combined. I tell you, we need a change.

How is he payin' for these short-term jobs? Reagan's economic recovery is being financed by deficit spending—$200 billion a year. Military spending, a major cause of this deficit, is projected, over the next five years, to be nearly $2 trillion and will cost about $40,000 for every taxpaying family. When the government borrows $200 billion annually to finance the deficit, this encourages the private sector to make its money off of interest rates, as opposed to development and economic growth.

Even money abroad—we don't have enough money domestically to finance the debt, so we are now borrowing money abroad from foreign banks, governments, and financial institutions: $40 billion in 1983; $70–80 billion in 1984, 40 percent of our total; over $100 billion, 50 percent of our total in 1985. By 1989 it is projected that 50 percent of all individual income taxes will be going just to pay for interest on that debt. The United States used to be the largest exporter of capital, but under Mr. Reagan we will quite likely become the largest debtor nation.

About two weeks ago, on July the fourth, we celebrated our Declaration of Independence, yet every

day supply-side economics[38] is making our nation more economically dependent and less economically free. Five to six percent of our gross national product is now being eaten up with President Reagan's budget deficits. To depend on foreign military powers to protect our national security would be foolish, making us dependent and less secure, yet Reaganomics has us increasingly dependent on foreign economic sources. This consumer-led but deficit-financed recovery[39] is unbalanced and artificial.

We have a challenge as Democrats to point a way out. Democracy guarantees opportunity, not success. Democracy guarantees the right to participate, not a license for either a majority or a minority to dominate. The victory for the Rainbow Coalition in the platform debates today was not whether we won or lost, but that we raised the right issues.[40] We could, we could afford to lose the vote; issues are nonnegotiable.[41] We could not afford to avoid raising the right questions. Our self-respect and our moral integrity were at stake. Our heads are perhaps bloody, but not bowed. Our back is straight. We can go home and face our people. Our vision is clear.

When we think on this journey from slave ship to championship, that we've gone from the planks of the Boardwalk in Atlantic City in 1964[42] to fighting to help write the planks in the platform in San Francisco in '84, there is a deep and abiding sense of joy in our souls in spite of the tears in our eyes. Though there are missing planks, there is a solid foundation upon which to build. Our party can win, but we must provide hope which will inspire people to struggle and achieve, provide

---

38. Central to fiscal policy during Reagan's presidency, supply-side economics called for reducing high marginal tax rates.

39. Jackson is referring to the economic recovery that had begun in 1983, following the recession of 1981–1982.

40. After losing platform votes on runoff primaries, military spending, and nuclear weapons, Jackson accepted a compromise on the affirmative action plank.

41. Jackson meant to say "negotiable."

42. Jackson is referring to the exclusion of the Mississippi Freedom Democratic Party delegation from the 1964 Democratic National Convention (see note 11 above).

a plan that shows a way out of our dilemma and then lead the way.

In 1984 my heart is made to feel glad because I know there is a way out—justice. The requirement for rebuilding America is justice. The linchpin of progressive politics in our nation will not come from the North; they in fact will come from the South. That is why I argue over and over again. We look from Virginia around to Texas, there's only one black Congressperson out of 115. Nineteen years later, we're locked out [of] the Congress, the Senate, and the Governor's mansion.

What does this large black vote mean? Why do I fight to win second primaries[43] and fight gerrymandering and annexation[44] and at-large?[45] Why do we fight over that? Because, I tell you, you cannot hold someone in the ditch unless you linger there with them—unless you linger there. If you want a change in this nation, you enforce that Voting Rights Act.[46] We'll get twelve to twenty black, Hispanic, female, and progressive Congresspersons from the South. We can save the cotton, but we got to fight the boll weevils.[47] We got to make a judgment. We've got to make a judgment.

It's not enough to hope ERA[48] will pass. How can we pass ERA? If blacks vote in great numbers, progressive whites win. It's the only way progressive whites win. If blacks vote in great numbers, Hispanics win. When blacks, Hispanics, and progressive whites vote, women win. When women win, children win. When women and children win, workers win. We must all come up together. We must come up together.

I tell you, for all, for all of our joy and excitement we must not save the world and lose our souls.[49] We should never short-circuit enforcing the Voting Rights Act at every level. When one of us rise[s], all of us will rise. Justice is a way out. Peace is a way out.

We should not act as if nuclear weaponry is negotiable and debatable. In this world in which we live, we dropped the bomb on Japan and felt guilty.[50] But in 1984 other folks also got bombs. This time, if we drop the bomb, six minutes later we, too, would be destroyed. It's not about droppin' the bomb on somebody. It's about droppin' the bomb on everybody. We must choose to develop minds over guided missiles, and think it out and not fight it out. It's time for a change.

Our foreign policy must be characterized by mutual respect, not by gunboat diplomacy, big-stick diplomacy, and threats. Our nation at its best feeds the hungry. Our nation at its worst, at its worst will mine the harbors of Nicaragua; at its worst will try to overthrow their government;[51] at its worst will cut aid to American education and increase the aid to El Salvador.[52] At its worst our nation will have partnership with South Africa.[53] That's a moral disgrace. It's a moral disgrace. It's a moral disgrace.

---

43. If no candidate received a majority of votes in a primary election, several Southern states required that the top two finishers face each other in a second, runoff primary to determine the winner. Arguing that runoff primaries were used to discriminate against African American candidates, Jackson fought unsuccessfully for a plank in the Democratic platform opposing them.

44. Methods of manipulating electoral districts so as to reduce the influence of African Americans and other minority voters.

45. "At-large" refers to convention delegates appointed by state party officials, as opposed to delegates elected on the basis of presidential primary votes.

46. The Voting Rights Act of 1965.

47. The boll weevil is an insect that caused severe damage to the Southern cotton crop through much of the 20th century. In politics, "boll weevil" was used to describe conservative Southern Democrats who voted against their party on racial, economic, or national defense issues.

48. Equal Rights Amendment providing for legal equality of the sexes. Although approved by Congress in 1971–1972, the amendment failed to achieve ratification by three-fourths of the states.

---

49. An allusion to Mark 8:36.

50. A reference to the atomic bombs dropped on Hiroshima and Nagasaki in August 1945.

51. It was revealed in April 1984 that the United States was supporting Contra rebels in Nicaragua by mining ports to prevent the arrival of military supplies to the government from Cuba and the Soviet Union. The mining was part of the Reagan administration's efforts to undermine Nicaragua's Leftist Sandinista government.

52. A reference to the Reagan administration's February 1984 request for $243 million in military aid for the government of El Salvador to resist Leftist guerrillas.

53. A criticism of Reagan's support of the proapartheid South African government as an American ally.

We look at Africa. We cannot just focus on apartheid in Southern Africa. We must fight for trade with Africa and not just aid to Africa. We cannot stand idly by and say we will not relate to Nicaragua unless they have elections there and then embrace military regimes in Africa overthrowing democratic governments in Nigeria and Liberia and Ghana.[54] We must fight for democracy all around the world and play the game by one set of rules.

Peace in this world: Our present formula for peace in the Middle East is inadequate. It will not work. There are twenty-two nations in the Middle East. Our nation must be able to talk and act and influence all of them. We must build upon Camp David[55] and measure human rights by one yardstick. In that region we have too many interests and too few friends.

There's a way out—jobs. Put America back to work. When I was a child growing up in Greenville, South Carolina, the Reverend Sample[56] used to preach ever so often a sermon relating to Jesus, and he said: "If I be lifted up, I'll draw all men unto me."[57] I didn't quite understand what he meant as a child growing up, but I understand a little better now. If you raise up truth, it's magnetic. It has a way of drawing people.

With all this confusion in this convention, the bright lights and parties and big fun, we must raise up the simple proposition: If we lift up a program to feed the hungry, they'll come running. If we lift up a program to study war no more, our youth will come running. If we lift up a program to put America back to work, and an alternative to welfare and despair, they will come working. If we cut that military budget without cutting our defense and use that money to rebuild bridges and put steelworkers back to work, and use that money and provide jobs for our cities,

and use that money to build schools and pay teachers and educate our children and build hospitals and train doctors and train nurses, the whole nation will come running to us.

As I leave you now and we vote in this convention and get ready to go back across this nation in a couple of days, in this campaign I tried to be faithful to my promise. I lived in the el barrios, ghettos, and in reservations and housing projects.[58]

I have a message for our youth. I challenge them to put hope in their brains and not dope in their veins. I told them that, like Jesus, I, too, was born in the slum. But just because you're born in the slum does not mean the slum is born in you, and you can rise above it if your mind is made up.

I told them in every slum there are two sides. When I see a broken window, that's the slummy side. Train some youth to become a glazier; that's the sunny side. When I see a missing brick, that's the slummy side. Let that child in a union and become a brick mason and build; that's the sunny side. When I see a missing door, that's the slummy side. Train some youth to become a carpenter; that's the sunny side. And when I see the vulgar words and hieroglyphics of destitution on the walls, that's the slummy side. Train some youth to become a painter and artist; that's the sunny side.

We leave this place lookin' for the sunny side because there's a brighter side somewhere. I am more convinced than ever that we can win. We have fought up the rough side of the mountain.[59] We can win.

I just want young America to do me one favor, just one favor. Exercise the right to dream. You must face reality—that which is. But then dream of the reality that ought to be, that must be. Live beyond the pain of reality with the dream of a bright tomorrow. Use hope and imagination as weapons of survival and progress. Use love to motivate you and obligate you to serve the human family.

---

54. All three countries experienced military coups during the early 1980s.

55. A reference to the Camp David Accords, a peace agreement between Israel and Egypt mediated by President Jimmy Carter and signed in September 1978.

56. D. S. Sample, preacher at the Long Branch Baptist Church.

57. Paraphrased from John 12:32.

58. Before the Connecticut primary in March 1984, Jackson said he would stay in the homes of poor people so as to focus attention on the problem of poverty in America.

59. An allusion to F. C. Barnes's song "The Rough Side of the Mountain."

Young America, dream. Choose the human race over the nuclear race. Bury the weapons and don't burn the people. Dream—dream of a new value system. Teachers who teach for life and not just for a living, teach because they can't help it. Dream—of lawyers more concerned about justice than a judgeship. Dream—of doctors more concerned about public health than personal wealth. Dream—of preachers and priests who will prophesy and not just profiteer.

Preach and dream. Our time has come. Our time has come. Suffering breeds character. Character breeds faith. In the end faith will not disappoint.[60]

Our time has come. Our faith, hope, and dreams will prevail. Our time has come. Weeping has endured for a night, but now joy cometh in the morning.[61]

Our time has come. No grave can hold our body down. Our time has come. No lie can live forever. Our time has come. We must leave racial battleground and come to economic common ground and moral higher ground. America, our time has come.

We've come from disgrace to amazing grace.[62] Our time has come. Give me your tired; give me your poor, your huddled masses who yearn to breathe free,[63] and come November there will be a change because our time has come.

Thank you, and God bless you.

---

60. An allusion to Romans 5:3–5: "We rejoice in our sufferings, knowing that suffering produces endurance, and endurance produces character, and character produces hope, and hope does not disappoint us" (Revised Standard Version).

61. Closely paraphrased from Psalm 30:5.

62. An allusion to John Newton's hymn "Amazing Grace" (1779).

63. Closely paraphrased from Emma Lazarus's "The New Colossus" (1883), which is engraved on the base of the Statue of Liberty.

Geraldine Ferraro

⧗

Speech Accepting the Democratic Vice-Presidential Nomination

San Francisco
July 19, 1984

WHEN WALTER MONDALE tabbed Geraldine Ferraro as his running mate in the 1984 presidential election, she became the first woman in American history to be nominated for Vice President by a major political party. A three-term Congresswoman from New York City, Ferraro also had experience as an assistant district attorney and had chaired the party's platform committee in the months leading up to the Democratic National Convention. Her selection capped a yearlong effort in which the National Organization for Women had pushed for a female vice-presidential candidate both as a matter of principle and as a way to make inroads against incumbent President Ronald Reagan.

Although it has since become hackneyed for convention speakers to begin by stating their name, it was novel when Ferraro stood before the delegates in San Francisco's Moscone Center and said, "Ladies and Gentlemen of the Convention: My name is Geraldine Ferraro. I stand before you to proclaim tonight: America is the land where dreams can come true for all of us." Unlike Barbara Jordan, who had referred explicitly to her unique standing as an African American keynoter in 1976 (pages 532–535), Ferraro merely alluded to her special situation. The effect, however, was equally electric, as the crowd chanted "Gerr-eee," "Gerr-eee." Many delegates brought their daughters or granddaughters onto the convention floor to see history being made, and Ferraro generated more excitement than Mondale did in his acceptance address the next night.

As it turned out, Ferraro's speech was the highlight of her campaign. She soon became embroiled in a dispute about her husband's financial dealings, followed by a row over abortion with Archbishop John O'Connor of New York. She acquitted herself capably in her vice-presidential debate with George Bush, and she proved to be a formidable fund-raiser, but Reagan swept to reelection, losing only Washington, D.C., and Mondale's home state of Minnesota. Ferraro's nomination, however, remains an important milestone, a reminder, as she said in her speech, that "If you work hard and play by the rules, you can earn your share of America's blessings."

◇◇◇

Ladies and Gentlemen of the Convention: My name is Geraldine Ferraro. I stand before you to proclaim tonight: America is the land where dreams can come true for all of us.

As I stand before the American people and think of the honor this great convention has bestowed upon me, I recall the words of Dr. Martin Luther King Jr., who made America stronger by making America more free. He said: "Occasionally in life there are moments…which cannot be completely explained by words. Their meaning can only be articulated by the inaudible language of the heart."[1]

Tonight is such a moment for me. My heart is filled with pride. My fellow citizens, I proudly accept your nomination for Vice President of the United States. And, and, and, and I am proud to run with a man who will be one of the great Presidents of this century, Walter F. Mondale.

Tonight, the daughter of a woman whose highest goal was a future for her children talks to our nation's oldest party about a future for us all. Tonight, the daughter of working Americans tells all Americans that the future is within our reach if we're willing to reach for it. Tonight, the daughter of an immigrant from Italy has been chosen, has been chosen to run for [Vice] President in the new land my father came to love.[2]

Our faith that we can shape a better future is what the American dream is all about. The promise of our country is that the rules are fair. If you work hard and play by the rules, you can earn your share of America's blessings. Those are the beliefs I learned from my parents. And those are the values I taught my students as a teacher in the public schools of New York City. At night I went to law school. I became

---

1. From King's speech of December 11, 1964, accepting the Nobel Peace Prize.

2. With regard to mistakenly saying that she was her party's presidential candidate, Ferraro wrote in her autobiography: "Luckily, I didn't notice my slipup at the time and kept right on going. Since Fritz [Mondale] didn't get upset about it later, I didn't either."

an assistant district attorney, and I put my share of criminals behind bars. I believe if you obey the law, you should be protected. But if you break the law, you must pay for your crime.

When I first ran for Congress, all the political experts said a Democrat could not win my home district in Queens. I put my faith in the people and the values that we shared. Together we proved the political experts wrong. In this campaign, Fritz Mondale and I have put our faith in the people. And we are going to prove the experts wrong again. We are going to win. We're going to win because Americans across this country believe in the same basic dream.

Last week I visited Elmore, Minnesota, the small town where—yea, Elmore[3]—the small town where Fritz Mondale was raised. And soon Fritz and Joan will visit our family in Queens. Nine hundred people live in Elmore. In Queens, there are 2,000 people on one block. You would think we'd be different, but we're not.

Children walk to school in Elmore past grain elevators; in Queens, they pass by subway stops. But no matter where they live, their future depends on education and their parents are willing to do their part to make those schools as good as they can be.

In Elmore, there are family farms; in Queens, small businesses. But the men and women who run them all take pride in supporting their families through hard work and initiative.

On the Fourth of July in Elmore, they hang flags out on Main Street; in Queens, they fly them over Grand Avenue. But all of us love our country and stand ready to defend the freedom that it represents.

Americans wanna live by the same set of rules. But under this administration, the rules are rigged against too many of our people.

It isn't right that every year the share of taxes paid by individual citizens is going up while the share paid by large corporations is getting smaller and smaller. The rules say everyone in our society should contribute their fair share.

It isn't right that this year Ronald Reagan will hand the American people a bill for interest on the national debt larger than the entire cost of the federal government under John F. Kennedy.[4] Our parents left us a growing economy. The rules say we must not leave our kids a mountain of debt.

It isn't right that a woman should get paid fifty-nine cents on the dollar for the same work as a man. If you play by the rules, you deserve a fair day's pay for a fair day's work.

It isn't right that if trends continue, by the year 2000 nearly all of the poor people in America will be women and children. The rules, the rules of a decent society say when you distribute sacrifice in times of austerity, you don't put women and children first.

It isn't right that young people today fear they won't get the Social Security they paid for and that older Americans fear they will lose what they have already earned.[5] Social Security is a contract between the last generation and the next, and the rules say you don't break contracts. We are going to keep faith with older Americans. We hammered out a fair compromise in the Congress to save Social Security.[6] Every group sacrificed to keep the system sound. It is time Ronald Reagan stopped scaring our senior citizens.

It isn't right that young couples question whether to bring children into a world of 50,000 nuclear warheads.

That isn't the vision for which Americans have struggled for more than two centuries. And our future doesn't have to be that way. Change is in the air just as surely as when John Kennedy beckoned America to a new frontier,[7] when Sally Ride rocketed into space,[8] and when Reverend Jesse Jackson ran for the

---

3. Ferraro is responding to cheering for Elmore from the Minnesota delegation.

4. Kennedy was President from January 20, 1961, to his assassination on November 22, 1963.

5. Ferraro misspoke this word as "learned."

6. Ferraro is referring to the Social Security Amendments of 1983, signed into law by President Reagan.

7. "The New Frontier" was Kennedy's campaign slogan during the 1960 presidential campaign.

8. The first American woman in space, Ride was a member of the 1983 *Challenger* flight.

office of President of the United States.[9] By choosing a woman to run for our nation's second-highest office, you send a powerful signal to all Americans: There are no doors we cannot unlock. We will place no limits on achievement. If we can do this, we can do anything.

Tonight, we reclaim our dream. We're going to make the rules of American life work fairly for all Americans again.

To an administration that would have us debate all over again whether the Voting Rights Act[10] should be renewed and whether segregated schools should be tax exempt, we say: "Mr. President, those debates are over." On the issue of civil rights, voting rights, and affirmative action for minorities, we must not go backwards. We must—and we will—move forward to open the doors of opportunity.

To those who understand that our country cannot prosper unless we draw on the talents of all Americans, we say: "We will pass the Equal Rights Amendment."[11] The issue is not what America can do for women, but what women can do for America.[12]

To the, to the Americans who will lead our country into the twenty-first century, we say: "We will not have a Supreme Court that turns the clock back to the nineteenth century."

To those, to those concerned about the strength of American family values, as I am, I say: "We are going to restore those values—love, caring, partnership—by including, and not excluding, those whose beliefs differ from our own." Because our own faith is strong,

we will fight to preserve the freedom of faith for others.

To those working Americans who fear that banks, utilities, and large special interests have a lock on the White House, we say: "Join us. Let's elect a people's President and let's have a government by and for the American people again."

To an administration that would savage student loans and education at the dawn of a new technological age, we say: "You fit the classic definition of a cynic; you know the price of everything, but the value of nothing."[13]

To our students and their parents, we say: "We will insist on the highest standards of excellence because the jobs of the future require skilled minds."

To young Americans who may be called to our country's service, we say: "We know your generation will proudly answer our country's call, as each generation before you." This past year, we remembered the bravery and sacrifice of Americans at Normandy.[14] And we finally paid tribute, as we should have done years ago, to that unknown soldier who represents all the brave young Americans who died in Vietnam.[15]

Let no one doubt: We will defend America's security and the cause of freedom around the world. But we want a President who tells us what America is fighting for, not just what we are fighting against. We want a President who will defend human rights, not just where it is convenient, but wherever freedom is at risk—from Chile to Afghanistan, from Poland to South Africa.

To those who have watched this administration's confusion in the Middle East, as it has tilted first toward one and then another of Israel's longtime enemies, and wonder, "Will America stand by her friends and sister democracy?" we say: "America knows who her friends are in the Middle East and around the world. America will stand with Israel always."

9. Jackson won 3.5 million votes in the 1984 Democratic primaries and came into the convention with the third-highest number of delegates. He addressed the convention two days before Ferraro (pages 584–593).

10. Ferraro is referring to the 1965 Voting Rights Act, which became law under President Lyndon B. Johnson.

11. Although the Equal Rights Amendment providing for legal equality of the sexes had failed to achieve ratification by three-fourths of the states by the deadline of June 30, 1982, it remained a campaign issue for Democrats in the 1984 election.

12. An allusion to President Kennedy's inaugural address, January 20, 1961: "Ask not what your country can do for you—ask what you can do for your country" (pages 341–344).

13. From Oscar Wilde, *Lady Windermere's Fan* (1892).

14. See Ronald Reagan's speech of June 6, 1984, at Pointe du Hoc, France, on the 40th anniversary of D-Day (pages 572–575).

15. A reference to the Vietnam Veterans Memorial in Washington, D.C., dedicated in November 1982.

Finally, finally we want a President who will keep America strong but use that strength to keep America and the world at peace. A nuclear freeze is not a slogan; it is a tool for survival in the nuclear age.[16] If we leave our children nothing else, let us leave them this earth as we found it—whole and green and full of life. I know in my heart that Walter Mondale will be that President.

A wise man once said, "Every one of us is given the gift of life, and what a strange gift it is. If it is preserved jealously and selfishly, it impoverishes and saddens, but if it is spent for others, it enriches and beautifies."[17] My fellow Americans, we can debate policies and programs. But in the end what separates the two parties in this election campaign is whether we use the gift of life for others or only ourselves.

Tonight, my husband, John, and our three children are in this hall with me. To my daughters, Donna and Laura, and my son, John Jr., I say: "My mother did not break faith with me, and I will not break faith with you." To all the children of America, I say: "The generation before ours kept faith with us, and, like them, we will pass on to you a stronger, more just America."

Thank you.

---

16. The nuclear-freeze campaign began in 1980 and called on the United States and the Soviet Union to mutually suspend testing, producing, and deploying nuclear weapons.

17. From Ignazio Silone, *Bread and Wine*, trans. Gwenda David and Eric Mosbacher (1937).

Mario Cuomo

Religious Belief and Public Morality

NOTRE DAME, INDIANA
SEPTEMBER 13, 1984

SHORTLY AFTER HIS acclaimed keynote speech at the 1984 Democratic National Convention (pages 576–583), Mario Cuomo found himself at the center of a simmering election-year debate on abortion and the role of religion in politics. Both issues had roiled American society since the 1973 Supreme Court decision in *Roe v. Wade* overturning state laws restricting or banning abortion. Among the multitude of questions raised in the wake of *Roe v. Wade* was the proper role of personal religious belief in the decision making of public officeholders. This question was especially acute for members of the Roman Catholic Church, which holds that abortion is a moral evil that must be opposed by all members of the church. When making political decisions involving abortion, how should an officeholder who is Catholic balance the dictates of the church with his or her responsibilities as a public servant?

As Governor of New York and a practicing Catholic, Cuomo had long wrestled with this question. Then, in late June 1984, Archbishop John J. O'Connor of New York City stated in a televised press conference that he did not see how any Catholic could in good conscience vote for a politician who supported abortion. When asked whether the church should excommunicate Cuomo, who was on record as being pro-choice, O'Connor demurred and refused to give a definitive answer, touching off a tempest that would engulf not only the Governor and the Archbishop, but much of the U.S. Catholic leadership and laity. After jousting with O'Connor in the press, Cuomo accepted an invitation to present his views in a mid-September address at the University of Notre Dame, the most prominent Catholic institution of higher education in the United States. By the time Cuomo took to the rostrum, his speech had become, in the words of Kenneth A. Briggs, "one of the most anticipated exercises in theology ever presented by a member of the laity."

Concurrently, the larger issue of religion in politics had assumed an increasingly prominent role in the presidential campaign, eventually drawing into the fray President Ronald Reagan and Vice President George H. W. Bush, as well as Democratic candidates Walter Mondale and Geraldine Ferraro. At Notre Dame, Cuomo sought not only to explain his views on abortion and his responsibilities as a Catholic officeholder but also to claim for liberalism a set of religious values that would make it politically competitive with Reagan's religiously tinctured brand of conservatism. As a Catholic, Cuomo explained, he believed abortion was morally wrong, but as a public official he had no right to impose his personal religious beliefs on public policy. In a pluralistic democracy based on majority rule, no one should "presume to speak for God or to claim God's sanction of our particular legislation and his rejection of all other positions. . . . God should not be made into a celestial party chairman" on abortion or any other issue. Indeed, Cuomo said, it would be tragic if the debate over abortion were to deter people from extending the spirit of Christian love where it "is most needed, among the poor and the weak and the dispossessed."

Cuomo received a standing ovation at the end of his fifty-three-minute address, which he had spent weeks preparing, but his responses in the question-and-answer period afterward drew both cheers and jeers. The larger national audience was also divided, though opinion polls showed that his message registered favorably among a majority of Catholics and non-Catholics alike. Despite warnings from his advisors against speaking on such an explosive topic, Cuomo demonstrated that there was room, even in the heated atmosphere of an election campaign, for thoughtful, even-tempered discourse. His speech at Notre Dame neither began nor ended deliberation about the place of religion in American public life, but it was an important moment in a dialogue that is as old as the republic itself.

◇◇◇

Thank you. Thank you. Thank you very much. Father Hesburgh,[1] Father McBrien,[2] all the distinguished clergy who are present, ladies and gentlemen:

I am very pleased to be at Notre Dame, and I feel very much at home, frankly.[3] Not just because you have seven or eight hundred students from New York State;[4] not just because, not just because Father McBrien's mother's name is Catherine Botticelli, a beautiful name; not just because Father Hesburgh is a Syracuse[5] native; but also because of your magnificent history of great football teams. Oh, the subway—they mean a lot to us, they, the great Fighting Irish. The subway alumni[6] of New York City have always been enthralled, and for years and years all over the state—Syracuse, north and south, out on Long Island—people on Saturdays would listen to their radio and now watch their television to watch the great Fighting Irish, wearing the Gaelic green. It's marvelous. The names of your great players reverberate back from the years: Nick Bouniconti, Nick Pietrosante, Angelo Bertelli. How about Ralph Guglielmi—what a great player he is.[7]

I want to begin this talk by drawing your attention to the title of the lecture: "Religious Belief and Public Morality: A Catholic Governor's Perspective." I was not invited to speak on "Church and State" generally, and certainly not to speak on "Mondale against Reagan."[8] The subject assigned to me is difficult enough. I'll not try to do more than I've been asked.

I'm honored by the invitation, but the record shows that I'm not the first Governor of New York State to appear at an event involving Notre Dame. One of my great predecessors, Al Smith,[9] went to the Army–Notre Dame football game each time it was played in New York. His fellow Catholics expected Smith to sit with Notre Dame; protocol required him to sit with Army because it was the home team. Protocol prevailed, but not without Smith noting the dual demands on his affections. "I'll take my seat with Army," he said, "but I commend my soul to Notre Dame."

Today, frankly, I'm happy I have no such problem. Both my seat and my soul are with Notre Dame. And as long as Father McBrien or Father Hesburgh doesn't invite me back to sit with him at the Notre Dame–St. John's[10] basketball game, I'm confident my loyalties will remain undivided.

And in a sense, it's a question of loyalty that Father McBrien has asked me here today to discuss. Specifically, must politics and religion in America divide our loyalties? Does the separation between church and state imply separation between religion and politics? Between morality and government? And are these different propositions? Even more specifically, what is the relationship of my Catholicism to my politics? Where does the one end and the other begin? Or are they divided at all? And if they're not, should they be?

These are hard questions. No wonder most of us in public life—at least until recently—preferred to stay away from them, heeding the biblical advice that if hounded and pursued in one city, we should flee to another.[11] Now, however, I think that it's too late to flee. The questions are all around us; the answers are coming from every quarter. Some of them have been simplistic, most of them fragmentary, and a few, spoken with a purely political intent, demagogic. There's been confusion and compounding of confusion, a blurring of the issue, entangling it in personalities and election strategies, instead of clarifying it for Catholics, as well as for others.

1. Theodore M. Hesburgh, president of Notre Dame.

2. Richard P. McBrien, chair of the theology department, who invited Cuomo to speak at Notre Dame.

3. Although not part of Cuomo's prepared text, this extemporized paragraph was warmly received by his audience, not least because he was speaking during football season.

4. Cuomo served as Governor of New York from 1983 to 1995.

5. City in central New York.

6. Popular name for Catholics across the United States who root for Notre Dame football, even though they did not attend the school and are not literally alumni.

7. Bertelli played for Notre Dame in the mid-1940s, Guglielmi and Pietrosante in the 1950s, and Bouniconti in the early 1960s.

8. Walter Mondale and Ronald Reagan were the Democratic and Republican presidential candidates in 1984.

9. Governor of New York, 1919–1921 and 1923–1929.

10. St. John's University, located in New York City.

11. An allusion to Matthew 10:23.

Today I'd like to try, just try, to help correct that. And, of course, I can offer you no final truths, complete and unchallengeable. But it's possible that this one effort will provoke other efforts—both in support and contradiction of my position—that will help all of us to understand our differences and perhaps even discover some basic agreement.

In the end, I am absolutely convinced that we will all benefit if suspicion is replaced by discussion, innuendo by dialogue; if the emphasis in our debate turns from a search for talismanic criteria and neat but simplistic answers to an honest, more intelligent attempt at describing the role that religion has in our public affairs and the limits placed on that role. And if we do it right—if we're not afraid of the truth even when the truth is complex—this debate, by clarification, can bring relief to untold numbers of confused, even anguished, Catholics, as well as to many others who want only to make our already great democracy even stronger than it is.

I believe the recent discussion in my own state has already produced some clearer definition. As you may know, in early summer an impression was created in some quarters that official church spokespeople would ask Catholics to vote for or against specific candidates on the basis of their political position on the abortion issue alone.[12] I was one of those that was given that impression. Thanks to the dialogue that ensued over the summer—only partially reported by the media— we learned that the impression was not accurate. Confusion had presented an opportunity for clarification, and we seized it. Now, all of us, all of us are saying one thing, in chorus, reiterating the statement of the National Conference of Catholic Bishops that they will not "take positions for or against specific political candidates" and that their stand, the stand of the bishops and the cardinals, on specific issues should not be perceived "as an expression of political partisanship."[13]

Now, of course, the bishops will teach—they must teach—more and more vigorously and more and more extensively. But they have said they will not use the power of their position, and the great respect it receives from all Catholics, to give an imprimatur to individual politicians or parties. Not that they couldn't do it if they wished to. Some religious leaders, as you know, do it; some are doing it at this very moment. And not that it would be a sin if they did—God does not insist on political neutrality. But because it is the judgment of the bishops, and most of us Catholic laypeople, that it is not wise for prelates and politicians to be too closely tied together.

Now, I think that getting this consensus in New York was an extraordinarily useful achievement. And now, with some trepidation, I take up your gracious invitation to continue the dialogue in the hope that it will lead to still further clarification.

Let me begin this part of the effort by underscoring the obvious. I do not speak as a theologian; I don't have that competence. I do not speak as a philosopher; to suggest that I could would be to set a new record for false pride. I don't presume to speak as a "good" person except in the ontological sense of that word. My principal credential is that I serve in a position that forces me to wrestle with the problems that you've come here to study and to debate.

I am by training a lawyer and by practice a politician. Now, both those professions make me suspect in many quarters, including, including some of my own coreligionists. Maybe there's no better illustration of the public perception of how politicians unite their faith and their profession than the story they tell in New York about Fishhooks McCarthy, a famous Democratic leader. He actually lived, Fishhooks McCarthy. Lived on the Lower East Side. He was right-hand man to Al Smith, the prototypical political person of his time.

Fishhooks, the story goes, was devout. So devout that every morning on his way to Tammany Hall[14] to do his political work, he stopped into St. James Church on Oliver Street in downtown Manhattan,

---

12. Cuomo is referring to the June 24, 1984, statement of John J. O'Connor, Archbishop of New York: "I do not see how a Catholic in conscience could vote for an individual explicitly expressing himself or herself as favoring abortion."

13. From a statement issued August 9, 1984, by James W. Malone, president of the National Conference of Catholic Bishops.

14. Popular name for the Democratic Party organization in New York City from the mid-19th century to the mid-20th century.

fell on his knees, and whispered every morning the same simple prayer: "Oh, Lord, give me health and strength. We'll steal the rest."

Fishhooks notwithstanding, I speak here as a politician. And also as a Catholic, a layperson baptized and raised in the pre–Vatican II[15] church, educated in Catholic schools, attached to the church first by birth, then by choice, now by love. An old-fashioned Catholic who sins, regrets, struggles, worries, gets confused, and most of the time feels better after confession. The Catholic Church is my spiritual home. My heart is there, and my hope.

But there is, of course, more to being a Catholic than a sense of spiritual and emotional resonance. Catholicism is a religion of the head as well as the heart, and to be a Catholic is to say "I believe" to the essential core of dogmas that distinguishes our faith. The acceptance of this faith requires a lifelong struggle to understand it more fully and to live it more truly, to translate truth into experience, to practice as well as to believe.

That's not easy. Applying religious belief to everyday life often presents difficult challenges, and it's always been that way. It certainly is today. The America of the late twentieth century is a consumer society, filled with endless distractions, where faith is more often dismissed than challenged, where the ethnic and other loyalties that once fastened us to our religion seem to be weakening.

In addition to all the weaknesses, all the dilemmas, all the temptations that impede every pilgrim's progress,[16] the Catholic who holds political office in a pluralistic democracy—a Catholic who is elected to serve Jews and Muslims and atheists and Protestants, as well as Catholics—bears special responsibility. He or she undertakes to help create conditions under which all can live with a maximum of dignity and with a reasonable degree of freedom; where everyone who chooses may hold beliefs different from

specifically Catholic ones, sometimes even contradictory to them; where the laws protect people's right to divorce, their right to use birth control devices, and even to choose abortion.

In fact, Catholic public officials take an oath to preserve the Constitution that guarantees this freedom. And they do so gladly. Not because they love what others do with their freedom, but because they realize that in guaranteeing freedom for all, they guarantee our right to be Catholics—our right to pray, our right to use the sacraments, to refuse birth control devices, to reject abortion, not to divorce and remarry if we believe it to be wrong.

The Catholic public official lives the political truth that most Catholics through most of American history have accepted and insisted on: the truth that to assure our freedom we must allow others the same freedom, even if occasionally it produces conduct by them which we would hold to be sinful. I protect my right to be a Catholic by preserving your right to be a Jew or a Protestant or a nonbeliever or anything else you choose. We know that the price of seeking to force our belief on others is that they might someday force their belief on us.

Now, this freedom is the fundamental strength of our unique experiment in government. In the complex interplay of forces and considerations that go into the making of our law and policies, its preservation—the preservation of freedom—must be a pervasive and dominant concern. But insistence on freedom is easier to accept as a general proposition than in its applications to specific situations because there are other valid general principles firmly embedded in our Constitution which, operating at the same time, create interesting and occasionally troubling problems.

Thus the same amendment of the Constitution that forbids the establishment of a state church affirms my legal right to argue that my religious belief would serve well as an article of our universal public morality.[17] I may use the prescribed processes of government, the legislative and executive and judicial processes, to convince my fellow citizens, Jews and

---

15. Called by Pope John XXIII, the Second Vatican Council met from 1962 to 1965 and instituted the most sweeping changes in the Catholic Church since the Council of Trent (1545–1563).

16. An allusion to John Bunyan's *The Pilgrim's Progress: From This World to That Which Is to Come* (1678).

---

17. Cuomo is referring to the First Amendment.

Protestants and Buddhists and nonbelievers, that what I propose is as beneficial for them as I believe it is for me—that it's not just parochial or narrowly sectarian, but fulfills a human desire for order, for peace, for justice, for kindness, for love, for any of the values that most of us agree are desirable even apart from their specific religious base or context.

I'm free to argue for a governmental policy for a nuclear freeze,[18] not just to avoid sin, but because I think my democracy should regard it as a desirable goal. I can, if I wish, argue that the state should not fund the use of contraceptive devices, not because the Pope demands it, but because I think that the whole community—for the good of the whole community—should not sever sex from an openness to the creation of life. And surely, I can, if I am so inclined, demand some kind of law against abortion, not because my bishops say it is wrong, but because I think that the whole community, regardless of its religious beliefs, should agree on the importance of protecting life—including life in the womb, which is at the very least potentially human and should not be extinguished casually.

Now, no law prevents us from advocating any of these things. I am free to do so. So are the bishops. So is Reverend Falwell.[19] In fact, the Constitution guarantees my right to try. And theirs. And his.

But should I? Is it helpful? Is it essential to human dignity? Would it promote harmony and understanding? Or does it divide us so fundamentally that it threatens our ability to function as a pluralistic community? When should I argue to make my religious value your morality? My rule of conduct your limitation? What are the rules and policies that should influence the exercise of this right to argue and to promote?

Now, I believe I have a salvific mission as a Catholic. Does that mean I am in conscience required to do everything I can as Governor to translate all my religious values into the laws and regulations of the state of New York or of the United States? Or be branded a hypocrite if I don't?

As a Catholic, I respect the teaching authority of my bishops. But must I agree with everything in the bishops' pastoral letter on peace[20] and fight to include it in party platforms? And will I have to do the same for the forthcoming pastoral on economics[21] even if I am an unrepentant supply-sider?[22]

Must I, having heard the Pope once again renew the church's ban on birth control devices as clearly as it's been done in modern times,[23] must I, as Governor, veto the funding of contraceptive programs for non-Catholics or dissenting Catholics in my state?

I accept the church's teaching on abortion. Must I insist that you do? By denying you Medicaid funding? By a constitutional amendment? And if by a constitutional amendment, which one? Would that be the best way to avoid abortions or to prevent them?

Now, these are only some of the questions for Catholics. People with other religious beliefs face similar problems. Let me try some answers.

Almost all Americans accept the religious values as part of our public life. We are a religious people, many of us descended from ancestors who came here expressly to live their religious faith free from coercion or repression. But we are also a people of many religions, with no established church, who hold different beliefs on many matters.

Our public morality, then—the moral standards we maintain for everyone, not just the ones we insist on in our private lives—depends on a consensus view of right and wrong. The values derived from religious belief will not—and should not—be accepted as part of the public morality unless they are shared by the

---

18. The nuclear-freeze campaign called on the United States and the Soviet Union to mutually suspend testing, producing, and deploying nuclear weapons.

19. Jerry Falwell, founder of the conservative Moral Majority.

20. *The Challenge of Peace: God's Promise and Our Response* (1983).

21. *Economic Justice for All: Pastoral Letter on Catholic Social Teaching and the U.S. Economy* (1986).

22. Supply-side economics, which called for reducing high marginal tax rates, was at the heart of fiscal policy during Ronald Reagan's presidency, 1981–1989.

23. On August 8, 1984, a month before Cuomo's speech, Pope John Paul II had reiterated his position that "all contraceptive means" are "morally wrong."

pluralistic community at large, by consensus. So that the fact that values happen to be religious values does not deny them acceptability as part of this consensus. But it does not require their acceptability either.

Think about it: The agnostics who joined the civil rights struggle were not deterred because that crusade's values had been nurtured and sustained in black Christian churches. And those on the political left are not perturbed today by the religious basis of the clergy and laypeople who join them in the protest against the arms race and hunger and exploitation. The arguments start when religious values are used to support positions which would impose on other people restrictions that they find unacceptable. Some people do object to Catholic demands for an end to abortion, seeing it as a violation of the separation of church and state. And some others, while they have no compunction about invoking the authority of Catholic bishops in regard to birth control and abortion, might reject out of hand their teaching on war and peace and social policy.

Ultimately, therefore, what this means is that the question [of] whether or not we admit religious values into our public affairs is too broad to yield to a single answer. Yes, we create our public morality through consensus, and in this country that consensus reflects to some extent the religious values of a great majority of Americans. But no, all religiously based values don't have an a priori place in our public morality. The community must decide if what is being proposed would be better left to private discretion than public policy; whether it restricts freedoms, and if so, to what end, to whose benefit; whether it will produce a good or bad result; whether overall it will help the community or merely divide it.

Now, the right answers to these terribly subtle and complex questions can be elusive. Some of the wrong answers, however, are quite clear. For example, there are those who say there is a simple answer to all these questions; they say that by history and by the practice of our people we were intended from the beginning to be—and should be today—a Christian country in law. But where would that leave the nonbelievers? And whose Christianity would be law—yours or mine?

This "Christian nation" argument should concern—even frighten—two groups in this society: non-Christians and thinking Christians. And I believe it does. I think it's already apparent that a good part of this nation understands, if only instinctively, that anything which seems to suggest that God favors a political party or the establishment of a state church is wrong and dangerous. Way down deep the American people are afraid of an entangling relationship between formal religions—or whole bodies of religious belief—and government. Apart from the constitutional law and apart from religious doctrine, there's a sense that tells us it's wrong to presume to speak for God or to claim God's sanction of our particular legislation and his rejection of all other positions. Most of us are offended when we see religion being trivialized by its appearance in political throwaway pamphlets.

The American people need no course in philosophy or political science or church history to know that God should not be made into a celestial party chairman. To most of us, the manipulative invoking of religion to advance a politician or a party is frightening and divisive. The American public will tolerate religious leaders taking positions for or against candidates, although I think the Catholic bishops are right in avoiding that position. But the American people are leery about large religious organizations, powerful churches, or synagogue groups engaging in such activities—again, not as a matter of law or doctrine, but because our innate wisdom and our democratic instinct teaches us these things are dangerous for both sides: dangerous for the religious institution, dangerous for the rest of our society.

Now, today there are a number of issues involving life and death that raise questions of public morality. And they are also questions of concern to most religions. Pick up a newspaper, almost any newspaper, and you're almost certain to find a bitter controversy over any one of these questions: Baby Jane Doe,[24] the right to die, artificial insemination, embryos in vitro,

---

24. Cuomo is referring to the controversy over a child born with spina bifida in New York in October 1983 whose parents chose to withhold treatment that would have prolonged her life.

abortion, birth control, not to mention nuclear war and the shadow that it throws across all of existence. Now, some of these issues touch the most intimate recesses of our lives, our roles as someone's mother or child or husband. Some affect women in a unique way. But they are also public questions for all of us. Public questions, not just religious one[s].

Put aside what God expects. Assume, if you like, that there is no God. Say that the Supreme Court has taken God entirely out of our civics. Then the greatest thing still left to us, the greatest value available to us, would be life—life itself. Even a radically secular world must struggle with the questions of when life begins, under what circumstances it can be ended, when it must be protected, by what authority. It, too, must decide what protection to extend to the helpless and the dying, to the aged and the unborn, to life in all of its phases.

Now, as a Catholic, I have accepted certain answers as the right ones for myself and for my family, and because I have, they have influenced me in special ways: as Matilda's husband, as a father of five children, as a son who stood next to his own father's deathbed trying to decide if the tubes and the needles no longer served a purpose. As a Governor, however, I'm involved in defining policies that determine other people's rights in these same areas of life and death. Abortion is one of these issues, and while it is only one issue among many, it is one of the most controversial and affects me in a special way as a Catholic public official. So let me spend a little time considering it.

I should start, I believe, by noting that the Catholic Church's actions with respect to the interplay of religious values and public policy make clear that there is no inflexible moral principle which determines what our political conduct should be. Think about it: On divorce and birth control, without changing its moral teaching, the church abides the civil law as it now stands, thereby accepting—without making much of a point of it—that in our pluralistic society we are not required to insist that all our religious values be the law of the land. The bishops are not demanding a constitutional amendment for birth control or on adultery.

Abortion is treated differently. Of course, there are differences both in degree and quality between abortion and some of the other religious positions that the church takes; abortion is a matter of life and death, and degree counts. But the differences in approach reveal a truth, I think, that is not well-enough perceived by Catholics and therefore still further complicates the process for us. That is, while we always owe our bishops' words respectful attention and careful consideration, the question whether to engage the political system in a struggle to have it adopt certain articles of our belief as part of the public morality is not a matter of doctrine—it is a matter of prudential political judgment. Recently, Michael Novak[25] put it succinctly. "Religious judgment and political judgment are both needed," he wrote. "But they are not identical."

Now, my church and my conscience require me to believe certain things about divorce, about birth control, about abortion. My church does not order me, under pain of sin or expulsion, to pursue my salvific mission according to a precisely defined political plan.

As a Catholic, I accept the church's teaching authority. And while in the past some Catholic theologians may appear to have disagreed on the morality of some abortions—it wasn't, I think, until 1869 that excommunication was attached to all abortions without distinction[26]—and while some theologians may still disagree, I accept the bishops' position that abortion is to be avoided.

As Catholics, my wife and I were enjoined never to use abortion to destroy the life we created, and we never have. We thought church doctrine was clear on this, and, more than that, both of us felt it in full agreement with what our own hearts and our own consciences told us. For me, for Matilda, life or fetal life in the womb should be protected, even if five of nine Justices of the Supreme Court and my neighbor disagree with me. A fetus is different from an appendix or a set of tonsils. At the very least, even if the argument is made by some scientists or theologians that in the early stages of fetal development we can't discern human life, the full potential of human life

25. Catholic author and philosopher.

26. The 1869 doctrine was pronounced by Pope Pius IX.

is indisputably there. That, to my less-subtle mind, by itself is enough to demand respect and caution—indeed, reverence.

But not everyone in our society agrees with me and Matilda. And those who don't—those who endorse legalized abortions—aren't a ruthless, callous alliance of anti-Christians determined to overthrow our moral standards. In many cases, the proponents of legal abortion are the very people who have worked with Catholics to realize the goals of social justice set out by Popes in encyclicals: the American Lutheran Church, the Central Conference of American Rabbis, the Presbyterian Church in the United States, B'nai B'rith Women, the Women of the Episcopal Church. And these are just a few of the religious organizations that don't share the Catholic Church's position on abortion.

Now, certainly we should not be forced to mold Catholic morality to conform to disagreement by non-Catholics, however sincere they are, however severe their disagreement. Our bishops should be teachers, not pollsters. They should not change what we Catholics believe in order to ease our consciences or please our friends or protect the church from criticism.

But if the breadth and intensity and sincerity of opposition to church teaching shouldn't be allowed to shape our Catholic morality, it can't help but determine our ability—our realistic, political ability—to translate our Catholic morality into civil law, a law not for the believers who don't need it, but for the disbelievers who reject it. And it's here, in our attempt to find a political answer to abortion—an answer beyond our private observance of Catholic morality—that we encounter controversy within and without the church over how and in what degree to press the case that our morality should be everybody else's morality.

I repeat, there is no church teaching that mandates the best political course for making our belief everyone's rule, for spreading this part of our Catholicism. There is neither an encyclical nor a catechism that spells out a political strategy for achieving legislative goals. And so the Catholic trying to make moral and prudent judgments in the political realm must discern which, if any, of the actions one could take would be the best.

This latitude of judgment is not something new in our Catholic Church; it's not a development that has arisen only with the abortion issue. Take, for example, a very popular illustration that I heard about again tonight two or three times and I'm told about often: the question of slavery. It has been argued that the failure to endorse a legal ban on abortions is equivalent to refusing to support the cause of abolition before the Civil War. This analogy has been advanced by bishops of my own state.

But the truth of the matter is, as I'm sure you know, few, if any, Catholic bishops spoke for abolition in the years before the Civil War. And it wasn't, I believe, that the bishops endorsed the idea of some humans owning and exploiting other humans—not at all. Pope Gregory XVI, in 1840, had condemned the slave trade.[27] Instead it was a practical political judgment that the bishops made. And they weren't hypocrites; they were realists. Remember, at the time the Catholics were a small minority, mostly immigrants, despised by much of the population, often vilified, and the object even of sporadic violence.

In the face of a public controversy that aroused tremendous passions and threatened to break the country apart, the bishops made a pragmatic decision. They believed their opinion would not change people's minds. Moreover, they knew that there were Southern Catholics, even some priests, who owned slaves. They concluded that, under the circumstances, arguing for a constitutional amendment against slavery would do more harm than good; so they were silent. As they have been, generally, in recent years on the question of birth control, and as the church has been on even more controversial issues in the past, even ones that dealt with life and death.

Now, what is relevant to this discussion is that the bishops were making judgments about translating Catholic teaching into public policy, not about the moral validity of the teachings. In so doing, they grappled with the unique political complexities of their time. The decision they made to remain silent on a constitutional amendment to abolish slavery or on

---

27. *In Supremo Apostolatus*, Pope Gregory's letter condemning the slave trade, was issued in December 1839.

the repeal of the Fugitive Slave Law[28] wasn't a mark of their moral indifference; it was a measured attempt to balance moral truths against political realities. Their decision reflected their sense of complexity, not their diffidence. And as history reveals, Lincoln[29] behaved with similar discretion.

Now, the parallel I want to draw here is not between or among what we Catholics believe to be moral wrongs. It is in the Catholic political response to those wrongs. Church teaching on abortion and slavery is clear. But in the application of those teachings—the exact way we translate them into political action, the specific laws we propose, the exact legal sanctions we seek—there was and is no one, clear, absolute route that the church says, as a matter of doctrine, we must follow.

The bishops' pastoral letter *The Challenge of Peace* speaks directly to this point. Quote: "We recognize," they wrote, "that the Church's teaching authority does not carry the same force when it deals with technical solutions involving particular means as it does when it speaks of principles or ends."[30] With regard to abortion, the American bishops have had to weigh Catholic moral teaching against the fact of a pluralistic country where our view is in the minority, acknowledging that what is ideally desirable isn't always feasible, that there can be different political approaches to abortion beside unyielding adherence to an absolute prohibition.

This is in the American-Catholic tradition of political realism. In supporting or opposing specific legislation, the church in this country has never retreated into a moral fundamentalism that will settle for nothing less than total acceptance of its views. Indeed, the bishops have already confronted the fact that an absolute ban on abortion doesn't have the support necessary to be placed in the Constitution. The bishops agreed to that. In 1981 they put aside their earlier efforts to describe a law that they could

accept and get passed and supported the Hatch Amendment[31] instead. They changed their view.

Some Catholics felt that the bishops had gone too far. You remember the discussion. Some Catholics felt that the bishops had not gone far enough. Such judgments weren't a rejection of the bishops' teaching authority; the bishops even disagreed among themselves about how to proceed. Catholics are allowed to disagree on their technical political questions without having to confess.

And so very respectfully, and after careful consideration of the position and the arguments of the bishops for a long time, I've concluded that the approach of a constitutional amendment is not the best way for us to seek to deal with abortion. I believe that the legal interdicting of abortion by either the federal government or the individual states is not a plausible possibility, and even if it could be obtained, it wouldn't work. Given present attitudes, it would be Prohibition revisited, legislating what couldn't be enforced and in the process creating a disrespect for law in general.[32]

And as much as I admire the bishops' hope that a constitutional amendment against abortion would be the basis for a full, new bill of rights for mothers and children, I disagree very respectfully that that would be the result. I believe that, more likely, a constitutional prohibition—which you can't get, but if you could—would allow people to ignore the causes of many abortions instead of addressing them, addressing the causes, much the way the death penalty is used to escape dealing more fundamentally and more rationally with the problem of violent crime.

Now, other legal options that have been proposed are, in my view, equally ineffective. The Hatch Amendment, by returning the question of abortion

---

28. Passed by Congress in 1850, the Fugitive Slave Law imposed stringent measures for the capture and return of slaves who escaped to the North.

29. Abraham Lincoln, U.S. President, 1861–1865.

30. See note 20 above.

31. An antiabortion amendment to the U.S. Constitution proposed by Senator Orrin Hatch and approved in December 1981 by the Senate Judiciary Committee. In June 1983 a revised version was voted on by the full Senate but did not receive the two-thirds support needed for passage.

32. Prohibition went into effect in 1920 with the Eighteenth Amendment to the U.S. Constitution, which forbade "the manufacture, sale, or transportation of intoxicating liquors." It was repealed in 1933 upon passage of the Twenty-first amendment.

to the various states,[33] would have given us a check-erboard of permissive and restrictive jurisdictions. In some cases people might have been forced to go elsewhere to have abortions; and that might have eased a few consciences here and there, but it would not have done what the church wants to do—it would not have created a deep-seated respect for life. Abortions would have gone on, millions of them.

Nor would a denial of Medicaid funding for abortion achieve our objectives. Given *Roe against Wade*,[34] it would be nothing more than an attempt to do indirectly what the law says cannot be done directly; and worse than that, it would do it in a way that would burden only the already disadvantaged. Removing funding from the Medicaid program would not prevent the rich and middle classes from having abortions. It would not even assure that the disadvantaged wouldn't have them; it would only impose financial burdens on poor women who want abortions.

And apart from that unevenness, there's a more basic question. Medicaid is designed to deal with health and medical needs. But the arguments for the cutoff of Medicaid abortion funds are not related to those needs. They're moral arguments. If we assume that there are health and medical needs, our personal view of morality ought not to be considered a relevant basis for discrimination.

We must keep in mind always that we are a nation of laws—when we like those laws, and when we don't. The Supreme Court has established a woman's constitutional right to abortion, whether we like it or not. The Congress has decided that the federal government doesn't have to provide federal funding. But that doesn't bind the states in the allocation of their own state funds. Under the law, the individual

states need not follow the federal lead, and in New York—I will speak only for New York, not for Indiana or any other state—in New York I believe we cannot follow the federal lead. The equal protection clause in New York's constitution has been interpreted by the courts as a standard of fairness that would preclude us from denying only the poor—indirectly, by a cutoff of funds—of the practical use of the constitutional right that's given to all women in *Roe against Wade*.

Look, in the end, even if after a long and divisive struggle we were able to remove all Medicaid funding for abortion and restore the law to what it was, even if we could put most abortions out of our sight, return them to the back rooms where they were performed for so long, I don't believe that our responsibility as Catholics would be any closer to being fulfilled than it is now with abortion guaranteed as a right for women.

The hard truth is that abortion is not a failure of government. No agency, no department of government forces women to have abortions, but abortions go on. Catholics, the statistics show, support the right to abortion in equal proportion to the rest of the population. Despite the teaching we've tried in our homes and our schools and our pulpits, despite the sermons and pleadings of parents and priests and prelates, despite all the efforts we've so far made at defining our opposition to what we call the sin of abortion, collectively we Catholics apparently believe—and perhaps act—little differently from those who don't share our commitment.[35] Are we asking government to make criminal what we believe to be sinful because we ourselves can't stop committing the sin? The failure here is not Caesar's.[36] This failure is our failure, the failure of the entire people of God.

Nobody has expressed this better than a bishop in my own state, Bishop Joseph Sullivan, a man who works with the poor in New York City, a man who is resolutely opposed to abortion and argues, with his

---

33. As approved by the Senate Judiciary Committee in December 1981 (see note 31 above), the Hatch Amendment read: "A right to abortion is not secured by this Constitution. The Congress and the several states shall have concurrent power to restrict and prohibit abortions: Provided, That a provision of law of a State which is more restrictive than a conflicting provision of a law of Congress shall govern."

34. The 1973 U.S. Supreme Court decision that overturned state laws restricting or banning abortion.

---

35. Cuomo is referring to public opinion polls showing that abortion rates among Catholics were similar to those among non-Catholics.

36. An allusion to Matthew 22:21, in which "Caesar" is used as a synecdoche for secular government.

fellow bishops, for a change of law. "The major problem the Church has is internal," the Bishop said last month in reference to abortion. "How do we teach? As much as I think we're responsible for advocating public policy issues, our primary responsibility is to teach our own people. We have not done that. We are asking politicians to do what we have not done effectively ourselves."[37]

I agree with Bishop Sullivan. I think our moral and social mission as Catholics must begin with the wisdom contained in the words, "Physician, heal thyself."[38] Unless we Catholics educate ourselves better to the values that define—and can ennoble—our lives, following those teachings better than we do now, unless we set an example that is clear and compelling, then we will never convince this society to change the civil laws to protect what we preach is precious human life.

Better than any law, better than any rule, better than any threat of punishment would be the moving strength of our own good example—demonstrating our lack of hypocrisy, proving the beauty and worth of our instruction. We must work to find ways to avoid abortions without otherwise violating our faith. We should provide funds and opportunity for young women to bring their child to term, knowing both of them will be taken care of if that is necessary. We should teach our young men better than we do now their responsibilities in creating and caring for human life.

It is this duty of the church to teach through its practice of love that Pope John Paul II has proclaimed so magnificently to all peoples. "The Church," he wrote in *Redemptor Hominis*,[39] "which has no weapons at her disposal apart from those of the spirit, of the word and of love, cannot renounce her proclamation of 'the word...in season and out of season.' For this reason she does not cease to implore...everybody in the name of God and in the name of man: Do not kill! Do not prepare destruction and extermination for each other. Think of your brothers and sisters who are suffering hunger and misery! Respect each one's dignity and freedom!"

The weapons of the word and of love are already available to us; we need no statute to provide them.

Now, I am not implying that we should stand by and pretend indifference to whether a woman takes a pregnancy to its conclusion or aborts it. I believe we should in all cases try to teach a respect for life. And I believe with regard to abortion that, despite *Roe against Wade*, we can, in practical, meaningful ways. And here, in fact, it seems to me that all of us can agree. Without lessening their insistence on a woman's right to an abortion, the people who call themselves pro-choice can support the development of government programs that present an impoverished mother with the full range of support that she needs to bear and raise her children—to have a real choice. And without dropping their campaign to ban abortion, those who gather under the banner of pro-life can join in developing and enacting a legislative bill of rights for mothers and children, as the bishops have already proposed.[40]

Remember this: While we argue over abortion, the United States' infant mortality rate places us sixteenth among the nations of the world—the United States, sixteenth among the nations of the world. Thousands of infants die each year because of inadequate medical care. Some are born with birth defects that, with proper treatment, could be prevented. Some are stunted in their physical and mental growth because of improper nutrition. If we want to prove our regard for life in the womb, for the helpless infant, if we care about women having real choices in their lives and not being driven to abortions by a sense of helplessness and despair about the future of their child, then there is work enough for all of us. Lifetimes of it.

In New York, we've put in place a number of programs to begin this work, assisting women in giving birth to healthy babies. This year we doubled

37. Quoted in the *New York Times*, August 11, 1984.

38. Luke 4:23.

39. Papal encyclical issued in 1979.

40. Cuomo is referring to "Testimony of United States Catholic Conference on Constitutional Amendment Protecting Unborn Human Life before the Sub-Committee on Constitutional Amendments of the Senate Committee on the Judiciary," March 7, 1974.

Medicaid funding to private-care physicians for prenatal and delivery services. We already spent twenty million dollars a year for prenatal care in outpatient clinics and for inpatient hospital care. One program is a favorite of mine. We call it New Avenues to Dignity, and it seeks to provide a teenage mother with the special services she needs to continue with her education, to train for a job, to become capable of standing on her own, to provide for herself and the child that she wants to bring into the world.

My dissent, then, from the contention that we can have effective and enforceable legal prohibitions on abortion is by no means an argument for religious quietism, for accepting the world's wrongs because that is our fate as "the poor banished children of Eve."[41] I don't accept that.

Let me make another point. Abortion has a unique significance but not a preemptive significance. Apart from the question of [the] efficacy of using legal weapons to make people stop having abortions, we know that our Christian responsibility doesn't end with any one law or amendment. It doesn't end with abortion. Because it involves life and death, abortion will always be central in our concern. But so will nuclear weapons and hunger and homelessness and joblessness—all the forces diminishing human life and threatening to destroy it. The "seamless garment" that Cardinal Bernardin has spoken of[42] is a challenge to all Catholics in public office, conservatives as well as liberals.

We cannot justify our aspiration to goodness as Catholics simply on the basis of the vigor of our demand for an elusive and questionable civil law declaring what we already know—that abortion is wrong. Approval or rejection of legal restrictions on abortion should not be the exclusive litmus test of Catholic loyalty. We should understand that whether abortion is outlawed or not, our work has barely begun:

the work of creating a society where the right to life doesn't end at the moment of birth; where an infant isn't helped into a world that doesn't care if it's fed properly and housed decently, educated adequately; where the blind or retarded child isn't condemned to exist rather than empowered to live.

The bishops stated this duty clearly in 1974. They said that a constitutional amendment was only the beginning of what we had to do,[43] and they were right. The bishops reaffirmed that view in 1976,[44] in 1980,[45] and again this year when the United States Catholic Committee asked Catholics to judge candidates on a wide range of issues—not just abortion, but also on food policy, on the arms race, on human rights, on education, on social justice, and military expenditures.[46] That's the bishops teaching us: Consider all things. The bishops have been consistently pro-life, and I respect them for that.

Ladies and gentlemen, the problems created by the matter of abortion are obviously complex and confounding. Nothing is clearer to me than my personal inadequacy to find compelling solutions to all of their moral, legal, and social implications. I, and many others like me, are eager for enlightenment, eager to learn new and better ways to manifest respect for the deep reverence for life, that deep reverence that is our religion and our instinct. I hope that this public attempt to describe the problems as I understand them will give impetus to the dialogue in the Catholic community. I'm delighted to hear Father Hesburgh speak of an ongoing effort.

However, it would be tragic if we let this dialogue over abortion become a prolonged, divisive argument that destroys or impairs our ability to practice any

41. From the "Hail, Holy Queen" prayer in the Rosary.

42. Joseph Bernardin, Archbishop of Chicago, first used the "seamless garment" metaphor for a consistent ethic of life in a question period after a lecture at Fordham University, December 6, 1983, and developed it more fully thereafter. The phrase is an allusion to the tunic Jesus wore before his crucifixion, which could not be divided by the soldiers because it was seamless (John 19:23).

43. See note 40 above.

44. "Testimony of United States Catholic Conference on Constitutional Amendments Protecting Unborn Human Life Before the Sub-Committee on Civil and Constitutional Rights of the House Committee on the Judiciary," March 24, 1976.

45. Likely a reference to deliberations of the National Conference of Catholic Bishops at its annual meeting, held in Washington, D.C., November 10–13, 1980.

46. "Political Responsibility: Choices for the '80s," issued March 22, 1984, by the Administrative Board of the United States Catholic Conference.

part of the morality given to us in the Sermon on the Mount[47] to touch, to heal, to affirm the human life that surrounds us. We Catholic citizens of the richest, most powerful nation that has ever existed are like the stewards made responsible over a great household: From those to whom so much has been given, much shall be required.[48] It is worth repeating that ours is not a faith that encourages its believers to stand apart from the world, seeking their salvation alone, separate from the salvation of those around them.

We speak of ourselves as a body. We come together in worship as companions in the ancient sense of that word—those who break bread together and who are obliged by the commitment that we share to help one another, everywhere, in all that we do, and, in the process, to help the whole human family. We see our mission to be the completion of the work of creation.[49]

And this is difficult work today. It presents us with many hard choices. The Catholic Church has come of age in America. The ghetto walls are gone; our religion is no longer a badge of irredeemable foreignness. And our newfound status is both an opportunity and a temptation. If we choose, we can give in to the temptation to become more and more assimilated into a larger, blander culture, abandoning the practice of the specific values that made us different, worshipping whatever gods the marketplace has to sell while we seek to rationalize our own laxity by urging the political system to legislate upon others a morality that we no longer practice ourselves.

Or we have another choice: We can remember where we come from, the journey of two millennia. We can cling to our personal faith, to its insistence on constancy and service and example and hope. We can live and practice the morality that Christ gave us, maintaining his truth in this world, struggling to embody his love, practicing it especially where that love is most needed, among the poor and the weak and the dispossessed. Not just by trying to make laws for other people to live by, but by living the laws already written for us by God in our minds and in our hearts.[50]

We can be fully Catholic, proudly, totally at ease with ourselves, a people in the world, transforming it, a light to this nation.[51] Appealing to the best in our people and not the worst. Persuading, not coercing. Leading people to truth by love. And still, all the while, respecting and enjoying our unique pluralistic democracy. And we can do it even as politicians.

Thank you for listening to me.

---

47. Matthew 5–7.

48. Paraphrased from Luke 12:48.

49. Perhaps a reference to *Gaudium et Spes*, promulgated in 1965 by Pope Paul VI, which refers to human beings as partners "in the work of bringing divine creation to perfection."

50. An allusion to Romans 2:15.

51. An allusion to John 9:5 and Acts 13:47.

Ronald Reagan

⌛

Address on the *Challenger* Explosion

T HE EXPLOSION OF the space shuttle *Challenger* on the morning of January 28, 1986, changed American perceptions of space flight and the risks attending it. Since the beginning of the shuttle program in 1981, twenty-three missions had been undertaken with no major problems. Then, seventy-three seconds into its flight, *Challenger* blew apart, killing all seven astronauts. It was, at the time, the single worst space tragedy in American history. Throughout the day, television replayed the footage over and over: the crew waving as they boarded the shuttle, the picture-perfect liftoff, the spacecraft breaking into pieces, the aftermath of jagged white contrails that scarred the bright blue sky.

Ronald Reagan postponed his State of the Union message, which was scheduled for that evening, and addressed the American people via television about the *Challenger* disaster. Speaking at the end of an emotionally draining day, he gave voice to the shock and grief of the nation, including the millions of schoolchildren who had tuned in to watch Christa McAuliffe become the first teacher in space. He also praised the courage of McAuliffe and the other astronauts who had lost their lives, expressed pride in the openness of the U.S. space program (implicitly contrasting it with the secretiveness of the Soviet Union's program), and confirmed that America would continue its quest in space. What made the speech unforgettable, however, were its closing strophes, in which Reagan linked the *Challenger* explosion with the death of the legendary explorer Sir Francis Drake 390 years earlier to the day. It was an unexpected twist that lent epic significance to the tragedy and set the stage for the eloquence of Reagan's final paean to the astronauts, who had "slipped the surly bonds of Earth" to "touch the face of God."

Composed principally by Peggy Noonan, the speech ran 649 words and lasted less than five minutes. Part elegy, part homily, part policy address, it bolstered America's sense of purpose and self-confidence even as it led the nation in mourning. Reagan's first reaction after the cameras were turned off was that he had not done the astronauts justice. He could not have been more wrong. The *Challenger* address was exactly what the nation needed, and it remains the most universally admired speech of Reagan's career.

◇◇◇◇◇◇◇◇◇◇◇◇◇◇◇◇◇◇◇◇◇◇◇◇◇◇◇◇◇◇◇◇◇◇◇◇

Ladies and Gentlemen: I'd planned to speak to you tonight to report on the State of the Union, but the events of earlier today have led me to change those plans. Today is a day for mourning and remembering.

Nancy[1] and I are pained to the core by the tragedy of the shuttle *Challenger*. We know we share this pain with all of the people of our country. This is truly a national loss.

Nineteen years ago, almost to the day, we lost three astronauts in a terrible accident on the ground.[2] But we've never lost an astronaut in flight; we've never had a tragedy like this. And perhaps we've forgotten the courage it took for the crew of the shuttle; but they, the *Challenger* Seven, were aware of the dangers, but overcame them and did their jobs brilliantly. We mourn seven heroes: Michael Smith, Dick Scobee, Judith Resnik, Ronald McNair, Ellison Onizuka, Gregory Jarvis, and Christa McAuliffe. We mourn their loss as a nation together.[3]

For the families of the seven, we cannot bear, as you do, the full impact of this tragedy. But we feel the loss, and we're thinking about you so very much. Your loved ones were daring and brave, and they had that special grace, that special spirit that says: "Give me a challenge and I'll meet it with joy." They had a hunger to explore the universe and discover its truths. They wished to serve, and they did. They served all of us.

We've grown used to wonders in this century. It's hard to dazzle us. But for twenty-five years the United States space program has been doing just that. We've grown used to the idea of space, and perhaps we forget that we've only just begun. We're still pioneers. They, the members of the *Challenger* crew, were pioneers.

And I want to say something to the schoolchildren of America who were watching the live coverage of the shuttle's takeoff. I know it's hard to understand, but sometimes painful things like this happen. It's all part of the process of exploration and discovery. It's all part of taking a chance and expanding man's horizons. The future doesn't belong to the fainthearted; it belongs to the brave. The *Challenger* crew was pulling us into the future, and we'll continue to follow them.

I've always had great faith in and respect for our space program, and what happened today does nothing to diminish it. We don't hide our space program. We don't keep secrets and cover things up.[4] We do it all up front and in public. That's the way freedom is, and we wouldn't change it for a minute.

We'll continue our quest in space. There will be more shuttle flights and more shuttle crews and, yes, more volunteers, more civilians, more teachers in space. Nothing ends here; our hopes and our journeys continue.

I want to add that I wish I could talk to every man and woman who works for NASA[5] or who worked on this mission and tell them: "Your dedication and professionalism have moved and impressed us for decades. And we know of your anguish. We share it."

There's a coincidence today. On this day 390 years ago, the great explorer Sir Francis Drake died aboard ship off the coast of Panama. In his lifetime the great frontiers were the oceans, and a historian later said, "He lived by the sea, died on it, and was buried in it."[6] Well, today we can say of the *Challenger* crew: Their dedication was, like Drake's, complete.

The crew of the space shuttle *Challenger* honored us by the manner in which they lived their lives. We will never forget them, nor the last time we saw them, this morning, as they prepared for their journey and waved goodbye and "slipped the surly bonds of earth" to "touch the face of God."[7]

Thank you.

----

1. First Lady Nancy Davis Reagan.

2. On January 27, 1967, Gus Grissom, Edward White, and Roger Chaffee were killed in a fire during a test of the *Apollo 1* spacecraft.

3. Reagan discussed each of the seven astronauts individually in his January 31 eulogy at the Johnson Space Center in Houston, Texas.

4. Reagan is referring to the Soviet Union's space program.

5. National Aeronautics and Space Administration.

6. From Thomas Fuller, *The Holy State and the Profane State* (1642).

7. From the poem "High Flight" by John Gillespie Magee Jr.

Ronald Reagan

Speech at the Brandenburg Gate

WEST BERLIN, GERMANY
JUNE 12, 1987

SOME OF THE most famous speeches in history are identified in public memory with a single compelling phrase: Patrick Henry's "Give me liberty or give me death," William Jennings Bryan's "You shall not crucify mankind upon a cross of gold," Franklin Roosevelt's "The only thing we have to fear is fear itself," Winston Churchill's "An iron curtain has descended across the Continent," Martin Luther King's "I have a dream," Sojourner Truth's "Ain't I a woman?" So, too, with Ronald Reagan's "Mr. Gorbachev, tear down this wall."

On June 12, 1987, as Reagan spoke at the Berlin Wall, with the monumental Brandenburg Gate rising behind him, these words provided one of the most unforgettable rhetorical moments of the Cold War. They were penned by speechwriter Peter Robinson after a conversation with Ingeborg Elze, the wife of a retired World Bank official in West Berlin. Referring to Soviet Premier Mikhail Gorbachev's announced policy of openness and reform, Elze said: "If this man Gorbachev is serious with his talk of glasnost and perestroika, he can prove it. He can get rid of this wall." When Reagan read the speech draft, he liked the line about tearing down the wall, but the State Department and the National Security Council insisted it was too inflammatory. For two weeks they did all they could to expunge it, yet Reagan never wavered. "The boys at State are going to kill me," he told Deputy Chief of Staff Kenneth Duberstein, "but it's the right thing to do."

Reagan delivered the speech in conjunction with the 750th anniversary of Berlin, and it was broadcast in much of Europe. Though the administration billed the speech as a major policy statement, it was the drama of Reagan's challenge to Gorbachev that dominated headlines. Moscow denounced it as "openly provocative" and "warmongering"; people throughout the Soviet bloc heard it as a call to freedom and liberation. In the West, it was shown over and over on television, not only at the time, but two years later, when the Berlin Wall fell, then again at Reagan's death in 2004, and countless times before and after. It became an iconic moment: an enduring representation of the Cold War, of Reagan's unflinching opposition to communism, and of the eventual collapse of Soviet control over Eastern Europe.

Thank you. Thank you very much. Chancellor Kohl, Governing Mayor Diepgen,[1] ladies and gentlemen: Twenty-four years ago, President John F. Kennedy visited Berlin, speaking to the people of this city and the world at the city hall.[2] Well, since then two other Presidents have come, each in his turn, to Berlin.[3] Today I, myself, make my second visit to your city.[4]

We come to Berlin, we American Presidents, because it's our duty to speak, in this place, of freedom. But I must confess, we're drawn here by other things as well: by the feeling of history in this city, more than five hundred years older than our own nation; by the beauty of the Grunewald and the Tiergarten;[5] most of all, by your courage and determination.

Perhaps the composer Paul Lincke[6] understood something about American Presidents. You see, like so many Presidents before me, I come here today because wherever I go, whatever I do, *Ich hab noch einen Koffer in Berlin.*[7]

Our gathering today is being broadcast throughout Western Europe and North America. I understand that it is being seen and heard as well in the East. To those listening throughout Eastern Europe, I extend my warmest greetings and the goodwill of the American people. To those listening in East Berlin, a special word: Although I cannot be with you, I address my remarks to you just as surely as to those standing here before me. For I join you, as I join your fellow countrymen in the West, in this firm, this unalterable belief: *Es gibt nur ein Berlin.*[8]

Behind me stands a wall that encircles the free sectors of this city, part of a vast system of barriers that divides the entire continent of Europe. From the Baltic south, those barriers cut across Germany in a gash of barbed wire, concrete, dog runs, and guard towers. Farther south, there may be no visible, no obvious wall. But there remain armed guards and checkpoints all the same—still a restriction on the right to travel, still an instrument to impose upon ordinary men and women the will of a totalitarian state.

Yet it is here in Berlin where the wall emerges most clearly; here, cutting across your city, where the news photo and the television screen have imprinted this brutal division of a continent upon the mind of the world. Standing before the Brandenburg Gate, every man is a German, separated from his fellow men. Every man is a Berliner, forced to look upon a scar.

President von Weizsäcker has said, "The German question is open as long as the Brandenburg Gate is closed."[9] Today, today I say: As long as this gate is closed, as long as this scar of a wall is permitted to stand, it is not the German question alone that remains open, but the question of freedom for all mankind.

Yet I do not come here to lament. For I find in Berlin a message of hope, even in the shadow of this wall, a message of triumph.

In this season of spring in 1945, the people of Berlin emerged from their air-raid shelters to find devastation. Thousands of miles away, the people of the United States reached out to help. And in 1947, Secretary of State—as you've been told[10]—George Marshall announced the creation of what would become known as the Marshall Plan.[11] Speaking precisely forty years ago this month, he said: "Our policy is directed not against any country or doctrine, but against hunger, poverty, desperation, and chaos."[12]

---

1. Helmut Kohl, Chancellor of West Germany; Eberhard Diepgen, Mayor of West Berlin.

2. See Kennedy's "Ich Bin ein Berliner," June 26, 1963 (pages 373–374).

3. Richard Nixon visited West Berlin in February 1969; Jimmy Carter, in July 1978.

4. Reagan's first visit occurred in June 1982.

5. Large, forested public parks in Berlin.

6. Popular German composer (1866–1946) whose songs established him as a symbol of Berlin.

7. "I still have a suitcase in Berlin," from the 1951 song of that title by Ralph Maria Siegel and Aldo Von Pinelli. Contrary to Reagan's implication, it was not composed by Paul Lincke, who died five years before the song was released.

8. "There is only one Berlin."

---

9. From a June 8, 1985, speech by Richard von Weizsäcker, President of West Germany.

10. A reference to comments by German Chancellor Helmut Kohl preceding Reagan's speech.

11. Officially titled the European Economic Recovery Program, the Marshall Plan was vital to rebuilding the Western European economies devastated by World War II.

12. From Marshall's speech of June 5, 1947 (pages 276–279).

In the Reichstag[13] a few moments ago, I saw a display commemorating this fortieth anniversary of the Marshall Plan. I was struck by the sign on a burnt-out, gutted structure that was being rebuilt. I understand that Berliners of my own generation can remember seeing signs like it dotted throughout the Western sectors of the city. The sign read simply: "The Marshall Plan is helping here to strengthen the free world." A strong free world in the West—that dream became real. Japan rose from ruin to become an economic giant. Italy, France, Belgium—virtually every nation in Western Europe—saw political and economic rebirth. The European Community was founded.

In West Germany and here in Berlin, there took place an economic miracle, the *Wirtschaftswunder*.[14] Adenauer,[15] Erhard,[16] Reuter,[17] and other leaders understood the practical importance of liberty—that just as truth can flourish only when the journalist is given freedom of speech, so prosperity can come about only when the farmer and businessman enjoy economic freedom. The German leaders, the German leaders reduced tariffs, expanded free trade, lowered taxes. From 1950 to 1960 alone, the standard of living in West Germany and Berlin doubled.

Where four decades ago there was rubble, today in West Berlin there is the greatest industrial output of any city in Germany—busy office blocks, fine homes and apartments, proud avenues, and the spreading lawns of parkland. Where a city's culture seemed to have been destroyed, today there are two great universities, orchestras and an opera, countless theaters, and museums. Where there was want, today there's abundance—food, clothing, automobiles, the wonderful goods of the *Ku'damm*.[18] From

devastation, from utter ruin, you Berliners have, in freedom, rebuilt a city that once again ranks as one of the greatest on earth. Now, the Soviets may have had other plans. But, my friends, there were a few things the Soviets didn't count on: *Berliner Herz, Berliner Humor, ja, und Berliner Schnauze*.[19]

In the 1950s, in the 1950s Khrushchev predicted: "We will bury you."[20] But in the West today we see a free world that has achieved a level of prosperity and well-being unprecedented in all human history. In the Communist world, we see failure, technological backwardness, declining standards of health, even want of the most basic kind—too little food. Even today the Soviet Union still cannot feed itself. After these four decades, then, there stands before the entire world one great and inescapable conclusion: Freedom leads to prosperity. Freedom replaces the ancient hatreds among the nations with comity and peace. Freedom is the victor.

And now, now the Soviets themselves may, in a limited way, be coming to understand the importance of freedom. We hear much from Moscow about a new policy of reform and openness. Some political prisoners have been released. Certain foreign news broadcasts are no longer being jammed. Some economic enterprises have been permitted to operate with greater freedom from state control.

Are these the beginnings of profound changes in the Soviet state? Or are they token gestures, intended to raise false hopes in the West, or to strengthen the Soviet system without changing it? We welcome change and openness, for we believe that freedom and security go together, that the advance of human liberty, the advance of human liberty can only strengthen the cause of world peace.

There is one sign the Soviets can make that would be unmistakable, that would advance dramatically the cause of freedom and peace. General Secretary Gorbachev,[21] if you seek peace, if you seek prosperity for

---

13. Building that houses the German Parliament.

14. Term used to refer to the economic rebirth of Germany following World War II.

15. Konrad Adenauer, Chancellor of West Germany, 1949–1963.

16. Ludwig Erhard, Chancellor of West Germany, 1963–1966.

17. Ernst Reuter, Mayor of West Berlin, 1948–1953, who led the city's opposition to the Soviet blockade of 1948–1949.

18. Popular name for fashionable Kurfürstendamm Boulevard.

19. "Berliner heart, Berliner humor, yes, and Berliner bluntness."

20. Soviet Premier Nikita Khrushchev made this boast at a reception at the Polish Embassy in Moscow on November 18, 1956.

21. Mikhail Gorbachev, General Secretary of the Communist Party of the Soviet Union.

the Soviet Union and Eastern Europe, if you seek liberalization, come here to this gate. Mr. Gorbachev, open this gate. Mr. Gorbachev, Mr. Gorbachev, tear down this wall.

I understand the fear of war and the pain of division that afflict this continent, and I pledge to you my country's efforts to help overcome these burdens. To be sure, we in the West must resist Soviet expansion. So we must maintain defenses of unassailable strength. Yet we seek peace; so we must strive to reduce arms on both sides.

Beginning ten years ago, the Soviets challenged the Western alliance with a grave new threat—hundreds of new and more deadly SS-20 nuclear missiles, capable of striking every capital in Europe. The Western alliance responded by committing itself to a counterdeployment unless the Soviets agreed to negotiate a better solution—namely, the elimination of such weapons on both sides. For many months, the Soviets refused to bargain in earnestness. As the alliance, in turn, prepared to go forward with its counterdeployment, there were difficult days—days of protests like those during my 1982 visit to this city[22]—and the Soviets later walked away from the table.

But through it all, the alliance held firm. And I invite those who protested then—I invite those who protest today[23]—to mark this fact: Because we remained strong, the Soviets came back to the table. And because we remained strong, today we have within reach the possibility not merely of limiting the growth of arms but of eliminating for the first time an entire class of nuclear weapons from the face of the earth.

As I speak, NATO ministers are meeting in Iceland to review the progress of our proposals for eliminating these weapons. At the talks in Geneva, we have also proposed deep cuts in strategic offensive weapons.[24]

And the Western allies have likewise made far-reaching proposals to reduce the danger of conventional war and to place a total ban on chemical weapons.

While we pursue these arms reductions, I pledge to you that we will maintain the capacity to deter Soviet aggression at any level at which it might occur. And in cooperation with many of our allies, the United States is pursuing the Strategic Defense Initiative[25]—research to base deterrence not on the threat of offensive retaliation, but on defenses that truly defend, on systems, in short, that will not target populations but shield them.

By these means we seek to increase the safety of Europe and all the world. But we must remember a crucial fact: East and West do not mistrust each other because we're armed. We're armed because we mistrust each other. And our differences are not about weapons but about liberty. When President Kennedy spoke at the city hall those twenty-four years ago, freedom was encircled, Berlin was under siege. And today, despite all the pressures upon this city, Berlin stands secure in its liberty. And freedom itself is transforming the globe.

In the Philippines, in South and Central America, democracy has been given a rebirth. Throughout the Pacific, free markets are working miracle after miracle of economic growth. In the industrialized nations, a technological revolution is taking place, a revolution marked by rapid, dramatic advances in computers and telecommunications. In Europe, only one nation and those it controls refuse to join the community of freedom. Yet in this age of redoubled economic growth, of information and innovation, the Soviet Union faces a choice: It must make fundamental changes, or it will become obsolete.

Today thus represents a moment of hope. We in the West stand ready to cooperate with the East to promote true openness, to break down barriers that separate people, to create a safer, freer world. And surely there is no better place than Berlin, the meeting place of East and West, to make a start.

---

22. More than 100,000 anti-American demonstrators took to the streets during Reagan's June 1982 stop in Berlin.

23. The day before Reagan's speech, 24,000 protesters had stormed through West Berlin, throwing bottles, smashing windows, and burning cars.

24. Reagan is referring to arms-control talks with the Soviet Union. They would result in a December 1987 treaty eliminating land-based intermediate-range and shorter-range nuclear missiles in Europe.

---

25. Program proposed by Reagan to develop laser weapons that could destroy intercontinental ballistic missiles while they were still in the upper atmosphere; opponents referred to it as "Star Wars."

Free people of Berlin: Today, as in the past, the United States stands for the strict observance and full implementation of all parts of the Four Power Agreement of 1971.[26] Let us use this occasion, the 750th anniversary of this city, to usher in a new era, to seek a still fuller, richer life for the Berlin of the future. Together, let us maintain and develop the ties between the Federal Republic and the Western sectors of Berlin, which is permitted by the 1971 agreement. And I invite Mr. Gorbachev: Let us work to bring the Eastern and Western parts of the city closer together so that all the inhabitants of all Berlin can enjoy the benefits that come with life in one of the great cities of the world.

To open Berlin still further to all Europe, East and West, let us expand the vital air access to this city, finding ways of making commercial air service to Berlin more convenient, more comfortable, and more economical. We look to the day when West Berlin can become one of the chief aviation hubs in all central Europe.

With, with our French and British partners, the United States is prepared to help bring international meetings to Berlin. It would be only fitting for Berlin to serve as the site of United Nations meetings, or world conferences on human rights and arms control or other issues that call for international cooperation.

There is no better way to establish hope for the future than to enlighten young minds, and we would be honored to sponsor summer youth exchanges, cultural events, and other programs for young Berliners from the East. Our French and British friends, I'm certain, will do the same. And it's my hope that an authority can be found in East Berlin to sponsor visits from young people of the Western sectors.

One final proposal, one close to my heart: Sport represents a source of enjoyment and ennoblement, and you may have noted that the Republic of Korea—South Korea—has offered to permit certain events of the 1988 Olympics to take place in the North.[27] International sports competitions of all kinds could take place in both parts of this city. And what better way to demonstrate to the world the openness of this city than to offer in some future year to hold the Olympic games here in Berlin, East and West?

In these four decades, as I have said, you Berliners have built a great city. You've done so in spite of threats—the Soviet attempts to impose the East Mark,[28] the blockade.[29] Today the city thrives in spite of the challenges implicit in the very presence of this wall. What keeps you here? Certainly there's a great deal to be said for your fortitude, for your defiant courage.

But I believe there's something deeper, something that involves Berlin's whole look and feel and way of life—not mere sentiment. No one could live long in Berlin without being completely disabused of illusions. Something instead that has seen the difficulties of life in Berlin but chose to accept them, that continues to build this good and proud city in contrast to a surrounding totalitarian presence that refuses to release human energies or aspirations. Something that speaks with a powerful voice of affirmation, that says yes to this city, yes to the future, yes to freedom. In a word, I would submit that what keeps you in Berlin is love—love both profound and abiding.

Perhaps this gets to the root of the matter, to the most fundamental distinction of all between East and West. The totalitarian world produces backwardness because it does such violence to the spirit, thwarting the human impulse to create, to enjoy, to worship. The totalitarian world finds even symbols of love and of worship an affront.

Years ago, before the East Germans began rebuilding their churches, they erected a secular structure—the television tower at Alexanderplatz.[30] Virtually ever since, the authorities have been working to correct what they view as the tower's one major

---

26. Signed by the United States, France, Great Britain, and the Soviet Union, this agreement aimed to ease travel restrictions and to improve communication between West Berlin and East Germany.

27. Held in Seoul, South Korea, the 1988 Summer Olympic Games were boycotted by North Korea.

28. East German currency.

29. The Soviet blockade of West Berlin in 1948–1949.

30. Historical plaza at the center of East Berlin.

flaw, treating the glass sphere at the top with paints and chemicals of every kind. Yet even today, when the sun strikes that sphere—that sphere that towers over all Berlin—the light makes the sign of the cross. There in Berlin, like the city itself, symbols of love, symbols of worship, cannot be suppressed.

As I looked out a moment ago from the Reichstag, that embodiment of German unity, I noticed words crudely spray-painted upon the wall, perhaps by a young Berliner. Quote: "This wall will fall. Beliefs become reality." Yes, across Europe, this wall will fall. For it cannot withstand faith; it cannot withstand truth. The wall cannot withstand freedom.

And I would like, before I close, to say one word. I have read, and I have been questioned since I've been here, about certain demonstrations against my coming. And I would like to say just one thing, and to those who demonstrate so. I wonder if they have ever asked themselves that if they should have the kind of government they apparently seek, no one would ever be able to do what they're doing again.

Thank you, and God bless you all. Thank you.

Ann Richards

⧗

Keynote Speech at the Democratic National Convention

ATLANTA, GEORGIA
JULY 18, 1988

A NN RICHARDS WAS Texas State Treasurer when she was chosen to deliver the keynote address at the 1988 Democratic National Convention. A native Texan, she was virtually unknown outside the Lone Star State, but she had a reputation there as a humorous, engaging, down-to-earth speaker. She attended Baylor University on a debate scholarship, became the first woman to win statewide office in fifty years when she was elected Treasurer in 1982, and would run a victorious campaign for Governor in 1990. The keynote marked her debut on the national stage. In addition to the usual challenges of energizing the delegates, articulating the party's principles, and winning over the television audience, Richards knew her effort would inevitably be measured against two recent masterpieces of the genre: Mario Cuomo's speech in San Francisco four years earlier (pages 576–583) and Barbara Jordan's 1976 address at Madison Square Garden (pages 532–535).

Richards arrived in Atlanta four days before the convention. She had worked on her speech for more than two weeks, but still it had not come together. She had consulted widely, seeking input from Kennedy speechwriter Ted Sorensen, humorist Erma Bombeck, and Texas politicos George Christian and Liz Carpenter, among others. Professional wordsmith John Sherman had been cranking out drafts, assisted by Richards's longtime speechwriter Suzanne Coleman and other members of her inner circle. It was not until early Sunday morning, the day before Richards was scheduled to speak, that a final text was ready.

The result was one of the most rollicking keynotes in convention history. Talking in her natural Texas twang and dotting her speech with folksy colloquialisms, Richards promised straight talk that would, as she put it, explain "how the cow ate the cabbage." (Although there is no way to capture Richards's twang on the printed page, we have tried to convey the tone of her address by printing her colloquialisms and informal parlance as delivered.) The primary object of her scorn was George H. W. Bush, Ronald Reagan's Vice President for the previous eight years and the Republican standard-bearer in 1988. Coming across, in the words of *New York Times* reporter Peter Applebome, as "a female Texas good ol' boy with a solicitous side." Richards was repeatedly interrupted with applause and laughter, but no line resonated more deeply than her explanation for Bush's behavior: "Poor George. He can't help it—he was born with a silver foot in his mouth." The delegates roared at the play on the old saw "Born with a silver spoon in his mouth." In a single line, Richards condensed Bush's patrician heritage, his tendency to misspeak, and the sense that he was somehow entitled to the presidency into one devastating image.

Republicans cried foul, but Richards's lampooning fell within the sometimes raucous bounds of rhetorical etiquette for convention speeches. In fact, the "silver foot" line had appeared two weeks earlier in a *New York Times* article quoting activist Heather Booth. A few days after Richards's speech, the line was claimed by writer David Kusnet, though he recollected hearing or reading it sometime during his youth. Soon thereafter, historian Arthur Schlesinger Jr. traced it to reporter Paul Crowell, quoted in a 1966 obituary of New York politician Newbold Morris. In her autobiography, Richards said she got the line from playwright Jane Wagner. Whatever the ultimate origins of Richards's quip, it has become indelibly associated with her, and the speech catapulted her overnight into the public limelight.

◇◇◇

Thank you, thank you, thank you very much. Good evening, ladies and gentlemen. *Buenas noches, mis amigos!*[1] I'm delighted to be here with you this evening because after listening to George Bush all these years, I figured you needed to know what a real Texas accent sounds like.

Twelve years ago, Barbara Jordan, another Texas woman, Barbara made the keynote address to this convention,[2] and two women in 160 years is about par for the course. But if you give us a chance, we can perform. After all, Ginger Rogers did everything that Fred Astaire did. She just did it backwards and in high heels.[3]

---

1. "Good evening, my friends."

2. Pages 532–535.

3. A legendary dance duo, Rogers and Astaire appeared together in nine films during the 1930s. The characterization of Rogers doing everything Astaire did in high heels and backwards has been traced to a 1982 "Frank and Ernest" comic strip by Bob Thaves.

I want to announce to this nation that in a little more than one hundred days, the Reagan-Meese-Deaver-Nofziger-Poindexter-North-Weinberger-Watt-Gorsuch-Lavelle-Stockman-Haig-Bork-Noriega–George Bush[4] [administration] will be over.

You know, tonight I feel a little like I did when I played basketball in the eighth grade. I thought I looked real cute in my uniform, and then I heard a boy yell from the bleachers, "Make that basket, bird legs." And my greatest fear is that same guy is somewhere out there in the audience tonight, and he's gonna cut me down to size. Because where I grew up, there really wasn't much tolerance for self-importance, people who put on airs.

I was born during the Depression in a little community just outside Waco, and I grew up listening to Franklin Roosevelt[5] on the radio. Well, it was back then that I came to understand the small truths and the hardships that bind neighbors together. Those were real people with real problems. And they had real dreams about getting out of the Depression.

I can remember summer nights when we'd put down what we called a Baptist pallet,[6] and we listened to the grown-ups talk. I can still hear the sound of the dominoes clickin' on the marble slab my daddy had found for a tabletop. I can still hear the laughter of the men tellin' jokes you weren't supposed to hear, talkin' about how big that ol' buck deer was, laughin' about mama puttin' Clorox in the well when the frog fell in. They talked about war and Washington and what this country needed. They talked straight talk. And it came from people who were living their lives as best they could. And that's what we're gonna do tonight—we're gonna tell how the cow ate the cabbage.[7]

I got a letter last week from a young mother in Lorena, Texas, and I wanna read part of it to you. She writes: "Our worries go from payday to payday, just like millions of others, and we have two fairly decent incomes. But I worry how I'm going to pay the rising car insurance and food. I pray my kids don't have a growth spurt from August to December so I don't have to buy new jeans. We buy clothes at the budget stores and we have them fray and fade and stretch in the first wash. We ponder and try to figure out how we're gonna pay for college and braces and tennis shoes. We don't take vacations and we don't go out to eat. Please don't think me ungrateful. We have jobs and a nice place to live, and we're healthy. We're the people you see every day in the grocery stores, and we obey the laws, we pay our taxes, we fly our flags on holidays. And we plod along, trying to make it better for ourselves and our children and our parents. We aren't vocal any more. I think maybe we're too tired. I believe that people like us are forgotten in America."

Well, of course, you believe you're forgotten—because you have been. This Republican administration treats us as if we were pieces of a puzzle that can't fit together. They've tried to put us into compartments and separate us from each other. Their political theory is divide and conquer. They've suggested time and time again that what is of interest to one group of Americans is not of interest to anyone else. We've been isolated. We've been lumped into that sad phraseology called "special interests."

They've told farmers that they were selfish, that they would drive up food prices if they asked the government to intervene on behalf of the family farm, and we watched farms go on the auction block while we bought food from foreign countries. Well, that's wrong.

They told working mothers it's all their fault that families are falling apart because they had to go to work to keep their kids in jeans and tennis shoes and college. And they're wrong.

They told American labor they were trying to ruin free enterprise by askin' for sixty days' notice of plant closings. And that's wrong.

And they told the auto industry and the steel industry and the timber industry and the oil industry—companies being threatened by foreign

---

4. Except for Manuel Noriega, the authoritarian leader of Panama, all these people were members of President Ronald Reagan's administration.

5. President of the United States, 1933–1945.

6. Originally a quilt or blanket on which babies and small children could sleep during evening church services.

7. Colloquial expression meaning to speak the unvarnished truth.

products flooding this country—that you're protectionist if you think the government should enforce our trade laws. And that is wrong.

When they belittle us for demanding clean air and clean water, for trying to save the oceans and the ozone layer, that's wrong.

No wonder we feel isolated and confused. We want answers, and their answer is that something is wrong with you. Well, nothing's wrong with you. Nothing's wrong with you that you can't fix in November.

We've been told, we've been told that the interests of the South and the Southwest are not the same interests as the North and the Northeast. They pit one group against the other. They've divided this country. And in our isolation we think government isn't gonna help us and that we're alone in our feelings. We feel forgotten.

Well, the fact is that we are not an isolated piece of their puzzle. We are one nation. We are the United States of America.

Now, we Democrats believe that America is still the country of fair play, that we can come out of a small town or a poor neighborhood and have the same chance as anyone else, and it doesn't matter whether we are black or Hispanic or disabled or[8] women.

We believe that America is a country where small-business owners must succeed because they are the bedrock, backbone of our economy.

We believe that our kids deserve good day care and public schools. We believe our kids deserve public schools where students can learn and teachers can teach.

And we wanna believe that our parents will have a good retirement—and that we will, too. We Democrats believe that Social Security is a pact that cannot be broken. We wanna believe that we can live out our lives without the terrible fear that an illness is going to bankrupt us and our children.

We Democrats believe that America can overcome any problem, including the dreaded disease called AIDS.

We believe that America is still a country where there is more to life than just a constant struggle for money.

And we believe that America must have leaders who show us that our struggles amount to something and contribute to something larger, leaders who want us to be all that we can be. We want leaders like Jesse Jackson.[9] Jesse Jackson is a leader and a teacher who can open our hearts and open our minds and stir our very souls. And he has taught us that we are as good as our capacity for caring—caring about the drug problem, caring about crime, caring about education, and caring about each other.

Now, in contrast, the greatest nation of the free world has had a leader for eight straight years that has pretended that he cannot hear our questions over the noise of the helicopters.[10] And we know he doesn't wanna answer. But we have a lot of questions. And when we get our questions asked, or there is a leak or an investigation, the only answer we get is "I don't know" or "I forgot."

But you wouldn't accept that answer from your children. I wouldn't. Don't tell me you "don't know" or you "forgot." We're not going to have the America that we want until we elect leaders who're gonna tell the truth—not most days, but every day. Leaders who don't forget what they don't wanna remember.

And for eight straight years George Bush hasn't displayed the slightest interest in anything we care about. And now that he's after a job that he can't get appointed to,[11] he's like Columbus discovering America. He's found child care. He's found education. Poor George. He can't help it—he was born with a silver foot in his mouth.

---

8. When delivering the speech, Richards mistakenly inserted "a" here.

9. Civil rights activist and candidate for the Democratic presidential nomination who addressed the convention two days after Richards's speech (pages 624–633).

10. Richards is referring to Ronald Reagan's habit of cupping his hand around his ear and shaking his head to indicate that he could not hear questions being shouted by the press corps as he walked toward the presidential helicopter.

11. Before becoming Reagan's Vice President, Bush had been appointed to a series of posts, including ambassador to the United Nations and head of the CIA, but his only elective office had been as a member of the U.S. House of Representatives, 1967–1971.

Well, no wonder, no wonder we can't figure it out. Because the leadership of this nation is telling us one thing on TV and doing something entirely different. They tell us, they tell us that they're fighting a war against terrorists. And then we find out that the White House is selling arms to the Ayatollah.[12] They, they tell us that they're fighting a war on drugs. And then people come on TV and testify that the CIA and the DEA[13] and the FBI knew they were flyin' drugs into America all along. And they're negotiating with a dictator who is shoveling cocaine into this country like crazy.[14] I guess that's their Central American strategy.

Now, they tell us that employment rates are great and that they're for equal opportunity. But we know it takes two paychecks to make ends meet today, when it used to take one. And the opportunity they're so proud of is low-wage, dead-end jobs. And there is no major city in America where you cannot see homeless men sitting in parking lots holding signs that say, "I will work for food."

Now, my friends, we really are at a crucial point in American history. Under this administration we have devoted our resources into making this country a military colossus, but we've let our economic lines of defense fall into disrepair. The debt of this nation is greater than it has ever been in our history. We fought a world war on less debt than the Republicans have built up in the last eight years. You know, it's kinda like that brother-in-law who drives a flashy new car, but he's always borrowin' money from you to make the payments.

Well, but let's take what they're proudest of—that is, their stand on defense. We Democrats are committed to a strong America. And, quite frankly, when our leaders say to us we need a new weapons

system, our inclination is to say, "Well, they must be right." But when we pay billions for planes that won't fly, billions for tanks that won't fire, and billions for systems that won't work, that old dog won't hunt. And you don't have to be from Waco[15] to know that when the Pentagon makes crooks rich and doesn't make America strong, that it's a bum deal.

Now, I'm gonna tell you I'm really glad that our young people missed the Depression and missed the great big war.[16] But I do regret that they missed the leaders that I knew—leaders who told us when things were tough and that we'd have to sacrifice and that these difficulties might last for a while. They didn't tell us things were hard for us because we were different or isolated or special interests. They brought us together and they gave us a sense of national purpose.

They gave us Social Security, and they told us they were setting up a system where we could pay our own money in, and when the time came for our retirement, we could take the money out. People in the rural areas were told that we deserved to have electric lights, and they were gonna harness the energy that was necessary to give us electricity so my grandmama didn't have to carry that old coal oil lamp around. And they told us that they were gonna guarantee when we put our money in the bank, that the money was gonna be there, and it was gonna be insured. They did not lie to us.

And I think one of the saving graces of Democrats is that we are candid. We talk straight talk. We tell people what we think. And that tradition, and those values, live today in Michael Dukakis, from Massachusetts.[17] Michael Dukakis knows that this country is on the edge of a great new era, that we're not afraid of change, that we're for thoughtful, truthful, strong leadership. Behind his calm there's an impatience to unify this country and to get on with the future. His instincts are deeply American; they're tough and they're generous. And personally I have

---

12. A reference to the Iran-Contra scandal, in which weapons were covertly sold to Iran, led by Ayatollah Ruhollah Khomeini, with the proceeds being used to fund the anti-Communist Contras in Nicaragua.

13. Drug Enforcement Administration.

14. Panama's Manuel Noriega, who would later be deported to the United States and convicted of racketeering and drug trafficking.

15. Texas town where Richards grew up.

16. World War II.

17. Democratic nominee for President in 1988.

to tell you that I have never met a man who had a more remarkable sense about what is really important in life.

And then there's my friend and my teacher for many years, Senator Lloyd Bentsen.[18] And I couldn't be prouder, both as a Texan and as a Democrat, because Lloyd Bentsen understands America—from the barrio to the boardroom. He knows how to bring us together by regions, by economics, and by example. And he's already beaten George Bush once.[19]

So when it comes right down to it, this election is a contest between those who are satisfied with what they have and those who know we can do better. That's what this election is really all about. It's about the American dream—those who wanna keep it for the few and those who know it must be nurtured and passed along.

I'm a grandmother now, and I have one nearly perfect granddaughter named Lily. And when I hold that grandbaby, I feel the continuity of life that unites us, that binds generation to generation, that ties us with each other. And sometimes I spread that Baptist pallet out on the floor and Lily and I roll a ball back and forth. And I think of all the families like mine, like the one in Lorena, Texas, like the ones that nurture children all across America. And as I look at Lily, I know that it is within families that we learn both

the need to respect individual human dignity and to work together for our common good.

Within our families, within our nation, it is the same. And as I sit there, I wonder if she'll ever grasp the changes I've seen in my life—if she'll ever believe that there was a time when blacks could not drink from public water fountains, when Hispanic children were punished for speaking Spanish in the public schools, and women couldn't vote.

I think of all the political fights I've fought and all the compromises I've had to accept as part payment. And I think of all the small victories that have added up to national triumphs. And all the things that would never have happened and all the people who would've been left behind if we had not reasoned and fought and won those battles together. And I will tell Lily that those triumphs were Democratic Party triumphs.

I want so much to tell Lily how far we've come, you and I. And as the ball rolls back and forth, I wanna tell her how very lucky she is. That for all of our difference[s], we are still the greatest nation on this good earth. And our strength lies in the men and women who go to work every day, who struggle to balance their family and their jobs, and who should never, ever be forgotten.

I just hope that, like her grandparents and her great-grandparents before, that Lily goes on to raise her kids with the promise that echoes in homes all across America: that we can do better. And that's what this election is all about.

Thank you very much.

---

18. Democratic nominee for Vice President in 1988.

19. Bentsen defeated Bush in a 1970 campaign for the U.S. Senate.

Jesse Jackson

Common Ground and Common Sense

ATLANTA, GEORGIA
JULY 19, 1988

UNLIKE JESSE JACKSON's 1984 run for the Democratic presidential nomination (see pages 584–593), which always had a quixotic air about it,
his 1988 campaign was a well-orchestrated enterprise that showed his
ability to transcend racial lines. When he won the Michigan caucuses on March
26 with 55 percent of the vote, he shocked the pundits and pulled into a neck-
and-neck contest with Massachusetts Governor Michael Dukakis. Although
Dukakis rebounded with victories in New York, Pennsylvania, and California
and arrived at the Democratic National Convention in Atlanta with more than
enough delegates to ensure nomination on the first ballot, Jackson was his closest challenger, with almost seven million votes and more than 1,200 delegates.
All told, Jackson finished first or second in forty-six primaries and caucuses, and
some two million of his votes came from whites.

Bolstered by his success in the primaries, as well as by a *U.S News and World
Report* poll that showed a Dukakis-Jackson ticket running ahead of Vice President
George H. W. Bush, the presumptive Republican candidate, Jackson pushed hard
for the vice-presidential nomination. When Dukakis opted instead for U.S. Senator
Lloyd Bentsen, Jackson made clear his displeasure. Departing from Chicago, he
set out for the convention in a seven-bus caravan dubbed the Rainbow Express. At
each stop he would sound the same refrain: "I cannot be asked to go out into the
field, pick up voters, bale them up, and deliver them to the big house where policy
is made and not be a part of the equation." After reaching Atlanta, he met with
Dukakis and received several concessions—none major—in return for endorsing
the ticket. As in 1984, he was also given a prime-time speaking slot at the convention. Some of his supporters thought he settled for too little.

Jackson faced a formidable task as he came to the podium at the Omni Center
on Tuesday, July 19. He needed to keep his own delegates in line and translate
their loyalty to him into support for the Dukakis-Bentsen ticket. Likewise, he
needed to motivate the voters who had turned out for him in the primaries, many
of whom had not participated in previous elections, to remain involved during the
fall campaign. Ideally, he would be able to do all this in a way that would appeal to
independents and other swing voters. Above all, he wanted to avouch his deeply
held beliefs about what he saw as the correct direction for the Democratic Party
and the nation. Jackson's address was the valedictory of his 1988 quest for the
presidency, and there was no guarantee he would be in such a position again.

Speaking in Atlanta, the heart of the Old South and the beacon of the New South, he began by honoring heroes of the civil rights movement, but he moved quickly from "racial battlegrounds" to "common ground"—a shared commitment to the greater good, "to working men and women, to the poor and the vulnerable, to the many in the world." Assailing the administration of outgoing President Ronald Reagan as "a long, dark night of reaction," he called for an end to "economic violence" in the United States and for international policy grounded on moral principle. "A master," as Garry Wills noted, "at wrapping a deeply felt conviction inside a one-liner," Jackson drew upon phrases, images, rhythms, and repetitions he had honed through the years. As his revival-style delivery lifted the crowd higher and higher, he concluded with a crescendo of exhortations to "never surrender" and to "keep hope alive." All told, he was interrupted by applause more than fifty times, including eighteen standing ovations.

Jackson's speech was the most dramatic moment of the convention, but its importance lay also in the fact that it was the first time an African American had taken to the rostrum having come so close to securing the presidential nomination of a major political party. Along the way, starting in 1984 and continuing in 1988, Jackson helped register millions of black voters and contributed indirectly to the election of dozens of black officials at the state and local levels. Willie Brown, who would later become the first African American Mayor of San Francisco, called him the Jackie Robinson of American politics.

◇◇

Thank you. Thank you. Thank you. Tonight we pause and give praise and honor to God for being good enough to allow us to be at this place at this time. When I look out at this convention, I see the face of America: red, yellow, brown, black, and white. We are all precious in God's sight[1]—the real rainbow coalition.[2]

All of us, all of us who are here think that we are seated, but we're really standing on someone's shoulders. Ladies and gentlemen: Mrs. Rosa Parks, the mother of the civil rights movement.[3]

I want to express my deep love and appreciation for the support my family has given me over these past months. They have endured pain, anxiety, threat, and fear. But they have been strengthened and made secure by our faith in God, in America, and in you. Your love has protected us and made us strong. To my wife, Jackie, the foundation of our family; to our five children, whom you met tonight; to my mother, Mrs. Helen Jackson, who is present tonight; and to our grandmother, Mrs. Matilda Burns; to my brother Chuck and his family; to my mother-in-law, Mrs. Gertrude Brown, who just last month at age sixty-one graduated from Hampton Institute—a marvelous achievement.

I offer my appreciation to Mayor Andrew Young, who has provided such gracious hospitality to all of us this week. And a special salute to President Jimmy Carter. President Carter, President Carter restored honor to the White House after

1. An echo of the hymn "Jesus Loves the Little Children," lyrics by C. Herbert Woolston.

2. Jackson is distinguishing all of God's creation from his organization, the National Rainbow Coalition.

3. On December 1, 1955, Parks was arrested for refusing to give up her seat on a bus in Montgomery, Alabama. Her act sparked the Montgomery bus boycott and helped inspire the civil rights movement that followed. When Jackson introduced her, she joined him on the podium.

Watergate.[4] He gave many of us a special opportunity to grow. For his kind words, for his unwavering commitment to peace in the world, and for the voters that came from his family, every member of his family, led by Billy and Amy,[5] I offer my special thanks to the Carter family.

My right and my privilege to stand here before you has been won, won in my lifetime, by the blood and the sweat of the innocent. Twenty-four years ago, the late Fannie Lou Hamer and Aaron Henry, who sits here tonight from Mississippi, were locked out onto the streets in Atlantic City, the head of the Mississippi Freedom Democratic Party.[6] But tonight a black and white delegation from Mississippi is headed by Ed Cole, a black man from Mississippi— twenty-four years later.

Many were lost in the struggle for the right to vote: Jimmie Lee Jackson, a young student, gave his life;[7] Viola Liuzzo, a white mother from Detroit, called "nigger lover" and brains blown out at point-blank range;[8] Schwerner, Goodman, and Chaney—two Jews and a black—found in a common grave, bodies riddled with bullets in Mississippi;[9] the four darling little girls in a church in Birmingham, Alabama.[10] They died that we might have a right to live.

Dr. Martin Luther King Jr. lies only a few miles from us tonight.[11] Tonight he must feel good as he looks down upon us. We sit here together, a rainbow, a coalition, the sons and daughters of slave masters and the sons and daughters of slaves sitting together around a common table[12] to decide the direction of our party and our country. His heart would be full tonight.

As a testament to the struggles of those who have gone before; as a legacy for those who will come after; as a tribute to the endurance, the patience, the courage of our forefathers and mothers; as an assurance that their prayers are being answered, that their work has not been in vain, and that[13] hope is eternal, tomorrow night my name will go in nomination for the presidency of the United States of America.

We meet tonight at the crossroads, a point of decision. Shall we expand, be inclusive, find unity and power, or suffer division and impotence? We've come to Atlanta, the cradle of the Old South, the crucible of the New South. Tonight there is a sense of celebration because we are moved, fundamentally moved, from racial battlegrounds by law to economic common ground. Tomorrow we'll challenge to move to higher ground.

Common ground. Think of Jerusalem, the intersection where many trails met. A small village that became the birthplace for three great religions: Judaism, Christianity, and Islam. Why was this village so blessed? Because it provided a crossroads where different people met—different cultures, different civilizations could meet and find common ground. When people come together, flowers always flourish, the air is rich with the aroma of a new spring.

Take New York, the dynamic metropolis. What makes New York so special? It's the invitation at the Statue of Liberty: "Give me your tired, your poor, your huddled masses who yearn to breathe free."[14]

---

4. Carter was President from 1977 to 1981.

5. President Carter's brother and daughter.

6. Jackson is referring to the exclusion of the Mississippi Freedom Democratic Party delegation, led by Hamer and Henry, from the 1964 Democratic National Convention in favor of the all-white Mississippi delegation.

7. Jackson's shooting by an Alabama state trooper in February 1965 was a catalyst for the march that resulted in the assault on civil rights supporters in Selma on March 7, an event that helped turn the tide in the battle for voting rights (see pages 427–433).

8. Liuzzo was murdered by the Ku Klux Klan outside Montgomery, Alabama, in March 1965.

9. Civil rights workers Michael Schwerner, Andrew Goodman, and James Chaney were killed in June 1964 near Philadelphia, Mississippi.

10. Jackson is referring to the September 15, 1963, bombing of the 16th Street Baptist Church in Birmingham, Alabama, that took the lives of four African American girls aged 11 to 14.

---

11. Assassinated in 1968, King is buried at the King Center in Atlanta, the city in which he was born.

12. An echo of King's "I Have a Dream," August 28, 1963 (pages 375–378).

13. Jackson misspoke this word as "the."

14. Closely paraphrased from Emma Lazarus's "The New Colossus" (1883), which is engraved on the base of the Statue of Liberty.

Not restricted to English only.[15] Many people, many cultures, many languages with one thing in common: They yearn to breathe free. Common ground.

Tonight in Atlanta, for the first time in this century, we convene in the South—a state where Governors once stood in schoolhouse doors,[16] where Julian Bond was denied his seat in the state legislature because of his conscientious objection to the Vietnam War,[17] a city that through its five black universities[18] has graduated more black students than any city in the world. Atlanta, now a modern intersection of the New South.

Common ground. That's the challenge of our party tonight—left wing, right wing. Progress will not come through boundless liberalism nor static conservatism, but at the critical mass of mutual survival— not at boundless liberalism nor static conservatism, but at the critical mass of mutual survival. It takes two wings to fly. Whether you're a hawk or a dove, you're just a bird living in the same environment, in the same world.

The Bible teaches that when lions and lambs lie down together, none will be afraid and there will be peace in the valley.[19] It sounds impossible. Lions eat lambs; lambs sensibly flee from lions. Yet even lions and lambs find common ground. Why? Because neither lion[s] nor lambs want the forest to catch on fire. Neither lions nor lambs want acid rain to fall. Neither lions nor lambs can survive nuclear war. If lions and lambs can find common ground, surely we can as well—as civilized people.

The only time that we win is when we come together. In 1960 John Kennedy, the late John Kennedy, beat Richard Nixon by only 112,000 votes— less than one vote per precinct. He won by the margin of our hope. He brought us together. He reached out. He had the courage to defy his advisors and inquire about Dr. King's jailing in Albany, Georgia.[20] We won by the margin of our hope, inspired by courageous leadership. In 1964 Lyndon Johnson brought both wings together—the thesis, the antithesis, and the creative synthesis—and together we won. In 1976 Jimmy Carter unified us again, and we won.[21]

When we do not come together, we never win. In 1968 the vision and despair in July led to our defeat in November.[22] In 1980 rancor in the spring and the summer led to Reagan in the fall.[23] When we divide, we cannot win. We must find common ground as the basis for survival and development and change and growth. Today when we debated, differed, deliberated, agreed to agree, agreed to disagree[24]—when we had the good judgment to argue a case and then not self-destruct—George Bush[25] was just a little further away from the White House and a little closer to private life.

Tonight I salute Governor Michael Dukakis.[26] He has run, he has run a well-managed and a dignified campaign. No matter how tired or how tried, he

---

15. A reference to the English Only movement advocating the establishment of English as the official U.S. language.

16. There is no record of a Georgia Governor standing in a schoolhouse door. In June 1963 George Wallace stood in the doorway to Foster Auditorium at the University of Alabama, symbolically blocking the entrance of African American students Vivian Malone and James Hood.

17. Three times during the mid-1960s Bond was elected and denied his seat; he entered the Georgia legislature in January 1967 after the U.S. Supreme Court ruled in his favor.

18. Clark Atlanta University, Spelman College, Interdenominational Theological Center, Morehouse College, and Morris Brown College.

19. An allusion to Isaiah 11:6.

20. Kennedy's phone call to Coretta Scott King to inquire about the jailing of her husband in October 1960 is often cited as one of the factors contributing to JFK's razor-thin victory.

21. Johnson won the presidency over Barry Goldwater; Carter defeated Gerald Ford.

22. Richard Nixon defeated Hubert H. Humphrey in the 1968 presidential election as Democrats divided among themselves over the war in Vietnam.

23. After a bitter battle with Senator Edward Kennedy, incumbent President Jimmy Carter secured the 1980 Democratic nomination but lost the election to Ronald Reagan.

24. Jackson is referring to the platform debates that took place earlier in the day, in which two of the planks he supported were defeated and a third was withdrawn before coming to a vote.

25. George H. W. Bush, Reagan's Vice President and the 1988 Republican presidential nominee.

26. Massachusetts Governor and the 1988 Democratic presidential nominee.

always resisted the temptation to stoop to demagoguery. I've watched a good mind fast at work, with steel nerves, guiding his campaign out of the crowded field without appeal to the worst in us. I've watched his perspective grow as his environment has expanded. I've seen his toughness and tenacity close up. I know his commitment to public service.

Mike Dukakis's parents were a doctor and a teacher; my parents a maid, a beautician, and a janitor. There's a great gap between Brookline, Massachusetts,[27] and Haney Street, the Fieldcrest Village housing projects in Greenville, South Carolina.[28] He studied law; I studied theology. There are differences of religion, region, and race, differences in experiences and perspectives. But the genius of America is that out of the many we become one.[29]

Providence has enabled our paths to intersect. His foreparents came to America on immigrant ships; my foreparents came to America on slave ships. But whatever the original ships, we're in the same boat tonight. Our ships could pass in the night if we have a false sense of independence, or they could collide and crash. We would lose our passengers. We can seek a higher reality and a greater good.

Apart, we can drift on the broken pieces of Reaganomics,[30] satisfy our baser instincts, and exploit the fears of our people. At our highest, we can call upon noble instincts and navigate this vessel to safety. The greater good is the common good. As Jesus said, "Not my will, but thine, be done."[31] It was his way of saying there's a higher good beyond personal comfort or position.

The good of our nation is at stake—its commitment to working men and women, to the poor and the vulnerable, to the many in the world. With so many guided missiles and so much misguided leadership, the stakes are exceedingly high. Our choice?

Full participation in a democratic government or more abandonment and neglect.

And so this night we choose not a false sense of independence, not our capacity to survive and endure. Tonight we choose interdependency and our capacity to act and unite for the greater good.

Common good is finding commitment to new priorities, to expansion and inclusion. A commitment to expanded participation in the Democratic Party at every level. A commitment to a shared national campaign strategy and involvement at every level. A commitment to new priorities that ensure that hope will be kept alive. A common-ground commitment to a legislative agenda for empowerment. For the John Conyers Bill—universal, on-site, same-day registration everywhere.[32] A commitment to D.C. statehood and empowerment—D.C. deserves statehood.[33] A commitment to economic set-asides.[34] A commitment to the Dellums Bill for comprehensive sanctions against South Africa.[35] A shared commitment to a common direction.

Common ground. Easier said than done. Where do you find common ground? At the point of challenge. This campaign has shown that politics need not be marketed by politicians, packaged by pollsters and pundits. Politics can be [a] moral arena where people come together to find common ground.

We find common ground at the plant gate that closes on workers without notice. We find common ground at the farm auction where a good farmer loses his or her land to bad loans or diminishing markets. Common ground at the schoolyard where teachers cannot get adequate pay and students cannot get a scholarship and can't make a loan. Common ground at the hospital admitting room where somebody tonight is dying because they cannot afford to go

27. Dukakis's birthplace.

28. Jackson's birthplace.

29. An echo of the motto on the Great Seal of the United States: *E Pluribus Unum.*

30. A term used by opponents of President Reagan's economic policies.

31. Luke 22:42.

32. Jackson is referring to a voter-registration bill introduced by Conyers in the U.S. House of Representatives.

33. The 1988 Democratic Party platform supported statehood for Washington, D.C.

34. Program requiring that a certain percentage of government funds and contracts be reserved for businesses owned by women or members of minority groups.

35. Jackson is referring to legislation proposed by U.S. Representative Ronald V. Dellums.

upstairs to a bed that's empty, waiting for someone with insurance to get sick. We are a better nation than that. We must do better.

Common ground. What is leadership if not present help in a time of crisis? And so I met you at the point of challenge—in Jay, Maine, where paper workers were striking for fair wages; in Greenville, Iowa, where family farmers struggle for a fair price; in Cleveland, Ohio, where working women seek comparable worth; in McFarland, California, where the children of Hispanic farm workers may be dying from poisoned land, dying in clusters with cancer; in the AIDS hospice in Houston, Texas, where the sick support one another, too often rejected by their own parents and friends.[36]

Common ground. America's not a blanket woven from one thread, one color, one cloth. When I was a child growing up in Greenville, South Carolina, and grandmama could not afford a blanket, she didn't complain and we did not freeze. Instead she took pieces of old cloth, patches—wool, silk, gabardine, croker sack—only patches, barely good enough to wipe off your shoes with. But they didn't stay that way very long. With sturdy hands and a strong cord she sewed them together into a quilt, a thing of beauty and power and culture. Now, Democrats, we must build such a quilt.

Farmers, you seek fair prices and you are right, but you cannot stand alone. Your patch is not big enough. Workers, you fight for fair wages. You are right, but your patch, labor, is not big enough. Women, you seek comparable worth and pay equity. You are right, but your patch is not big enough.

Women, mothers, who seek Head Start[37] and day care and prenatal care on the front side of life, rather than jail care and welfare on the back side of life, you are right, but your patch is not big enough. Students, you seek scholarships. You are right, but your patch is not big enough. Blacks and Hispanics, when we fight for civil rights, we are right, but our patch is not big enough.

Gays and lesbians, when you fight against discrimination and [for] a cure for AIDS, you are right, but your patch is not big enough. Conservatives and progressives, when you fight for what you believe—right wing, left wing, hawk, dove—you are right, from your point of view, but your point of view is not enough.

But don't despair. Be as wise as my grandmama. Pull the patches and the pieces together, bound by a common thread. When we form a great quilt of unity and common ground, we'll have the power to bring about health care and housing and jobs and education and hope to our nation. We, the people,[38] can win.

We stand at the end of a long, dark night of reaction. We stand tonight united in the commitment to a new direction. For almost eight years we've been led by those who view social good coming from private interest, who viewed public life as a means to increase private wealth. They have been prepared to sacrifice the common good of the many to satisfy the private interests and the wealth of a few.

We believe in a government that's a tool of our democracy in service to the public, not an instrument of the aristocracy in search of private wealth. We believe in government with the consent of the governed of, for, and by the people.[39] We must now emerge into a new day with a new direction.

Reaganomics: based on the belief that the rich had too much money—too little money—and the poor had too much. That's classic Reaganomics. They believe that the poor had too much money and the rich had too little money, so they engaged in reverse Robin Hood[40]—took from the poor, gave to the rich, paid for by the middle class. We cannot stand four more years of Reaganomics in any version, in any disguise.

How do I document that case? Seven years later, the richest 1 percent of our society pays 20 percent

---

36. During his campaign, Jackson visited all the locations mentioned in this paragraph.

37. Federal program for preschool children from low-income families.

38. Jackson is invoking the opening words of the U.S. Constitution.

39. An allusion to Abraham Lincoln's Gettysburg Address, November 19, 1863.

40. Medieval English folk hero touted for robbing the rich to help the poor.

less in taxes. The poorest 10 percent pay 20 percent more. Reaganomics. Reagan gave the rich and the powerful a multi-billion-dollar party. Now the party is over, he expects the people to pay for the damage. I take this principled position: Convention, let us not raise taxes on the poor and the middle class; but those who had the party, the rich and the powerful, must pay for the party.

I just want to take common sense to high places. We're spending $150 billion a year defending Europe and Japan forty-three years after the war is over. We have more troops in Europe tonight than we had seven years ago. Yet the threat of war is ever more remote. Germany and Japan are now creditor nations; that means they've got a surplus. We are a debtor nation—means we are in debt. Let them share more of the burden of their own defense. Use some of that money to build decent housing. Use some of that money to educate our children. Use some of that money for long-term health care. Use some of that money to wipe out these slums and put America back to work.

I just want to take common sense to high places. If we can bail out Europe and Japan,[41] if we can bail out Continental Bank[42] and Chrysler[43]—and Mr. Iacocca[44] make[s] $8,000 an hour—we can bail out the family farmer.

I just want to make common sense. It does not make sense to close down 650,000 family farms in this country while importing food from abroad subsidized by the U.S. government. Let's make sense.

It does not make sense to be escorting all our tankers up and down the Persian Gulf paying $2.50 for every $1 worth of oil we bring out, while oil wells are capped in Texas, Oklahoma, and Louisiana. I just want to make sense.

Leadership must meet the moral challenge of its day. What's the moral challenge of our day? We have public accommodations. We have the right to vote. We have open housing. What's the fundamental challenge of our day? It is to end economic violence. Plant closings without notice—economic violence. Even the greedy do not profit long from greed—economic violence.

Most poor people are not lazy. They're not black. They're not brown. They're mostly white and female and young. But whether white, black, or brown, a hungry baby's belly turned inside out is the same color. Color it pain; color it hurt; color it agony.

Most poor people are not on welfare. Some of them are illiterate and can't read the want-ad sections. And when they can, they can't find a job that matches the address. They work hard every day. I know; I live amongst them. I'm one of them. I know they work; I'm a witness. They catch the early bus—they work every day. They raise other people's children—they work every day. They clean the streets—they work every day. They drive dangerous cabs—they work every day. They change the beds you slept in in these hotels last night and can't get a union contract—they work every day.

No, no, they are not lazy. Someone must defend them because it's right and they cannot speak for themselves. They work in hospitals. I know they do. They wipe the bodies of those who are sick with fever and pain. They empty their bedpans. They clean out their commode. No job is beneath them, and yet when they get sick, they cannot lie in the bed they made up every day. America, that is not right. We are a better nation than that. We are a better nation than that.

We need a real war on drugs. You can't just say no.[45] It's deeper than that. You can't just get a palm reader or an astrologer.[46] It's more profound than that. We are spending $150 billion on drugs a year. We've gone from ignoring it to focusing on the children. Children cannot buy $150 billion worth of drugs a

41. A reference to American support for the reconstruction of Germany and Japan after World War II.

42. In May 1984 the Federal Deposit Insurance Corporation announced that it would intervene to prevent the possible collapse of Continental Bank of Illinois, the 7th-largest bank in the United States.

43. In 1980 Congress provided $1.5 billion in loan guarantees to prevent Chrysler Corporation from falling into bankruptcy.

44. Lee Iacocca, chairman of Chrysler Corporation.

45. The "Just Say No" campaign was championed by First Lady Nancy Reagan as part of the Reagan administration's efforts to reduce drug use.

46. An allusion to press reports that Nancy Reagan used the advice of an astrologer to schedule the President's travel dates.

year. A few high-profile athletes—athletes are not laundering $150 billion a year; bankers are.

I met the children in Watts who, unfortunately in their despair, their grapes of hope have become raisins of despair, and they're turning on each other and they're self-destructing. But I stayed with them all night long. I wanted to hear their case.

They said, "Jesse Jackson, as you challenge us to say no to drugs, you're right; and to not sell them, you're right; and not use these guns, you're right." By the way, the promise of CETA: They displaced CETA; they did not replace CETA.[47] "We have neither jobs nor houses nor services nor training—no way out. Some of us take drugs as anesthesia for our pain. Some take drugs as a way of pleasure, good short-term pleasure and long-term pain. Some sell drugs to make money. It's wrong, we know, but you need to know that we know. We can go and buy the drugs by the boxes at the port. If we can buy the drugs at the port, don't you believe the federal government can stop it if they want to?"

They say, "We don't have Saturday night specials any more." They say, "We buy AK-47s and Uzis, the latest make of weapons. We buy them across the counter along this boulevard."

You cannot fight a war on drugs unless and until you're gonna challenge the bankers and the gun sellers and those who grow them. Don't just focus on the children; let's stop drugs at the level of supply and demand. We must end the scourge on the American culture.

Leadership. What difference will we make? Leadership cannot just go along to get along. We must do more than change Presidents. We must change direction.

Leadership must face the moral challenge of our day. The nuclear war buildup is irrational. Strong leadership cannot desire to look tough and let that stand in the way of the pursuit of peace. Leadership must reverse the arms race. At least we should pledge no first use. Why? Because first use begets first

retaliation, and that's mutual annihilation. That's not a rational way out; no use at all. Let's think it out and not fight it out because it's an unwinnable fight. Why hold a card that you can never drop? Let's give peace a chance.

Leadership. We now have this marvelous opportunity to have a breakthrough with the Soviets. Last year 200,000 Americans visited the Soviet Union. There's a chance for joint ventures into space—not Star Wars[48] and the war arms escalation, but a space defense initiative. Let's build in the space together and demilitarize the heavens. There's a way out.

America, let us expand. When Mr. Reagan and Mr. Gorbachev[49] met, there was a big meeting. They represented together one-eighth of the human race. Seven-eighths of the human race was locked out of that room. Most people in the world tonight—half are Asian, one-half of them are Chinese. There are twenty-two nations in the Middle East. There's Europe. Forty million Latin Americans next door to us. The Caribbean. Africa, a half billion people. Most people in the world today are yellow or brown or black, non-Christian, poor, female, young, and don't speak English in the real world.

This generation must offer leadership to the real world. We're losing ground in Latin America, Middle East, South Africa because we're not focusing on the real world, that real world. We must use basic principles, support international law. We stand the most to gain from it. Support human rights; we believe in that. Support self-determination; we're built on that. Support economic development; you know it's right. Be consistent and gain our moral authority in the world. I challenge you tonight, my friends, let's be bigger and better as a nation and as a party.

We have basic challenges. Freedom in South Africa: We've already agreed as Democrats to declare South Africa to be a terrorist state.[50] But don't just

---

47. Enacted in 1973 to train needy workers and provide them with public-service jobs, the Comprehensive Employment and Training Act (CETA) was superseded by the Job Training Partnership Act of 1982.

48. Phrase used by opponents to belittle President Reagan's plan to develop laser weapons that could destroy intercontinental ballistic missiles while they were still in the upper atmosphere.

49. Soviet leader Mikhail Gorbachev.

50. Jackson is referring to language in the 1988 Democratic Party platform.

stop there. Get South Africa out of Angola; free Namibia; support the Frontline States.[51] We must have a new humane, human rights–consistent policy in Africa.

I'm often asked, "Jesse, why do you take on these tough issues? They're not very political. We can't win that way." If an issue is morally right, it will eventually be political. It may be political and never be right. Fannie Lou Hamer didn't have the most votes in Atlantic City, but her principles have outlasted every delegate who voted to lock her out. Rosa Parks did not have the most votes, but she was morally right. Dr. King didn't have the most votes about the Vietnam War, but he was morally right.[52] If we are principled first, our politics will fall in place.

"Jesse, why do you take these big, bold initiatives?" A poem by an unknown author went something like this: "We've mastered the air, we've conquered the sea, annihilated distance and prolonged life, but we're not wise enough to live on this earth without war and without hate."[53]

As for Jesse Jackson: "I'm tired of sailing my little boat, far inside the harbor bar. I want to go out where the big ships float, out on the deep where the great ones are. And should my frail craft prove too slight for waves that sweep those billows o'er, I'd rather go down in the stirring fight than drowse to death at the sheltered shore."[54] We've got to go out, my friends, where the big boats are.

And, then, for our children. Young America, hold your head high now. We can win. We must not lose you to the drugs and violence, premature pregnancy, suicide, cynicism, pessimism, and despair. We can win.

Wherever you are tonight, I challenge you to hope and to dream. Don't submerge your dreams.

Exercise above all else. Even on drugs, dream of the day you're drug free. Even in the gutter, dream of the day that you'll be up on your feet again. You must never stop dreaming.

Face reality, yes, but don't stop with the way things are. Dream of things as they ought to be. Dream. Face pain, but love, hope, faith, and dreams will help you rise above the pain. Use hope and imagination as weapons of survival and progress, but you keep on dreaming, young America.

Dream of peace. Peace is rational and reasonable. War is irrationable[55] in this age, and unwinnable. Dream of teachers who teach for life and not for a living. Dream of doctors who are concerned more about public health than private wealth. Dream of lawyers more concerned about justice than a judgeship. Dream of preachers who are concerned more about prophecy than profiteering. Dream on the high road with sound values.

And then, America, as we go forth to September, October, November, and then beyond, America must never surrender to a high moral challenge. Do not surrender to drugs. The best drug policy is a "no first use."[56] Don't surrender with needles and cynicism. Let's have no first use on the one hand or clinics on the other. Never surrender, young America. Go forward.

America must never surrender to malnutrition. We can feed the hungry and clothe the naked.[57] We must never surrender. We must go forward. We must never surrender to illiteracy. Invest in our children. Never surrender, and go forward.

We must never surrender to inequality. Women cannot compromise ERA[58] or comparable worth. Women are making sixty cents on the dollar to what a man makes. Women cannot buy meat cheaper. Women cannot buy bread cheaper. Women cannot

---

51. Founded in 1974, the Frontline States promoted black liberation in Africa. Members at the time of Jackson's speech were Angola, Botswana, Mozambique, Tanzania, Zambia, and Zimbabwe.

52. See King's speech at Riverside Church, April 4, 1967 (pages 453–463).

53. From Benjamin E. Mays, *Disturbed About Man* (1969).

54. Jackson is quoting from an often-printed poem, the author of which is unknown.

---

55. Jackson meant to say "irrational."

56. This phrase was usually associated with nuclear weapons; Jackson appropriated it for a different cause.

57. An allusion to Matthew 25:35–36.

58. Equal Rights Amendment providing for legal equality of the sexes. Though approved by Congress in 1971–1972, the amendment failed to achieve ratification by three-fourths of the states.

buy milk cheaper. Women deserve to get paid for the work that you do. It's right, and it's fair.

Don't surrender, my friends. Those who have AIDS tonight, you deserve our compassion. Even with AIDS, you must not surrender.

In your wheelchairs, I see you sitting here tonight in those wheelchairs. I've stayed with you. I've reached out to you across our nation. And don't you give up. I know it's tough sometime[s]. People look down on you. It took you a little more effort to get here tonight. And no one should look down on you, but sometimes mean people do. The only justification we have for lookin' down on someone is that we're gonna stop and pick them up.

But even in your wheelchairs, don't you give up. We cannot forget fifty years ago, when our backs were against the wall, Roosevelt was in a wheelchair.[59] I would rather have Roosevelt in a wheelchair than Reagan and Bush on a horse. Don't you surrender and don't you give up. Don't surrender and don't give up.

Why can I challenge you this way? "Jesse Jackson, you don't understand my situation. You be on television. You don't understand. I see you with the big people. You don't understand my situation."

I understand. You see me on TV, but you don't know the me that makes me me. They wonder, "Why does Jesse run?" Because they see me running for the White House, they don't see the house I'm running from.

I have a story. I wasn't always on television. Writers were not always outside my door. When I was born late one afternoon, October 8, in Greenville, South Carolina, no writers asked my mother her name. Nobody chose to write down our address. My mama was not supposed to make it, and I was not supposed to make it. You see, I was born to a teenage mother, who was born to a teenage mother.

I understand. I know abandonment and people being mean to you and saying you're nothing and nobody and can never be anything.

I understand. Jesse Jackson is my third name. I'm adopted. When I had no name, my grandmother gave me her name. My name was Jesse Burns 'til I was twelve. So I wouldn't have a blank space, she gave me a name to hold me over. I understand when nobody knows your name. I understand when you have no name.

I understand. I wasn't born in the hospital. Mama didn't have insurance. I was born in bed, at house. I really do understand. Born in a three-room house, bathroom in the backyard, slop jar by the bed, no hot and cold running water. I understand. Wallpaper used for decoration? No, for a windbreaker.

I understand. I'm a workin' person's person. That's why I understand you whether you're black or white— I understand work. I was not born with a silver spoon in my mouth. I had a shovel programmed for my hand. My mother, a workin' woman. So many days she went to work early, with runs in her stockings. She knew better, but she wore runs in her stockings so that my brother and I could have matching socks and not be laughed at at school.

I understand. At three o'clock on Thanksgiving Day, we couldn't eat turkey because mama was preparing somebody else's turkey at three o'clock. We had to play football to entertain ourselves. And then around six o'clock she would get off the Alta Vista bus and we would bring up the leftovers and eat our turkey—leftovers, the carcass, the cranberries— around eight o'clock at night.

I really do understand. Every one of these funny labels they put on you, those of you who are watching this broadcast tonight in the projects, on the corners, I understand. Call you outcast, low down, you can't make it, you're nothing, you're from nobody, subclass, underclass. When you see Jesse Jackson, when my name goes in nomination, your name goes in nomination.

I was born in the slum, but the slum was not born in me. And it wasn't born in you. And you can make it. Wherever you are tonight, you can make it. Hold your head high. Stick your chest out. You can make it. It gets dark sometimes, but the morning comes. Don't you surrender. Suffering breeds character, character breeds faith. In the end, faith will not disappoint.

You must not surrender. You may or may not get there, but just know that you are qualified. And you hold on and hold out. We must never surrender. America will get better and better. Keep hope alive. Keep hope alive. Keep hope alive. On tomorrow night and beyond, keep hope alive.

I love you very much. I love you very much.

---

59. Franklin D. Roosevelt, President of the United States, 1933–1945, was confined to a wheelchair because of polio.

Barbara Bush

✕

Choices and Change

WELLESLEY, MASSACHUSETTS
JUNE 1, 1990

W HEN BARBARA BUSH accepted an invitation to give the 1990 commencement address at Wellesley College, she had no idea it would
soon explode into a major controversy. In protest of Bush's selection,
about 150 students—roughly one-fourth of the graduating class—signed a petition charging that she was not a good role model for career-oriented women and
had "gained recognition through the achievements of her husband," President
George H. W. Bush. Throughout the month before Bush's speech, educators,
newspaper columnists, politicians, and others debated the petition and the larger
issue of women's role in American society. The media spotlight became so bright
that Bush's speech was broadcast live by all the major television networks. Adding
to the occasion was the presence of Raisa Gorbachev, wife of Russian President
Mikhail Gorbachev, who was in the country for a state visit.

   With a blend of grace and humor, Bush explained the choices she had made
in her life, talked about the importance of friends and family, and stressed the
values of tolerance, diversity, and compassion. Acknowledging that Alice Walker,
author of *The Color Purple*, had been the students' first choice for speaker. Bush
joked that instead they had ended up with her, "known for the color of my
hair!" She capped off the speech by suggesting that someone in the audience
might follow in her footsteps and one day preside over the White House as the
President's spouse. "I wish *him* well," she added, to resounding cheering and
applause.

   Although Bush had expressed many of the same ideas in earlier appearances
that spring at St. Louis University and the University of Pennsylvania—including
the line about the President's spouse—the speech was carefully reworked to meet
the situation she faced at Wellesley, where it received rave reviews. The *Boston
Globe* deemed it "a brilliant performance," the *New York Times* called it "a triumph," and NBC anchor Tom Brokaw said it was "one of the best commencement speeches I've ever heard." Many of the students who had been critical of
Bush beforehand were also impressed. "She was wonderful and funny," one of
them stated. "She could have addressed more women's issues, but she was sincere
and she won our hearts." The speech went over so well that it even changed a
cherished Wellesley tradition. Originally it had been held that the winner of the
annual hoop race would be the first woman in her class to marry. Later it was

634

said she would be the first to become a CEO. Ever since Bush suggested this modification in her speech, the winner has been deemed the first to attain her dreams, whatever they may be.

Most published versions of the speech are based on the text released to the press. The version printed here was taken from a recording and includes the comments Bush extemporized, mostly at the beginning of her address.

◇◇

Thank you very, very much, President Keohane;[1] Mrs. Gorbachev;[2] trustees; faculty; parents; and, I should say, Julia Porter, class president; and certainly my new best friend, Christine Bicknell.[3] And, of course, the Class of 1990. I'm really thrilled to be here today and very excited, as I know all of you must be, that Mrs. Gorbachev could join us. These, these are exciting times. They're exciting in Washington, and I had really looked forward to coming to Wellesley. I thought it was gonna be fun; I never dreamt it would be this much fun. So thank you for that.

More than ten years ago, when I was invited here to talk about our experiences in the People's Republic of China,[4] I was struck by both the natural beauty of your campus and the spirit of this place. Wellesley, you see, is not just a place, but an idea—an experiment in excellence in which diversity is not just tolerated but is embraced.

The essence of this spirit was captured in a moving speech about tolerance given last year by a student body president of one of your sister colleges.[5] She related the story by Robert Fulghum about a young pastor [who], finding himself in charge of some very energetic children, hits upon the game called Giants, Wizards, and Dwarfs.[6] "You have to decide now," the pastor instructed the children, "which you are—a giant, a wizard, or a dwarf." At that, a small girl tugging at his pants leg asks, "But where do the mermaids stand?" And the pastor tells her there are no mermaids. And she says, "Oh yes there are; I am a mermaid."

Now, this little girl knew what she was, and she was not about to give up on either her identity or the game. She intended to take her place wherever mermaids fit into the scheme of things. Where do the mermaids stand—all of those who are different, those who do not fit the boxes and the pigeonholes? "Answer that question," wrote Fulghum, "and you can build a school, a nation, or a whole world."

As that very wise young woman said, "Diversity, like anything worth having, requires effort."[7] Effort to learn about and respect difference, to be compassionate with one another, to cherish our own identity, and to accept unconditionally the same in others. You should all be very proud that this is the Wellesley spirit.

1. Nan Keohane, president of Wellesley.

2. Raisa Gorbachev, wife of Soviet leader Mikhail Gorbachev, spoke after Bush.

3. Bicknell, who delivered the student commencement speech, had been one of those who objected to Bush's selection as speaker. In her memoir, Bush explains that she received a fax from Bicknell on May 30 thanking her for being understanding of the protesters in comments to the press. In response, Bush telephoned Bicknell and had "a warm, nice talk." According to Bicknell, when she met Bush on graduation day, the First Lady "threw her arms open and said, 'Oh, hi,' like we had known each other forever, . . . and then she gave me a big hug."

4. The Bushes were in China from 1974 to 1976, when George H. W. Bush served as chief of the U.S. Liaison Office.

5. Bush is referring to a speech presented by Farah Pandith, president of the Student Government Association at Smith College, on September 6, 1989. The occasion was Smith's opening convocation, at which Bush received an honorary Doctor of Humane Letters degree.

6. From Fulghum's *All I Ever Needed to Know I Learned in Kindergarten* (1986).

7. From Farah Pandith's remarks at Smith College (see note 5 above).

Now, I know your first choice today was Alice Walker—guess how I know!—known for *The Color Purple*.[8] Instead you got me—known for the color of my hair.[9] Alice Walker's book has a special resonance here. At Wellesley, each class is known by a special color. For four years the class of '90 has worn the color purple. Today you meet on Severance Green[10] to say goodbye to all of that, to begin a new and a very personal journey to search for your own true colors.[11]

In the world that awaits you beyond the shores of Lake Waban,[12] no one can say what your true colors will be. But this I do know: You have a first-class education from a first-class school. And so you need not, probably cannot, live a paint-by-numbers life. Decisions are not irrevocable. Choices do come back. And as you set off from Wellesley, I hope that many of you will consider making three very special choices.

The first is to believe in something larger than yourself, to get involved in some of the big ideas of our time. I chose literacy[13] because I honestly believe that if more people could read, write, and comprehend, we would be that much closer to solving so many of the problems that plague our nation and our society.

And early on I made another choice which I hope you'll make as well. Whether you're talking about education, career, or service, you're talking about life, and life really must have joy. It's supposed to be fun. One of the reasons I made the most important decision of my life—to marry George Bush—is because he made me laugh. It's true, sometimes we've laughed through our tears, but that shared laughter has been one of our strongest bonds. Find the joy in life because, as Ferris Bueller said on his day off,

"Life moves pretty fast, and [if] you don't stop and look around once in a while, you're gonna miss it."[14] (I'm not gonna tell George you clapped more for Ferris than you clapped for George!)

The third choice that must not be missed is to cherish your human connections, your relationships with family and friends. For several years you've had impressed upon you the importance to your career of dedication and hard work—and, of course, that's true. But as important as your obligations as a doctor, a lawyer, a business leader will be, you are a human being first, and those human connections—with spouses, with children, with friends—are the most important investment you will ever make. At the end of your life, you will never regret not having passed one more test, winning one more verdict, or not closing one more deal. You will regret time not spent with a husband, a child, a friend, or a parent.

We are in a transitional period right now. We are in a transitional period right now, fascinating and exhilarating times, learning to adjust to changes and the choices we—men and women—are facing. As an example, I remember what a friend said on hearing her husband complain to his buddies that he had to babysit. Quickly setting him straight, my friend told her husband that when it's your own kids, it's not called babysitting.

Now, maybe we should adjust faster; maybe we should adjust slower. But whatever the era, whatever the times, one thing will never change: Fathers and mothers, if you have children, they must come first. You must read to your children and you must hug your children and you must love your children. Your success as a family, our success as a society, depends not on what happens in the White House, but on what happens inside your house.

For over fifty years, it was said that the winner of Wellesley's annual hoop race would be the first to get married. Now they say the winner will be the first to become a CEO. Both of those stereotypes show too little tolerance for those who want to know where the mermaids stand. So, so I want to offer a

8. Walker's book received the 1983 National Book Award and Pulitzer Prize for Fiction.

9. A reference to Bush's distinctively white hair.

10. Large expanse of lawn and tree-lined walks, where the graduation ceremonies were held.

11. A reference to the song *True Colors*, originally released in 1986 by Cyndi Lauper.

12. Located on the Wellesley campus.

13. Bush's work in behalf of literacy included the Barbara Bush Foundation for Family Literacy, founded in 1989.

14. From the movie *Ferris Bueller's Day Off* (1986).

new legend: The winner of the hoop race will be the first to realize her dream. Not society's dreams—her own personal dream.[15] And who knows? Somewhere out in this audience may even be someone who will

one day follow in my footsteps and preside over the White House as the President's spouse. And I wish him well!

Well, the controversy ends here, but our conversation is only beginning. And a worthwhile conversation it has been. So as you leave Wellesley today, take with you deep thanks for the courtesy and the honor you have shared with Mrs. Gorbachev and with me. Thank you. God bless you. And may your future be worthy of your dreams.

---

15. The hoop-rolling race is held among seniors and usually takes place about a week before graduation. Ever since Bush suggested the change in her speech, it has been said that the winner will be the first to attain her dreams, whatever they may be.

Anita F. Hill

Statement to the Senate Judiciary Committee

Washington, D.C.
October 11, 1991

WHEN PRESIDENT GEORGE H. W. Bush nominated Clarence Thomas to become an Associate Justice of the U.S. Supreme Court in July 1991, he anticipated a tough battle over confirmation in the Senate, which was under Democratic control. Thomas would be replacing Thurgood Marshall, the first black Justice to serve on the Court and one of its most liberal members. Although Thomas, too, was African American, he had a conservative judicial philosophy and was an outspoken opponent of affirmative action, which Marshall had championed. The NAACP, the Urban League, and most other civil rights groups lined up against Thomas, as did the National Organization of Women.

On September 10 the Senate Judiciary Committee began public hearings on Thomas's nomination. Unable to reach a majority for or against confirmation, on September 27 the committee sent the nomination to the Senate floor without endorsement. A vote was scheduled for October 8, and every indication was that Thomas would be confirmed. But on Sunday, October 6, *Newsday* and National Public Radio reported that the FBI had uncovered evidence during its background check of Thomas that he had been accused of sexual harassment by Anita Hill, an African American law professor at the University of Oklahoma who had worked under Thomas in two government posts during the early 1980s.

The Judiciary Committee had received Hill's charges long before they became public but had not investigated further, partly because she had asked that her name be kept confidential. Now that her affidavit had been leaked to the press, on October 11 the Judiciary Committee reopened its hearings, which were broadcast live by all the major television networks. For three days, the nation watched spellbound as Hill, Thomas, and their supporters and detractors testified in front of the committee. There had been nothing like it since the Watergate hearings of 1974. Thomas spoke first, adamantly denying all accusations of sexual harassment and charging that his character and integrity were being falsely destroyed. He was followed by Hill, who detailed her allegations and stated that she had "no personal vendetta" against Thomas. "It would have been more comfortable to remain silent," she said, but "I felt that I had to tell the truth."

There was no way to prove or disprove what had happened in private between Hill and Thomas. When was all said and done, the Senate voted 52–48 in favor of confirmation, and Thomas took his seat on the Supreme Court. The aftershocks, however, continued to rattle American life. Although opinion polls taken at the time showed that most Americans believed Thomas, they later shifted in Hill's direction. Propelled partly by what was called "the Anita Hill effect," a record forty-six women were elected to the U.S. House of Representatives in 1992 and the number of sexual harassment charges filed with the Equal Employment Opportunity Commission jumped by more than 50 percent. Hill's speech contained few traces of eloquence, and its graphic portrayal of Thomas shocked more than a few listeners, but it brought the issue of sexual harassment to national attention in a new way.

◇◇

Mr. Chairman,[1] Senator Thurmond,[2] members of the committee: My name is Anita F. Hill, and I am a professor of law at the University of Oklahoma. I was born on a farm in Okmulgee County, Oklahoma, in 1956. I am the youngest of thirteen children. I had my early education in Okmulgee County. My father, Albert Hill, is a farmer in that area. My mother's name is Erma Hill. She is also a farmer and a housewife.

My childhood was one of a lot of hard work and not much money, but it was one of solid family affection as represented by my parents. I was reared in a religious atmosphere in the Baptist faith, and I have been a member of the Antioch Baptist Church in Tulsa, Oklahoma, since 1983. It is a very warm part of my life at the present time.

For my undergraduate work, I went to Oklahoma State University and graduated from there in 1977. I am attaching to this statement a copy of my resumé for further details of my education.

Senator Biden: It will be included in the record.

Hill: Thank you. I graduated from the university with academic honors and proceeded to the Yale Law School, where I received my J.D. degree in 1980.

Upon graduation from law school, I became a practicing lawyer with the Washington, D.C., firm of Wald, Harkrader, and Ross. In 1981 I was introduced to now Judge Thomas by a mutual friend. Judge Thomas told me that he was anticipating a political appointment, and he asked if I would be interested in working with him. He was in fact appointed as

1. Senator Joseph Biden, chairman of the Senate Judiciary Committee.

2. J. Strom Thurmond, ranking Republican on the committee.

Assistant Secretary of Education for Civil Rights.[3] After he had taken that post, he asked if I would become his assistant, and I accepted that position.

In my early period there, I had two major projects. The first was an article I wrote for Judge Thomas's signature on the education of minority students. The second was the organization of a seminar on high-risk students, which was abandoned because Judge Thomas transferred to the EEOC,[4] where he became the chairman of that office. During this period at the Department of Education, my working relationship with Judge Thomas was positive. I had a good deal of responsibility and independence. I thought he respected my work and that he trusted my judgment.

After approximately three months of working there, he asked me to go out socially with him. What happened next and telling the world about it are the two most difficult things—experiences—of my life. It is only after a great deal of agonizing consideration and a great number of sleepless nights that I am able to talk of these unpleasant matters to anyone but my close friends.

I declined the invitation to go out socially with him and explained to him that I thought it would jeopardize [what] at the time I considered to be a very good working relationship. I had a normal social life with other men outside of the office. I believed then, as now, that having a social relationship with a person who was supervising my work would be ill-advised. I was very uncomfortable with the idea and told him so.

I thought that by saying no and explaining my reasons, my employer would abandon his social suggestions. However, to my regret, in the following few weeks he continued to ask me out on several occasions. He pressed me to justify my reasons for saying no to him. These incidents took place in his office or mine. They were in the form of private conversations which would not have been overheard by anyone else.

My working relationship became even more strained when Judge Thomas began to use work situ-

ations to discuss sex. On these occasions he would call me into his office for reports on education issues and projects, or he might suggest that because of the time pressures of his schedule we go to lunch to a government cafeteria. After a brief discussion of work, he would turn the conversation to a discussion of sexual matters. His conversations were very vivid. He spoke about acts that he had seen in pornographic films involving such matters as women having sex with animals, and films showing group sex or rape scenes. He talked about pornographic materials depicting individuals with large penises or large breasts involved in various sex acts. On several occasions Thomas told me graphically of his own sexual prowess.

Because I was extremely uncomfortable talking about sex with him at all, and particularly in such a graphic way, I told him that I did not want to talk about these subjects. I would also try to change the subject to education matters or to nonsexual personal matters, such as his background or his beliefs. My efforts to change the subject were rarely successful.

Throughout the period of these conversations, he also from time to time asked me for social engagements. My reaction to these conversations was to avoid them by eliminating opportunities for us to engage in extended conversations. This was difficult because, at the time, I was his only assistant at the Office of Education—or Office for Civil Rights.

During the latter part of my time at the Department of Education, the social pressures and any conversation of his offensive behavior ended. I began both to believe and hope that our working relationship could be a proper, cordial, and professional one.

When Judge Thomas was made chair of the EEOC, I needed to face the question of whether to go with him. I was asked to do so, and I did. The work itself was interesting, and, at that time, it appeared that the sexual overtures which had so troubled me had ended. I also faced the realistic fact that I had no alternative job. While I might have gone back to private practice, perhaps in my old firm or at another, I was dedicated to civil rights work and my first choice was to be in that field. Moreover, at that time the Department of Education itself was a dubious

3. Thomas held this position during 1981–1982.

4. Equal Employment Opportunity Commission, on which Thomas served from 1982 to 1989.

venture. President Reagan was seeking to abolish the entire department.[5]

For my first months at the EEOC, where I continued to be an assistant to Judge Thomas, there were no sexual conversations or overtures. However, during the fall and winter of 1982 these began again. The comments were random and ranged from pressing me about why I didn't go out with him to remarks about my personal appearance. I remember his saying that someday I would have to tell him the real reason that I wouldn't go out with him. He began to show displeasure in his tone and voice and his demeanor in his continued pressure for an explanation. He commented on what I was wearing in terms of whether it made me more or less sexually attractive. The incidents occurred in his inner office at the EEOC.

One of the oddest episodes I remember was an occasion in which Thomas was drinking a Coke in his office. He got up from the table at which we were working, went over to his desk to get the Coke, looked at the can, and asked, "Who has put pubic hair on my Coke?" On other occasions he referred to the size of his own penis as being larger than normal, and he also spoke on some occasions of the pleasures he had given to women with oral sex.

At this point, late 1982, I began to feel severe stress on the job. I began to be concerned that Clarence Thomas might take out his anger with me by degrading me or not giving me important assignments. I also thought that he might find an excuse for dismissing me.

In January of 1983 I began looking for another job. I was handicapped because I feared that if he found out, he might make it difficult for me to find other employment and I might be dismissed from the job I had. Another factor that made my search more difficult was that there was a period—this was during a period—of a hiring freeze in the government.

In February 1983 I was hospitalized for five days on an emergency basis for acute stomach pain, which I attributed to stress on the job. Once out of the hospital, I became more committed to find other employment

and sought further to minimize my contact with Thomas. This became easier when Allyson Duncan became office director[6] because most of my work was then funneled through her and I had contact with Clarence Thomas mostly in staff meetings.

In the spring of 1983 an opportunity to teach at Oral Roberts University opened up. I participated in a seminar, taught an afternoon session in a seminar, at Oral Roberts University. The dean of the university saw me teaching and inquired as to whether I would be interested in furthering—pursuing—a career in teaching, beginning at Oral Roberts University. I agreed to take the job in large part because of my desire to escape the pressures I felt at the EEOC due to Judge Thomas.

When I informed him that I was leaving in July, I recall that his response was that now I would no longer have an excuse for not going out with him. I told him that I still preferred not to do so. At some time after that meeting, he asked if he could take me to dinner at the end of the term. When I declined, he assured me that the dinner was a professional courtesy only and not a social invitation. I reluctantly agreed to accept that invitation, but only if it was at the very end of a working day.

On, as I recall, the last day of my employment at the EEOC in the summer of 1983, I did have dinner with Clarence Thomas. We went directly from work to a restaurant near the office. We talked about the work I had done both at Education and at the EEOC. He told me that he was pleased with all of it except for an article and speech that I had done for him while we were at the Office for Civil Rights. Finally, he made a comment that I will[7] vividly remember. He said that if I ever told anyone of his behavior, that it would ruin his career. This was not an apology; nor was it an explanation. That was his last remark about the possibility of our going out, or reference to his behavior.

In July of 1983 I left [the] Washington, D.C., area and have had minimal contacts with Judge Clarence Thomas since.

---

5. During the 1980 presidential campaign, Ronald Reagan had pledged to dismantle the Department of Education.

6. Duncan worked at the EEOC from 1978 to 1986.

7. Hill meant to say "still."

I am, of course, aware from the press that some questions have been raised about conversations I had with Judge Clarence Thomas after I left the EEOC. From 1983 until today I have seen Judge Thomas only twice. On one occasion I needed to get a reference from him, and on another he made a public appearance in Tulsa. On one occasion he called me at home and we had an inconsequential conversation. On one occasion he called me without reaching me, and I returned the call without reaching him, and nothing came of it. I have, on at least three occasions, been asked to act as a conduit to him for others.

I knew his secretary, Diane Holt. We had worked together at both EEOC and Education. There were occasions on which I spoke to her, and on some of these occasions undoubtedly I passed on some casual comment to then Chairman Thomas.

There were a series of calls in the first three months of 1985, occasioned by a group in Tulsa which wished to have a civil rights conference. They wanted Judge Thomas to be the speaker and enlisted my assistance for this purpose. I did call in January and February to no effect and finally suggested to the person directly involved, Susan Cahall, that she put the matter, that she put the matter into her own hands and call directly. She did so in March of 1985. In connection with that March invitation, Ms. Cahall wanted conference materials for the seminar, and some research was needed. I was asked to try to get the information and did attempt to do so. There was another call about another possible conference in July of 1985.

In August 1987 I was in Washington, D.C., and I did call Diane Holt. In the course of this conversation she asked me how long I was going to be in town, and I told her. It is recorded in the message

as August 15th; it was in fact August 20. She told me about Judge Thomas's marriage,[8] and I did say, "Congratulate him."

It is only after a great deal of agonizing consideration that I am able to talk of these unpleasant matters to anyone except my closest friends. As I've said before, these last few days have been very trying and very hard for me, and it hasn't just been the last few days this week. It has actually been over a month now that I have been under the strain of this issue. Telling the world is the most difficult experience of my life, but it is very close to having to live through the experience that occasioned this meeting.

I may have used poor judgment early on in my relationship with this issue. I was aware, however, that telling at any point in my career could adversely affect my future career, and I did not want, early on, to burn all the bridges to EEOC. As I said, I may have used poor judgment. Perhaps I should have taken angry or even militant steps, both when I was in the agency or after I left it, but I must confess to the world that the course that I took seemed the better, as well as the easier, approach.

I declined any comment to newspapers. But later, when Senate staff asked me about these matters, I felt I had a duty to report. I have no personal vendetta against Clarence Thomas. I seek only to provide the committee with information which it may regard as relevant. It would have been more comfortable to remain silent. It took no initiative to inform anyone—I took no initiative to inform anyone. But when I was asked by a representative of this committee to report my experience, I felt that I had to tell the truth. I could not keep silent.

---

8. Thomas was married on May 30, 1987.

Elizabeth Glaser

AIDS: A Personal Story

NEW YORK, NEW YORK
JULY 14, 1992

BY 1982, WHEN the term AIDS was first used, the disease was responsible for 160 known deaths in the United States. By 1987 the figure had grown to 25,000 and would swell to more than 200,000 by the end of 1992. Despite mounting evidence that AIDS affected every segment of society, many Americans persisted in stigmatizing it as an affliction of drug addicts and gay men. Discrimination against AIDS victims could be seen in every corner of the land; one poll showed that 34 percent of Americans thought people with AIDS should be quarantined from the rest of the population. Although wholesale changes in public attitudes were slow in coming, one important development occurred in the summer of 1992, when, for the first time, the Democratic and Republican national conventions featured speakers who acknowledged having AIDS.

Elizabeth Glaser was one of two such speakers at the Democratic convention. She had contracted AIDS from a blood transfusion, passed it on to her children, and would lose her life to it in 1994. She helped found the Pediatric AIDS Foundation after her daughter, Ariel, died of AIDS at the age of seven. By 1992 the foundation had raised $13 million. Glaser was chosen to address the convention after telling the campaign manager for presidential nominee Bill Clinton, "I have words inside me that I have to share."

As Glaser spoke to the delegates at New York's Madison Square Garden, the usual hubbub of the convention came to a halt. Weaving her personal narrative with a plea for new leadership in Washington, Glaser emphasized that AIDS is "everyone's problem" and that the nation faced "a crisis of caring." Her somber words, delivered slowly and deliberately, were underscored by her gaunt physical condition and had a powerful emotional impact. The most memorable speech of the convention, it dramatized the fact that anyone could get AIDS and that urgent measures were needed to bring it under control.

◇◇◇◇◇◇◇◇◇◇◇◇◇◇◇◇◇◇◇◇◇◇◇◇◇◇◇◇◇◇◇◇◇◇◇◇

I'm Elizabeth Glaser. Eleven years ago, while giving birth to my first child, I hemorrhaged and was transfused with seven pints of blood. Four years later, I found out that I had been infected with the AIDS virus and had unknowingly passed it to my daughter, Ariel, through my breast milk, and my son, Jake, in utero. Twenty years ago, I wanted to be at the Democratic convention because it was a way to participate in my country. Today, I am here because it's a matter of life and death.

Exactly, exactly four years ago my daughter died of AIDS. She did not survive the Reagan administration.[1] I am here because my son and I may not survive four more years of leaders who say they care but do nothing. I, I am in a race with the clock. This is not about being a Republican or an independent or a Democrat. It's about the future for each and every one of us.

I started out just a mom, fighting for the life of her child. But along the way I learned how unfair America can be today, not just for people who have HIV, but for many, many people—poor people, gay people, people of color, children. A strange spokesperson for such a group—a well-to-do white woman. But I have learned my lesson the hard way, and I know that America has lost her path and is at risk of losing her soul. America, wake up. We are all in a struggle between life and death.

I understand, I understand the sense of frustration and despair in our country because I know firsthand about shouting for help and getting no answer. I went to Washington to tell Presidents Reagan and Bush[2] that much, much more had to be done for AIDS research and care and that children couldn't be forgotten. The first time when nothing happened, I thought they just didn't hear me. The second time when nothing happened, I thought maybe I didn't shout loud enough. But now I realize they don't hear because they don't want to listen.

When you cry for help and no one listens, you start to lose your hope. I began to lose faith in America. I felt my country was letting me down—and it was. This is not the America I was raised to be proud of. I was raised to believe that others' problems were my problems as well. But when I tell most people about HIV in hopes that they will help and care, I see the look in their eyes. "It's not my problem," they're thinking.

Well, it's everyone's problem. And we need a leader who will tell us that. We need a visionary to guide us—to say it wasn't all right for Ryan White to be banned from school because he had AIDS,[3] to say it wasn't all right for a man or a woman to be denied a job because they're infected with this virus. We need a leader who is truly committed to educating us.

I believe in America, but not with a leadership of selfishness and greed, where the wealthy get health care and insurance and the poor don't. Do you know, do you know how much my AIDS care costs? Over $40,000 a year. Someone without insurance can't afford this. Even the drugs that I hope will keep me alive are out of reach for others. Is their life any less valuable? Of course not. This is not the America I was raised to be proud of, where rich people get care and drugs that poor people can't. We need health care for all. We need a leader who will say this and do something about it.

I believe in America, but not a leadership that talks about problems but is incapable of solving them. Two HIV commission reports with recommendations about what to do to solve this crisis,[4] sitting on shelves, gathering dust. We need a leader who will not only listen to these recommendations but implement them.

I believe in America, but not with a leadership that doesn't hold government accountable. I go to Washington, to the National Institutes of Health, and say, "Show me what you're doing on HIV." They hate it when I come because I try to tell them how to do it better. But that's why I love being a taxpayer—because it's my money and they must feel accountable.

I believe in an America where our leaders talk straight. When anyone tells President Bush that the battle against AIDS is seriously underfunded, he juggles the numbers to mislead the public into thinking

1. Ronald Reagan was President of the United States from 1981 to 1989.

2. George H. W. Bush, President from 1989 to 1993.

3. Ryan White was a teenager in Kokomo, Indiana, who learned in 1983 that he had contracted the AIDS virus through contaminated blood products he took to treat his hemophilia. He became a national figure when the community turned against him and education officials tried to keep him from returning to school. In 1990, the year of his death, Congress passed the Ryan White CARE Act to provide health care for people with HIV.

4. Glaser is referring to *Report of the Presidential Commission on the Human Immunodeficiency Virus Epidemic* (June 1988) and *America Living with AIDS: Report of the National Commission on Acquired Immune Deficiency Syndrome* (September 1991).

we're spending twice as much as we really are. While they play games with numbers, people are dying.

I believe in America, but an America where there is a light in every home. A thousand points of light[5] just wasn't enough. My house has been dark for too long.

Once every generation, history brings us to an important crossroads. Sometimes in life there is that moment when it's possible to make a change for the better. This is one of those moments. For me, this is not politics. This is a crisis of caring.

In this hall is the future—women, men of all colors saying, "Take America back." We are, we are just real people wanting a more hopeful life. But words and ideas are not enough. Good thoughts won't save my family. What's the point of caring if we don't do something about it? A President and a Congress that can work together so we can get out of this gridlock and move ahead, because I don't win my war if the President cares and the Congress doesn't, or if the Congress cares and the President doesn't support the ideas. The people in this hall this week, the Democratic Party, all of us can begin to deliver that partnership. And in November, we can all bring it home.

My daughter lived seven years, and in her last year, when she couldn't walk or talk, her wisdom shone through. She taught me to love when all I wanted to do was hate. She taught me to help others when all I wanted to do was help myself. She taught me to be brave when all I felt was fear. My daughter and I loved each other with simplicity. America, we can do the same.

This was the country that offered hope. This was the place where dreams could come true—not just economic dreams, but dreams of freedom, justice, and equality. We all need to hope that our dreams can come true. I challenge you to make it happen. Because all our lives, not just mine, depend on it.

Thank you.

---

5. A reference to language used by George H. W. Bush in his speech accepting the 1988 Republican presidential nomination to symbolize the diversity of American communities and voluntary organizations.

Mary Fisher

⧖

A Whisper of AIDS

HOUSTON, TEXAS
AUGUST 19, 1992

ONE MONTH AFTER Elizabeth Glaser's speech on AIDS at the Democratic National Convention (pages 642–644), Mary Fisher addressed the Republican convention on the same subject. A former staff assistant to President Gerald Ford, Fisher had contracted the AIDS virus from her ex-husband. She resolved to do all she could to fight the disease and became an outspoken advocate of the need for public understanding and resources. After telling her story to the Republican Platform Committee in May 1992, she was invited to address the party's convention that summer. Whereas Glaser had the luxury of facing an audience already sympathetic to her cause, Fisher faced a much tougher task. Feeling, as she said later, like "the only HIV-positive Republican," she was deeply concerned how her message of compassion and awareness would be received.

It did not take long for Fisher's listeners to realize they were hearing a special speech. Her clear, calm voice spelled out the brutal reality of AIDS and the dangers it posed to all Americans. "The AIDS virus," she reminded, "is not a political creature. It does not care whether you are Democrat or Republican. It does not ask whether you are black or white, male or female, gay or straight, young or old." Nor, she declared, did victims of AIDS deserve to be treated as outcasts. They were no less God's creatures than anyone else. It was not they who should feel shame, but rather those "who tolerate ignorance and practice prejudice." "If it is true that HIV inevitably turns to AIDS," she stated matter-of-factly, "then my children will inevitably turn to orphans." Pledging to her sons that she would not give in, she called on the nation to "set aside prejudice and politics to make room for compassion and sound policy."

Within a few minutes, a hush settled over the Astrodome as the delegates stopped chatting and gave Fisher their undivided attention. Some were moved to tears. Across the United States, millions watched on television, captivated by Fisher's poignant words and heartfelt delivery. She reached out to both audiences, speaking at the level of principle rather than partisanship. Her language was elevated, even elegant, her prose lucid and uncluttered, her pacing confident and unhurried. Although some critics caviled that a well-to-do white woman from a privileged family was not representative of most people with AIDS, there can be no gainsaying the artistry or impact of her speech. As the *New York Times* stated, she "took the crusade for decency and compassion into the lion's den. She spoke the message to the people who were most in need of hearing it. For that she has earned our gratitude."

◇◇◇◇◇◇◇◇◇◇◇◇◇◇◇◇◇◇◇◇◇◇◇◇◇◇◇◇◇◇◇◇◇◇

Less than three months ago, at platform hearings in Salt Lake City, I asked the Republican Party to lift the shroud of silence which has been draped over the issue of HIV and AIDS. I have come tonight to bring our silence to an end.

I bear a message of challenge, not self-congratulation. I want your attention, not your applause. I would never have asked to be HIV-positive. But I believe that in all things there is a purpose, and I stand before you and before the nation, gladly.

The reality of AIDS is brutally clear. Two hundred thousand Americans are dead or dying; a million more are infected. Worldwide forty million, sixty million, or a hundred million infections will be counted in the coming few years. But despite science and research, White House meetings and congressional hearings, despite good intentions and bold initiatives, campaign slogans and hopeful promises—it is, despite it all, the epidemic which is winning tonight.

In the context of an election year, I ask you—here in this great hall or listening in the quiet of your home—to recognize that [the] AIDS virus is not a political creature. It does not care whether you are Democrat or Republican. It does not ask whether you are black or white, male or female, gay or straight, young or old.

Tonight I represent an AIDS community whose members have been reluctantly drafted from every segment of American society. Though I am white and a mother, I am one with a black infant struggling with tubes in a Philadelphia hospital. Though I am female and contracted this disease in marriage and enjoy the warm support of my family, I am one with the lonely gay man sheltering a flickering candle from the cold wind of his family's rejection.

This is not a distant threat; it is a present danger. The rate of infection is increasing fastest among women and children. Largely unknown a decade ago, AIDS is the third-leading killer of young adult Americans today—but it won't be third for long. Because, unlike other diseases, this one travels. Adolescents don't give each other cancer or heart disease because they believe they are in love. But HIV is different, and we have helped it along. We have killed each other with our ignorance, our prejudice, and our silence.

We may take refuge in our stereotypes, but we cannot hide there long. Because HIV asks only one thing of those it attacks: Are you human? And this is the right question: Are you human? Because people with HIV have not entered some alien state of being. They are human. They have not earned cruelty and they do not deserve meanness. They don't benefit from being isolated or treated as outcasts. Each of them is exactly what God made: a person. Not evil, deserving of our judgment; not victims, longing for our pity. People. Ready for support and worthy of compassion.

My call to you, my party, is to take a public stand no less compassionate than that of the President[1] and Mrs. Bush. They have embraced me and my family in memorable ways. In the place of judgment, they have shown affection. In difficult moments, they have raised our spirits. In the darkest hours, I have seen them reaching not only to me but also to my parents, armed with that stunning grief and special grace that comes only to parents who have themselves leaned too long over the bedside of a dying child.[2]

With the President's leadership, much good has been done; much of the good has gone unheralded; and, as the President has insisted, "Much remains to be done." But we do the President's cause no good if we praise the American family but ignore a virus that destroys it. We must be consistent if we are to be believed. We cannot love justice and ignore prejudice, love our children and fear to teach them. Whatever our role, as parent or policy maker, we must act as eloquently as we speak—else we have no integrity.

My call to the nation is a plea for awareness. If you believe you are safe, you are in danger. Because I was not hemophiliac, I was not at risk. Because I was not gay, I was not at risk. Because I did not inject drugs, I was not at risk.

My father has devoted much of his lifetime [to] guarding against another Holocaust.[3] He is part of the generation who heard Pastor Niemöller come out of the Nazi death camps to say:[4] "They came after the Jews, and I was not a Jew, so I did not protest. They came after the trade unionists, and I was not a trade unionist, so I did not protest. Then they came after the Roman Catholics, and I was not a Roman Catholic, so I did not protest. Then they came after me, and there was no one left to protest."[5]

The lesson history teaches is this: If you believe you are safe, you are at risk. If you do not see this killer stalking your children, look again. There is no family or community, no race or religion, no place left in America that is safe. Until we genuinely embrace this message, we are a nation at risk.

Tonight, HIV marches resolutely toward AIDS in more than a million American homes, littering its

---

1. George H. W. Bush and Barbara Bush.

2. The Bushes' second child, Pauline Robinson Bush, died from leukemia shortly before her fourth birthday.

3. Max M. Fisher, businessman, philanthropist, and advisor to U.S. Presidents, headed a number of major Jewish organizations, national and international.

4. Lutheran pastor and theologian Martin Niemöller was imprisoned in Dachau and Sachsenhausen concentration camps from 1937 to 1945.

5. These exact words have not been found in Niemöller's writings. Over the years, there has been considerable debate about his statement, and many versions, some seriously corrupted, have gained currency.

pathway with the bodies of the young—young men, young women, young parents, and young children. One of the families is mine. If it is true that HIV inevitably turns to AIDS, then my children will inevitably turn to orphans.

My family has been a rock of support. My eighty-four-year-old father, who has pursued the healing of the nations, will not accept the premise that he cannot heal his daughter. My mother refuses to be broken; she still calls at midnight to tell wonderful jokes that make me laugh. Sisters and friends and my brother Phillip, whose birthday is today—all have helped carry me over the hardest places. I am blessed, richly and deeply blessed, to have such a family.

But not all of you, but not all of you have been so blessed. You are HIV-positive but dare not say it. You have lost loved ones, but you dared not whisper the word AIDS. You weep silently; you grieve alone.

I have a message for you: It is not you who should feel shame, it is we—we who tolerate ignorance and practice prejudice, we who have taught you to fear. We must lift our shroud of silence, making it safe for you to reach out for compassion. It is our task to seek safety for our children—not in quiet denial, but in effective action.

Someday our children will be grown. My son Max, now four, will take the measure of his mother. My son Zachary, now two, will sort through his memories. I may not be here to hear their judgments, but I know already what I hope they are.

I want my children to know that their mother was not a victim. She was a messenger. I do not want them to think, as I once did, that courage is the absence of fear. I want them to know that courage is the strength to act wisely when most we are afraid. I want them to have the courage to step forward when called by their nation or their party and give leadership—no matter what the personal cost. I ask no more of you than I ask of myself or of my children.

To the millions of you who are grieving, who are frightened, who have suffered the ravages of AIDS firsthand: Have courage and you will find support.

To the millions who are strong, I issue the plea: Set aside prejudice and politics to make room for compassion and sound policy.

To my children, I make this pledge: I will not give in, Zachary, because I draw my courage from you. Your silly giggle gives me hope. Your gentle prayers give me strength. And you, my child, give me the reason to say to America: "You are at risk." And I will not rest, Max, until I have done all I can to make your world safe. I will seek a place where intimacy is not the prelude to suffering. I will not hurry to leave you, my children. But when I go, I pray that you will not suffer shame on my account.

To all within sound of my voice, I appeal: Learn with me the lessons of history and of grace, so my children will not be afraid to say the word AIDS when I am gone. Then their children, and yours, may not need to whisper it at all.

God bless the children, and God bless us all. Good night.

Bill Clinton

Speech for Victims of the Oklahoma City Bombing

OKLAHOMA CITY, OKLAHOMA
APRIL 23, 1995

O N APRIL 19, 1995, a 5,000-pound truck bomb made of ammonium nitrate and nitromethane was detonated in front of the Alfred P. Murrah Federal Office Building in Oklahoma City, killing 168 people and wounding hundreds more. Because the Murrah Building housed a day-care center, nineteen of the victims were children. Although people immediately suspected international terrorists, it was soon discovered that the attack had been planned and executed by a right-wing American extremist named Timothy McVeigh. The blast was so powerful that it was felt thirty miles away. "Everything just went black," recalled one survivor. "It was like somebody had turned out the lights. . . . And then it seemed like the whole world ended." It was, to that point in time, the worst attack on American soil since Pearl Harbor.

Four days after the blast, President Bill Clinton arrived in Oklahoma City to speak at a memorial service. Twelve thousand people attended the service, held at the State Fair Arena, and many more watched it on national television. Clinton commingled a New Testament spirit of compassion for the victims with an Old Testament vow of revenge for the perpetrators. Those who lost their lives, he said, "now belong to God. Someday we will be with them. But until that happens, their legacy must be our lives." Calling the bombing a "terrible sin," he pledged to bring to justice "those who did this evil. . . . Let us teach our children that the God of comfort is also the God of righteousness. Those who trouble their own house will inherit the wind."

Clinton's eulogy honored the dead, assuaged the living, and assured the nation that justice would be done. In conjunction with his other words and deeds in response to the bombing, it marked a turning point in his first administration. Speaking for the whole nation in a time of crisis, he seemed for the first time, in the eyes of many Americans, to be genuinely presidential. As with chief executives before and since, his adroit rhetorical response to tragic events enhanced his political stature at the same time that it salved the nation's wounds.

Thank you. Thank you. Thank you very much. Governor Keating and Mrs. Keating;[1] Reverend Graham;[2] to the families of those who have been lost and wounded; to the people of Oklahoma City, who have endured so much, and the people of this wonderful state; to all of you who are here as our fellow Americans: I am honored to be here today to represent the American people. But I have to tell you that Hillary[3] and I also come as parents, as husband and wife, as people who were your neighbors for some of the best years of our lives.[4]

Today our nation joins with you in grief. We mourn with you. We share your hope against hope that some may still survive. We thank all those who have worked so heroically to save lives and to solve this crime—those here in Oklahoma and those who are all across this great land and many who left their own lives to come here to work hand in hand with you. We pledge to do all we can to help you heal the injured, to rebuild this city, and to bring to justice those who did this evil.

This terrible sin took the lives of our American family: innocent children in that building only because their parents were trying to be good parents as well as good workers, citizens in the building going about their daily business, and many there who served the rest of us—who worked to help the elderly and the disabled, who worked to support our farmers and our veterans, who worked to enforce our laws and to protect us. Let us say clearly: They served us well, and we are grateful.

But for so many of you they were also neighbors and friends. You saw them at church or the PTA meetings, at the civic clubs, at the ballpark. You know them in ways that all the rest of America could not. And to all the members of the families here present who have suffered loss, though we share your grief, your pain is unimaginable, and we know that. We cannot undo it. That is God's work.

Our words seem small beside the loss you have endured. But I found a few I wanted to share today. I've received a lot of letters in these last terrible days. One stood out because it came from a young widow and a mother of three whose own husband was murdered with over two hundred other Americans when Pan Am 103 was shot down.[5] Here is what that woman said I should say to you today: "The anger you feel is valid, but you must not allow yourselves to be consumed by it. The hurt you feel must not be allowed to turn into hate, but instead into the search for justice. The loss you feel must not paralyze your own lives. Instead, you must try to pay tribute to your loved ones by continuing to do all the things they left undone, thus ensuring they did not die in vain." Wise words from one who also knows.

You have lost too much, but you have not lost everything. And you have certainly not lost America, for we will stand with you for as many tomorrows as it takes. If ever we needed evidence of that, I could only recall the words of Governor and Mrs. Keating. If anybody thinks that Americans are mostly mean and selfish, they ought to come to Oklahoma. If anybody thinks Americans have lost the capacity for love and caring and courage, they ought to come to Oklahoma.[6]

To all my fellow Americans beyond this hall, I say: One thing we owe those who have sacrificed is the duty to purge ourselves of the dark forces which

1. Frank Keating, Governor of Oklahoma, and his wife, Cathy.

2. Evangelist Billy Graham.

3. First Lady Hillary Clinton.

4. Clinton was born and raised in Arkansas, which borders on Oklahoma; he was elected Governor five times before winning the presidency in 1992.

5. Pan American World Airways Flight 103 was destroyed by a bomb over Lockerbie, Scotland, on December 21, 1988, killing 259 people on the plane and 11 on the ground.

6. Although many printed versions of the speech represent this and the preceding sentence as direct quotations from the Keatings, neither Governor nor Mrs. Keating used such words in their remarks at the prayer service. Clinton may have been inspired in some fashion by the Keatings, but the exact words appear to have been his creation and were extemporized from notes written by hand in the margin of his prepared text. Given his admiration of President John F. Kennedy, it is probably not coincidental that his repetition of "they ought to come to Oklahoma" echoes the repetition of "Let them come to Berlin" in Kennedy's Berlin Wall speech of June 26, 1963 (pages 373–374).

gave rise to this evil. They are forces that threaten our common peace, our freedom, our way of life. Let us teach our children that the God of comfort is also the God of righteousness. Those who trouble their own house will inherit the wind.[7] Justice will prevail.

Let us let our own children know that we will stand against the forces of fear. When there is talk of hatred, let us stand up and talk against it. When there is talk of violence, let us stand up and talk against it. In the face of death, let us honor life. As St. Paul admonished us, let us not be overcome by evil, but overcome evil with good.[8]

Yesterday, Hillary and I had the privilege of speaking with some children of other federal employees, children like those who were lost here. And one little girl said something we will never forget. She said we should all plant a tree in memory of the children. So this morning, before we got on the plane to come here, at the White House we planted that tree in honor of the children of Oklahoma. It was a dogwood, with its wonderful spring flower and its deep, enduring roots. It embodies the lesson of the Psalms—that the life of a good person is like a tree whose leaf does not wither.[9]

My fellow Americans, a tree takes a long time to grow, and wounds take a long time to heal. But we must begin. Those who are lost now belong to God. Someday we will be with them. But until that happens, their legacy must be our lives.

Thank you all, and God bless you.

---

7. An echo of Proverbs 11:29.

8. From Romans 12:21.

9. An allusion to Psalm 1:3.

Hillary Rodham Clinton

Women's Rights Are Human Rights

BEIJING, CHINA
SEPTEMBER 5, 1995

THE MOST CONTROVERSIAL First Lady of the twentieth century after Eleanor Roosevelt, Hillary Clinton headed the U.S. delegation to the United Nations' Fourth World Conference on Women, held in Beijing, China, in September 1995. Unlike the previous three conferences, which proceeded in relative obscurity, this one became a major international event—partly because of Clinton's participation, partly because of strained relations between the United States and China over human rights issues. Knowing, as Clinton said later, that "one wrong word in this speech might lead to a diplomatic brouhaha," she continued to revise it through the night on the flight to Beijing.

Clinton did not mention China by name when she spoke, but there could be no doubt that her remarks about the enforced sterilization of women and the right of people to disagree with their government were directed at leaders in Beijing—as well as at public opinion in the United States. Nor could there be any doubt whom the Chinese Foreign Ministry had in mind when it stated the next day that "some people from some countries made some unwarranted remarks or criticism of other countries. We would like to caution these people to pay more attention to the problems in their own countries." Beyond this verbal jousting, however, Chinese-American relations continued on their normal path.

For all the attention paid at the time to the diplomatic aspects of Clinton's speech, its lasting impact has come from its powerful words about the rights and material conditions of women. In an effort to move women's issues from the margins of international dialogue to the center, Clinton made two pivotal linkages in the speech. First, she connected the condition of women to "economic and political progress around the globe." Communities and nations flourish, she held, when women are healthy, educated, free from violence, and able to work as equal partners in society. Second, she coupled women's rights with human rights, thereby making them a matter of transnational concern. She cited a litany of abuses suffered by women and girls in all parts of the globe, concluding that "the potential of the human family to create a peaceful, prosperous world will not be realized" until all governments accept "their responsibility to protect and promote internationally recognized human rights."

Casting aside diplomatic restraint, the 2,500 delegates at the Beijing International Convention Center responded enthusiastically to Clinton's address. Although some feminists complained that it did not go far enough, it was as forceful as diplomatic constraints would allow and proved to be a signal document in the international women's movement.

◇◇

Thank you very much, Gertrude Mongella,[1] for your dedicated work that has brought us to this point, distinguished delegates, and guests. I would like to thank the Secretary General[2] for inviting me to be part of this important United Nations Fourth World Conference on Women. This is truly a celebration, a celebration of the contributions women make in every aspect of life—in the home, on the job, in the community, as mothers, wives, sisters, daughters, learners, workers, citizens, and leaders.

It is also a coming together, much the way women come together every day in every country. We come together in fields and factories, in village markets and supermarkets, in living rooms and boardrooms. Whether it is while playing with our children in the park or washing clothes in a river or taking a break at the office water cooler, we come together and talk about our aspirations and concerns.

And time and again our talk turns to our children and our families. However different we may appear, there is far more that unites us than divides us. We share a common future. And we are here to find common ground so that we may help bring new dignity and respect to women and girls all over the world—and in so doing, bring new strength and stability to families as well.

By gathering in Beijing, we are focusing world attention on issues that matter most in our lives, the lives of women and their families—access to education, health care, jobs, and credit; the chance to enjoy

1. Tanzanian diplomat who served as chair of the Beijing conference.

2. UN Secretary-General Boutros Boutros-Ghali.

basic legal and human rights and to participate fully in the political life of our countries.

There are some who question the reason for this conference. Let them listen to the voices of women in their homes, neighborhoods, and workplaces. There are some who wonder whether the lives of women and girls matter to economic and political progress around the globe. Let them look at the women gathered here and at Huairou[3]—the homemakers and nurses, the teachers and lawyers, the policy makers and women who run their own businesses. It is conferences like this that compel governments and peoples everywhere to listen, look, and face the world's most pressing problems. Wasn't it, after all, after the women's conference in Nairobi ten years ago[4] that the world focused for the first time on the crisis of domestic violence?

Earlier today, I participated in a World Health Organization forum. In that forum, we talked about ways that government officials, NGOs,[5] and individual citizens are working to address the health problems of women and girls. Tomorrow, I will attend a gathering of the United Nations Development Fund for Women. There the discussion will focus on local—and highly successful—programs that give hardworking women access to credit so they can improve their own lives and the lives of their families.

What we are learning around the world is that if women are healthy and educated, their families will flourish. If women are free from violence, their families will flourish. If women have a chance to work and earn as full and equal partners in society, their families will flourish. And when families flourish, communities and nations do as well. That is why every woman, every man, every child, every family, and every nation

on this planet does have a stake in the discussion that takes place here.

Over the past twenty-five years, I have worked persistently on issues relating to women, children, and families. Over the past two and a half years, I've had the opportunity to learn more about the challenges facing women in my own country and around the world.

I have met new mothers in Indonesia who come together regularly in their village to discuss nutrition, family planning, and baby care.

I have met working parents in Denmark who talk about the comfort they feel in knowing that their children can be cared for in safe and nurturing after-school centers.

I have met women in South Africa who helped lead the struggle to end apartheid and are now helping to build a new democracy.

I have met with the leading women of my own hemisphere who are working every day to promote literacy and better health care for children in their countries.

I have met women in India and Bangladesh who are taking out small loans to buy milk cows or rickshaws or thread in order to create a livelihood for themselves and their families.

I have met the doctors and nurses in Belarus and Ukraine who are trying to keep children alive in the aftermath of Chernobyl.[6]

The great challenge of this conference is to give voice to women everywhere whose experiences go unnoticed, whose words go unheard.

Women comprise more than half the world's population, 70 percent of the world's poor, and two-thirds of those who are not taught to read and write. We are the primary caretakers for most of the world's children and elderly. Yet much of the work we do is not valued—not by economists, not by historians, not by popular culture, not by government leaders.

At this very moment, as we sit here, women around the world are giving birth, raising children, cooking meals, washing clothes, cleaning houses, planting crops, working on assembly lines, running

---

3. Located 35 miles outside Beijing, Huairou was the site of a nongovernmental forum on women held concurrently with the UN conference and attended by thousands of activists. Clinton addressed the Huairou meeting the day after her speech in Beijing.

4. The World Conference to Review and Appraise the Achievements of the United Nations Decade for Women, Nairobi, Kenya, July 1985.

5. Nongovernmental organizations.

6. Site of a nuclear power plant that exploded in April 1986, contaminating a region inhabited by some two million people.

companies, and running countries. Women also are dying from diseases that should have been prevented or treated. They are watching their children succumb to malnutrition caused by poverty and economic deprivation. They are being denied the right to go to school by their own fathers and brothers. They are being forced into prostitution, and they are being barred from the bank lending offices and banned from the ballot box.

Those of us who have the opportunity to be here have the responsibility to speak for those who could not. As an American, I want to speak for women in my own country—women who are raising children on the minimum wage, women who can't afford health care or child care, women whose lives are threatened by violence, including violence in their own homes. I want to speak up for mothers who are fighting for good schools, safe neighborhoods, clean air, and clean airwaves; for older women, some of them widows, who find that after raising their families, their skills and life experiences are not valued in the marketplace; for women who are working all night as nurses, hotel clerks, or fast-food chefs so that they can be at home during the day with their children; and for women everywhere who simply don't have time to do everything they are called upon to do each and every day.

Speaking to you today, I speak for them—just as each of us speaks for women around the world who are denied the chance to go to school or see a doctor or own property or have a say about the direction of their lives simply because they are women. The truth is that most women around the world work both inside and outside the home, usually by necessity.

We need to understand there is no one formula for how women should lead our lives. That is why we must respect the choices that each woman makes for herself and her family. Every woman deserves the chance to realize her own God-given potential.

But we must recognize that women will never gain full dignity until their human rights are respected and protected. Our goals for this conference—to strengthen families and societies by empowering women to take greater control over their own destinies—cannot be fully achieved unless all governments, here and around the world, accept their responsibility to protect and promote internationally recognized human rights.

The international community has long acknowledged, and recently reaffirmed at Vienna,[7] that both women and men are entitled to a range of protections and personal freedoms, from the right of personal security to the right to determine freely the number and spacing of the children they bear. No one, no one should be forced to remain silent for fear of religious or political persecution, arrest, abuse, or torture.

Tragically, women are most often the ones whose human rights are violated. Even now, in the late twentieth century, the rape of women continues to be used as an instrument of armed conflict. Women and children make up a large majority of the world's refugees, and when women are excluded from the political process, they become even more vulnerable to abuse.

I believe that now, on the eve of a new millennium, it is time to break the silence. It is time for us to say, here in Beijing and for the world to hear, that it is no longer acceptable to discuss women's rights as separate from human rights. These abuses have continued because, for too long, the history of women has been a history of silence. Even today there are those who are trying to silence our words. But the voices of this conference and of the women at Huairou must be heard loudly and clearly:

It is a violation of human rights when babies are denied food or drowned or suffocated or their spines broken simply because they are born girls.

It is a violation of human rights when women and girls are sold into the slavery of prostitution for human greed, and the kinds of reasons that are used to justify this practice should no longer be tolerated.

It is a violation of human rights when women are doused with gasoline, set on fire, and burned to death because their marriage dowries are deemed too small.

It is a violation of human rights when individual women are raped in their own communities and when thousands of women are subjected to rape as a tactic or prize of war.

---

7. Clinton is referring to the World Conference on Human Rights, held at Vienna, Austria, June 14–25, 1993.

It is a violation of human rights when a leading cause of death worldwide among women ages fourteen to forty-four is the violence they are subjected to in their own homes by their own relatives.

It is a violation of human rights when young girls are brutalized by the painful and degrading practice of genital mutilation.

It is a violation of human rights when women are denied the right to plan their own families—and that includes being forced to have abortions or being sterilized against their will.

If there is one message that echoes forth from this conference, let it be that human rights are women's rights and women's rights are human rights once and for all.

And among those rights are the right to speak freely and the right to be heard. Women must enjoy the rights to participate fully in the social and political lives of their countries if we want freedom and democracy to thrive and endure. It is indefensible that many women in nongovernmental organizations who wished to participate in this conference have not been able to attend or have been prohibited from fully taking part.

Let me be clear. Freedom means the right of people to assemble, organize, and debate openly. It means respecting the views of those who may disagree with the views of their governments. It means not taking citizens away from their loved ones and jailing them, mistreating them, or denying them their freedom or dignity because of the peaceful expression of their ideas and opinions.

In my country, we recently celebrated the seventy-fifth anniversary of women's suffrage. It took one hundred and fifty years after the signing of our Declaration of Independence for women to win the right to vote.[8] It took seventy-two years of organized struggle before that happened, on the part of many courageous women and men.[9] It was one of America's most divisive philosophical wars. But it was a bloodless war. Suffrage was achieved without a shot being fired.

But we have also been reminded, in V-J Day[10] observances last weekend, of the good that comes when men and women join together to combat the forces of tyranny and to build a better world. We have seen peace prevail in most places for a half century. We have avoided another world war. But we have not solved older, deeply rooted problems that continue to diminish the potential of half the world's population.

Now it is the time to act on behalf of women everywhere. If we take bold steps to better the lives of women, we will be taking bold steps to better the lives of children and families too. Families rely on mothers and wives for emotional support and care, families rely on women for labor in the home, and, increasingly, everywhere families rely on women for income needed to raise healthy children and care for other relatives. As long as discrimination and inequities remain so commonplace everywhere in the world—as long as girls and women are valued less, fed less, fed last, overworked, underpaid, not schooled, subjected to violence in and outside their homes—the potential of the human family to create a peaceful, prosperous world will not be realized.

Let, let this conference be our—and the world's—call to action. Let us heed that call so we can create a world in which every woman is treated with respect and dignity, every boy and girl is loved and cared for equally, and every family has the hope of a strong and stable future.

That is the work before you. That is the work before all of us who have a vision of the world we want to see for our children and our grandchildren. The time is now. We must move beyond rhetoric, we must move beyond recognition of problems, to working together to have the common efforts to build that common ground we hope to see.

God's blessings on you, your work, and all who will benefit from it. Godspeed, and thank you very much.

---

8. The right of women to vote was established in 1920, with ratification of the Nineteenth Amendment to the U.S. Constitution.

9. Clinton is referring to the time between 1920 and the 1848 women's rights convention in Seneca Falls, New York.

10. Victory in Japan Day, marking the official surrender of Japan in World War II.

Elie Wiesel

The Perils of Indifference

WASHINGTON, D.C.
APRIL 12, 1999

FEW PEOPLE IN the twentieth century could speak with greater moral authority than Elie Wiesel. In 1944, when Wiesel was fifteen years old, he and his family were uprooted from their home in Romania and transported to Nazi death camps. His mother and younger sister perished at Auschwitz, his father at Buchenwald. Wiesel survived beatings, forced marches, disease, and starvation at the hands of the Germans before he was freed by the Allies at the end of World War II. After working in Paris as a journalist, he settled in the United States, where he became an internationally acclaimed writer, lecturer, human rights activist, and witness to the horrors of the Holocaust. In 1986 he received the Nobel Peace Prize for his work "as one of the most important spiritual leaders and guides in an age when violence, repression, and racism continue to characterize the world."

In April 1999 Wiesel presented "The Perils of Indifference" as a Millennial Lecture at the White House. His audience included some 200 people in the East Room and millions more via satellite and the Internet. At the time, war was raging in Kosovo, where the world saw the same kind of hatred and genocide that, on a much larger scale, had produced the massacre of six million Jews during Wiesel's childhood. Against this backdrop, he blended autobiography, historical narrative, and jeremiad to produce a powerful plea for moral awareness and involvement. To be indifferent to suffering, he warned, is to lose one's humanity: "The political prisoner in his cell, the hungry children, the homeless refugees—not to respond to their plight, not to relieve their solitude by offering them a spark of hope, is to exile them from human memory. And in denying their humanity, we betray our own."

Looking back on the twentieth century and forward to the twenty-first, Wiesel concluded eloquently with a measure of optimism tempered by the harsh realities of history. "Once again," he said, referring to his childhood, "I think of the young Jewish boy from the Carpathian Mountains. He has accompanied the old man I have become throughout these years of quest and struggle. And together we walk towards the new millennium, carried by profound fear and extraordinary hope." Few words captured better the feelings of people the world over at century's end.

Mr. President, Mrs. Clinton, members of Congress, Ambassador Holbrooke,[1] Excellencies, friends: Fifty-four years ago to the day, a young Jewish boy from a small town in the Carpathian Mountains woke up, not far from Goethe's[2] beloved Weimar,[3] in a place of eternal infamy called Buchenwald.[4] He was finally free,[5] but there was no joy in his heart. He thought there never would be again.

Liberated a day earlier by American soldiers, he remembers their rage at what they saw. And even if he lives to be a very old man, he will always be grateful to them for that rage, and also for their compassion. Though he did not understand their language, their eyes told him what he needed to know—that they, too, would remember and bear witness. And now I stand before you, Mr. President—commander in chief of the army that freed me and tens of thousands of others—and I am filled with a profound and abiding gratitude to the American people.

Gratitude is a word that I cherish. Gratitude is what defines the humanity of the human being. And I am grateful to you, Hillary—or Mrs. Clinton—for what you said[6] and for what you are doing for children in the world, for the homeless, for the victims of injustice, the victims of destiny and society. And I thank all of you for being here.

We are on the threshold of a new century, a new millennium. What will the legacy of this vanishing century be? How will it be remembered in the new millennium? Surely it will be judged, and judged severely, in both moral and metaphysical terms. These failures have cast a dark shadow over humanity: two world wars, countless civil wars, a senseless chain of assassinations—Gandhi, the Kennedys, Martin Luther King, Sadat, Rabin[7]—bloodbaths in Cambodia and Algeria, India and Pakistan, Ireland and Rwanda, Eritrea and Ethiopia, Sarajevo and Kosovo;[8] the inhumanity in the gulag;[9] and the tragedy of Hiroshima.[10] And on a different level, of course, Auschwitz and Treblinka.[11] So much violence, so much indifference.

What is indifference? Etymologically, the word means "no difference." A strange and unnatural state in which the lines blur between light and darkness, dusk and dawn, crime and punishment, cruelty and compassion, good and evil.

What are its courses and inescapable consequences? Is it a philosophy? Is there a philosophy of indifference conceivable? Can one possibly view indifference as a virtue? Is it necessary at times to practice it simply to keep one's sanity, live normally, enjoy a fine meal and a glass of wine as the world around us experiences harrowing upheavals?

Of course, indifference can be tempting—more than that, seductive. It is so much easier to look away from victims. It is so much easier to avoid such rude interruptions to our work, our dreams, our hopes. It is, after all, awkward, troublesome, to be involved in another person's pain and despair. Yet for the person who is indifferent, his or her neighbor[s] are of no consequence. And, therefore, their lives are meaningless. Their hidden or even visible anguish is of no interest. Indifference reduces the other to an abstraction.

Over there, behind the black gates of Auschwitz, the most tragic of all prisoners were the Muselmänner,

---

1. Richard C. Holbrooke, U.S. ambassador to the United Nations.

2. Johann Wolfgang von Goethe (1749–1832), German poet and dramatist.

3. A German cultural center since the 16th century, Weimar is located 13 miles east of Frankfurt.

4. Nazi concentration camp during World War II.

5. Wiesel was liberated from Buchenwald in April 1945.

6. First Lady Hillary Clinton made remarks introducing Wiesel before his speech.

7. Mahatma Gandhi, Indian leader killed in 1948; John F. Kennedy and Robert F. Kennedy, killed in 1963 and 1968, respectively; civil rights leader Martin Luther King, killed in 1968; Egyptian President Anwar Sadat, killed in October 1981; Israeli Prime Minister Yitzhak Rabin, killed in November 1995.

8. More than six million people are estimated to have lost their lives in these countries during the 20th century as a result of political or sectarian conflicts.

9. The system of prisons and labor camps in the former Soviet Union.

10. The United States dropped an atomic bomb on Hiroshima, Japan, in August 1945.

11. Nazi concentration camps during World War II.

as they were called.[12] Wrapped in their torn blankets, they would sit or lie on the ground, staring vacantly into space, unaware of who or where they were, strangers to their surroundings. They no longer felt pain, hunger, thirst. They feared nothing. They felt nothing. They were dead and did not know it.

Rooted in our tradition, some of us felt that to be abandoned by humanity then was not the ultimate. We felt that to be abandoned by God was worse than to be punished by him. Better an unjust God than an indifferent[13] one. For us to be ignored by God was a harsher punishment than to be a victim of his anger. Man can live far from God—not outside God. God is wherever we are. Even in suffering? Even in suffering.

In a way, to be indifferent to that suffering is what makes the human being inhuman. Indifference, after all, is more dangerous than anger and hatred. Anger can at times be creative. One writes a great poem, a great symphony, one does something special for the sake of humanity because one is angry at the injustice that one witnesses. But indifference is never creative. Even hatred at times may elicit a response. You fight it. You denounce it. You disarm it. Indifference elicits no response. Indifference is not a response.

Indifference is not a beginning; it is an end. And, therefore, indifference is always the friend of the enemy, for it benefits the aggressor—never his victim, whose pain is magnified when he or she feels forgotten. The political prisoner in his cell, the hungry children, the homeless refugees—not to respond to their plight, not to relieve their solitude by offering them a spark of hope, is to exile them from human memory. And in denying their humanity, we betray our own.

Indifference, then, is not only a sin, it is a punishment. And this is one of the most important lessons of this outgoing century's wide-ranging experiments in good and evil.

In the place that I come from, society was composed of three simple categories: the killers, the victims, and the bystanders. During the darkest of times

inside the ghettos and death camps—and I'm glad that Mrs. Clinton mentioned that we are now commemorating that event, that period, that we are now in the Days of Remembrance[14]—but then we felt abandoned, forgotten. All of us did.

And our only miserable consolation was that we believed that Auschwitz and Treblinka were closely guarded secrets, that the leaders of the free world did not know what was going on behind those black gates and barbed wire, that they had no knowledge of the war against the Jews that Hitler's armies and their accomplices waged as part of the war against the Allies. If they knew, we thought, surely those leaders would have moved heaven and earth to intervene. They would have spoken out with greater outrage and conviction. They would have bombed the railways leading to Birkenau[15]—just the railways, just once.

And now we knew, we learned, we discovered that the Pentagon knew, the State Department knew. And the illustrious occupant of the White House then, who was a great leader, and I say it with some anguish and pain because today is exactly fifty-four years marking his death; Franklin Delano Roosevelt died on April the twelfth, 1945. So he's very much present to me and to us. No doubt, he was a great leader. He mobilized the American people and the world, going into battle, bringing hundreds and thousands of valiant and brave soldiers in America to fight fascism, to fight dictatorship, to fight Hitler. And so many of the young people fell in battle. And nevertheless his image in Jewish history—I must say it—his image in Jewish history is flawed.

The depressing tale of the *St. Louis* is a case in point. Sixty years ago, its human cargo—maybe one thousand Jews—was turned back to Nazi Germany.[16]

---

12. "Muselmänner" was used in the concentration camps to refer to people who were near death from privation and starvation.

13. Wiesel misspoke this word as "undifferent."

14. An annual set of weeklong activities established by Congress in 1980 in commemoration of Holocaust victims.

15. Nazi extermination camp established in 1941 near Auschwitz.

16. In May 1939 the *St. Louis* departed from Germany with more than 900 Jewish refugees. After being denied entry to Cuba, despite having landing certificates for Havana, the refugees sought entrance to the United States but were refused there as well. Forced to return to Europe, most were eventually killed in the Holocaust.

And that happened after the Kristallnacht, after the first state-sponsored pogrom, with hundreds of Jewish shops destroyed, synagogues burned, thousands of people put in concentration camps.[17] And that ship, which was already in the shores of the United States, was sent back.

I don't understand. Roosevelt was a good man, with a heart. He understood those who needed help. Why didn't he allow these refugees to disembark? A thousand people—in America, the great country, the greatest democracy, the most generous of all new nations in modern history. What happened? I don't understand. Why the indifference, on the highest level, to the suffering of the victims?

But, then, there were human beings who were sensitive to our tragedy. Those non-Jews, those Christians that we call the "Righteous Gentiles," whose selfless acts of heroism saved the honor of their faith. Why were they so few? Why was there a greater effort to save SS murderers[18] after the war than to save their victims during the war? Why did some of America's largest corporations continue to do business with Hitler's Germany until 1942? It has been suggested, and it was documented, that the Wehrmacht[19] could not have conducted its invasion of France without oil obtained from American sources. How is one to explain their indifference?

And yet, my friends, good things have also happened in this traumatic century: the defeat of Nazism, the collapse of communism, the rebirth of Israel on its ancestral soil, the demise of apartheid, Israel's peace treaty with Egypt, the peace accord in Ireland.[20] And

let us remember the meeting, filled with drama and emotion, between Rabin and Arafat that you, Mr. President, convened in this very place.[21] I was here and I will never forget it. And then, of course, the joint decision of the United States and NATO to intervene in Kosovo[22] and save those victims, those refugees, those who were uprooted by a man whom I believe that, because of his crimes, should be charged with crimes against humanity.[23] But this time, the world was not silent. This time, we do respond. This time, we intervene.

Does it mean that we have learned from the past? Does it mean that society has changed? Has the human being become less indifferent and more human? Have we really learned from our experiences? Are we less insensitive to the plight of victims of ethnic cleansing and other forms of injustices in places near and far? Is today's justified intervention in Kosovo, led by you, Mr. President, a lasting warning that never again will the deportation, the terrorization of children and their parents, be allowed anywhere in the world? Will it discourage other dictators in other lands to do the same?

What about the children? Oh, we see them on television, we read about them in the papers, and we do so with a broken heart. Their fate is always the most tragic, inevitably. When adults wage war, children perish. We see their faces, their eyes. Do we hear their pleas? Do we feel their pain, their agony? Every minute, one of them dies of disease, violence, famine. Some of them—so many of them—could be saved.

And so, once again, I think of the young Jewish boy from the Carpathian Mountains. He has accompanied the old man I have become throughout these years of quest and struggle. And together we walk towards the new millennium, carried by profound fear and extraordinary hope.

---

17. Kristallnacht, "Night of Broken Glass," occurred on November 9–10, 1938.

18. The Schutzstaffel, known as the SS, included more than 250,000 troops and were responsible, among other duties, for running the concentration camps.

19. Armed forces of the German Third Reich.

20. Wiesel is referring to the Allies' victory over Germany in World War II, the dissolution of the Soviet Union in 1991, the creation of the state of Israel in 1948, the abolition of apartheid in South Africa in the early 1990s, the March 1979 treaty in which Egypt became the first Arab state officially to recognize Israel, and the April 1998 agreement that halted violence between Catholics and Protestants in Northern Ireland.

21. A reference to the October 1993 meeting at the White House between Israeli Prime Minister Yitzhak Rabin and Yasser Arafat, chairman of the Palestine Liberation Organization.

22. The Kosovo intervention took place March–June 1999.

23. Wiesel is referring to Slobodan Milosevic, President of Serbia, 1989–1997, and of the Federal Republic of Yugoslavia, 1997–2000. Milosevic was charged with genocide by the United Nations war crimes tribunal in November 2001.

Note on Sources

Unless otherwise indicated, all speech texts are transcribed from audio or video recordings. Here we list bibliographic information for texts for which we had only printed sources or a combination of printed and recorded sources. Editorial procedures are explained in the Introduction.

Russell H. Conwell, *Acres of Diamonds* (Cleveland, Ohio: F. M. Barton [1905]).

William Jennings Bryan, *Imperialism: Being the speech of Hon. William Jennings Bryan in response to the committee appointed to notify him of his nomination to the Presidency of the United States, Delivered at Indianapolis, August 8th, 1900* (n.p.: [1900]), except for the second paragraph, which is from the *Indianapolis Journal*, August 9, 1900.

Theodore Roosevelt, The Man with the Muckrake, *New York Times*, April 15, 1906.

Eugene Debs, The Issue, *Appeal to Reason*, May 23, 1908.

Woodrow Wilson, First Inaugural Address, *Inaugural Address of President Wilson and Vice-President Thomas R. Marshall* (Washington, D.C.: Government Printing Office, 1913), 3–6, with minor corrections from the typescript copy in the Papers of Woodrow Wilson in the Library of Congress.

Anna Howard Shaw, The Fundamental Principle of a Republic, *Ogdensburg Advance and St. Lawrence Weekly Democrat*, July 1, 1915.

Carrie Chapman Catt, The Crisis, *Woman's Journal and Suffrage News*, September 16, 1916, with minor corrections from the partial typescript of Catt's speech in the New York Public Library.

Woodrow Wilson, War Message, Printed Reading Copy, Woodrow Wilson Papers, Library of Congress.

Emma Goldman, Address to the Jury, *Mother Earth* (July 1917), 150–61.

Robert La Follette, Freedom of Speech in Wartime, *Congressional Record: Containing the Proceedings and Debates of the First Session of the Sixty-Fifth Congress of* the United States of America, Volume 55 (Washington, D.C.: Government Printing Office, 1917), 7878–86.

Carrie Chapman Catt, *An Address to the Congress of the United States* (New York: National Woman Suffrage Publishing Company, 1917).

Woodrow Wilson, The Fourteen Points, Printed Reading Copy, Woodrow Wilson Papers, Library of Congress.

Eugene Debs, Statement to the Court, *The Debs Case: A Complete History* (Chicago: National Socialist Office, [1919]), 111–17.

Crystal Eastman, Now We Can Begin, *The Liberator* (December 1920), 23–24.

Woodrow Wilson, Des Moines Address for the League of Nations, *Des Moines Register,* September 7, 1919, with minor corrections from *Addresses of President Wilson . . . on His Western Tour, September 4 to September 25, 1919* (Washington, D.C.: Government Printing Office, 1919), 59–70.

Woodrow Wilson, Pueblo Address for the League of Nations, *Addresses of President Wilson . . . on His Western Tour, September 4 to September 25, 1919* (Washington, D.C.: Government Printing Office, 1919), 359–70, with minor corrections from the *Pueblo Chieftain*, September 26, 1919.

Clarence Darrow, Plea for Leopold and Loeb: Day one from People of the State of Illinois vs. Nathan F. Leopold Jr. and Richard Loeb, Criminal Court of Cook County, Before Honorable John R. Caverly, Trial Transcript, August 22, 1924, pages 3879–3936; days two and three from *Attorney Clarence Darrow's Plea for Mercy and Prosecutor Robert E. Crowe's Demand for the Death Penalty in the Loeb-Leopold Case* (Chicago:

Wilson Publishing Company, [1924]), with corrections from stenographic accounts in the Chicago newspapers of August 22–26, 1924.

Margaret Sanger, The Children's Era, typescript in the American Birth Control League Papers, Houghton Library, Harvard University, with minor corrections from *International Neo-Malthusian and Birth Control Conference Proceedings*, vol. 4 (New York: American Birth Control League, 1926), 53–58.

Franklin D. Roosevelt, Address to the Commonwealth Club, *New York Times*, September 24, 1932.

Huey Long, Every Man a King: Printed portions from *Congressional Record: Proceedings and Debates of the Second Session of the Seventy-Third Congress of the United States of America, Volume 78, Part 4* (Washington, D.C.: Government Printing Office, 1934), 3450–53; audio portions from a recording of Long's address as presented on NBC Radio, February 23, 1934.

John L. Lewis, Labor and the Nation, *New York Times*, September 4, 1937, with minor corrections from John L. Lewis, "Guests at Labor's Table," *Vital Speeches of the Day*, 3 (September 15, 1937), 731–33, and John L. Lewis, *Labor and the Nation* (Washington, D.C.: Committee for Industrial Organization, 1937).

Lou Gehrig, Farewell to Baseball, *Sporting News*, July 12, 1939, with additions from Eleanor Gehrig and Joseph Durso, *My Luke and I: Mrs. Lou Gehrig's Joyous and Tragic Love for the "Iron Man of Baseball"* (New York: Crowell, 1976), 221–22, and from recorded fragments of the speech.

Eleanor Roosevelt, The Struggle for Human Rights: Printed portions from *Human Rights and Genocide: Selected Statements, United Nations Resolutions, September 21–December 12, 1948*. Department of

State Publication 3416; International Organization and Conference Series III, 25 (Washington, D.C.: Government Printing Office, 1949), 1–12; audio portions from the Institut National de l'Audiovisuel, Paris, France, translated by Rob Lewis and Mary Louise Roberts.

Eleanor Roosevelt, Adoption of the Declaration of Human Rights, *Human Rights and Genocide: Selected Statements, United Nations Resolutions, September 21–December 12, 1948*. Department of State Publication 3416; International Organization and Conference Series III, 25 (Washington, D.C.: Government Printing Office, 1949), 24–29.

Margaret Chase Smith, Declaration of Conscience, *Congressional Record: Proceedings and Debates of the 81st Congress, Second Session, Volume 96, Part 6* (Washington, D.C.: Government Printing Office, 1950), 7894–95.

Elizabeth Gurley Flynn, Statement to the Court, United States District Court, Southern District of New York, *United States of America vs. Elizabeth Gurley Flynn, et al, Defendants, Before Hon. Edward J. Dimock, D.J., and a Jury. Stenographer's Minutes*, pages 16386–435.

Mario Savio, An End to History, *Humanity: An Arena of Critique and Commitment* (December 1964), 1–4.

Cesar Chavez, Speech on Breaking His Fast, United Farm Workers Papers, Walter P. Reuther Library, Wayne State University.

Shirley Chisholm, For the Equal Rights Amendment, *Congressional Record: Proceedings and Debates of the 91st Congress, Second Session, Volume 116, Part 21* (Washington, D.C.: Government Printing Office, 1970), 28028–29.

Ursula K. Le Guin, A Left-Handed Commencement Address, *Mills Quarterly* (August 1983), 4–5.

Permissions

Index of Names and Subjects

Index of Speech Types and Occasions

"*Words of a Century* is simply the best anthology of its kind. It is edited by two of the best rhetorical critics in the business, and the speeches were chosen on the basis of their artistry and impact through a survey of 137 communication scholars. The headnotes are insightful and historically accurate, and the texts have been painstakingly authenticated—a rarity in such works. There is no comparable collection of great American speeches. No serious student of rhetoric should be without it."

—J. Michael Hogan, *Pennsylvania State University*

"Moments of political crisis beget some of the best and most memorable instances of political oratory. This magnificently researched and carefully annotated collection reminds us just how close the connection is between our shared political life and our public speech. This volume is a unique and invaluable resource for students and scholars alike on the history, politics, and oratory of the twentieth century."

—Mary E. Stuckey, *Georgia State University*

Boldly breaking the mold of previous anthologies, *Words of a Century: The Top 100 American Speeches, 1900–1999* contains the complete—and authentic—texts of the best American speeches of the twentieth century as delivered to their immediate audiences. It features a remarkable array of speakers, from Woodrow Wilson, Clarence Darrow, and Carrie Chapman Catt to Martin Luther King, Ronald Reagan, John F. Kennedy, and Barbara Jordan.

As diverse in type as they are in subject matter, the speeches open a unique window on the twentieth century, and many continue to resonate in our own time. Each is preceded by a headnote with background on the speaker, the occasion, and the impact of the speech. More than 2,000 annotations identify people, events, and textual references that help bring the speeches to life for today's readers.

This exceptional anthology is ideal for courses in rhetoric, political communication, and twentieth century American history, as well as for anyone interested in the artistry and impact of the spoken word.

ABOUT THE EDITORS

Stephen E. Lucas is Evjue-Bascom Professor in the Humanities, Department of Communication Arts, University of Wisconsin.

Martin J. Medhurst is Distinguished Professor of Rhetoric and Communication at Baylor University.

Cover design: Eve Siegel

ISBN 978-0-19-516805-1

90000

9 780195 168051

OXFORD
UNIVERSITY PRESS
www.oup.com/us/he